R.2002 D.P.L.

D1111342

THE WALL STREET JOURNAL. ALMANAC

1999

The Staff of
THE WALL STREET JOURNAL.

Ronald J. Alsop
EDITOR

BALLANTINE BOOKS · NEW YORK

Sale of this book without a front cover may be unauthorized. If this book is coverless, it may have been reported
to the publisher as "unsold or destroyed" and neither the
author nor the publisher may have received payment for it.

Copyright © 1998 by Dow Jones & Company, Inc.

All rights reserved under International and Pan-American
Copyright Conventions. Published in the United States by
Ballantine Books, a division of Random House, Inc., New
York, and simultaneously in Canada by Random House of
Canada Limited, Toronto.

http://www.randomhouse.com

A record for this book is found at the Library of Congress

ISBN: 0-345-41102-1

Manufactured in the United States of America

First Edition: November 1998

10   9   8   7   6   5   4   3   2   1

CONTENTS

(This Contents lists articles [in italics] and broad subject categories. For more detail, consult the Index beginning on page 877.)

Year-End News

DEMOCRATIC RESURGENCE

The Democratic Party made a surprisingly strong showing in the November midterm elections, an outcome that seemed likely to hinder Republicans' attempts to drive President Clinton from office.

A largely contented electorate returned Republicans to control of both houses of Congress and a majority of the nation's governorships. But Democrats knocked off two key GOP Senate incumbents—Alfonse D'Amato of New York and Lauch Faircloth of North Carolina—picked up two Southern governorships in Alabama and South Carolina, and snatched the biggest prize of the year by winning the California governorship.

Democrats also defied the trend that the party controlling the White House loses seats in Congress in the midterm elections. Republicans had expected to add to their House majority, but ended up with a net loss of at least four seats. And the GOP had hoped to pick up the five seats in the Senate necessary for a filibuster-proof majority, but the party split remained the same—55 Republicans to 45 Democrats.

The GOP's weak performance represented a disappointment for the party, considering its immense advantage in campaign funds and the yearlong sex scandal that rocked the Clinton White House. The results sent waves of doubt and recrimination through a GOP riven by ideological fissures, leadership disputes and tactical disagreements over how to handle President Clinton's potential impeachment.

"We didn't have a national Republican message this year," said Sal Russo, a top adviser to GOP Senate candidate Matt Fong, who lost his bid to unseat liberal Democratic Senator Barbara Boxer of California. "Because we were so focused on [scandal], we didn't develop our issues." Michigan-based pollster Fred Steeper added that GOP leaders in Washington "lost their edge. . . . They got obsessed with Clinton's sex life, which was not a winning message for us this fall." By contrast, Mr. Steeper noted, some high-profile Republican governors won big victories with activist programs that "are actually trying to solve problems."

Texas Governor George W. Bush, son of the former president, displayed impressive strength among Hispanic voters in winning a landslide re-election that may serve as a springboard for his own White House bid in 2000; his younger brother Jeb Bush, meanwhile, won the governorship of Florida, another Sun Belt powerhouse. Popular Republican incumbents also swept to additional statehouse terms in New York, Pennsylvania, Michigan, Wisconsin and Connecticut.

But Democrats won the California governorship for the first time in 20 years, as Gray Davis defeated his Republican rival Dan Lungren. Amid reports of heavy black turnout, Mr. Clinton's party also snatched back territory from its old Southern base, defeating incumbent GOP Governors David Beasley of South Carolina and Fob James of Alabama in elections framed by the Democrats' support for state lotteries to fund education improvements. Democrats also captured the statehouse in Iowa for the first time in 30 years, amid a weak farm economy.

Mr. Gingrich, who has presidential ambitions of his own in 2000, is clearly anxious now for the House to stake out more of an aggressive legislative agenda. Mr. Gingrich stressed that the GOP still maintained control of the House in three consecutive elections for the first time in 70 years, which he characterized as a historic achievement.

It was clear from election-day polls that voters were generally satisfied with the state of the economy. That feeling contributed to a widespread embrace of the status quo, which favored many incumbents. Those same voters reported mixed views of Mr. Clinton, while shrugging off the idea that the election represented a referendum on the president.

MIDTERM ELECTIONS 1998

1998 State Governor Races

Here are the preliminary results for Democrats, Republicans and other major candidates in state governor contests. (i=incumbent)

ALABAMA
Donald Siegelman (D) 747,541 - 58%
Fob James (R) (i) 542,531 - 42%

ALASKA
Tony Knowles (D) (i) 95,731 - 65%
John Lindauer (R) 32,229 - 22%

ARIZONA
Paul Johnson (D) 328,268 - 36%
Jane Dee Hull (R) (i) 554,353 - 61%

ARKANSAS
Bill Bristow (D) 261,943 - 39%
Mike Huckabee (R) (i) 397,033 - 59%

CALIFORNIA
Gray Davis (D) 4,290,572 - 58%
Daniel Lungren (R) 2,837,215 - 38%

COLORADO
Gail Schoettler (D) 621,801 - 49%
Bill Owens (R) 626,559 - 49%

CONNECTICUT
Barbara Kennelly (D) 341,671 - 35%
John Rowland (R) (i) 607,997 - 63%

FLORIDA
Kenneth "Buddy" MacKay (D) 1,768,742 - 45%
John Ellis "Jeb" Bush (R) 2,179,571 - 55%

GEORGIA
Roy Barnes (D) 908,083 - 53%
Guy Millner (R) 743,243 - 43%

HAWAII
Ben Cayetano (D) (i) 197,639 - 50%
Linda Lingle (R) 192,582 - 49%

IDAHO
Robert Huntley (D) 107,415 - 29%
Dirk Kempthorne (R) 250,250 - 68%

ILLINOIS
Glenn Poshard (D) 1,557,157 - 47%
George Ryan (R) 1,681,319 - 51%

IOWA
Tom Vilsack (D) 497,729 - 52%
Jim Lightfoot (R) 442,473 - 47%

KANSAS
Tom Sawyer (D) 163,502 - 23%
Bill Graves (R) (i) 529,208 - 73%

MAINE
Thomas Connolly (D) 46,541 - 12%
James Longley (R) 73,291 - 19%
Angus King (Ind) (i) 226,067 - 59%

MARYLAND
Parris Glendening (D) (i) 826,609 - 56%
Ellen Sauerbrey (R) 662,554 - 44%

MASSACHUSETTS
Scott Harshbarger (D) 862,193 - 48%
Argeo Paul Cellucci (R) (i) 918,861 - 51%

MICHIGAN
Geoffrey Fieger (D) 1,122,275 - 38%
John Engler (R) (i) 1,868,191 - 62%

MINNESOTA
Hubert Humphrey III (D) 565,461 - 28%
Norm Coleman (R) 693,448 - 34%
Jesse Ventura (Ind) 745,307 - 37%

NEBRASKA
Bill Hoppner (D) 236,670 - 46%
Mike Johanns (R) 277,312 - 54%

NEVADA
Jan Jones (D) 181,344 - 42%
Kenny Guinn (R) 222,698 - 52%

NEW HAMPSHIRE
Jeanne Shaheen (D) (i) 209,626 - 66%
Jay Lucas (R) 97,802 - 31%

NEW MEXICO
Martin Chavez (D) 205,888 - 46%
Gary Johnson (R) (i) 240,180 - 54%

NEW YORK
Peter Vallone (D) 1,458,563 - 33%
George Pataki (R) (i) 2,395,176 - 54%

OHIO
Lee Fisher (D) 1,471,348 - 45%
Bob Taft (R) 1,650,404 - 50%

OKLAHOMA
Laura Boyd (D) 364,637 - 41%
Frank Keating (R) (i) 512,572 - 58%

OREGON
John Kitzhaber (D) (i) 265,078 - 63%
Bill Sizemore (R) 129,500 - 31%

PENNSYLVANIA
Ivan Itkin (D) 931,810 - 31%
Thomas Ridge (R) (i) 1,726,748 - 57%

RHODE ISLAND
Myrth York (D) 124,435 - 42%
Lincoln Almond (R) (i) 150,787 - 51%

SOUTH CAROLINA
Jim Hodges (D) 555,657 - 53%
David Beasley (R) (i) 473,984 - 45%

SOUTH DAKOTA
Bernie Hunhoff (D) 84,789 - 33%
William Janklow (R) (i) 165,181 - 64%

TENNESSEE
John Hooker (D) 287,052 - 30%
Don Sundquist (R) (i) 667,689 - 69%

TEXAS
Garry Mauro (D) 1,157,574 - 31%
George W. Bush (R) (i) 2,569,195 - 69%

VERMONT
Howard Dean (D) (i) 117,490 - 56%
Ruth Dwyer (R) 86,571 - 41%

WISCONSIN
Ed Garvey (D) 658,383 - 38%
Tommy Thompson (R) (i) 1,036,450 - 60%

WYOMING
John Vinich (D) 70,661 - 40%
Jim Geringer (R) (i) 97,299 - 56%

1998 U.S. House Races

Here are the preliminary results for Democrats, Republicans and other major candidates in the 435 races for the U.S. House of Representatives. (i=incumbent)

ALABAMA
District 1
Sonny Callahan (R) (i) Uncontested

District 2
Joe Fondren (D) 58,075 - 31%
Terry Everett (R) (i) 131,216 - 69%

District 3
Joe Turnham (D) 73,296 - 42%
Bob Riley (R) (i) 101,490 - 58%

District 4
Don Bevill (D) 80,224 - 44%
Robert Aderholt (R) (i) 100,744 - 56%

District 5
Bud Cramer (D) (i) 134,696 - 70%
Gil Aust (R) 58,507 - 30%

District 6
Donna Smalley (D) 57,448 - 28%
Spencer Bachus (R) (i) 145,270 - 72%

District 7
Earl Hilliard (D) (i) Uncontested

ALASKA
At-Large
Jim Duncan (D) 64,629 - 35%
Don Young (R) (i) 116,338 - 63%

ARIZONA
District 1
David Mendoza (D) 47,667 - 36%
Matt Salmon (R) (i) 85,081 - 64%

District 2
Ed Pastor (D) (i) 48,848 - 67%
Ed Barron (R) 20,977 - 29%

District 3
Stuart Starky (D) 61,697 - 33%
Bob Stump (R) (i) 124,275 - 67%

District 4
Eric Ehst (D) 43,820 - 32%
John Shadegg (R) (i) 88,716 - 64%

District 5
Tom Volgy (D) 83,992 - 45%
Jim Kolbe (R) (i) 96,144 - 52%

District 6
Steve Owens (D) 80,011 - 44%
J.D. Hayworth (R) (i) 95,207 - 53%

ARKANSAS
District 1
Marion Berry (D) (i) Uncontested

District 2
Vic Snyder (D) (i) 100,281 - 58%
Phil Wyrick (R) 72,749 - 42%

District 3
Asa Hutchinson (R) (i) 131,857 - 80%
No Democratic candidate

District 4
Judy Smith (D) 67,286 - 43%
Jay Dickey (R) (i) 90,955 - 57%

CALIFORNIA
District 1
Mike Thompson (D) 110,099 - 62%
Mark Luce (R) 58,104 - 33%

District 2
Roberts Braden (D) 64,254 - 34%
Wally Herger (R) (i) 115,120 - 61%

District 3
Sandra Dunn (D) 81,211 - 45%
Douglas Ose (R) 95,551 - 53%

District 4
David Shapiro (D) 76,071 - 35%
John Doolittle (R) (i) 136,946 - 62%

District 5
Robert Matsui (D) (i) 123,067 - 72%
Robert Dinsmore (R) 44,641 - 26%

District 6
Lynn Woolsey (D) (i) 144,998 - 58%
Ken McAuliffe (R) 63,481 - 26%

District 7
George Miller (D) (i) 117,423 - 77%
Norman Reece (R) 35,534 - 23%

District 8
Nancy Pelosi (D) (i) 119,583 - 86%
David Martz (R) 16,053 - 12%

District 9
Barbara Lee (D) (i) 126,232 - 83%
Claiborne Sanders (R) 19,978 - 13%

District 10
Ellen Tauscher (D) (i) 114,938 - 53%
Charles Ball (R) 94,200 - 44%

District 11
Robert Figueroa (D) 52,491 - 36%
Richard Pombo (R) (i) 88,307 - 61%

District 12
Tom Lantos (D) (i) 106,661 - 74%
Robert Evans (R) 30,094 - 21%

District 13
Fortney Stark (D) (i) 91,911 - 71%
James Goetz (R) 34,496 - 27%

District 14
Anna Eshoo (D) (i) 111,973 - 69%
John "Chris" Haugen (R) 46,543 - 28%

District 15
Dick Lane (D) 61,018 - 38%
Tom Campbell (R) (i) 96,493 - 60%

District 16
Zoe Lofgren (D) (i) 73,689 - 73%
Horace Thayn (R) 23,737 - 23%

District 17
Sam Farr (D) (i) 91,687 - 64%
Bill McCampbell (R) 46,558 - 33%

District 18
Gary Condit (D) (i) 104,094 - 87%
No Republican candidate

District 19
George Radanovich (R) (i) 110,103 - 80%
No Democratic candidate

District 20
Cal Dooley (D) (i) 50,637 - 61%
Cliff Unruh (R) 32,596 - 39%

District 21
Bill Thomas (R) (i) 107,913 - 79%
No Democratic candidate

District 22
Lois Capps (D) (i) 70,932 - 57%
Tom Bordonaro (R) 51,151 - 41%

District 23
Daniel Gonzalez (D) 53,641 - 40%
Elton Gallegly (R) (i) 79,420 - 60%

District 24
Brad Sherman (D) (i) 89,925 - 58%
Randy Hoffman (R) 58,842 - 38%

District 25
Howard McKeon (R) (i) 101,019 - 75%
No Democratic candidate

District 26
Howard Berman (D) (i) 62,099 - 82%
No Republican candidate

District 27
Barry Gordon (D) 65,413 - 47%
James Rogan (R) (i) 70,210 - 50%

District 28
Janice Nelson D 55,626 - 39%
David Dreier (R) (i) 81,314 - 58%

District 29
Henry Waxman (D) (i) 116,213 - 74%
Mike Gottlieb (R) 34,871 - 22%

District 30
Xavier Becerra (D) (i) 52,358 - 82%
Patricia Parker (R) 11,677 - 18%

District 31
Matthew Martinez (D) (i) 55,402 - 71%
Frank Moreno (R) 17,621 - 22%

District 32
Julian Dixon (D) (i) 100,291 - 87%
Larry Ardito (R) 12,881 - 11%

District 33
Lucille Roybal-Allard (D) (i) 39,708 - 87%
Wayne Miller (R) 5,736 - 13%

District 34
Grace Napolitano (D) 69,598 - 68%
Edward Perez (R) 29,252 - 28%

District 35
Maxine Waters (D) (i) 71,111 - 89%
No Republican candidate

District 36
Janice Hahn (D) 75,434 - 47%
Steven Kuykendall (R) 78,686 - 49%

District 37
Juanita Millender-McDonald (D) (i) 64,381 - 85%
Saul Lankster (R) 11,203 - 15%

District 38
Peter Mathews (D) 54,012 - 44%
Steve Horn (R) (i) 64,083 - 53%

District 39
A. Groom (D) 47,428 - 34%
Ed Royce (R) (i) 87,262 - 63%

District 40
Robert Conaway (D) 45,736 - 32%
Jerry Lewis (R) (i) 92,991 - 65%

District 41
Eileen Ansari (D) 47,785 - 41%
Gary Miller (R) 61,725 - 53%

District 42
George Brown (D) (i) 59,297 - 55%
Elia Pirozzi (R) 43,091 - 40%

District 43
Mike Rayburn (D) 51,017 - 38%
Ken Calvert (R) (i) 74,226 - 55%

District 44
Ralph Waite (D) 52,872 - 36%
Mary Bono (R) (i) 88,079 - 60%

District 45
Patricia Neal (D) 52,421 - 38%
Dana Rohrabacher (R) (i) 81,680 - 58%

District 46
Loretta Sanchez (D) (i) 40,346 - 56%
Robert Dornan (R) 28,227 - 39%

District 47
Christina Avalos (D) 50,354 - 30%
Christopher Cox (R) (i) 114,452 - 67%

District 48
Ron Packard (R) (i) 114,022 - 77%
No Democratic candidate

District 49
Christine Kehoe (D) 72,510 - 46%
Brian Bilbray (R) (i) 76,566 - 49%

District 50
Bob Filner (D) (i) Uncontested

District 51
Daniel Kripke (D) 60,330 - 35%
Randy Cunningham (R) (i) 106,086 - 61%

District 52
Duncan Hunter (R) (i) 100,424 - 76%
No Democratic candidate

COLORADO
District 1
Diana DeGette (D) (i) 116,544 - 67%
Nancy McClanahan (R) 52,401 - 30%

District 2
Mark Udall (D) 113,933 - 50%
Bob Greenlee (R) 108,379 - 47%

District 3
Reed Kelley (D) 69,274 - 31%
Scott McInnis (R) (i) 146,289 - 66%

District 4
Susan Kirkpatrick (D) 75,588 - 40%
Robert Schaffer (R) (i) 111,745 - 60%

District 5
Ken Alford (D) 55,275 - 26%
Joel Hefley (R) (i) 155,167 - 73%

District 6
Henry Strauss (D) 85,614 - 43%
Tom Tancredo (R) 110,090 - 55%

CONNECTICUT
District 1
John Larson (D) 80,992 - 59%
Kevin O'Connor (R) 55,874 - 41%

District 2
Sam Gejdenson (D) (i) 90,000 - 61%
Gary Koval (R) 51,687 - 35%

District 3
Rosa DeLauro (D) (i) 107,999 - 71%
Martin Reust (R) 41,782 - 28%

District 4
Jonathan Kantrowitz (D) 40,047 - 31%
Christopher Shays (R) (i) 89,816 - 68%

District 5
James Maloney (D) (i) 70,409 - 50%
Mark Nielsen (R) 67,409 - 48%

District 6
Charlotte Koskoff (D) 57,816 - 38%
Nancy Johnson (R) (i) 89,051 - 59%

DELAWARE
At-Large
Dennis Williams (D) 57,847 - 32%
Michael Castle (R) (i) 120,605 - 66%

FLORIDA
District 1
Joe Scarborough (R) (i) Uncontested

District 2
Allen Boyd (D) (i) Uncontested

District 3
Corrine Brown (D) (i) 66,363 - 56%
Bill Randall (R) 53,075 - 44%

District 4
Tillie Fowler (R) (i) Uncontested

District 5
Karen Thurman (D) (i) 131,892 - 66%
No Republican candidate

District 6
Clifford Stearns (R) (i) Uncontested

District 7
John Mica (R) (i) Uncontested

District 8
Al Krulick (D) 54,187 - 34%
Bill McCollum (R) (i) 104,146 - 66%

District 9
Michael Bilirakis (R) (i) Uncontested

District 10
Bill Young (R) (i) Uncontested

District 11
Jim Davis (D) (i) 85,167 - 65%
Joe Chillura (R) 46,107 - 35%

District 12
Charles Canady (R) (i) Uncontested

District 13
Dan Miller (R) (i) Uncontested

District 14
Porter Goss (R) (i) Uncontested

District 15
David Golding (D) 75,639 - 37%
Dave Weldon (R) (i) 129,232 - 63%

District 16
Mark Foley (R) (i) Uncontested

District 17
Carrie Meek (D) (i) Uncontested

District 18
Ileana Ros-Lehtinen (R) (i) Uncontested

District 19
Robert Wexler (D) (i) Uncontested

District 20
Peter Deutsch (D) (i) Uncontested

District 21
Patrick Cusack (D) 28,378 - 25%
Lincoln Diaz-Balart (R) (i) 84,003 - 75%

District 22
Clay Shaw (R) (i) Uncontested

District 23
Alcee Hastings (D) (i) Uncontested

GEORGIA
District 1
Jack Kingston (R) (i) Uncontested

District 2
Sanford Bishop (D) (i) 76,123 - 57%
Joseph McCormick (R) 56,692 - 43%

District 3
Michael "Mac" Collins (R) (i) Uncontested

District 4
Cynthia McKinney (D) (i) 95,320 - 63%
Sunny Warren (R) 55,091 - 37%

District 5
John Lewis (D) (i) 85,449 - 80%
John H. Lewis (R) 21,907 - 20%

District 6
Gary Pelphrey (D) 61,944 - 30%
Newt Gingrich (R) (i) 144,339 - 70%

District 7
James Williams (D) 59,394 - 44%
Bob Barr (R) (i) 74,761 - 56%

District 8
Ronald Cain (D) 52,473 - 38%
Saxby Chambliss (R) (i) 86,257 - 62%

District 9
Nathan Deal (R) (i) Uncontested

District 10
Denise Freeman (D) 59,448 - 40%
Charles Norwood (R) (i) 88,177 - 60%

District 11
Vincent Littman (D) 49,682 - 31%
John Linder (R) (i) 108,413 - 69%

HAWAII
District 1
Neil Abercrombie (D) (i) 113,686 - 62%
Gene Ward (R) 66,661 - 36%

District 2
Patsy Mink (D) (i) 139,005 - 69%
Carol Douglass (R) 48,791 - 24%

IDAHO
District 1
Dan Williams (D) 88,471 - 45%
Helen Chenoweth (R) (i) 108,691 - 55%

District 2
Richard Stallings (D) 75,959 - 45%
Mike Simpson (R) 89,439 - 53%

ILLINOIS
District 1
Bobby Rush (D) (i) 136,970 - 86%
Marlene White Ahimaz (R) 17,704 - 11%

District 2
Jesse Jackson Jr. (D) (i) 142,608 - 89%
Robert Gordon (R) 15,611 - 10%

District 3
William Lipinski (D) (i) 112,679 - 72%
Robert Marshall (R) 43,301 - 28%

District 4
Luis Gutierrez (D) (i) 51,803 - 82%
John Birch (R) 10,120 - 16%

District 5
Rod Blagojevich (D) (i) 91,399 - 74%
Alan Spitz (R) 32,465 - 26%

District 6
Thomas Cramer (D) 49,603 - 30%
Henry Hyde (R) (i) 111,115 - 67%

District 7
Danny Davis (D) (i) 125,798 - 93%
No Republican candidate

District 8
Mike Rothman (D) 47,268 - 31%
Philip Crane (R) (i) 103,459 - 69%

District 9
Janice Schakowsky (D) 104,809 - 74%
Herbert Sohn (R) 32,771 - 23%

District 10
John Porter (R) (i) Uncontested

District 11
Gary Mueller (D) 66,618 - 41%
Jerry Weller (R) (i) 95,864 - 59%

District 12
Jerry Costello (D) (i) 99,606 - 60%
William Price (R) 65,409 - 40%

District 13
Susan Hynes (D) 77,712 - 39%
Judy Biggert (R) 121,736 - 61%

District 14
Robert Cozzi (D) 50,837 - 30%
J. Dennis Hastert (R) (i) 117,291 - 70%

District 15
Laurel Prussing (D) 64,477 - 39%
Thomas Ewing (R) (i) 102,901 - 61%

District 16
Donald Manzullo (R) (i) Uncontested

District 17
Lane Evans (D) (i) 100,128 - 52%
Mark Baker (R) 94,072 - 48%

District 18
Ray LaHood (R) (i) Uncontested

District 19
David Phelps (D) 123,249 - 58%
Brent Winters (R) 90,185 - 42%

District 20
Rich Verticchio (D) 76,475 - 39%
John Shimkus (R) (i) 121,103 - 61%

INDIANA
District 1
Peter Visclosky (D) (i) 90,656 - 73%
Michael Petyo (R) 32,503 - 26%

District 2
Sherman Boles (D) 62,052 - 38%
David McIntosh (R) (i) 98,938 - 61%

District 3
Tim Roemer (D) (i) 84,260 - 58%
Daniel Holtz (R) 60,665 - 42%

District 4
Mark Wehrle (D) 53,862 - 37%
Mark Souder (R) (i) 92,881 - 63%

District 5
David Steele (D) 58,032 - 36%
Steve Buyer (R) (i) 101,141 - 63%

District 6
Bob Kern (D) 31,185 - 17%
Dan Burton (R) (i) 133,235 - 72%

District 7
Samuel Hillenburg (D) 44,550 - 28%
Edward Pease (R) (i) 109,511 - 69%

District 8
Gail Riecken (D) 81,882 - 46%
John Hostettler (R) (i) 91,297 - 52%

District 9
Baron Hill (D) 93,075 - 51%
Jean Leising (R) 87,978 - 48%

District 10
Julia Carson (D) (i) 65,951 - 58%
Gary Hofmeister (R) 44,919 - 39%

IOWA
District 1
Bob Rush (D) 79,559 - 42%
Jim Leach (R) (i) 106,350 - 57%

District 2
Rob Tully (D) 82,441 - 44%
Jim Nussle (R) (i) 103,667 - 55%

District 3
Leonard Boswell (D) (i) 106,638 - 57%
Larry McKibben (R) 77,017 - 41%

District` 4
Jon Dvorak (D) 66,059 - 34%
Greg Ganske (R) (i) 126,124 - 65%

District 5
Tom Latham (R) (i) Uncontested

KANSAS
District 1
James Phillips (D) 36,113 - 19%
Jerry Moran (R) (i) 151,028 - 81%

District 2
James Clark (D) 68,960 - 39%
Jim Ryun (R) (i) 107,590 - 61%

District 3
Dennis Moore (D) 102,299 - 52%
Vince Snowbarger (R) (i) 92,801 - 48%

District 4
James Lawing (D) 61,432 - 38%
Todd Tiahrt (R) (i) 94,092 - 59%

KENTUCKY
District 1
Thomas Barlow (D) 77,219 - 45%
Edward Whitfield (R) (i) 94,815 - 55%

District 2
Bob Evans (D) 62,419 - 35%
Ron Lewis (R) (i) 112,657 - 64%

District 3
Chris Gorman (D) 92,865 - 48%
Anne Northup (R) (i) 100,690 - 52%

District 4
Kenneth Lucas (D) 92,803 - 53%
Gex Williams (R) 80,824 - 47%

District 5
Sidney Bailey-Bamer (D) 38,900 - 22%
Harold Rogers (R) (i) 138,846 - 78%

District 6
Ernesto Scorsone (D) 89,665 - 46%
Ernie Fletcher (R) 103,381 - 53%

LOUISIANA
District 1
Robert Livingston (R) (i) Uncontested

District 2
William Jefferson (D) (i) 102,056 - 86%
No Republican candidate

District 3
Billy Tauzin (R) (i) Uncontested

District 4
Jim McCrery (R) (i) Uncontested

District 5
John Cooksey (R) (i) Uncontested

District 6
Marjorie McKeithen (D) 94,172 - 49%
Richard Baker (R) (i) 96,944 - 51%

District 7
Chris John (D) (i) Uncontested

MAINE
District 1
Thomas Allen (D) (i) 117,292 - 61%
Ross Connelly (R) 68,567 - 35%

District 2
John Baldacci (D) (i) 139,095 - 76%
Jon Reisman (R) 42,875 - 24%

MARYLAND
District 1
Irving Pinder (D) 58,320 - 31%
Wayne Gilchrest (R) (i) 130,087 - 69%

District 2
Kenneth Bosley (D) 62,709 - 31%
Robert Ehrlich (R) (i) 140,644 - 69%

District 3
Benjamin Cardin (D) (i) 134,941 - 78%
Colin Harby (R) 38,378 - 22%

District 4
Albert Wynn (D) (i) 126,755 - 86%
John Kimble (R) 20,619 - 14%

District 5
Steny Hoyer (D) (i) 123,339 - 66%
Robert Ostrom (R) 64,637 - 34%

District 6
Timothy McCown (D) 71,047 - 37%
Roscoe Bartlett (R) (i) 122,434 - 63%

District 7
Elijah Cummings (D) (i) 112,546 - 86%
Kenneth Kondner (R) 18,049 - 14%

District 8
Ralph Neas (D) 83,997 - 40%
Constance Morella (R) (i) 127,833 - 60%

MASSACHUSETTS
District 1
John Olver (D) (i) 114,878 - 72%
Gregory Morgan (R) 44,605 - 28%

District 2
Richard Neal (D) (i) Uncontested

District 3
James McGovern (D) (i) 99,508 - 58%
Matthew Amorello (R) 69,972 - 41%

District 4
Barney Frank (D) (i) Uncontested

District 5
Martin Meehan (D) (i) 99,594 - 69%
David Coleman (R) 44,493 - 31%

District 6
John Tierney (D) (i) 104,712 - 55%
Peter Torkildsen (R) 81,426 - 42%

District 7
Edward Markey (D) (i) 137,032 - 71%
Patricia Long (R) 56,901 - 29%

District 8
Michael Capuano (D) 97,181 - 82%
Philip Hyde (R) 13,302 - 11%

District 9
Joe Moakley (D) (i) Uncontested

District 10
William Delahunt (D) (i) 132,537 - 70%
Eric Bleicken (R) 57,771 - 30%

MICHIGAN
District 1
Bart Stupak (D) (i) 129,672 - 59%
Michelle McManus (R) 87,455 - 40%

District 2
Bob Shrauger (D) 63,161 - 30%
Peter Hoekstra (R) (i) 146,802 - 69%

District 3
John Ferguson (D) 49,432 - 25%
Vernon Ehlers (R) (i) 146,201 - 73%

District 4
Dave Camp (R) (i) 154,052 - 91%
No Democratic candidate

District 5
James Barcia (D) (i) 134,507 - 71%
Donald Brewster (R) 51,061 - 27%

District 6
Clarence Annen (D) 45,345 - 28%
Fred Upton (R) (i) 113,254 - 70%

District 7
Jim Berryman (D) 71,952 - 40%
Nick Smith (R) (i) 103,127 - 57%

District 8
Debbie Stabenow (D) (i) 125,167 - 57%
Susan Munsell (R) 84,255 - 39%

District 9
Dale Kildee (D) (i) 105,262 - 56%
Tom McMillin (R) 78,797 - 42%

District 10
David Bonior (D) (i) 107,861 - 52%
Brian Palmer (R) 93,326 - 45%

District 11
Travis Reeds (D) 76,097 - 34%
Joseph Knollenberg (R) (i) 144,247 - 64%

District 12
Sander Levin (D) (i) 104,742 - 56%
Leslie Touma (R) 79,342 - 42%

District 13
Lynn Rivers (D) (i) 95,456 - 58%
Thomas Hickey (R) 64,870 - 40%

District 14
John Conyers (D) (i) 116,197 - 87%
Vendella Collins (R) 15,404 - 11%

District 15
Carolyn Kilpatrick (D) (i) 100,055 - 86%
Chrysanthea Boyd-Fields (R) 12,542 - 11%

District 16
John Dingell (D) (i) 115.595 - 67%
William Morse (R) 53,678 - 31%

MINNESOTA
District 1
Tracy Beckman (D) 108,091 - 45%
Gil Gutknecht (R) (i) 130,760 - 55%

District 2
David Minge (D) (i) 148,246 - 57%
Craig Duehring (R) 99,434 - 38%

District 3
Stanley Leino (D) 66,196 - 24%
Jim Ramstad (R) (i) 202,698 - 72%

District 4
Bruce Vento (D) (i) 126,094 - 54%
Dennis Newinski (R) 93,455 - 40%

District 5
Martin Sabo (D) (i) 139,081 - 67%
Frank Taylor (R) 58,045 - 28%

District 6
William Luther (D) (i) 148,016 - 51%
John Kline (R) 135,755 - 47%

District 7
Collin Peterson (D) (i) 166,036 - 72%
Aleta Edin (R) 64,550 - 28%

District 8
James Oberstar (D) (i) 170,375 - 66%
Jerry Shuster (R) 69,184 - 27%

MISSISSIPPI
District 1
Rex Weathers (D) 29,894 - 31%
Roger Wicker (R) (i) 65,761 - 67%

District 2
Bennie Thompson (D) (i) 79,156 - 71%
No Republican candidate

District 3
Charles Pickering (R) (i) 81,826 - 85%
No Democratic candidate

District 4
Ronnie Shows (D) 71,132 - 53%
Delbert Hosemann (R) 60,595 - 45%

District 5
Gene Taylor (D) (i) 77,030 - 78%
Randy McDonnell (R) 19,003 - 19%

MISSOURI
District 1
William Clay (D) (i) 91,702 - 73%
Richmond Soluade (R) 30,746 - 24%

District 2
John Ross (D) 57,565 - 28%
James Talent (R) (i) 142,313 - 70%

District 3
Richard Gephardt (D) (i) 98,281 - 56%
William Federer (R) 74,002 - 42%

District 4
Ike Skelton (D) (i) 128,156 - 70%
Cecilia Noland (R) 50,994 - 28%

District 5
Karen McCarthy (D) (i) 101,215 - 66%
Penny Bennett (R) 47,558 - 31%

District 6
Pat Danner (D) (i) 136,776 - 71%
Jeff Bailey (R) 51,679 - 27%

District 7
Marc Perkel (D) 43,389 - 24%
Roy Blunt (R) (i) 129,588 - 73%

District 8
Anthony Heckemeyer (D) 59,485 - 36%
Jo Ann Emerson (R) (i) 104,320 - 63%

District 9
Linda Vogt (D) 66,684 - 36%
Kenny Hulshof (R) (i) 116,195 - 62%

MONTANA
At-Large
Dusty Deschamps (D) 145,793 - 44%
Rick Hill (R) (i) 173,925 - 53%

NEBRASKA
District 1
Don Eret (D) 47,830 - 26%
Doug Bereuter (R) (i) 133,015 - 74%

District 2
Michael Scott (D) 50,169 - 34%
Lee Terry (R) 96,510 - 66%

District 3
Bill Barrett (R) (i) 138,604 - 85%
No Democratic candidate

NEVADA
District 1
Shelley Berkley (D) 79,315 - 49%
Don Chairez (R) 73,540 - 46%

District 2
Jim Gibbons (R) (i) 199,296 - 81%
No Democratic candidate

NEW HAMPSHIRE
District 1
Peter Flood (D) 50,091 - 33%
John E. Sununu (R) (i) 101,265 - 67%

District 2
Mary Rauh (D) 71,700 - 45%
Charles Bass (R) (i) 84,806 - 53%

NEW JERSEY
District 1
Robert Andrews (D) (i) 89,297 - 73%
Ronald Richards (R) 27,467 - 22%

District 2
Derek Hunsberger (D) 43,269 - 31%
Frank LoBiondo (R) (i) 92,196 - 66%

District 3
Steven Polansky (D) 54,626 - 35%
Jim Saxton (R) (i) 96,328 - 62%

District 4
Larry Schneider (D) 51,782 - 35%
Christopher Smith (R) (i) 91,924 - 62%

District 5
Mike Schneider (D) 52,783 - 32%
Marge Roukema (R) (i) 100,002 - 60%

District 6
Frank Pallone (D) (i) 77,722 - 57%
Michael Ferguson (R) 55,011 - 40%

District 7
Maryanne Connelly (D) 64,268 - 44%
Bob Franks (R) (i) 75,809 - 52%

District 8
William Pascrell (D) (i) 79,403 - 62%
Matthew Kirnan (R) 45,624 - 36%

District 9
Steven Rothman (D) (i) 88,423 - 65%
Steve Lonegan (R) 46,111 - 34%

District 10
Donald Payne (D) (i) 78,705 - 83%
Stan Wnuck (R) 10,316 - 11%

District 11
John Scollo (D) 43,919 - 30%
Rodney Frelinghuysen (R) (i) 100,625 - 68%

District 12
Rush Holt (D) 91,573 - 50%
Mike Pappas (R) (i) 86,448 - 47%

District 13
Robert Menendez (D) (i) 68,501 - 80%
Theresa de Leon (R) 14,221 - 17%

NEW MEXICO
District 1
Phillip Maloof (D) 61,250 - 43%
Heather Wilson (R) (i) 66,164 - 46%

District 2
Shirley Baca (D) 61,040 - 42%
Joe Skeen (R) (i) 84,158 - 58%

District 3
Thomas Udall (D) 83,265 - 53%
William Redmond (R) (i) 66,856 - 43%

NEW YORK
District 1
William Holst (D) 52,136 - 36%
Michael Forbes (R) (i) 93,664 - 64%

District 2
John Bace (D) 36,394 - 30%
Rick Lazio (R) (i) 81,119 - 66%

District 3
Kevin Langberg (D) 60,302 - 35%
Peter King (R) (i) 112,418 - 65%

District 4
Carolyn McCarthy (D) (i) 86,157 - 52%
Gregory Becker (R) 76,874 - 47%

District 5
Gary Ackerman (D) (i) 92,490 - 65%
David Pinzon (R) 47,802 - 33%

District 6
Gregory Meeks (D) (i) Uncontested

District 7
Joseph Crowley (D) 45,398 - 66%
James Dillon (R) 19,332 - 28%

District 8
Jerrold Nadler (D) (i) 101,493 - 86%
Theodore Howard (R) 17,028 - 14%

District 9
Anthony Weiner (D) 64,761 - 66%
Louis Telano (R) 23,500 - 24%

District 10
Edolphus Towns (D) (i) 77,630 - 92%
Ernestine Brown (R) 5,337 - 6%

District 11
Major Owens (D) (i) 70,541 - 90%
David Greene (R) 7,105 - 9%

District 12
Nydia Velazquez (D) (i) 50,387 - 82%
Rosemarie Markgraf (R) 7,966 - 13%

District 13
Eugene Prisco (D) 38,044 - 33%
Vito Fossella (R) (i) 74,484 - 66%

District 14
Carolyn Maloney (D) (i) 101,848 - 77%
Stephanie Kupferman (R) 30,426 - 23%

District 15
Charles Rangel (D) (i) 82,973 - 93%
David Cunningham (R) 5,116 - 6%

District 16
Jose Serrano (D) (i) 64,509 - 95%
Thomas Bayley (R) 2,396 - 4%

District 17
Eliot Engel (D) (i) 75,443 - 88%
Peter Fiumefreddo (R) 10,592 - 12%

District 18
Nita Lowey (D) (i) 83,583 - 83%
No Republican candidate

District 19
Richard Collins (D) 52,503 - 33%
Sue Kelly (R) (i) 98,512 - 63%

District 20
Paul Feiner (D) 59,555 - 40%
Benjamin Gilman (R) (i) 86,814 - 58%

District 21
Michael McNulty (D) (i) 138,913 - 74%
Lauren Ayers (R) 48,404 - 26%

District 22
Jean Bordewich (D) 76,339 - 42%
John Sweeney (R) 100,743 - 55%

District 23
Sherwood Boehlert (R) (i) 104,846 - 80%
No Democratic candidate

District 24
Neil Tallon (D) 28,329 - 21%
John McHugh (R) (i) 106,949 - 79%

District 25
Yvonne Rothenberg (D) 51,156 - 31%
James Walsh (R) (i) 114,798 - 69%

District 26
Maurice Hinchey (D) (i) 101,762 - 62%
William Walker (R) 51,299 - 31%

District 27
Bill Cook (D) 71,461 - 42%
Thomas Reynolds (R) 99,427 - 58%

District 28
Louise Slaughter (D) (i) 113,742 - 64%
Richard Kaplan (R) 54,871 - 31%

District 29
John LaFalce (D) (i) 89,792 - 57%
Chris Collins (R) 63,616 - 41%

District 30
Crystal Peoples (D) 52,716 - 32%
Jack Quinn (R) (i) 110,327 - 68%

District 31
Caleb Rossiter (D) 38,112 - 25%
Amo Houghton (R) (i) 103,561 - 68%

NORTH CAROLINA
District 1
Eva Clayton (D) (i) 84,927 - 62%
Ted Tyler (R) 50,175 - 37%

District 2
Bob Etheridge (D) (i) 96,765 - 57%
Dan Page (R) 71,163 - 42%

District 3
Jon Williams (D) 49,472 - 37%
Walter Jones (R) (i) 82,517 - 62%

District 4
David Price (D) (i) 127,919 - 57%
Thomas Roberg (R) 92,685 - 42%

District 5
Michael Robinson (D) 54,736 - 32%
Richard Burr (R) (i) 116,939 - 68%

District 6
Howard Coble (R) (i) 110,484 - 89%
No Democratic candidate

District 7
Mike McIntyre (D) (i) 122,838 - 91%
No Republican candidate

District 8
Mike Taylor (D) 63,558 - 48%
Robin Hayes (R) 67,059 - 51%

District 9
Rory Blake (D) 46,370 - 30%
Sue Myrick (R) (i) 107,579 - 69%

District 10
Cass Ballenger (R) (i) 117,738 - 86%
No Democratic candidate

District 11
David Young (D) 73,675 - 42%
Charles Taylor (R) (i) 100,153 - 57%

District 12
Melvin Watt (D) (i) 81,150 - 56%
Scott Keadle (R) 61,482 - 42%

NORTH DAKOTA
At-Large
Earl Pomeroy (D) (i) 119,077 - 56%
Kevin Cramer (R) 87,137 - 41%

OHIO
District 1
Roxanne Qualls (D) 79,016 - 47%
Steve Chabot (R) (i) 90,060 - 53%

District 2
Charles Sanders (D) 48,141 - 24%
Rob Portman (R) (i) 150,740 - 76%

District 3
Tony Hall (D) (i) 111,890 - 69%
John Shondel (R) 49,594 - 31%

District 4
Paul McClain (D) 62,537 - 36%
Michael Oxley (R) (i) 109,948 - 64%

District 5
Susan Davenport Darrow (D) 61,085 - 33%
Paul Gillmor (R) (i) 122,360 - 67%

District 6
Ted Strickland (D) (i) 101,231 - 57%
Nancy Hollister (R) 76,949 - 43%

District 7
Donald Minor (D) 49,058 - 28%
Dave Hobson (R) (i) 118,729 - 67%

District 8
John Griffin (D) 51,980 - 29%
John Boehner (R) (i) 125,645 - 71%

District 9
Marcy Kaptur (D) (i) 128,844 - 81%
Edward Emery (R) 30,117 - 19%

District 10
Dennis Kucinich (D) (i) 107,854 - 67%
Joseph Slovenec (R) 53,836 - 33%

District 11
Stephanie Tubbs Jones (D) 110,931 - 79%
James Hereford (R) 18,728 - 13%

District 12
Edward Brown (D) 67,583 - 37%
John Kasich (R) (i) 114,413 - 63%

District 13
Sherrod Brown (D) (i) 115,168 - 62%
Grace Drake (R) 71,789 - 38%

District 14
Thomas Sawyer (D) (i) 104,243 - 63%
Thomas Watkins (R) 62,027 - 37%

District 15
Adam Miller (D) 44,986 - 26%
Deborah Pryce (R) (i) 100,419 - 59%

District 16
Peter Ferguson (D) 64,631 - 36%
Ralph Regula (R) (i) 114,770 - 64%

District 17
James Traficant (D) (i) 122,157 - 68%
Paul Alberty (R) 57,116 - 32%

District 18
Robert Burch (D) 73,678 - 40%
Bob Ney (R) (i) 111,988 - 60%

District 19
Elizabeth Kelley (D) 62,993 - 34%
Steven LaTourette (R) (i) 124,388 - 66%

OKLAHOMA
District 1
Howard Plowman (D) 56,309 - 38%
Steve Largent (R) (i) 91,031 - 62%

District 2
Kent Pharaoh (D) 65,271 - 40%
Tom Coburn (R) (i) 93,114 - 57%

District 3
Walt Roberts (D) 55,163 - 38%
Wes Watkins (R) (i) 89,801 - 62%

District 4
Ben Odom (D) 52,107 - 38%
J.C. Watts (R) (i) 83,272 - 62%

District 5
M.C. Smothermon (D) 48,182 - 32%
Ernest Istook (R) (i) 103,217 - 68%

District 6
Paul Barby (D) 43,555 - 33%
Frank Lucas (R) (i) 84,901 - 65%

OREGON
District 1
David Wu (D) 39,816 - 52%
Molly Bordonaro (R) 34,188 - 45%

District 2
Kevin Campbell (D) 38,719 - 35%
Greg Walden (R) 67,988 - 61%

District 3
Earl Blumenauer (D) (i) 46,334 - 84%
No Republican candidate

District 4
Peter DeFazio (D) (i) 71,872 - 68%
Steve Webb (R) 33,113 - 31%

District 5
Darlene Hooley (D) (i) 35,485 - 55%
Marylin Shannon (R) 25,933 - 40%

PENNSYLVANIA
District 1
Robert Brady (D) (i) 76,570 - 81%
William Harrison (R) 15,977 - 17%

District 2
Chaka Fattah (D) (i) 102,126 - 86%
Anne Marie Mulligan (R) 16,082 - 14%

District 3
Robert Borski (D) (i) 67,064 - 60%
Charles Dougherty (R) 44,666 - 40%

District 4
Ron Klink (D) (i) 103,190 - 64%
Mike Turzai (R) 58,320 - 36%

District 5
John Peterson (R) (i) 99,795 - 85%
No Democratic candidate

District 6
Tim Holden (D) (i) 84,573 - 61%
John Meckley (R) 53,551 - 39%

District 7
Martin D'Urso (D) 46,545 - 28%
Curt Weldon (R) (i) 119,163 - 72%

District 8
Bill Tuthill (D) 48,281 - 33%
Jim Greenwood (R) (i) 93,762 - 63%

District 9
Bud Shuster (R) (i) Uncontested

District 10
Patrick Casey (D) 83,419 - 48%
Donald Sherwood (R) 84,015 - 49%

District 11
Paul Kanjorski (D) (i) 88,461 - 67%
Stephen Urban (R) 43,850 - 33%

District 12
John Murtha (D) (i) 100,264 - 68%
Timothy Holloway (R) 46,210 - 32%

District 13
Joseph Hoeffel (D) 94,464 - 52%
Jon Fox (R) (i) 85,110 - 47%

District 14
William Coyne (D) (i) 82,746 - 60%
Bill Ravotti (R) 52,747 - 38%

District 15
Roy Afflerbach (D) 66,598 - 45%
Patrick Toomey (R) 81,472 - 55%

District 16
Robert Yorczyk (D) 40,037 - 29%
Joseph Pitts (R) (i) 95,801 - 71%

District 17
George Gekas (R) (i) Uncontested

District 18
Michael Doyle (D) (i) 97,643 - 68%
Richard Walker (R) 46,764 - 32%

District 19
Linda Ropp (D) 40,614 - 29%
William Goodling (R) (i) 96,268 - 68%

District 20
Frank Mascara (D) (i) Uncontested

District 21
Larry Klemens (D) 54,866 - 37%
Philip English (R) (i) 93,452 - 63%

RHODE ISLAND
District 1
Patrick Kennedy (D) (i) 89,940 - 67%
Ronald Santa (R) 36,882 - 27%

District 2
Robert Weygand (D) (i) 106,903 - 72%
John Matson (R) 36,719 - 25%

SOUTH CAROLINA
District 1
Mark Sanford (R) (i) 114,555 - 91%
No Democratic candidate

District 2
Jane Frederick (D) 81,204 - 41%
Floyd Spence (R) (i) 116,337 - 58%

District 3
Lindsey Graham (R) (i) Uncontested

District 4
Glenn Reese (D) 73,224 - 40%
James DeMint (R) 104,965 - 58%

District 5
John Spratt (D) (i) 87,416 - 57%
Mike Burkhold (R) 62,232 - 41%

District 6
James Clyburn (D) (i) 110,825 - 73%
Gary McLeod (R) 38,506 - 25%

SOUTH DAKOTA
At-Large
Jeff Moser (D) 63,878 - 25%
John Thune (R) (i) 192,742 - 75%

TENNESSEE
District 1
Kay White (D) 30,595 - 31%
William Jenkins (R) (i) 68,644 - 69%

District 2
John Duncan (R) (i) 91,450 - 89%
No Democratic candidate

District 3
James Lewis (D) 35,491 - 31%
Zach Wamp (R) (i) 75,863 - 66%

District 4
Jerry Cooper (D) 42,663 - 40%
Van Hilleary (R) (i) 62,869 - 60%

District 5
Bob Clement (D) (i) 74,533 - 83%
No Republican candidate

District 6
Bart Gordon (D) (i) 74,758 - 55%
Walt Massey (R) 62,217 - 45%

District 7
Ed Bryant (R) (i) Uncontested

District 8
John Tanner (D) (i) Uncontested

District 9
Harold Ford Jr. (D) (i) 75,428 - 79%
Claude Burdikoff (R) 18,078 - 19%

TEXAS
District 1
Max Sandlin (D) (i) 80,118 - 59%
Dennis Boerner (R) 54,895 - 41%

District 2
Jim Turner (D) (i) 81,824 - 58%
Brian Babin (R) 57,180 - 41%

District 3
Sam Johnson (R) (i) 103,391 - 91%
No Democratic candidate

District 4
Ralph Hall (D) (i) 83,985 - 58%
Jim Lohmeyer (R) 58,944 - 41%

District 5
Victor Morales (D) 45,950 - 44%
Pete Sessions (R) (i) 58,628 - 56%

District 6
Ben Boothe (D) 39,700 - 26%
Joe Barton (R) (i) 112,035 - 73%

District 7
Bill Archer (R) (i) 110,999 - 93%
No Democratic candidate

District 8
Kevin Brady (R) (i) 123,359 - 91%
No Democratic candidate

District 9
Nick Lampson (D) (i) 86,051 - 64%
Tom Cottar (R) 49,105 - 36%

District 10
Lloyd Doggett (D) (i) 116,111 - 85%
No Republican candidate

District 11
Chet Edwards (D) (i) 71,956 - 83%
No Republican candidate

District 12
Tom Hall (D) 39,084 - 36%
Kay Granger (R) (i) 66,737 - 62%

District 13
Mark Harmon (D) 36,776 - 31%
William Thornberry (R) (i) 80,594 - 68%

District 14
Loy Sneary (D) 67,897 - 44%
Ron Paul (R) (i) 84,443 - 55%

District 15
Ruben Hinojosa (D) (i) 48,282 - 59%
Tom Haughey (R) 33,018 - 41%

District 16
Silvestre Reyes (D) (i) 67,477 - 88%
No Republican candidate

District 17
Charles Stenholm (D) (i) 79,491 - 54%
Rudy Izzard (R) 66,717 - 45%

District 18
Sheila Jackson Lee (D) (i) 82,079 - 90%
No Republican candidate

District 19
Sidney Blankenship (D) 21,141 - 16%
Larry Combest (R) (i) 108,249 - 84%

District 20
Charlie Gonzalez (D) 50,343 - 63%
James Walker (R) 28,324 - 36%

District 21
Lamar Smith (R) (i) 161,971 - 91%
No Democratic candidate

District 22
Hill Kemp (D) 45,381 - 34%
Tom DeLay (R) (i) 87,806 - 65%

District 23
Charles Jones (D) 40,308 - 35%
Henry Bonilla (R) (i) 73,273 - 64%

District 24
Martin Frost (D) (i) 52,931 - 58%
Shawn Terry (R) 37,358 - 41%

District 25
Ken Bentsen (D) (i) 58,444 - 58%
John Sanchez (R) 41,620 - 41%

District 26
Dick Armey (R) (i) 113,095 - 88%
No Democratic candidate

District 27
Solomon Ortiz (D) (i) 61,337 - 63%
Erol Stone (R) 34,301 - 35%

District 28
Ciro Rodriguez (D) (i) 71,844 - 91%
No Republican candidate

District 29
Gene Green (D) (i) 44,276 - 93%
No Republican candidate

District 30
Eddie Bernice Johnson (D) (i) 46,291 - 70%
Carrie Kelleher (R) 19,270 - 29%

UTAH
District 1
Steve Beierlein (D) 49,186 - 30%
James Hansen (R) (i) 109,370 - 68%

District 2
Lily Eskelsen (D) 76,865 - 43%
Merrill Cook (R) (i) 93,367 - 53%

District 3
Christopher Cannon (R) (i) 99,983 - 77%
No Democratic candidate

VERMONT
At-Large
Mark Candon (R) 69,405 - 33%
Bernard Sanders (Ind) (i) 135,209 - 64%
No Democratic candidate

VIRGINIA
District 1
Herbert Bateman (R) (i) 76,468 - 77%
No Democratic candidate

District 2
Owen Pickett (D) (i) Uncontested

District 3
Robert Scott (D) (i) 48,132 - 77%
No Republican candidate

District 4
Norman Sisisky (D) (i) Uncontested

District 5
Virgil Goode (D) (i) Uncontested

District 6
David Bowers (D) 40,070 - 31%
Robert Goodlatte (R) (i) 89,488 - 69%

District 7
Thomas Bliley (R) (i) 57,507 - 74%
No Democratic candidate

District 8
James Moran (D) (i) 97,336 - 67%
Demaris Miller (R) 48,064 - 33%

District 9
Rick Boucher (D) (i) 87,090 - 61%
Joseph Barta (R) 55,942 - 39%

District 10
Cornell Brooks (D) 36,294 - 25%
Frank Wolf (R) (i) 102,187 - 71%

District 11
Thomas Davis (R) (i) 90,982 - 83%
No Democratic candidate

WASHINGTON
District 1
Jay Inslee (D) 80,294 - 51%
Rick White (R) (i) 68,187 - 43%

District 2
Margarethe Cammermeyer (D) 79,700 - 45%
Jack Metcalf (R) (i) 97,368 - 55%

District 3
Brian Baird (D) 100,868 - 55%
Don Benton (R) 83,043 - 45%

District 4
Gordon Pross (D) 34,851 - 25%
Richard "Doc" Hastings (R) (i) 96,075 - 69%

District 5
Brad Lyons (D) 62,336 - 38%
George Nethercutt (R) (i) 92,764 - 57%

District 6
Norman Dicks (D) (i) 106,620 - 68%
Bob Lawrence (R) 49,057 - 32%

District 7
Jim McDermott (D) (i) 118,511 - 89%
No Republican candidate

District 8
Heidi Behrens Benedict (D) 56,925 - 42%
Jennifer Dunn (R) (i) 78,909 - 58%

District 9
Adam Smith (D) (i) 76,274 - 65%
Ron Taber (R) 41,422 - 35%

WEST VIRGINIA
District 1
Alan Mollohan (D) (i) 104,054 - 85%
No Republican candidate

District 2
Robert Wise (D) (i) 98,397 - 73%
Sally Anne Kay (R) 28,785 - 21%

District 3
Nick Rahall (D) (i) 76,866 - 86%
No Republican candidate

WISCONSIN
District 1
Lydia Spottswood (D) 82,926 - 43%
Paul Ryan (R) 111,938 - 57%

District 2
Tammy Baldwin (D) 114,185 - 53%
Josephine Musser (R) 99,730 - 47%

District 3
Ronald Kind (D) (i) 126,666 - 72%
Troy Brechler (R) 50,115 - 28%

District 4
Jerry Kleczka (D) (i) 105,850 - 58%
Thomas Reynolds (R) 76,397 - 42%

District 5
Thomas Barrett (D) (i) 117,581 - 78%
Jack Melvin (R) 32,290 - 22%

District 6
Thomas Petri (R) (i) 143,470 - 93%
No Democratic candidate

District 7
David Obey (D) (i) 115,621 - 61%
Scott West (R) 74,943 - 39%

District 8
Jay Johnson (D) (i) 92,552 - 46%
Mark Green (R) 110,016 - 54%

District 9
James Sensenbrenner (R) (i) 182,931 - 91%
No Democratic candidate

WYOMING
At-Large
Scott Farris (D) 67,398 - 39%
Barbara Cubin (R) (i) 100,657 - 58%

1998 U.S. Senate Races

Here are the preliminary results for the Democrats and Republicans running for the U.S. Senate. (i=incumbent)

ALABAMA
Clayton Suddith (D) 468,438 - 37%
Richard Shelby (R) (i) 800,830 - 63%

ALASKA
Joseph Sonneman (D) 36,827 - 20%
Frank Murkowski (R) (i) 140,746 - 75%

ARIZONA
Ed Ranger (D) 250,890 - 28%
John McCain (R) (i) 622,710 - 68%

ARKANSAS
Blanche Lincoln (D) 381,237 - 56%
Fay Boozman (R) 285,889 - 42%

CALIFORNIA
Barbara Boxer (D) (i) 3,907,461 - 53%
Matthew Fong (R) 3,149,003 - 43%

COLORADO
Dottie Lamm (D) 451,680 - 35%
Ben Nighthorse Campbell (R) (i) 802,125 - 62%

CONNECTICUT
Christopher Dodd (D) (i) 567,130 - 65%
Gary Franks (R) 277,698 - 32%

FLORIDA
Bob Graham (D) (i) 2,428,840 - 63%
Charles Crist (R) 1,455,621 - 37%

GEORGIA
Michael Coles (D) 782,038 - 45%
Paul Coverdell (R) (i) 899,832 - 52%

HAWAII
Daniel Inouye (D) (i) 305,410 - 79%
Crystal Young (R) 68,371 - 18%

IDAHO
Bill Mauk (D) 104,241 - 28%
Mike Crapo (R) 255,022 - 70%

ILLINOIS
Carol Moseley-Braun (D) (i) 1,565,265 - 47%
Peter Fitzgerald (R) 1,691,994 - 51%

INDIANA
Evan Bayh (D) 999,665 - 63%
Paul Helmke (R) 553,514 - 35%

IOWA
David Osterberg (D) 291,899 - 31%
Charles Grassley (R) (i) 640,233 - 68%

KANSAS
Paul Feleciano (D) 227,702 - 32%
Sam Brownback (R) (i) 469, 632 - 65%

KENTUCKY
Scotty Baesler (D) 560,888 - 49%
Jim Bunning (R) 567,951 - 50%

LOUISIANA
John Breaux (D) (i) 619,219 - 64%
Jim Donelon (R) 306,081 - 32%

MARYLAND
Barbara Mikulski (D) (i) 1,034,814 - 71%
Ross Pierpont (R) 426,499 - 29%

MISSOURI
Jeremiah Nixon (D) 690,687 - 44%
Christopher Bond (R) (i) 830,800 - 53%

NEVADA
Harry Reid (D) (i) 207,606 - 48%
John Ensign (R) 207,067 - 48%

NEW HAMPSHIRE
George Condodemetraky (D) 88,679 - 28%
Judd Gregg (R) (i) 213,150 - 68%

NEW YORK
Charles Schumer (D) 2,358,196 - 54%
Al D'Amato (R) (i) 1,924,403 - 44%

NORTH CAROLINA
John Edwards (D) 993,567 - 51%
Lauch Faircloth (R) (i) 912,786 - 47%

NORTH DAKOTA
Byron Dorgan (D) (i) 133,520 - 63%
Donna Nalewaja (R) 74,267 - 35%

OHIO
Mary Boyle (D) 1,458,210 - 44%
George Voinovich (R) 1,887,342 - 56%

OKLAHOMA
Don Carroll (D) 274,889 - 31%
Don Nickles (R) (i) 578,604 - 66%

OREGON
Ronald Wyden (D) (i) 247,985 - 57%
John Lim (R) 151,244 - 35%

PENNSYLVANIA
William Lloyd (D) 1,018,821 - 35%
Arlen Specter (R) (i) 1,803,018 - 61%

SOUTH CAROLINA
Ernest Hollings (D) (i) 541,283 - 52%
Bob Inglis (R) 475,245 - 46%

SOUTH DAKOTA
Thomas Daschle (D) (i) 161,544 - 62%
Ron Schmidt (R) 94,918 - 36%

UTAH
Scott Leckman (D) 162,481 - 33%
Robert Bennett (R) (i) 315,070 - 64%

VERMONT
Patrick Leahy (D) (i) 147,357 - 72%
Fred Tuttle (R) 47,838 - 23%

WASHINGTON
Patty Murray (D) (i) 807,499 - 58%
Linda Smith (R) 576,674 - 42%

WISCONSIN
Russell Feingold (D) (i) 863,201 - 50%
Mark Neumann (R) 833,780 - 49%

Senators Whose Terms Expire in 2000 or 2002

ALABAMA
Jeff Sessions (R) 2002

ALASKA
Ted Stevens (R) 2002

ARIZONA
Jon L. Kyl (R) 2000

ARKANSAS
Tim Hutchinson (R) 2002

CALIFORNIA
Dianne Feinstein (D) 2000

COLORADO
Wayne Allard (R) 2002

CONNECTICUT
Joseph I. Lieberman (D) 2000

DELAWARE
William V. Roth, Jr. (R) 2000
Joseph R. Biden, Jr. (D) 2002

FLORIDA
Connie Mack (R) 2000

GEORGIA
Max W. Cleland (D) 2002

HAWAII
Daniel K. Akaka (D) 2000

IDAHO
Larry E. Craig (R) 2002

ILLINOIS
Richard J. Durbin (D) 2002

INDIANA
Richard G. Lugar (R) 2000

IOWA
Tom Harkin (D) 2002

KANSAS
Pat Roberts (R) 2002

KENTUCKY
Mitch McConnell (R) 2002

LOUISIANA
Mary Landrieu (D) 2002

MAINE
Olympia J. Snowe (R) 2000
Susan M. Collins (R) 2002

MARYLAND
Paul S. Sarbanes (D) 2000

MASSACHUSETTS
Edward M. Kennedy (D) 2000
John F. Kerry (D) 2002

MICHIGAN
Carl Levin (D) 2002
Spencer Abraham (R) 2000

MINNESOTA
Paul David Wellstone (D) 2002
Rod Grams (R) 2000

MISSISSIPPI
Thad Cochran (R) 2002
Trent Lott (R) 2000

MISSOURI
John Ashcroft (R) 2000

MONTANA
Max Baucus (D) 2002
Conrad Burns (R) 2000

NEBRASKA
J. Robert Kerrey (D) 2000
Chuck Hagel (R) 2002

NEVADA
Richard H. Bryan (D) 2000

NEW HAMPSHIRE
Robert C. Smith (R) 2002

NEW JERSEY
Frank R. Lautenberg (D) 2000
Robert G. Torricelli (D) 2002

NEW MEXICO
Pete V. Domenici (R) 2002
Jeff Bingaman (D) 2000

NEW YORK
Daniel Patrick Moynihan (D) 2000

NORTH CAROLINA
Jesse Helms (R) 2002

NORTH DAKOTA
Kent Conrad (D) 2000

OHIO
Mike DeWine (R) 2000

OKLAHOMA
James M. Inhofe (R) 2002

OREGON
Gordon Smith (R) 2002

PENNSYLVANIA
Rick Santorum (R) 2000

RHODE ISLAND
John H. Chafee (R) 2000
Jack Reed (D) 2002

SOUTH CAROLINA
Strom Thurmond (R) 2002

SOUTH DAKOTA
Tim Johnson (D) 2002

TENNESSEE
Fred Thompson (R) 2002
Bill Frist (R) 2000

TEXAS
Phil Gramm (R) 2002
Kay Bailey Hutchison (R) 2000

UTAH
Orrin G. Hatch (R) 2000

VERMONT
Jim M. Jeffords (R) 2000

VIRGINIA
John W. Warner (R) 2002
Charles S. Robb (D) 2000

WASHINGTON
Slade Gorton (R) 2000

WEST VIRGINIA
Robert C. Byrd (D) 2000
John D. Rockefeller IV (D) 2002

WISCONSIN
Herbert H. Kohl (D) 2000

WYOMING
Craig Thomas (R) 2000
Michael B. Enzi (R) 2002

October News

Federal Reserve Chairman Alan Greenspan painted a frightening picture of the damage that Long-Term Capital Management LP's failure could have inflicted, as he defended its rescue. He said the hedge fund's collapse could have "triggered the seizing up of markets and could have potentially impaired the economies of many nations, including our own." He also suggested that more such threats may lurk in the markets. A group of banks and brokerage firms agreed in September to shore up Long-Term Capital by putting $3.6 billion into the faltering fund.

Stock prices continued to slump early in the month as investors said their gloom had deepened over lack of progress in dealing with the global financial crisis. But the market began to rally toward the middle of October, and a surprise interest-rate cut by the Federal Reserve helped propel the Dow Jones Industrials toward the 8500 mark.

The Justice Department accused Visa and MasterCard of stifling competition and innovation in an antitrust lawsuit that could reshape the credit-card industry. The government is seeking to break up the joint ownership of Visa and MasterCard, the nation's two largest credit-card networks, by the same group of banks.

The House of Representatives voted 258-176 to begin an open-ended impeachment inquiry. The vote marked only the third time Congress has weighed removing a president. The Republicans' counsel, alleging a "deliberate and direct" assault on the justice system, laid out 15 possible charges against President Clinton. They emphasize obstruction of justice and allege that former White House intern Monica Lewinsky was a co-conspirator in that endeavor. Mr. Clinton had a sexual relationship with Ms. Lewinsky, that he tried unsuccessfully to conceal.

Matthew Shepard, a gay University of Wyoming student who died after a savage bias-related beating, sparked outrage throughout the country and inspired people—both gay and straight—to hold candlelight vigils and protest marches. He had been lured from a bar by two young men who said they, too, were gay. They allegedly pistol-whipped him, robbed him and tied him to a fence in near freezing temperatures. President Clinton urged Congress to pass legislation making it easier for prosecution of such hate crimes.

The National Basketball Association canceled the first two weeks of its season, from Nov. 3 to Nov. 16. The unprecedented cancellation came after collective bargaining talks between owners and players broke off after 3½ hours. The NBA later canceled all November games.

American Home Products and Monsanto canceled their $35.08 billion merger, unable to agree on how to blend two companies with dramatically different cultures and chief executives.

The supermarket business continued its consolidation. First, Safeway agreed to buy Dominick's Supermarkets for $1.2 billion plus the assumption of about $646.2 million of debt. Then, Kroger reached a pact to acquire Fred Meyer, creating the largest U.S. supermarket chain. That transaction was valued at about $7.4 billion plus the assumption of $4.9 billion in debt.

The United States charged Eric Robert Rudolph, one of the FBI's 10 most-wanted fugitives, with the 1996 bombing at the Olympics and two other attacks in Atlanta. Mr. Rudolph was earlier charged with bombing an Alabama abortion clinic.

Former Chilean dictator Augusto Pinochet was arrested in London following extradition requests from Spanish judges. Mr. Pinochet faced charges of genocide, terrorism and torture. But his lawyers argued in a British court that his arrest was illegal because he has immunity from prosecution for acts committed in an "official capacity."

McKesson, the nation's largest drug wholesaler, agreed to acquire medical-software supplier HBO & Co. for stock valued at $14.46 billion in a deal that would create a new category of health-care giant. The stock prices of McKesson and HBO tumbled on news of their proposed merger, and the value of the deal fell to about $12 billion.

As the Microsoft antitrust trial began, the government challenged Bill Gates's credibility under oath and charged that Mr. Gates personally directed a campaign to crush rival Netscape.

BankAmerica's president, David Coulter, resigned following more than $1.4 billion in write-downs and losses from global markets that sent the bank's quarterly earnings plunging.

Congress adjourned after sending President Clinton its big election-year spending bill. Mr. Clinton quickly signed the measure, which tops $520 billion. The catch-all measure shattered spending caps adopted in 1997 and is loaded with election-year favors for constituents. Democrats tout more education funds, while Republicans point to billions more for defense and the war on drugs.

An ex-Communist was sworn in as prime minister of Italy. Massimo D'Alema, leader of the Democratic Left, will head a center-left government that includes two Marxist ministers, the first since 1947. Romano Prodi had submitted his resignation after losing a parliamentary confidence motion by a single vote.

Texas floods claimed 29 lives. Damage from the Hill Country flooding after two feet of rain was estimated at nearly $500 million.

Benjamin Netanyahu and Yasser Arafat struck a peace agreement after nine grueling days of negotiations at a conference center in Maryland. The summit meeting produced a plan for Israel to withdraw from an additional 13 percent of the West Bank over the next three months and for Mr. Arafat to step up efforts to prevent terrorist attacks against Israel. Opposition to the accord spilled onto the streets as an Israeli security guard was killed in Hebron. Hours later, a Palestinian farmer was found dead near Nablus.

Serbia won a reprieve from NATO airstrikes as it pulled troops from Kosovo. The Western alliance said the troop withdrawal was sufficient, but extended the threat of military action indefinitely to try to prevent further attacks on ethnic Albanians.

Ohio Senator John Glenn at age 77 returned to space aboard the shuttle *Discovery*, 36 years after becoming the first American to orbit the Earth.

Notable Deaths: **Gene Autry**, 91, singing cowboy on TV and in movies . . . **Roddy McDowall**, 70, actor in such movies as *Lassie Come Home* and *Planet of the Apes* . . . **Clark Clifford**, 91, adviser to four Democratic presidents . . . **Mary S. Calderone**, 94, early advocate of childhood sex education . . . **Eric Ambler**, 89, innovative author of spy thrillers . . . **Ted Hughes**, 68, Britain's poet laureate whose life was shadowed by the suicide of his first wife, American poet Sylvia Plath.

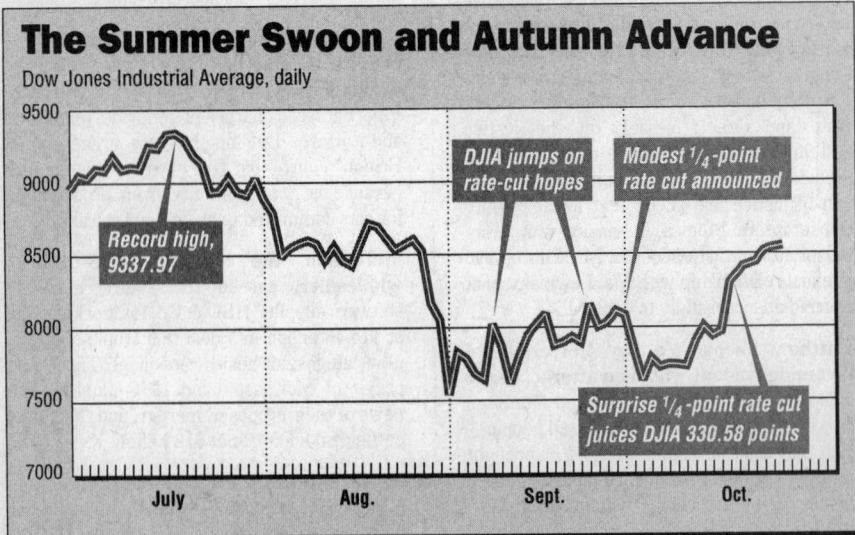

The Summer Swoon and Autumn Advance

Dow Jones Industrial Average, daily

Record high, 9337.97

DJIA jumps on rate-cut hopes

Modest 1/4-point rate cut announced

Surprise 1/4-point rate cut juices DJIA 330.58 points

1998 Major League Baseball Playoffs

American League Division Series

NY Yankees vs. Texas

NY Yankees	2	Texas	0
NY Yankees	3	Texas	1
NY Yankees	4	Texas	0

(NY Yankees won series 3-0)

Cleveland vs. Boston

Boston	11	Cleveland	3
Cleveland	9	Boston	5
Cleveland	4	Boston	3
Cleveland	2	Boston	1

(Cleveland won series 3-1)

American League Championship Series

NY Yankees vs. Cleveland

NY Yankees	7	Cleveland	2	
Cleveland	4	NY Yankees	1	(12 inn.)
Cleveland	6	NY Yankees	1	
NY Yankees	4	Cleveland	0	
NY Yankees	5	Cleveland	3	
NY Yankees	9	Cleveland	5	

(NY Yankees won series 4-2)

National League Division Series

Atlanta vs. Chicago Cubs

Atlanta	7	Chicago Cubs	1	
Atlanta	2	Chicago Cubs	1	(10 inn.)
Atlanta	6	Chicago Cubs	2	

(Atlanta won series 3-0)

San Diego vs. Houston

San Diego	2	Houston	1
Houston	5	San Diego	4
San Diego	2	Houston	1
San Diego	6	Houston	1

(San Diego won series 3-1)

National League Championship Series

Atlanta vs. San Diego

San Diego	3	Atlanta	2	(10 inn.)
San Diego	3	Atlanta	0	
San Diego	4	Atlanta	1	
Atlanta	8	San Diego	3	
Atlanta	7	San Diego	6	
San Diego	5	Atlanta	0	

(San Diego won series 4-2)

World Series

NY Yankees vs. San Diego

NY Yankees	9	San Diego	6
NY Yankees	9	San Diego	3
NY Yankees	5	San Diego	4
NY Yankees	3	San Diego	0

(NY Yankees won series 4-0)

1998 WORLD SERIES

So, are the 1998 New York Yankees the best team in baseball history? After beating the San Diego Padres four games to none in the World Series, the Cleveland Indians, 4–2, and the Texas Rangers, 3–0, in the American League Playoffs, and after winning 114 regular-season games, it was a question certainly worth asking.

George Steinbrenner's Yankees had everything—pitching: David Wells, David Cone, Orlando "El Duque" Hernandez, closer Mariano Rivera; hitting: Bernie Williams, the AL batting champion, plus Tino Martinez and Paul O'Neill; speed: shortstop Derek Jeter and second baseman Chuck Knaublach; depth: five left fielders; good fortune: third baseman Scot Brosius starting the year as an unknown from the Oakland Athletics but finishing as the World Series MVP; and emotion: Darryl Strawberry's apparently successful surgery for colon cancer during the first round of the playoffs. All this and the Bronx Bombers were—get this—a hard bunch not to like.

But perhaps the best argument for their best-ever claim is this double barrel: They were expected to win it all from opening day, and they did. Can there be anything more difficult to accomplish in professional sports

Final 1998 Major League Baseball Regular-Season Standings

National League

	Won	Lost	Pct.	GB
Eastern Division				
Atlanta	106	56	.654	–
NY Mets	88	74	.543	18
Philadelphia	75	87	.463	31
Montreal	65	97	.401	41
Florida	54	108	.333	52
Central Division				
Houston	102	60	.630	–
Chicago Cubs*	90	73	.552	12.5
St Louis	83	79	.512	19
Cincinnati	77	85	.475	25
Milwaukee	74	88	.457	28
Pittsburgh	69	93	.426	33
Western Division				
San Diego	98	64	.605	–
San Francisco	89	74	.546	9.5
Los Angeles	83	79	.512	15
Colorado	77	85	.475	21
Arizona	65	97	.401	33

American League

	Won	Lost	Pct.	GB
Eastern Division				
NY Yankees	114	48	.704	–
Boston*	92	70	.568	22
Toronto	88	74	.543	26
Baltimore	79	83	.488	35
Tampa Bay	63	99	.389	51
Central Division				
Cleveland	89	73	.549	–
Chi White Sox	80	82	.494	9
Kansas City	72	89	.447	16.5
Minnesota	70	92	.432	19
Detroit	65	97	.401	24
Western Division				
Texas	88	74	.543	–
Anaheim	85	77	.525	3
Seattle	76	85	.472	11.5
Oakland	74	88	.457	14

*Wild Card qualifier for playoffs.
Source: Major League Baseball

than to win when you're supposed to? And in the playoffs, they turned the other teams and players into just so many subplots and supporting actors.

But give the Cleveland Indians some credit: They provided the Yankees Postseason Coronation Tour with its only real moments of drama. In Game Two at Yankee Stadium, a Tino Martinez throw on a bunt by Travis Fryman hit Fryman in the back as both ball and runner reached first base. Chuck Knaublach, covering at first, argued heatedly with the umpire rather than retrieve the ball, which had trickled into short right field, and allowed a player to score. It was one game apiece going to Cleveland for games three, four and five. At Jacobs Field, the Indians won game three on a couple of colossal blasts from first baseman Jim Thome, and suddenly it was 2–1, Cleveland. For Game Four, Yankees manager Joe Torre gave the ball to Orlando Hernandez, who just 10 months before was floating away from Cuba on a leaky raft. Hernandez pitched a beautiful, high-kicking gem,

the Yanks won 4–0 and, really, never looked back.

The World Series was all formality. The Padres were a worthy if overmatched opponent. On the plus side, it was good to see the Padres' meticulous batsman, Tony Gwynn, back in the Series for the first time since 1984. But the Series itself was over by the end of the seventh inning of the first game. The Yankees entered the bottom half down 3–0 with Padres ace Kevin Brown on the mound. By the time the inning had ended, a two-run homer by Chuck Knaublach and a grand slam by Tino Martinez (the goats of the Cleveland Game-Two debacle) had put the Yanks on their way to a 9–3 win. Goodnight, Padres.

A business note. For all the trumpeting of this baseball season as the best ever (McGwire, Sosa, Ripken, Yankees), the World Series, on Fox, was the lowest rated Fall Classic ever. If the Yankees were indeed history's darlings, it appears not a whole lot of people bothered to watch.

Steve McKee

1998 Nobel Laureates

(Winners of the Nobel Prize in all categories since 1901 appear on pages 700 to 707.)

Physics
Robert B. Laughlin of Stanford University in California; Horst L. Stormer of Columbia University in New York and Bell Laboratories in Murray Hill, New Jersey; and Daniel C. Tsui of Princeton University in New Jersey, for discovering that electrons acting together in strong magnetic fields can form new types of "particles" with charges that are fractions of electron charges. Their research was cited as "yet another breakthrough in our understanding of quantum physics."

Chemistry
Walter Kohn of the University of California at Santa Barbara and John A. Pople of Northwestern University in Evanston, Illinois, for their work in the area of quantum chemistry. Dr. Kohn was cited for development of the density-functional theory, which is used in calculating the geometrical structure of molecules and in mapping chemical reactions. Dr. Pople was honored for his development of computer-based calculation methods.

Physiology or Medicine
Robert F. Furchgott of the State University of New York in Brooklyn; Louis J. Ignarro of the University of California at Los Angeles; and Ferid Murad of the University of Texas medical school in Houston, for their discoveries concerning nitric oxide as a signaling molecule in the cardiovascular system. The findings have led to research and new treatments for heart disease, shock, cancer and impotence, including the drug Viagra.

Literature
Jose Saramago, a Portuguese writer, for his novels which display "imagination, compassion and irony." His works include *Baltasar and Blimunda*, *The Stone Raft* and *The History of the Siege of Lisbon*.

Peace
John Hume, head of the Catholic Social Democratic and Labor Party in Northern Ireland, and David Trimble, leader of the Protestant Ulster Unionist Party, for their efforts to find a peaceful solution to the country's national, religious and social conflict, which has claimed more than 3,500 lives over the past 30 years. Other leaders in Northern Ireland and the governments of Great Britain, Ireland and the United States also were cited for their positive contributions to the peace process.

Economic Sciences
Amartya Sen, an Indian-born professor at Trinity College in Cambridge, England, for his contributions to welfare economics, including indexes of welfare and poverty and studies of famine. He was cited for combining tools from economics and philosophy to restore "an ethical dimension to the discussion of vital economic problems."

1999 SOCIAL SECURITY CHANGES

Cost-of-Living Adjustment (COLA)

Based on the increase in the Consumer Price Index (CPI-W) from the third quarter of 1997 through the third quarter of 1998, recipients of Social Security benefits and Supplemental Security Income payments received a 1.3% COLA for 1999.

	1998	1999
Tax Rate		
Employee	7.65%*	7.65%*
Self-Employed	15.30%	15.30%

*The Social Security portion is 6.2% on earnings up to the maximum taxable amount; the Medicare portion is 1.45% on all earnings.

Maximum Earnings Taxable

	1998	1999
Social Security	$68,400	$72,600
Medicare	No limit	No limit

Retirement Earnings Exempt Amounts

	1998	1999
Age 65–69	$14,500/yr ($1,209/mo)	$15,500/yr ($1,292/mo)
Under age 65	$9,120/yr ($760/mo)	$9,600/yr ($800/mo)

Note: For people 65 through 69, $1 in benefits will be withheld for every $3 in earnings above the limit. For people under 65, $1 will be withheld for every $2 in earnings above the limit.

Maximum Social Security Benefit

(for workers retiring at age 65 in January) $1,342/mo $1,373/mo

Estimated Average Monthly Social Security Benefits Before and After the December 1998 COLA:

	Before 1.3% COLA	After 1.3% COLA
All Retired Workers	$770	$780
Aged Couple, Both Receiving Benefits	$1,293	$1,310
Widowed Mother and Two Children	$1,534	$1,554
Aged Widow(er) Alone	$740	$749
Disabled Worker, Spouse and One or More Children	$1,202	$1,217
All Diabled Workers	$724	$733

Federal Income Tax Rates

The U.S. tax code requires that federal income tax brackets and other figures be adjusted for inflation annually. The Internal Revenue Service usually releases official numbers in December each year. CCH Inc.'s 1999 tax year projections, which are compared to official 1998 tax year figures, appear below.

MARRIED FILING JOINTLY (& SURVIVING SPOUSE)

1998 Taxable Income	Tax Rate	1999 Taxable Income
$0–$42,350	15%	$0–43,050
$42,350–$102,300	28%	$43,050–$104,050
$102,300–$155,950	31%	$104,050–$158,550
$155,950–$278,450	36%	$158,550–$283,150
over $278,450	39.6%	over $283,150

MARRIED FILING SEPARATELY

1998 Taxable Income	Tax Rate	1999 Taxable Income
$0–$21,175	15%	$0–$21,525
$21,175–$51,150	28%	$21,525–$52,025
$51,150–$77,975	31%	$52,025–$79,275
$77,975–$139,225	36%	$79,275–$141,575
over $139,225	39.6%	over $141,575

SINGLE FILERS

1998 Taxable Income	Tax Rate	1999 Taxable Income
$0–$25,350	15%	$0–$25,750
$25,350–$61,400	28%	$25,750–$62,450
$61,400–$128,100	31%	$62,450–$130,250
$128,100–$278,450	36%	$130,250–$283,150
over $278,450	39.6%	over $283,150

HEAD OF HOUSEHOLD

1998 Taxable Income	Tax Rate	1999 Taxable Income
$0–$33,950	15%	$0–$34,550
$33,950–$87,700	28%	$34,550–$89,150
$87,700–$142,000	31%	$89,150–$144,400
$142,000–$278,450	36%	$144,400–$283,150
over $278,450	39.6%	over $283,150

STANDARD DEDUCTION AMOUNTS

Filing Status	1998	1999	Increase
Married Filing Jointly			
(& Surviving Spouse)	$7,100	$7,200	$100
Married Filing Separately	$3,550	$3,600	$50
Single	$4,250	$4,300	$50
Head of Household	$6,250	$6,350	$100

STANDARD DEDUCTION FOR DEPENDENTS ("KIDDIE" STANDARD DEDUCTION)

1998	1999	Increase
$700	$700	$0

INCOME LEVEL AT WHICH THREE-PERCENT ITEMIZED DEDUCTION LIMITATION TAKES EFFECT
(ADJUSTED GROSS INCOME)

Filing Status	1998	1999	Increase
Married Filing Jointly			
(& Surviving Spouse)	$124,500	$126,600	$2,100
Married Filing Separately	$62,250	$63,300	$1,050
Single	$124,500	$126,600	$2,100
Head of Household	$124,500	$126,600	$2,100

PERSONAL EXEMPTION AMOUNTS

1998	1999	Increase
$2,700	$2,750	$50

THRESHOLD FOR PERSONAL EXEMPTION PHASEOUT

Filing Status	1998	1999	Increase
Married Filing Jointly			
(& Surviving Spouse)	$186,800	$189,950	$3,150
Married Filing Separately	$93,400	$94,975	$1,575
Single	$124,500	$126,600	$2,100
Head of Household	$155,650	$158,300	$2,650

GIFT TAX EXEMPTION

Gift Status	1998	1999	Increase
Amount of Gift Per Donee	$10,000	$10,000	$0

Source: CCH Inc., Riverwoods, Illinois

1999

JANUARY

S	M	T	W	T	F	S
					1	2
3	4	5	6	7	8	9
10	11	12	13	14	15	16
17	18	19	20	21	22	23
24	25	26	27	28	29	30
31						

1 New Year's Day
15 Martin Luther King, Jr.'s Birthday
18 Martin Luther King, Jr. Day

FEBRUARY

S	M	T	W	T	F	S
	1	2	3	4	5	6
7	8	9	10	11	12	13
14	15	16	17	18	19	20
21	22	23	24	25	26	27
28						

12 Lincoln's Birthday
14 Valentine's Day
15 Washington's Birthday-Observed
17 Ash Wednesday
22 Washington's Birthday

MARCH

S	M	T	W	T	F	S
	1	2	3	4	5	6
7	8	9	10	11	12	13
14	15	16	17	18	19	20
21	22	23	24	25	26	27
28	29	30	31			

17 St. Patrick's Day
28 Palm Sunday

APRIL

S	M	T	W	T	F	S
				1	2	3
4	5	6	7	8	9	10
11	12	13	14	15	16	17
18	19	20	21	22	23	24
25	26	27	28	29	30	

1 Passover
2 Good Friday
4 Easter Sunday
4 Daylight Saving Time begins
21 Professional Secretaries Day

MAY

S	M	T	W	T	F	S
						1
2	3	4	5	6	7	8
9	10	11	12	13	14	15
16	17	18	19	20	21	22
23	24	25	26	27	28	29
30	31					

9 Mother's Day
15 Armed Forces Day
24 Victoria Day (Canada)
30 Memorial Day
31 Memorial Day-Observed

JUNE

S	M	T	W	T	F	S
		1	2	3	4	5
6	7	8	9	10	11	12
13	14	15	16	17	18	19
20	21	22	23	24	25	26
27	28	29	30			

14 Flag Day
20 Father's Day
24 St-Jean (Québec)

JULY

S	M	T	W	T	F	S
				1	2	3
4	5	6	7	8	9	10
11	12	13	14	15	16	17
18	19	20	21	22	23	24
25	26	27	28	29	30	31

1 Canada Day (Canada)
4 Independence Day

AUGUST

S	M	T	W	T	F	S
1	2	3	4	5	6	7
8	9	10	11	12	13	14
15	16	17	18	19	20	21
22	23	24	25	26	27	28
29	30	31				

SEPTEMBER

S	M	T	W	T	F	S
			1	2	3	4
5	6	7	8	9	10	11
12	13	14	15	16	17	18
19	20	21	22	23	24	25
26	27	28	29	30		

6 Labor Day
11 Rosh Hashanah
20 Yom Kippur

OCTOBER

S	M	T	W	T	F	S
					1	2
3	4	5	6	7	8	9
10	11	12	13	14	15	16
17	18	19	20	21	22	23
24	25	26	27	28	29	30
31						

11 Columbus Day-Observed
11 Thanksgiving Day (Canada)
12 Columbus Day
24 United Nations Day
31 Halloween
31 Daylight Saving Time ends

NOVEMBER

S	M	T	W	T	F	S
	1	2	3	4	5	6
7	8	9	10	11	12	13
14	15	16	17	18	19	20
21	22	23	24	25	26	27
28	29	30				

2 Election Day
11 Veterans Day
11 Remembrance Day (Canada)
25 Thanksgiving Day

DECEMBER

S	M	T	W	T	F	S
			1	2	3	4
5	6	7	8	9	10	11
12	13	14	15	16	17	18
19	20	21	22	23	24	25
26	27	28	29	30	31	

4 Hanukkah
25 Christmas Day
26 Boxing Day (Canada)

THE YEAR IN REVIEW

"Lifestyle" Drugs

The drug industry doesn't just want to cure you anymore. It wants to make you look better, feel cheerier—even improve your sex life. Sales of "lifestyle" drugs—pills that give chrome-domes hair, make shy people more social and turn aging baby-boomers into the Casanovas of their youth—have fattened the bottom line of a pharmaceutical industry that is going gangbusters. And there's no letup in sight.

In fact, researchers say we have only seen the beginning. New drugs to improve memory, antidepressants to target specific personality quirks and pills to fend off the diseases associated with aging are all in the works. These drugs, some doctors say, could give us the ability not just to be normal, but supernormal.

But that idea raises some tough ethical questions. Even if we have a pill that can eradicate "undesirable" traits in someone who is aloof, obnoxious or flaky, should we use it? If a kid acts up at home, should we figure out what is wrong, or just throw a pill at him? Because all drugs have side effects, could millions of healthy people taking enhancement drugs lead to some unforeseen medical nightmare? And in a world of finite resources, should drug companies be spending million of dollars on drugs to enhance life rather than focusing on medicines that will save lives?

"The entire trend in research is to enhance our lives rather than dealing with our health. That's where the money is," says Sherwin B. Nuland, a clinical professor of surgery at Yale University. "We seem to have no tolerance for any irritation in our lives. Those of us who have the money, we need to look for a pill for it."

The number of antidepressant prescriptions has skyrocketed in the last few years, partly because better medications are available, but also because doctors are more willing to prescribe pills to any patient who is feeling a little grumpy or down. Sales of SSRIs—the class of antidepressants that includes Prozac, Zoloft and Paxil—reached $4.6 billion in 1997, up from $1.4 billion in 1993, according to IMS Health Inc., a health-care information company in Plymouth Meeting, Pennsylvania.

A study published this year in the Archives of General Psychiatry showed that the number of psychiatric patients who received prescriptions for antidepressants jumped from 23 percent in 1985 to almost 50 percent in 1994. "There has clearly been a substantial growth in the use of antidepressants in a population where there isn't well established scientific evidence to support their use," says Dr. Mark Olfson, an associate professor of clinical psychiatry at Columbia University and the lead author of the study.

But the science may slowly be catching up, showing what clinicians say they already know—that antidepressants can make people who aren't really sick happier or less stressed. A recent study of SmithKline Beecham PLC's

Paxil published in the American Journal of Psychiatry showed that the drug made healthy people less irritable and more cooperative

Perhaps the most controversial part of the antidepressant boom is the surge in prescriptions to children. While there are still no medications approved by the Food and Drug Administration to treat depression in kids, that hasn't stopped doctors from offering the pills to thousands of youngsters "off-label." But critics warn that it is difficult to discern true depression from the normal ups and down of childhood. Stressed-out parents, they say, may prefer to reach for a pill than deal with normal kids' tantrums. Novartis AG's Ritalin for hyperactivity has come under similar fire, with many doctors saying it also is grossly overprescribed to lively children who are within the normal range.

Even aging, which used to be looked upon as inevitable and normal, is now seen by some as just another disease to be cured. The specialty of "anti-aging medicine" even has its own board certification and peer-reviewed journal. The American Academy of Anti-Aging Medicine started in 1993 with 12 doctors, but has ballooned to more than 5,500 today. Its members, who include plastic surgeons, gynecologists and specialists in sports medicine, believe in the use of antioxidant supplements (such as vitamins C and E and grape seed extract) and hormone replacement to fend off aging. "We're looking at aging as an illness," says Dr. Ronald Klatz, the organization's president. "We're saying it is not inevitable."

Already, consumers are snapping up products that promise to combat two of the most visible signs of aging—baldness and wrinkles. Johnson & Johnson's Renova wrinkle cream has pulled in $56 million since it was launched in January 1996, while Merck & Co.'s hair-sprouting Propecia has generated $31.4 million in sales since its January 1998 debut.

The notion that we can be better than healthy also is fueling an explosion in the market for nutritional supplements and herbs. Herbal supplements are a $2 billion business, propelled largely by youth-seeking baby boomers. While the science is often sketchy, the herbal products industry has a treasure trove of products' it claims can give you an edge: gingko biloba if you are forgetful, St.-John's-wort if you are bummed out, kava kava if you are stressed. Herbal remedies have some fierce critics.

There are very few clinical studies to show that the products are efficacious or safe. And regulation of the industry is so spotty that sometimes the contents listed on the label don't match what is in the bottle.

Federal regulations do bar herbal manufacturers from claiming that their products can cure a disease or treat a medical condition. Companies can only make "structure/function" claims—basically that a particular product affects a certain system in the body. But many manufacturers come close to crossing that line. And there are no restrictions on what the myriad independent books and pamphlets about herbs can say. What's more, the Internet is full of fantastic herbal claims, touting the substances as cure-alls for everything from AIDS to cancer.

Perhaps the most powerful example of the new fountain-of-youth drugs is Pfizer Inc.'s Viagra. While certainly a godsend to impotent men, Viagra has morphed from a medical breakthrough into a social phenomenon. And that phenomenon has been fueled by a legion of men just looking for a sexual boost.

The little blue pill is being passed out at birthday parties, swallowed by young hipsters at urban nightclubs and sold on the black market for as much as 10 times the $10-per-pill retail price. It has been sold over the Internet, on Web sites with names like penispill.com. And prescriptions have been churned out by opportunistic doctors and diet clinics turned Viagra dispensers.

"It is getting more common for men than aspirin," says William Granzig, president of the American Board of Sexology. Pfizer says four million Viagra prescriptions were written in the first six months after the drug was approved by the FDA. And some analysts predict sales will reach $700 million in 1998.

Researchers and urologists say Viagra can indeed help healthy men achieve an erection more quickly and, after intercourse, get a second erection faster. The drug also can compensate for the natural lessening of erectile function that urologists say happens with age. That is why some healthy but Viagra-enhanced middle-aged men say the pill makes them feel like a teenager. Mark Issacs-Ward says he has no problem getting an erection but that the half dozen times he tried Viagra were pretty miraculous. "It was fun to revisit my youth," says the 47-year-old director of the Barron Centers, a sexual-health facility in

Beverly Hills, California. "To feel sort of like a stud once again is nice."

So Viagra may seem to be the perfect "performance" drug, with a huge potential market in healthy men looking for better sex lives, but Pfizer has been loath to talk about Viagra's effects on those who are not impotent. The FDA, the company points out, only approves drugs based on whether they treat a specific illness. Also, insurance companies are already looking for reasons not to cover the pricey drug. If Viagra is considered a party pill, companies could easily rationalize not paying for it.

This quandary—how to responsibly market a drug that can enhance normal functions—is one that pharmaceutical companies will continue to face as science creates more drugs that can turn back the clock.

It is an issue that Barry Gordon already thinks a lot about. Dr. Gordon is conducting clinical trials for a number of pharmaceutical companies on drugs that can improve memory. Already, he says, doctors are prescribing Alzheimer's drugs to patients who have normal age-related memory loss. And he sees the day, not too far in the future, when we will have a pill that can give normal people super memories—or at least wipe out the forgetfulness that occurs as we age. But he isn't convinced that when we get them we should freely use them. "It will raise another issue about when you should apply these drugs and how you actually know if they are doing any good," he says.

And in an era of "enhancement drugs," we could create a society of pharmaceutical haves and have nots. Those who can pay for enhancing drugs will be calmer, more beautiful and mentally sharper. Their poorer neighbors will have no choice but to age less than gracefully.

Andrea Petersen, staff reporter for *The Wall Street Journal* in New York

Asian Crisis

Asia's economic and political crisis has turned globalization from a buzzword into a very real and potentially dangerous dynamic.

The region's travails mutated from a currency crisis in 1997 into full-blown economic recession and political turmoil in 1998. As the storm of stock-market upheaval and monetary devaluation swept through Asia and then jumped to emerging markets such as Latin America, Russia and elsewhere and even to the industrialized world, including Europe and the United States, it cast an ominous new light on the global economy.

Trouble in Asian economies spread into the political arena. Governments toppled in Thailand, South Korea, Japan and, most dramatically, Indonesia.

The crisis that had started with overvalued currencies and excessive borrowing in the likes of Thailand, Indonesia and Korea claimed a wider circle of victims in Asia as investors reacted negatively in Japan, Malaysia, Singapore, the Philippines, Hong Kong and Taiwan.

The Asian crisis helped push Russia into economic and political crisis and caused great volatility in the U.S. stock market.

With commodities prices plunging, numbing the economies of resource-rich countries such as Canada, Mexico, Venezuela, Brazil, Australia and South Africa, and stock markets around the world stumbling, talk of a coming global recession took on more adherents.

In Asia, expectations that recovery was on the way fizzled quickly. One turnaround scenario after another failed to materialize, and each lull in the carnage gave way to fresh jitters in some new hot spot. Prospects for attracting the capital needed to rebuild Asia are fading. Few economists now expect the region to return to normalcy in fewer than five years.

Even the gospel of unrestricted capital flows as an unalloyed good has come under question. Investors, from speculators such as George Soros to pensioners in Peoria, had poured their money into Asia's emerging markets, driving the rapid expansion of these economies. Their sudden departure from Asia and other emerging markets rocked these rickety financial structures and stretched the resources of the International Monetary Fund and other parts of the world's financial emergency-response system. More than a year after it began its work in Asia, the IMF could point to precious little progress among its patients, despite multibillion-dollar bail-outs and plenty of advice. Indeed, critics charged that in many cases the economies were sicker than when the IMF stepped in.

To be sure, some troubled nations rejected the IMF money and made attempts of their own design at financial stability. Charging that the free market had failed Malaysia, Prime Minister Mahathir Mohamad put foreign investors and speculators on a short leash, freezing trade in the Malaysian currency and limiting the ability of foreign shareholders to sell off their shares.

Hong Kong, whose huge holdings of foreign currencies made an IMF bailout unnecessary, nevertheless attempted to fight off pressure to devalue its U.S.-dollar-pegged currency by propping up its stock market with a massive and controversial buying spree. By doing so, the former British colony, which reverted to Chinese sovereignty in 1997, tarnished its record as a bastion of laissez-faire economics—though economists noted that even in British days, the government closely managed major sectors of the economy.

The year had started with a victory for the forces of stability, as the IMF and a handful of big-country central banks came to South Korea's rescue. The IMF engineered a $57 billion bailout, and twisted international bankers' arms to roll over $100 billion in short-term debts.

Combined with newly elected President Kim Dae Jung's hearty embrace of IMF-imposed reforms, the Korean rescue seemed to signal a shift for the better. A wave of U.S. money rolled into Asian financial markets in January and February, lifting stock markets and spirits alike. But it didn't change Asia's fundamental problems, and as economies continued to slump, the money rushed back out, leaving Asian markets at fresh lows. Across the region, unemployment and inflation were on the rise; recession was on the way.

It became clear, finally, that Asia was suf-fering from something far worse than a currency crisis. As in the savings-and-loan crisis in the United States, poorly supervised banks had funded ill-conceived projects unlikely to thrive under the best of conditions; as economies slumped, ritzy real-estate developments and hot new nightspots went cold. They left behind piles of bad loans that weighed on banks, exacerbating a credit crunch and worsening conditions for marginal businesses that needed capital to keep going. The United States and the IMF, among others, argued that what was needed was an S&L-style cleanup: close out the bad loans, force the irresponsible bank owners and borrowers to share the pain by liquidating their collateral, and then make taxpayers pay for the rest.

But it wasn't so easy in Asia. Bankruptcy laws—or the will to enforce them—were missing; many loans had been made at the government's behest or to well-connected players. And the size of the hole in the banking systems was much larger than in the United States. Where would the money for recapitalization come from? In the closing days of 1998, with global investors more nervous than ever about emerging markets, that question loomed ever larger.

The need to solve Asia's banking crisis was obscured through much of the spring and summer as the economic crisis swept into the political arena. The interruption of decades of economic growth, and the restructuring required to restart it, challenged Asia's political order. The people and parties who have translated that economic growth into decades of rule, offering prosperity in exchange for power, have come under pressure. Some fell victim to the crisis.

Soon after the crisis started, Thailand made one of its frequent changes in government, bringing Prime Minister Chuan Leekpai and his Democratic Party to power. Not long after, South Korea swept to power long-suffering pro-democracy activist Kim Dae Jung, replacing Kim Young Sam.

But most dramatic was the collapse of the 32-year reign of President Suharto of Indonesia. Initially thought to be a certain survivor of the crisis, by January 1998 Indonesia was in desperate shape. Investors, advisers, even the World Bank, which had been singing Indonesia's praises as it lent it $25 billion over three decades, concluded they had been deluding themselves: Much of Indonesia's miracle was built on corruption and easy credit.

Student-led demonstrations against Mr. Suharto and his family's extensive business interests grew in May, eventually exploding into violent clashes with police and a week of bloody riots followed by an even bloodier crackdown. But the students prevailed as Mr. Suharto's supporters deserted him and he was forced to cede power to his vice president, B. J. Habibie. The dismantling of the vast business empires of his family and friends and the search for the national assets they are accused of misappropriating started immediately but may take years to complete.

Japan held far closer to the status quo, and in doing so created even more havoc in financial markets than collapsing Indonesia. Japanese voters delivered a mid-year electoral pummeling to the ruling Liberal Democratic Party that cost Prime Minister Ryutaro Hashimoto his job. But the LDP survived basically intact, and proceeded to appoint the unpopular party insider Keizo Obuchi as Mr. Hashimoto's successor.

Japan's inability to act decisively had repercussions far beyond its own economy. The world's second-largest economy and a key investor and trading partner throughout Asia, Japan should have been helping pull Asia's damaged economies out of their slump. Instead, it was in a funk of its own, with a stagnant economy, a battered banking system and a slumping currency that exacerbated the rest of Asia's woes—"a crisis within the crisis," IMF Managing Director Michel Camdessus called it.

It fell to China to fill the leadership vacuum. China's defense of its currency and that of Hong Kong's, both of which are pegged to the U.S. dollar, became a linchpin in containing the crisis. The farther Japan's currency slid, the more China had to sacrifice its own economic competitiveness to keep its currency pegged and the more points it won on the world stage. But there are limits to China's tolerance; the question has become when, not whether, China will devalue—making the answer one of the key global issues for 1999.

Assuming no fresh catastrophes—a dangerous assumption, by 1998's measure—Asia now faces a long, difficult process of restructuring. Social and political structures that created easy wealth for cronies in Indonesia, Thailand and Malaysia, blanket job security for workers in Korea and Japan and artificially high real-estate values around the region will have to be dismantled. Capital—when it's available again—will go to companies that show they know how to use it. And more likely than not, Asians will have to learn to live with a far bigger role for foreigners in their key industries.

Darren McDermott,
staff reporter for
The Wall Street Journal
in Singapore

What Was News
Top National and International News Stories of 1998

THE MONICA LEWINSKY SCANDAL

Monica Lewinsky

The sex scandal involving President Clinton and former White House intern Monica Lewinsky kept the nation riveted throughout the past year.

The affair came to light in January in the Paula Jones sexual-harassment lawsuit against the president and reached its high point in September with the release of Independent Counsel Kenneth Starr's graphic report to Congress about the sexual relationship between Mr. Clinton and Ms. Lewinsky. Mr. Starr charged that there were 11 grounds for considering impeachment, including perjury and obstruction of justice, as well as abuse of power. The House began an impeachment inquiry, but some government officials believed some type of censure of the president would be more suitable.

Many politicians and newspapers called for Mr. Clinton's resignation, but the public didn't seem to agree. While many people found the affair distasteful and were disappointed by Mr. Clinton's denial of the relationship for so many months, Americans continued to give the president a favorable job-performance rating.

EMBASSY BOMBINGS

The U.S. embassies in Kenya and Tanzania were bombed in early August, killing more than 250 people. In retaliation, President Clinton two weeks later ordered missile strikes against terrorist training camps in Afghanistan and a suspected chemical-weapons factory in Sudan that were linked to alleged terrorist-financier Osama bin Laden.

Osama bin Laden

Mr. Clinton said there was "compelling evidence" that Mr. bin Laden's terrorist network was planning further attacks against U.S. embassies and other facilities overseas. U.S. officials had identified Mr. bin Laden as the prime suspect within hours of the embassy bombings, but decided there was little chance of prying him out of Afghanistan, either through diplomacy or by ruse.

Mr. bin Laden, the disavowed son of a Saudi construction billionaire, has few friends in the moderate Arab world. Saudi Arabia, which stripped him of citizenship in 1994, has linked him to a 1995 bombing of a U.S. military training site in Riyadh.

ASIAN CONTAGION

The Asian Contagion couldn't be contained.

Throughout 1998, Asia was beset with one economic calamity after another in a growing list of countries, including South Korea, Thailand, Indonesia, Malaysia, the Philippines and Japan. Among the many problems: plunging currencies, troubled banking systems, shrinking gross domestic products and tumbling stock market values.

Some countries also faced political upheaval. After ruling Indonesia for 32 years, President Suharto resigned under great pressure following months of economic turmoil and civil unrest. And in Japan, Ryutaro Hashimoto resigned as prime minister after the ruling Liberal Democrats suffered a humiliating election defeat.

Asia's troubles were felt in the United States, as exports to Asia dropped and some American companies' international sales and profits suffered. But strong consumer spending, business investment and home building offset the ill winds from Asia and kept the U.S. economy expanding.

CONFRONTATION WITH IRAQ

Saddam Hussein

Saddam Hussein created international tension repeatedly during 1998 by preventing United Nations representatives from searching Iraq for possible weapons of mass destruction.

Early in the year, the United States appeared poised to launch massive air strikes against Iraq. But in late February, U.N. Secretary-General Kofi Annan negotiated an agreement with Baghdad that called for Iraq to provide "immediate, unconditional and unrestricted" access to weapons inspectors.

By summer, however, Mr. Hussein was again being defiant. Iraq demanded that the U.N.'s monitoring commission be radically overhauled to lessen alleged U.S. domination before inspections could resume. The U.N. Security Council denounced Iraq's actions as "totally unacceptable," but didn't suggest any new punishments for the defiance. Bill Richardson, the U.S. ambassador to the U.N., said the real punishment is that "economic sanctions will remain in perpetuity" unless Baghdad lives up to all of the U.N.'s demands.

KIDS AS KILLERS

America was stunned repeatedly in 1998 by the murderous acts of teenagers and children.

One of the most notorious and most calculated shootings occurred on March 24 at Westside Middle School in Jonesboro, Arkansas. Two boys, ages 11 and 13, pulled a false fire alarm, and as students and teachers piled out of the building, they opened fire, killing four young girls and a 32-year-old teacher. "It's the babies that are dead, and babies that did it," said one teacher after the Jonesboro incident.

In some cases, school authorities were criticized for not responding to warnings from the young shooters. For example, Kipland Kinkel, a 15-year-old at Thurston High School in Springfield, Oregon, was obsessed with guns and bombs and announced to his literature class that he planned to "shoot everybody." But his behavior wasn't taken seriously enough, and he brought a rifle to school in May and killed two students and wounded 23 others in the cafeteria.

American society takes most of the blame for the killings. The juvenile shooting spree is considered the product of a violent U.S. culture—from the easy availability of guns to the bloody content of movies and television programs. "A nation that glorifies guns should not be shocked when children act out their dearest fantasies with those very same weapons," said gun-control lobbyist Sara Brady.

RUSSIAN ROULETTE

Russia faced political and financial turmoil in August, as the ruble plunged in value and President Boris Yeltsin fired his entire government.

Amid a growing clamor for Mr. Yeltsin to step down, he dismissed the government of Sergei Kiriyenko in August and installed as acting prime minister Viktor Chernomyrdin, a veteran Soviet-era industrialist whom he had sacked from the post only five months earlier. But the parliament rejected Mr. Chernomyrdin, and Yevgeny Primakov was ultimately confirmed as prime minister.

The political shake-up followed a de facto devaluation of the ruble and a de facto default on $40 billion of government debt. As the ruble continued to drop, Russians were scrambling to get their money out of banks. But many were turned away.

"The mood is one of despair, there is no other way to characterize it," John Paul Smith, an analyst with Morgan Stanley Dean Witter & Co., told *The Wall Street Journal*. "The speed at which the whole system has unraveled is sensational."

To try to convey a message of stability, Russian leaders said neither the economic crisis nor political bargaining with Communist legislators foreshadowed a return to Soviet-style fiscal policy.

NEW NUCLEAR THREAT

India and Pakistan reawakened fears of nuclear conflict in May when first India, then Pakistan tested nuclear devices. The tests immediately drew condemnation from other nations and threats of economic sanctions.

The sudden addition of both India and Pakistan to the world's nuclear club focused American attention on security concerns that had largely been ignored since the end of the Cold War.

India's tests of three nuclear devices showed that its new Hindu-nationalist-led government means business when it says it wants to make India a world power. But they also entail serious risks: diplomatic wrath, trade sanctions at a time when the country needs foreign investment, possible damage to budding ties with the United States and a deadly arms race with China and Pakistan.

Two weeks after India's tests, Pakistan followed suit by setting off five nuclear blasts of its own, despite a late-night phone call of concern from President Clinton to Pakistani Prime Minister Nawaz Sharif. Pakistan said the tests evened the score with India.

By September, however, both India and Pakistan said they intended to sign an international treaty banning nuclear testing.

SURPRISE SURPLUS

Washington ended its fiscal year on September 30, with the first federal budget surplus in nearly 30 years.

Budget analysts estimated a surprising surplus of about $70 billion for fiscal 1998, the first such surplus since 1969. Originally, a deficit of $5 billion to $10 billion had been expected in  *Bill Clinton* fiscal 1998, with the first surplus coming in fiscal 1999. But tax revenues flowed at an astounding rate into the Treasury's coffers in 1998 because of the robust economy and strong stock market.

Now, the question becomes how to use the surplus from 1998 and future years. President Clinton adamantly argues that it should be used to shore up the troubled Social Security program. But House Republican leaders are pushing to use a big chunk for tax cuts.

PROGRESS IN THE WAR ON CANCER

The war against cancer, marked by years of failure and frustration, advanced on several fronts in 1998.

Most notable was the report that two cancer drugs had eradicated tumors in mice. Wall Street and Main Street alike went wild as cancer patients gained a new sense of hope and investors immediately bid up the stock of little-known EntreMed Inc., the manufacturer of the new drugs, by 330 percent. The stock price later dropped back.

The new drugs blocked the blood vessels of the tumors, thereby halting the nourishment and growth of the tumors. But scientists cautioned that the therapy, which uses a technique called anti-angiogenesis, might not work as well in humans as it did in mice.

Even further along in development: a whole new generation of gene-based drugs for a broad range of cancers. They take direct aim at the genetic machinery inside malignant cells to disable defective or mutated genes that provide the marching orders for unchecked growth.

"This is the dawn of the future of cancer therapy," declared Richard Klausner, director of the National Cancer Institute. Even more ebullient was J. Michael Bishop, a Nobel laureate in cancer research: "For the first time in my life, I believe we will eventually be able to conquer cancer."

WEIRD WEATHER

Extreme weather became the norm in 1998.

People in much of the northeastern United States enjoyed one of the mildest winters ever, while Canada suffered its worst ice storm ever. Floridians battled wildfires, the tornado season was the deadliest in many years and Texans endured a fatal heat wave and severe drought. To top it all off, July was declared the hottest month on record.

The severe weather was attributed primarily to El Niño, the warming phenomenon in the Pacific Ocean. But other climatologists believe global warming caused by industrial emissions, especially carbon dioxide, may be a more fundamental cause of the weird weather.

The U.S. National Climatic Data Center in Asheville, North Carolina, may decide the new records should lead to a redefinition of "normal" weather patterns. Such a shift has multibillion-dollar consequences for business because it means changes in weather norms used for building codes, highway construction, the utility industry, flood insurance and the nation's protective levees and dams.

"This is a pretty exciting time," said Tom Karl, who directs the National Climatic Data Center and has become a frequent White House visitor, explaining the weather records to Vice President Al Gore.

MEDIA MISTAKES

"Whom do you believe?" seemed the appropriate question following a string of goofs by the news media in 1998.

The media have withstood journalistic embarrassments in the past, of course. But an unusually large number of major news organizations were caught with egg on their faces during the past year, straining their already fragile credibility with the public.

Cable News Network and *Time* magazine weathered the harshest attack over their reports that American military forces used nerve gas on U.S. defectors during the Vietnam War. The story's accuracy was quickly challenged, and CNN, which reported the story, and *Time*, which carried it, eventually issued retractions.

There also was the fabricated reporting of *New Republic* writer Stephen Glass. And the *Cincinnati Enquirer* published an extraordinary front-page apology to Chiquita Brands International Inc., renouncing a series of articles accusing the banana company of improper business practices in Latin America.

The Boston Globe suffered a double whammy. First, columnist Patricia Smith was dismissed after the paper learned she had invented people and quotations in columns. Then, columnist Mike Barnicle caused a furor by refusing to resign over close similarities between jokes printed in one of his columns and a book by comedian George Carlin. Mr. Barnicle ultimately quit over a 1995 column about two young cancer patients because he couldn't substantiate facts he reported.

GAY DEBATE

Is coming out of the closet a choice?

Republican politicians and religious groups stirred up national debate over that question during the summer of 1998 through a series of anti-gay moves. First, Senate Majority Leader Trent Lott compared homosexuality to kleptomania and alcoholism and blocked a vote to allow James Hormel,

Trent Lott

who is gay, to become ambassador to Luxembourg. Next came a major advertising campaign featuring people who claimed that they had converted from a gay to a straight lifestyle and were now happy with themselves.

Gay-rights organizations feared that after years of advances by the gay community, this right-wing backlash would stir up more homophobia throughout the country.

After all the rhetoric, though, no one could adequately answer one of the core questions in the gay debate: What makes a person a homosexual? Experts still don't know the relative contributions of genetics and environment to a person's sexual orientation, although many psychologists believe that it isn't a choice and that trying to switch from being gay to straight is extremely difficult and can be quite damaging.

CARNAGE IN KOSOVO

Violence spread during 1998 through the Serb province of Kosovo, where ethnic Albanian rebels were battling to secede from Serbia, the dominant republic in the Yugoslav Federation. Hundreds were killed in the fighting, and more than 200,000 were displaced from their homes after the Serbs cracked down on the rebels early in the year.

Hoping to end the Serb attacks in Kosovo, the North Atlantic Treaty Organization canvassed members in August to see which would join in air strikes against Serbian targets. As NATO moved closer to a bombing campaign, officials were unsure whether military action would force Yugoslav President Slobodan Milosevic and the Kosovo Albanian separatists to the bargaining table.

Mr. Milosevic stripped Kosovo, which is 90 percent Albanian, of its autonomy in 1989. The United States and its allies oppose independence for Kosovo, fearing it would lead to the unraveling of other states in the Balkans. They argue that the only solution is diplomatic negotiations to restore full political and cultural autonomy.

IRISH PEACE ACCORD

Catholic and Protestant factions in Northern Ireland reached a sweeping peace accord on Good Friday, but as the year progressed, violence flared in the troubled region.

Gerry Adams

The agreement, the result of negotiations led by former U.S. Senator George J. Mitchell, offered at least a paper peace. It established a Belfast-based assembly in which Catholics and Protestants will share day-to-day governing authority and formed a North-South Council, which will coordinate policies of mutual interest with the Republic of Ireland. Northern Ireland will retain its status as part of the United Kingdom, at least until a majority of Northern Irish people decide otherwise.

After Irish voters in the north and south voted overwhelmingly for the peace pact in May, Catholic militant Gerry Adams said, "If God spares me to live long enough, I hope to grow old in a united Ireland."

By August, that prospect seemed less likely. A car bomb killed 29 people and injured more than 200 in Omagh, a town west of Belfast, in what authorities believed was a move by the group known as the "Real IRA" to spark a backlash against the peace agreement.

HOME-RUN RACE

By mid-summer, it was no longer a matter of *if*, but rather a question of *when* Roger Maris's single-season home-run record of 61 from 1961 would be broken.

Fans kept a running tally of the home runs of two baseball players throughout the season. Finally on September 8, Mark McGwire, first baseman for the St. Louis Cardinals, hit his 62nd ball out of the park. It was Mr. McGwire's shortest homer of the season, barely clearing the wall at Busch Stadium in St. Louis.

Just five days later, Sammy Sosa of the Chicago Cubs hit two homers in a game against the Milwaukee Brewers and tied Mr. McGwire.

It became a race to the finish, and by the end of the regular season, Mr. McGwire held the record with 70 home runs to Mr. Sosa's 66.

What Was News
Top Business and Economic News Stories of 1998

RESILIENT ECONOMY

The U.S. economy continued its strong run in 1998, but some economists and business executives started talking of a recession on the horizon.

The statistics generally remained very upbeat: unemployment and consumer confidence the best they have been in nearly 30 years, stock price indexes and the housing market bouncing around all-time records, and inflation and interest rates still low and stable. In fact, Federal Reserve Chairman Alan Greenspan pronounced the economy to be as good as he has seen in 50 years of watching it.

But the nagging fear of Mr. Greenspan and others is that the odds of a downturn, though still less than 50-50, are rising. Economists believe the longer the Asian contagion rages, the greater the danger of a destructive erosion in business and consumer confidence in the United States. The trade deficit already was growing due to falling exports to struggling Asian economies and rising imports fueled by the strong dollar.

The biggest check on American business pessimism has been American consumer optimism. Household spending remained strong because of plentiful jobs, rising incomes and unprecedented gains in the stock market.

STOCK MARKET JITTERS

The bull market stampeded on in 1998, with the Dow Jones Industrial Average topping the 9000 mark for the first time on April 6 and reaching as high as 9337.97 on July 17 before a late-summer slump took its toll.

The stock market came close to entering bear-market territory when the Dow Jones Industrial Average fell nearly 20% from the July peak. The market rebounded a bit in mid-September but was falling again in early October.

Despite the continuing Asian turmoil and instability in Russia, some analysts didn't believe a bear market was necessarily in sight. They noted that in almost all the bear markets in the postwar period, the prime cause has been a rise in the U.S. inflation rate and an accompanying increase in interest rates, often leading to recession. And that wasn't the case in late summer.

MERGER MANIA

Merger mania continued in 1998, with bigger and bigger price tags.

John Reed

The granddaddy of deals was the $83 billion combination of Travelers Group Inc. and Citicorp. Not only was it the biggest merger of all time, but it also may be the trigger for the formal end of legislation preventing full-fledged unions among insurance companies, banks and brokerage firms. In fact, the merger is based on the assumption that Congress will dismantle the Depression-era law separating the banking and brokerage industries.

Behind the formation of the new company—Citigroup Inc.—is a bold bet that "cross-selling" products will finally work. Travelers is eager to sell mutual funds, annuities and insurance to customers of Citicorp. In turn, Citicorp wants to offer student loans, mortgages and trust services to clients of Travelers and its units, including Salomon Smith Barney.

"The customer doesn't want to shop from place to place and be sold time and again," said Citicorp Chairman John Reed, who will serve as co-chairman and chief executive of the merged company along with Travelers Chairman Sanford Weill. But financial supermarkets have never really worked well: High-profile attempts by American Express Co. and Sears, Roebuck & Co. to cross-sell with Wall Street partners failed.

UNITED STATES VS. MICROSOFT

Bill Gates

In a landmark antitrust lawsuit, the U.S. Department of Justice charged Microsoft Corp. with crushing competition and stifling innovation in the software industry.

The Justice Department and 20 state attorneys general sued Microsoft in May, accusing it of illegally maintaining and extending a software monopoly by tying its operating systems to its World Wide Web software. The suits charged that Microsoft undermined Netscape Communications Corp.'s business and prevented it from threatening Microsoft's Windows franchise.

The government called for a preliminary injunction forcing Microsoft to separate its Internet software from Windows so computer makers can freely choose between Microsoft and Netscape.

In seeking to demonstrate Microsoft's anticompetitive intent, the government suits cited Microsoft electronic-mail messages and internal documents to show that Chairman Bill Gates and other executives were obsessed with the threat from Netscape and had concluded that Microsoft couldn't boost its share of the browser market without technical ties between that product and the operating system. The suits also attacked a series of Microsoft contract agreements with computer on-line and Internet services, PC makers and other partners that limited their ability to use or promote Netscape's browser.

Microsoft denied the antitrust charges and sought to dismiss the suits, arguing in court filings that its Internet initiatives helped consumers and didn't prevent Netscape from marketing rival products.

GM'S LONG, HOT SUMMER

In its determination to create a leaner manufacturing operation, General Motors Corp. endured one of its longest strikes during the summer.

The strike, which continued for 54 days after the first walkout began in Flint, Michigan, was the longest, costliest labor disruption in the U.S. auto industry since the United Auto Workers union's epic 67-day national strike against GM in 1970. The strike began over a clash about company investment in a Flint metal-stamping plant and archaic work rules and productivity, and ended up costing GM at least $2 billion in lost production. The company's willingness to sacrifice that much underscores the depth of management's resolve to carry out a fundamental restructuring of operations in North America.

The settlement gives GM assurances of future labor peace and gives the union promises of more investment by GM in U.S. plants. But company executives privately vowed to continue "riding the attrition curve" as older workers retire, eliminating 50,000 more jobs in the next few years. That's a certain recipe for more battles with the UAW, which is digging in its heels to resist further erosion of its membership rolls.

"Nobody really won," said UAW President Stephen Yokich, after the settlement was reached. "We had to strike over what we already negotiated for."

UP IN SMOKE

Senate Republicans killed landmark tobacco legislation in June, reflecting a growing belief within the GOP that the public cared less about the bill than Democrats and public-health officials claimed.

The bill, which would have raised cigarette prices $1.10 a pack and broadened regulatory oversight of tobacco, was sent back to the panel where it started, the Senate Commerce Committee. But Senator John McCain of Arizona, committee chairman and the bill's author, said he had no plans to rewrite the bill to make it palatable to his colleagues.

One factor in the bill's defeat was an advertising blitz by the tobacco industry, which spent tens of millions of dollars to brand the bill as, among other things, "a tax giveaway to trial lawyers."

Democrats accused the Senate leadership of acting to protect Republicans in the House, where all members faced reelection in the fall. The tobacco industry has showered Republicans with millions of dollars in campaign contributions, including $4.4 million in 1997.

HMO ILLS

HMOs and other managed-care companies suffered financial ills and faced criticism from patients, politicians and corporate customers alike in 1998.

Corporate America was resisting steep rate increases and stepping up pressure on HMOs to cut their costs the way other industries have done.

Meanwhile in Washington, members of Congress debated how HMOs should be regulated and agreed at least some reforms are needed to give patients more freedom to choose doctors and easier access to emergency-room care.

Amid all the criticism, big managed-care companies like Oxford Health Plans Inc. and United HealthCare Corp. were ailing financially. Oxford reported a second-quarter loss of $507.6 million, including charges related to restructuring and other special items. And United HealthCare took a $900 million charge against second-quarter earnings, partly because of unexpectedly high costs in HMO plans for Medicare patients.

POTENT VIAGRA

The blockbuster drug Viagra brought impotence out of the bedroom and made it part of everyday conversation in 1998.

Viagra, which offered new hope to an estimated 20 million to 30 million men suffering from impotence, has become one of the best-selling drugs in history. Other treatments must be injected directly into the penis, but men merely have to pop one of the blue-diamond Viagra pills in their mouth to help them achieve an erection.

Indeed, because Viagra is so simple to use and effective, men who aren't suffering from any dysfunction also are trying it out, hoping to increase their sexual stamina. The drug entered questionable distribution channels thanks to opportunistic doctors, entrepreneurs and Web sites and even began turning up in discos and at parties.

Viagra isn't risk-free, however. The drug's label cautions against combining Viagra with nitrate heart medications like nitroglycerin, which can lead to dangerous drops in blood pressure. In late summer, the Food and Drug Administration said it had received reports of 123 deaths among patients who had received a Viagra prescription and had confirmed 69 of them. Eighteen deaths occurred during or immediately after sexual intercourse. Only five deaths occurred among Viagra users who had no history of heart disease or other risk factors.

The FDA and Pfizer Inc., the drug's maker, maintain that Viagra is safe and effective.

"CHAINSAW AL" GETS AXED

It was sweet revenge for thousands of workers who had lost their jobs at the hands of Albert J. Dunlap, aka "Chainsaw Al." The feared CEO got a taste of his own medicine in June, when the board of Sunbeam Corp. fired him for failing to turn around the ailing appliance maker. Directors said they lost confidence in his leadership and his financial forecasts.

Albert Dunlap

Mr. Dunlap's two-year tenure as Sunbeam's chief executive left the company in tatters, with a Securities and Exchange Commission investigation, a slew of shareholder suits and 1997 financial results that nobody can agree on. Trying to fix the mess is financier Ronald Perelman's longtime turnaround artist, Jerry Levin, Sunbeam's new CEO.

Mr. Dunlap had achieved a reputation as the ultimate "downsizer," having cut thousands of jobs at such companies as Lily-Tulip Co. and Scott Paper Co. At Scott, for example, he eliminated 11,000 jobs and set up the company for sale to Kimberly-Clark Corp. in 1995.

After slashing jobs at Sunbeam, Mr. Dunlap went into his victory dance far too soon. "We took a company that was an absolute basket case and restructured it in seven months," he declared in the paperback edition of his autobiography, *Mean Business.*

CHRYSLER-MERCEDES MARRIAGE

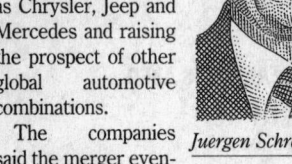

Chrysler Corp. and Daimler-Benz AG, two of the world's premier car makers, announced a surprising $38 billion merger agreement in May, bringing together such disparate brands as Chrysler, Jeep and Mercedes and raising the prospect of other global automotive combinations.

Juergen Schrempp

The companies said the merger eventually would result in annual savings and revenue gains of at least $3 billion. "When two of the most successful players are combining, it's a massive signal for the others that further combinations are needed to increase scale and reduce costs," John Casesa, an auto industry analyst, told *The Wall Street Journal*.

Industry experts were enthusiastic about the merger because of the global reach of the two companies, combined with the almost total lack of competing markets.

Juergen Schrempp, Daimler's chief executive, and Robert Eaton, Chrysler's CEO, will be co-chairmen and chief executives of the new company, DaimlerChrysler. After three years, Mr. Eaton will step down, and Mr. Schrempp will continue to run the company.

SINKING OIL PRICES

Crude oil prices dropped to their lowest level in more than a decade, benefiting consumers at the gas pump and helping spark a big industry merger.

Lower Asian demand, an unusually mild winter and burgeoning oil inventories sent prices sinking to 12-year lows. Prices hovered in the $13-a-barrel range in late summer, compared with more than $20-a-barrel as recently as the fall of 1997. The Organization of Petroleum Exporting Countries agreed in June to cut production to try to shore up prices, but it appeared unlikely that any significant price rebound would occur in 1998. Prior to the 1998 oil glut, OPEC as a group hadn't cut production in about a decade.

Spurred by the low prices, British Petroleum PLC agreed to acquire Amoco Corp. in a $48 billion deal. The mammoth merger came at a time when oil companies had all but run out of ways to boost their bottom lines as they struggled with low oil and chemical prices. The major companies have been cutting costs in the 1990s to the point where little fat remains, leaving mergers as one of the only routes to higher profits.

MARKET MERGERS

Companies weren't the only ones merging at warp speed in 1998. Three major mergers of securities markets were also announced during the year.

The biggest combination brings together the American Stock Exchange and the National Association of Securites Dealers, parent of the Nasdaq Stock Market. In addition, they also agreed to join forces with a third party, the Philadelphia Stock Exchange. The other merger would unite the Chicago Board Options Exchange and the Pacific Exchange, the nation's No. 1 and No. 3 options-trading markets.

Meanwhile, exchanges in Europe were also forming alliances, and even the New York Stock Exchange said it was exploring opportunities to become a partner with the Paris Bourse and other exchanges.

The mergers are driven by a number of factors, including the punitive cost of technology and the pressure from securities firms, themselves consolidating, to cut costs.

COOKING THE BOOKS

Cendant Corp., a little-known company with some famous brand names, gained much greater notoriety in 1998, thanks to allegations of a major accounting fraud.

Cendant, created by the $14 billion merger of HFS Inc. and CUC International Inc., said it uncovered evidence of wide-ranging fraud and estimated that about $500 million of revenue reported by CUC from 1995 to 1997 was simply invented and that 61 percent of CUC's 1997 net income was fake. Two former CUC managers blew the whistle by detailing in sworn affidavits how they had been told by superiors to record millions of dollars of phony orders and cook the books in other ways.

Walter Forbes, CUC's founder, resigned under pressure as Cendant's chairman, though he said he know of no accounting problems.

Walter Forbes

The Cendant saga is a tale of missed—or ignored—warning signs and deep mistrust in a corporate marriage that seems to have had as much to do with the desire to keep stock prices climbing as with fundamental business sense.

The HFS half of Cendant includes such powerhouse brand names as Ramada hotels and Avis rental cars, while CUC is a hodge-podge of businesses, including software, advertising publications and an on-line venture.

BANKING BEHEMOTHS

In banking, size matters. That became clearer than ever in 1998 as big banks gobbled up big banks and reshaped the industry.

During the same week in April, for example, BankAmerica Corp. agreed to join with NationsBank Corp. in a $60 billion deal, while Banc One Corp. and First Chicago NBD Corp. said they would combine in a stock swap valued at about $30 billion. The BankAmerica-NationsBank merger will create the closest thing yet to a truly national U.S. bank, spanning 24 states and Washington, D.C., and boasting $570 billion of assets, nearly 5,000 branches and roughly 15,000 automated-teller machines.

The industry consolidation started more than a decade ago, but it has evolved from regional and superregional banking in which the drive was for cost savings and efficiency. Now, it's a race to build empires that can ramp up revenue while having the geographic and customer diversity to withstand local economic downturns.

Such cross-country combinations raise some thorny issues: Are financial organizations of such scale manageable, either by the bankers who run them or the regulators who oversee them? And will the mergers reduce competition to the extent that the new giants are unresponsive to their smallest customers?

Major Global Hot Spots in 1998 and 1999

RUSSIA

Russia has entered the turbulent end game of President Boris Yeltsin's rule. The collapse of its financial markets and the appointment of a new government stacked with Soviet-era apparatchiks have terminated an era that began in 1991 when Mr. Yeltsin clambered onto a tank to defeat a hard-line putsch and bury the Soviet Union.

Boris Yeltsin

An already threadbare consensus over Russia's direction crumbled with the country's currency and stock market, leading to the September confirmation as prime minister of Yevgeny Primakov, a former foreign minister and onetime spy master. A compromise choice, Mr. Primakov has pledged to continue economic reforms but says Russia's free-market experiment must be corrected to halt "wild capitalism."

What will be put in its place, though, is uncertain. Mr. Yeltsin vows to serve out his term but has ruled out running again in presidential elections due in 2000. His ebbing authority has emboldened the communist party, which controls the largest bloc of votes in parliament as well as the country's only nationwide political organization. Both Mr. Yeltsin and his communist foes, however, share the same handicap—deep public disenchantment with the country's entire political elite.

A lurch back toward Soviet-style central planning is unlikely. There is little support for such a shift outside the communist party's avowedly Marxist fringe, and the Russian state is simply too weak to make its implementation possible.

Instead, Russia is groping toward a new model that will somehow mix markets and state control. Underpinning such a hybrid will be a robust nationalism, albeit one constrained by Russia's slight economic and hence geopolitical weight. As foreign minister, Mr. Primakov sought to enhance Russia's influence by making mischief, resisting U.S. policy in the Balkans, cozying up to Saddam Hussein in Iraq and selling missiles to Cyprus. But, after much noisy complaining, he also accepted the expansion of NATO into eastern Europe.

Russia's muddled direction will come into clearer focus with elections for a new parliament, due at the end of 1999. The communists will do well but are unlikely to expand their support beyond a traditional base that accounts for less than a third of the electorate. More important will be a race already under way to succeed Mr. Yeltsin. Communist party leader Gennady Zyuganov has a solid constituency, but it is too small to give him a majority. Better placed are relative outsiders such as Alexander Lebed, a former general now running the Siberian region of Krasnoyarsk, and Yuri Luzhkov, the mayor of Moscow. Both offer a pugnacious cocktail of nationalism and state-supervised market economics.

Russia's financial blowout discredited a free-market model that guided seven years of fitful reform. It turned what was the world's best performing emerging market in 1996 and 1997 into a virtual untouchable among foreign investors. In the first nine months of 1998, Russian shares fell by nearly 90 percent. The ruble went into freefall. The government announced a de facto default on $40 billion in domestic debt. But while the wreckage buries the reform ideal pursued by Mr. Yeltsin, it also limits the room for maneuver of his potential successors. Whatever their creed, their policies will be tethered by the same immovable fact that helped topple the Soviet Union and then undermined free-market reform: Russia, for all its oil, gas and other vast resources, is broke.

Andrew Higgins

JAPAN

If there is an epicenter in the emerging global economic crisis, Japan is it. Nearly every negative trend that battered economies around the world in 1998, from sinking currencies and stock markets to deflation and deep recession, can be traced at least in part to Japan's own stubborn economic problems. The government's agenda for 1999 is simple: to craft a credible and effective solution to the mess.

It isn't going to be easy.

Japan's problems begin with its troubled banking sector, which is burdened by $600 billion in problem loans. Facing both tougher reserve requirements and the need to set aside additional funds to deal with their bad loans, banks have throttled back their lending at home and abroad, which in turn has put the squeeze on businesses throughout Asia and deepened Japan's own serious recession.

The government's intended "soft landing" for the sector is designed both to speed a workout of the bad-debt problem and to protect the nation's 19 largest banks from bankruptcy, but it could take years to work. In the meantime, while the economy may stage a mild recovery in 1999 from an expected 2% contraction in 1998, unemployment and corporate bankruptcies—both at near-record levels—are likely to continue worsening.

Japan's much-vaunted trade surplus can't help it much, either. Any slowdown in the United States or Europe is likely to deal a serious blow to the nation's exporters, which are about the only bright spot in the entire economy. In the meantime, huge capital outflows are also likely to weaken the yen further; many economists expect to see the Japanese currency hit levels of 160 to the dollar or lower in the coming year. A weak yen makes it even less likely that Japan will import the goods Asian nations need to export for their own recoveries.

Making matters worse, Japanese politics are in disarray. Angry voters turned against the ruling Liberal Democratic Party, or LDP, in mid-1998 upper-house elections, costing Prime Minister Ryutaro Hashimoto his job. But the party itself, which has been in power almost continuously since 1955, managed to survive nearly unscathed. Its opposition remains divided, and new elections don't have to be held until 2000. That's one reason the LDP is still dragging its feet on structural economic reform in hopes that matters will get better on their own.

David P. Hamilton

AFRICA

A mix of old and new conflicts spreading across Africa, combined with a bleak economic forecast for 1999, dashed hopes for the continent of a new era of stability and prosperity.

War and political violence in 1998 rocked Algeria, Angola, Congo (formerly Zaire), Eritrea, Ethiopia, Guinea Bissau, Lesotho,

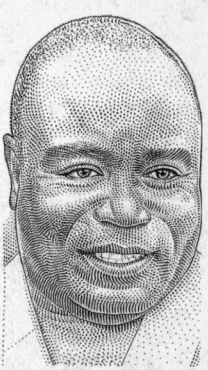

Laurent-Desire Kabila

Rwanda, Senegal, Sierra Leone, Somalia and Sudan. Driven in some cases by combinations of ethnic hatred, religious zeal, political rivalries, border disputes and economic mismanagement, many of these conflicts show no signs of long-term resolution, confounding predictions by world leaders that an African renaissance was in the offing.

Much of that hope was generated in May 1997 when rebel chieftain Laurent-Desire Kabila overthrew Zaire's dying dictator, Mobutu Sese Seko, declared himself president and promised to rebuild a mineral-rich state ravaged by decades of misrule. But the optimism was fleeting in the country Mr. Kabila renamed Congo.

After 15 months in power, he had taken few concrete steps to restore the economy and rebuild crumbling infrastructure. Mr. Kabila had cracked down on dissent. Government purges and random imprisonments, rumors of massacres and heated ethnic tensions fed disaffection both inside the country and outside until it erupted into an ethnic rebellion in August 1998 that sucked in Congo's neighbors.

In the absence of genuine efforts to address the problems of Congo's diverse ethnic groups and its moribund economy, the Central African behemoth will remain a source of regional instability.

Strife-torn Angola had also been expected to be on the mend, yet peace remained elusive. Fabulously rich in oil and diamonds, the country is nevertheless mired in poverty and instability after three decades of war between the government and the rebel Unita movement. A fragile peace signed in 1994 finally broke down in 1998.

Ethnic tensions between majority Hutus and minority Tutsis are still ripping Rwanda and Burundi apart and spilling over into neighboring countries. Violent conflict over trade and national borders between two of Africa's "new breed" leaders in Ethiopia and Eritrea dealt another blow to hopes of economic and political integration in East Africa. And in North Africa, Algeria's government is still fighting with Islamic extremists in a murderous war in which civilians are often the primary targets.

Analysts agree that Africa will never break out of the cycle of poverty and violence until it achieves a level of sustainable good governance that gives foreign investors confidence. But with the meltdown of the world's financial markets in 1998 and a slump in the price of commodities on which most of Africa depends, even those countries that have made progress, such as South Africa, are in for a rough and unpredictable year.

Robert Block

THAILAND, SOUTH KOREA AND INDONESIA

When Asia's financial turmoil erupted in Thailand in the spring of 1997, no one expected it to eventually engulf the entire region—and then to jump Asia's borders and slam Russia, Latin America, even the United States. Even as it spread, many observers expected that 1998 would be a year of recovery. Instead, it was a year of carnage.

The crisis claimed the governments of Thailand, South Korea and, most dramatically, Indonesia, where President Suharto's 32-year rule collapsed after a week of bloody rioting. Painful as those changes were, they may at least have paved the way for new governments to challenge the cronies and entrenched political structures that helped cause the crisis.

The trouble had started when speculators targeted Thailand's currency in May 1997. Thailand had borrowed billions of dollars and invested much of it in ill-conceived real-estate projects that earned Thai baht, not the hard currencies needed to repay the debt, when they earned anything at all. When the baht's peg to the dollar broke, the value of those dollar loans soared, plunging the nation into debt.

Upon reflection, speculators realized that much of Southeast Asia shared many of the same problems. Indonesia, Malaysia and the Philippines soon found their currencies under massive selling pressure, while once-plentiful foreign bank lending disappeared, exacerbating the demand for dollars and ensuring economic turmoil. Interest rates spiked, stock and property prices plunged, and wobbly banks keeled over. South Korea, which for years had been directing its banks to make loans for reasons that had little to do with the economic viability of the projects involved, and hiding the inevitable effects, couldn't stand up for long as its own citizens piled out of its currency.

By the beginning of 1998, the International Monetary Fund's three primary patients were under treatment. Thailand had been handed a $17 billion bailout; Korea, with a much bigger economy, had signed on for $56 billion and begun the process of a rescue from near default on sovereign-debt payments; and Indonesia had signed the first agreement for a $40 billion bailout. Its pact would be renegotiated and re-signed four times by June. A fourth patient, the Philippines, has been under IMF care for 12 years and remained so as the crisis swept over it.

Yet as 1998 came to a close, all four nations were still slipping further into recession, raising questions about how much longer they would submit to such painful treatment.

Darren McDermott

CHINA AND TAIWAN

China's world image underwent a radical makeover in 1998. Its leaders had gained the ugly title "Butchers of Beijing" in some quarters after soldiers gunned down hundreds of protesters at Tiananmen Square in June 1989. But in 1998, the phrase "Bulwark of Stability" was heard more often as China's economic stewardship amid Asia's tumult won praise around the world.

China pledged not to let its currency devalue, while most of its Asian trade competitors did, and it put its own export competitiveness at risk. A wholesale overhaul of its state sector, in contrast with laggards from Tokyo to Moscow, also cast China in the unaccustomed role of good guy. And a June visit by President Clinton showcased a fast-changing country with a growing middle-class, less the police state of the Tiananmen era than a profit center for a growing number of multinationals.

But the goodwill gained by China is bad news for the relatively wealthy island of Taiwan. Half a century after a civil war split the two sides, the 80-mile-wide Taiwan Strait marks the faultline of the longest-running conflict of the Cold War. Chinese missiles are no longer flying—as they did most recently in 1996 when Beijing fired warning missiles near Taiwan—but Beijing stands by its threat to use force to reclaim the island where Nationalist leader Chiang Kai-shek brought his Republic of China in 1949.

The United States put itself squarely in Beijing's camp in 1998, reiterating its opposition to independent status for the island. The peaceful transition of Hong Kong to Chinese rule in 1997, where Beijing has since been conspicuous only in its absence, is prodding Taiwan to cut a similar deal on its own future.

In 1999, the economy tops the agenda of China's rulers. They must maintain enough growth to absorb millions of Chinese made jobless by economic reforms, while fixing an insolvent banking system that unnervingly resembles those of Asia's other troubled economies. But Beijing is also impatient to bring Taiwan back into the fold. An offer of more generous terms for the island to reunify with China could pressure Taipei to make concessions. Such moves would be just the thing to cap off celebrations in 1999 marking the 50th anniversary of the Communist takeover.

Leslie Chang

THE BALKANS

No country in Europe has caused more havoc in this decade than Yugoslavia, and its tendency for violent unrest is likely to continue well beyond 1999.

The country's bloody breakup starting in 1991 left about 200,000 dead and nearly two million homeless as the war spread from Croatia into Bosnia. For the first time since World War II, Europe faced the reality of concentration camps and mass killings based on ethnicity.

A U.S.-brokered peace agreement in 1995 has brought a shaky calm to Bosnia, but it will

take years to heal the ethnic rifts and stitch the place into a stable country. For now Bosnia remains a virtual protectorate held together by tens of thousands of in-ternational troops, diplomats and human-rights workers.

The region's worst trauma has shifted south to Kosovo, a com- *Slobodan Milosevic*
bustible province of Serbia in what remains of Yugoslavia. Fighting in Kosovo exploded in early 1998 and raged through the summer as Serbian forces moved to crush an independence drive among the province's ethnic Albanians, who make up 90 percent of Kosovo's two million people.

The Albanian population has lived for years under heavy-handed Serb rule as Serbian strongman Slobodan Milosevic ran the province as a virtual police state, purging Albanians from schools and government jobs. The Albanians responded at first with peaceful resistance, but events turned violent in 1998 with the rise of the militant Kosovo Liberation Army. A Serb campaign to wipe out the militants has killed hundreds of civilians and torched more than 20,000 homes.

Bringing lasting peace to Kosovo and the rest of the Balkans won't be easy. A U.S.-led diplomatic effort hopes to achieve a respite by pushing Serbia to grant the province limited self-rule. But true calm will depend largely on whether the Serbian government can become more democratic and less brutal.

Experts have long warned that war in Kosovo could renew fighting throughout the Balkans, engulfing neighboring states like Macedonia, Albania, Bulgaria and Greece. That nightmare hasn't happened, but 1999 could be crucial in tilting the region toward peace or deeper into war.

Neil King Jr.

NORTHERN IRELAND

It was the best of times and the worst of times in Northern Ireland in 1998, with the year bringing the historic passage of the Good Friday peace agreement in April, and four months later, the bombing in the town of Omagh that killed 29 people. It was the province's worst atrocity in 30 years of troubles, but by all appearances, the Omagh tragedy represents a dying routine.

Northern Ireland is inching into a new era that is blissfully uncharted, where age-old grudges don't travel as well. The Belfast-based Assembly provided for in the agreement will assume broad powers from London in 1999, and with its all-party representation, including political wings of paramilitary groups, it has an authority that previous bodies lacked.

It has always been the details that tripped up peace efforts in Northern Ireland, and here, too, important unfinished business remains. Topping the list is the decommissioning of the Irish Republican Army's weapons, some 100 tons of guns, ammunition and explosives that are buried in dumps in Northern Ireland and the Republic of Ireland. The Good Friday Agreement requires the IRA to surrender the arms by 2000, and with negotiations under way, steady progress is crucial to the credibility of the IRA-allied political party, Sinn Fein, which leads one of the assembly's four main voting blocs. Another bit of unresolved business is the restructuring of the province's Protestant-dominated police force, which many Roman Catholics deeply distrust.

If the peace agreement is momentous for its tone of reconciliation and compromise, it calls for all sides to sacrifice something dear, especially extremists on both sides. Perhaps its most threatening provision is the all-Ireland body that will be formed to consider shared interests in the north and the south, such as transportation and tourism.

That's a long way from the republican dream of a united Ireland, but it's a chilling foreboding for Protestants who remain loyal to union with the United Kingdom.

Shailagh Murray

SOUTH ASIA

Nawaz Sharif

Just a year after India and Pakistan made tentative diplomatic steps to reduce tensions, these South Asian rivals are back on Cold War footing following their tit-for-tat nuclear weapons tests in May and June 1998. Though they merely confirmed both of their long-suspected nuclear capabilities, the detonations heightened concerns about peace and stability in this impoverished region.

Neither India nor Pakistan appeared inclined to fight another war; they have fought three since gaining independence from Britain in 1947. But there are fears that miscalculations between the distrustful neighbors could lead to a military conflict. After the first bilateral summit since the nuclear tests ended in acrimony in July, Indian and Pakistani prime ministers met again in September to ease tensions. They agreed to resume diplomatic talks, activate a telephone hotline linking their offices and reduce artillery shelling in the disputed territory of Kashmir. Both leaders told the United Nations they intended to sign a U.N.-sponsored nuclear test-ban treaty, but they each attached conditions to help them in their separate negotiations with the U.S.

The heightened tensions followed the rise of the Hindu-nationalist Bharatiya Janata Party, which formed India's government in March 1998. The BJP traditionally has taken a hard line toward Pakistan and favored making India a nuclear power. Relations with Washington soured over the tests, but U.S. sanctions had little direct impact on the economy.

For Pakistan, the nuclear tests triggered a domestic crisis that threatened the government of Prime Minister Nawaz Sharif. He spurned offers of billion of dollars of foreign aid in order to match India's nuclear might, and then was hit with U.S. sanctions that brought Pakistan to the brink of default on its foreign debt. Fearing that an economic collapse would destabilize the region, the United States softened sanctions and supported emergency International Monetary Fund aid for Pakistan.

The economic woes bred a political crisis for Mr. Sharif. And, after the United States sent cruise missiles flying over Pakistan to attack suspected terrorist bases in Afghanistan, Mr. Sharif came under pressure from Islamist opposition parties. To placate them and consolidate his power, Mr. Sharif introduced a constitutional amendment to make Islamic law supreme in Pakistan. But that move did little to buoy his sinking popularity, or his credibility with the military, which has ruled Pakistan for half of its 51-year history. Pakistani commentators said the military didn't want to rule again directly, but might move to replace Mr. Sharif if public order broke down.

The outlook for India's BJP-led coalition was precarious, as well. The initial euphoria over the nuclear tests wore off quickly amid power shortages and rising inflation, and Prime Minister Atal Bihari Vajpayee's minority coalition appeared vulnerable to fickle regional allies.

Jonathan Karp

MIDDLE EAST

The Middle East is likely to remain a center of anti-American sentiment as long as Israeli-Palestinian peace talks are in suspended animation. But some movement, toward peace or war, seems inevitable this year, as Palestinian leaders have threatened to declare an independent state by May 1999.

Syria, tired of being ignored since talks over Israel's withdrawal from the Golan Heights ended in 1995, is pushing for more leverage as sympathetic European officials take over some of Washington's role as negotiator. An Israeli withdrawal from South Lebanon, however, could reduce Syria's bargaining power: Lebanese support for Syria-backed Hizbolla would evaporate if it didn't have an Israeli army to fight.

Meanwhile, the region's economic insularity has let it avoid much of the turmoil in global markets, but if Arab states can't assert control over oil prices, tensions among them are bound to rise.

In some Arab countries, including Syria, any succession battle against long-serving leaders could bring volatile strife among ethnic groups. In Iraq, such fears for years had made the United States wary of any change in Baghdad. But the policy seemed to shift in 1998, when the Clinton administration asked Congress to let it wage covert war on Saddam Hussein, and started courting Iranian-backed groups fighting the Iraqi regime. Arab allies no longer backed the policy of fighting Saddam Hussein with sanctions and the constant threat of military strikes. To the United States, the danger after eight years of privation in Iraq is that civil society could be too weakened to allow a transition from dictatorship.

Some former archenemies might drift closer to the United States in 1999. Libya's Muammar Gadhafi, despite periodically slandering Western figures, has more to fear from Islamist opponents at home. Sudan, while indignant that a Khartoum pharmaceuticals plant was sacrificed in America's proclaimed war on terrorism, maintained its hopes for rapprochement. And Iran's President Mohammed Khatami, elected two years ago, will be looking for some payback for his softer line toward the West. Local elections this year could strengthen his support, but economic drift could prove his Achilles' heel.

Daniel Pearl

MEXICO

Mexicans are praying that the political and economic crisis that usually occurs in the last year of the Mexican president's six-year term doesn't come early this time around.

The signs aren't reassuring. President Ernesto Zedillo, who took office in December 1994, has taken steps to prevent an economic

Ernesto Zedillo

and financial crisis by floating the currency, running an austere fiscal policy and limiting the country's overseas indebtedness. Despite these steps, Mexico is at the mercy of international financial forces beyond its control. Growth in the second half of 1998 was slowing as a result of low prices for Mexico's main export, petroleum. And because of the world-wide flight of capital from emerging markets, Mexican authorities raised interest rates to hold on to more of it. By midyear, the turbulence had pushed the peso down nearly 20 percent against the dollar and made Mexico's stock market one of the world's worst-performing outside of Asia and Russia.

The slowdown, expected to last throughout 1999, will have unpleasant social consequences. It will probably contribute to a surge in crime, which has already reached epidemic proportions in Mexico's larger cities. And it could ignite new labor unrest as workers struggle to keep their wages ahead of inflation.

The campaign for Mexico's presidency in the year 2000 will be in full swing in 1999. Expected to be the most competitive in modern Mexican history, it will complicate matters for Mr. Zedillo, widely viewed as a weak chief executive with limited ability to inspire confidence. The president will continue to face a Congress where his ruling Institutional Revolutionary Party doesn't command a majority and where the center-right National Action Party, which in the past has cooperated with the PRI, may be less inclined to do so.

Further complicating the political scene, the United States will be entering the presidential-election season as well, possibly translating into shrill criticism of Mexico by the U.S. Congress on hot-button issues such as drug-trafficking and immigration.

The Zapatista guerrillas in the poor and backward state of Chiapas remain a wild card. The government is unlikely to reach a settlement with the rebels, who pose no military threat but have in the past caused the Zedillo team political and social headaches. The country's other guerrilla group, the shadowy Ejercito Popular Revolucionario, or EPR, which operates in Oaxaca and Guerrero states, could also decide to take advantage of the political season to attempt some flamboyant military raids. Both groups will take advantage of the economic slowdown to lure recruits.

Jose DeCordoba

What Was News
National and International News, 1997–1998

OCTOBER 1997

Members of a Christian men's group left Washington after a massive rally at which they pledged to be better fathers and husbands. No official tally was given for the size of the Promise Keepers event, but estimates put it at more than 500,000.

Attorney General Janet Reno criticized the White House for its tardy release of fund-raising tapes. She said she was "very disturbed" about the sudden appearance of videotapes long sought by campaign investigators. She also rebuffed claims that she had prematurely exonerated President Clinton in the affair, and said her investigation continues. Separately, House campaign hearings opened as three witnesses told lawmakers they helped launder donations to the Democrats.

A hurricane struck Mexico's west coast, killing more than 230 around Acapulco. Destruction caused by the storm, called Pauline, was extensive. Waves were more than 30 feet high and winds exceeded 100 mph at the resort city. The Pacific warm-water phenomenon called El Niño was blamed for increasing the hurricane's strength.

Childproof handgun locks will be provided with many major brands under an agreement announced by President Clinton and several big firearms manufacturers. Critics want a blanket requirement, but the president said the pact will affect 80 percent of sales.

Planned EPA rules could force utilities in 22 states in the Midwest, South and on the East Coast to cut emissions of nitrogen oxide, a smog ingredient, an average of 85 percent. The program is expected to cost utilities about $2 billion to implement by 2005.

A bill banning late so-called "partial-birth" abortions was vetoed by President Clinton, who demands an exemption when a mother's health is endangered.

A bus crash in Canada killed 43 people when the bus plunged into a ravine about 60 miles northeast of Quebec near St. Joseph-de-la-Rive, police said. The bus, traveling from the Beauce region southeast of Quebec, was carrying a senior citizens club on a sightseeing excursion for Canada's Thanksgiving.

Northern Ireland Protestants jeered and jostled Britain's Tony Blair, calling him a "traitor" after he shook hands with Sinn Fein leader Gerry Adams at Belfast peace talks. Police had to intervene. Mr. Blair is the first British prime minister in 76 years to have contact with the Irish nationalist group.

The army named Command Sgt. Maj. Robert Hall as its senior enlisted soldier, succeeding Gene McKinney as sergeant major of the army. Mr. McKinney was stripped of the title because he was to be court-martialed on charges of sex abuse.

Italy's president reinstated Prime Minister Romano Prodi after Communists completed their about-face and gave support to the government's 1998 budget. They rejected the budget over spending cuts they opposed, touching off a political crisis and threatening Italy's entry into the economic and monetary union, or EMU.

An Egyptian suspect said he was hoping to kill Jews when he and his brother shot nine German tourists to death in Cairo on Sept. 18, 1997. The man, whom Egypt described as a mental patient, and his brother were to be tried along with seven alleged accomplices.

The CIA disclosed the U.S. budget for spy services, which also includes funding for other agencies, was $26.6 billion for fiscal 1997. The disclosure came in response to a declassification suit by the Federation of American Scientists. Spending has fallen by at least $5 billion since the Cold War's end.

The Cassini spacecraft blasted off without incident from Cape Canaveral for a seven-year journey to Saturn. Protesters had tried to block the launch, fearing a mishap involving its plutonium fuel source.

British driver Andy Green set a land speed record in the supersonic range for the first time,

a two-run average of 763.035 mph. He broke the sound barrier earlier, but a glitch kept that speed out of record books.

A Georgia woman gave birth after being impregnated with frozen donor eggs in what may be the first such case in the United States. Pregnancies from frozen embryos, or fertilized eggs, are no longer rare, but frozen eggs were thought too fragile to fertilize after thawing. The Reproductive Biology Associates clinic in Atlanta performed the procedure.

The Supreme Court refused to give judges more say in minors' abortions. Justices voted 8–1 to turn away a Louisiana case involving a parental-consent law that was tougher than most states' and let stand a lower-court ruling overturning the requirement. The court also refused an appeal by a Texas death-row inmate, but four justices criticized the state for prohibiting juries from being told a convicted murderer would have no chance of parole if sentenced to life. The court agreed to hear a case involving the 1986 tax overhaul that could mean an added $1 billion in tax liability for property-casualty insurers.

President Clinton unveiled his three-stage plan to combat global warming, a proposal relying on industry cooperation, technical innovation and a trading system for carbon-dioxide emissions. It was presented to treaty negotiators in Germany, and was criticized by European Union leaders. Business and environmental groups were split over the plan.

Two air force jets collided over Edwards Air Force Base in California, killing two aboard a T-38 trainer that crashed. The other plane involved in the collision, an F-16, managed to land safely with two crewmen.

Black women marched in Philadelphia in a show of solidarity. Winnie Madikizela-Mandela, ex-wife of South Africa's president, gave the keynote speech. There was no official figure, but the crowd was estimated at 300,000 to one million.

President Clinton's nominee ended his bid to head the Veterans Affairs Department after senators scheduled a hearing on sexual-misconduct allegations against him. Hershel Gober denied the allegations.

The budget deficit narrowed to $22.6 billion, the lowest since 1974. Higher-than-expected tax revenue due to the robust economy, combined with slower spending on benefit programs, helped cut the gap, which contrasts sharply with forecasts of more than $120 billion made at the start of the fiscal year by Congress, the White House and most economists. Washington couldn't fully explain how $46 billion—money largely responsible for shrinking the deficit in the last year—ended up in Treasury coffers.

The air force released a report ruling that A-10 pilot Capt. Craig Button committed suicide when he crashed into a Colorado mountain in April 1997. But the accident panel couldn't provide a reason for his decision.

The U.N. said human-rights chief Mary Robinson would meet with Algeria's envoy in Geneva amid growing horror at the massacre of civilians in the North African nation, where 75,000 have died in a civil war. Some 30,000 Algerians marched through their capital in the largest antigovernment protest since the military voided a Muslim fundamentalist election victory in 1992. Protesters, including opposition as well as progovernment parties, charged fraud in the recent government victory in local voting.

President Clinton and Jiang Zemin met, clashing on human rights but sealing a nuclear accord. Mr. Clinton, while promising to continue the U.S. policy of engagement, said the United States had a "profound disagreement" with Beijing on freedom and human rights. Business deals were unveiled during the U.S. visit of China's president, including an accord to let Westinghouse and other firms develop nuclear power in China and a larger-than-expected $3 billion Boeing order. Separately, China promised the United States it would cut its average tariff to 10 percent. The reduction by 2005, a cut of more than half, was a response to U.S. calls for Beijing to open its vast domestic market and whittle the big trade imbalance.

Postmaster General Marvin Runyon agreed to pay $27,550 to settle Justice Department conflict-of-interest charges. The case involved his participation in talks on a deal to put Coca-Cola vending machines in post offices. Mr. Runyon held $350,000 of Coke stock at the same time.

NOVEMBER 1997

The Supreme Court refused to review California's affirmative-action ban. While setting no precedent, the court's rejection of a challenge to the 1996 ballot initiative was expected to galvanize the movement to pass similar legislation in other states and cities. If such efforts are successful, justices are almost certain to be asked to revisit the issue. The law, which passed as Proposition 209, bars race and gender preferences in government hiring, education and contracting.

The trial of Terry Nichols opened as the prosecution laid out its case against the accused accomplice in the 1995 Oklahoma City bombing. Prosecutors said Mr. Nichols helped buy and hide bomb parts, stole money to fund the plot and helped put a getaway car in place. The defense denied such a role, and said Mr. Nichols was in Kansas during the attack.

Republicans won the governorship of Virginia and a House race in New York. James Gilmore, a former state attorney general, defeated Lt. Gov. Don Beyer in the Virginia race. In Staten Island, Vito Fossella won the special election for the seat vacated when GOP Rep. Susan Molinari took a TV job. New Jersey Gov. Christine Whitman held off a little-known but unexpectedly strong Democrat, James McGreevey, in a very tight race. And New York Mayor Ruldolph Giuliani defeated Democratic challenger Ruth Messinger.

The House of Representatives approved a bill to restructure the Internal Revenue Service by a vote of 426 to 4. The legislation would create a board to oversee the agency, give taxpayers new powers in disputes and attempt to shift the bureaucracy away from law enforcement and toward customer service. The administration, which initially resisted the measure, now wants the role of its champion.

Senate Judiciary Chairman Orrin Hatch said the nomination of Bill Lann Lee to head the Justice Department's civil-rights division is dead and that he will not hold a hearing to allow Mr. Lee to answer charges he backs racial and gender preferences. The top Democrat on the panel said Republicans want to kill the nomination as a "trophy."

Thailand named Chuan Leekpai prime minister, a move expected to combat perceptions of economic mismanagement. The new prime minister, who ruled from 1992 to 1995, must meet terms of an IMF bailout after a financial crisis that brought down predecessor Chavilit Yongchaiyudh.

Flooding in Somalia killed an estimated 1,300 people and displaced 400,000 people. A month of torrential rains, blamed on the Pacific phenomenon known as El Niño, ravaged much of coastal East Africa. Meanwhile, a Somali militia freed five foreign aid workers who were kidnapped in the nation's northeast.

President Clinton conceded defeat on "fast track" trade legislation in a harsh blow to his prestige. Faced with a loss in the House on legislation to renew his authority to negotiate trade accords on an expedited basis, the president agreed to pull the bill. While he insists the setback is temporary, reviving the bill in 1998, an election year, will be hard, Senate leader Trent Lott said. Defeat diminishes Mr. Clinton's clout here and abroad and threatens to make him a lame duck early in his second term. Victory went to House Democratic leader Richard Gephardt, who kept opposition firm under great pressure.

A Massachusetts judge freed a British au pair whom a jury convicted of second-degree murder for the death of a baby in her care. The judge, in a rare move, said the evidence compelled him to reduce the jury's verdict to involuntary manslaughter and set sentence at 279 days already served. Both the prosecution and defense planned appeals.

Defense Secretary William Cohen announced plans to cut 28,000 of 140,000 civilian administrative positions over five years and put thousands of defense service jobs out for competitive bidding. He also called for two or more rounds of base closings in a bid to save $6 billion a year, but congressional opposition to further closings was fierce.

A Pakistani man was convicted of shooting two CIA employees to death and wounding three as he walked down a line of stopped cars outside the agency's Virginia headquarters in 1993. Mir Aimal Kasi was captured in a remote border area of Pakistan in June 1997. Following the conviction, five employees of Union Texas Petroleum Holdings were killed by gunmen in Karachi, apparently in retaliation. U.S. diplomats in Pakistan warned Americans further violence was

possible after a U.S. jury's decision to sentence the Pakistani to death.

Ramzi Yousef was convicted of leading the 1993 bombing of the World Trade Center that killed six and injured more than 1,000. Eyad Ismoil was convicted of driving the bomb into a parking garage under the New York landmark. Mr. Yousef was arrested in Pakistan in 1995, and an FBI agent testified he boasted of his role in the plot on the flight back to the U.S. Mr. Ismoil was arrested in Jordan, also in 1995. Prosecutors said a third defendant in the Yousef-Ismoil indictment was also being hunted.

President Clinton said Iraq's decision to carry out threats to expel American arms inspectors was "clearly unacceptable," and the United States beefed up its military presence in the Persian Gulf region. Later in the month, Saddam Hussein promised the U.N. Security Council that inspectors, including American members, would be allowed back. The United States insisted on unimpeded inspections before Iraq sanctions would be lifted, but Defense Secretary William Cohen said Baghdad had ruled off-limits 63 sites, including 47 presidential compounds, to U.N. inspectors. Meanwhile, U.N. inspectors reported to the Security Council that banned weapons remain concealed and recommended a stricter inspections regime.

Dormant AIDS-virus cells were found in patients whose bloodstreams were thought free of the virus after getting new combination therapies, two teams of researchers said. One prominent AIDS scientist had argued a three-drug combination could wipe out the virus, but his view was attacked as overly optimistic.

Vietnamese leaders mourned victims of Typhoon Linda, which was the nation's most destructive storm since 1904. At least 3,406 people, many at sea on fishing boats, were presumed killed.

Chinese dissident Wei Jingsheng arrived in the United States after being released from a Chinese prison, in a major human-rights concession just weeks after Chinese President Jiang Zemin met with President Clinton. Mr. Wei said his need for medical care was the only reason he left China.

A federal judge in California ruled, for the second time, that much of the state's proposed ban on benefits to illegal immigrants is unconstitutional. The ban, approved as a ballot initiative called Proposition 187, has been tied up in court since 1994.

Ron Carey was disqualified from running for Teamsters chief in 1998. The decision by a federal overseer left the field to Detroit labor lawyer James P. Hoffa, son of the longtime union boss. The decision was based on the same allegations that led to the August 22 overturning of Mr. Carey's 1996 victory, namely that his campaign, styled as a reform movement, ran a $750,000 illegal fund-raising scheme. Later in the month, a review panel charged Mr. Carey with financial improprieties, and he said he would take an "unpaid leave of absence" to fight allegations he took part in the scheme to divert union funds to his 1996 election campaign.

The FBI formally closed the criminal investigation into the TWA crash. The bureau said it followed 3,000 leads, conducted 7,000 interviews and spent as much as $20 million to determine if a bomb or missile brought down the Paris-bound Boeing 747 off New York on July 17, 1996. Assistant Director James Kallstrom said no such evidence had been found. The focus shifted to federal safety officials, who were to hold hearings in December on the hunt for a mechanical cause.

Egyptian Islamic militants claimed responsibility for the killing of 62 people, mostly foreign tourists, at a temple near Luxor, and said the attack was meant to force the United States to free Sheik Omar Abdel-Rahman. The blind Muslim cleric is serving a life term in the United States for his involvement in a plot to bomb New York City landmarks.

The American Medical Association said it planned to create a seal of approval for physicians who meet certain quality criteria, drawing immediate criticism from skeptics who question how the group can rate its own members. The AMA says the accreditations will ease consumer fears about cost-cutting. Collected data are to be sold to health plans.

Russian President Boris Yeltsin removed deputy premiers Anatoly Chubais and Boris Nemtsov from second positions as finance minister and energy minister, respectively. The move averted a showdown with Russian lawmakers who threatened to derail the 1998

budget, in the wake of a book-advance scandal implicating Mr. Chubais. Mr. Yeltsin named Mikhail Zadornov, a well-regarded Duma budget-panel member, as finance chief. But Mr. Chubais remained deputy premier in charge of economic reform.

An Iowa woman gave birth to four boys and three girls, the second set of septuplets known to be born alive. The babies, from 2 pounds, 5 ounces, to 3 pounds, 4 ounces, were delivered by Caesarean section. The parents, Bobbi and Kenny McCaughey, had taken fertility drugs and refused suggestions that some of the fetuses be aborted.

Affirmative-action laws remain unsettled after civil-rights groups agreed to contribute more than $300,000 to settle a white New Jersey school teacher's complaint. The U.S. Supreme Court had been set to hear the case, and experts say no other case is likely to be taken up by the court soon in its place.

A onetime lobbyist was convicted of giving illegal gratuities to former Agriculture chief Mike Espy, but acquitted of making illegal contributions to Mr. Espy's brother. Prosecutors told a jury that Richard Douglas acted at the behest of Sun-Diamond Growers, which relies heavily on government purchases.

Car use will be banned at the Grand Canyon, Yosemite and Zion national parks under a plan to reduce overcrowding. Visitors would ride buses and light-rail systems instead. Interior Secretary Bruce Babbitt said the changes, beginning in 2000, would be a model for other popular national parks.

Boeing 747s should be fitted with shields to guard against possible electrical surges near the jumbo jets' center fuel tanks, the FAA said. While no cause has been determined for the 1996 TWA explosion, speculation centers on an electrical spike near Flight 800's center fuel tank.

Israel's cabinet approved Prime Minister Benjamin Netanyahu's West Bank pullback in principle. No decision was taken on the withdrawl's extent or timetable. Media reports put the planned pullout at 6 percent to 8 percent of the West Bank, which Palestinians reject as inadequate. The pullback is conditional upon Palestinian action to fight terrorism and agreement to move to a final settlement, a cabinet spokesman said. The cabinet decision came a day after widespread Palestinian-Israeli clashes, the worst in months, left more than 40 demonstrators and troops injured.

India's government collapsed for the second time in seven months, threatening a further blow to the rupee and delays in market reforms needed to attract investment. The Congress Party, which brought the government down, was bidding to form a new coalition, but new parliamentary elections could be called.

DECEMBER 1997

A federal jury convicted former Agriculture Secretary Mike Espy's onetime chief of staff, Ronald Blackley, of lying to hide more than $22,000 in payments from Mississippi agribusiness interests. Separately, Tyson Foods agreed to pay $6 million to settle charges in the Espy case. In return, the poultry firm received protection from prosecution for top executives and avoided any possible suspension from government contracts. It admitted giving $12,000 in illegal gratuities to Mr. Espy.

Attorney General Janet Reno rejected seeking an independent counsel for an inquiry into fund-raising by President Clinton and Vice President Al Gore. Later in the month, under questioning by a House panel, the attorney general defended her rejection, but FBI Director Louis Freeh wouldn't explain why he had urged appointment of an outside prosecutor. Mr. Freeh did say some agents were frustrated by the Justice Department's decision.

The FDA approved irradiation as a safe way to rid meat of bacteria. The agency allowed use of gamma rays in low dosages on beef and other red meats such as lamb, and changed the dosage levels for pork. But few meat processors seem willing to be the first to bring irradiated beef, lamb or pork products to market.

Pakistan's president resigned and its chief justice was ousted, both victims of a power struggle with Prime Minister Nawaz Sharif that forced the army to step in as mediator. The developments appeared to bolster Mr. Sharif, who battled President Farooq Leghari and the judiciary in pushing for Parliament's supremacy.

More than 120 nations began signing a treaty to ban antipersonnel land mines. The United States, which sent observers to the two-day Ottawa proceeding, has said it could sign the treaty only if exemptions were made to protect its troops in Korea. Other countries not signing include Russia, China and Iraq.

Winnie Madikizela-Mandela denied allegations of murder and assault but said she was "deeply sorry" that "things went horribly wrong," after South African commission chairman Desmond Tutu begged her to offer an apology. She insisted most witnesses had lied.

Mars at one time was more like Earth than previously imagined, astronomers said in reporting data in the journal *Science* from the Mars Pathfinder mission. Water once flowed on the planet's surface, creating boulders, pebbles and sand. It has a molten core similar to Earth's, and it has clouds.

The Medicare program made "excessive payments" for prescription drugs totaling $447 million in 1996, according to federal investigators. Medicare inspectors also found widespread problems in a part of the program that provides durable equipment such as wheelchairs. Inspectors said 41 percent of suppliers and 40 percent of new applicants fail to meet the program's requirements, including maintaining an address.

President Clinton ordered the Pentagon to maintain hundreds of troops in Haiti, to keep the nation from falling back into chaos. Canadian and Pakistani troops had already pulled out.

M. Larry Lawrence's widow said she would have the body of the late ambassador to Switzerland and prominent Democratic contributor removed from Arlington National Cemetery and taken to San Diego. She told President Clinton that the burial controversy, after questions were raised about Mr. Lawrence's wartime service, would preclude his resting "in peace."

Talks on a Korean peace began for the first time since a 1953 armistice ended the Korean War. But swift progress wasn't likely, as representatives of the North and South, China and the United States sat down in Geneva. Meanwhile, relief workers reported North Korea's famine had doubled death rates among young children.

World diplomats approved a sweeping global-warming agreement. More than 160 nations endorsed the treaty, which binds industrial nations to cut emissions of so-called greenhouse gases by 6 to 8 percent from 1990 levels, starting in 2008. But negotiators fell short of a key U.S. goal: to get developing nations to commit to "meaningful" targets. An industry spokesman said "business, labor and agriculture will campaign hard and defeat it."

Britain rejected Spain's proposal for shared sovereignty over tiny but strategically important Gibraltar. U.K. officials said people living in the Mediterranean territory must decide its future status.

Former Housing and Urban Development chief Henry Cisneros was indicted on 18 counts of conspiracy, obstructing justice and making false statements about payments to a former mistress. His attorney said Mr. Cisneros will "defend himself vigorously" and expects to be exonerated. Three other people, including the ex-mistress, were also charged.

The Internal Revenue Service unveiled modest new protections for taxpayers after an internal audit criticized a management "climate" that "could affect" fair treatment. One change limiting agents' discretion requires them to consult with an IRS "taxpayer advocate" if a delinquent citizen says a property seizure would cause "hardship."

President Clinton named Bill Lann Lee to the top civil-rights post, bypassing the Senate. The president, acting weeks after Congress adjourned without voting on his controversial nominee for the Justice Department job, appointed the California NAACP lawyer "acting" assistant attorney general. That designation was intended to hold down criticism from Republican leaders while allowing Mr. Lee to serve for the rest of Mr. Clinton's term.

Defense Secretary William Cohen ordered all 1.5 million men and women in uniform to be inoculated against anthrax, citing a growing global threat of biological warfare. Treatment involves six shots over 18 months, then annual boosters. Iraq, Russia and as many as 10 other nations are believed to have weapons capable of delivering anthrax.

Iraq refused to allow U.N. inspectors to enter any of Saddam Hussein's palaces, the chief arms inspector said after two days of talks in Baghdad. Richard Butler said the Iraqis told him permission will never be granted. Separately, the Security Council demanded that Iraq allow inspectors into all suspected weapons sites, saying failure to do so was "unacceptable."

Nelson Mandela resigned as head of South Africa's ruling African National Congress. The move began the gradual winding down of Mr. Mandela's presidency, which ends in 1999, and the transfer of power to his designated successor, Thabo Mbeki. In a farewell address, Mr. Mandela made a surprisingly bitter attack on whites for their reluctance to embrace and their efforts to undermine a three-year-old black-led government.

Czech President Vaclav Havel named Josef Tosovsky, a central bank governor, to succeed Prime Minister Vaclav Klaus, who quit in a campaign scandal.

Gay and unmarried couples reached a settlement with New Jersey giving them the right to jointly adopt children, which, according to gay-rights activists, makes it the only state to grant such status. Many states let individuals in such relationships adopt, but require second petitions from partners.

A Japanese TV network canceled the cartoon *Pokemon* after hundreds of young viewers were taken to hospitals with convulsions and nausea. Health experts said the show's flashing lights or sheer intensity may have been to blame.

Kim Dae Jung won the presidency of South Korea. The election of the 72-year-old longtime dissident marked the first shift away from the ruling elite. He drew 40.3 percent of the vote, while Lee Hoi Chang of the renamed ruling party got 38.7 percent.

U.S. troops will stay in Bosnia indefinitely, President Clinton announced, adding he was wrong to have promised a June 1998 withdrawal. The president said NATO will determine the size and scope of the extended mission. Mr. Clinton made a one-day trip to Bosnia, touring Sarajevo and visiting troops.

Scottish cloning scientists produced two lambs that contain a human gene, giving their milk a blood-clotting protein that can be extracted for use in treating hemophilia. Polly and Molly continue the line of research that started with Dolly, the first large mammal to be cloned.

Despite charges of voting fraud, electoral authorities in Serbia proclaimed Milan Milutinovic, protégé of strongman Slobodan Milosevic, winner of the presidential election.

Terry Nichols was found guilty of conspiracy in the Oklahoma City bombing. Jurors, however, decided that he didn't play a direct role in carrying out the April 19, 1995, attack that killed 168 people. Mr. Nichols was acquitted of murder in the deaths of eight federal agents in the attack, with the jury instead convicting him of involuntary manslaughter.

Gunmen in Mexico massacred 45 Indians in the southern state of Chiapas. Eleven villagers were wounded in the attack, which survivors said was carried out by local loyalists of the PRI, Mexico's ruling party. Government critics said Mexico's leaders deserve some blame, and the attorney general promised to question officials about their response to warnings an attack appeared imminent. Sporadic violence has gripped Chiapas since Zapatista rebels began a revolt early in 1994.

"Carlos the Jackal" was convicted in France of the 1975 murders of two French investigators and a Lebanese man. He faces a life term. Ilich Ramirez Sanchez, captured in Sudan in 1994, was linked to such 1970s political attacks as the Entebbe hijacking.

Hong Kong ordered all chickens slaughtered as fear of a deadly flu rose. An estimated 1.2 million chickens, and any other birds that came in contact with them, were to be gassed and buried in three big landfills. The extraordinary measures were ordered after a fourth person was confirmed to have died of the mysterious avian disease, for a total of 12 cases. The cases, the first known instances of an avian flu directly infecting humans, alarmed health officials in the United States.

Air turbulence killed a Japanese woman and injured 87 of the 412 people aboard a United Air flight from Tokyo to Honolulu. The FAA said the Boeing 747, flying at 33,000 feet about 925 miles east of Tokyo, dropped suddenly and sent those whose seat belts weren't fastened into the overhead luggage bins.

JANUARY 1998

California smokers began life under a ban covering bars and casinos, among the last public places they could light up legally. Many people ignored the ban when it took effect January 1, but an antismoking group said enforcement and compliance would grow.

Israel's foreign minister quit, putting the Netanyahu government in peril. David Levy's announcement left the Likud-led governing coalition with a one-vote majority in the Knesset, and the opposition Labor Party said it would try to force early elections. Mr. Levy had been at odds with his colleagues over the stalled peace process and cited budget cuts in his announcement.

Kenyan election officials declared President Moi the winner of a chaotic presidential vote, giving him another five-year term. Mr. Moi, 73, has ruled since 1978 as criticism of his regime's corruption has mounted. He dismissed his rivals' charges of vote-rigging.

Lithuanians elected Valdas Adamkus, 72, a retired Chicago-area EPA administrator, as president. Mr. Adamkus won by a hair in runoff elections, taking 49.9 percent of the vote to 49.3 percent for challenger Arturas Paulauskas, 44, former top prosecutor. Mr. Adamkus seeks better ties to the West.

President Clinton proposed the biggest expansion of Medicare in its 31-year history. The main thrust of the plan is to let uninsured people age 62 through 64 buy Medicare coverage for $300 a month. Two other significant provisions were also unveiled: One would give workers 55 and older who are laid off the ability to buy coverage for $400 a month. The other would let retirees 55 and older buy into former employers' health plans until age 65 if firms cancel benefits.

NASA launched *Lunar Prospector*, a $63 million mission to map the moon for a year and hunt for water and minerals that could be useful in future exploration efforts. The last U.S. lunar mission was *Apollo 17* in late 1972.

President Clinton's use of the line-item veto was overturned by a federal judge in a case involving pension plans for federal workers. The judge accepted an administration-union deal restoring workers' ability to switch plans later in 1998. Two other legal challenges to the new veto powers were pending.

Terry Nichols was spared execution in the Oklahoma City bombing case. Jurors, after two days of deliberations, failed to agree on a sentence and handed the decision to a federal judge in Denver, who, under federal law, can't impose the death sentence in the absence of a jury verdict.

Iran's president called for cultural exchanges with the United States to ease two decades of hostility, but stopped short of offering political negotiations at this time. Cultural exchanges with Iran will be considered, the White House said, but the State Department said it favors a political dialogue and wants issues such as terrorism to be addressed.

Ramzi Yousef was sentenced to life in prison for the 1994 bombing of a Philippines airliner and 240 years for masterminding the 1993 World Trade Center bombing. The judge, calling him "an apostle of evil," recommended he be kept in solitary confinement. "Yes, I am a terrorist and I am proud of it," Mr. Yousef declared at the hearing.

Federal climate researchers said 1997 was the warmest year on record, and for the first time said human activities are playing a role. The head of the National Oceanic and Atmospheric Administration noted reports that oceans have risen six inches this century and Alaska's permafrost is softening.

Canada and the northeastern United States dug out from a destructive ice storm. Millions were without power, and search parties combed remote areas for people stranded by the storm. Thousands took to shelters as temperatures plunged after the five-day storm let up. At least 12 deaths were reported in Canada, five in New York state and two in Maine.

The death toll from an earthquake in China rose to 47, and officials said destruction was more widespread than initially thought. About 11,400 people were injured and 44,000 left homeless after the quake, centered near the Great Wall 150 miles north of Beijing and measured at 6.2 on the Richter scale.

The Asian financial crisis shook up U.S. foreign policy in areas from defense cuts by allies to South Korean funding for a reactor project meant to stop North Korea's nuclear-arms bid. Defense Secretary William Cohen toured the region to reassure leaders of U.S. support and discuss revising arms-acquisition plans.

A human-cloning ban was signed by 19 European nations, which called the technique a misuse of science. Britain and Germany balked. President Clinton urged Congress to pass such a ban after a Chicago physicist said he would try to clone a child.

Bob Dole registered with the Justice Department as a foreign agent for Taiwan, but his law firm insisted the former Senate leader won't be lobbying Congress. Instead, the firm said, he will provide "strategic advice" under a $30,000-a-month contract.

Israel's cabinet voted to keep permanent control over much of the West Bank, including its eastern and western edges, areas near Jerusalem, and all settlements, major roads, water sources and historical sites. The decision further threatened any prospect of meaningful peace talks. Separately, President Clinton met with both Israeli Prime Minister Benjamin Netanyahu and Palestinian leader Yasser Arafat in Washington, but little progress was made in reviving the peace process.

John Glenn was scheduled to travel back into space on a shuttle mission set for October, 36 years after he became the first American to orbit Earth. The senator has long lobbied for a return flight, and his role on the 10-day mission was to be as a subject in tests on the effects of weightlessness on the elderly.

Henry Cisneros's onetime mistress pleaded guilty to criminal charges linked to payments the former HUD secretary made to her after they ended their affair. Mr. Cisneros was awaiting trial on charges that he lied to federal investigators about the payments.

Police in Guatemala arrested four suspects and were seeking three more for raping five women in the daylight armed robbery of a busload of U.S. college students. The bus was forced off a road during a tour of local cultural and historical sites.

Three calves were cloned by University of Massachusetts researchers, who genetically altered them in a move that significantly enhances the economics of making medicine in animal milk. Cows make more milk than sheep, the only large mammal cloned until now.

Zimbabwe called out the army to quell two days of rioting over rising food prices, and President Mugabe threatened a state of emergency. It was the first time troops have been used to control civil unrest since the former Rhodesia's independence in 1980.

President Clinton was hit with allegations of an affair with a young White House intern. Responding to reports that the Whitewater prosecutor has expanded his investigation to include the new accusations, Mr. Clinton denied having a sexual relationship with Monica Lewinsky, 24, and said he never told her to lie to lawyers in the Paula Jones sexual-harassment suit. Ms. Lewinsky denied an affair in an affidavit taken in the case, but a former White House aide reportedly secretly taped her discussing the affair.

Pope John Paul II arrived in Cuba and said the United States should change its 35-year economic embargo against the Communist island. The pope told Fidel Castro that Cuba needs to make "progress in the order of human freedom" and criticized the country's relaxed attitude toward abortion. He also called for Mr. Castro to free political prisoners.

Theodore Kaczynski admitted that he is the Unabomber in a deal to escape execution. The antitechnology hermit, who conducted an 18-year bombing campaign that included elaborately made explosive devices he sent through the mail, entered the plea just before his trial was to have started and after the judge denied his request to act as his own attorney. The agreement resolves all federal charges arising from the bombing spree, which killed three people and injured 29 across the United States. He will serve life in prison without parole.

President Clinton told Congress of his spending plans and gave Iraq a tough warning in his State of the Union address. He called for new education, health and environmental initiatives, and an increase in the minimum wage. Mr. Clinton also said he wants to use $200 billion in surpluses expected over five years for Social Security alone. He told Saddam Hussein, "You cannot defy the will of the world," and vowed the United States would prevent Iraq from ever using weapons of mass destruction. In the GOP response, Senate leader Trent Lott called for tax cuts and a ban on some late-term abortions.

India sentenced 26 people to hang for the 1991 assassination of Rajiv Gandhi. The leader of the Tamil Tigers rebel group in Sri Lanka and two top aides were convicted in absentia by the court in southern Tamil Nadu state, site of the prime minister's killing. Only two defendants were convicted of murder; the rest were tried under special terrorist laws. Mr. Gandhi and 17 others were killed at a rally near Poonamallee when a suicide bomber offered him flowers, then set off a pound of explosives.

An abortion clinic was bombed in Birmingham, Alabama, killing an off-duty police officer moonlighting as a security guard and critically injuring a nurse. It was the first fatal bombing of a U.S. abortion clinic.

Interior Secretary Bruce Babbitt appeared before the House campaign committee and angrily denied that political contributions to Democrats played any role in his 1995 rejection of a Wisconsin Indian tribe's casino.

The navy was ordered by a federal judge to reinstate a sailor dismissed after he was accused of being a homosexual based on America Online's identification of him as the author of a pseudonymous profile. A lawyer for Timothy R. McVeigh said the 17-year veteran feared for his safety.

FEBRUARY

President Clinton proposed a $1.733-trillion budget, the first in 30 years with no deficit. The president said his fiscal 1999 spending plan, projecting a nearly $10 billion surplus, marks the end of an era of shortfalls "that have shackled our economy, paralyzed our politics and held our people back." It calls for $135 billion over five years in new and increased spending, as well as tax breaks for education, technology, research, job training and fighting crime and drugs, among other things. Critics said it marks the return of big government.

U.S. AIDS deaths fell 44 percent in the first half of 1997, the Centers for Disease Control and

Prevention said. The big decline was attributed to new combination therapies. AIDS deaths totaled 12,040 in the period, compared with 21,460 in the 1996 first half. Separately, AIDS scientists pinpointed what they believe is the earliest known case of the disease, an African man who died of it in 1959.

Former Arizona Gov. Fife Symington drew a 2½-year prison term after being convicted of lying to get big loans to shore up his collapsing real-estate empire. The judge, saying the harm to lenders had been "significantly overstated," ordered a sentence for the two-term Republican that was much lighter than prosecutors had requested.

Texas executed Karla Faye Tucker for the 1983 pickax slayings of two people during a break-in. She is the first woman put to death in the state since 1863, and the first in the United States since 1984.

A U.S. warplane struck a cable carrying a gondola to a mountaintop ski resort in northern Italy, and 20 people died when the car fell hundreds of feet in the Dolomite Mountains near Trento.

Sgt. Maj. Gene McKinney pleaded innocent to charges of sexual misconduct against six women as jury selection began in the court-martial of the army's former top enlisted man.

Yah Lin "Charlie" Trie pleaded innocent to charges that he raised illegal campaign contributions for the Democrats and obstructed Justice Department and congressional inquiries. The Clinton associate, who returned to the United States from Macau, also denied through his lawyer that he had ever served as a spy for a foreign country. Separately, Maria Hsia, a Democratic fund-raiser, pleaded innocent to charges she laundered Clinton-Gore campaign funds through a Buddhist temple in California.

An earthquake in Afghanistan left as many as 5,000 dead in northern Takhar province. The quake measured 6.1 on the Richter scale and struck where the Hindu Kush and Pamir mountains meet.

Rebels in Colombia blew up the nation's main oil pipeline, spilling 15,000 gallons of crude oil and forcing the suspension of pumping. The attack, 285 miles north of Bogota near the town of El Carmen, was the seventh on an oil pipeline so far this year.

France's National Assembly gave initial approval to a bill to cut the workweek to 35 hours from 39 starting in 2000, a measure the Socialist government hoped would create jobs amid unrest over the nation's 12.2 percent unemployment rate. Employers argued it would make them less competitive in world markets.

A U.N. food agency said 10 million people in East Africa need emergency aid because of crop damage from floods linked to the El Niño weather phenomenon. Kenya said the floods boosted mosquito populations, and malaria killed 354 people in recent weeks.

An abortion-clinic arsonist pleaded guilty to setting fire to seven clinics over three years in California, Montana, Idaho and Wyoming. Under the plea agreement, Richard T. Andrews of Washington state is to serve nearly seven years in prison.

Attorney General Janet Reno asked for an independent counsel to investigate Interior Secretary Bruce Babbitt. It was the first appointment of a special prosecutor in the campaign fund-raising affair. Mr. Babbitt was accused of misleading Congress about his role in the 1995 rejection of Wisconsin Indian tribes' casino plan. Republicans charge he was influenced by casino opponents' donations to the Democrats. Mr. Babbitt denies such influence, and said the local community opposed the casino.

A Maine gay-rights law was repealed at referendum, losing by a two-point margin with 30 percent of the registered voters taking part. The Christian Coalition, which backed the repeal drive, said similar efforts may be made in the 10 other states, plus the District of Columbia, that have laws barring discrimination in jobs, housing and other areas.

The EPA proposed requiring private and municipal water systems to tell customers of pollutants in drinking water and list their sources and health risks. Such information would be provided in annual reports, the first of which are due in October 1999. The rules would apply to 56,000 water systems across the nation.

The line-item veto was ruled unconstitutional by a U.S. District Court judge in Washington in a case brought by New York and an Idaho farmers group over Clinton vetoes affecting them. The administration said it would appeal on an expedited basis to the Supreme Court.

Nigerian-led troops in Sierra Leone said they captured the presidential residence in Freetown and were mopping up resistance by the junta that overthrew President Kabbah. A Belgian aid group said 250 people died and 5,000 others fled during the recent fighting for the city. Later in the month, Sierra Leone's second city was captured by troops pursuing forces loyal to the junta.

A Taiwan jet crash killed all 196 aboard, including the central bank leaders. Seven people were reported killed on the ground when the China Air plane crashed short of the runway while trying to land in fog at Chiang Kai-Shek airport near Taipei after a flight from Bali.

Indonesia's President Suharto installed a new military chief in a bid to maintain stability amid growing unrest brought on by the nation's economic crisis. Later in the month, Indonesia imposed a 25-day ban on street protests to quell rising discontent about higher prices. Human-rights groups said five people died and 13 were missing in rioting in February.

The FBI arrested two men suspected of possessing anthrax, a biological-warfare agent, in Nevada, but the case was dropped after tests showed the substance was actually a vaccine. One suspect, however, was charged with violating probation from his 1995 conviction for buying bubonic plague material by mail. Larry Wayne Harris, a reputed white supremacist, was accused of threatening to possess anthrax to use as a weapon.

Barnes & Noble said it will plead not guilty to Alabama charges that it is violating child-pornography laws by selling two books containing photos of nude children. The chain said it won't take the books off shelves before any verdict.

Cuba said it had freed 299 prisoners in response to a plea by Pope John Paul II during his recent visit to the Communist island. Political dissidents said they were able to confirm release of only 136.

U.N. Secretary-General Kofi Annan announced a deal was reached in Baghdad after talks with Saddam Hussein and other top Iraq officials. President Clinton cautiously endorsed the accord, but warned of "serious consequences" if Baghdad reneges on its agreement to give unrestricted access to U.N. arms inspectors. He credited the U.S. military force in the Persian Gulf with producing the deal. But Senate leader Trent Lott complained the deal with Baghdad "does not adequately address the threat posed by Saddam Hussein."

Former Arkansas Governor Jim Guy Tucker agreed to cooperate with the Whitewater prosecutor in a plea bargain that spared him a potential prison sentence. Mr. Tucker, who resigned in 1996 after a conviction in an unrelated case, pleaded guilty to conspiring to avoid taxes through a sham bankruptcy.

Sinn Fein, the IRA-allied party, was ejected from Northern Ireland peace talks. Britain called for the expulsion after two recent killings were blamed on the IRA. Sinn Fein leaders vowed to challenge the move.

The 18th Winter Olympics ended with ceremonies in Nagano, Japan, and the flag was passed to Salt Lake City, the host for the 2002 Games. Germany won the most medals, 12 gold, nine silver and eight bronze. Norway placed second with 10, 10 and five, while Russia was third with nine, six and three.

The Supreme Court refused to hear a double-jeopardy challenge to New Jersey's Megan's Law, which requires that communities be told of the whereabouts of sex offenders who have served their sentences. Most states have similar laws.

El Niño storms made this the wettest winter this century for California, which suffered from severe floods and mudslides. Meanwhile, tornadoes in Florida killed an estimated 40 people and caused about $100 million in damage.

U.S. high-school seniors ranked near the bottom of the industrialized world in international mathematics and science tests. While doing slightly better in science, the United States placed ahead of only Cyprus and South Africa in math among the 21 countries that had participated.

Rep. Bill Paxon announced that he wouldn't seek re-election. The New York Republican played a central role in the 1997 failed effort to topple House Speaker Newt Gingrich, and was openly moving to challenge Majority Leader Richard Armey in leadership elections.

The Senate deadlocked on campaign reform, burying the issue. In a final test vote on the bipartisan McCain-Feingold bill to ban unregulated "soft money" contributions, supporters fell eight votes short of the 60 needed to end a Republican filibuster.

Oprah Winfrey was found not liable for damages in a Texas lawsuit brought by cattlemen claiming the TV talk-show host's 1996 comments about "mad cow" disease caused beef prices to plunge. Ms. Winfrey said the case was an attempt to "muzzle" her.

MARCH

South Korea's president named his cabinet over fierce opposition in the National Assembly to Kim Jong Pil, nominee for prime minister. After a vote was blocked, he was named acting premier. Other choices were viewed by some as ill-suited for an economic overhaul.

The Supreme Court ruled that workers can sue for same-sex harassment. In a unanimous decision with big implications for U.S. workplaces, justices overruled lower courts and found a suit filed by a worker on an offshore oil rig, who claimed male supervisors harassed him to the point he feared rape, was covered by civil-rights laws. The court also put new constraints on harassment suits of all kinds, urging judges to use common sense in deciding whether to let them proceed.

Ezer Weizman won election to a second five-year term as Israel's president in a 63–49 Knesset defeat of Prime Minister Netanyahu's choice, Shaul Amor.

A California court ruled parenthood isn't just genes in a test-tube age. The appellate panel said a man who consented to a high-tech baby-making procedure before divorcing must pay support even though neither he nor his wife are genetically related to the child. They arranged in 1994 to make an embryo from a donor egg and sperm, and have it carried to term by a surrogate. Experts expect the case to reverberate beyond California, a bellwether in the emerging area of reproductive law.

A U.S. special envoy to Serbia accused Belgrade of "brutal, disproportionate and overwhelming" force against ethnic Albanians in Kosovo province. A mass viewing was held for some of the estimated 85 people killed in a Serb crackdown. Separately, President Clinton warned the recent killings in Kosovo province could escalate into a Bosnia-style war.

Miami election results were reversed by a federal appeals court, which restored Joe Carollo to the mayor's office four months after he was beaten by Xavier Suarez in a vote later voided because of fraudulent absentee ballots.

An asteroid will miss the Earth by at least 600,000 miles, astronomers at NASA's Jet Propulsion Laboratory said. The finding came a day after other astronomical groups warned of a possible collision in 2028. A JPL official said chances of that are "zero."

President Clinton faced fresh legal and political problems arising from the sex scandal. Paula Jones's lawyers' release of 700 pages of documents did little to bolster her sex-discrimination case, but lurid new allegations of sexual misconduct could hurt the president in the eyes of the public. Another blow was delivered by a CBS-TV interview with Kathleen Willey, who claims Mr. Clinton groped her during a 1993 White House meeting. He later denied the charge.

Sgt. Maj. Gene McKinney was ordered reprimanded and demoted one rank by an army jury that convicted him of obstruction of justice but cleared him of sexual misconduct. The army's former top enlisted man faced a maximum five-year sentence. Four of his six accusers said the army had "sacrificed" them and their reputations.

The Vatican expressed remorse for the cowardice of some Roman Catholics during the Holocaust, but rejected accusations that Pope Pius XII turned a blind eye to Nazi attempts to exterminate the Jews in World War II. The long-promised document drew criticism from many Jewish leaders. Israel's chief rabbi called it "too little, too late."

China's Legislature named Zhu Rongji as premier, continuing on a reformist path after appointing Hu Jintao, 55, as the youngest vice president in modern Chinese history. Zhu's predecessor, Li Peng, earlier was named chairman of the National People's Congress, but faced an unusual level of opposition.

India's Congress Party elected Sonia Gandhi chairman, which makes her leader of the Congress parliamentary delegation. The new title was added to that of party president, which she won earlier. But India's new government got off to a rocky start as members of the disparate Hindu nationalist-led coalition haggled over cabinet posts. Prime Minister Atal Bihari Vajpayee was also named foreign minister.

President Clinton eased some restrictions on humanitarian aid and travel to Cuba. The new regulations roll back punishments imposed after Havana shot down two private planes in 1996. One U.S. official said the moves are intended to bolster the Roman Catholic Church and opposition groups after Pope John Paul II's recent visit. Some direct flights from the United States will resume, and Cuban-American households will be allowed to send $1,200 a year.

President Clinton flew to sub-Saharan Africa, the first president to visit in 20 years. The 11-day tour, the longest foreign trip of his presidency, was intended to promote investment. While in Uganda, he declared slavery was wrong, but stopped short of the full apology African-Americans want.

Russian President Boris Yeltsin fired his government, including the man considered heir apparent. In dismissing the prime minister, Mr. Yeltsin, just back from an absence blamed on illness, told Viktor Chernomyrdin to concentrate on preparing for the 2000 election. But analysts believe his candidacy will now flag, and the move renewed talk Mr. Yeltsin may want another term.

The Supreme Court let stand California term limits for state legislators. In a boost to the cause, justices turned away an appeal of a ballot initiative limiting Assembly members to three two-year terms and state Senate members to two four-year terms. On the federal level, the court ruled in 1995 that term limits can't be imposed on Congress without a constitutional amendment.

Two boys, ages 11 and 13, shot 15 people at an Arkansas school, killing five. A false fire alarm,

believed set by a third boy, sent schoolmates and teachers streaming out of the Westside Middle School in Jonesboro, and the boys opened fire from nearby woods.

Oregon's assisted-suicide law was used for the first time by an elderly woman with breast cancer who took a lethal dose of barbiturates prescribed by a doctor, an advocacy group said. The state wouldn't confirm the case, saying it would make a report after 10 suicides have taken place.

Four Marine airmen were charged with negligent homicide, involuntary manslaughter and dereliction of duty after their jet clipped a ski-lift cable in Italy on February 3, killing 20.

El Niño made February 1998 the world's warmest February since record-keeping began in 1856 and the Northern Hemisphere's warmest since 1950, the World Meteorological Organization said.

APRIL

Minority admissions fell at California colleges as affirmative action ended. The number of blacks, Hispanics and Native Americans plummeted in the next freshman class, the first affected by a 1995 Board of Regents decision and a 1996 ballot initiative banning affirmative-action programs.

The Paula Jones suit was thrown out by a federal judge in a big break for President Clinton. U.S. District Judge Susan Webber Wright, a Bush appointee, ruled that even if Ms. Jones's allegations of a crude 1991 proposition by Mr. Clinton were true, she had failed to back up sexual-harassment claims.

A giant highway bill passed the House 337–80, calling for spending $218 billion on transportation projects over six years. The measure, a version of which had already cleared the Senate, was loaded with pork-barrel items and touched off Republican criticism that it mocks the party's advocacy of less government.

An artificial sweetener was approved by the FDA, the first such product the agency has endorsed in 10 years. It is called Sucralose and its maker, Johnson & Johnson, hopes it will become a major player in the market for sugar-free foods and drinks, which are now consumed by 144 million people in the United States.

Coretta Scott King, Martin Luther King Jr.'s widow, called for a national commission to investigate the civil-rights leader's killing. She was joined by former U.N. envoy Andrew Young in saying she believes confessed killer James Earl Ray was a scapegoat in a wider plot.

U.N. arms inspectors left Iraq after the first-ever searches of eight of Saddam Hussein's palaces turned up no evidence of banned materials. More detailed inspections were possible, one participant said after the first test of a February pact that averted a military confrontation.

A Palestinian man drew a 240-year prison sentence for driving the truck bomb that killed six people in New York's World Trade Center in 1993. Eyad Ismoil was arrested in Jordan in 1995 and convicted with plot mastermind Ramzi Yousef.

President Clinton issued an executive order permanently barring importation of 58 models of assault weapons. The foreign-made guns, such as the Uzi and the AK-47, were prohibited in 1994 but many were modified for sport shooting to get around the ban. The NRA immediately vowed a campaign to persuade Congress to overturn the new regulation.

Pakistan tested a missile with a range of 900 miles that is believed capable of carrying a nuclear warhead. India accused China of helping build the weapon. India's new Hindu nationalist government recently refused to rule out further nuclear-arms development.

Higher Social Security taxes were rejected by President Clinton at the first of four town-hall meetings to seek ideas on bolstering the program's solvency. The president, however, didn't rule out raising the ceiling on wages subject to the tax. The popularity of allowing private investments was reflected in public comments.

Tornadoes swept the South, killing 38 people and causing significant damage. The twisters, which touched down in Alabama, Georgia and Mississippi, were described as unusually strong, with winds of 250 mph, and they cut mile-wide swaths. The National Storm Prediction Center in Oklahoma said this is the deadliest tornado season in 14 years, with at least 95 deaths so far. There were 122 in 1984.

An Irish peace accord was hammered out in marathon talks, but both Catholic and Protestant extremists in Northern Ireland remained a threat to the agreement. Sinn Fein leader Gerry Adams told a nationalist rally it was time for Britain to withdraw its troops, and said the struggle for a united Ireland is far from over. The peace accord was rejected by hard-line Protestant leaders, but Britain's prime minister urged Northern Ireland voters to ignore such voices.

Virginia executed a Paraguayan man despite International Court of Justice and State Department pleas for a stay. Secretary of State Albright argued the issue involved, the right to contact one's consulate when facing prosecution, could affect Americans abroad. But Governor Jim Gilmore and the Supreme Court, voting 6–3, refused to block the injection.

Pol Pot's body was put on display by Khmer Rouge guerrillas in Cambodia. The viewing was meant to dispel doubts about early reports that one of the century's worst mass murderers died in his sleep of natural causes. The timing, with capture imminent and a trial for genocide being discussed, remains suspicious. But there is little question his death marks the end of the Khmer Rouge, blamed for nearly two million deaths from 1975 to 1979.

The FAA proposed mandatory changes in older Boeing 737s' fuel-system vents and wiring to prevent explosions such as the one believed to have brought down TWA Flight 800 in 1996. The changes are similar to those urged recently for 747s. The FAA was reviewing all Boeing and Airbus jetliners with center fuel tanks.

President Clinton finished a summit with 33 other North and South American leaders. The group, which met in Chile, officially kicked off talks for a new hemispheric free trade area by 2005, and worked to formulate a consensus position in areas such as the war on drugs. The trade agenda was dimmed, however, by the U.S. president's lack of "fast-track" negotiating authority. Some leaders, in fact, used the gathering to strengthen regional or bilateral accords that exclude the United States.

A top Chinese dissident arrived at a Detroit hospital, freed ahead of a visit by President Clinton. Wang Dan, a Tiananmen Square student leader, was given a clean bill of health. The United States hailed the release as a validation of its human-rights efforts, but dissident Wei Jing-sheng, freed in 1997, said Wang was a pawn in Beijing's bid to quell criticism.

The RICO law was used to convict three organizers of antiabortion protests. A federal jury in Chicago found the men engaged in 21 acts of extortion to shut down clinics. The jury also found that the Pro-Life Action League and Operation Rescue were part of the scheme. They were ordered to pay $258,000. The ruling opens the door for claims by as many as 1,000 clinics.

A U.N. panel rejected a U.S.-led bid to cite Cuba for violations of human rights. The move ends seven years of censure of Havana's policies, and reflects an erosion of support for Washington's hard-line stance toward the Communist island.

The Supreme Court ruled white defendants can challenge indictments based on alleged discrimination against blacks in the selection of grand-jury members. The unanimous decision in the appeal of a Louisiana murder case builds on a series of rulings beginning in 1986 that prohibit the exclusion of jurors because of their race or gender.

Russia's new premier faced a battle to prove himself after a bruising confirmation fight that ended when the Duma gave in and approved Sergei Kiriyenko's candidacy rather than face dissolution by President Boris Yeltsin. The premier named eight cabinet members after a meeting with Mr. Yeltsin. Seven return from the government abruptly fired by the Russian president in March, including Boris Nemtsov as deputy premier and Yevgeny Primakov as foreign minister, indicating no change of course for Moscow.

The Internal Revenue Service named a former FBI chief for an internal inquiry as new hearings began. William Webster, who was brought in by Ronald Reagan to clean up the CIA in the 1980s, will scrutinize the criminal-investigation unit. The administration was working to shift the focus from Senate hearings, which opened with a former Treasury investigator telling of one IRS worker who "misappropriated" cars seized from taxpayers, and another who threatened to audit a state trooper who arrested him.

A Whitewater grand jury saw a videotape of testimony given by Hillary Clinton in a five-hour session that focused on work she did as a lawyer for the now-defunct Madison Guaranty S&L. Her lawyer confirmed that she had refused to answer two questions on grounds of marital privilege.

MAY

Webster Hubbell was indicted by a Whitewater grand jury on tax-fraud charges, along with his wife and two associates. The 10-count indictment alleges the former top Justice Department aide tried to evade $894,000 in taxes. Separately, Susan McDougal was indicted for refusing to talk to prosecutors. The Clintons' former Whitewater partner, who already has spent 18 months in jail for her refusal to testify, was charged with contempt of court and obstructing justice.

Theodore Kaczynski was sentenced to life in prison without parole under a plea agreement in his 18-year bombing spree that killed three.

The pope's top bodyguard, Alois Estermann, was shot and killed, along with his wife and a colleague, on the same day he was appointed head of the Swiss Guards. Vatican officials said a member of the Swiss Guards was driven by bitterness when he killed his new commander, the commander's wife and then himself. They said the man had been reprimanded and left off a list of guards to be honored by the pope.

The FBI offered a $1 million reward for Eric Robert Rudolph, a suspect in the January 1998 bombing of a Birmingham, Alabama, abortion clinic that killed a guard. Officials also want to question him about the 1996 Olympics bombing and two other attacks in Atlanta.

The Senate approved a sweeping overhaul of the Internal Revenue Service. The 97–0 vote in the Senate followed a similarly lopsided 426–4 vote on IRS reform legislation in the House in the fall of 1997. Sponsors say the changes will make the agency more efficient and more concerned with taxpayer service than law enforcement.

The FAA grounded many older 737s, disrupting flight plans for 100,000 people. The agency, after discovering worn fuel-tank wiring during inspections, idled 179 jetliners and ordered examinations of 282 newer 737s. The action was part of the FAA's plan to raise safety standards following the 1996 TWA Flight 800 crash, in which an electrical spark is suspected of igniting fuel-tank vapors in the 747.

India exploded three atomic bombs, boosting tensions with Pakistan and China. The tests came seven weeks after a Hindu nationalist-led government took power in New Delhi, and drew immediate international condemnation, including economic sanctions from the United States. Later in the month, Pakistan set off nuclear bombs in tests it said evened the score with India. Hours after the underground explosions, which also drew international condemnation and sanctions, Islamabad declared a state of emergency and suspended civil rights in response to what it called a threat of "external aggression" from an unidentified source.

Attorney General Janet Reno asked for an independent counsel to investigate the secretary of labor. The allegations against Alexis Herman included influence-peddling and violations of campaign-finance laws. The attorney general, after a preliminary review, found evidence that "potentially" corroborates a Cameroon businessman's accusations that Ms. Herman, while a White House aide, agreed to a kickback scheme. Ms. Herman denied any impropriety and said she was "baffled" by Ms. Reno's decision.

A serviceman's remains were unearthed from the Tomb of the Unknowns at Arlington National Cemetery for DNA testing that could identify the person buried there in 1984. Secretary of Defense William Cohen said the removal came "with profound reluctance" but from a need to identify the nation's war dead.

The United States and European Union agreed to end a dispute on Cuba, Iran and Libya sanctions. The penalties against foreign firms doing business with those nations have constituted the most contentious trade spat between Washington and its European allies. The agreement would waive such penalties, and specifically exempts the $2-billion contract for Total SA of France, Gazprom of Russia and Petronas of Malaysia to develop an Iranian oil field. The EU agreed to curb sensitive technology exports to Iran and Libya and will try to "inhibit" purchases of Cuban properties seized by the Castro regime.

Suharto quit as Indonesia's president, naming B.J. Habibie, the vice president, to serve out his term. Mr. Habibie agreed to hold elections in 1999. Suharto's 32-year reign crumbled in the face of student protests and rioting over price increases imposed amid a financial crisis.

A satellite failure brought communications disruptions across the United States. Most pager customers were affected, as well as some radio and TV broadcasts, airline flights, retail telecommunications and self-service gasoline pumps. PanAmSat, 81 percent-owned by General Motors Corp.'s Hughes unit, said it would require several days to restore service.

A 15-year-old Orgeon boy killed one and wounded 19 in a shooting spree at a school. The boy, who had been suspended the day before for bringing a gun to Thurston High School in Springfield, opened fire on about 400 schoolmates in the cafeteria.

The Northern Ireland peace accord received overwhelming approval at referendums. It passed by 71 percent in the north and 94 percent in the republic.

Russian President Boris Yeltsin held crisis talks on the economy as Russia fought to defend the ruble. The Central Bank raised interest rates by 100 points, to 150 percent, and the currency held fairly steady. But investors remained fearful, with stocks plunging more than 10 percent and yields on short-term government debt soaring. The immediate catalyst was the failure of the privatization of the Rosneft oil firm. Moscow had hoped the sale of a 75 percent stake would give it at least $2.1 billion to pay debt and back wages to protesting coal miners.

An Oklahoma bombing-case figure was sentenced to 12 years in prison for not warning of the 1995 attack that killed 168. Michael Fortier, the star government witness against Timothy McVeigh and Terry Nichols, said he was "completely ashamed" of his inaction. Victims' relatives had pleaded for the maximum term of 23 years.

JUNE

Rescue workers in Afghanistan searched for survivors of the May 30 earthquake that killed 3,000 to 5,000 people. Aftershocks from the main quake, which measured 6.9 on the Richter scale, continued to rock the northern region. Landslides blocked roads, and an estimated 45,000 were homeless.

A train crash killed more than 100 in Germany's worst postwar rail accident. The luxury high-speed Inter City Express train, carrying mostly businesspeople on a midmorning Munich-Hamburg run, derailed and jackknifed at 125 mph as it neared a station in Eschede.

California voted to end bilingual classes. Proposition 227, to halt 30 years of bilingual instruction, passed by 61 percent, but was challenged in court.

Terry Nichols was sentenced to life in prison for helping Timothy McVeigh carry out the 1995 Oklahoma City bombing, which killed 168. He refused an opportunity to tell what he knows about the plot. The sentence was the maximum the judge could impose after the jury deadlocked on the death penalty.

The FAA ordered retraining for 10,000 air-traffic controllers after two planes almost collided over New York's La Guardia Airport in April and after a sharp increase in errors by air-traffic controllers nationwide. The retraining covered everything from takeoffs and runway clearance to landings.

Nigerian dictator Sani Abacha died unexpectedly of a heart attack, leaving the oil-rich West African country that he ruled ruthlessly for five years in uncertainty. The military quickly picked army Gen. Abdulsalam Abubakar, the defense chief of staff, as his successor, hoping to avert a power vacuum.

Defense chief William Cohen ordered an investigation into a report that U.S. forces used nerve gas in Vietnam, including against defectors. He said he knew of no evidence to support the allegations, which appeared in a report by CNN and Time magazine. In early July, CNN retracted the report.

American Honda and Ford agreed to pay nearly $25 million to settle allegations that they altered some vehicles' emissions mechanisms in violation of the Clean Air Act. American Honda paid $17.1 million, the largest civil penalty in the act's 28-year history, and Ford agreed to pay $7.8 million in civil penalties.

The shuttle Discovery pulled away from Mir, marking the end of America's partnership with the Russian space station and the transition to a new era of space flight: an international space station on which construction was scheduled to begin in orbit in November 1998.

Southern Baptists adopted the first change to their statement of beliefs in 35 years, defining marriage exclusively in heterosexual terms and asking women to "submit graciously" to their husbands.

Pakistan declared a moratorium on nuclear tests in a move to ease tensions and allay the threat of international sanctions. Nevertheless, the United States unveiled sanctions over the earlier atomic tests by both India and Pakistan. The administration's broad package will probably cost the two nations billions of dollars in loans and millions in trade annually.

President Clinton added 10 years to the ban on new offshore oil drilling, extending it to 2012. The extension was one of $224 million in initiatives for rescuing ocean resources that he announced in California.

NATO jets held war games near Kosovo. The show of force over Albania and Macedonia by 85 aircraft from 13 nations was intended to press Serbia to halt a violent crackdown on ethnic Albanians, but live-fire exercises were scrapped after objections by Moscow. Later in the month, Albania's prime minister said his nation was "on the eve of war" with Serbia, and reiterated his call for NATO to intervene to keep the conflict in Kosovo from spreading.

A British au pair was free to return home after the Massachusetts high court upheld a judge's decision to reduce a sentence by a jury that convicted her of second-degree murder of a child in her care. Louise Woodward faced 15 years until the judge lowered her conviction to manslaughter and cut her sentence to the 279 days already served.

Tobacco legislation was killed in Senate votes guided by GOP leaders. A bid to move the bill toward final passage, joined by 14 Republicans, fell three votes short of the 60 needed. The defeat of the measure, which would have boosted cigarette prices $1.10 a pack and increased tobacco regulation, promised to be an issue in fall elections.

AIDS-drug makers agreed to cut prices as much as 75 percent in poor nations for combination therapies. While discounts could make accessible to poorer nations some of the medications that have so improved treatment in the West, they are likely to generate debate because of unsolved distribution problems in the developing world, home to more than 90 percent of those infected with HIV. Separately, a U.N. official said AIDS has killed 12 million and infected 31 million, and is spreading to 16,000 a day.

Iraq sanctions were renewed by the U.N. Security Council despite a threat by Baghdad of unspecified action against arms inspectors if they weren't lifted. Rancor rose after a U.S. lab found nerve gas in a missile-warhead evidence inspectors collected.

Russia received a long-awaited $690 million installment of an IMF loan, but the international lending agency said further aid would have to be negotiated. Premier Kiriyenko presented an austerity plan including spending cuts and improvements in collecting taxes.

Florida wildfires threatened to converge near Daytona Beach as weary firefighters manned breaks and planes dropped pellets to set backfires. There were about 280 fires statewide. About 118,000 acres had been burned and 116 homes destroyed since May, making the fire season the worst in 50 years.

The Supreme Court rejected 6–3 the line-item veto, ruled 5–4 that a federal ban on bias against the disabled covers people with HIV even if they have no AIDS symptoms, and backed, 8–1, a law allowing the National Endowment for the Arts to deny grants for work it deems indecent. The court said a constitutional amendment is required to give presidents authority to excise individual items from spending bills.

Susan McDougal was ordered freed by a federal judge, who cited her back problem. Ms. McDougal served 18 months for refusing to answer a Whitewater grand jury's questions before beginning a two-year jail term for fraud in March.

President Clinton traveled to China and challenged the nation's leaders on human rights in a Beijing University speech. All people have basic rights, the president said, and China's 1.2 billion people must be "free to reach the fullness of their potential." Separately, China and the United States agreed to stop aiming nuclear weapons at each other, and Beijing pledged to allow tighter U.S. inspections in technology exports.

The Tomb of the Unknowns at Arlington National Cemetery is unlikely to again hold the remains of a Vietnam War soldier or those of future wars because of advances in DNA technology, Defense Secretary William Cohen said. The Pentagon identified the remains of a Vietnam War airman recently exhumed from the Tomb of the Unknowns as those of Michael J. Blassie, a pilot shot down in 1972 near An Loc.

Colombian rebels offered to hold peace talks with Andres Pastrana after he becomes president in August. The National Liberation Army, the second-largest rebel group, also said it would hold preliminary talks in July that may lead to an early cease-fire.

JULY

U.S. District Judge James Robertson threw out tax charges against Webster Hubbell, his wife and two associates. The judge was sharply critical of the Whitewater prosecutor's tactics in ruling that Kenneth Starr exceeded his authority by bringing a case not directly tied to his inquiry.

President Clinton's China trip gave Beijing's leaders a new aura of respectability. Winding up his nine-day visit in Hong Kong, Mr. Clinton praised President Jiang's government as "the right leadership at the right time." The effects of the visit were felt elsewhere in Asia. Taiwan was rattled when the president used China's wording to describe U.S. opposition to its independence. But a U.S. official said Beijing was warned reunification must occur peacefully.

A big teachers-union merger failed when National Education Association delegates voted to reject linking up with the smaller American Federation of Teachers. The merged union would have had 3.3 million members and been a powerful labor force, but members were concerned about losing their independence.

CNN said it would establish a watchdog unit to prevent situations such as the recent apology and retraction of a story claiming the United States used nerve gas against Vietnam War defectors. Three producers left the Time Warner unit, and star reporter Peter Arnett was reprimanded.

Florida evacuees were allowed to return to Flagler County. About 40,000 were ordered out as wildfires advanced, but conditions improved and some rain fell. State officials estimated $300 million in damage, but residential claims were expected to be less.

Nigeria's top dissident died after meeting U.S. aides seeking his release. News of the death of Moshood Abiola, winner of 1993 presidential elections annulled by the military, sparked rioting that killed as many as 45. The regime said Mr. Abiola died of a heart attack, which was confirmed by an autopsy. Separately, Nigeria's military ruler vowed civilian rule would be restored by May 29, 1999.

Congress passed legislation to overhaul the Internal Revenue Service. The bill was approved by the Senate 96–2, and President Clinton signed the measure, which puts taxpayers in a stronger position when dealing with the agency. Separately, the IRS said it would review property seizures made in the past nine months for possible agency wrongdoing and would make restitution to certain taxpayers whose rights had been violated.

Ryutaro Hashimoto resigned as Japanese prime minister after the ruling Liberal Democrats' humiliating election defeat. Keizo Obuchi was confirmed later in the month as the new prime minister. Meanwhile, the new finance minister, Kiichi Miyazawa, expressed a reluctance to intervene in support of the yen.

Russia was scheduled to receive $22.6 billion from the IMF, the World Bank and Japan by the end of 1999. The substantially larger-than-expected assistance depends on Moscow's promise to deliver on reforms to boost tax revenue, narrow its budget deficit and encourage competition.

The first half of 1998 was the warmest six months ever recorded on Earth, and July was expected to set a record as well. A Southwest heat wave that had killed 110 people since May led President Clinton to order $100 million in emergency funds to help people pay utility bills and buy air conditioners and fans. He also ordered disaster aid for Texas farms.

President Clinton sought authorization for covert operations against Saddam Hussein. The administration asked for broad new authority from Congress to plan and mount covert operations against the Iraqi dictator. The secret initiative would go far beyond past CIA efforts to encourage resistance inside Iraq.

Tidal waves killed thousands and razed five Papua New Guinea villages. The tsunami, consisting of three waves nearly 30 feet high, washed over the coast 370 miles northwest of Port Moresby after an earthquake, measuring 7.0 on the Richter scale, struck 18 miles out to sea.

President Clinton attacked Republican tax-cut plans as "a return to irresponsibility." He opposed using surpluses for that purpose until a plan to shore up Social Security is in place. But House leaders, undaunted, endorsed a plan for $702 billion in cuts and $698 billion for the retirement program over 10 years. Senate Republicans and Fed chief Alan Greenspan were less enthusiastic about cuts that big.

A Senate panel rejected President Clinton's nominee for Air Force secretary in a 9–9 vote. The Armed Services Committee heard testimony raising questions about the Air Force Reserve safety record of Daryl Jones, a Florida state senator and former fighter pilot. He would have been the first black in the post.

The Senate voted 90–10 to ban on-line gambling in an effort to strengthen prosecutors' fight against illegal betting and "virtual casino" operations overseas. The Senate also voted to require schools and libraries to block indecent Internet material.

The House revived an abortion debate, voting 296–132 to override President Clinton's veto of a ban on certain late-term abortions.

Attorney General Janet Reno promised a careful review of a task force's recommendation that she request an independent counsel to investigate fund-raising abuses by the Clinton campaign. The long-awaited report by Reno deputy Charles La Bella revived Republican calls for such an appointment.

Pope John Paul II tightened control over national bishops conferences, requiring them to agree unanimously before issuing doctrinal declarations. The Vatican must grant any exceptions. The rules may curb bishops from addressing divisive issues.

A California firm pleaded guilty to criminal charges for distributing apple juice contaminated with E. coli bacteria and agreed to pay a $1.5 million fine, the largest ever in a food-injury case. Odwalla's juice was blamed for the 1996 death of a girl.

Two Capitol police officers were shot by a gunman attempting to storm into the Washington landmark. The gunman, Russell Eugene Weston of Montana and Illinois, and a tourist were wounded. The incident revived debate over increasing security at the Capitol.

A federal Teamsters board expelled Ron Carey from the union and barred him from ever associating with it because of charges that his 1996 presidential re-election campaign embezzled union funds. William Hamilton, the former political director, drew similar sanctions.

Former White House intern Monica Lewinsky agreed to cooperate with Kenneth Starr in return for immunity from prosecution, and President Clinton said he would give videotaped testimony in the case on Au-gust 17. Ms. Lewinsky was expected to testify that she had an intimate relationship with Mr. Clinton.

Serb forces drove ethnic Albanian rebels from a stronghold 25 miles south of Kosovo's capital and stepped up pressure on a village along the Albanian border through which rebel arms are smuggled. The U.N. estimated the war had displaced 107,000 people.

Adultery by military personnel will be prosecuted only when it hurts order and discipline or discredits the military, the Pentagon said after a year-long study prompted by a rash of sex scandals. The army was ordered to bring its looser rules on fraternization in line with other services.

AUGUST

A campaign-reform bill passed the House 237–186, a rebuff to GOP leaders. The vote on the bipartisan measure, which bans unregulated "soft-money" donations, set the stage for a showdown with a less-restrictive bill that would exempt such contributions at the state level. Though 51 Republicans broke ranks on the issue, GOP leaders oppose the ban because their party gets the biggest share of soft money.

A Congo revolt broke out as troops near the Rwanda border declared themselves in opposition to the Kabila regime and a curfew was imposed to quell fighting in Kinshasa. But by the end of the month, Congo and its foreign allies, including Angola and Zimbabwe, had driven Tutsi-led rebels from their last strongholds in the nation's southwest, including a hydroelectric dam that supplies power to Kinshasa.

Iraq suspended U.N. arms inspections, a sign of a fresh crisis brewing. Reviving an issue that nearly led to a military confrontation with the United States earlier in 1998, Baghdad demanded the inspections commission be overhauled to lessen U.S. domination. Iraq could begin rebuilding its chemical-arms arsenal in six months if U.N. inspections don't resume, Scott Ritter, a U.S. arms inspector who quit in protest, said in a TV interview.

Portugal and Indonesia agreed to discuss limited autonomy for East Timor, the former Portuguese colony seized by Jakarta in 1976. The accord came after U.N.-sponsored talks in New York. But Nobel peace laureate Bishop Carlos Belo said most East Timorese are still wary of Indonesia's proposals.

Anglican bishops voted 526–70 to declare homosexuality incompatible with scripture, to oppose ordination of gay clerics and to affirm that sex is allowed only within marriage. The bishops' conference can't enforce the decision, but wields great moral authority.

Monica Lewinsky testified before the grand jury investigating sex allegations against President Clinton for the first time after reaching an immunity deal for herself and her family. Later in the month, Mr. Clinton admitted misleading people about his relationship with Ms. Lewinsky, a former White House intern. In a brief televised address following his unprecedented testimony to the grand jury, the president admitted they had an inappropriate relationship and that he hadn't been forthcoming about it in his deposition in the Paula Jones suit. But he denied committing perjury or asking others to lie.

Oil drilling in Alaska will be permitted on more than four million acres in an environmentally sensitive area under a plan announced by the Interior Department. The North Slope parcel, thought to hold 2.2 billion barrels, is part of a naval petroleum reserve set aside in 1923.

Bombing attacks on U.S. embassies in the capitals of Kenya and Tanzania claimed 257 lives, and at least 5,500 people were injured, the majority in Nairobi. In retaliation, President Clinton ordered attacks on Sudan and Afghanistan. Cruise missiles struck Afghan camps that the United States said were used by terrorists and a suspected chemical-arms plant in Khartoum. The United States also laid the groundwork to arrest the chief bombing suspect, Osama bin Laden, whose Muslim extremist group was the target of the U.S. cruise-missile attacks. He was charged in a sealed indictment handed up in an inquiry related to the 1993 World Trade Center bombing. Two other suspects flew to the United States for trial in the Kenya bombing.

A Marine air-squadron commander was relieved of his post over errors uncovered in the investigation of the February 3 crash of a warplane into a ski-lift cable in Italy that killed 20. A second officer was reprimanded. Neither officer will lose rank or benefits.

Colombia's new president replaced the military's top leaders after a recent rebel offensive that killed more than 140. The U.S. drug czar, following the inauguration of Andres Pastrana, accused rebels of supporting cocaine trafficking.

Afghanistan's Taliban militia appeared to be in control of Mazar-e-Sharif, the last city held by the opposition. The city has changed hands several times, but the current Taliban offensive appears much better planned. The nation has been in constant turmoil since the Taliban drove the former government from the capital in 1996.

The IRS "taxpayer advocate" will be W. Val Oveson, Utah's chief tax collector. The post got new clout under recent legislation to overhaul the agency, and the choice of an outsider is unprecedented.

Two Arkansas boys were ordered held in a juvenile facility, perhaps until they are 21, for shooting a teacher and four schoolmates to death at a Jonesboro middle school on March 24. The judge said the two, 12 and 14 years old, should spend 90 days in an adult prison if juvenile officials free them before age 21.

Comedian Bill Cosby's son's convicted killer was sentenced to life in prison without parole. Ukrainian immigrant Mikail Markhasev shot Ennis Cosby during a botched robbery off a Los Angeles freeway in 1997.

Swiss banks and Jewish groups agreed on a $1.2 billion settlement of claims that the banks kept money deposited by Holocaust victims. It is to be paid out to survivors and heirs over four years. The accord came after sometimes bitter negotiations and a threat of sanctions by some U.S. cities and states.

Drought in parts of the United States will cut the cotton crop by 24 percent in 1998, according to the Agriculture Department, which also slashed its forecasts for wheat, cattle and hog prices. Meanwhile, President Clinton signed legislation intended to speed $5.5 billion in subsidy payments to farmers.

The federal milk-pricing system was upheld by an appeals court panel in St. Louis after a lower court ruled in 1997 that the regulations were "arbitrary and capricious." The price dairy farmers can charge is set according to how far the farm is from Eau Claire, Wisconsin.

A car bomb killed 29 people and injured more than 200 in Northern Ireland. An IRA splinter group claimed responsibility for the bombing in Omagh, which was seen as a bid to turn public opinion against the fragile Irish peace accord. The atrocity was the most murderous single incident in three decades of fighting between pro-Irish Catholic nationalists and pro-British Protestant unionists.

NATO troops opened a five-day military exercise in Albania intended to show the alliance's resolve in containing the conflict in Serbia's Kosovo province. Meanwhile, diplomats pressed Belgrade to open talks with ethnic Albanian leaders in the province as Serb troops began a drive to clear rebels from three villages in the area around Pec. But Albanian leaders refused to open peace talks with Serbia until attacks on ethnic Albanians in the restive province cease. More than 500 people had died and 231,000 had been driven from their homes in six months of fighting.

U.S. balloonist Steve Fossett was rescued from a raft 500 miles east of Australia after storms wrecked his craft at the 15,200-mile mark of his attempt to circle the Earth. He told Australian TV he doesn't know how he survived the descent from 29,000 feet.

Quebec secessionists were handed a setback by Canada's Supreme Court, which ruled the province can't unilaterally separate from the rest of the country. Secession, the court said, must be negotiated with the rest of Canada if Quebec votes for independence.

A former Ku Klux Klan leader was found guilty by a Mississippi jury of the 1966 firebomb murder of civil-rights activist Vernon Dahmer. It was the fifth time Samuel Bowers was tried for the crime. He drew a mandatory life prison sentence.

An appeals court barred the use of statistical sampling in the 2000 census. Siding with congressional Republicans and dealing a setback to the administration, the three-judge panel said the Constitution calls for an "actual enumeration." The GOP fears sampling will help Democrats in drawing congressional districts. Democrats argue that sampling would help end undercounts of immigrants and minorities, which cut federal aid to cities and reduce urban clout in Congress.

A bombing in South Africa killed one and injured 25 at a Cape Town Planet Hollywood restaurant. A little-known Muslim group said the attack was revenge for U.S. strikes on Sudan and Afghanistan, but the United States said it had no evidence of political motive.

Seven Cuban-Americans were charged by a federal grand jury in Puerto Rico with plotting to kill Castro. Several were arrested in 1997 on their way to a summit the Cuban leader was attending in Venezuela. One is a leader of the Cuban American National Foundation, a prominent U.S. exile group.

Russia's government reeled as the financial system went into a tailspin. President Boris Yeltsin fired his government leaders and resurrected Acting Prime Minister Viktor Chernomyrdin in hopes of restoring calm. But calling his economic program "a deadly policy under the thumb of the West," Communist leaders in the Duma stepped up demands for Mr. Yeltsin to resign and rejected Mr. Chernomyrdin's appointment.

Attorney General Janet Reno began a new review of fund-raising issues involving Vice President Al Gore. The issue is whether the vice president answered questions accurately in an earlier review of his fund-raising calls from the White House. A document emerged raising questions about Mr. Gore's assertion that calls were to seek only unregulated funds.

Libya issued a statement saying it would deal "positively" with a United States-British offer of a compromise on the venue for a trial of two suspects in the 1988 Lockerbie bombing. But Tripoli gave no indication when it would turn them over for trial in The Hague by Scottish-court rules. The United States called Libya's reply inadequate.

Floods in China killed more than 3,000 people, according to a vice premier, who put much of the blame on erosion caused by heavy logging. President Jiang ordered 178,000 police and soldiers guarding Yangtze River dikes placed on alert as a fresh flood surge entered a critical phase.

The Martin Luther King assassination will be the subject of a limited Justice Department review, Attorney General Janet Reno said, but not an inquiry by a national commission that the slain civil-rights leader's family favors. The family believes a conspiracy was behind the 1968 murder, to which the late James Earl Ray confessed.

Cambodians paralyzed Phnom Penh with a demonstration calling for a bigger role for opposition parties after July 26 elections. Opposition leaders held rallies every day for a week to protest fraud by the Hun Sen regime. The government ordered the protests halted, calling them illegal.

North Korea fired a two-stage missile that passed over Japan's main island before landing in the Pacific, a test that could point to development of a weapon capable of reaching Alaska or Hawaii.

SEPTEMBER

President Clinton met with Boris Yeltsin, who said he remains committed to reforming Russia. During Mr. Clinton's visit to Russia, Mr. Yeltsin said U.S. support for reforms could help lure back investors driven off by the country's financial crisis.

The annual U.N. population survey said the global growth rate has slowed to 1.4 percent a year from 2 percent in 1960, and the biggest increases are occurring among the very old and the very young. The report predicts the world's population will rise to about 9.4 billion in 2050 from six billion in mid-1999.

The 1998 SAT scores barely budged from 1997's, the College Board said, with the average math score rising one point to 512 and the verbal section flat at 505. Gaps between whites and blacks and suburban and inner-city students widened further.

An Internet child-pornography ring was the target of an international crackdown as police in the U.S. and 13 other nations made simultaneous raids on about 100 suspected members. U.S. customs agents served warrants in 22 states.

A Swissair jet crashed off Nova Scotia, killing 229. The Geneva-bound MD-11 reported smoke in the cockpit shortly after takeoff from New York, and was attempting an emergency landing in Halifax. Investigators said the cockpit-voice recorder stopped six minutes before the crash, as did the flight-data recorder. The findings bolstered the suspicion that the MD-11 had a massive electrical failure.

Japan and South Korea put their military forces on alert after Tokyo received unspecified information that North Korea was preparing another missile test. Later in the month, the United States said North Korea's missile test was a failed attempt to launch a satellite. Despite the reassessment, officials said the test shows Pyongyang is developing a three-stage rocket that could threaten the United States.

Flooding in northern India was the worst since 1938, according to a Red Cross official who said contamination of drinking water was a serious threat. More than 2,000 people had died in flooding and mudslides.

The number of executions in China fell 31 percent to about 3,000 in 1997 from 4,367 in 1996, according to a report by Amnesty International. China, however, remains the world's heaviest user of the death penalty.

Attorney General Janet Reno began a 90-day review of whether an independent counsel should investigate President Clinton's role in 1996 Democratic Party advertising. Federal auditors question the legality of $46.5 million in "issue" ads because they effectively promoted Mr. Clinton and were coordinated with his campaign staff.

Timothy McVeigh's conviction was upheld by a federal appeals court, which ruled the jury wasn't improperly swayed by testimony by relatives of the 168 victims of the 1995 Oklahoma City bombing. The court also rejected eight other avenues of appeal.

Mark McGwire broke baseball's record for home runs in a season on Sept. 8, hitting his 62nd in a game with the Chicago Cubs. The St. Louis Cardinals' first baseman left the field to hug the family of the 1961 record-setter, Roger Maris. The ball fell out of fans' reach and was to go to Mr. McGwire.

Kenneth Starr delivered his impeachment report, putting President Clinton in severe peril. Mr. Starr's office said it contains "substantial and credible" evidence that may be grounds for impeachment. The Whitewater prosecutor's graphic 445-page report was distributed over the Internet, the airwaves and in newspaper supplements. The White House said the report is nothing more than an attempt to use the Monica Lewinsky sex scandal, detailed with "pornographic specificity," to destroy the president. Polls indicated the public was opposed to removing Mr. Clinton from office. Later in the month, Americans watched television broadcasts of Mr. Clinton's grand-jury testimony. The four-hour videotape of the president's August 17 questioning before the panel contained sexually graphic language, but mostly consisted of legalistic jousting.

Iraq sanctions won't be reconsidered until Baghdad ends resistance to U.N. arms inspections, the Security Council decided in a unanimous vote. The end of sanctions reviews was a victory for the White House, which had been accused of softening its policy on Iraq. Secretary of State Madeleine Albright strongly rejected the charge.

Three diet-drug studies provided the strongest evidence yet linking long-term use of Redux and fenfluramine to heart-valve problems. But all three found the problems affect significantly fewer than the 30 percent of users estimated by the FDA when it asked American Home Products to withdraw the drugs in 1997.

Student protests in Indonesia escalated, with demonstrators demanding the ouster of President Habibie during his visit to Surabaya. The unrest, which paralyzed the nation's second-largest city, echoed May protests that helped topple Suharto, and markets were roiled.

The Justice Department and EPA gave details on an initiative to crack down on pollution in the Mississippi River system. It consists of 142 cases against polluters that have resulted in 54 convictions and $29 million in fines.

Russian President Boris Yeltsin named Yevgeny Primakov, the foreign minister, as premier. Backing down in a confrontation with the Duma over his first choice, Viktor Chernomyrdin, the president picked the former high KGB official as more palatable to the Communists who dominate the legislature. The United States endorsed the nomination, but Mr. Primakov has challenged Washington's power and policy in Iraq, Iran, Kosovo and other places.

The Pentagon planned to request a big rise in the defense budget to improve morale, boost readiness and pay for weapons acquisitions. No figure was expected to be specified, but several annual increases of as much as $15 billion apiece were thought necessary by the military chiefs.

Algeria faced uncertainty following President Zeroual's unexpected announcement that he will cut short his term and hold elections in February, nearly two years early. Some analysts say he was pushed into the move by hard-liners in the army, which dominates Algeria.

Sammy Sosa tied the record set by the St. Louis Cardinals' Mark McGwire for home runs in a season. The 61st and 62nd by the Chicago Cubs outfielder, in a Milwaukee Brewers game, set up a race to the finish.

Health-care costs will double to $2.1 trillion by 2007, a study by the federal agency that runs Medicare and Medicaid predicted. The surge would be in contrast to five years of low growth under managed care, and most of the acceleration is expected in the private sector.

House Speaker Newt Gingrich said he will pay his $300,000 penalty for ethics violations without a loan from former Senate leader Bob Dole. Mr. Gingrich is to use personal funds for final payments, in November and January.

Geraldine Ferraro was defeated by Rep. Charles Schumer for the New York Demo-

cratic nomination to challenge Sen. Alfonse D'Amato, who ran unopposed in the GOP primary, in November. The 1984 vice presidential nominee lost by a wide margin.

U.S. teen sexual activity fell 11 percent from 1991 to 1997 after two decades of increases, the Centers for Disease Control and Prevention said. The reports said 48.4 percent of high school students in 1997 reported having had sex, compared with 54.1 percent in 1991.

Nuclear-processing plant owners were ordered by a federal jury to pay $36.5 million to eight cancer-stricken residents of Apollo, Pa. The suit by residents said radiation from the plant, run by Babcock & Wilcox and Atlantic Richfield, caused the cluster.

Sweden's Social Democrats won another four years at the head of a minority government backed by smaller leftist parties, according to parliamentary election results. Prime Minister Goran Persson claimed victory, but his party's 37 percent showing was the lowest since World War II.

A new AIDS drug was approved by the FDA, and it could cut the number of daily pills patients must take if it lives up to its promise. DuPont's Sustiva blocks viral replication in a different way than protease inhibitors or AZT.

Cal Ripken of the Baltimore Orioles took himself out of the lineup against the New York Yankees, and his record for consecutive games played likely will stay at 2,632. He beat Lou Gehrig's mark of 2,130 in 1995.

Afghanistan's capital was hit with a second day of rocket barrages, which killed at least 10 people. At least 50 were killed and 200 injured in earlier attacks on Kabul. The Taliban, who rule most of the country, blamed a northern opposition alliance. The opposition denied launching the rockets.

Secretary of State Madeleine Albright met with her Iranian counterpart, the highest-level contact in 29 years, as part of a six-nation effort to avert an Iran-Afghanistan war. Iran's president, whose army is on the border, also met with Pakistan's premier on the issue.

Northern Ireland bombing suspects were seized in dawn raids in both the British province and the republic. The nine were arrested under tough new antiterrorist laws but their alleged role in the August 15 Omagh bombing that killed 29 wasn't specified.

A minimum-wage increase was blocked in a 55-44 Senate vote, largely on party lines. It would have raised the wage to $6.15 an hour from $5.15 in two 50-cent increments.

Iran's President Khatami called for U.S. investment in Iran, but added Tehran remains cautious about improving ties with Washington. He said the U.S. must first end its hostile stance. Separately, Mr. Khatami said Iran, which has 200,000 troops on the Afghan border, is doing its best to avoid a war.

U.S. median household income passed the 1990 level in 1997, marking a symbolic turning point though falling short of the 1989 record, the Census Bureau said. Poverty fell to its lowest point since 1990, but this decade's expansion has been criticized for mainly benefiting the rich.

New EPA smog rules were unveiled, and they require reductions of an average 28 percent by 2007 in emissions of nitrogen oxide in 22 states. The $1.7 billion plan attempts to address a dispute between the Midwest and East Coast, but business doesn't like it.

India's prime minister said he was ready to adhere to the nuclear test-ban treaty within a year, following Pakistan's lead by a day. A U.S. official called both nations' moves helpful but insufficient to bring an end to sanctions.

Helmut Kohl lost the chancellorship of Germany after 16 years in power. Conceding victory to Social Democrat Gerhard Schroeder and stepping down as Christian Democratic leader, Mr. Kohl was defeated amid economic uncertainty. His loss reinforces Europe's swing to the left. Mr. Schroeder, the first member of the postwar generation in the office, ran on a platform of social justice and economic modernization. A strong showing by smaller parties played a decisive role.

President Clinton went on the offensive against Congress in a battle over tax cuts. The House approved the measure, providing $80 billion in cuts over five years, by 229-195 in an unusual Saturday vote. The president reiterated his threat to veto the bill because it would use

the budget surplus, which he wants for Social Security.

"Fast track" legislation failed in a 243-180 vote in the House that the White House claimed was held only to divide Democrats before elections. President Clinton favors the bill, giving him authority to negotiate trade pacts on an expedited basis, but many in his party don't.

Malaysian protests continued despite warnings by police, who banned all demonstrations in central Kuala Lumpur. About 10,000 gathered outside the capital to protest a crackdown on dissent by the Mahathir regime. Separately, Malaysia's top dissident was arraigned on corruption and sex charges, his first public appearance since his September 20 arrest. Ousted Deputy Premier Anwar complained he had been beaten unconscious by police and denied care.

People lacking health insurance made up 16.1 percent of the population in 1997, up from 15.6 percent in 1996, the Census Bureau said. Those most likely to be without coverage include young adults, Hispanics, part-timers, the less-educated and those born elsewhere.

Mark McGwire hit his 70th home run, putting him four ahead in the competition for the record with the Chicago Cubs' Sammy Sosa. The St. Louis Cardinal slugger got five in three games in a season-ending series with Montreal.

Hurricane Georges killed hundreds in the Caribbean and claimed at least four lives in the United States. After causing extensive damage in the Florida Keys, Georges headed for the Gulf Coast. It flooded some areas with 20 inches of rain but spared New Orleans a direct hit.

House-Senate negotiators agreed to emergency farm aid totaling more than $4.1 billion, to be funded by budget surpluses. President Clinton, muddying his call to keep surpluses for Social Security, has proposed spending $3 billion more.

Liberia's leader said his regime prevailed in clashes following a deal with the United States to let a rival warlord leave the country. Roosevelt Johnson, who had taken refuge in the U.S. Embassy, was in Nigeria.

The Supreme Court's new term was expected again to focus on sex harassment and bias. The court announced 12 cases it would hear, including two involving those issues. In one, a fifth-grader said she was sexually harassed by a classmate and is seeking damages from the school. The other case involves gender bias in college athletics.

Palestinian leader Yasser Arafat accepted a plan for an Israeli pullout from 13 percent of the West Bank, including Israel's demand that a nature preserve count in the total, after talks with President Clinton.

Albania's opposition Democrats called for an interim government to be set up and early elections scheduled following the resignation of Fatos Nano as premier. But the ruling Socialists proceeded with plans to install Pandeli Majko as Mr. Nano's successor.

A Sri Lanka battle claimed 1,300 lives, the largest toll in years of conflict. Claims by both the government and Tamil separatist rebels are often exaggerrated, but the Red Cross said rebels turned over the bodies of 600 of Colombo's troops. The military said 262 others were killed, along with more than 400 rebels. The battle began as the army tried to take a highway linking the capital and Jaffna, in rebel territory. The road's capture would be a turning point in the 15-year-old war.

Kosovo massacres by Serbs drew international condemnation and renewed threats of NATO action. Britain called for an emergency U.N. Security Council meeting after Western diplomats viewed mutilated bodies of at least 20 ethnic Albanian civilians killed in recent days. Serb police denied they were responsible.

A Democratic fund-raiser was indicted on 17 counts of illegal contributions to the 1996 Clinton-Gore campaign and other races. Miami businessman Mark Jimenez allegedly had employees make donations, then reimbursed them.

Business and Economic News, 1997–1998

OCTOBER 1997

Raytheon won conditional approval from the U.S. Justice Department to buy the defense lines of General Motors' Hughes Electronics. As expected, Raytheon had to shed certain businesses that make high-tech sensors used in weapons systems.

Occidental Petroleum agreed to buy the majority of the U.S. government's Naval Petroleum Reserve for $3.65 billion and said it planned to sell its MidCon natural-gas pipeline unit to cover most of the cost. The sale, ordered by Congress because the navy no longer needs the reserves, is the largest privatization in U.S. history, the Department of Energy said.

Sun Microsystems sued Microsoft alleging the software giant was trying to disrupt development of Java, a software language that could compete with Microsoft's Windows operating system. Sun wanted to force Microsoft to distribute a version of Java that is compatible with the version adopted by much of the rest of the industry. Sun contended that Microsoft aimed to balkanize Java into different versions, in particular one that runs best on Windows. Microsoft filed a countersuit against Sun.

Union Pacific's service problems began to hurt a number of industries. The No. 1 railroad's clogged network triggered everything from production slowdowns to a scramble to switch to other forms of transportation. And Union Pacific faced claims from some companies seeking damages for the service problems. Late in the month, regulators said Union Pacific's delays posed a "transportation emergency in the West," and ordered the company to temporarily open part of its Houston business to a rival.

CoreStates Financial rejected an $18 billion, or $88-a-share, takeover bid by Mellon Bank, and Mellon withdrew its proposal. But CoreStates said it remained open to takeover offers.

Gencor and Goldfields planned to merge their South African gold-mining operations in a

$3.6 billion deal to create the largest producer of gold in the world.

IBM planned to fold its two-year-old consumer division into its business-PCs unit, a setback for the computing giant, which was blindsided by the popularity of under-$1,000 machines. Separately, IBM began offering a voluntary job buyout plan to most of its 241,000 employees in a cost-cutting move that could eliminate several thousand positions.

Avis was accused by Pennsylvania's attorney general of discriminating against minority car-renters. The company also came under investigation by the U.S. Justice Department for such alleged practices.

GTE offered $28 billion for MCI, a deal that would have been the largest cash purchase ever. GTE hoped to topple WorldCom's bid as well as MCI's pact to be bought by British Telecom.

Zurich Insurance said it would merge with the financial-services arm of B.A.T in a multibillion-dollar deal. The agreement cleared the way for B.A.T to break off its tobacco operations into a separate company. The combined Anglo-Swiss concern would be a powerful force with a significant share of the U.S. market and a network of companies to sell and distribute financial products.

AT&T chose C. Michael Armstrong, chief executive officer of Hughes Electronics, to run the telecommunications giant. The board also decided that Chairman Robert E. Allen would resign within weeks, while Vice Chairman John D. Zeglis would become president. Hughes named Michael T. Smith, the company vice chairman, to replace Mr. Armstrong as it faces rising competition in its satellite and DirecTV businesses. Separately, AT&T said it planned to sell its Universal credit card and a customer-service business.

Coca-Cola named its No. 2 executive M. Douglas Ivester chairman and CEO following the death of CEO Roberto C. Goizueta.

Ernst & Young said it agreed to merge with KPMG Peat Marwick in a deal to create the world's largest accounting and consulting firm, with $18.3 billion in global revenue.

ITT agreed to be acquired by REIT Starwood Lodging for $9.8 billion in cash and stock, plus $3.5 billion in assumed debt. The deal was intended to keep ITT out of the hands of hostile bidder Hilton Hotels and create the world's largest hotel company.

Microsoft was charged with violating a 1995 antitrust pact with the Justice Department, which asked a federal judge to stop the software giant from bundling its Windows 95 operating system with its Internet browser. The suit called for a fine of $1 million a day as long as the practice continued.

Seagram agreed to merge a big part of Universal Television, including cable giant USA Network, with Barry Diller's HSN. Mr. Diller was expected to use a revamped USA to expand. Separately, HSN made an unsolicited $285 million bid to acquire the slightly more than 50 percent of Ticketmaster it didn't already own.

Sunbeam said it hired Morgan Stanley to find potential suitors or takeover targets, 16 months into a major restructuring engineered by its aggressive CEO, Albert J. Dunlap.

U S West announced it would split its phone and cable businesses into two companies. The move underscored the fact that the much sought-after convergence between the two industries failed to materialize.

As Hong Kong was swept up into Asia's financial turmoil, stock prices plummeted on Oct. 27. The continuing sell-off eliminated about $1.2 trillion in global market value. Trading in the United States was halted early for the first time under the Big Board's circuit-breaker rules after the Dow Jones industrials sank 554.26, or 7.18 percent, to 7161.15. It was the Dow's biggest point drop ever, while only the 12th worst in percentage terms. The next day, stocks bounced back as volume topped a billion shares on both the Big Board and Nasdaq for the first time. The Dow Jones industrials surged 337.17 points, or 4.71 percent to 7498.32, their largest point gain ever.

Rolls-Royce Motor Cars was put on the block by British engineering group Vickers. Analysts said a sale of the luxury car maker could fetch about $650 million.

PhyCor said it agreed to acquire MedPartners in a stock swap valued at about $6.98 billion, plus the assumption of about $1.2 billion in debt. The merger would bring together the nation's top two physician-management concerns. PhyCor shares fell 19 percent a day after the plan was unveiled, while MedPartners' stock dropped 17 percent.

Silicon Graphics CEO Edward McCracken stepped down under pressure, and the computer company said it would cut its work force by as many as 1,000 people as part of a restructuring plan.

Crude-oil futures advanced 25 cents to $20.71 a barrel amid rising tensions between the United States and Iraq.

DuPont said John Krol would give up his president's title immediately and his CEO job on February 1, 1998, to executive vice president Charles Holliday.

Amtrak reached a settlement with its track-workers union, averting a crippling strike. But the accord appeared to solve few of the passenger railroad's long-term problems.

R.J. Reynolds won a legal victory as a Florida state-court jury refused to blame the cigarette maker for the lung cancer of a former smoker.

NOVEMBER 1997

Levi Strauss said it would close 11 of its 37 plants in the United States and Canada and cut 6,395 workers. The blue-jeans maker said the move would reduce overcapacity, not send jobs overseas.

Oxford Health posted a wider-than-expected quarterly loss and sharply scaled back 1998 projections. The HMO's loss was $13 million more than it forecast October 27 when its stock plunged 62 percent as it disclosed a computer problem that caused it to lose control of its billing and claims paying. Andrew B. Cassidy, Oxford's financial chief, resigned after the loss was announced.

Manufacturers can cap the prices retailers charge for their products as long as they can show they aren't stifling competition, the Supreme Court ruled. The unanimous decision reverses a 30-year-old ruling and could lead to lower prices for consumers.

Krupp and Thyssen said they plan a $12 billion merger of the German steel giants, six months after Krupp's hostile takeover bid for Thyssen failed.

Metropolitan Life Insurance was being investigated by Florida regulators for allegedly misleading sales practices that are similar to charges made in recent years against Prudential. The accusations of so-called churning, selling new policies to customers while draining the value of their existing policies to pay for the coverage, have spawned civil suits in several states. A spokesman said Metropolitan Life believes that any problems would be found to be isolated.

Some Wall Street economists cut estimates for 1998 economic growth by 0.5 percentage point or more, because of the turmoil in Southeast Asia and also due to some domestic concerns.

Philip Morris planned to roll out an ultralow-tar version of its Marlboro cigarette in early 1998. The move raised speculation the firm was scrambling to launch the product because Congress might pass sweeping tobacco legislation.

Chancellor Media's pact to buy four stations from SFX drew a lawsuit from the Justice Department, its first legal move against a radio merger.

MCI accepted a sweetened takeover offer from WorldCom of $51 a share, or $37 billion, in WorldCom stock. The huge offer was expected to vanquish rival, and far bigger, suitors GTE and British Telecom.

Walt Disney and former studio chief Jeffrey Katzenberg reached a "partial settlement" of Mr. Katzenberg's contentious $250 million breach-of-contract suit. The accord canceled an upcoming trial.

Eastman Kodak said it would cut 10,000 jobs and take a pretax restructuring charge of at least $1 billion, moving to address its high costs and lagging profitability. Some investors were disappointed the cuts weren't deeper, and the company's shares fell 6.1 percent.

NBC and Turner Sports will air more games with slimmer profits under their new agreements with the National Basketball Association, valued at a total of $2.64 billion. NBC paid $1.75 billion, and Turner, $890 million, to retain exclusive television rights through the 2001–02 season.

ITT shareholders rejected Hilton Hotels' slate of directors in a proxy vote, dealing Hilton's 10-month hostile bid for ITT a crushing blow. ITT directors then approved a revised merger agreement with Starwood Lodging, providing for ITT shareholders to receive Starwood's $85-a-share cash and stock offer.

The Securities and Exchange Commission and the National Association of Securities Dealers launched inquiries into investment banks' allocation of initial-public-offering shares to corporate officials in an apparent bid for business from the executives' companies.

Hicks Muse agreed to buy United Artists theaters for $300 million plus $550 million in assumed debt. The buyout firm said it plans to become a major investor in movie houses.

Westinghouse Electric said it would change its name to CBS, reflecting a transformation that began with its purchase of the television and radio network in 1995. The company also said Siemens agreed to buy its power-generation business for $1.53 billion.

Stocks surged on November 17, led by a 7.96 percent rally in Japan. The Dow Jones industrials jumped 125.74, or 1.66 percent, to 7698.22, their highest close since the 554.26-point drop on October 27. Banking and technology stocks were the biggest gainers, with the Nasdaq composite surging 30.60, or 1.93 percent, to 1614.11. Tokyo's buying spree was spurred by Japan's decision to allow a top lender, Hokkaido Takushoku Bank, to fail. The news raised hopes that Tokyo will move aggressively to resolve its financial and economic problems.

French ad group Publicis made an unsolicited offer for True North Communications in a transaction that values the Chicago firm at $700 million. True North shares jumped 11 percent.

First Union agreed to acquire CoreStates Financial for $81.40 a share in stock, or $16.3 billion, making it the largest bank merger ever. The deal came less than two months after Mellon unsuccessfully bid for CoreStates. First Union defended the acquisition, which provides the bank with a solid franchise from Connecticut to Florida. Still, analysts called the deal's price high relative to CoreStates' book value.

Germany's Allianz agreed to buy Assurances Generales de France is an attempt to reclaim the lead in European insurance. The $10.35-billion friendly deal would snatch AGF from Italy's Assicurazioni Generali.

Smith Barney agreed to high goals for hiring and promoting women under a class-action pact, but they will be hard to reach, industry experts said. The settlement plan calls for the Travelers Group unit to spend $15 million over four years on programs aimed at increasing the diversity of its work force.

Merrill Lynch said it would buy Mercury Asset Management, a London-based money manager, for $5.3 billion in the biggest overseas acquisition by a U.S. securities firm. The deal would catapult Merrill to No. 4 in the ranks of global asset managers, with $450 billion in assets under management. It also signaled Merrill's bet on the future of international investing, despite recent volatility centered in Southeast Asia.

IBM's Louis Gerstner said he agreed to stay on at least five more years as chairman and CEO. In return, the board is granting him options for two million shares, nearly as many as he has received so far. Mr. Gerstner said that despite the gains since he took over the computer maker in 1993, IBM is only at the midpoint of its comeback.

Nabisco said H. John Greeniaus, its chairman and CEO, would resign for health reasons and be succeeded by James Kilts, a former Philip Morris executive vice president.

The trade gap swelled 17 percent to $11.1 billion in September, the widest deficit since January, amid a surge of imported toys and other holiday products from China and elsewhere in Asia.

Yamaichi Securities told Japanese authorities that the nation's No. 4 securities firm would shut down, in the largest corporate failure in Japan since World War II. The collapse raised the question of whether other large shutdowns are in store at Japan's banks, insurers and brokerage firms, which have been weakened by a seven-year fall in land and stock prices and a resulting bad-loan crisis. Japanese officials and bankers sought to assure global investors that their banking system remains stable. Still, Japanese lenders continued to face a credit squeeze in international markets, amid fears of more failures in the financial system.

The New York Stock Exchange proposed that the market's circuit-breakers be activated after stock prices fall 10 percent and 20 percent, almost tripling the current point moves required to halt trading.

Knoll Pharmaceutical's new obesity drug won FDA approval. Meridia, made by the BASF unit, is believed to be similar in efficacy to Redux, but there's no evidence of heart or lung side effects.

Prince al-Waleed bin Talal, a billionaire Saudi Arabian investor, paid a total of about $850 million for stakes in News Corp., Netscape Communications and Motorola, as part of a push into global media and technology.

President Clinton joined other Pacific Rim leaders in endorsing IMF bailout efforts in Asia's worst financial crisis in years. But they substantively did little more than try to boost confidence. In a communique from the 18-nation Asia-Pacific Economic Cooperation forum, the leaders backed an accord reached in Manila keeping the IMF at the center of the rescue and seeking ways to make it easier for the fund to lend large sums to countries facing currency crises.

A federal grand jury indicted 19 people, including five alleged organized crime figures, in a stock-manipulation scheme as prosecutors step up inquires into whether the mob has tried to infiltrate parts of Wall Street.

Gold prices fell through the $300-an-ounce mark on November 26, the first time since March 1985. December gold futures on the Comex slid $3.60 to $296.90 a troy ounce, a 12½-year low.

OPEC's accord to lift the group's production cap by a larger-than-expected 2.5 million barrels a day was expected to lead to more oil on world markets and potentially lower prices.

DECEMBER 1997

Stocks surged on December 1, sending the Dow Jones industrials to their first close above 8000 since October 15. The industrials soared 189.98 points, or 2.4 percent, to 8013.11, amid renewed confidence that Asian governments would control the region's financial problems.

The yen bounced back from a 5½-year low against the dollar after top Japanese finance officials warned the currency has fallen too far and said Tokyo was prepared to support it. Separately, Japanese Prime Minister Ryutaro Hashimoto announced an income-tax cut valued at $15.4 billion in a bid to revive the nation's economy, sparking a sharp sell-off of the dollar in Tokyo.

South Korea agreed to a broad dismantling of its interlocked financial and industrial system as the price for a record $55-billion International Monetary Fund bailout. Separately, banks in the United States, Europe and Japan were considering extending as much as $10 billion in new credit to the South Korean government. The banks also agreed to extend the repayment terms on the bulk of their short-term loans to South Korean banks.

GE Capital CEO Gary Wendt must share with his ex-wife certain stock options, on top of other payments, in a divorce case that set off a debate over the role of corporate wives.

Chrysler named Thomas T. Stallkamp president, essentially anointing him heir apparent to Robert J. Eaton, the No. 3 U.S. auto maker's chairman and CEO. Mr. Stallkamp is best known as a cost-cutter; he also oversaw Chrysler's key minivan operations.

A $25-billion merger between Union Bank of Switzerland and Swiss Bank created a new global powerhouse in financial services that will force U.S. banks to reassess their strategies. The combined firm, the world's No. 2 bank and No. 1 asset manager, could spur a new wave of U.S. megamergers, analysts said.

AT&T said it will sell back its stake in Hughes Electronics' DirecTV, a satellite-based rival to cable TV. The move could free AT&T to pursue grander alliances with cable firms.

Dow Jones and General Electric's NBC announced plans for a television alliance that includes the consolidation of their business-news channels in Europe and Asia, and a close collaboration between CNBC and *The Wall Street Journal* in the United States.

Oracle's shares tumbled 29 percent as more than 171 million shares changed hands, a record for any stock trading for over $1, after the No. 2

software company released disappointing earnings. The report hurt other technology issues and rattled Wall Street's confidence in Oracle's future market growth, technological prowess and management skill.

Oxford Health Plans said it expects to post a quarterly loss of $120 million as it adds to its medical-claims reserves, a sign the HMO's problems are even more serious than it disclosed six weeks before.

Gold futures fell to $282.80 a troy ounce, the fourth new 12½-year low the December contract hit this month.

Avon Products appointed Charles Perrin chief operating officer, with plans to name him CEO. Previously, the company had signaled it might name a female executive to the CEO post.

Microsoft was ordered by a federal judge to stop bundling its Internet browser with its Windows operating systems, dealing at least a temporary blow to the software giant's plans to dominate the hotly contested market. Microsoft said it would appeal.

A World Trade Organization pact to liberalize financial services was approved after Asian nations agreed to sign. Under the landmark accord, 102 nations will open their banks, insurance firms and other financial institutions to foreigners.

Citicorp and AT&T reached an agreement under which the nation's biggest credit-card issuer will acquire the phone giant's Universal Card for about $4 billion.

Chase Manhattan announced a management shakeup that created an unusual power-sharing structure in which President Thomas Labrecque would be an equal partner to Walter Shipley, its chairman and CEO.

RJR Nabisco Holdings said it planned to cut its total work force by nearly 10 percent and take a $390-million pretax charge in a restructuring that would primarily affect its overseas tobacco business. Separately, Polaroid said it would slash about 1,500 jobs, or 15 percent of its world-wide work force, and take a $310-million pretax charge in the fourth quarter as part of a broad cost-cutting effort.

Boeing was criticized by air-safety regulators for congestion at its factories. At one point, FAA employees warned that conditions for inspecting planes were "out of control," agency documents show. The FAA complaints support the notion that the commercial jet maker's rapid drive toward record production was a far bigger worry for regulators than they had indicated publicly.

Partners of Andersen Consulting unanimously agreed to break away from parent Andersen Worldwide. The vote was the culmination of a feud between the consulting partners and the firm's Arthur Andersen accounting unit.

General Motors said it has the technology to make some of its gasoline-powered cars 99 percent emission-free as soon as the 1999 model year if a new national emissions standard is adopted by more states and auto makers.

Eastman Kodak raised its projected fourth-quarter restructuring charge by 50 percent to $1.5 billion and sharply increased its layoff target to 19,900 employees by the end of 1999.

Wal-Mart Stores agreed to acquire German "hypermarket" retailer Wertkauf, giving it a foothold in the European market for the first time.

Allegheny Teledyne offered to buy rival steelmaker Lukens for $456 million, topping a Bethlehem Steel bid that Lukens agreed to earlier.

Colgate-Palmolive launched a $100 million ad campaign in the United States for Total, a toothpaste that contains a germ-fighting ingredient found in a number of soaps and deodorants.

Comedian Jerry Seinfeld said this would be the final season for his highly rated and very profitable half-hour comedy. The loss of *Seinfeld* came at a time when NBC was facing other issues challenging its position as prime-time king, including a renegotiation to keep medical drama *ER*.

True North shareholders voted to buy Bozell Jacobs Kenyon & Eckhardt, creating the world's sixth-largest advertising agency and handing a defeat to France's Publicis, which was angling for control of True North.

China's economy grew 8.8 percent in 1997, the country's statistical agency said, missing growth projections of 10 percent.

JANUARY 1998

Offerings of new bonds and stocks jumped 33 percent to $1.29 trillion in 1997, exceeding the $1-trillion mark for the first time since 1993. An additional $254 billion was raised through private placements, pushing the total issuance to more than $1.5 trillion.

Bond prices surged in early January, sending the 30-year Treasury to a record-low yield of 5.72 percent, while comparable government-bond yields reached their lowest levels since the 1960s. The rally was in large part due to comments by Federal Reserve Chairman Alan Greenspan that the markets interpreted as raising the chance the economy could soon face deflationary pressures. Prices of mortgage-backed securities tumbled as investors braced for a wave of home refinancings.

SBC Communications agreed to buy Southern New England Telecom for $4.26 billion in stock, in an aggressive move to become the first Baby Bell to offer long-distance services. The pact would give the Texas-based Bell a strong foothold in the Mid-Atlantic and Northeast.

DNA Plant Technology was accused of conspiring with Brown & Williamson to develop a tobacco with high nicotine content. The criminal charge was the first to emerge from the Justice Department's three-year investigation of the tobacco industry.

PhyCor and MedPartners called off their proposed $6.25-billion merger, blaming "significant operational and strategic differences" between the big physician management companies.

Indonesia faced hoarding and fears of social unrest, amid concerns the International Monetary Fund would suspend its $43-billion rescue package if Jakarta doesn't conform to IMF policies. But later in the month, Indonesian President Suharto signed an accord with the IMF that was expected to accelerate economic reforms and erode business breaks enjoyed by his friends and family members.

AT&T said it will acquire Teleport Communications for $11.3 billion in stock, an expensive but crucial move to penetrate local-phone markets. For Tele-Communications, Cox Enterprises and Comcast, the big cable firms selling their controlling stake in Teleport, the deal offers a graceful exit from the phone business, while preserving the option to return.

Retail sales rose a healthy 4.4 percent in December 1997, as last-minute holiday shoppers and post-Christmas bargain hunters helped save what had appeared to be a weak holiday season.

Walt Disney agreed to pay more than $9 billion over the next eight years for its ABC and ESPN subsidiaries to be able to carry National Football League games. And CBS returned to the football business, agreeing to pay at least $4 billion over eight years to carry the NFL. General Electric's NBC was sidelined after broadcasting NFL games since 1965.

Peregrine Investments officially filed for court liquidation, and the firm's chairman said the Hong Kong investment house was exploring offers from mainland Chinese entities and other parties for certain operations.

NBC struck an $850-million deal to keep the nation's top-rated show, *ER*. The deal marked a rapid recovery for the General Electric unit after failing to keep rights to NFL games.

Seagate Technology said it planned to lay off about 10,000 workers in response to its continuing troubles in the computer disk-drive business.

Tobacco firms agreed to pay Texas $15.3 billion over 25 years to avoid a trial in the state's suit to recover health-care costs. The industry already settled with Mississippi and Florida for a combined total of $14.4 billion.

Hicks, Muse, Tate & Furst and Kohlberg Kravis Roberts agreed to combine the movie-theater chains they were acquiring and planned to purchase Regal Cinemas in a transaction that would create the biggest chain in the United States. The two leveraged-buyout rivals valued the transaction at $3 billion, including the assumption of debt. The surprise move would form a company with 5,347 screens in 727 locations. That is an estimated 17 percent of the screens in the country.

Auto-insurance rates started falling for the first time in more than 20 years. Insurers passed along savings as baby boomers drive more cautiously, buy safer cars and buckle up.

Two Russian oil giants agreed to merge to form the world's third-largest private oil company. Yukos and Sibneft didn't disclose terms of the deal.

The five Baby Bells attempted to catch up with cable TV's move into high-speed data access by supporting a rival technology standard backed by Microsoft, Intel and Compaq Computer.

Ciba Specialty Chemicals said it would buy U.K. chemicals firm Allied Colloids for $2.31 billion, trumping Hercules's hostile bid and ending a takeover battle.

Microsoft settled a legal dispute with the Justice Department, but the company's tactics set the stage for what may be a costly war. Microsoft agreed to give PC makers the right to ship Windows 95 on their machines without also having to install Microsoft's Internet-browser software. But federal investigators were building a new antitrust case against the software giant.

Royal Bank of Canada and Bank of Montreal announced plans for a $12.12-billion merger. The combined bank, with $312 billion in assets, would edge out Citicorp to be North America's second-largest, after Chase Manhattan.

The Kennedy family agreed to sell Chicago's Merchandise Mart, along with other properties, to Vornado Realty Trust for $575 million and the assumption of debt.

Compaq Computer agreed to acquire Digital Equipment for $8.55 billion, or $57.40 a share, in cash and stock, placing the world's biggest seller of PCs in a position to vie directly with IBM and Hewlett-Packard. The move gives Compaq the ability to expand into high-end computing and services for large companies. Digital's missteps had turned the former powerhouse into a second-tier player.

Northwest Airlines and Continental Airlines formed an alliance, ending Delta's bid to buy Continental. Northwest agreed to pay $519 million in cash and stock, or $60.80 a share, to an investor group for a 14 percent stake with 51 percent of voting rights.

AT&T's chairman C. Michael Armstrong announced a major revamping that could entail as many as 18,000 new job cuts and up to $1.2 billion in charges against earnings.

Union Pacific Resources said it would buy Norcen Energy Resources of Canada for $2.55 billion and the assumption of $900 million in debt. The deal follows the Texas firm's failed attempt to buy Pennzoil.

Deutsche Bank set aside $2.1 billion for restructuring costs and potential Asian losses. The move pleased investors, but raised fears about such losses at other European banks. Credit Lyonnais put its Southeast Asian exposure at $5 billion, but said any losses would be confined to $2 billion of Thai and Indonesian loans.

South Korea reached a deal with international creditors to restructure most short-term foreign-currency debt of the country's banks as longer-term, government-backed loans.

Compaq Computer won a three-year deal to supply PCs for Tandy's 6,800 Radio Shack stores, a further blow to IBM, which saw its U.S. retail-market share decrease to 5.9 percent in November 1997 from 10.3 percent in the previous year.

A bribery scandal in Japan intensified as the finance minister resigned, two other Finance Ministry officials offered to quit, and one was found dead in an apparent suicide. Earlier, two bank examiners for the finance ministry were arrested for allegedly accepting bribes to help hide problem loans at banks they inspected.

Bethlehem Steel won a bidding war for steelmaker Lukens by coupling its $30-a-share stock-and-cash offer with a deal to sell some Lukens assets to rival suitor Allegheny Teledyne.

Omnicom Group of New York agreed to acquire GGT Group of London for $235 million, and the resulting company seems likely to become the world's largest advertising concern.

Fed Chairman Alan Greenspan signaled that he would hold interest rates steady for the foreseeable future, partly because the impact of the Asian economic crisis remained unclear. He described the U.S. economy as "exceptionally healthy" in testimony before a Senate committee. His words sent the bond market soaring and helped buoy stocks.

Three big tobacco companies became subjects of a Justice Department criminal antitrust probe. The agency was investigating whether Brown & Williamson, R.J. Reynolds and Philip Morris colluded on the price of tobacco leaf.

AirTouch Communications agreed to acquire the domestic wireless operations of U S West Media Group in a deal valued at $4.3 billion, plus the assumption of $1.4 billion of debt. The agreement came six months after an earlier deal fell apart because of the elimination of a federal tax loophole.

Reuters of Britain said a grand jury in New York was investigating whether a U.S.-based bond-analysis subsidiary improperly took information from rival Bloomberg. Reuters put three executives on paid leave.

SmithKline Beecham and Glaxo Wellcome said they were having merger talks to create the world's largest drug maker. The proposed deal between the two British companies was tentatively valued at $65 billion to $70 billion, and the combined firm would have annual sales of over $25 billion. The talks scuttled months of merger discussions between SmithKline and American Home Products.

The framework of a new aviation pact was announced by U.S. and Japanese officials. The accord will bring radical changes to the trans-Pacific passenger market, challenging Northwest Airlines' pre-eminent position.

FEBRUARY

Attorneys general from 11 states issued new subpoenas in their antitrust probe of Microsoft, widening their inquiry to include Windows 98. Separately, the Justice Department also issued new subpoenas in its antitrust probe of Microsoft that focused on exclusive deals the software giant may have cut with some Internet publishers.

PacifiCorp reached a sweetened $6.53-billion agreement to buy Energy Group, Britain's largest electric utility, betting that the increased price would discourage competing bids.

Berkshire Hathaway said it owned 129.7 million ounces of silver, an amount valued at around $858.6 million. After Berkshire's heavy buying, silver prices rose and the metal was in tight supply, forcing London's metal exchange to loosen deadlines for delivery.

Netscape focused on deals involving its Web site and software businesses, industry executives and analysts said, as it considered its options, including the sale of the company. Its stock rose $2.6875, or 14 percent, to $21.9375.

The New York Stock Exchange adopted circuit breakers that would automatically close markets for the day only after a 30 percent stock-market drop.

The Federal Trade Commission was preparing to end decades of leniency toward the cigar industry. Alarmed about cigars' booming sales and popularity among teenagers, regulators were considering such steps as requiring big cigar makers to report how much they spend on advertising and promotions, including product placements in movies.

Thailand's central bank seized two more banks. Their estimated losses raised questions about the government's ability to contain the crisis.

CVS agreed to acquire Arbor Drugs, a Michigan chain, for $1.48 billion, in a move that pits it against Walgreen for leadership in the consolidating drugstore industry. The acquisition of Arbor, a regional leader, will bolster CVS's growing dominance in markets east of the Mississippi.

America Online said it would boost its monthly charge 10 percent, potentially clearing the way for a wave of price increases throughout the Internet-access industry. The move sent AOL's stock soaring 12 percent to a record high.

An insurance-industry study found that people in cars that are hit broadside by large pickup trucks or sport-utility vehicles are 27 times as likely to die as the trucks' occupants.

Frito-Lay started rolling out a new line of chips called Wow!, as part of a national launch of the PepsiCo division's snack foods made with the fake fat olestra.

China's government approved a Royal Dutch/Shell Group plan to construct a $4.5-billion petrochemical plant, the biggest foreign investment in the nation to date.

DFS Group said it wouldn't pursue an acquisition of Barney's after reaching a stalemate with creditors and Barney's management over the value of the upscale clothing-store chain.

The Dow Jones industrials set their first record in six months on February 10, overcoming anxiety about Asia-related turmoil, with a gain of 115.09 points, or 1.41 percent, to 8295.61. Standard & Poor's 500-stock index reached a new high as well.

Canadian National Railway announced an agreement to buy Illinois Central for $39 a share in cash and stock, or $2.4 billion. The deal would create the fifth-largest railroad in North America.

Columbia/HCA defrauded the Medicare system of tens of millions of dollars through its home-health operations, investigators charged in newly released portions of an FBI affidavit.

Computer Sciences rejected Computer Associates' hostile $9.18-billion takeover bid, setting the stage for a battle over control of the computer-services company.

Reuters's chief executive conceded that it was "possible" employees may have misinterpreted company policy and stolen information from Bloomberg amid competitive pressures.

Prudential Insurance was proceeding with steps to convert to stock ownership, shedding its status as a policyholder-owned company. The move was driven by Prudential's desire to tap into the equity market and take part in a merger wave that has been altering the financial-services world.

The planned merger of KPMG Peat Marwick and Ernst & Young collapsed and the head of KPMG blamed Ernst & Young, saying that the deal could have been successfully sealed despite regulatory and client issues.

Major U.S. companies posted profit growth of 1.3 percent for the 1997 fourth quarter, extending their streak of gains to two years. But analysts expected the momentum to slow as labor costs edged up and Asia's troubles started to hit home.

Beneficial put itself up for sale amid pressure from Wall Street, and Household International said it would be interested in acquiring its consumer-finance rival. Beneficial's shares soared $30.625, or 37 percent, to $112.875, for a value of $6.15 billion.

Gasoline prices slid below $1 a gallon in some U.S. cities. Crude-oil prices were lower, and supplies were growing amid warm winter weather.

Echlin reacted coolly to SPX's hostile-takeover offer of $3 billion, as investors bid up the auto-parts maker's shares, anticipating a richer offer.

CBS conceded that the Winter Olympics were disappointing, and it offered free time to advertisers to make up for the Games' lackluster ratings.

SBC Warburg's negotiations to take over Christie's collapsed, the London-based auction house said.

Simon DeBartolo Group agreed to pay $4.8 billion for Corporate Property Investors, which owns two dozen malls and New York's General Motors Building. The purchase firmly established Simon DeBartolo as the largest U.S. owner of retail properties and signaled that the commercial real-estate market was heating up again.

Caterpillar and UAW leaders suffered a rebuke when workers at Caterpillar's factories rejected a tentative contract agreement that would have ended a six-year dispute.

Hicks, Muse, Tate & Furst terminated its $300-million agreement to purchase United Artists, a move that will reduce the size of the theater chain that Hicks Muse is building together with Kohlberg Kravis Roberts.

SmithKline Beecham broke off merger talks with Glaxo Wellcome over differences about who would manage the company, scuttling what would have been a $70-billion deal. SmithKline said officials of Glaxo, which didn't comment, reneged on previously agreed terms of the deal.

Oxford Health Plans unveiled a $700 million recapitalization package and named an industry veteran as its CEO. But Oxford's shares fell as its quarterly loss proved unexpectedly big and Kohlberg Kravis Roberts withdrew from the refinancing.

Four drug wholesalers' mergers drew antitrust opposition from the FTC staff. The news hurt the shares of McKesson, AmeriSource Health, Cardinal Health and Bergen Brunswig.

Halliburton reached an accord to buy Dresser Industries for about $7.7 billion in stock, bringing together the two big oil-field-services concerns. The union of the Dallas-based rivals will form a giant with $16.3 billion in revenue that will leap over Schlumberger to become the No. 1 energy-services concern in the world.

Eight Big Board floor brokers were charged in federal court with illegally profiting from information that the brokers picked up on the exchange floor. A small brokerage firm and two of its owners also were charged.

Two big British insurers unveiled an $11.72 billion merger. The deal between Commercial Union and General Accident came as the industry consolidated ahead of the euro's launch.

Toys "R" Us named Robert Nakasone as its new CEO, replacing Michael Goldstein, and announced another earnings disappointment.

Michael Milken agreed to pay $47 million to settle federal charges that he violated a lifetime ban from the securities business. The SEC civil suit covered the former financier's role as a consultant in two deals involving MCI, News Corp. and New World Communications.

Apple Computer said it was killing its Newton hand-held computer as part of a plan to focus resources on its Macintosh line.

MARCH

Sunbeam announced agreements to buy Coleman, along with the makers of Mr. Coffee machines and First Alert smoke alarms, for $1.8 billion, plus the assumption of $700 million of debt. The moves marked the first time Sunbeam's chairman, Albert Dunlap, used acquisitions to build the household-products concern since its restructuring began 18 months ago.

PacifiCorp raised its offer for Energy Group 7.2 percent to $7 billion, just hours after Texas Utilities said it had won approval from the British utility's board for its initial $6.9-billion offer.

Mark Whitacre was sentenced to nine years in prison for swindling $9.5 million from ADM at the same time he was helping a federal price-fixing probe of his superiors at the company.

CA ended its pursuit of Computer Sciences, saying it would rather walk away than prolong an acrimonious takeover battle. CA said it would look for smaller acquisitions to boost its computer-services capabilities.

Transport firms raised prices for the first time in a decade, as the strong economy filled the nation's trucks, ships and trains with cargo.

Qwest said it would acquire LCI International, a larger competitor, for $4.43 billion in stock, in a transaction that would form the fourth-largest long-distance company in the country.

The Supreme Court limited copyright protection for companies that export their products. The ruling hurts U.S. firms fighting the gray market, in which their products are bought, often abroad, and resold in the U.S.

Reed Elsevier and Wolters Kluwer called off merger plans that would have created a publishing giant.

USA Waste said it would merge with giant trash hauler Waste Management in a stock transaction valued at about $13.47 billion. Waste Management shareholders would end up with about 60 percent of the combined company.

PG&E won a contract to manage $2 billion in electricity and natural-gas purchases for San Antonio-based Ultramar, in the largest national retail power deal announced to date.

The boards of the Nasdaq Stock Market and the American Stock Exchange unanimously approved a preliminary merger agreement that would join the nation's second-largest and third-largest securities markets.

Warren Buffett said he doesn't believe U.S. stocks are overvalued. He also said, in a report to shareholders, that Berkshire has sold a sizable piece of its McDonald's stake, but he made scant mention of his silver holdings.

Omnicom Group closed Wells BDDP, its recently acquired ad agency, and divided up Wells's clients among other Omnicom shops.

The nation's largest shipyard said it would abort its bid to build commercial cargo ships. Newport News's move was a blow to U.S. hopes of returning to the world shipbuilding market.

Washington Mutual agreed to acquire H.F. Ahmanson in a stock swap valued at $10.03 billion, a transaction that would combine the nation's two largest thrift companies. The accord, which could trigger mergers among smaller thrifts, creates the country's seventh-largest banking company.

The Beardstown Ladies said a Price Waterhouse audit shows their 10-year average annual rate of return was 9.1 percent, not the 23.4 percent touted on the cover of their bestselling book.

ITT Industries said it was considering selling most of its $4.7 billion automotive business, which accounted for more than half of the company's 1997 sales. The manufacturer said it was weighing its options in the face of tough competition in the auto-parts market.

Hewlett-Packard said it planned to market its own variant of Java software, breaking with Sun Microsystems and opening a rift in the industry alliance against Microsoft. H-P said it developed specifications and software for running programs written in the Java language on a range of electronic devices, including its widely used computer printers.

Cigarette makers aren't liable for the death of a nonsmoking nurse, a jury in Muncie, Indiana, ruled in a case seen as a test of whether secondhand-smoke cases could be successfully brought against the industry.

Caterpillar's UAW workers ratified a revised labor agreement. The contract's approval by 54 percent of UAW members ended a six-year dispute between the union and the company.

Germany's Bertelsmann said it planned to buy Random House, creating a company that would dominate book publishing and wield great clout over retailers, agents and Hollywood.

The Justice Department asked a federal court to block Lockheed's $8.3-billion purchase of Northrop on antitrust grounds, and the companies vowed to fight to protect their deal.

Intel's Andrew Grove said he would yield the position of CEO to his top lieutenant, Craig Barrett, in May, ending an era for the computer-chip colossus. Meanwhile, Intel faced problems including slower PC sales, falling computer prices, Asia's financial crisis and an FTC antitrust probe.

Pfizer's impotence pill, Viagra, received FDA approval, clearing the way for a drug that's being touted as a simple treatment for men with the condition as well as a potential bestseller.

Apple Computer's board said it would let Steve Jobs stay for as long as he likes as interim CEO, which could make its search for a permanent leader less urgent.

OPEC agreed to cut crude-oil production by 1.25 million barrels a day, after a meeting that yielded specific pledges about how much each country will now produce. Still, the cuts, about 1.5 million including cuts by non-OPEC producers, fell short of amounts promised March 22 and weren't expected to boost oil prices immediately.

Sony Pictures folded its TriStar Pictures unit into sister company Columbia Pictures, in an attempt to make its operations more efficient.

Bacardi said it would buy the Dewar's Scotch whisky and Bombay gin brands from Diageo in a $1.94-billion deal.

BMW agreed to buy Rolls-Royce from Vickers for $572 million. Volkswagen had also bid for Rolls-Royce.

APRIL

Woolworth said it planned to change its name to Venator Group in an effort to convey its current identity as a retailer of sports shoes and apparel.

GTE unveiled a major program to cut costs and raise cash in an effort to give it more financial flexibility to fund its expansion. The phone company said it would take more than $800 million in first-quarter charges, raise up to $3 billion in cash by selling assets and slash costs by $500 million annually.

Citicorp and Travelers Group said they were merging in an $82.9-billion deal, the biggest corporate combination ever. The new company, Citigroup, would be a behemoth of banking, brokerage services and insurance, with assets of nearly $700 billion. The merger will test the idea of one-stop shopping for financial services.

Pratt & Whitney told 15 airlines, including United, Delta and Northwest, that it improperly serviced many jet-engine blades and urged airlines to remove engines with the suspect parts from planes immediately.

Conseco agreed to acquire Green Tree Financial, a subprime-market lender, in a stock swap valued at $6.44 billion. Meanwhile, Household International emerged as the winning bidder for Beneficial, agreeing to a $7.7 billion stock acquisition. The two deals reflect the continued consolidation of the financial-services industry.

Xerox said it plans to cut about 9,000 jobs, or about 10 percent of its work force, over two years and take a $1 billion restructuring charge as the company tries to rein in its costs.

Ford Motor's Lincoln passed General Motors' Cadillac for the first time in luxury-vehicle sales. Lincoln's car and truck sales grew 63 percent so far this year.

The chief executive of RJR Nabisco Holdings declared the tobacco deal dead. Steven Goldstone said his company would fight efforts to pass a tobacco bill and will no longer negotiate with Congress, the White House or the state attorneys general with whom RJR hashed out the proposed settlement. Other tobacco makers followed suit, a week after a Senate panel passed a bill toughening the deal.

The United States and France agreed to deregulate air traffic between them, authorizing 40 percent growth in trans-Atlantic service during a five-year phase-in.

Investors put a record $37.5 billion in net new cash into mutual funds in March, according to an official estimate. That represents about $1.7 billion a day, most of it going into stock funds. Some analysts cautioned that the surge showed investors are overenthusiastic about the market.

BankAmerica agreed to merge with Nations-Bank in a deal valued at $60 billion that would create the closest thing yet to a national bank, spanning 24 states coast to coast. Separately, Banc One said it would merge with First Chicago in a stock swap valued at $30 billion.

The SEC cleared "circuit breaker" trigger levels that would halt trading after one-day drops in the Dow Jones industrials of 10 percent, 20 percent and 30 percent.

Apple Computer exceeded analysts' profit estimates for the second straight quarter and reported its first increase in Macintosh unit shipments in two years.

Cendant said it found "potential accounting irregularities" that will require it to reduce 1997 operating income and will hurt 1998 earnings. In response, Cendant's stock plunged 46.5 percent, knocking $14 billion off its market value. The company dismissed a senior finance executive as more details of the accounting problems emerged.

The Justice Department cleared the $1-billion merger of Cineplex Odeon and Sony's Loews after the companies agreed to sell theaters.

Eli Lilly's Evista may prevent breast cancer, clinical trials indicated. What's more, Evista, currently approved as an osteoporosis drug, may work without the higher rates of uterine cancer associated with tamoxifen, the most recent breast-cancer breakthrough. Trials of Evista to combat cancer go back only two years. But word of the unreleased results boosted Lilly's shares $5.125 to $68.375.

Two big Canadian banks planned to merge. The $14.3-billion union of CIBC and Toronto Dominion will create a giant with a solid presence in the United States.

Pfizer's impotence pill quickly became one of the fastest-selling drugs ever, with doctors writing tens of thousands of Viagra prescriptions a day.

Bank of New York made public a proposal to acquire Mellon Bank for stock valued at about $23.8 billion, in an effort to pressure the bank to sell itself. Mellon promptly rejected the "bear hug," but its shares rose 12 percent. The move came four months after merger discussions between the two banks collapsed.

Delta Air Lines and United Airlines said they would form a massive marketing partnership, while separately, American Airlines and US Airways announced plans to begin a marketing alliance. The two agreements reflect the quickening pace of consolidation in the airline industry in the wake of January's ambitious accord between Northwest and Continental.

Transportation officials were investigating whether big airlines use their growing control of landing rights and gate leases at major airports to stifle competition from start-up carriers.

A junk-bond deal from Level 3 raised $2 billion, equaling the largest corporate junk-bond deal so far in the 1990s. The sale renewed worry about overheating in the junk-bond market.

Times Mirror said it would sell its Matthew Bender legal-publishing unit and its 50 percent interest in Shepard's to Reed Elsevier for $1.65 billion, moving to further focus on its core newspaper business.

Boeing unveiled an ambitious production plan for its new 717 jetliners, projecting that as many as 10 a month eventually may be built at a plant that Boeing inherited from McDonnell.

Liggett Group agreed to cooperate fully with the Justice Department's criminal investigation of the tobacco industry. The Brooke Group unit didn't receive any promise of immunity from prosecution on any charges against tobacco companies that could emerge. The agreement marked a turning point in the government's effort to build a case against the biggest U.S. tobacco makers.

IBM boosted its quarterly dividend by 10 percent and announced a $3.5-billion stock-repurchase plan, extending a three-year buyback strategy that has helped lift its per-share earnings.

Ziff-Davis sold 25.8 million shares at $15.50 each in its initial public offering, raising $399.9 million in the second-biggest IPO so far this year.

MAY

The European Union moved closer to launching a common currency, as EU leaders picked the new monetary union's 11 founding members and set exchange rates. The weekend summit saw a bitter battle over who should lead the new European Central Bank, underscoring the challenges Europe faces.

Dana agreed to acquire Echlin for stock currently valued at $3.42 billion, creating one of the world's largest auto-parts suppliers. The deal tops a hostile takeover offer by SPX for Echlin. The definitive agreement, in which Dana would also assume $570 million in debt, was approved by both companies' boards.

EntreMed's shares more than quadrupled on reports that, in about 12 to 18 months, EntreMed may begin human tests of two experimental drugs that have destroyed tumors in mice.

Chrysler's directors approved a $38.3-billion merger with Daimler-Benz, while the German company's management board also ratified the accord. News of the deal boosted their stocks, along with those of several foreign auto makers, as industry executives said the merger could force more combinations in the global auto business.

Vickers agreed to sell Rolls-Royce to Germany's Volkswagen for $713 million, after it had first agreed to sell the luxury-car maker to BMW.

PepsiCo sued Coca-Cola, accusing it of violating antitrust law by trying to keep Pepsi out of the business of selling soft drinks in restaurants and theaters served by independent distributors. Coca-Cola said there is nothing illegal about its business practices.

Minnesota won a $6.6-billion settlement of its suit to recover health-care costs linked to smoking, along with numerous concessions limiting how cigarettes can be marketed in the state.

SBC Communications announced plans to acquire Ameritech for $56.18 billion in stock, setting off a torrent of criticism from rival carriers and regulators. The transaction would create a local-service behemoth with more than $40 billion in revenue. Analysts hailed the union as a melding of two lean operators, but scrutiny from federal and state regulators could disappoint the Texas-based Bell's hopes to close the deal in about a year.

DuPont planned to shed Conoco and use most of the estimated $25 billion proceeds to invest in its life-sciences business. The chemical company is expected to raise about $5 billion in an IPO of as much as 20 percent of the oil unit.

Monsanto agreed to buy two crop-biotech concerns for a total of about $4.2 billion in cash and stock, shifting the power balance in the field. Separately, Monsanto formed a joint venture with crop processor Cargill and said each company will invest about $100 million a year in the venture.

The Justice Department sued to block Primestar's purchase of a satellite slot owned by MCI and News Corp. The government said the deal would thwart competition by giving the cable companies that back Primestar the last available satellite-TV capacity.

Two ex-Texaco executives were acquitted of obstruction of justice, despite secret tapes that the government contended showed the men agreeing to withhold and destroy evidence sought in a race-discrimination case.

The House voted 214–213 to pass a landmark reform bill that would eliminate many of the barriers separating banks, brokerage firms and insurers.

Pearson agreed to purchase Simon & Schuster's educational and reference operations for $4.6 billion from Viacom, and to sell the reference business to investment firm Hicks, Muse, Tate & Furst for about $1 billion.

Genentech said its drug Herceptin slows a form of breast cancer that afflicts as many as 30 percent of U.S. women annually diagnosed with the disease.

Microsoft was accused of seeking to destroy software-industry rivals in landmark antitrust lawsuits filed by the United States and 20 states. A government victory could mean that new computers would display links to products and services placed there by the computer maker, not by Microsoft.

Federal prosecutors alleged that three of eight Big Board floor brokers charged in February with illegal trading also engaged in criminal "front-running," or trading ahead of clients.

Columbia/HCA planned to sell 22 hospitals to a consortium of not-for-profit hospitals. The $1.2-billion transaction, involving eight separate buyers in four states, marks a major turnabout for the once-aggressive acquirer.

Royal Ahold planned to acquire Giant Food for about $2.7 billion, strengthening the Dutch company's position among the top U.S. food retailers. Ahold, which acquired Stop & Shop in 1996 and Bi-Lo in 1997, said it is seeking further U.S. acquisitions.

DuPont said it will pay $2.6 billion for Merck's 50 percent stake in a pharmaceutical joint venture, in a move to further expand its presence in life sciences.

AT&T invited regional Baby Bells to sell its long-distance service in their local markets. Such alliances would mark the first between AT&T and the Bells since the regional companies were spawned in 1984's breakup of AT&T.

Bank of New York withdrew its $22.1-billion bid for Mellon Bank, blasting the Pittsburgh concern's dismissive stance. Mellon said it lacked faith in BONY's chairman, Thomas Renyi.

Seagram said it will sell its Tropicana juice unit for an estimated $3.5 billion to $4 billion to help pay for its $10.6-billion cash-and-stock acquisition of music powerhouse PolyGram. That deal would make entertainment, not liquor sales, Seagram's main focus for the first time in its 74-year history.

Tyco International agreed to acquire U.S. Surgical for about $3.3 billion in stock. The deal will make Tyco one of the world's biggest providers of disposable medical products.

ABN Amro offered to buy Generale Bank of Belgium for $12.3 billion in stock and cash, topping a bid by Fortis. ABN's offer is the biggest ever unsolicited bid for a European bank.

Gateway 2000 will modify Windows 98 to emphasize its own Internet service and offer consumers a choice of Web-browsing software, taking a defiant stance toward Microsoft. Starting with its first Windows 98–based systems in June, Gateway will install Netscape's Navigator browser on its PCs as well as Microsoft's Internet Explorer browser.

Louisiana-Pacific agreed to pay $37 million in fines and pleaded guilty in federal court to 18 felony criminal charges, including fraud, conspiracy and various Clean Air Act violations.

United Healthcare agreed to buy Humana for about $5.38 billion in stock, creating what will be the largest managed-care company in the United States and continuing an industry consolidation. The combined company will have $27 billion in annual revenue and will provide full-risk managed-care coverage for 10.4 million people.

Huffy will close its largest U.S. bicycle factory and dismiss 950 workers, fighting competition from bikes made in Asia. Huffy is among the last major bike makers with U.S. production.

JUNE

American Home agreed to buy Monsanto in a $35.08-billion stock swap, driven by the race to turn genetics advances into new drugs and agricultural products. The proposed deal, pooling both companies' research facilities, would create a powerhouse in the pharmaceutical, nutrition and agriculture industries.

Merrill Lynch agreed to pay $437.1 million to resolve the damage claims lodged against it by Orange County, California, and local governments. Merrill aimed to end more than three years of litigation stemming from its role in the county's bankruptcy-law filing.

The Food and Drug Administration permitted the nation's first large-scale test of an AIDS vaccine. VaxGen, a company led by pioneering virologist Donald Francis, will carry out the three-year trial.

Tellabs said it agreed to buy Ciena for stock valued at $6.9 billion, joining two makers of network equipment for phone and data services.

Motorola said it is taking radical steps to stanch the erosion of its profits and market share. They include a layoff of 10 percent of its work force, or 15,000 workers, and a $1.95 billion charge to pay for the firings and a consolidation of its semiconductor and paging operations.

France's Alcatel said it was buying phone-equipment maker DSC Communications in a $4.4-billion stock swap that will almost double Alcatel's presence in the U.S. telecom market and accelerate the industry's consolidation.

The United Auto Workers struck an important General Motors parts factory in Flint, Michigan, as a long-simmering dispute over job security and productivity erupted. Other plant closings followed, and GM dealers grew increasingly concerned that they would run out of vehicles to sell in a red-hot market.

A major shipping cartel said it will raise rates 15 percent on shipments from the United States to Asia, the biggest boost since the mid-1980s, affecting rates on about $70 billion of U.S. goods a year.

Intel was hit with antitrust charges from the Federal Trade Commission, which alleged the chip maker stifled innovation and competition by retaliating against companies that challenged it over their rights to technology.

Norwest and Wells Fargo agreed to a $31.4-billion merger that will form the nation's seventh-largest bank while joining two very different cultures.

The dollar rose above 140 yen for the first time in seven years, and the United States intervened in the currency markets to support the yen. The United States's yen purchases marked its first move in foreign-exchange markets since August 1995 and signaled that it believes Tokyo can't regain the confidence of financial markets without help. Japan also bought yen and promised to take more aggressive measures to fix its economy.

The Philadelphia Stock Exchange agreed to join the American Stock Exchange and National Association of Securities Dealers, which themselves plan to merge. The Philadelphia exchange rejected a competing proposal from the Chicago Board Options Exchange.

General Electric's NBC network said it is buying a stake in the on-line news company CNET and intends to take control of its Snap! directory service, staking out a portal to the Web.

Mitsubishi Motor Manufacturing of America will pay $34 million to settle a sexual-harassment case the Equal Employment Opportunity Commission filed on behalf of women workers at its only U.S. auto factory. The record settlement will conclude the largest sexual-harassment case in legal history.

Sunbeam's board ousted Albert Dunlap, known for his layoffs and cost-cutting tactics, concluding that he was failing to turn around the company. Directors named Peter Langerman, who represents Michael Price on the board, to succeed Mr. Dunlap as chairman, and appointed Revlon's chairman, Jerry Levin, as acting CEO.

Nortel agreed to acquire Bay Networks, which makes equipment that helps companies manage data traffic, for $7.68 billion in stock.

Oil prices slid, touching an 11½ year low of $11.40 and fueling talk of futures falling below $10. Later in the month, OPEC nations agreed to cut output by 1.4 million barrels a day to try to shore up oil prices.

Goldman, Sachs confirmed plans to sell a 10 percent to 15 percent stake in the firm, in an IPO that could raise $2.5 billion or more. The move will transform the last big Wall Street private partnership into a publicly owned firm.

Atlantic Richfield reached an agreement to sell its Arco Chemical division to Lyondell Petrochemical for $5.6 billion.

Texas Instruments said it will sell its struggling memory-chip business to Micron Technology and lay off about 8 percent of its workforce, reflecting an overcapacity of chips that has sent prices plunging. The sale will leave Micron and IBM as the last U.S.-based makers of DRAMs, the most widely used memory-chip type.

Walt Disney said it will buy a 43 percent stake in Infoseek, an on-line search and directory service, vaulting Disney into the Internet portal business. It will give Infoseek its ownership position in Web-site developer Starwave plus $70 million.

Berkshire Hathaway agreed to pay $23.5 billion in stock for General Re, in an acquisition that vaults Warren Buffett into the realm of high-profile megadeals.

Tobacco companies won a big victory as a Florida appeals court reversed a two-year-old jury verdict against Brown & Williamson and ordered the case dismissed. The court said Grady Carter's case shouldn't have been allowed to go to trial because he waited longer than four years after learning he might have lung cancer to sue.

American Home withdrew Duract, a pain reliever launched in July 1997, after four patients died and eight needed liver transplants while taking it.

A butter shortage lifted the price of milk butterfat, a major dairy-product ingredient, to record levels. As a result, ice cream, cream cheese and milk were becoming more expensive.

Microsoft won a solid victory as a federal appeals court struck down a judge's injunction against the company and gave it ammunition to fight the Justice Department's antitrust case.

AT&T said it agreed to acquire cable giant TCI for $37.3 billion in cash and stock, in a sweeping combination of the country's most powerful long-distance company and the biggest cable operator. The deal paves the way for AT&T to go after the $100 billion local-phone market after years of unsuccessful attempts on its own.

The Supreme Court said employers can be sued over acts of sexual harassment they didn't know about, clearing the way for the possibility of more such cases.

News Corp. said it plans to spin off 20 percent of its Fox Group entertainment operations in an initial public stock offering that analysts said could raise as much as $4 billion.

Hilton Hotels agreed to acquire Grand Casinos and split into separate hotel and casino companies, after months of seeking a major deal.

JULY

Proffitt's agreed to acquire Saks Holdings, the New York–based holding company for Saks Fifth Avenue, in a stock transaction valued at $2.14 billion. The acquisition would add the well-known department stores to a growing collection of chains Proffitt's is compiling from its base in Birmingham, Alabama.

Chip makers fell into a global slump, caused by problems in Asia, a glut of production capacity and pricing pressures. Global chip sales in May fell nearly 13 percent from a year earlier to $9.99 billion, the Semiconductor Industry Association said.

U.S. auto sales shot up 14 percent in June to one of the most robust levels of the decade, as buyers rushed to cash in on discounts.

Dow Corning reached a tentative pact with negotiators for women with silicone breast implants on a $3.2 billion bankruptcy-reorganization plan that would end most of the litigation. The $3.2 billion would be paid to about 400,000 people with injury and illness claims far faster than under an earlier proposal by Dow Corning.

Nearly three dozen Wall Street securities firms were in preliminary settlement talks with the SEC over alleged trading violations in the past on the Nasdaq Stock Market. The SEC was telling the firms and more than 100 traders—a higher number than originally expected—that it was preparing civil charges against them.

Tina Brown quit her post as editor of the *New Yorker* magazine to become chairman of a new multimedia unit of Disney's Miramax Films. Advance Publications tapped David Remnick, a *New Yorker* staff writer and book author, to succeed her.

UPS nullified an agreement to create 2,000 full-time jobs by the end of the month, putting the package-delivery company back on a collision course with the Teamsters. The accord was a key part of the settlement that ended its 1997 strike.

Four drug companies set a tentative agreement to pay about $350 million to settle class-action price-fixing litigation. Abbott, a unit of Hoechst, a unit of Rhone-Poulenc and Pharmacia & Upjohn are in the settlement.

Electricity-market deregulation faced new questions after a meltdown in late June left utilities short of power and sent wholesale-electricity prices soaring. Some players wondered if the industry is ready for deregulation.

Cendant said accounting fraud at the company was far deeper than thought and included widespread booking of fictitious revenue, among other deceptions. Cendant Chairman Walter Forbes resigned in the face of mounting pressure from investors and his own top executives.

America West agreed to pay the FAA a $2.5 million penalty, the highest fine ever against an air carrier, for maintenance and operations lapses.

The farm economy faced problems ranging from low prices for wheat, corn and soybeans to a Southern drought that was expected to stunt cotton and peanut harvests. Meanwhile, Asia's turmoil cut into demand. Some farmers were retrenching, sending shivers through the farm-equipment industry and causing concern among bankers and farm-policy makers.

Lockheed Martin abandoned its proposed merger with Northrop Grumman, conceding defeat in one of the largest antitrust cases brought by the United States.

The Dow Jones Industrial Average crossed the 9300 mark for the first time on July 16 and set an all-time record of 9337.97 on July 17.

Tobacco makers won a victory in their battle against public-smoking restrictions as a federal judge declared that a 1993 EPA study overstated the proven link between secondhand smoke and cancer. The EPA findings have helped spur regulations curbing smoking in public buildings, workplaces and restaurants.

PepsiCo agreed to pay $3.3 billion to buy Tropicana, Seagram's juice business, which had been in play for months. The deal opened a new front in Pepsi's battle with Coca-Cola, which owns Tropicana rival Minute Maid.

SunTrust Banks agreed to acquire Crestar for stock valued at $8.61 billion, creating the nation's tenth-largest bank and extending the consolidation of the U.S. banking industry.

Alan Greenspan said the Fed was more concerned about inflation than about a recession and warned that Asia's turmoil won't end soon. The Fed chairman's carefully balanced congressional testimony suggested the Federal Reserve was unlikely to make any interest-rate move soon.

Joseph Jett was cleared of the most serious charge against him, as an SEC administrative-law judge ruled that the former Kidder trader didn't commit securities fraud. But Mr. Jett was sanctioned on a lesser charge.

PepsiCo's board authorized the company to study taking public a "significant portion" of its bottling business, responding to investors' calls.

The CBOE and Pacific Exchange agreed in principle to merge, a move that would join the country's No. 1 and No. 3 options-trading markets.

Moody's said it would review for possible downgrade Japan's triple-A sovereign debt rating. The move knocked down the yen.

AT&T agreed with British Telecommunications to form a venture with $11 billion in annual revenue that will provide voice, data and video services to multinational customers.

General Motors and the United Auto Workers reached a tentative agreement to settle the long-running strikes. The proposed pact gives GM assurances of labor peace and offers the union promises of more investment in U.S. plants. UAW members voted to endorse the GM settlement as the automaker sought to justify the most expensive labor confrontation in its history.

Bell Atlantic and GTE said they planned to merge in a $52.55 billion stock swap. But GTE shareholders already were balking at the transaction, which prices their company below the recent trading level of GTE shares.

BMW bought the rights to the Rolls-Royce name, leaving Volkswagen with the less-prominent Bentley marque despite its recent purchase of the company that now makes both brands.

Brazil's government sold its remaining stake in telecommunications giant Telebras for $18.85 billion, surpassing its expectations, in an auction dominated by European buyers.

AUGUST

The Senate ratified a treaty aimed at fighting bribery of foreign officials. Many U.S. companies hope that the Justice Department can use the pact to police their foreign competitors.

Albertson's agreed to acquire American Stores, a bigger but weaker competitor, for about $8.4 billion in stock, in a deal that will create the nation's largest supermarket company. The combined companies will operate more than 2,470 stores in 37 states and have total sales of about $36 billion.

Philip Morris raised cigarette prices by roughly six cents a pack. It was the fifth increase in 12 months, but tobacco marketers were compensating by offering many price promotions.

AlliedSignal surprised the market with an unsolicited bid of $9.8 billion for AMP, a large maker of electronic connectors. AlliedSignal's offer sent AMP's share price soaring 49 percent. AMP rejected the hostile bid and appointed Robert Ripp to be its new chairman and CEO, taking the unusual step of changing leaders amid a takeover battle.

Amazon announced deals that signal ambitions beyond books. It planned to buy PlanetAll, a provider of on-line address books, for about $90 million, and Junglee, which offers Internet shopping services, for $180 million.

The FTC launched a broad new investigation of alcohol advertising and forced a beer and a liquor company to yank two ads from television.

IBM pulled out as a worldwide sponsor of the Olympic Games, severing a 38-year marketing relationship and underscoring the high cost of linking corporate marketing to sports.

United HealthCare's acquisition of Humana, once valued at $5.5 billion, collapsed because a drop in United HealthCare's stock value significantly lessened the value of the deal to Humana's shareholders. They would have received only $3.12 billion of United HealthCare stock, instead of the originally announced amount. The stock price fell after United HealthCare took a $900 million charge against earnings.

Goldman Sachs's partners voted overwhelmingly to sell as much as a 15-percent stake in an initial public stock offering, paving the way for the investment bank to go public in the fall.

Ford Motor said the average sticker price of its 1999-model cars and trucks in the United States will be 0.3 percent lower than prices on 1998 models, in Ford's first average price decrease in more than 30 years.

Livent suspended ex-CEO Garth Drabinsky and another top executive and is restating earnings because of "serious irregularities" in its financial records.

British Petroleum agreed to buy Amoco in a $48.2 billion deal. The combined company, BP Amoco, is expected to rank No. 2 in reserves and oil-and-gas production. The move came as the industry grappled with low oil prices. The new partners hope for $2 billion in annual cost savings by the end of the year 2000.

Bell Atlantic reached a tentative two-year agreement with the Communications Workers of America, ending a two-day strike. The accord guarantees the union a role in growing operations such as data networking.

British Telecom agreed to buy MCI's 24.9 percent stake in their Concert Communications venture for $1 billion, effectively severing ties between the one-time merger partners. The announcement came just weeks after British Telecom agreed to form a new global venture with MCI rival AT&T.

The Food and Drug Administration lacks authority to regulate the tobacco industry, a federal appeals court ruled. The 2–1 decision capped a string of legal victories for tobacco companies and thrust the debate over teenage smoking back before a reluctant Congress. President Clinton said the Justice Department would ask the full appeals court to review the case.

AIG agreed to buy SunAmerica, an industry leader in annuities, in a stock deal valued at $16.5 billion. The price tag was nearly six times book value, roughly double the level for other recent purchases of annuity-based businesses. But the ranks of annuity-firm targets for subsequent deals are thin.

Union Pacific said it would restructure its railroad management, putting more authority in the field and changing the centralized system that added to its massive service problems. Separately, Union Pacific agreed to buy back 107 miles of track and save as much as several hundred miles of other track it had planned to abandon.

Monsanto said it is the first to genetically engineer corn to resist root-worm, an insect that causes $1 billion in damages annually to crops.

Moody's stripped Toyota of its triple-A rating, showing that Japan's economic problems are hurting the credit-worthiness of top companies.

Barnes & Noble planned to sell a 20 percent stake in its Internet unit to the public, following the success of Amazon.com and of Internet IPO stocks in general.

Wendy's picked Coke as its exclusive soft-drink supplier for the next 10 years, in a setback to Pepsi's efforts to breach Coke's dominance in the sale of fountain-dispensed soft drinks.

Sunbeam's new chief executive unveiled a turnaround strategy for the appliance maker and said it could take until late 1999 to eliminate a glut of inventory at the company. Jerry Levin also gave a reprieve to four plants that were set to close and said he is decentralizing the management. The moves amount to a repudiation of the cost-cutting plan unveiled in May by former CEO Albert Dunlap.

Quark proposed buying Adobe Systems, a much larger maker of electronic-publishing software that suffers from slow sales and a declining stock price. Adobe rejected the offer.

Russia's central bank said it would stop intervening to support the ruble, allowing the currency to plunge. The central bank also canceled dollar trading on the Moscow currency exchange. Those moves followed Russia's earlier decision to allow the ruble to fall by as much as 34 percent in a de facto devaluation, and to delay repayment of billions of dollars of debt. Global markets tumbled on speculation that President Boris Yeltsin would resign and fears that Russia would partially return to Soviet-style economics.

U.S. corporate profits slid 1.5 percent in the second quarter, the first year-to-year decline in nearly a decade. Meanwhile, the GDP expanded at a revised 1.6 percent annual rate in the quarter, the smallest increase in three years.

A Cendant probe criticized former Chairman Walter Forbes but didn't directly link him to an accounting fraud. The company said it would delay filing revised results for 1995 to 1997 because of a disagreement with the SEC.

A Northwest Airlines' pilots strike hit business travelers in markets the airline dominates, amid little hope for a quick settlement. Meanwhile, Northwest's imminent negotiations with other unions complicated talks with the pilots.

Insurers put damage claims from Hurricane Bonnie at $375 million, according to an insurance trade group.

The Dow Jones industrials fell 512.61 points, or 6.37 percent, to 7539.07 on August 31, wiping out what remained of the year's gains. Blue-chip stocks were down 19.26 percent from their July high, just short of the 20 percent that commonly defines a bear market. Amid the economic and political turmoil in Russia, more investors started pulling cash out of stock mutual funds and moving into money-market funds.

U S West and the Communications Workers of America reached a tentative contract agreement that reduces mandatory overtime for union workers but retains a version of the telephone company's controversial performance-based pay plan. The settlement ended a contentious 15-day strike by 34,000 telephone operators, technicians and other union employees.

SEPTEMBER

The Dow Jones industrials rebounded on September 1, by 288.36 points, or 3.82 percent, to 7827.43. The gyrations continued through the month as investors hoped for a cut in interest rates but worried about financial troubles abroad and the Clinton sex scandal.

Malaysia announced sweeping currency controls, including an end to trading its currency abroad. The move sent Malaysia's stocks down 13 percent. Meanwhile, Prime Minister Mahathir fired his finance minister, a proponent of free-market tactics.

By early September, financial firms had lost more than $8 billion in the fallout from Russia's financial collapse.

Rupert Murdoch was preparing to launch a $960.5 million offer for a popular British soccer team, Manchester United.

Kellogg launched an evaluation of its over 2,000 North American employees, setting the stage for a possible round of white-collar job cuts. Later in the month, Kellogg North America lost its president, in the second resignation of a top Kellogg executive within a week.

U.S. steelmakers were accelerating plans to file complaints claiming that Japan, Russia and other countries were dumping steel at unfairly low prices.

Procter & Gamble unveiled a major corporate restructuring and said it would elevate Durk Jager, chief operating officer, to CEO sooner than planned. As the company warned of weaker-than-expected sales, its shares declined 9.7 percent.

A rocket carrying satellites built by Loral for the Globalstar mobile-phone system exploded after liftoff in Russia, dealing another blow to the satellite industry and rattling investors.

Intel disclosed that demand for personal computers was recovering in the third quarter, boosting the chip giant's expected revenue for the period as much as 10 percent above its previous estimates.

Venator Group called off plans to acquire Sports Authority, citing adverse stock-market conditions. Separately, Venator said it would close two weak shoestore chains, Kinney Shoe and Footquarters, in another step to bolster flagging results and narrow its focus.

Northwest pilots approved a new four-year contract. But the strike's effects were likely to linger, as Northwest said it expects to post losses

in the third and fourth quarters and for all of 1998. The airline began recalling workers who had been temporarily laid off and announced a plan to return to its full schedule by September 21.

Ford Motor installed a leadership team led by William Clay Ford Jr. and Jacques Nasser, giving the company added stability and a clearer succession picture than its domestic rivals.

Japan's GDP fell 0.8 percent in the April-to-June quarter from the previous period. The nation's longest contraction in decades raised fears of a deflationary spiral.

AlliedSignal said holders of 72 percent of AMP shares accepted its $9.99 billion takeover offer, and it took steps to increase the pressure on AMP management. At the end of the month, AMP announced a $1.65 billion buyback, offering to pay $55 a share for as much as 14 percent of its stock, as the company tried to win over investors backing AlliedSignal's hostile bid.

Quark dropped its bid to acquire Adobe Systems, its much larger competitor in electronic-publishing software, ending one of the more unlikely takeover proposals of the year.

Tellabs' plan to acquire Ciena was called off after weeks of concerns over Ciena's prospects. Ciena shares plunged 17 percent, leaving them down 77 percent from June 3. Tellabs stock fell 16 percent.

Microsoft passed General Electric to take the top spot on the list of the world's most valuable companies. Microsoft had a market capitalization of $261.1 billion, while GE was valued at $257.3 billion.

General Motors launched an all-out marketing push, including financing deals and cash rebates of up to $3,000 a vehicle, in an effort to force its U.S. market share back up to 30 percent of light-vehicle sales. The No. 1 auto maker also said dealer supplies of popular models, depleted during the strikes in June and July, had been rebuilt.

Toys 'R' Us said it would take a $495 million charge to slash inventories, cut its work force by as much as 3,000, or 2.6 percent, and close 59 toy stores.

Citigroup expected to cut about 8,000 jobs by year end, or 5 percent of the work force of the financial-services giant being formed by the merger of Citicorp and Travelers Group.

Three former Archer-Daniels-Midland executives were found guilty by a federal jury in a landmark price-fixing case. The decision was reached after a week of deliberations in the two-month trial.

France rejected Coke's proposed $880 million purchase of Orangina from Pernod on antitrust grounds, dealing a blow to the global ambitions of the U.S. soft-drink maker.

The global financial hurricane swept through Latin America in September: Colombia allowed its peso to drop more than 5 percent, Ecuador let its currency fall nearly 10 percent, and Chile eliminated a key capital control and widened the trading band for its peso in order to reduce interest-rate volatility. Meanwhile, the IMF opened negotiations with Brazil over what could become a multi-billion-dollar rescue package.

Lockheed agreed to buy Comsat in a two-step deal valued at $2.7 billion. The big aerospace and defense concern is hoping to take advantage of Comsat's control of key access to the global satellite network and its experience in satellite communications. The proposed acquisition was certain to face tough scrutiny by federal antitrust regulators and the FCC.

Brokerage firms were set to report their worst quarterly earnings since the fourth quarter of 1994 amid big trading losses and a dearth of stock and bond deals. That prospect had some major securities firms, including Merrill Lynch and Salomon Smith Barney, considering layoffs.

Investors pulled as much as $9 billion more from stock funds than they put in during August, the first month of net redemptions since 1990, according to fund data collectors' estimates.

President Clinton pressed Japan's prime minister to move more quickly to fix the country's banking system. But Mr. Clinton came away without much optimism about Japan's ability to solve its economic woes. The talks came as the latest Japanese bank bailout plan seemed to unravel amid parliamentary infighting in Tokyo.

Energy regulators found no "direct evidence" that the electricity market was manipulated in the Midwest in June, but investigators did identify some questionable practices.

Wall Street power brokers agreed to shore up Long-Term Capital Management by putting more than $3.5 billion into the faltering hedge fund. The rescue was the result of intense negotiations among the hedge fund's lenders, dealers and the Federal Reserve. The bailout sent shock waves through financial institutions' stocks.

The Senate approved an overhaul of the bankruptcy code that is easier on debtors than House legislation. With only weeks for the two chambers to reach a compromise, the prospects for reform in 1998 remained cloudy.

Japan's second-largest leasing firm filed for bankruptcy-court protection, with liabilities of more than $16 billion. It marked one of the biggest failures in Japan's postwar history.

The founder of Domino's agreed to sell the pizza-delivery chain to Bain Capital, a private investment company, for an estimated $1 billion.

Goldman Sachs said it would shelve indefinitely its plan to go public, perhaps until mid-1999, amid unsettled U.S. financial markets.

Gillette planned to close 14 factories, lay off 11 percent of its work force and take a $350 million charge to third-quarter earnings amid a slowdown overseas.

The FCC rejected two Baby Bells' plans to market Qwest's long-distance service, in a blow to the Bells' efforts to enter the long-distance market.

The Federal Reserve cut a key short-term rate by one-quarter percentage point, in a pre-emptive strike against recession. It was the first rate decrease since January 1996, but some investors were disappointed the cut wasn't bigger. Major banks subsequently reduced their prime lending rates by 0.25 percentage point to 8.25 percent, the first reduction in 2 1/2 years. But the move was considered too small to have much of an impact on borrowing.

CBS beat recent ratings champion NBC during the first week of the new fall TV season, as its gamble on pro football showed signs of paying off.

Bonds surged on September 30, as declining global stock markets and signs of domestic financial stress had investors seeking safety. The 30-year Treasury gained 2 7/32, and its yield slid to 4.954 percent, marking the first time that long-term yields had dropped below 5 percent since 1967. The Dow Jones industrials plunged 237.90 points, or 2.94 percent, to 7842.62, capping their worst quarterly performance in eight years.

AT&T said it was in talks to acquire IBM's Global Network operation, showing its eagerness to gain ground in the data-networking arena.

What Was News
Notable Deaths, 1997–1998

OCTOBER 1997

John Denver, 53, singer who composed songs about love and nature's wonders.

Harold Robbins, 81, author of steamy bestsellers.

James Michener, 90, author of popular novels such as *Centennial* and *Hawaii*.

Roberto C. Goizueta, 65, Cuban immigrant who rose to chairman of Coca-Cola Co.

NOVEMBER 1997

Baron Edmond de Rothschild, 71, financier and member of the banking dynasty.

Sir Isaiah Berlin, 88, Latvia-born philosopher who in a 60-year career at Oxford University specialized in the history of political ideas.

Georges Marchais, 77, longtime leader of the French Communist Party.

Eddie Arcaro, 81, only jockey to ride two horses to Triple Crowns.

Jorge Mas Canosa, 58, Cuban exile leader who dominated U.S. policy toward Havana.

Harold Geneen, 87, ITT Corp. head who acquired some 250 firms during his 1959–1977 tenure.

Robert Lewis, 88, co-founder of the Actors Studio and teacher of Marlon Brando.

Coleman A. Young, 79, Detroit's first black mayor, who served five terms.

DECEMBER 1997

John E. Moss, 82, former California congressman who forged the landmark Freedom of Information Act.

Stubby Kaye, 79, rotund comedian and singer best known for his role in *Guys and Dolls*.

Anthony Ulasewicz, 79, Nixon campaign aide who spread Watergate hush money.

Denise Levertov, 74, English-born American poet who confronted many social and political issues.

Toshiro Mifune, 77, Japanese actor whose work in films such as *Rashomon* and *The Seven Samurai* won him acclaim.

Michael Kennedy, 39, son of the late Senator Robert F. Kennedy.

JANUARY 1998

Sonny Bono, 62, entertainer who in 1994 became a Republican congressman from California.

Carl Perkins, 65, rock music pioneer best known for *Blue Suede Shoes*.

Jack Lord, 77, television actor who played tough-guy roles.

Shinichi Suzuki, 99, pioneer of a way of teaching toddlers the violin by imitation and repetition.

Joseph Alioto, 81, mayor of San Francisco from 1968 to 1976.

FEBRUARY

Carl Wilson, 51, a founder of the pop group the Beach Boys.

Enoch Powell, 85, British Conservative known for anti-immigrant views.

Harry Caray, 77, broadcaster for baseball's Chicago Cubs and other teams.

Bob Merrill, 77, who wrote music and lyrics for shows such as *Funny Girl*.

Abraham Ribicoff, 87, former senator, Connecticut governor and President Kennedy's secretary of health, education and welfare.

Henny Youngman, 91, comic king of one-liners.

MARCH

Henry Steele Commager, 95, American historian, professor and a champion of the Constitution.

Fred Friendly, 82, CBS News ex-president and TV documentary pioneer.

Lloyd Bridges, 85, actor known best for TV's *Sea Hunt*.

Benjamin Spock, 94, pediatrician whose book *Baby and Child Care* urged parents of the baby-boom generation to be flexible.

Ferdinand Porsche Jr., 88, founder of the sports-car firm who, in 1930s Germany, helped his father design the Volkswagen Beetle.

Bella Abzug, 77, colorful feminist and Democratic House member from 1971 to 1977.

APRIL

Tammy Wynette, 55, country singer known for "Stand by Your Man."

Maurice Stans, 90, Nixon administration commerce secretary who pleaded guilty to minor fund-raising charges.

Pol Pot, 73, Khmer Rouge leader held responsible for the deaths of at least one million Cambodians herded into "killing fields" in the 1970s.

Terry Sanford, 80, former senator, North Carolina governor and Democratic presidential candidate.

Octavio Paz, 84, Mexican poet-essayist who won a Nobel Prize for literature.

Constantine Caramanlis, 91, Greek leader who rebuilt democracy after a 1967–1974 junta.

James Earl Ray, 70, convicted of the 1968 assassination of Martin Luther King Jr.

Nguyen Van Linh, 82, former Vietnamese Communist Party boss who imposed free-market reforms.

Linda Eastman McCartney, 56, photographer and wife of ex-Beatle Paul McCartney.

MAY

Eldridge Cleaver, 62, former Black Panther leader.

Frank Sinatra, 82, singer and actor whose voice and craft made him popular music's "Chairman of the Board."

Telford Taylor, 90, a top prosecutor at the Nuremberg trials of Nazi leaders.

Barry Goldwater, 89, former Arizona Republican senator whose failed 1964 presidential bid planted the seeds of later conservative victories.

JUNE

Alfred Kazin, 83, influential critic and writer.

Shirley Povich, 92, longtime *Washington Post* sports columnist.

Sam Yorty, 88, 1961–1973 mayor of Los Angeles who switched to the Republican Party in 1972.

Agostino Casaroli, 83, Italian cardinal and 1979–1990 Vatican secretary of state whose diplomacy helped renew church freedom in Eastern Europe.

Maureen O'Sullivan, 87, an Irish-born U.S. actress best known for playing Jane in Tarzan films.

JULY

Roy Rogers, 86, singing cowboy on television and in the movies.

Nguyen Ngoc Loan, 67, South Vietnamese general photographed shooting a prisoner through the head on a Saigon street in 1968.

Alan Shepard, 74, first American in space, 1961, fifth man on the moon, 1971.

Robert Young, 91, actor best known for TV's *Father Knows Best* and *Marcus Welby, M.D.*

William McChesney Martin, 91, chairman of the Federal Reserve, 1951–1970.

Zbigniew Herbert, 73, Polish poet who opposed Communist rule.

Jerome Robbins, 79, choreographer best known for his work on *West Side Story.*

"Buffalo Bob" Smith, 80, host of one of television's first hit programs, *The Howdy Doody Show.*

AUGUST

Shari Lewis, 65, TV puppeteer and ventriloquist.

Alfred Schnittke, 63, Soviet composer.

Todor Zhivkov, 86, Bulgaria's Communist dictator, 1954–1989.

Lewis F. Powell, 90, Supreme Court justice 1971–87 and a swing vote in many cases.

E.G. Marshall, 84, TV and movie actor.

SEPTEMBER

Akira Kurosawa, 88, influential Japanese director whose 30-film career included such classics as "The Seven Samurai," "Kagemusha" and "Rashomon."

George C. Wallace, 79, former Alabama governor who built his career on segregation but later denied he was a racist.

Florence Griffith Joyner, 38, track star in the 1988 Olympics.

Betty Carter, 69, jazz singer whose bands nurtured many young players.

Tom Bradley, 80, first black mayor of Los Angeles, serving from 1973 to 1993.

Looking to 1999 and Beyond

The Wall Street Journal Almanac 1999 asked three companies that focus on the future to offer their assessment of the most important trends and issues affecting consumers and companies as we head into the twenty-first century. Here are their views:

Marita Wesely-Clough, director of creative strategy development at Hallmark Cards Inc., Kansas City, Missouri.

• **Vision, Vision, Who's Got the Vision?** In a fast-track, computer-cluttered world of deals and pseudo deal-makers, visibility is near zero. Those with a clear vision and with the ability to inspire will be winners. In demand will be people who can "head 'em up and move 'em out" toward the vision, who can formulate clear, communicable ideas in a complex world.

• **Age of the Broker (Beyond the Deal).** As the marketplace shifts and realigns, there are even bigger deals to be made. The role of the broker is becoming increasingly important. The person with the "A" list of contacts, whether for financial backing, marketable content or talent, will be in high demand. The broker of the twenty-first century sees which alliances can yield mutually profitable synergies and brings these value-added players together.

• **The Five-Second Spin.** In the age of the sound bite, spinning has become a valued skill, a necessity in a litigious society. Serious positioning will pass for reality. Glib, facile interpretations of fact will proliferate. Everything becomes relative, including winning or losing, depending upon whom you listen to.

• **Women with Options.** There is something on the horizon ... women forming new relationships and setting out on new adventures. Women are creating their own destinies in realms beyond business competence. They quest for new mastery, new freedom, new exploration. Women are seeking excitement, whether daily life intensified, a new joy in the home or unusual solo travel. Women also look to the camaraderie of their friends and create shared time for renewal and emotional support.

• **The Boiling Cauldron.** Suppressed anger boils, simmers and spills out everywhere. It is inescapable. Road rage has moved into government offices, the workplace, high schools, grade schools—and, sadly, into our homes. Places once thought to be havens no longer provide safe refuge for adults or children. Rage morphs as it permeates society. MY anger becomes YOUR problem. Look out. None of us is immune.

• **American Mosaic.** The face of America is changing. Individuals, communities and businesses that embrace and understand that the mosaic of American life is rapidly evolving will thrive in the new millennium. There will be heightened recognition of and appreciation for ethnic and cultural communication and lifestyles.

• **Men Sorting It Out.** Men are searching for their place in society. Forty years ago, life was good, roles were defined and expectations were clear. This has changed. What we all "know for sure" is less than we once knew. Rigid stereotypes will give way to an even broader spectrum of career and lifestyle options.

• **Slicing the Pie.** Traditional demographics are too simplistic to describe consumers in the millennium. Shared values, communities of like minds and sets of common interests are more relevant and will identify potential new consumer niches or consumer needs.

• **Having Less, Being More.** Money is what it buys; life is about trade-offs; you can't have it all; moving out of the fast lane is okay—it's your choice. People will be reclaiming their lives in new numbers. They will want the time of their life to be about something worthwhile—savoring moments, creating, giving back.

• **Simplify and Clarify.** Return on consumer investment of time and energy as well as dollars will be a must. Consumers are weary ... weary of leading such busy lives, weary of so many choices and so little time. Retailers who can help consumers edit, limit and clarify shopping options will be rewarded with dollars.

• **Techno Heartbeat.** Web users are savvy, experienced consumers who can spot hype a mile away. On-line service must connect with consumers on an emotional, intuitive level to succeed. Distinctiveness, emotional reach and even humor in delivery will be important for Web offerings.

- **Return of the Retirees.** Many individuals who were encouraged to retire will be invited back to the companies they left to provide their critical skills that were acquired through years of work experience. These folks have knowledge and skills that have not yet been honed in young workers.
- **Age of the Assistant.** Real and virtual assistants will help people organize their lives: work, social responsibilities, houses, closets, file cabinets . . . the list is endless. A well-managed, organized life will allow more time for the experiences and relationships that really matter.
- **The Zen Spirit.** With the ascent of the Pacific Rim and China's vast economic potential receiving the global nod, our spirituality and sensibilities are subtly influenced by Eastern trade winds. Western food, thinking and even aesthetics have been altered. Sought after by maxed-out, loud-living Westerners will be the expression of "shibui"—restrained elegance—in its many dimensions.

Vickie Abrahamson, Mary Meehan and Larry Samuel, co-founders of Iconoculture Inc., a Minneapolis-based consultancy, and co-authors of The Future Ain't What It Used to Be.

- **Wisewoman.** Feminism has shifted from the bra burning 1970s into a more personal, less public, and for many, a more powerful sisterhood. Women of every age are recognizing their full potential through an individual combination of spirituality, environmentalism, femininity (yes, it's true) and personal power. Wisewoman strength will be a force to reckon with in businesses spanning women's/girls' sports, health research and products and media.
- **Chi.** America has thrown its borders wide open to spiritual and physical alternatives from the East. This Easternization of America centers on realizing greater energy, more balance and a higher consciousness. Talk about mainstream—one in three adults uses alternative medical therapies and the corner drugstore is selling cold remedies with gingseng and echinacea as key ingredients.
- **Culture Shock.** Around the world the bedrock of society is being shaken. The gap between the haves and the have-nots is widening. The erosion of faith in the system

is breeding an atmosphere of social and cultural uneasiness and accelerating our desire to protect ourselves and our loved ones from harm. Whether it's a presidential scandal, El Niño or schoolkids being killed by classmates, we're being shaken right down to our roots. On whom and on what can we depend?

- **Zentrepreneurism.** A combination of the introspection of Zen and the entrepreneurial spirit, Zentrepreneurism is the concept of making business a force for positive change on the planet. Zentrepreneurism is the fusion of one's personal vision with one's professional mission, and it has surfaced all over the world, from the Body Shop to Ben & Jerry's. Twentysomethings are already showing themselves to be the zentrepreneurial heroes of the next millennium.
- **Cultural Infidelity.** Instant communication, cyber everything and booming immigration are the cultural waves eroding our geographic borders. This blurring of boundaries is fueling a tsunami-sized interest in other cultures—everything from fusion cuisine to world music to Mongolian supermodels.
- **Technomorphing.** Who can't see the quantum effects that warp speed technology is having on our lives? We love dialing up a movie on demand, but we hate how the phone/fax/e-mail reach us on command. Technology in everyday life is only going to intensify, and with the Y2K apocalyptic bug ready to bring the world to its knees, it won't be subsiding anytime soon. Technology companies can help consumers reconcile this love-hate relationship through user-friendly design, applications and terminology.
- **Unplugged.** Simplify, pare down, disengage, cut back, tune out, streamline—these are the verbs that describe the unplugged values shift in process. For some, the decision to slough possessions, positions, relationships and out-of-reach/out-of-whack goals is a voluntary tack. For others, corporate downsizing is the catalyst that forces them to reinvent their lives. Whatever the push, it has come to shove.
- **Gaia.** As we watch the ozone hole grow, the polar ice cap melt, and the rainforests shrink, who can still say our industrial ways have had no ill effect on our planet? Gaia is the ancient philosophy defining our relationship with Earth as symbiotic—how we treat Earth will in turn affect the quality of our lives. Expect a stronger voice for Native American values and the gaian reverence and responsi-

bility for the health and longevity of the planet.

• **Soul Searching.** Has your soul had enough chicken soup? Maybe it's because the baby boomers are finally facing their mortality or maybe it's because after spending to the limit, they still feel something's missing. But one thing is for sure: The search is on for meaningful relationships with yourself, with others or with a higher power. Classes on Kabbala, books on finding your soul mate, television specials on angels and magazines on Buddhism are the guiding lights for this soul-searching era.

• **Money to Burn.** Pockets are deep. Pockets are full. Both the rich and the little guys have been running with the bulls. When the stampeding market hits the wall, there will be plenty of time to enjoy all the luxury souvenirs collected along the way. No compromise on quality or spending—$900 fountain pens, luxe Lexus and Mercedes SUVs, crocodile handbags, "sport yachts" and second and third vacation homes are raising the bar on what now defines the good life. The trendwinds are blowing with a cocky confidence in America the Beautiful . . . and Rich. Companies can take goods and services to new heights of quality and price as the quest for the best rages on.

Stephen M. Millett, leader, the Breakthrough Center at Battelle, a research and development organization in Columbus, Ohio.

• **Human Genetic Profiles and Genetic-Based Drugs.** While human cloning may be decades away, the Human Genome Project and associated research will provide a basic map of human genetics. Personalized genetic profiles will be available and will become a part of routine physical exams. Preventive medicine will take on a whole new meaning, and pharmaceutical companies will offer revolutionary new products to address and perhaps delay the symptoms of genetic diseases. Long before there are cloned people there will be cloned organs for transplants.

• **Packaged Energy.** Thirty years after the Energy Crisis, the United States will enter a new era of energy utilization. The breakthrough will be in packaged energy forms—advanced batteries, fuel cells, solar panels and small power generators. Packaged energy will offer new opportunities in transportation and mobile consumer electronics, while miniatur-

ized electric generators will provide supplementary power to homes, heating/cooling systems and major appliances.

• **Agrogenetics.** The breakthrough in agricultural genetic engineering, both plant and animal, will come sooner than the breakthrough in human genetics. Many crops will be engineered to resist disease, insects and weeds; they will also be designed to increase nutritional value to humans. Plant genetics may be altered to make them suitable for a variety of growing conditions, ranging from very wet rain forests to very dry deserts. Likewise, animals will be genetically engineered to increase protein value while reducing harmful fats.

• **Convergence of Entertainment and Information in the Home.** The race to "own the home" will be won by the companies that control the primary consumer interface: the television. Personal computers and Internet access will increase to 95% home penetration through the digital, high-definition TV displayed on large flat panel display screens. The TV will also provide videoconferencing capabilities at home for occasional use. The business opportunity is to make entertainment more informational and information more entertaining. Another challenge will be how to make new systems affordable to average Americans. The answer will likely be leasing and pay-for-use.

• **Personalized Electronics.** Miniaturization of electronics and packaged power will take cellular phones down to the size of a wristwatch, à la Dick Tracy. Personal computers will become personalized computers, the size of a wallet or a purse. The palm computer will have wireless telecommunications linkages to send and receive data (portable e-mail, data and phone messages). The traditional keyboard will be replaced by symbols and a stylus, and there will be voice-command operations.

• **Hybrid Fuel Systems for Transportation.** By 2010, most cars and trucks in the United States will have converted from one engine–one fuel system to hybrid fuels. A small internal combustion engine will run on reformulated, low-emissions gasoline for start up and rapid acceleration. In the cruise mode, the driver will shift to another fuel, which might be electricity from solar cells and advanced batteries, or forms of natural gas. The impact of hybrid fuel systems, for both private and public transportation, will be enormous: reduced reliance on foreign oil imports and less environmental pollution. But it will not be cheap. We are still decades away from the hydrogen fuels economy.

• **Virtual and Actual Shopping.** There was a virtual explosion of electronic commerce in 1998. People are becoming more comfortable shopping over the Internet, and transactions are becoming more secure. Traditional retailers will have to add value in the face of e-competition. Two ways are service and entertainment. When people shop in person, they will demand more personal attention, product information and a pleasing situation.

• **Global Positioning Systems as Consumer Products.** We are just beginning to identify commercial applications for global positioning systems. Long-distance, wireless communications and geographical locating via satellites will become extremely popular worldwide. Cars, trucks and boats will enjoy highly accurate navigation systems, showing where the vehicle is in relation to desired destinations. Global positioning systems will be available to bikers, hikers and explorers, and they will be used to track objects of high value, especially vehicles. They may also be used to track high-value people, especially small children.

• **Indoor Health Quality and Waste Management.** If people are concerned about the quality of the air they breathe outside, wait until they learn what they are breathing at home. The quality of air inside homes is compromised by pollen, dust, pet dander and bad bacteria. There will be an explosion in the market for clean air filters and devices. People will want to vacuum living-room air, not just cover up odors. They will also be increasingly concerned about the quality of water and food. Devices to detect deadly bacteria will become very popular in response to continuous food-health scares.

• **Home Health and Wellcare.** The center of health care is shifting from centralized hospitals to decentralized clinics to homes. Home care offers lower overhead costs, more privacy and more comfort. People will demand home health monitors as easy to use as the bathroom scales, but providing data on multiple physical parameters. Genetic profiles will create a huge market opportunity for reliable home health monitors. The TV-computer-telephone convergence will provide home access to doctors and information sources around the world. There will be visiting nurses and doctors—a return to house calls! At the same time, people, especially baby boomers, will try to delay old age and prevent major illness through nutrition, exercise (once in a while) and preventive medicines, including ancient herbs and concoctions. Foods, especially genetic designer foods, will compete with pharmaceuticals.

POLITICS & POLICY

President Clinton entered 1998, the sixth year of his presidency, hoping to make it a period of significant legislative achievements. His goal was nothing less than securing his place in history as a new kind of activist Democratic leader. But in his darkest moments, he couldn't have imagined what transpired instead. Before the first month of 1998 had passed, Mr. Clinton found himself embroiled in a personal scandal that would overshadow all else, undermine his quest for substantive achievements and ultimately threaten his very tenure in office.

The sixth year of a two-term presidency is, in many respects, the last time a chief executive can hope to make significant strides to put his mark on the nation. By the end of that year, congressional elections begin to distract lawmakers. And after that, a president becomes a true lame duck, as attention and political jockeying increasingly turns on the question of who will take his place.

But before Mr. Clinton could even make a State of the Union address detailing his dreams of significant new education programs, health-care reforms and historic legislation combating tobacco use, he was wounded by the scandal that soon dominated the capital. On January 21, the *Washington Post* ran a story across its front page saying that Kenneth Starr, the independent counsel investigating a variety of charges against the president, had expanded his probe. His new quest: to determine whether the president had encouraged a 24-year-old former White House intern to lie under oath about a sexual affair with the president.

Ultimately, Mr. Clinton would see his hopes of landmark tobacco legislation dashed, his education and child-care initiatives shredded, and his dream of a patient bill of rights shrunk by a Republican Congress that increasingly

sensed his political weakness. His decisive air attacks to punish terrorist groups blamed for bombing U.S. embassies in Africa were clouded by suspicions that he had acted to distract attention from his domestic problems.

More troubling for Mr. Clinton, the scandal prompted Congress to oil up the machinery for considering impeachment of a president, largely unused since the Watergate affair. The House seriously debated whether impeachment would be justified, or whether some public censure of Mr. Clinton would be more appropriate. Dozens of Republican lawmakers called for his resignation, as did more that 100 newspapers. Amid such talk, his hopes of achieving more in the remainder of his term dwindled.

All this transpired because of a sex scandal. As it turned out, the former White House intern, Monica Lewinsky, had told of her intimate relationship with the president during the course of 20 hours of secretly taped phone conversations with a friend and administration colleague, Linda Tripp. Eventually, those tapes were obtained by Mr. Starr and his investigators.

Yet when called to testify in a sexual-harassment lawsuit against the president, Ms. Lewinsky denied a sexual relationship. And when Mr. Clinton himself was secretly questioned on January 17 in the sexual-harassment lawsuit filed against him by a former Arkansas state employee named Paula Jones, he also denied under oath that he had engaged in "sexual relations" with Ms. Lewinsky. Nine days after giving that testimony, Mr. Clinton gave a finger-wagging public statement in which he declared that he never had "sexual relations with that woman," Ms. Lewinsky.

As the president would grudgingly acknowledge seven months later, he wasn't being truthful. He finally admitted to having what he called an "inappropriate" relationship with Ms. Lewinsky.

But ultimately, the nature of the Clinton-Lewinsky relationship was probably less important than questions about the president's honesty under oath, and the long-term damage he may have inflicted on his office. Those became central issues because of the dogged pursuit of the president by Mr. Starr, the president's main nemesis.

He put his investigators, and two grand juries, to work on the Lewinsky affair. His main questions: Had the president lied under oath about a sexual relationship with Ms. Lewinsky, and did he get others to lie for him? Mr. Starr attempted to strike a deal with Ms. Lewinsky to win her voluntary testimony in return for immunity. The dance between Ms. Lewinsky and her lawyers dragged on for months, until the end of July, before such a deal was struck. In the end, associates said, Ms. Lewinsky told the grand jury of specific sexual encounters in the White House.

Earlier, Mr. Starr summoned presidential friend Vernon Jordan to see whether he had tried to secure a new job for Ms. Lewinsky in return for her silence. He called the president's secretary, Betty Currie, to see whether she had retrieved presidential gifts from Ms. Lewinsky so investigators couldn't find them. In unprecedented fashion, he summoned Mr. Clinton's Secret Service guards to find what they knew of the relationship, and presidential counselors to probe for any conspiracy to obstruct justice.

Finally, Mr. Starr subpoenaed the president himself to testify before the grand jury. Rather than resist, Mr. Clinton agreed to appear voluntarily. On August 17, he spent more than four hours answering questions in the White House Map Room from Mr. Starr and his aides, while a grand jury watched by closed-circuit television hookup to a court-room. Then, in dramatic fashion, he went before a nationally televised audience and vaguely acknowledged a relationship with Ms. Lewinsky that was "wrong." He maintained his original testimony about the affair had been evasive but "legally accurate"—because, as it turned out, he considered his sexual activities with Ms. Lewinsky to be of a different nature than implied in the questions originally posed to him. And he flatly denied asking anyone to lie. Appearing less contrite than his foes demanded and his friends hoped, the president also launched a thinly veiled attack on Mr. Starr, saying his inquiry had gone on too long and become too intrusive.

The president's public acknowledgment of an affair hardly brought the matter to a close. In fact, it was merely a prelude to an explosion of public obsession with the issue. In September, Mr. Starr filed a report to Congress on the Lewinsky matter, charging that there were 11 grounds for considering impeachment of the president. They included perjury and obstruction of justice, as well as abuse of power. Within days, the Republican-controlled House made the entire Starr report public, and shortly thereafter released a videotape of the president's grand jury testimony and thousands of pages of documents gathered by investigators. Almost overnight, the whole world knew every detail of the Lewinsky affair, including some graphic details that many critics charged were released by the Republicans running Congress solely to undermine the president.

Remarkably, through it all, Americans continued to give Mr. Clinton high marks for his performance on the job. Beneath the surface, though, the scandal seemed to be slowly taking a toll on Mr. Clinton's personal popularity—and his political clout. The Congress, long wary of Mr. Clinton's political prowess and powers of public persuasion, seemed to be slowly losing its fear of crossing him.

In a significant foreign-policy victory for the White House, the Senate did overcome some initial misgivings and approve the Clinton request to expand the North Atlantic Treaty Organization by adding Poland, Hungary and the Czech Republic. But on domestic issues, Mr. Clinton was finding more resistance. His White House spent the spring pushing for a big and tough anti-tobacco bill, one that would regulate tobacco in new ways, sharply curtail cigarette marketing, and add a tax of $1 or more to each pack of cigarettes to force down consumption. Clintonites thought they were on the verge of victory when Republicans in Congress turned on the bill in late June. Bolstered by a tobacco-industry advertising campaign attacking the bill as an exercise in big government and high taxes, the Republican Senate strangled the legislation.

Republicans gave short shrift to Mr. Clinton's plan for education spending to reduce classroom sizes. Instead, they passed a bill creating tax-preferred savings accounts for elementary and secondary education expenses, forcing Mr. Clinton to veto it to satisfy Democratic constituencies maintaining it would undermine public schools. They pushed through a bill reforming the Internal Revenue Service so rapidly that the Clinton administration overcame its initial misgivings and backed it fully. For months, GOP lawmakers resisted the administration's calls to approve almost $18 billion in new American commitments to the International Monetary Fund. The Congress refused to approve "fast track" legislation giving the president more power to negotiate trade deals.

All along the way, a second investigation, into the financing of Mr. Clinton's 1996 presidential campaign, was being conducted by the Justice Department, raising the specter of additional scandal problems for the president and Vice President Al Gore.

Of potentially deeper significance, both Clinton allies and critics worried that the investigation of Mr. Clinton may have set precedents that weaken the presidency itself. At the outset, the Supreme Court ruled that a civil lawsuit—in this case, the Paula Jones sexual-harassment suit—could go forward against a sitting president. During the course of the investigation, federal courts and the Supreme Court variously ruled that Secret Service agents could be forced to testify about their work for presidents, that the secrecy of conversations between the president and his aides isn't protected by claims of executive privilege, and that even conversations between a president and White House lawyers aren't shielded from disclosure by attorney-client privilege. The rulings hurt Mr. Clinton, but also are sobering developments for his successors.

Gerald F. Seib,
deputy Washington bureau
chief and columnist for
The Wall Street Journal

A PRIMER ON
THE CLINTON SCANDALS

Within months of coming to power, the Clinton administration was rocked by scandals with startling regularity, from the ever-present Whitewater imbroglio to the Monica Lewinsky affair. Keeping them straight and understanding where they overlap can be mind-bending. Here's a primer, in chronological order:

March 8, 1992: *The New York Times* breaks the Whitewater story with an exposé on Bill and Hillary Clinton's land deal with a savings-and-loan operator named James McDougal. Mr. Clinton oversaw the regulation of financial institutions in Arkansas as governor, and Mr. McDougal seemed to have suffered more losses from the deal than his high-powered partner. The story creates a minor panic in the campaign, which launches its vaunted damage-control operation. The story dies down, but explodes into controversy nearly two years later and leads to the appointment of Independent Counsel Kenneth Starr, a Republican former judge. He spends the subsequent years investigating Whitewater and secures convictions of numerous Clinton associates.

May 19, 1993: The White House fires the staff of its travel office—the people who arranged for the press to travel with the president—amid indications that officials wanted to give the business to friends of the First Family. The head of the office, Billy Dale, is later indicted on corruption charges but is acquitted. Mr. Starr's investigation is later expanded to include the travel office firings.

July 20, 1993: White House lawyer Vince Foster is found dead of a gunshot wound. Repeated official inquiries later declare it a suicide, but questions about his death linger and right-wing conspiracy theorists voice suspicions about a possible murder. In the panicked aftermath of his death, White House officials fail to fully cooperate with investigators looking into the matter. Later reports that Whitewater papers were spirited out of Mr. Foster's office lead to Mr. Starr's appointment to investigate the land deal and Mr. Foster's death.

December 1993: The *Los Angeles Times* and *American Spectator* magazine publish exposés alleging that when Mr. Clinton was governor of Arkansas, he used state troopers to arrange sexual liaisons with numerous women. The magazine story includes a cryptic reference to a woman named "Paula" who allegedly had been summoned to the president's hotel room one day in 1991. The trooper who allegedly brought her to the room is quoted as saying she was willing to be Mr. Clinton's girlfriend. Paula Corbin Jones denies the story and later sues the president and the trooper, alleging that Mr. Clinton had exposed himself and crudely propositioned her. Mr. Clinton tries to get the case delayed until after he leaves office, but the Supreme Court refuses in a landmark decision. A federal judge in Arkansas dismisses Ms. Jones's suit in 1998, but her lawyers appeal the decision.

March 1994: Webster Hubbell, a Clinton friend from Arkansas, resigns from a top post at the Justice Department and later pleads guilty to defrauding his former law firm and goes to prison in a cooperation deal with Mr. Starr. Mr. Hubbell was involved in early Whitewater damage control efforts and is considered key to unraveling the complex transaction. After his release from prison, Mr. Hubbell frustrates Mr. Starr, who finds him uncooperative and launches an investigation into lucrative consulting fees arranged for him by numerous Clinton friends, including lobbyist Vernon Jordan. Unable to prove a quid pro quo, Mr. Starr has Mr. Hubbell indicted on tax charges, which are later dismissed by a federal judge.

September 10, 1994: Donald Smaltz is named independent counsel to investigate Agriculture Secretary Mike Espy's alleged acceptance of gifts from people with business before his department. After Mr. Smaltz secures convictions against several individuals and businesses involved in the matter, a grand jury indicts Mr. Espy himself.

May 24, 1995: David Barrett is appointed independent counsel to investigate whether Housing Secretary Henry Cisneros lied to FBI agents during his pre-nomination background check about payments to his former mistress. Mr. Cisneros is later indicted.

July 6, 1995: Daniel Pearson is appointed

independent counsel to investigate questionable business transactions involving Commerce Secretary Ron Brown. Mr. Brown later dies in a plane crash, and the probe is turned back over to the Justice Department.

June 1996: Inquiries from Congress force the White House to disclose that it requested FBI background files on former travel office chief Billy Dale. The administration insists Mr. Dale wasn't singled out and calls the incident an innocent mistake in which files were inadvertently requested on hundreds of former White House employees, including numerous prominent Republicans. The firestorm later prompts Attorney General Janet Reno to move to expand Mr. Starr's jurisdiction.

Fall 1996: Reports in *The Wall Street Journal* and elsewhere reveal numerous campaign finance improprieties at the Democratic National Committee, especially in efforts by DNC fund-raiser John Huang to secure money from Asian-Americans. The DNC is forced to return millions of dollars that were illegally contributed through straw donors or that were otherwise questionable. The fund-raising scandal dogs the administration for years in the face of relentless congressional investigations into various campaign finance matters: the use of the White House and Air Force One as fund-raising tools; Vice President Al Gore's Buddhist temple fund-raiser; allegations that the Chinese tried to funnel money into U.S. campaigns; the alleged trading of various perks and policies for donations; Messrs. Clinton and Gore's use of White House phones to make fund-raising calls; and the use of nonprofit groups for political purposes. A Justice Department campaign finance task force secures guilty pleas and indictments against a number of Democratic fund-raisers. Ms. Reno rejects calls by FBI Director Louis Freeh, the head of the task force and Republicans for an independent counsel to investigate the whole mess. She considers an independent investigation into fund-raising phone calls by Messrs. Clinton and Gore, rejects the idea as too trivial and then reopens the matter when documents raise questions about the accuracy of Mr. Gore's statements to investigators. Ms. Reno

initially refuses to seriously consider an independent inquiry into allegations that President Clinton sought to evade campaign spending limits by using DNC "soft money" for pro-Clinton television ads. But she opens a formal preliminary investigation after Federal Election Commission auditors say the ads may have been illegal.

August 22, 1997: A federal overseer nullifies the re-election of Teamsters' President Ron Carey after finding that his underlings had used union donations to leverage contributions to his campaign. Democratic fund-raisers are implicated in the affair, and several Carey associates later plead guilty to federal charges, while Mr. Carey is barred from running for Teamsters president again.

January 16, 1998: Mr. Starr's investigation is expanded to include allegations that President Clinton was involved in obstructing justice in the Paula Jones case. The independent counsel had received tapes of former White House intern Monica Lewinsky saying she had an affair with President Clinton and felt compelled to deny it under oath. At the same time, she was also getting job assistance from presidential friend Vernon Jordan, the same lawyer who helped Webster Hubbell. The president denies the affair for months but faced with a mountain of evidence later admits it while insisting he had been "legally accurate" in denying a sexual relationship under oath in the Jones case. After months of pitched legal battles with the administration over efforts to question White House lawyers and the Secret Service, Mr. Starr recommends that the House consider impeaching the president in a lurid report recounting the details of numerous sexual liaisons between Ms. Lewinsky and the president.

February 11, 1998: In an offshoot of the campaign finance scandal, Ms. Reno asks for the appointment of an independent counsel to investigate Interior Secretary Bruce Babbitt. Mr. Babbitt had made contradictory statements to Congress about efforts to help a group of Native American major donors in a dispute over a proposed casino.

Phil Kuntz

1996 Official Presidential Election Results

State	Clinton	Dole	Perot	Electoral vote Clinton	Electoral vote Dole
Alabama	662,165	769,044	92,149	-	9
Alaska	80,380	122,746	26,333	-	3
Arizona	653,288	622,073	112,072	8	-
Arkansas	475,171	325,416	69,884	6	-
California	5,119,835	3,828,380	697,847	54	-
Colorado	671,152	691,848	99,629	-	8
Connecticut	735,740	483,109	139,523	8	-
Delaware	140,355	99,062	28,719	3	-
District of Columbia	158,220	17,339	3,611	3	-
Florida	2,546,870	2,244,536	483,870	25	-
Georgia	1,053,849	1,080,843	146,337	-	13
Hawaii	205,012	113,943	27,358	4	-
Idaho	165,443	256,595	62,518	-	4
Illinois	2,341,744	1,587,021	346,408	22	-
Indiana	887,424	1,006,693	224,299	-	12
Iowa	620,258	492,644	105,159	7	-
Kansas	387,659	583,245	92,639	-	6
Kentucky	636,614	623,283	120,396	8	-
Louisiana	927,837	712,586	123,293	9	-
Maine	312,788	186,378	85,970	4	-
Maryland	966,207	681,530	115,812	10	-
Massachusetts	1,571,763	718,107	227,217	12	-
Michigan	1,989,653	1,481,212	336,670	18	-
Minnesota	1,120,438	766,476	257,704	10	-
Mississippi	394,022	439,838	52,222	-	7
Missouri	1,025,935	890,016	217,188	11	-
Montana	167,922	179,652	55,229	-	3

State	Clinton	Dole	Perot	Electoral vote Clinton	Electoral vote Dole
Nebraska	236,761	363,467	71,278	-	5
Nevada	203,974	199,244	43,986	4	-
New Hampshire	246,214	196,532	48,390	4	-
New Jersey	1,652,329	1,103,078	262,134	15	-
New Mexico	273,495	232,751	32,257	5	-
New York	3,756,177	1,933,492	503,458	33	-
North Carolina	1,107,849	1,225,938	168,059	-	14
North Dakota	106,905	125,050	32,515	-	3
Ohio	2,148,222	1,859,883	483,207	21	-
Oklahoma	488,105	582,315	130,788	-	8
Oregon	649,641	538,152	121,221	7	-
Pennsylvania	2,215,819	1,801,169	430,984	23	-
Rhode Island	233,050	104,683	43,723	4	-
South Carolina	506,283	573,458	64,386	-	8
South Dakota	139,333	150,543	31,250	-	3
Tennessee	909,146	863,530	105,918	11	-
Texas	2,459,683	2,736,167	378,537	-	32
Utah	221,633	361,911	66,461	-	5
Vermont	137,894	80,352	31,024	3	-
Virginia	1,091,060	1,138,350	159,861	-	13
Washington	1,123,323	840,712	201,003	11	-
West Virginia	327,812	233,946	71,639	5	-
Wisconsin	1,071,971	845,029	227,339	11	-
Wyoming	77,934	105,388	25,928	-	3
Total	47,402,357	39,198,755	8,085,402	379	159
	49.24%	40.71%	8.40%	Total electoral vote = 538 Total electoral vote needed to win = 270	

Source: Federal Election Commission and State Elections Offices

National Voter Turnout in Federal Elections

Year	Voting age population	Registration	Turnout	% Turnout of voting age population
1968	120,328,186	81,658,180	73,211,875	60.84%
1970	124,498,000	82,496,747*	58,014,338	46.60
1972	140,776,000	97,328,541	77,718,554	55.21
1974	146,336,000	96,199,020**	55,943,834	38.23
1976	152,309,190	105,037,986	81,555,789	53.55
1978	158,373,000	103,291,265	58,917,938	37.21
1980	164,597,000	113,043,734	86,515,221	52.56
1982	169,938,000	110,671,225	67,615,576	39.79
1984	174,466,000	124,150,614	92,652,680	53.11
1986	178,566,000	118,399,984	64,991,128	36.40
1988	182,778,000	126,379,628	91,594,693	50.11
1990	185,812,000	121,105,630	67,859,189	36.52
1992	189,529,000	133,821,178	104,405,155	55.09
1994	193,650,000	130,292,822	75,105,860	38.78
1996	196,511,000	146,211,960	96,456,345	49.08

*Registrations from Iowa and Missouri not included.
**Registrations from Iowa not included.
Source: Federal Election Commission

Voter Registration and Turnout - 1996

State	1996 voting age population	1996 registered voters	% REG of VAP	Turnout	% T/O of VAP
Alabama	3,220,000	2,470,766	76.73%	1,534,349	47.65%
Alaska	425,000	414,815	97.60	241,620	56.85
Arizona	3,145,000	2,244,672	71.37	1,404,405	44.66
Arkansas	1,873,000	1,369,459	73.12	884,262	47.21
California	22,826,000	15,662,075	68.62	10,019,484	43.90
Colorado	2,862,000	2,346,253	81.98	1,510,704	52.78
Connecticut	2,479,000	1,881,323	75.89	1,392,614	56.18
Delaware	548,000	421,710	76.95	270,810	49.42
District of Columbia	422,000	361,419	85.64	185,726	44.01
Florida	11,043,000	8,077,877	73.15	5,300,927	48.00
Georgia	5,418,000	3,811,284	70.34	2,298,899	42.43
Hawaii	890,000	544,916	61.23	360,120	40.46
Idaho	858,000	700,430	81.64	489,481	57.05
Illinois	8,754,000	6,663,301	76.12	4,311,391	49.25
Indiana	4,374,000	3,488,088	79.75	2,135,431	48.82
Iowa	2,138,000	1,776,433	83.09	1,234,075	57.72
Kansas	1,897,000	1,436,418	75.72	1,063,452	56.06
Kentucky	2,928,000	2,396,086	81.83	1,387,999	47.40
Louisiana	3,131,000	2,559,352	81.74	1,783,959	56.98
Maine	945,000	1,001,292*	105.96	679,499	71.90
Maryland	3,820,000	2,587,978	67.75	1,780,870	46.62
Massachusetts	4,649,000	3,459,193	74.41	2,556,459	54.99
Michigan	7,072,000	6,677,079	94.42	3,848,844	54.42
Minnesota	3,422,000	3,067,802	89.65	2,192,640	64.07
Mississippi	1,967,000	1,715,913	87.24	893,857	45.44
Missouri	3,995,000	3,342,849	83.68	2,158,065	54.02
Montana	656,000	590,751	90.05	407,083	62.06
Nebraska	1,211,000	1,015,056	83.82	677,415	55.94
Nevada	1,212,000	778,092	64.20	464,279	38.31
New Hampshire	871,000	754,771	86.66	499,053	57.30
New Jersey	6,034,000	4,320,866	71.61	3,075,860	50.98
New Mexico	1,224,000	851,479	69.57	556,074	45.43
New York	13,564,000	10,162,156	74.92	6,439,129	47.47
North Carolina	5,519,000	4,318,008	78.24	2,515,807	45.58
North Dakota	476,000	N/A	N/A	266,411	55.97
Ohio	8,347,000	6,879,687	82.42	4,534,434	54.32
Oklahoma	2,426,000	1,979,017	81.58	1,206,713	49.74
Oregon	2,411,000	1,962,155	81.38	1,377,760	57.14
Pennsylvania	9,197,000	6,805,612	74.00	4,506,118	49.00
Rhode Island	751,000	602,692	80.25	390,247	51.96
South Carolina	2,771,000	1,814,777	65.49	1,151,689	41.56
South Dakota	535,000	459,971	85.98	323,826	60.53
Tennessee	4,035,000	2,849,910	70.63	1,894,105	46.94
Texas	13,597,000	10,540,678	77.52	5,611,644	41.27
Utah	1,333,000	1,050,452	78.80	665,629	49.93
Vermont	445,000	385,328	86.59	258,449	58.08
Virginia	5,083,000	3,322,135	65.36	2,416,642	47.54
Washington	4,115,000	3,078,128	74.80	2,253,837	54.77
West Virginia	1,417,000	970,745	68.51	636,459	44.92
Wisconsin	3,824,000	N/A	NA	2,196,169	57.43
Wyoming	356,000	240,711	67.62	211,571	59.43
United States	**196,511,000**	**146,211,960**	**74.40%**	**96,456,345**	**49.08%**

*Maine's system of election-day registration results in over-representation of registered voters.
Source: Federal Election Commission

The Electoral College

The Electoral College was established by the founding fathers as a compromise between election of the president by Congress and election by popular vote. The electors are a popularly elected body chosen by the states and the District of Columbia on the Tuesday after the first Monday in November. The Electoral College consists of 538 electors (one for each of 435 members of the House of Representatives and 100 Senators; and 3 for the District of Columbia by virtue of the 23rd Amendment). Each state's allotment of electors is equal to the number of House members to which it is entitled plus two Senators. The decennial census is used to reapportion the number of electors allocated among the states.

The electors meet in each state on the first Monday after the second Wednesday in December. A majority of 270 electoral votes is required to elect the President and Vice President. No constitutional provision or federal law requires electors to vote in accordance with the popular vote in their state. But some state laws require electors to cast their votes according to the popular vote.

Source: Office of the Federal Register

States and Electoral College Votes

(Total: 538; Majority Needed to Elect: 270)

Alabama - 9	Illinois - 22	Montana - 3	Rhode Island - 4
Alaska - 3	Indiana - 12	Nebraska - 5	South Carolina - 8
Arizona - 8	Iowa - 7	Nevada - 4	South Dakota - 3
Arkansas - 6	Kansas - 6	New Hampshire - 4	Tennessee - 11
California - 54	Kentucky - 8	New Jersey - 15	Texas - 32
Colorado - 8	Louisiana - 9	New Mexico - 5	Utah - 5
Connecticut - 8	Maine - 4	New York - 33	Vermont - 3
Delaware - 3	Maryland - 10	North Carolina - 14	Virginia - 13
District of Columbia - 3	Massachusetts - 12	North Dakota - 3	Washington - 11
Florida - 25	Michigan - 18	Ohio - 21	West Virginia - 5
Georgia - 13	Minnesota - 10	Oklahoma - 8	Wisconsin - 11
Hawaii - 4	Mississippi - 7	Oregon - 7	Wyoming - 3
Idaho - 4	Missouri - 11	Pennsylvania - 23	

Source: Office of the Federal Register

"Soft Money" Surge

National party committees raised $115,774,161 in soft money during the first eighteen months of the 1998 election cycle – more than double the $50.1 million they raised during the comparable period in 1994, the last nonpresidential election cycle, according to a Common Cause analysis.

Political Party Fund Raising

Party Committee	Jan. 1993 – June 1994	Jan. 1997 – June 1998
Democratic National Committee (DNC)	$25,983,379	$27,871,872
Democratic Congressional Dinner Committee*	803,375	0
Democratic Senatorial Campaign Committee (DSCC)	65,500	8,906,320
Democratic Congressional Campaign Committee (DCCC)	3,271,864	8,998,698
Total Democratic Soft Money	30,124,118	45,776,890
Republican National Committee (RNC)	10,693,155	34,550,113
Republican Senate-House Dinner Committee*	4,879,350	12,486,144
National Republican Senatorial Committee (NRSC)	2,409,870	11,765,424
National Republican Congressional Committee (NRCC)	2,013,253	11,195,590
Total Republican Soft Money	19,995,628	69,997,271

*The Democratic Congressional Dinner Committee divides its donations between the DSCC and DCCC. The Republican Senate-House Dinner Committee divides its donations between the NRSC and NRCC.
Source: Common Cause

Congressional Campaign Finances

A survey of campaign disclosure reports found that Senate and House campaigns raised a total of $484.3 million between January 1, 1997, and June 30, 1998, an increase of 8% over the same period in 1995–96. Spending during this period totaled $301.6 million, an increase of only 3%.

Top 10 Senate Receipts, Jan. 1, '97 – June 30, '98

Candidate	State	Party		Net receipts	Candidate	State	Party		Net receipts
1 Darrell E. Issa	CA	R	C	$13,582,767	6 Charles Owen	KY	D	O	$6,725,629
2 Alfonse M. D'Amato	NY	R	I	12,354,451	7 Arlen Specter	PA	R	I	4,900,829
3 Charles E. Schumer	NY	D	C	12,083,014	8 Carol Moseley Braun	IL	D	I	4,535,895
4 Peter G. Fitzgerald	IL	R	C	11,517,903	9 Duncan M. Faircloth	NC	R	I	4,500,074
5 Barbara Boxer	CA	D	I	8,011,988	10 Thomas A. Daschle	SD	D	I	4,367,422

Top 10 Senate Contributions From Individuals, Jan. 1, '97 – June 30, '98

Candidate	State	Party		Individual contributions	Candidate	State	Party		Individual contributions
1 Alfonse M. D'Amato	NY	R	I	$9,995,427	6 Carol Moseley Braun	IL	D	I	$3,475,454
2 Barbara Boxer	CA	D	I	6,314,395	7 Duncan M. Faircloth	NC	R	I	3,218,185
3 Charles E. Schumer	NY	D	C	6,215,570	8 George V. Voinovich	OH	R	O	3,198,764
4 Matthew K. Fong	CA	R	C	3,779,930	9 Thomas A. Daschle	SD	D	I	2,778,814
5 Arlen Specter	PA	R	I	3,579,386	10 Christopher S. Bond	MO	R	I	2,587,413

Top 10 Senate Contributions From PACs and Other Committees, Jan. 1, '97 – June 30, '98

Candidate	State	Party		Contributions	Candidate	State	Party		Contributions
1 Thomas A. Daschle	SD	D	I	$1,526,477	6 Arlen Specter	PA	R	I	$1,054,793
2 Alfonse M. D'Amato	NY	R	I	1,331,230	7 Richard C. Shelby	AL	R	I	985,415
3 Christopher S. Bond	MO	R	I	1,263,002	8 Christopher J. Dodd	CT	D	I	956,139
4 John B. Breaux	LA	D	I	1,224,053	9 Paul D. Coverdell	GA	R	I	930,007
5 Duncan M. Faircloth	NC	R	I	1,112,771	10 Barbara Boxer	CA	D	I	875,812

Top 10 Senate Disbursements, Jan. 1, '97 – June 30, '98

Candidate	State	Party		Net disbursements	Candidate	State	Party		Net disbursements
1 Darrell E. Issa	CA	R	C	$13,549,659	6 Charles E. Schumer	NY	D	C	$4,871,263
2 Peter G. Fitzgerald	IL	R	C	10,780,168	7 John R. Edwards	NC	D	C	3,957,815
3 Alfonse M. D'Amato	NY	R	I	7,126,946	8 Matthew K. Fong	CA	R	C	3,793,953
4 Charles Owen	KY	D	O	6,763,843	9 Carol Moseley Braun	IL	D	I	3,463,090
5 Barbara Boxer	CA	D	I	5,129,103	10 Thomas A. Daschle	SD	D	I	2,606,888

Note: I - incumbent; C - challenger; O - open seat.

Top 10 House Receipts, Jan. 1, '97 – June 30, '98

Candidate	State	Party		Net receipts	Candidate	State	Party		Net receipts
1 Newton L. Gingrich	GA	R	I	$4,878,472	6 Christopher F. Gabrieli	MA	D	O	$1,964,921
2 Richard A. Gephardt	MO	D	I	4,219,583	7 Jay R. Pritzker	IL	D	O	1,897,872
3 Phillip J. Maloof*	NM	D	O	2,570,539	8 Lois Capps*	CA	D	O	1,734,261
4 Loretta Sanchez	CA	D	I	2,366,962	9 Richard K. Armey	TX	R	I	1,670,138
5 Robert K. Dornan	CA	R	C	2,003,243	10 Bob Riley	AL	R	I	1,439,567

Top 10 House Contributions From Individuals, Jan. 1, '97 – June 30, '98

Candidate	State	Party		Individual contributions	Candidate	State	Party		Individual contributions
1 Newton L. Gingrich	GA	R	I	$4,135,480	6 Richard K. Armey	TX	R	I	$1,204,164
2 Richard A. Gephardt	MO	D	I	2,123,012	7 Ronald E. Paul	TX	R	I	1,120,981
3 Robert K. Dornan	CA	R	C	2,003,243	8 Lois Capps*	CA	D	O	1,035,684
4 Loretta Sanchez	CA	D	I	1,879,616	9 Nita M. Lowey	NY	D	I	927,738
5 Noach Dear	NY	D	O	1,311,242	10 John R. Kasich	OH	R	I	827,222

Top 10 House Contributions From PACs and Other Committees, Jan. 1, '97 – June 30, '98

Candidate	State	Party		Contributions	Candidate	State	Party		Contributions
1 Richard A. Gephardt	MO	D	I	$1,033,279	6 Lois Capps*	CA	D	O	$611,178
2 Martin Frost	TX	D	I	766,825	7 Thomas D. Delay	TX	R	I	600,890
3 Newton L. Gingrich	GA	R	I	681,026	8 Charles W. Stenholm	TX	D	I	562,325
4 Nancy L. Johnson	CT	R	I	661,344	9 Thomas J. Bliley Jr.	VA	R	I	533,669
5 John D. Dingell	MI	D	I	620,662	10 Vito J. Fossella Jr.	NY	R	O	500,629

Top 10 House Disbursements, Jan. 1, '97 – June 30, '98

Candidate	State	Party		Net disbursements	Candidate	State	Party		Net disbursements
1 Newton L. Gingrich	GA	R	I	$4,752,113	6 Richard A. Gephardt	MO	D	I	$1,721,056
2 Phillip J. Maloof*	NM	D	O	2,501,830	7 Lois Capps*	CA	D	O	1,602,656
3 Robert K. Dornan	CA	R	C	2,053,544	8 Jonathan H. Newman	PA	R	C	1,368,442
4 Jay R. Pritzker	IL	D	O	1,919,968	9 Richard K. Armey	TX	R	I	1,358,389
5 Christopher F. Gabrieli	MA	D	O	1,838,712	10 Loretta Sanchez	CA	D	I	1,304,990

*Special election activity.
Note: I - incumbent; C - challenger; O - open seat.
Source: Federal Election Commission

Annual Salaries of U.S. Government Officials

- The President's salary is $200,000 per year plus expense allowance.
- The Vice President receives a salary of $171,500.
- The Chief Justice of the Supreme Court receives $175,400. The associate justices earn $167,900.

- Cabinet-level officials receive $151,800.
- The Speaker of the House of Representatives receives $171,500. The President Pro Tempore of the Senate earns $148,400. The Majority and Minority Leaders of the House and Senate each receive $148,400. Other Senators and Representatives have a yearly salary of $133,600.

THE EXECUTIVE BRANCH

As required by the U.S. Constitution, the President must be a natural-born citizen and at least 35 years old. The President can serve no more than two four-year terms.

The President of the United States: Bill Clinton of Arkansas, born August 19, 1946.
The Vice President of the United States: Al Gore of Tennessee, born March 31, 1948.

Presidential Staff

DEPUTY CHIEF OF STAFF: John Podesta
DEPUTY CHIEF OF STAFF: Maria Echaveste
COUNSELOR TO THE PRESIDENT: Douglas Sosnik
COUNSEL TO THE PRESIDENT: Charles Ruff
SENIOR ADVISER FOR POLICY DEVELOPMENT: Ira Magaziner
ASSISTANT TO THE PRESIDENT FOR DOMESTIC POLICY: Bruce Reed
NATIONAL SECURITY ADVISER: Samuel Berger
ASSISTANT TO THE PRESIDENT FOR ECONOMIC POLICY, DIRECTOR OF NATIONAL ECONOMIC COUNCIL: Gene Sperling
PRESS SECRETARY: Joseph Lockhart
ASSISTANT TO THE PRESIDENT, COORDINATOR OF STRATEGIC PLANNING: Sidney Blumenthal
ASSISTANT TO THE PRESIDENT, DIRECTOR OF COMMUNICATIONS: Ann Lewis
ASSISTANT TO THE PRESIDENT, LEGISLATIVE AFFAIRS: Larry Stein
ASSISTANT TO THE PRESIDENT, MANAGEMENT AND ADMINISTRATION: Virginia Apuzzo
ASSISTANT TO THE PRESIDENT, DIRECTOR OF POLITICAL AFFAIRS: Craig T. Smith
ASSISTANT TO THE PRESIDENT, DIRECTOR OF PRESIDENTIAL PERSONNEL: Bob Nash
ASSISTANT TO THE PRESIDENT, DIRECTOR OF PUBLIC LIAISON: Minyon Moore
ASSISTANT TO THE PRESIDENT, STAFF SECRETARY: Todd Stern

Executive Agencies

COUNCIL OF ECONOMIC ADVISERS: Janet L. Yellen, chair
COUNCIL OF ENVIRONMENTAL QUALITY: Kathleen McGinty, chair
OFFICE OF ADMINISTRATION: Ada Posey, director
OFFICE OF MANAGEMENT AND BUDGET: Jacob J. Lew, director
OFFICE OF NATIONAL DRUG CONTROL POLICY: Barry R. McCaffrey, director
OFFICE OF SCIENCE AND TECHNOLOGY POLICY: Neal Lane, director
OFFICE FOR WOMEN'S INITIATIVES AND OUTREACH: Audrey Tayse Haynes, director
FOREIGN INTELIGENCE ADVISORY BOARD: Warren Rudman, vice chairman
U.S. TRADE REPRESENTATIVE: Charlene Barshefsky

The Cabinet

DEPARTMENT OF AGRICULTURE
Secretary—Dan Glickman
DEPARTMENT OF COMMERCE
Secretary—William Daley
DEPARTMENT OF DEFENSE
Secretary—William Cohen
DEPARTMENT OF EDUCATION
Secretary—Richard Riley
DEPARTMENT OF ENERGY
Secretary—Bill Richardson
DEPARTMENT OF HEALTH AND HUMAN SERVICES
Secretary—Donna Shalala

DEPARTMENT OF HOUSING AND URBAN DEVELOPMENT
Secretary—Andrew M. Cuomo
DEPARTMENT OF INTERIOR
Secretary—Bruce Babbitt
DEPARTMENT OF JUSTICE
Attorney General—Janet Reno
DEPARTMENT OF LABOR
Secretary—Alexis Herman

DEPARTMENT OF STATE
Secretary—Madeleine Albright
DEPARTMENT OF TRANSPORTATION
Secretary—Rodney Slater
DEPARTMENT OF THE TREASURY
Secretary—Robert Rubin
DEPARTMENT OF VETERANS' AFFAIRS
Secretary—Togo D. West Jr.

Heads of Selected U.S. Government Agencies

BUREAU OF ALCOHOL, TOBACCO, AND FIREARMS—John Magaw
BUREAU OF ENGRAVING AND PRINTING—Thomas Ferguson (acting)
CENSUS BUREAU—James F. Holmes (acting)
CENTERS FOR DISEASE CONTROL AND PREVENTION—Dr. Jeffrey P. Koplan
CENTRAL INTELLIGENCE AGENCY—George Tenet
COMMODITY FUTURES TRADING COMMISSION—Brooksley Born
CONSUMER PRODUCT SAFETY COMMISSION—Kathleen Begala
CORPORATION FOR PUBLIC BROADCASTING—President and Chief Executive Officer—Robert T. Coonrod
DRUG ENFORCEMENT ADMINISTRATION—Thomas Constantine
ENVIRONMENTAL PROTECTION AGENCY—Carol Browner
EQUAL EMPLOYMENT OPPORTUNITY COMMISSION—Paul M. Igasaki (acting)
EXPORT-IMPORT BANK OF THE UNITED STATES—James A. Harmon
FARM CREDIT ADMINISTRATION—Marsha Pyle Martin
FEDERAL AVIATION ADMINISTRATION—Jane Garvey
FEDERAL BUREAU OF INVESTIGATION—Louis Freeh
FEDERAL COMMUNICATIONS COMMISSION—William Kennard
FEDERAL DEPOSIT INSURANCE CORPORATION—Donna Tanoue
FEDERAL ELECTION COMMISSION—Darryl Wold
FEDERAL EMERGENCY MANAGEMENT AGENCY—James L. Witt
FEDERAL ENERGY REGULATORY COMMISSION—James Hoecker
FEDERAL MEDIATION AND CONCILIATION SERVICE—C. Richard Barnes (acting)
FEDERAL RESERVE SYSTEM—Alan Greenspan
FEDERAL TRADE COMMISSION—Robert Pitofsky

FOOD AND DRUG ADMINISTRATION—Michael Friedman (lead deputy commissioner)
GENERAL ACCOUNTING OFFICE—James F. Hinchman (acting)
GENERAL SERVICES ADMINISTRATION—David J. Barram
GOVERNMENT PRINTING OFFICE—Michael DiMario
IMMIGRATION AND NATURALIZATION SERVICE—Doris Meissner
INTERNAL REVENUE SERVICE—Charles O. Rossotti
INTERNATIONAL TRADE COMMISSION—Lynn Bragg
NATIONAL AERONAUTICS AND SPACE ADMINISTRATION—Daniel Goldin
NATIONAL ENDOWMENT FOR THE ARTS—William J. Ivey
NATIONAL HIGHWAY TRAFFIC SAFETY ADMINISTRATION—Dr. Ricardo Martinez
NATIONAL INSTITUTE OF MENTAL HEALTH—Dr. Steven Hyman
NATIONAL INSTITUTE OF STANDARDS AND TECHNOLOGY—Raymond Kammer
NATIONAL INSTITUTES OF HEALTH—Dr. Harold Varmus
NATIONAL LABOR RELATIONS BOARD—position open
NATIONAL PARK SERVICE—Robert G. Stanton
NATIONAL TRANSPORTATION SAFETY BOARD—James Hall
NUCLEAR REGULATORY COMMISSION—Dr. Shirley Ann Jackson
OCCUPATIONAL SAFETY AND HEALTH ADMINISTRATION—Charles N. Jeffress
PATENT AND TRADEMARK OFFICE—Bruce Lehman
PEACE CORPS—Mark Gearan
POSTAL SERVICE—William J. Henderson
SECURITIES AND EXCHANGE COMMISSION—Arthur Levitt
SMALL BUSINESS ADMINISTRATION—Aida Alvarez
SMITHSONIAN INSTITUTION—I. Michael Heyman
SOCIAL SECURITY ADMINISTRATION—Kenneth S. Apfel
SURGEON GENERAL—Dr. David Satcher
U.S. FISH AND WILDLIFE SERVICE—Jamie Rappaport Clark
U.S. FOREST SERVICE—Dr. Michael Dombeck

U.S. Presidents and Vice Presidents

	President	Party	Vice President	Years served
1	George Washington	Federalist	John Adams	1789–1797
2	John Adams	Federalist	Thomas Jefferson	1797–1801
3	Thomas Jefferson	Dem.-Rep.	Aaron Burr (1801–1805)	1801–1809
			George Clinton	
4	James Madison	Dem.-Rep.	George Clinton (died 1812)	1809–1817
			Elbridge Gerry (died 1814)	
5	James Monroe	Dem.-Rep.	Daniel D. Tompkins	1817–1825
6	John Quincy Adams	Dem.-Rep.	John C. Calhoun	1825–1829
7	Andrew Jackson	Democratic	John C. Calhoun (resigned 1832)	1829–1837
			Martin Van Buren	
8	Martin Van Buren	Democratic	Richard M. Johnson	1837–1841
9	William Henry Harrison*	Whig	John Tyler	1841
10	John Tyler	Whig	vacant	1841–1845
11	James Knox Polk	Democratic	George M. Dallas	1845–1849
12	Zachary Taylor*	Whig	Millard Fillmore	1849–1850
13	Millard Fillmore	Whig	vacant	1850–1853
14	Franklin Pierce	Democratic	William R. King (died 1853)	1853–1857
15	James Buchanan	Democratic	John C. Breckinridge	1857–1861
16	Abraham Lincoln**	Republican	Hannibal Hamlin (1861–1865)	1861–1865
			Andrew Johnson (1865)	
17	Andrew Johnson	Democratic	vacant	1865–1869
18	Ulysses Simpson Grant	Republican	Schuyler Colfax (1869–1873)	1869–1877
			Henry Wilson (died 1875)	
19	Rutherford Birchard Hayes	Republican	William A. Wheeler	1877–1881
20	James Abram Garfield**	Republican	Chester Alan Arthur	1881
21	Chester Alan Arthur	Republican	vacant	1881–1885
22	Grover Cleveland	Democratic	Thomas A. Hendricks (died 1885)	1885–1889
23	Benjamin Harrison	Republican	Levi P. Morton	1889–1893
24	Grover Cleveland	Democratic	Adlai E. Stevenson	1893–1897
25	William McKinley**	Republican	Garret A. Hobart (died 1899)	1897–1901
			Theodore Roosevelt	
26	Theodore Roosevelt	Republican	Charles W. Fairbanks (1905–1909)	1901–1909
27	William Howard Taft	Republican	James S. Sherman (died 1912)	1909–1913
28	Woodrow Wilson	Democratic	Thomas R. Marshall	1913–1921
29	Warren Gamaliel Harding*	Republican	Calvin Coolidge	1921–1923
30	Calvin Coolidge	Republican	Charles G. Dawes (1925–1929)	1923–1929
31	Herbert Clark Hoover	Republican	Charles Curtis	1929–1933
32	Franklin Delano Roosevelt*	Democratic	John N. Garner (1933–1941)	1933–1945
			Henry A. Wallace (1941–1945)	
			Harry S Truman	
33	Harry S Truman	Democratic	Alben W. Barkley (1949–1953)	1945–1953
34	Dwight David Eisenhower	Republican	Richard M. Nixon	1953–1961
35	John Fitzgerald Kennedy**	Democratic	Lyndon B. Johnson	1961–1963
36	Lyndon Baines Johnson	Democratic	Hubert H. Humphrey (1965–1969)	1963–1969
37	Richard Mihous Nixon†	Republican	Spiro T. Agnew (resigned 1973)	1969–1974
			Gerald R. Ford	
38	Gerald Rudolph Ford	Republican	Nelson A. Rockefeller	1974–1977
39	James Earl Carter	Democratic	Walter F. Mondale	1977–1981
40	Ronald Reagan	Republican	George Bush	1981–1989
41	George Bush	Republican	Dan Quayle	1989–1993
42	Bill Clinton	Democratic	Al Gore	1993–

*Died in office of natural causes.
**Assassinated.
† Resigned.

THE CONGRESS

The Senate is composed of 100 members—two from each state, irrespective of population or area—elected by the people in conformity with the provisions of the 17th Amendment to the Constitution. That amendment changed the former constitutional method under which senators were chosen by the respective state legislatures. A senator must be at least 30 years of age, have been a citizen of the United States for nine years, and, when elected, be a resident of the state for which the senator is chosen. The term of office is six years, and one-third of the total membership of the Senate is elected every second year.

The House of Representatives includes 435 members elected every two years from among the 50 states, apportioned to their total populations. A representative must be at least 25 years of age, have been a citizen of the United States for seven years, and, when elected, be a resident of the state in which the representative is chosen. In addition to the representatives from each of the states, there is a resident commissioner from the Commonwealth of Puerto Rico, as well as delegates from the District of Columbia, American Samoa, Guam and the Virgin Islands. The resident commissioner and the delegates have most of the prerogatives of representatives, with the important exception of the right to vote on matters before the House.

A Congress lasts for two years, commencing in January of the year following the biennial election of members, and is divided into two sessions. Unlike some other parliamentary bodies, both the Senate and the House have equal legislative functions and powers, except that only the House can initiate revenue bills. The chief function of Congress is the making of laws. In addition, the Senate has the function of advising and consenting to treaties and to certain nominations by the President.

Number of Women in the U.S. Congress

CONGRESS	YEARS	TOTAL	HOUSE	SENATE
96th	1979–1981	17	16	1
97th	1981–1983	23	21	2
98th	1983–1985	24	22	2
99th	1985–1987	25	23	2
100th	1987–1989	25	23	2
101st	1989–1991	31	29	2
102nd	1991–1993	33	30	3
103rd	1993–1995	55	48	7
104th	1995–1997	58	49	9
105th	1997–1999	62	53	9

Number of Black Members in the U.S. Congress

CONGRESS	YEARS	TOTAL	HOUSE	SENATE
96th	1979–1981	17	17	0
97th	1981–1983	19	19	0
98th	1983–1985	21	21	0
99th	1985–1987	21	21	0
100th	1987–1989	23	23	0
101st	1989–1991	24	24	0
102d	1991–1993	27	27	0
103d	1993–1995	40	39	1
104th	1995–1997	41	40	1
105th	1997–1999	40	39	1

Source: Congressional Research Service

Major Actions by the Congress in 1998

NATO Expansion: The Senate in April approved a treaty that will add three former Warsaw Pact members to the North Atlantic Treaty Organization. By a vote of 80–19, 14 more than the two-thirds majority needed for ratification, the Senate agreed to admit Central Europe's most robust new democracies, Poland, Hungary and the Czech Republic. Before the final vote, senators rejected an amendment requiring a three-year waiting period before taking any more new members into the alliance. The Senate also refused to consider a separate amendment that would have restricted NATO's future participation in Bosnia-style peacekeeping and other "out of area" missions.

Transportation Spending: A landmark $216 billion transportation bill cleared Congress in May, just in time for the summer highway-construction season. Some legislators, including House Budget Committee Chairman John Kasich of Ohio, opposed the measure, which far exceeds the spending levels assumed in the 1997 balanced-budget plan. On average, states would receive a 44 percent increase in federal highway aid under the new transportation bill, which was quickly embraced by President Clinton despite the measure's image as a monument to pork-barrel politics. There are literally thousands of "earmarks" and set-asides parsed out among members and totaling nearly $14 billion over the six-year life of the measure.

IRS Overhaul: Congress passed legislation restructuring the Internal Revenue Service and putting taxpayers in a stronger position when dealing with the agency. The wide-ranging measure, which includes new taxpayer protections against overzealous IRS agents, was signed by President Clinton in July. The legislation received strong bipartisan support, with only eight House members and two senators voting against it.

Credit Unions: President Clinton in August signed a bill to expand credit-union membership, making credit unions more directly competitive with banks. Congress passed the legislation to address a Supreme Court ruling earlier in 1998 that restricted credit-union membership. Under the legislation, federally chartered credit unions would be permitted to include more than one group in their memberships, as long as each group doesn't exceed 3,000 people.

Bankruptcy: The Senate in September overwhelmingly approved a sweeping overhaul of the federal Bankruptcy Code aimed at curbing the sharp rise in American households that have turned to the courts to avoid paying debts. But the Senate bill is easier on debtors—and tougher on creditors—than legislation that passed in the House in June, and the prospects for the first major bankruptcy reform in two decades remained cloudy. The main point of both the House and Senate bills is to make it harder for debtors to file for relief under Chapter 7 of the U.S. Bankruptcy Code, under which they can fairly easily wipe out unsecured debts, such as credit-card debt. Both bills would instead try to push more debtors into Chapter 13, which requires a repayment plan.

THE U.S. SUPREME COURT

The Supreme Court is the highest tribunal for all cases and controversies arising under the Constitution or laws of the United States. The court also has "original jurisdiction" in a very small number of cases arising out of disputes between states or between a state and the federal government. When the Supreme Court rules on a constitutional issue, that judgment is virtually final. Its decisions can be altered only by the rarely used procedure of constitutional amendment or by a new ruling of the court. However, when the court interprets a statute, new legislative action can be taken.

A term of the Supreme Court begins, by statute, on the first Monday in October. Usually, court sessions continue until late June or early July. The term is divided between "sittings," when the justices hear cases and deliver opinions, and intervening "recesses," when they consider the business before the court and write opinions. More than 6,500 cases are filed in the Supreme Court each year from the various state and federal courts. Plenary review, with oral arguments by attorneys, is granted in only 120 to 150 cases per term. Formal written opinions are delivered in 115 to 130 cases. About 75 to 100 additional cases are disposed of without granting plenary review.

The nine members of the Supreme Court are appointed by the President, subject to the approval of the U.S. Senate. To ensure an independent judiciary and to protect judges from partisan pressures, the Constitution provides that the justices serve during "good Behaviour," which has generally meant life terms.

HIGHLIGHTS OF THE 1997–98 SUPREME COURT TERM

Clinton vs. New York: The court voted 6–3 to strike down the presidential line-item veto. The justices said the U.S. Constitution bars the president from vetoing or amending individual pieces of legislation.

Faragher vs. Boca Raton and Burlington Industries vs. Ellerth: In a pair of landmark sexual-harassment decisions, a seven-member majority of the court set out a new rule that presumes companies are to blame when supervisors create a sexually hostile workplace. But the court said employers can defend themselves by showing they took steps to root out harassment and that the complaining employee failed to use internal grievance procedures.

Swidler & Berlin vs. U.S.: The justices ruled 6–3 that conversations with a lawyer should remain confidential even after the client dies. The decision grew out of a request by Independent Counsel Kenneth Starr for notes taken by a lawyer for the late White House deputy counsel Vincent Foster.

Hudson vs. U.S.: The court ruled that people fined by federal agencies can also be criminally prosecuted for the same misdeeds that led to their civil fines. The 5–4 decision made it harder for defendants to prove that such prosecutions amount to the kind of "double jeopardy" forbidden by the Constitution.

Phillips vs. Washington Legal Foundation: Voting 5–4, the justices dealt a blow to a major method of funding legal aid for the poor, but stopped short of wiping it out. The case challenged state programs that fund such services by taking interest payments that lawyers earn while they hold onto clients' money.

State Oil Co. vs. Khan: The justices unanimously ruled that manufacturers may cap the prices retailers charge for their products. The decision reversed a 30-year-old decision that had forbidden such limits, citing antitrust laws.

Oncale vs. Sundowner: The justices ruled unanimously that workers can file discrimination suits claiming sexual harassment by people of their own gender. The court said "same-sex" harassment is covered by federal civil-rights law.

General Electric Co. vs. Joiner: The court strengthened the power of trial judges to keep controversial scientific evidence out of their courtrooms. The unanimous decision said trial judges who bar such evidence can be overruled only if they have clearly abused their discretion.

U.S. vs. Best Foods: The court granted relief to companies facing so-called Superfund liability in environmental-cleanup lawsuits. The unanimous decision ruled that a parent company is liable for pollution caused by a subsidiary only if the parent was directly involved in running the polluting facility.

National Credit Union Administration vs. First National Bank: The court sided with banks in their long-running effort to restrict membership in federal credit unions. But the 5–4 decision was later reversed when Congress changed the law in question, which had limited the membership of individual credit unions to people with a shared occupation or community.

Baker vs. General Motors Corp.: The court prevented GM from enforcing a settlement pact that restricted a former employee's right to testify against it in product-liability cases. The unanimous ruling is likely to unleash more whistle-blowers on corporate America.

Justices of the U.S. Supreme Court

Name	Appointed by President	Judicial oath taken
Chief Justice		
William H. Rehnquist (born October 1, 1924)	Reagan	September 26, 1986*
Associate Justices		
John Paul Stevens (born April 20, 1920)	Ford	December 19, 1975
Sandra Day O'Connor (born March 26, 1930)	Reagan	September 25, 1981
Antonin Scalia (born March 11, 1936)	Reagan	September 26, 1986
Anthony M. Kennedy (born July 23, 1936)	Reagan	February 18, 1988
David H. Souter (born September 17, 1939)	Bush	October 9, 1990
Clarence Thomas (born June 23, 1948)	Bush	October 23, 1991
Ruth Bader Ginsburg (born March 15, 1933)	Clinton	August 10, 1993
Stephen G. Breyer (born August 15, 1938)	Clinton	August 3, 1994

*Mr. Rehnquist was appointed to the court by President Nixon and took the oath as an associate justice January 7, 1972.

Past Members of the U.S. Supreme Court

Name	Appointed by President	Judicial oath taken	Date service terminated
Chief Justices			
John Jay	Washington	October 19, 1789	June 29, 1795
John Rutledge	Washington	August 12, 1795	December 15, 1795
Oliver Ellsworth	Washington	March 8, 1796	December 15, 1800
John Marshall	John Adams	February 4, 1801	July 6, 1835
Roger Brooke Taney	Jackson	March 28, 1836	October 12, 1864
Salmon Portland Chase	Lincoln	December 15, 1864	May 7, 1873
Morrison Remick Waite	Grant	March 4, 1874	March 23, 1888
Melville Weston Fuller	Cleveland	October 8, 1888	July 4, 1910
Edward Douglass White	Taft	December 19, 1910	May 19, 1921
William Howard Taft	Harding	July 11, 1921	February 3, 1930
Charles Evans Hughes	Hoover	February 24, 1930	June 30, 1941
Harlan Fiske Stone	Franklin D. Roosevelt	July 3, 1941	April 22, 1946
Fred Moore Vinson	Truman	June 24, 1946	September 8, 1953
Earl Warren	Eisenhower	October 5, 1953	June 23, 1969
Warren Earl Burger	Nixon	June 23, 1969	September 26, 1986
Associate Justices			
John Rutledge	Washington	February 15, 1790	March 5, 1791
William Cushing	Washington	February 2, 1790	September 13, 1810
James Wilson	Washington	October 5, 1789	August 21, 1798
John Blair	Washington	February 2, 1790	October 25, 1795
James Iredell	Washington	May 12, 1790	October 20, 1799
Thomas Johnson	Washington	August 6, 1792	January 16, 1793
William Paterson	Washington	March 11, 1793	September 9, 1806
Samuel Chase	Washington	February 4, 1796	June 19, 1811
Bushrod Washington	John Adams	February 4, 1799	November 26, 1829
Alfred Moore	John Adams	April 21, 1800	January 26, 1804
William Johnson	Jefferson	May 7, 1804	August 4, 1834
Henry Brockholst Livingston	Jefferson	January 20, 1807	March 18, 1823
Thomas Todd	Jefferson	May 4, 1807	February 7, 1826
Gabriel Duvall	Madison	November 23, 1811	January 14, 1835
Joseph Story	Madison	February 3, 1812	September 10, 1845
Smith Thompson	Monroe	September 1, 1823	December 18, 1843
Robert Trimble	John Quincy Adams	June 16, 1826	August 25, 1828
John McLean	Jackson	January 11, 1830	April 4, 1861
Henry Baldwin	Jackson	January 18, 1830	April 21, 1844
James Moore Wayne	Jackson	January 14, 1835	July 5, 1867
Philip Pendleton Barbour	Jackson	May 12, 1836	February 25, 1841
John Catron	Van Buren	May 1, 1837	May 30, 1865
John McKinley	Van Buren	January 9, 1838	July 19, 1852
Peter Vivian Daniel	Van Buren	January 10, 1842	May 31, 1860
Samuel Nelson	Tyler	February 27, 1845	November 28, 1872
Levi Woodbury	Polk	September 23, 1845	September 4, 1851
Robert Cooper Grier	Polk	August 10, 1846	January 31, 1870
Benjamin Robbins Curtis	Fillmore	October 10, 1851	September 30, 1857
John Archibald Campbell	Pierce	April 11, 1853	April 30, 1861
Nathan Clifford	Buchanan	January 21, 1858	July 25, 1881
Noah Haynes Swayne	Lincoln	January 27, 1862	January 24, 1881
Samuel Freeman Miller	Lincoln	July 21, 1862	October 13, 1890
David Davis	Lincoln	December 10, 1862	March 4, 1877
Stephen Johnson Field	Lincoln	May 20, 1863	December 1, 1897
William Strong	Grant	March 14, 1870	December 14, 1880
Joseph P. Bradley	Grant	March 23, 1870	January 22, 1892

Name	Appointed by President	Judicial oath taken	Date service terminated
Associate Justices			
Ward Hunt	Grant	January 9, 1873	January 27, 1882
John Marshall Harlan	Hayes	December 10, 1877	October 14, 1911
William Burnham Woods	Hayes	January 5, 1881	May 14, 1887
Stanley Matthews	Garfield	May 17, 1881	March 22, 1889
Horace Gray	Arthur	January 9, 1882	September 15, 1902
Samuel Blatchford	Arthur	April 3, 1882	July 7, 1893
Lucius Quintus C. Lamar	Cleveland	January 18, 1888	January 23, 1893
David Josiah Brewer	Harrison	January 6, 1890	March 28, 1910
Henry Billings Brown	Harrison	January 5, 1891	May 28, 1906
George Shiras, Jr.	Harrison	October 10, 1892	February 23, 1903
Howell Edmunds Jackson	Harrison	March 4, 1893	August 8, 1895
Edward Douglass White	Cleveland	March 12, 1894	December 18, 1910*
Rufus Wheeler Peckham	Cleveland	January 6, 1896	October 24, 1909
Joseph McKenna	McKinley	January 26, 1898	January 5, 1925
Oliver Wendell Holmes	Theodore Roosevelt	December 8, 1902	January 12, 1932
William Rufus Day	Theodore Roosevelt	March 2, 1903	November 13, 1922
William Henry Moody	Theodore Roosevelt	December 17, 1906	November 20, 1910
Horace Harmon Lurton	Taft	January 3, 1910	July 12, 1914
Charles Evans Hughes	Taft	October 10, 1910	June 10, 1916
Willis Van Devanter	Taft	January 3, 1911	June 2, 1937
Joseph Rucker Lamar	Taft	January 3, 1911	January 2, 1916
Mahlon Pitney	Taft	March 18, 1912	December 31, 1922
James Clark McReynolds	Wilson	October 12, 1914	January 31, 1941
Louis Dembitz Brandeis	Wilson	June 5, 1916	February 13, 1939
John Hessin Clarke	Wilson	October 9, 1916	September 18, 1922
George Sutherland	Harding	October 2, 1922	January 17, 1938
Pierce Butler	Harding	January 2, 1923	November 16, 1939
Edward Terry Sanford	Harding	February 19, 1923	March 8, 1930
Harlan Fiske Stone	Coolidge	March 2, 1925	July 2, 1941*
Owen Josephus Roberts	Hoover	June 2, 1930	July 31, 1945
Benjamin Nathan Cardozo	Hoover	March 14, 1932	July 9, 1938
Hugo Lafayette Black	Franklin D. Roosevelt	August 19, 1937	September 17, 1971
Stanley Forman Reed	Franklin D. Roosevelt	January 31, 1938	February 25, 1957
Felix Frankfurter	Franklin D. Roosevelt	January 30, 1939	August 28, 1962
William Orville Douglas	Franklin D. Roosevelt	April 17, 1939	November 12, 1975
Frank Murphy	Franklin D. Roosevelt	February 5, 1940	July 19, 1949
James Francis Byrnes	Franklin D. Roosevelt	July 8, 1941	October 3, 1942
Robert Houghwout Jackson	Franklin D. Roosevelt	July 11, 1941	October 9, 1954
Wiley Blount Rutledge	Franklin D. Roosevelt	February 15, 1943	September 10, 1949
Harold Hitz Burton	Truman	October 1, 1945	October 13, 1958
Tom Campbell Clark	Truman	August 24, 1949	June 12, 1967
Sherman Minton	Truman	October 12, 1949	October 15, 1956
John Marshall Harlan	Eisenhower	March 28, 1955	September 23, 1971
William J. Brennan, Jr.	Eisenhower	October 16, 1956	July 20, 1990
Charles Evans Whittaker	Eisenhower	March 25, 1957	March 31, 1962
Potter Stewart	Eisenhower	October 14, 1958	July 3, 1981
Byron Raymond White	Kennedy	April 16, 1962	June 28, 1993
Arthur Joseph Goldberg	Kennedy	October 1, 1962	July 25, 1965
Abe Fortas	Lyndon Johnson	October 4, 1965	May 14, 1969
Thurgood Marshall	Lyndon Johnson	October 2, 1967	October 1, 1991
Harry A. Blackmun	Nixon	June 9, 1970	August 3, 1994
Lewis F. Powell, Jr.	Nixon	January 7, 1972	June 26, 1987

*Named Chief Justice.

Military Might ☆

Active-Duty Military Personnel Strength Levels

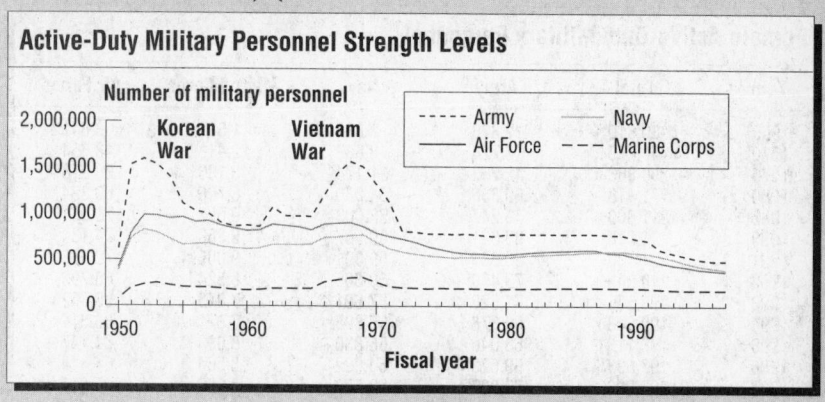

Number of military personnel

Korean War Vietnam War

- - - - Army   ——— Navy
——— Air Force - - - Marine Corps

Fiscal year

Active-Duty Military Personnel*

Year	Total	Army	Navy	Marine Corps	Air Force
1950	1,459,462	593,167	380,739	74,279	411,277
1955	2,935,107	1,109,296	660,695	205,170	959,946
1960	2,475,438	873,078	616,987	170,621	814,752
1965	2,653,926	969,066	669,985	190,213	824,662
1970	3,064,760	1,322,548	691,126	259,737	791,349
1975	2,128,120	784,333	535,085	195,951	612,751
1980	2,050,627	777,036	527,153	188,469	557,969
1985	2,151,032	780,787	570,705	198,025	601,515
1990	2,043,705	732,403	579,417	196,652	535,233
1991	1,985,555	710,821	570,262	194,040	510,432
1992	1,807,177	610,450	541,883	184,529	470,315
1993	1,705,103	572,423	509,950	178,379	444,351
1994	1,610,490	541,343	468,662	174,158	426,327
1995	1,518,224	508,559	434,617	174,639	400,409
1996	1,471,722	491,103	416,735	174,883	389,001
1997	1,438,562	491,707	395,564	173,906	377,385

*Military personnel on extended or continuous active duty. Excludes reserves on active duty for training.
Source: U.S. Defense Department

Women in Uniform

Female Active-Duty Military Personnel

Year	Total	Army	Navy	Marine Corps	Air Force
1965	30,610	12,326	7,862	1,581	8,841
1970	41,479	16,724	8,683	2,418	13,654
1975	96,868	42,295	21,174	3,186	30,213
1980	171,418	69,338	34,980	6,706	60,394
1985	211,606	79,247	52,603	9,695	70,061
1990	227,018	83,621	59,907	9,356	74,134
1991	221,138	80,306	59,391	9,005	72,436
1992	210,048	73,430	59,305	8,524	68,789
1993	203,506	71,328	57,601	7,845	66,732
1994	199,688	69,878	55,825	7,671	66,314
1995	196,116	68,046	55,830	8,093	64,147
1996	197,693	69,623	54,692	8,564	64,814
1997	200,526	72,827	52,578	9,286	65,835

Source: U.S. Defense Department

Women and Minority Officers

The percentage of women and minority officers in the military has grown significantly since 1980.

	Army	Navy	Air Force	Marines
1980				
Black	7.1%	2.5%	4.6%	3.9%
Hispanic	1.0	0.7	1.6	1.0
Other minority	2.8	1.6	2.3	0.9
Total minority	11.0	4.9	8.5	5.8
Female	7.7	7.7	8.7	2.7
1997				
Black	11.6%	6.2%	6.0%	6.7%
Hispanic	3.6	3.7	2.2	4.4
Other minority	4.9	4.1	4.5	2.9
Total minority	20.2	14.1	12.6	13.9
Female	13.1	13.8	16.3	4.6

Source: U.S. Defense Department

America at War

U.S. Military Personnel Serving and Casualties in Principal Wars[a]

War/conflict	Branch of service	Number serving	Battle deaths	Other deaths	Wounds not mortal[b]
Revolutionary War	Total	–[c]	4,435	–	6,188
1775–1783	Army	–	4,044	–	6,004
	Navy	–	342	–	114
	Marines	–	49	–	70
War of 1812	Total	286,730	2,260	–	4,505
1812–1815	Army	–	1,950	–	4,000
	Navy	–	265	–	439
	Marines	–	45	–	66
Mexican War	Total	78,718	1,733	11,550	4,152
1846–1848	Army	–	1,721	11,550	4,102
	Navy	–	1	–	3
	Marines	–	11	–	47
Civil War	Total	2,213,363	140,414	224,097	281,881
(Union Forces only)	Army	2,128,948	138,154	221,374	280,040
1861–1865[d]	Navy	–	2,112	2,411	1,710
	Marines	84,415	148	312	131
Spanish–American War	Total	306,760	385	2,061	1,662
1898	Army	280,564	369	2,061	1,594
	Navy	22,875	10	–	47
	Marines	3,321	6	–	21
World War I	Total	4,734,991	53,402	63,114	204,002
1917–1918	Army	4,057,101	50,510	55,868	193,663
	Navy	599,051	431	6,856	819
	Marines	78,839	2,461	390	9,520
World War II	Total	16,112,566	291,557	113,842	671,846
1941–1946	Army	11,260,000	234,874	83,400	565,861
	Navy	4,183,466	36,950	25,664	37,778
	Marines	669,100	19,733	4,778	68,207
Korean Conflict	Total	5,720,000	33,651	3,262	103,284
1950–1953	Army	2,834,000	27,709	2,452	77,596
	Navy	1,177,000	475	173	1,576
	Marines	424,000	4,269	339	23,744
	Air Force	1,285,000	1,198	298	368
Vietnam Conflict	Total	8,744,000	47,378	10,799	153,303
1964–1973	Army	4,368,000	30,922	7,273	96,802
	Navy	1,842,000	1,631	931	4,178
	Marines	794,000	13,084	1,753	51,392
	Air Force	1,740,000	1,741	842	931

[a]Data prior to World War I are based on incomplete records in many cases. Casualty data are confined to dead and wounded and, therefore, exclude personnel captured or missing in action who were subsequently returned to military control.

[b]Marine Corps data for World War II, the Spanish–American War, and prior wars represent the number of individuals wounded, whereas all other data in this column represent the total number (incidence) of wounds.

[c]Not known, but estimates range from 184,000 to 250,000.

[d]Authoritative statistics for the Confederate forces are not available. Estimates of the number who served range from 600,000 to 1,500,000. The final report of the Provost Marshal General, 1863–1866, indicated 133,821 Confederate deaths (74,524 battle and 59,297 other) based upon incomplete returns. In addition, an estimated 26,000 to 31,000 Confederate personnel died in Union prisons.

Source: U.S. Defense Department

Military Spending

U.S. spending for military operations has declined in the post-Cold War era.

Military Outlays
(In billions of dollars)

Military Outlays
(In millions of dollars)

1987	$273,966
1988	281,935
1989	294,880
1990	289,755
1991	262,389
1992	286,892
1993	278,561
1994	268,622
1995	259,442
1996	253,300
1997	258,300
1998*	253,400
1999*	254,800

*Estimate.
Source: Office of Management and Budget

Top Defense Contractors

Recipients of the Largest Dollar Volume of Prime Contract Awards From the U.S. Defense Department in 1997

Rank	Contractor	Total (In thousands)
1	Lockheed Martin	$11,637,526
2	Boeing	9,644,855
3	Northrop Grumman	3,475,752
4	General Dynamics	3,012,018
5	Raytheon	2,863,236
6	General Motors	2,829,943
7	United Technologies	1,810,297
8	General Electric	1,677,067
9	Litton Industries	1,602,659
10	Textron	1,445,066
11	Science Applications Intl.	1,094,560
12	GTE	889,899
13	ITT Industries	789,618
14	TRW	781,999
15	CBS	777,325
16	Newport News Shipbuilding	719,991
17	Computer Sciences	704,328
18	Foundation Health Systems	655,884
19	Avondale Industries	622,329
20	Humana	621,449
21	United Defense	610,986
22	Tracor	554,663
23	AlliedSignal	547,030
24	Exxon	538,621
25	DynCorp	534,754
26	Texas Instruments	528,904
27	Standard Missile	471,932
28	Rockwell International	453,764
29	BDM International	380,523
30	Alliant Techsystems	378,035
31	United States Dept. of Energy	375,543
32	Massachusetts Inst. of Tech.	368,290
33	Electronic Data Systems	358,777
34	Longbow	338,015
35	Logicon	336,602
36	Sverdrup	328,222
37	FMC	325,176
38	Renco Group	313,805
39	Motorola	310,840
40	Mitre	304,358
41	Aerospace Corp.	297,682
42	OHM	293,795
43	Shell Oil	293,291
44	Halliburton	290,497
45	Federal Express	289,324
46	Nassco Holdings	287,783
47	Johnson Controls	284,011
48	Chevron	278,096
49	Stewart & Stevenson Services	267,650
50	Bechtel Group	266,508

Source: U.S. Defense Department

The United States Budget

Receipts by Source
(In millions of dollars)

Fiscal year	Individual income taxes	Corporate income taxes	Social insurance taxes and contributions	Excise taxes	Other	Total receipts
1987	$392,557	$ 83,926	$303,318	$32,457	$42,137	$ 854,396
1990	466,884	93,507	380,047	35,345	56,186	1,031,969
1996	656,417	171,824	509,414	54,014	61,393	1,453,062
1997	737,500	182,300	539,400	56,900	63,200	1,579,300
1998*	810,500	187,700	575,400	55,600	74,600	1,703,800
1999*	832,600	187,000	602,500	72,600	89,500	1,784,300

Spending
(In millions of dollars)

	1987	1990	1996	1997	1998*	1999*
National defense	$281,999	$299,331	$265,748	$270,500	$266,100	$267,600
International affairs	11,648	13,764	13,496	15,200	14,700	15,000
General space, science, technology	9,216	14,444	16,709	17,200	17,100	17,600
Energy	4,115	3,341	2,836	1,500	600	-1,000
Natural resources and environment	13,363	17,080	21,614	21,400	24,000	23,200
Agriculture	26,606	11,958	9,159	9,000	11,300	11,400
Commerce and housing credit	6,435	67,600	-10,646	-14,600	3,600	4,900
Transportation	26,222	29,485	39,565	40,800	41,500	42,600
Community and regional development	5,051	8,498	10,685	11,000	10,900	11,700
Education, training, employment, and social services	29,724	38,755	52,001	53,000	54,600	59,300
Health	39,967	57,716	119,378	123,800	131,800	141,900
Medicare	75,120	98,102	174,225	190,000	197,700	210,300
Income security	123,282	147,076	225,989	230,900	236,800	251,500
Social security	207,353	248,623	349,676	365,300	379,500	393,000
Veterans benefits and services	26,750	29,058	36,985	39,300	43,100	43,300
Administration of justice	7,553	9,993	17,548	20,200	22,300	25,600
General government	7,565	10,734	11,892	12,800	12,900	17,200
Net interest	138,652	184,221	241,090	244,000	244,100	235,700
Allowances	–	–	–	–	–	1,400
Undistributed offsetting receipts	-36,455	-36,615	-37,620	-50,000	-48,000	-42,300
Total outlays	1,004,164	1,253,163	1,560,330	1,601,200	1,664,700	1,730,000
Deficit or surplus	-149,769	-221,194	-107,268	-21,900	39,100	54,200

*Estimate.
Source: Office of Management and Budget

United States Budget Trend

Budget analysts expected a surplus in 1998, the first since 1969.

Government Receipts, Outlays, and Surpluses or Deficits

	Total (In millions of dollars)				Total (In millions of dollars)		
Year	Receipts	Outlays	Surplus or deficit (-)	Year	Receipts	Outlays	Surplus or deficit (-)
1955	65,451	68,444	-2,993	1979	463,302	504,032	-40,729
1956	74,587	70,640	3,947	1980	517,112	590,947	-73,835
1957	79,990	76,578	3,412	1981	599,272	678,249	-78,976
1958	79,636	82,405	-2,769	1982	617,766	745,755	-127,989
1959	79,249	92,098	-12,849	1983	600,562	808,380	-207,818
1960	92,492	92,191	301	1984	666,499	851,888	-185,388
1961	94,388	97,723	-3,335	1985	734,165	946,499	-212,334
1962	99,676	106,821	-7,146	1986	769,260	990,505	-221,245
1963	106,560	111,316	-4,756	1987	854,396	1,004,164	-149,769
1964	112,613	118,528	-5,915	1988	909,303	1,064,489	-155,187
1965	116,817	118,228	-1,411	1989	991,190	1,143,671	-152,481
1966	130,835	134,532	-3,698	1990	1,031,969	1,253,163	-221,194
1967	148,822	157,464	-8,643	1991	1,055,041	1,324,400	-269,359
1968	152,973	178,134	-25,161	1992	1,091,279	1,381,681	-290,402
1969	186,882	183,640	3,242	1993	1,154,401	1,409,414	-255,013
1970	192,807	195,649	-2,842	1994	1,258,627	1,461,731	-203,104
1971	187,139	210,172	-23,033	1995	1,351,830	1,515,729	-163,899
1972	207,309	230,681	-23,373	1996	1,453,062	1,560,330	-107,268
1973	230,799	245,707	-14,908	1997	1,579,300	1,601,200	-21,900
1974	263,224	269,359	-6,135	1998	1,704,000	1,665,000	39,000
1975	279,090	332,332	-53,242	1999	1,784,000	1,730,000	54,000
1976	298,060	371,792	-73,732	2000	1,835,000	1,774,000	61,000
1977	355,559	409,218	-53,659	2001	1,902,000	1,820,000	83,000
1978	399,561	458,746	-59,186	2002	1,990,000	1,843,000	148,000

The Shrinking U.S. Deficit

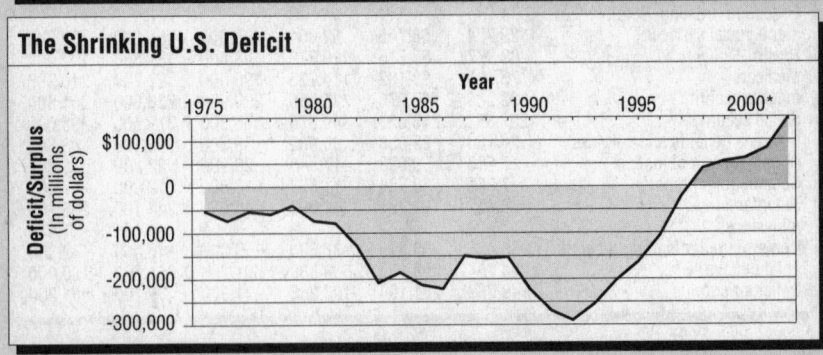

*Estimates, 1998–2002.
Sources: U.S. Treasury Department and Office of Management and Budget

The Federal Debt

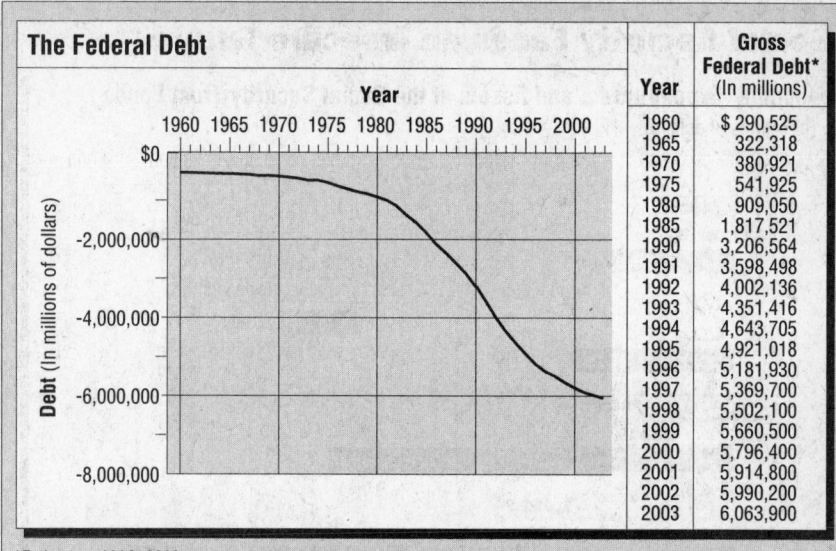

Year	Gross Federal Debt* (In millions)
1960	$ 290,525
1965	322,318
1970	380,921
1975	541,925
1980	909,050
1985	1,817,521
1990	3,206,564
1991	3,598,498
1992	4,002,136
1993	4,351,416
1994	4,643,705
1995	4,921,018
1996	5,181,930
1997	5,369,700
1998	5,502,100
1999	5,660,500
2000	5,796,400
2001	5,914,800
2002	5,990,200
2003	6,063,900

*Estimates, 1998–2003.
Sources: Bureau of the Public Debt and Office of Management and Budget

Social Security Faces an Insecure Future

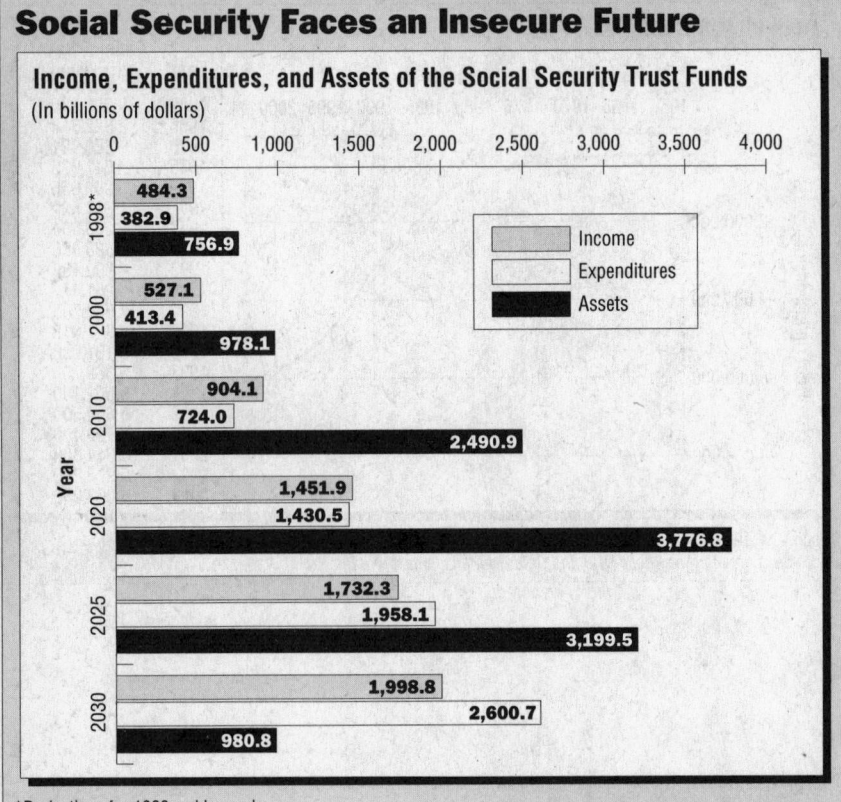

Income, Expenditures, and Assets of the Social Security Trust Funds
(In billions of dollars)

Legend:
- Income
- Expenditures
- Assets

Year	Income	Expenditures	Assets
1998*	484.3	382.9	756.9
2000	527.1	413.4	978.1
2010	904.1	724.0	2,490.9
2020	1,451.9	1,430.5	3,776.8
2025	1,732.3	1,958.1	3,199.5
2030	1,998.8	2,600.7	980.8

*Projections for 1998 and beyond.

Income, Expenditures, and Assets of the Social Security Trust Funds
(In billions of dollars)

Year	Income	Expenditures	Assets (end of year)	Year	Income	Expenditures	Assets (end of year)
1960	$ 12.4	$ 11.8	$ 22.6	1998*	$ 484.3	$ 382.9	$ 756.9
1965	17.9	19.2	19.8	1999	503.7	396.3	864.4
1970	37.0	33.1	38.1	2000	527.1	413.4	978.1
1975	67.6	69.2	44.3	2001	553.2	433.0	1,098.3
1980	119.7	123.6	26.5	2002	581.1	454.8	1,224.6
1985	203.5	190.6	42.2	2003	611.1	478.2	1,357.4
1990	315.4	253.1	225.3	2004	643.9	504.2	1,497.2
1991	329.7	274.2	280.7	2005	680.9	533.1	1,645.0
1992	342.6	291.9	331.5	2010	904.1	724.0	2,490.9
1993	355.6	308.8	378.3	2015	1,169.2	1,014.1	3,354.9
1994	381.1	323.0	436.4	2020	1,451.9	1,430.5	3,776.8
1995	399.5	339.8	496.1	2025	1,732.3	1,958.1	3,199.5
1996	424.5	353.6	567.0	2030	1,998.8	2,600.7	980.8
1997	457.7	369.1	655.5				

*Projections for 1998 and beyond.
Note: The trust funds are expected to become exhausted in 2032.
Source: Social Security Administration

Living Longer

People are expected to live longer in the 21st century, putting added pressure on the Social Security and Medicare systems. Here are Census Bureau projections of life expectancy at age 65 and the growing percentage of people over 65.

Life Expectancy at 65

Year	Total	
	Male	Female
1997	15.6	19.3
2000	15.9	19.5
2010	16.8	20.0
2020	17.6	20.6
2030	18.5	21.2
2040	19.3	21.8
2050	20.3	22.4

Elderly Population by Age:
1900 to 2050 (Numbers in thousands)

	65 and over	
Census date	Number	% of total population
1900	3,080	4.1%
1910	3,949	4.3
1920	4,933	4.7
1930	6,634	5.4
1940	9,019	6.8
1950	12,269	8.1
1960	16,560	9.2
1970	19,980	9.8
1980	25,550	11.3
1990	31,235	12.5
2000	34,709	12.6
2010	39,408	13.2
2020	53,220	16.5
2030	69,379	20.0
2040	75,233	20.3
2050	78,859	20.0

Source: U.S. Census Bureau

The Ailing Medicare Program

The Hospital Insurance program, also referred to as Medicare Part A, covers specified inpatient hospital services, skilled nursing care after hospitalization, home health services and hospice care for aged and disabled people. The financially troubled program is funded primarily by payroll taxes paid by workers and employers.

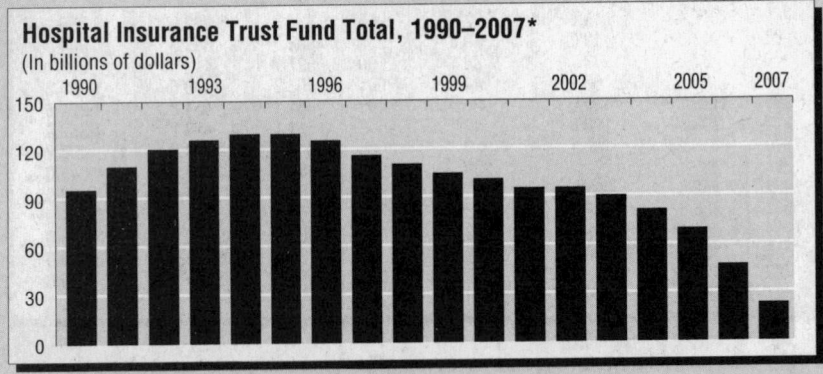

Hospital Insurance Trust Fund Total, 1990–2007*

(In billions of dollars)

*Estimates for years 1998 and beyond.
Source: U.S. Health Care Financing Administration

Operations of the Hospital Insurance Trust Fund During Fiscal Years 1970–2007

(In millions)

Fiscal year	Payroll taxes	Income from taxation of benefits	Railroad retirement account transfers	Reimbursement for uninsured persons	Premiums from voluntary enrollees	Payments for military wage credits	Interest and other income	Total income
1970	$ 4,785	–	$ 64	$617	–	$ 11	$ 137	$ 5,614
1975	11,291	–	132	481	$ 6	48	609	12,568
1980	23,244	–	244	697	17	141	1,072	25,415
1985	46,490	–	371	766	38	86	3,182	50,933
1986	53,020	–	364	566	40	-714	3,167	56,442
1987	57,820	–	368	447	40	94	3,982	62,751
1988	61,901	–	364	475	42	80	5,148	68,010
1989	67,527	–	379	515	42	86	6,567	75,116
1990	70,655	–	367	413	113	107	7,908	79,563
1991	74,655	–	352	605	367	-1,011	8,969	83,938
1992	80,978	–	374	621	484	86	10,133	92,677
1993	83,147	–	400	367	622	81	12,484	97,101
1994	92,028	$1,639	413	506	852	80	10,676	106,195
1995	98,053	3,913	396	462	998	61	10,963	114,847
1996	106,934	4,069	401	419	1,107	-2,293	10,496	121,135
1997	112,725	3,558	419	481	1,279	70	9,970	128,501
1998*	119,941	5,071	413	34	1,315	64	9,264	136,102
1999	123,529	5,116	413	652	1,333	64	8,783	139,890
2000	129,116	5,435	414	194	1,368	63	8,062	144,652
2001	134,314	5,774	415	154	1,422	63	7,502	149,644
2002	140,202	6,168	417	137	1,497	63	6,992	155,476
2003	146,413	6,612	428	134	1,591	63	6,733	161,974
2004	153,109	7,111	440	132	1,715	63	6,120	168,690
2005	162,448	7,664	454	137	1,837	63	5,302	177,905
2006	169,903	8,288	468	142	1,976	63	4,184	185,024
2007	179,181	8,977	483	146	2,121	63	2,639	193,610

Fiscal year	Disbursements			Trust fund	
	Benefits payments	Administrative expenses	Total disbursements	Net increase in fund	Fund at end of year
1970	$ 4,804	$ 149	$ 4,953	$ 661	$ 2,677
1975	10,353	259	10,612	1,956	9,870
1980	23,790	497	24,288	1,127	14,490
1985	47,841	813	48,654	4,103	21,277
1986	49,018	667	49,685	17,370	38,648
1987	49,967	836	50,803	11,949	50,596
1988	52,022	707	52,730	15,281	65,877
1989	57,433	805	58,238	16,878	82,755
1990	65,912	774	66,687	12,876	95,631
1991	68,705	934	69,638	14,299	109,930
1992	80,784	1,191	81,974	10,703	120,633
1993	90,738	866	91,604	5,497	126,131
1994	101,535	1,235	102,770	3,425	129,555
1995	113,583	1,300	114,883	-36	129,520
1996	124,088	1,229	125,317	-4,182	125,338
1997	136,175	1,613	137,789	-9,287	116,050
1998*	139,639	1,929	141,568	-5,466	110,584
1999	143,792	2,022	145,814	-5,924	104,660
2000	146,352	2,108	148,460	-3,808	100,852
2001	153,046	2,220	155,266	-5,622	95,230
2002	153,067	2,333	155,400	76	95,306
2003	164,619	2,448	167,067	-5,093	90,213
2004	175,026	2,499	177,525	-8,835	81,378
2005	187,192	2,559	189,751	-11,846	69,532
2006	204,978	2,630	207,608	-22,584	46,948
2007	214,735	2,713	217,448	-23,838	23,110

*Estimates for years 1998 and beyond.
Source: U.S. Health Care Financing Administration

Medicare's Healthier Side

The Supplementary Medical Insurance program, also known as Medicare Part B, covers part of the cost of physicians' services, outpatient hospital care and related services. This program is funded primarily by transfers from the general fund of the U.S. Treasury and by monthly premiums paid by beneficiaries, and is expected to continue to be adequately financed because the law provides for automatic increases in premiums and government contributions to meet expected costs.

Operations of the Supplementary Medical Insurance Trust Fund (Cash Basis) During Fiscal Years 1970–2007
(In millions)

Fiscal year*	Income				Disbursements			Balance at end of year
	Premium from enrollees	Government contributions	Interest and other income	Total income	Benefit payments	Administrative expenses	Total disbursements	
1970	$ 936	$ 928	$ 12	$ 1,876	$ 1,979	$ 217	$ 2,196	$ 57
1975	1,887	2,330	105	4,322	3,765	405	4,170	1,424
1980	2,928	6,932	415	10,275	10,144	593	10,737	4,532
1985	5,524	17,898	1,155	24,577	21,808	922	22,730	10,646
1986	5,699	18,076	1,228	25,003	25,169	1,049	26,218	9,432
1987	6,480	20,299	1,018	27,797	29,937	900	30,837	6,392
1988	8,756	25,418	828	35,002	33,682	1,265	34,947	6,447
1989	11,548	30,712	1,022	43,282	36,867	1,450	38,317	11,412
1990	11,494	33,210	1,434	46,138	41,498	1,524	43,022	14,527

	Income				Disbursements			
Fiscal year*	Premium from enrollees	Government contri-butions	Interest and other income	Total income	Benefit payments	Adminis-trative expenses	Total disburse-ments	Balance at end of year
1991	11,807	34,730	1,629	48,166	45,514	1,505	47,019	15,675
1992	12,748	38,684	1,717	53,149	48,627	1,661	50,288	18,535
1993	14,683	44,227	1,889	60,799	54,214	1,845	56,059	23,276
1994	16,895	38,355	2,118	57,368	58,006	1,718	59,724	20,919
1995	19,244	36,988	1,937	58,169	63,491	1,722	65,213	13,874
1996	18,931	61,702	1,392	82,025	67,176	1,771	68,946	26,953
1997	19,141	59,471	2,193	80,806	71,133	1,420	72,553	35,206
1998*	19,241	59,375	2,423	81,039	76,824	1,411	78,235	38,011
1999	20,548	63,431	2,287	86,266	84,878	1,460	86,338	37,939
2000	22,752	70,187	2,246	95,185	93,536	1,509	95,045	38,079
2001	25,134	77,739	2,224	105,097	105,682	1,565	107,247	35,929
2002	27,626	86,009	2,216	115,851	111,148	1,622	112,770	39,010
2003	30,496	95,423	2,226	128,145	125,194	1,682	126,876	40,279
2004	33,975	104,070	2,270	140,315	137,513	1,748	139,261	41,333
2005	37,315	113,453	2,295	153,063	150,275	1,822	152,097	42,299
2006	41,264	125,408	2,342	169,014	167,842	1,900	169,742	41,571
2007	45,516	138,378	2,553	186,447	179,667	1,982	181,649	46,369

*Estimates for years 1998 and beyond.
Source: U.S. Health Care Financing Administration

Major Welfare Programs

Aid to Families with Dependent Children

The AFDC program, which was changed to Temporary Assistance for Needy Families (TANF), has helped families with at least one child under 18 and is financed with both federal and state funds.

Year	Recipients	Federal and state benefits
1975	11,165,185	$ 8,153,448,850
1980	10,597,445	12,061,790,697
1985	10,812,625	14,644,559,007
1990	11,460,382	18,641,562,487
1995	13,652,232	22,031,584,208
1996	12,648,859	23,258,868,000
1997	10,936,298	27,698,739,000

Source: U.S. Health and Human Services Department

Supplemental Security Income

The SSI program, which includes both federal and state funds, pays monthly checks to needy people who are blind, have a disability, or are 65 or older. People who receive SSI also usually receive food stamps and Medicaid.

Year	Recipients	Federal and state payments
1975	4,359,625	$ 5,878,224,000
1980	4,194,100	7,940,734,000
1985	4,200,177	11,060,476,000
1990	4,888,180	16,598,680,000
1995	6,515,753	27,827,658,000
1996	6,676,729	28,791,924,000
1997	6,494,985	28,370,568,871

Source: Social Security Administration

Food Stamps

Year	Number of Participants	Program cost	Average benefit per person per month
1980	21,100,000	$ 9,100,000,000	$39.47
1985	19,900,000	11,600,000,000	44.99
1986	19,400,000	11,600,000,000	45.59
1987	19,100,000	11,600,000,000	45.49
1988	18,600,000	12,400,000,000	49.83
1989	18,800,000	12,900,000,000	51.85
1990	20,100,000	15,500,000,000	58.91
1991	22,600,000	18,500,000,000	63.86
1992	25,400,000	22,500,000,000	68.57
1993	26,900,000	23,700,000,000	67.96
1994	27,500,000	24,500,000,000	69.01
1995	26,400,000	24,600,000,000	71.27
1996	25,533,302	24,325,836,730	73.24
1997	22,850,063	21,488,214,832	71.35

Source: U.S. Agriculture Department

Health Insurance for the Poor

The Medicaid law (Title XIX of the Social Security Act) authorizes federal matching funds to assist the states in providing health care for low-income people. The program has grown considerably, with total medical-assistance payments of about $160 billion a year to about 36 million individuals.

Medicaid Medical Assistance Payments*

(Fiscal years; in billions)

	1980	1990	1993	1994	1995	1996	1997
Federal share	$13.3	$38.9	$72.3	$78.8	$86.5	$87.0	$90.8
States' share	10.7	29.8	53.5	58.8	65.3	65.9	69.5
Total	24.0	68.7	125.8	137.6	151.8	152.9	160.3

*Excluding state administrative costs.

Medicaid Recipients

(Fiscal years; in millions)

Category*	1975	1980	1985	1990	1995	1997[†]	1998[†]
Total	22.0	21.6	21.8	25.3	36.3	36.2	36.7
Aged	3.6	3.4	3.1	3.2	4.2	4.5	4.6
Blind/Disabled	2.5	2.9	3.0	3.7	6.0	6.6	6.8
Children	9.6	9.3	9.8	11.2	17.6	16.9	17.1
Adults	4.5	4.9	5.5	6.0	7.8	7.4	7.5
Other	1.8	1.5	1.2	1.0	0.6	0.7	0.7

*Prior to 1991, recipient categories do not add to total because recipients could be reported in more than one category. Totals after 1990 may not add due to rounding.
[†]Estimates for years 1997 and 1998.
Source: Health Care Financing Administration

Coming to America

Immigration Fiscal Years 1820–1996

Years	Number	Years	Number
1820–1996	63,140,227	1901–1910	8,795,386
		1911–1920	5,735,811
1821–1830	143,439	1921–1930	4,107,209
1831–1840	599,125	1931–1940	528,431
1841–1850	1,713,251	1941–1950	1,035,039
1851–1860	2,598,214	1951–1960	2,515,479
1861–1870	2,314,824	1961–1970	3,321,677
1871–1880	2,812,191	1971–1980	4,493,314
1881–1890	5,246,613	1981–1990	7,338,062
1891–1900	3,687,564	1991–1996	6,146,213

Immigration to the U.S. 1981–1996

(In thousands)

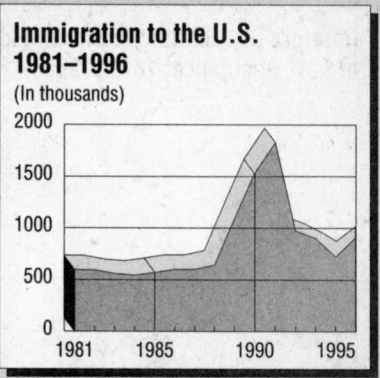

Immigrants Admitted from Top 20 Countries of Birth, Fiscal Years 1995-96

Country	1996	1995	Change Number	Change Percent
All countries	915,900	720,461	195,439	27.1
1. Mexico	163,572	89,932	73,640	81.9
2. Philippines	55,876	50,984	4,892	9.6
3. India	44,859	34,748	10,111	29.1
4. Vietnam	42,067	41,752	315	0.8
5. China, People's Republic	41,728	35,463	6,265	17.7
6. Dominican Republic	39,604	38,512	1,092	2.8
7. Cuba	26,466	17,937	8,529	47.5
8. Ukraine	21,079	17,432	3,647	20.9
9. Russia	19,668	14,560	5,108	35.1
10. Jamaica	19,089	16,398	2,691	16.4
11. Haiti	18,386	14,021	4,365	31.1
12. Korea	18,185	16,047	2,138	13.3
13. El Salvador	17,903	11,744	6,159	52.4
14. Canada	15,825	12,932	2,893	22.4
15. Poland	15,772	13,824	1,948	14.1
16. Colombia	14,283	10,838	3,445	31.8
17. United Kingdom	13,624	12,427	1,197	9.6
18. Taiwan	13,401	9,377	4,024	42.9
19. Peru	12,871	8,066	4,805	59.6
20. Pakistan	12,519	9,774	2,745	28.1
Other	289,123	243,693	45,430	18.6

Source: U.S. Immigration and Naturalization Service

Country of Origin

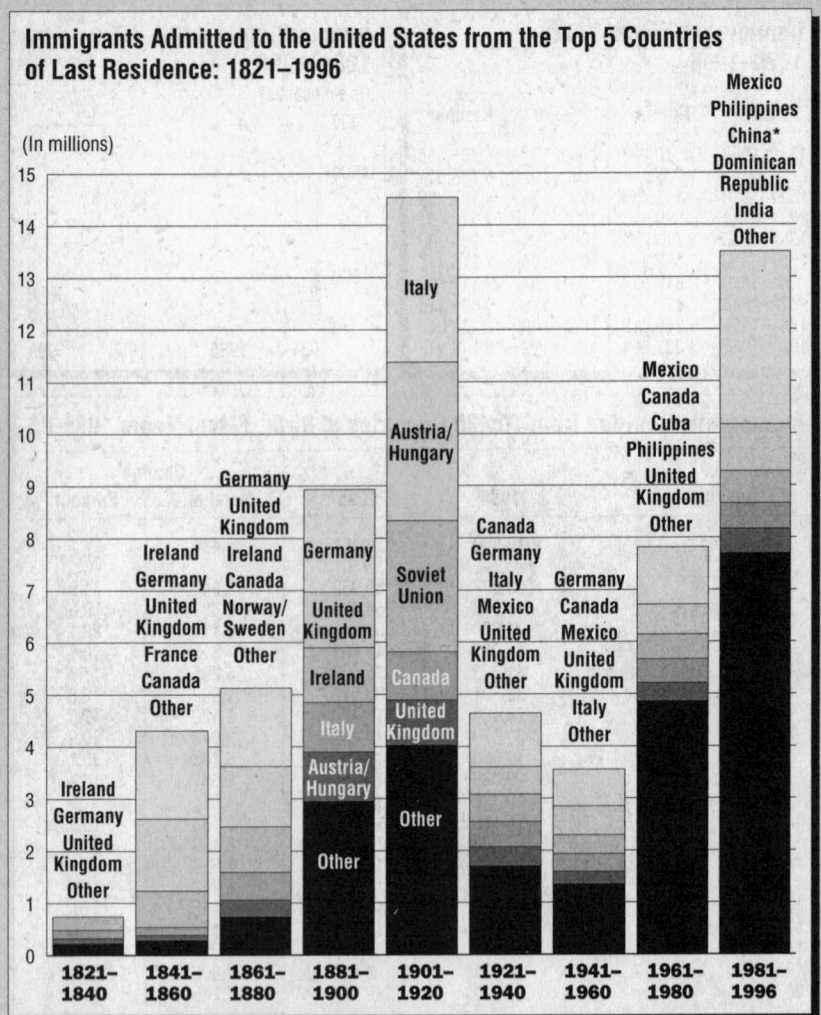

Immigrants Admitted to the United States from the Top 5 Countries of Last Residence: 1821–1996

(In millions)

*China includes People's Republic of China and Taiwan.
Source: U.S. Department of Justice, Immigration and Naturalization Service

Estimated Illegal Immigrant Population for Top 20 Countries of Origin and Top 20 States of Residence: October 1996

Country of origin	Population		State of residence	Population
All Countries	5,000,000		All States	5,000,000
1 Mexico	2,700,000		1 California	2,000,000
2 El Salvador	335,000		2 Texas	700,000
3 Guatemala	165,000		3 New York	540,000
4 Canada	120,000		4 Florida	350,000
5 Haiti	105,000		5 Illinois	290,000
6 Philippines	95,000		6 New Jersey	135,000
7 Honduras	90,000		7 Arizona	115,000
8 Dominican Republic	75,000		8 Massachusetts	85,000
9 Poland	70,000		9 Virginia	55,000
10 Nicaragua	70,000		10 Washington	52,000
11 Bahamas	70,000		11 Colorado	45,000
12 Colombia	65,000		12 Maryland	44,000
13 Ecuador	55,000		13 Michigan	37,000
14 Trinidad & Tobago	50,000		14 Pennsylvania	37,000
15 Jamaica	50,000		15 New Mexico	37,000
16 Pakistan	41,000		16 Oregon	33,000
17 India	33,000		17 Georgia	32,000
18 Ireland	30,000		18 District of Columbia	30,000
19 Peru	30,000		19 Connecticut	29,000
20 Korea	30,000		20 Nevada	24,000
Other	744,000		Other	330,000

3

THE U.S. ECONOMY

Through the mid-1990s, pundits liked to talk of America's perfectly balanced "Goldilocks economy."

Like the porridge that the girl of fable devoured, it was not too hot and not too cold, but just right. And while everybody acknowledged that dangers would, from time to time, threaten the U.S. economy, many serious observers began to argue that the country had so insulated itself from harm that it would always, like Goldilocks at the end of the tale, be able to elude the grasp of any growling menaces. The boom, it seemed, would never end.

As the summer of 1998 wore on, however, the Dow Jones Industrial Average was swooning, corporate profits were getting pinched, and layoffs were mounting. A fear spread across trading pits, factory floors and farms: Had the bears finally caught Goldilocks?

In late August, Columbia University's Center of International Business Cycle Research reported that its boom-bust index was showing the first, albeit "very tentative," warning "of a possibly serious slowdown." AMP Inc., a leading maker of electronic components, saw profits in mid-1998 collapse to half the year-earlier level, and was forced to close factories, lay off workers, and cut capital spending plans. William J. Hudson, then the chief executive of the Harrisburg, Pennsylvania, maker of electronic components told *The Wall Street Journal*: "From our standpoint, we're seeing a recession."

At first blush, the very notion seemed farfetched. The unemployment rate in August stood at 4.5 percent. Excluding a slightly lower rate earlier in the year, that was the lowest level since the Nixon era. Interest rates hovered near 5 percent, the lowest since the late 1960s. The inflation rate, by some measures, was well below 1 percent, a price stability unseen since the 1950s. For the first time in years, household incomes across the board were rising.

"The fundamentals of the United States economy are strong," Treasury Secretary Robert Rubin insisted in a hastily arranged press conference called to inject some calm after the Dow plunged more than 500 points one late August day. "The prospects for growth with low inflation and low unemployment continue to be strong," he vowed.

Indeed, there was little doubt that the great 1990s expansion, officially begun in March 1991, would continue at the very least through the fall of 1998, passing the seven-year-eight-month stretch in the 1980s that previously had been America's longest peacetime expansion. In the September survey of 50 leading forecasters conducted by Blue Chip Economic Indicators, the average projected growth rate for 1999 was a decent 2.2 percent. In other words, no downturn in sight. And if these wise men and women are even close to right, the 1990s would break the record-long growth enjoyed during the 1960s.

But forecasters, for all their sophisticated models, are notoriously bad at calling economic turning points. "Nobody has a good record of predicting when a recession comes," Milton Friedman, the Nobel laureate economist, pointed out. "If you look at the historical record, the first quarters of most recessions have been regarded by most commentators at the time as a continuation of prosperity." And while the consensus among experts was that continued growth remained the most likely scenario, most acknowledged that the odds of a more dire outlook were rising. It was becoming clear that key sources of 1990s growth—globalization and financial market expansion at home and abroad—had huge risks as well as rewards.

The biggest cloud looming over the U.S. economy was the Asian crisis, which began with the seemingly innocuous devaluation of the Thai baht in the summer of 1997 and had, within a year, helped plunge a third of the world's economies into recessions and depressions.

Emblematic of the good luck and optimism that has graced the United States of late, the region's woes actually appeared for a time to *benefit* American business and consumers. Oil prices plunged as worldwide demand fell. Prices for Asian-manufactured imports also dropped, the result of falling Asian currencies vs. the dollar. So while Indonesians were struggling with painful price hikes, the combined impact of their travails was still-lower inflation for Americans. Meanwhile, the flight of global investor capital from shattered financial markets to the so-called safe haven of U.S. Treasuries helped push down interest rates. While South Koreans suffered from sharp interest-rate hikes, American consumers enjoyed new income through a wave of mortgage refinancings and kicked off a new home-buying boom.

The once high-flying Asian economies were literally shrinking. But from January through March of 1998, U.S. Gross Domestic Product grew at an eye-popping 5.5 percent annual rate, adjusted for inflation. The most vivid image capturing this phenomenon was that invoked famously by Abby Joseph Cohen, Goldman Sachs's irrepressible market strategist: "Supertanker America," she called the U.S. economy, a sturdy ship largely immune to the rough seas around the world.

But the potential damage to the United States from the Asian crisis became increasingly obvious as the year wore on. Exporters lost sales to a key market, while companies faced more intense import competition. Manufacturing was hit particularly hard and

the sector started to contract by midyear. Farmers and oil producers saw a worldwide glut for their products, and their prices collapsed, even if they didn't themselves sell to the region. Companies as diverse as shoemaker Nike Inc. and semiconductor equipment manufacturer Applied Materials Inc. announced plans to cut at least 1,000 jobs each from their payrolls. Corporate profit growth for 1998 had eased to the slowest pace since 1991, the last time the country had felt a recession.

All of that was *before* the Asian flu had spread late in the summer beyond the immediate region to a raft of other emerging markets, from Russia to leading Latin American economies such as Brazil, Venezuela and Mexico.

The disease was transmitted in part through conventional links: a drop in Asian industrial production pushed down demand for commodities like oil, which hurt oil exporters from Russia to Mexico. But the turmoil was also spread through ways unseen before the days of global capital markets. Because investors tend to invest in worldwide "emerging market" funds, trouble in one such country can force massive sell-offs in another, as bondholders scramble to cover losses. That's why Russia's ruble devaluation and debt rescheduling pushed up interest rates as far away as Latin America.

As more and more dominoes fell, it became harder and harder to argue that the United States had little to fear. "It is just not credible that the United States can remain an oasis of prosperity unaffected by a world that is experiencing greatly increased stress," Federal Reserve Chairman Alan Greenspan warned in an early September speech at the University of California at Berkeley.

The first concrete sign of a changing psychology about the U.S. economy was the stock market's summer plunge. After hitting a peak of 9337.97 in July, the Dow fell toward 7400 in September—a 20 percent drop, the level that is officially considered a correction.

Of course, the market isn't the economy. Despite widespread fears at the time, the 1987 crash had no lasting discernible impact on growth. Yet the 1990s may well be different. The sustained bull market has produced more than 10 trillion dollars of new wealth, and it has been spread around more widely than before, through the expansion of

Real U.S. Gross Domestic Product

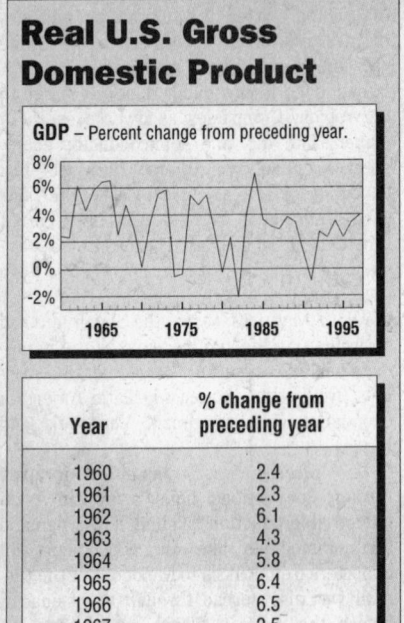

GDP – Percent change from preceding year.

Year	% change from preceding year
1960	2.4
1961	2.3
1962	6.1
1963	4.3
1964	5.8
1965	6.4
1966	6.5
1967	2.5
1968	4.7
1969	3.0

Year	% change from preceding year
1970	0.1
1971	3.3
1972	5.5
1973	5.8
1974	-0.6
1975	-0.4
1976	5.4
1977	4.7
1978	5.4
1979	2.8
1980	-0.3
1981	2.3
1982	-2.1
1983	4.0
1984	7.0
1985	3.6
1986	3.1
1987	2.9
1988	3.8
1989	3.4
1990	1.2
1991	-0.9
1992	2.7
1993	2.3
1994	3.5
1995	2.3
1996	3.4
1997	3.9

Source: U.S. Commerce Department, Bureau of Economic Analysis

mutual-fund retirement plans and employee stock-ownership programs. The Commerce Department reported that by June 1998, the average household savings rate—the percentage of after-tax wages and salaries that wasn't spent—had dropped to an all-time low of 0.2 percent. That meant Americans were no longer relying on earned income for savings and increasingly counting on capital gains for their needed financial cushion.

Nobody really knew how much a stock market drop would induce consumers to cut sharply their spending to make up for a drop in anticipated investment profits. If the response were big, that would certainly stall the economy, since consumer spending was the main engine for growth in 1998.

Most economists played down the dangers. Joel Prakken, head of St. Louis-based Macroeconomic Advisers said that, in his model, even "a 20% sustained decline doesn't produce a recession."

But economics is as much psychology as math. Nobody can fully explain the great 1990s boom. Much of it, of course, has resulted from improved business practices and wise economic policies. Some unknown part, however, has been fueled by optimism itself: a confidence that stock markets would rise, jobs would be plentiful and that the global march to capitalism could continue quickly and smoothly. Good news persuaded businesses and consumers to behave in ways—investing in new factories, hiring more workers, shopping for more products— that produced more good news.

In 1998, some of those happy assumptions were being questioned. The Asian miracle, a central part of the endless-growth scenarios, had been dashed. Scudder Kemper Invest-

Real Gross Domestic Product
(Billions of chained 1992 dollars)

Year	GDP	Personal consumption expenditures	Gross private domestic investment	Exports and imports of goods and services		Government	GDP (% change)
				Exports	Imports		
1960	$2,262.9	$1,432.6	$270.5	$86.8	$108.1	$617.2	2.4%
1961	2,314.3	1,461.5	267.6	88.3	107.3	647.2	2.3
1962	2,454.8	1,533.8	302.1	93.0	119.5	686.0	6.1
1963	2,559.4	1,596.6	321.6	100.0	122.7	701.9	4.3
1964	2,708.4	1,692.3	348.3	113.3	129.2	715.9	5.8
1965	2,881.1	1,799.1	397.2	115.6	143.0	737.6	6.4
1966	3,069.2	1,902.0	430.6	123.4	164.2	804.6	6.5
1967	3,147.2	1,958.6	411.8	126.1	176.2	865.6	2.5
1968	3,293.9	2,070.2	433.3	135.3	202.5	892.4	4.7
1969	3,393.6	2,147.5	458.3	142.7	214.0	887.5	3.0
1970	3,397.6	2,197.8	426.1	158.1	223.1	866.8	0.1
1971	3,510.0	2,279.5	474.9	159.2	235.0	851.0	3.3
1972	3,702.3	2,415.9	531.8	172.0	261.0	854.1	5.5
1973	3,916.3	2,532.6	595.5	209.6	272.6	848.4	5.8
1974	3,891.2	2,514.7	546.5	229.8	265.3	862.9	-0.6
1975	3,873.9	2,570.0	446.6	228.2	235.4	876.3	-0.4
1976	4,082.9	2,714.3	537.4	241.6	281.5	876.8	5.4
1977	4,273.6	2,829.8	622.1	247.4	311.6	884.7	4.7
1978	4,503.0	2,951.6	693.4	273.1	338.6	910.6	5.4
1979	4,630.6	3,020.2	709.7	299.0	344.3	924.9	2.8
1980	4,615.0	3,009.7	628.3	331.4	321.3	941.4	-0.3
1981	4,720.7	3,046.4	686.0	335.3	329.7	947.7	2.3
1982	4,620.3	3,081.5	587.2	311.4	325.5	960.1	-2.1
1983	4,803.7	3,240.6	642.1	303.3	366.6	987.3	4.0
1984	5,140.1	3,407.6	833.4	328.4	455.7	1,018.4	7.0
1985	5,323.5	3,566.5	823.8	337.3	485.2	1,080.1	3.6
1986	5,487.7	3,708.7	811.8	362.2	526.1	1,135.0	3.1
1987	5,649.5	3,822.3	821.5	402.0	558.2	1,165.9	2.9
1988	5,865.2	3,972.7	828.2	465.8	580.2	1,180.9	3.8
1989	6,062.0	4,064.6	863.5	520.2	603.0	1,213.9	3.4
1990	6,136.3	4,132.2	815.0	564.4	626.3	1,250.4	1.2
1991	6,079.4	4,105.8	738.1	599.9	622.2	1,258.0	-0.9
1992	6,244.4	4,219.8	790.4	639.4	669.0	1,263.8	2.7
1993	6,389.6	4,343.6	863.6	658.2	728.4	1,252.1	2.3
1994	6,610.7	4,486.0	975.7	712.4	817.0	1,252.3	3.5
1995	6,761.7	4,605.6	966.0	792.6	889.0	1,254.5	2.3
1996	6,994.8	4,752.4	1,050.6	860.0	971.2	1,268.2	3.4
1997	7,269.8	4,913.5	1,138.0	970.0	1,106.1	1,285.0	3.9

Note: Users of this table are cautioned that for periods before 1982, comparisons across the chained (1992) dollar components of GDP may be misleading.
Source: U.S. Commerce Department, Bureau of Economic Analysis

ments Inc. chief economist Maureen Allyn scoffed at the various forecasters who tried to minimize the impact of Asia's troubles on the U.S. economy, simply by invoking the rela- tively small percentage of American exports that get sent across the Pacific. For years, "every corporate executive who came into our office talked about their growth prospects

Boom and Bust Times
Business Cycle Expansions and Contractions

Business cycle reference dates		Duration in months			
				Cycle	
Trough	Peak	Contraction (trough from previous peak)	Expansion (trough to peak)	Trough from previous trough	Peak from previous peak
December 1854	June 1857	—	30	—	—
December 1858	October 1860	18	22	48	40
June 1861	April 1865	8	**46**	30	**54**
December 1867	June 1869	**32**	18	**78**	50
December 1870	October 1873	18	34	36	52
March 1879	March 1882	65	36	99	101
May 1885	March 1887	38	22	74	60
April 1888	July 1890	13	27	35	40
May 1891	January 1893	10	20	37	30
June 1894	December 1895	17	18	37	35
June 1897	June 1899	18	24	36	42
December 1900	September 1902	18	21	42	39
August 1904	May 1907	23	33	44	56
June 1908	January 1910	13	19	46	32
January 1912	January 1913	24	12	43	36
December 1914	August 1918	23	**44**	35	**67**
March 1919	January 1920	**7**	10	**51**	17
July 1921	May 1923	18	22	28	40
July 1924	October 1926	14	27	36	41
November 1927	August 1929	13	21	40	34
March 1933	May 1937	43	50	64	93
June 1938	February 1945	13	**80**	63	**93**
October 1945	November 1948	**8**	37	**88**	45
October 1949	July 1953	**11**	**45**	48	**56**
May 1954	August 1957	**10**	39	55	49
April 1958	April 1960	8	24	47	32
February 1961	December 1969	10	**106**	34	**116**
November 1970	November 1973	**11**	36	**117**	47
March 1975	January 1980	16	58	52	74
July 1980	July 1981	6	12	64	18
November 1982	July 1990	16	92	28	108
March 1991	—	8	—	100	—

Note: Figures printed in bold are the wartime expansions (Civil War, World War I and II, Korean War, and Vietnam War), the postwar contractions, and the full cycles that include the wartime expansions.
Source: National Bureau of Economic Research, Inc., Cambridge, MA

for Asia," she said. "They have an empty part of their presentation now."

The global financial crisis, meanwhile, was causing a backlash against unfettered capital markets. The world's 1990s boom—and hopes for a continued golden twenty-first century—included the massive channeling of investor funds into countries that had never before tapped into world financial markets.

That was happily welcomed when the funds poured in. But when Western money quickly pulled out in 1997 and 1998, enthusiasm soured. "The free market has failed disastrously," Malaysian Prime Minister Mahatir Mohamed proclaimed as he declared that his country would no longer let its currency trade outside its borders. Other countries, such as Russia, were also contemplating controls.

The U.S. Work Force

The labor force grew 96% between 1960 and 1997, reflecting both population growth and a higher percentage of women working.

Civilian Labor Force (Persons 16 Years of Age and Over)
(Numbers in thousands)

Year	Total	Percent of population	Total employed	Total unemployed	Total not in labor force
1960	69,628	59.4%	65,778	3,852	47,617
1965	74,455	58.9	71,088	3,366	52,058
1970	82,771	60.4	78,678	4,093	54,315
1975	93,774	61.2	85,846	7,929	59,377
1980	106,940	63.8	99,302	7,637	60,806
1985	115,461	64.8	107,150	8,312	62,744
1986	117,834	65.3	109,597	8,237	62,752
1987	119,865	65.6	112,440	7,425	62,888
1988	121,669	65.9	114,968	6,701	62,944
1989	123,869	66.5	117,342	6,528	62,523
1990	125,840	66.5	118,793	7,047	63,324
1991	126,346	66.2	117,718	8,628	64,578
1992	128,105	66.4	118,492	9,613	64,700
1993	129,200	66.3	120,259	8,940	65,638
1994	131,056	66.6	123,060	7,996	65,758
1995	132,304	66.6	124,900	7,404	66,280
1996	133,943	66.8	126,708	7,236	66,647
1997	136,297	67.1	129,558	6,739	66,837

U.S. Unemployment Rate

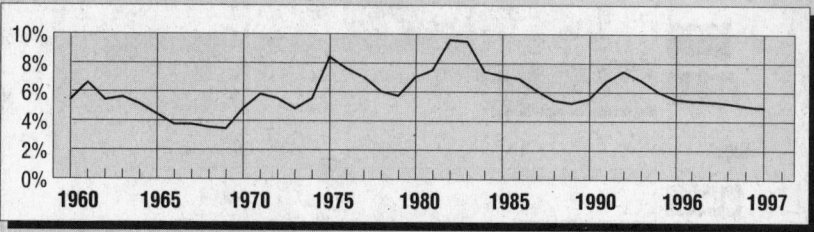

Persons 16 years of age and over

Year	% of labor force unemployed	Year	% of labor force unemployed	Year	% of labor force unemployed	Year	% of labor force unemployed
1960	5.5	1970	4.9	1980	7.1	1990	5.6
1961	6.7	1971	5.9	1981	7.6	1991	6.8
1962	5.5	1972	5.6	1982	9.7	1992	7.5
1963	5.7	1973	4.9	1983	9.6	1993	6.9
1964	5.2	1974	5.6	1984	7.5	1994	6.1
1965	4.5	1975	8.5	1985	7.2	1995	5.6
1966	3.8	1976	7.7	1986	7.0	1996	5.4
1967	3.8	1977	7.1	1987	6.2	1997	4.9
1968	3.6	1978	6.1	1988	5.5		
1969	3.5	1979	5.8	1989	5.3		

Source: U.S. Bureau of Labor Statistics

Age, Color and Unemployment

Annual Unemployment Rate in the U.S., by Age, Race, and Hispanic Origin

Percent of labor force unemployed, 1997

☐ Total unemployed 16 years and older   ■ 16–19 years old

Total

	0	10	20	30	40

4.9%
16.0%

Men

	0	10	20	30	40

4.9%
16.9%

Women

	0	10	20	30	40

5.0%
15.0%

White

	0	10	20	30	40

4.2%
13.6%

Black

	0	10	20	30	40

10.0%
32.4%

Hispanic

	0	10	20	30	40

7.7%
21.6%

Source: U.S Bureau of Labor Statistics

Adding to economic fears was mounting political instability in key nations, from Russian President Boris Yeltsin's travails to a sharp electoral setback to Japan's ruling Liberal Democratic Party to President Clinton's sex scandal troubles. At a time of world economic crisis, the leaders charged with attempting to address the troubles were weakened or preoccupied.

In the summer of 1998, Washington, D.C.,

The Dwindling Dollar

The purchasing power of the dollar, based on changes in the Consumer Price Index. The base period is 1982–1984, and the data show how much more a dollar would have purchased in earlier years and how much less it would have bought in later years.

Annual Average Purchasing Power of the Dollar as Measured by CPI*
(1982–1984=$1.00)

Year		Year		Year	
1950	$4.151	1966	$3.080	1982	$1.035
1951	3.846	1967	2.993	1983	1.003
1952	3.765	1968	2.873	1984	0.961
1953	3.735	1969	2.726	1985	0.928
1954	3.717	1970	2.574	1986	0.913
1955	3.732	1971	2.466	1987	0.880
1956	3.678	1972	2.391	1988	0.846
1957	3.549	1973	2.251	1989	0.807
1958	3.457	1974	2.029	1990	0.766
1959	3.427	1975	1.859	1991	0.734
1960	3.373	1976	1.757	1992	0.713
1961	3.340	1977	1.649	1993	0.692
1962	3.304	1978	1.532	1994	0.675
1963	3.265	1979	1.380	1995	0.656
1964	3.220	1980	1.215	1996	0.638
1965	3.166	1981	1.098	1997	0.623

*Obtained by dividing the average price index for the 1982–84=100, CPI base period by the price index for a given period and expressing the result in dollars and cents. Annual figures are based on average of monthly data.
Source: U.S. Bureau of Labor Statistics

stationery stores sold a bumper sticker cheekily imploring: "Forget Paula Jones, How's Dow Jones?" The implication: as long as times were good, nobody cared about other problems. But in September, the Dow plunged nearly 300 points the day after Congress received an impeachment report against Mr. Clinton. Just as everything for the U.S. economy seemed to be going right a year earlier, all of a sudden even seemingly unrelated matters appeared to become threats.

**Jacob M. Schlesinger,
economics reporter for
The Wall Street Journal**

Consumer Price Index
All Urban Consumers (CPI-U), Annual % Change

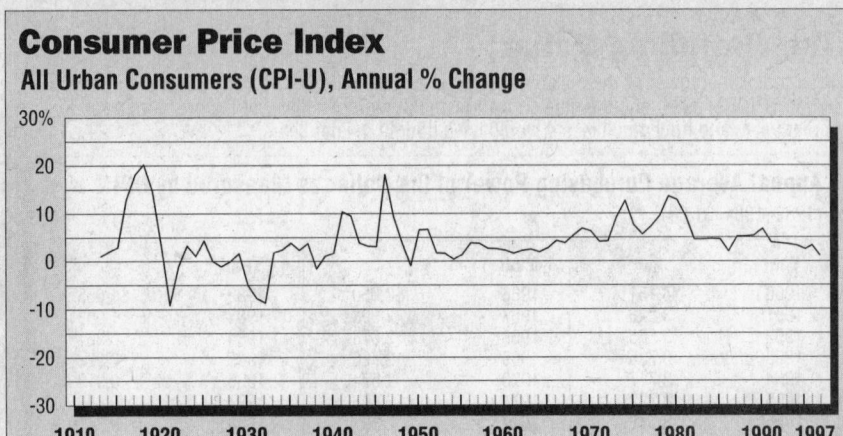

Year	% change	Year	% change	Year	% change	Year	% change
1914	1.0%	1936	1.4%	1958	1.8%	1980	12.5%
1915	2.0	1937	2.9	1959	1.7	1981	8.9
1916	12.6	1938	-2.8	1960	1.4	1982	3.8
1917	18.1	1939	0.0	1961	0.7	1983	3.8
1918	20.4	1940	0.7	1962	1.3	1984	3.9
1919	14.5	1941	9.9	1963	1.6	1985	3.8
1920	2.6	1942	9.0	1964	1.0	1986	1.1
1921	-10.8	1943	3.0	1965	1.9	1987	4.4
1922	-2.3	1944	2.3	1966	3.5	1988	4.4
1923	2.4	1945	2.2	1967	3.0	1989	4.6
1924	0.0	1946	18.1	1968	4.7	1990	6.1
1925	3.5	1947	8.8	1969	6.2	1991	3.1
1926	-1.1	1948	3.0	1970	5.6	1992	2.9
1927	-2.3	1949	-2.1	1971	3.3	1993	2.7
1928	-1.2	1950	5.9	1972	3.4	1994	2.7
1929	0.6	1951	6.0	1973	8.7	1995	2.5
1930	-6.4	1952	0.8	1974	12.3	1996	3.3
1931	-9.3	1953	0.7	1975	6.9	1997	1.7
1932	-10.3	1954	-0.7	1976	4.9		
1933	0.8	1955	0.4	1977	6.7		
1934	1.5	1956	3.0	1978	9.0		
1935	3.0	1957	2.9	1979	13.3		

Source: U.S. Bureau of Labor Statistics

Consumer Price Index

CPI-U, U.S. City Average, by Commodity and Service Group
(1982–84 = 100, unless otherwise noted)

Commodity and service group	Unadjusted indexes for December								
	1989	1990	1991	1992	1993	1994	1995	1996	1997
All items	126.1	133.8	137.9	141.9	145.8	149.7	153.5	158.6	161.3
Commodities	118.2	126.0	127.5	130.1	132.0	135.1	137.0	141.4	141.7
Food and beverages	127.2	133.9	137.3	139.5	143.3	147.2	150.3	156.6	159.1
Commodities less food and beverages	112.6	121.1	121.5	124.3	125.1	127.6	128.9	132.1	131.2
Nondurables less food and beverages	112.0	125.8	124.5	127.4	126.5	128.1	128.8	133.7	133.5
Apparel products	117.1	123.0	127.2	128.7	129.7	127.2	127.1	126.5	127.7
Nondurables less food, beverages, and apparel	112.0	130.1	126.0	129.6	127.7	131.5	132.7	140.5	139.5
Durables	113.5	114.5	117.2	120.1	123.3	126.9	129.0	129.9	128.0
Services	134.6	142.3	148.8	154.2	160.0	164.7	170.4	176.1	181.0
Rent of shelter*	140.9	148.4	154.2	158.7	163.5	168.3	174.2	179.3	185.3
Household services less rent of shelter*	119.0	122.2	127.8	131.4	134.9	135.9	138.6	143.4	145.7
Transportation services	138.6	150.0	153.7	159.2	166.9	171.1	176.3	184.1	186.0
Medical care services	154.1	169.3	182.8	195.6	207.1	218.2	227.8	235.0	241.8
Other services	145.1	154.5	164.1	172.8	181.6	188.9	197.3	205.0	213.1
Special indexes									
All items less food	125.8	133.7	138.1	142.5	146.4	150.2	154.2	159.0	161.8
Energy	93.2	110.1	101.9	103.9	102.4	104.7	103.3	112.2	108.4
All items less energy	130.6	137.4	142.8	147.1	151.7	155.7	160.2	164.8	168.3
All items less food and energy	131.5	138.3	144.4	149.2	153.9	157.9	162.7	167.0	170.7

Commodity and service group	Percent change from previous December								
	1989	1990	1991	1992	1993	1994	1995	1996	1997
All items	4.6	6.1	3.1	2.9	2.7	2.7	2.5	3.3	1.7
Commodities	4.1	6.6	1.2	2.0	1.5	2.3	1.4	3.2	0.2
Food and beverages	5.5	5.3	2.5	1.6	2.7	2.7	2.1	4.2	1.6
Commodities less food and beverages	3.3	7.5	0.3	2.3	0.6	2.0	1.0	2.5	-0.7
Nondurables less food and beverages	4.8	12.3	-1.0	2.3	-0.7	1.3	0.5	3.8	-0.1
Apparel products	0.7	5.0	3.4	1.2	0.8	-1.9	-0.1	-0.5	0.9
Nondurables less food, beverages, and apparel	7.2	16.2	-3.2	2.9	-1.5	3.0	0.9	5.9	-0.7
Durables	1.2	0.9	2.4	2.5	2.7	2.9	1.7	0.7	-1.5
Services	5.1	5.7	4.6	3.6	3.8	2.9	3.5	3.3	2.8
Rent of shelter*	4.9	5.3	3.9	2.9	3.0	2.9	3.5	2.9	3.3
Household services less rent of shelter*	2.4	2.7	4.6	2.8	2.7	0.7	2.0	3.5	1.6
Transportation services	4.9	8.2	2.5	3.6	4.8	2.5	3.0	4.4	1.0
Medical care services	8.6	9.9	8.0	7.0	5.9	5.4	4.4	3.2	2.9
Other services	6.5	6.5	6.2	5.3	5.1	4.0	4.4	3.9	4.0
Special indexes									
All items less food	4.5	6.3	3.3	3.2	2.7	2.6	2.7	3.1	1.8
Energy	5.1	18.1	-7.4	2.0	-1.4	2.2	-1.3	8.6	-3.4
All items less energy	4.6	5.2	3.9	3.0	3.1	2.6	2.9	2.9	2.1
All items less food and energy	4.4	5.2	4.4	3.3	3.2	2.6	3.0	2.6	2.2

*Indexes on a December 1982 = 100 base.

Consumer Price Index

CPI-U, U.S. City Average, by Selected Expenditure Categories

Expenditure category	Percent change from previous December								
	1989	1990	1991	1992	1993	1994	1995	1996	1997
Food and beverages	5.5	5.3	2.5	1.6	2.7	2.7	2.1	4.2	1.6
Food	5.6	5.3	1.9	1.5	2.9	2.9	2.1	4.3	1.5
Food at home	6.2	5.8	1.3	1.5	3.5	3.5	2.0	4.9	1.0
Food away from home	4.6	4.5	2.9	1.4	1.9	1.9	2.2	3.1	2.6
Alcoholic beverages	4.8	4.2	9.9	2.9	1.5	1.0	2.0	3.6	2.2
Housing	3.9	4.5	3.4	2.6	2.7	2.2	3.0	2.9	2.4
Shelter	4.9	5.2	3.9	2.9	3.0	3.0	3.5	2.9	3.4
Fuel and other utilities	3.2	4.0	2.9	2.3	2.5	0.2	1.4	4.6	0.5
Household furnishings and operation	1.0	1.8	2.3	1.6	1.8	0.4	2.5	1.0	0.1
Housefurnishings	-0.4	0.6	0.9	1.5	1.5	0.0	0.7	-0.1	-1.4
Housekeeping supplies	5.6	3.2	1.8	-0.2	1.9	0.8	5.2	1.1	1.4
Housekeeping services	1.5	4.0	5.8	3.8	2.2	1.4	4.5	3.3	2.4
Apparel and upkeep	1.0	5.1	3.4	1.4	0.9	-1.6	0.1	-0.2	1.0
Apparel products	0.7	5.0	3.4	1.2	0.8	-1.9	-0.1	-0.5	0.9
Apparel services	3.6	6.8	3.4	3.3	2.7	1.7	0.8	2.4	1.4
Transportation	4.0	10.4	-1.5	3.0	2.4	3.8	1.5	4.4	-1.4
Private	3.9	9.8	-1.4	2.7	1.5	4.9	1.3	3.7	-1.2
New vehicles	2.4	2.0	3.2	2.3	3.3	3.3	1.9	1.8	-0.9
Used cars	-0.4	-2.2	2.6	7.4	8.0	8.8	4.4	-1.6	-4.9
Motor fuel	6.8	36.5	-16.0	1.8	-5.4	5.9	-4.0	12.7	-6.2
Automobile maintenance and repair	4.4	4.4	4.5	3.5	3.1	2.8	2.5	3.1	2.6
Public transportation	4.1	17.2	-3.0	5.6	11.6	-6.2	3.1	11.2	-2.9
Airline fares	5.3	22.7	-6.0	6.6	17.0	-9.5	1.8	14.7	-4.8
Other intercity transportation	1.7	6.6	2.4	0.1	-2.8	2.3	0.8	1.7	0.7
Intracity public transportation	2.1	7.7	3.8	5.0	2.8	1.0	7.6	5.8	1.1
Medical care	8.5	9.6	7.9	6.6	5.4	4.9	3.9	3.0	2.8
Medical care products	8.2	8.4	7.5	5.2	3.1	3.0	1.8	2.6	2.3
Prescription drugs	9.5	9.9	9.4	5.7	3.3	3.3	2.0	3.2	2.5
Nonprescription drugs and medical supplies	5.8	5.5	3.6	3.9	2.7	2.3	1.4	1.3	1.7
Medical care services	8.6	9.9	8.0	7.0	5.9	5.4	4.4	3.2	2.9
Professional medical services	6.5	6.7	6.1	5.7	4.5	4.6	4.0	3.5	3.1
Hospital and related services	11.3	11.3	8.9	8.8	7.6	5.5	4.6	4.1	3.2
Entertainment	5.1	4.3	3.9	2.8	2.8	2.3	3.3	2.9	1.4
Entertainment products	3.5	3.0	3.5	1.8	1.9	1.8	2.9	2.4	-0.1
Entertainment services	6.8	5.4	4.4	3.7	3.5	2.7	3.7	3.4	2.5
Other goods and services	8.2	7.6	8.0	6.5	2.7	4.2	4.3	3.6	5.2
Tobacco and smoking products	14.7	10.8	11.1	8.1	-5.9	3.0	2.7	2.7	7.2
Personal care	3.8	4.2	2.5	2.9	2.5	1.9	2.1	1.1	2.3
Personal and educational expenses	7.2	7.5	8.4	6.9	6.5	5.4	5.5	4.6	5.2
College tuition	8.1	8.2	12.1	10.0	7.9	6.3	5.7	5.3	4.6

Source: U.S. Bureau of Labor Statistics

CPI Market Basket

Percentage weight given to different goods and services in the Consumer Price Index.

Housing 39.6%

Food and drinks 16.3%

Transportation 17.6%

Other 4.3%

5.5%

6.1%

4.9%

5.6%

Medical care

Apparel and Upkeep

Entertainment

Education and Communication

Source: U.S. Bureau of Labor Statistics

Producer Price Trend

Annual Percent Changes for Major Categories of the Producer Price Index, by Stage of Processing

Index	Annual percent changes						
	1991	1992	1993	1994	1995	1996	1997
Finished goods							
Total	-0.1	1.6	0.2	1.7	2.3	2.8	-1.2
Foods	-1.5	1.6	2.4	1.1	1.9	3.4	-0.8
Energy	-9.6	-0.3	-4.1	3.5	1.1	11.7	-6.4
Other	3.1	2.0	0.4	1.6	2.6	0.6	0.0
Intermediate materials, supplies, and components							
Total	-2.6	1.0	1.0	4.4	3.3	0.7	-0.8
Foods	-0.2	-0.5	5.5	-4.5	10.3	2.1	-1.7
Energy	-11.6	0.7	-4.2	2.9	1.1	11.2	-7.0
Other	-0.8	1.2	1.6	5.2	3.2	-0.9	0.3
Crude materials for further processing							
Total	-11.6	3.3	0.1	-0.5	5.5	14.7	-11.3
Foods	-5.8	3.0	7.2	-9.4	12.9	-1.0	-4.0
Energy	-16.6	2.3	-12.3	-0.1	3.7	51.2	-23.1
Other	-7.6	5.7	10.7	17.3	-4.2	-5.5	0.0

Source: U.S. Bureau of Labor Statistics

Index of Leading Economic Indicators

The index of leading economic indicators is based on 10 different measures and is considered a signal to the direction of the U.S. economy.

Leading Index (1992=100)				Leading Index – Percent change from preceding quarter			
	IQ	IIQ	IIIQ	IVQ	IQ	IIQ	IIIQ	IVQ

	IQ	IIQ	IIIQ	IVQ	IQ	IIQ	IIIQ	IVQ
1988	100.2	100.5	100.3	100.2	0.1	0.3	-0.2	-0.1
1989	100.0	99.5	99.5	99.6	-0.2	-0.5	0.0	0.1
1990	99.8	99.7	99.2	98.1	0.2	-0.1	-0.5	-1.1
1991	98.2	99.1	99.6	99.3	0.1	0.9	0.5	-0.3
1992	99.7	99.9	99.9	100.5	0.4	0.2	0.0	0.6
1993	100.5	100.3	100.3	100.7	0.0	-0.2	0.0	0.4
1994	101.1	101.3	101.3	101.4	0.4	0.2	0.0	0.1
1995	100.9	100.4	100.8	101.0	-0.5	-0.5	0.4	0.2
1996	101.1	102.0	102.3	102.5	0.1	0.9	0.3	0.2
1997	103.2	103.5	104.1	104.5	0.7	0.3	0.6	0.4
1998	104.9	105.2			0.4	0.3		

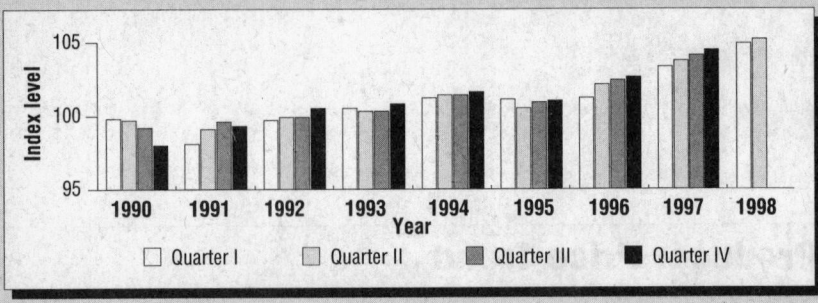

Note: Quarterly data are averages of monthly figures.
Source: Conference Board

Leading Index Components

		Factor
1	Average weekly hours, manufacturing	.222
2	Average weekly initial claims for unemployment insurance	.025
3	Manufacturers' new orders, consumer goods and materials	.047
4	Vendor performance, slower deliveries diffusion index	.026
5	Manufacturers' new orders, nondefense capital goods	.012
6	Building permits, new private housing units	.017
7	Stock prices, 500 common stocks	.031
8	Money supply, M2	.293
9	Interest rate spread, 10-year Treasury bonds less federal funds	.310
10	Index of consumer expectations	.017

Source: Conference Board

Corporate Profits

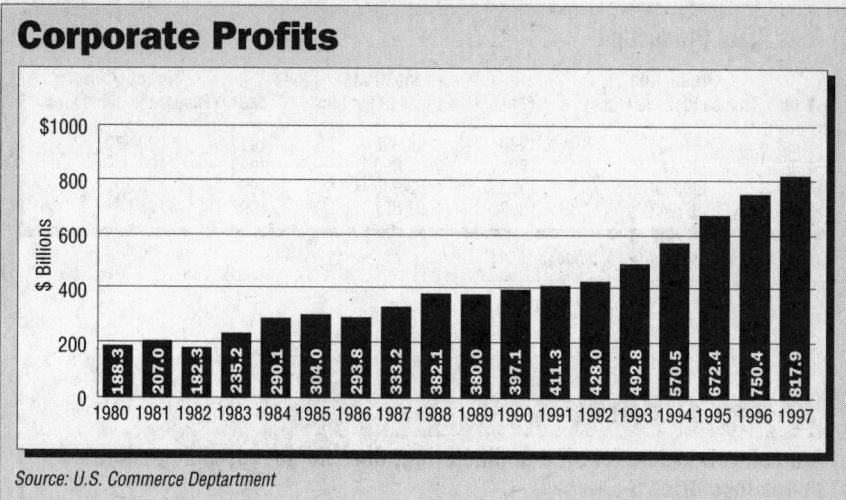

Year	$ Billions
1980	188.3
1981	207.0
1982	182.3
1983	235.2
1984	290.1
1985	304.0
1986	293.8
1987	333.2
1988	382.1
1989	380.0
1990	397.1
1991	411.3
1992	428.0
1993	492.8
1994	570.5
1995	672.4
1996	750.4
1997	817.9

Source: U.S. Commerce Deptartment

Industrial Production and Capacity Utilization

Industrial Production

Annual % Change by Year:

Year	Annual % Change
1985	1.6
1986	1.1
1987	4.6
1988	4.5
1989	1.8
1990	-0.2
1991	-2.0
1992	3.1
1993	3.6
1994	5.4
1995	4.9
1996	3.5
1997	5.0

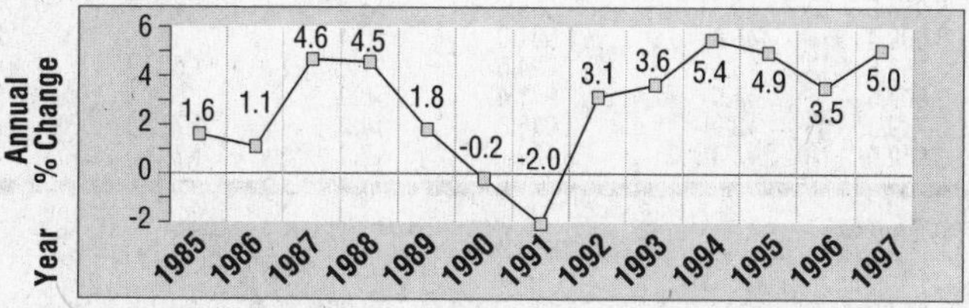

Industrial Capacity Utilization

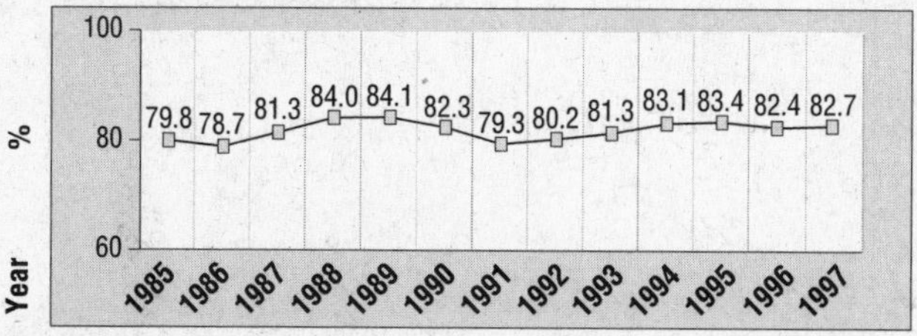

Year	%
1985	79.8
1986	78.7
1987	81.3
1988	84.0
1989	84.1
1990	82.3
1991	79.3
1992	80.2
1993	81.3
1994	83.1
1995	83.4
1996	82.4
1997	82.7

Source: Federal Reserve System

Raw Steel Production

Year	Production (Thousands of net tons)	Year	Production (Thousands of net tons)	Year	Production (Thousands of net tons)
1986	81,606	1990	98,906	1994	100,579
1987	89,151	1991	87,896	1995	104,930
1988	99,924	1992	92,949	1996	105,309
1989	97,943	1993	97,877	1997	108,561

Source: American Iron & Steel Institute

Factory Orders

Annual new orders for all manufacturing, durable goods, and nondurable goods industries ($ billions)

Year	All manufacturing Amount	% change	Durable goods Amount	% change	Nondurable goods Amount	% change
1987	$2,512.7	+7.3	$1,329.7	+6.9	$1,183.0	+7.7
1988	2,739.2	+9.0	1,464.9	+10.2	1,274.3	+7.7
1989	2,874.9	+5.0	1,512.7	+3.3	1,362.2	+6.9
1990	2,934.1	+2.1	1,507.0	-0.4	1,427.1	+4.8
1991	2,865.7	-2.3	1,438.2	-4.6	1,427.5	–
1992	2,978.5	+3.9	1,515.7	+5.4	1,462.9	+2.5
1993	3,092.4	+3.8	1,597.0	+5.4	1,495.4	+2.2
1994	3,356.8	+8.6	1,794.5	+12.4	1,562.3	+4.5
1995	3,607.6	+7.5	1,941.4	+8.2	1,666.2	+6.7
1996	3,749.3	+3.9	2,036.5	+4.9	1,712.8	+2.8
1997	3,952.0	+5.4	2,180.7	+7.1	1,771.3	+3.4

Source: U.S. Census Bureau

Capital Spending

Capital Expenditures for Companies with Five or More Employees

	1993		1994		1995		1996	
	$ millions	%	$ millions	%	$ millions	%	$ millions	%
Total structures	144,918	29.6	168,101	30.6	183,111	30.5	196,317	30.5
Total equipment	338,444	69.1	376,340	68.5	417,736	69.5	446,630	69.5
Other	6,320	1.3	4,833	0.9	277	—	2	—
Total	489,682	100	549,274	100	601,124	100	642,949	100

Capital Expenditures for Structures and Equipment by Selected Industry Sectors, 1996 ($ billions)

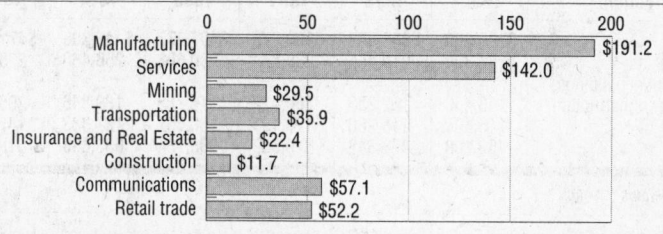

Manufacturing	$191.2
Services	$142.0
Mining	$29.5
Transportation	$35.9
Insurance and Real Estate	$22.4
Construction	$11.7
Communications	$57.1
Retail trade	$52.2

Source: U.S. Census Bureau

Worker Productivity

Changes in Productivity, or Output per Hour Worked, in Nonfarm Businesses

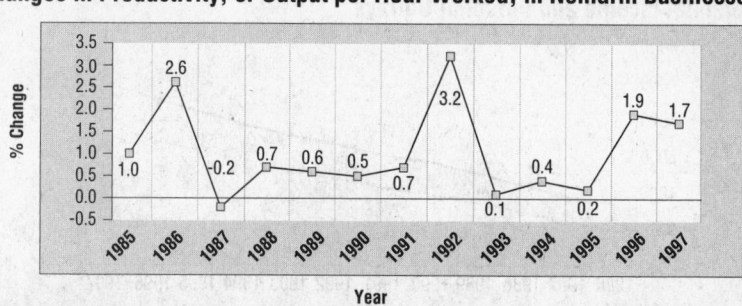

Year	% Change
1985	1.0
1986	2.6
1987	-0.2
1988	0.7
1989	0.6
1990	0.5
1991	0.7
1992	3.2
1993	0.1
1994	0.4
1995	0.2
1996	1.9
1997	1.7

Source: U.S. Bureau of Labor Statistics

Construction Spending

Value of New Construction Put in Place ($ millions)

Type of construction	1986	1987	1988	1989	1990	1991
Private	$345,300	$351,000	$360,900	$371,600	$361,100	$314,100
Residential	187,100	194,700	198,100	196,600	182,900	157,800
Nonresidential buildings and other construction	158,200	156,300	162,800	175,100	178,200	156,200
Public	84,600	90,600	94,700	98,200	107,500	110,100
Total	429,900	441,600	455,600	469,800	468,500	424,200

Type of construction	1992	1993	1994	1995	1996	1997
Private	$336,200	$362,688	$399,346	$407,477	$446,306	$471,159
Residential	187,800	210,455	238,874	230,688	256,460	265,610
Nonresidential buildings and other construction	148,400	152,233	160,472	176,788	189,846	205,548
Public	115,800	115,960	120,193	130,657	137,333	147,058
Total	452,100	478,648	519,539	538,134	583,638	618,217

Source: U.S. Census Bureau

Personal Income: Where It Goes

Personal Income and Personal Outlays

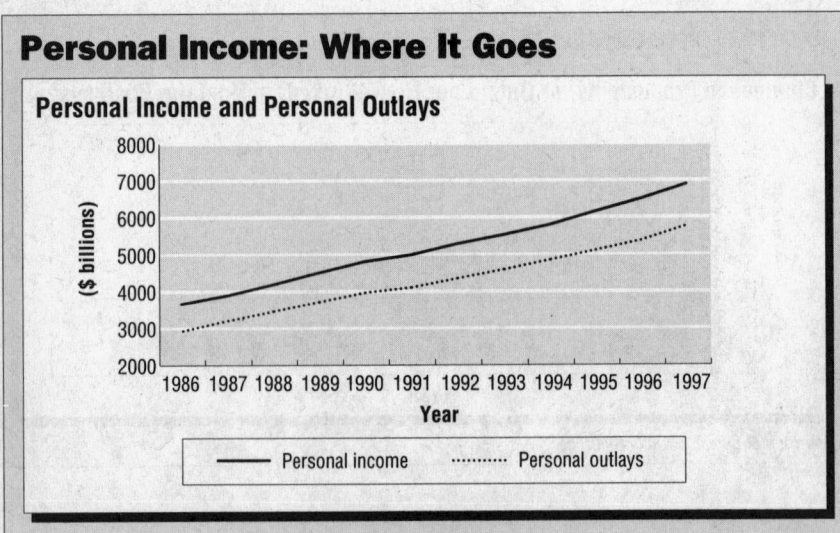

Source: U.S. Commerce Department, Bureau of Economic Analysis

U.S. Personal Income

Year	Personal income ($ billions)	Disposable personal income after taxes ($ billions)	Personal outlays ($ billions)	Personal savings ($ billions)
1986	3,658.4	3,198.5	2,991.1	207.4
1987	3,888.7	3,374.6	3,194.7	179.9
1988	4,184.6	3,652.6	3,451.7	200.9
1989	4,501.0	3,906.1	3,706.7	199.4
1990	4,804.2	4,179.4	3,958.1	221.3
1991	4,981.6	4,356.8	4,097.4	259.5
1992	5,277.2	4,626.7	4,341.0	285.6
1993	5,519.2	4,829.2	4,580.7	248.5
1994	5,757.9	5,018.9	4,842.1	176.8
1995	6,072.1	5,277.0	5,097.2	179.8
1996	6,425.2	5,534.7	5,376.2	158.5
1997	6,784.0	5,795.1	5,674.1	121.0

Source: U.S. Commerce Department, Bureau of Economic Analysis

Consumer Spending

Personal Consumption Expenditures
(In billions)

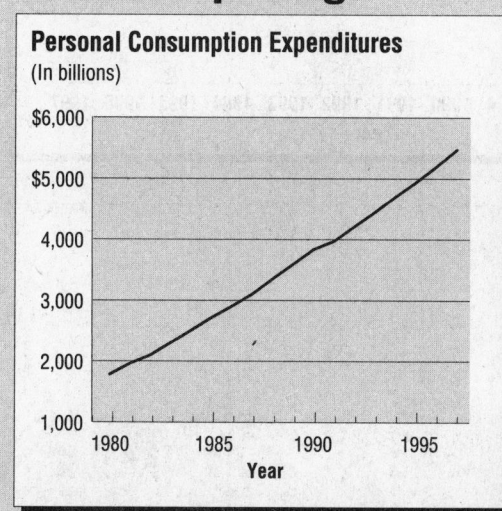

Year	Personal consumption expenditures (In billions)
1980	$1,760.4
1981	1,941.3
1982	2,076.8
1983	2,283.4
1984	2,492.3
1985	2,704.8
1986	2,892.7
1987	3,094.5
1988	3,349.7
1989	3,594.8
1990	3,839.3
1991	3,975.1
1992	4,219.8
1993	4,459.2
1994	4,717.0
1995	4,953.9
1996	5,215.7
1997	5,493.7

Source: U.S. Commerce Department, Bureau of Economic Analysis

Retail Sales

Retail Sales by Type of Business ($ millions)

	1986	1990	1995	1996	1997
Retail sales total	$1,449,636	$1,844,611	$2,329,310	$2,461,196	$2,566,209
Durable goods total	540,688	668,835	939,730	1,008,531	1,058,235
Nondurable goods total	908,948	1,175,776	1,389,580	1,452,665	1,507,974
Kind of business					
Building materials stores	$ 77,104	$ 94,640	$ 130,109	$ 140,250	$ 150,494
Automotive dealers	326,138	387,605	556,708	599,667	625,682
Furniture stores	75,714	91,545	130,348	137,897	146,679
General merchandise stores	169,397	215,514	297,962	313,231	331,496
Food stores	297,019	368,333	407,392	420,980	429,805
Gasoline service stations	102,093	138,504	149,555	157,645	158,693
Apparel and accessory stores	75,626	95,819	110,936	114,635	117,826
Eating and drinking places	139,415	190,149	222,081	228,172	236,159

Total Retail Sales ($ millions)

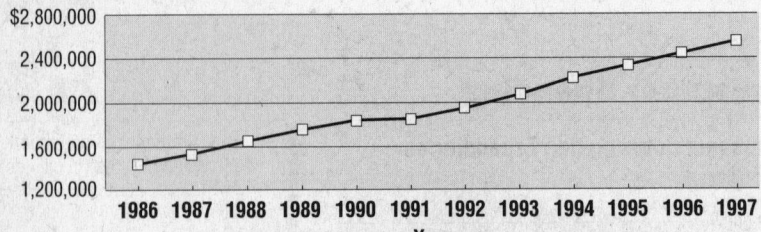

Source: U.S. Census Bureau

Consumer Confidence Index

Consumer confidence levels reflect people's feelings about general business conditions, employment opportunities and their own income prospects (1985=100).

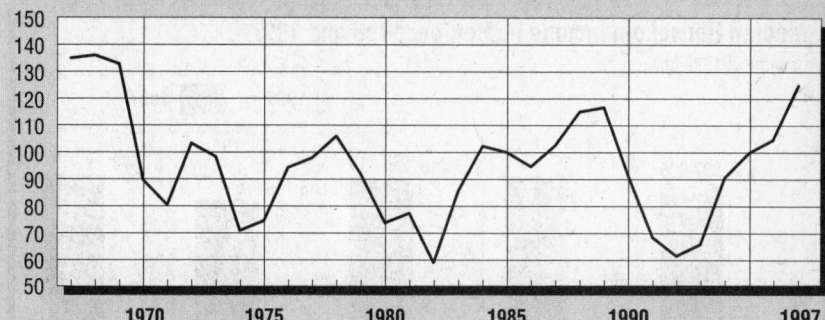

Year	Annual average	Year	Annual average	Year	Annual average
1967	135.0	1978	106.0	1989	116.8
1968	136.1	1979	91.9	1990	91.5
1969	132.9	1980	73.8	1991	68.5
1970	89.6	1981	77.4	1992	61.6
1971	80.4	1982	59.0	1993	65.9
1972	103.3	1983	85.7	1994	90.6
1973	98.3	1984	102.3	1995	100.0
1974	70.9	1985	100.0	1996	104.6
1975	74.5	1986	94.7	1997	125.4
1976	94.3	1987	102.6		
1977	97.9	1988	115.2		

Source: Conference Board

Making Up Lost Ground

Median household income, adjusted for inflation, is increasing, and has nearly caught up with the levels of the late 1980s.

Median Household Income by Region: 1996 and 1997

(Income in 1997 dollars)

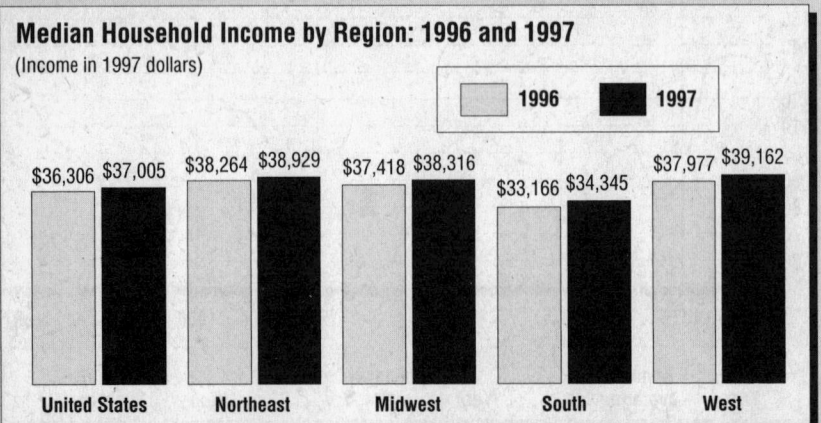

	1996	1997
United States	$36,306	$37,005
Northeast	$38,264	$38,929
Midwest	$37,418	$38,316
South	$33,166	$34,345
West	$37,977	$39,162

Median Household Income in 1997 Dollars, by Race and Hispanic Origin

Year	All races	White	Black	Hispanic origin
1967	$31,583	$32,936	$19,123	–
1968	32,964	34,322	20,239	–
1969	34,173	35,664	21,558	–
1970	33,942	35,353	21,518	–
1971	33,619	35,165	20,772	–
1972	35,053	36,774	21,465	$27,751
1973	35,745	37,462	22,052	27,693
1974	34,627	36,213	21,536	27,542
1975	33,699	35,241	21,156	25,317
1976	34,278	35,907	21,351	25,856
1977	34,467	36,245	21,388	27,039
1978	35,819	37,236	22,377	28,065
1979	35,703	37,433	21,978	28,287
1980	34,538	36,437	20,992	26,622
1981	33,978	35,900	20,145	27,255
1982	33,864	35,453	20,093	25,482
1983	33,869	35,508	20,100	25,451
1984	34,626	36,529	20,809	26,248
1985	35,229	37,154	22,105	26,051
1986	36,460	38,331	22,083	26,875
1987	36,820	38,794	22,142	27,319
1988	36,937	39,048	22,260	27,621
1989	37,415	39,356	23,406	28,374
1990	36,770	38,352	22,934	27,421
1991	35,501	37,201	22,162	26,739
1992	35,047	36,846	21,455	25,850
1993	34,700	36,610	21,696	25,420
1994	34,942	36,852	22,772	25,365
1995	35,887	37,667	23,583	24,075
1996	36,306	38,014	24,021	25,477
1997	37,005	38,972	25,050	26,628

Source: U.S. Census Bureau

The Rich Get Richer...

The top-earning households claim a very large share of the total household income in America.

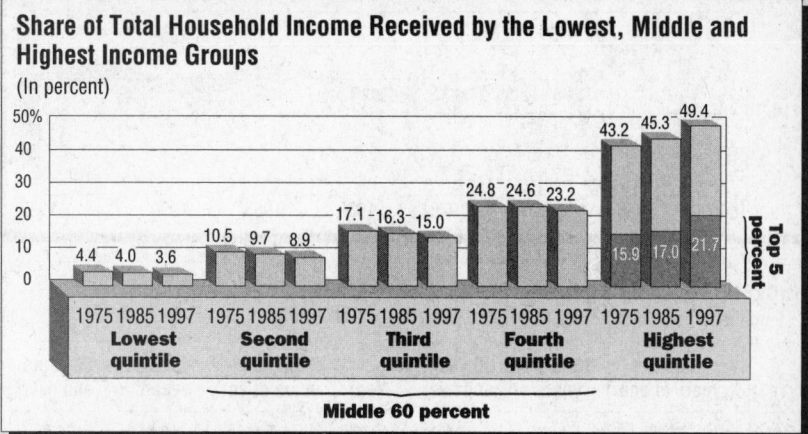

Share of Total Household Income Received by the Lowest, Middle and Highest Income Groups
(In percent)

Share of Total Income Received by Each Fifth and Top 5 Percent of Households
(Income in 1997 dollars)

	Upper limit of each fifth (dollars)				Lower limit of top 5 percent (dollars)	Share of aggregate income					
Year	Lowest	Second	Third	Fourth		Lowest	Second	Third	Fourth	Highest	Top 5 %
1980	$14,736	$27,498	$42,143	$61,821	$100,434	4.3	10.3	16.9	24.9	43.7	15.8
1981	14,536	26,781	41,677	61,635	100,290	4.2	10.2	16.8	25.0	43.8	15.6
1982	14,304	26,879	41,233	61,564	102,591	4.1	10.1	16.6	24.7	44.5	16.2
1983	14,503	27,029	41,443	62,682	104,099	4.1	10.0	16.5	24.7	44.7	16.4
1984	14,830	27,657	42,490	64,262	107,500	4.1	9.9	16.4	24.7	44.9	16.5
1985	14,916	28,120	43,290	65,347	109,282	4.0	9.7	16.3	24.6	45.3	17.0
1986	15,168	28,971	44,745	67,539	114,555	3.9	9.7	16.2	24.5	45.7	17.5
1987	15,259	28,963	45,211	68,330	114,339	3.8	9.6	16.1	24.3	46.2	18.2
1988	15,442	29,169	45,458	68,641	116,190	3.8	9.6	16.0	24.3	46.3	18.3
1989	15,657	29,770	45,755	69,520	118,757	3.8	9.5	15.8	24.0	46.8	18.9
1990	15,350	29,057	44,454	67,792	116,351	3.9	9.6	15.9	24.0	46.6	18.6
1991	14,834	28,282	43,684	66,887	113,599	3.8	9.6	15.9	24.2	46.5	18.1
1992	14,414	27,616	43,357	66,359	113,277	3.8	9.4	15.8	24.2	46.9	18.6
1993	14,403	27,412	43,088	66,977	116,225	3.6	9.0	15.1	23.5	48.9	21.0
1994	14,540	27,291	43,428	68,057	118,936	3.6	8.9	15.0	23.4	49.1	21.2
1995	15,165	28,344	44,234	68,585	119,006	3.7	9.1	15.2	23.3	48.7	21.0
1996	15,107	28,397	45,016	69,576	122,283	3.7	9.0	15.1	23.3	49.0	21.4
1997	15,400	29,200	46,000	71,500	126,550	3.6	8.9	15.0	23.2	49.4	21.7

Source: U.S. Census Bureau.

Poverty's Burden

Percentage of All Persons Below Poverty Level

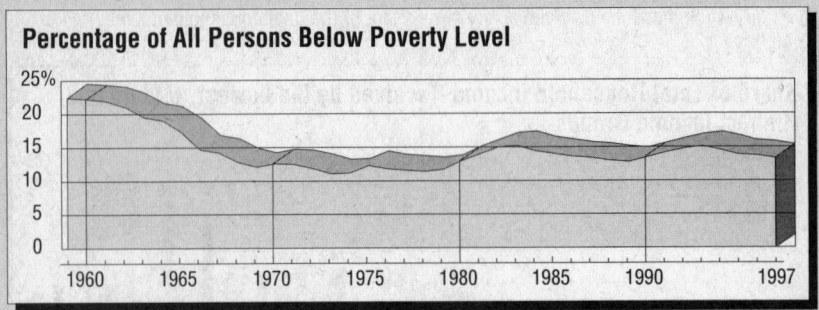

Poverty Rates by Age
(Percent)

Year	Under 18 years of age	18 to 64 years	65 years and over	Year	Under 18 years of age	18 to 64 years	65 years and over
1959	27.3	17.0	35.2	1979	16.4	8.9	15.2
1960	26.9	—	—	1980	18.3	10.1	15.7
1961	25.6	—	—	1981	20.0	11.1	15.3
1962	25.0	—	—	1982	21.9	12.0	14.6
1963	23.1	—	—	1983	22.3	12.4	13.8
1964	23.0	—	—	1984	21.5	11.7	12.4
1965	21.0	—	—	1985	20.7	11.3	12.6
1966	17.6	10.5	28.5	1986	20.5	10.8	12.4
1967	16.6	10.0	29.5	1987	20.3	10.6	12.5
1968	15.6	9.0	25.0	1988	19.5	10.5	12.0
1969	14.0	8.7	25.3	1989	19.6	10.2	11.4
1970	15.1	9.0	24.6	1990	20.6	10.7	12.2
1971	15.3	9.3	21.6	1991	21.8	11.4	12.4
1972	15.1	8.8	18.6	1992	22.3	11.9	12.9
1973	14.4	8.3	16.3	1993	22.7	12.4	12.2
1974	15.4	8.3	14.6	1994	21.8	11.9	11.7
1975	17.1	9.2	15.3	1995	20.8	11.4	10.5
1976	16.0	9.0	15.0	1996	20.5	11.4	10.8
1977	16.2	8.8	14.1	1997	19.9	10.9	10.5
1978	15.9	8.7	14.0				

Poverty Rates by Age: 1959–1997

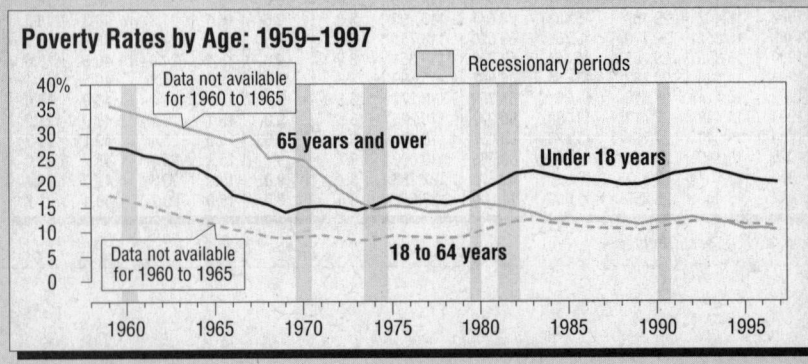

Source: U.S. Census Bureau

Persons Below Poverty Level by Race and Hispanic Origin
(Numbers in thousands)

Year	Total Number	Total Percent	White Number	White Percent	Black Number	Black Percent	Hispanic Origin* Number	Hispanic Origin* Percent
1959	39,490	22.4%	28,484	18.1%	9,927	55.1%	–	–
1960	39,851	22.2	28,309	17.8	–	–	–	–
1965	33,185	17.3	22,496	13.3	–	–	–	–
1966	28,510	14.7	19,290	11.3	8,867	41.8	–	–
1970	25,420	12.6	17,484	9.9	7,548	33.5	–	–
1975	25,877	12.3	17,770	9.7	7,545	31.3	2,991	26.9%
1980	29,272	13.0	19,699	10.2	8,579	32.5	3,491	25.7
1985	33,064	14.0	22,860	11.4	8,926	31.3	5,236	29.0
1990	33,585	13.5	22,326	10.7	9,837	31.9	6,006	28.1
1991	35,708	14.2	23,747	11.3	10,242	32.7	6,339	28.7
1992	38,014	14.8	25,259	11.9	10,827	33.4	7,592	29.6
1993	39,265	15.1	26,226	12.2	10,877	33.1	8,126	30.6
1994	38,059	14.5	25,379	11.7	10,196	30.6	8,416	30.7
1995	36,425	13.8	24,423	11.2	9,872	29.3	8,574	30.3
1996	36,529	13.7	24,650	11.2	9,694	28.4	8,697	29.4
1997	35,574	13.3	24,396	11.0	9,116	26.5	8,308	27.1

*Persons of Hispanic origin may be of any race.

Persons in Poverty by Region: 1996 and 1997

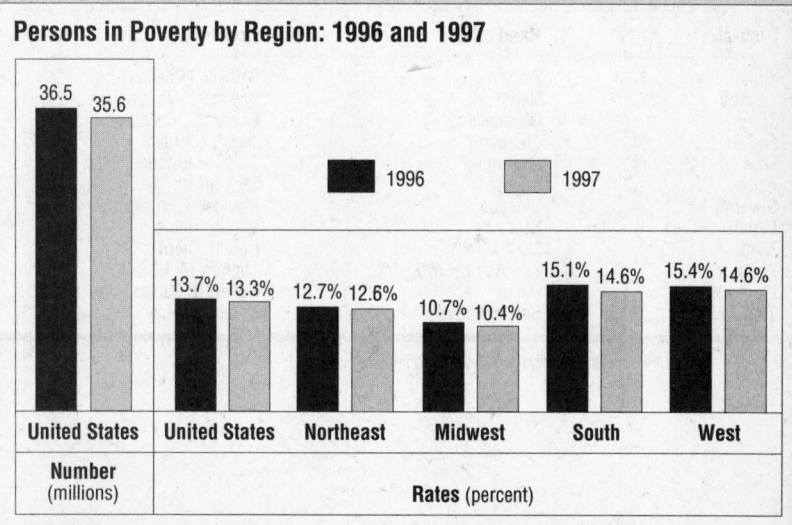

	United States	United States	Northeast	Midwest	South	West
1996	36.5	13.7%	12.7%	10.7%	15.1%	15.4%
1997	35.6	13.3%	12.6%	10.4%	14.6%	14.6%

Number (millions) — Rates (percent)

Poverty Thresholds by Size of Family in 1997

	One person	Two persons	Three persons	Four persons	Five persons	Six persons
(In dollars)	$8,183	$10,473	$12,802	$16,400	$19,380	$21,886

Source: U.S. Census Bureau

Members of the Board of Governors of the Federal Reserve System

Name	Appointed by President	Term expires
Alan Greenspan, Chairman	Reagan and Bush	January 31, 2006*
Alice Rivlin, Vice Chairman	Clinton	January 31, 2010**
Laurence Meyer	Clinton	January 31, 2002
Edward W. Kelley Jr.	Reagan and Bush	January 31, 2004
Edward M. Gramlich	Clinton	January 31, 2008
Roger W. Ferguson Jr.	Clinton	January 31, 2000

*In 1996, Mr. Greenspan was reappointed as chairman until the year 2000, but his term as a Fed governor runs until 2006. **Ms. Rivlin was named vice chairman for a four-year term, ending in 2000, but her term as a Fed governor continues until 2010.

Presidents of the Federal Reserve Banks

District	Head office	President*
First	Boston	Cathy E. Minehan
Second	New York	William J. McDonough
Third	Philadelphia	Edward G. Boehne
Fourth	Cleveland	Jerry L. Jordan
Fifth	Richmond	J. Alfred Broaddus, Jr.
Sixth	Atlanta	Jack Guynn
Seventh	Chicago	Michael H. Moskow
Eighth	St. Louis	William Poole
Ninth	Minneapolis	Gary H. Stern
Tenth	Kansas City, MO	Thomas M. Hoenig
Eleventh	Dallas	Robert D. McTeer, Jr.
Twelfth	San Francisco	Robert T. Parry

*All the presidents are serving five-year terms that end Feb. 28, 2001.

The Money Supply

Money Stock and Liquid Assets
(Billions of dollars, seasonally adjusted)

Year (December)	M1	M2	M3	L
1980	$408.9	$1,601.1	$1,992.2	$2,330.0
1981	436.8	1,756.2	2,240.9	2,601.8
1982	474.7	1,910.9	2,442.3	2,846.0
1983	521.2	2,127.7	2,684.9	3,150.7
1984	552.3	2,312.3	2,979.8	3,518.7
1985	619.9	2,497.7	3,198.4	3,827.1
1986	724.4	2,734.0	3,486.4	4,122.4
1987	749.7	2,832.7	3,672.7	4,340.0
1988	787.0	2,996.4	3,913.1	4,663.7
1989	794.2	3,161.0	4,066.3	4,893.2
1990	825.8	3,279.6	4,126.8	4,977.5
1991	897.3	3,379.9	4,182.1	5,008.0
1992	1,025.0	3,434.7	4,193.5	5,081.4
1993	1,129.9	3,487.5	4,258.9	5,173.0
1994	1,150.7	3,503.0	4,333.6	5,315.8
1995	1,128.7	3,651.2	4,595.6	5,702.2
1996	1,082.8	3,826.1	4,935.5	6,088.3
1997	1,076.0	4,040.2	5,382.6	6,626.5

M1: Sum of currency, demand deposits, travelers checks, and other checkable deposits.
M2: M1 plus retail money-market mutual fund balances, savings deposits (including money-market deposit accounts) and small time deposits.
M3: M2 plus large time deposits, repurchase agreements, Euro-dollars, and institution-only money-market mutual fund balances.
L: M3 plus other liquid assets.
Source: Federal Reserve System

Key Interest Rates (Average of daily figures)

Year	Discount rate	Federal funds rate	Prime rate
1977	5.46%	5.54%	6.83%
1978	7.46	7.94	9.06
1979	10.29	11.20	12.67
1980	11.77	13.35	15.26
1981	13.42	16.39	18.87
1982	11.01	12.24	14.85
1983	8.50	9.09	10.79
1984	8.80	10.23	12.04
1985	7.69	8.10	9.93
1986	6.32	6.80	8.33
1987	5.66	6.66	8.21
1988	6.20	7.57	9.32
1989	6.93	9.21	10.87
1990	6.98	8.10	10.01
1991	5.45	5.69	8.46
1992	3.25	3.52	6.25
1993	3.00	3.02	6.00
1994	3.60	4.21	7.15
1995	5.21	5.83	8.83
1996	5.02	5.30	8.27
1997	5.00	5.46	8.44

Source: Federal Reserve System

U.S. International Trade

U.S. Balance of Trade (In millions)

Year	Exports		Imports		Balance		
	Goods	Services	Goods	Services	Goods	Services	Total
1980	224,250	47,584	-249,750	-41,491	-25,500	6,093	-19,407
1981	237,044	57,354	-265,067	-45,503	-28,023	11,852	-16,172
1982	211,157	64,079	-247,642	-51,749	-36,485	12,329	-24,156
1983	201,799	64,307	-268,901	-54,973	-67,102	9,335	-57,767
1984	219,926	71,168	-332,418	-67,748	-112,492	3,419	-109,073
1985	215,915	73,155	-338,088	-72,862	-122,173	294	-121,880
1986	223,344	86,312	-368,425	-81,836	-145,081	4,476	-140,605
1987	250,208	98,553	-409,765	-92,349	-159,557	6,204	-153,353
1988	320,230	111,024	-447,189	-99,965	-126,959	11,059	-115,900
1989	362,120	127,142	-477,365	-104,185	-115,245	22,957	-92,288
1990	389,307	147,824	-498,337	-120,019	-109,030	27,805	-81,225
1991	416,913	164,236	-490,981	-121,195	-74,068	43,041	-31,027
1992	440,352	177,154	-536,458	-120,255	-96,106	56,899	-39,207
1993	456,832	186,711	-589,441	-126,403	-132,609	60,308	-72,301
1994	502,398	197,248	-668,590	-135,472	-166,192	61,776	-104,416
1995	575,871	218,739	-749,431	-147,036	-173,560	71,703	-101,857
1996	612,069	236,764	-803,239	-156,634	-191,170	80,130	-111,040
1997	678,150	253,220	-877,125	-167,929	-198,975	85,291	-113,684

Source: U.S. Commerce Department

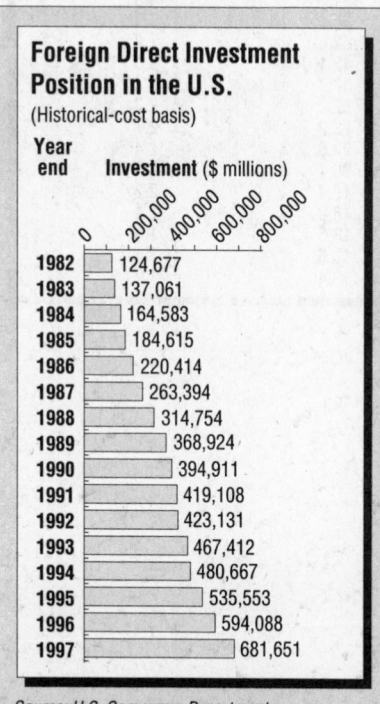

Foreign Direct Investment Position in the U.S.
(Historical-cost basis)

Year end — Investment ($ millions)

Year end	Investment
1982	124,677
1983	137,061
1984	164,583
1985	184,615
1986	220,414
1987	263,394
1988	314,754
1989	368,924
1990	394,911
1991	419,108
1992	423,131
1993	467,412
1994	480,667
1995	535,553
1996	594,088
1997	681,651

Source: U.S. Commerce Department

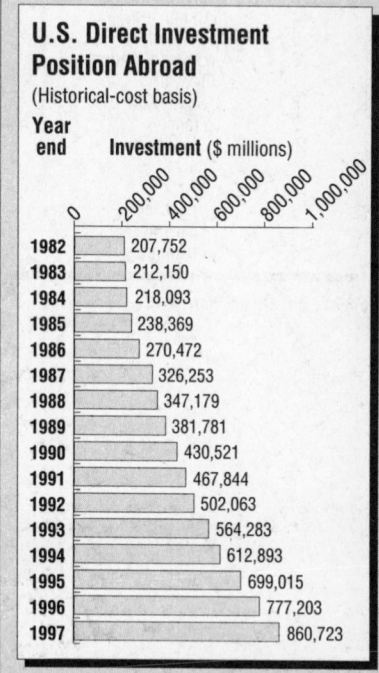

U.S. Direct Investment Position Abroad
(Historical-cost basis)

Year end — Investment ($ millions)

Year end	Investment
1982	207,752
1983	212,150
1984	218,093
1985	238,369
1986	270,472
1987	326,253
1988	347,179
1989	381,781
1990	430,521
1991	467,844
1992	502,063
1993	564,283
1994	612,893
1995	699,015
1996	777,203
1997	860,723

Source: U.S. Commerce Department

Major U.S. Trading Partners

Top 15 Trading Partners - Exports of Goods in 1997

Rank	Country	($ billions)	% of total
1	Canada	$151.8	22.0%
2	Mexico	71.4	10.4
3	Japan	65.5	9.5
4	United Kingdom	36.4	5.3
5	South Korea	25.0	3.6
6	Germany	24.5	3.6
7	Taiwan	20.4	3.0
8	Netherlands	19.8	2.9
9	Singapore	17.7	2.6
10	France	16.0	2.3
11	Brazil	15.9	2.3
12	Hong Kong	15.1	2.2
13	Belgium	13.4	1.9
14	China	12.9	1.9
15	Australia	12.1	1.8

Top 15 Trading Partners - Imports of Goods in 1997

Rank	Country	($ billions)	% of total
1	Canada	$168.2	19.3%
2	Japan	121.7	14.0
3	Mexico	85.9	9.9
4	China	62.6	7.2
5	Germany	43.1	5.0
6	United Kingdom	32.7	3.8
7	Taiwan	32.6	3.7
8	South Korea	23.2	2.7
9	France	20.6	2.4
10	Singapore	20.1	2.3
11	Italy	19.4	2.2
12	Malaysia	18.0	2.1
13	Venezuela	13.5	1.6
14	Thailand	12.6	1.4
15	Philippines	10.4	1.2

Source: U.S. Census Bureau

BUSINESS & INDUSTRY

There were the big mergers: *American Home Products bought Monsanto for $35 billion, and Norwest snapped up Wells Fargo for more than $30 billion.*

Then there were the gigantic mergers: BankAmerica and NationsBank spanned North America with a $60-billion deal, and Travelers Group and Citicorp shocked Wall Street with their $83-billion agreement to merge. And finally there were the international mergers, highlighted by the stunning agreement for Germany's Daimler-Benz to buy Chrysler Corp. for $38 billion.

Certainly 1998 was the year of the colossal mergers, deals that broke all previous records for size. But size was only one facet of the dealmaking that took place. The frenzied maneuvering took on a decided international tone, as well, with more transnational mergers than ever. And with the increased size and geographic scope of merger activity, more attention was focused on the question that won't be answered for years to come: Can managements make these enormous and complex transactions work or are they caught up in some mania, taking on too much, too fast?

In many ways, of course, the record-breaking volume of mergers and acquisitions that occurred in 1998 was simply an extension of what went before. For several years now, experts have been calling the 1990s an era of strategic mergers, pairings of like-minded companies that made business sense. That has been in sharp contrast to the merger mania that was characteristic of the 1980s, when hostile bidders issued billions of dollars of junk bonds to buy companies that would then be stripped of their assets to repay all that debt.

There is no question that many deals made a great deal of sense. Norwest, a Midwestern bank, merged with Wells Fargo because it wanted to tap the lucrative California market, a strategy shared by Charlotte, North Carolina-based NationsBank, which agreed to merge with San Francisco-based BankAmerica. Similarly, Ameritech was looking to extend the geographic reach of its telecommunications network when it merged with SBC Communications. Given the limited range of their ambitions and the similarities of their businesses, it isn't hard to believe that such pairings can be made to work effectively for shareholders and customers alike.

But what of such marriages as AT&T's merger with TCI? Can an old-line telephone company, which earlier spun off some of its most innovative engineering talent such as Lucent, really make more of a progressive cable company than TCI's own management could have? It may be worth noting that AT&T's stock price fell after the deal was disclosed, hardly an endorsement from Wall Street.

Does it make sense for Travelers Group, which peddles insurance, stocks and bonds, to merge with Citicorp, one of the globe's premier banks? The answer the merger partners give is that cross-selling—simply put, selling insurance, stocks and bonds from bank branches—will make the combined entity more efficient and profitable than either could be separately. But even if cross-selling works (and it hasn't been an especially effective strategy for other financial institutions), can two men of such widely differing temperaments as Travelers' volatile Sanford Weill and Citicorp's mercurial John Reed really function together as co-chairmen for very long?

Finally, what to make of the mega-merger that brings together Germany's Daimler-Benz, a maker of extremely expensive luxury cars, with Chrysler Corp., a maker of unremarkable sedans, minivans purchased mostly by middle-class suburbanites and relatively inexpensive sport-utility vehicles? Even if Chrysler dealers can sell pricey Mercedes-Benz cars, can two such different managements and workforces cooperate at every level, a necessity if the combined organization is to become more efficient and competitive?

The Daimler-Chrysler merger commanded much of the attention focused on cross-border mergers, but it was far from the only one. The German publishing company Bertelsmann A.G. bought Random House in a deal that raised a hue and cry among America's literati, who feared that profit-minded German executives would discourage publication of all but certified bestsellers, leaving many authors of merit with no outlet for their works.

And American companies weren't the target of all cross-border mergers. The economic and financial troubles plaguing the Pacific Rim created shopping opportunities for many acquisitive-minded U.S. companies. Merrill Lynch and Travelers Group, for example, both took advantage of the virtual depression gripping Japan to snap up lucrative parts of Japanese financial services concerns, and there was a flurry of shopping by American and European companies amid Southeast Asia's economically ravaged nations. Even staid utility companies demonstrated an international flair, albeit with a decidedly British accent, when Texas Utilities bought the U.K.'s Energy Group and Houston Industries snapped up that country's PowerGen.

The urge to merge spread beyond the corporate realm, too. Even as many of the companies that trade on the Nasdaq market were merging or at least thinking about merging, the National Association of Securities Dealers, which runs that market, was cutting a deal with the long-beleaguered American Stock Exchange to merge in an attempt to reduce costs and become more competitive with the New York Stock Exchange. That, in turn, inspired the Chicago Board Options Exchange to buy the Pacific Exchange for the same reasons.

Despite the magnitude and number of deals done in 1998, the U.S. government played a muted role, at best. The only significant merger that it stopped was a proposed combination of Lockheed Martin Corp. with Northrop Grumman Corp. The Pentagon complained that a combination of the two defense contractors would be too concentrated. But merger experts argued that the government's antitrust suits against Microsoft and Intel, while not merger-related, raised red flags about how the government may view future mergers that create mighty new companies.

Much of the merger activity that took place in 1998 occurred in the first half, before Asia's economic turmoil and the virtual collapse of Russia's economy began to hit home in the U.S. stock market. Since the vast majority of mergers in the United States were done as stock transactions rather than outright purchases, the sharp plunge in share values that began in August brought a pause to much merger action as executives and investment bankers reassessed the outlook for their own companies and those of potential partners. Not only did many analysts believe that the market turmoil would result in fewer deals, but they also predicted that the nature of the deals would change: more cash deals and more hostile deals and fewer friendly stock transactions.

Douglas R. Sease,
deputy editor,
Money and Investing, at
The Wall Street Journal

Corporate Shopping Spree

Merger and acquisition activity heated up again in the mid-1990s.

Total Value of Mergers and Acquisitions in the U.S.

(In billions)

Value and Number of Mergers and Acquisitions in the U.S.

Announcement date	Value (In millions)	Number of mergers and acquisitions
1985	$203,928.5	2,254
1986	228,293.6	3,151
1987	224,059.9	3,320
1988	349,639.3	3,921
1989	303,589.5	5,449
1990	182,352.2	5,654
1991	135,861.9	5,275
1992	150,050.1	5,505
1993	234,517.4	6,310
1994	342,370.1	7,575
1995	509,278.9	9,117
1996	624,417.6	10,346
1997	905,853.0	11,128

The Largest U.S. Corporate Mergers, Acquisitions and Spinoffs
(As of 9/15/98)

Target name	Acquirer name	Date announced	Value of transaction* (In millions)
Citicorp	Travelers Group Inc.	04/06/98	$72,558.2
Ameritech Corp.	SBC Communications Inc.	05/11/98	72,356.5
GTE Corp.	Bell Atlantic Corp.	07/28/98	70,873.6
Tele-Communications Inc.	AT&T Corp.	06/24/98	69,896.5
BankAmerica Corp.	NationsBank Corp.	04/13/98	61,633.4
Amoco Corp.	British Petroleum Co. PLC	08/11/98	54,333.1
MCI Communications Corp.	WorldCom Inc.	10/01/97	43,351.9
Chrysler Corp.	Daimler-Benz AG	05/07/98	40,466.5
Monsanto Co.	American Home Products Corp.	06/01/98	39,134.7
Wells Fargo & Co.	Norwest Corp.	06/08/98	34,352.6
US WEST Media Group	Shareholders	10/27/97	31,710.9
NYNEX Corp.	Bell Atlantic Corp.	04/22/96	30,786.1
Electronic Data Systems Corp.	Shareholders	08/07/95	29,687.7
First Chicago NBD Corp.	Banc One Corp.	04/13/98	29,616.0
RJR Nabisco Inc.	Kohlberg Kravis Roberts & Co.	10/24/88	29,406.8
Associates First Capital Corp.	Shareholders	10/08/97	26,624.6
Lucent Technologies Inc.	Shareholders	09/20/95	24,067.1
Pacific Telesis Group	SBC Communications Inc.	04/01/96	22,421.0
General Re Corp.	Berkshire Hathaway Inc.	06/19/98	22,337.9
Waste Management Inc.	USA Waste Services Inc.	03/11/98	19,971.4
Capital Cities/ABC Inc.	Walt Disney Co.	07/31/95	18,280.4
SunAmerica Inc.	American International Group	08/20/98	18,117.0
CoreStates Financial Corp.	First Union Corp.	11/18/97	17,122.2
McCaw Cellular Commun Inc.	AT&T Corp.	08/16/93	16,699.7
McDonnell Douglas Corp.	Boeing Co.	12/17/96	15,782.0
Warner Communications Inc.	Time Inc.	03/04/89	15,113.4
MFS Communications Co.	WorldCom Inc.	08/26/96	14,885.5
Barnett Banks	NationsBank Corp.	08/29/97	14,821.7
Kraft Inc.	Philip Morris	10/17/88	13,654.2
ITT Corp.	Starwood Hotels & Resorts	10/20/97	13,502.2

*Securities Data includes assumption of debt in its calculation of the value.
Source: Securities Data Co.

Largest Announced U.S. Mergers, Acquisitions and Spinoffs in 1998
(As of 9/15/98)

Target name	Acquirer name	Date announced	Value of transaction* ($ millions)
Citicorp	Travelers Group Inc.	04/06/98	$72,558.2
Ameritech Corp.	SBC Communications Inc.	05/11/98	72,356.5
GTE Corp.	Bell Atlantic Corp.	07/28/98	70,873.6
Tele-Communications Inc.	AT&T Corp.	06/24/98	69,896.5
BankAmerica Corp.	NationsBank Corp.	04/13/98	61,633.4
Amoco Corp.	British Petroleum Co. PLC	08/11/98	54,333.1
Chrysler Corp.	Daimler-Benz AG	05/07/98	40,466.5
Monsanto Co.	American Home Products Corp.	06/01/98	39,134.7
Wells Fargo & Co.	Norwest Corp.	06/08/98	34,352.6
First Chicago NBD Corp.	Banc One Corp.	04/13/98	29,616.0
General Re Corp.	Berkshire Hathaway Inc.	06/19/98	22,337.9
Waste Management Inc.	USA Waste Services Inc.	03/11/98	19,971.4
SunAmerica Inc.	American International Group	08/20/98	18,117.0
American Stores Co.	Albertson's Inc.	08/03/98	11,833.0
Teleport Communications Group	AT&T Corp.	01/08/98	11,030.8
AMP Inc.	AlliedSignal Inc.	08/04/98	10,055.6
IMS International Inc.	Shareholders	01/15/98	9,669.6
Crestar Financial Corp.	SunTrust Banks Inc.	07/20/98	9,603.1
HF Ahmanson & Co.	Washington Mutual	03/17/98	9,015.5
Bay Networks Inc.	Northern Telecom Ltd.	06/15/98	9,009.0
Beneficial Corp.	Household International Inc.	04/07/98	8,703.8
Digital Equipment Corp.	Compaq Computer Corp.	01/26/98	8,680.5
Dresser Industries Inc.	Halliburton Co.	02/26/98	8,426.5
Green Tree Financial Corp.	Conseco Inc.	04/07/98	7,358.8
Firstar Corp.	Star Banc Corp.	07/01/98	7,217.6
Excel Communications Inc.	Teleglobe Inc.	06/15/98	6,915.6
ARCO Chemical Co.	Lyondell Petrochemical Co.	06/18/98	6,512.7
360 Communications Co.	ALLTEL Corp.	03/16/98	6,021.6
Corporate Property Investors	Simon DeBartolo Group Inc.	02/19/98	5,781.0
Southern New England Telecomm	SBC Communications Inc.	01/05/98	5,759.6

*Securities Data includes assumption of debt in its calculation of the value.
Source: Securities Data Co.

Largest Global Mergers, Acquisitions and Spinoffs
(As of 9/15/98)

Target name	Acquirer name	Date announced	Value of transaction (In millions)*
Citicorp	Travelers Group Inc.	04/06/98	$72,558.2
Ameritech Corp.	SBC Communications Inc.	05/11/98	72,356.5
GTE Corp.	Bell Atlantic Corp.	07/28/98	70,873.6
Tele-Communications Inc.	AT&T Corp.	06/24/98	69,896.5
BankAmerica Corp.	NationsBank Corp.	04/13/98	61,633.4
Amoco Corp.	British Petroleum Co. PLC	08/11/98	54,333.1
MCI Communications Corp.	WorldCom Inc.	10/01/97	43,351.9
Chrysler Corp.	Daimler-Benz AG	05/07/98	40,466.5
Monsanto Co.	American Home Products Corp.	06/01/98	39,134.7
Wells Fargo & Co.	Norwest Corp.	06/08/98	34,352.6
Bank of Tokyo Ltd.	Mitsubishi Bank Ltd.	03/27/95	33,787.7
US West Media Group	Shareholders	10/27/97	31,710.9
NYNEX Corp.	Bell Atlantic Corp.	04/22/96	30,786.1
Electronic Data Systems Corp.	Shareholders	08/07/95	29,687.7
First Chicago NBD Corp.	Banc One Corp.	04/13/98	29,616.0
RJR Nabisco Inc.	Kohlberg Kravis Roberts & Co.	10/24/88	29,406.8
Ciba-Geigy AG	Sandoz AG	03/07/96	28,000.7
Associates First Capital Corp.	Shareholders	10/08/97	26,624.6
Lucent Technologies Inc.	Shareholders	09/20/95	24,067.1
Taiyo Kobe Bank Ltd.	Mitsui Bank Ltd.	08/28/89	23,016.8
Schweizerischer Bankverein	Union Bank of Switzerland	12/08/97	23,008.7
Pacific Telesis Group	SBC Communications Inc.	04/01/96	22,421.0
General Re Corp.	Berkshire Hathaway Inc.	06/19/98	22,337.9
Waste Management Inc.	USA Waste Services Inc.	03/11/98	19,971.4
BAT Industries PLC-Financial	Zurich Versicherungs GmbH	10/13/97	18,354.6
Guinness PLC	Grand Metropolitan PLC	05/12/97	18,290.4
Capital Cities/ABC Inc.	Walt Disney Co.	07/31/95	18,280.4
SunAmerica Inc.	American International Group	08/20/98	18,117.0
CoreStates Financial Corp.	First Union Corp.	11/18/97	17,122.2
McCaw Cellular Commun Inc.	AT&T Corp.	08/16/93	16,699.7

*Securities Data includes assumption of debt in its calculation of the value.
Source: Securities Data Co.

Total Announced Worldwide Mergers and Acquisitions

Year	Value ($ millions)	Number of deals
1985	$242,658.0	2,805
1986	286,916.0	4,076
1987	336,802.5	5,321
1988	523,689.3	7,873
1989	567,633.4	10,856
1990	454,071.8	11,343
1991	367,048.7	15,985
1992	364,594.5	15,596
1993	456,243.5	16,710
1994	559,962.1	19,135
1995	943,251.4	22,153
1996	1,102,973.7	23,266
1997	1,611,737.1	23,638

Source: Securities Data Co.

Largest Announced Global Mergers, Acquisitions and Spinoffs in 1998
(As of 9/15/98)

Target name	Acquirer name	Date announced	Value of transaction* ($ millions)
Citicorp	Travelers Group Inc.	04/06/98	$72,558.2
Ameritech Corp.	SBC Communications Inc.	05/11/98	72,356.5
GTE Corp.	Bell Atlantic Corp.	07/28/98	70,873.6
Tele-Communications Inc.	AT&T Corp.	06/24/98	69,896.5
BankAmerica Corp.	NationsBank Corp.	04/13/98	61,633.4
Amoco Corp.	British Petroleum Co. PLC	08/11/98	54,333.1
Chrysler Corp.	Daimler-Benz AG	05/07/98	40,466.5
Monsanto Co.	American Home Products Corp.	06/01/98	39,134.7
Wells Fargo & Co.	Norwest Corp.	06/08/98	34,352.6
First Chicago NBD Corp.	Banc One Corp.	04/13/98	29,616.0
General Re Corp.	Berkshire Hathaway Inc.	06/19/98	22,337.9
Waste Management Inc.	USA Waste Services Inc.	03/11/98	19,971.4
SunAmerica Inc.	American International Group	08/20/98	18,117.0
Toronto-Dominion Bank	Canadian Imperial Bank of Commerce	04/17/98	15,397.6
Bank of Montreal	Royal Bank of Canada	01/23/98	12,543.1
Generale de Banque SA	Fortis AG	05/18/98	12,298.5
American Stores Co.	Albertson's Inc.	08/03/98	11,833.0
General Accident PLC	Commercial Union PLC	02/25/98	11,152.5
Teleport Communications Group	AT&T Corp.	01/08/98	11,030.8
Unicredito SpA	Credito Italiano SpA	04/15/98	10,959.0
AMP Inc.	AlliedSignal Inc.	08/04/98	10,055.6
IMS International Inc.	Shareholders	01/15/98	9,669.6
Crestar Financial Corp.	SunTrust Banks Inc.	07/20/98	9,603.1
Istituto Mobiliare Italiano	Istituto Bancario San Paolo	04/27/98	9,492.4
HF Ahmanson & Co.	Washington Mutual	03/17/98	9,015.5
Bay Networks Inc.	Northern Telecom Ltd.	06/15/98	9,009.0
Energy Group PLC	Texas Utilities Co.	03/02/98	8,844.7
Beneficial Corp.	Household International Inc.	04/07/98	8,703.8
Digital Equipment Corp.	Compaq Computer Corp.	01/26/98	8,680.5
Dresser Industries Inc.	Halliburton Co.	02/26/98	8,426.5

*Securities Data includes assumption of debt in its calculation of the value.
Source: Securities Data Co.

300 Largest U.S. Companies in the Dow Jones Global Indexes

Company Name	Fiscal Year	Sales ($ Millions)	Net Income ($ Millions)
1 General Motors	12/31/97	$178,174.00	$6,698.00
2 Ford Motor	12/31/97	153,627.00	6,920.00
3 Exxon	12/31/97	120,279.00	8,460.00
4 Wal-Mart Stores	1/31/98	117,958.00	3,526.00
5 General Electric	12/31/97	89,110.99	8,203.00
6 IBM	12/31/97	78,508.00	6,093.00
7 Mobil	12/31/97	75,370.00	3,272.00
8 Chrysler	12/31/97	61,147.00	2,805.00
9 Philip Morris	12/31/97	56,114.00	6,310.00
10 AT&T	12/31/97	51,319.00	4,638.00
11 Boeing	12/31/97	45,800.00	(178.00)
12 Texaco	12/31/97	45,187.00	2,664.00
13 Hewlett-Packard	10/31/97	42,895.00	3,119.00
14 Sears, Roebuck	12/30/97	41,296.00	1,188.00
15 DuPont	12/31/97	39,730.00	2,405.00
16 Travelers	12/31/97	37,609.00	3,104.00
17 Procter & Gamble	6/30/98	37,154.00	3,780.00
18 Chevron	12/31/97	35,009.00	3,256.00
19 Citicorp	12/31/97	34,697.00	(2,361.00)
20 Kmart	1/28/98	32,183.00	298.00
21 Amoco	12/31/97	31,910.00	2,720.00
22 Merrill Lynch	12/26/97	31,731.00	1,906.00
23 J.C. Penney	1/31/98	30,546.00	566.00
24 Chase Manhattan	12/31/97	30,323.00	3,708.00
25 Bell Atlantic	12/31/97	30,193.90	2,454.90
26 Motorola	12/31/97	29,794.00	1,180.00
27 Lockheed Martin	12/31/97	28,069.00	(526.00)
28 Dayton Hudson	1/31/98	27,757.00	751.00
29 Fannie Mae	12/31/97	27,652.00	3,056.00
30 American International	12/31/97	27,246.03	3,332.33
31 Morgan Stanley, Dean Witter	11/30/97	27,132.00	2,586.00
32 Kroger	12/27/97	26,567.35	411.66
33 Lucent Technologies	9/30/97	26,360.00	541.00
34 Intel	12/27/97	25,070.00	6,945.00
35 Allstate	12/31/97	24,949.00	3,144.00
36 SBC Communications	12/31/97	24,856.00	1,474.00
37 United Technologies	12/31/97	24,713.00	1,072.00
38 Compaq Computer	12/31/97	24,584.00	1,855.00
39 Home Depot	1/27/98	24,156.00	1,160.00
40 ConAgra	5/31/98	23,840.50	613.20
41 Merck	12/31/97	23,636.90	4,614.10
42 BankAmerica	12/31/97	23,372.00	3,210.00
43 GTE	12/31/97	23,260.00	2,806.00
44 Johnson & Johnson	12/28/97	22,629.00	3,303.00
45 Safeway	12/30/97	22,483.80	557.40
46 Walt Disney	9/30/97	22,473.00	1,966.00
47 Costco	9/2/97	21,874.40	312.20
48 NationsBank	12/31/97	21,734.00	3,077.00
49 PepsiCo	12/27/97	20,917.00	2,142.00
50 McKesson	3/31/98	20,857.30	161.10
51 BellSouth	12/31/97	20,561.00	3,261.00
52 Enron	12/31/97	20,273.00	174.00
53 International Paper	12/31/97	20,096.00	(151.00)
54 CIGNA	12/31/97	20,038.00	1,086.00
55 Dow Chemical	12/31/97	20,018.00	1,808.00
56 Loews	12/31/97	20,014.50	793.60
57 Sara Lee	6/30/97	19,734.00	1,009.00
58 MCI Communications	12/31/97	19,653.00	209.00
59 American Stores	2/1/98	19,138.88	280.62
60 American Express	12/31/97	18,958.00	1,991.00
61 Caterpillar	12/31/97	18,925.00	1,665.00
62 Coca-Cola	12/31/97	18,868.00	4,129.00
63 Columbia/HCA Healthcare	12/31/97	18,819.00	(305.00)
64 Atlantic Richfield	12/31/97	18,684.00	1,771.00
65 AMR	12/31/97	18,570.00	985.00
66 Aetna	12/31/97	18,540.20	901.10
67 Xerox	12/31/97	18,166.00	1,452.00
68 Morgan	12/31/97	17,701.00	1,465.00
69 UAL	12/31/97	17,378.00	954.00
70 Supervalu	2/28/98	17,201.38	230.76
71 CNA Financial	12/31/97	17,072.00	966.00
72 Lehman Brothers	11/30/97	16,883.00	647.00
73 Bristol-Myers Squibb	12/31/97	16,701.00	3,205.00
74 Duke Energy	12/31/97	16,308.90	974.40
75 Archer-Daniels-Midland	6/30/98	16,108.63	403.61
76 Ameritech	12/31/97	15,998.00	2,325.00
77 FDX	5/31/98	15,872.80	503.03
78 Federated Department Stores	1/31/98	15,668.00	536.00
79 USX-Marathon	12/31/97	15,665.26	456.00
80 PG&E	12/31/97	15,400.00	716.00
81 Sysco	6/27/98	15,327.54	296.77

Company Name	Fiscal Year	Sales ($ Millions)	Net Income ($ Millions)
82 Electronic Data Systems	12/31/97	15,235.60	730.60
83 Phillips Petroleum	12/31/97	15,210.00	1,041.00
84 3M	12/31/97	15,070.00	2,121.00
85 Sprint	12/31/97	14,873.90	952.50
86 Albertson's	1/29/98	14,689.51	516.81
87 Eastman Kodak	12/31/97	14,538.00	5.00
88 Microsoft	6/30/98	14,484.00	4,490.00
89 AlliedSignal	12/31/97	14,472.00	1,170.00
90 First Union	12/31/97	14,329.00	1,896.00
91 FHLMC	12/31/97	14,299.00	1,395.00
92 Fluor	10/31/97	14,298.54	146.19
93 Ashland	9/30/97	14,200.00	279.00
94 American Home Products	12/31/97	14,196.03	2,043.12
95 Delta Air Lines	6/30/98	14,133.00	1,001.00
96 Raytheon	12/30/97	13,673.00	527.00
97 Walgreen	8/31/97	13,363.00	436.00
98 Alcoa	12/31/97	13,319.20	805.10
99 Hartford Financial Services	12/31/97	13,305.00	1,332.00
100 Time Warner	12/31/97	13,294.00	246.00
101 Banc One	12/31/97	13,219.10	1,305.70
102 Winn-Dixie Stores	6/25/97	13,218.71	204.44
103 Viacom	12/31/97	13,206.10	793.60
104 Goodyear Tire & Rubber	12/31/97	13,155.10	558.70
105 Georgia-Pacific Group	12/31/97	13,094.00	69.00
106 Cardinal Health	6/30/98	12,926.78	241.90
107 Deere	10/31/97	12,791.40	960.10
108 CVS	12/31/97	12,738.20	37.70
109 May Department Stores	2/2/98	12,685.00	775.00
110 Kimberly-Clark	12/31/97	12,546.60	901.50
111 Pfizer	12/31/97	12,504.00	2,213.00
112 Southern	12/31/97	12,463.00	1,135.00
113 Dell Computer	1/30/98	12,327.00	944.00
114 Emerson Electric	9/30/97	12,298.60	1,121.90
115 Bankers Trust	12/31/97	12,176.00	866.00
116 Marriott International	12/30/97	12,034.00	335.00
117 Abbott Laboratories	12/31/97	11,883.46	2,094.46
118 United Healthcare	12/31/97	11,794.00	460.00
119 McDonald's	12/31/97	11,408.80	1,642.50
120 Rite Aid	3/4/98	11,375.11	316.44
121 Coca-Cola Enterprises	12/31/97	11,278.00	171.00
122 Weyerhaeuser	12/28/97	11,210.00	342.00
123 Johnson Controls	9/30/97	11,145.40	288.50
124 Union Pacific	12/31/97	11,079.00	432.00
125 Anheuser-Busch	12/31/97	11,066.20	1,169.20
126 Toys 'R' Us	1/31/98	11,038.00	490.00
127 CSX	12/26/97	10,859.00	799.00
128 TRW	12/31/97	10,831.00	(49.00)
129 Schlumberger	12/31/97	10,647.59	1,295.70
130 Textron	12/30/97	10,544.00	584.00
131 Sun	12/31/97	10,464.00	263.00
132 Republic Industries	12/31/97	10,305.60	439.70
133 Northwest Airlines	12/31/97	10,225.80	596.50
134 Food Lion	12/30/97	10,194.38	172.25
135 Lowe's	1/30/98	10,136.89	357.48
136 First Chicago NBD	12/31/97	10,098.00	1,525.00
137 West	12/31/97	10,083.00	1,252.00
138 Gillette	12/31/97	10,062.00	1,427.00
139 Tenet Healthcare	5/31/98	9,895.00	261.00
140 Sun Microsystems	6/30/98	9,790.84	762.86
141 Texas Instruments	12/31/97	9,750.00	1,849.00
142 Tricon Global Restaurants	12/27/97	9,681.00	(111.00)
143 Equitable Companies	12/31/97	9,666.10	561.00
144 Norwest	12/31/97	9,659.70	1,351.00
145 Coastal	12/31/97	9,653.10	301.50
146 Wells Fargo	12/31/97	9,608.00	1,155.00
147 Entergy	12/31/97	9,561.72	322.21
148 Nike	5/31/98	9,553.10	399.60
149 Edison International	12/31/97	9,235.00	743.00
150 Heinz	4/29/98	9,209.28	801.57
151 Limited	1/31/98	9,188.80	217.39
152 Waste Management	12/31/97	9,188.58	(1,176.10)
153 Northrop Grumman	12/31/97	9,153.00	407.00
154 Colgate-Palmolive	12/31/97	9,056.70	740.40
155 PacifiCare Health Systems	12/31/97	8,982.68	(21.70)

Company Name	Fiscal Year	Sales ($ Millions)	Net Income ($ Millions)
156 American General	12/31/97	8,927.00	542.00
157 Circuit City	2/28/98	8,870.80	104.30
158 Halliburton	12/31/97	8,818.60	454.40
159 ITT Industries	12/31/97	8,777.10	108.10
160 Nabisco	12/31/97	8,734.00	405.00
161 Whirlpool	12/31/97	8,617.00	(15.00)
162 Dana	12/31/97	8,529.40	369.10
163 Eli Lilly	12/31/97	8,517.60	(385.10)
164 US Airways	12/31/97	8,513.82	1,024.70
165 Crown Cork & Seal	12/31/97	8,494.60	294.00
166 Cisco Systems	7/25/98	8,458.78	1,878.99
167 Burlington Northern	12/31/97	8,409.00	929.00
168 Best Foods	12/30/97	8,400.00	344.00
169 Best Buy	2/28/98	8,358.21	94.45
170 Associates First Capital	12/31/97	8,278.60	1,031.70
171 General Re	12/31/97	8,251.00	968.00
172 Amerada Hess	12/31/97	8,233.72	7.50
173 Warner-Lambert	12/31/97	8,179.80	869.50
174 Honeywell	12/31/97	8,027.50	471.00
175 Occidental Petroleum	12/31/97	8,016.00	(390.00)
176 Campbell Soup	7/30/97	7,964.00	713.00
177 Texas Utilities	12/31/97	7,945.61	758.14
178 Fleet Financial	12/31/97	7,920.00	1,303.00
179 Humana	12/31/97	7,880.00	173.00
180 Arrow Electronics	12/31/97	7,763.95	163.66
181 Rockwell International	9/30/97	7,762.00	644.00
182 Tele-Communications	12/31/97	7,570.00	(626.00)
183 Eaton	12/31/97	7,563.00	518.00
184 Washington Mutual	12/31/97	7,524.36	481.78
185 Dominion Resources	12/31/97	7,521.00	447.10
186 Monsanto	12/31/97	7,514.00	739.00
187 Dresser Industries	10/31/97	7,419.10	318.00
188 TJX	1/31/98	7,389.07	304.82
189 PPG Industries	12/31/97	7,379.00	714.00
190 WorldCom	12/31/97	7,351.35	383.65
191 Lear	12/31/97	7,342.90	207.20
192 Fort James	12/31/97	7,259.00	(27.00)
193 Manpower	12/31/97	7,258.50	163.88
194 Tenneco	12/31/97	7,220.00	315.00
195 Oracle	5/31/98	7,143.87	813.70
196 Consolidated Edison	12/31/97	7,121.25	712.82
197 Ingersoll-Rand	12/31/97	7,103.30	380.50
198 Unicom	12/31/97	7,083.02	(763.50)
199 Apple Computer	9/26/97	7,081.00	(1,045.00)
200 AFLAC	12/31/97	6,983.48	585.02
201 Bancorp	12/31/97	6,899.40	838.50
202 Reynolds Metals	12/31/97	6,881.00	136.00
203 Houston Industries	12/31/97	6,873.39	449.60
204 PNC Bank	12/31/97	6,859.00	1,052.00
205 Kellogg	12/31/97	6,830.10	546.00
206 Seagate Technology	6/30/98	6,819.00	(530.00)
207 USX-U.S. Steel	12/31/97	6,815.00	462.00
208 Schering-Plough	12/31/97	6,778.00	1,444.00
209 Paccar	12/31/97	6,763.70	344.60
210 Office Depot	12/27/97	6,717.51	159.68
211 Chubb	12/31/97	6,664.00	769.50
212 Paine-Webber	12/31/97	6,656.95	415.45
213 Unisys	12/31/97	6,636.00	(853.60)
214 Dillard	1/31/98	6,631.75	258.33
215 Venator Group	1/31/98	6,624.00	(10.00)
216 Computer Sciences	3/31/98	6,600.84	260.37
217 Tyco International	6/30/97	6,597.63	419.00
218 Pharmacia & Upjohn	12/31/97	6,586.00	323.00
219 KeyCorp	12/31/97	6,568.00	919.00
220 Gap	1/30/98	6,507.83	533.90
221 Union Carbide	12/31/97	6,502.00	659.00
222 Public Service Enterprise	12/31/97	6,370.00	619.00
223 FPL	12/31/97	6,369.00	637.00
224 Tyson Foods	9/29/97	6,355.70	185.80
225 Med-Partners	12/31/97	6,331.15	(820.62)
226 Navistar International	10/31/97	6,321.00	150.00
227 Gateway 2000	12/31/97	6,293.68	109.80
228 PacifiCorp	12/31/97	6,278.00	663.70

Company Name	Fiscal Year	Sales ($ Millions)	Net Income ($ Millions)
229 St. Paul	12/31/97	6,219.27	705.47
230 American Electric Power	12/31/97	6,161.37	747.63
231 Baxter International	12/31/97	6,138.00	300.00
232 Bear Stearns	6/30/97	6,077.28	613.33
233 Marsh & McLennan	12/31/97	6,008.60	399.40
234 Genuine Parts	12/31/97	6,005.24	342.40
235 Avnet	6/26/98	5,916.30	151.40
236 Case	12/31/97	5,796.00	403.00
237 Browning-Ferris	9/30/97	5,782.97	265.21
238 Unocal	12/31/97	5,781.00	581.00
239 Aon	12/31/97	5,750.60	298.80
240 AMP	12/31/97	5,745.23	473.09
241 Champion International	12/31/97	5,735.50	(548.50)
242 Transamerica	12/31/97	5,726.50	793.80
243 Consolidated Natural Gas	12/31/97	5,710.02	304.38
244 Bank of New York	12/31/97	5,697.00	1,104.00
245 El Paso Energy	12/31/97	5,638.00	186.00
246 Cummins Engine	12/31/97	5,625.00	212.00
247 General Mills	5/25/97	5,609.30	445.40
248 Household International	12/31/97	5,503.10	686.60
249 Boise Cascade	12/31/97	5,493.82	(30.42)
250 3Com	5/31/98	5,420.37	30.21
251 Tandy	12/31/97	5,372.20	186.90
252 CBS	12/30/97	5,363.00	549.00
253 Hilton Hotels	12/31/97	5,316.00	250.00
254 Cendant	1/31/98	5,314.70	55.40
255 Cooper Industries	12/31/97	5,288.80	394.60
256 Wachovia	12/31/97	5,269.61	592.81
257 First Data	12/31/97	5,234.50	356.70
258 VF	12/30/97	5,222.25	350.94
259 Illinois Tool Works	12/31/97	5,220.43	586.95
260 Staples	2/2/98	5,181.04	130.95
261 Bank Boston	12/31/97	5,164.00	879.00
262 National City	12/31/97	5,152.08	807.43
263 Mellon Bank	12/31/97	5,134.00	771.00
264 Ikon Office Solutions	9/30/97	5,128.43	130.36
265 Avon	12/31/97	5,079.40	338.80
266 Mead	12/31/97	5,077.40	150.10
267 Columbia Energy Group	12/31/97	5,053.60	273.30
268 Inland Steel	12/31/97	5,046.80	119.30
269 US West Media	12/31/97	5,043.00	(480.00)
270 Quaker Oats	12/31/97	5,015.70	(930.90)
271 Black & Decker	12/31/97	4,940.50	227.20
272 Comcast	12/30/97	4,912.60	(238.70)
273 Lincoln National	12/31/97	4,898.48	933.99
274 Ryder System	12/31/97	4,893.90	175.69
275 Sherwin-Williams	12/31/97	4,881.10	260.61
276 Nordstrom	1/31/98	4,851.62	186.21
277 Donnelley & Sons	12/31/97	4,850.03	130.63
278 Stone Container	12/31/97	4,849.10	(417.70)
279 Mattel	12/31/97	4,834.62	285.18
280 Automatic Data Processing	6/30/98	4,798.06	605.30
281 CMS Energy	12/31/97	4,787.00	311.00
282 Praxair	12/30/97	4,735.00	405.00
283 Gannett	12/28/97	4,729.49	712.68
284 Computer Associates	3/31/98	4,719.00	1,169.00
285 Safeco	12/31/97	4,709.30	444.80
286 Eastman Chemical	12/31/97	4,678.00	286.00
287 Owens-Illinois	12/31/97	4,658.50	167.90
288 Air Products and Chemicals	9/30/97	4,637.80	429.30
289 Parker Hannifin	6/30/98	4,633.02	323.23
290 Bethlehem Steel	12/31/97	4,631.20	280.70
291 PECO Energy	12/31/97	4,617.90	(1,497.11)
292 Progressive	12/31/97	4,608.20	400.00
293 SunTrust Banks	12/31/97	4,584.98	667.25
294 Dover	12/31/97	4,547.66	405.43
295 MBNA	12/31/97	4,523.89	622.50
296 Ralston Purina	9/30/97	4,486.80	423.70
297 Union Camp	12/31/97	4,476.76	81.07

Company Name	Fiscal Year	Sales ($ Millions)	Net Income ($ Millions)	Company Name	Fiscal Year	Sales ($ Millions)	Net Income ($ Millions)
298 LTV	12/31/97	4,446.00	30.00	300 Owens			
299 Williams	12/31/97	4,409.60	271.40	Corning	12/31/97	4,373.00	58.00

Source: Dow Jones Global Indexes

100 Largest World Companies in the Dow Jones Global Indexes

	Company Name	Country	Fiscal Year	Sales (US$ Millions)	Net Income (US$ Millions)
1	General Motors	United States	12/31/97	$178,174	$6,698
2	Royal Dutch / Shell Group	Netherlands/UK	12/31/97	171,657	7,753
3	Ford Motor	United States	12/31/97	153,627	6,920
4	Mitsui	Japan	3/31/98	134,157	253
5	Mitsubishi	Japan	3/31/98	121,842	425
6	Exxon	United States	12/31/97	120,279	8,460
7	Itochu	Japan	3/31/98	119,060	(728)
8	Wal-Mart Stores	United States	1/31/98	117,958	3,526
9	Marubeni	Japan	3/31/98	104,477	13
10	Sumitomo	Japan	3/31/98	96,273	197
11	Toyota Motor	Japan	3/31/98	89,449	3,480
12	General Electric	United States	12/31/97	89,111	8,203
13	IBM	United States	12/31/97	78,508	6,093
14	Nissho Iwai	Japan	3/31/98	76,997	23
15	Mobil	United States	12/31/97	75,370	3,272
16	AXA-UAP	France	12/31/97	74,006	1,317
17	Nippon Telegraph and Telephone	Japan	3/31/98	72,381	2,220
18	British Petroleum	United Kingdom	12/31/97	71,858	4,084
19	Daimler-Benz	Germany	12/31/97	68,947	4,470
20	Hitachi	Japan	3/31/98	64,467	27
21	Volkswagen	Germany	12/31/97	62,942	744
22	Chrysler	United States	12/31/97	61,147	2,805
23	Matsushita Electric Industrial	Japan	3/31/98	60,437	717
24	Siemens	Germany	9/30/97	59,432	1,331
25	Allianz	Germany	12/31/97	56,204	1,129
26	Philip Morris	United States	12/31/97	56,114	6,310
27	Sony	Japan	3/31/98	51,742	1,701
28	Shell Transport & Trading	United Kingdom	12/31/97	51,735	3,132
29	AT&T	United States	12/31/97	51,319	4,638
30	Fiat	Italy	12/31/97	50,358	1,367
31	Nissan Motor	Japan	3/31/98	50,283	(107)
32	Unilever Group	Netherlands/UK	12/31/97	48,721	5,568
33	CS Holding	Switzerland	12/31/97	48,203	271
34	Nestle	Switzerland	12/31/97	47,851	2,738
35	Honda Motor	Japan	3/31/98	45,954	1,996
36	Boeing	United States	12/31/97	45,800	(178)
37	Texaco	United States	12/31/97	45,187	2,664
38	Hewlett-Packard	United States	10/31/97	42,895	3,119

	Company Name	Country	Fiscal Year	Sales (US$ Millions)	Net Income (US$ Millions)
39	Elf Aquitaine	France	12/31/97	$42,279	$931
40	VEBA	Germany	12/31/97	42,278	1,562
41	Toshiba	Japan	3/31/98	41,808	56
42	Sears, Roebuck	United States	12/30/97	41,296	1,188
43	Tomen	Japan	3/31/98	40,805	(168)
44	Deutsche Bank	Germany	12/31/97	40,715	531
45	Tokyo Electric Power	Japan	3/31/98	40,426	1,036
46	RWE	Germany	6/30/98	40,129	778
47	DuPont	United States	12/31/97	39,730	2,405
48	Fujitsu	Japan	3/31/98	38,185	43
49	Philips Electronics	Netherlands	12/31/97	37,736	2,830
50	Travelers	United States	12/31/97	37,609	3,104
51	Deutsche Telekom	Germany	12/31/97	37,545	1,836
52	NEC	Japan	3/31/98	37,539	316
53	HSBC Holdings plc	United Kingdom/ Hong Kong	12/31/97	37,449	5,492
54	Procter & Gamble	United States	6/30/98	37,154	3,780
55	Prudential	United Kingdom	12/31/97	37,135	1,384
56	ING	Netherlands	12/31/97	36,609	2,026
57	ENI	Italy	12/31/97	35,609	2,894
58	Chevron	United States	12/31/97	35,009	3,256
59	Citicorp	United States	12/31/97	34,697	(2,361)
60	Renault	France	12/31/97	34,566	902
61	BMW	Germany	12/31/97	33,424	693
62	Kmart	United States	1/28/98	32,183	298
63	BASF	Germany	12/31/97	32,114	1,798
64	Amoco	United States	12/31/97	31,910	2,720
65	Total	France	12/31/97	31,768	1,275
66	Merrill Lynch	United States	12/26/97	31,731	1,906
67	Suez Lyonnaise	France	12/31/97	31,658	667
68	Metro	Germany	12/31/97	31,592	308
69	Peugeot	France	12/31/97	31,053	(460)
70	Alcatel Alsthom	France	12/31/97	30,901	776
71	Bayer	Germany	12/31/97	30,572	1,635
72	J.C. Penney	United States	1/31/98	30,546	566
73	Chase Manhattan	United States	12/31/97	30,323	3,708
74	Bell Atlantic	United States	12/31/97	30,194	2,455
75	Motorola	United States	12/31/97	29,794	1,180
76	Mitsubishi Electric	Japan	3/31/98	29,116	(811)
77	Hoechst	Germany	12/31/97	28,957	746
78	Mitsubishi Motors	Japan	3/31/98	28,609	(780)
79	Carrefour	France	12/31/97	28,141	596
80	Lockheed Martin	United States	12/31/97	28,069	(526)
81	Societe Generale	France	12/31/97	27,866	1,016
82	Dayton Hudson	United States	1/31/98	27,757	751
83	Fannie Mae	United States	12/31/97	27,652	3,056
84	ABN-Amro	Netherlands	12/31/97	27,562	1,902
85	Bank of Tokyo-Mitsubishi	Japan	3/31/98	27,558	(4,016)
86	Japan Tobacco	Japan	3/31/98	27,550	444
87	Viag	Germany	12/31/97	27,537	478
88	Vivendi	France	12/31/97	27,438	897
89	American International	United States	12/31/97	27,246	3,332
90	Morgan Stanley, Dean Witter	United States	11/30/97	27,132	2,586
91	Kroger	United States	12/27/97	26,567	412
92	Lucent Technologies	United States	9/30/97	26,360	541
93	Tesco	United Kingdom	2/28/98	26,314	835

	Company Name	Country	Fiscal Year	Sales (US$ Millions)	Net Income (US$ Millions)
94	Zurich Insurance	Switzerland	12/31/97	$26,248	$1,221
95	France Telecom	France	12/31/97	26,057	2,471
96	Bankinter	Spain	12/31/97	25,910	1,605
97	BT	United Kingdom	3/31/98	25,860	2,821
98	Intel	United States	12/27/97	25,070	6,945
99	Banque Nationale de Paris	France	12/31/97	25,062	991
100	Ahold	Netherlands	12/28/97	24,960	461

Source: Dow Jones Global Indexes

Top 50 Employers With Headquarters in the U.S.

Rank	Name	City	State	Number of Employees
1	Government of United States	Washington	District of Columbia	1,936,786
2	Manpower Inc.	Milwaukee	Wisconsin	1,610,200
3	Wal-Mart Stores Inc.	Bentonville	Arkansas	728,000
4	United States Postal Service	Washington	District of Columbia	700,000
5	Kelly Services Inc	Troy	Michigan	669,800
6	General Motors Corp.	Detroit	Michigan	608,000
7	Interim Services Inc.	Fort Lauderdale	Florida	414,000
8	Ford Motor Co.	Dearborn	Michigan	371,702
9	United Parcel Service of America Inc.	Atlanta	Georgia	336,000
10	Tricon Global Restaurants Inc.	Louisville	Kentucky	335,000
11	Sears Roebuck and Co.	Hoffman Estates	Illinois	334,000
12	State of Texas	Austin	Texas	304,993
13	Columbia/HCA Healthcare Corp.	Nashville	Tennessee	285,000
14	General Electric Co.	Fairfield	Connecticut	276,000
15	Kmart Corp.	Troy	Michigan	265,025
16	J C Penney Co.	Plano	Texas	252,000
17	International Business Machines Corp.	Armonk	New York	241,000
18	City of New York	New York	New York	237,181
19	McDonalds Corp.	Hinsdale	Illinois	237,000
20	State of New York	Albany	New York	231,631
21	Dayton Hudson Corp.	Minneapolis	Minnesota	218,000
22	Boeing Co.	Seattle	Washington	215,000
23	Kroger Co.	Cincinnati	Ohio	212,000
24	State of California	Sacramento	California	200,972
25	Accustaff Inc.	Jacksonville	Florida	187,000
26	United Technologies Corp.	Hartford	Connecticut	180,100
27	FDX Corp.	Memphis	Tennessee	173,500
28	Lockheed Martin Corp.	Bethesda	Maryland	173,000
29	Robert Half International	Menlo Park	California	164,300
30	Philip Morris Cos.	New York	New York	154,000
31	Aramark Corp.	Philadelphia	Pennsylvania	150,000
32	Motorola Inc.	Schaumburg	Illinois	150,000
33	State of Florida	Tallahassee	Florida	148,697
34	Safeway Inc.	Pleasanton	California	147,000
35	Carlson Holdings Inc.	Minneapolis	Minnesota	145,000
36	PepsiCo Inc.	Purchase	New York	142,000
37	Bell Atlantic Corp.	New York	New York	141,000
38	Sara Lee Corp.	Chicago	Illinois	141,000
39	Winn-Dixie Stores Inc.	Jacksonville	Florida	136,000
40	Lucent Technologies Inc.	New Providence	New Jersey	134,000

41	AT&T Corp.	New York	New York	128,000
42	American Stores Co.	Salt Lake City	Utah	127,000
43	University of California	Oakland	California	125,000
44	City of New York Board of Education	Brooklyn	New York	123,906
45	Limited Inc.	Columbus	Ohio	123,100
46	Hewlett-Packard Co.	Palo Alto	California	121,900
47	Chrysler Corp.	Auburn Hills	Michigan	121,544
48	State of Georgia	Atlanta	Georgia	120,000
49	SBC Communications Inc.	San Antonio	Texas	118,340
50	Federated Dept. Stores Inc.	Cincinnati	Ohio	117,100

Source: Dun & Bradstreet

Top 50 Employers With Headquarters Outside the U.S.

Rank	Name	Country	Number of Employees
1	National Health Service	England	1,000,000
2	Government of Canada	Canada	600,000
3	ABF Holdings Ltd.	England	500,000
4	Governo do Estado de Minas Gerais	Brazil	493,000
5	Siemens AG	Germany	382,000
6	The People's Construction Bank of China	China Peoples Rep	307,000
7	Deutsche Bahn AG	Germany	306,241
8	Deutsche Post AG	Germany	292,027
9	Daimler-Benz AG	Germany	290,029
10	Poste (la)	France	289,354
11	Volkswagen AG	Germany	274,575
12	Matsushita Electric Industrial Co. Ltd.	Japan	270,651
13	State Bank of India	India	250,000
14	Shougang Corporation (PR CHINA)	China Peoples Rep	250,000
15	Deutsche Telekom AG	Germany	236,812
16	Jardine Matheson Holdings Ltd.	Hong Kong	200,000
17	The Post Office	England	193,633
18	Steel Authority of India Ltd.	India	189,506
19	Maybank Securities (Holdings) SDN BHD	Malaysia	186,000
20	Nippon Telegraph & Telephone Corp.	Japan	182,482
21	Chemins de Fer Francais (St. Nationale des)	France	177,890
22	Metro AG	Germany	176,518
23	South West Water Services Ltd.	England	176,500
24	Ente Poste	Italy	175,000
25	Robert Bosch GmbH	Germany	172,359
26	J Sainsbury PLC	England	165,992
27	BAT Industries PLC	England	163,854
28	Hoechst AG	Germany	151,486
29	Bayer AG	Germany	144,728
30	Tesco PLC	England	143,694
31	Tesco Stores Ltd.	England	143,614
32	Ardouin Pierre	France	139,733
33	British Railways Board	England	137,729
34	RWE AG	Germany	137,070
35	Pakistan Railways	Pakistan	137,000
36	Myer Emporium Ltd.	Australia	136,195
37	Pakistan Water & Power Development Authority	Pakistan	135,500
38	Penneys PTY Ltd.	Australia	135,000

Rank	Name	Country	Number of Employees
39	Coles Myer Ltd.	Australia	135,000
40	G J Coles & Coy PTY Ltd.	Australia	135,000
41	Coles Myer International PTY Ltd.	Australia	135,000
42	Financial Network Card Services PTY Ltd.	Australia	135,000
43	Myer Properties (WA) Ltd.	Australia	135,000
44	Coles Myer Queensland Ltd.	Australia	135,000
45	Compass Group PLC	England	130,548
46	Guinness Ltd.	England	130,100
47	Jardine Strategic Holdings Ltd.	Hong Kong	130,000
48	British Telecommunications PLC	England	129,600
49	Veba AG	Germany	126,734
50	Banco Do Brasil SA	Brazil	125,894

Source: Dun & Bradstreet

Number of Insured Banks and Number of Failures, 1980–1997
(Assets in millions of dollars)

Year	Number of insured commercial banks	Total assets	Number of failures	Failed bank assets
1980	14,435	$1,855,695	11	$8,189
1981	14,408	2,029,151	7	104
1982	14,446	2,193,867	34	1,862
1983	14,460	2,341,955	45	4,137
1984	14,483	2,508,871	79	36,394
1985	14,407	2,730,672	118	3,034
1986	14,199	2,940,699	144	7,609
1987	13,703	2,999,949	201	7,538
1988	13,123	3,130,796	221	52,620
1989	12,709	3,299,362	206	28,507
1990	12,343	3,389,490	159	10,739
1991	11,921	3,430,682	108	43,552
1992	11,462	3,505,663	100	16,915
1993	10,958	3,706,164	42	2,588
1994	10,451	4,010,516	11	825
1995	9,940	4,312,680	6	753
1996	9,528	4,578,291	5	186
1997	9,143	5,014,884	1	27

Number of Insured Savings Institutions and Number of Failures, 1980–1997 (Assets in millions of dollars)

Year	Number of insured savings institutions	Total assets	Number of failures	Failed institution assets
1980	4,328	$ 773,191	11	$ 1,351
1981	4,116	814,388	31	16,332
1982	3,664	854,829	84	32,575
1983	3,477	989,887	57	25,435
1984	3,418	1,144,247	28	6,391
1985	3,626	1,262,654	37	13,100
1986	3,677	1,386,866	52	24,570
1987	3,622	1,502,111	49	12,676
1988	3,438	1,606,489	222	110,761
1989	3,087	1,427,512	330	136,250
1990	2,815	1,259,178	223	134,628
1991	2,561	1,113,002	163	98,545
1992	2,390	1,030,214	81	72,729
1993	2,262	1,000,891	8	6,938
1994	2,152	1,008,568	4	707
1995	2,030	1,025,742	2	456
1996	1,924	1,028,289	1	34
1997	1,779	1,026,219	0	0

Source: Federal Deposit Insurance Corp.

Top 100 World Banking Companies in Total Assets (in millions)

RANK DEC. 1997		TOTAL ASSETS DEC. 31, 1997	DEC. 31, 1996
1	Bank of Tokyo-Mitsubishi Ltd., Tokyo, Japan	$691,920.3	$648,161.0
2	Deutsche Bank AG, Frankfurt, Germany	580,069.0	575,072.0
3	Sumitomo Bank Ltd., Osaka, Japan	483,730.4	426,103.0
4	Credit Suisse Group, Zurich, Switzerland	473,829.8	463,751.4
5	HSBC Holdings, Plc., London, United Kingdom	471,037.8	404,979.0
6	Dai-Ichi Kangyo Bank Ltd., Tokyo, Japan	433,102.9	434,115.0
7	Sanwa Bank Ltd., Osaka, Japan	427,979.6	427,689.0
8	Credit Agricole Mutual, Paris, France	419,763.2	479,963.0
9	Fuji Bank Ltd., Tokyo, Japan	414,173.0	432,992.0
10	ABN-AMRO Bank N.V., Amsterdam, Netherlands	412,771.9	341,916.0
11	Societe Generale, Paris, France	410,842.2	341,867.0
12	Sakura Bank Ltd., Tokyo, Japan	399,491.5	423,017.0
13	Union Bank of Switzerland, Zurich, Switzerland	395,086.5	326,190.0
14	Norin Chunkin Bank, Tokyo, Japan	392,553.5	375,210.0
15	BarclaysBank Plc., London, United Kingdom	385,950.3	308,710.0
16	Dresdner Bank, Frankfurt, Germany	371,371.0	358,829.0
17	Industrial Bank of Japan Ltd., Tokyo, Japan	369,954.0	350,468.0
18	Chase Manhattan Corp., New York, United States	365,521.0	333,777.0
19	Banque Nationale de Paris, France	339,648.2	357,322.0
20	Westdeutsche Landesbank Girozentrale, Duesseldorf, Germany	335,816.2	298,455.0
21	Citicorp, New York, United States	310,897.0	278,941.0
22	ING Bank, Amsterdam, Netherlands	307,559.6	178,886.0
23	NatWest Group, London, United Kingdom	304,941.8	317,295.0
24	Swiss Bank Corporation, Basel, Switzerland	300,259.1	268,519.0
25	Commerzbank, Frankfurt, Germany	286,946.6	290,300.0
26	Mitsubishi Trust & Banking Corp., Tokyo, Japan	269,524.4	284,528.0
27	NationsBank Corp., Charlotte, N.C., United States	264,562.0	184,886.0
28	Tokai Bank Ltd., Nagoya, Japan	262,423.7	273,430.0
29	JP Morgan & Co. Inc., New York, United States	262,159.0	221,814.0
30	BankAmerica Corp., San Francisco, United States	260,159.0	247,892.0
31	Lloyds TSB Group Inc., London, United Kingdom	260,042.8	252,292.0
32	Sumitomo Trust & Banking Co. Ltd., Osaka, Japan	254,189.7	248,418.0
33	Credit Lyonnais, Paris, France	250,149.9	311,747.0
34	Bayerische Vereinsbank AG, Munich, Germany	249,830.6	260,848.0
35	Abbey National Plc., London, United Kingdom	248,040.3	212,307.0
36	Compagnie Financiere de Paribas, Paris, France	245,061.1	292,320.0
37	Mitsui Trust & Banking Co., Ltd., Tokyo, Japan	241,916.0	254,189.0
38	Bayerische Landesbank Girozentrale, Munich, Germany	241,714.0	223,496.0
39	Asahi Bank Ltd., Tokyo, Japan	219,939.4	230,080.0
40	Halifax Plc., Leeds, United Kingdom	215,625.4	175,111.0
41	Rabobank Group, Utrecht, Netherlands	208,739.6	180,960.0
42	Deutsche Genossenschaftsbank, Frankfurt, Germany	207,768.9	212,061.0
43	Bayerische Hypotheken-und Wechsel-Bank AG, Munich, Germany	203,567.0	218,294.0
44	Dexia Belgium, Brussels, Belgium	202,958.5	117,793.0
45	Bankgesellschaft Berlin AG, Berlin, Germany	197,364.8	218,226.0
46	Long Term Credit Bank of Japan, Tokyo, Japan	188,497.4	231,761.0
47	Royal Bank of Canada, Toronto, Canada	171,218.5	157,264.0
48	Grupo Santander, Spain	170,927.0	149,881.0
49	Canadian Imperial Bank of Commerce, Toronto, Canada	166,472.4	142,160.0
50	Yasuda Trust & Banking Co. Ltd., Tokyo, Japan	165,784.2	196,520.0

RANK DEC. 1997		TOTAL ASSETS	
		DEC. 31, 1997	DEC. 31, 1996
51	Cassa di Risparmio delle Provincle Lombarde, Milan, Italy	$163,361.9	$126,808.0
52	Generale Bank, Brussels, Belgium	160,811.5	174,639.0
53	Toyo Trust & Banking Co. Ltd., Tokyo, Japan	159,346.0	192,802.0
54	First Union Corp., Charlotte, N.C., United States	157,274.0	151,847.4
55	Istituto Bancario San Paolo di Torino, Turin, Italy	145,738.3	172,540.0
56	Bank of Montreal, Canada	145,381.9	123,580.0
57	National Australia Bank Ltd., Melbourne, Australia	145,217.9	123,734.0
58	Norddeutsche Landesbank Girozentrale, Hannover, Germany	140,402.7	140,493.0
59	Bankers Trust New York Corp., United States	140,102.0	120,235.0
60	Banco Bilbao Viscaya, Bilbao, Spain	138,666.1	132,492.0
61	Bank of Nova Scotia, Toronto, Canada	136,508.8	113,033.0
62	Sudwestdeutsche Landesbank, Stuttgart, Germany	128,069.0	133,452.0
63	Zenshinren Bank, Tokyo, Japan	127,537.3	130,630.0
64	Daiwa Bank Ltd., Osaka, Japan	125,828.9	212,967.0
65	Bank Austria AG, Vienna, Austria	123,638.0	69,463.0
66	Banca di Roma, Rome, Italy	117,847.0	91,824.0
67	Royal Bank of Scotland Group Plc., Edinburgh, United Kingdom	117,119.9	95,341.0
68	Banc One Corp., Columbus, Ohio, United States	115,901.3	101,848.1
69	Banca Commerciale Italiana, Milan, Italy	115,637.8	116,271.0
70	Toronto-Dominion Bank, Toronto, Canada	114,613.5	93,856.0
71	Deutsche Pfandbriefanstalt-und Hypothekenbank, Weisbaden, Germany	114,131.3	111,390.0
72	First Chicago NBD Bancorp Inc., United States	114,096.0	104,619.0
73	Fortis AG, Brussels, Belgium	113,516.1	123,600.6
74	Kredietbank NV, Brussels, Belgium	112,365.5	114,140.0
75	Bank Bruxelles Lambert, Brussels, Belgium	111,442.1	113,532.0
76	Groupe des Banques Populaires, Paris, France	111,141.2	116,080.0
77	Shoko Chukin Bank, Tokyo, Japan	109,065.2	125,442.0
78	Svenska Handelsbanken, Stockholm, Sweden	108,600.7	65,165.0
79	Monte del Paschi di Siena, Italy	107,419.9	93,841.0
80	Compagnie Financiere de CIC et de L'Union Europeenne, Paris, France	105,604.6	115,975.0
81	Landesbank Hessen-Thuringen-Girozentrale, Frankfurt, Germany	104,935.8	103,693.0
82	Banca Nazionale del Lavoro, Rome, Italy	103,172.9	90,472.0
83	Credito Italiano, Milan, Italy	100,463.6	115,914.0
84	Australian & New Zealand Banking Group Ltd., Melbourne, Australia	99,396.8	89,850.0
85	Westpac Banking Corp., Sydney, Australia	97,827.9	87,260.0
86	Banco do Brasli, SA, Brasilla, Brazil	97,560.0	75,564.0
87	Wells Fargo & Co., San Francisco, United States	97,456.0	108,888.3
88	Landesbank Schieswig-Holstein Girozentrale, Kiel, Germany	95,599.7	66,423.0
89	Nippon Credit Bank Ltd., Tokyo, Japan	91,903.4	114,104.0
90	Chuo Trust & Banking Corp., Tokyo, Japan	91,860.5	101,271.0
91	Bank of Scotland, Edinburgh, United Kingdom	89,962.5	85,095.0
92	Norwest Corp., Minneapolis, United States	88,540.2	80,175.4
93	Commonwealth Bank of Australia, Sydney, Australia	86,355.2	78,293.0
94	Fleet Financial Group Inc., Boston, United States	85,535.0	85,517.7
95	Skandinaviska Enskilda Banken, Stockholm, Sweden	84,544.6	79,841.0
96	ASLK-CGER Bank, Brussels, Belgium	81,945.5	82,634.0
97	Bank of Yokohama Ltd., Yokohama, Japan	80,579.2	91,509.0
98	Standard Chartered Plc, London, United Kingdom	77,600.6	72,140.0
99	Banco Central Hispanoamericano S.A., Madrid, Spain	77,339.8	61,135.0
100	Danske Bank, Copenhagen, Denmark	76,891.1	75,895.0

Source: American Banker

The Securities Industry

Securities Industry Profitability

Year	Total revenue (In millions)	Pre-tax profits (In millions)	Pre-tax profit margin (%)
1965	$2,320	$473	20.4%
1966	2,851	578	20.3
1967	3,992	1,022	25.6
1968	5,403	1,328	24.6
1969	4,534	565	12.5
1970	3,972	591	14.9
1971	5,510	1,331	24.2
1972	5,990	789	13.2
1973	4,811	-72	-1.5
1974	4,620	36	0.8
1975	5,867	804	13.7
1976	6,884	979	14.2
1977	6,730	416	6.2
1978	8,832	684	7.7
1979	11,233	1,100	9.8
1980	16,030	2,262	14.1
1981	19,796	2,144	10.8
1982	23,210	3,035	13.1
1983	29,566	3,824	12.9
1984	31,216	1,608	5.2
1985	38,621	4,140	10.7
1986	50,082	5,512	11.0
1987	50,837	1,133	2.2
1988	51,829	2,492	4.8
1989	59,537	1,842	3.1
1990	54,034	-162	-0.3
1991	60,718	5,849	9.6
1992	62,840	6,186	9.8
1993	73,182	8,600	11.8
1994	71,355	1,128	1.6
1995	96,303	7,405	7.7
1996	120,249	11,272	9.4
1997	145,004	12,209	8.4

Source: Securities Industry Association

Largest Securities Firms

Ranking based on each firm's capital, which is the sum of ownership equity and subordinated liabilities unless otherwise noted.

Firm	1998 rank	January 1, 1998 capital (000)	1997 rank	January 1, 1997 capital (000)
Merrill Lynch & Co.*	1	$51,419,000	1	$32,994,000
Morgan Stanley Dean Witter & Co.*	2	39,747,000[1]	2	21,901,000[2]
Salomon Smith Barney Holdings Inc.*	3	27,592,000	4	18,992,000
Lehman Brothers Holdings Inc.*	4	24,784,000[3]	3	19,796,000[4]
Goldman Sachs Group L.P.*	5	21,774,000	5	17,685,000
Bear Stearns Companies Inc.*	6	14,789,047	6	9,467,710
Paine Webber Group Inc.*	7	5,911,342	7	4,894,774
Donaldson, Lufkin & Jenrette Inc.	8	4,513,347	9	3,388,979
Credit Suisse First Boston	9	3,736,126	10	2,786,474
BT Alex. Brown Inc.	10	2,360,000	26	603,945
UBS Securities LLC	11	2,161,700	12	1,681,004
NationsBanc Montgomery Securities LLC	12	1,838,530	—	N/A
Chase Securities Inc.	13	1,778,868	13	1,560,000
Prudential Securities Inc.	14	1,660,098	14	1,506,947
Charles Schwab Corp.	15	1,506,166	17	1,138,371
J.P. Morgan Securities Inc.	16	1,453,942	16	1,151,636
A.G. Edwards Inc.	17	1,414,148	15	1,211,866
SBC Warburg Dillon Read Inc.	18	1,412,211	22	819,699
D.E. Shaw & Co.*	19	1,384,779	20	885,133
Deutsche Bank Securities Inc.	20	1,370,709	21	865,281
CIBC Oppenheimer Corp.	21	1,331,873	32	488,919
Nomura Securities International Inc.	22	1,094,881	19	932,513
Bank of Tokyo-Mitsubishi Trust Co.	23	1,067,533	18	973,288
Daiwa Securities America Inc.	24	945,522	25	617,007
Societe Generale Securities Corp.	25	888,278	28	555,933
Spear, Leeds & Kellogg	26	700,000	29	550,000
Fidelity Brokerage	27	683,075	31	499,371
Citicorp Securities Inc.	28	669,595	27	584,408
ING Baring Furman Selz LLC	29	666,822	36	439,955
Zions First National Bank	30	575,861	—	N/A
Legg Mason Inc.*	31	574,217	30	505,577
Allen & Company Inc.	32	499,997	38	362,023
Edward Jones	33	491,449	34	465,083
TD Securities (USA) Inc.	34	462,632	44	311,870
Raymond James Financial Inc.	35	444,893	40	343,531
ABN AMRO Inc.	36	415,709	35	444,880
Alliance Capital Management L.P.	37	398,051	61	187,256
Jefferies Group Inc.*	38	392,046	52	248,432
OppenheimerFunds Distributor Inc.	39	364,275	51	266,952
American Express Financial Advisors Inc.	40	344,221	49	272,698
EVEREN Securities Inc.	41	340,826	47	295,294
Dain Rauscher Corp.	42	334,750	45	303,176
Nesbitt Burns Inc.	43	328,524	33	488,819
Waterhouse Investor Services Inc.	44	321,799	73	158,491
John Nuveen Co.	45	318,120	50	271,894
HSBC Securities Inc.	46	316,695	43	327,634
Paribas Corp.	47	311,681	42	330,646
Midland Walwyn Capital Inc.	48	273,777	39	347,312
Arnhold and S. Bleichroeder Inc.	49	255,439	57	224,584
First Marathon Inc.	50	254,131	53	236,279

[1]Data as of 11/30/97   [2]Data as of 11/30/96   [3]Data as of 11/30/97   [4]Data as of 11/30/96
*Firm's capital is the sum of long-term borrowings and ownership equity.

Source: Securities Industry Association

World's Top 20 Advertising Organizations (In millions of U.S. dollars)

Rank 1997	Rank 1996	Ad organization	Headquarters	Worldwide gross income 1997	Worldwide gross income 1996	% change
1	1	Omnicom Group	New York	$4,154.3	$3,750.8	10.8%
2	2	WPP Group	London	3,646.6	3,430.2	6.3
3	3	Interpublic Group of Cos.	New York	3,384.5	3,037.1	11.4
4	4	Dentsu	Tokyo	1,987.8	1,929.9	3.0
5	5	Young & Rubicam	New York	1,497.9	1,356.4	10.4
6	7	True North Communications	Chicago	1,211.5	996.7	21.6
7	6	Grey Advertising	New York	1,143.0	1,027.7	11.2
8	8	Havas Advertising	Paris	1,033.1	974.3	6.0
9	10	Leo Burnett Co.	Chicago	878.0	866.3	1.4
10	9	Hakuhodo	Tokyo	848.0	897.7	-5.5
11	11	MacManus Group	New York	842.6	756.2	11.4
12	13	Saatchi & Saatchi	London	657.0	616.9	6.5
13	12	Publicis Communication	Paris	625.0	672.4	-7.1
14	14	Cordiant Communications Group	London	596.7	577.0	3.4
15	17	Carlson Marketing Group	Minneapolis	285.2	255.8	11.5
16	18	TMP Worldwide	New York	274.1	222.5	23.2
17	15	Asatsu	Tokyo	263.1	268.2	-1.9
18	19	Tokyu Agency	Tokyo	204.5	214.0	-4.4
19	16	Daiko Advertising	Tokyo	204.4	256.7	-20.4
20	23	Abbott Mead Vickers	London	187.3	145.8	28.4

Source: Advertising Age, Crain Communications, Inc.

Largest Accounting Firms

National Accounting Firms

Rank by U.S. revenue	Firm	FY97 U.S. net revenue ($ million)	% change from FY 96	No. of partners	Rev./ partner ($000)	Global revenue FY 97 net revenue ($ million)	Global revenue % change from FY 96
1	Andersen Worldwide*	$5,445	21.0%	1,673	$3,255	$11,300	19.0%
2	Ernst & Young	4,416	23.7	2,172	2,033	9,100	17.4
3	Deloitte & Touche	3,600	23.1	1,719	2,094	7,400	13.8
4	KPMG Peat Marwick	2,698	18.2	1,600	1,686	8,219	11.1
5	Coopers & Lybrand**	2,504	18.4	1,277	1,961	7,500	10.7
6	Price Waterhouse**	2,344	16.0	1,062	2,207	5,630	12.2
7	Grant Thornton	289	8.7	278	1,040	1,403	9.2
8	McGladrey & Pullen	270	5.5	381	709	1,060	12.3
9	BDO Seidman	240	13.7	217	1,106	1,450	9.0
	National Firms	21,806	20.0	10,379	2,101	53,062	13.9

*Includes Arthur Andersen and Andersen Consulting
**Coopers & Lybrand and Price Waterhouse merged in 1998.
Source: Public Accounting Report

Legion of Lawyers

The number of lawyers has tripled in the last 27 years.

Numbers and Percentage of Lawyers by Types of Employment

Year	Total active lawyers
1970	326,842
1975	404,772
1980	574,810
1985	653,686
1990	755,694
1991	777,119
1992	799,760
1993	846,036
1994	862,954
1995	896,140
1996	946,449
1997	985,900

Employment setting	1980	1991
Private practice	68.3%	72.9%
Federal judicial department	0.5	0.4
Other federal government	3.7	3.5
State/local judicial department	3.1	2.3
Other state/local government	5.6	4.7
Private industry	10.1	8.8
Private association	0.8	0.7
Legal aid or public defender	1.5	1.1
Education	1.2	1.0
Retired or inactive	5.3	4.6

Sources: American Bar Association and American Bar Foundation

Top Law Firms Ranked by Gross Revenue, 1997

Rank	Firm	Size (Lawyers/Equity partners)	Gross revenue
1	Skadden, Arps, Slate, Meagher & Flom	1,074/257	$ 826,000,000
2	Baker & McKenzie	2,094/515	696,500,000
3	Jones, Day, Reavis & Pogue	1,146/263	490,000,000
4	Latham & Watkins	723/248	420,500,000
5	Sullivan & Cromwell	410/114	395,000,000
6	Davis Polk & Wardwell	447/118	390,000,000
7	Sidley & Austin	709/236	360,000,000
8	Morgan, Lewis & Bockius	838/301	359,000,000
9	Shearman & Sterling	566/130	356,000,000
10	Weil, Gotshal & Manges	600/167	354,000,000
11	Cleary, Gottlieb, Steen & Hamilton	463/130	341,000,000
12	Mayer, Brown & Platt	685/260	340,000,000
13	Gibson, Dunn & Crutcher	570/212	336,000,000
14	McDermott, Will & Emery	653/219	333,500,000
15	White & Case	653/161	318,000,000
16	Simpson Thacher & Bartlett	459/114	315,000,000
17	O'Melveny & Myers	561/197	284,000,000
18	Cravath, Swaine & Moore	341/71	273,000,000
19	Fulbright & Jaworski	603/293	265,500,000
20	Kirkland & Ellis	486/112	255,000,000
21	Vinson & Elkins	509/243	255,000,000
22	Akin, Gump, Strauss, Hauer & Feld	635/204	246,000,000
23	Morrison & Foerster	553/165	242,000,000
24	Foley & Lardner	617/274	234,000,000
25	Dewey Ballantine	400/115	227,500,000

Top Law Firms Ranked by Profits Per Partner, 1997

Rank	Firm	Profits per partner	Size (Lawyers/Equity partners)	% change from 1996
1	Wachtell, Lipton, Rosen & Katz	$ 2,200,000	139/64	22.2%
2	Cravath, Swaine & Moore	1,790,000	341/71	18.1
3	Sullivan & Cromwell	1,450,000	410/114	7.5
4	Cahill Gordon & Reindel	1,445,000	189/55	3.3
5	Davis Polk & Wardwell	1,295,000	447/118	15.3
6	Skadden, Arps, Slate, Meagher & Flom	1,290,000	1,074/257	30.6
7	Simpson Thacher & Bartlett	1,285,000	459/114	11.3
8	Debevoise & Plimpton	1,105,000	360/89	8.1
9	Cleary, Gottlieb, Steen & Hamilton	1,060,000	463/130	8.5
10	Robins, Kaplan, Miller & Ciresi	1,010,000	230/60	207.0
11	Kirkland & Ellis	975,000	486/112	15.4
12	Shearman & Sterling	920,000	566/130	12.7
13	Willkie Farr & Gallagher	900,000	359/102	-1.7
14	Paul, Weiss, Rifkind, Wharton & Garrison	865,000	343/90	16.3
15	Milbank, Tweed, Hadley & McCloy	860,000	335/84	17.4
16	Latham & Watkins	825,000	723/248	8.5
17	Weil, Gotshal & Manges	805,000	600/167	9.3
18	Cadwalader, Wickersham & Taft	785,000	249/67	21.5
19	Dewey Ballantine	780,000	400/115	19.9
20	Gibson, Dunn & Crutcher	710,000	570/212	23.2
21	McDermott, Will & Emery	705,000	653/219	14.2
22	Schulte Roth & Zabel	670,000	210/50	10.2
23	Jones, Day, Reavis & Pogue	655,000	1,146/263	35.6
24	Rogers & Wells	645,000	363/84	22.4
25	White & Case	625,000	653/161	11.2

Source: The American Lawyer, American Lawyer Media, L.P.

Total Gross Revenue of Top 100 Law Firms

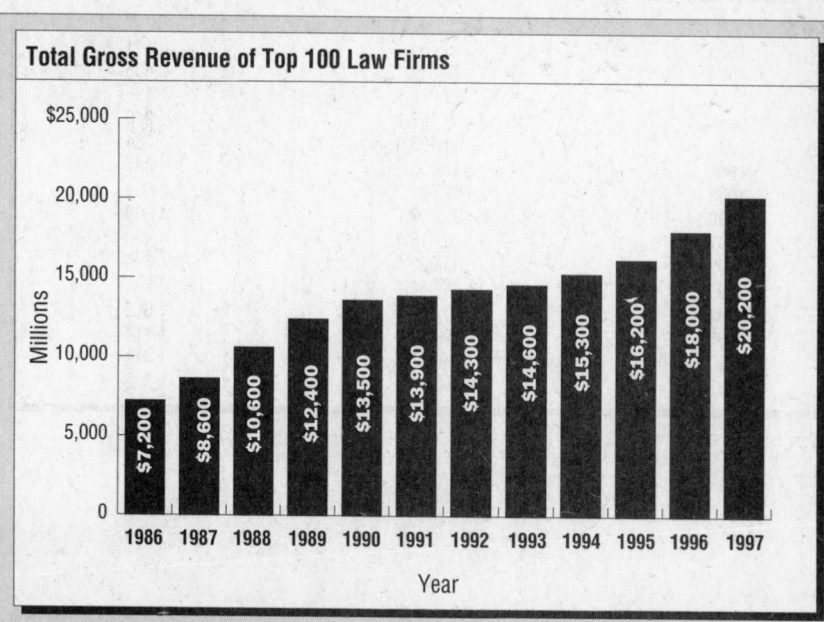

Year	Millions
1986	$7,200
1987	$8,600
1988	$10,600
1989	$12,400
1990	$13,500
1991	$13,900
1992	$14,300
1993	$14,600
1994	$15,300
1995	$16,200
1996	$18,000
1997	$20,200

Source: The American Lawyer, American Lawyer Media, L.P.

Corporate Earnings

Year-to-year percentage change in net income for companies in the DJ U.S. Market Index

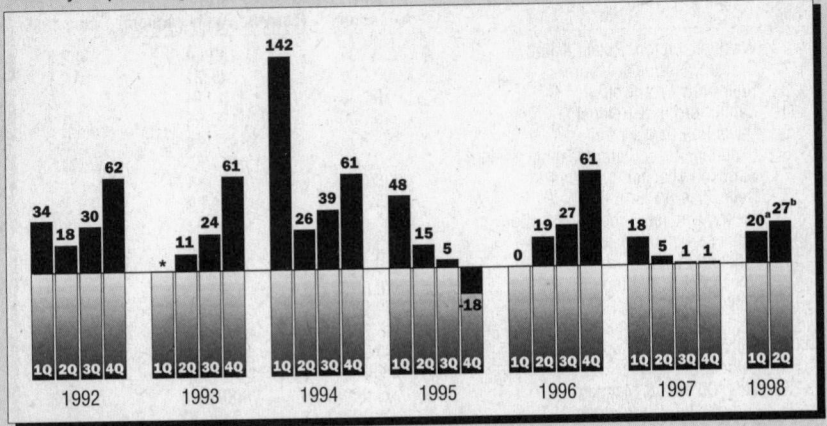

*Loss in 1992 quarter
[a] Rose 2.5% without one-time Ford Motor $15.96 billion gain from sale
[b] Fell 1.5% without one-time Media One Group $24.5 billion gain from US West transaction

Stock Buyback Boom

Announced corporate stock repurchases

Announcement date	Value ($ millions)	Number of deals
1983	$ 6,764.9	141
1984	27,346.1	435
1985	20,275.1	195
1986	28,167.1	240
1987	54,993.8	884
1988	37,355.7	327
1989	63,671.7	634
1990	36,087.7	1,009
1991	20,416.2	438
1992	35,623.1	600
1993	38,341.7	606
1994	73,808.8	1,013
1995	99,579.3	1,114
1996	176,577.7	1,474
1997	189,900.0	1,362

Source: Securities Data Co.

IPO Volume

Number and Proceeds from Initial Public Offerings*

Year	Proceeds ($ millions)	Number of issues
1985	$6,284.8	332
1986	17,738.8	694
1987	16,745.7	518
1988	6,111.7	222
1989	6,082.0	209
1990	4,519.0	172
1991	16,283.2	366
1992	23,379.8	512
1993	34,461.1	667
1994	22,771.9	571
1995	29,270.8	575
1996	48,789.8	865
1997	38,970.0	609

*Excludes closed-end funds and real estate investment trusts.
Source: Securities Data Co.

Largest U.S. Initial Public Offerings
(As of 9/15/98)

Issuer	Offer date	Amount ($ millions)	Offer price (Dollars)
British Petroleum Co. PLC	10/30/87	$2,864.1	$67.950
Lucent Technologies Inc.	04/03/96	2,647.0	27.000
Allstate Corp.	06/02/93	1,849.5	27.000
Associates First Capital Corp.	05/07/96	1,651.6	29.000
Deutsche Telekom AG	11/17/96	1,605.7	18.890
Consolidated Rail Corp.	03/26/87	1,456.0	28.000
USEC	07/22/98	1,282.5	14.250
YPF SA	06/28/93	1,235.0	19.000
TeleDanmark A/S	04/27/94	1,219.6	23.526
Henley Group Inc.	05/20/86	1,190.0	21.250
Wellcome PLC	07/27/92	1,067.5	15.250
Republic Services Inc.	06/30/98	1,056.0	24.000
Coca-Cola Enterprises	11/21/86	1,001.4	16.500
PacTel Corp.	12/02/93	966.0	23.000
Lyondell Petrochemical Co.	01/18/89	960.0	30.000
Nabisco Holdings Corp.	01/19/95	882.0	24.500
CIT Group Holdings Inc.	11/12/97	850.5	27.000
France Telecom SA	10/20/97	836.1	31.690
Fireman's Fund Corp.	10/23/85	824.0	25.750
Heller Financial Inc.	04/03/98	814.1	27.000

Source: Securities Data Co.

Largest U.S. Initial Public Offerings of 1998
(As of 9/15/98)

Issuer	Offer date	Amount ($ millions)	Offer price (Dollars)
USEC	07/22/98	$1,282.5	$14.250
Republic Services Inc.	06/30/98	1,056.0	24.000
Heller Financial Inc.	04/30/98	814.1	27.000
Alstom	06/22/98	712.2	34.220
Capstar Broadcasting Corp.	05/26/98	471.2	19.000
UniCapital Corp.	05/14/98	425.6	19.000
Waddell & Reed Financial Inc.	03/04/98	399.3	23.000
Young & Rubicam Inc.	05/12/98	332.0	25.000
Ziff-Davis Inc. (Softbank Corp.)	04/28/98	319.9	15.500
Global Crossing Ltd.	08/13/98	319.2	19.000
Amkor Technology Inc.	04/30/98	308.0	11.000
SFX Entertainment	05/20/98	302.8	43.250
Capital Automotive REIT	02/13/98	300.0	15.000
Anthracite Capital	03/24/98	300.0	15.000
Equant NV	07/20/98	282.2	27.000
Steelcase Inc.	02/18/98	272.2	28.000
Federated Investors	05/13/98	266.9	19.000
Maxtor Corp. (Hyundai)	07/30/98	266.0	7.000
Enterprise Products Partners	07/27/98	264.0	22.000
Aurora Foods Inc.	06/25/98	258.8	21.000

Source: Securities Data Co.

American Enterprise

Post-War New Business Incorporations

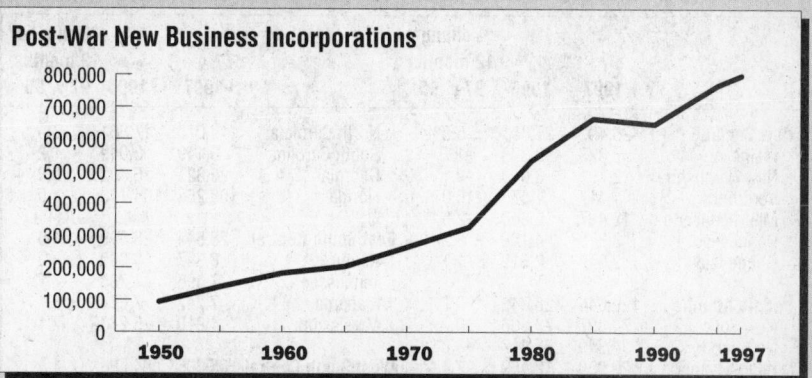

Annual U.S. Business Starts

Year	Starts	% change	Employment	% change
1985	249,770	—	1,657,383	—
1986	253,092	1.3%	1,650,537	-0.4%
1987	233,710	-7.7	1,552,708	-5.9
1988	199,091	-14.8	1,333,426	-14.1
1989	181,645	-8.8	1,212,464	-9.1
1990	158,930	-12.5	827,012	-31.8
1991	155,672	-2.0	731,621	-11.5
1992	164,086	5.4	800,827	9.5
1993	166,154	1.3	780,804	-2.5
1994	188,387	13.4	758,134	-2.9
1995	168,158	-10.7	738,606	-2.6
1996	170,475	1.4	846,973	14.7
1997	166,740	-2.2	939,310	10.9

Note: Dun & Bradstreet provides two different types of data measuring entrepreneurial activity in the U.S. Incorporations may include "idea" enterprises not yet actively doing business, businesses that have recently begun operation, and existing companies filing for various reasons. Business starts reflect companies that have recently been introduced into Dun & Bradstreet's commercial credit information database.

Annual New Business Incorporations

Year	Number
1946	132,916
1950	93,092
1955	139,915
1960	182,713
1965	203,897
1970	264,209
1975	326,345
1980	533,520
1985	664,235
1986	702,738
1987	685,572
1988	685,095
1989	676,565
1990	647,366
1991	628,604
1992	666,800
1993	706,537
1994	741,657
1995	768,180
1996	786,482
1997	798,917 *

Source: Dun & Bradstreet

*Estimate.

New Business Incorporations by State and Geographic Regions

	1997	1996	% change 12 months 97 v. 96		1997	1996	% change 12 months 97 v. 96
New England	25,492	27,071*	-5.8%	North Carolina	19,078	17,861	6.8%
Maine	2,823	2,873	-1.7	South Carolina	8,149*	8,049*	1.2
New Hampshire	2,791	3,070	-9.1	Georgia	29,321	26,902	9.0
Vermont	1,417	1,575	-10.0	Florida	108,268	104,113	4.0
Massachusetts	12,437	12,808*	-2.9				
Connecticut	3,375	4,126	-18.2	**East South Central**	28,544	28,819	-1.0
Rhode Island	2,649	2,619	1.1	Kentucky	8,397	8,060	4.2
				Tennessee	7,495	7,785	-3.7
Middle Atlantic	129,646	128,742	0.7	Alabama	7,742	7,686	0.7
New York	74,397	73,866	0.7	Mississippi	4,910	5,288	-7.1
New Jersey	34,349	35,417	-3.0				
Pennsylvania	20,900	19,459	7.4	**West South Central**	65,606*	64,684	1.4
				Arkansas	6,994*	6,010	16.4
East North Central	108,150*	109,888	-1.6	Louisiana	11,152	11,531	-3.3
Ohio	20,105*	20,517	-2.0	Oklahoma	8,162	8,105	0.7
Indiana	12,734	12,620	0.9	Texas	39,298	39,038	0.7
Illinois	36,090	36,210	-0.3				
Michigan	31,260	31,994	-2.3	**Mountain**	72,126*	68,457	5.4
Wisconsin	7,961	8,547	-6.9	Montana	3,219	2,325	38.5
				Idaho	2,489	2,504	-0.6
West North Central	38,366	37,909	1.2	Wyoming	2,267	2,167	4.6
Minnesota	12,655	12,639	0.1	Colorado	15,670	16,749	-6.4
Iowa	4,695	4,589	2.3	New Mexico	2,919	3,042	-4.0
Missouri	10,273	10,545	-2.6	Arizona	11,262	12,153	-7.3
North Dakota	933	925	0.9	Nevada	26,999	23,222	16.3
South Dakota	1,440	1,382	4.2	Utah	7,301*	6,295	16.0
Nebraska	3,523	3,453	2.0				
Kansas	4,847	4,376	10.8	**Pacific**	73,686*	71,159*	3.6
				Alaska	1,063	1,103	-3.6
South Atlantic	257,301*	249,753*	3.0	Washington	12,487	12,954	-3.6
Maryland	18,066	18,632	-3.0	Oregon	9,289	9,267	0.2
Delaware	52,184	51,272	1.8	California	47,055	44,043	6.8
Washington, DC	1,462	1,497*	-2.3	Hawaii	3,792*	3,792*	0.0
Virginia	18,704	19,047	-1.8				
West Virginia	2,069*	2,380*	-13.1	**Total U.S.**	798,917*	786,482*	1.6

*Includes some or all estimated monthly figures.
Source: Dun & Bradstreet

Business Starts by Industry

	Business starts 1996	Business starts 1997	Change	Employment 1996	Employment 1997	Change
Agriculture/ forestry/ fishing	2,295	2,275	-0.9%	7,794	10,001	28.3%
Mining	589	655	11.2	4,697	4,248	-9.6
Construction	18,624	18,513	-0.6	64,478	82,336	27.7
Manufacturing	12,908	13,144	1.8	108,644	125,007	15.1
Transportation/ utilities	7,993	8,741	9.4	50,072	59,144	18.1
Wholesale	16,019	15,780	-1.5	69,001	73,281	6.2
Retail	38,407	36,377	-5.3	200,354	211,007	5.3
Finance/ insurance/ real estate	11,222	12,198	8.7	61,185	70,982	16.0
Services	50,077	50,253	0.4	278,292	299,137	7.5
Nonclassifiable	12,341	8,804	-28.7	2,456	4,167	69.7
Total	170,475	166,740	-2.2	846,973	939,310	10.9

NOTE: This compilation covers all businesses with a 1995, 1996 or 1997 starting date added to the Dun & Bradstreet business data file in 1997. It includes newly opened establishments. It does not include changes in ownership of previously operating businesses or changes in name, location, legal type or mergers.
Source: Dun & Bradstreet

Business Starts by State

	Business starts 1996	Business starts 1997	Change	Employment 1996	Employment 1997	Change
New England	8,960	7,979	-10.9%	45,936	45,272	-1.4%
Maine	712	570	-19.9	3,131	3,231	3.2
New Hampshire	852	718	-15.7	4,079	3,772	-7.5
Vermont	278	291	4.7	1,586	1,874	18.2
Massachusetts	4,351	3,766	-13.4	22,480	22,241	-1.1
Connecticut	2,207	2,123	-3.8	12,219	11,579	-5.2
Rhode Island	560	511	-8.8	2,441	2,575	5.5
Middle Atlantic	30,137	28,381	-5.8	130,404	141,817	8.8
New York	15,174	14,450	-4.8	67,314	72,856	8.2
New Jersey	7,911	7,481	-5.4	32,403	34,023	5.0
Pennsylvania	7,052	6,450	-8.5	30,687	34,938	13.9
East North Central	23,280	21,971	-5.6	111,205	131,097	17.9
Ohio	5,468	5,122	-6.3	28,875	30,427	5.4
Indiana	2,955	2,928	-0.9	13,778	17,636	28.0
Illinois	6,860	6,525	-4.9	32,226	39,040	21.1
Michigan	5,489	4,881	-11.1	23,416	28,777	22.9
Wisconsin	2,508	2,515	0.3	12,910	15,217	17.9

Business Starts by State

	Business starts 1996	Business starts 1997	Change	Employment 1996	Employment 1997	Change
West North Central	8,390	8,268	-1.5%	46,775	54,003	15.5%
Minnesota	2,286	2,336	2.2	12,632	14,974	18.5
Iowa	1,087	1,199	10.3	6,795	8,155	20.0
Missouri	2,502	2,435	-2.7	13,102	14,857	13.4
North Dakota	233	255	9.4	1,448	1,924	32.9
South Dakota	307	286	-6.8	1,955	1,811	-7.4
Nebraska	725	648	-10.6	3,848	4,402	14.4
Kansas	1,250	1,109	-11.3	6,995	7,880	12.7
South Atlantic	32,142	34,307	6.7	160,654	186,690	16.2
Maryland	3,310	3,668	10.8	15,668	18,534	18.3
Delaware	534	602	12.7	2,675	2,661	-0.5
District of Columbia	595	696	17.0	2,757	3,457	25.4
Virginia	3,591	3,779	5.2	18,557	21,852	17.8
West Virginia	569	555	-2.5	2,682	4,239	58.1
North Carolina	4,007	4,578	14.3	19,504	25,464	30.6
South Carolina	1,903	2,014	5.8	10,175	11,236	10.4
Georgia	5,334	5,383	0.9	28,627	29,859	4.3
Florida	12,299	13,032	6.0	60,009	69,388	15.6
East South Central	7,994	8,749	9.4	43,063	50,940	18.3
Kentucky	1,725	1,859	7.8	9,446	10,761	13.9
Tennessee	3,055	3,239	6.0	16,772	20,137	20.1
Alabama	2,138	2,480	16.0	11,140	13,383	20.1
Mississippi	1,076	1,171	8.8	5,705	6,659	16.7
West South Central	17,240	16,569	-3.9	97,423	103,766	6.5
Arkansas	1,258	1,183	-6.0	5,801	6,928	19.4
Oklahoma	1,543	1,499	-2.9	8,999	8,685	-3.5
Louisiana	2,110	2,028	-3.9	11,890	13,692	15.2
Texas	12,329	11,859	-3.8	70,733	74,461	5.3
Mountain	12,262	11,996	-2.2	60,575	68,244	12.7
Montana	397	419	5.5	1,510	2,136	41.5
Idaho	789	784	-0.6	3,372	3,689	9.4
Wyoming	281	247	-12.1	1,087	1,249	14.9
Colorado	3,424	3,276	-4.3	16,892	17,575	4.0
New Mexico	952	961	0.9	4,308	5,156	19.7
Arizona	3,362	3,110	-7.5	17,460	20,146	15.4
Utah	1,523	1,527	0.3	7,940	8,672	9.2
Nevada	1,534	1,672	9.0	8,006	9,621	20.2
Pacific	30,070	28,520	-5.2	150,938	157,481	4.3
Alaska	235	267	13.6	1,303	1,503	15.3
Hawaii	618	696	12.6	3,470	3,987	14.9
Washington	3,165	3,223	1.8	16,170	16,961	4.9
Oregon	2,065	1,837	-11.0	10,097	9,355	-7.3
California	23,987	22,497	-6.2	119,898	125,675	4.8
Total	170,475	166,740	-2.2	846,973	939,310	10.9

Note: This compilation covers all businesses with a 1995, 1996 or 1997 starting date added to the Dun & Bradstreet business data file in January-December 1997. It includes newly opened establishments. It does not include changes in ownership of previously operating businesses or changes in name, location, legal type or mergers.

Source: Dun & Bradstreet

Out of Business

Number of Business Failures in the U.S.

Year	Failures
1984	52,078
1985	57,253
1986	61,616
1987	61,111
1988	57,097
1989	50,361
1990	60,747
1991	88,140
1992	97,069
1993	86,133
1994	71,558
1995	71,128
1996	71,931
1997*	83,384

*Preliminary.
Source: Dun & Bradstreet

Business Failures by State and Region

	1996 failures	1996 liabilities	1997 failures	1997 liabilities	Failures % change	Liabilities % change
New England	**3,064**	**$1,149,267,713**	**3,445**	**$1,672,116,056**	**12.4%**	**45.5%**
Maine	299	42,842,018	395	81,501,575	32.1	90.2
New Hampshire	375	74,880,098	417	119,609,159	11.2	59.7
Vermont	108	212,584,739	148	29,120,810	37.0	-86.3
Massachusetts	1,612	321,100,570	1,667	607,290,594	3.4	89.1
Connecticut	536	482,706,580	635	809,409,903	18.5	67.7
Rhode Island	134	15,153,708	183	25,184,015	36.6	66.2
Middle Atlantic	**10,328**	**7,685,728,382**	**10,819**	**7,054,266,262**	**4.8**	**-8.2**
New York	4,946	5,689,206,537	5,054	3,358,190,346	2.2	-41.0
New Jersey	2,460	588,322,558	2,641	1,935,434,495	7.4	229.0
Pennsylvania	2,922	1,408,199,287	3,124	1,760,641,421	6.9	25.0
East North Central	**8,191**	**3,517,839,503**	**10,221**	**9,925,745,565**	**24.8**	**182.2**
Ohio	2,280	886,005,030	2,823	2,508,389,235	23.8	183.1
Indiana	850	1,003,767,748	852	664,447,696	0.2	-33.8
Illinois	2,568	794,926,416	3,407	6,039,046,177	32.7	659.7
Michigan	1,559	545,421,042	1,934	581,293,261	24.1	6.6
Wisconsin	934	287,719,267	1,205	132,569,196	29.0	-53.9
West North Central	**3,841**	**1,032,540,641**	**5,326**	**896,147,687**	**38.7%**	**-13.2%**
Minnesota	596	443,439,048	1,183	73,599,234	98.5	-83.4
Iowa	458	81,634,765	506	118,469,018	10.5	45.1
Missouri	1,060	163,679,764	1,490	238,888,370	40.6	45.9
North Dakota	81	7,327,005	138	19,069,729	70.4	160.3
South Dakota	159	14,146,730	281	136,106,743	76.7	862.1
Nebraska	392	53,707,353	479	42,374,565	22.2	-21.1
Kansas	1,095	268,605,976	1,249	267,640,028	14.1	-0.4
South Atlantic	**8,541**	**3,579,154,354**	**8,010**	**7,846,486,050**	**-6.2**	**119.2**
Maryland	1,621	431,580,675	1,480	1,668,013,176	-8.7	286.5
Delaware	49	140,569,984	33	40,320,598	-32.7	-71.3
District of Columbia	121	59,210,818	93	1,537,678,416	-23.1	2,497.0
Virginia	1,058	215,083,474	877	251,052,142	-17.1	16.7
West Virginia	300	325,404,069	319	577,786,268	6.3	77.6
North Carolina	1,038	521,100,456	1,031	238,885,289	-0.7	-54.2
South Carolina	372	28,535,834	413	192,690,125	11.0	575.3
Georgia	1,306	532,822,986	1,181	417,701,147	-9.6	-21.6
Florida	2,676	1,324,846,058	2,583	2,922,358,889	-3.5	120.6

	1996 failures	1996 liabilities	1997 failures	1997 liabilities	Failures % change	Liabilities % change
East South Central	**2,698**	**$335,666,985**	**3,067**	**$494,508,765**	**13.7%**	**47.3%**
Kentucky	642	47,942,029	568	130,515,186	-11.5	172.2
Tennessee	1,331	118,037,039	1,717	349,763,688	29.0	196.3
Alabama	542	141,808,946	635	7,275,481	17.2	-94.9
Mississippi	183	27,878,971	147	6,954,410	-19.7	-75.1
West South Central	**8,895**	**3,844,018,620**	**10,285**	**1,925,823,581**	**15.6**	**-49.9**
Arkansas	1,005	314,961,010	1,117	94,375,060	11.1	-70.0
Oklahoma	1,560	297,144,222	1,546	84,549,438	-0.9	-71.5
Louisiana	272	53,475,102	300	33,086,300	10.3	-38.1
Texas	6,058	3,178,438,286	7,322	1,713,812,783	20.9	-46.1
Mountain	**5,381**	**1,776,463,690**	**7,152**	**869,170,963**	**32.9**	**-51.1**
Montana	179	15,578,331	189	41,781,170	5.6	168.2
Idaho	539	1,741,648	677	3,363,657	25.6	93.1
Wyoming	122	154,114	137	372,952	12.3	142.0
Colorado	2,254	1,591,288,868	3,082	551,758,741	36.7	-65.3
New Mexico	423	46,462,013	645	76,780,972	52.5	65.3
Arizona	1,010	40,876,525	1,207	5,912,393	19.5	-85.5
Utah	378	21,334,849	581	5,073,973	53.7	-76.2
Nevada	476	59,027,342	634	184,127,105	33.2	211.9
Pacific	**20,992**	**6,648,051,831**	**25,059**	**6,752,669,735**	**19.4**	**1.6**
Alaska	184	2,436,749	177	86,370	-3.8	-96.5
Hawaii	395	109,920,949	630	137,618,165	59.5	25.2
Washington	2,695	980,454,794	2,977	653,204,969	10.5	-33.4
Oregon	839	119,676,772	1,186	249,275,754	41.4	108.3
California	16,879	5,435,562,567	20,089	5,712,484,477	19.0	5.1
Total U.S.	**71,931**	**29,568,731,719**	**83,384**	**37,436,934,664**	**15.9**	**26.6**

Source: Dun & Bradstreet

Business Failures by Industry

Industry	1996 failures	1997 failures	% change	1996 liabilities	1997 liabilities	% change
Agriculture/forestry/ fishing	2,723	2,945	8.2%	$436,653,066	$ 456,771,235	4.6%
Mining	189	163	-13.8	70,836,256	173,915,870	145.5
Construction	9,801	10,867	10.9	1,291,258,410	2,021,220,115	56.5
Manufacturing	4,093	4,207	2.8	4,237,239,216	3,670,906,401	-13.4
Transportation/utilities	3,362	4,345	29.2	1,697,521,171	10,114,930,255	495.9
Wholesale	3,957	3,874	-2.1	2,344,983,919	1,863,302,221	-20.5
Retail	13,476	15,035	11.6	5,060,452,369	8,902,340,239	75.9
Finance/insurance/ real estate	4,138	4,586	10.8	7,581,673,649	3,581,379,502	-52.8
Services	22,928	29,359	28.0	5,782,144,935	5,067,541,910	-12.4
Nonclassifiable	7,264	8,003	10.2	1,065,968,728	1,584,626,916	48.7
Total	**71,931**	**83,384**	**15.9**	**29,568,731,719**	**37,436,934,664**	**26.6**

Source: Dun & Bradstreet

Women Entrepreneurs

Women owned more than 6.4 million businesses in 1992, generating $1.6 trillion in revenues, according to a Census Bureau survey. Here are the metropolitan areas with the most women-owned firms:

Metropolitan area	Number of firms in 1992
Los Angeles-Long Beach	232,723
New York	187,525
Chicago	163,883
Washington, DC	122,007
Philadelphia	95,441
Houston	87,303
Boston	86,133
Atlanta	82,821
Dallas	80,830
Detroit	80,673

Source: U.S. Census Bureau

Largest Women-Controlled Businesses in 1997

Rank	Company, location	Name, title	Sales ($ million)	Employees
1	JM Family Enterprises, Deerfield Beach, FL	Pat Moran, President, CEO	5,400.0	3,000
2	Fidelity Investments, Boston, MA	Abigail Johnson, Sr. VP, Equities	5,000.0	25,000
3	Ingram Industries, Nashville, TN	Martha Ingram, Chair, CEO	2,350.0	5,300
4	Carlson Cos., Minneapolis, MN	Marilyn Carlson, Vice Chair, CEO	2,300.0	44,000
5	Little Caesar Enterprises, Detroit, MI	Marian Ilitch, Vice Chair	2,100.0	8,100
6	Mary Kay Cosmetics, Dallas, TX	Mary Kay Ash, Chair Emeritus	2,000.0	3,000
7	Raley's, West Sacramento, CA	Joyce Raley Teal, Co-chair	1,957.0	12,900
8	Washington Post Co., Washington, DC*	Katharine Graham, Chair, Exec. Committee	1,937.5	7,010
9	Alberto-Culver Co., Melrose Park, IL*	Bernice Lavin, Vice Chair Carol Bernick, Exec. VP	1,775.3	11,000
10	84 Lumber, Eighty-Four, PA	Maggie Hardy Magerko, President, COO	1,600.0	4,500
11	Roll International, Los Angeles, CA	Lynda Resnick, Co-owner, Vice Chair	1,511.0	7,500
12	Warnaco Group, New York, NY*	Linda Wachner, Chair, President, CEO	1,436.0	17,323
13	Frank Consolidated Enterprises, Des Plaines, IL	Elaine S. Frank, Chair	1,435.7	600
14	Axel Johnson Group, Stamford, CT	Antonia Axson Johnson, Chair	1,400.0	2,000
15	Cumberland Farms, Canton, MA	Lily Bentas, President, CEO	1,155.0	7,100
16	Sutherland Lumber, Kansas City, MO	Donna Sutherland Pearson, CEO	990.0	3,000
17	Minyard Food Stores, Coppell, TX	Gretchen Minyard Williams, Co-chair Liz Minyard, Co-chair	984.2	7,700
18	Printpack, Atlanta, GA	Gay Love, Chair	899.0	4,000
19	Software Spectrum, Garland, TX*	Judy Sims, Chair, President, CEO	860.2	1,650
20	J. Crew, New York, NY	Emily Woods, Chair	830.0	6,300

*Public company.
Note: For a company to make the list, a woman must be the largest individual shareholder. At public companies, she must hold at least 5% of the stock; at private companies, at least 10%. If she shares ownership equally with a partner or family member, she qualifies. If a business is family-owned and the woman is chairman, president or CEO, she is included, even if her exact ownership stake could not be determined.
Source: Working Woman *magazine, MacDonald Communications Corp.*

Top Black-Owned Companies

Black Enterprise magazine's ranking of the largest industrial and service companies that are at least 51% black-owned.

1997 rank	1996 rank	Company and location	Type of business	Year started	No. of employees	1997 revenues ($ thousands)
1	1	TLC Beatrice International Holdings Inc., New York, NY	Manufacturing and distribution of grocery products	1987	4,500	$1,400,000
2	2	Johnson Publishing Co. Inc., Chicago, IL	Publishing, broadcasting, TV production, cosmetics, hair care	1942	2,877	361,112
3	3	Philadelphia Coca-Cola Bottling Co., New York, NY	Soft-drink bottling	1985	1,500	357,000
4	–	Active Transportation, Louisville, KY	Transportation services, hauling of cars and trucks to dealers	1987	1,600	250,000
5	11	The Bing Group, Detroit, MI	Steel processing, steel stamping, full seat assembly, foam manufacturing	1980	594	183,000
6	7	Granite Broadcasting Corp., New York, NY	Company sells commercial time primarily to retail businesses	1988	1,200	181,083
7	10	BET Holdings Inc., Washington, DC	Cable television programming and magazine publishing	1982	563	170,000
8	5	H.J. Russell & Co., Atlanta, GA	Construction, property mgt., airport concessions, real estate development	1952	1,862	155,300
9	4	Pulsar Data Systems Inc., Lanham, MD	Computer systems (sales, design, support, installation)	1983	85	151,000
10	13	Anderson-Dubose Co., Solon, OH	Food, paper products and operating supplies distributor	1991	88	138,700
11	–	World Wide Technology, Inc., St. Louis, MO	Distribution of computer hardware/software/services	1990	175	135,000
12	17	Mays Chemical Co. Inc., Indianapolis, IN	Stocking distributor and inventory management of raw materials	1980	132	123,000
13	16	Midwest Stamping Co., Bowling Green, OH	Automotive metal stamping and assemblies	1993	545	121,000
14	18	Barden Co. Inc., Detroit, MI	Casino gaming, interactive training, real estate development	1981	1,600	110,000
15	–	Simeus Foods International, Mansfield, TX	Custom food manufacturing for national chain account restaurant	1996	400	105,000
16	19	Essence Communications Inc., New York, NY	Magazine publishing and entertainment	1969	136	104,822
17	25	Spiral, Inc., Chandler, AZ	Supplies and services to grocery stores and amusement entertainment facilities	1989	6	100,000
18	20	Soft Sheen Products Inc., Chicago, IL	Manufacturer of ethnic hair care products	1964	395	95,000
18	21	Wesley International Inc., Bloomfield Hills, MI	Coatings and castings	1983	800	95,000
20	22	Thomas Madison Inc., Detroit, MI	Metal fabricator and full line steel service center to automotive manufacturers	1990	650	90,000

Source: Black Enterprise

Boom in Black-Owned Businesses

Number of Black-Owned Firms in the U.S.

46% Increase

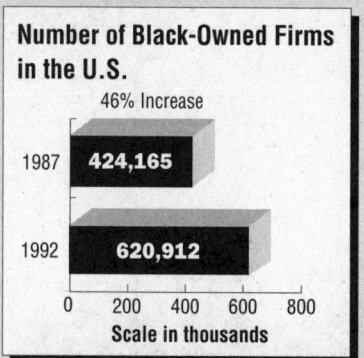

1987	424,165
1992	620,912

0   200   400   600   800
Scale in thousands

Revenues of Black-Owned Firms in the U.S. (In billions)

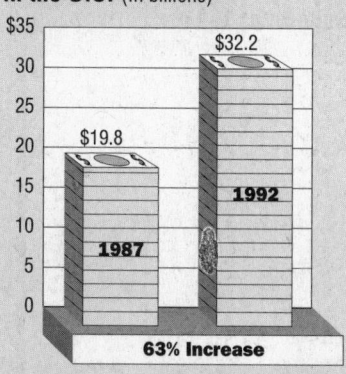

$35 — $32.2 (1992)
$19.8 (1987)

63% Increase

Metropolitan Areas with the Most Black-Owned Firms

Metropolitan area	Number of firms in 1992
New York	39,404
Washington, DC	37,988
Los Angeles-Long Beach	32,645
Chicago	24,644
Atlanta	23,488
Houston	18,840
Philadelphia	13,956
Detroit	13,910
Baltimore	12,492
Dallas	11,395

Source: U.S. Census Bureau

Hispanic-Owned Firms Flourish

Hispanic-Owned Businesses in the U.S.

76% Increase

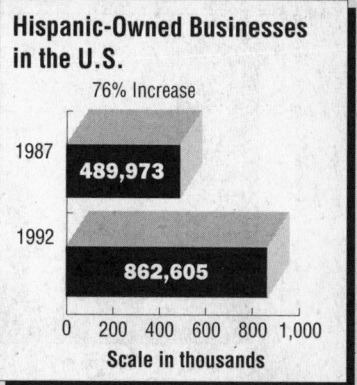

1987	489,973
1992	862,605

0   200   400   600   800   1,000
Scale in thousands

Revenues of Hispanic-Owned Firms in the U.S. (In billions)

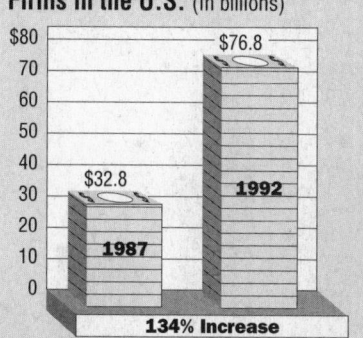

$80 — $76.8 (1992)
$32.8 (1987)

134% Increase

Metropolitan Areas with the Most Hispanic-Owned Firms

Metropolitan area	Number of firms in 1992
Los Angeles-Long Beach	109,104
Miami	77,300
New York	39,175
Houston	33,765
Riverside-San Bernardino, CA	21,380
San Antonio	21,244
Orange County, CA	19,270
San Diego	18,983
Chicago	16,663
Dallas	14,791

Source: U.S. Census Bureau

Hispanic-Owned Business Revenues, by Subgroup, 1992 (In billions)

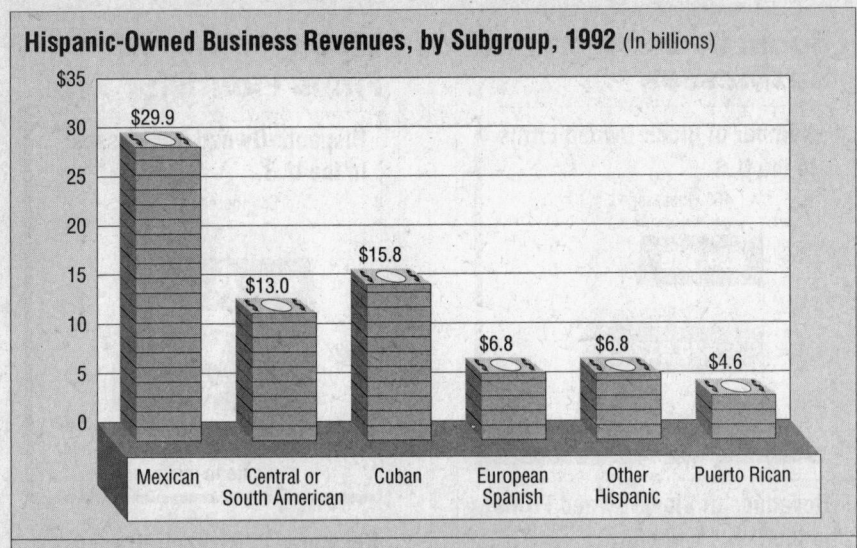

Number of Hispanic-Owned Businesses, by Subgroup, 1992

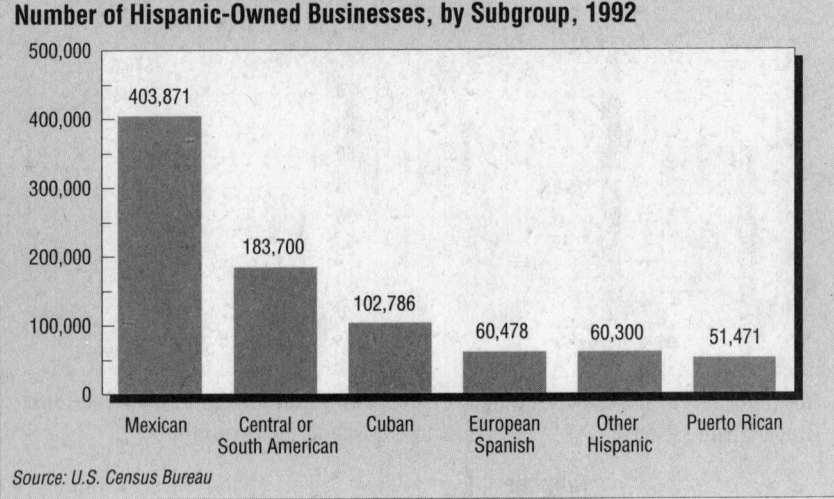

Source: U.S. Census Bureau

Top Hispanic-Owned Companies

Hispanic Business magazine's ranking of the largest companies that are at least 51% owned by Hispanic U.S. citizens.

1997 rank	1996 rank	Company and location	Type of business	Year started	No. of employ- ees	1997 revenues ($ thousands)
1	5	Vincam Group Inc., Coral Gables, FL	Employment services	1984	550	$983,630
2	1	Burt Automotive Network, Englewood, CO	Automotive sales and services	1939	875	866,560
3	3	MasTec Inc., Miami, FL	Telecommunications infrastructure construction	1969	8,800	703,400
4	2	Goya Foods Inc., Secaucus, NJ	Hispanic food manufacturing and marketing	1936	500	620,000
5	7	Ancira Enterprises Inc., San Antonio, TX	Automotive sales and services	1983	520	412,250
6	11	International Bancshares Corp., Laredo, TX	Banking services	1965	1,276	312,510
7	6	Troy Ford, Troy, MI	Automotive sales and services	1967	108	308,500
8	10	AJ Contracting Co. Inc., New York, NY	Construction management/ contracting	1917	205	276,000
9	9	Sedano's Supermarkets, Miami, FL	Supermarket chain	1962	1,700	271,000
10	12	IFS Financial Corp., Wilmington, DE	Financial services	1995	1,597	234,700
11	15	Lloyd A. Wise Cos., Oakland, CA	Automotive sales and services	1914	253	223,500
12	4	de la Cruz Cos., Miami, FL	Beer wholesaler	1984	750	218,450
13	20	Precision Trading Corp., Miami, FL	Consumer electronics wholesaler	1979	55	181,000
14	18	Mexican Industries in Michigan Inc., Detroit, MI	Automotive soft trim manufacturing	1979	1,478	167,090
15	26	Rosendin Electric Inc., San Jose, CA	Electrical contracting	1919	1,350	167,000
16	21	Lopez Foods Inc., Oklahoma City, OK	Meat products manufacturing	1989	265	161,290
17	19	Supreme International Corp., Miami, FL	Men's apparel design and wholesaler	1967	336	155,710
18	27	HUSCO International Inc., Waukesha, WI	Hydraulic controls manufacturing	1985	770	145,000
19	33	Physicians Healthcare Plans Inc., Coral Gables, FL	Managed health care services	1993	521	130,000
20	23	Avanti/Case-Hoyt, Miami, FL	Commercial printing services	1965	1,000	125,000

Source: Hispanic Business Inc., Santa Barbara, CA

Growth of Firms Owned by Asian and Native Americans

Asian– and Pacific Islander– Owned Businesses in the U.S.

56% Increase

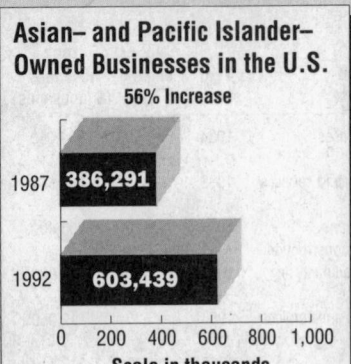

1987 — 386,291

1992 — 603,439

0   200   400   600   800   1,000

Scale in thousands

American Indian– and Alaska Native– Owned Businesses in the U.S.

93% Increase

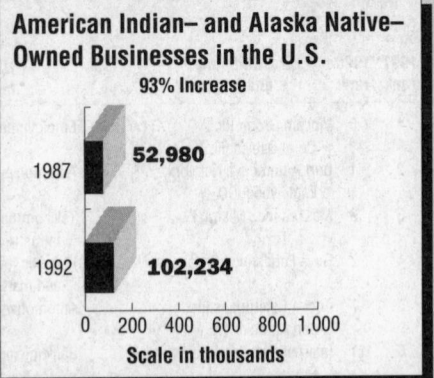

1987 — 52,980

1992 — 102,234

0   200   400   600   800   1,000

Scale in thousands

Revenues of Asian– and Pacific Islander–Owned Firms in the U.S. (In billions)

163% Increase

$100
90
80
70
60
50
40
30
20
10
0

$36.5 (1987) $96.0 (1992)

Revenues of American Indian– and Alaska Native–Owned Firms in the U.S. (In billions)

115% Increase

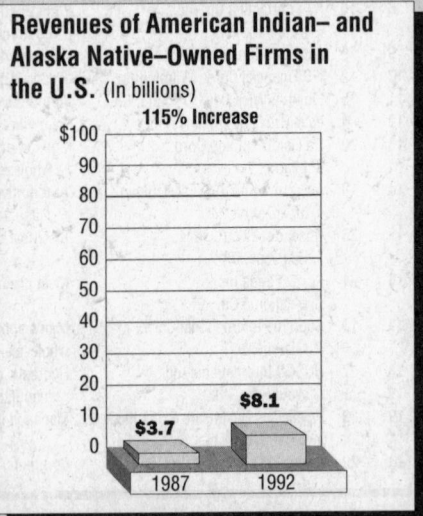

$100
90
80
70
60
50
40
30
20
10
0

$3.7 (1987) $8.1 (1992)

Metropolitan Areas With the Most Asian–, Pacific Islander–, American Indian–, and Alaska Native–Owned Firms

Metropolitan area	Number of firms, 1992	Metropolitan area	Number of firms, 1992
Los Angeles-Long Beach	92,209	Oakland	19,758
New York	50,283	Washington, DC	19,722
Honolulu	29,940	Chicago	19,706
Orange County, CA	27,252	San Jose	19,113
San Francisco	24,185	Houston	15,010

Source: U.S. Census Bureau

Asian and Pacific Islander–Owned Business Revenue, by Subgroup, 1992

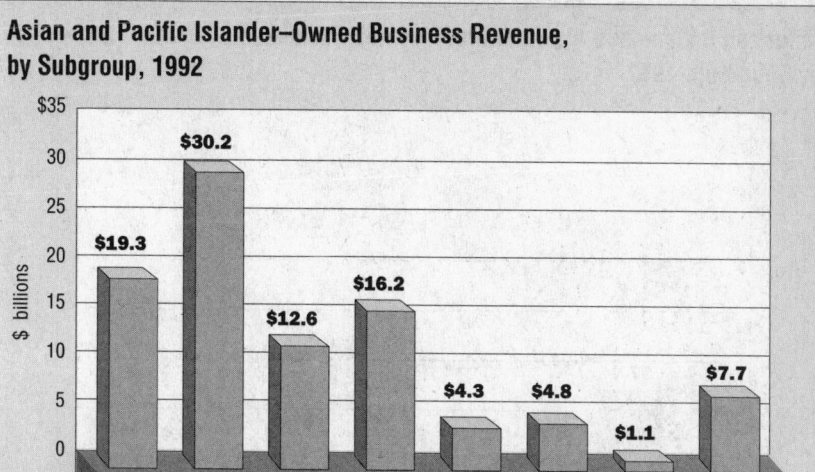

Number of Asian– and Pacific Islander–Owned Buisinesses, by Subgroup, 1992

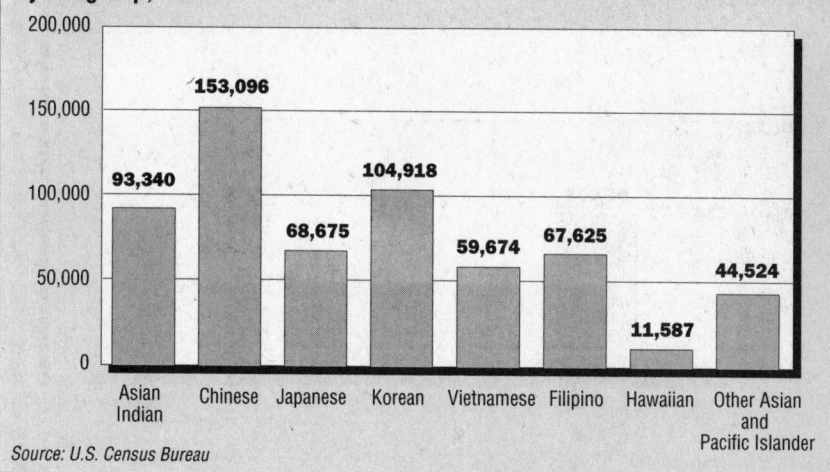

Source: U.S. Census Bureau

American Indian– and Alaska Native– Owned Business Revenue, by Subgroup, 1992

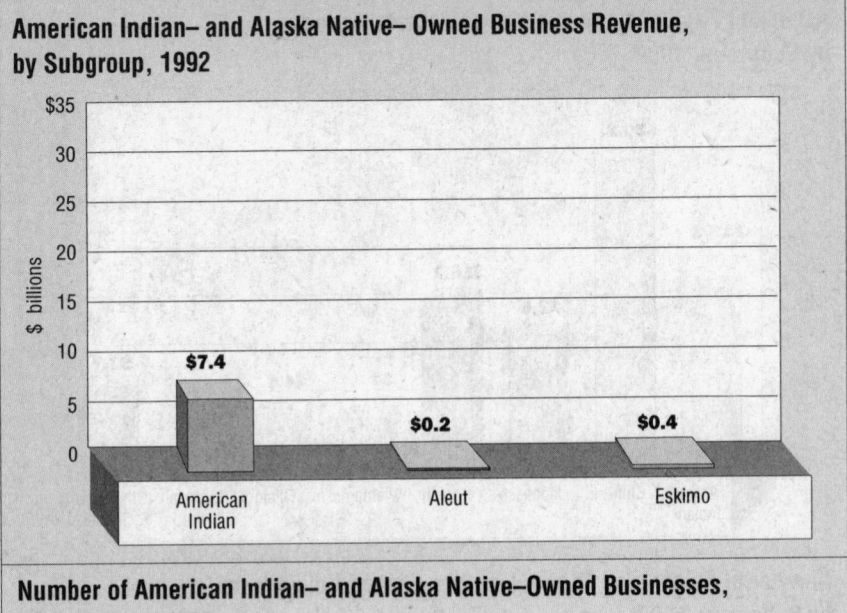

Number of American Indian– and Alaska Native–Owned Businesses, by Subgroup, 1992

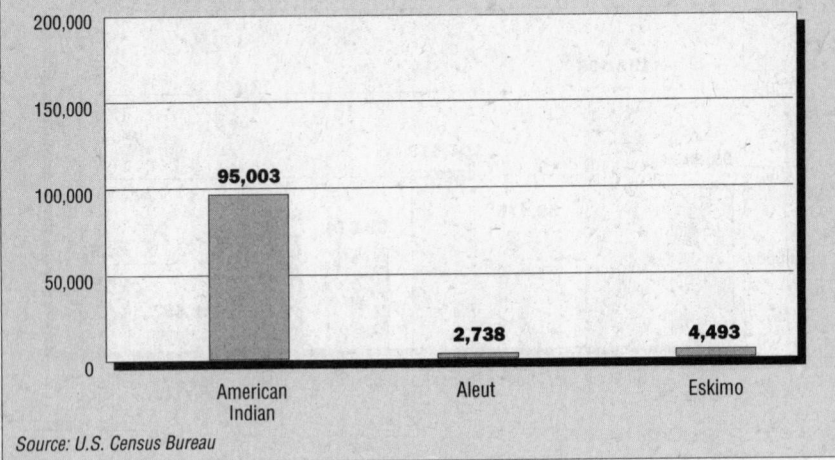

Source: U.S. Census Bureau

Job Creation by Small Business
Number of Jobs Created, by Size of Business

U.S. Job Growth, 1992–1996

Source: U.S. Small Business Administration

Entrepreneurial Ventures

Top 20 Types of Business Start-Ups in 1997

RANK	DESCRIPTION	TOTAL	RANK	DESCRIPTION	TOTAL
1	Retail Stores	37,122	11	Beauty Salons	12,158
2	Construction	32,320	12	Painters	8,855
3	Computer Services	27,114	13	Gift Shops	8,533
4	Business Consultants	23,170	14	Marketing Programs & Services	8,125
5	General Contractors	23,067	15	Crafts	7,640
6	Restaurants	21,644	16	Trucking	7,556
7	Cleaning Service	17,134	17	Health Services	6,481
8	Landscape Contractors	17,025	18	Vending Machines	5,579
9	Real Estate	16,290	19	Graphic Designers	5,565
10	Automobile Repairing & Service	14,078	20	Importers	5,376

Source: County Data Corp.

Venture Dollars and Deals

The number of companies backed by venture capital has continued to rise throughout the 1990s, with the share of venture capital going to information-technology companies increasing to 62% of the total in 1997 from 47% in 1992.

Total Venture Capital and Deals

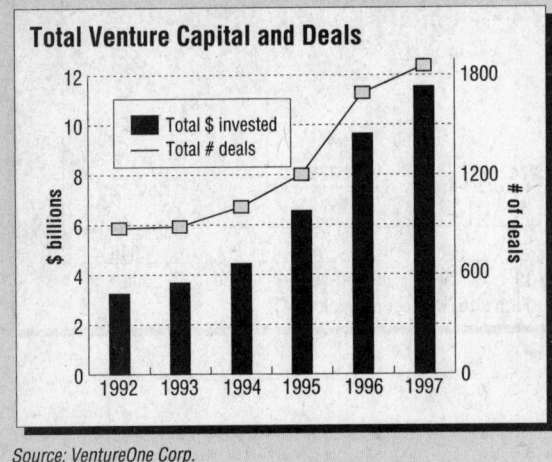

1997 Venture Dollars Invested by Industry Group

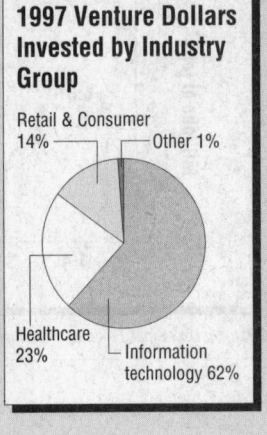

Source: VentureOne Corp.

FRANCHISE EMPIRES

At first glance, Bill Byrne seems the quintessential franchising success story: One-time Iowa farm boy with no restaurant experience opens Taco John's outlet, works hard, passes operation over to son.

But a closer look at Mr. Byrne's business reveals the type of larger, sophisticated operation that is moving franchising beyond its mom-and-pop stereotypes. Since opening his first restaurant in 1973, he has added 13 more Taco John's in and around Des Moines, all supported by the same advertising and accounting systems. "The future money is going to develop for those who can quickly set up economies of scale," says Mr. Byrne.

These days, Mr. Byrne resides in South Dakota and has another home overlooking a lake in Colorado. He's set up a small company—Taco John's of Iowa Inc. in Des Moines—to run the 14 restaurants. Among the administrators there: a director of human resources, a job that like many others he once handled himself.

National statistics show operations like Mr. Byrne's are becoming more common. At Frandata, a franchise tracking firm in Washington, D.C., 40 percent of the 219,714 franchised units in its database are owned by franchisees who operate at least two outlets.

Some franchisees are even branching into more than one concept. In Southern California, franchisee Blair Taylor owns five Athlete's Foot shops and one Mail Boxes Etc. outlet and is building another Mail Boxes. One economy of scale: The shoe stores' printing and mailing needs are taken care of by his Mail Boxes operations.

Frandata says an increasing number of franchise chains are selling development rights only to multi-unit franchisees. And why not? These franchisees pay the same royalties, have more experience and give the franchisers fewer people to deal with. "We're easy money. One call does it all," says Mr. Byrne.

As for the nation's largest outlet owners, they keep getting larger. In 1997 the top 200 restaurant franchisees operated 14,170 units, up 10.3 percent from the 12,846 they operated in 1996, according to the *Restaurant Finance Monitor*, a Roseville, Minnesota-based newsletter. The total revenue of the top 200 was $13.1 billion, up 12 percent from $11.7 billion in 1996.

Topping the list is RTM Restaurant Group,

Atlanta, which has 150 central employees who occupy a two-story office building. RTM owns 706 Arby's Roast Beef outlets and seven Del Taco outlets. RTM even owns two entire restaurant chains—Lee's Famous Recipe Chicken and Mrs. Winner's Chicken and Biscuits—becoming a franchiser in its own right.

It's getting harder for ground-floor entrepreneurs to enter this big-time market. Consider the case of Tricon Global Restaurant Inc.'s Taco Bell chain, which sells new restaurants only to its existing outlet owners who want to expand. As for anyone who wants to join the chain, they must purchase at least three existing, company-owned outlets. And the minimum requirements for these prospects is strictly large scale: investment of $2 million to $3 million, net worth of $600,000, exclusive of personal residence and property, and multi-unit restaurant experience of at least three years.

Such standards at the large chains make it even more imperative that the smaller franchisee be willing to grow. In Des Moines, Mr. Byrne says he's been able to compete so well against Taco Bell because he has enough outlets that when banded together, they can create advertising to match the larger players. Relying heavily on television advertising, "We can make noise at the right decibel level," Mr. Byrne says, noting that his

Taco John's units typically bring in 30 to 35 percent more than the $410,000 in revenue at the average Taco John's outlet.

The 54-year-old says that in the restaurant game, capital costs have gone up in the last 10 years while menu prices have essentially stayed the same. With margins decreasing, market penetration becomes even more important. So Mr. Byrne recommends that those wanting to open just one unit do so in an area so small that it takes only one outlet to penetrate the entire market.

"At the moment, I think the little guy is best off in the little markets; I think the little guy has to be very cautious these days," says Mr. Byrne, whose 1992 book *Habits of Wealth* has been translated into eight different languages.

Of course, it's possible for a single-unit operator to survive in a larger market. But often that's all they do—and end up investing their life savings simply to buy themselves a job, one that has them at it 12 hours a day, seven days a week.

Or they'll buy themselves an even bigger problem. Mr. Byrne cites his own experience. When he tried to open a check-cashing franchise outlet in Omaha, Nebraska, he couldn't make enough money to expand into more outlets. Nor did he get much support from the chain itself. "Basically, I think it was two fools getting together," he concedes, saying he

Franchising Field

Estimated Number of Franchise Establishments in the U.S.

Year	Franchisee owned	Total (incl. company owned units)
1981	356,000	442,000
1982	353,000	440,000
1983	355,000	441,000
1984	357,000	444,000
1985	369,000	455,000
1986	374,000	463,000
1987	390,000	479,000
1988	386,844	480,789
1989	404,269	498,780
1990	435,191	532,959
1991	442,000	542,496
1992	465,691	571,574
1993	498,057	611,298
1994	540,342	663,197

Source: International Franchise Association

Office Space

Office Building Vacancy Rates and Rental Rates, Second Quarter 1998

Region/ area/ market	Overall vacancy rates		Average rental rates (per square foot)		
	Central business district	Non-central business district	Central business district	Non-central business district	Overall
Atlanta, GA	14.7%	13.7%	$18.34	$22.64	$22.01
Boston, MA	6.1	9.2	38.35	25.04	28.62
Southern NH	*	15.6	*	16.32	16.32
Hartford, CT	18.0	14.6	22.90	18.54	20.74
New Haven, CT	22.0	15.3	21.62	22.76	22.44
New England area totals:	8.3	10.9			
Downtown, NY	9.2	*	36.48	*	36.48
Midtown, NY	7.5	*	42.90	*	42.90
Midtown South, NY	7.2	*	30.26	*	30.26
Brooklyn, NY	9.0	*	25.06	*	25.06
Long Island, NY	*	10.8	*	26.69	26.69
Central NJ	*	12.8	*	23.08	23.08
Northern NJ	*	12.2	*	27.35	27.35
Westchester County, NY	25.3	12.7	26.51	26.90	26.74
Fairfield County, CT	5.2	10.4	31.21	24.88	25.77
New York area totals:	8.2	12.0			
Baltimore, MD	18.5	8.2	23.39	18.86	20.36
Northern VA	*	4.8	*	26.31	26.31
Suburban MD	*	11.7	*	22.83	22.83
Washington, DC	9.8	*	37.11	*	37.11
Philadelphia, PA	16.2	9.2	23.58	20.28	22.11
Mid-Atlantic area totals:	12.5	7.8			
Ft. Lauderdale, FL	11.1	13.5	27.55	22.74	23.59
West Palm Beach, FL	20.3	11.7	30.41	24.50	25.36
Miami, FL	16.0	12.5	27.36	24.07	26.59
Tampa, FL	16.5	12.0	20.72	20.81	20.78
St. Petersburg/Clearwater, FL	*	10.2	*	16.61	16.61
Orlando, FL	8.0	8.9	24.24	19.87	20.52
Florida area totals:	14.4	11.7			

eventually lost about $50,000 before shutting down.

By comparison, his Taco John's have fared well because he's steadily expanded. When he opened in 1973 he had only enough money to acquire a $39,500 single unit—a 12-foot-wide, 32-foot-long modular structure that arrived on the back of a truck. His first day, he made $353. "I had in my pocket the finances of a single-unit operator, but I had in my head the vision of a fairly sophisticated operation," Mr. Byrne says.

With his current 14 outlets, he says he has more than reached a critical mass. But even with as few as four to six units, he says, "We'd be a bit player on the margin of failure. We could be gone—or wish we were."

Dan Morse

Region/ area/ market	Overall vacancy rates		Average rental rates (per square foot)		
	Central business district	Non-central business district	Central business district	Non-central business district	Overall
Dallas, TX	29.1%	9.4%	$20.96	$24.43	$22.80
Houston, TX	17.4	13.4	20.26	20.63	20.47
Denver, CO	10.4	11.4	21.05	21.17	21.14
Texas/Denver area totals:	19.6	11.4			
Chicago, IL	12.5	11.2	29.09	25.89	27.66
Detroit, MI	16.1	8.0	18.24	23.16	21.07
St. Louis, MO	16.1	9.1	19.76	21.06	20.44
Midwest area totals:	13.2	9.8			
Seattle, WA	4.8	9.7	26.20	16.13	21.82
Bellevue, WA	4.8	3.1	28.65	27.48	27.83
Portland, OR	8.0	7.9	20.30	19.98	20.18
Pacific Northwest area totals:	5.9	6.3			
San Francisco, CA	4.9	8.2	45.60	33.96	39.72
Oakland, CA	15.1	13.0		28.20	24.96
SF Peninsula, CA	*	4.9	24.24	39.60	39.60
Contra Costa, CA	*	6.1	*	24.36	24.36
San Jose, CA	6.3	6.0	*	36.12	36.00
Northern California area totals:	6.9	7.0			
Los Angeles, CA	21.7	26.2	34.20	18.24	19.80
Los Angeles-North, CA	*	17.2	21.12	23.28	23.28
Los Angeles-South, CA	*	19.4	*	20.76	20.76
Los Angeles-West, CA	*	11.4	*	30.36	30.36
Los Angeles-Tri-Cities, CA	*	13.0	*	26.64	26.64
Ontario, CA	*	26.2	*	19.56	19.56
Orange County, CA	11.9	12.4	27.72	21.84	26.28
Southern California area totals:	16.5	17.3			
Phoenix, AZ	12.0	8.8	21.09	22.70	22.32
National totals:	11.0	11.1			

*Not applicable.
Note: Rental rates are for office space offered through the landlord and are weighted by the amount of available space at each rental rate.
Source: Cushman & Wakefield Inc.

Farm Erosion

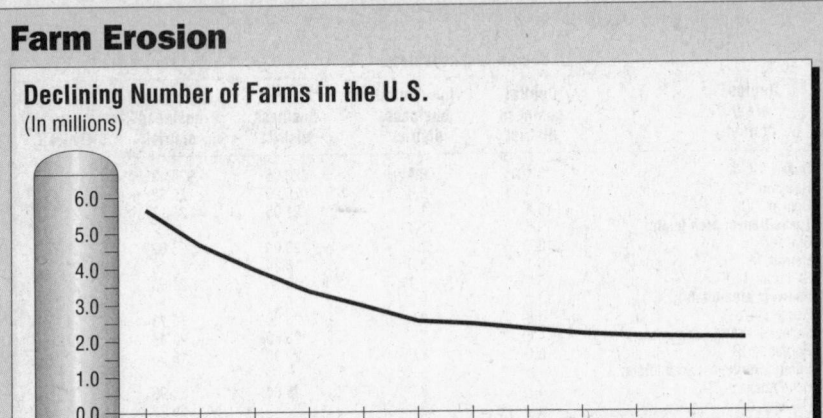

Declining Number of Farms in the U.S.
(In millions)

Fewer But Bigger Farms

Year	Number of Farms	Land in Farms (1,000 acres)	Average size (acres)	Year	Number of Farms	Land in Farms (1,000 acres)	Average size (acres)
1950	5,647,800	1,202,019	213	1974	2,795,460	1,084,433	388
1951	5,427,600	1,203,500	222	1975	2,521,420	1,059,420	420
1952	5,197,500	1,204,740	232	1976	2,497,270	1,054,075	422
1953	4,983,600	1,205,740	242	1977	2,455,830	1,047,785	427
1954	4,798,200	1,206,355	251	1978	2,436,250	1,044,790	429
1955	4,653,800	1,201,840	258	1979	2,437,300	1,043,195	428
1956	4,514,100	1,197,070	265	1980	2,439,510	1,038,885	426
1957	4,371,700	1,191,340	273	1981	2,439,920	1,034,190	424
1958	4,232,900	1,184,944	280	1982	2,406,550	1,027,795	427
1959	4,104,520	1,182,563	288	1983	2,378,620	1,023,425	430
1960	3,962,520	1,175,646	297	1984	2,333,810	1,017,803	436
1961	3,825,410	1,167,699	305	1985	2,292,530	1,012,073	441
1962	3,692,410	1,159,383	314	1986	2,249,820	1,005,333	447
1963	3,572,200	1,151,572	322	1987	2,212,960	998,923	451
1964	3,456,690	1,146,106	332	1988	2,200,940	994,423	452
1965	3,356,170	1,139,597	340	1989	2,174,520	990,723	456
1966	3,257,040	1,131,844	348	1990	2,145,820	986,850	460
1967	3,161,730	1,123,456	355	1991	2,116,760	981,736	464
1968	3,070,860	1,115,231	363	1992	2,107,840	978,503	464
1969	3,000,180	1,107,811	369	1993	2,083,430	976,463	469
1970	2,949,140	1,102,371	374	1994	2,064,720	973,403	471
1971	2,902,310	1,096,863	378	1995	2,071,520	972,253	469
1972	2,859,880	1,092,065	382	1996	2,063,910	970,048	470
1973	2,823,260	1,087,923	385	1997	2,057,910	968,338	471

Source: U.S. Agriculture Department

Farm Income (In billions)

Income of farm operators from farming

Year	Gross farm income					Production expenses	Net farm income
		Cash marketing receipts			Value of inventory changes**		
	Total*	Total	Livestock and products	Crops			
1945	$25.4	$21.7	$12.0	$ 9.7	$-0.04	$13.1	$12.3
1950	33.1	28.5	16.1	12.4	0.8	19.5	13.6
1955	33.5	29.5	16.0	13.5	0.2	22.2	11.3
1960	38.6	34.0	19.0	15.0	0.4	27.4	11.2
1965	46.5	39.4	21.9	17.5	1.0	33.6	12.9
1970	58.8	50.5	29.5	21.0	0.0	44.5	14.4
1975	100.6	88.9	43.1	45.8	3.4	75.0	25.5
1980	149.3	139.7	68.0	71.7	-6.3	133.1	16.1
1981	166.3	141.6	69.2	72.5	6.5	139.4	26.9
1982	164.1	142.6	70.3	72.3	-1.4	140.3	23.8
1983	153.9	136.8	69.6	67.2	-10.9	139.6	14.2
1984	168.0	142.8	72.9	69.9	6.0	142.0	26.0
1985	161.2	144.1	69.8	74.3	-2.3	132.6	28.6
1986	156.1	135.4	71.6	63.8	-2.2	125.2	30.9
1987	168.4	141.8	76.0	65.8	-2.3	131.0	37.4
1988	177.9	151.2	79.6	71.6	-4.1	139.9	38.0
1989	191.9	160.8	83.9	76.9	3.8	146.7	45.3
1990	198.2	169.5	89.2	80.3	3.3	153.4	44.8
1991	191.9	167.9	85.8	82.1	-0.2	153.3	38.5
1992	200.6	171.3	85.6	85.7	4.2	152.5	48.0
1993	204.2	177.6	90.2	87.5	-4.5	160.5	43.6
1994	215.8	181.2	88.2	93.1	8.3	167.5	48.3
1995	210.1	188.1	87.0	101.0	-5.1	174.1	36.0
1996	235.8	199.6	93.0	106.6	7.8	182.4	53.4
1997	238.3	208.7	96.6	112.1	-0.4	188.4	49.8
1998†	229.2	199.1	94.4	104.8	-1.1	187.2	42.0

*Cash marketing receipts and inventory changes plus government payments, other farm cash income, and nonmoney income furnished by farms.
**Physical changes in end-of-period inventory of crop and livestock commodities valued at average prices during the period.
†Projections.

Ranking of 10 Leading States in Cash Receipts for Top 10 Commodities, 1996

	Commodity	Value $ millions	State and dollars (In millions)									
			1	2	3	4	5	6	7	8	9	10
1	Cattle & calves	$31,138	$5,331 TX	$4,082 NE	$3,995 KS	$2,072 CO	$1,461 IA	$1,446 OK	$1,145 CA	$946 SD	$925 MN	$656 MT
2	Dairy products	22,834	3,717 CA	3,262 WI	1,693 NY	1,662 PA	1,362 MN	921 TX	807 MI	788 WA	653 ID	651 OH
3	Corn	21,573	4,290 IA	3,546 IL	2,491 NE	1,784 IN	1,704 MN	947 OH	783 KS	707 WI	684 TX	670 MO
4	Soybeans	16,211	2,892 IA	2,784 IL	1,618 MN	1,453 IN	1,126 OH	996 MO	828 NE	763 AR	561 SD	455 KS
5	Broilers	13,906	2,205 GA	2,122 AR	1,635 AL	1,310 NC	1,197 MS	726 TX	524 DE	513 MD	466 VA	457 CA
6	Hogs	12,644	3,004 IA	1,749 NC	1,116 MN	1,039 IL	856 NE	830 IN	652 MO	398 OH	328 KS	325 SD
7	Greenhouse & nursery	10,887	2,224 CA	1,140 FL	889 NC	838 TX	517 OH	442 OR	422 MI	318 PA	273 GA	263 OK
8	Wheat	9,956	1,607 ND	1,184 KS	861 MT	775 WA	520 SD	484 ID	413 MN	398 OK	391 CO	338 NE
9	Cotton	7,461	1,810 TX	1,191 CA	782 GA	726 MS	625 AR	520 LA	343 NC	341 AZ	276 TN	260 AL
10	Chicken eggs	4,757	367 CA	359 OH	348 GA	320 IN	300 AR	295 PA	291 TX	247 IA	225 AL	218 NC
	Livestock & products	92,814	7,758 TX	6,213 CA	5,457 IA	5,277 NE	4,570 KS	4,427 NC	4,288 WI	4,168 MN	3,357 AR	3,279 GA
	Crops	109,425	17,096 CA	7,396 IA	6,989 IL	5,295 TX	4,942 FL	4,641 MN	4,177 NE	4,017 WA	3,663 IN	3,404 NC
	Total	202,339	23,310 CA	13,053 TX	12,853 IA	9,454 NE	9,050 IL	8,809 MN	7,869 KS	7,831 NC	6,131 FL	6,062 WI

Spirit of Generosity

Total amount of money given to different causes in current and inflation-adjusted dollars

(In billions)

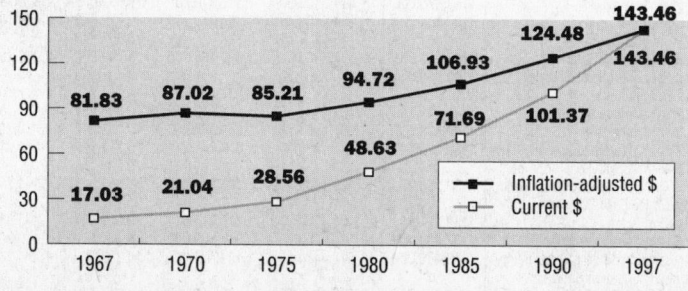

Source: American Association of Fund-Raising Counsel Trust for Philanthropy

50 Largest U.S. Recipients of Private Charitable Contributions, 1996

	Income		Expenses		
	Private support	Total	Program services	Fund raising	Total
1 Salvation Army	$1,012,403,000	$2,055,320,000	n/a	n/a	n/a
2 American Red Cross	479,928,282	1,806,593,892	$1,604,021,713	$72,069,898	$1,756,331,785
3 American Cancer Society	426,695,000	510,632,000	296,776,000	91,001,000	415,886,000
4 Emory University	415,406,381	1,645,065,469	1,088,721,017	6,797,232	1,095,518,249
5 Catholic Charities USA	386,545,894	2,154,506,918	1,871,332,111	28,698,031	2,053,507,893
6 Second Harvest*	351,376,162	353,486,271	351,850,796	496,777	352,954,746
7 YMCA of the USA	340,337,000	2,473,023,000	1,994,564,000	28,274,000	2,383,642,000
8 Habitat for Humanity International	334,737,000	336,542,000	227,522,000	20,350,000	270,889,000
9 Boys and Girls Clubs of America	321,757,180	437,764,871	346,961,996	21,922,265	421,582,012
10 Stanford University	312,887,120	2,022,226,608	1,465,071,308	20,757,270	1,674,334,861
11 Harvard University	309,360,000	2,769,240,457	1,271,357,915	35,188,810	1,369,907,489
12 Fidelity Investments Charitable Gift Fund	298,186,219	342,851,472	114,987,277	1,253,253	118,788,458
13 American Heart Association	273,989,000	345,230,000	251,600,000	43,819,000	321,699,000
14 YWCA of the USA	265,352,445	510,829,407	417,291,916	11,952,375	493,879,144
15 Gifts in Kind International*	223,871,836	226,757,463	208,180,703	41,299	208,619,370
16 Boy Scouts of America	233,230,000	553,471,000	404,595,000	34,101,000	500,750,000
17 Shriners Hospitals for Children	220,123,000	721,317,000	318,451,000	2,501,000	334,624,000
18 Cornell University	219,746,000	1,641,918,000	1,222,310,000	19,609,000	1,314,247,000
19 Campus Crusade for Christ International	212,794,000	240,934,000	208,816,000	17,757,000	226,573,000
20 Nature Conservancy	203,886,056	337,533,794	260,462,868	30,794,077	316,108,987
21 University of Wisconsin at Madison	186,694,596	1,593,637,298	1,333,446,383	3,777,461	1,494,420,076
22 World Vision	184,662,922	303,566,772	234,702,690	33,645,246	296,257,319
23 Duke University	181,258,000	1,535,468,063	1,391,024,666	7,932,669	1,413,114,230
24 AmeriCares Foundation*	174,208,751	174,572,611	170,871,251	2,055,748	174,062,793
25 ALSAC/St. Jude Children's Research Hospital	174,131,722	303,857,816	126,721,909	29,413,902	178,483,604

	Income		Expenses		
	Private support	Total	Program services	Fund raising	Total
26 Yale University	$172,165,000	$1,566,328,554	$915,549,917	$25,734,904	$956,800,088
27 New York Community Trust	165,554,617	263,188,007	83,863,095	589,845	89,457,506
28 Columbia University	163,870,000	1,641,918,000	1,222,310,000	19,609,000	1,314,247,000
29 Jewish Communal Fund	160,354,678	184,446,843	65,050,503	213,793	66,184,688
30 University of Washington	154,601,039	n/a	n/a	5,607,640	n/a
31 University of Pennsylvania	153,133,291	2,369,868,000	1,930,165,000	5,785,000	2,069,485,000
32 University of California at Berkeley	141,835,000	n/a	n/a	n/a	n/a
33 Osmond Foundation (Children's Miracle Network)	141,341,143	151,569,935	144,812,816	6,868,553	151,681,369
34 University of Minnesota	140,538,015	1,967,156,128	1,264,365,000	10,453,233	1,713,298,000
35 University of California at Los Angeles	139,820,823	1,981,423,000	1,873,707,271	15,211,729	1,888,919,000
36 United Jewish Appeal–Federation of Jewish Philanthropies of New York	139,356,279	175,194,011	125,271,059	21,650,584	161,736,621
37 March of Dimes Birth Defects Foundation	139,221,834	151,407,008	110,815,511	25,609,407	147,040,570
38 Goodwill Industries International	137,300,000	1,200,000,000	987,900,000	5,100,000	1,109,500,000
39 Massachusetts Institute of Technology	132,456,000	1,542,448,000	1,144,437,000	14,222,000	1,244,139,000
40 Community Foundation Serving Richmond and Central Virginia	132,375,870	143,410,795	26,519,642	47,742	26,594,186
41 Indiana University	131,147,335	n/a	n/a	n/a	n/a
42 Public Broadcasting Service*	129,097,184	330,309,869	313,376,965	326,850	317,503,852
43 National Association for the Exchange of Industrial Resources*	128,769,487	138,967,490	98,458,014	0	100,345,388
44 University of Southern California	128,566,000	1,189,433,000	907,781,000	14,537,000	1,001,675,000
45 University of Chicago	126,953,000	989,777,042	697,710,509	8,192,478	763,552,320
46 Larry Jones International Ministries/Feed the Children*	126,348,045	128,123,961	121,257,782	9,552,032	134,052,638
47 University of California at San Francisco	126,303,000	n/a	n/a	n/a	n/a
48 Johns Hopkins University	125,871,764	1,696,175,000	1,407,574,000	14,452,000	11,500,220,000
49 Ohio State University	124,076,806	1,891,914,000	n/a	9,000,000	1,613,781,000
50 Planned Parenthood Federation of America	122,700,000	504,000,000	385,500,000	24,200,000	477,800,000

n/a: not available.
*Noncash gifts make up 50 percent or more of private support.
Source: The Chronicle of Philanthropy

The 50 largest U.S. grantmaking foundations (ranked by total giving)

RANK	NAME	TOTAL GIVING	FISCAL YEAR END DATE
1.	The Ford Foundation	$332,412,106	09/30/96
2.	W.K. Kellogg Foundation	255,259,633	08/31/97
3.	Robert W. Woodruff Foundation, Inc.	253,271,554	12/31/96
4.	The Robert Wood Johnson Foundation	229,275,359	12/31/96
5.	The Pew Charitable Trusts	175,059,312	12/31/96
6.	Lilly Endowment, Inc.	168,322,607	12/31/96
7.	John D. and Catherine T. MacArthur Foundation	137,291,138	12/31/96
8.	The Andrew W. Mellon Foundation	113,698,038	12/31/96
9.	The David and Lucile Packard Foundation	102,778,997	12/31/96
10.	The Annenberg Foundation	97,190,186	06/30/97
11.	Open Society Institute	96,842,289	12/31/96
12.	Joseph B. Whitehead Foundation	90,567,439	12/31/96
13.	The Rockefeller Foundation	85,050,008	12/31/96
14.	The New York Community Trust	83,863,095	12/31/96

RANK	NAME	TOTAL GIVING	FISCAL YEAR END DATE
15.	The Kresge Foundation	77,145,110	12/31/96
16.	The Duke Endowment	72,952,931	12/31/96
17.	Bella Mabury Trust	72,631,764	09/30/96
18.	The Annie E. Casey Foundation	71,313,976	12/31/96
19.	The William and Flora Hewlett Foundation	69,280,500	12/31/96
20.	The McKnight Foundation	68,338,819	12/31/96
21.	Charles Stewart Mott Foundation	66,929,823	12/31/96
22.	Carnegie Corporation of New York	60,452,696	09/30/96
23.	The California Endowment	57,990,000	02/28/97
24.	The Harry and Jeanette Weinberg Foundation, Inc.	56,998,815	02/28/97
25.	Richard King Mellon Foundation	53,362,171	12/31/96
26.	The Starr Foundation	51,629,658	12/31/96
27.	Alfred P. Sloan Foundation	47,389,062	12/31/96
28.	The San Francisco Foundation	45,610,852	06/30/97
29.	Houston Endowment, Inc.	45,434,752	12/31/96
30.	F.W. Olin Foundation, Inc.	43,508,000	12/31/96
31.	Robert R. McCormick Tribune Foundation	43,218,118	12/31/96
32.	The Whitaker Foundation	42,892,208	12/31/96

RANK	NAME	TOTAL GIVING	FISCAL YEAR END DATE
33.	Weingart Foundation	40,353,859	06/30/97
34.	The James Irvine Foundation	40,019,400	12/31/96
35.	Donald W. Reynolds Foundation	39,896,778	06/30/97
36.	The Freedom Forum	38,123,440	05/31/96
37.	The William Penn Foundation	38,073,460	12/31/96
38.	AT&T Foundation	37,738,769	12/31/96
39.	John S. and James L. Knight Foundation	36,558,533	12/31/96
40.	The California Wellness Foundation	36,035,436	12/31/96
41.	Ewing Marion Kauffman Foundation	34,711,656	06/30/97
42.	DeWitt Wallace-Reader's Digest Fund, Inc.	34,054,181	12/31/96
43.	The Brown Foundation, Inc.	34,008,622	06/30/96
44.	W. M. Keck Foundation	33,125,894	12/31/96
45.	The Wal-Mart Foundation	32,571,556	01/31/96
46.	California Community Foundation	32,082,319	06/30/97
47.	The Greater Kansas City Community Foundation and Affiliated Trusts	32,027,000	12/31/96
48.	Arthur S. DeMoss Foundation	31,755,330	12/31/95
49.	The Ahmanson Foundation	31,168,451	10/31/96
50.	The Columbus Foundation and Affiliated Organizations	30,871,043	12/31/96

Source: The Foundation Center

Marketplace

Peek inside your kitchen and bathroom cabinets. Chances are they're filled with products that are New! Improved! Better Tasting! Softer! Longer Lasting! and Faster Acting!

That's because consumers in the past few years have been inundated with an unprecedented proliferation of new products from the world's packaged goods companies. Products ranging from lipstick to potato chips have been reformulated using high-tech ingredients aimed at making life easier and tastier for consumers, while sporting premium prices that fatten the bottom lines of the world's consumer-goods makers.

Procter & Gamble Co., which makes Tide detergent, Crest toothpaste and Folger's coffee, says it has more new products in its pipeline that at any other time in its history. Soon consumers may be dry cleaning at home with the company's Dryel cleaning kits, sweeping up with the Swiffer Sweeper, easing their aches and pains with ThermaCare heat wraps and washing their fruits and vegetables with Fit produce cleaner.

At Colgate-Palmolive Co., nearly one-third of the dish and toothpaste maker's $9.1 billion in annual sales comes from products introduced in the past five years. Food makers such as Philip Morris Cos.' Kraft unit and PepsiCo Inc.'s Frito-Lay are battling for consumers' stomachs with new foods like Oscar Mayer Lunchables and Wow! fat-free snack chips made with the new fake-fat olestra.

Even the Avon lady is chiming in: Avon Products Inc. led the new products pack in 1997 with 768 new products, accounting for 16 percent of the new products introduced by the 25 most prolific consumer goods companies, according to Marketing Intelligence Service. Among those same companies, new product launches, which averaged 13 a day, jumped 60 percent between 1995 and 1997.

What's behind the new product binge? One reason is that an aging population of baby boomers is demanding more products that make them look and feel younger. As a result, products like Avon's Anew alpha-hydroxy-based skin creams have started a revolution in skin care. Toothpaste companies have been cashing in on boomers' obsession with pearly whites, offering products such as SmithKline Beecham's Aquafresh Whitening toothpaste. And food makers are pushing good-for-you foods like RJR Nabisco Holdings Corp.'s low-fat Snackwell products and Campbell Soup Co.'s vitamin-fortified V-8 Splash juice drink.

Other factors are fueling the new-product boom. Time-strapped consumers, many of whom are members of two-career households, are looking for products that make their lives easier. Food makers have responded with "home meal replacements"—a hybrid of the old frozen TV dinner and a traditional home-cooked meal. Tyson Foods Inc., for instance, now offers a line of meals that are refrigerated, not frozen, so they heat up faster. And with home-style flavors such as meat loaf with mashed potatoes and gravy, Mom can trick the family into thinking they really are eating a homemade meal.

Food isn't the only thing that's gotten easier. Cosmetics companies have unveiled a range of new products that promise fast makeovers. Forget makeup brushes, messy liquids and foundation sponges; Estee Lauder Cos. now sells foundation-on-a-stick, while Revlon Inc. has boosted sales with its popular "won't-kiss-off" lipstick.

But perhaps the biggest driver of the new-product push is the fact that many companies are trying to boost sales and profits in slow-growing mature markets such as the United States and Europe. P&G has promised to double sales to $70 billion by the year 2005, meaning it needs 9 percent annual sales growth. Gillette Co., meanwhile, is gunning for 15 percent annual earnings growth. It's unlikely the growth can come simply by raising prices. In recent years, boosting prices has been a challenge for consumer-goods makers because shoppers have grown accustomed to the bargains offered by big discount chains like Wal-Mart. Moreover, competition from fast-food restaurants has kept food prices low at the grocery store.

But tack new-and-improved on the label

and watch what happens. Replacement blades for Gillette's new Mach 3 razor cost about 35 percent to 50 percent more than earlier Gillette blades. Colgate Total, a toothpaste that promises to prevent gum disease, has been one of the hottest new products in the past few years, even though it costs about 25 percent more than other toothpastes.

A marketing sleight of hand helps ensure that consumers won't experience sticker shock: Although most toothpaste comes in 6.2 or 6.4 ounce tubes, a Colgate Total tube is just 6 ounces or as much as 6 percent smaller, something most people won't notice. Kimberly-Clark Corp. has pulled off the same trick with its Kleenex-Cottonelle toilet paper, which costs about 50 cents a roll, the same as other brands. But take a closer look. Each square of the toilet paper has shrunk by 0.4 inches, which amounts to a 9 percent price increase.

One of the biggest new product launches in decades has been P&G's new fake-fat olestra, which took 25 years and $200 million to develop. P&G hopes olestra, which has the brand name Olean, one day will become a grocery-store staple that can turn foods like greasy french fries into fat-free, guilt-free indulgences—much as Nutrasweet transformed the soft drink industry. "I think it will become a household word," said P&G chairman John E. Pepper.

According to P&G, olestra is made from soybean oil, cottonseed oil and sugar. In a process that includes more than 100 patents, olestra is created by rearranging the fatty acids in the ingredients and attaching them to the sugar. The resulting product has the taste and texture of real fat, but the molecules are too large to digest and pass through the body unabsorbed. P&G says consumers who eat a one-ounce bag of chips at lunch would cut eight pounds of fat out of their diet annually if they switched to an olestra chip. In addition to being fat free, chips and snacks made with olestra contain about half the calories of regular chips. But some consumers have been afraid to try the chips because of a label, required by the Food and Drug Administration, that tells consumers that olestra may cause "abdominal cramping and loose stools."

Marketers say the new product boom may begin to taper off, as grocery stores literally run out of room for more new items. According to *American Demographics* magazine, the grocery stores of the 1950s carried about 3,000 items, but stores today offer as many as 30,000 products.

Nonetheless, analysts say growth-hungry consumer-goods companies are expected to continue cooking up a variety of new products to sell to eager shoppers. "Consumers are still willing to give new things a try," said Lynn Dornblaser, editorial director of *New Product News* in Chicago. "They're particularly looking for things that make their lives easier one way or another."

Tara Parker-Pope

SUPERMARKET SHOPPING BASKET

Billion-Dollar Products

The 50 largest product categories in food stores in 1997 and percentage change from 1996.

CATEGORY	1997 SALES	CHG VS. 1996	CATEGORY	1997 SALES	CHG VS. 1996
Carbonated Beverages	$11,747,164,160	1.2%	Frozen Dinners/Entrees	$4,541,018,112	2.8%
Milk	9,234,837,504	−0.3	Ice Cream/Sherbet	3,857,171,712	4.0
Cold Cereal	7,049,482,240	−5.2	Juice/Beverage-Rfg	3,514,383,360	5.5
Fresh Bread & Rolls	6,848,995,328	2.3	Soup	3,408,095,488	1.4
Cheese	6,474,141,696	3.0	Cookies	3,388,698,112	−1.0
Salty Snacks	5,673,877,504	3.0	Coffee	3,372,947,456	6.3
Beer & Ale	5,464,752,128	3.9	Luncheon Meats	2,931,889,664	0.5
Cigarettes	5,293,129,728	−3.3	Crackers	2,915,554,560	2.2
			Laundry Detergent	2,832,596,480	0.6

CATEGORY	1997 SALES	CHG VS. 1996
Dog Food	$2,785,677,056	2.4%
Bottled Juices-shelf stable	2,648,135,168	4.0
Wine	2,641,510,912	10.0
Dinners	2,512,268,288	3.7
Toilet Tissue	2,323,080,192	−1.5
Vegetables	2,112,347,392	3.4
Breakfast Meats	2,068,490,240	6.9
Baby Formula/ Electrolytes	1,989,415,680	0.3
Fresh Eggs	1,977,989,376	−1.3
Cat Food	1,951,378,432	1.3
Frozen Pizza	1,884,119,808	9.8
Diapers	1,869,971,200	−2.8
Frozen Novelties	1,717,510,400	0.7
Yogurt	1,714,863,104	2.6
Entree/Side Dishes	1,703,211,008	13.6
Chocolate Candy (Non-Seasonal)	1,650,536,704	2.4
Frozen Plain Vegetables	1,619,613,696	0.0
Paper Towels	1,619,109,632	−0.6

CATEGORY	1997 SALES	CHG VS. 1996
Seafood-shelf stable	$1,554,074,624	−1.0%
Shortening & Oil	1,489,160,192	−1.9
Frankfurters	1,473,739,008	3.2
Canned/Bottled Fruit	1,467,240,704	1.7
Spices/Seasonings	1,466,142,976	0.7
Household Cleaner	1,431,380,736	−0.6
Food & Trash Bags	1,408,475,392	0.5
Spaghetti/Italian Sauce	1,378,231,808	0.7
Pickles/Relish/Olives	1,328,303,360	0.8
Frozen Poultry	1,310,006,016	10.5
Salad Dressings-shelf stable	1,275,040,512	1.7
Pasta	1,250,642,176	−1.8
Margarine/Spreads/ Butter Blends	1,245,782,016	−1.9
Juices-Frozen	1,203,809,280	−10.0
Dough/Biscuit Dough-Rfg	1,199,278,336	8.0

Source: Information Resources Inc.

Price Check

Price changes in 1997 for some of the largest product categories in food stores.

CATEGORY	AVG PRICE PERCENT CHANGE IN 1997
Fresh Breads & Rolls	2.9%
Cheese	1.8%
Milk	1.1%
Yogurt	0%
Refrigerated Juice	5.4%
Breakfast Meats	7.6%
Cold Cereal	−2.3%
Cookies	2.4%
Crackers	4.1%
Chips & Snacks	4.6%
Soup	2.7%
Baby Formula/Electrolytes	8.1%
Coffee	12.8%

CATEGORY	AVG PRICE PERCENT CHANGE IN 1997
Ice Cream	4.4%
Toothpaste	2.7%
Diapers	8.7%
Laundry Detergent	5.0%
Toilet Tissue	6.2%
Paper Towels	4.5%
Cat Food	3.5%
Cigarettes	1.0%
Beer & Ale	3.2%
Wine	6.9%
Bottled Water	−0.8%
Carbonated Beverages	2.4%
Batteries	5.7%

Source: Information Resources Inc.

Product Proliferation

Total number of new consumer packaged-goods products

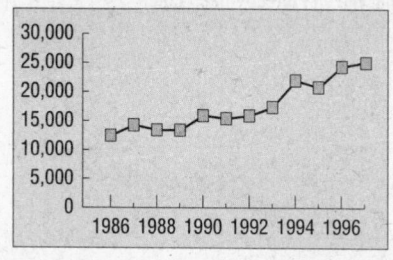

Year	New products
1986	12,436
1987	14,254
1988	13,421
1989	13,382
1990	15,879
1991	15,401
1992	15,886
1993	17,363
1994	21,986
1995	20,808
1996	24,496
1997	25,261

Categories with the Largest Increase and Largest Decrease in New Products

Biggest gainers	No. of new products 1997	1996	Biggest decliners	No. of new products 1997	1996
Deodorizers & air fresheners	742	315	Coffee	311	1,098
Fingernail products	720	510	Spices, extracts & seasonings	417	536
Soap & body cleansers	680	476	Bread & bread products	298	413
Lipsticks	906	705	Milk, non-dairy milk & yogurt drinks	114	210
Skin care	1,201	1,028	Cheese	274	366
Miscellaneous soft drinks	299	133	Soup	242	330
Dog food	330	170	Chewing gum	94	175
Facial cosmetics & accessories	562	424	Bath products	451	522
Hair styling products	288	160	Ice cream, novelties & frozen yogurt	561	630
Fragrances for men & women	489	373	Pastries & baked products	311	376

Companies With the Most New Products, 1997

1	Avon Products, Inc.	768	15	Estee Lauder Inc.	119
2	L'Oreal	429	16	Now Foods	117
3	Unilever U.S. Inc.	323	17	Frederic Fekkai Beaute	115
4	Revlon, Inc.	306	18	McAuley's, Inc.	110
5	Garden Botanika	286	19	Lancaster Colony Co.	101
6	Philip Morris Inc.	262	20	Del Laboratories, Inc.	99
7	Procter & Gamble Co.	215		PepsiCo, Inc.	99
8	Nestle	172	22	Dean Foods Co.	98
9	Paradiso Ltd.	162		Source Naturals	98
10	Tsumura International, Inc.	148	24	CPC International, Inc.	95
11	Grand Metropolitan Inc.	145		MGM Productions, Inc.	95
12	Pavion Ltd.	123			
13	ConAgra, Inc.	120		**Total Top 25 Companies**	**4,725**
	Sara Lee Corp.	120		**% All New Products**	**18.7%**

Source: Marketing Intelligence Service, Ltd.

The Name Game

Along with the proliferation of new products has come a surge in the number of trademark applications filed with the U.S. Patent and Trademark Office. That is making it harder for companies to think up catchy brand names that haven't already been taken.

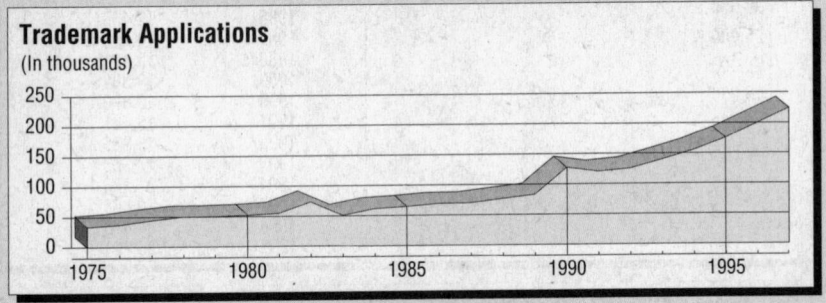

Trademark Applications
(In thousands)

Trademark Applications Filed and Registrations Issued

Fiscal Year	Applications	Registrations	Fiscal Year	Applications	Registrations
1975	33,898	27,324	1993	139,735	74,349
1980	52,149	14,614	1994	155,376	59,797
1985	64,677	63,122	1995	175,307	65,662
1990	127,294	56,515	1996	200,640	78,674
1991	120,365	43,152	1997	224,355	97,294
1992	125,237	62,067			

Source: U.S. Patent and Trademark Office

Blockbuster Brands

The American consumer's heart still belongs to big-name brands. While people are buying more store brands in some product categories, private-label merchandise accounts for only about 14% of total packaged-goods sales in food, drug, and mass-merchandise stores. Here is an assortment of some of the best-selling consumer products in the U.S.

Top Beverage Brands and Companies, Market Share and Volume

Brands	1997 share	1996 share	1997 cases (millions)	1996 cases (millions)	Volume % change
Coke Classic	20.6 %	20.8 %	1,978.2	1,929.2	+2.5 %
Pepsi-Cola	14.5	14.9	1,391.5	1,384.6	+0.5
Diet Coke	8.5	8.7	819.0	811.4	+0.9
Mountain Dew	6.3	5.8	605.2	535.6	+13.0
Sprite	6.2	5.8	598.0	541.5	+10.4
Dr Pepper	5.9	5.8	566.1	536.9	+5.4
Diet Pepsi	5.5	5.7	524.5	529.8	-1.0
7UP	2.3	2.3	216.7	217.7	-0.5
Caffeine-free Diet Coke	1.8	1.9	172.8	180.1	-4.1
Caffeine-free Diet Pepsi	1.0	1.0	94.0	94.6	-0.6

Companies	1997 share	1996 share	1997 cases (millions)	1996 cases (millions)	Volume % change
Coca-Cola	43.9 %	43.1 %	4,208.6	4,006.1	+5.1 %
Pepsi-Cola	30.9	31.0	2,965.7	2,880.6	+3.0
Dr. Pepper/Seven Up	14.5	14.7	1,392.3	1,366.8	+1.9
Cott Corp.	3.2	2.9	305.0	265.0	+15.1
National Beverage	2.0	1.9	188.0	180.0	+4.4
Royal Crown	1.7	1.9	160.2	176.2	-9.1
Monarch	1.3	1.5	128.3	140.5	-8.7
Big Red	0.3	0.3	30.4	28.3	+7.4
Double Cola	0.3	0.3	29.5	31.2	-5.4
Private label/other	1.9	2.4	182.0	215.3	-15.5
Industry totals			**9,590.0**	**9,290.0**	**+3.2**

Source: Beverage Digest/Maxwell Report

Top Cereal Brands, Based on 1997 Food Store Sales

Brands	Sales	Dollar market share
General Mills Cheerios	$293,590,976	4.12%
Kelloggs Frosted Flakes	254,627,872	3.57
Kelloggs Corn Flakes	206,722,592	2.90
General Mills Honey Nut Cheerios	189,867,392	2.66
Kelloggs Raisin Bran	185,673,632	2.60
Kelloggs Froot Loops	161,206,720	2.26
Kelloggs Rice Krispies	160,914,720	2.26
General Mills Lucky Charms	146,911,088	2.06
Kelloggs Special K	145,337,008	2.04
Kelloggs Frosted Mini Wheats, bite-size	133,410,816	1.87

Top Regular Ground Coffee Brands, Based on 1997 Food Store Sales

Brands	Sales	Dollar market share
Folgers	$485,966,080	24.0%
Maxwell House	401,283,072	19.8
Private Label	201,816,400	10.0
Folgers Coffee House	137,221,728	6.8
Maxwell House Master Blend	131,551,376	6.5
Hills Brothers	76,403,296	3.8
Chock Full O' Nuts	58,718,560	2.9
Maxwell House Lite	57,310,016	2.8
Yuban	52,018,176	2.6
Folgers Coffee Singles	43,733,248	2.2

Top Analgesic Brands, Based on 1997 Sales in Food, Drug and Mass-Merchandise Stores

Brands	Sales	Dollar market share
Private label	$596,074,752	23.8%
Tylenol	569,132,160	22.8
Advil	350,270,336	14.0
Aleve	140,402,352	5.6
Excedrin	140,381,600	5.6
Tylenol PM	109,135,088	4.4
Bayer	108,020,592	4.3
Motrin IB	87,240,304	3.5
Excedrin PM	45,470,024	1.8
Ecotrin	43,533,616	1.7

Top Toothpaste Brands, Based on 1997 Sales in Food, Drug and Mass-Merchandise Stores

Brands	Sales	Dollar market share
Crest	$370,436,864	24.5%
Colgate	321,084,416	21.2
Aquafresh	177,988,832	11.8
Mentadent	170,630,496	11.3
Arm & Hammer	109,512,288	7.2
Rembrandt	52,066,960	3.4
Sensodyn	50,133,408	3.3
Listerine	40,106,864	2.6
Closeup	32,009,456	2.1
Ultrabrite	25,358,464	1.7

Top Laundry Detergent Brands, Based on 1997 Sales in Food, Drug and Mass-Merchandise Stores

Brands	Sales	Dollar market share
Tide	$1,625,852,160	37.5%
Cheer	335,963,584	7.7
Wisk	318,887,968	7.3
All	308,340,096	7.1
Surf	235,170,384	5.4
Purex	229,123,984	5.3
Gain	226,950,992	5.2
Arm & Hammer	198,045,616	4.6
Era	152,386,544	3.5
Xtra	125,900,528	2.9

Top Brands of Potato Chips, Based on 1997 Food Store Sales

Brands	Sales	Dollar market share
Lays	$440,373,504	24.5%
Ruffles	364,419,072	20.3
Private label	175,227,952	9.7
Frito Lay	121,427,088	6.8
Wavy Lays	76,663,008	4.3
Ruffles Choice	60,318,576	3.4
Wise	54,375,296	3.0
Utz	49,692,592	2.8
Herrs	36,052,736	2.0
Jays	33,062,736	1.8

Source: Information Resources, Inc.

Top Brands of Diapers/Training Pants, Based on 1997 Sales in Food, Drug and Mass-Merchandise Stores

Brands	Sales	Dollar market share
Huggies	$1,506,468,096	41.3 %
Pampers	935,054,592	25.6
Private label	577,999,808	15.8
Luvs	442,491,680	12.1
Drypers	121,895,896	3.3
Fitti	33,139,844	0.9

Top Brands of Cookies, Based on 1997 Food Store Sales

Brands	Sales	Dollar market share
Private label	$462,322,176	12.7 %
Oreos	360,535,264	9.9
Chips Ahoy	302,345,216	8.3
Snackwells	170,182,144	4.7
Newtons	154,331,296	4.2
Chips Deluxe	139,342,720	3.8
Fudge Shoppe	99,563,040	2.7
Pepperidge Farm Distinctive	85,096,328	2.3
Nilla	75,202,088	2.1
Murray's	65,002,460	1.8

Top Brands of Refrigerated Orange Juice, Based on 1997 Food Store Sales

Brands	Sales	Dollar market share
Tropicana Pure Premium	$747,196,928	31.1%
Private label	578,929,664	24.1
Minute Maid Premium	325,527,552	13.5
Florida's Natural	175,435,984	7.3
Tropicana Seasons Best	159,126,640	6.6
Minute Maid	140,052,016	5.8
Tropicana Pure Premium Plus	40,785,664	1.7
Florida Gold	34,114,832	1.4
Citrus World Donald Duck	17,067,136	0.7
Florida's Natural Growers Pride	14,858,481	0.6

Source: Information Resources Inc.

Largest Restaurant Chains

1997 Rank	Chain	1997 U.S. Sales ($000)	% Sales Change vs. 1996	1997 U.S. Units	% Unit Change vs. 1996
1	McDonald's	$17,124,700	4.6%	12,380	2.4%
2	Burger King	7,860,867	5.0	7,539	6.8
3	Taco Bell	4,800,000	4.3	6,768	1.9
4	Pizza Hut	4,700,000	−4.4	8,698	0.0
5	Wendy's	4,603,000 *	7.4	4,575	4.7
6	KFC	4,000,000	2.6	5,120	0.2
7	Subway	2,900,000	7.4	11,165	2.9
8	Dairy Queen	2,685,000 *	3.2	5,069	0.7
9	Hardee's	2,684,346	−10.2	2,944	−8.7
10	Domino's Pizza	2,482,000	7.9	4,431	3.0
11	Arby's	2,050,000 *	7.0	2,925 *	2.3
12	Denny's	1,871,000	1.1	1,592	3.3
13	Little Caesar	1,775,000 *	−1.4	4,825 *	0.3
14	Applebee's	1,771,502	21.0	945	14.8
15	Dunkin' Donuts	1,762,508	13.3	3,436	5.8
16	Red Lobster	1,755,200	−1.2	649	−5.0

1997 Rank	Chain	1997 U.S. Sales ($000)	% Sales Change vs. 1996	1997 U.S. Units	% Unit Change vs. 1996
17	Jack in the Box	$1,355,136	9.3%	1,319	5.5%
18	Olive Garden	1,307,134	5.5	460	−3.2
19	Cracker Barrel	1,231,640	19.6	327	15.5
20	Outback Steakhouse	1,226,000	20.1	445	19.6
21	Boston Market	1,197,000	8.8	1,166	7.3
22	Chili's Grill and Bar	1,195,634	15.5	520	7.0
23	Sonic Drive-Ins	1,191,786	17.7	1,725	8.7
24	Shoney's	1,057,772 *	−12.6	760	−10.0
25	T.G.I. Friday's	1,016,264	8.6	343	7.5
26	Papa John's	867,609	40.1	1,517	30.8
27	IHoP	861,140 *	13.8	740	8.0
28	Starbucks	859,060	38.2	1,327	35.7
29	Long John Silver's	829,466	−7.1	1,395	−3.9
30	Big Boy	780,000 *	4.0	700 *	0.0
31	Golden Corral	768,365	8.4	452	3.2
32	Popeyes	723,621	8.6	944	5.7
33	Perkins Family Restaurants	690,700	4.8	460	1.5
34	Carl's Jr.	684,150	8.6	686	6.7
35	Chick-fil-A	671,510	17.9	761	6.4
36	Ryan's	635,696	6.4	295	5.0
37	Bob Evans	632,254	7.0	406	6.3
38	Ruby Tuesday	611,409 *	14.3	345	9.9
39	Friendly Ice Cream	607,700	1.8	696	−1.6
40	Church's	574,863	9.2	1,070	8.1
41	Baskin-Robbins	570,554	−1.3	2,677	4.5
42	Ponderosa	550,000 *	−9.8	493	−5.4
43	Hardee's (Advantica)	546,000	−9.4	557	−4.0
44	Old Country Buffet	539,000 *	−1.2	246	−4.3
45	Arby's (RTM)	516,000 *	125.3	700	122.9
46	Lone Star	509,504	14.2	265	29.3
47	Captain D's	505,380 *	7.9	601	0.5
48	Luby's Cafeterias	497,831	7.3	232	4.5
49	Whataburger	480,000 *	9.1	550	3.8
50	Bennigan's	465,000 *	3.3	220	−0.5

*Technomic estimate.

Source: Technomic, Inc.

WHAT'S FOR DINNER?

Percent of Dinner Orders Made at Restaurants that Include Item

Item	% of orders	Item	% of orders
Regular Soft Drink	25.2%	Tap Water	9.1%
French Fries	24.8%	Diet Soft Drink	7.9%
Pizza	24.1%	Iced Tea	6.3%
Hamburger/Cheeseburger	16.7%	Alcohol	5.7%
Side Dish Salad	16.3%	Fried Chicken	5.6%

Source: NPD Group's CREST service

Top Toys

Top Selling Toys Ranked by Dollar Sales, December 1997

Rank	Description	Manufacturer	Average retail price
1	Giga Pets Asst.	Tiger Electronics	$9.98
2	Tamagotchi Virtual Pet Asst.	Bandai America	13.99
3	Sesame Street Tickle Me Elmo	Tyco Preschool	27.60
4	Super Talk! Barbie Sun Jammer 4 x 4	Fisher-Price	215.64
5	Sesame Street Tickle Me Elmo Asst. 11"	Tyco Preschool	14.23
6	Barbie Folding Pretty House	Mattel	48.29
7	Sesame Street Sing & Snore Ernie	Tyco Preschool	28.49
8	Holiday Barbie '97	Mattel	26.93
9	Barbie and Ginger	Mattel	28.20
10	Barbie Motorhome	Mattel	46.86
11	My Size Rapunzel Barbie Doll	Mattel	110.51
12	Jeep Wrangler	Fisher-Price	181.97
13	Easy Bake Oven & Snack Center	Hasbro	18.04
14	Barney Actimates	Microsoft	97.61
15	Cool Shoppin' Barbie Doll	Mattel	17.52
16	Laser Challenge: Team Force Set	Toymax	34.73
17	Talking Nano Asst.	Playmates Toys	19.53
18	Kawasaki Ninja ATV	Fisher-Price	166.56
19	6V Jet Turbo Asst.	Mattel	58.11
20	Nano Virtual Pet Asst.	Playmates Toys	14.85

Top Selling Toys Ranked by Dollar Sales, June 1998

Rank	Description	Manufacturer	Average retail price
1	Family Swim Center Pool (120")	Intex	$43.45
2	Spice Girls Fashion Dolls Asst.	Galoob	13.00
3	Teletubbies Talking Asst.	Hasbro	25.02
4	XP-70 Super Soaker	Hasbro	9.00
5	CPS-1000 Super Soaker	Hasbro	18.57
6	Crazy Daisy	Fisher-Price	9.50
7	Funnoodle Float Asst.	Kidpower	1.60
8	CPS-2500 Super Soaker	Hasbro	29.05
9	Hot Wheels Vehicles	Mattel	0.92
10	8 ft. Waterworld Rainbow Snapset Pool	Intex	15.76
11	Rectangular Pool 120" x 72" x 24"	Tony Trading	43.67
12	King Kool Lounge	Intex	7.87
13	Super Talk! Barbie Sun Jammer 4 x 4	Fisher-Price	227.66
14	90" Aquarium Pool	Intex	42.96
15	XP-110 Super Soaker	Hasbro	13.81
16	Jeep Wrangler	Fisher-Price	194.89
17	Super Crocodile Mile	Empire	29.44
18	Family Swim Center Pool (144")	Intex	92.28
19	Bass Fishin'	Radica	17.60
20	CPS-1500 Super Soaker	Hasbro	24.69

Source: NPD Group, Inc.

"Coolest" Brands for U.S. Teenagers

Percentage of teens naming the brand as one of three "coolest."

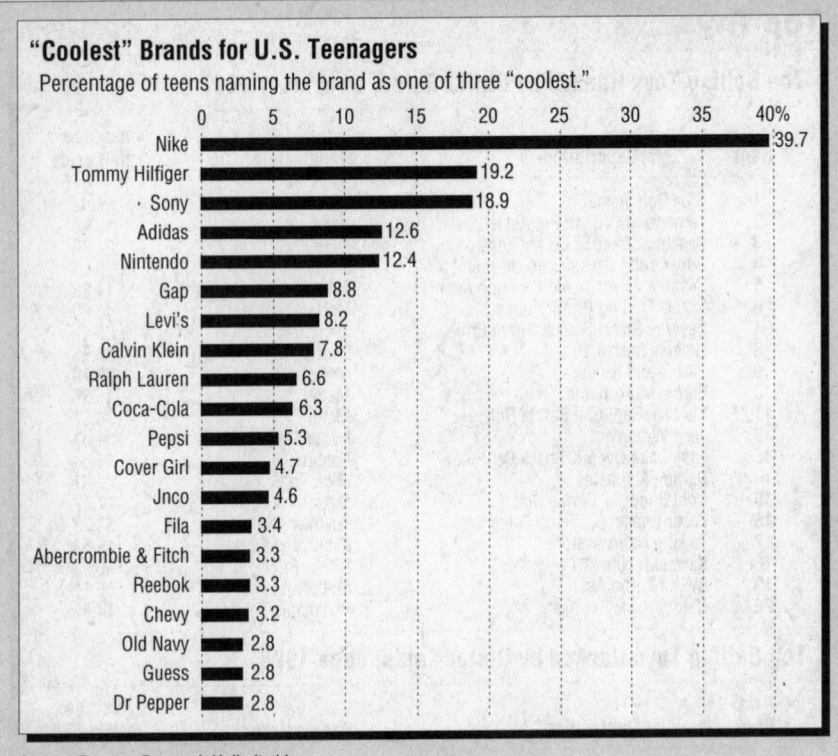

Source: Teenage Research Unlimited Inc.

Alcoholic-Beverage Market

The alcoholic-beverage business went flat in the first half of the 1990s, but showed slight growth in 1996 and 1997.

Alcoholic Beverages Entering U.S. Distribution Channels by Category
(In millions of gallons)

Category	1970	1975	1980	1985	1990	1991	1992	1993	1994	1995	1996	1997
Beer	3,804	4,659	5,515	5,664	5,986	5,854	5,836	5,836	5,803	5,754	5,828	5,855
Wine	267	368	478	493	421	410	440	424	437	451	481	501
Distilled spirits	388	447	452	428	385	346	350	342	333	329	325	326
Low-alcohol refreshers	–	–	*	98	107	92	90	101	124	108	91	85
Cider	*	*	*	*	*	*	1	1	1	4	6	8
Total	4,459	5,474	6,445	6,683	6,899	6,702	6,717	6,704	6,698	6,646	6,731	6,775

*Less than 500,000 gallons.

Share of Market
Alcoholic Beverages Entering U.S. Distribution Channels by Category

Category	1970	1980	1990	1997
Beer	85.3%	85.6%	86.8 %	86.4%
Wine	6.0	7.4	6.1	7.4
Distilled spirits	8.7	7.0	5.6	4.8
Low-alcohol refreshers	–	*	1.6	1.3
Cider	*	*	*	0.1
Total	100.0	100.0	100.0	100.0

*Less than 0.05%.
Source: Impact's Annual Beer, Wine and Distilled Spirits Report

Top 10 Wine Brands

(thousands of nine-liter cases)

Rank	Brand	Company	Origin/Type	Depletions 1997
1	Franzia	The Wine Group	California Table	18,000
2	Carlo Rossi	E. & J. Gallo Winery	California Table	11,400
3	Gallo Livingston Cellars	E. & J. Gallo Winery	California Table	9,800
4	Wine Cellars of Ernest & Julio Gallo	E. & J. Gallo Winery	California Table	8,690
5	Almaden	Canandaigua Wine Company	California Table	7,600
6	Sutter Home	Sutter Home Winery, Inc.	California Table	6,600
7	Inglenook	Canandaigua Wine Company	California Table	6,500
8	Woodbridge	Robert Mondavi Winery	California Table	4,240
9	Vendange	Sebastiani Vineyards	California Table	3,800
10	Beringer	Beringer Wine Estates	California Table	3,725
	Total Top 10			80,355

Source: Impact Databank

Top 10 Distilled Spirit Brands[1]

(thousands of nine-liter cases)

Rank	Brand	Distiller/Importer	Category	Depletions 1997
1	Bacardi[2]	Bacardi-Martini USA, Inc.	Rum	6,000
2	Smirnoff[3]	UDV NA (Diageo)	Vodka	5,655
3	Absolut[3]	The House of Seagram	Vodka	3,525
4	Seagram's Gin	The House of Seagram	Gin	3,250
5	Jack Daniel's Black	Brown Forman Beverages Worldwide	Tennessee Whiskey	3,085
6	Jim Beam	Jim Beam Brands Co. (Fortune Brands)	Bourbon	3,020
7	E & J	E & J Gallo Winery	Brandy	2,850
8	Seagram's 7 Crown	The House of Seagram	Blended Whiskey	2,850

Rank	Brand	Distiller/Importer	Category	Depletions 1997
9	Jose Cuervo[4]	UDV NA (Diageo)	Tequila	2,830
10	Canadian Mist	Brown Forman Beverages Worldwide	Canadian Whiskey	2,620
	Total Top 10			35,685

[1] Excludes distilled spirits-based low-alcohol refreshers.
[2] Includes Light, Dark, 151, Black, Reserve, and Anejo.
[3] Includes flavored vodkas.
[4] Includes Cuervo 1800, Jose Cuervo Mistico, and Tradicional.

Source: Impact Databank

Top 10 Beer Brands[1]

(millions of barrels)

Rank	Brand	Brewer/Importer	Segment	Depletions 1997
1	Budweiser	Anheuser-Busch, Inc.	Premium	35.6
2	Bud Light	Anheuser-Busch, Inc.	Light Premium	22.8
3	Miller Lite	Miller Brewing Co. (Philip Morris)	Light Premium	16.2
4	Coors Light	Coors Brewing Co.	Light Premium	13.5
5	Busch	Anheuser-Busch, Inc.	Sub-Premium	7.9
6	Natural Light	Anheuser-Busch, Inc.	Light Sub-Premium	7.1
7	Miller Genuine Draft	Miller Brewing Co. (Philip Morris)	Premium	5.5
8	Miller High Life	Miller Brewing Co. (Philip Morris)	Sub-Premium/Premium	4.7
9	Busch Light	Anheuser-Busch, Inc.	Light Sub-Premium	4.5
10	Milwaukee's Best	Miller Brewing Co. (Philip Morris)	Sub-Premium	3.9
	Total Top 10			121.7

[1] Excludes commercial exports and shipments to Puerto Rico, U.S. possessions and armed forces overseas, including U.S. armed forces post exchanges.

Source: Impact Databank

Cigarette Market

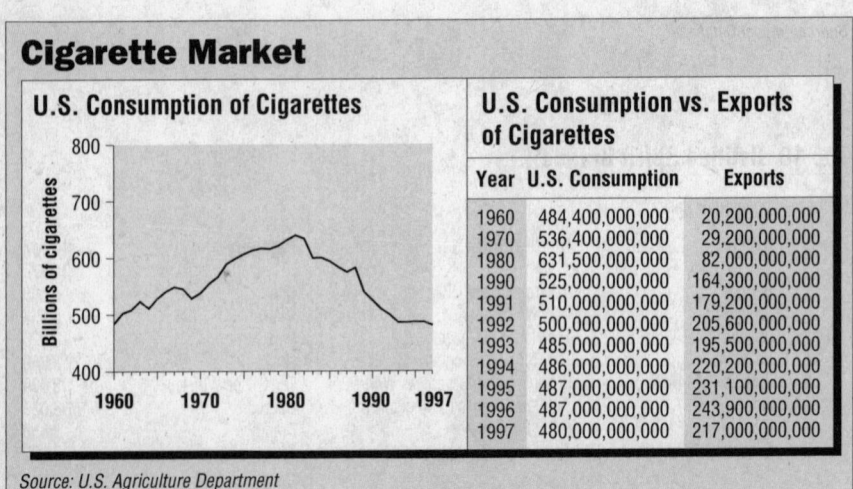

U.S. Consumption of Cigarettes

U.S. Consumption vs. Exports of Cigarettes

Year	U.S. Consumption	Exports
1960	484,400,000,000	20,200,000,000
1970	536,400,000,000	29,200,000,000
1980	631,500,000,000	82,000,000,000
1990	525,000,000,000	164,300,000,000
1991	510,000,000,000	179,200,000,000
1992	500,000,000,000	205,600,000,000
1993	485,000,000,000	195,500,000,000
1994	486,000,000,000	220,200,000,000
1995	487,000,000,000	231,100,000,000
1996	487,000,000,000	243,900,000,000
1997	480,000,000,000	217,000,000,000

Source: U.S. Agriculture Department

Top Tobacco Brands

Twelve Month Unit Volume Comparisons for the Leading U.S. Cigarette Brands

	1996			1997			
	Billions of cigarettes	Share	Ranking	Billions of cigarettes	Share	Percent volume change	Ranking
Philip Morris							
Marlboro	156.21	32.2%	1	163.98	34.0%	5.0%	1
Basic	23.17	4.8	6	23.52	4.9	1.5	7
Virginia Slims	11.57	2.4	10	11.53	2.4	-0.3	10
Merit	11.33	2.3	11	10.67	2.2	-5.8	11
Benson & Hedges	11.11	2.3	12	10.66	2.2	-4.1	12
RJR Nabisco							
Doral	28.57	5.9	3	30.03	6.2	5.1	3
Winston	25.40	5.2	5	25.14	5.2	-1.0	5
Camel*	22.47	4.6	7	23.58	4.9	4.9	6
Salem	17.33	3.6	8	16.48	3.4	-4.9	8
Lorillard							
Newport	29.30	6.0	2	31.43	6.5	7.3	2
Brown & Williamson							
GPC	28.10	5.8	4	29.18	6.0	3.8	4
Kool*	17.21	3.5	9	16.39	3.4	-4.6	9
Total leading brands	381.77	78.7		392.59	81.4	2.8	

*Includes filter and nonfilter.
Source: The Maxwell Consumer Report, Davenport & Co.

Cigar Revival in the U.S.

Year	Annual cigar consumption	Per capita cigar consumption Total pop.	Per capita cigar consumption Male pop.	Year	Annual cigar consumption	Per capita cigar consumption Total pop.	Per capita cigar consumption Male pop.
1920	8,502,008,000	80	269	1985	4,335,448,000	18	55
1925	7,391,824,000	64	216	1986	3,948,894,000	16	50
1930	6,583,431,000	53	177	1987	3,919,987,000	16	49
1935	5,215,948,000	41	131	1988	3,706,702,000	15	45
1940	5,709,686,000	43	136	1989	3,620,630,000	15	44
1945	5,114,339,000	39	130	1990	3,553,659,000	14	42
1950	5,607,939,000	37	116	1991	3,530,432,000	14	42
1955	6,077,966,000	37	121	1992	3,518,098,000	14	41
1960	7,103,334,000	39	136	1993	3,423,424,000	13	40
1965	8,948,594,000	46	163	1994	3,718,115,000	14	43
1970	8,881,120,000	44	152	1995	4,040,277,000	16	46
1975	8,645,540,000	41	136	1996	4,588,612,000	18	52
1980	5,374,436,000	24	75	1997	5,174,600,000	20	58

Source: Cigar Association of America

Post-War Advertising Boom

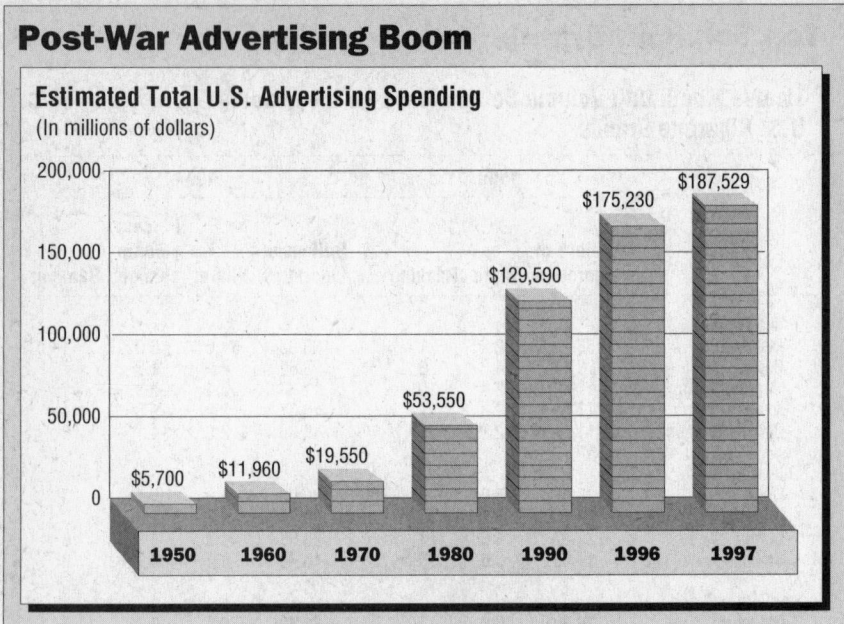

Estimated Total U.S. Advertising Spending
(In millions of dollars)

	1950	1960	1970	1980	1990	1996	1997
	$5,700	$11,960	$19,550	$53,550	$129,590	$175,230	$187,529

Estimated Annual U.S. Advertising Expenditures
(In millions of dollars)

	1990	1991	1992	1993	1994	1995	1996	1997
Television	$29,073	$28,189	$30,450	$31,698	$35,435	$37,828	$42,484	$44,519
Newspapers	32,281	30,409	30,737	32,025	34,356	36,317	38,402	41,670
Direct Mail	23,370	24,460	25,391	27,266	29,638	32,866	34,509	36,890
Radio	8,726	8,476	8,654	9,457	10,529	11,338	12,269	13,491
Yellow Pages	8,926	9,182	9,320	9,517	9,825	10,236	10,849	11,423
Magazines	6,803	6,524	7,000	7,357	7,916	8,580	9,010	9,821
Other	20,411	20,230	21,098	22,220	23,981	25,765	27,707	29,715
Total	129,590	127,470	132,650	139,540	151,680	162,930	175,230	187,529

Source: Robert J. Coen, McCann-Erickson

Top 25 Advertisers in 1997
($ in thousands)

Company	Total	Company	Total
1 General Motors Corp.	$2,226,933.5	15 Toyota Motor Corp.	$592,327.2
2 Procter & Gamble Co.	1,703,053.3	16 McDonald's Corp.	580,802.4
3 Philip Morris Cos. Inc.	1,319,015.9	17 Federated Dept. Stores Inc.	532,544.6
4 Chrysler Corp.	1,311,789.2	18 General Motors Corp.	512,113.0
5 Ford Motor Co.	973,127.7	Dealer Assn.	
6 Pepsico Inc.	797,405.4	19 Sony Corp.	493,344.4
7 Time Warner Inc.	779,108.1	20 AT&T Corp.	475,857.0
8 Walt Disney Co.	746,296.9	21 General Motors Corp.	469,032.1
9 Johnson & Johnson	738,702.4	local dealers	
10 Sears Roebuck & Co.	734,145.5	22 MCI Communications Corp.	455,381.6
11 Diageo PLC	685,044.9	23 Nissan Motor Co. Ltd.	452,708.8
12 Unilever	618,975.9	24 National Amusements Inc.	450,607.2
13 News Corp. Ltd.	613,822.9	25 May Dept. Stores Co.	445,958.0
14 Ford Motor Co. local dealers	609,455.1		

Source: Competitive Media Reporting and Publishers Information Bureau

TV Commercial Stars

Consumers rated these sports and entertainment celebrities as the most credible product endorsers in 1997.

Sports Presenters

1. Michael Jordan
2. Tiger Woods
3. Dennis Rodman
4. Shaquille O'Neal
5. Scottie Pippen
6. Grant Hill
7. Dan Marino
8. George Foreman
9. Charles Barkley
10. Cal Ripken

Entertainment Presenters

1. Candice Bergen
2. Jerry Seinfeld
3. Paul Reiser
4. Rosie O'Donnell
5. Bill Cosby
6. Cindy Crawford
7. James Earl Jones
8. Tim Allen
9. Elizabeth Taylor
10. Oprah Winfrey

Source: Video Storyboard Tests Inc.

Top 25 Television Advertising Campaigns of 1997

Advertising campaigns that consumers considered the most "outstanding" they had seen. Ranking based on surveys of about 20,000 people, primarily at shopping malls.

1997 rank	1996 rank	Brand	1997 rank	1996 rank	Brand
1	8	Nissan	14	19	Taco Bell
2	1	Budweiser	15	–	Snickers
3	2	Pepsi	16	6	Bud Light
4	7	Milk	17	23	Burger King
5	3	McDonald's	18	20	AT&T
6	5	Coca-Cola	19	–	Texaco
7	9	Little Caesars	20	–	Sprite
8	12	M&M's	21	–	Wendy's
9	16	Ford	22	–	Miracle Whip
10	18	Levi's	23	–	Toyota
11	4	Dryer's/Edy's	24	15	Pizza Hut
12	11	Nike	25	–	Volkswagen
13	–	Miller			

Source: Video Storyboard Tests Inc.

Marketers Take the Direct Route

Largest Industries by Direct-Marketing Sales Volume in the Consumer Marketplace (In billions)

	1997	2002*	Compound Annual Growth through 2002
Non-store retailers	$92.253	$129.690	7.05%
Real estate	46.555	55.494	3.58
General merchandise stores	39.812	57.700	7.70
Auto dealers & service stations	36.751	51.465	6.97
Food & kindred products	33.416	45.350	6.30
Membership-based organizations	31.134	41.710	6.02
Health services	30.724	63.660	15.70
Depository institutions	30.425	53.093	11.80
Insurance carriers/agents	29.857	40.009	6.03
Food stores	23.623	27.826	3.34

* Projected.
Source: Direct Marketing Association

Direct-Marketing Sales by Medium (In billions)

	1992	1996	1997	1998	2002	Compound Annual Growth '92-'97	'97-2002
Direct Mail	**$260.2**	**$359.5**	**$390.0**	**$421.2**	**$589.8**	**8.4%**	**8.6%**
Consumer	167.6	227.4	244.3	261.1	352.8	7.8	7.6
Business-to-business	92.5	132.1	145.7	160.2	237.0	9.5	10.2
Telephone marketing	**293.0**	**391.2**	**424.5**	**460.3**	**666.3**	**7.7**	**9.4**
Consumer	134.8	174.0	185.9	198.8	272.7	6.6	8.0
Business-to-business	158.3	217.2	238.6	261.5	393.6	8.6	10.5
Newspaper	**122.5**	**161.7**	**173.2**	**185.0**	**248.5**	**7.2**	**7.5**
Consumer	82.0	105.7	112.1	118.6	152.1	6.5	6.3
Business-to-business	40.4	56.0	61.0	66.4	96.4	8.6	9.6
Magazine	**45.5**	**60.6**	**65.5**	**70.5**	**95.0**	**7.6**	**7.7**
Consumer	25.0	32.5	34.7	36.9	47.8	6.8	6.6
Business-to-business	20.6	28.1	30.9	33.6	47.2	8.4	8.8
Television	**52.2**	**77.7**	**84.4**	**91.4**	**126.7**	**10.1**	**8.5**
Consumer	33.0	48.4	52.0	55.8	74.5	9.5	7.5
Business-to-business	19.2	29.3	32.4	35.7	52.2	11.0	10.0
Radio	**18.2**	**28.5**	**30.9**	**33.7**	**47.8**	**11.2**	**9.1**
Consumer	10.6	16.4	17.6	19.0	26.2	10.7	8.3
Business-to-business	7.6	12.1	13.3	14.7	21.7	11.8	10.3
Other	**38.8**	**53.5**	**57.6**	**61.8**	**84.4**	**8.2**	**7.9**
Consumer	26.5	35.6	38.0	40.3	52.7	7.5	6.8
Business-to-business	12.3	17.9	19.6	21.5	31.7	9.8	10.1
Total	**830.4**	**1,132.7**	**1,226.2**	**1,324.0**	**1,858.7**	**8.1**	**8.7**
Consumer	**479.5**	**640.0**	**684.6**	**730.5**	**978.8**	**7.4**	**7.4**
Business-to-business	**350.9**	**492.6**	**541.6**	**593.5**	**879.9**	**9.1**	**10.2**

Source: Direct Marketing Association

How to Curtail the Catalogs and Sales Calls

It's impossible to stop all junk mail and telemarketing calls, but frustrated consumers can reduce the volume by contacting the Direct Marketing Association, an industry trade group. To have their names removed from telephone lists, consumers should write to Telephone Preference Service, Direct Marketing Association, P.O. Box 9014, Farmingdale, NY, 11735-9014. To get off mailing lists, people should contact the Mail Preference Service, Direct Marketing Association, P.O. Box 9008, Farmingdale, NY, 11735-9008.

Largest Catalog Marketers

Rank	Company	1997 sales ($ millions)	1996 sales ($ millions)	Market segment
1	Dell Computer Corp.	$11,946.3	$7,553.8	Computer hardware, software and peripherals
2	Gateway 2000	6,293.7	5,035.2	Computer hardware, software and peripherals
3	J.C. Penney Co.	3,880.0	3,744.0	General merchandise
4	International Business Machines	3,000.0*	2,300.0*	Computer hardware, software and peripherals
5	Micro Warehouse	2,126.0	1,916.0	Computer hardware, software and peripherals
6	Fingerhut Cos.	1,530.0	1,638.0	General merchandise
7	Spiegel	1,522.0	1,674.7	General merchandise
8	Henry Schein	1,518.1	1,231.8	Medical, dental and veterinary supplies
9	Viking Office Products	1,382.9	1,182.3	Office supplies
10	Brylane	1,279.0	705.0	Apparel
11	CDW Computer Centers	1,276.9	927.9	Computer hardware, software and peripherals
12	Lands' End	1,244.6	1,112.0	Apparel and home goods
13	Global DirectMail Corp.	1,145.4	911.9	Computer, industrial and office supplies
14	L.L. Bean	926.0	908.0	Outdoor gear and apparel
15	Intimate Brands (Victoria's Secret catalog)	734.0	684.0	Women's apparel
16	Insight Enterprises	627.7	410.9	Computer hardware, software and peripherals
17	Damark International	594.6	513.7	Computers, home goods, electronics, fitness gear
18	Newark Electronics	576.3	543.2	Industrial electronics
19	Hanover Direct	557.6	700.3	Apparel, home goods and gifts
20	PC Connection	550.6	333.0	Computer hardware, software and peripherals

*Estimate.
Source: Catalog Age

Licensed Merchandise Sales

Whether it's Mickey Mouse or the Olympics, licensed merchandise is a huge business, generating retail sales in 1997 of more than $73 billion.

Licensed Product Retail Sales
U.S. & Canada, by Property Type, 1996-1997
($ in billions)

Property type	1997	1996	% change 1996/1997	% of total 1997
Art	$5.25	$5.20	1%	7%
Celebrities/estates	2.61	2.57	2	4
Entertainment/character	16.13	16.70	-3	22
Fashion	13.16	12.60	4	18
Music	1.00	1.03	-3	1
Non-profit	0.72	0.70	3	1
Publishing	1.57	1.64	-4	2
Sports	13.65	13.79	-1	19
Trademarks/brands	16.06	15.11	6	22
Toys/games	2.81	2.71	4	4
Other	0.27	0.23	18	<1
Total	73.23	72.28	1	100

Source: The Licensing Letter

Marketing Patrons

More marketers are paying to link their corporate and brand names to sporting and entertainment events, arts programs, and charitable causes.

Sponsorship Spending in North America

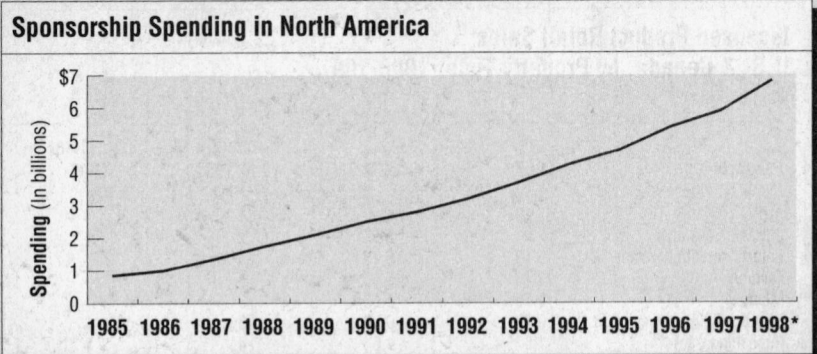

*Projected.

Sponsorship Spending by Type of Property (In millions)

	1996	1997	1998*
Sports	$3,540	$3,840	$4,550
Pop music/entertainment tours	566	650	675
Festivals, fairs, annual events	512	558	578
Causes	485	535	544
Arts	323	354	413
Total	5,426	5,937	6,760

*Projected.
Source: IEG Sponsorship Report

Sponsored By . . .

The Largest Corporate Sponsors in 1997

1. Philip Morris	$140–145 million
2. Anheuser-Busch	$130–135 million
3. Coca-Cola	$110–115 million
4. General Motors	$90–95 million
5. PepsiCo	$75–80 million
6. Nike	$60–65 million
7. Eastman Kodak	$55–60 million
AT&T	$55–60 million
9. Chrysler	$45–50 million
IBM	$45–50 million
RJR Nabisco	$45–50 million
McDonald's	$45–50 million

Source: IEG Sponsorship Report.

Shop Till You Drop

Growth in number of shopping centers, total retailing space, retailing space per capita, and annual sales.

Year	Total square footage	Number of centers	Square feet per capita	Sales
1964*	1,010,000,000	7,600	5.3	$ 78,700,000,000
1972	1,649,972,000	13,174	7.9	123,159,000,000
1976	2,338,210,000	17,523	10.7	211,504,000,000
1980	2,962,701,000	22,050	13.0	385,501,000,000
1984	3,375,632,000	25,508	14.2	475,130,000,000
1988	3,947,025,000	32,563	16.1	641,097,000,000
1991	4,563,800,000	37,975	18.1	716,913,000,000
1992	4,678,527,000	38,966	18.3	768,220,248,000
1993	4,770,700,000	39,633	18.5	806,645,004,000
1994	4,860,920,000	40,274	18.7	875,900,000,000
1995	4,967,160,000	41,145	18.9	916,800,000,000
1996	5,100,000,000	42,045	19.2	970,300,000,000
1997	5,230,000,000	42,874	19.5	1,019,300,000,000

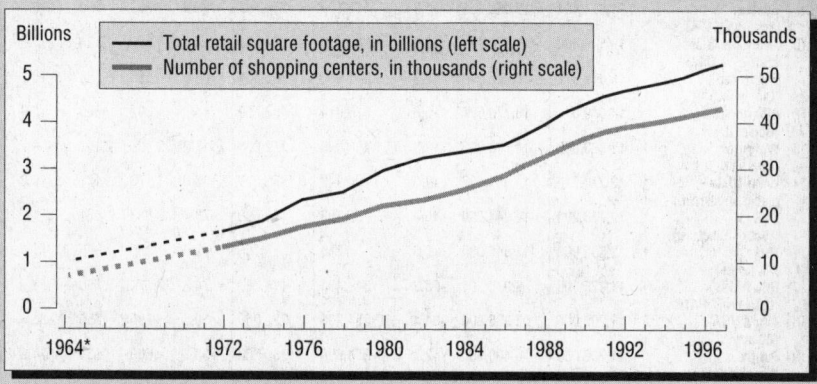

*Estimated.
Source: International Council of Shopping Centers

Ten Largest U.S. Shopping Centers (Gross Leasable Area)

Name & location	Size (square feet)	Name & location	Size (square feet)
Mall of America Bloomington, MN	4,200,000 (2,574,525 retail GLA)	**Aventura Mall** Aventura, FL	2,300,000
Del Amo Fashion Center Torrance, CA	3,000,000	**Roosevelt Field Mall** Garden City, NY	2,100,000
South Coast Plaza/ Crystal Court Costa Mesa, CA	2,918,236	**The Galleria** Houston, TX	2,100,000
Woodfield Mall Schaumburg, IL	2,700,000	**King of Prussia Plaza** King of Prussia, PA	2,099,000
Sawgrass Mills Sunrise, FL	2,350,000	**Oak Brook Shopping Center** Paramus, NJ	2,013,000

Source: National Research Bureau and International Council of Shopping Centers

Retail Giants

Top 50 Retailers

	Company (Headquarters)	Volume (000)			Earnings (loss) (000)			Units		
		1997	1996	Change	1997	1996	Change	1997	1996	Change
1	Wal-Mart (Bentonville, AR)	$117,958,000	$104,859,000	+12.5%	$3,526,000	$3,056,000	+15.4	3,408	3,054	+11.6%
2	Sears, Roebuck (Hoffman Estates, IL)	41,469,000	38,236,000	+8.5	1,188,000	1,271,000	-6.5	3,530	3,371	+4.7
3	Kmart (Troy, MI)	32,183,000	31,437,000	+2.4	249,000	(220,000)	—	2,136	2,419	-11.7
4	JCPenney (Plano,TX)	30,546,000	23,471,000	+30.1	566,000	565,000	+0.2	3,927	1,883	+108.6
5	Dayton Hudson (Minneapolis)	27,757,000	25,371,000	+9.4	751,000	463,000	+62.2	1,130	1,100	+2.7
6	Kroger (Cincinnati)	26,567,348	25,170,909	+5.5	411,657	349,873	+17.7	2,198	2,187	—
7	Home Depot (Atlanta)	24,155,746	19,535,503	+23.7	1,159,960	937,739	+23.7	624	512	+21.9
8	Safeway (Pleasanton, CA)	22,483,800	17,269,000	+30.2	621,500	460,600	+34.9	1,368	1,052	+30.0
9	Costco (Issaquah, WA)	21,874,404	19,566,456	+11.8	312,197	248,793	+25.5	269	252	+6.7
10	American Stores (Salt Lake City)	19,138,880	18,678,129	+2.5	280,620	287,221	-2.3	1,557	1,529	+1.8
11	Federated (Cincinnati)	15,668,312	15,228,999	+2.9	535,950	265,864	+101.6	555	554	+0.2
12	Albertsons (Boise, ID)	14,689,511	13,776,678	+6.6	516,814	493,779	+4.7	892	826	+8.0
13	Walgreen (Deerfield, IL)	13,363,000	11,778,000	+13.5	436,000	372,000	+17.2	2,405	2,193	+9.7
14	Winn-Dixie (Jacksonville, FL)	13,218,715	12,955,488	+2.0	204,443	255,634	-20.0	1,176	1,178	-0.2
15	CVS (Woonsocket, RI)	12,738,200	10,944,800	+16.4	37,700	176,600	-78.7	3,888	1,431	+171.7
16	May (St. Louis)	12,352,000	11,546,000	+7.0	775	755	+2.6	369	365	+1.1
17	Rite Aid (Camp Hill, PA)	11,375,105	6,970,201	+63.2	316,435	115,377	+174.3	2,774	2,759	—
18	Ahold USA (Atlanta)	11,200,000	8,335,800	+34.4	354,200	222,000	+59.5	895	655	+36.6
19	Publix (Lakeland, FL)	11,200,000	10,400,000	+7.7	354,600	265,200	+33.7	560	534	+4.9
20	Toys "R" Us (Paramus, NJ)	11,037,800	9,932,400	+11.1	490,100	427,400	+14.7	1,454	1,372	+6.0
21	A&P (Montvale, NJ)	10,262,243	10,089,014	+1.7	63,042	73,032	-13.7	936	1,014	-7.7
22	Food Lion (Salisbury, NC)	10,194,385	9,005,932	+13.2	179,488	206,070	-12.9	1,157	1,112	+4.0
23	Lowe's (N. Wilkesboro, NC)	10,136,890	8,600,241	+17.9	357,484	292,150	+22.4	446	402	+10.9
24	Limited (Columbus, OH)	9,188,804	8,644,791	+6.3	217,390	434,208	-49.9	3,774	5,298	-28.8
25	Circuit City (Richmond, VA)	8,870,797	7,663,811	+15.7	104,311	136,414	-23.5	556	448	+24.1

	Company (Headquarters)	Volume (000)			Earnings (loss) (000)			Units		
		1997	1996	Change	1997	1996	Change	1997	1996	Change
26	**Best Buy** (Minneapolis)	$8,358,212	$7,770,683	+7.6%	$94,453	$1,748	+5,303.5%	272	247	+10.1%
27	**TJX** (Framingham, MA)	7,389,069	6,689,410	+10.5	304,815	363,123	-16.1	1,171	1,136	+3.1
28	**Southland** (Dallas)	7,060,557	6,955,263	+1.5	70,042	89,476	-21.7	5,423	5,422	—
29	**Office Depot** (Delray Beach, FL)	6,717,514	6,068,598	+10.7	159,676	129,042	+23.7	560	570	-1.8
30	**Dillard** (Little Rock, AR)	6,632,000	6,227,600	+6.5	258,000	238,600	+8.1	270	250	+8.0
31	**Venator Group** (formerly **Woolworth**) (New York)	6,624,000	7,017,000	-5.6	(10,000)	169,000	—	7,333	7,746	-5.3
32	**Meijer** (Grand Rapids, MI)	6,600,000	6,000,000	+10.0	NA	NA	—	112	110	+1.8
33	**Gap** (San Francisco)	6,507,825	5,284,381	+23.2	533,901	452,859	+17.9	2,130	1,854	+14.9
34	**H.E.B.** (San Antonio, TX)	6,000,000	5,500,000	+9.1	NA	NA	—	245	235	+4.3
35	**Montgomery Ward** (Chicago)	5,700,000	6,600,000	-13.6	(1,170,000)	(237,000)	—	300	398	-2.1
36	**Ralphs** (Compton, CA)	5,500,000	4,250,000	+29.4	NA	NA	—	409	418	+2.0
37	**Fred Meyer** (Portland, OR)	5,481,087	3,724,839	+47.1	12,094	58,545	-79.3	518	218	+1.4
38	**Tandy** (Fort Worth, TX)	5,372,200	6,285,500	-14.5	186,900	(91,571)	—	6,996	6,999	—
39	**Staples** (Westborough, MA)	5,181,035	3,967,665	+30.6	130,949	106,420	+23.0	742	574	+29.3
40	**Supervalu Retail** (Eden Prairie, MN)	4,877,290	4,719,079	+3.4	117,576	93,662	+25.5	328	300	+9.3
41	**Nordstrom** (Seattle)	4,851,624	4,453,063	+9.0	186,213	147,505	+26.2	93	83	+12.0
42	**CompUSA** (Dallas)	4,610,523	3,829,786	+20.4	93,886	59,665	+57.4	127	106	+19.8
43	**Giant Food** (Landover, MD)	4,230,640	3,880,959	+9.0	71,190	85,504	-16.7	179	174	+2.9
44	**Hechinger/Builders Sq.** (Largo, MD)	4,117,600	4,740,000	-13.1	NA	NA	—	260	280	-7.1
45	**Consolidated Stores** (Columbus, OH)	4,055,300	3,420,200	+18.6	85,900	129,000	-33.4	1,798	861	+108.8
46	**OfficeMax** (Shaker Heights, OH)	3,765,444	3,179,274	+18.4	89,620	68,805	+30.3	722	574	+25.8
47	**Pathmark** (Carteret, NJ)	3,695,900	3,710,500	-0.4	(35,700)	(20,800)	—	135	145	-6.9
48	**Service Merchandise** (Nashville, TN)	3,662,778	3,955,016	-7.4	(91,600)	39,330	—	357	400	-10.8
49	**Fleming Retail** (Oklahoma City)	3,620,000	3,627,140	-0.2	NA	NA	—	310	350	-11.4
50	**Intimate Brands** (Columbus, OH)	3,617,856	2,997,340	+20.7	288,936	258,210	+11.9	1,710	1,609	+6.3

Source: National Retail Federation

Estimated Annual Apparel Sales

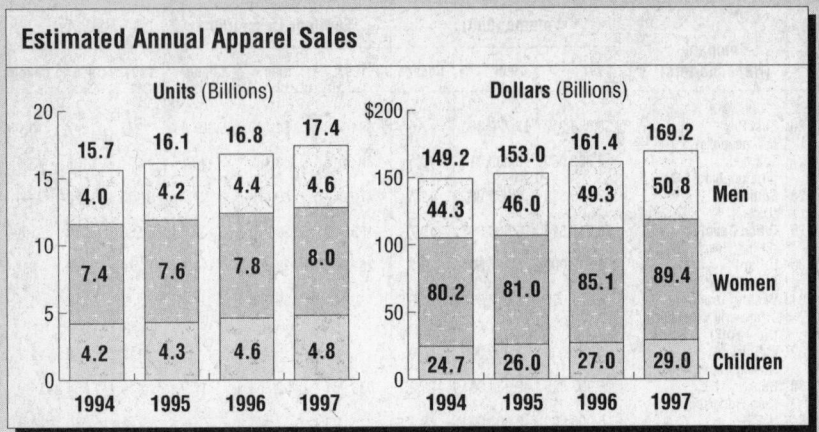

Units (Billions)

	1994	1995	1996	1997
Total	15.7	16.1	16.8	17.4
Men	4.0	4.2	4.4	4.6
Women	7.4	7.6	7.8	8.0
Children	4.2	4.3	4.6	4.8

Dollars (Billions)

	1994	1995	1996	1997
Total	149.2	153.0	161.4	169.2
Men	44.3	46.0	49.3	50.8
Women	80.2	81.0	85.1	89.4
Children	24.7	26.0	27.0	29.0

Changing Apparel Market Shares, by Type of Retailer

Discount stores have improved their clothing lines and stolen share from other retailers.

	Unit share (%)				Dollar share (%)			
	1994	1995	1996	1997	1994	1995	1996	1997
Department stores	10.1%	9.7%	9.4%	9.2%	19.5%	19.0%	18.5%	18.5%
Specialty stores	11.8	11.5	11.4	11.7	21.7	21.9	21.2	21.6
Major mass merchandise chains	14.7	14.7	14.6	14.3	16.8	16.7	16.9	16.8
Discount stores	39.3	41.1	42.2	43.1	19.2	19.7	19.8	19.8
Off-price retailers	5.6	5.5	5.6	5.3	6.8	6.4	6.5	6.4
Factory outlets	4.3	4.3	4.1	4.4	4.0	4.3	4.2	4.0
Direct mail	4.0	3.8	3.8	3.4	5.7	5.6	6.3	6.1
Other outlets	10.2	9.4	9.0	8.6	6.3	6.3	6.6	6.8

Source: NPD Group Inc.

Loyalty to Labels

In the fickle world of fashion, shoppers are most loyal to these brands:

Top Men's Brands Ranked by Repurchase Intent

1994	1996	1998
1. Levi's	1. Levi's	1. Levi's
2. Starter	2. Land's End	2. Dockers
3. Dockers	3. L.L. Bean	3. Starter
4. Russell Athletic	4. Nike	4. London Fog
5. Hanes	5. Gold Toe	4. Timberland
5. Gold Toe	5. London Fog	4. Tommy Hilfiger
7. Fruit of the Loom	5. Reebok	7. Nike
8. Lee	8. Champion	7. Reebok
8. Reebok	9. Arizona	9. Fruit of the Loom
10. Champion	9. Disney	9. Lee
	9. Hanes	

Top Women's Brands Ranked by Repurchase Intent

1994	1996	1998
1. Levi's	1. Levi's	1. Tommy Hilfiger
2. London Fog	2. Hanes	2. Hanes
3. Hanes Her Way	3. Reebok	3. Victoria's Secret
4. Hanes	4. Hanes Her Way	4. L.L. Bean
5. Reebok	5. L.L. Bean	5. Eddie Bauer
6. Dockers	6. Arizona	5. Hanes Her Way
6. Fruit of the Loom	7. Fruit of the Loom	5. Timberland
8. Just My Size	7. Lee	8. Alfred Dunner
9. Nike	7. London Fog	8. Dockers
10. Lee	10. Disney	8. Levi's
		8. Nike

Sources: Kurt Salmon Associates and NPD Group Inc.

Top Selling "Prestige" Fragrance Brands, 1997

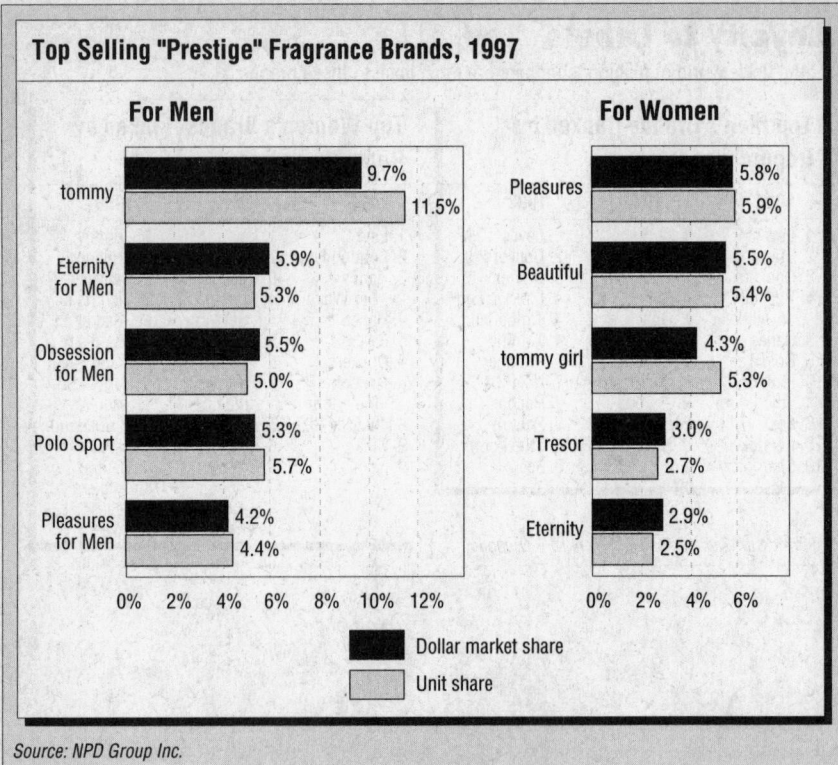

For Men

Brand	
tommy	9.7% / 11.5%
Eternity for Men	5.9% / 5.3%
Obsession for Men	5.5% / 5.0%
Polo Sport	5.3% / 5.7%
Pleasures for Men	4.2% / 4.4%

0% 2% 4% 6% 8% 10% 12%

For Women

Brand	
Pleasures	5.8% / 5.9%
Beautiful	5.5% / 5.4%
tommy girl	4.3% / 5.3%
Tresor	3.0% / 2.7%
Eternity	2.9% / 2.5%

0% 2% 4% 6%

■ Dollar market share
▢ Unit share

Source: NPD Group Inc.

Lost Sales

Shoplifting and employee theft are the two major causes of "inventory shrinkage" for the retailing industry.

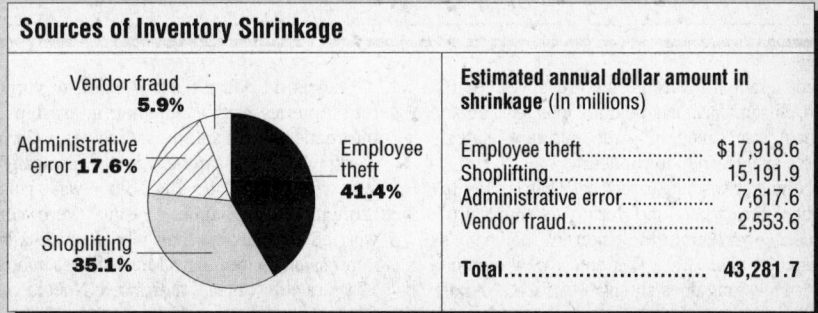

Sources of Inventory Shrinkage

Vendor fraud **5.9%**
Administrative error **17.6%**
Employee theft **41.4%**
Shoplifting **35.1%**

Estimated annual dollar amount in shrinkage (In millions)

Employee theft	$17,918.6
Shoplifting	15,191.9
Administrative error	7,617.6
Vendor fraud	2,553.6
Total	**43,281.7**

Sources: National Retail Federation and Center for Retailing Education, University of Florida

Customer Dissatisfaction

These businesses provoked the most consumer complaints to Better Business Bureaus in 1997.

1997 rank	Type of business	No. of complaints
1	Franchised auto dealers	13,200
2	Auto repair (mechanical) shops	8,760
3	Home remodeling contractors	8,330
4	Computer sales and service	6,730
5	Home furnishing stores	5,825
6	Telephone companies	5,220
7	Roofing and gutter contractors	5,100
8	Used auto dealers	4,650
9	Dry cleaners	4,630
10	Catalog and mail order	4,130

Source: Council of Better Business Bureaus

Workplace

Since graduating from Harvard seven years ago, Susan Carls has held six jobs, earned an M.B.A. and lived in three different states. She's also learned to windsurf.

Now, her winding career path has led her to Yahoo! Inc., where she works as a senior producer, overseeing the Internet company's classified ads, auto sales and a new auction site. How long does she plan to stick around? "I can definitely understand the logic of staying until my options vest," Ms. Carls says. Even so, money isn't going to tie her down. "I'll stay as long as the people are fun and we're building interesting products," she says.

When the 29-year-old Ms. Carls does leave—and it is when, not if—she plans to try her hand at fish farming or some other agribusiness pursuit. "There are worlds to be conquered," she says.

Ms. Carls and others about her age—the 52.5 million Americans known collectively as Generation X—have entered a job market transformed by the competitive pressures of globalization and quantum leaps in technology. They switch jobs much more often and move around more than previous generations.

The result: Their attitudes toward work are vastly different from those of their parents. They are less loyal to employers, and they see work as a transaction. In exchange for their labor, they expect to gain new skills, win immediate rewards and be recognized for their contributions. "This is a generation that thinks of themselves as the sole proprietor of their skills and abilities," says Bruce Tulgan, founder of Rainmaker Thinking, a New Haven, Connecticut, consultancy that specializes in Generation X in the workplace. "Wherever they work, they feel like they're in business for themselves."

The Gen Xers' approach to their jobs, in turn, is reconfiguring the workplace, making it less hierarchical, less formal and more flexible. They are helping forge a new covenant between workers and companies. The changes extend beyond the office, too, as Gen Xers' work habits affect their personal and civic lives, straining friendships and making ties to geographic communities more tenuous.

Francis de Souza's introduction to corporate America was a summer internship at International Business Machines Corp., working with researchers in the company's superconductor lab. Big Blue was going through a tough time. "People were very worried about losing their jobs. It made a big impression on me," says Mr. de Souza, who is 27 years old. "I mean, there were Nobel Prize winners in that group."

An electrical engineer educated at the Massachusetts Institute of Technology, Mr. de Souza decided he never wanted to be in that position, stuck "working on the wrong problem" and not one essential to the company's survival. So, after graduation he took a job as a management consultant. He traveled across the country and around the world advising clients, primarily telecommunications companies, for Gemini Consulting. In South Africa, he helped the government plan the installation of the country's communications infrastructure.

After three years, he and a Gemini vice president left to start VenCom Group, a $100 million investment fund that took equity stakes in telecommunications and high-tech startups. He worked with an on-line apartment-marketing venture and a company that sold bundled communications services to apartment blocks.

Then, Mr. de Souza got an idea for an Internet company of his own: instant-messaging technology. He got together with a group of MIT friends and started Flash. "It was the most intense experience of my life," Mr. de Souza says. "For 61 days, we didn't leave the office." In February 1998, he sold the company to Microsoft Corp. and went to work at the software giant's Redmond, Washington, headquarters.

Mr. de Souza has followed a Generation X pattern that Rainmaker's Mr. Tulgan describes as "retiring early and often." People change employers, change disciplines and sometimes start their own companies. It is not uncommon, Mr. Tulgan says, "to see people work like dogs for a couple of years and then just bail out. People just don't have such a stake in a long-term relationship with a company."

The expectation of frequent job changes means that, instead of investing time and effort in hopes of a future payoff in increased responsibilty and rewards, Generation Xers look for more immediate payback. Money is important. And in the booming U.S. economy in recent years, competition for labor has been so intense that workers switching employers often have been able to bump their salaries up by 30 to 50 percent. And workers who stay put expect to see frequent increases as well.

Brian Harniman, a 26-year-old Web master at Priceline.com Inc., an electronic-commerce company based in Stamford, Connecticut, has received three raises of 10 to 12 percent in his 19 months at the company. "I want to be shown and I want to be told that I'm doing well," he says.

There is also a great thirst for training and responsibility. "It's all about me, what this job is going to do for me," says Susan O'Connor, manager of technical staffing at Gartner Group's Gartner Research Advisory Services unit. "They want you to provide an environment where they can grow, educate themselves and develop skills." A recent Gallup survey found that 80 percent of Generation Xers considered the availability of company-sponsored training as a factor in deciding whether to take a job. Fifty-eight percent of workers 32 years old and under said training was useful to prepare them for higher level jobs, compared with 42 percent of older workers.

Gen Xers also expect flexibility on the part of their employers, and hunger for the ability to work from home and take time off to be with friends and family. Gail Murray, a human-resources executive at Xerox Corp., says younger applicants "have no problem telling you that they plan to have a life, that they're not going to work every weekend."

But for many, the workplace becomes an important community, even as they seek to achieve a balance between work and private life. Priceline's Mr. Harniman, for example, practically lives at work. He comes in at 8 or 9 in the morning and often stays until 10 at night, scrambling to supervise work on two Web sites plus the company's affiliate program, which gives Priceline a presence on other companies' Web pages. Most days he eats lunch and dinner at the office, food that the company provides free.

After hours, his life revolves around Priceline as well. He's lead singer in the five-person company band, performing at Priceline's Monday morning staff meetings and other company functions. On weekends, he plays softball and basketball with friends from work. "We tend to stick together," Mr. Harniman says. "The off time is when some of our best brainstorming takes place."

Priceline management tries hard to foster this sense of community. The company videotapes employees at work and play, creating "home movies" that are shown at meetings and parties. The chief operating officer, Jesse Fink, once rented an ice-cream truck and handed out treats in front of the office. Another time, Mr. Fink and other executives dressed up in Star Trek uniforms and "beamed" employees up to work in the elevators. "The energy level at work is very important," Mr. Harniman says. "I think Priceline and I will be together for a very long time."

Mr. Harniman doesn't have much of a tie to his new hometown, however. He's not registered to vote in Connecticut and says he's not very interested in local politics. To have fun, he's more likely to go to Yankee Stadium or somewhere else in nearby New York City.

Ms. Carls from Yahoo! plays on soccer and ultimate-frisbee teams in Mountain View, California, her new home. "I do have a library card," Ms. Carls says. "But I'm not very connected." Mr. de Souza, likewise, is still settling in to his first house in Kirkland, Washington, near Microsoft headquarters. Seven months after moving in, he and his girlfriend are starting to buy furniture.

Many of Mr. de Souza's best friends came with him to Microsoft when the company bought Flash. But he still has close friends scattered around the globe—in Boston, London and South Africa. "My friendships are maintained by e-mail and phone," Mr. de Souza says.

Some think that as Gen Xers grow older, have children and settle down, their peripatetic lifestyles will change. But many experts, including Rainmaker's Mr. Tulgan, think the new workplace attitudes are here to stay. The reason is that the source of job security has changed. Investing in a lengthy relationship with a company is risky. "People who enhance their skills and mobility have the most security," Mr. Tulgan says. "It's about options, not long-term commitments."

Gordon Fairclough

Changing Complexion of the U.S. Workplace

The shifting racial and ethnic makeup of the U.S. work force: number of workers by race and ethnic origin and their share of the total civilian labor force.

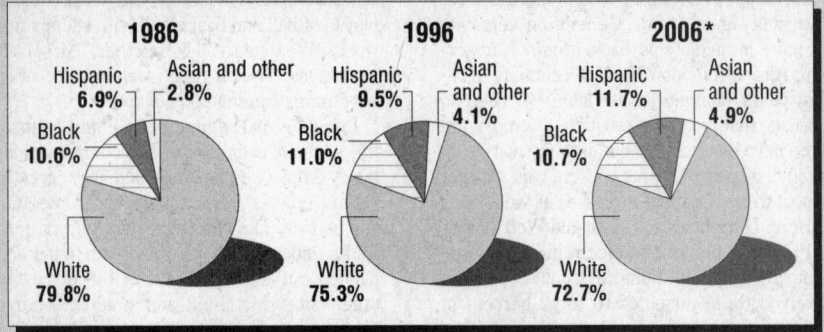

Numbers (thousands)	1986	1996	2006*	Percent	1986	1996	2006*
Total	**117,834**	**133,944**	**148,847**	**Total**	**100.0%**	**100.0%**	**100.0%**
Men	65,422	72,087	78,226	Men	55.5	53.8	52.6
Women	52,412	61,857	70,620	Women	44.5	46.2	47.4
White, non-Hispanic	**94,026**	**100,915**	**108,166**	**White, non-Hispanic**	**79.8**	**75.3**	**72.7**
Men	52,442	54,451	56,856	Men	44.5	40.7	38.2
Women	41,583	46,464	51,310	Women	35.3	34.7	34.5
Black, non-Hispanic	**12,483**	**14,795**	**15,983**	**Black, non-Hispanic**	**10.6**	**11.0**	**10.7**
Men	6,279	7,091	7,347	Men	5.3	5.3	4.9
Women	6,204	7,704	8,636	Women	5.3	5.8	5.8
Hispanic origin	**8,076**	**12,774**	**17,401**	**Hispanic origin**	**6.9**	**9.5**	**11.7**
Men	4,948	7,646	10,235	Men	4.2	5.7	6.9
Women	3,128	5,128	7,166	Women	2.7	3.8	4.8
Asian and other, non-Hispanic	**3,249**	**5,459**	**7,296**	**Asian and other, non-Hispanic**	**2.8**	**4.1**	**4.9**
Men	1,753	2,899	3,788	Men	1.5	2.2	2.5
Women	1,496	2,561	3,508	Women	1.3	1.9	2.4

*Projected.
Source: U.S. Bureau of Labor Statistics

At Your Service

Jobs in service-producing businesses have grown at a much faster pace than those in the goods-producing industries.

Percentages of Nonfarm Jobs in Service and Goods-Producing Industries

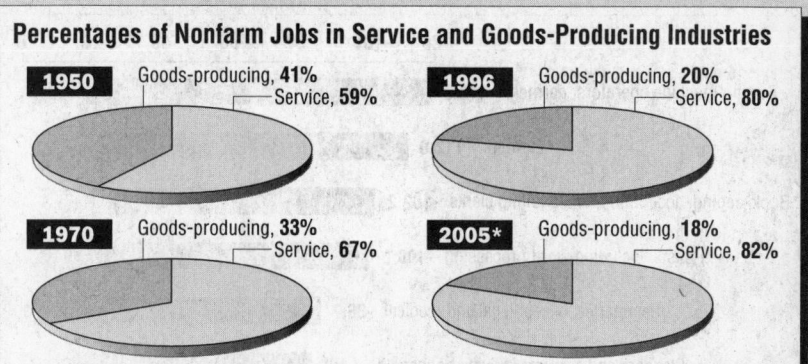

1950 Goods-producing, **41%** — Service, **59%**

1996 Goods-producing, **20%** — Service, **80%**

1970 Goods-producing, **33%** — Service, **67%**

2005* Goods-producing, **18%** — Service, **82%**

Number of Employees on Nonfarm Payrolls

(In thousands)

Annual averages			Annual averages			
Year	Total	Goods-producing	Service-producing	Year	Total	Goods-producing	Service-producing
1946	41,652	17,248	24,404	1988	105,209	25,125	80,084
1950	45,197	18,506	26,691	1989	107,884	25,254	82,631
1955	50,641	20,513	30,128	1990	109,403	24,905	84,497
1960	54,189	20,434	33,755	1991	108,249	23,745	84,504
1965	60,765	21,926	38,839	1992	108,601	23,231	85,370
1970	70,880	23,578	47,302	1993	110,713	23,352	87,361
1975	76,945	22,600	54,345	1994	114,163	23,908	90,256
1980	90,406	25,658	64,748	1995	117,191	24,265	92,925
1985	97,387	24,842	72,544	1996	119,523	24,431	95,092
1986	99,344	24,533	74,811	1997	122,259	24,739	97,520
1987	101,958	24,674	77,284	2005*	130,185	22,930	107,256

*Projection.
Source: U.S. Bureau of Labor Statistics

Changing Jobs

Occupations with the Largest Numerical Job Decline, 1996–2006

(Projections in thousands)

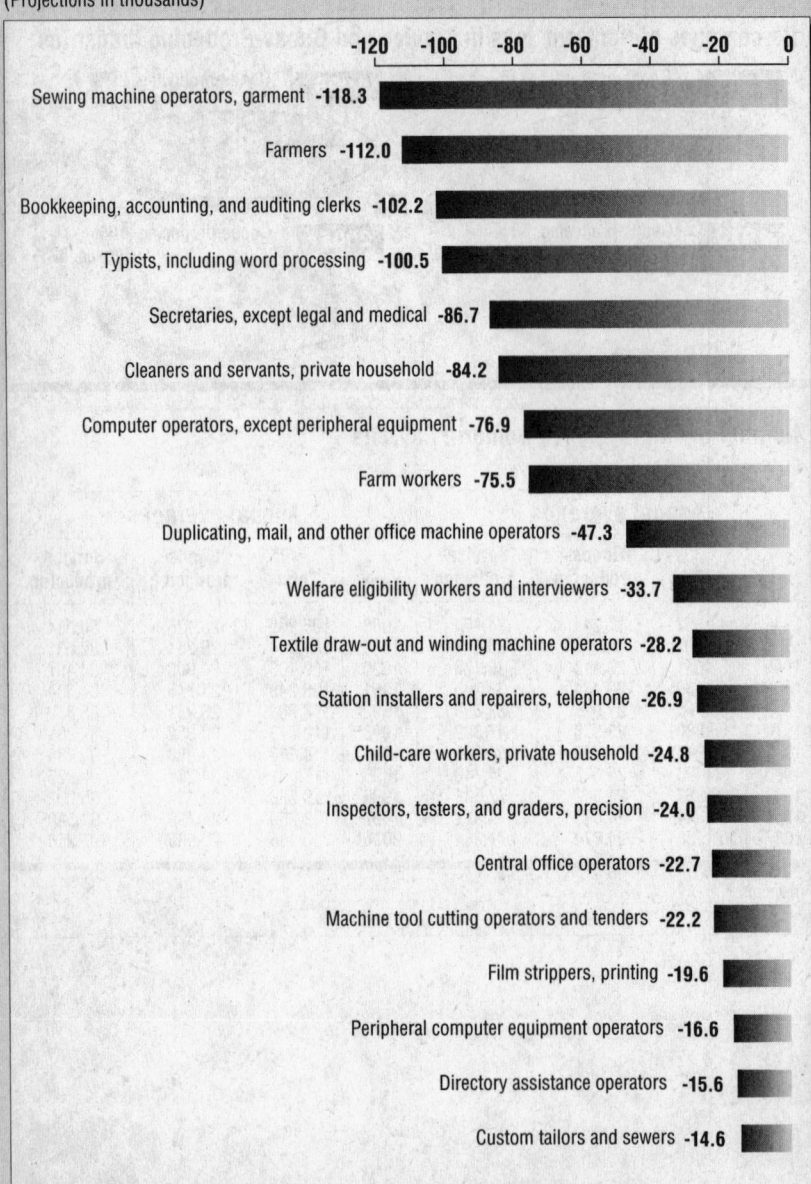

Occupation	Decline
Sewing machine operators, garment	-118.3
Farmers	-112.0
Bookkeeping, accounting, and auditing clerks	-102.2
Typists, including word processing	-100.5
Secretaries, except legal and medical	-86.7
Cleaners and servants, private household	-84.2
Computer operators, except peripheral equipment	-76.9
Farm workers	-75.5
Duplicating, mail, and other office machine operators	-47.3
Welfare eligibility workers and interviewers	-33.7
Textile draw-out and winding machine operators	-28.2
Station installers and repairers, telephone	-26.9
Child-care workers, private household	-24.8
Inspectors, testers, and graders, precision	-24.0
Central office operators	-22.7
Machine tool cutting operators and tenders	-22.2
Film strippers, printing	-19.6
Peripheral computer equipment operators	-16.6
Directory assistance operators	-15.6
Custom tailors and sewers	-14.6

Source: U.S. Bureau of Labor Statistics

Occupations with the Largest Numerical Job Growth, 1996–2006

(Projections in thousands)

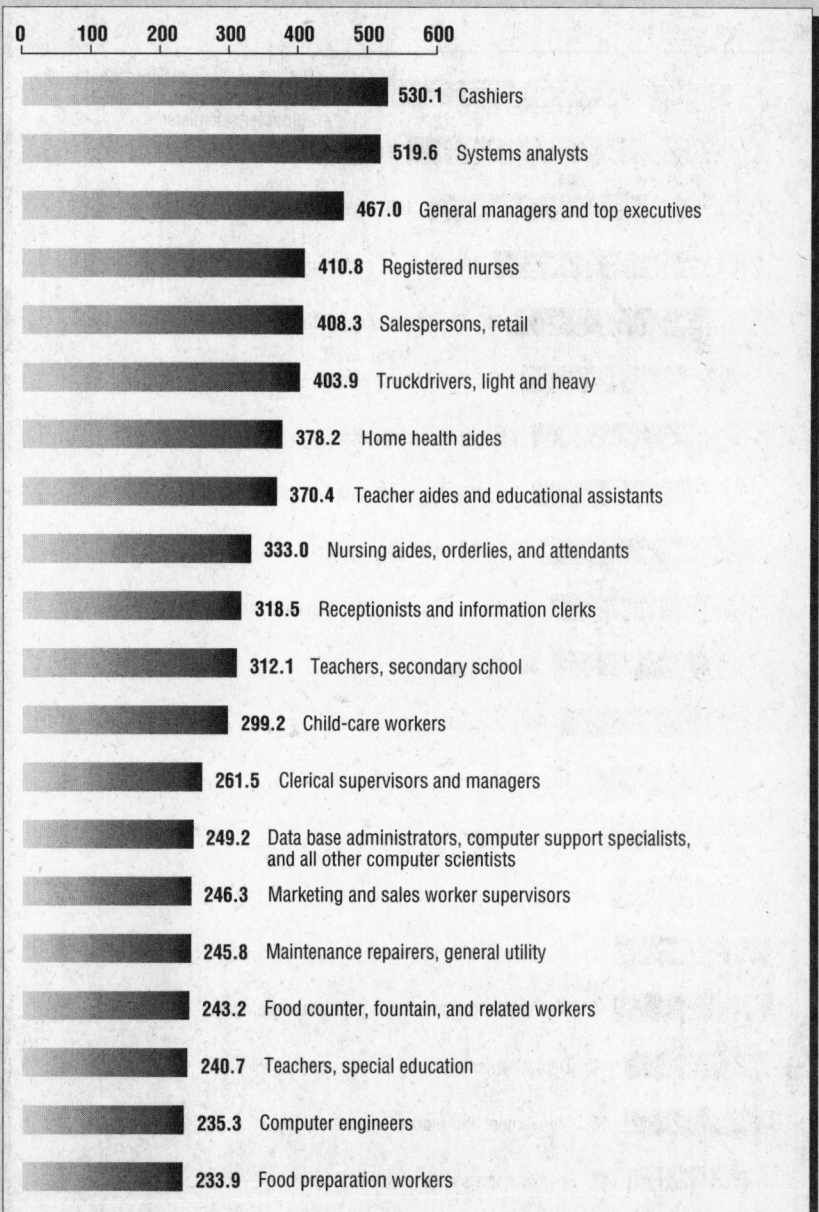

530.1	Cashiers
519.6	Systems analysts
467.0	General managers and top executives
410.8	Registered nurses
408.3	Salespersons, retail
403.9	Truckdrivers, light and heavy
378.2	Home health aides
370.4	Teacher aides and educational assistants
333.0	Nursing aides, orderlies, and attendants
318.5	Receptionists and information clerks
312.1	Teachers, secondary school
299.2	Child-care workers
261.5	Clerical supervisors and managers
249.2	Data base administrators, computer support specialists, and all other computer scientists
246.3	Marketing and sales worker supervisors
245.8	Maintenance repairers, general utility
243.2	Food counter, fountain, and related workers
240.7	Teachers, special education
235.3	Computer engineers
233.9	Food preparation workers

Source: U.S. Bureau of Labor Statistics

Fastest Growing Occupations, 1996–2006

(Projected percentage increase)

```
0      20      40      60      80      100     120
```

118 Data base administrators, computer support specialists, and all other computer scientists

109 Computer engineers

103 Systems analysts

85 Personal and home care aides

79 Physical and corrective therapy assistants and aides

77 Home health aides

74 Medical assistants

74 Desktop publishing specialists

71 Physical therapists

69 Occupational therapy assistants and aides

68 Paralegals

66 Occupational therapists

59 Teachers, special education

55 Human services workers

52 Data processing equipment repairers

51 Medical records technicians

51 Speech-language pathologists and audiologists

48 Dental hygienists

48 Amusement and recreation attendants

47 Physician assistants

Source: U.S. Bureau of Labor Statistics

Work Time

Louis Harris & Associates' surveys of Americans show an increase in the amount of time devoted to work activities and about the same amount of time for leisure as in 1980. Work includes working for pay, keeping house and going to school.

Year	Median number of hours of work per week	Median number of hours of leisure per week
1973	40.6	26.2
1975	43.1	24.3
1980	46.9	19.2
1984	47.3	18.1
1987	46.8	16.6
1989	48.7	18.8
1993	50.0	18.8
1994	50.7	19.5
1995	50.6	19.2
1997	50.8	19.5

Source: Louis Harris & Associates

Percentage of Non-Farm Workers, by Hours on the Job Per Week in 1997

Hours of work	Percent distribution
1 to 34 hours	24.8%
1 to 4 hours	1.0
5 to 14 hours	3.9
15 to 29 hours	12.3
30 to 34 hours	7.5
35 hours and over	75.2
35 to 39 hours	7.0
40 hours	36.4
41 hours and over	31.9
41 to 48 hours	11.6
49 to 59 hours	11.7
60 hours and over	8.5

Average hours, total at work................................. 39.5
Average hours, persons who usually work full time.............43.4

Source: U.S. Bureau of Labor Statistics

Stressed Out

The most and least stressful jobs, based on such factors as quotas and deadlines, long work weeks, the hazards involved, level of competitiveness, physical demands, environmental conditions, contact with the public, need for precision, and amount of stamina required.

Most Stressful Jobs

1. U.S. President
2. Firefighter
3. Senior corporate executive
4. Race car driver (Indy class)
5. Taxi driver
6. Surgeon
7. Astronaut
8. Police officer
9. Football player (NFL)
10. Air traffic controller
11. Highway patrol officer
12. Public relations executive
13. Mayor
14. Jockey
15. Basketball coach (NCAA)
16. Advertising account executive
17. Real estate agent
18. Photojournalist
19. Member of Congress
20. Stockbroker
21. Fisherman
22. Airplane pilot
23. Lumberjack
24. Emergency medical technician
25. Architect

Least Stressful Jobs

1. Medical records technician
2. Janitor
3. Forklift operator
4. Musical instrument repairer
5. Florist
6. Actuary
7. Appliance repairer
8. Medical secretary
9. Librarian
10. Bookkeeper
11. File clerk
12. Piano tuner
13. Photographic process worker
14. Dietitian
15. Paralegal assistant
16. Vending machine repairer
17. Bookbinder
18. Barber
19. Medical laboratory technician
20. Electrical technician
21. Typist/Word processor
22. Broadcast technician
23. Mathematician
24. Dental hygienist
25. Jeweler

Source: The Wall Street Journal, National Business Employment Weekly Jobs Rated Almanac

Benefits Coverage

The percentage of small companies providing each of the following benefits compared with the percentage of larger concerns.

Benefit	Small	Medium & Large
Vacations	88%	96%
Holidays	82	89
Health insurance	66	77
Life insurance	61	87
Jury duty leave	58	85
Sick leave	50	58
Funeral leave	50	80
Retirement plans	42	80
Dental insurance	28	57
401(k) plans with employer contribution	20	45
Long-term disability insurance	20	42
Personal leave	13	22

Note: Figures are for 1994 for small companies and for 1995 for medium and large concerns.

Source: U.S. Bureau of Labor Statistics

Wage and Benefit Growth

The growth of wages, salaries and benefits slowed in the first half of the 1990s, as measured by the Labor Department's Employment Cost Index. But the growth rate for wages rebounded somewhat in 1996 and 1997.

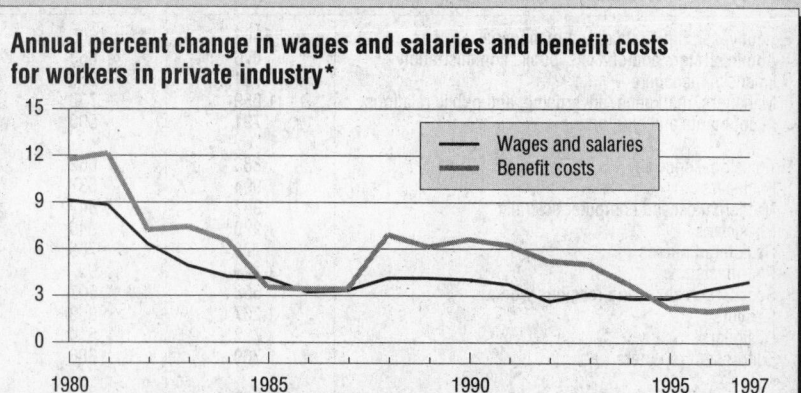

Annual percent change in wages and salaries and benefit costs for workers in private industry*

Percent Change in Wages, Salaries, and Benefit Costs of Private Industry Workers Based on Employment Cost Index

Year	Wages and Salaries			Year	Benefit Costs		
	Private industry*	White-collar occupations	Blue-collar occupations		Private industry*	White-collar occupations	Blue-collar occupations
1980	9.1%	8.6%	9.6%	1980	11.7%	12.1%	11.1%
1981	8.8	9.1	8.5	1981	12.1	12.5	11.8
1982	6.3	6.5	5.6	1982	7.2	6.8	7.3
1983	4.9	6.0	3.8	1983	7.4	7.5	7.3
1984	4.2	4.3	3.6	1984	6.5	7.2	5.9
1985	4.1	4.9	3.4	1985	3.5	4.2	2.5
1986	3.2	3.4	2.6	1986	3.4	3.6	3.1
1987	3.3	3.7	3.0	1987	3.4	3.7	3.4
1988	4.1	4.7	3.2	1988	6.9	6.3	7.4
1989	4.1	4.7	3.5	1989	6.1	6.7	5.3
1990	4.0	4.1	3.5	1990	6.6	6.9	6.2
1991	3.7	3.8	3.4	1991	6.2	6.1	6.1
1992	2.6	2.7	2.6	1992	5.2	4.8	5.6
1993	3.1	3.3	2.9	1993	5.0	4.6	5.5
1994	2.8	2.8	2.8	1994	3.7	4.5	2.8
1995	2.8	2.9	2.9	1995	2.2	2.6	1.7
1996	3.4	3.5	3.0	1996	2.0	2.2	1.7
1997	3.9	4.3	3.2	1997	2.3	2.6	1.5

*Excludes farm and household workers.
Source: U.S. Bureau of Labor Statistics

Earnings by Occupation

Median Weekly Earnings of Full-Time Workers, 1997

Occupation	Men	Women
Executive, administrative, and managerial	$868	$605
Administrators and officials, public administration	876	653
Financial managers	991	660
Managers, marketing, advertising, and public relations	1,059	736
Accountants and auditors	791	590
Professional specialty	883	662
Engineers	994	837
Mathematical and computer scientists	947	842
Physicians	1,220	946
Registered nurses	778	705
Pharmacists	1,129	907
Social, recreation, and religious workers	558	502
Lawyers	1,267	959
Designers	792	514
Editors and reporters	769	606
Health technologists and technicians	553	466
Computer programmers	869	742
Sales occupations	603	352
Real estate sales	685	523
Securities and financial services sales	858	550
Sales workers, retail and personal services	392	266
Administrative support, including clerical	514	403
Computer equipment operators	526	422
Bookkeepers, accounting and auditing clerks	446	418
Mail carriers, postal service	691	610
Insurance adjusters, examiners, and investigators	655	473
Police and detectives	628	547
Waiters and waitresses	328	268
Cooks, except short order	300	245
Janitors and cleaners	330	275
Mechanics and repairers, except supervisors	570	475
Construction trades	538	445
Precision metalworking occupations	597	399
Machine operators, assemblers, and inspectors	449	313
Truck drivers	509	399
Farm workers	276	247

Source: U.S. Bureau of Labor Statistics

EARNINGS GAP

Median Weekly Earnings of Full-time Wage and Salary Workers

The gap between men's and women's earnings narrowed through the early 1990s, but widened slightly in recent years. Still, women have made progress, with their earnings averaging 74% of men's in 1997, compared with 69% in 1986. But the gap grew between whites and minorities: the median weekly earnings for blacks were 77% of whites' earnings, down from 79% in 1986; Hispanics earned 68% of what whites earned, compared with 75% in 1986.
(Annual averages in current dollars)

	1980	1986	1990	1995	1996	1997
Men	$312	$419	$485	$538	$557	$579
Women	201	290	348	406	418	431
White	268	370	427	494	506	519
Black	212	291	329	383	387	400
Hispanic	–	277	307	329	339	351

Source: U.S. Bureau of Labor Statistics

Tracking the Minimum Wage

The hourly federal minimum wage and its purchasing power in 1997 dollars

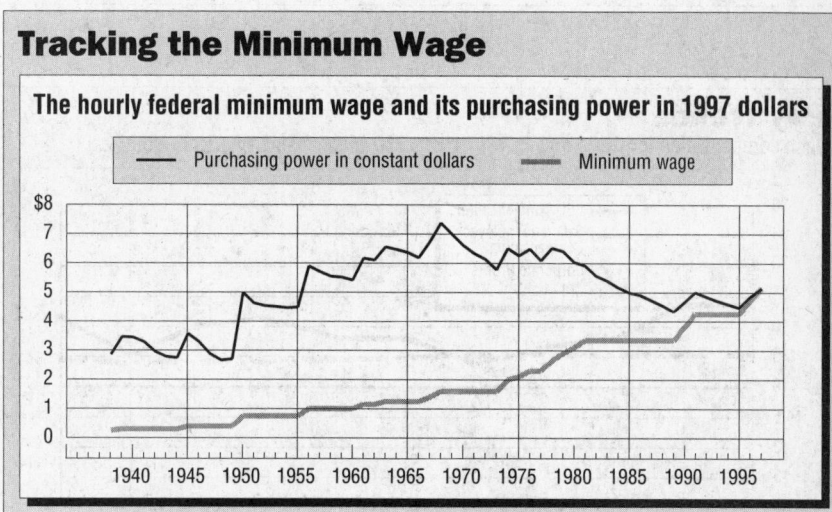

Year	Minimum wage	Purchasing Power in 1997 dollars using CPI-U	Year	Minimum wage	Purchasing Power in 1997 dollars using CPI-U
1938	$0.25	$2.85	1980	$3.10	$6.04
1939	0.30	3.46	1981	3.35	5.92
1940	0.30	3.44	1982	3.35	5.57
1945	0.40	3.57	1983	3.35	5.40
1950	0.75	4.99	1984	3.35	5.17
1955	0.75	4.49	1985	3.35	5.00
1956	1.00	5.90	1986	3.35	4.91
1960	1.00	5.42	1987	3.35	4.73
1961	1.15	6.17	1988	3.35	4.55
1963	1.25	6.56	1989	3.35	4.34
1965	1.25	6.37	1990	3.80	4.67
1967	1.40	6.73	1991	4.25	5.01
1968	1.60	7.38	1992	4.25	4.86
1970	1.60	6.62	1993	4.25	4.72
1974	2.00	6.51	1994	4.25	4.60
1975	2.10	6.26	1995	4.25	4.48
1976	2.30	6.49	1996	4.75	4.86
1977	2.30	6.09	1997	5.15	5.15
1978	2.65	6.52			
1979	2.90	6.41			

Source: U.S. Bureau of Labor Statistics

Pay Trends

Cash compensation for CEOs rose in 1997 by 11.7%, much faster than 1996's 5.2%.

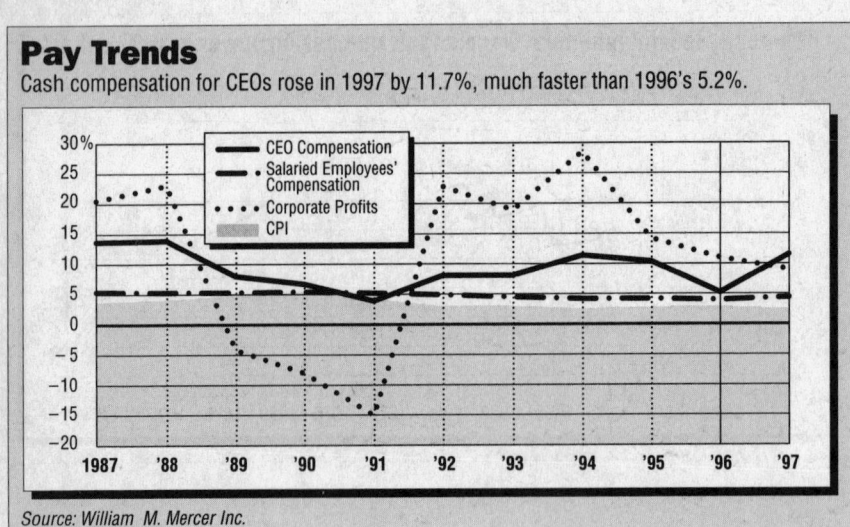

Source: William M. Mercer Inc.

10 Highest Paid CEOs in 1997

Based on an analysis of proxy statements from 350 of the largest U.S. businesses

Company	Executive	Salary & bonus	Gain on option exercise	Restricted stock grants	Long term incentive payouts	Total direct compensation
Travelers Group Inc.	Sanford I. Weill	$ 9,525,000	$220,162,892	$ 777,322	$0	$230,465,214
Morgan Stanley, Dean Witter & Co.	Philip J. Purcell	10,473,750	36,397,538	3,135,577	0	50,006,865
Monsanto Co.	Robert B. Shapiro	1,765,000	46,741,110	0	750,365	49,256,475
General Electric Co.	John F. Welch Jr.	8,000,000	31,825,020	0	0	39,825,020
American Express Co.	Harvey Golub	3,200,000	27,132,498	0	2,856,231	33,188,729
Bristol-Myers Squibb Co.	Charles A. Heimbold Jr.	2,802,635	25,286,763	0	1,121,900	29,211,298
AlliedSignal Inc.	Lawrence A. Bossidy	5,150,000	23,082,225	0	0	28,232,225
Pfizer Inc.	William C. Steere Jr.	3,861,800	15,402,984	0	8,837,500	28,102,284
Colgate-Palmolive Co.	Reuben Mark	3,846,555	18,164,302	704,769	2,674,716	25,390,342
Merrill Lynch & Co.	David H. Komansky	7,728,863	14,398,750	1,524,325	0	23,651,938

Source: Study conducted by William M. Mercer Inc. for The Wall Street Journal

Payday for Junior

A survey by *Zillions*, the magazine for kids from *Consumer Reports*, found that 9-to-14 year olds collect the following median weekly income from their parents as allowances, handouts, and payments for chores. The median weekly allowance for 9-and-10 year olds has risen 50 cents since 1994, but it hasn't budged for older kids since 1991. Like many of their elders in the work force, two out of three kids said they asked for an increase but didn't get one.

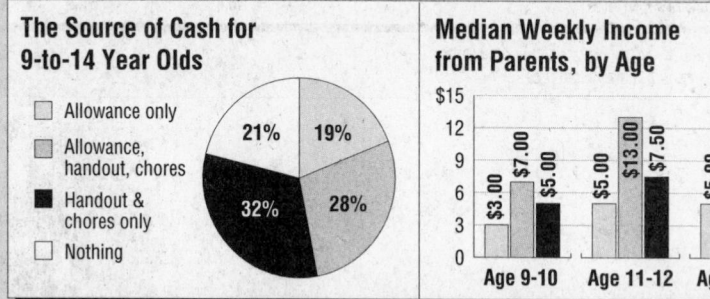

The Source of Cash for 9-to-14 Year Olds

- Allowance only — 19%
- Allowance, handout, chores — 28%
- Handout & chores only — 32%
- Nothing — 21%

Median Weekly Income from Parents, by Age

	Age 9-10	Age 11-12	Age 13-14
Allowance only	$3.00	$5.00	$5.00
Allowance, handout, chores	$7.00	$13.00	$15.00
Handout & chores only	$5.00	$7.50	$12.00

Source: Consumer Reports and Zillions

Women in the Executive and Professional Ranks

Percentage of Employees in Selected Occupations Who Were Women

Occupation	1983	1997
Total work force, 16 years and over	43.7%	46.2%
Executive, administrative, and managerial	32.4	44.3
Officials and administrators, public administration	38.5	49.5
Financial managers	38.6	49.3
Personnel and labor relations managers	43.9	63.4
Purchasing managers	23.6	40.9
Managers, marketing, advertising, and public relations	21.8	34.6
Managers, medicine and health	57.0	76.8
Accountants and auditors	38.7	56.6
Management analysts	29.5	42.0
Professional specialty	48.1	53.3
Architects	12.7	17.9
Engineers	5.8	9.6
Mathematical and computer scientists	29.6	30.4
Natural scientists	20.5	31.0
Physicians	15.8	26.2
Dentists	6.7	17.3
Teachers, college and university	36.3	42.7
Economists	37.9	52.2
Psychologists	57.1	59.3
Lawyers	15.3	26.6
Authors	46.7	53.6
Musicians and composers	28.0	36.6
Editors and reporters	48.4	51.2

*Data for 1983 and 1997 are not strictly comparable.
Source: U.S. Bureau of Labor Statistics

Women and Men in the Work Force

Percent of Population in the Civilian Labor Force

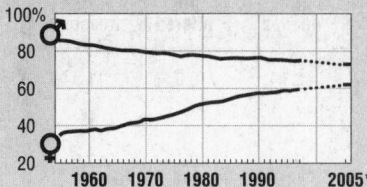

Year	% of population	
	Women	Men
1955	35.7%	85.4%
1960	37.7	83.3
1965	39.3	80.7
1970	43.3	79.7
1975	46.3	77.9
1980	51.5	77.4
1985	54.5	76.3
1990	57.5	76.4
1995	58.9	75.0
1996	59.3	74.9
1997	59.8	75.0
2005*	61.7	72.9

*Projected.
Source: U.S. Bureau of Labor Statistics

Working Mothers

Percentage of mothers in the labor force, by age of their children

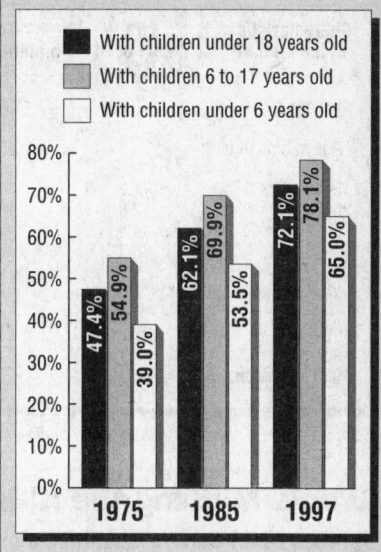

■ With children under 18 years old
▨ With children 6 to 17 years old
□ With children under 6 years old

Source: U.S. Bureau of Labor Statistics

Maternity Leave

Percentage of women, 15 to 44 years of age, by use of maternity leave for the most recent birth

Characteristic of the mother	Not employed	Took maternity leave	Did not take maternity leave		
			Not needed	Not offered	Other reasons
All women	48.0 %	37.3 %	2.3 %	0.9 %	11.6 %
Age at time of birth					
15–19 years	71.9	14.8	0.7	0.1	12.5
20–24 years	52.8	29.8	1.3	1.3	14.9
25–29 years	44.8	41.1	2.7	0.8	10.5
30–44 years	38.3	48.3	3.5	0.8	9.1
Year of child's birth					
1991–95	43.2	43.5	2.2	0.9	10.3
1981–90	47.4	37.2	2.7	0.8	11.8
1980 and before	61.5	22.0	1.6	0.9	14.0

Source: Centers for Disease Control and Prevention, National Center for Health Statistics

Who's Minding the Kids?

Primary Child-Care Arrangements of Preschoolers Under Age 5

Changes in Selected Child Care Arrangements: 1988–1994

(Percent of preschoolers of working mothers in selected arrangements)

■ 1988   ▨ 1991   □ 1994

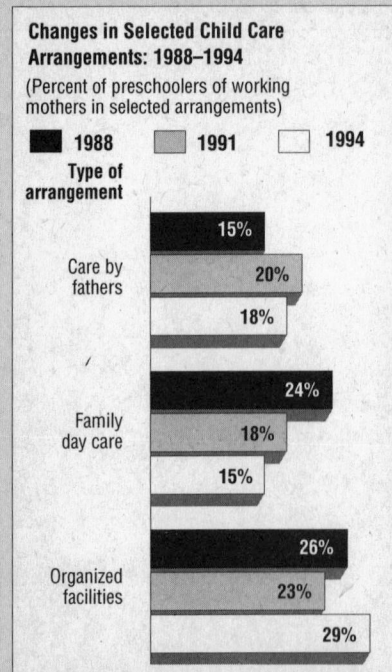

Type of arrangement

Care by fathers
15%
20%
18%

Family day care
24%
18%
15%

Organized facilities
26%
23%
29%

Type of arrangement 1994	All preschoolers with working mothers	
	Number (Thousands)	Percent
All Preschoolers	10,288	100.0%
Care in child's home	3,381	33.0
By father	1,898	18.5
By grandparent	604	5.9
By other relative	355	3.5
By nonrelative	524	5.1
Care in provider's home	3,219	31.3
By grandparent	1,068	10.4
By other relative	565	5.5
By nonrelative	1,586	15.4
Organized child care facilities	3,019	29.4
Day/group care center	2,218	21.6
Nursery/preschool	801	7.8
Mother cares for child at work*	563	5.5
Other**	107	1.1

*Includes women working at home or away from home.

**Includes preschoolers in kindergarten and school-based activities.

Source: U.S. Census Bureau

Employment of Blacks and Persons of Hispanic Origin in Selected Occupations, 1983 and 1997*

(Minorities as a percentage of total employed)

Occupation	Blacks 1983	Blacks 1997	Hispanic origin 1983	Hispanic origin 1997
Total work force, 16 years and over	9.3%	10.8%	5.3%	9.3%
Executive, administrative, and managerial	4.7	6.9	2.8	5.4
Officials and administrators, public administration	8.3	11.9	3.8	5.6
Financial managers	3.5	5.6	3.1	5.1
Personnel and labor relations managers	4.9	7.5	2.6	2.9
Purchasing managers	5.1	6.4	1.4	4.6
Managers, marketing, advertising, and public relations	2.7	3.7	1.7	4.8
Managers, medicine and health	5.0	7.4	2.0	4.3
Accountants and auditors	5.5	7.9	3.3	5.0
Management analysts	5.3	3.6	1.7	3.0
Professional specialty	6.4	7.8	2.5	4.5
Architects	1.6	1.7	1.5	5.1
Engineers	2.7	3.9	2.2	3.8
Mathematical and computer scientists	5.4	7.5	2.6	3.1
Natural scientists	2.6	5.1	2.1	2.2
Physicians	3.2	4.2	4.5	4.8
Dentists	2.4	2.6	1.0	1.1
Teachers, college and university	4.4	6.5	1.8	3.4
Economists	6.3	6.6	2.7	3.7
Psychologists	8.6	9.2	1.1	4.5
Lawyers	2.6	2.7	0.9	3.8
Authors	2.1	1.7	0.9	2.1
Musicians and composers	7.9	10.5	4.4	9.3
Editors and reporters	2.9	4.8	2.1	1.7

*Data for 1983 and 1997 are not strictly comparable.
Source: U.S. Bureau of Labor Statistics

Displaced Workers

Number of People Who Lost a Job Between January 1993 and December 1995
(In thousands)

Total workers who lost jobs
Total, 20 years and older	9,367
Men	5,315
Women	4,052

Age
20 to 24 years	1,117
25 to 54 years	7,310
55 to 64 years	707
65 years and older	233

Occupation
Managerial and professional specialty	2,021
Technical, sales, and administrative support	2,806
Service occupations	921
Precision production, craft, and repair	1,351
Operators, fabricators, and laborers	2,013
Farming, forestry, and fishing	112

Industry of job loss
Mining	91
Construction	974
Manufacturing	2,166
Durable goods	1,312
Nondurable goods	854
Transportation and public utilities	607
Wholesale and retail trade	2,042
Wholasale trade	412
Retail trade	1,630
Finance, insurance, and real estate	599
Services	2,012
Agriculture wage and salary workers	132
Government workers	498

Reason for job loss
Plant or company closed down or moved	3,404
Insufficient work	3,500
Position or shift abolished	2,463

Source: U.S. Bureau of Labor Statistics

Discrimination Complaints

Number of complaints received, number of cases resolved, and amount of monetary benefits for different types of workplace discrimination.

	1993	1994	1995	1996	1997
Race					
Complaints received	31,695	31,656	29,986	26,287	29,199
Resolutions	27,440	25,253	31,674	35,127	36,419
Monetary benefits (millions)	$ 33.3	$ 39.7	$ 30.1	$ 37.2	$ 41.8
Sex					
Complaints received	23,919	25,860	26,181	23,813	24,728
Resolutions	21,606	21,545	26,726	30,965	32,836
Monetary benefits (millions)	$ 44.0	$ 44.1	$ 23.6	$ 47.1	$ 72.5
Disabilities					
Complaints received	15,274	18,859	19,798	18,046	18,108
Resolutions	4,502	12,523	18,900	23,451	24,200
Monetary benefits (millions)	$ 15.9	$ 32.6	$ 38.7	$ 38.7	$ 36.1
Age					
Complaints received	19,809	19,618	17,416	15,719	15,785
Resolutions	19,761	13,942	17,033	17,699	18,279
Monetary Benefits (millions)	$ 40.7	$ 42.3	$ 29.4	$ 31.5	$ 44.3
Sexual Harassment					
Complaints received	11,908	14,420	15,549	15,342	15,889
Resolutions	9,971	11,478	13,802	15,861	17,333
Monetary benefits (millions)	$ 25.1	$ 22.5	$ 24.3	$ 27.8	$ 49.5
National Origin					
Complaints received	7,454	7,414	7,035	6,687	6,712
Resolutions	6,788	6,453	7,619	9,047	8,795
Monetary benefits (millions)	$ 8.8	$ 15.5	$ 10.5	$ 10.5	$ 9.1

Source: U.S. Equal Employment Opportunity Commission

Alternative Work Styles

About 10% of the American work force is employed under an alternative arrangement, particularly as independent contractors.

Employed Workers with Alternative Work Arrangements by Occupation and Industry, 1997 (Percent distribution)

Characteristic	Workers with alternative arrangements			
	Independent contractors	On-call workers	Temporary help agency workers	Workers provided by contract firms
Total, 16 years and over (thousands)	8,456	1,996	1,300	809
Occupation				
Executive, administrative, and managerial	20.7%	2.7%	6.9%	8.1%
Professional specialty	17.9	21.2	6.6	19.8
Technicians and related support	0.8	4.1	5.8	7.2
Sales occupations	17.9	6.7	1.7	2.8
Administrative support, including clerical	3.9	8.6	34.1	5.2
Services	9.1	20.4	9.0	27.7
Precision production, craft, and repair	17.9	14.7	5.2	19.8
Operators, fabricators, and laborers	6.8	18.8	29.1	9.2
Farming, forestry, and fishing	5.1	2.8	1.6	0.2
Industry				
Agriculture	5.7	3.4	–	0.2
Mining	0.2	0.4	0.6	2.1
Construction	20.7	14.4	2.2	4.6
Manufacturing	4.7	5.3	27.7	19.0
Transportation and public utilities	5.1	8.6	5.3	12.9
Wholesale trade	3.5	1.7	3.8	1.5
Retail trade	10.1	12.5	3.4	6.3
Finance, insurance, and real estate	8.4	1.5	7.4	7.5
Services	41.4	47.5	36.6	26.5
Public administration	0.2	4.0	–	13.1

Source: U.S. Bureau of Labor Statistics

HOME-BUSINESS BOOM

A few years ago, people working from their homes would go to great lengths to hide that fact from clients. They'd use private mailboxes at the local Mail Boxes Etc. or add a "suite" number to their home addresses. Many made it a policy to always visit clients rather than invite them over, fearful they wouldn't be taken seriously.

But as the number of home businesses has skyrocketed, the stigma has faded. In fact, successful home-based business people have become such advocates, they often attract other office-bound colleagues into the fold. "All I use now are other home-based businesses, and I've converted quite a few, too," says Joy Klan, an Atlanta-based event planner who works with a bevy of independent composers, dress designers, florists and choreographers.

An estimated 21.5 million people, or about 18 percent of the U.S. workforce, did some job-related work at home in 1997, according to the Bureau of Labor Statistics. Of the 21.5 million, nearly 20 percent operated home-based businesses.

Lower technology costs, greater Internet access and the strong economy have been major catalysts for home-business formation. A fax machine, copier and PC could easily top $5,000 earlier this decade. Now, all that can be had for under $1,500. The Internet "allows people to function independently," says Tom Miller, vice president of Cyber Dialogue, a New York consulting group that tracks home-based businesses. "It's communication on steroids."

The last time there was a big jump in home business formation was the early 1990s when voice mail became popular, Mr. Miller says.

Catherine Clegg of Tulsa, Oklahoma, has worked out of her home on and off for 30 years, running businesses ranging from a janitorial service to interior decorating. More recently, this mother of four has turned to real-estate investing, an ideal home business because she can do much of her work on computer.

Ms. Clegg says e-mail makes it easy for her to stay in touch with dozens of people with minimal hassle. She also can study land records in Tulsa with direct Internet access

to the city courthouse. Otherwise, "I'd have to drive my car down to the courthouse and spend hours going through stacks and stacks of files," she says. "Boring!"

Many people work at home for the flexibility, and few seem to follow the old nine-to-five routine. "We can work until 2 or 3 A.M. in the morning brainstorming or planning, and it's more comfortable for everyone than being at the office," Ms. Klan says. At the same time, she says she can work 15 hours a day for a week, then take several days off, no questions asked.

Omar Sultan says having an infant was a factor in his leaving Pacific Bell in 1998 to start his own information-technology consultancy business out of his Alameda, California, home, working in partnership with Leslee Mesick, who also has a small child. "We didn't want to pour our lives into these big faceless companies and never spend time with the kids," Mr. Sultan says. "If it's a slow week, we can pick them up at day care and go to the park."

Though there are plenty of benefits in running a home-based business, it's not for everyone, warns Beverly Williams, president of the nonprofit group, the American Association of Home-Based Businesses in Rockville, Maryland. "People need to be self-motivated and have to be able to function without too many distractions," she says. When she first started a home-based desktop publishing business a few years ago, she says, "I felt pulled in two directions: I wanted to paint the room, do the laundry. It came down to the balance in the checking account. If I don't work, there's no money."

Ms. Clegg, a single mother, says her kids know that when the door is closed to her home office, a converted fifth bedroom, they shouldn't enter "unless the house is on fire or you're bleeding."

Home-based businesspeople also have to learn to live without as much face-to-face interaction and forgo the water-cooler gossip. Some make regular trips to the local Mail Boxes Etc. or Kinko's to alleviate their feeling of isolation.

Rene Siegel, co-owner of a company based near Silicon Valley that hooks up home-based public relations people with large companies, tries to solve the loneliness problem by bringing together fellow home-based workers to schmooze at quarterly lunches at local restaurants. Many of the people who meet used to work together at big high-tech companies.

"It's like a reunion," says Cheri Goodman, a fellow home-based Silicon Valley consultant. "People talk up a storm."

The work-at-home trend has come so far that Ms. Klan, the event planner, says she now uses her home status as a selling point to clients, which include many Fortune 500 companies. "I tell them we don't have the overhead big event-planning companies do, so we can spend on the event itself," she says. "I invite them over to my place, I cook for them, have lunch. The conference room is my living room."

Rodney Ho

Home Work

Number of People Doing Job-Related Work at Home

Characteristic	Number (thousands)	Rate*	Wage & Salary		Self-Employed	
			Paid	Unpaid	Total	Home-based Business
Total, 16 years and over	21,478	17.8%	17.0%	51.5%	30.1%	19.2%
With no children under 18	12,179	16.1	16.3	52.0	30.3	19.0
With own children under 18	9,299	20.5	17.8	50.9	29.9	19.5
With own children under 6	3,885	19.6	18.8	47.6	31.6	22.3
Men, 16 years and over	11,202	17.3	15.0	50.1	33.8	19.3
With no children under 18	6,259	15.4	16.0	47.1	35.8	21.3
With own children under 18	4,943	20.5	13.8	54.0	31.2	16.7
With own children under 6	2,118	18.8	14.2	55.5	28.7	16.3
Women, 16 years and over	10,275	18.3	19.1	53.1	26.2	19.2
With no children under 18	5,920	17.0	16.7	57.2	24.6	16.6
With own children under 18	4,356	20.4	22.4	47.4	28.3	22.7
With own children under 6	1,767	20.8	24.3	38.1	35.0	29.6

*Refers to the number of persons working at home as a percent of the total at work.
Source: U.S. Bureau of Labor Statistics

Top 10 States For Small Offices/Home Offices 1998

		Number of small home offices
1	California	126,957
2	Texas	92,549
3	New York	76,708
4	Illinois	65,404
5	Florida	65,322
6	Pennsylvania	62,033
7	Michigan	59,043
8	Washington	51,073
9	Minnesota	48,116
10	Ohio	47,830

Source: Dun & Bradstreet's Cottage Industry Indicator

Where the Jobs Are Moving

Job Migration 1991–1995

	State	Jobs Entering	Jobs Exiting	Net Gain or Loss
1	Georgia	55,667	20,603	35,064
2	Texas	72,129	54,501	17,628
3	Tennessee	42,527	26,537	15,990
4	Colorado	25,239	11,331	13,908
5	Delaware	20,192	6,691	13,501
6	Virginia	45,631	32,187	13,444
7	Ohio	46,630	33,418	13,212
8	New Jersey	74,099	61,209	12,890
9	Florida	54,665	42,163	12,502
10	Maryland	46,305	34,822	11,483
11	Connecticut	35,514	25,729	9,785
12	Massachusetts	33,444	24,566	8,878
13	Arizona	19,480	11,132	8,348
14	North Carolina	27,214	19,575	7,639
15	Nevada	12,432	5,185	7,247
16	South Carolina	17,334	10,577	6,757
17	Utah	9,090	4,497	4,593
18	Indiana	20,203	15,618	4,585
19	Oregon	14,244	9,661	4,583
20	Kansas	16,311	13,983	2,328
21	Arkansas	11,888	9,736	2,152
22	Idaho	5,822	3,879	1,943
23	Washington	14,603	13,157	1,446
24	Missouri	24,293	22,874	1,419
25	New Mexico	4,484	3,107	1,377
26	Alaska	1,443	700	743
27	Alabama	9,025	8,638	387
28	New Hampshire	8,994	8,623	371
29	Nebraska	4,881	4,551	330
30	South Dakota	2,379	2,118	261
31	Kentucky	16,414	16,318	96
32	Virgin Islands	159	158	1
33	Rhode Island	5,568	5,594	-26
34	Montana	1,203	1,332	-129
35	Vermont	1,706	1,853	-147
36	Wyoming	1,697	1,892	-195
37	Puerto Rico	424	945	-521
38	North Dakota	1,223	2,166	-943
39	Hawaii	1,013	2,535	-1,522
40	Oklahoma	9,347	10,904	-1,557
41	Mississippi	4,428	6,128	-1,700
42	Wisconsin	11,244	14,178	-2,934
43	Minnesota	13,283	16,269	-2,986
44	Iowa	5,669	8,885	-3,216
45	Michigan	19,227	22,567	-3,340
46	West Virginia	3,554	7,290	-3,736
47	Maine	1,847	6,663	-4,816
48	Louisiana	6,109	11,517	-5,408
49	Pennsylvania	45,554	52,122	-6,568
50	Illinois	42,795	51,045	-8,250
51	Washington, D.C.	16,749	40,339	-23,590
52	California	48,661	128,499	-79,838
53	New York	62,150	145,619	-83,469
	Total	**1,096,186**	**1,096,186**	**0**

Source: Dun & Bradstreet

Labor Unions' Waning Influence

Percentage of Wage and Salary Employees Who Were Union or
Employee Association Members

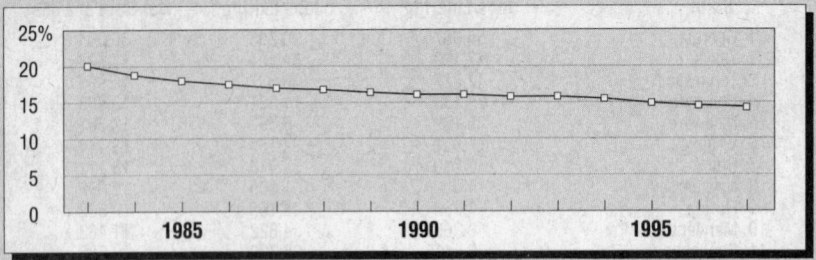

Year	Union or employee association members (thousands)	Union or association members as percent of wage and salary employment
1983	17,717	20.1%
1984	17,340	18.8
1985	16,996	18.0
1986	16,975	17.5
1987	16,913	17.0
1988	17,002	16.8
1989	16,960	16.4
1990	16,740	16.1
1991	16,568	16.1
1992	16,390	15.8
1993	16,598	15.8
1994	16,748	15.5
1995	16,360	14.9
1996	16,269	14.5
1997	16,110	14.1

Source: U.S. Bureau of Labor Statistics

Changing Membership of the 10 Largest Affiliates of the AFL-CIO
(Ranking based on 1997 membership; numbers in thousands)

Organizations	1955	1965	1975	1991	1997
International Brotherhood of Teamsters	—	—	—	1,379	1,276
American Federation of State, County and Municipal Employees	99	237	647	1,191	1,242
Service Employees International Union	—	—	480	881	1,037
United Food and Commercial Workers International Union	—	—	—	997	986
Automobile, Aerospace and Agricultural Implement Workers of America*	1,260	1,150	—	840	766
American Federation of Teachers	40	97	396	573	682
International Brotherhood of Electrical Workers	460	616	856	730	657
United Steelworkers of America	980	876	1,062	459	503
Communications Workers of America	249	288	476	492	480
International Association of Machinists and Aerospace Workers	627	663	780	534	411

*Disaffiliated in 1968 and reaffiliated in 1981.
Source: AFL-CIO

A Striking Trend
Number of Work Stoppages Involving 1,000 or More Workers

Number of work stoppages

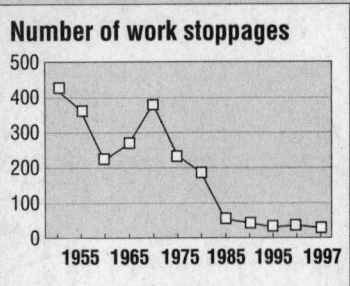

	Stoppages		Days Idle
Year	Number	Workers involved (thousands)	Number (thousands)
1950	424	1,698	30,390
1955	363	2,055	21,180
1960	222	896	13,260
1965	268	999	15,140
1970	381	2,468	52,761
1975	235	965	17,563
1980	187	795	20,844
1985	54	324	7,079
1990	44	185	5,926
1995	31	192	5,771
1996	37	273	4,889
1997	29	339	4,497

Source: U.S. Bureau of Labor Statistics

The Top Countries for International Transfers

1997		1996	
1. United States	6. China	1. England	6. Japan
2. United Kingdom	7. Indonesia	2. Mexico	7. Hong Kong
3. Singapore	8. Canada	3. Belgium	8. Singapore
4. Mexico	9. India	4. Germany	9. France
5. Hong Kong	10. Saudi Arabia	5. Australia	10. India

Source: PHH Relocation

How Affordable Is Working Abroad?

Worldwide Cost-of-Living Index (Standard City, USA = 100.0)

Expensive Locations		Less Expensive Locations	
Tokyo, Japan	285.1	Montreal, Canada	90.8
Seoul, South Korea	276.1	Mexico City, Mexico	105.1
Moscow, Russia	221.2	Melbourne, Australia	116.2
Geneva, Switzerland	178.0	Madrid, Spain	117.1
London, England	155.3	Sydney, Australia	125.5

The table above is based on a U.S. expatriate family of two with a base salary of $75,000. Total annual costs are based on a combination of housing, transportation, and goods and services. Taxes are not included.

Annual Housing Costs in Selected Cities

Bombay, India	$63,418
Dusseldorf, Germany	26,719
Hong Kong, China	143,378
London, England	61,726
Madrid, Spain	30,638
New York, NY	58,425
Paris, France	35,551
San Francisco, CA	40,216
Singapore	73,386
Sydney, Australia	29,604
Tokyo, Japan	78,848

The annual rental housing costs are based on a U.S. expatriate family of two earning $75,000 and residing in a four-to-six room unit. Utilities and renter's insurance are included.
Source: Runzheimer International

1997/1998 Business Travel Costs in Selected U.S. Cities

	Per Diem Total
New York, NY	$342
Chicago, IL	281
Nashville, TN	199
San Diego, CA	194
Atlanta, GA	192
Los Angeles, CA	192
Dallas, TX	191
Anaheim, CA	186
Las Vegas, NV	175
St. Louis, MO	170
Orlando, FL	160

Note: The per diem totals represent average costs for the typical business traveler, and include breakfast, lunch and dinner in business-class restaurants and single-rate lodging in business-class hotels and motels.

Source: Runzheimer International

1997/1998 Overseas Business Travel Costs

LOCATION	Per Diem Total
Hong Kong	$452
Moscow, Russia	415
Buenos Aires, Argentina	409
Tokyo, Japan	406
Paris, France	349
Edinburgh, Scotland	237
Mexico City, Mexico	225
Munich, Germany	206
Panama City, Panama	154
Johannesburg, S. Africa	148
Ottawa, Canada	128

Source: Runzheimer International

Violence in the Workplace

Crimes of violence on the job	Number in 1994	Percent of total crimes of this type
Simple assault	1,264,230	20.9%
Aggravated assault	315,520	14.9
Robbery	81,280	6.7
Rape/sexual attack	16,480	3.9
Total	1,677,510	17.1

Source: U.S. Justice Department

Occupations with High Risk of Work-Related Homicides, 1996

Occupation	All fatalities	Number of homicides	Rate of homicides per 100,000 employed
Taxi drivers	65	46	22.7
Guards	97	50	6.2
Police and detectives	114	54	5.6
Sales counter clerks	14	11	5.5
Managers, food and lodging	75	61	4.4
Bartenders	11	11	3.5
Sales, supervisors and proprietors	225	147	3.3
Cashiers	94	85	2.9
Stock handlers and baggers	22	12	1.1
Truck drivers	785	27	0.9

Source: U.S. Bureau of Labor Statistics

Injury-Prone Businesses

Nonfatal Occupational Injuries: Number of Cases and Incidence Rates per 100 Full-Time Workers, for Industries with 100,000 or More Injury Cases, 1996

Industry	Total cases (Thousands)	Incidence rate
Eating and drinking places	309.7	6.1
Hospitals	300.2	10.0
Nursing and personal care facilities	221.9	16.2
Grocery stores	211.6	9.7
Department stores	172.8	9.8
Trucking and courier services, except air	153.3	10.2
Motor vehicles and equipment	148.9	14.9
Air transportation, scheduled	148.4	18.6
Hotels and motels	118.3	8.9

Source: U.S. Bureau of Labor Statistics

Dangerous Occupations

Index of Relative Risk and Number of Occupational Fatalities Resulting from 1996 Injuries, for 10 High-Risk Occupations (Index for All Workers = 1.0)

Occupation	Index of relative risk	Number of fatalities	Major deadly event
Fishers	37.5	66	drowning (74%)
Timber cutters	33.1	118	struck by object (76%)
Airplane pilots	18.5	100	airplane crash (100%)
Structural metal workers	17.9	52	fall (77%)
Extractive jobs	14.1	87	vehicular (26%)
Water transportation jobs	12.8	42	fall from ship (36%)
Garbage collectors	10.3	21	vehicular (81%)
Public transportation attendants	8.4	38	airplane crash (92%)
Construction laborers	7.5	291	vehicular (29%)
Taxicab drivers and chauffeurs	6.7	65	homicide (71%)

Source: U.S. Bureau of Labor Statistics

5

MONEY & INVESTING

A fter eight years of stunning gains, the bull market in stocks suffered a near-death experience as the summer of 1998 drew to a close: the Dow Jones Industrial Average twice swooped within a hair's breadth of falling 20 percent from the all-time high it set in July, a decline that would have marked the first bear market since 1990.

Throughout the first half of 1998, individual investors—for years the life force of the bull market—continued their love affair with stocks, pouring billions of dollars into individual stocks and stock mutual funds. By midsummer the Dow industrials hit a record 9337.97, a gain of 18 percent from the beginning of the year. Some analysts were predicting that Dow 10000 would be at hand before the year ended.

Then Russia collapsed, touching off a wave of global economic chaos that finally penetrated even to the heart of the world's most powerful and dynamic economy. Mystified by the events that had plunged much of Asia into recession, that had raised anew concerns about Latin America's emerging markets and that took a toll on the earnings of such stock market stalwarts as Intel and Boeing, individual investors who had stood by their stock portfolios through thick and thin for eight years began to hesitate, then to retreat. In previous market frights, while professionals bolted and ran, it was the individual who consistently saved the day by "buying the dips." But this time was different: Rather than buying the dips, individual investors instead chose to sell the rallies.

The result: precipitous declines in both the Dow industrials and Standard & Poor's 500-stock index, the two barometers that tell most of America what is happening to stock prices. The drops threatened to end the third-longest bull market in history, even as the U.S. economy was perking along at a good pace, inflation was low and interest rates were falling.

In reality, though, many investors had been suffering from the effects of a bear market for much of 1998. While the 30 big blue-chip companies that are the Dow and the mighty technology companies that dominate the S&P 500 were moving higher through the first half of 1998, thousands of smaller stocks had long been in eclipse. By late summer, for example, the average New York Stock Exchange stock was down 24.3 percent from its 52-week high. Since May 1998, more stocks had been making new lows than had reached new highs. And on the Nasdaq Stock Market, home of thousands of smaller stocks, more than half the issues traded there were down more than 50 percent from their 52-week highs by late summer.

Analysts had various explanations for how such a "stealth" bear market had developed. The most likely cause, they argued, was that as huge amounts of money flowed into the stock market via mutual funds, the fund managers tended to look for big, liquid stocks in which they could put the money to work quickly. And that seemed apparent in the performance of such issues as Microsoft, Lucent Technologies, General Electric, Wal-Mart Stores and Pfizer. Together, those five stocks provided a quarter of the S&P 500's gains by the end of July. Another issue: A slowing global economy was expected to take a greater toll on small companies' profits than on large companies, which had more options to offset slower growth.

The decline in both small and large stocks nevertheless was puzzling in some ways. To be sure, there were plenty of things to keep investors worried throughout the year: The worsening economic situation in Asia, the virtual meltdown of Russia's economy and the accelerating scandal surrounding the Clinton Administration were just the most obvious of many. Yet at the same time the economic climate surrounding the stock market slump was unusual. Most bear markets begin with rising inflation and rising interest rates. The slump of 1998 began in quite different circumstances. As blue-chip stocks began their slide in August, the U.S. economy was growing at a healthy pace, inflation and interest rates were low and falling, and employment in the country was at unusually high levels—all signs of continued prosperity.

Extraordinarily high prices for stocks help explain how that could happen. Before the slide began in mid-summer, some of the most popular stocks were trading at prices that defied common sense. Microsoft, Lucent and Cisco Systems, for example, all sported price-to-earnings ratios of more than 60, and the S&P 500 as a whole had a price-to-earnings ratio of 28, far above the 20 or so that many market experts regard as richly priced and nearly double the historical average of about 15. Those kinds of prices can only be sustained under perfect conditions, and as 1998 wore on, conditions were far from perfect.

While the stock market suffered its worst declines in years, bond investors—at least those who invested in Treasury bonds—had a field day. The combination of world-wide market and economic turmoil and a slumping stock market set the stage for a massive flight to quality as investors in America and abroad sought safety in U.S. government bonds. Reflecting the extraordinary demand for safety, the yield on the Treasury's benchmark 30-year bond tumbled to less than 5.2 percent by early fall, a level last seen some 30 years ago.

But not everybody who owned bonds was happy. While Treasury bonds benefited from the safe haven syndrome, most other kinds of bonds, including corporate and municipal issues, suffered from concerns about a slowing economy and the ability of companies and cities to repay their debts. And, not surprisingly, emerging markets bonds, once the darling of investors seeking high yields, were punished worst of all.

Some of the most painful losses were inflicted on some of the investing world's highest flyers. Hedge funds, which are essentially mutual funds for sophisticated, high-rolling investors, are free to make all sorts of bets in an effort to capture big gains. And for much of the bull market they had been remarkably successful: The best had returned 50 percent or more annually to their investors through complex strategies that involved borrowing money to make bets on currency, commodity, stock and bond moves around the globe.

But in August, some of those big bets came unhinged. One of the more remarkable bad bets made by some big hedge funds: Global investors, eager for high returns, would sell such low-yielding instruments as Treasury bonds and would buy high-yielding mortgage-backed bonds. The exact opposite happened, catching the hedge funds in an extraordinary squeeze that cost some more than half of their capital base.

Commodity markets fared poorly in 1998, too, the result of weakening global demand and burgeoning supplies of such products as metals, lumber, cattle and grain. Mid-American grain farmers enjoyed some of the best weather in years, yielding huge crops even as demand from economically ravaged Asia and other foreign buyers seemed to virtually dry up. Indeed, in mid-summer, prices for so many commodities were falling so low that analysts began to talk about the looming threat not of *inflation*, but of *deflation*, a condition in which it becomes difficult or impossible for companies to raise prices and boost profits. The one beneficiary in the commodities markets from all the doom and gloom was gold. Long regarded as a storehouse of value in turbulent times, gold seemed to have lost that cachet through much of the 1990s. But as Russia, Asia and the Clinton Administration all found themselves deeply in trouble, gold prices began to creep back up toward the $300-an-ounce level.

How long the stock market's woes will last is anyone's guess. Pessimists predicted that the extraordinarily powerful and long-lasting bull market had set the stage for a longer or deeper than usual bear market. If so, that would truly be bad news, since the average bear market during the past century lasted 418 days. But optimists suggested that the favorable economic underpinnings that were in place as the market slumped into bear ter-

ritory would make this one painful, but short. Only time will tell.

Douglas R. Sease
deputy editor,
Money and Investing,
at *The Wall Street Journal*

The Dow Jones Industrial Average Through History

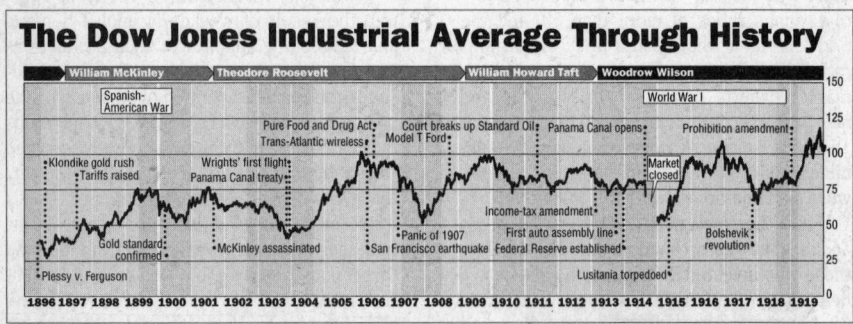

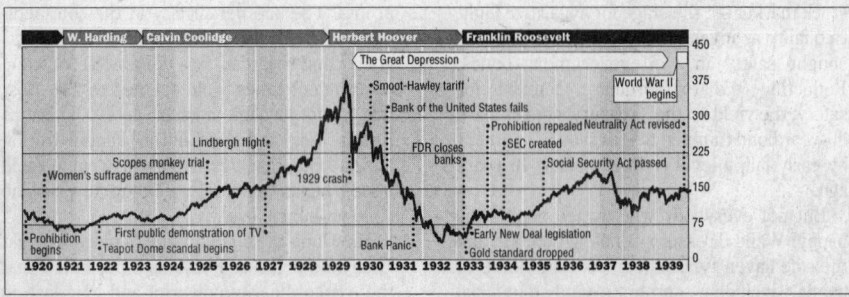

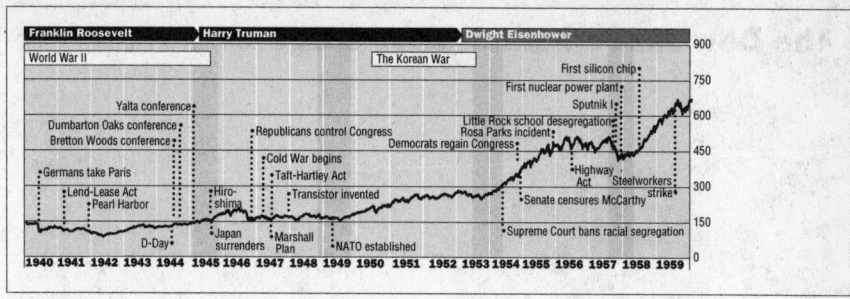

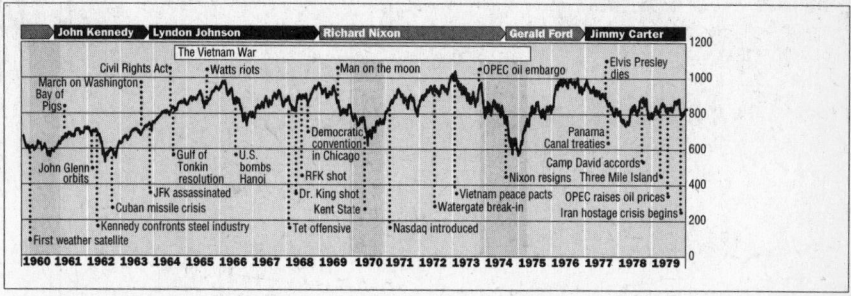

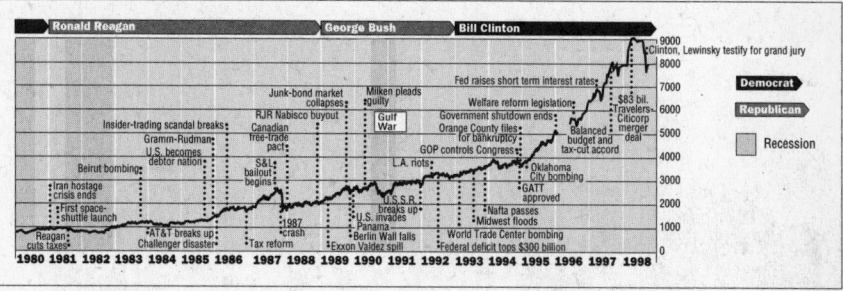

The Dow Jones Industrial Average

Dow Milestones

Milestone	Date	Comment
40.94	May 26, 1896	The index of 12 stocks (now 30), is launched by Wall Street Journal co-founder Charles Dow and distributed by hand.
100.00	Jan. 12, 1906	DJIA's first century mark comes 10 years after launch. But the news, greeted with little fanfare, doesn't make the front page of *The Wall Street Journal*.
500.00	March 12, 1956	After taking a quarter century to go from 300 to 400, the average speeds through 500 in little more than a year.
1000.00	Nov. 14, 1972	After near-misses at crossing this mark for the previous six years, the public gapes but reaction is muted in *The Wall Street Journal*. A front-page article attaches "little market significance" to it.
2000.00	Jan. 8, 1987	New Year's rally pushes index past milestone after four years of a bull market.
3000.00	April 17, 1991	Rally after Gulf War propels stocks past milestone, nine months after just missing.
4000.00	Feb. 23, 1995	Optimism about interest rates pushes DJIA ahead, more than a year after first flirting with the mark.
5000.00	Nov. 21, 1995	Just in time for Thanksgiving, DJIA surges past milestone just nine months after breaking 4000.
6000.00	Oct. 14, 1996	Shrugging off a summer pullback that included two 100-point-or-more drops, the DJIA breaks barrier as inflation fears ebb.
7000.00	Feb. 13, 1997	Quickest-ever vault of a 1000 point milestone continues a long bull market despite increasing warnings about high valuations.
8000.00	July 16, 1997	DJIA recovers from 9.8% plunge in March and April to continue the bull market.
9000.00	April 6, 1998	DJIA , propelled by low interest rates and good corporate profits, tops 9000 after $83 billion Travelers Group–Citicorp merger is announced.

Source: Wall Street Journal research

Defined Bull Markets

Beginning		Ending			
Date	DJIA	Date	DJIA	% Gain	Days
9/24/00	38.80	6/17/01	57.33	47.8	266
11/09/03	30.88	1/19/06	75.45	144.4	802
11/15/07	38.83	11/19/09	73.64	89.7	735
9/25/11	53.43	9/30/12	68.97	29.1	371
12/24/14	53.17	11/21/16	110.15	107.2	698
12/19/17	65.95	11/03/19	119.62	81.4	684
8/24/21	63.90	3/20/23	105.38	64.9	573
10/27/23	85.76	9/03/29	381.17	344.5	2,138
11/13/29	198.69	4/17/30	294.07	48.0	155
7/08/32	41.22	9/07/32	79.93	93.9	61
2/27/33	50.16	2/05/34	110.74	120.8	343
7/26/34	85.51	3/10/37	194.40	127.3	958
3/31/38	98.95	11/12/38	158.41	60.1	226
4/08/39	121.44	9/12/39	155.92	28.4	157
4/28/42	92.92	5/29/46	212.50	128.7	1,492
5/17/47	163.21	6/15/48	193.16	18.4	395
6/13/49	161.60	1/05/53	293.79	81.8	1,302
9/14/53	255.49	4/06/56	521.05	103.9	935
10/22/57	419.79	1/05/60	685.47	63.3	805
10/25/60	566.05	12/13/61	734.91	29.8	414
6/26/62	535.76	2/09/66	995.15	85.7	1,324
10/07/66	744.32	12/03/68	985.21	32.4	788
5/26/70	631.16	4/28/71	950.82	50.6	337
11/23/71	797.97	1/11/73	1051.70	31.8	415
12/06/74	577.60	9/21/76	1014.79	75.7	655
2/28/78	742.12	9/08/78	907.74	22.3	192
4/21/80	759.13	4/27/81	1024.05	34.9	371
8/12/82	776.92	11/29/83	1287.20	65.7	474
7/24/84	1086.57	8/25/87	2722.42	150.6	1,127
10/19/87	1738.74	7/16/90	2999.75	72.5	1,001
10/11/90	2365.10				

A Bull Market requires a 30% rise in the Dow Jones Industrial Average after 50 calendar days or a 13% rise after 155 calendar days. Reversals of 30% in the Value Line Composite since 1965 also qualify. The NYSE was closed from 7/31/14 to 12/11/14 due to World War I. DJIA was then adjusted to reflect the composition change from 12 to 20 stocks.
Source: Ned Davis Research, Inc.

Defined Bear Markets

Beginning		Ending			
Date	DJIA	Date	DJIA	% Decline	Days
6/17/01	57.33	11/09/03	30.88	-46.1	875
1/19/06	75.45	11/15/07	38.83	-48.5	665
11/19/09	73.64	9/25/11	53.43	-27.4	675
9/30/12	68.97	7/30/14	52.32	-24.1	668
11/21/16	110.15	12/19/17	65.95	-40.1	393
11/03/19	119.62	8/24/21	63.90	-46.6	660
3/20/23	105.38	10/27/23	85.76	-18.6	221
9/03/29	381.17	11/13/29	198.69	-47.9	71
4/17/30	294.07	7/08/32	41.22	-86.0	813
9/07/32	79.93	2/27/33	50.16	-37.2	173
2/05/34	110.74	7/26/34	85.51	-22.8	171
3/10/37	194.40	3/31/38	98.95	-49.1	386
11/12/38	158.41	4/08/39	121.44	-23.3	147
9/12/39	155.92	4/28/42	92.92	-40.4	959
5/29/46	212.50	5/17/47	163.21	-23.2	353
6/15/48	193.16	6/13/49	161.60	-16.3	363
1/05/53	293.79	9/14/53	255.49	-13.0	252
4/06/56	521.05	10/22/57	419.79	-19.4	564
1/05/60	685.47	10/25/60	566.05	-17.4	294
12/13/61	734.91	6/26/62	535.76	-27.1	195
2/09/66	995.15	10/07/66	744.32	-25.2	240
12/03/68	985.21	5/26/70	631.16	-35.9	539
4/28/71	950.82	11/23/71	797.97	-16.1	209
1/11/73	1051.70	12/06/74	577.60	-45.1	694
9/21/76	1014.79	2/28/78	742.12	-26.9	525
9/08/78	907.74	4/21/80	759.13	-16.4	591
4/27/81	1024.05	8/12/82	776.92	-24.1	472
11/29/83	1287.20	7/24/84	1086.57	-15.6	238
8/25/87	2722.42	10/19/87	1738.74	-36.1	55
7/16/90	2999.75	10/11/90	2365.10	-21.2	87

A Bear Market requires a 30% drop in the Dow Jones Industrial Average after 50 calendar days or a 13% decline after 145 calendar days. Reversals of 30 % in the Value Line Composite also qualify. This applied to the 1990 high and low. (The table uses corresponding high and low dates and values for DJIA). The NYSE was closed from 7/31/14 to 12/11/14 due to World War I. DJIA was then adjusted to reflect the composition change from 12 to 20 stocks. *Source: Ned Davis Research, Inc.*

Biggest Drops in the Dow Jones Industrial Average (As of 9/30/98)

Days with Greatest Net Loss

Rank	Date	Close	Net change	% change
1	10/27/97	7161.15	-554.26	-7.18
2	08/31/98	7539.07	-512.61	-6.37
3	10/19/87	1738.74	-508.00	-22.61
4	08/27/98	8165.99	-357.36	-4.19
5	08/04/98	8487.31	-299.43	-3.41
6	09/10/98	7615.54	-249.48	-3.17
7	08/15/97	7694.66	-247.37	-3.11
8	09/30/98	7842.62	-237.90	-2.94
9	01/09/98	7580.42	-222.20	-2.85
10	09/17/98	7873.77	-216.01	-2.67

Days with Greatest Percentage Loss

Rank	Date	Close	Net change	% change
1	10/19/87	1738.74	-508.00	-22.61
2	10/28/29	260.64	-38.33	-12.82
3	10/29/29	230.07	-30.57	-11.73
4	11/06/29	232.13	-25.55	-9.92
5	12/18/99	58.27	-5.57	-8.72
6	08/12/32	63.11	-5.79	-8.40
7	03/14/07	76.23	-6.89	-8.29
8	10/26/87	1793.93	-156.83	-8.04
9	07/21/33	88.71	-7.55	-7.84
10	10/18/37	125.73	-10.57	-7.75

Biggest Jumps in the Dow Jones Industrial Average (As of 9/30/98)

Days with Greatest Net Gain

Rank	Date	Close	Net change	% change
1	09/08/98	8020.78	380.53	4.98
2	10/28/97	7498.32	337.17	4.71
3	09/01/98	7827.43	288.36	3.82
4	09/02/97	7879.78	257.36	3.38
5	09/23/98	8154.41	257.21	3.26
6	11/03/97	7674.39	232.31	3.12
7	02/02/98	8107.78	201.28	2.55
8	12/01/97	8013.11	189.98	2.43
9	10/21/87	2027.85	186.84	10.15
10	09/11/98	7795.50	179.96	2.36

Days with Greatest Percentage Gain

Rank	Date	Close	Net change	% change
1	10/06/31	99.34	12.86	14.87
2	10/30/29	258.47	28.40	12.34
3	09/21/32	75.16	7.67	11.36
4	10/21/87	2027.85	186.84	10.15
5	08/03/32	58.22	5.06	9.52
6	02/11/32	78.60	6.80	9.47
7	11/14/29	217.28	18.59	9.36
8	12/18/31	80.69	6.90	9.35
9	02/13/32	85.82	7.22	9.19
10	05/06/32	59.01	4.91	9.08

Best Years for the Dow Jones Industrial Average

The Dow's Best Years

Rank	Date	Close	% change
1	1915	99.15	81.66
2	1933	99.90	66.69
3	1928	300.00	48.22
4	1908	86.15	46.64
5	1954	404.39	43.96
6	1904	69.61	41.74
7	1935	144.13	38.53
8	1975	852.41	38.32
9	1905	96.20	38.20
10	1958	583.65	33.96

Worst Years for the Dow Jones Industrial Average

The Dow's Worst Years

Rank	Date	Close	% change
1	1931	77.90	-52.67
2	1907	58.75	-37.73
3	1930	164.58	-33.77
4	1920	71.95	-32.90
5	1937	120.85	-32.82
6	1914	54.58	-30.72
7	1974	616.24	-27.57
8	1903	49.11	-23.61
9	1932	59.93	-23.07
10	1917	74.38	-21.71

Source: Dow Jones & Co.

The Dow Jones Averages

The Dow Jones Industrial Average is an index of 30 "blue chip" U.S. stocks. At 100 plus years, it is the oldest continuing U.S. market index. It is called an "average" because it originally was computed by adding up stock prices and dividing by the number of stocks. (The very first average price of industrial stocks, on May 26, 1896, was 40.94.) The methodology remains the same today, but the divisor has been changed to preserve historical continuity. The DJIA is the best-known market indicator in the world, partly because it is old enough that many generations of investors have become accustomed to quoting it, and partly because the U.S. stock market is the biggest.

Dow Jones & Co. most recently changed the components of the DJIA, effective with trading on March 17, 1997.

The 30 stocks in the Dow Jones Industrial Average are:

AT&T Corp.	Goodyear Tire & Rubber Co.
AlliedSignal Inc.	Hewlett-Packard Co.
Aluminum Co. of America	International Business Machines Corp.
American Express Co.	International Paper Co.
Boeing Co.	Johnson & Johnson
Caterpillar Inc.	McDonald's Corp.
Chevron Corp.	Merck & Co.
Citigroup	Minnesota Mining & Manufacturing Co.
Coca-Cola Co.	J.P. Morgan & Co.
Walt Disney Co.	Philip Morris Cos.
DuPont Co.	Procter & Gamble Co.
Eastman Kodak Co.	Sears, Roebuck & Co.
Exxon Corp.	Union Carbide Corp.
General Electric Co.	United Technologies Corp.
General Motors Corp.	Wal-Mart Stores Inc.

The 20 stocks in the Dow Jones Transportation Average are:

AMR Corp.	CSX Corp.
J.B. Hunt Transport Services	Airborne Freight Corp.
Alexander & Baldwin Inc.	Burlington Northern Santa Fe Corp.
CNF Transportation Inc.	Roadway Express Inc.
Delta Air Lines Inc.	FDX Corp.
GATX Corp.	Norfolk Southern Corp.
Ryder System Inc.	Southwest Airlines Co.
UAL Corp.	Union Pacific Corp.
US Airways Group Inc.	USFreightways
Northwest Airlines	Yellow Corp.

The 15 stocks in the Dow Jones Utility Average are:

American Electric Power Co.	Columbia Energy Group
Consolidated Edison Inc.	Consolidated Natural Gas Co.
Duke Energy Corp.	Edison International
Enron Corp.	Houston Industries Inc.
Peco Corp.	PG&E Corp.
Public Service Enterprise Group	Southern Co.
Texas Utilities Co.	Unicom Corp.
Williams Cos.	

The Original 12 Stocks in the Dow Jones Industrial Average

American Cotton Oil
American Sugar
American Tobacco
Chicago Gas
Distilling & Cattle Feeding
General Electric

Laclede Gas
National Lead
North American
Tennessee Coal & Iron
U.S. Leather preferred
U.S. Rubber

Long-Term Investment Performance

Average Annual Rates of Return, 1926–1997

S&P 500	11.0%
Small Company Stocks	12.7
Long-Term Corporate Bonds	5.7
Long-Term Government Bonds	5.2
Intermediate-Term Government Bonds	5.3
U.S. Treasury Bills	3.8
Inflation	3.1

Source: Ibbotson Associates, www.ibbotson.com

Dow Jones Global Indexes

The Dow Jones Global Indexes are a broad indicator of more than 3,000 companies worldwide, representing more than 80% of the equity capital on 34 stock markets around the globe. The indexes are market capitalization weighted—that is both the stock price and number of shares outstanding enter into the computation. This means a particular stock's effect on the indexes is proportionate to its value in the marketplace. The indexes are broken down by country and region, as well as by nine broad market sectors.

Quarter	World	United States	Americas	Europe	Asia/Pacific
03/31/93	101.34	429.09	108.43	99.72	94.64
06/30/93	106.46	427.84	108.33	98.98	109.55
09/30/93	111.07	436.78	110.28	107.74	114.67
12/31/93	111.08	442.19	112.18	116.08	106.76
03/31/94	111.80	422.69	107.00	113.87	116.43
06/30/94	114.60	420.28	105.93	111.69	127.21
09/30/94	116.11	437.13	110.91	115.39	123.12
12/30/94	113.91	433.07	108.53	115.70	119.39
03/31/95	117.67	472.01	117.07	121.55	116.15
06/30/95	122.21	514.49	127.63	128.66	111.97
09/29/95	127.96	553.41	136.97	132.44	114.95
12/29/95	133.46	581.43	143.61	136.54	119.80
03/29/96	138.01	610.77	150.93	141.40	121.18
06/29/96	141.31	633.63	156.50	143.89	122.91
09/30/96	142.45	653.06	161.08	148.52	118.02
12/31/96	147.57	700.56	173.40	162.41	108.93
03/31/97	146.71	713.69	176.48	168.23	98.23
06/30/97	167.53	831.56	205.34	181.80	115.57
09/30/97	173.18	896.92	221.92	192.62	101.19
12/31/97	166.63	922.34	227.09	191.64	77.93
03/31/98	188.95	1043.56	256.16	229.00	81.33
06/30/98	192.34	1072.34	264.12	243.39	73.21
09/30/98	168.06	960.81	233.99	207.65	64.24

Note: Indexes based on 6/30/82=100 for U.S., 12/31/91 =100 for World.

Stock Indexes

Dow Jones Industrials

The Dow Jones Industrial Average is a price-weighted average of 30 actively traded blue-chip stocks. The number of shares outstanding isn't taken into account, so higher-priced issues wield greater influence than lower-priced ones.

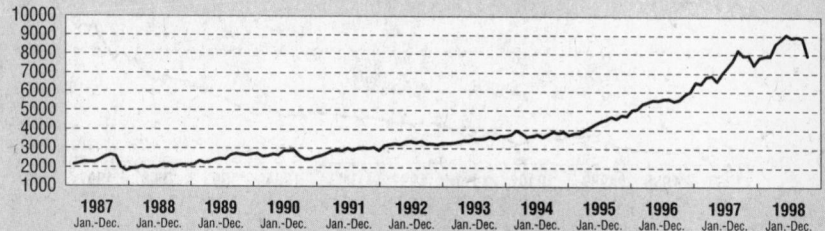

Dow Jones Transportation

The Dow Jones Transportation Average is a price-weighted average of the stocks of 20 large companies in the transportation industry.

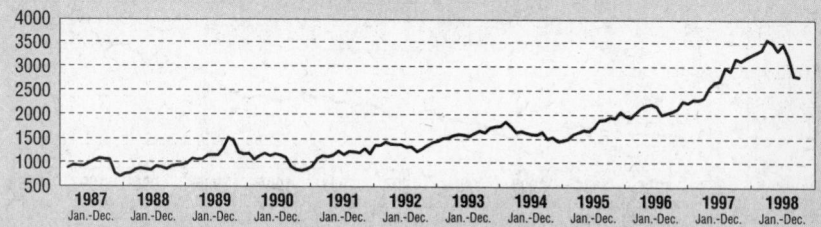

Dow Jones Utilities

The Dow Jones Utilities Average is a price-weighted average composed of 15 utility companies.

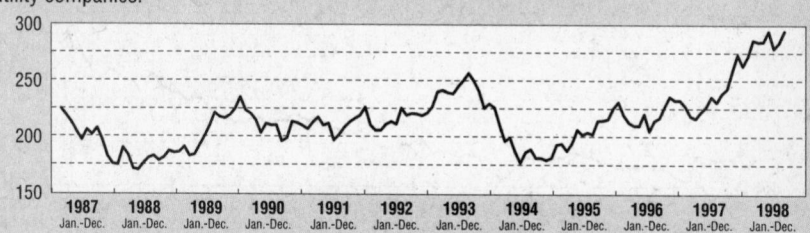

Dow Jones Composite

The Dow Jones Composite Average includes the 30 industrial stocks, 20 transportation stocks and 15 utility stocks in the other three averages

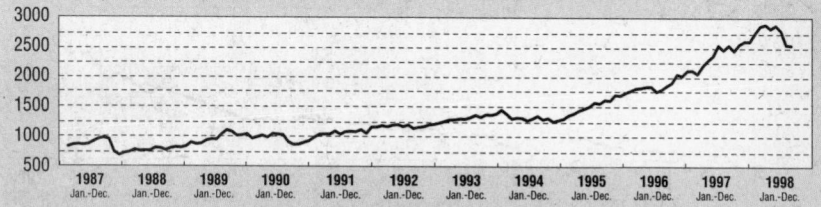

Standard & Poor's 500

The Standard & Poor's 500 Index is a market-value weighted index that includes 500 stocks chosen for market size, liquidity and industry group representation. The stock price is multiplied by the number of shares outstanding so that an issue's weight in the index is proportionate to its market value.

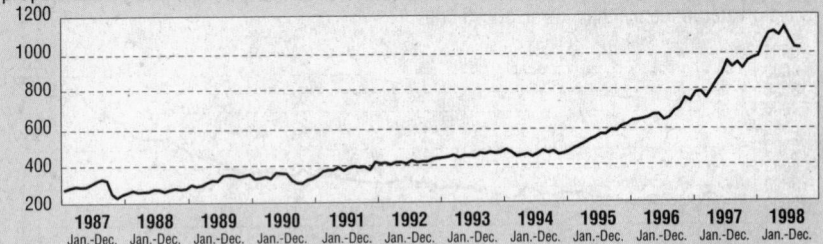

Nasdaq Composite

The Nasdaq Composite Index is a market-value weighted measure of all the common stocks listed on the Nasdaq Stock Market.

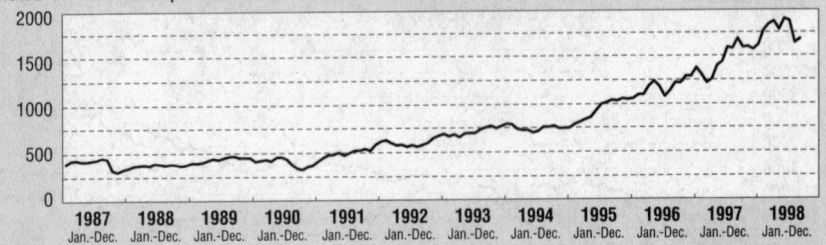

Russell 2000

The Russell 2000 Index represents the smallest two-thirds of the 3,000 largest U.S. companies, based on total market capitalization.

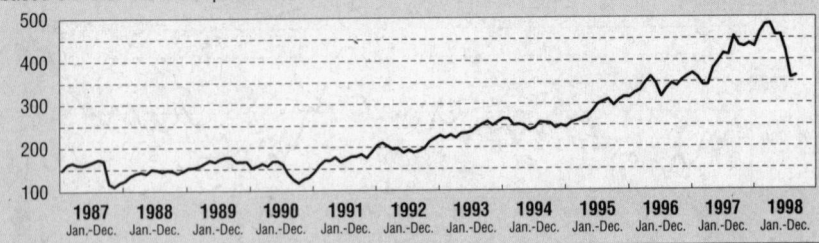

Wilshire 5000

The Wilshire 5000 Index, the broadest stock-market index, includes the equity securities of all U.S.-based companies with readily available price data.

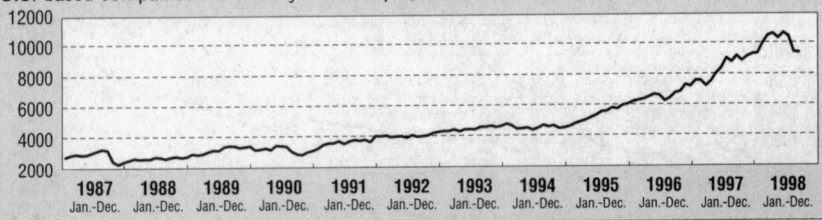

New York Stock Exchange Composite

The New York Stock Exchange Composite Index is a market value-weighted index of all common stocks traded on the Big Board. There are four subgroup indices, shown below.

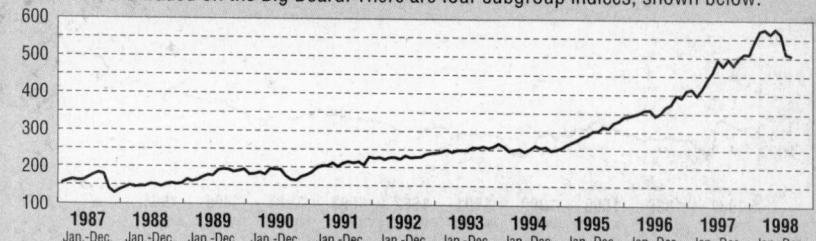

New York Stock Exchange Industrials

New York Stock Exchange Utilities

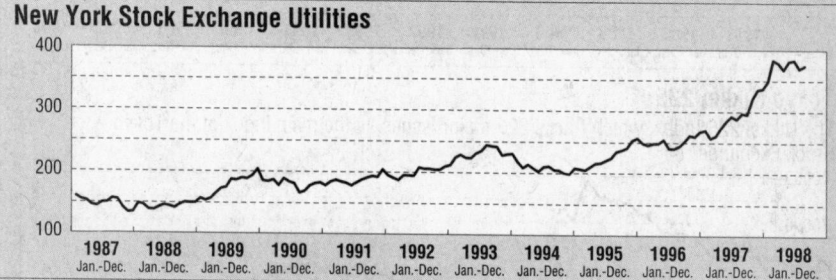

New York Stock Exchange Transportation

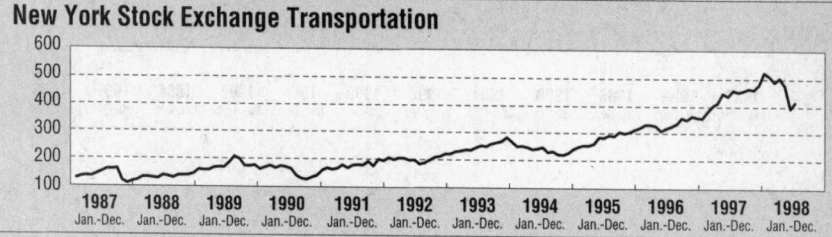

New York Stock Exchange Finance

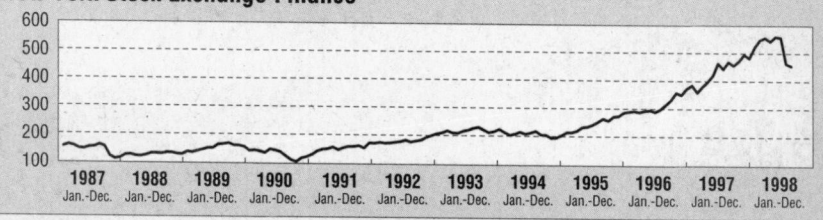

Value-Line Composite

The Value-Line Composite Index follows the performance of about 1,700 common stocks.

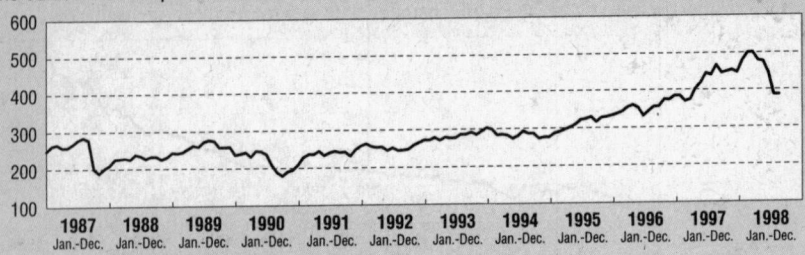

London FT-SE 100

The FT-SE 100 Index, which contains the stocks of Britain's 100 largest companies ranked by market capitalization, is the most widely quoted index for tracking the London Stock Exchange.

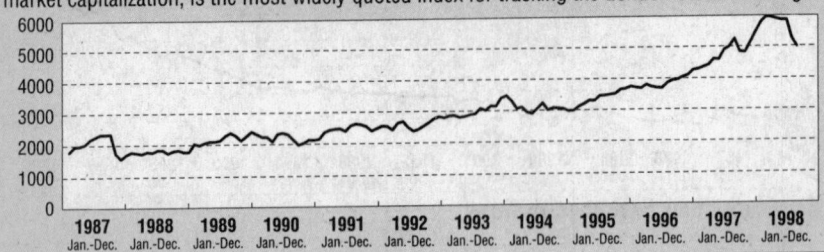

Tokyo Nikkei 225

The Nikkei 225 Index, which tracks 225 major issues, is the main index of the Tokyo Stock Exchange.

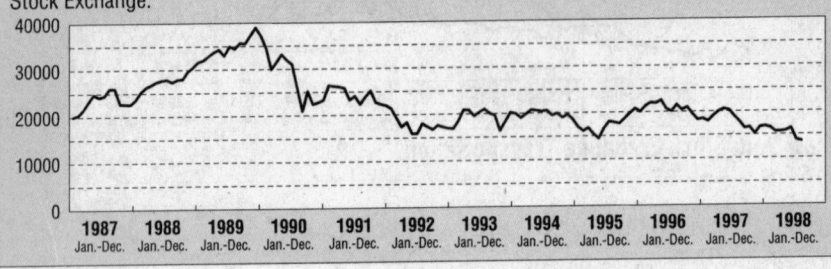

Foreign Currency Exchange Data

Japanese Yen
Japanese yen per U.S. dollar

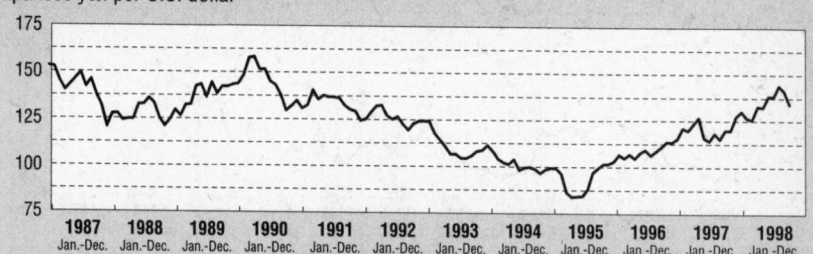

German Mark
German marks per U.S. dollar

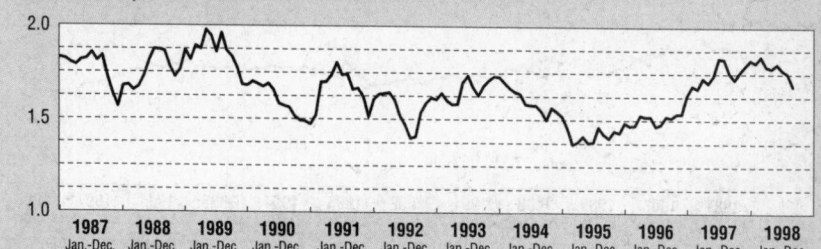

British Pound
British pound in U.S. dollars

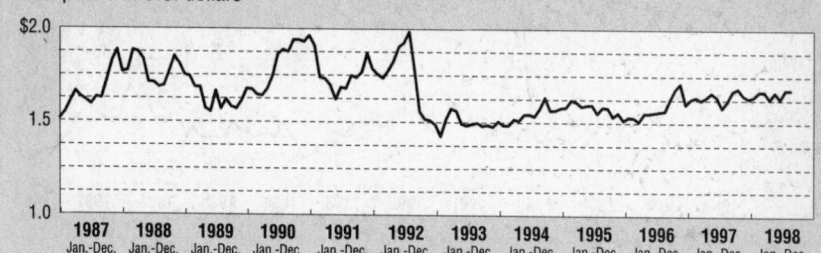

Canadian Dollar
Canadian dollar in U.S. dollars

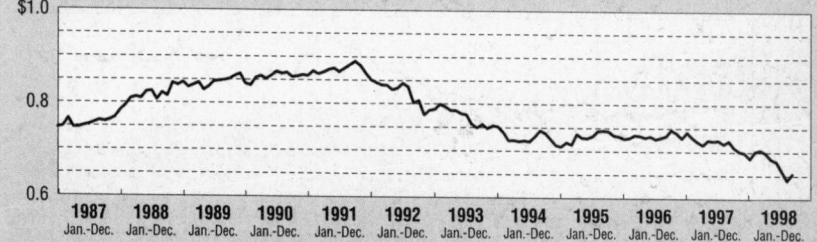

Commodities
Wheat
Price of Kansas City wheat per bushel

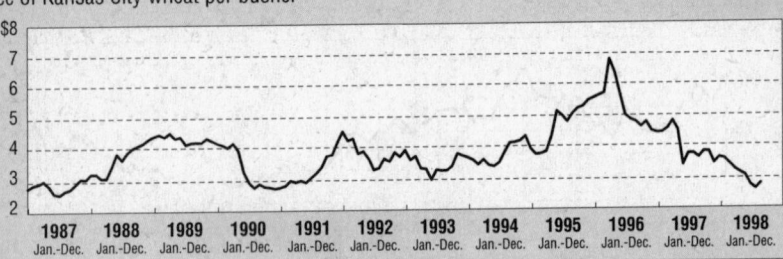

Gold
Comex spot price per troy oz.

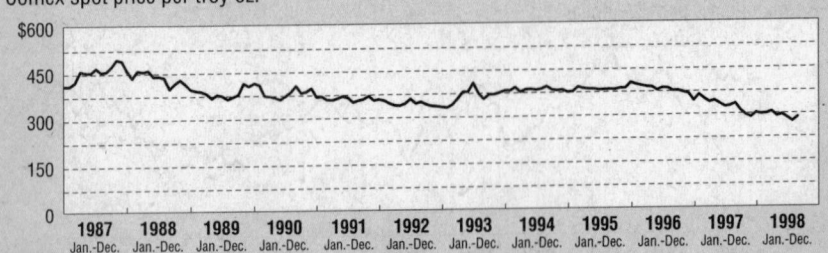

Crude Oil
West Texas intermediate crude, price per barrel

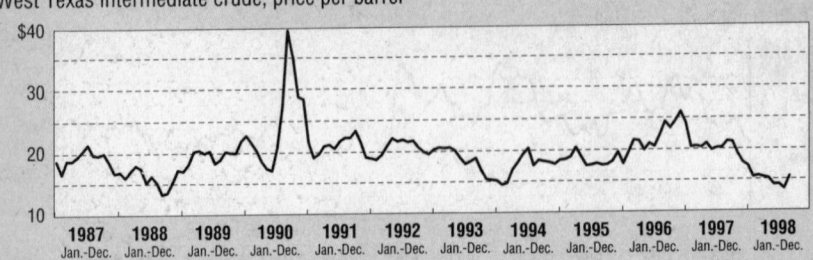

Bond Indexes

Dow Jones 10 Industrial Bonds
Dow Jones 10 Industrial Bonds tracks the bonds of 10 of the largest U.S. industrial companies.

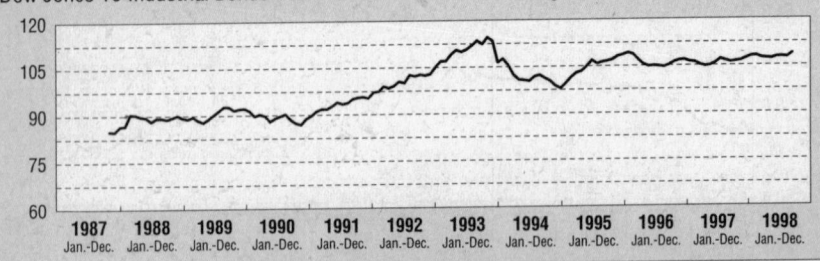

Dow Jones 10 Utility Bonds

Dow Jones 10 Utility Bonds includes the bonds of 10 large utility companies.

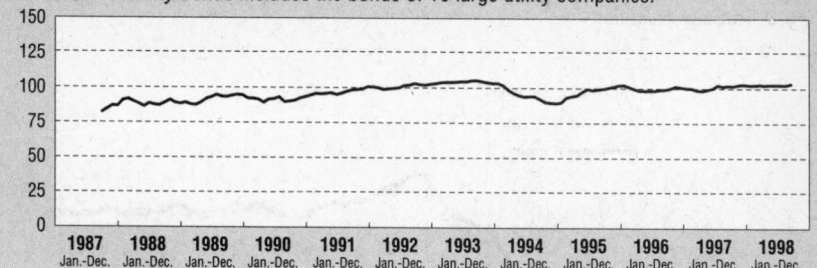

Dow Jones 20 Bond

Dow Jones 20 Bond Average represents the combination of the 10 utility bonds and 10 industrial bonds.

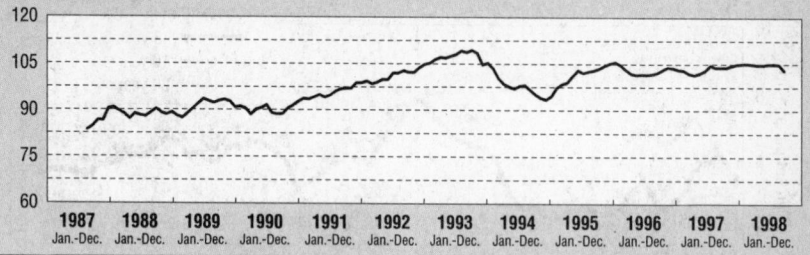

Merrill Lynch Corporate Bond

The Merrill Lynch Corporate Bond Index includes securities issued in the U.S. market with an outstanding face value of at least $100 million and a year or more left to final maturity.

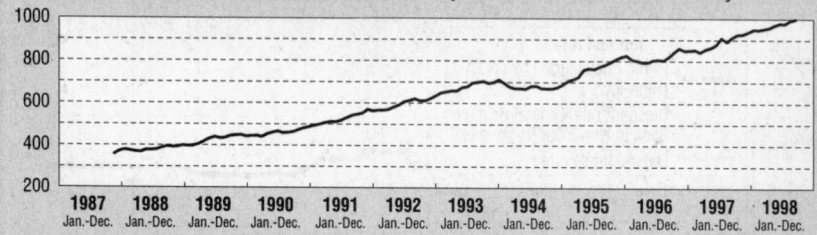

Lehman Long Treasury Bond

The Lehman Brothers Long Treasury Bond Index is a weighted average of all Treasury securities with maturities of 10 years and longer.

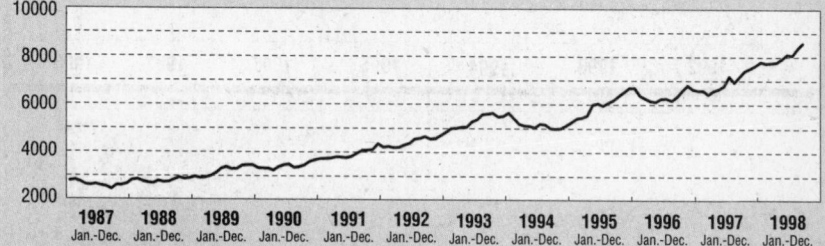

Bond Yields and Interest Rates

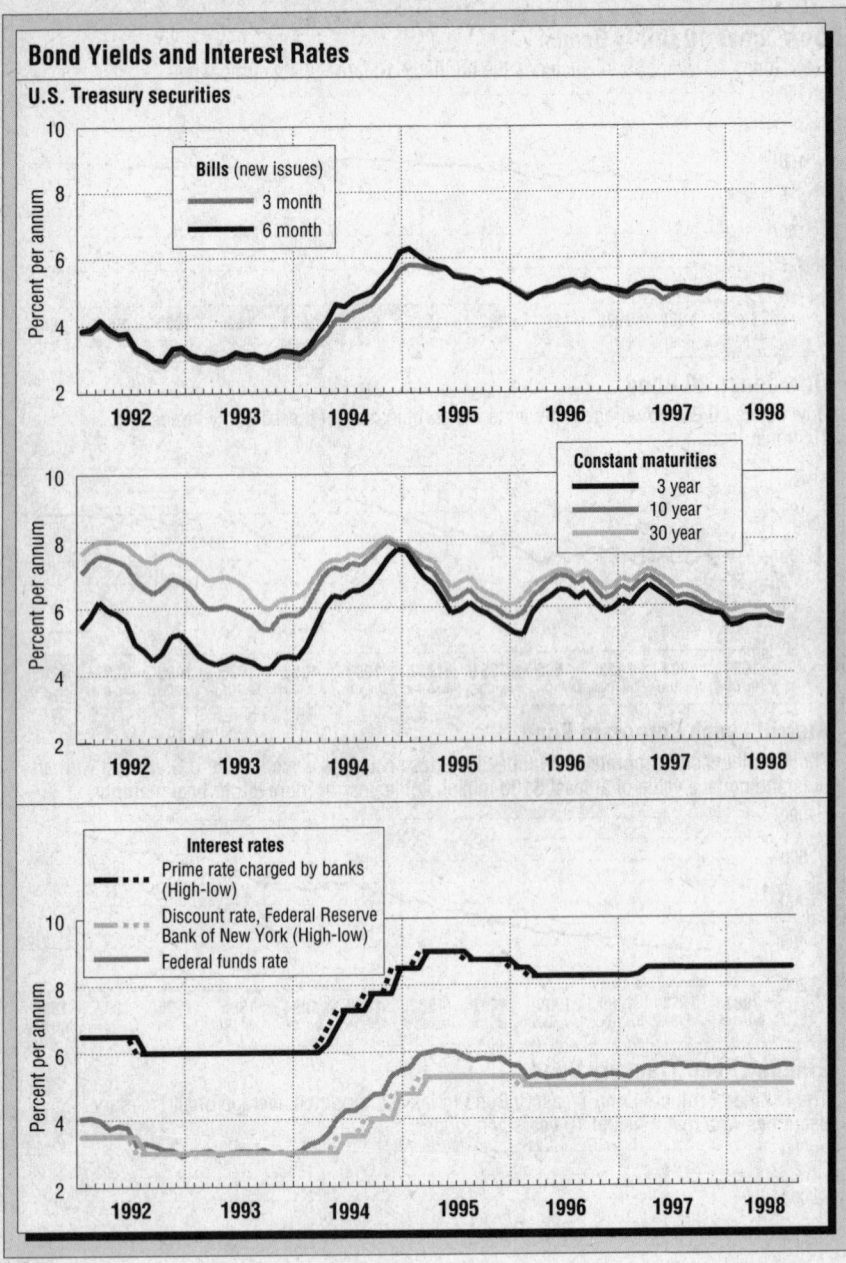

U.S. Treasury securities

Bills (new issues)
— 3 month
— 6 month

Constant maturities
— 3 year
— 10 year
— 30 year

Interest rates
----- Prime rate charged by banks (High-low)
----- Discount rate, Federal Reserve Bank of New York (High-low)
— Federal funds rate

Yields on Treasury Securities and Bonds (Percent per annum)

Year	U.S. Treasury securities					Corporate bonds (Moody's)		High-grade municipal bonds (Standard & Poor's)
	Bills (new issues)		Constant maturities					
	3-month	6-month	3-yr	10-yr	30-yr	Aaa	Baa	
1980	11.506	11.374	11.55	11.46	11.27	11.94	13.67	8.51
1981	14.029	13.776	14.44	13.91	13.45	14.17	16.04	11.23
1982	10.686	11.084	12.92	13.00	12.76	13.79	16.11	11.57
1983	8.630	8.750	10.45	11.10	11.18	12.04	13.55	9.47
1984	9.580	9.800	11.89	12.44	12.41	12.71	14.19	10.15
1985	7.480	7.660	9.64	10.62	10.79	11.37	12.72	9.18
1986	5.980	6.030	7.06	7.68	7.78	9.02	10.39	7.38
1987	5.820	6.050	7.68	8.39	8.59	9.38	10.58	7.73
1988	6.690	6.920	8.26	8.85	8.96	9.71	10.83	7.76
1989	8.120	8.040	8.55	8.49	8.45	9.26	10.18	7.24
1990	7.510	7.470	8.26	8.55	8.61	9.32	10.36	7.25
1991	5.420	5.490	6.82	7.86	8.14	8.77	9.80	6.89
1992	3.450	3.570	5.30	7.01	7.67	8.14	8.98	6.41
1993	3.020	3.140	4.44	5.87	6.59	7.22	7.93	5.63
1994	4.290	4.660	6.27	7.09	7.37	7.97	8.63	6.19
1995	5.510	5.590	6.25	6.57	6.88	7.59	8.20	5.95
1996	5.020	5.090	5.99	6.44	6.71	7.37	8.05	5.75
1997	5.070	5.180	6.10	6.35	6.61	7.27	7.87	5.55

Sources: U.S. Treasury Department, Board of Governors of the Federal Reserve System, Federal Housing Finance Board, Moody's Investors Service, and Standard & Poor's Corp.

Profile of Stock Owners

Stock ownership has grown dramatically in the 1990s. From 1965 to 1990, stock ownership among Americans doubled from 10.4% to 21.1%. In the next seven years, it doubled again, standing today at about 43% of adult Americans.

Investing in mutual funds has tripled over the past seven years, from 13% of all adults in 1990 to 40% today. Fully 88% of investors now own shares in one or more mutual funds (up from 60% in 1990). Indeed, nearly half (46%) of all investors own all their stock through mutual funds.

Of those who own shares in mutual funds, 69% say their holdings exceed $10,000. Among those who own individual stocks, 59% claim holdings in excess of $10,000. (These groups overlap.) And two-thirds of all investors say that their stock and fund shares make up more than 20% of their total investments. The following is based on a survey of more than 1,200 investors.

Sex

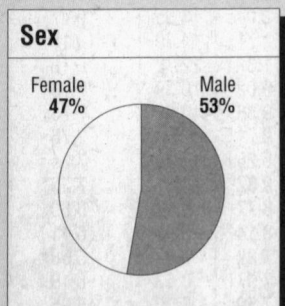

Female 47%
Male 53%

Highest Educational Level Reached

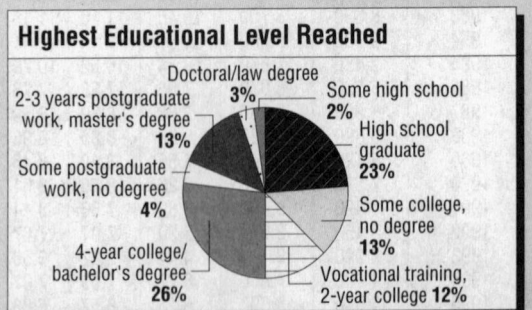

Doctoral/law degree 3%
2-3 years postgraduate work, master's degree 13%
Some postgraduate work, no degree 4%
4-year college/bachelor's degree 26%
Some high school 2%
High school graduate 23%
Some college, no degree 13%
Vocational training, 2-year college 12%

Age

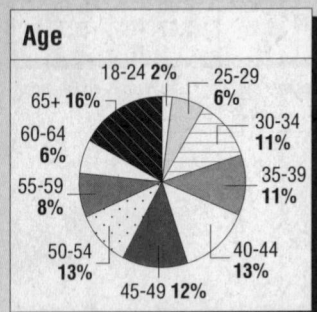

18-24 2%
25-29 6%
30-34 11%
35-39 11%
40-44 13%
45-49 12%
50-54 13%
55-59 8%
60-64 6%
65+ 16%

Occupation

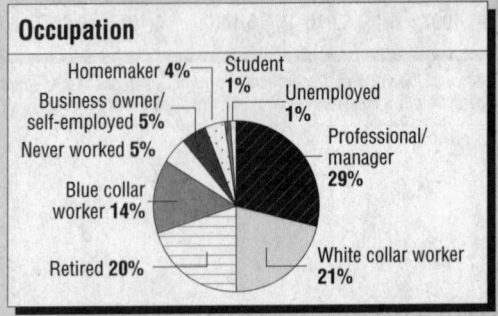

Homemaker 4%
Student 1%
Business owner/self-employed 5%
Unemployed 1%
Never worked 5%
Professional/manager 29%
Blue collar worker 14%
Retired 20%
White collar worker 21%

Race or Ethnic Origin

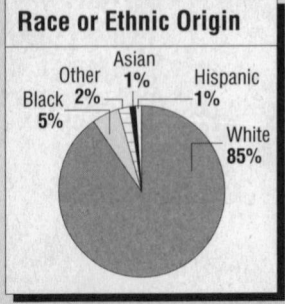

Asian 1%
Other 1%
Hispanic 1%
Black 2%
5%
White 85%

Household Income

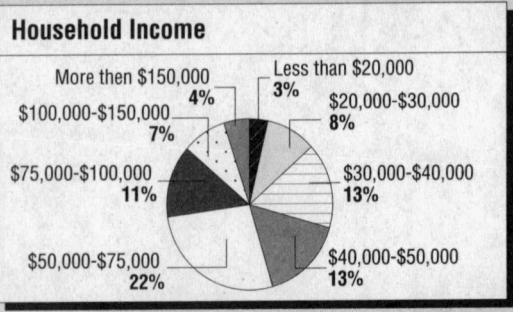

More then $150,000 4%
$100,000-$150,000 7%
$75,000-$100,000 11%
$50,000-$75,000 22%
Less than $20,000 3%
$20,000-$30,000 8%
$30,000-$40,000 13%
$40,000-$50,000 13%

Note: Percentages may not add up to 100% because some survey respondents did not provide all the information or said they were not sure.

Sources: Study by Peter D. Hart Research Associates for the Nasdaq Stock Market

Growth of Investment Clubs

1956	1,967
1960	5,608
1965	7,642
1970	13,678
1975	7,137
1980	3,642
1985	6,300
1990	7,085
1991	7,360
1992	8,267
1993	10,033
1994	12,429
1995	16,054
1996	25,409
1997	34,618

Profile of Investment Club Members

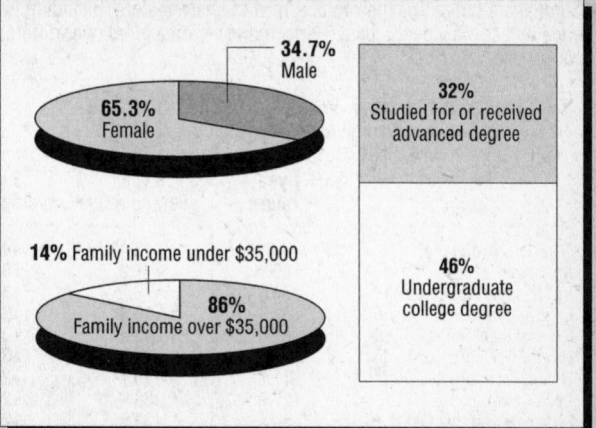

34.7% Male

65.3% Female

14% Family income under $35,000

86% Family income over $35,000

32% Studied for or received advanced degree

46% Undergraduate college degree

Source: National Association of Investment Clubs

Most Popular Stocks with Investment Clubs

Rank by no. of investment clubs holding	Company	Number of clubs holding stock
1	PepsiCo, Inc.	11,388
2	Intel Corp.	11,019
3	Motorola, Inc.	9,863
4	Tricon Global Restaurants	9,168
5	Merck & Co., Inc.	8,687
6	AFLAC Inc.	6,796
7	Diebold, Inc.	6,552
8	McDonald's Corp.	6,498
9	Coca-Cola Co.	6,101
10	Lucent Technologies	5,563
11	Home Depot, Inc.	5,414
12	Clayton Homes, Inc.	5,390
13	RPM, Inc.	5,033
14	Cisco Systems, Inc.	4,541
15	General Electric Co.	4,507
16	Johnson & Johnson	4,464
17	Microsoft Corp.	4,152
18	Wendy's International, Inc.	4,150
19	Walt Disney Co.	3,999
20	AT&T Corp.	3,619

Source: National Association of Investment Clubs

The Wall Street Journal Shareholder Scoreboard

Companies ranked by their total return to shareholders, including both change in the stock price and any dividends paid. Performance is measured over different time periods, ended Dec. 31, 1997.

30 Stocks in the Dow Jones Industrial Average
Ranked on five-year average returns through Dec. 31,1997

Company name	1 year return	3 year average return	5 year average return	10 year average return
Travelers Group Inc	+79.9%	+73.4%	+48.3%	+32.5%
American Express Co	+59.9	+47.2	+36.0	+19.7
Intl Business Mach Corp	+39.3	+43.2	+35.1	+9.4
Caterpillar Inc	+31.3	+23.3	+31.4	+14.0
General Electric Co	+51.0	+45.4	+31.2	+24.3
Hewlett-Packard Co	+25.3	+37.0	+30.4	+16.8
United Technologies Corp	+11.7	+35.1	+28.0	+19.3
Coca-Cola Co	+27.9	+38.9	+27.8	+32.6
Procter & Gamble Co	+50.5	+39.6	+26.9	+25.2
Sears, Roebuck & Co	+.01	+28.5	+25.4	+18.6
DuPont (E.I.) de Nemours	+30.3	+32.4	+24.2	+19.3
Union Carbide Corp	+6.8	+15.6	+23.9	+21.6
Johnson & Johnson	+34.3	+36.1	+23.5	+24.0
AlliedSignal Inc	+17.4	+33.7	+22.7	+22.3
Merck & Co	+35.6	+43.7	+22.7	+22.6
Chevron Corp	+22.1	+24.2	+21.8	+19.6
Boeing Co	-7.1	+29.5	+21.7	+22.0
Exxon Corp	+28.4	+30.9	+19.6	+17.5
Disney (Walt) Co	+42.9	+30.0	+18.9	+21.7
General Motors Corp	+19.4	+18.6	+17.7	+12.2
Philip Morris Cos	+24.6	+39.0	+17.3	+25.2
Eastman Kodak Co	-22.7	+10.9	+16.9	+ 8.5
Aluminum Co of America	+11.9	+19.7	+16.7	+14.7
Morgan (J.P.) & Co	+19.4	+31.0	+15.8	+16.6
Goodyear Tire & Rubber Co	+26.3	+26.4	+15.5	+10.7
McDonald's Corp	+5.9	+18.5	+15.2	+16.9
AT&T Corp	+53.2	+24.7	+14.9	+16.3
Minnesota Mining & Mfg. Co	+1.2	+20.2	+14.4	+13.8
Intl Paper Co	+ 8.7	+7.0	+ 7.8	+10.3
Wal-Mart Stores Inc	+74.7	+23.9	+5.0	+20.5
30 Stocks in Dow Jones Industrials	**+27.0**	**+30.9**	**+22.6**	**+19.0**

Sources: LEK/Alcar Consulting Group LLC, IDD/Tradeline, Media General Financial Services Inc.

The Best Performers in the Shareholder Scoreboard

1 year

Company name	Stock symbol	Average return	Company name	Stock symbol	Average return
Yahoo Inc	YHOO	+511.0%	Keane Inc	KEA	+155.9%
Arterial Vascular Energy Inc	AVEI	+420.0	CompuWare Corp	CPWR	+155.4
Best Buy Co Inc	BBY	+247.1	ICN Pharmaceuticals Inc	ICN	+152.5
Dell Computer Corp	DELL	+216.2	Allied Waste Inds Inc	AWIN	+152.0
Cablevision Systems Cl A	CVC	+212.7	Barnes & Noble Inc	BKS	+147.2
Chancellor Media Corp	AMFM	+198.5	Royal Carib Cruises Ltd	RCL	+131.6
Heftel Broadcasting Cl A	HBCCA	+196.8	Donaldsn Lufkin & Jenrette	DLJ	+123.2
Immunex Corp	IMNX	+176.9	National-Oilwell Inc	NOI	+122.4
America Online Inc	AOL	+172.2	Rexall Sundown Inc	RXSD	+122.1
Navistar International	NAV	+171.9	Cincinnati Financial Corp	CINF	+121.2
Airborne Freight Corp	ABF	+167.7	Coca-Cola Enterprises	CCE	+120.7
US Airways Group Inc	U	+167.4	Clear Channel Com	CCU	+119.9
Caliber Systems Inc	CBB	+158.0			

5 years

Company name	Stock symbol	Average return	Company name	Stock symbol	Average return
Tellabs Inc	TLAB	+91.3%	Peoples Bank Br'port CT	PBCT	+63.8%
Iomega Corp	IOM	+90.8	Global Marine Inc	GLM	+63.1
America Online Inc	AOL	+90.0	Schwab (Charles) Corp	SCH	+62.3
Clear Channel Com	CCU	+89.4	Republic Industries Inc	RII	+60.7
PeopleSoft Inc	PSFT	+85.7	Networks Associates Inc	NETA	+60.0
Corrections Corp of Amer	CXC	+84.8	EVI Inc	EVI	+60.0
Robert Half Intl Inc	RHI	+78.5	Altera Corp	ALTR	+59.4
Starwood Lodging Trust	HOT	+74.8	McKesson Corp	MCK	+58.2
HBO & Co	HBOC	+72.4	Reading & Bates Corp	RB	+58.0
Ensco International Inc	ESV	+71.7	Safeway Inc	SWY	+57.6
Dell Computer Corp	DELL	+69.5	Maxim Integrated Products	MXIM	+56.4
Keane Inc	KEA	+69.3	EMC Corp/ma	EMC	+56.0
Dura Pharmaceuticals Inc	DURA	+66.1			

10 years

Company name	Stock symbol	Average return	Company name	Stock symbol	Average return
Keane Inc	KEA	+65.8%	Microsoft Corp	MSFT	+45.6%
Iomega Corp	IOM	+60.7	Nabors Industries	NBR	+43.2
Clear Channel Com	CCU	+60.4	Comair Holdings Inc	COMR	+42.6
Schwab (Charles) Corp	SCH	+54.2	Harley-Davidson Inc	HDI	+42.5
Conseco Inc	CNC	+52.4	Sealed Air Corp	SEE	+42.1
HBO & Co	HBOC	+51.8	SunAmerica Inc.	SAI	+42.0
United Healthcare Corp	UNH	+49.3	Home Depot Inc	HD	+41.8
Concord EFS Inc	CEFT	+48.8	WorldCom Inc/ga Cl A	WCOM	+41.4
Dollar General	DG	+47.9	Fastenal Co	FAST	+41.1
Intl Game Technology	IGT	+47.8	Price (T. Rowe) Associates	TROW	+40.5
Tellabs Inc	TLAB	+47.1	Corrections Corp of Amer	CXC	+40.5
Adaptec Inc	ADPT	+46.5	Cardinal Health Inc	CAH	+40.2
EVI Inc	EVI	+46.0			

Sources: LEK/Alcar Consulting Group, IDD/Tradeline, Media General Financial Services Inc.

The Worst Performers in the Shareholder Scoreboard

1 year

Company name	Stock symbol	Average return	Company name	Stock symbol	Average return
Boston Chicken Inc	BOST	-82.1%	Tupperware Corp	TUP	-46.5%
Informix Corp	IFMX	-76.7	Freeport-McMoran Cl B	FTX	-45.6
Oxford Health Plans Inc	OXHP	-73.4	Nine West Group Inc	NIN	-44.1
Amax Gold Inc	AU	-63.7	Atmel Corp	ATML	-44.0
Ascend Communications Inc	ASND	-60.6	Nu Skin Asia Pacific Cl A	NUS	-40.9
Netscape Comm Corp	NSCP	-57.1	Circus Circus Entp Inc	CIR	-40.4
Cabletron Systems	CS	-54.9	Fluor Corp	FLR	-39.5
3Com Corp	COMS	-52.4	Readers Digest Assn Cl A	RDA	-38.6
Silicon Graphics Inc	SGI	-51.7	Pacificare Health Sys Cl B	PHSYB	-38.6
Seagate Technology	SEG	-51.3	Apple Computer Inc	AAPL	-37.1
Atlas Air Inc	CGO	-49.7	Homestake Mining	HM	-37.0
Zenith Electronics Corp	ZE	-49.4	Getchell Gold Corp	GGO	-36.2
Pittston Co-Minerals Group	PZM	-48.5			

5 years

Company name	Stock symbol	Average return	Company name	Stock symbol	Average return
Apple Computer Inc	AAPL	-25.6%	Northeast Utilities	NU	-9.2%
Novell Inc	NOVL	-23.4	Hecla Mining Co	HL	-8.6
Amax Gold Inc	AU	-23.0	Niagara Mohawk Power	NMK	-7.9
U.S. Surgical Corp	USS	-15.3	Great Lakes Chem Corp	GLK	-7.6
Informix Corp	IFMX	-12.1	Stone Container Corp	STO	-7.2
Readers Digest Assn Cl A	RDA	-12.1	Louisiana-Pacific Corp	LPX	-6.8
Fruit of the Loom Inc Cl A	FTL	-12.0	Alza Corp	AZA	-6.7
Sybase Inc	SYBS	-11.6	Woolworth Corp	Z	-6.5
Circus Circus Entp Inc	CIR	-11.5	Dillards Inc Cl A	DDS	-6.3
KMart Corp	KM	-11.5	Armco Inc	AS	-6.1
Bethlehem Steel Corp	BS	-11.5	Cooper Tire & Rubber	CTB	-5.4
Cyprus Amax Minerals Co	CYM	-10.6	Waste Management Inc	WMX	-5.3
Stride Rite Corp	SRR	-9.9			

10 years

Company name	Stock symbol	Average return	Company name	Stock symbol	Average return
Amax Gold Inc	AU	-17.9%	Sun Energy Partners LP	SLP	-2.5%
Digital Equipment	DEC	-12.1	U.S. Filter Corp	USF	-1.8
Apple Computer Inc	AAPL	-10.2	Boise Cascade Corp	BCC	-0.1
Battle Mountain Gold Co	BMG	-10.2	Reading & Bates Corp	RB	+0.3
Hecla Mining Co	HL	-9.6	KMart Corp	KM	+1.0
Zenith Electronics Corp	ZE	-9.5	Asarco Inc	AR	+1.1
Unisys Corp	UIS	-7.5	USF&G Corp	FG	+1.4
Armco Inc	AS	-7.1	Yellow Corp	YELL	+1.5
Stone Container Corp	STO	-5.8	Newmont Mining Corp	NEM	+1.7
Bethlehem Steel Corp	BS	-5.8	Food Lion Inc Cl A	FDLNA	+1.8
Homestake Mining	HM	-5.5	Cyprus Amax Minerals Co	CYM	+2.5
Navistar International	NAV	-5.2	Northeast Utilities	NU	+2.6
Inland Steel Industries Inc	IAD	-4.3			

Sources : LEK/Alcar Consulting Group, IDD/Tradeline, Media General Financial Services Inc.

Mutual Funds Review

Largest Stock and Balanced Funds
Percentage gains for periods ended June 30, 1998; assets as of May 31, 1998

	Assets ($ millions)	Performance 2nd quarter	12 months	5 years
Fidelity Magellan Fund	$71,534.5	+3.37%	+28.97%	+141.87%
Vanguard Index:500 Port	60,840.6	+3.29	+30.05	+180.85
Washington Mutual Inv	45,766.6	+0.34	+27.23	+165.36
Investment Co Of America	43,951.7	+1.58	+24.38	+144.52
Fidelity Growth & Income	43,567.8	+2.99	+27.96	+169.00
Fidelity Contrafund	33,581.2	+4.46	+29.70	+152.65
Vanguard Windsor II	29,866.8	+1.80	+30.43	+173.52
Amer Cent:TC Ultra;Inv	25,548.2	+6.95	+31.15	+146.68
Vanguard Wellington Fund	24,689.2	+1.01	+19.06	+116.47
Fidelity Puritan	24,671.9	+2.56	+18.95	+106.68
Fidelity Equity-Inc	24,581.7	-0.12	+23.20	+150.50
Fidelity Adv Gr Opp;T	23,431.0	+1.23	+24.52	+154.56
Vanguard Windsor	22,439.3	-2.29	+17.01	+138.91
Income Fund Of America	22,233.9	-0.47	+18.12	+97.16
Janus Fund	21,523.9	+6.12	+31.99	+141.58
Europacific Growth	21,277.8	-0.19	+7.61	+105.95
Putnam Gro & Inc;A	19,238.5	-1.00	+17.75	+139.57
New Perspective Fund	19,199.2	+2.64	+18.36	+136.54
Fidelity Equity-Inc II	18,502.2	+3.12	+26.99	+143.35
Vanguard Instl IX;Inst	18,259.0	+3.32	+30.20	+182.66
MSDW Div Gro;B	17,806.6	+0.83	+22.35	+133.52
Putnam Gro & Inc;B	16,395.0	-1.19	+16.83	+130.76
Fidelity Blue Chip Grow	15,796.3	+4.22	+29.27	+171.35
Janus Worldwide	14,720.6	+7.19	+26.36	+188.49
Templeton Fds:For;I	14,514.7	-7.35	-1.58	+74.45
AIM Eq:Consteltn;Rtl A	14,435.3	+1.47	+17.99	+124.53
T Rowe Price Equ Income	14,173.9	-2.35	+19.39	+144.67
Templeton Growth;I	14,023.6	-5.32	+5.84	+109.15
Growth Fund Of America	13,500.1	+2.43	+29.10	+138.60
Putnam Voyager;A	13,366.6	+1.88	+32.14	+167.99
Fidelity Asset Manager	12,531.7	+0.52	+18.82	+83.89
Fidelity Sprt US Eq Indx	12,312.6	+3.24	+29.84	+179.20
Fundamental Investors	12,052.6	+1.56	+22.42	+153.13
Fidelity Low-Price	11,662.1	-1.38	+21.92	+156.84
T Rowe Price Int:Stock	10,589.2	+0.13	+4.38	+85.78
American Mutual	10,378.2	-0.98	+20.02	+118.63
Vanguard PRIMECAP	10,246.5	+1.34	+26.47	+199.23
Fidelity Growth Company	10,195.1	+1.57	+21.04	+133.44
IDS New Dimensions;A	10,033.8	+3.43	+28.04	+157.92
Vanguard World:US Growth	9,893.9	+7.27	+32.91	+194.08
Putnam New Oppty;A	9,475.7	+2.91	+32.75	+193.46
Templeton Fds:World;I	9,473.9	-4.61	+8.57	+125.85
Merrill Glbl Alloc;B	9,327.7	-2.92	+6.60	+70.22
Smallcap World Fund	9,306.6	-4.29	+9.24	+104.85
Oakmark Fund	8,756.8	-2.70	+18.38	+169.42
AVERAGE U.S. STOCK FUND	—	-0.29	+22.62	+133.19
S&P 500 (with dividends)	—	+3.30	+30.15	+182.43

Source: Lipper Analytical Services

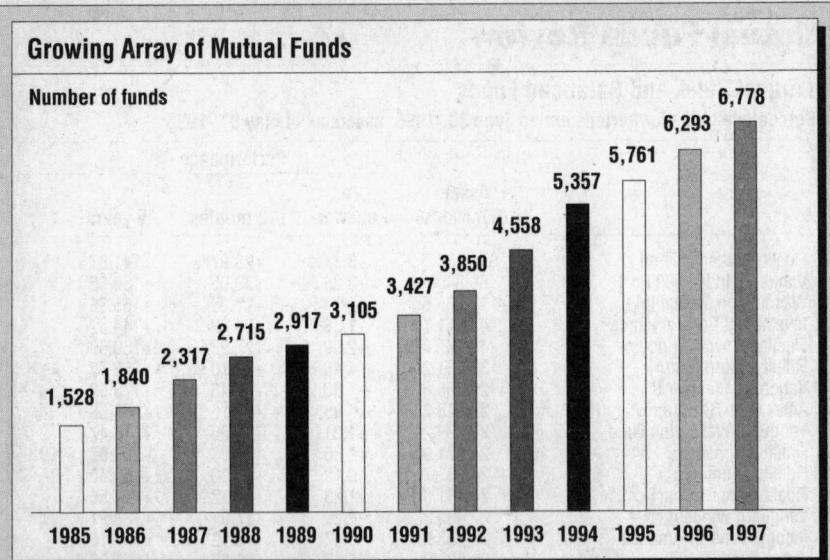

Growing Array of Mutual Funds

Number of funds

1985	1986	1987	1988	1989	1990	1991	1992	1993	1994	1995	1996	1997
1,528	1,840	2,317	2,715	2,917	3,105	3,427	3,850	4,558	5,357	5,761	6,293	6,778

Total Assets of Mutual Funds (In billions)

Year end	All funds	Equity funds*	Bond & Income funds	Taxable money markets	Tax-exempt money markets
1979	$ 94.5	$ 35.9	$ 13.1	$ 45.2	$ 0.3
1980	134.8	44.4	14.0	74.5	1.9
1981	241.4	41.2	14.0	181.9	4.3
1982	296.7	53.7	23.2	206.6	13.2
1983	292.9	77.0	36.6	162.5	16.8
1984	370.7	83.1	54.0	209.7	23.8
1985	495.5	116.9	134.8	207.5	36.3
1986	716.3	161.5	262.6	228.3	63.8
1987	769.9	180.7	273.1	254.7	61.4
1988	810.3	194.8	277.5	272.3	65.7
1989	982.0	249.0	304.8	358.7	69.4
1990	1,066.9	245.8	322.7	414.7	83.6
1991	1,395.5	411.6	441.4	452.6	89.9
1992	1,646.3	522.8	577.3	451.4	94.8
1993	2,075.4	749.0	761.1	461.9	103.4
1994	2,161.5	866.4	684.0	500.4	110.6
1995	2,820.4	1,269.0	798.3	629.7	123.3
1996	3,539.2	1,750.9	886.5	761.8	140.1
1997	4,489.7	2,399.3	1,031.5	898.1	160.8

*Equity funds include Aggressive Growth, Growth, Growth & Income, Precious Metals, International, Global-Equity, Income-Equity and Option/Income.

Source: Investment Company Institute

Mutual-Fund Performance Yardsticks
How Fund Categories Stack Up on a Total Return Basis

Investment objective	2nd quarter	One year	3 years (Annualized)	5 years (Annualized)	10 years (Annualized)
Growth & Income	+0.58%	+23.54%	+25.33%	+19.44%	+15.86%
Equity Income	-0.97	+20.95	+23.21	+17.64	+14.72
Sector	-2.45	+17.03	+22.77	+18.55	+18.30
Utility	-1.60	+25.93	+19.13	+12.30	+13.44
Growth	+1.85	+25.38	+24.18	+19.25	+16.50
Latin America	-19.01	-24.20	+9.09	+4.60	N.A.
Health & Biotechnology	-1.73	+17.97	+24.42	+21.64	+21.78
Small Cap	-4.12	+18.13	+20.06	+16.97	+15.45
Capital Appreciation	+0.29	+22.12	+21.04	+16.82	+15.13
Mid-Cap	-1.40	+22.22	+20.63	+16.95	+15.85
Balanced	+1.15	+17.58	+17.82	+13.97	+12.86
European Region	+6.30	+33.00	+24.03	+21.18	+12.40
Stock & Bond Funds	+0.49	+14.96	+16.08	+12.68	+11.53
Science & Technology	+2.92	+25.43	+19.52	+21.72	+19.73
Global Funds	-0.08	+12.88	+16.91	+15.12	+12.14
International	+0.80	+8.17	+12.95	+12.23	+10.31
Natural Resources	-10.46	-10.98	+9.98	+8.25	+9.11
Emerging Markets	-19.71	-31.86	-4.09	-0.53	N.A.
Pacific Region	-19.55	-44.77	-13.37	-5.23	+1.01
Gold	-16.04	-34.97	-17.10	-10.61	-3.89
High-Yield Taxable Bond	+0.29	+11.44	+12.36	+9.93	+10.30
High-Yield Municipal Bond	+1.48	+9.48	+7.86	+6.47	+7.93
General Taxable Bond	+0.37	+7.73	+9.60	+7.48	+9.24
L-T Inv. Grade Corp. Bond	+2.24	+10.42	+7.86	+6.95	+9.05
L-T US Treas./Govt Bond	+2.44	+10.97	+7.14	+6.12	+8.42
General Municipal Debt	+1.33	+8.39	+7.32	+5.78	+7.97
Single State Muni. Debt	+1.34	+8.13	+7.20	+5.67	+7.78
Int. Inv. Grade Corp. Bond	+2.06	-9.43	+7.09	+6.13	+8.32
Insured Municipal Debt	+1.30	+8.01	+7.15	+5.72	+7.86
Int. Term US Treas./Govt	+2.01	+9.10	+6.58	+5.52	+7.78
Mortgage	+1.53	+7.61	+6.74	+5.62	+7.93
Inter Term Muni. Debt	+1.13	+6.56	+6.02	+5.15	+6.87
Short Term US Treas./Govt	+1.43	+6.52	+5.79	+4.94	+7.01
Short Term Inv. Grade Corp.	+1.47	+6.59	+6.01	+5.35	+6.97
Short Term Muni. Debt	+0.93	+4.90	+4.57	+4.26	+5.49
World Bond	-0.77	+3.65	+8.40	+5.86	+7.43

Benchmarks for Mutual-Fund Investors on a Total Return Basis

Investment objective	2nd quarter	One year	3 years (Annualized)	5 years (Annualized)	10 years (Annualized)
DJIA (w/divs)	+2.14 %	+18.68 %	+27.77 %	+23.35%	+18.72 %
S&P 500 (w/divs)	+3.30	+30.15	+30.24	+23.08	+18.56
Small-Co. Index Fund[1]	-5.00	+16.94	+20.06	+17.04	+13.71
Lipper Index: Europe	+5.18	+33.88	+25.19	+21.20	N.A.
Lipper Index: Pacific	-13.64	-39.43	-11.07	-4.09	N.A.
Lipper L-T Gov't[2]	+2.17	+9.95	+6.95	+5.58	+7.71
AVG. STOCK FUND	-0.29	+22.62	+23.13	+18.45	+15.87
AVG. BOND FUND	+1.56	+8.98	+7.56	+6.33	+8.56

Note: Final data, as of July 2, 1998
[1]Vanguard's; tracks Russell 2000.
[2]Includes government agency debt.
Source: Lipper Analytical Services

Second-Quarter and 12-Month Winners and Losers

Best- and worst-performing stock funds for the periods ended June 30, 1998; assets are figured as of May 31, 1998. Performance data are total returns, which include both share prices and reinvested dividends.

Second-Quarter Best Performers

Fund name	Assets ($ millions)	2nd quarter	12 months	5 years
IAI Value Fund	$29.8	+24.80%	+44.80 %	+142.72%
Grand Prix Fund	1.2	+21.77	N.A.	N.A.
Deutche:German Eqty;A	0.2	+18.07	N.A.	N.A.
WEBS;Belgium	30.2	+17.66	+34.89	N.A.
WEBS;Germany	55.1	+17.40	+44.71	N.A.
Profunds:Ultaotc;Inv	11.2	+17.04	N.A.	N.A.
Transam Prem:Sm Co;Inv	26.8	+16.79	+76.11	N.A.
Wright Equi:Belg/Lux	2.4	+16.71	+33.50	N.A.
Fidelity Germany	22.8	+16.28	+44.22	N.A.
Munder:Netnet;Y	12.7	+14.85	+87.32	N.A.
Janus Twenty	8,131.6	+14.53	+47.21	+188.39
ASAF:Jan Cap Gro;B	17.6	+13.99	N.A.	N.A.
Transam Prem:Agg Gro;Inv	40.3	+13.97	+77.10	N.A.
IDEX:Growth;A	745.2	+13.89	+43.60	+160.76
AIM Intl:Euro Devel;A	39.7	+13.82	N.A.	N.A.
Berkshire Cap:Grow&Val	0.1	+13.42	N.A.	N.A.
PIMCO:Innovation;C	190.9	+12.92	+46.97	N.A.
Deutsche:Euro Mid Cp;A	0.9	+12.61	N.A.	N.A.
Orbitex:Info-Tech/Comm	2.3	+12.35	N.A.	N.A.
WEBS:France	38.1	+12.24	+41.88	N.A.
Fidelity France	14.8	+12.16	+40.94	N.A.
Dresdner RCM:Glbl Tech	8.7	+11.88	+52.07	N.A.
Managers:Capital Aprrec	66.4	+11.74	+43.11	+149.01
Marsico Inv Fd:Focus	352.9	+11.70	N.A.	N.A.
PIMCO:Intl Growth;Inst	6.7	+11.25	N.A.	N.A.
Sm Barney Wld:Europe;B	39.3	+11.23	+29.74	N.A.
Fidelity Sel Computer	686.0	+11.18	+26.36	+283.03
Potomac:OTC Plus	11.5	+11.12	N.A.	N.A.
Nations:Mars Fe;Inv B	49.6	+10.82	N.A.	N.A.
IAI Balanced Fund	32.7	+10.80	+24.50	+104.59
Sm Barney Inv:Lc Gr;B	343.0	+10.74	N.A.	N.A.
Waddell&Reed:Intl Gr;B	97.0	+10.64	+37.03	+109.53
Janus Olympus Fund	789.3	+10.48	+39.46	N.A.
Fidelity Nordic	149.5	+10.43	+32.92	N.A.
IDEX:Agg Growth;A	40.7	+10.38	+36.98	N.A.
Amerindo:Technology;D	45.8	+10.37	+36.46	N.A.
Janus Mercury	2,150.7	+10.32	+37.16	+195.13
ICAP:Euro Select Equity	27.3	+10.30	N.A.	N.A.
Federated Intl Sm Co;B	192.3	+10.23	+29.82	N.A.
Excelsior:Large Cap Grow	66.2	+10.22	N.A.	N.A.
Montgomery II:Gl L-S;A	23.5	+10.19	N.A.	N.A.
Reserve Prv:Inf Inv	4.3	+10.18	+27.54	N.A.
Caldwell & Orkin:Mkt Opp	180.1	+10.13	+34.15	+140.91
WM:Growth;A	111.2	+10.07	+35.42	+149.48
Nich-App:Glbl Blue Chip	7.7	+9.99	N.A.	N.A.
Schroder Cap:Intl SC;Inv	6.7	+9.98	+9.48	N.A.
PBHG:Large Cap 20;PBHG	222.4	+9.95	+52.65	N.A.
Rydex:OTC Fund	239.5	+9.83	+40.63	N.A.
Ridgeway Millnnium	9.6	+9.79	N.A.	N.A.
Alliance Technology;B	1,248.3	+9.75	+28.10	+220.57

N.A.: Not applicable; fund is too new.
Note: For funds with multiple share classes only the largest is shown.
Source: Lipper Analytical Services

Second-Quarter Worst Performers

		Performance		
Fund name	Assets ($ millions)	2nd quarter	12 months	5 years
Lexington Trka Russia	$58.6	-55.02 %	-62.38%	N.A.%
WEBS:Malaysia	63.5	-46.01	-73.96	N.A.
Citifunds Em Asia Mk	1.4	-41.88	-75.61	N.A.
Matthews Intl:Korea;I	80.0	-36.51	-69.33	N.A.
WEBS:Singapore	59.0	-36.28	-60.06	N.A.
Guinness Flght:Asia SC	54.0	-34.87	-62.67	N.A.
Ivy:Asia Pacific;A	2.1	-34.21	-58.20	N.A.
Newport Grtr China;A	56.6	-33.77	-52.46	N.A.
Montgomery:Em Asia;R	27.7	-33.68	-63.44	N.A.
INVESCO Sp:Asian Growth	13.5	-33.46	-60.08	N.A.
Newcap Contrarian Fund	1.4	-33.22	-29.10	N.A.
Kemper Asian Growth;A	3.9	-33.05	-52.49	N.A.
DFA Grp:Pac Rim Small Co	92.1	-32.29	-59.01	-38.58
Matthews Intl:P Tigr;I	45.1	-31.95	-60.01	N.A.
Newport Tiger;B	275.5	-31.36	-56.26	N.A.
Colonial Nwprt T-Cub;A	5.3	-31.27	-50.41	N.A.
Lexington Crosby SC Asia	14.2	-30.75	-64.74	N.A.
GAM:Asian Capital;A	0.5	-29.75	-55.24	N.A.
Guinness Flght:Mnld Ch	15.8	-29.59	N.A.	N.A.
Ivy:China Region;A	10.0	-29.46	-51.59	N.A.
US Glbl:China Reg Opp	20.8	-29.36	-52.06	N.A.
Salomon Bros:Asia Gr;B	6.7	-29.06	-52.53	N.A.
GMO:Evolving Cntry;III	51.9	-28.87	N.A.	N.A.
Merrill Emer Tigers;A	44.9	-28.83	-61.60	N.A.
Pilgrim Amer:Asia-Pc;A	12.8	-28.53	-59.65	N.A.
Tocqueville:Intl Value	73.2	-28.47	-43.12	N.A.
US Glbl:Gold Shares	47.3	-28.30	-58.72	-82.37
GMO:Emerging Mkts;III	801.7	-28.24	-40.07	N.A.
Abn Amro:Asian Tigr;Com	26.4	-28.21	-53.16	N.A.
Stein Roe Emerg Mkts	19.7	-28.21	-51.67	N.A.
Wright Equi:Hng Kng Chna	4.7	-27.70	-54.52	-38.47
Fidelity Soeast Asia	216.5	-27.59	-52.73	-24.94
Sm Barney Wld:Em Mk;B	11.1	-27.53	-42.01	N.A.
Eaton Vance Grtr Ch;B	111.6	-27.37	-54.24	-21.36
Pac Cap:New Asia Gr;Y	15.4	-27.22	-46.38	N.A.
Alliance Gtr China97;B	2.2	-27.13	N.A.	N.A.
WEBS:Hong Kong	50.8	-27.04	-50.36	N.A.
CVO Greater China;I	14.6	-26.97	-46.11	N.A.
Guinness Flght:China	204.2	-26.85	-49.43	N.A.
Goldman:Asia Gr;A	75.3	-26.76	-56.71	N.A.
Guinness Flght:Asia Bc	7.3	-26.75	-52.45	N.A.
Glenmede:Emerg Mkts	74.9	-26.33	-42.61	N.A.
Scudder Pacific Oppty	116.7	-26.20	-51.72	-35.70
Painewbr Asia Pac Gr;B	15.4	-26.13	-53.37	N.A.
Delaware Emerg Mkt;A	8.8	-26.03	-36.91	N.A.
AIM Intl:Asian Gro;A	6.5	-25.67	N.A.	N.A.
Merrill Dragon Fund;B	265.9	-25.51	-58.17	-34.78
Govett:Asia;A	1.1	-25.38	-55.77	N.A.
Ivy:Dev Nations;B	7.8	-25.36	-47.35	N.A.
BT Inv:Pacific Basin	12.9	-25.29	-55.27	N.A.

N.A.: Not applicable; fund is too new.
Source: Lipper Analytical Services

12-Month Best Performers

Fund name	Assets ($ millions)	Performance		
		2nd quarter	12 months	5 years
Munder:Netnet;Y	$12.7	+14.85%	+87.32%	N.A.%
Transam Prem:Agg Gro;Inv	40.3	+13.97	+77.10	N.A.
Transam Prem:Sm Co;Inv	26.8	+16.79	+76.11	N.A.
Weitz:Hickory	131.1	+9.61	+61.99	+270.55
Delaware Aggr Gro;A	37.4	+1.82	+60.77	N.A.
WEBS;Italy	70.2	-2.02	+60.49	N.A.
Fidelity Sel Brokerage	910.8	+7.37	+57.72	+240.92
FMI:Focus Fund	18.5	-0.95	+54.91	N.A.
PBHG:Large Cap 20;PBHG	222.4	+9.95	+52.65	N.A.
Fidelity Sel Retailing	200.6	+6.91	+52.38	+157.91
Dresdner RCM:Glbl Tech	8.7	+11.88	+52.07	N.A.
MAS Fds:Midcap Gro;Inst	529.0	+3.46	+52.03	+198.01
GAM:Gamerica Capital;A	8.8	+3.49	+51.91	N.A.
Fidelity Sel Leisure	290.3	+6.33	+51.58	+182.52
Scudder Greater Europe	978.5	+8.57	+51.17	N.A.
Flag Inv Comm;A	745.7	+3.13	+51.06	+160.87
Weitz Partners:Value	171.7	+6.15	+49.31	N.A.
Sequoia Fund	4,477.5	+8.03	+48.24	+231.82
Waddell&Reed:Growth;B	332.3	+6.48	+48.10	+179.06
TIP:Turner Mid Cap Gro	21.6	+5.85	+47.87	N.A.
Weitz:Value	493.5	+6.20	+47.81	+181.86
Gabelli Gl:Couch Potato	73.9	+5.71	+47.79	N.A.
Janus Twenty	8,131.6	+14.53	+47.21	+188.39
T Rowe Price Media/Tele	194.6	+1.60	+47.13	N.A.
Nich-App:Lg C Gr Inst	2.4	+7.88	+47.11	N.A.
BEA Gl Telecomm;Adv	1.1	+4.44	+47.03	N.A.
PIMCO:Innovation;C	190.9	+12.92	+46.97	N.A.
WEBS:Spain	28.5	+2.77	+46.71	N.A.
Heritage Cap Apprec;A	109.9	+4.50	+46.67	+172.09
MFS Strategic Growth;B	160.6	+3.98	+46.48	N.A.
Fidelity Sel Air Trans	99.1	+5.30	+46.31	+137.86
Artisan:Mid Cap	12.9	-0.73	+46.07	N.A.
ICON:South Europe Reg	15.7	+3.31	+45.85	N.A.
Excelsior Inst:Opt Gr;In	52.4	+9.33	+45.70	N.A.
MFS Mass Invest Gro;A	2,536.1	+3.56	+45.60	+199.92
Montgomery:Glbl Comm;R	252.1	+5.99	+45.47	+141.86
Jundt Opportunity;I	7.6	+6.87	+45.45	N.A.
Information Tech 100	5.0	+7.86	+45.17	N.A.
INVESCO Sp:Wrld Commun	212.4	+2.40	+44.84	N.A.
IAI Value Fund	29.8	+24.80	+44.80	+142.72
WEBS:Germany	55.1	+17.40	+44.71	N.A.
SAFECO Growth;No Ld	1,573.3	-1.05	+44.63	+217.95
MSDW Finl Svc;B	370.1	+4.48	+44.59	N.A.
Oakmark Select Fund	1,483.6	+1.91	+44.30	N.A.
INVESCO Intl:European	645.5	+9.19	+44.28	+181.01
Fidelity Germany	22.8	+16.28	+44.22	N.A.
IDEX:Growth;A	745.2	+13.89	+43.60	+160.76
TCW Galileo:Midcap Gro	87.6	+8.47	+43.43	N.A.
Bjurman:Micro-Cap Growth	7.3	+2.25	+43.41	N.A.
Gabelli Value Fund	742.0	+3.10	+43.37	+176.87

N.A.: Not applicable; fund is too new.
Source: Lipper Analytical Services

12-Month Worst Performers

Fund name	Assets ($ millions)	Performance 2nd quarter	12 months	5 years
Citifunds Em Asia Mk	$1.4	-41.88%	-75.61%	N.A.%
WEBS:Malaysia	63.5	-46.01	-73.96	N.A.
Matthews Intl:Korea;I	80.0	-36.51	-69.33	N.A.
Lexington Crosby SC Asia	14.2	-30.75	-64.74	N.A.
Montgomery:Em Asia;R	27.7	-33.68	-63.44	N.A.
Guinness Flght:Asia SC	54.0	-34.87	-62.67	N.A.
Lexington Trka Russia	58.6	-55.02	-62.38	N.A.
Morg Stan In:Asia Eq;A	69.5	-24.63	-61.78	-38.60
Merrill Emer Tigers;A	44.9	-28.83	-61.60	N.A.
Morg Stan Fd:Asian;A	53.5	-22.42	-60.57	-42.39
INVESCO Sp:Asian Growth	13.5	-33.46	-60.08	N.A.
WEBS:Singapore	59.0	-36.28	-60.06	N.A.
Matthews Intl:P Tigr;I	45.1	-31.95	-60.01	N.A.
Pilgrim Amer:Asia-Pc;A	12.8	-28.53	-59.65	N.A.
DFA Grp:Pac Rim Small Co	92.1	-32.29	-59.01	-38.58
US Glbl:Gold Shares	47.3	-28.30	-58.72	-82.37
Ivy:Asia Pacific;A	2.1	-34.21	-58.20	N.A.
Merrill Dragon Fund;B	265.9	-25.51	-58.17	-34.78
Goldman:Asia Gr;A	75.3	-26.76	-56.71	N.A.
Newport Tiger;B	275.5	-31.36	-56.26	N.A.
Govett:Asia;A	1.1	-25.38	-55.77	N.A.
BT Inv:Pacific Basin	12.9	-25.29	-55.27	N.A.
GAM:Asian Capital;A	0.5	-29.75	-55.24	N.A.
Delaware New Pac;A	6.6	-25.16	-54.58	N.A.
Wright Equi:Hng Kng Chna	4.7	-27.70	-54.52	-38.47
AIM New Pacific Gr;A	98.6	-22.45	-54.39	-38.93
Eaton Vance Grtr Ch;B	111.6	-27.37	-54.24	-21.36
MSDW Pac Gro;B	468.3	-25.02	-53.73	-35.51
Midas Fund	106.4	-22.12	-53.57	-47.19
Painewbr Asia Pac Gr;B	15.4	-26.13	-53.37	N.A.
Abn Amro:Asian Tigr;Com	26.4	-28.21	-53.16	N.A.
Chasevista:SE Asia;A	3.8	-25.12	-53.14	N.A.
Schroder:All-Asia;A	61.3	-22.53	-52.93	N.A.
Fidelity Soeast Asia	216.5	-27.59	-52.73	-24.94
Salomon Bros:Asia Gr;B	6.7	-29.06	-52.53	N.A.
Kemper Asian Growth;A	3.9	-33.05	-52.49	N.A.
Newport Grtr China;A	56.6	-33.77	-52.46	N.A.
Guinness Flght:Asia Bc	7.3	-26.75	-52.45	N.A.
INVESCO Strat:Gold	114.5	-23.64	-52.21	-54.67
US Glbl:China Reg Opp	20.8	-29.36	-52.06	N.A.
Franklin Intl:Pac Gr;I	39.7	-23.78	-51.72	-27.85
Scudder Pacific Oppty	116.7	-26.20	-51.72	-35.70
Stein Roe Emerg Mkts	19.7	-28.21	-51.67	N.A.
Ivy:China Region;A	10.0	-29.46	-51.59	N.A.
T Rowe Price New Asia	653.6	-24.62	-50.61	-27.59
Colonial Nwprt T-Cub;A	5.3	-31.27	-50.41	N.A.
WEBS:Hong Kong	50.8	-27.04	-50.36	N.A.
Guinness Flght:China	204.2	-26.85	-49.43	N.A.
Nations:Pac Gro;Prm A	42.7	-22.53	-49.40	N.A.
Fidelity Emerging Mkts	399.2	-21.06	-49.11	-32.44

N.A.: Not applicable; fund is too new.
Source: Lipper Analytical Services

Five-Year Winners and Losers

Best- and worst-performing stock funds for the periods ended June 30, 1998; assets are figured as of May 31, 1998. Performance data are total returns, which include both share prices and reinvested dividends.

Five-Year Best Performers

Fund name	Assets ($ millions)	Performance		
		2nd quarter	12 months	5 years
Fidelity Sel Home Fin	$1,759.2	-2.93 %	+26.69 %	+295.00 %
Fidelity Sel Computer	686.0	+11.18	+26.36	+283.03
Fidelity Sel Health	2,165.7	+7.29	+32.30	+279.03
Fidelity Sel Elctronic	1,980.2	-7.50	+0.19	+275.92
Weitz:Hickory	131.1	+9.61	+61.99	+270.55
Legg Mason Value Tr;Prm	5,275.4	+5.21	+38.45	+262.59
Pilgrim Am Bk&Thrift;A	530.0	-1.61	+41.93	+258.30
Seligman Communictn;A	3,301.9	-2.09	+19.13	+251.35
White Oak Growth Stock	648.3	+6.83	+31.36	+250.03
MFS Instl:Em Equities	492.0	+0.48	+23.51	+248.50
Vanguard Spl:Health	6,257.7	+5.63	+27.77	+245.11
Fidelity Sel Brokerage	910.8	+7.37	+57.72	+240.92
Enterprise:Growth;A	602.7	+6.73	+31.05	+233.79
Sequoia Fund	4,477.5	+8.03	+48.24	+231.82
Fidelity Dividend Growth	6,433.6	+4.14	+34.59	+228.81
Davis:Financial;A	425.9	+4.50	+33.93	+228.00
Fidelity Sel Regl Bnks	1,385.3	+1.47	+35.97	+227.58
Fidelity Sel Financial	664.4	+4.28	+42.25	+226.42
Excelsior:Val & Restruct	504.5	-1.25	+26.56	+225.91
J Hancock Reg Bnk;B	5,611.9	-1.58	+34.74	+223.86
Spectra Fund	149.0	+9.43	+32.28	+223.86
Torray Fund	1,452.0	+0.99	+37.16	+223.47
Putnam Cap Apprec;A	1,528.4	-1.58	+22.95	+223.30
Alliance Technology;B	1,248.3	+9.75	+28.10	+220.57
Morg Stan In:Eqty Gr;A	733.0	-0.96	+33.53	+219.09
Franklin Str:CA Gro;I	704.7	-1.32	+19.18	+218.08
SAFECO Growth;No Ld	1,573.3	-1.05	+44.63	+217.95
Putnam Hlth Sciences;A	2,380.2	+1.56	+26.88	+213.79
GAM:Global;A	116.8	+5.18	+32.18	+212.18
Oak Value Fund	352.4	+3.40	+34.56	+211.96
Vanguard Index:Growth	3,710.8	+5.86	+34.73	+207.38
FPA Capital	819.4	+0.18	+22.56	+206.82
Alliance Premier Gr;B	1,633.9	+7.50	+42.30	+206.51
Pioneer Growth Shrs;A	864.1	+7.14	+40.90	+206.27
INVESCO Strat:Financial	1,586.3	+4.23	+38.25	+204.98
T Rowe Price Blue Chip	3,091.3	+3.05	+29.75	+204.19
PIMCO:Micro Cp Gr;Inst	253.0	-2.31	+33.95	+204.03
Accessor:Growth	110.8	+6.51	+34.20	+202.85
Robrtsn Stph:Val+Gro;A	703.8	+4.58	+18.32	+201.92
Harbor:Capital Apprec	3,709.9	+5.12	+34.90	+201.29
Painewbr Finl Svc Gr;A	226.6	+0.27	+30.66	+201.04
Lord Abbett Dev Gro;A	627.4	-2.94	+23.82	+200.48
MSDW Euro Gro;B	2,217.0	+4.78	+30.09	+200.12
MFS Mass Invest Gro;A	2,536.1	+3.56	+45.60	+199.92
Vanguard PRIMECAP	10,246.5	+1.34	+26.47	+199.23
SIFE Trust Fund;A-I	1,073.9	+0.39	+33.11	+198.67
Wright Equi:Netherland	19.7	+5.90	+24.99	+198.56
Pioneer Europe;A	324.6	+4.01	+38.23	+198.42
Papp America-Abroad	352.0	+0.31	+14.08	+198.35
MAS Fds:Midcap Gro;Inst	529.0	+3.46	+52.03	+198.01

Source: Lipper Analytical Services

Five-Year Worst Performers

Fund name	Assets ($ millions)	Performance 2nd quarter	12 months	5 years
US Glbl:Gold Shares	$47.3	-28.30 %	-58.72 %	-82.37 %
Frontier:Equity Fund	0.5	-21.78	-35.60	-71.40
Bull&Bear Gold Investors	9.0	-16.40	-43.45	-63.56
DFA Grp:Japan Small Co	113.8	-7.17	-45.56	-61.45
Monterey:Ocm Gold	5.6	-13.89	-28.01	-60.98
PIMCO Prec Metals;C	15.8	-16.67	-40.69	-54.85
INVESCO Strat:Gold	114.5	-23.64	-52.21	-54.67
Lexington Strat Invments	21.8	-11.48	-38.40	-49.73
Amer Cent:AC Gl Gold;Inv	257.4	-15.80	-31.72	-47.25
Midas Fund	106.4	-22.12	-53.57	-47.19
MSDW Prec Mtl;B	31.8	-16.91	-37.07	-47.17
Van Eck:Intl Gold;A	250.6	-15.30	-30.58	-45.30
Van Eck:Gold/Res;A	63.0	-14.36	-31.05	-44.77
Barr Rosen:Japan;Inst	0.8	-3.39	-39.52	-43.87
Comstock Cap Value;A	62.2	-2.77	-27.67	-43.82
Morg Stan Fd:Asian;A	53.5	-22.42	-60.57	-42.39
USAA Gold Fund	93.1	-14.01	-28.89	-41.84
Pioneer Gold Shares;A	21.8	-14.76	-32.55	-41.26
Steadman Amer Industry	0.9	+6.17	-19.44	-41.10
Evergreen Prc MT;B	29.5	-17.70	-34.14	-40.84
Fidelity Sel Prec Mtls	161.3	-20.88	-38.87	-40.15
Lexington Goldfund	57.7	-13.52	-32.81	-39.90
Vanguard Spl:Gold	330.6	-14.99	-33.02	-39.32
AIM New Pacific Gr;A	98.6	-22.45	-54.39	-38.93
Morg Stan In:Asia Eq;A	69.5	-24.63	-61.78	-38.60
DFA Grp:Pac Rim Small Co	92.1	-32.29	-59.01	-38.58
Wright Equi:Hng Kng Chna	4.7	-27.70	-54.52	-38.47
American Heritage Fund	16.9	-3.80	-24.00	-37.16
Capstone Japan Fund	2.1	-4.62	-31.00	-36.12
Scudder Pacific Oppty	116.7	-26.20	-51.72	-35.70
MSDW Pac Gro;B	468.3	-25.02	-53.73	-35.51
Merrill Dragon Fund;B	265.9	-25.51	-58.17	-34.78
Franklin Gold Fund;I	218.8	-14.84	-30.79	-34.56
Fidelity Sel Gold	205.1	-20.17	-36.73	-33.32
Fidelity Emerging Mkts	399.2	-21.06	-49.11	-32.44
Van Eck:Asia Dynsty;A	9.8	-23.96	-47.09	-30.56
Centurion TAA Fund;C	6.8	-4.31	-3.20	-29.75
T Rowe Price Int:Japan	143.7	-5.41	-32.24	-29.07
INVESCO Intl:Pacific	42.1	-9.31	-46.42	-28.18
Franklin Intl:Pac Gr;I	39.7	-23.78	-51.72	-27.85
T Rowe Price New Asia	653.6	-24.62	-50.61	-27.59
US Glbl:World Gold	131.6	-19.51	-37.45	-27.46
Oppenheimer Gld & Sp;A	84.9	-15.29	-30.23	-27.04
Vanguard Intl Idx:Pac	896.3	-8.93	-35.22	-26.37
Fidelity Soeast Asia	216.5	-27.59	-52.73	-24.94
Ivy:Canada Fund;A	6.8	-20.11	-31.50	-24.89
Excelsior:Pacific/Asia	35.6	-20.25	-45.87	-23.56
The Japan Fund	281.2	+0.70	-22.09	-22.66
Newport Tiger;T	56.7	-31.16	-55.80	-22.54
J Hancock Pac Bsn;A	14.1	-17.20	-46.88	-22.38

Source: Lipper Analytical Services

Bullish on Stocks

As Americans increasingly invest in stocks, the New York Stock Exchange maintains its dominance.

Share and Dollar Volume by Exchanges (In percentage)

Year	Total Share Volume (In thousands)	NYSE	AMEX	CHIC	PSE	PHLX	BSE	CSE	Others
1960	1,441,120	68.47	22.27	2.20	3.11	0.88	0.38	0.04	2.65
1970	4,834,887	71.28	19.03	3.16	3.68	1.63	0.51	0.02	0.69
1980	15,587,986	79.94	10.78	3.84	2.80	1.54	0.57	0.32	0.21
1985	37,187,567	81.52	5.78	6.12	3.66	1.47	1.27	0.15	0.03
1990	53,746,087	81.86	6.23	4.68	3.16	1.82	1.71	0.53	0.01
1991	58,290,641	82.01	5.52	4.66	3.59	1.60	1.77	0.86	0.01
1992	65,705,037	81.34	5.74	4.62	3.19	1.72	1.57	1.83	0.01
1993	83,056,237	82.90	5.53	4.57	2.81	1.55	1.47	1.17	0.00
1994	90,786,603	84.55	4.96	3.88	2.37	1.42	1.39	1.42	0.01
1995	107,069,656	84.49	4.78	3.67	2.56	1.39	1.45	1.66	0.00
1996	125,922,577	85.95	4.29	3.37	2.40	1.28	1.29	1.42	0.00

Year	Total Dollar Volume ($ in thousands)	NYSE	AMEX	CHIC	PSE	PHLX	BSE	CSE	Others
1960	$ 45,309,825	83.80	9.35	2.72	1.94	1.03	0.60	0.07	0.49
1970	131,707,946	78.44	11.11	3.76	3.81	1.99	0.67	0.03	0.19
1980	476,500,688	83.53	7.33	4.33	2.27	1.61	0.52	0.40	0.01
1985	1,200,127,848	85.25	2.23	6.59	3.06	1.49	1.20	0.18	0.00
1990	1,616,798,075	86.15	2.33	4.58	2.77	1.79	1.63	0.74	0.00
1991	1,778,154,074	86.20	2.31	4.34	3.05	1.54	1.72	0.83	0.01
1992	2,032,684,135	86.47	2.07	4.28	2.87	1.70	1.52	1.09	0.00
1993	2,610,504,390	87.21	2.08	4.10	2.38	1.52	1.35	1.37	0.00
1994	2,817,671,150	88.08	2.01	3.49	2.09	1.34	1.31	1.68	0.00
1995	3,507,991,171	87.71	2.10	3.26	2.24	1.27	1.43	1.99	0.00
1996	4,511,779,836	88.91	1.91	3.01	2.03	1.19	1.32	1.63	0.00

Key to abbreviations: NYSE, New York Stock Exchange; AMEX, American Stock Exchange; CHIC, Chicago Stock Exchange; PSE, Pacific Stock Exchange; PHLX, Philadelphia Stock Exchange; BSE, Boston Stock Exchange; and CSE, Cincinnati Stock Exchange.

Source: U.S. Securities and Exchange Commission

Sizing Up the Big Board

Daily Average Share Volume on the New York Stock Exchange

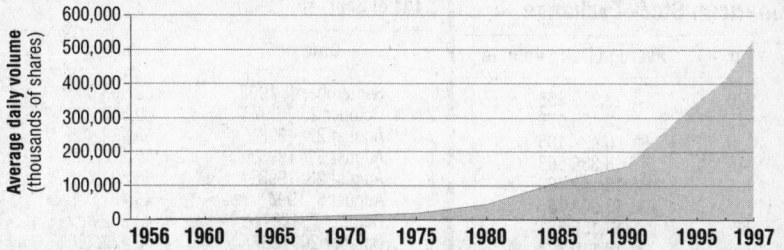

Average daily volume (thousands of shares)

600,000 — 500,000 — 400,000 — 300,000 — 200,000 — 100,000 — 0

1956 1960 1965 1970 1975 1980 1985 1990 1995 1997

Most Active Trading Days on the NYSE
(As of Sept. 15, 1998)

Date	Volume (millions)
September 1, 1998	1,216
October 28, 1997	1,201
August 27, 1998	938
August 31, 1998	917
September 2, 1998	894
September 10, 1998	880
September 3, 1998	880
August 5, 1998	859
August 4, 1998	852
August 28, 1998	841

NYSE Membership Prices

Year	High	Low	Year	High	Low
1945	$95,000	$49,000	1988	$820,000	$580,000
1955	90,000	80,000	1989	675,000	420,000
1960	162,000	135,000	1990	430,000	250,000
1965	250,000	190,000	1991	440,000	345,000
1970	320,000	130,000	1992	600,000	410,000
1975	138,000	55,000	1993	775,000	500,000
1980	275,000	175,000	1994	830,000	760,000
1985	480,000	310,000	1995	1,050,000	785,000
1986	600,000	455,000	1996	1,450,000	1,225,000
1987	1,150,000	605,000	1997	1,750,000	1,175,000

Listings on the NYSE

End of year	Number of companies	Number of issues	Shares listed (millions) Number	Market value
1977	1,575	2,177	26,093	$ 796,639
1980	1,570	2,228	33,709	1,242,803
1985	1,541	2,298	52,427	1,950,332
1990	1,774	2,284	90,732	2,819,778
1991	1,885	2,426	99,622	3,712,835
1992	2,088	2,658	115,839	4,035,100
1993	2,361	2,904	131,053	4,540,850
1994	2,570	3,060	142,281	4,448,284
1995	2,675	3,126	154,719	6,012,971
1996	2,907	3,285	176,944	7,300,351
1997	3,047	3,358	207,089	9,413,109

Source: New York Stock Exchange

Activity on the Amex

Average Daily Volume on the American Stock Exchange

Year	Average Daily Volume
1970	3,319,355
1975	2,138,079
1980	6,427,165
1985	8,336,568
1990	13,157,780
1991	13,308,784
1992	14,156,651
1993	18,110,724
1994	17,945,357
1995	20,128,255
1996	22,158,216
1997	24,388,515

Most Active Trading Days on the Amex
(As of Sept. 15, 1998)

Date	Volume
September 1, 1998	60,903,040
October 28, 1997	60,347,770
August 27, 1998	53,472,455
August 31, 1998	50,218,560
August 28, 1998	48,521,425
August 5, 1998	46,481,050
October 7, 1997	43,942,875
October 20, 1987	43,432,760
October 15, 1993	42,940,750
October 8, 1997	42,180,600

Amex Membership Prices

Year	High	Low	Year	High	Low
1960	$60,000	$51,000	1989	$215,000	$155,000
1965	80,000	55,000	1990	170,000	83,500
1970	185,000	70,000	1991	120,000	80,000
1975	72,000	34,000	1992	110,000	76,000
1980	252,000	95,000	1993	163,000	92,000
1985	160,000	115,000	1994	205,000	155,000
1986	285,000	145,000	1995	152,000	105,000
1987	420,000	265,000	1996	210,000	150,000
1988	280,000	180,000	1997	420,000	200,000

Listings on the Amex

Year-end	Number of equity issues	Number of shares outstanding	Total Market Value
1970	1,222	2,857,275,369	$39,535,679,374
1975	1,267	3,180,800,830	29,365,930,815
1980	973	4,179,545,476	82,916,682,074
1985	940	6,339,768,349	87,013,822,402
1990	1,063	9,767,749,621	102,301,457,254
1991	1,055	10,814,101,577	124,454,193,457
1992	943	10,177,908,769	109,354,448,986
1993	1,005	10,611,665,000	135,106,852,386
1994	981	10,924,697,000	113,600,509,489
1995	936	10,493,013,000	137,272,115,187
1996	896	11,011,105,039	135,058,498,619
1997	893	10,889,273,005	162,162,957,875

Source: American Stock Exchange

Trading on Nasdaq

Daily Average Volume on the Nasdaq

Year	Average daily share volume (In millions)	Number of active securities
1985	82.1	4,784
1990	131.9	4,706
1991	163.3	4,684
1992	190.8	4,764
1993	263.0	5,393
1994	295.0	5,761
1995	401.4	5,955
1996	543.7	6,384
1997	647.8	6,208

Most Active Trading Days on the Nasdaq
(As of Sept. 15, 1998)

Date	Share volume
October 28, 1997	1,354,164,600
September 1, 1998	1,258,678,800
April 22, 1998	1,026,054,200
August 31, 1998	1,003,780,300
October 1, 1997	970,684,200
August 27, 1998	959,264,000
April 21, 1998	938,570,300
September 2, 1998	938,301,700
October 24, 1997	936,235,800
June 24, 1998	927,393,400

Source: National Association of Securities Dealers

Most Active Stocks on the New York Stock Exchange in 1997

Issue	Reported share volume
Compaq Computer	1,231,586,100
Philip Morris	1,107,800,100
AT&T	1,052,683,300
Micron Technology	1,003,272,800
PepsiCo	879,810,600
Int'l Business Machines	875,730,500
General Electric	840,512,600
Coca-Cola	753,484,100
Wal-Mart Stores	736,662,400
Columbia/HCA Healthcare	700,830,800

Source: New York Stock Exchange

Most Active Stocks on the American Stock Exchange in 1997

	Issue	Share volume (In millions)
1	Viacom (Class B)	223.1
2	Trans World Airlines	222.8
3	Harken Energy	214.5
4	Echo Bay Mines	188.7
5	JTS	177.0
6	Nabors Industries	172.9
7	Hasbro	159.1
8	Royal Oak Mines	140.6
9	Grey Wolf Industries	132.9
10	IVAX	132.5

Source: American Stock Exchange

Most Active Nasdaq National Market Securities in 1997

	Company name	Share volume
1	Intel	3,887,851
2	Cisco Systems	2,693,288
3	3Com	2,200,433
4	Microsoft	2,097,889
5	Oracle	1,970,157
6	Ascend Communications	1,945,994
7	Dell Computer	1,859,496
8	Applied Materials	1,804,235
9	WorldCom	1,784,807
10	Sun Microsystems	1,490,324

Source: Nasdaq Stock Market

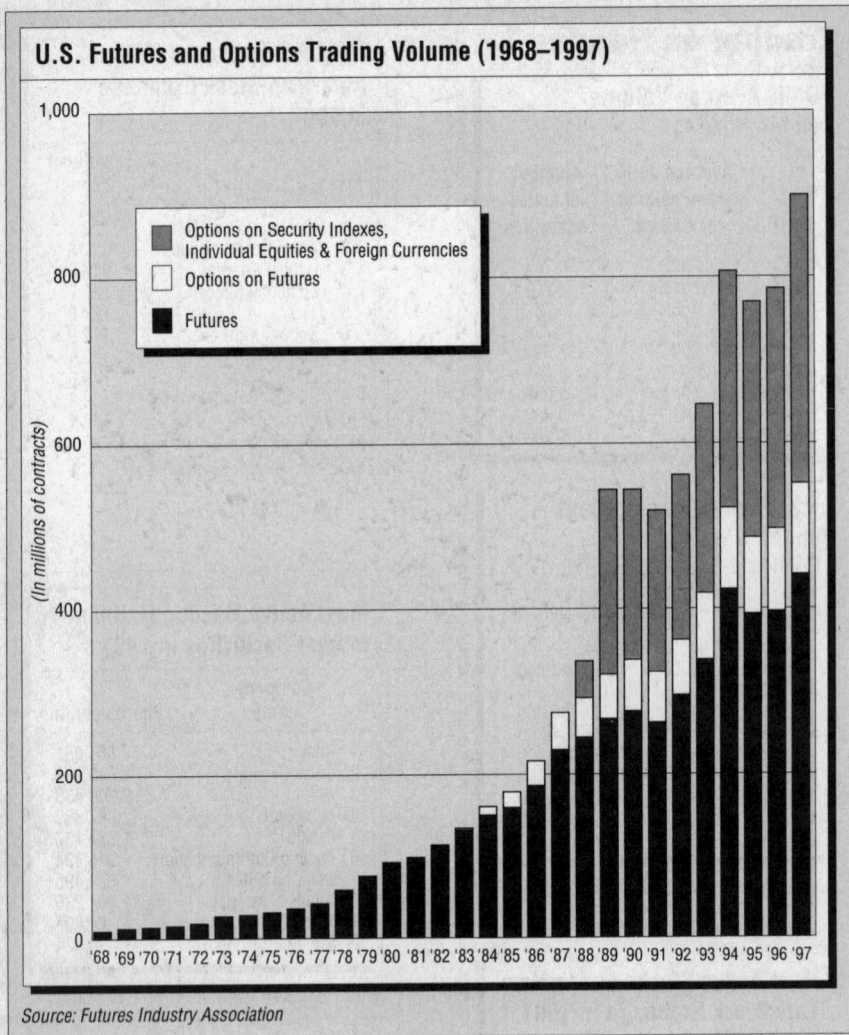

U.S. Futures and Options Trading Volume (1968–1997)

Legend:
- Options on Security Indexes, Individual Equities & Foreign Currencies
- Options on Futures
- Futures

(In millions of contracts)

Source: Futures Industry Association

Total U.S. Futures and Options on U.S. Futures (1972–1990)

Number of contracts

1972	Total U.S. Futures	18,332,055
1973	Total U.S. Futures	25,826,747
1974	Total U.S. Futures	27,733,328
1975	Total U.S. Futures	32,200,106
1976	Total U.S. Futures	36,875,727
1977	Total U.S. Futures	42,847,064
1978	Total U.S. Futures	58,462,172
1979	Total U.S. Futures	75,966,471
1980	Total U.S. Futures	92,096,109
1981	Total U.S. Futures	98,522,371

1982	U.S. Futures	112,400,879
	Options on U.S. Futures	177,350
	(Began trading in 1982)	
	Total	**112,578,229**

1983	U.S. Futures	139,924,940
	Options on U.S. Futures	2,646,865
	Total	**142,571,805**

1984	U.S. Futures	149,372,225
	Options on U.S. Futures	9,928,141
	Total	**159,300,366**

1985	U.S. Futures	158,696,578
	Options on U.S. Futures	20,044,744
	Total	**178,741,322**

1986	U.S. Futures	184,354,496
	Options on U.S. Futures	31,770,613
	Total	**216,125,109**

1987	U.S. Futures	228,876,684
	Options on U.S. Futures	46,185,985
	Total	**275,062,669**

1988	U.S. Futures	245,871,290
	Options on U.S. Futures	49,137,490
	Total	**295,008,780**

1989	U.S. Futures	267,386,263
	Options on U.S. Futures	55,446,130
	Options on U.S. Securities Indexes, Individual Equities & Foreign Currencies	226,657,728
	Total	**549,490,121**

1990	U.S. Futures	276,536,280
	Options on U.S. Futures	64,103,094
	Options on U.S. Securities Indexes, Individual Equities & Foreign Currencies	209,747,484
	Total	**550,386,858**

Source: Futures Industry Association

Total Volume on U.S. Futures, Options on U.S. Futures, and Options on U.S. Securities Indexes and Foreign Currencies (1991–1997)

		Number of contracts
1991	U.S. Futures	262,895,551
	Options on U.S. Futures	62,201,905
	Options on U.S. Securities Indexes, Individual Equities & Foreign Currencies	198,257,932
	Total	**523,355,388**
1992	U.S. Futures	295,292,042
	Options on U.S. Futures	69,244,775
	Options on U.S. Securities Indexes, Individual Equities & Foreign Currencies	201,970,675
	Total	**566,507,492**
1993	U.S. Futures	339,075,626
	Options on U.S. Futures	81,858,635
	Options on U.S. Securities Indexes, Individual Equities & Foreign Currencies	231,377,310
	Total	**652,311,571**
1994	U.S. Futures	426,307,942
	Options on U.S. Futures	100,881,506
	Options on U.S. Securities Indexes, Individual Equities & Foreign Currencies	280,678,941
	Total	**807,868,389**
1995	U.S. Futures	395,313,480
	Options on U.S. Futures	94,208,810
	Options on U.S. Securities Indexes, Individual Equities & Foreign Currencies	287,113,818
	Total	**776,636,108**
1996	U.S. Futures	397,402,153
	Options on U.S. Futures	101,973,807
	Options on U.S. Securities Indexes, Individual Equities & Foreign Currencies	294,256,755
	Total	**793,632,715**
1997	U.S. Futures	443,653,757
	Options on U.S. Futures	111,059,345
	Options on U.S. Securities Indexes, Individual Equities & Foreign Currencies	350,442,359
	Total	**905,155,461**

Source: Futures Industry Association

Top 20 Futures Contracts Traded in 1997

1997 rank	Futures	1997 contracts	%	1996 contracts	%	1996 rank
1	T-bonds, CBOT	99,827,659	22.50	84,725,128	21.32	2
2	Eurodollar, CME	99,770,237	22.49	88,883,119	22.37	1
3	Crude oil, NYMEX	24,771,375	5.58	23,487,821	5.91	3
4	T-notes (10 year), CBOT	23,961,819	5.40	21,939,725	5.52	4
5	S&P 500 index, CME	21,294,584	4.80	19,899,999	5.01	5
6	Corn, CBOT	16,984,951	3.83	19,620,188	4.94	6
7	Soybeans, CBOT	14,539,766	3.28	14,236,295	3.58	7
8	T-notes (5 year), CBOT	13,488,725	3.04	11,463,640	2.88	8
9	Natural gas, NYMEX	11,923,628	2.69	8,813,867	2.22	10
10	Gold (100 oz.), COMEX Div. of NYMEX	9,541,904	2.15	8,902,179	2.24	9
11	#2 heating oil, NYMEX	8,370,964	1.89	8,341,877	2.10	11
12	Unleaded regular gas, NYMEX	7,475,145	1.68	6,312,339	1.59	12
13	Deutschemark, CME	7,044,783	1.59	5,979,464	1.50	13
14	Soybean meal, CBOT	6,424,945	1.45	5,955,977	1.50	14
15	Japanese Yen, CME	6,034,565	1.36	5,101,819	1.28	16
16	Soybean oil, CBOT	5,284,994	1.19	4,980,277	1.25	19
17	Sugar #11, CSC	5,284,971	1.19	4,751,852	1.20	18
18	Wheat, CBOT	5,058,645	1.14	5,385,967	1.36	15
19	Silver (5,000 oz.), COMEX Div. of NYMEX	4,893,520	1.10	4,870,808	1.23	17
20	Swiss Franc, CME	4,222,268	0.95	3,929,225	0.99	20

Source: Futures Industry Association

U.S. Futures Exchange Volume

1997 rank	Exchange	1997 contracts	%	1996 contracts	%	1996 rank
1	Chicago Board of Trade	190,056,287	42.84	171,134,185	43.06	1
2	Chicago Mercantile Exchange	159,975,955	36.06	141,600,469	35.63	2
3	New York Mercantile Exchange (incl. Comex Division)	70,634,699	15.92	64,223,291	16.16	3
4	Coffee Sugar & Cocoa Exchange	10,022,427	2.26	9,102,029	2.29	4
5	New York Cotton Exchange	6,201,235	1.40	4,967,176	1.25	5
6	MidAmerica Commodity Exchange	3,500,791	0.79	3,229,710	0.81	6
7	Kansas City Board of Trade	2,192,694	0.49	2,084,493	0.52	7
8	Minneapolis Grain Exchange	1,040,594	0.23	1,012,598	0.25	8
9	Philadelphia Board of Trade	29,075	0.01	48,202	0.01	9
	Total	**443,653,757**	**100.00**	**397,402,153**	**100.00**	

Source: Futures Industry Association

Volume of Options Traded on U.S. Futures Exchanges

1997 rank	Exchange	1997 contracts	%	1996 contracts	%	1996 rank
1	Chicago Board of Trade	52,642,632	47.40	51,304,320	50.31	1
2	Chicago Mercantile Exchange	40,738,473	36.68	35,421,726	34.74	2
3	New York Mercantile Exchange (incl. Comex Division)	13,216,647	11.90	11,576,001	11.35	3
4	Coffee Sugar & Cocoa Exchange	3,043,615	2.74	2,287,750	2.24	4
5	New York Cotton Exchange	1,232,052	1.11	1,261,109	1.24	5
6	Kansas City Board of Trade	103,879	0.09	68,479	0.07	6
7	Minneapolis Grain Exchange	47,710	0.04	26,891	0.03	8
8	MidAmerica Commodity Exchange	34,337	0.03	27,531	0.03	7
	Total	**111,159,345**	**99.97**	**101,973,807**	**99.97**	

Volume of Options Traded on U.S. Securities Exchanges

1997 rank	Exchange	1997 contracts	%	1996 contracts	%	1996 rank
1	Chicago Board Options Exchange	187,243,742	53.43	173,944,877	59.11	1
2	American Stock Exchange	88,107,842	25.14	61,584,907	20.93	2
3	Pacific Stock Exchange	43,367,640	12.38	33,388,258	11.35	3
4	Philadelphia Stock Exchange	30,351,028	8.66	21,949,833	7.46	4
5	New York Stock Exchange	1,372,107	0.39	3,388,880	1.15	5
	Total	**350,442,359**	**100.00**	**294,256,755**	**100.00**	

Source: Futures Industry Association

Top 20 Options Contracts Traded in 1997*

1997 rank	Options	1997 contracts	%	1996 contracts	%	1996 rank
1	S&P 100 Index, CBOE	36,595,576	7.93	54,929,246	13.86	1
2	T-bonds, CBOT	30,805,885	6.68	25,930,661	6.54	2
3	Eurodollar, CME	29,595,246	6.41	22,234,888	5.61	4
4	S&P 500 Index, CBOE	26,494,543	5.74	24,884,808	6.28	3
5	T-notes (10 year), CBOT	6,032,088	1.31	7,907,650	2.00	5
6	Crude oil, NYMEX	5,790,333	1.25	5,271,456	1.33	7
7	Soybeans, CBOT	5,339,936	1.16	5,135,124	1.30	8
8	Corn, CBOT	4,963,603	1.08	6,602,010	1.67	6
9	S&P 500 Index, CME	4,734,950	1.03	4,636,236	1.17	9
10	T-notes (5 year), CBOT	2,105,792	0.46	2,723,525	0.69	12
11	Natural gas, NYMEX	2,079,607	0.45	1,234,691	0.31	18
12	Gold (1,000 oz.), COMEX Div. of NYMEX	2,064,883	0.45	2,079,663	0.52	13
13	NASDAQ 100, CBOE	2,061,379	0.45	3,216,041	0.81	10
14	Morgan Stanley High Tech 35 Index, AMEX	1,764,963	0.38	1,539,719	0.39	17
15	Dow Jones Industrial Index, CBOE	1,750,485	0.38	—	—	—
16	Wheat, CBOT	1,698,969	0.37	1,886,909	0.48	14
17	Japanese Yen, CME	1,661,417	0.36	1,734,186	0.44	16
18	Deutschemark, CME	1,411,110	0.31	1,822,649	0.46	15
19	Sugar, CSC	1,369,465	0.30	1,094,879	0.28	21
20	Coffee, CSC	1,272,767	0.28	856,710	0.22	24

*Excludes options on individual equities.
Source: Futures Industry Association

Top Works of Art at Auction

Paintings that sold for the highest prices.

Artist	Title	Sale date	Hammer price	With premium
Vincent van Gogh	Portrait du Dr. Gachet (1890)	05/15/90	$75,000,000	$82,500,000
Pierre-Auguste Renoir	Au Moulin de la Galette (1876)	05/17/90	71,000,000	78,100,000
Pablo Picasso	Les Noces de Pierrette (1905)	11/30/89	49,200,000	49,200,000
Vincent van Gogh	Irises (1889)	11/11/87	49,000,000	53,900,000
Pablo Picasso	La Reve (1932)	11/10/97	44,000,000	48,402,500
Pablo Picasso	Yo Picasso (c.1901)	05/09/89	43,500,000	47,850,000
Pablo Picasso	Au Lapin Agile (1905)	11/15/89	37,000,000	40,700,000
Vincent van Gogh	Sunflowers (1889)	03/30/87	36,292,500	39,921,750
Pablo Picasso	Acrobate et Jeune Arlequin (1905)	11/28/88	34,960,000	38,456,000
Pontormo	Portrait of Duke Cosimo I de Medici	05/31/89	32,000,000	35,200,000
Claude Monet	Bassin aux Nympheas et Sentier au Bord de l'Eau (1900)	06/30/98	30,000,600	33,003,160
Pablo Picasso	Les Femmes d'Alger (Version "0") (1955)	11/10/97	29,000,000	31,902,500
Pablo Picasso	Angel Fernandez de Soto (1903)	05/08/95	26,500,000	29,152,500
Paul Cezanne	Nature Morte: Les Grosses Pommes (c.1890)	05/11/93	26,000,000	28,602,500
Vincent van Gogh	Sous-bois (1890)	11/08/95	24,500,000	26,952,500
Vincent van Gogh	Autoportrait (1888)	05/15/90	24,000,000	26,400,000
Édouard Manet	La Rue Mosnier aux Drapeaux (1878)	11/14/89	24,000,000	26,400,000
Pablo Picasso	Le Miroir (1932)	11/15/89	24,000,000	26,400,000
Pablo Picasso	Femme Assisedans un Fauteuil (Eva) (1913)	11/10/97	22,500,000	24,752,500
Pablo Picasso	Maternité (1901)	11/14/88	22,500,000	24,750,000
Claude Monet	Dans la Prairie (1876)	06/28/88	22,230,000	24,453,000
Paul Gauguin	Mata Mua (1892)	05/09/89	22,000,000	24,200,000
Pablo Picasso	Les Tuileries (1901)	06/25/90	21,612,500	23,773,750
Gustav Klimt	Schloss Kammer Am Attersee II	10/09/97	21,442,080	23,588,725
Paul Cezanne	Madame Cezanne au Fauteuil Jaune (1888)	05/12/97	21,000,000	23,102,500

Source: Sotheby's Holdings Inc.

The Art Market

Sales at the two major auction houses have rebounded from the low levels of the early 1990's.

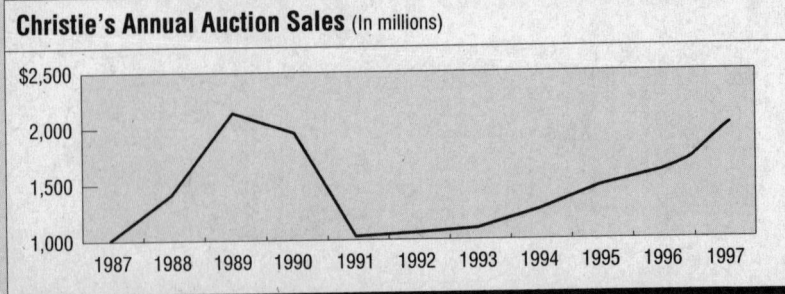

Christie's Annual Auction Sales (In millions)

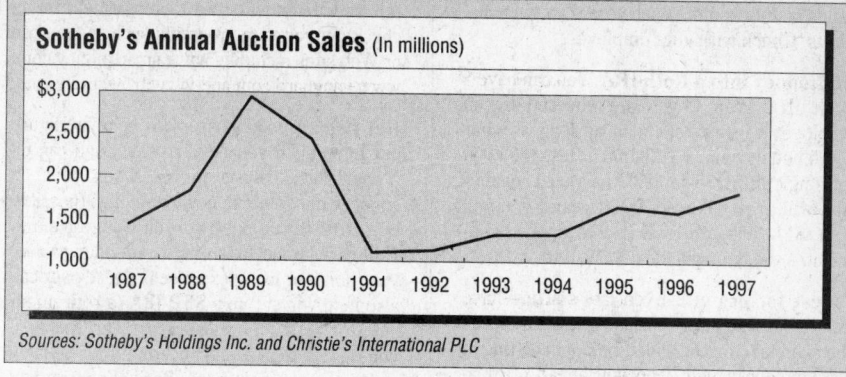

Sotheby's Annual Auction Sales (In millions)

Sources: Sotheby's Holdings Inc. and Christie's International PLC

Personal Finance

Failing to save for retirement is the new midlife crisis of the 1990s.

Plenty of baby boomers in their 40s and 50s are waking up to the fact that they have only 10 or 20 years to save for retirement. Instead of preparing for their golden years, they have been too busy paying for everything else— a home, medical bills, child care, their kids' college.

But retirees of the twenty-first century can still make a huge difference in their standard-of-living after they leave the workplace. On the plus side, many are in their peak earning years and still have time on their side.

Consider: If you are in your 40s, you have 20 to 25 years before retirement, and another 20 to 30 years in retirement. (It's not as if the savings clock stops when people hit 65.) That's 50 years in which your savings could grow and compound. If you are able to save, say, $100 a week, in 20 years you will have $297,830, assuming a 10 percent return. Would you want to turn 65 with zero savings, or $297,830?

Some things to consider if you are just starting:

Downsize your home. If your home has appreciated greatly in value, consider selling it and moving to a less-expensive one now. The new tax law allows you to take as much as $500,000 in capital gains tax free, which you can invest. (The old law allowed only a one-time exclusion of $125,000 in gains from a home sale.) You had to be 55 or older to qualify for that; under the new law, there isn't any age restriction. The new law allows people to take their gains tax free after only two years in a new home. So you could sell the smaller home in a few years when you retire—and again capture the gains tax free.

Restructure your debts. Even if you can't sell your home, consider refinancing your mortgage. People with high credit-card debts might consider consolidating them under a home-equity loan, which could lower their payments and make their interest deductible.

Contribute to your 401(k). If you have a 401(k) or any type of plan at work that lets you set aside pretax pay, contribute as much as you are allowed, if you can afford it. A 401(k) lets you put in up to $10,000 a year (the limit may be lower at your company). The contributions lower your taxable income. And if your employer matches a portion of your contributions, it's like getting a huge boost in your return. (A 50 percent match would be like getting a 50 percent return on your money. Only the most hairy-knuckle investments could give you a return like that. They will also give you a heart attack.) If you are a teacher or nonprofit worker, take advantage of a major break some of these plans offer older workers: They let you make "catch-up" contributions that can be thousands of dollars more each year than the usual limits. Check with your employer.

Put money into a Roth IRA. You can have a Roth IRA even if you are covered by an employer's retirement plan as long as your combined income is $150,000 or less ($95,000 for single filers). The $2,000-a-year contribution will grow tax free. In 20 years, you will have $114,550, tax free. If your spouse contributes too, you will have $229,100.

Invest for growth. Even late-starters have long-term investing horizons, which means they can take on the added risk of investing in stocks. Stocks will keep you ahead of inflation, which historically has run 3 percent a year. But resist the temptation to bet on the riskiest investments in an effort to catch up. You can't afford that kind of risk. Lower-to-moderate-risk stock funds include equity income funds, growth and income funds, balanced funds and utilities funds.

Take stock. Even if you have saved nothing, you are probably not starting out with zero. A middle-income couple in their mid-40s will receive roughly $30,000 a year in retirement from Social Security. (Ignore the hysterical predictions of the system's demise.) Currently, Social Security replaces approximately one-third to 40 percent of average annual pre-retirement income for individuals who earn from $30,000 to $60,000 a year. If that couple has managed to accumulate something by now—whether it is in IRAs, pensions, home equity, a small business—these assets could also generate income in retirement. To figure out how much your assets will generate, and how much you will need to supplement them, check out software programs such as Quicken or Web sites including www.smartmoney.com, www.vanguard.com and www.troweprice.com.

Get help. A good adviser can help you figure out how much you need to save, and can do a cash-flow analysis to see when you can squeeze out some money for savings (possibly by restructuring debt, consolidating or eliminating insurance coverage, and downsizing your home or living expenses). An adviser can also help you set up a SEP-IRA (a retirement plan for self-employed persons) or Keogh if you're self-employed, check out your pension and figure out how much Social Security you are likely to get. For a list of fee-only advisers in your area, call 1-888-333-6659, or check out the Web site www.napfa.org.

Aim to save 10 percent of your gross income. Between your employer's savings plan and IRAs, try to save at least 10 percent of your pretax income. The 401(k) will be easiest because contributions will be taken automatically from your paycheck. To make saving for an IRA easier, set up an automatic-investing program in which a set amount, say $100, is shifted monthly from your credit union or bank account into a mutual fund.

Make it a priority. Don't wait until you have paid off debts or put the kids through college. Some people come up with an annual excuse for why they can't save. Maybe they want to fix up the house on the Cape. Maybe their daughter's getting married. There's always a good reason not to save. Ignore it.

Ellen E. Schultz

Deeper in Debt

Growth of consumer credit in the 1990s, with revolving credit now accounting for a larger share of the total than auto loans.

Consumer Credit Outstanding*
(In billings)

Legend:
- Total
- Automobile
- Revolving
- Other**

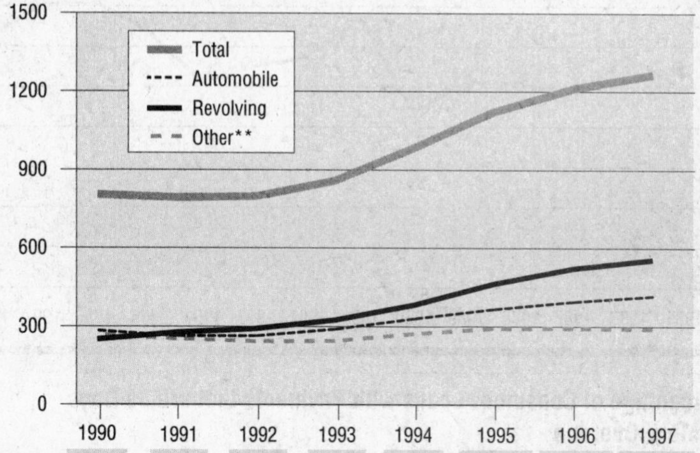

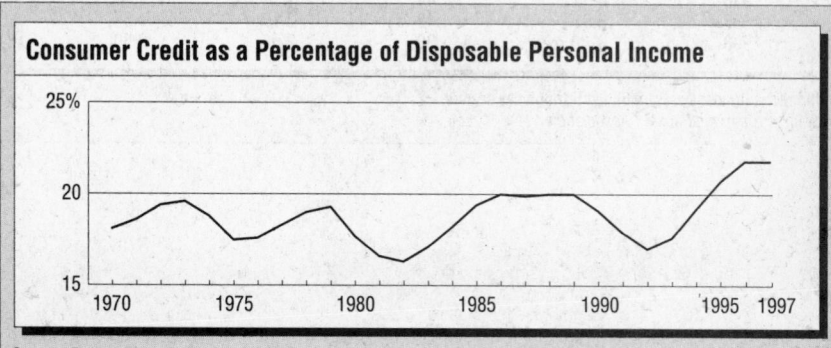

Amount in Dec. of year (In billions)	1990	1991	1992	1993	1994	1995	1996	1997
Total	$805.1	$794.5	$798.3	$859.0	$983.9	$1,122.8	$1,211.6	$1,264.1
Automobile	283.9	264.2	264.0	289.8	330.2	367.1	395.6	417.0
Revolving	250.9	277.1	292.0	325.0	383.2	464.1	522.9	555.9
Other**	270.3	253.2	242.3	244.2	270.5	291.6	293.1	291.3

*Covers most short- and intermediate-term consumer credit, excluding loans secured by real estate.
**Loans for mobile homes, education, vacations and other purposes.
Source: Federal Reserve Board

Consumer Credit as a Percentage of Disposable Personal Income

Source: Federal Reserve Board

Falling Behind

Percentage of Bank Credit Card Accounts with Payments that are 30 Days or More Overdue

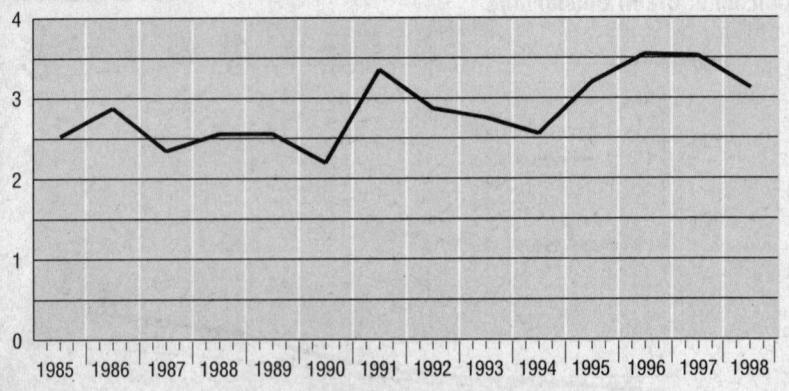

Percentage of Consumer Loans with Payments that are 30 Days or More Overdue

Year, 1st quarter	Bank credit card	Home equity loans	Auto direct	Auto indirect*
1985	2.51%	2.07%	1.63%	2.15%
1986	2.86	1.95	1.82	2.04
1987	2.33	1.66	1.76	2.13
1988	2.54	1.77	1.75	2.04
1989	2.54	1.51	1.73	2.40
1990	2.18	1.47	1.94	2.43
1991	3.34	1.75	2.14	2.66
1992	2.86	1.73	2.37	2.61
1993	2.74	1.48	2.00	2.31
1994	2.54	1.51	1.53	1.64
1995	3.18	1.25	1.45	1.76
1996	3.53	1.44	1.74	2.13
1997	3.51	1.38	2.10	2.55
1998	3.11	1.30	2.06	2.50

*Indirect auto loans are originated through car dealers.
Source: American Bankers Association

Bankruptcy Filings

Total, Business, and Consumer Bankruptcy Filings

Calendar year	Total filings	Business cases	Consumer cases
1982	380,251	69,300	310,951
1983	348,880	62,436	286,444
1984	348,521	64,004	284,517
1985	412,510	71,277	341,233
1986	530,438	81,235	449,203
1987	577,999	82,446	495,553
1988	613,465	63,853	549,612
1989	679,461	63,235	616,226
1990	782,960	64,853	718,107
1991	943,987	71,549	872,438
1992	971,517	70,643	900,874
1993	875,202	62,304	812,898
1994	832,829	52,374	780,455
1995	926,601	51,959	874,642
1996	1,178,555	53,549	1,125,006
1997	1,404,145	54,027	1,350,118

Bankruptcy Filings by Decade

Decade	Total filings
1900–1909	173,298
1910–1919	215,296
1920–1929	410,475
1930–1939	614,938
1940–1949	296,021
1950–1959	584,272
1960–1969	1,695,416
1970–1979	2,086,189
1980–1989	4,586,432
1990–1997	7,915,796

Bankruptcy Filing Trends by State

State	1984	1997	% change	State	1984	1997	% change
Alabama	9,950	34,176	243.48	Montana	948	3,572	276.79
Alaska	433	1,373	217.09	Nebraska	2,565	5,949	131.93
Arizona	4,839	25,069	418.06	Nevada	2,776	13,427	383.68
Arkansas	3,720	15,643	320.51	New Hampshire	497	4,902	886.32
California	61,882	209,499	238.55	New Jersey	6,744	42,434	529.21
Colorado	6,475	19,146	195.69	New Mexico	1,585	7,560	376.97
Connecticut	1,852	13,499	628.89	New York	13,902	74,718	437.46
Delaware	442	2,646	498.64	North Carolina	4,871	26,203	437.94
Dist. of Columbia	636	2,530	297.80	North Dakota	654	1,961	199.85
Florida	8,230	73,483	792.87	Ohio	19,704	53,770	172.89
Georgia	13,090	62,789	379.67	Oklahoma	6,568	22,569	243.62
Hawaii	614	4,463	626.87	Oregon	6,149	18,197	195.93
Idaho	2,233	6,973	212.27	Pennsylvania	9,180	42,967	368.05
Illinois	24,988	63,954	155.94	Rhode Island	713	5,472	667.46
Indiana	11,950	36,808	208.02	South Carolina	2,033	11,232	452.48
Iowa	3,913	9,843	151.55	South Dakota	867	2,366	172.90
Kansas	4,417	13,131	197.28	Tennessee	14,018	52,784	276.54
Kentucky	6,660	21,687	225.63	Texas	14,597	72,729	398.25
Louisiana	6,927	23,158	234.31	Utah	3,583	12,147	239.02
Maine	599	4,218	604.17	Vermont	213	1,911	797.18
Maryland	3,783	31,991	745.65	Virginia	8,531	43,119	405.44
Massachusetts	2,251	23,892	961.40	Washington	10,280	33,337	224.29
Michigan	8,939	39,609	343.10	West Virginia	1,862	8,542	358.75
Minnesota	5,076	20,225	298.44	Wisconsin	7,652	19,197	150.89
Mississippi	4,627	19,269	316.45	Wyoming	979	2,031	107.46
Missouri	6,984	26,115	273.93				

Source: American Bankruptcy Institute

Less Thrift in the '90s

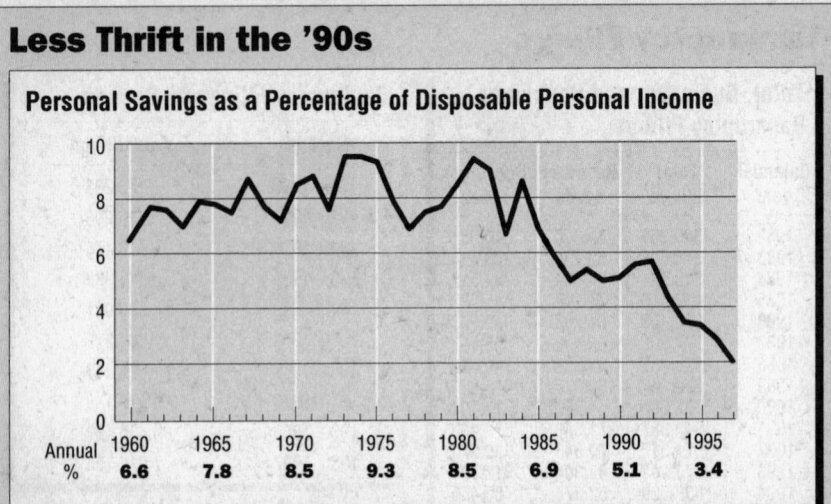

Personal Savings as a Percentage of Disposable Personal Income

Annual %	1960	1965	1970	1975	1980	1985	1990	1995
	6.6	7.8	8.5	9.3	8.5	6.9	5.1	3.4

Source: U.S. Commerce Department, Bureau of Economic Analysis

Family Finances

The Federal Reserve System's 1995 Survey of Consumer Finances reveals that consumers' incomes grew from their depressed 1992 levels, but still lagged 1989 levels. Median net worth reported in 1995 returned to a level nearly equal to that in 1989, but mean net worth remained below the 1989 level. Among family assets, stocks and retirement accounts assumed a bigger share. And as for debt, mortgages grew strongly as a share of family debt, while more families used credit cards and reported higher balances outstanding.

Before-tax Family Income for Previous Year, by Selected Characteristics of Families, 1989, 1992, and 1995, and Percentage of Families Who Saved, 1992 and 1995 (Thousands of 1995 dollars except as noted)

Family characteristics	1989			1992				1995			
	Median	Mean	Percentage of families	Median	Mean	Percentage of families who saved	Percentage of families	Median	Mean	Percentage of families who saved	Percentage of families
All families	$31.8	$49.8	100.0%	$29.1	$43.5	57.1%	100.0%	$30.8	$44.3	55.0%	100.0%
Age of head (years)											
Less than 35	25.8	35.4	27.2	26.8	33.1	59.3	25.8	26.7	31.9	56.4	24.8
35–44	46.3	61.8	23.4	39.1	50.8	57.1	22.8	39.1	48.3	54.1	23.2
45–54	45.7	77.4	14.4	45.5	61.5	59.0	16.2	41.1	64.8	57.6	17.8
55–64	32.1	52.7	13.9	31.6	53.3	59.0	13.2	36.0	52.9	58.5	12.5
65–74	19.3	38.6	12.0	19.3	31.4	53.8	12.6	19.5	37.0	49.6	11.9
75 and more	16.7	28.5	9.0	14.9	25.3	49.2	9.4	17.3	27.3	51.5	9.8
Education of head											
No high school diploma	16.7	23.8	24.3	13.4	19.0	38.3	20.4	15.7	21.9	42.7	19.0
High school diploma	27.3	36.2	32.1	25.8	32.7	56.9	29.9	26.7	35.2	50.9	31.6
Some college	36.0	50.3	15.1	30.5	40.3	59.9	17.7	29.8	39.9	54.2	19.0
College degree	51.4	87.0	28.5	48.6	70.8	67.8	31.9	46.3	70.4	67.5	30.5
Current work status of head											
Professional, managerial	55.5	76.6	16.9	50.9	69.8	68.9	16.8	54.4	72.7	67.9	15.9
Technical, sales, clerical	35.2	43.6	13.4	35.8	41.6	64.5	14.8	34.4	46.2	56.3	14.9
Precision production	47.6	50.9	9.6	36.1	43.4	65.6	7.0	41.1	43.8	60.0	8.2
Machine operators and laborers	30.9	35.4	10.6	29.1	34.1	57.6	10.0	32.9	35.6	60.9	13.1
Service occupations	19.3	25.8	6.6	21.3	28.7	51.5	6.2	21.1	27.2	50.2	6.6
Self-employed	48.1	111.0	11.2	48.6	82.2	59.2	10.9	39.0	79.0	62.3	9.7
Retired	17.3	28.4	25.0	16.5	24.9	48.0	26.0	17.5	27.3	46.1	25.0
Other not working	9.0	17.6	6.7	12.3	22.9	41.6	8.2	12.3	19.9	31.4	6.5
Net Worth (1995 dollars)											
Less than 10,000	13.9	19.2	27.8	14.8	19.8	39.3	27.0	15.4	18.9	36.0	25.8
10,000–24,999	27.1	29.5	9.3	26.2	29.5	52.5	10.4	25.7	28.4	54.1	10.0
25,000–49,999	29.6	33.6	10.1	25.8	30.4	50.0	11.4	32.0	33.9	48.2	11.6
50,000–99,999	36.0	39.5	14.6	32.8	35.9	61.3	15.3	35.2	38.2	57.8	16.9
100,000–249,999	42.9	52.2	21.6	40.9	48.0	67.6	20.7	39.4	47.6	64.4	21.3
250,000 and more	72.0	128.4	16.5	70.0	106.5	78.6	15.2	68.4	111.6	78.2	14.4

Source: Federal Reserve System

Family Net Worth, by Selected Characteristics of Families, 1989, 1992, and 1995 (Thousands of 1995 dollars except as noted)

Family characteristics	1989			1992			1995		
	Median	Mean	Percentage of families	Median	Mean	Percentage of families	Median	Mean	Percentage of families
All families	$56.5	$216.7	100.0%	$52.8	$200.5	100.0%	$56.4	$205.9	100.0%
*Income (1995 dollars)**									
Less than 10,000	1.6	26.1	15.4	3.3	30.9	15.5	4.8	45.6	16.0
10,000–24,999	25.6	77.9	24.3	28.2	71.2	27.8	30.0	74.6	26.5
25,000–49,999	56.0	121.8	30.3	54.8	124.4	29.5	54.9	119.3	31.1
50,000–99,999	128.1	229.5	22.3	121.2	240.8	20.0	121.1	256.0	20.2
100,000 and more	474.7	1,372.9	7.7	506.1	1,283.6	7.1	485.9	1,435.2	6.1
Age of head (years)									
Less than 35	9.2	66.3	27.2	10.1	50.3	25.8	11.4	47.2	24.8
35–44	69.2	171.3	23.4	46.0	144.3	22.8	48.5	144.5	23.2
45–54	114.0	338.9	14.4	83.4	287.8	16.2	90.5	277.8	17.8
55–64	110.5	334.4	13.9	122.5	358.6	13.2	110.8	356.2	12.5
65–74	88.4	336.8	12.0	105.8	308.3	12.6	104.1	331.6	11.9
75 and more	83.2	250.8	9.0	92.8	231.0	9.4	95.0	276.0	9.8
Education of head									
No high school diploma	28.5	92.1	24.3	21.6	75.8	20.4	26.3	87.2	19.0
High school diploma	43.4	134.4	32.1	41.4	120.6	29.9	50.0	138.2	31.6
Some college	56.4	213.8	15.1	62.6	185.4	17.7	43.2	186.6	19.0
College degree	132.1	416.9	28.5	103.1	363.3	31.9	104.1	361.8	30.5

*For the calendar year preceding the survey.
Source: Federal Reserve System

Family Holdings of Financial Assets, 1995

Family characteristic	Transaction accounts	CDs	Savings bonds	Bonds	Stocks	Mutual funds	Retirement accounts	Life insurance	Other managed	Other financial	Any financial asset
	Percentage of families holding asset										
All families	87.1%	14.1%	22.9%	3.0%	15.3%	12.0%	43.0%	31.4%	3.8%	11.0%	90.8%
Income (1995 dollars)											
Less than 10,000	61.1	7.2	5.9	–	2.5	1.8	5.9	15.8	–	8.9	68.1
10,000–24,999	82.3	16.0	11.8	–	9.2	4.9	24.2	25.2	3.2	8.6	87.6
25,000–49,999	94.7	13.7	27.4	3.2	14.3	12.4	52.6	33.1	4.2	13.2	97.8
50,000–99,999	98.6	15.6	39.9	4.8	26.0	20.9	69.8	42.5	5.3	11.3	99.5
100,000 and more	100.0	21.1	36.3	14.5	45.2	38.0	84.6	54.1	8.0	15.2	100.0
Age of head (years)											
Less than 35	80.8	7.1	21.1	0.5	11.1	8.8	39.2	22.3	1.6	13.5	87.0
35–44	87.4	8.2	31.0	1.6	14.5	10.5	51.5	28.9	3.4	10.5	92.0
45–54	88.9	12.5	25.1	4.6	17.5	16.0	54.3	37.5	2.9	13.0	92.4
55–64	88.2	16.2	19.6	2.9	14.9	15.2	47.2	37.5	7.1	9.0	90.5
65–74	91.9	23.9	17.0	5.1	18.0	13.7	35.0	37.0	5.6	10.4	92.0
75 and more	93.0	34.1	15.3	7.0	21.3	10.4	16.5	35.1	5.7	5.3	93.8
	Median value of holdings for families holding asset (Thousands of 1995 dollars)										
All families	$2.1	$10.0	$1.0	$26.2	$8.0	$19.0	$15.6	$5.0	$30.0	$3.0	$13.0
Income (1995 dollars)											
Less than 10,000	0.7	7.0	0.4	–	2.0	25.0	3.5	1.5	–	2.0	1.2
10,000–24,999	1.4	10.0	0.8	–	5.7	8.0	6.0	3.0	19.7	2.0	5.4
25,000–49,999	2.0	10.0	0.7	29.0	6.9	12.5	10.0	5.0	25.0	2.5	12.1
50,000–99,999	4.5	13.0	1.2	9.4	5.7	15.0	23.0	7.0	35.0	3.0	40.7
100,000 and more	15.8	15.6	1.5	58.0	30.0	48.0	85.0	12.0	62.5	23.0	214.5
Age of head (years)											
Less than 35	1.2	6.0	0.5	2.0	3.7	5.0	5.2	3.4	3.8	1.0	5.3
35–44	2.0	6.0	1.0	11.0	4.0	10.0	12.0	5.0	10.8	2.0	11.6
45–54	2.7	12.0	1.0	17.0	10.0	17.5	25.0	6.5	43.0	5.0	24.8
55–64	3.0	14.0	1.1	10.0	17.0	55.0	32.8	6.0	42.0	9.0	32.3
65–74	3.0	17.0	1.5	58.0	15.0	50.0	28.5	5.0	26.0	9.0	19.1
75 and more	5.0	11.0	4.0	40.0	25.0	50.0	17.5	5.0	100.0	35.0	20.9

Source: Federal Reserve System

Family Holdings of Debt, 1995

Family characteristic	Mortgage and home equity	Installment	Other lines of creit	Credit card	Investment real estate	Other debt	Any debt
	Percentage of families holding debt						
All families	41.1%	46.5%	1.9%	47.8%	6.3%	9.0%	75.2%
Income (1995 dollars)							
Less than 10,000	8.9	25.9	–	25.4	1.6	6.6	48.5
10,000–24,999	24.8	41.3	1.4	41.9	2.5	8.7	67.3
25,000–49,999	47.3	54.3	2.0	56.7	5.8	8.5	83.9
50,000–99,999	68.7	60.7	3.2	62.8	9.5	10.0	89.9
100,000 and more	73.6	37.0	4.0	37.0	27.9	15.8	86.4
Age of head (years)							
Less than 35	32.9	62.2	2.6	55.4	2.6	7.8	83.8
35–44	54.1	60.7	2.2	55.8	6.5	11.1	87.2
45–54	61.9	54.0	2.3	57.3	10.4	14.1	86.5
55–64	45.8	36.0	1.4	43.4	12.5	7.5	75.2
65–74	24.8	16.7	1.3	31.3	5.0	5.5	54.5
75 and more	7.1	9.6	–	18.3	1.5	3.6	30.1
	Median value of holdings for families holding debt (Thousands of 1995 dollars)						
All families	$51.0	$6.1	$3.5	$1.5	$28.0	$2.0	$22.5
Income (1995 dollars)							
Less than 10,000	14.0	2.9	–	0.6	15.0	2.0	2.6
10,000–24,999	26.0	3.9	3.0	1.2	18.3	1.2	9.2
25,000–49,999	46.0	6.6	3.0	1.4	25.0	1.5	23.4
50,000–99,999	68.0	9.0	2.2	2.2	34.0	2.5	65.0
100,000 and more	103.4	8.5	19.5	3.0	36.8	7.0	112.2
Age of head (years)							
Less than 35	63.0	7.0	1.4	1.4	22.8	1.5	15.2
35–44	60.0	5.6	2.0	1.8	30.0	1.7	37.6
45–54	48.0	7.0	5.7	2.0	28.1	2.5	41.0
55–64	36.0	5.9	3.5	1.3	26.0	4.0	25.8
65–74	19.0	4.9	3.8	0.8	36.0	2.0	7.7
75 and more	15.9	3.9	–	0.4	8.0	3.0	2.0

Source: Federal Reserve System

Bringing Up Baby

Estimated Annual Expenditures on a Child by Husband-Wife Families in 1997

Age of child	Total	Housing	Food	Transpor-tation	Clothing	Health care	Child care and education	Miscel-laneous*
Before-tax income: Less than $35,500 (Average = $22,100)								
0–2	$5,820	$2,220	$ 830	$ 730	$370	$400	$690	$580
3–5	5,920	2,190	920	700	360	380	780	590
6–8	6,070	2,120	1,190	820	410	440	460	630
9–11	6,090	1,910	1,420	890	450	480	280	660
12–14	6,880	2,130	1,490	1,000	760	480	200	820
15–17	6,790	1,720	1,610	1,350	670	510	330	600
Before-tax income: $35,500 to $59,700 (Average = $47,200)								
0–2	$8,060	$3,000	$ 990	$1,090	$440	$520	$1,130	$ 890
3–5	8,270	2,970	1,140	1,060	430	500	1,260	910
6–8	8,350	2,900	1,460	1,180	480	570	810	950
9–11	8,320	2,700	1,710	1,250	530	620	530	980
12–14	9,050	2,920	1,730	1,360	890	620	390	1,140
15–17	9,170	2,500	1,920	1,720	790	660	660	920
Before-tax income: More than $59,700 (Average = $89,300)								
0–2	$11,990	$4,770	$1,310	$1,520	$580	$600	$1,710	$1,500
3–5	12,230	4,740	1,480	1,490	570	580	1,860	1,510
6–8	12,180	4,670	1,790	1,610	620	660	1,280	1,550
9–11	12,090	4,470	2,080	1,680	680	710	890	1,580
12–14	12,930	4,690	2,180	1,790	1,120	710	690	1,750
15–17	13,260	4,270	2,300	2,180	1,020	750	1,210	1,530

*Miscellaneous expenses include personal care items, entertainment, and reading materials.

Total Estimated Expenditures on Children Born in 1997 to Age 18, by Income Group

Lowest	Middle	Highest
$178,840	$242,890	$353,130

Source: U.S. Agriculture Department

CD and Money Market Rates (National average)

Date	Money market	Certificates of Deposit				
		3 month CD	6 month CD	1 year CD	2 year CD	5 year CD
June 1998	3.48	4.01	4.64	4.90	5.02	5.23
March 1998	3.39	4.03	4.65	4.89	5.03	5.26
December 1997	3.45	4.11	4.80	5.06	5.25	5.47
September 1997	3.47	4.13	4.78	5.06	5.31	5.55
June 1997	3.50	4.17	4.81	5.11	5.39	5.64
March 1997	3.45	4.08	4.71	4.96	5.18	5.47
December 1996	3.47	4.06	4.69	4.95	5.15	5.44
September 1996	3.46	4.10	4.72	4.99	5.23	5.50
June 1996	3.46	4.06	4.65	4.90	5.11	5.38

Source: BanxQuote Inc., www.banx.com

Consumer Loan Rates (National average)

| | Mortgage loans | | | | | | Car loans | | | | | |
| | Conforming | | | Jumbo | | | New | | | Used | | |
Date	15 year	30 year	1 year ARM	15 year	30 year	1 year ARM	36 month	48 month	60 month	1 year old	2 year old	3 year old
June 1998	6.75	7.05	6.07	7.01	7.34	6.26	9.35	9.43	9.49	—	10.18	10.40
March 1998	6.78	7.13	6.03	7.11	7.44	6.25	9.23	9.30	9.37	9.92	10.07	10.29
December 1997	6.90	7.23	6.04	7.20	7.53	6.06	9.25	9.32	9.40	9.90	10.09	10.31
September 1997	7.11	7.48	5.92	7.40	7.66	5.93	9.27	9.35	9.44	9.92	10.10	10.32
June 1997	7.50	7.88	6.06	7.67	7.99	6.11	9.36	9.43	9.51	10.05	10.19	10.41
March 1997	7.68	8.11	6.05	7.85	8.21	6.09	9.27	9.33	9.40	9.93	10.10	10.33
December 1996	7.35	7.81	5.79	7.58	7.98	5.89	9.26	9.34	9.42	9.90	10.10	10.31
September 1996	7.94	8.40	6.23	8.21	8.62	6.36	9.26	9.33	9.42	9.90	10.10	10.31
June 1996	7.93	8.41	6.25	8.24	8.73	6.35	9.24	9.32	9.41	9.90	10.09	10.32

| | Boat loan | RV loan | Credit cards | | | | Home equity | | | Unsecured |
| | New | New | Standard | | Gold | | Loan | | Line | Personal loan |
Date	Rate	Rate	Fixed rate	Var. rate	Fixed rate	Var. rate	5 year fixed	10 year fixed	Adj. rate	Rate
June 1998	10.20	10.43	15.41	15.83	14.85	15.29	9.06	9.28	9.35	13.96
March 1998	10.27	10.40	16.23	15.61	15.92	15.27	9.09	9.30	9.44	14.01
December 1997	10.50	10.62	16.51	15.71	16.24	15.00	9.35	9.53	9.52	14.13
September 1997	10.40	10.51	17.07	15.84	16.84	15.07	9.54	9.73	9.61	14.21
June 1997	10.55	10.73	16.94	15.72	16.70	15.10	9.64	9.89	9.71	14.16
March 1997	10.47	10.63	16.91	15.66	16.44	14.82	9.55	9.86	9.60	13.91
December 1996	10.44	10.57	16.69	15.69	16.18	14.85	9.59	9.89	9.62	13.89
September 1996	10.45	10.54	16.74	15.68	16.17	14.83	9.57	9.89	9.72	13.65
June 1996	10.43	10.60	16.74	15.61	16.17	14.74	9.53	9.85	9.60	13.89

Source: BanxQuote Inc., www.banx.com

Charge It

Charge Volume and Market Share of Major Credit Card Brands
($ billions charge volume)

Year	Visa	Market share	MasterCard	Market share	American Express	Market share	Discover	Market share	Total
1986	$ 85.2	44.5%	$ 57.3	30.0%	$ 46.8	24.5%	$ 2.0	1.0%	$191.3
1987	98.1	43.4	68.4	30.3	53.5	23.7	5.9	2.6	225.9
1988	116.1	44.5	74.9	28.7	61.2	23.4	8.8	3.4	261.0
1989	128.2	43.3	83.4	28.1	71.9	24.3	12.8	4.3	296.3
1990	151.2	44.7	93.1	27.5	77.6	22.9	16.5	4.9	338.4
1991	163.4	45.3	99.1	27.5	76.7	21.2	21.8	6.0	361.0
1992	180.9	44.9	112.3	27.9	82.4	20.4	27.5	6.8	403.1
1993	215.4	45.2	138.6	29.1	89.8	18.8	32.9	6.9	476.7
1994	273.4	46.8	170.8	29.2	101.2	17.3	39.4	6.7	584.8
1995	340.5	48.6	198.0	28.2	115.2	16.4	47.5	6.8	701.2
1996	393.1	49.2	220.6	27.6	131.0	16.4	53.6	6.7	798.3
1997	431.8	48.7	246.2	27.8	150.5	17.0	56.7	6.4	885.2

Source: CardWeb Inc.'s CardData, www.carddata.com

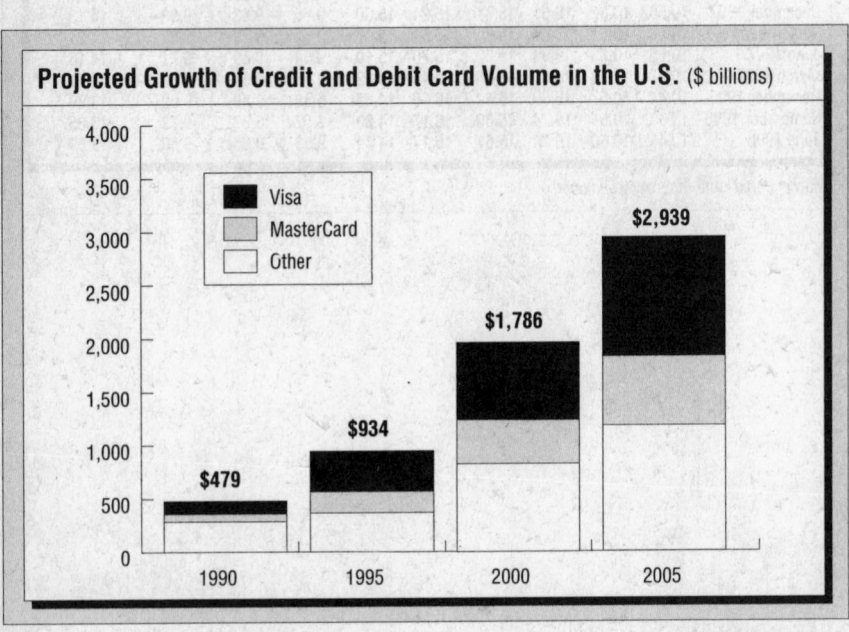

Projected Growth of Credit and Debit Card Volume in the U.S. ($ billions)

Legend: Visa, MasterCard, Other

1990: $479
1995: $934
2000: $1,786
2005: $2,939

Debit Card Growth in 1997

	Visa		MasterCard		Total	
Cards (In thousands)	58,056	+27%	22,400	+44%	80,456	+32%
Transactions (In millions)	2,052.8	+66%	412.4	+93%	2,465.2	+70%
Total Volume (In billions)	$93.69	+72%	$16.75	+93%	$110.44	+75%

20 Largest Bank Credit Card Issuers in the U.S. – 1997, Ranked by Amount Outstanding

Issuer	'97 rank	'96 rank	Amount outstanding	Change vs. '96	'97 rank	'96 rank	Charge volume	Change vs. '96	'97 rank	'96 rank	Credit cards	Change vs. '96
Citibank	1	1	$48,200,000,000	+3%	1	1	$102,800,000,000	+7%	1	1	39,600,000	+4%
MBNA America	2	2	41,707,000,000	+18	2	2	58,076,652,000	+24	4	3	27,319,100	+13
Bank One/First USA	3	4	38,483,500,000	+19	4	8	41,813,524,000	+17	2	7	31,998,700	+15
Chase Manhattan	4	3	32,500,000,000	+29	5	5	39,800,000,000	+22	3	2	30,100,000	+24
First Chicago NBD	5	6	18,081,345,112	0	3	3	47,081,653,214	+4	7	5	21,113,141	-7
Household Bank	6	5	17,314,186,000	-5	6	4	34,232,106,000	+2	6	6	21,184,000	+3
AT&T Universal	7	7	15,300,000,000	+13	7	6	27,700,000,000	+10	5	4	24,200,000	+5
Capital One	8	9	13,620,701,000	+9	11	13	19,816,565,853	+38	8	9	17,503,030	+37
Advanta	9	8	11,244,601,000	-11	12	12	12,243,000,000	-18	11	13	10,959,053	+49
Bank of America	10	10	10,444,000,000	+3	10	9	21,842,000,000	+10	9	10	14,427,900	+17
NationsBank	11	12	9,084,639,000	+2	9	7	23,186,637,000	+13	12	11	9,865,400	+6
Providian	12	14	7,800,000,000	+13	14	15	8,700,000,000	+7	15	21	6,140,000	+31
Wells Fargo	13	13	7,345,169,246	+3	13	14	11,284,298,214	+18	14	16	6,536,962	+2
First Union	14	15	6,292,755,414	-5	17	19	6,840,164,674	+3	16	15	6,018,292	-6
US Bancorp	15	20	6,037,200,000	+37	8	10	25,937,400,000	+36	19	25	4,587,273	+37
Wachovia Bank	16	16	6,002,561,067	+11	16	18	7,940,324,055	+18	17	19	5,577,117	+13
Associates Nat'l	17	19	5,833,422,450	+19	18	21	6,370,004,450	+17	10	12	13,985,250	+53
GE Capital	18	22	5,379,000,000	+50	21	23	5,752,800,000	+23	13	14	8,856,400	+31
Chevy Chase FSB	19	18	5,100,000,000	+4	19	20	6,171,900,000	+5	21	24	3,735,256	+1
PNC Bank	20	25	3,834,528,460	+38	20	42	5,760,524,901	+253	20	20	4,387,308	-9

Source: The Nilson Report

Credit Reports

Consumer advocates urge people to review their credit reports at least once a year to detect any errors and make sure they are up-to-date. Here are the three major credit-reporting agencies:

Equifax P.O. Box 105873 Atlanta, GA 30348	800-685-1111	Free if credit has been denied; otherwise, $8 per report in most states
Experian P.O. Box 2104 Allen, TX 75013-2104	800-682-7654	Free if credit has been denied; otherwise, $8 per report in most states
Trans Union Corp. P.O. Box 390 Springfield, PA 19064-0390	800-888-4213	Free if credit has been denied; otherwise, $8 per report in most states

Tax Report

The wide-ranging tax legislation enacted July 22, 1998, is a grab bag of goodies for investors, many homeowners and other individuals.

One significant provision will cut by a third the length of time an investor must hold a stock, bond or other investment to qualify for the most favorable capital-gains tax rate. Another will effectively wipe out most or all taxes for many people who make a profit on selling a home they have owned for fewer than two years.

Other provisions will mean significant changes in the way some people interact with the Internal Revenue Service. Separated or divorced taxpayers will find it easier to avoid getting hit by tax debts run up by a spouse or ex-spouse. Taxpayers in general will have more defenses against overzealous IRS agents.

But the legislation also has some losers. Among those will be any investor who thought lawmakers would actually allow people to take advantage of a change in the 1997 tax law that would have given savers an unintended windfall.

Here is a closer look at some of the more significant provisions:

CAPITAL GAINS. The bill reduces the capital-gains holding period, effective retroactively to January 1, 1998, eliminating a complex timing requirement introduced by the 1997 tax law. As a result, investors will no longer be required to hold stocks, bonds and certain other types of investments for more than 18 months to pay taxes on their profits at the most favorable rates. The new holding period will now be more than 12 months, as it was before the 1997 tax law.

The 1997 law created a wide variety of capital-gains tax rates. Generally, that law cut the top, long-term capital-gains rate to 20 percent from 28 percent, although the rate is only 10 percent for gains that would otherwise be in the 15 percent income-tax bracket.

Reducing the holding period to 12 months isn't expected to have a big impact on the stock market. But some analysts say it could make stocks, especially riskier stocks, mar-

ginally more attractive. It also could encourage some investors to take profits sooner, thereby leading to more short-term trading.

HOME SALES. Under the 1997 law, married couples generally may exclude a gain of as much as $500,000 from the sale of their principal residence. For singles, the limit is $250,000. To qualify for that full exclusion, you must have owned your home and lived in it for at least two of the five years prior to the sale.

But what if you sell a home you have owned for less than two years? The 1997 law didn't provide a clear answer, but the new legislation does. It says you are entitled to partial relief based on a fraction of the maximum exclusion (that's the $500,000 for married couples, $250,000 for singles), rather than a fraction of your actual realized profit.

While that may sound arcane and confusing, it can also make an enormous difference, as illustrated by the following hypothetical examples:

Winners. A couple buys a house in early 1997 for $250,000 and sells a year later, because of a job change, for $275,000, making a quick $25,000 profit. Because they have lived there for a year, they are eligible for half of the $500,000 exemption they would have qualified for if they had remained in the house for two years. Because that amount is greater than their actual gain of $25,000, they owe no tax on the sale. If the alternative interpretation had applied, they would have been able to exclude only half their actual $25,000 gain, requiring them to pay tax on the remaining $12,500.

Losers. A woman pays $1.5 million for her home in early 1997 in a hot real-estate market. She switches jobs a year later and sells the home for $1.9 million, collecting a hefty $400,000 profit. The house was her principal residence for one year, so she is eligible for only half of the $250,000 exemption for singles. Thus, she may exclude $125,000 of her gain, resulting in a taxable gain of $275,000. If the alternative interpretation had applied, she would have excluded half of her actual $400,000 gain, resulting in a taxable gain of only $200,000. So she would have been better off if Congress hadn't made this fix.

Congress agreed to make this provision generally effective for sales and exchanges after May 6, 1997.

IRA LOOPHOLE. A potentially significant blooper in the 1997 law would have allowed some people to yank money out of tax-deferred accounts without getting hit by the usual 10 percent penalty on early withdrawals.

Under the 1997 law, taxpayers making $100,000 a year or less could convert an existing individual retirement account into a Roth IRA starting in 1998. They could then close the new Roth IRA right away, spread their tax payments over four years and avoid the 10 percent penalty. Congress now has slammed that door shut.

There is some consolation, though. Taxpayers converting an existing IRA to a Roth IRA will no longer be required to spread the taxes over four years. This may be a benefit for people who expect to be in higher tax brackets in years to come and, thus, would like to pay their tax bill in the year of conversion, says Martin Nissenbaum, national director of personal income-tax planning at Ernst & Young in New York.

Tom Herman

Federal Tax Collections
(In thousands of dollars)

Fiscal year	Total Internal Revenue collections	Total income and profit taxes	Corporation income and profit taxes	Individual income taxes	Employment taxes	Estate and gift taxes	Excise taxes
1970	$195,722,096	$138,688,568	$35,036,983	$103,651,585	$37,449,188	$3,680,076	$15,904,264
1975	293,822,726	202,146,097	45,746,660	156,399,437	70,140,809	4,688,079	16,847,741
1980	519,375,273	359,927,392	72,379,610	287,547,782	128,330,480	6,498,381	24,619,021
1985	742,871,541	474,072,327	77,412,769	396,659,558	225,214,568	6,579,703	37,004,944
1986	782,251,812	497,406,391	80,441,620	416,964,771	243,978,380	7,194,956	33,672,086
1987	886,290,590	568,311,471	102,858,985	465,452,486	277,000,469	7,667,670	33,310,980
1988	935,106,594	583,349,120	109,682,554	473,666,566	318,038,990	7,784,445	25,934,040
1989	1,013,322,133	632,746,069	117,014,564	515,731,504	345,625,586	8,973,146	25,977,333
1990	1,056,365,652	650,244,947	110,016,539	540,228,408	367,219,321	11,761,939	27,139,445
1991	1,086,851,401	660,475,445	113,598,569	546,876,876	384,451,220	11,473,141	30,451,596
1992	1,120,799,558	675,673,952	117,950,796	557,723,156	400,080,904	11,479,116	33,565,587
1993	1,176,685,625	717,321,668	131,547,509	585,774,159	411,510,516	12,890,965	34,962,476
1994	1,276,466,776	774,023,837	154,204,684	619,819,153	443,831,352	15,606,793	43,004,794
1995	1,375,731,835	850,201,510	174,422,173	675,779,337	465,405,305	15,144,394	44,980,627
1996	1,486,546,674	934,368,068	189,054,791	745,313,276	492,365,178	17,591,817	42,221,611
1997	1,623,272,071	1,029,513,216	204,492,336	825,020,880	528,596,833	20,356,401	44,805,621

Source: Internal Revenue Service

Assessing the Tax Burden

Tax Freedom Day

Tax Freedom Day denotes the number of days that the average American must work each year to pay all federal, state and local taxes.

Year	Tax Freedom Day	Year	Tax Freedom Day	Year	Tax Freedom Day
1902	January 31	1950	April 3	1995	May 6
1913	January 30	1960*	April 16	1996*	May 7
1922	February 17	1970	April 26	1997	May 9
1930	February 13	1980*	May 1		
1940*	March 8	1990	May 2		

*Leap year makes Tax Freedom Day appear a day earlier.

Total Taxes as a Percentage of Total Income

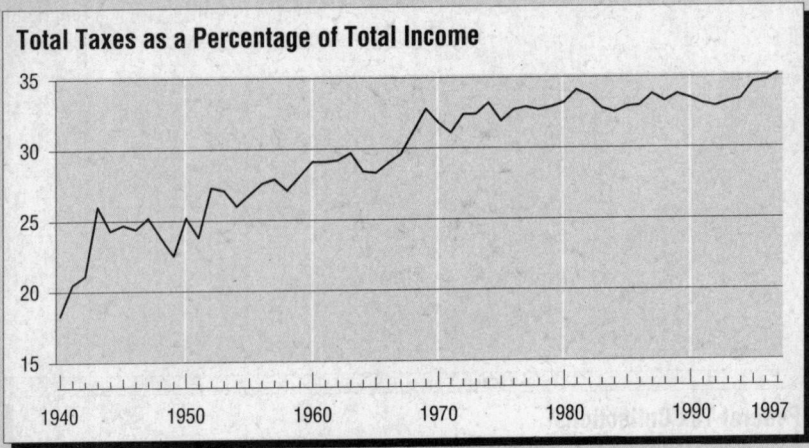

Total Taxes as a Percentage of Total Income

Year	%	Year	%	Year	%
1940	18.3	1970	31.7	1992	32.9
1945	24.7	1975	31.9	1993	33.3
1950	25.2	1980	33.3	1994	33.8
1955	26.8	1985	32.7	1995	34.4
1960	29.2	1990	33.2	1996	34.9
1965	28.3	1991	33.2	1997	35.2

Source: Tax Foundation

Taxes Per Capita and as a Percent of Income, 1997

	Per Capita Taxes				Taxes as a Percent of Income		
	Total	Federal	State & local	Per capita income	Total	Federal	State & local
United States	$9,205	$6,127	$3,078	$26,187	35.2%	23.4%	11.8%
Alabama	6,982	4,923	2,060	21,732	32.1	22.7	9.5
Alaska	8,922	6,780	2,142	25,954	34.4	26.1	8.3
Arizona	8,114	5,239	2,875	23,709	34.2	22.1	12.1
Arkansas	6,780	4,523	2,257	20,766	32.6	21.8	10.9
California	9,321	6,287	3,034	27,117	34.4	23.2	11.2
Colorado	9,705	6,521	3,184	27,624	35.1	23.6	11.5
Connecticut	13,709	9,091	4,618	35,341	38.8	25.7	13.1
Delaware	9,939	6,798	3,141	29,752	33.4	22.8	10.6
Florida	9,172	6,286	2,886	26,438	34.7	23.8	10.9
Georgia	8,393	5,666	2,727	25,370	33.1	22.3	10.8
Hawaii	9,609	6,070	3,539	26,504	36.3	22.9	13.4
Idaho	7,389	4,861	2,529	21,779	33.9	22.3	11.6
Illinois	10,271	7,042	3,229	28,390	36.2	24.8	11.4
Indiana	8,243	5,717	2,526	24,003	34.3	23.8	10.5
Iowa	8,295	5,286	3,009	23,611	35.1	22.4	12.7
Kansas	8,780	5,742	3,038	24,520	35.8	23.4	12.4
Kentucky	7,324	4,757	2,568	21,415	34.2	22.2	12.0
Louisiana	6,750	4,660	2,090	21,321	31.7	21.9	9.8
Maine	7,811	5,063	2,747	22,247	35.1	22.8	12.3
Maryland	10,474	7,044	3,431	29,297	35.8	24.0	11.7
Massachusetts	11,027	7,600	3,427	31,617	34.9	24.0	10.8
Michigan	9,533	6,409	3,124	26,934	35.4	23.8	11.6
Minnesota	9,997	6,358	3,638	27,512	36.3	23.1	13.2
Mississippi	6,397	4,084	2,313	18,924	33.8	21.6	12.2
Missouri	8,421	5,674	2,747	24,554	34.3	23.1	11.2
Montana	7,355	4,809	2,546	20,502	35.9	23.5	12.4
Nebraska	8,518	5,528	2,991	24,611	34.6	22.5	12.2
Nevada	10,440	6,975	3,465	29,237	35.7	23.9	11.9
New Hampshire	9,643	6,944	2,699	28,803	33.5	24.1	9.4
New Jersey	11,942	8,282	3,660	33,342	35.8	24.8	11.0
New Mexico	7,011	4,647	2,365	20,614	34.0	22.5	11.5
New York	11,859	7,188	4,671	30,461	38.9	23.6	15.3
North Carolina	8,158	5,419	2,739	24,648	33.1	22.0	11.1
North Dakota	7,387	4,908	2,479	20,741	35.6	23.7	12.0
Ohio	8,829	5,818	3,010	25,222	35.0	23.1	11.9
Oklahoma	6,835	4,630	2,206	20,775	32.9	22.3	10.6
Oregon	9,062	5,799	3,263	24,918	36.4	23.3	13.1
Pennsylvania	9,229	6,216	3,013	26,194	35.2	23.7	11.5
Rhode Island	9,317	6,300	3,017	26,362	35.3	23.9	11.4
South Carolina	7,067	4,832	2,235	21,407	33.0	22.6	10.4
South Dakota	7,371	4,976	2,396	22,516	32.7	22.1	10.6
Tennessee	7,574	5,460	2,114	23,748	31.9	23.0	8.9
Texas	8,118	5,538	2,580	24,145	33.6	22.9	10.7
Utah	7,341	4,699	2,642	21,298	34.5	22.1	12.4
Vermont	8,164	5,460	2,704	23,878	34.2	22.9	11.3
Virginia	9,421	6,365	3,056	26,908	35.0	23.7	11.4
Washington	9,881	6,572	3,309	27,086	36.5	24.3	12.2
West Virginia	6,425	4,305	2,119	19,518	32.9	22.1	10.9
Wisconsin	9,165	5,825	3,340	25,105	36.5	23.2	13.3
Wyoming	8,119	5,896	2,223	22,639	35.9	26.0	9.8
District of Columbia	13,219	8,608	4,611	36,142	36.6	23.8	12.8

Source: Tax Foundation

Tax Bite in the Eight-Hour Day by State, 1997 (Hours:Minutes)

The hours and minutes in an eight-hour day devoted to paying taxes.

	Total taxes	Federal taxes	State/ local taxes
United States	2:49	1:53	0:56
Alabama	2:34	1:49	0:45
Alaska	2:45	1:46	0:58
Arizona	2:44	1:41	0:56
Arkansas	2:37	1:45	0:52
California	2:45	1:51	0:54
Colorado	2:49	1:53	0:55
Connecticut	3:06	2:03	1:03
Delaware	2:40	1:50	0:51
Florida	2:47	1:54	0:52
Georgia	2:39	1:47	0:52
Hawaii	2:54	1:50	1:04
Idaho	2:43	1:47	0:56
Illinois	2:54	1:59	0:55
Indiana	2:45	1:54	0:51
Iowa	2:49	1:47	1:01
Kansas	2:52	1:52	0:59
Kentucky	2:44	1:47	0:58
Louisiana	2:32	1:45	0:47
Maine	2:49	1:49	0:59
Maryland	2:52	1:55	0:56
Massachusetts	2:47	1:55	0:52
Michigan	2:50	1:54	0:56
Minnesota	2:54	1:51	1:03
Mississippi	2:42	1:44	0:59
Missouri	2:45	1:51	0:54
Montana	2:52	1:53	1:00
Nebraska	2:46	1:48	0:58
Nevada	2:51	1:55	0:57
New Hampshire	2:41	1:56	0:45
New Jersey	2:52	1:59	0:53
New Mexico	2:43	1:48	1:14
New York	3:07	1:53	1:17
North Carolina	2:39	1:46	0:53
North Dakota	2:51	1:54	0:57
Ohio	2:48	1:51	0:57
Oklahoma	2:38	1:47	0:51
Oregon	2:55	1:42	1:03
Pennsylvania	2:49	1:54	0:55
Rhode Island	2:50	1:55	0:55
South Carolina	2:38	1:48	0:50
South Dakota	2:37	1:46	0:51
Tennessee	2:33	1:50	0:43
Texas	2:41	1:50	0:51
Utah	2:45	1:46	1:00
Vermont	2:44	1:50	0:54
Virginia	2:48	1:54	0:55
Washington	2:55	1:56	0:59
West Virginia	2:38	1:46	0:52
Wisconsin	2:55	1:51	1:04
Wyoming	2:52	2:05	0:47
District of Columbia	2:56	1:54	1:01

Source: Tax Foundation

Balance of Payments

The balance of payments between the federal government and individual states varies widely. In some states, there is a large surplus because the federal government spends significantly more in those states than it collects from them in taxes. On the other hand, some states run big deficits, paying much more in taxes than the federal government returns to them in defense spending, grants, payments to the elderly, disabled, and poor, federal employees' wages, and other expenditures.

Balance of Payments, Fiscal Year 1996
(Per capita)

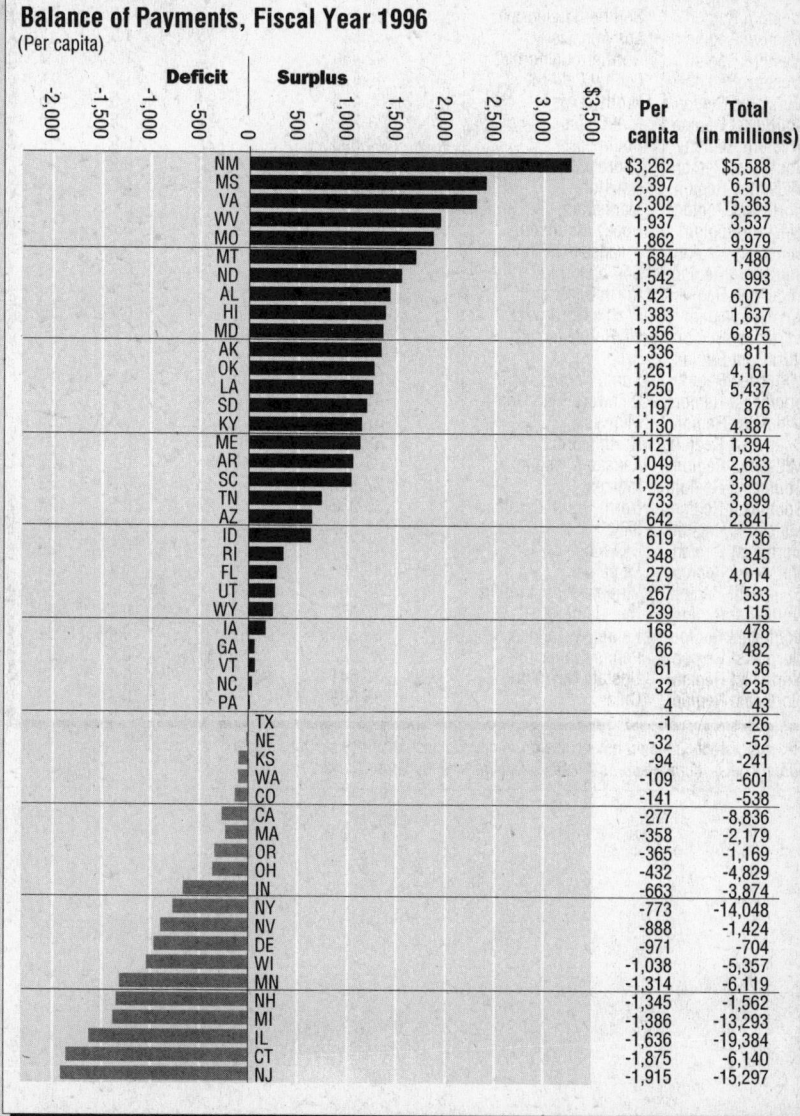

State	Per capita	Total (in millions)
NM	$3,262	$5,588
MS	2,397	6,510
VA	2,302	15,363
WV	1,937	3,537
MO	1,862	9,979
MT	1,684	1,480
ND	1,542	993
AL	1,421	6,071
HI	1,383	1,637
MD	1,356	6,875
AK	1,336	811
OK	1,261	4,161
LA	1,250	5,437
SD	1,197	876
KY	1,130	4,387
ME	1,121	1,394
AR	1,049	2,633
SC	1,029	3,807
TN	733	3,899
AZ	642	2,841
ID	619	736
RI	348	345
FL	279	4,014
UT	267	533
WY	239	115
IA	168	478
GA	66	482
VT	61	36
NC	32	235
PA	4	43
TX	-1	-26
NE	-32	-52
KS	-94	-241
WA	-109	-601
CO	-141	-538
CA	-277	-8,836
MA	-358	-2,179
OR	-365	-1,169
OH	-432	-4,829
IN	-663	-3,874
NY	-773	-14,048
NV	-888	-1,424
DE	-971	-704
WI	-1,038	-5,357
MN	-1,314	-6,119
NH	-1,345	-1,562
MI	-1,386	-13,293
IL	-1,636	-19,384
CT	-1,875	-6,140
NJ	-1,915	-15,297

Source: Harvard University, Kennedy School of Government

Odds of Being Audited by the IRS

Odds of IRS District Tax Audit 1996 (Percent is based on individual returns)

Region	District	Average adjusted gross income reported	Income rank	Percent audited	Audit rank
–	United States	$35,213	–	0.7%	–
Western Region	Southern California	38,299	15	1.6	1
Western Region	Los Angeles	38,034	16	1.6	2
Western Region	Northern California	42,456	5	1.2	3
Western Region	Central California	40,575	9	1.2	4
Midstates Region	North Texas	36,458	24	1.0	5
Southeast Region	Gulf Coast	31,272	31	0.8	6
Western Region	Southwest	34,898	27	0.8	7
Southeast Region	Georgia	36,749	22	0.8	8
Midstates Region	Houston	39,003	11	0.8	9
Northeast Region	Manhattan	53,031	1	0.7	10
Western Region	Rocky Mountain	37,013	21	0.7	11
Midstates Region	Arkansas-Oklahoma	30,461	32	0.7	12
Southeast Region	South Florida	37,142	19	0.7	13
Midstates Region	North Central	38,950	12	0.7	14
Western Region	Pacific Northwest	38,853	13	0.6	15
Northeast Region	CT-Rhode Island	48,347	2	0.6	16
Northeast Region	Brooklyn	40,531	10	0.6	17
Midstates Region	South Texas	29,672	33	0.5	18
Southeast Region	Delaware-Maryland	42,864	4	0.5	19
Midstates Region	Midwest	37,036	20	0.5	20
Southeast Region	North Florida	33,137	30	0.5	21
Midstates Region	Kansas-Missouri	36,340	25	0.5	22
Southeast Region	Indiana	37,337	18	0.5	23
Southeast Region	North-South Carolina	33,935	28	0.5	24
Midstates Region	Illinois	42,266	6	0.5	25
Northeast Region	New England	41,681	7	0.5	26
Northeast Region	Michigan	40,823	8	0.4	27
Southeast Region	Virginia-West Virginia	38,766	14	0.4	28
Northeast Region	New Jersey	47,973	3	0.4	29
Southeast Region	Kentucky-Tennessee	33,605	29	0.4	30
Northeast Region	Pennsylvania	38,022	17	0.4	31
Northeast Region	Upstate New York	36,541	23	0.4	32
Northeast Region	Ohio	35,583	26	0.3	33

Note: IRS district audits do not include tax audits conducted by IRS service centers.
Source: Transactional Records Access Clearinghouse, Syracuse University

Tax Refunds

The number of federal income-tax refunds issued to individuals and the average amount.

Tax year	Number of refunds (In millions)	Average amount
1990	80.5	$ 970.00
1991	82.4	1,020.00
1992	77.8	1,013.00
1993	79.3	1,069.00
1994	79.3	1,178.00
1995	80.4	1,244.00
1996	82.3	1,302.00
1997*	81.4	1,332.00

*As of Aug. 21, 1998.
Source: Internal Revenue Service

The Home Front

Barbara and Patrick Ratliff spent several weeks and more than a little money readying their three-bedroom ranch house in Shawnee, Kansas, for sale. Perhaps they shouldn't have bothered—the two sold the house less than a week after they put it up for sale. "It was a couple in their early 20s," says Ms. Ratliff, a restaurant employee. "Hey, if they're that young and they can do it, that's great."

It's a housing boom, '90s style. The U.S. Census Bureau says the nation's home ownership rate stands at 65 percent, matching highs set in the early 1980s. The National Association of Realtors estimates that by the end of 1998 about 4.7 million existing homes will have changed hands—a level never seen since the group began tracking such numbers 20 years before. Meanwhile, new-home starts reached a seasonally adjusted annual rate of 1.6 million in July, a level last reached during the heady building and buying spurts of the mid-1980s, according to the U.S. Department of Commerce.

In many markets, homes are being snapped up as soon as the "For Sale" sign is hammered into the front lawn. Wall Street millionaires with paper gains are snapping up vacation homes. In the New York area, mul-

tiple bids aren't uncommon. In Dallas, home builders have begun building subdivisions within the city limits—something almost unheard of in any major metropolitan city. And just outside San Francisco, home builders that are already putting up homes as fast as they can have raised prices in hopes of actually quelling demand. All of this may be good news for homeowners, home builders and real-estate agents. But for some economists, they're reasons to feel uneasy. They soberly remember the last housing boom—the one in the 1980s, when speculation drove the market. Some areas of the country, particularly in California, still haven't fully recovered from the burst of that bubble.

With that in mind, economists and others in the real-estate industry have probed the nation's housing markets for evidence of speculation, unjustified home appreciation or any other signs of a housing bubble. The good news: So far, the nation's real-estate market is unusually well-balanced. "Demand for housing is extraordinary," says Mark Zandi, an economist with Regional Financial Associates of West Chester, Pennsylvania. "Everything's just working in the right direction."

According to a home-price index compiled

by mortgage buyers Fannie Mae and Freddie Mac, home values rose 5.3 percent between June 1997 and June 1998—well above the Consumer Price Index. True, home-value increases of 5 percent still won't compete with stocks as an investment, but that appreciation rate is a marked improvement over the 2 percent annual increases of the early 1990s.

That's not to say some markets aren't poised for a fall. *Local Market Monitor*, an economic and housing forecast publication, predicts flattening economic growth in Des Moines, Iowa, can't sustain the 35 percent rise in home values it has seen in the past five years. Detroit, the unlikely home of a 50 percent rise in median home prices since 1994, could also cool if a weakening economy eats into demand for automobiles. "Whether, and how far, home prices will fall in these markets depends on how much the local economy falls," says Ingo Winzer, editor of the *Local Market Monitor*, in Wellesley, Massachusetts. "A U.S. recession or a steep fall in financial markets will put additional downward pressure on home prices."

Still, in most of the nation, the building spurt has met an equal spurt in demand. The prime instigators are, of course, the baby boomers, who have better jobs, growing families and a need to buy bigger, better houses. Younger and lower-income Americans, also enjoying a strong economy and low unemployment, are snapping up the starter homes the boomers are leaving behind.

There are also more families chasing houses. Twentysomethings who might have waited another 10 years before buying a house and starting a family suddenly found themselves with enough wealth and job security to take the plunge anyway. Meanwhile, the wave of 1980s immigrants, now better paid and more acclimated to American life, began families of their own. Regional Financial Associates estimates 1.3 million households a year were being formed in the mid-1990s, between 200,000 and 300,000 more than expected.

And when they bought their homes, they found one of the best environments for interest rates since the 1960s. In 1995, the average rate for a plain vanilla 30-year fixed-rate mortgage danced just below 8 percent. In 1998, after a few ups and downs, it held close to 7 percent, according to HSH Associates, a Butler, New Jersey, firm that tracks mortgage rates. That difference can add up: On a $200,000 house with a 7 percent loan, monthly principal and interest payments total $1,330.60, compared with $1,467.53 under an 8 percent loan. Loans were also easier to get. Mortgages that once required up to 20 percent down now sometimes require only 3 percent down—and under certain programs, that downpayment can be a gift from somebody in the buyer's family. Meanwhile, immigrants and others with non-existent credit records found lenders willing to accept as criteria for a loan a short history of paying bills on time.

As a result, just about every sector of the housing business had begun to perk up by 1998. Even in Los Angeles's notoriously down-and-out neighborhood of South Central, the site of riots in 1992, housing activity is beginning to stir. Malcolm Bennett, a local real-estate broker and property manager, saw his moribund single-family home business perk up about two years ago. Since then, median home prices in the neighborhood haven't budged, but he's hopeful. "We're going to continue to see not a price increase in South Central, but more sales activity as demand increases. And then, maybe, we'll see some appreciation," he says.

No boom lasts forever, and this one will be no exception. Analysts already foresee a slowdown in housing activity during 1999 and 2000, when the nation's economy is predicted to cool. Household formation also is expected to drop to 1.1 million households. Perhaps the biggest reason for an expected slowdown is the sheer amount of activity seen between 1995 and 1998; by now, Americans may feel they've moved enough.

Still for now, business remains brisk. Steve Stephenson, a real-estate agent in suburban Overland Park, Kansas, continues to scan his daily newspaper for garage-sale advertisements. He says garage sales indicate a family ready to move, which is good news for him because he needs houses for his customers. "I just pop in and leave my card," he says. "Ninety percent of the time, they sell."

Carlos Tejada

Suburban Sprawl

Metropolitan and Nonmetropolitan Distribution of Housing Units: 1940 and 1990

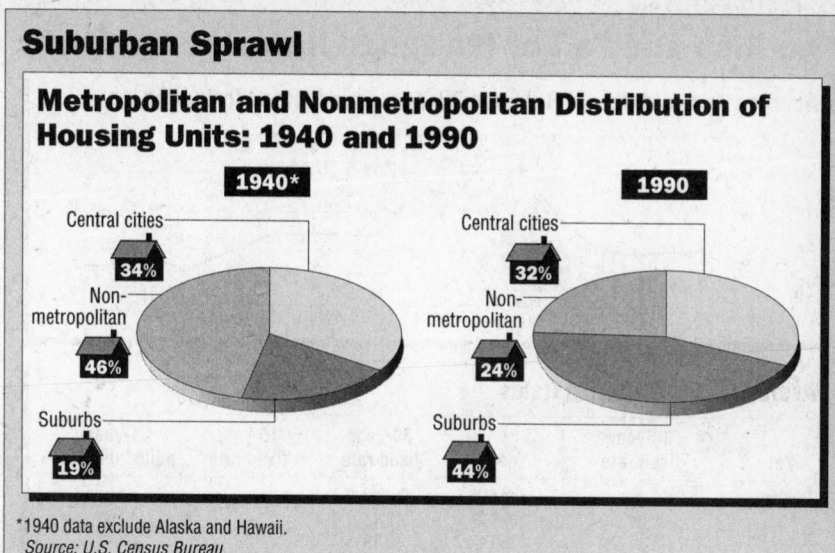

*1940 data exclude Alaska and Hawaii.
Source: U.S. Census Bureau

Home, Sweet Home

Percentage of People who are Homeowners, by Race or Hispanic Origin

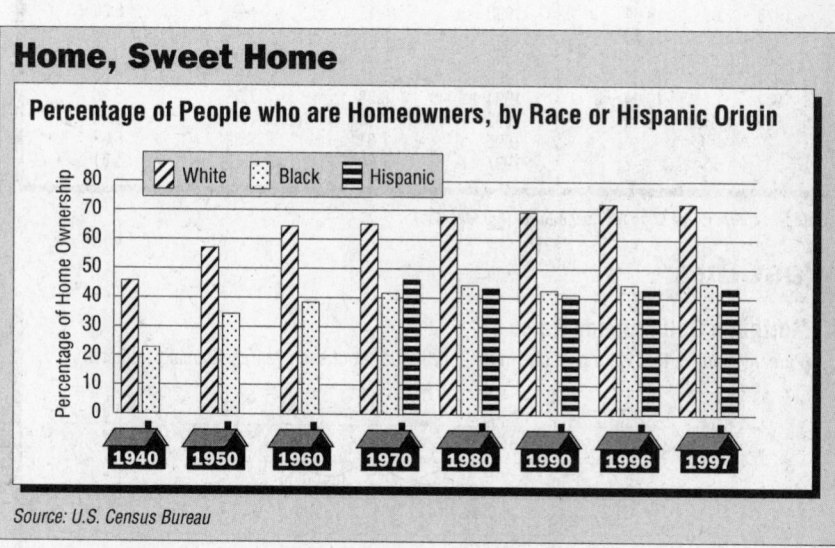

Source: U.S. Census Bureau

The Rise and Fall of Mortgage Rates

Average Annual Interest Rates on 30-Year Fixed-Rate Mortgages

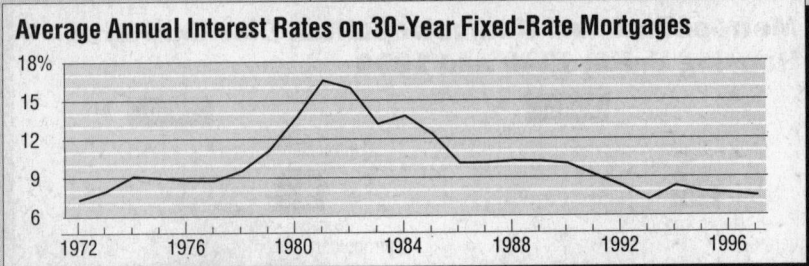

Average Annual Interest Rates

Year	30-year fixed rate	Year	30-year fixed rate	15-year fixed rate	1-year adjustable rate
1972	7.38%	1984	13.88%	—	11.51%
1973	8.04	1985	12.43	—	10.05
1974	9.19	1986	10.19	—	8.43
1975	9.05	1987	10.21	—	7.83
1976	8.87	1988	10.34	—	7.90
1977	8.85	1989	10.32	—	8.80
1978	9.64	1990	10.13	—	8.36
1979	11.20	1991	9.25	—	7.09
1980	13.74	1992	8.39	7.96%	5.62
1981	16.63	1993	7.31	6.83	4.58
1982	16.04	1994	8.38	7.86	5.36
1983	13.24	1995	7.93	7.48	6.06
		1996	7.81	7.32	5.67
		1997	7.60	7.13	5.61

Source: Federal Home Loan Mortgage Corp. (Freddie Mac)

Past Due

Mortgage Delinquency Rates
(Percent of loans that were past due in the fourth quarter of each year, seasonally adjusted)

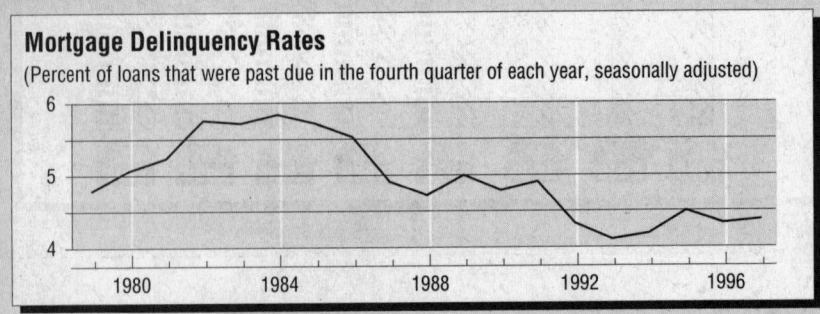

Source: Mortgage Bankers Association of America

Mortgage Payment Table
Principal and interest for a fixed-rate, 15-year loan

Loan amount	5.0%	5.5%	6.0%	6.5%	7.0%	7.5%	8.0%	8.5%	9.0%	9.5%	10.0%
$ 5,000	$ 40	$ 41	$ 42	$ 44	$ 45	$ 46	$ 48	$ 49	$ 51	$ 52	$ 54
10,000	79	82	84	87	90	93	96	98	101	104	107
15,000	119	123	127	131	135	139	143	148	152	157	161
20,000	158	163	169	174	180	185	191	197	203	209	215
25,000	198	204	211	218	225	232	239	246	254	261	269
30,000	237	245	253	261	270	278	287	295	304	313	322
35,000	277	286	295	305	315	324	334	345	355	365	376
40,000	316	327	338	348	360	371	382	394	406	418	430
45,000	356	368	380	392	404	417	430	443	456	470	484
50,000	395	409	422	436	449	464	478	492	507	522	537
55,000	435	449	464	479	494	510	526	542	558	574	591
60,000	474	490	506	523	539	556	573	591	609	627	645
65,000	514	531	549	566	584	603	621	640	659	679	698
70,000	554	572	591	610	629	649	669	689	710	731	752
75,000	593	613	633	653	674	695	717	739	761	783	806
80,000	633	654	675	697	719	742	765	788	811	835	860
85,000	672	695	717	740	764	788	812	837	862	888	913
90,000	712	735	759	784	809	834	860	886	913	940	967
95,000	751	776	802	828	854	881	908	936	964	992	1,021
100,000	791	817	844	871	899	927	956	985	1,014	1,044	1,075

Mortgage Payment Table
Principal and interest for a fixed-rate, 30-year loan

Loan amount	5.0%	5.5%	6.0%	6.5%	7.0%	7.5%	8.0%	8.5%	9.0%	9.5%	10.0%
$ 5,000	$ 27	$ 28	$ 30	$ 32	$ 33	$ 35	$ 37	$ 38	$ 40	$ 42	$ 44
10,000	54	57	60	63	67	70	73	77	80	84	88
15,000	81	85	90	95	100	105	110	115	121	126	132
20,000	107	114	120	126	133	140	147	154	161	168	176
25,000	134	142	150	158	166	175	183	192	201	210	219
30,000	161	170	180	190	200	210	220	231	241	252	263
35,000	188	199	210	221	233	245	257	269	282	294	307
40,000	215	227	240	253	266	280	294	308	322	336	351
45,000	242	256	270	284	299	315	330	346	362	378	395
50,000	268	284	300	316	333	350	367	384	402	420	439
55,000	295	312	330	348	366	385	404	423	443	462	483
60,000	322	341	360	379	399	420	440	461	483	505	527
65,000	349	369	390	411	432	454	477	500	523	547	570
70,000	376	397	420	442	466	489	514	538	563	589	614
75,000	403	426	450	474	499	524	550	577	603	631	658
80,000	429	454	480	506	532	559	587	615	644	673	702
85,000	456	483	510	537	566	594	624	654	684	715	746
90,000	483	511	540	569	599	629	660	692	724	757	790
95,000	510	539	570	600	632	664	697	730	764	799	834
100,000	537	568	600	632	665	699	734	769	805	841	878

Note: For mortgages over $100,000, add the appropriate figures. For example, the principal and interest on a 30-year, $100,000 mortgage at 8 percent is $734 and the principal and interest on a 30-year, $50,000 mortgage at 8 percent is $367, making the total principal and interest payment on a $150,000 mortgage $734 plus $367, or $1,101 per month.
Source: National Association of Home Builders

New Homes

New Privately Owned Housing Units Started
(In thousands)

Year	Total units	Structures with:			Region			
		One unit	2 to 4 units	5 or more units	Northeast	Midwest	South	West
1970	1,434	813	85	536	218	294	612	311
1975	1,160	892	64	204	149	294	442	275
1980	1,292	852	110	331	125	218	643	306
1985	1,742	1,072	93	576	252	240	782	468
1990	1,193	895	37	260	131	253	479	329
1991	1,014	840	36	138	113	233	414	254
1992	1,200	1,030	31	139	127	288	497	288
1993	1,288	1,126	29	133	126	298	562	302
1994	1,457	1,198	35	224	138	329	639	351
1995	1,354	1,076	34	244	118	290	615	331
1996	1,477	1,161	45	271	132	322	662	361
1997	1,476	1,134	44	298	137	303	672	364

New Privately Owned One-Family Houses Sold, by Region
(In thousands)

Year	Total sales	Region			
		Northeast	Midwest	South	West
1970	485	61	100	203	121
1972	718	96	130	305	187
1974	519	69	103	207	139
1976	646	72	128	247	199
1978	817	78	145	331	262
1980	545	50	81	267	145
1982	412	47	48	219	99
1984	639	94	76	309	160
1986	750	136	96	322	196
1988	676	101	97	276	202
1990	534	71	89	225	149
1991	509	57	93	215	144
1992	610	65	116	259	170
1993	666	60	123	295	188
1994	670	61	123	295	191
1995	667	55	125	300	187
1996	757	74	137	337	209
1997	800	79	139	362	220

Source: U.S. Census Bureau and U.S. Department of Housing and Urban Development

Dream Homes

Characteristics of New Privately Owned One-Family Houses Completed
(Percent distribution)

Financing

1970
- Cash or equivalent: 16
- FHA-insured: 30
- Conventional: 47
- VA-guaranteed: 7

1997
- Conventional: 77
- Rural Housing Service: 1
- VA-Guaranteed: 4
- Cash or equivalent: 10
- FHA-insured: 9

Number of stories

1970
- Two or more: 17
- Split level: 10
- One: 74

1997
- Two or more: 49
- Split level: 2
- One: 49

Bedrooms

1970
- Four or more: 24
- Two or less: 13
- Three: 63

1997
- Four or more: 31
- Two or less: 13
- Three: 56

Bathrooms

1970
- 2 1/2 or more: 16
- 1 1/2 or less: 52
- Two: 32

1997
- 1 1/2 or less: 9
- 2 1/2 or more: 50
- Two: 41

Heating fuel

1970
- Oil: 8
- Other: 1
- Electricity: 28
- Gas: 62

1997
- Oil: 3
- Other: 1
- Electricity: 26
- Gas: 69

Central air conditioning

1970
- With: 34
- Without: 66

1997
- Without: 18
- With: 82

Fireplaces

1970
- One or more: 35
- No fireplace: 65

1997
- No fireplace: 39
- One or more: 61

Parking facilities

1970
- No garage or carport: 25
- Carport: 17
- Garage: 58

1997
- Carport: 1
- No garage or carport: 13
- Garage: 85

Square footage

	Average floor area		Median floor area	
	1970	1997	1970	1997
Square footage	1,500	2,150	1,385	1,975

Source: U.S. Census Bureau and U.S. Department of Housing and Urban Development

New Home Prices

Median Sales Prices of New Privately Owned One-Family Houses Sold, by Region

(In thousands)

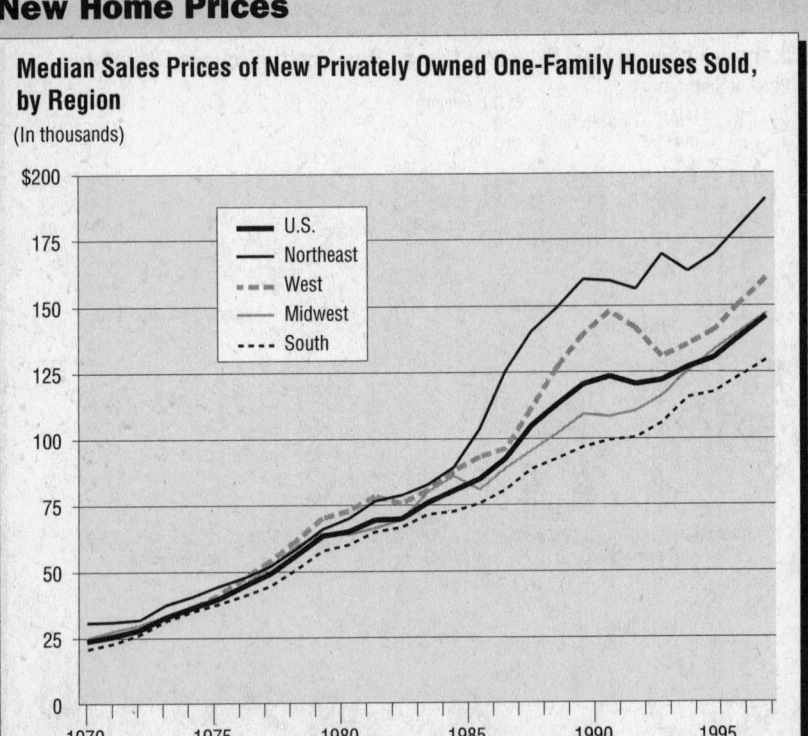

1970	1975	1980	1985	1990	1995
U.S. $23,400	$39,300	$64,600	$84,300	$122,900	$133,900

Legend:
- U.S.
- Northeast
- West
- Midwest
- South

Source: U.S. Census Bureau and U.S. Department of Housing and Urban Development

Older Homes

Median Sales Price of Existing Single-Family Homes

Year	United States	Northeast	Midwest	South	West
1970	$23,000	$25,2000	$20,100	$22,200	$24,300
1972	26,700	29,800	23,900	26,400	28,400
1974	32,000	35,800	27,700	32,300	34,800
1976	38,100	41,800	32,900	36,500	46,100
1978	48,700	47,900	42,200	45,100	66,700
1980	62,200	60,800	51,900	58,300	89,300
1982	67,800	63,500	55,100	67,100	98,900
1984	72,400	78,700	57,100	71,300	95,800
1986	80,300	104,800	63,500	78,200	100,900
1988	89,300	143,000	68,400	82,200	124,900
1990	95,500	141,200	74,000	85,900	139,600
1991	100,300	141,900	77,800	88,900	147,200
1992	103,700	140,000	81,700	92,100	143,800
1993	106,800	139,500	85,200	95,100	142,600
1994	109,800	139,100	87,900	96,000	146,700
1995	113,100	136,900	93,600	97,800	148,300
1996	118,200	140,900	99,800	102,800	152,900
1997	124,100	145,100	106,100	109,000	160,300

Median Sales Price of Existing Homes

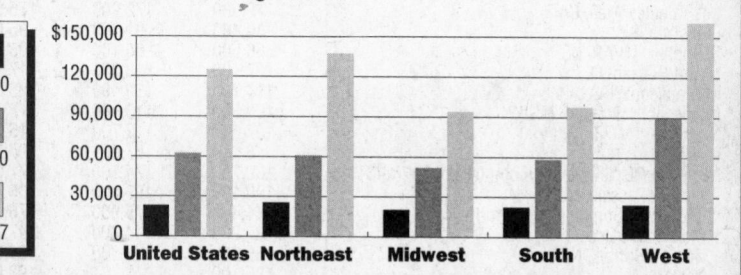

Legend: 1970, 1980, 1997

Existing Single-Family Home Sales

(In thousands)

Year	Total sales	North-east	Mid-west	South	West	Year	Total sales	North-east	Mid-west	South	West
1970	1,612	251	501	568	292	1988	3,513	606	865	1,224	817
1972	2,252	361	630	788	473	1990	3,211	469	831	1,202	709
1974	2,272	354	645	839	434	1991	3,220	479	840	1,199	702
1976	3,064	439	881	1,033	712	1992	3,520	534	939	1,292	755
1978	3,986	516	1,144	1,416	911	1993	3,802	571	1,007	1,416	808
1980	2,973	403	806	1,092	672	1994	3,946	592	1,027	1,464	863
1982	1,990	354	490	780	366	1995	3,812	577	992	1,431	813
1984	2,829	478	720	1,006	624	1996	4,087	611	1,048	1,516	912
1986	3,474	635	922	1,145	773	1997	4,215	632	1,067	1,575	942

Source: National Association of Realtors

Home Values

Median Sales Price of Existing Single-Family Homes for Major Metropolitan Areas

Metropolitan area	1995	1996	1997
Atlanta, GA	$97,500	$100,700	$108,400
Austin/San Marcos, TX	101,400	108,100	118,000
Boston, MA	179,000	189,300	196,200
Buffalo/Niagara Falls, NY	81,300	82,900	82,000
Charlotte/Gastonia/Rock Hill, NC/SC	107,800	116,800	124,200
Chicago, IL	147,900	153,200	158,900
Cincinnati, OH/KY/IN	100,400	104,800	110,500
Cleveland, OH	104,700	111,900	116,800
Columbus, OH	99,100	108,200	117,600
Dallas, TX	96,400	103,500	112,000
Dayton/Springfield, OH	88,300	95,100	96,700
Denver, CO	127,300	133,400	140,600
Detroit, MI	98,200	111,400	119,600
Grand Rapids, MI	80,600	87,200	93,600
Greensboro/Winston-Salem/High Point, NC	102,500	112,700	117,300
Hartford, CT	133,400	139,200	138,100
Houston, TX	79,200	84,700	90,900
Indianapolis, IN	94,600	98,000	103,700
Jacksonville, FL	83,100	88,400	86,400
Kansas City, MO/KS	91,700	98,800	106,800
Las Vegas, NV	113,500	118,500	123,200
Los Angeles Area, CA	179,900	172,900	176,500
Louisville, KY	86,400	91,300	96,800
Memphis, TN/AR/MS	86,500	96,100	103,700
Miami/Hialeah, FL	107,100	113,200	117,700
Milwaukee, WI	114,700	119,400	125,300
Minneapolis/St. Paul, MN/WI	106,800	113,900	118,400
Nashville, TN	107,300	112,700	115,200
New Orleans, LA	78,000	87,000	93,300
New York/N. New Jersey/Long Island, NY/NJ/CT	169,700	174,500	177,900
Bergen/Passaic, NJ	190,100	199,400	205,400
Middlesex/Somerset/Hunterdon, NJ	171,400	175,900	176,700
Monmouth/Ocean, NJ	137,200	144,700	147,700
Nassau/Suffolk, NY	155,300	159,800	164,000
Newark, NJ	185,100	*	193,000
Norfolk/Virginia Beach/Newport News, VA	104,400	110,200	*
Oklahoma City, OK	70,400	74,600	77,000
Orlando, FL	89,200	92,400	94,500
Philadelphia, PA/NJ	118,700	*	*
Phoenix, AZ	96,800	105,300	113,700
Pittsburgh, PA	82,100	84,800	87,000
Portland, OR	128,400	141,500	152,400
Providence, RI	115,600	118,100	119,600
Raleigh/Durham, NC	127,000	*	152,800
Rochester, NY	85,000	86,200	86,800
Sacramento, CA	119,500	115,200	116,100
Saint Louis, MO/IL	87,700	91,200	96,900
Salt Lake City/Ogden, UT	113,700	122,700	128,600
San Antonio, TX	80,800	84,900	86,800
San Diego, CA	171,600	174,500	185,200
San Francisco Bay Area, CA	254,400	266,400	292,600
Seattle, WA	159,000	164,600	171,300
Tampa/St. Petersburg/Clearwater, FL	78,300	81,300	83,900
Washington, DC/MD/VA	156,500	160,700	166,300
W. Palm Beach/Boca Raton/Delray Beach, FL	121,300	126,600	133,400

*Not available.
Source: National Association of Realtors

Metros With Greatest Home Price Growth

Quarterly Median Sales Price, Percent Change From Last Year

Metro area	1st qtr. 1998	% change from last year
Champaign/Urbana/Rantoul, IL	$ 90,600	18.4 %
Bradenton, FL	100,200	15.8
Lansing/East Lansing, MI	95,500	15.3
Omaha, NE/IA	102,100	15.2
Charleston, SC	113,400	15.1
Louisville, KY/IN	105,700	14.9
Gary/Hammond, IN	101,000	14.6
Ocala, FL	67,000	14.1
Detroit, MI	128,900	13.2
Orange County, CA	243,200	13.0
Charlotte/Gastona/Rock Hill, NC/SC	131,800	12.5
San Francisco Bay Area, CA	303,600	12.0
Boston, MA	205,200	11.9
Saginaw/Bay City/Midland, MI	76,000	11.8
Springfield, MA	114,700	11.4
Sarasota, FL	120,700	11.2
Lexington/Fayette, KY	106,200	11.1
Des Moines, IA	104,000	11.1
Oklahoma City, OK	81,200	10.8
Baton Rouge, LA	97,100	10.5
Dallas, TX	116,400	10.2
Tallahassee, FL	115,600	9.7
Springfield, IL	85,900	9.1
Shreveport, LA	81,900	9.1
San Diego, CA	192,300	9.0

Source: National Association of Realtors

Most Expensive Residential Real Estate Markets, According to Coldwell Banker Home Price Comparison Index, 1998

City	Average sale price*
Beverly Hills, CA	$812,225
Greenwich, CT	694,161
San Francisco, CA	670,824
Brentwood, CA	634,940
San Mateo, CA	578,450
La Jolla, CA	545,900
Wellesley, MA	537,160
Newport Beach, CA	530,332
Darien, CT	522,518
Palos Verdes, CA	481,505
Chicago/Lincoln Park, IL	473,265
Lexington, IL	465,902
Monterey Peninsula, CA	455,400
Westport, CT	454,660
Fremont, CA	448,308
Pasadena, CA	446,790
San Jose, CA	445,611
San Rafael, CA	439,875
Pleasanton, CA	400,479
Oakland/Monclair, CA	396,558
Bergen County, NJ	388,940
Somerset County, NJ	383,216
Ridgefield, CT	382,480
Queens North Shore, NY	382,248
Honolulu, HI	374,100
Walnut Creek, CA	370,108
Stamford, CT	358,679
Hudson River Valley, NY	357,385
Vancouver, BC	344,705
Long Beach, CA	336,550
Hollywood Hills, CA	334,669
Torrance, CA	330,623
Norwalk, CT	328,104
Agoura Hills, CA	327,275
Barrington, IL	326,553
Acton, MA	322,359
Union County, NJ	316,670
Westchester County, NY	313,933
Mercer County, NJ	304,506
Philadelphia Mainline/Suburb West, PA	300,190
Bellevue, WA	299,886
Western Essex County, NJ	289,821
Nassau, N. Shore, NY	288,411
Hunterdon County, NJ	287,205
Framingham, MA	283,551
Northern Virginia, VA	283,339
Deerfield, IL	283,170
Morris County, NJ	281,533
Encinatas, CA	281,430
Mission Viejo, CA	276,660

*Subject homes are single-family dwellings, approximately 2,200 square feet, 4 bedrooms, 2.5 baths, family room (or equivalent) and two-car garage. Homes and neighborhoods surveyed are typical for corporate middle-management transferees.
Source: Coldwell Banker

Most Affordable Housing Markets

Ranking of the most affordable housing markets, based on the proportion of homes that a family earning the median income in that market could afford to buy. For example, the housing opportunity index in Binghamton, NY, the most affordable Northeast market in the fourth quarter of 1997, was 84.8, meaning that families earning the median income could have purchased 84.8% of all the homes sold in the quarter.

Most Affordable Markets	Housing Opportunity Index	1997 median family income	Median sale price (000s)	1997 Q4 affordability rank	
Metro area	1997 Q4	(000s)	1997 Q4	National	Regional
Northeast					
Binghamton, NY	84.8	$41.0	$70	6	1
Vineland-Millville-Bridgeton, NJ	83.4	43.0	85	11	2
Utica-Rome, NY	83.0	37.2	65	12	3
Jamestown, NY	81.9	36.0	58	18	4
Nashua, NH	81.7	59.6	119	21	5
Syracuse, NY	81.2	43.6	79	22	6
Hartford, CT	80.9	58.9	122	23	7
Springfield, MA	79.6	45.5	97	30	8
Elmira, NY	79.2	38.8	66	35	9
Nassau-Suffolk, NY	79.0	68.5	136	36	10
Midwest					
Kokomo, IN	95.3	46.9	79	1	1
Elkhart-Goshen, IN	86.6	46.1	98	3	2
Duluth-Superior, MN-WI	85.9	40.6	77	4	3
Rockford, IL	84.8	47.1	85	6	4
Lima, OH	83.5	42.3	70	10	5
Des Moines, IA	83.0	50.6	94	12	6
Davenport-Moline-Rock Island, IA-IL	82.9	43.6	65	14	7
Springfield, IL	82.4	49.9	88	17	8
Dayton-Springfield, OH	81.8	46.4	90	19	9
Peoria-Pekin, IL	81.8	46.0	79	19	9
South					
Baton Rouge, LA	87.4	42.6	92	2	1
Lakeland-Winter Haven, FL	85.1	37.2	77	5	2
Wilmington-Newark, DE-MD	84.7	57.6	125	8	3
Melbourne-Titusville-Palm Bay, FL	84.2	44.5	87	9	4
Beaumont-Port Arthur, TX	82.6	40.9	74	16	5
Daytona Beach, FL	80.9	37.4	79	23	6
Pensacola, FL	79.9	38.0	90	28	7
Ocala, FL	79.5	33.3	74	32	8
Oklahoma City, OK	79.5	40.8	80	32	8
Punta Gorda, FL	77.4	36.9	84	42	10
West					
Anchorage, AK	82.8	58.6	133	15	1
Bakersfield, CA	76.2	37.7	87	48	2
Modesto, CA	73.8	41.0	114	64	3
Riverside-San Bernardino, CA	69.5	44.8	119	100	4
Reno, NV	68.3	52.5	145	110	5
Denver, CO	67.9	54.9	140	112	6
Phoenix-Mesa, AZ	66.0	47.5	120	123	7
Las Vegas, NV-AZ	65.5	46.1	129	126	8
Sacramento, CA	65.5	48.4	138	126	8
Pueblo, CO	64.8	34.8	90	129	10

Source: National Association of Home Builders

Buying the American Dream

Changing Characteristics of Home Buyers in Major Metropolitan Areas

Characteristics	1976	1989	1997
Median price of home purchased	$43,340	$129,800	$159,700
First-time buyers	37,670	105,200	135,400
Repeat buyers	50,090	144,700	178,700
Average monthly payment	$329	$1,054	$1,114
First-time buyers	313	969	1,020
Repeat buyers	342	1,118	1,197
Average monthly payment as % of after-tax income	24.0%	31.8%	32.8%
First-time buyers	23.0	34.1	35.0
Repeat buyers	24.9	30.0	31.0
Average age of first-time buyers	28.1	29.6	32.1
Average age of repeat buyers	35.9	39.4	41.1
Down payment as % of sales price			
Average down payment	25.2%	24.4%	20.3%
First-time buyers	18.0	15.8	13.7
Repeat buyers	30.8	30.3	26.1
Median household income	$20,840	$58,700	$66,100
First-time buyers	20,480	50,700	53,800
Repeat buyers	21,080	64,400	76,900

Highs and Lows for Major Metropolitan Housing Markets

Characteristics	Metropolitan market	High	Metropolitan market	Low
Median price of home purchased	San Francisco	$289,700	Orlando	$103,300
First-time buyers	San Francisco	269,400	Houston	77,500
Repeat buyers	San Francisco	316,700	Houston	118,200
Average monthly payment	San Francisco	$1,632	Orlando	$841
First-time buyers	San Francisco	1,491	Phoenix	733
Repeat buyers	San Francisco	1,787	Cleveland	925
Average monthly payment as % of after-tax income	New York City	37.5%	Minneapolis-St. Paul	29.0%
First-time buyers	San Francisco	40.1	Minneapolis-St. Paul	29.8
Repeat buyers	New York City	35.1	Minneapolis-St. Paul	27.9
Down payment as % of sales price	New York City	27.8%	Washington, DC	15.8%
First-time buyers	New York City/Boston	20.6	Denver	10.7
Repeat buyers	New York City	35.0	Washington, DC	18.8
Average time to save down payment (years)	San Francisco	4.0	Memphis	1.1
Median household income	San Francisco	$86,600	Orlando	$53,800
First-time buyers	San Francisco	78,500	Orlando	45,500
Repeat buyers	San Francisco	95,400	Orlando	63,400

Source: Chicago Title & Trust Co.

Biggest Builders

Professional Builder magazine's 1997 ranking of the largest home builders in the U.S., based on the companies' housing revenue.

Rank	Company/Headquarters	Housing revenue	Closings	Starts	Total revenues
1	**Pulte Corp.**/Bloomfield Hills, MI	$2,479,171,000	15,322	15,541	$2,487,203,000
2	**Centex Corp.**/Dallas, TX	2,273,477,786	11,981	16,858	3,787,402,975
3	**Kaufman & Broad**/Los Angeles, CA	1,827,274,000	11,443	12,042	1,876,271,000
4	**Champion Enterprises Inc.**/ Auburn Hills, MI	1,675,053,000	—	64,285	1,675,053,000
5	**Lennar Corp.**/Miami, FL	1,658,493,000	8,943	9,696	1,692,083,000
6	**Ryland Group Inc.**/Columbia, MD	1,527,100,000	8,377	8,493	1,557,300,000
7	**Fleetwood Enterprises Inc.**/Riverside, CA	1,439,936,000	—	64,262	1,439,936,000
8	**U.S. Home Corp.**/Houston, TX	1,278,315,000	7,496	7,893	1,319,752,000
9	**NVR Inc.**/McLean, VA	1,154,000,000	6,107	6,107	1,188,200,000
10	**Del Webb Corp.**/Phoenix, AZ	1,144,089,000	6,206	5,600	1,186,262,000
11	**Toll Brothers Inc.**/Huntingdon Valley, PA	968,253,000	2,517	2,609	971,660,000
12	**Oakwood Homes Corp.**/Greensboro, NC	952,704,000	—	25,135	1,070,051,000
13	**M.D.C. Holdings Inc.**/Denver, CO	939,016,000	5,223	5,769	969,562,000
14	**D.R. Horton Inc.**/Arlington, TX	924,052,000	5,593	7,291	925,214,000
15	**Beazer Homes USA Inc.**/Atlanta, GA	844,285,000	5,710	5,690	845,866,000
16	**Lincoln Property Co.**/Dallas, TX	823,000,000	5,462	6,386	1,398,500,000
17	**Clayton Homes Inc.**/Knoxville, TN	822,906,000	—	32,714	1,021,703,000
18	**A.G. Spanos Cos.**/Stockton, CA	809,500,000	7,920	11,560	964,000,000
19	**Shea Homes**/Walnut, CA	759,586,000	3,049	3,411	1,001,412,000
20	**K. Hovnanian Enterprises Inc.**/Red Bank, NJ	731,807,000	3,717	4,202	784,136,000
21	**Weyerhaeuser Real Estate**/ Federal Way, WA	717,005,000	3,238	3,254	960,811,000
22	**Continental Homes Holding**/ Scottsdale, AZ	710,393,000	5,204	5,755	741,609,000
23	**JPI**/Irving, TX	676,413,615	4,269	5,965	676,413,615
24	**Standard Pacific Corp.**/Costa Mesa, CA	600,273,799	1,946	1,698	640,938,191
25	**Lewis Homes Group of Cos.**/Upland, CA	594,821,457	3,290	3,890	732,366,747

Source: Professional Builder's Annual Report of Housing's Giants

TOP REAL-ESTATE SELLERS

Real-estate brokerage firms with the largest dollar-volume of closed sales in 1997

COMPANY	SALES VOLUME	AVERAGE PRICE
NRT, Inc.	$50,031,000,000	$243,826
Weichert, Realtors	$13,000,000,000	$204,724
Long & Foster Real Estate, Inc.	$7,791,115,419	$174,642
Burnet Financial Group	$6,603,045,114	$175,926
Prudential Florida Realty	$4,927,000,000	$170,002
Fred Sands Realtors	$4,410,000,000	$366,950
Edina Realty, Inc.	$4,055,492,250	$137,349
John L. Scott Real Estate	$3,721,140,406	$188,708
Coldwell Banker Hunneman & Co.	$3,700,000,000	$272,600
DeWolfe New England	$3,593,000,000	$209,248
Prudential California Realty	$3,439,028,065	$310,830
Realty Executives	$3,354,909,508	$137,756
Fox & Roach Realtors	$3,194,179,477	$179,489
Realty One, Inc.	$2,711,960,437	$135,071
O'Conor, Piper & Flynn	$2,711,077,860	$127,466
Baird & Warner, Inc.	$2,400,000,000	$200,000
Gundaker Realtors/Better Homes and Gardens	$2,210,000,000	$120,844
Ebby Halliday, Realtors	$2,164,372,686	$166,465
Prudential Connecticut Realty	$2,140,000,000	$221,349
Coldwell Banker Premier Van Schaack, Inc.	$2,023,707,421	$156,404
Crye-Leike, Inc.	$1,968,657,431	$125,568
Henry S. Miller Co., Realtors	$1,917,763,040	$157,452
Smythe, Cramer Co.	$1,912,236,631	$156,114
RE/MAX North Atlanta Inc.	$1,844,584,363	$174,280
Pacific Union Residential Brokerage Co.	$1,829,136,680	$438,852

Source: REAL Trends, Dallas, TX

Modern Conveniences

Percent of U.S. Households with Appliances in 1997

Central air conditioner	47.1%	Waterbed heater	8.3%	Ceiling fans	60.1%
Clothes washer	77.4	Hot tub or spa	3.9	Range	99.2
Clothes dryer	71.1	Aquarium	3.8	Refrigerator	99.9
Dishwasher	50.2	Stereo equipment	68.8	Microwave oven	83.0
Freezer	33.2	Rechargeable tools/ appliances	43.7	Outdoor grill	28.5

Usage of Home Appliances (Percent of U.S. households in 1997)

Loads of laundry washed each week

Use of clothes washer	77.4%
1 load or less	5.2
2 to 4 loads	29.4
10 to 15 loads	10.0
More than 15 loads	3.3
No washing machine	22.6

Dishwasher use each week

Use a dishwasher	50.2
Less than 4 times	28.3
4 to 6 times	12.7
At least once each day	9.2
No dishwasher	49.8

Number of hot meals cooked in the home

3 or more a day	6.9%
2 a day	25.3
Once a day	41.6
A few per week	20.1
About once a week	3.0
Less than once a week	3.0

Amount of food cooked in microwave oven

Use a microwave oven	83.0
Most or all	7.2
About half	18.1
Some or very little	21.9
Only for defrosting, reheating, or snacks	35.6
No microwave oven	17.0

Source: U.S. Energy Department, Energy Information Administration

Fixing Up

As the U.S. housing stock ages, the remodeling industry is expected to remain strong and grow about 5% a year through 2005.

Residential Remodeling (In billions of dollars)

Year	Total	Maintenance/repair	Improvements
1980	$ 46.3	$ 15.2	$ 31.2
1985	80.3	35.4	44.9
1990	106.8	51.3	55.5
1991	97.5	49.8	47.7
1992	103.7	45.2	58.6
1993	108.3	41.7	66.6
1994	115.0	43.0	72.1
1995	111.7	42.0	69.6
1996	114.9	37.0	77.9
1997	121.1	41.0	80.1
Projected			
1998	127.9	44.9	83.0
2000	138.8	50.5	88.3
2005	166.8	63.6	103.2

The Age of Homes in the U.S.

Year built	Total housing units		Owner occupied		Renter occupied	
	Number built (In thousands)	%	Number built (In thousands)	%	Number built (In thousands)	%
Before 1920	10,019	9	5,039	8	3,632	11
1920–1949	20,497	19	10,700	17	7,424	22
1950–1969	29,375	27	18,147	29	8,518	25
1970–1979	23,717	22	13,347	21	7,685	23
1980–1989	17,290	16	10,001	16	5,412	16
1990–1995	8,559	8	6,310	10	1,478	4
Total	**109,457**	**100**	**63,544**	**100**	**34,149**	**100**
Median Age	**28 years**		**27 years**		**30 years**	

Sources: U.S. Census Bureau and National Association of Home Builders

Apartment Living

Average Monthly Apartment Rent*

Some of the most expensive apartment rents in the U.S. (New York City is not included in the survey.)

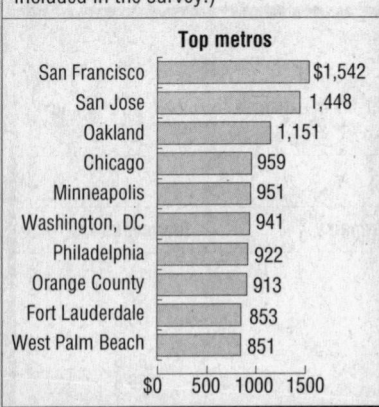

Top metros

San Francisco	$1,542
San Jose	1,448
Oakland	1,151
Chicago	959
Minneapolis	951
Washington, DC	941
Philadelphia	922
Orange County	913
Fort Lauderdale	853
West Palm Beach	851

$0   500 1000 1500

*First quarter 1998.
Source: M/PF Research, Inc.

Apartment Residents

(Number of U.S. apartment households in millions)

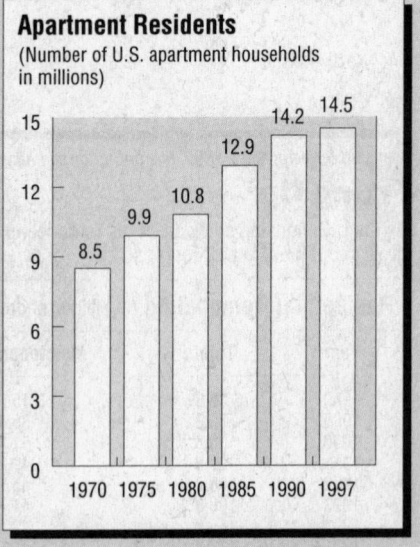

Year	Value
1970	8.5
1975	9.9
1980	10.8
1985	12.9
1990	14.2
1997	14.5

Sources: U.S. Census Bureau and National Multi Housing Council

Business and Economy Glossary

arbitrage The practice of simultaneously buying and selling a security in separate markets to take advantage of slight differences in price. Arbitrage is a high-volume undertaking: Because any discrepancy in price is usually razor-thin, a transaction must involve a great number of shares to generate significant profit. The term also refers to the activities of those who speculate in the stocks of companies thought to be takeover targets; they are said to engage in "risk arbitrage."

balance of payments A statistical record of economic transactions between one country and the rest of the world, which represents the flow of money into and out of the nation. No single figure represents an overall balance.
Current Account Balance: Also known as the current balance or balance of payments on current account, it is the most widely used figure. It is the net balance on trade in goods and services plus remittances (which are unilateral transfers such as Social Security payments to a recipient outside the country) and government grants to other countries. It doesn't include long-term loans.
Balance on Goods and Services: This is the difference between the value of imports of goods and services and exports.
Balance of Trade: Also known as the balance of merchandise trade, this is the difference between the value of imports of goods only and exports.

Bankruptcy Code The U.S. Bankruptcy Code is divided into chapters that provide different types of relief to debtors:
Chapter 7 governs liquidation, rather than reorganization. A debtor can voluntarily file for Chapter 7, or creditors can file an involuntary petition against a debtor to force the debtor into bankruptcy proceedings. A trustee, elected by the creditors, collects and liquidates all the debtor's property and examines creditors' claims against the property. If the debtor has not been guilty of any misconduct, the federal bankruptcy court will grant a discharge releasing the debtor from most or all pre-bankruptcy petition debts. Once the debtor obtains the discharge, a creditor is forbidden from taking any steps to collect the discharged debt.
Chapter 9 provides for municipal debt adjustments. To obtain relief under Chapter 9, the municipality must be insolvent or unable to meet its debts, and it ordinarily must show some prior efforts to negotiate a settlement with its various creditors. A municipality may not liquidate under Chapter 7; it must attempt to formulate a plan under Chapter 9 and then, only if the state involved allows, resort to federal bankruptcy law.
Chapter 11 relief is generally available to individuals, partnerships and corporations. It is not necessary that a company be insolvent to qualify for Chapter 11. The absence of an insolvency requirement has enabled debtors having problems other than an inability to meet current obligations—such as a massive potential liability—to seek relief under the bankruptcy code. Chapter 11 is the provision under which most corporate reorganizations occur. Ordinarily, the debtor will continue to operate its business as a "debtor in possession" after filing under Chapter 11. The filing automatically stays unilateral action by any creditor to enforce or secure a lien on the debtor's property. A secured creditor is given assurance under the code that the value of its collateral will be maintained and that at the end of the proceedings it will receive the value of its interest in the collateral. The proceeding culminates in a plan of reorganization that classifies the claims against the debtor and provides for satisfaction of those claims, as far as possible. A plan of reorganization must be approved by the court.

bond A certificate issued by a corporation or a government that states the amount of a loan, the interest to be paid, the time for repayment and the collateral pledged if payment cannot be made. In the case of a bond, repayment generally isn't due for a long period, generally seven years or more—as distinguished from a note, which has a shorter life span.

bond rating A rating is an assessment of the stability and strength of an issue. The rating is made by an independent agency such as Moody's Investors Service or Standard & Poor's Ratings Group. The agency, which is hired by the issuer, investigates the risk of default.

For a bond investor, a lower rating generally means greater risk and a higher yield, while a higher rating offers more security and usually a lower yield. An issuer with a sturdy reputation and higher bond rating can offer lower interest rates and still find customers for its debt. Ratings agencies periodically re-evaluate their assessments, either issuing "upgrades" or "downgrades," or "affirming" a debt rating. An agency may also put a company's ratings under review.

book-to-bill ratio A measure of sales trends in a company or industry. For the North American semiconductor industry, for example, the monthly figure is used as the leading economic indicator. A figure above 1 indicates an expanding market, and a number below 1 is a contracting market. For example, a book-to-bill ratio of 1.03 means that for every $100 of products shipped, $103 in new orders was received.

book value The difference between a company's assets and its liabilities, usually expressed in per-share terms. It takes into account all money invested in the company since its founding, as well as retained earnings. Book value is also referred to as stock-holders' equity and is calculated by subtracting liabilities from assets and dividing the result by the number of shares outstanding.

Bundesbank Germany's central bank. It controls monetary policy and money supply. Its U.S. counterpart is the Federal Reserve System.

capital gains tax A tax levied on the difference between the purchase price and the sale price of an asset—including real estate, stocks, bonds and other securities—when the asset is sold for a profit.

commercial paper The document that describes the details of a short-term corporate loan with a maturity typically between 30 and 90 days.

common stock An investment in common stock represents an ownership stake in a company. Dividends may be paid to common stock holders, and they may be increased or lowered as the company's earnings rise and fall. When preferred or preference classes of stock are also outstanding, the common stock holders are the last to receive dividends and the last to receive payments if the company is dissolved.

composite trading Composite trading figures, which appear in *The Wall Street Journal*'s stock tables and articles, take into account a stock's action on exchanges other than its primary one. For instance, a stock listed on the New York Stock Exchange may also be traded on regional stock exchanges, such as those in Boston or Cincinnati.

Comptroller of the Currency An office of the U.S. government that charters and oversees nationally chartered banks. It also has the power to declare an institution insolvent and to liquidate it. The comptroller is appointed by the President.

consumer confidence This closely watched statistic, generated by the Conference Board, a private research organization, measures consumers' feelings about the economy. It is based on their responses to questions about current and future business conditions, employment opportunities and family income.

consumer prices, Consumer Price Index (CPI) The CPI is a measure of change in prices of consumer goods, and therefore a main gauge of inflation. The figures, released monthly by the U.S. Labor Department, are based on a list of specific goods and services as purchased in urban areas. Components include food, housing, apparel, transportation, medical care and entertainment. The change in consumer prices is usually reported in terms of a percentage increase or decrease. The reason: The actual index is in the form of a number, but the figure by itself is abstract and makes sense only when compared with a previous period's CPI. Because it is an important indicator of the presence or absence of inflation, the CPI is often used as a benchmark for cost-of-living adjustments in retirement benefits and employment contracts.

currency depreciation, currency devaluation A nation's money depreciates when its value falls in relation to the currencies of other nations or in relation to its own prior value. A nation's money is devalued when its government deliberately reduces its value in relation to the currencies of other nations. When a country devalues its currency, the goods it imports become more expensive, while its exports become less costly abroad and thus more competitive.

deflation The opposite of inflation, deflation is an actual decline in prices.

derivatives Financial instruments with returns that move in response to some underlying asset or index. Futures contracts, for instance, "derive" their value from an underlying commodity such as gold or pork bellies. Other derivatives are based variously on bonds, currencies or intricate formulas that take into account changes in the prime rate or certain benchmark indexes.

discount rate The interest rate at which banks are able to borrow money from a central bank to loan to their customers. It is one of the key tools in a central bank's role as traffic cop for a nation's money supply; the higher the rate, the more expensive it becomes for businesses and individuals to borrow, and therefore spend money.

disinflation This slowing of price increases usually occurs during a recession when retailers are unable to pass higher prices along to consumers.

disposable personal income This is the income that a person retains after income taxes, Social Security deductions, property taxes and other payments to the various levels of government.

dividend The amount paid per share to holders of common stock. Payouts are generally made in quarterly installments. The dividend usually amounts to a portion of earnings. However, if a company shows no profit during a given period, it may be able to use earnings retained from profitable periods to pay its dividend on schedule.

Dow Jones Averages The Dow Jones Industrial, Transportation, Utilities and Composite Averages are widely used indicators of stock-market performance and sentiment. The industrial average is based on 30 major industrial issues listed on the New York Stock Exchange. The stocks are selected by

editors of *The Wall Street Journal*, and the average is found by adding the stocks' closing prices and dividing by an adjusted denominator. The average is price-weighted—that is, number of shares outstanding isn't taken into account, so higher-priced issues wield greater influence than lower-priced ones. It was first calculated in 1884 by Charles Dow, a founder of *The Wall Street Journal*.

The Dow Jones transportation, utilities and composite averages are calculated by the same method as the industrial average. The transportation average tracks 20 stocks, while the utilities average includes 15.

The Dow Jones Composite Average reflects the 65 stocks that together constitute the industrials, transportation and utilities averages.

The four averages are published daily in the *Journal*.

Dow Jones U.S. Index A broad indicator of movement in the stock market based on stocks in more than 120 industry groups in nine industry sectors: basic materials, consumer cyclical, consumer noncyclical, energy, financial, industrial, technology, utilities and independent (large companies with wide-ranging interests). Altogether, the stocks in the index represent about 80% of U.S. market capitalization. The index includes more than 700 issues that trade on the New York Stock Exchange, the American Stock Exchange and the Nasdaq Stock Market. The index is market-capitalization weighted—that is, both the stock price and number of shares outstanding enter into the computation. The effect is that a given stock's influence on the index is proportionate to its value in the market. The index's base date is June 30, 1982, which is equal to 100.

Dow Jones Global Indexes A broad indicator of more than 3,000 companies worldwide, representing more than 80% of the equity capital on 34 stock markets around the globe. The indexes are market-capitalization weighted—that is, both the stock price and number of shares outstanding enter into the computation. This means a particular stock's effect on the indexes is proportionate to its value in the marketplace. The indexes are structured to make adjustments for mergers, acquisitions, spinoffs, corporate restructurings, noncash distributions and other out-of-the-ordinary events. Companies are selected to represent about 80% of a country's market capitalization. The Dow Jones U.S. Index is the U.S. component of the Global Indexes, which are broken down by country and region, as well as by nine broad economic sectors and more than 120 industry groups. The base date is Dec. 31, 1991, which is equal to 100.

Export-Import Bank of the U.S. The Ex-Im Bank assists in the financing, insuring and guaranteeing of certain aspects of the import-export business, its general goal being to encourage international trade with the U.S. The bank itself, which is independent of the government but was federally chartered in 1934, finances its workings by borrowing from the U.S. Treasury.

federal-funds rate The interest rate charged for the overnight loans banks make to one another. It is named for federal funds—the money banks are required by the Federal Reserve to keep on hand to back up deposits. A bank that has more federal funds than necessary may lend the excess to a bank that needs it to meet requirements. The Fed sets a recommended federal-funds rate, but the rate itself is negotiated daily by the parties to a particular loan. That's why it is regarded as an important gauge of interest-rate trends.

Federal Home Loan Bank System This network of regional Federal Home Loan Banks provides loans to savings banks, savings and loans and other institutions that are important providers of mortgage loans. The FHLB's role is much like the Federal Reserve's among larger, commercial banks.

Federal Home Loan Mortgage Corp. Known as Freddie Mac, it helps to provide banks and other lenders with money for home loans by buying from them the mortgages they issue. It pools the mortgages, then sells securities backed by the interest and principal payments produced by those mortgage pools. Freddie Mac was chartered by the U.S. government but is now publicly owned; its shares trade on the New York Stock Exchange.

Federal National Mortgage Association Known as Fannie Mae, it buys mortgages from banks and lenders and repackages them as investment securities. Its purpose is to improve liquidity in the secondary market for such mortgages. Fannie Mae was chartered by the U.S. government but is now publicly owned; its shares trade on the New York Stock Exchange.

Federal Open Market Committee The policy-making arm of the Federal Reserve Board, this committee sets monetary policy geared to achieving the larger objectives of the Fed as regulator of money supply and credit. The FOMC's chief tool is the purchase and sale of government securities to increase or decrease the money supply, respectively. It also sets key interest rates, such as the discount rate and the federal-funds rate. The FOMC, which meets monthly, is made up of Federal Reserve governors and the presidents of several Federal Reserve Banks.

Federal Reserve System/Bank/Board The Federal Reserve System is the nation's central bank. It is responsible for regulating banking and credit in the U.S. economy. It was formed in 1913 by an act of Congress in the wake of a financial scare and a severe run on banks. The Fed controls the money supply, holds the federal government's savings accounts and acts as examiner for national-chartered and state-chartered banks. (Other institutions, such as savings banks and savings and loans, are regulated by the Federal Home Loan Bank System.)

The Federal Reserve System includes the 12 regional Federal Reserve Banks, and its policies are established by the Federal Reserve Board. That panel's seven members are appointed by the President to 14-year, staggered terms.

Financial Accounting Standards Board Chief rule-making body for U.S. accountants.

futures contract A futures contract is an agreement to buy or sell an asset—such as pork bellies or U.S. Treasury bonds—at a set time in the future at an agreed-upon price. Futures contracts may also be based on other types of financial instruments or on certain stock-market indexes.

Activity in the futures market is an important measure of market sentiment because it indicates the direction investors believe prices of real commodities, financial instruments and other assets are headed.

Government National Mortgage Association Known as Ginnie Mae, it is a middleman in residential mortgages, particularly those for low-income housing. It is owned by the Department of Housing and Urban Development and has a two-part role: It helps to provide lenders with money for home loans by buying mortgages they issue, and it guarantees interest and principal payments on certain mortgage-backed securities.

gross domestic product The total value of goods and services produced by a nation. In the U.S., the GDP is calculated by the Commerce Department, and it is the main measure of U.S. economic output.

hedge An investment strategy designed to limit the risk of loss. It can be as simple as putting money in a bank account instead of a mattress; by earning interest, the investor hedges against losses of purchasing power due to inflation. More complex strategies take the form of a series of investments set up so that one balances another. For example, an investor might buy some stock while simultaneously investing in a "put option" for the same stock. (The option grants its holder the right but not the obligation to sell shares at a specified price by a certain date.) As a result, the investor makes money if his shares rise in value. However, the option can be exercised to limit losses if the share price falls. Hedging is also a driving force behind the commodities futures market.

hedge fund A little-regulated, private investment partnership that invests huge sums in global currency, bond and stock markets in search of profit. To avoid regulation as a mutual fund in the U.S., such funds must have 99 or fewer U.S. investors. Therefore, they are private investment clubs for the well-to-do—although some hedge funds trade publicly abroad. Hedge funds typically require minimum investments that start in the hundreds of thousands of dollars. Despite the name, many hedge funds don't necessarily hedge. Indeed, the spectacular returns and mighty tumbles for which they are known often result from mammoth, leveraged one-way bets in the market. They got the name because the funds often are pitched as producing high returns and—courtesy of sophisticated strategies that are rarely revealed—little risk of loss.

historical cost A valuation method for direct investment that values assets and liabilities at their book value.

housing starts An estimate of the number of houses on which construction began in a certain period, such as a month or a year. It is one of the leading gauges of the health and direction of the U.S. economy and the level of consumer confidence. The figure also indicates the pace of future sales of lumber and materials, and of big-ticket consumer items such as furnishings and appliances.

inflation A rise in prices. Inflation may be caused by an increase in the money supply; when there are more dollars available to spend, each dollar buys less. It may also be caused by rising manufacturing costs, a decrease in supply of goods or a combination of factors.

initial public offering (IPO) The first offering of stock that a company makes to the public.

International Monetary Fund The IMF makes loans and provides other services intended to stabilize world currencies and foster orderly and balanced trade. Its pool of money is funded and supported by subscriptions of member nations, and IMF aid typically comes with conditions that a recipient country take certain steps to stabilize its economy by reducing inflation or its trade deficit.

junk bonds Debt issues that are considered risky investments. To attract investors, they typically offer higher yields than bonds with investment-grade ratings. If a junk bond carries a rating at all, it is set below triple-B by Standard & Poor's Ratings Group and below Baa by Moody's Investors Service Inc.

leading economic indicators A composite index of important economic measures used to forecast likely changes in the economy as a whole. Some of the factors taken into consideration: length of work week, unemployment claims, orders for consumer goods, building permits, plant and equipment orders, stock prices, money supply and consumer expectations. The monthly index is compiled by the Conference Board.

leveraged buyout The purchase of a company that is financed largely by borrowed money. Ultimately, the debt is paid with funds generated by the acquired company's operations or by the sale of its assets.

limited partnership A type of partnership in which general partners are responsible for the running of the firm, while limited partners have no say in its operation. However, general partners carry the burden of full liability. The limited partners' liability is no greater than the capital they contributed to the venture.

loss In corporate reports, the excess of expenses over revenue during a company's fiscal period.

money-supply measures There are three basic categories for measuring the supply of money in the U.S. economy.

The basic money-supply gauge is M1. It consists of funds that are readily available for spending, including cash and checking accounts. (M1 is sometimes broken down into M1-A and M1-B. M1-A is the total private checking-account deposits at commercial banks plus cash in public hands. M1-B is cash plus checking-type deposits at all financial institutions, including credit unions and savings-and-loan associations.)

M2 consists of cash and private deposits, such as CDs, but not large ones that tie up funds for a length of time. It also includes certain short-term assets, such as the amounts held in money-market mutual funds.

M3 includes cash and all private deposits, as well as other financial instruments, such as large-denomination time deposits.

most-favored nation A status bestowed by the U.S. on trading partners with which it has a good relationship. Most-favored nation standing gives a country the same privileges and tariff levels that the U.S. grants to the vast majority of its trading partners. Considering this, the term is somewhat misleading. Rather than being a special, select status, MFN is actually the term for a normal trading relationship between countries.

mutual fund A fund run by an investment company that provides a way for small investors to pool their money so that together they can afford to hire a professional money manager. Though a fund is owned by its shareholders, it is usually established, managed and distributed by the fund's invest-

ment adviser and its affiliated companies. Among the many types of mutual funds are these:

Balanced Fund: This fund invests in a combination of stocks and bonds, with a typical combination being 60% stocks and 40% bonds.

Closed-End Fund: Mutual fund that sells a limited number of shares, after which the fund is closed to investors and the shares are listed on a stock exchange. After that, the only way new investors can get in is to buy some of the exchange-traded shares.

Index Fund: A fund that tries to mimic the performance of a stock-market or bond-market index by buying all or many of the securities that make up the index. However, because of fund-management fees, its returns never quite match those of the index. But fees for index funds are typically much lower than for "actively managed" funds.

Money-Market Fund: A type of mutual fund that invests in stable, short-term securities. Money funds are designed to be easily converted into cash, and are structured to maintain an unchanging value of $1 a share. The yield fluctuates.

Nasdaq Stock Market A system set up for the trading of so-called over-the-counter stocks, those not listed on major exchanges. Unlike the New York Stock Exchange and other major markets, there is no Nasdaq trading floor. All trading takes place on a computer network. "Nasdaq" began as an acronym for National Association of Securities Dealers Automated Quotations, but now doesn't stand for anything but itself, Nasdaq insists. The system is operated by the National Association of Securities Dealers.

National Association of Securities Dealers A membership organization for securities brokers and underwriters in the U.S. that promise to abide by association rules. It sets guidelines for ethics and standardized industry practices, and has a disciplinary structure for looking into allegations of rules violations. The NASD also operates the Nasdaq Stock Market.

net asset value For a mutual fund, the NAV is the value of all investments held by the fund, usually expressed in per-share terms. The NAV is calculated daily at the close of markets in a process called "marking to market," or the valuing of all a fund's investments at current market prices.

net income, profit, earnings The amount left after a company pays taxes and all other expenses. A portion may be committed to pay preferred dividends. Some of what remains may, at the company's discretion, be paid in dividends to holders of common stock. The rest may be invested to obtain interest revenue or spent to acquire new buildings or equipment to increase the company's ability to make a future profit.

North American Free Trade Agreement, NAFTA Nafta phases out tariffs among the U.S., Canada and Mexico over 15 years and greatly eases investment across borders. Passed by Congress in late 1993, it took effect Jan. 1, 1994.

note A certificate issued by a corporation or a government that states the amount of a loan, the interest to be paid, the time for repayment and the collateral pledged if payment cannot be made. The repayment date is generally more than a year after issue but not more than seven or eight years later. This is the primary distinction between a note and a bond, which has a longer life span.

operating profit/loss Net income excluding income derived from sources other than the company's regular activities. It is calculated before income deductions, including taxes. Also called net operating income/loss.

option This agreement allows an investor to buy or sell something—such as shares of stock—within a specified period and at a set price. Options can be bought and sold as investments, but they are also important to some companies' executive-compensation plans.

Purchasers of options speak in terms of "calls" and "puts"—which are options to buy and sell, respectively. They may be purchased either to hedge against stock-market risks or to speculate in the market. Because calls can rise more sharply than an underlying stock's price, some investors expecting a stock to jump will use them to maximize returns. Similarly, puts often appreciate quickly as a stock falls. Options may also be based on the value of certain stock indexes, and on futures contracts.

As for executive compensation: By paying executives in stock options, a company can argue it is giving its management an incentive to boost corporate performance. If the stock price rises, executives get to cash in. Their options let them purchase shares at a lower-than-market price, which they can turn around and sell for a gain.

Organization for Economic Cooperation and Development Founded in 1961 to replace the Organization for European Economic Cooperation, which was set up in connection with the Marshall Plan, the OECD is a forum for its members to discuss and attempt to coordinate economic policies. The 29 members of the Paris-based group include Australia, Austria, Belgium, Canada, Czech Republic, Denmark, Finland, France, Germany, Greece, Hungary, Iceland, Ireland, Italy, Japan, Luxembourg, Mexico, Netherlands, New Zealand, Norway, Poland, Portugal, South Korea, Spain, Sweden, Switzerland, Turkey, the United Kingdom and the U.S.

Organization of Petroleum Exporting Countries Established in 1960 to link countries whose main source of export earnings is petroleum, it is based in Vienna. The 11 members of OPEC: Algeria, Indonesia, Iran, Iraq, Kuwait, Libya, Nigeria, Qatar, Saudi Arabia, United Arab Emirates and Venezuela.

prime rate The interest rate banks use as a base for a wide range of loans to businesses and to individuals. Changes in the prime rate typically don't have an immediate effect on consumer rates, such as mortgages and personal loans.

producer prices, producer price index The producer price index is a measure of change in prices paid by producers of goods. Actually there are three producer price indexes. The main one is the index for finished goods. As its name implies, it tracks prices of goods that are ready for sale to consumers. The other two are for intermediate materials and for crude materials. The indexes are based on specific "baskets" of goods as purchased by producers.

The three indexes are considered guides to future inflation because they chart the production costs of goods that will reach the consumer market a few months later.

proxy fight A battle for control of a company in which several groups seek proxies from the company's shareholders. (A proxy is an authorization for someone else to vote on behalf of a shareholder.) The winner is the one who collects enough proxies to guarantee it can vote the majority of shares outstanding in its own favor.

purchasing power parity A calculation method for other countries' gross domestic product that involves the use of international dollar price weights, which are applied to the quantities of goods and services produced in a given economy. This is an alternative to using conversions at official currency exchange rates and is considered a better way to compare the economic well-being of countries.

recession A downturn in economic activity, it is defined broadly by many economists as at least two consecutive quarters of decline in a nation's gross domestic product.

recovery In a business cycle, it is the period after a downturn or recession when economic activity picks up and the gross domestic product grows. It leads into the expansion phase of the business cycle.

revenue The amount of money a company took in during a fiscal period. The figure includes interest earned and receipts from services provided, sales, rents and royalties.

revenue passenger mile A calculation used by airlines to measure traffic. It is one paying passenger carried one mile.

revolving credit line A line of credit that may be used repeatedly up to a specific total, with periodic full or partial repayment.

sales In a corporate report, the money a company received in a fiscal period for goods and services sold.

Securities and Exchange Commission The SEC enforces securities laws and sets standards for disclosure about publicly traded securities, including mutual funds. It was created in 1934 and is made up of five commissioners, who are appointed by the President to staggered terms.

short sale, cover A short sale is a bet that the price of a stock will fall. A short seller borrows stock he thinks is overvalued, then sells it, hoping that before long other investors will see what he has seen and sell their shares, driving down the price. The short seller will then "short cover," or buy back shares to replace the borrowed ones, and pocket the difference between the higher selling price and the lower repurchase price.

Standard & Poor's 500 index The S&P 500 is made up of large-capitalization stocks and leading companies within major industries in the U.S. economy. The index is market-value weighted. That is, a stock price is multiplied by number of shares outstanding so that an issue's weight in the index is proportionate to its market value. The main criteria for a stock's inclusion in the index are market value and industry-group representation, along with liquidity, operating condition and proportion of closely held ownership. The S&P 500 includes issues traded in the three major U.S. markets, the New York Stock Exchange, the American Stock Exchange and Nasdaq Stock Market

Student Loan Marketing Association Known as Sallie Mae, it is a middleman in student loans. It helps to provide money for such loans by buying them from lenders. It then repackages the loans and sells them on a secondary market, and provides related services to financial and educational institutions. Sallie Mae was chartered by the U.S. government, but now its shares are traded on the New York Stock Exchange.

tariff A tax levied on imported goods that makes them more expensive and less appealing to consumers. Tariffs are sometimes imposed on imports that are hurting a domestic industry's sales.

tender offer An offer to acquire stock of a company for cash, stock of another company, bonds, other types of securities or a combination of these. A tender offer can be used to obtain control of a company.

Treasury bill/note/bond A Treasury bill is a certificate representing a short-term loan to the federal government that matures in three, six or 12 months. A Treasury note matures in two to 10 years. A Treasury bond matures in more than 10 years. Among bonds, the 30-year issue is considered a key indicator of trends in long-term interest rates, so its performance is regularly cited.

The yield on Treasury issues fluctuates—if their prices rise, yields fall. It works this way: A given bond pays a set interest rate and carries a set face value. But once it begins to trade, its price is set by market conditions. If the market expects interest rates to rise, the bond's price will fall because the rate it pays is less desirable.

underwriter An underwriter is a company that—for a fee—brings an issue of stocks, bonds or other securities to market. The underwriter buys all or most of the issue, then resells it to individual investors or other buyers. It makes money by purchasing the securities at one price and reselling them at a higher price (a difference known as the "underwriting spread.") Issuers turn to underwriters to minimize the risk of taking a security to market and to benefit from an underwriter's sales and marketing staff. Underwriting is an important source of income for investment banks and securities firms.

unemployment rate The unemployment rate is the percentage of people in the work force who aren't working and are looking for jobs. The numbers are compiled monthly by the Labor Department.

World Bank An organization created to make loans primarily in developing countries, with the stipulation that the country's government must guarantee the loan. The full name is International Bank for Reconstruction and Development.

6

TECHNOLOGY & SCIENCE

I*n 1998, millions more people started watching the Internet. They also began to realize the Internet is watching back.*

Privacy concerns, once the province of a small cadre of activists, became one of the most pressing issues in cyberspace. Suddenly, the masses began to realize that the vast network of computers that make up the Internet can track their every action, from the books they buy to the Web sites they browse to the comments they make in chat rooms. Combining these observations on Net surfing habits with the files already in marketers' databases could result in a significant loss of privacy.

Concerns of what will happen if Web sites abuse the personal information they collect from users range from the pesky (an increasing flood of unwanted junk e-mail) to the sobering (health insurance companies finding out an insured customer was surfing a cancer Web site). Even more alarming is the worry that children will be taken advantage of or preyed upon if private information about them becomes available.

A decorated sailor named Timothy R. McVeigh became the poster child for privacy advocates in January, when it was reported that he was inadvertently "outed" by an America Online Inc. representative. Mr. McVeigh owned an anonymous AOL account in which he identified himself as gay. When questioned, an AOL employee told a Navy investigator that Mr. McVeigh owned the account; Mr. McVeigh was given a dishonorable discharge from the Navy.

He sued the Navy and AOL and eventually settled with both parties and retired from the Navy with full benefits. But the case sent shock waves through the on-line privacy community.

It demonstrated the worst-case scenario for what can happen when on-line information isn't carefully guarded. AOL said the incident was a result of human error and that the employee violated company policy by releasing any customer information, but privacy activists argued that this case called for the government to take a closer look at on-line privacy issues.

The Clinton administration has long advocated a hands-off policy when it comes to the Internet. Supporters of this approach argue that the Internet's explosive growth resulted from its freewheeling culture and that heavy-handed regulation would slow the new medium's growth.

As an alternative to regulation, though, the White House has encouraged the Internet industry to put its own voluntary restrictions in place. As a model for this type of watchdog organization, it points to the efforts of the advertising and direct marketing industries. But the administration's patience with the industry is showing signs of wearing thin. "One year from now, you're going to be liable" whether it be under self-regulation or government requirement, Ira Magaziner, President Clinton's senior adviser on Internet policy, warned at an IBM-sponsored privacy conference in New York in May.

The government has been keeping a close eye on the industry throughout 1998. In March, the Federal Trade Commission conducted a sweep of more than 100 Web sites to see if they had posted privacy policies. The agency issued a report in June berating the

Internet sites for their lax controls with sensitive information. And administration officials from the FTC and the White House have warned repeatedly that if the industry doesn't come up with some concrete solutions to the privacy problem, they will step in.

Congress, in fact, seems anxious to legislate privacy protections in cyberspace. At least a dozen bills concerning privacy on the Internet were proposed in the 105th Congress, targeting everything from junk e-mail to the types of information Web sites can collect from consumers.

The watershed event of the year came in August, when the Federal Trade Commission cracked down on Web sites that violate privacy policies. The agency settled a privacy-violation complaint with GeoCities Inc., one of the Web's most popular sites, and issued a sternly worded release in which it accused the company of turning over to advertisers confidential data that it had promised would be kept secret. The stock price of GeoCities, which had just issued a wildly successful initial public offering, plummeted on the news.

The settlement highlighted one of the key privacy problems on the Internet. Many Web sites offer an amazing array of free services and information, but there is a hidden price: registration forms that require all kinds of data, from e-mail addresses to Social Security numbers to personal income information.

While there still are no federal laws requiring Web sites to post privacy laws, the FTC took an unprecedented move with the Geo-Cities action: It cracked down on the site because it didn't follow the privacy policy it had voluntarily posted on its site, something the agency has jurisdiction over because it constitutes a deceptive practice.

Following the release of the FTC report in June and the crackdown on GeoCities in August, industry players scrambled to come up with solutions to reassure consumers—and stave off legislation. The on-line industry knows it must deal with privacy protection or risk losing consumers. That's a bigger threat to the medium's growth than any stifling laws or regulations, some industry experts say.

Two groups—the Council of Better Business Bureaus Inc. and the Online Privacy Alliance, a group of about 50 companies and trade groups—have announced self-regulatory guidelines. Both of the industry proposals require member Web sites to in-

form consumers about the kind of information they are gathering and how it will be used. They also require sites to have opt-out policies, allowing consumers to request that they be removed from marketers' lists.

Even more important, both plans require strict protections for children, one of the galvanizing issues that few marketers are arguing with. The Online Privacy Alliance, for example, is requiring that all Web sites get permission from a parent before gathering any information from children.

It isn't just Americans who are grappling with privacy issues on the Internet. The European Union has taken an even more stringent approach and has threatened to block data from being transmitted between the United States and Europe unless America passes laws designed to protect privacy on-line. White House officials say they are confident they will be able to get Europe to back down from that threat as long as the industry proves it can regulate itself.

Even with the industry efforts and increased government involvement, some advocates say personal privacy remains in jeopardy. Privacy groups such as the Electronic Privacy Information Center, the Center for Democracy and Technology and the Electronic Frontier Foundation continue to push for stringent government standards. Self-regulatory efforts, some of these advocates argue, are inherently flawed because they typically contain no provision for ensuring that companies follow the rules.

Web sites that post privacy policies don't go far enough, they say, arguing that these policies often merely spell out the multitude of ways in which the site plans to use visitors' personal data. "They're just telling people their privacy is going to be invaded. That's not privacy protection," says David Banisar, legal director for the Electronic Privacy Information Center in Washington, D.C.

While governments and business chew over these issues, privacy advocates also encourage consumers to take a closer look at the ways they can protect themselves. Their suggestions range from the highly technical (reconfigure browsers so that Web sites can't read who you are or where you've been) to the sneaky (don't ever give a Web site accurate information about yourself). One industry group even began an advertising campaign with television commercials warning parents that the Internet is not a safe place for kids to visit alone.

The most obvious precaution, it turns out,

is also the one that is most often ignored: Don't put it on the Internet if you don't want someone to read it. That includes e-mail, personal profiles, chat room conversations and postings on electronic bulletin boards.

The most closely watched event of the year—the release of the Starr report—illustrated the fact that e-mail is far from a confidential means of communication. Included in the 2,800 pages of evidence the independent prosecutor released were scads of e-mail messages Monica Lewinsky had sent to friends about her relationship with President Clinton. Some of these messages were voluntarily turned over by Ms. Lewinsky; others were recovered from her computer by the FBI.

The messages—many of which divulged details of her encounters with Mr. Clinton—were a startling reminder to the public that once something is transformed into digital bits, there's no way to completely erase it.

Not only are copies of e-mail messages likely to remain in the sender's personal computer, but there also is no way of knowing exactly who can see them once they're sent through cyberspace. When e-mail is sent, it bounces from one routing computer to another as it makes its way across the Internet. A message can go through a dozen or so routing computers before it ends up in the recipient's e-mailbox, and each one of those computers is another place prying eyes can peek at the message.

Even if no one sees the message the moment it flits across the network, it could get caught by an instant replay. One of the top priorities for system administrators is to make sure they never lose any important information on their computer networks. So, most of them frequently make backup tapes to record all the information on the network. That way, if the network crashes, there is a copy of all the data that have moved over the computers. That's great if a user loses an important file—but not so great for someone trying to erase embarrassing messages.

The only surefire way to protect confidential information is to keep it off the Internet entirely, experts say. "When you send e-mail, it's kind of like sending a postcard," says Sarah Reardon, a spokeswoman for the Electronic Messaging Association in Roslyn, Virginia. "The problem is, people feel it's safer than writing a letter."

Rebecca Quick, staff reporter for *The Wall Street Journal* in New York

The Technology Culture

A Gadget Generation

Share of U.S. households with the following:

Television	98%
Radio	98
Cordless phone	70
Telephone answering device	69
Stereo component system	55
Home CD player	52
Personal computer	42
Computer printer	40
Cellular phone	39
Camcorder	30
Pager	29
Electronic car alarm	29
Computer with CD-ROM	26
Modem or fax/modem	24
Caller-ID equipment	18
Direct-view satellite dish	11
Fax machine	10

Note: Figures are for January 1998
Source: Consumer Electronics Manufacturers Assn.

The Speed of Change

How many years it took each of these technologies to spread to 25% of the U.S. population*

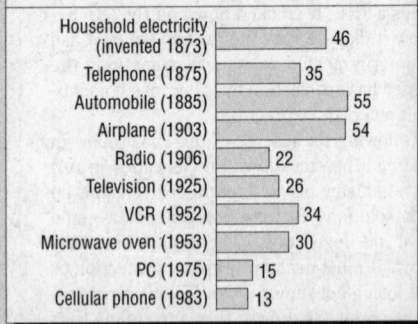

Household electricity (invented 1873)	46
Telephone (1875)	35
Automobile (1885)	55
Airplane (1903)	54
Radio (1906)	22
Television (1925)	26
VCR (1952)	34
Microwave oven (1953)	30
PC (1975)	15
Cellular phone (1983)	13

*Defined as 25% of households, except for airplane, automobile and cell phone. Airplane: 25% of the 1996 level of air miles traveled per capita. Automobile: The number of motor vehicles reached 25% of the number of people age 16 and older. Cellular phone: The number of cellular phones reached 25% of the number of registered passenger automobiles.
Source: Dallas Federal Reserve Bank

THE YEAR 2000 BUG

It's called the Year 2000 bug, and, depending on whom you ask, it is either the biggest issue to face companies and government agencies in years—or the most overhyped marketing event of all time.

This much is clear: Come January 1, 2000, some percentage of the world's computers will malfunction because they will think it is January 1, 1900. The result could be chaos—or a delay in getting your electric bill.

The "Y2K" (for Year 2000) bug stems from a decades-old practice by software writers to represent years as just two digits in computer programs, as well as in some computer chips. Representing 1980 as "80" saved data-storage space, which was vital back when giant mainframe computers had less storage capacity than your average laptop computer does today.

But now that memory-saving trick has come back to haunt the industry. Each time a computer program stores a date, it could turn into a time bomb. And programs store millions of dates—when a bill was sent to a customer, when a customer paid, when an airline reservation expires and when an assembly line last was lubricated—just to name a few. Remarkably, some software sold just a year or two ago still stored dates as two digits.

If a computer mistakenly thinks that the year 2000, represented as "00," is 1900, all sorts of things could go wrong. The computer at your mortgage company may calculate that you haven't sent in a payment for 100 years and start to foreclose on your house. Your reservation for that flight to Chicago may be wiped out because the computer believes it was made 100 years ago. Elevators may think they haven't received maintenance work for

Going On-Line

The projected number of U.S. households with personal computers, modems and on-line services.

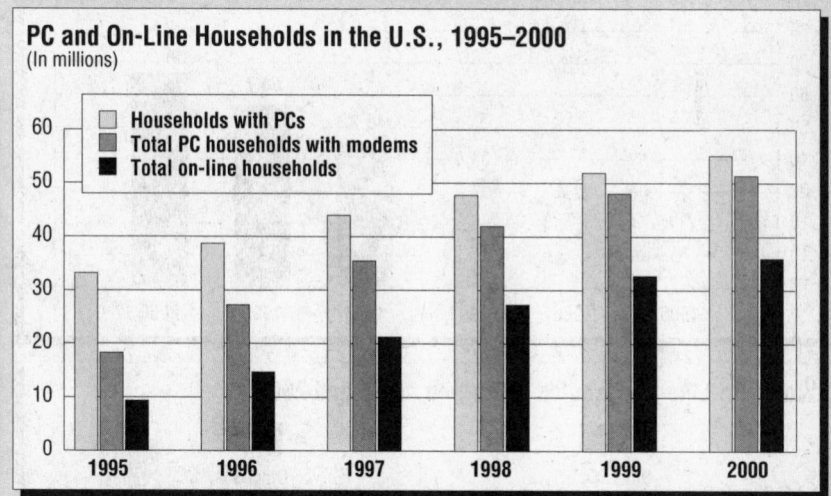

PC and On-Line Households in the U.S., 1995–2000
(In millions)

Legend:
- Households with PCs
- Total PC households with modems
- Total on-line households

	1995	1996	1997	1998	1999	2000
Households in the U.S.	97.7	98.9	99.9	101.0	102.1	103.2
Households with PCs	33.2	38.7	44.0	47.8	51.9	55.1
Households with PCs and modems	18.3	27.2	35.5	42.0	48.1	51.4
On-line households	9.4	14.7	21.3	27.3	32.7	36.0

Source: Jupiter Communications

100 years and shut themselves down. And a food-processing plant whose inventory-control system thinks the flour and butter are over 100 years old may stop churning out the hot-dog rolls and crackers.

But things could get even worse, according to the doomsday scenarios painted by the most pessimistic observers of the millennium bug. They reason that since computers are such an integral part of the economy—running everything from the air-traffic control system to power and water networks to food-delivery operations—something dire is likely to occur.

These pessimists say cities could go dark, planes could fall from the sky, and a global banking crisis prompted by the inability to transfer money electronically could send the world spiraling into depression. Some Y2K sages have advocated that people store money under their mattresses and stock up with enough food and water to last for months. A few fanatics even say they will head for the hills—literally—out of fear that urban areas could devolve into lawless chaos.

It isn't just software that could be affected. Millions of computer chips that are found in everything from factory equipment to hospital medical gear to cars and microwave ovens could be affected by the same date problem. Finding and fixing these chips is, in some cases, tougher than rectifying the software issue. That's because chips are often buried deep inside equipment, and tracing which chips have problems is thorny. The manufacturer that originally sold the electronic sub-

The World On-Line Market

The estimated number of on-line households around the world and the changing regional breakdown.

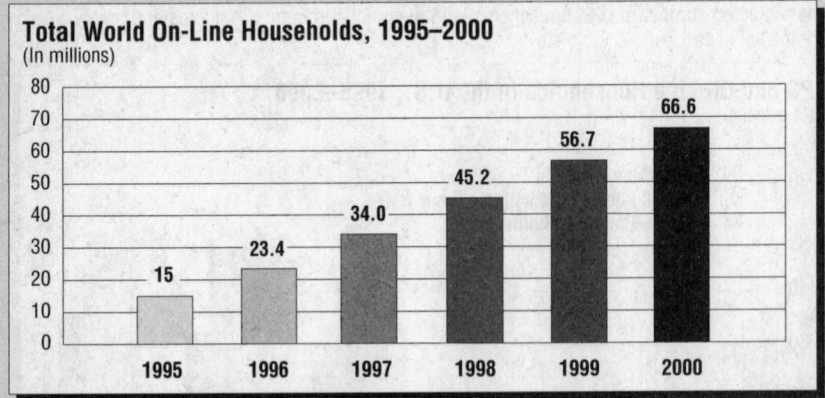

Total World On-Line Households, 1995–2000
(In millions)

Year	Households
1995	15
1996	23.4
1997	34.0
1998	45.2
1999	56.7
2000	66.6

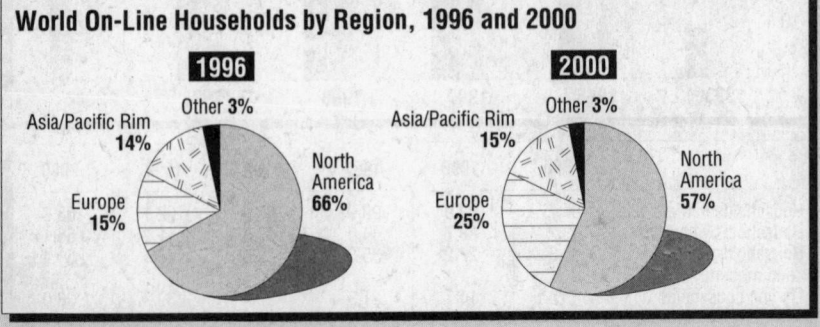

World On-Line Households by Region, 1996 and 2000

1996
- Other 3%
- Asia/Pacific Rim 14%
- Europe 15%
- North America 66%

2000
- Other 3%
- Asia/Pacific Rim 15%
- Europe 25%
- North America 57%

Source: Jupiter Communications

Cyberspace Demographics

Demographic Characteristics of On-Line Users, or "Cybercitizens"

Gender		Income	
Male	60%	Under $50,000	48%
Female	40	$50,000 or more	52
Age		**Number in household**	
16-29	31	2 or fewer	33
30-49	52	3 or more	67
50 +	17		
Education		**Employment**	
High school or less	31	Employed	76
Beyond high school	69	Not employed	24
Marital status		**Race**	
Married	52	White	76
Not married	48	Non-white	24

Source: Yankelovich Partners Inc.

assembly holding the chip may have, in turn, sold that circuit board to a wholesaler, who in turn sold it to the equipment maker. Whom do you contact about the chip?

Overall, fixing the glitch is taking longer and is costing more than many anticipated. A key reason is that it is a labor-intensive process to sort through millions of lines of software code just to find those elusive dates. Then the software has to be tested, and tested again.

According to Gartner Group, a computer-industry consulting firm, fixing the glitch will cost at least $600 billion world-wide. And that's just for the software part of the problem. Gartner hasn't added in the cost of fixing chips. Despite all this spending, as many as 20 percent of U.S. companies will still be faced with serious problems from the bug when the calendar turns to 2000, "and they don't even know it," says Manny Fernandez, Gartner's chairman and chief executive officer. That's because the problem is so elusive, and pervasive.

Things are more serious abroad. Gartner projects that as many as 35 percent of European companies will have serious Y2K-related computer failures, and in parts of Asia and Latin America, the majority of businesses are at risk. Third-world companies and governments in particular will have problems since they haven't had the money or programming resources to fix the bug, experts say. Asian companies, dogged by that region's

dire economic downturn, have had far more pressing issues to address—such as their very survival. And everywhere, smaller businesses are at greater risk of trouble because many seem ill-informed about the issue.

Yet others say the bug has been overhyped. Consulting firms that stand to benefit by selling their Y2K "remediation" services—including Gartner—have whipped up an unwarranted frenzy, these observers say. Sure, there's a problem, but it is being addressed.

Most big companies and major government agencies have been working to fix the bug for several years. The most aggressive ones are long past the fixing phase and have been testing their computers to see how they interact with those of suppliers and customers. Companies are too smart to let their vital systems be in jeopardy of failure, these experts say. Critical systems aren't likely to collapse, and manual overrides would allow airlines to keep flying and power to keep flowing if computers in these operations are affected, the optimists say.

Whatever the actual outcome, the issue won't necessarily go away once the calendar turns January 1, 2000. Software and chips that aren't fixed may make it past that date but could face problems later in 2000, as calculations keyed to certain dates kick in—and the computer thinks it is 1900.

Bart Ziegler

Information-Technology Industry

Worldwide sales estimates and projections for the information-technology industry, including computer and data-communications equipment, packaged software, and such services as consulting, operations management, maintenance and training. Projections and growth rate are based on 1997 currency conversion rates.

Information Technology Sales and Percent Change From Previous Year
(Dollars in billions)

Year	Hardware		Software		Services		Total	
	Sales	Change	Sales	Change	Sales	Change	Sales	Change
1996	$319	–	$112	–	$248	–	$679	–
1997	337	10 %	121	14%	259	11 %	717	11%
1998	367	9	142	17	283	9	793	11
1999	404	10	163	15	307	9	874	10
2000	443	10	186	14	333	9	962	10
2001	481	9	208	12	361	8	1,050	9

Source: International Data Corp.

Top Companies in the PC Market

Apple Computer and IBM, the leading personal-computer makers in the U.S. market in 1992, have seen their shares fall and have lost their dominant positions to Compaq and Dell.

Top 10 Marketers of Personal Computers (U.S. Shipments)

Rank	1992			1996			1997		
	Vendor	Shipments	Market share	Vendor	Shipments	Market share	Vendor	Shipments	Market share
1	Apple	1,550,000	13.2%	Compaq	3,417,360	12.9%	Compaq	5,035,118	16.0%
2	IBM	1,374,600	11.7	Packard Bell NEC	3,030,398	11.4	Dell	2,930,235	9.3
3	Compaq	675,820	5.7	IBM	2,196,318	8.3	Packard Bell NEC	2,776,144	8.8
4	Packard Bell	623,500	5.3	Dell	1,790,755	6.8	IBM	2,738,588	8.7
5	Dell	438,994	3.7	Apple	1,687,161	6.4	Gateway 2000	2,219,395	7.1
6	Gateway 2000	428,180	3.6	Gateway 2000	1,666,706	6.3	Hewlett-Packard	2,063,383	6.6
7	Tandy	330,000	2.8	Hewlett-Packard	1,404,216	5.3	Toshiba	1,460,920	4.6
8	AST	320,000	2.7	Toshiba	1,334,380	5.0	Apple	1,276,249	4.1
9	Toshiba	242,950	2.1	Acer	1,240,230	4.7	Acer	1,108,852	3.5
10	NEC	173,450	1.5	AST	633,005	2.4	Micron	684,222	2.2
	Others	5,603,538	47.6	Others	8,079,796	30.5	Others	9,185,697	29.2
	All Vendors	11,761,032	100.0	All Vendors	26,480,326	100.0	All Vendors	31,477,603	100.0

Top 10 Marketers of Personal Computers (Worldwide Shipments)

Rank	1992			1996			1997		
	Vendor	Shipments	Market share	Vendor	Shipments	Market share	Vendor	Shipments	Market share
1	IBM	3,210,153	10.4%	Compaq	7,211,350	10.4%	Compaq	10,145,946	12.7%
2	Apple	2,780,055	9.0	IBM	6,175,644	8.9	IBM	7,226,293	9.0
3	Compaq	1,555,510	5.1	Packard Bell NEC	4,230,011	6.1	Dell	4,716,411	5.9
4	NEC	1,375,700	4.5	Apple	3,750,686	5.4	Hewlett-Packard	4,468,429	5.6
5	Packard Bell	700,000	2.3	Dell	2,995,889	4.3	Packard Bell NEC	4,173,368	5.2
6	Dell	697,523	2.3	Hewlett-Packard	2,983,736	4.3	Toshiba	3,271,674	4.1
7	Toshiba	629,557	2.0	Acer	2,808,781	4.1	Fujitsu	2,967,119	3.7
8	AST	594,052	1.9	Toshiba	2,691,815	3.9	Acer	2,814,177	3.5
9	Olivetti	551,857	1.8	NEC (Japan)	2,663,088	3.8	Gateway 2000	2,689,170	3.4
10	Groupe Bull/ZDS	499,081	1.6	Fujitsu	2,581,580	3.7	Apple	2,668,470	3.2
	Others	18,159,512	59.0	Others	31,228,391	45.0	Others	34,844,801	43.6
	All Vendors	30,753,000	100.0	All Vendors	69,320,970	100.0	All Vendors	79,885,856	100.0

Source: International Data Corp.

Growth of the Personal Computer

U.S. and Worldwide Shipments of Personal Computers

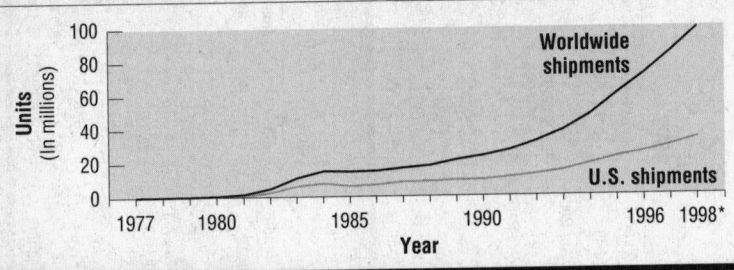

*Estimates

Personal Computer Shipments and Revenues

	Worldwide shipments (Thousands)	Worldwide revenue (Millions of U.S. $)	U.S. shipments (Thousands)	U.S. revenue (Millions of U.S. $)
Pre 1977	17		16.3	
1977	48		43	
1978	189		158	
1979	350		274	
1980	609		490	
1981	1,631		764	
1982	4,893		2,567	
1983	11,123	$11,019	6,199	$6,497
1984	15,044	18,496	7,768	10,683
1985	14,705	22,765	6,072	11,980
1986	15,064	22,968	6,814	12,092
1987	16,676	24,975	8,391	13,821
1988	18,061	33,367	8,616	17,361
1989	21,327	40,435	9,330	19,700
1990	23,738	46,000	9,430	18,898
1991	26,966	57,580	10,903	24,589
1992	32,411	64,095	12,544	25,858
1993	38,851	73,561	14,775	29,663
1994	47,894	94,457	18,605	37,339
1995	60,171	123,643	22,583	47,749
1996	71,065	150,414	25,650	60,129
1997	82,400	162,834	30,989	70,086
1998*	97,321	181,544	35,550	69,698

*Estimates
Source: Dataquest

Top Software Publishers

Publishers, Ranked by Dollar Sales

Publisher	1997 $	1997 units	Mkt share $	Mkt share units
Microsoft	$943,796,288	9,560,114	20.16%	8.42%
Cendant Software	375,021,906	13,672,070	8.01	12.04
Intuit	264,705,162	4,907,076	5.65	4.32
Symantec	208,395,616	2,740,680	4.45	2.41
Broderbund	205,720,968	5,739,808	4.39	5.05
Learning Co.	186,147,261	8,437,873	3.98	7.43
Electronic Arts	149,726,992	4,872,815	3.20	4.29
Adobe	139,027,479	753,543	2.97	0.66
GT Interactive	122,415,211	6,739,356	2.61	5.94
Corel	96,115,205	923,162	2.05	0.81
Mindscape	85,341,440	2,787,778	1.82	2.46
Disney	72,169,658	2,412,071	1.54	2.12
Hasbro Interactive	70,789,558	2,372,441	1.51	2.09
LucasArts	60,671,190	1,693,945	1.30	1.49
Network Associates	58,109,280	1,286,204	1.24	1.13
Virgin	56,380,312	1,698,592	1.20	1.50
Activision	51,938,477	1,549,917	1.11	1.36
Cybermedia	47,695,920	1,362,651	1.02	1.20
Apple	47,188,424	529,355	1.01	0.47
Mattel	46,558,591	1,468,995	0.99	1.29
	$3,287,914,938	75,508,446		
Total Software Sales	$4,682,021,664	113,549,959		

Source: PC Data

Most Popular CD-ROM Titles

Top Selling CD-ROMs Ranked by Unit Sales, in 1997

No.	Title	Publisher	Unit sales	Dollar sales	Avg. price
1	Microsoft Windows 95 Upgrade	Microsoft	941,483	$84,998,376	$90.28
2	Riven: The Sequel to Myst	Broderbund	915,413	39,858,835	43.54
3	Myst	Broderbund	869,774	18,931,830	21.77
4	Microsoft Flight Simulator	Microsoft	813,830	37,665,103	46.28
5	Diablo	Cendant Software	670,155	30,056,390	44.85
6	Turbo Tax Deluxe Final	Intuit	471,394	22,537,414	47.81
7	VirusScan 3	Network	431,597	17,411,374	40.34
8	Monopoly Game	Hasbro Interactive	397,864	12,781,528	32.13
9	NASCAR II	Cendant Software	388,473	17,136,275	44.11
10	Barbie Fashion Designer	Mattel	363,541	14,394,588	39.60
11	Command & Conquer: Red Alert	Virgin	363,207	17,091,677	47.06
12	Barbie Magic Hair Styler	Mattel	361,141	11,881,561	32.90
13	Microsoft Office Pro 97/ Bkshlf Comp/Ver	Microsoft	359,494	112,519,827	313.00
14	Trophy Bass	Cendant Software	356,280	3,722,931	10.45
15	Printmaster Gold Deluxe	Mindscape	336,284	14,448,413	42.96
16	Quicken Deluxe	Intuit	324,035	18,596,745	57.39
17	Lego Island	Mindscape	323,085	11,882,223	36.78
18	Microsoft Greetings Workshop	Microsoft	313,822	7,701,557	24.54
19	Print Shop Deluxe III	Broderbund	309,431	8,029,834	25.95
20	Microsoft Publisher	Microsoft	306,632	21,994,067	71.73

Source: PC Data

TELECOM TUMULT

The pipe dream of turning the simple telephone line into a conduit for data, movies and, oh yes, cheap telephone calls, is inching closer to reality.

Fueled by the explosive growth of Internet traffic, telephone companies are looking for ways to efficiently deliver such services to homes and businesses. The local telephone companies, including the Baby Bells, are teaming up with the computer industry to promote new technology that turns traditional copper wires into fat pipes, allowing consumers to surf the Internet at faster speeds. Meanwhile, a new generation of carriers is changing the way telephone networks are designed, eschewing the old "circuit switched" model in favor of a more efficient design based on Internet technology.

Carriers want to sell customers a complete package of telecommunications services: Long-distance, local, Internet, wireless and even video services. But regulatory and logistical barriers remain, despite the enactment of sweeping telecommunications legislation a few years ago. The Baby Bell telephone companies still have not won permission to enter the long-distance market. The long-distance companies haven't brought widespread competition to the local-telephone market, as expected. They say the Bells, which control much of the local-service architecture, have made it difficult and costly to lease parts of the network needed to deliver local service.

As a way of end-running the Bells and other local carriers, AT&T Corp. announced plans to acquire cable-telephone company Tele-Communications Inc. for $37 billion. TCI's cables could provide an alternative to the copper wires that extend into most homes, enabling AT&T to offer local, long-distance and entertainment services via a single pipeline. Some cable-television companies have begun offering telephone service to compete with the Bells in a handful of markets. "This will combine the best brand in the industry with the best broadband company in the industry," C. Michael Armstrong, AT&T's chairman, said when the deal was announced.

Still, AT&T will have to spend billions to turn TCI's infrastructure into a phone network— and the network would reach only a portion of American homes. While big questions still remain about the viability of the TCI acquisition, AT&T's plan clearly signaled its emergence from nearly two years of crisis and confusion. Under the leadership of Mr. Armstrong, the former Hughes Electronics Corp. chief, the company has made a series of bold moves, including the purchase of local carrier Teleport Communications Group, in an effort to maintain its leadership position in the rapidly changing telecommunications industry.

The Bells are bulking up, too. SBC Communications Inc., the Texas-based Bell, announced plans to acquire neighbor Ameritech Corp. for more than $56 billion. Bell Atlantic Corp. agreed to a $52 billion merger with GTE Corp. The carriers have promised to use their scale to bring local competition to markets outside their home territories. The mergers also underscore the fact that local-telephone service remains a good business: Residential customers continue to add second, third and even fourth telephone lines, and phone companies make fat profits on services such as voice mail, call waiting and three-way calling.

Even with the onslaught of "competitive local exchange carriers," or "CLECs," which primarily aim to take business customers away from the Bells, incumbent local carriers still control about 98 percent of the telephone lines in the United States.

The Bells face big challenges, of course. They need to figure out how to gracefully make the transition away from their traditional

The Telephone's Reach

The percentage of U.S. households with telephones has increased, but phone service still isn't universal primarily because many low-income people cannot afford it.

Year	Percentage of households with telephones
1920	35.0%
1930	40.9
1940	36.9
1950	61.8
1960	78.3
1970	90.5
1980	92.9
1990	94.8
1997	93.9

Source: U.S. Census Bureau and Federal Communications Commission

"circuit switched" architecture, designed to accommodate five-minute telephone calls, to a "packet switched" network—based on Internet protocols—that ships calls, data or images in digital bits. And they must maintain and train an emboldened union workforce, even as their competitors hire nonunion labor. During contract negotiations in 1998, Bell Atlantic was hit with a two-day work stoppage while U S West Inc. faced a 15-day strike.

Telecommunications executives also say their companies need to get bigger to compete globally. Indeed, all the large carriers have their eyes on serving multinational corporations, which have operations around the globe. British Telecommunications PLC, which bowed out of the takeover battle for MCI Communications Corp., is teaming up with AT&T to sell calling and data services to international clients. WorldCom, which ultimately acquired MCI, is pursuing international customers using a new European network. International carriers, meanwhile, are looking for new ways to enter the lucrative American market.

The Baby Bells say they need to be able to offer long-distance services before they truly can participate in the global trend. The Telecommunications Act of 1996 requires the Bells to open their markets to competitors before regulators grant them permission to offer long-distance services in their local markets. The Bells challenged the constitutionality of the law, which doesn't apply the same open-market test to other local carriers such as GTE. A Texas judge declared parts of the Act unconstitutional in a stunning decision, only to have a federal appeals court overturn the decision.

That likely means that the Bells aren't going to get any shortcuts to long-distance entry. Instead, they're probably going to have to make some concessions to competitors. Regulators say the companies have started to make progress, and some analysts predict at least one Bell will be in the long-distance business in early 1999.

"Cable, long distance and local telephone companies all said that they were going to enter each other's businesses. Entry turned out to be harder and more costly than expected," William Kennard, chairman of the Federal Communications Commission, said in a speech to the Federal Communications Bar Association in June 1998. "But the rise of the Internet has changed business plans again.

Telecommunications Industry Revenue

Telecommunications Industry Revenue Reached $222 Billion in 1996 and Grew 11.6% from 1995 (Amounts in millions)

	1992	1993	1994	1995	1996
Local service					
Local exchange	$39,235	$40,176	$42,245	$45,194	$48,717
Local private line	1,049	1,088	1,138	1,226	1,616
Cellular, PCS, paging & other mobile	7,285	10,237	14,293	18,759	26,049
Other local	7,687	8,002	8,302	10,428	10,543
Total local service	55,256	59,503	65,977	75,607	86,924
Interstate & intrastate access service	29,353	30,832	32,759	33,911	35,641
Long distance service					
Operator (including pay telephone & card)	9,465	10,772	10,539	11,170	10,975
Non-operator switched toll	54,300	58,294	60,819	64,431	71,467
Long distance private line	7,783	8,067	9,043	9,719	10,665
Other long distance	4,196	5,392	4,078	4,309	6,583
Total long distance	75,744	82,525	84,478	89,629	99,691
Total reported revenue	160,353	172,860	183,214	199,147	222,256

Source: Federal Communications Commission

The Long-Distance Market

The fourth-quarter market shares of the major long-distance telephone companies, based on their quarterly shareholder reports.

Market Share

	AT&T	MCI	SPRINT	WORLDCOM	Others
4Q84	87.7%	4.9%	3.0%	–	4.4%
4Q85	85.7	6.3	3.2	–	4.8
4Q86	81.5	7.9	5.1	–	5.6
4Q87	78.3	9.0	6.2	–	6.5
4Q88	73.9	11.7	7.2	0.1%	7.1
4Q89	68.9	13.7	8.9	0.2	8.2
4Q90	66.5	15.1	9.1	0.3	9.0
4Q91	63.9	15.9	8.8	1.2	10.2
4Q92	60.6	17.2	9.3	1.3	11.6
4Q93	57.5	18.1	9.3	2.3	12.9
4Q94	55.4	18.2	9.2	3.1	14.2
4Q95	53.2	18.5	9.1	4.4	14.9
4Q96	50.2	18.7	9.4	5.3	16.3
4Q97	47.0	18.7	9.5	6.2	18.4

Source: Federal Communications Commission

Companies can now compete to sell high speed Internet access ... Internet and digital technology have the potential to renew the promise of the Telecom Act."

Stephanie N. Mehta

Phone Prices

Percent Change From December of Previous Year Through December of the Year Shown

Year	Telephone services	Local services	Interstate toll service	Intrastate toll service
1980	4.6%	7.0%	3.4%	-0.6%
1981	11.7	12.6	14.6	6.2
1982	7.2	10.8	2.6	4.2
1983	3.6	3.1	1.5	7.4
1984	9.2	17.2	-4.3	3.6
1985	4.7	8.9	-3.7	0.6
1986	2.7	7.1	-9.4	0.3
1987	-1.3	3.3	-12.4	-3.0
1988	1.3	4.5	-4.2	-4.2
1989	-0.3	0.6	-1.3	-2.6
1990	-0.4	1.0	-3.7	-2.2
1991	3.5	5.1	1.3	-1.5
1992	-0.3	0.5	-1.3	-2.4
1993	1.8	1.0	6.5	0.2
1994	0.7	-0.3	5.4	-1.0
1995	1.2	2.6	0.1	-3.8
1996	2.1	0.9	3.7	6.1
1997	0.2	1.0	-4.3	2.8

Source: U.S. Bureau of Labor Statistics

Cell Phone Callers

As the number of people using cell phones has soared, the average local monthly bill has declined.

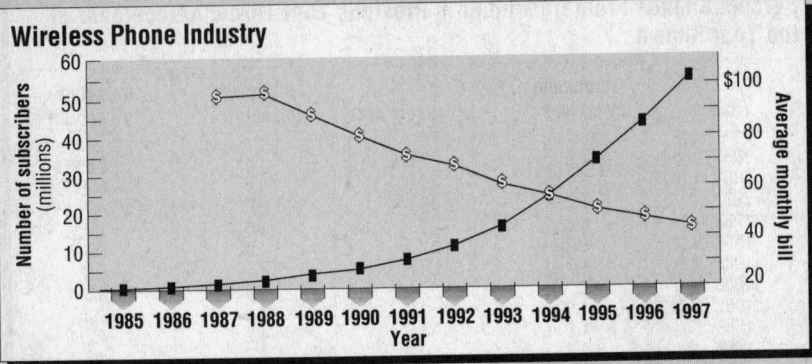

Wireless Phone Industry

Year	Subscribers	Annual revenues	Average local monthly bill
1985	340,213	$482,428,000	–
1986	681,825	823,052,000	–
1987	1,230,855	1,151,519,000	$96.83
1988	2,069,441	1,959,548,000	98.02
1989	3,508,944	3,340,595,000	89.30
1990	5,283,055	4,548,820,000	80.90
1991	7,557,148	5,708,522,000	72.74
1992	11,032,753	7,822,726,000	68.68
1993	16,009,461	10,892,175,000	61.48
1994	24,134,421	14,229,922,000	56.21
1995	33,785,661	19,081,239,000	51.00
1996	44,042,992	23,634,971,000	47.70
1997	55,312,293	27,485,633,000	42.78

Source: Cellular Telecommunications Industry Association

Research Report

U.S. Expenditures for Research & Development by Source of Funds and Performer

		Source of funds - Millions of current dollars				
	Total	Federal Government	Industry	Universities & colleges	Other nonprofits	Nonfederal government
1970	26,235	14,970	10,446	251	340	228
1975	35,565	18,437	15,823	424	542	340
1980	63,076	29,857	30,926	877	911	505
1985	114,344	52,493	58,013	1,680	1,365	793
1990	151,655	61,456	83,374	3,096	2,367	1,361
1997	205,742	62,745	133,308	4,457	3,411	1,821

		Source of funds - Millions of constant 1992 dollars				
	Total	Federal Government	Industry	Universities & colleges	Other nonprofits	Nonfederal government
1970	85,842	48,982	34,181	820	1,112	746
1975	84,358	43,732	37,530	1,006	1,284	806
1980	104,464	49,448	51,219	1,453	1,509	836
1985	145,559	66,824	73,850	2,139	1,737	1,009
1990	161,957	65,631	89,038	3,307	2,527	1,454
1997	182,217	55,571	118,066	3,947	3,021	1,612

	Performer - Millions of current dollars						
	Federal Government	Industry	Industry FFRDCs*	Universities & colleges	Univ. & college FFRDCs*	Other nonprofits	Nonprofit FFRDCs*
1970	4,154	17,594	473	2,376	732	677	230
1975	5,561	23,460	727	3,489	1,027	1,076	225
1980	7,831	43,228	1,277	6,259	2,306	1,700	475
1985	13,093	82,376	1,863	9,997	3,616	2,736	663
1990	15,671	107,404	2,323	16,610	4,894	4,117	636
1997	16,450	151,418	2,273	24,031	5,405	5,520	644

	Performer - Millions of constant 1992 dollars						
	Federal Government	Industry	Industry FFRDCs*	Universities & colleges	Univ. & college FFRDCs*	Other nonprofits	Nonprofit FFRDCs*
1970	13,590	57,568	1,548	7,775	2,394	2,214	753
1975	13,191	55,645	1,724	8,276	2,436	2,552	534
1980	12,969	71,593	2,115	10,366	3,819	2,816	787
1985	16,667	104,864	2,372	12,726	4,603	3,483	843
1990	16,736	114,700	2,481	17,738	5,226	4,397	679
1997	14,569	134,105	2,013	21,283	4,787	4,889	571

*FFRDC = federally funded research and development center.
Source: National Science Foundation

Top Patent Recipients

Corporations Receiving the Most Patents for Inventions 1969–1997

	Total 1969–1997	1997
General Electric	24,440	664
International Business Machines	20,926	1,724
Hitachi	16,951	903
Canon	15,061	1,381
Toshiba	14,511	862
AT&T	14,409	46
Eastman Kodak	13,916	795
U.S. Philips	13,115	473
DuPont	13,004	311
Siemens	11,976	454
Westinghouse Electric	11,878	72
Bayer	11,467	357
Mitsubishi	11,274	892
Motorola	11,084	1,058
General Motors	11,080	277
Fuji Photo Film	10,315	467
Xerox	10,204	606
Dow Chemical	9,731	163
Matsushita Electric Industrial	9,696	746
NEC	8,995	1,095
Ciba-Geigy	8,527	238

Foreign Countries Receiving the Most Patents for Inventions 1963–1997

	Total 1963–1997	1997
Japan	359,496	23,178
Germany	202,663	7,008
United Kingdom	90,975	2,678
France	77,904	2,958
Canada	47,671	2,378
Switzerland	40,756	1,090
Italy	29,357	1,239
Sweden	25,660	867
Netherlands	24,215	809
Taiwan	13,186	2,057

Source: U.S. Patent and Trademark Office

Increasing Innovation

Number of Patents Granted for Inventions 1983–1997

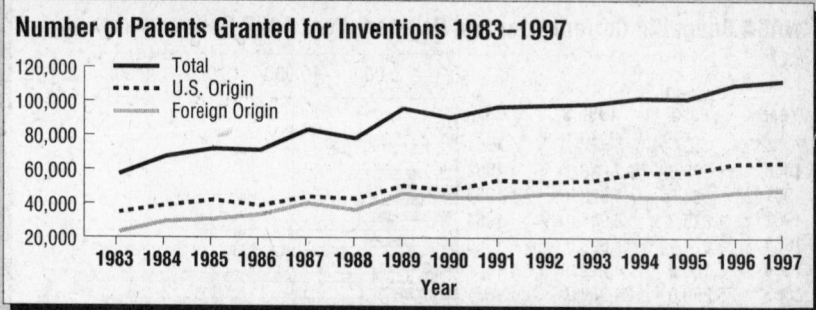

Total
U.S. Origin
Foreign Origin

Number of Patents Granted by Type of Recipient 1983–1997

Recipients	1983	1985	1988	1991	1994	1995	1996	1997
U.S. Corporations	25,677	31,181	31,437	39,133	44,036	44,035	48,741	50,229
U.S. Government	1,048	1,139	733	1,183	1,258	1,028	923	935
U.S. Individuals	7,574	9,265	10,122	13,207	12,805	12,885	13,729	12,914
Foreign Corporations	19,246	25,957	30,960	37,594	38,788	38,688	41,476	42,908
Foreign Government	339	483	453	472	296	245	259	273
Foreign Individuals	2,976	3,636	4,219	4,924	4,493	4,538	4,518	4,725
Total	56,860	71,661	77,924	96,513	101,676	101,419	109,646	111,984

Source: U.S. Patent and Trademark Office

Space Program Spending

NASA Budget in Current Year and Constant Year 1996 Dollars (In millions)

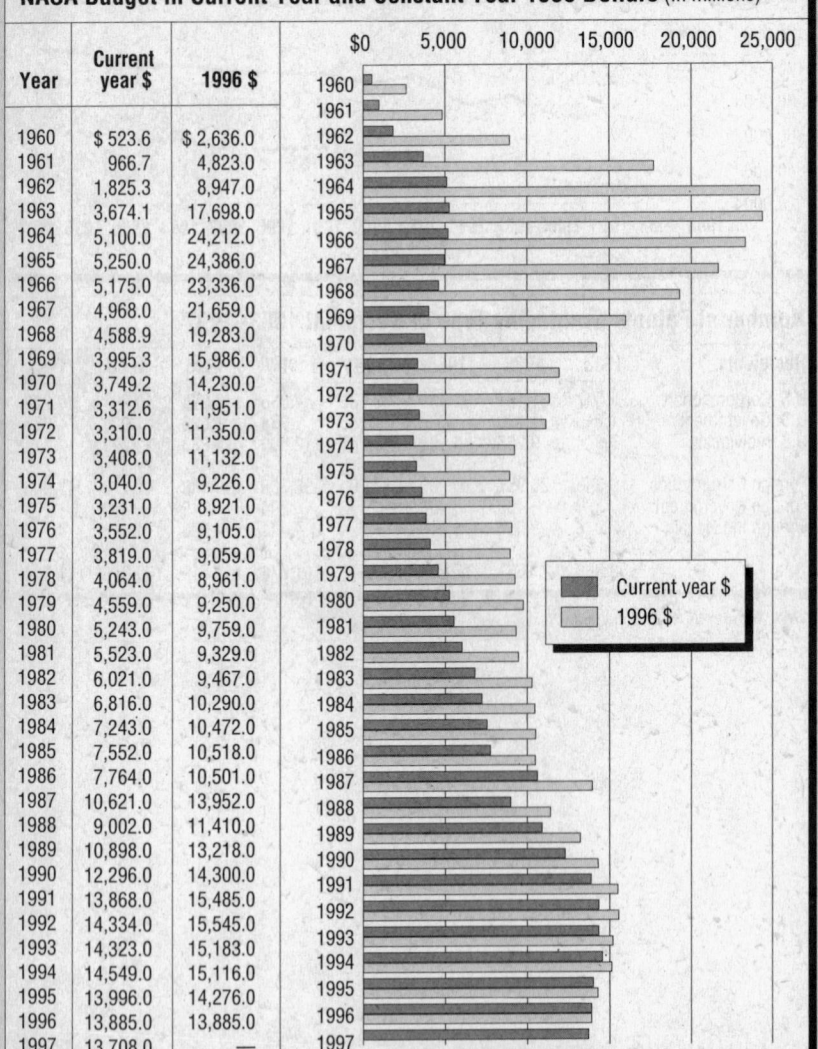

Year	Current year $	1996 $
1960	$ 523.6	$ 2,636.0
1961	966.7	4,823.0
1962	1,825.3	8,947.0
1963	3,674.1	17,698.0
1964	5,100.0	24,212.0
1965	5,250.0	24,386.0
1966	5,175.0	23,336.0
1967	4,968.0	21,659.0
1968	4,588.9	19,283.0
1969	3,995.3	15,986.0
1970	3,749.2	14,230.0
1971	3,312.6	11,951.0
1972	3,310.0	11,350.0
1973	3,408.0	11,132.0
1974	3,040.0	9,226.0
1975	3,231.0	8,921.0
1976	3,552.0	9,105.0
1977	3,819.0	9,059.0
1978	4,064.0	8,961.0
1979	4,559.0	9,250.0
1980	5,243.0	9,759.0
1981	5,523.0	9,329.0
1982	6,021.0	9,467.0
1983	6,816.0	10,290.0
1984	7,243.0	10,472.0
1985	7,552.0	10,518.0
1986	7,764.0	10,501.0
1987	10,621.0	13,952.0
1988	9,002.0	11,410.0
1989	10,898.0	13,218.0
1990	12,296.0	14,300.0
1991	13,868.0	15,485.0
1992	14,334.0	15,545.0
1993	14,323.0	15,183.0
1994	14,549.0	15,116.0
1995	13,996.0	14,276.0
1996	13,885.0	13,885.0
1997	13,708.0	—

Source: National Aeronautics and Space Administration

Principal NASA Contractors

The 50 contractors that received the largest dollar value of NASA direct awards to business firms during fiscal year 1997.

Contractor	(In thousands)	(Percent)
Total awards to businesses	**$9,817,157**	**100.00%**
Boeing Co.	1,661,705	16.93
United Space Alliance LLC	1,314,367	13.39
Lockheed Martin Corp.	1,048,698	10.68
Thiokol Corp.	424,393	4.32
Lockheed Martin Engineering & Science Co.	376,179	3.83
McDonnell Douglas Corp.	354,079	3.61
AlliedSignal Technical Services	333,172	3.39
TRW Inc.	281,349	2.87
Boeing North America Inc.	236,587	2.41
Computer Sciences Corp.	162,853	1.66
EG&G Florida Inc.	156,106	1.59
Hughes Aircraft Co.	153,403	1.56
USBI Booster Production Co.	146,863	1.50
United Technologies Corp.	139,537	1.42
Hughes Information Tech. Corp.	117,003	1.19
Boeing Commercial Airplane Group	90,341	.92
Lockheed Martin Aerospace Corp.	71,763	.73
General Electric Co.	68,664	.70
Swales & Associates Inc.	67,815	.69
Johnson Controls World Services	62,370	.64
Science Applications International Corp.	57,631	.59
Bamsi Inc.	55,233	.56
Ball Aerospace & Tech. Corp.	51,802	.53
Silicon Graphics Inc.	51,437	.52
Grumman Aerospace Corp.	46,579	.47
Cortez III Service Corp.	44,190	.45
Hughes Training Inc.	43,016	.44
Hughes STX Corp.	41,210	.42
Santa Barbara Research Center	40,677	.41
Aerojet General Corp.	39,157	.40
NYMA Inc.	38,515	.39
Johnson Engineering Corp.	35,680	.36
ITT Corp.	35,129	.36
Sterling Software US Inc.	33,015	.34
Government Micro Resources	32,767	.33
Wang Government Services Inc.	30,772	.31
Lockheed Space Operations Co.	27,106	.28
Sverdrup Technology Inc.	26,767	.27
Spacehab Inc.	26,284	.27
Unisys Corp.	25,741	.26
Raytheon Service Co.	24,918	.25
Space Systems Loral Inc.	24,670	.25
NSI Technology Services Corp.	24,464	.25
Calspan Corp.	24,304	.25
Jackson & Tull Inc.	23,010	.23
Bionetics Corp.	20,615	.21
EG&G Langley Inc.	20,218	.21
Orbital Sciences Corp.	19,449	.20
Micro Craft Inc.	19,163	.20
General Electric UTC JV	19,025	.19

Source: National Aeronautics and Space Administration

THE WORLD

Skeptics were finally forced to admit in 1998 that Europe's biggest experiment ever, economic and monetary union, or EMU, could fly.

EMU was officially set to begin on January 1, 1999, after heads of state nailed down the final details, including the initial members, at a special May summit. To be sure, marks, francs, lire and other currencies won't disappear until 2002, when the new *euro* bills and coins start circulating. But once exchange rates are fixed for perpetuity on New Year's Day, economists say the deed is as good as done. The ramifications are mind-boggling.

EMU has been 41 years in the making, ever since former archenemies Germany and France plus four other nations signed the Treaty of Rome and gave birth to the old Common Market. The new treaty is on a far grander scale. Eleven countries have signed on for EMU: Germany, France, Italy, Spain, Belgium, the Netherlands, Luxembourg, Ireland, Finland, Portugal and Austria. Four members of the European Union have opted out, at least for the initial round, or didn't meet the membership criteria of low inflation, interest rates, government deficits and overall debt. Danish voters rejected EMU in a 1992 referendum; Sweden and the United Kingdom say they want to wait and see, though the U.K. is expected to reverse course early in the next century. An ambitious Greece hopes to meet the criteria at the end of 1999 in order to join in 2001.

The permanent fixing of exchange rates is designed to eliminate the competitive devaluations that have scarred Europe's economies for decades. But for these new rates to hold, policymakers had to undergo a funda-

mental rethink of fiscal and monetary policy. Governments have been forced to tighten their belts to an extent unheard of only a few years ago and are now privatizing everything from telephone companies to airports. Countries where double-digit inflation is a recent memory now have prices rising less than 2 percent annually.

And once EMU takes hold, there will be only one monetary policy for all of Euroland, the Disneyesque term coined for the new grouping. National central banks will continue to exist but have a far less important role. Interest rates will now be set by 18 men and women who head up a new institution called the European Central Bank and based in Frankfurt, Germany's financial capital. Like the Federal Reserve does for all 50 U.S. states, the ECB will set monetary policy for all of Euroland—an area of 290 million people and economic output totaling $6.3 trillion.

Dramatic changes are in store for companies, which will find it much tougher to justify substantial price differences across national borders for everything from shampoo to cars. Euroland stock markets were to quote all their prices in euros as soon as dealing began in 1999, well before the currency actually exists in wallets. One result should be hefty portfolio shifts as insurance companies, some of the biggest investors in European markets, suddenly have a much bigger "home currency" in which to invest.

The disappearance of exchange-rate risk

means bond-market investors will pay more attention to borrowers' credit quality as a way of boosting returns. The European bond market is expected to swell to more than $10 trillion in five years, rivaling that of the United States in size. The euro already has unleashed a fury of mergers and acquisitions as companies bulk up to compete in a market similar in size to the United States.

Of course, this wouldn't be Europe if there wasn't plenty of *sturm und drang* up to the very end. Indeed, the springtime battle over just who would head up the ECB, the most important job under EMU, seemed all too familiar to those who have watched Europe try to unite in the past. France, Germany and the Netherlands were locked in a bitter dispute that pushed what was supposed to be Europe's finest hour into 12 hours of overtime in early May. Only shortly after midnight did French President Jacques Chirac, U.K. Prime Minister Tony Blair and Wim Duisenberg, the Dutchman picked to head up the new central bank, emerge from a closed-door arm-twisting session. Mr. Duisenberg, the candidate backed by the Netherlands, Germany and most other European Union governments, was given the job only after agreeing to retire early, following the introduction of notes and coins, in favor of a Frenchman. (He's since suggested that he might serve out the full term.)

Italy, one of the original Treaty of Rome signatories, was forced to lobby its case for admission well into 1998 as skeptics, led by the Germans, questioned just how deeply and lastingly it was reducing its mountain of debt.

Optimists see EMU as the dawn of an era of unprecedented growth and prosperity, putting an end to the old high-tax, high-spending politics that have characterized Europe for decades. Countries like Spain, Italy and Ireland already are booming in large part because interest rates are at unprecedented low levels. "EMU will create big incentives for structural reforms," said Paul Mortimer-Lee, chief economist at Banque Paribas in London.

The continent certainly still faces plenty of challenges once monetary union starts. The biggest question is whether its economies can stay in synch or whether politicians will start backsliding now that the hard work of qualifying for EMU is done. Former U.K. Prime Minister Margaret Thatcher has predicted EMU won't last even three years. Unlike the United States, there is no pan-European fiscal policy or taxation, no system of redistributing government monies to areas that are suffering from high unemployment. Private economists dismiss the so-called stability pact, devised by the Germans to punish governments for fiscal profligacy, as toothless.

Most European governments have yet to seriously tackle the excesses of the welfare state, which has defined Europe since World War II and makes it different—in its eyes, better—than other parts of the world. This is why long-term unemployed French workers demonstrated and occupied government offices in 1998 in an ultimately successful bid to get more benefits.

Labor mobility remains a dramatic handicap in tackling Euroland's unemployment rate of more than 11%. Unlike the United States, there's no single language or qualifications system for everything from carpenters to doctors that makes it easier to find a job in another part of the EMU.

Finally, politicians are still struggling to build support for their great experiment. Just months before the launch of the single currency, polls regularly found that a plurality of Germans still opposed giving up the stability of the mark for the unknown of the euro.

But economists say breaking up EMU would be too costly to even contemplate, and that fact should keep governments fairly honest. Any country that would leave the single currency, willingly or unwillingly, would find its borrowing costs skyrocketing, its currency weakening and its economy suffering. After going through so much pain to achieve the opposite, they aren't likely to want to go through it again.

**Silvia Ascarelli,
staff reporter for
The Wall Street Journal
in London**

THE BIG GUYS

*Major Trading Blocs
and Trade Organizations*

WORLD TRADE ORGANIZATION (WTO)

The WTO includes 132 countries that agree to rules that govern a set of global trade and economic policies. The organization has a dispute-settlement body that has emerged as the leading international arbiter of trade spats.

EUROPEAN UNION (EU)

A free-trade and economic-policy bloc of 15 European nations: Austria, Belgium, Denmark, Finland, France, Germany, Greece, Ireland, Italy, Luxembourg, Netherlands, Portugal, Spain, Sweden, and the United Kingdom. It was launched as the European Economic Community in 1958. Next on the EU's agenda is a step that would take it far further than any trade group has gone before: a unified common currency, which is supposed to go into effect by 1999. The impact on business—including American firms operating in Europe—would be profound: Currency-exchange markets would probably be decimated; export-transaction costs should fall; psychological price barriers between nations would vanish; contracts would have to be rewritten.

NORTH AMERICAN FREE TRADE AGREEMENT (NAFTA)

A free-trade bloc grouping the U.S., Canada, and Mexico, begun in 1994. Nafta has led to a big increase in trade between the U.S. and Mexico, but the pact's scope is less ambitious than the EU's—no common currency here. The countries of the Western Hemisphere, except Cuba, have agreed to negotiate an even bigger trade zone, the Free Trade Area of the Americas, by 2005.

ASIA-PACIFIC ECONOMIC COOPERATION (APEC)

Eighteen countries in a consultative body, begun in 1993, that tries to promote cooperation on trade and investment. A smaller, weaker, Asian version of the WTO. Members: Australia, Brunei, Canada, Chile, China, Hong Kong, Indonesia, Japan, South Korea, Malaysia, Mexico, New Zealand, Papua New Guinea, Philippines, Singapore, Taiwan, Thailand, and the U.S.

ASSOCIATION OF SOUTHEAST ASIAN NATIONS (ASEAN)

Set up in 1967 to promote stability and economic growth in Southeast Asia. Functions as a trade group, and though trade by the individual members has been greater with the U.S. and Japan, intra-Asean trade is growing fast. Members are Brunei, Indonesia, Malaysia, Philippines, Singapore, Thailand, Vietnam and Burma.

SOUTHERN COMMON MARKET (MERCOSUR)

Mercosur, established in 1991, groups four South American trading partners in a free-trade zone: Argentina, Brazil, Paraguay, and Uruguay. Chile and Bolivia have signed free-trade deals with the group.

GROUP OF SEVEN (G-7)

The members are the U.S., Japan, Germany, France, Italy, Britain, and Canada. The group tries to coordinate macroeconomic policy, which mainly involves talking up or down the dollar's value against other currencies—with limited success.

World Population Growth

Population by Country or Area (In thousands)

Region and country or area	1998	2020*	Region and country or area	1998	2020*
World	**5,926,467**	**7,584,821**	**North Africa**	**140,950**	**202,587**
Less Developed Countries	4,749,637	6,365,695	Algeria	30,481	44,783
More Developed Countries	1,176,830	1,219,126	Egypt	66,050	92,234
Africa	**760,771**	**1,206,597**	Libya	5,691	12,157
Sub-Saharan Africa	**619,820**	**1,004,010**	Morocco	29,114	40,839
Angola	10,865	19,207	Tunisia	9,380	12,216
Benin	6,101	11,920	Western Sahara	234	357
Bostwana	1,448	1,601	**Near East**	**164,974**	**271,157**
Burkina Faso	11,266	19,239	Bahrain	616	870
Burundi	5,537	9,432	Cyprus	749	855
Cameroon	15,029	26,059	Gaza Strip	1,054	2,448
Cape Verde	400	512	Iraq	21,722	39,713
Central African Republic	3,376	5,133	Israel	5,644	7,439
Chad	7,360	12,831	Jordan	4,435	7,511
Comoros	546	1,022	Kuwait	1,913	3,351
Congo (Brazzaville)	2,658	3,945	Lebanon	3,506	4,613
Congo (Kinshasa)	49,001	92,852	Oman	2,364	4,680
Côte d'Ivoire	15,446	25,268	Qatar	697	1,160
Djibouti	441	751	Saudi Arabia	20,786	43,255
Equatorial Guinea	454	783	Syria	16,673	28,926
Eritrea	3,842	7,471	Turkey	64,567	85,643
Ethiopia	58,390	89,943	United Arab Emirates	2,303	3,286
Gabon	1,208	1,675	West Bank	1,557	2,725
Gambia, The	1,292	2,399	Yemen	16,388	34,682
Ghana	18,497	26,516	**Asia**	**3,362,994**	**4,247,079**
Guinea	7,477	11,836	Afghanistan	24,792	43,050
Guinea-Bissau	1,206	1,925	Bangladesh	127,567	172,098
Kenya	28,337	33,936	Bhutan	1,908	3,035
Lesotho	2,090	2,625	Brunei	315	490
Liberia	2,772	5,737	Cambodia	11,340	19,164
Madagascar	14,463	25,988	China	1,265,530	1,430,806
Malawi	9,840	12,052	Mainland	1,236,915	1,397,434
Mali	10,109	19,677	Hong Kong	6,707	7,869
Mauritania	2,511	4,765	Taiwan	21,908	25,504
Mauritius	1,168	1,440	India	984,004	1,340,865
Mayotte	142	321	Indonesia	212,942	276,017
Mozambique	18,641	30,392	Iran	68,960	104,282
Namibia	1,622	2,154	Japan	125,932	123,076
Niger	9,672	17,983	Laos	5,261	8,923
Nigeria	110,532	183,962	Macau	429	607
Reunion	705	962	Malaysia	20,933	31,583
Rwanda	7,956	11,304	Maldives	290	554
Saint Helena	7	8	Mongolia	2,579	3,393
Sao Tome and Principe	150	292	Myanmar	47,305	64,280
Senegal	9,723	19,497	Nepal	23,698	38,859
Seychelles	79	89	North Korea	21,234	24,937
Sierra Leone	5,080	9,690	Pakistan	135,135	198,723
Somalia	6,842	13,312	Philippines	77,726	112,963
South Africa	42,835	48,983	Singapore	3,490	4,137
Sudan	33,551	58,621	South Korea	46,417	53,451
Swaziland	966	1,434	Sri Lanka	18,934	23,338
Tanzania	30,609	46,693	Thailand	60,037	69,298
Togo	4,906	10,146	Vietnam	76,236	99,153
Uganda	22,167	42,772	**Latin America and**		
Zambia	9,461	14,695	**the Caribbean**	**507,551**	**664,366**
Zimbabwe	11,044	12,162	Anguilla	11	16

*Projection.

Population by Country or Area (In thousands)

Region and country or area	1998	2020*	Region and country or area	1998	2020*
Antigua and Barbuda	64	66	Greece	10,662	10,740
Argentina	36,265	46,345	Guernsey	65	79
Aruba	68	74	Iceland	271	296
Bahamas, The	280	355	Ireland	3,619	3,910
Barbados	259	275	Italy	56,783	52,209
Belize	230	356	Jersey	89	94
Bolivia	7,826	11,245	Liechtenstein	32	36
Brazil	169,807	204,187	Luxembourg	425	455
Cayman Islands	38	81	Malta	380	396
Chile	14,788	18,159	Man, Isle of	75	84
Colombia	38,581	54,626	Monaco	32	34
Costa Rica	3,605	5,044	Netherlands	15,731	16,085
Cuba	11,051	11,721	Norway	4,420	4,609
Dominica	66	65	Portugal	9,928	9,239
Dominican Republic	7,999	11,085	San Marino	25	27
Ecuador	12,337	16,876	Spain	39,134	37,850
El Salvador	5,752	7,852	Sweden	8,887	9,197
French Guiana	163	251	Switzerland	7,260	7,209
Grenada	96	141	United Kingdom	58,970	60,177
Guadeloupe	416	490	**Eastern Europe**	**121,686**	**122,938**
Guatemala	12,008	20,283	Albania	3,331	4,155
Guyana	708	714	Bosnia and		
Haiti	6,781	9,600	Herzegovina	3,366	3,565
Honduras	5,862	8,182	Bulgaria	8,240	7,515
Jamaica	2,635	3,213	Croatia	4,672	4,469
Martinique	407	473	Czech Republic	10,286	10,309
Mexico	98,553	134,387	Hungary	10,208	9,604
Montserrat	13	13	Macedonia, The		
Netherlands Antilles	206	238	Former Yugoslav		
Nicaragua	4,583	7,479	Republic of	2,009	2,167
Panama	2,736	3,619	Montenegro	680	696
Paraguay	5,291	8,960	Poland	38,607	40,344
Peru	26,111	36,898	Romania	22,396	21,789
Puerto Rico	3,857	4,180	Serbia	10,526	10,669
Saint Kitts and Nevis	42	57	Slovakia	5,393	5,739
Saint Lucia	152	194	Slovenia	1,972	1,917
Saint Vincent and			**New Independent**		
the Grenadines	120	146	**States**	**291,117**	**297,821**
Suriname	428	461	Baltics	7,407	6,765
Trinidad and Tobago	1,117	1,075	Estonia	1,421	1,271
Turks and Caicos Islands	16	29	Latvia	2,385	2,030
Uruguay	3,285	3,811	Lithuania	3,600	3,464
Venezuela	22,803	30,876	**Commonwealth of**		
Virgin Islands	118	141	**Independent States**	**283,710**	**291,056**
Virgin Islands, British	19	28	Armenia	3,422	3,416
Europe and the New			Azerbaijan	7,856	9,082
Independent States	**799,401**	**798,448**	Belarus	10,409	10,387
Western Europe	**386,599**	**377,689**	Georgia	5,109	4,767
Andorra	65	89	Kazakhstan	16,847	18,127
Austria	8,134	8,006	Kyrgyzstan	4,522	5,764
Belgium	10,175	9,762	Moldova	4,458	4,783
Denmark	5,334	5,401	Russia	146,861	141,311
Faroe Islands	42	26	Tajikistan	6,020	8,890
Finland	5,149	5,093	Turkmenistan	4,298	6,084
France	58,805	58,710	Ukraine	50,125	46,061
Germany	82,079	77,848	Uzbekistan	23,784	32,383
Gibraltar	29	30			

*Projection.

Population by Country or Area (In thousands)

Region and country or area	1998	2020*	Region and country or area	1998	2020*
North America	**301,115**	**360,094**	Marshall Islands	63	144
Bermuda	62	68	Micronesia, Federated States of	130	143
Canada	30,675	36,897	Nauru	11	12
Greenland	59	69	New Caledonia	194	255
Saint Pierre and Miquelon	7	8	New Zealand	3,625	4,326
United States	270,312	323,052	Northern Mariana Islands	67	124
Oceania	**29,659**	**37,080**	Palau	18	24
American Samoa	62	96	Papua New Guinea	4,600	7,044
Australia	18,613	21,696	Samoa	225	341
Cook Islands	20	24	Solomon Islands	441	767
Fiji	803	1,037	Tonga	108	128
French Polynesia	238	320	Tuvalu	10	15
Guam	148	204	Vanuatu	185	266
Kiribati	84	98	Wallis and Futuna	15	18

*Projection.
Source: U.S. Census Bureau

World Population by Region and Development Category (In millions)

Region	1950	1970	1990	1998	2020*
World	**2,556**	**3,707**	**5,279**	**5,926**	**7,585**
Less Developed Countries	1,749	2,703	4,136	4,750	6,366
More Developed Countries	807	1,004	1,143	1,177	1,219
Africa	**228**	**360**	**621**	**761**	**1,207**
Sub-Saharan Africa	184	289	502	620	1,004
North Africa	44	71	119	141	203
Near East	**44**	**75**	**135**	**165**	**271**
Asia	**1,368**	**2,038**	**2,987**	**3,363**	**4,247**
Latin America and the Caribbean	**166**	**286**	**443**	**508**	**664**
Europe and the New Independent States	**572**	**703**	**788**	**799**	**798**
Western Europe	304	352	376	387	378
Eastern Europe	88	108	122	122	123
New Independent States	180	242	289	291	298
North America	**166**	**227**	**278**	**301**	**360**
Oceania	**12**	**19**	**27**	**30**	**37**
Excluding China (Mainland and Taiwan):					
World	1,983	2,868	4,114	4,661	6,154
Less Developed Countries	1,176	1,864	2,971	3,484	4,935
Asia	795	1,199	1,823	2,097	2,816
Less Developed Countries	711	1,094	1,699	1,972	2,693

Share of World Population (Percent)

Region	1998	2020*
Less Developed Countries	80.0%	83.9%
More Developed Countries	19.9	16.1
Sub-Saharan Africa	10.5	13.2
Near East and North Africa	5.2	6.3
China (Mainland and Taiwan)	21.4	18.9
Other Asia	33.2	35.5
Latin America and the Caribbean	8.6	8.8
Eastern Europe and the New Independent States	7.0	5.5
Rest of the World	14.2	11.8

NOTE: Other Asia excludes China and Japan. Rest of the World includes Western Europe, North America, Japan, and Oceania.
*Projection
Source: U.S. Census Bureau

Distribution of World Births by Country

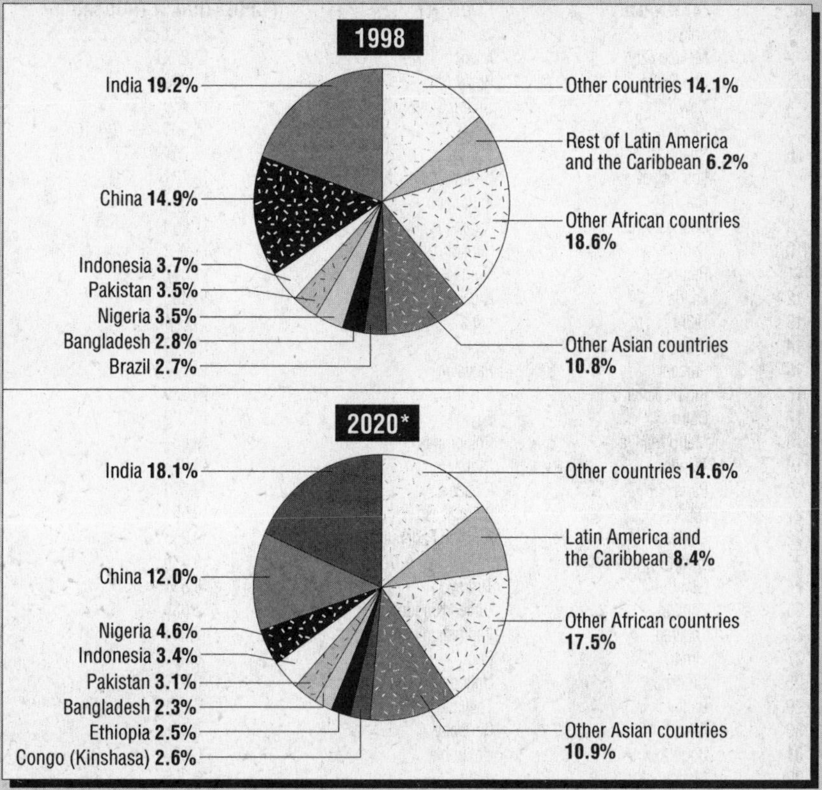

1998

India **19.2%**

China **14.9%**

Indonesia **3.7%**
Pakistan **3.5%**
Nigeria **3.5%**
Bangladesh **2.8%**
Brazil **2.7%**

Other countries **14.1%**

Rest of Latin America and the Caribbean **6.2%**

Other African countries **18.6%**

Other Asian countries **10.8%**

2020*

India **18.1%**

China **12.0%**

Nigeria **4.6%**
Indonesia **3.4%**
Pakistan **3.1%**
Bangladesh **2.3%**
Ethiopia **2.5%**
Congo (Kinshasa) **2.6%**

Other countries **14.6%**

Latin America and the Caribbean **8.4%**

Other African countries **17.5%**

Other Asian countries **10.9%**

*Projection.
Source: U.S. Census Bureau

World's 50 Largest Urban Areas in 1997

RANK	CITY-NAME	COUNTRY	POPULATION IN THOUSANDS
1	Tokyo	Japan	27,481
2	Mexico City	Mexico	17,263
3	Sao Paulo	Brazil	17,036
4	New York	United States of America	16,450
5	Bombay	India	16,306
6	Shanghai	China	13,757
7	Los Angeles	United States of America	12,731
8	Calcutta	India	12,307
9	Buenos Aires	Argentina	12,058
10	Seoul	Republic of Korea	11,902
11	Beijing	China	11,547
12	Lagos	Nigeria	11,495
13	Delhi	India	10,644
14	Osaka	Japan	10,619
15	Karachi	Pakistan	10,517
16	Rio de Janeiro	Brazil	10,339
17	Cairo	Egypt	10,119
18	Metro Manila	Philippines	9,881
19	Tianjin	China	9,716
20	Paris	France	9,579
21	Dhaka	Bangladesh	9,501
22	Moscow	Russian Federation	9,295
23	Jakarta	Indonesia	9,069
24	Istanbul	Turkey	8,511
25	London	United Kingdom	7,639
26	Teheran	Iran (Islamic Rep. of)	7,034
27	Lima	Peru	6,985
28	Chicago	United States of America	6,879
29	Bangkok	Thailand	6,811
30	Essen	Germany	6,520
31	Bogotá	Colombia	6,392
32	Madras	India	6,255
33	Hyderabad	India	6,018
34	Hong Kong	Hong Kong	5,955
35	Lahore	Pakistan	5,396
36	Shenyang	China	5,328
37	St. Petersburg	Russian Federation	5,136
38	Bangalore	India	5,101
39	Santiago	Chile	5,044
40	Hangzhou	China	5,034
41	Harbin	China	4,861
42	Guangzhou	China	4,749
43	Chengdu	China	4,701
44	Changchun	China	4,698
45	Kinshasa	Congo	4,559
46	Baghdad	Iraq	4,496
47	Toronto	Canada	4,474
48	Wuhan	China	4,437
49	Philadelphia	United States of America	4,339
50	Milan	Italy	4,223

Source: United Nations

Man-Made Marvels

Highest Bridge
Royal Gorge, Arkansas River, CO, U.S.; 1,053 feet (321 m) above water

Longest Bridge Span
Humber Estuary, Hull, England; 4,626 feet (1,410 m)

Longest Big Ship Canal
Suez Canal, Egypt, links the Red Sea and the Mediterranean; 100.6 miles (162 km)

Biggest Dam (Concrete)
Grand Coulee, Columbia River, WA, U.S.; 10,585,000 cubic yards (8,093,000 cu m)

Biggest Dam (Earthfill)
Pati Pavana River, Argentina; 311,527,000 cubic yards (238,193,544 cu m)

Tallest Dam
Nurek, Tajikistan; 984 feet (300 m)

Great Pyramid of Cheops
Giza, Egypt; 450 feet (137 m) high; base covers 13.1 acres (5.3 ha)

Great Wall of China
3,930 miles (6,325 km) long; averages 25 feet (7.6 m) high; 15 feet (4.6 m) wide at top;
25 feet (7.6 m) wide at base

Largest Artificial Lake
Lake Volta, formed by the Akosombo Dam on the Volta River, Ghana; 3,500 square miles
(9,065 sq km)

Tallest Office Building
Petronas Towers, Kuala Lumpur, Malaysia; 1,483 feet (452 m); 88 stories

Longest Railroad
Trans-Siberian Railroad, Moscow to Nakhodka, near Vladivostok, Russia; 5,864 miles (9,437 km)

Tallest Tower (Freestanding)
Canadian National Railroad Tower, Toronto, Canada; 1,815.5 feet (553.3 m)

Longest Rail Tunnel
Seikan Undersea Tunnel, from Honshu to Hokkaido, Japan; 33.46 miles (53.85 km)

Longest Road Tunnel
St. Gotthard, from Göschenen to Airolo, Switzerland; 10.1 miles (16.3 km)

Longest Artificial Waterway
St. Lawrence Seaway, on the St. Lawrence River from Montreal, Canada, to Lake Ontario;
189 miles (304 km)

Deepest Water Well
Stensvad Well 11-W1, Rosebud County, MT, U.S.; 7,320 feet (2,231 m)

Source: National Geographic Society

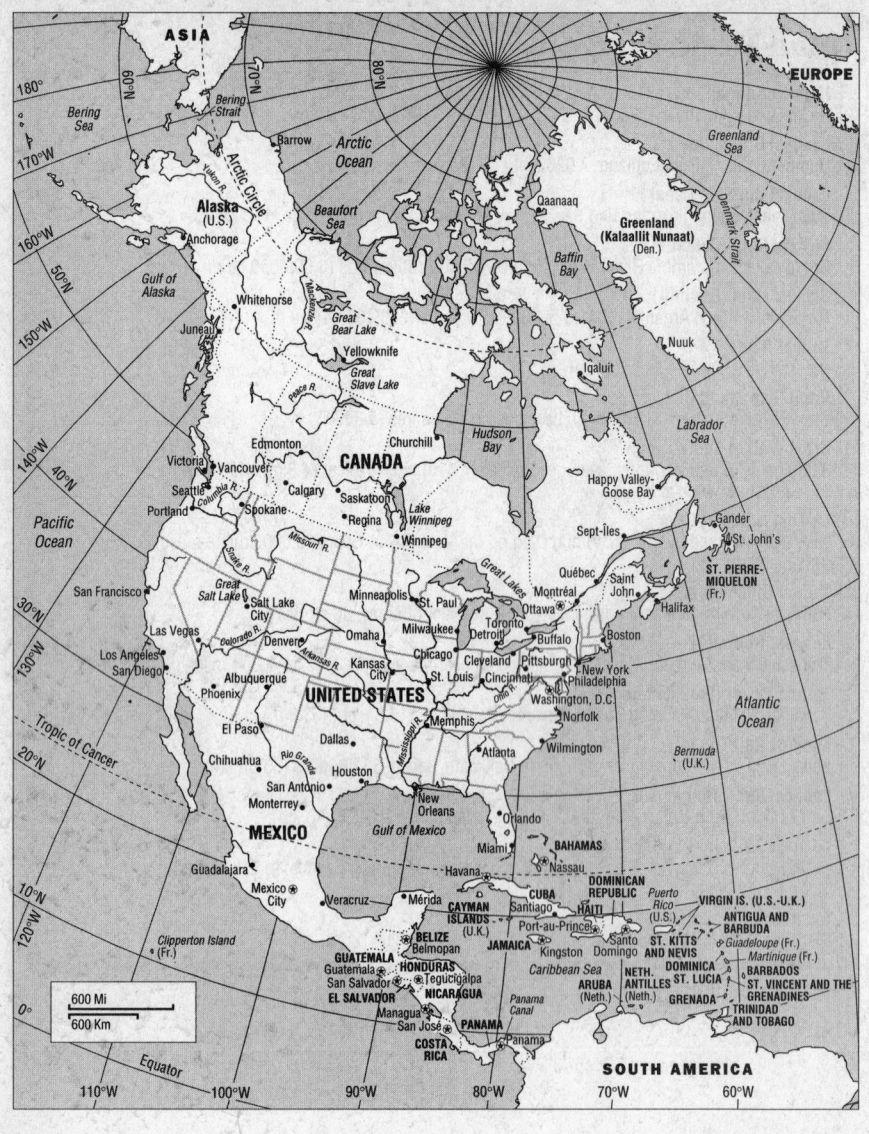

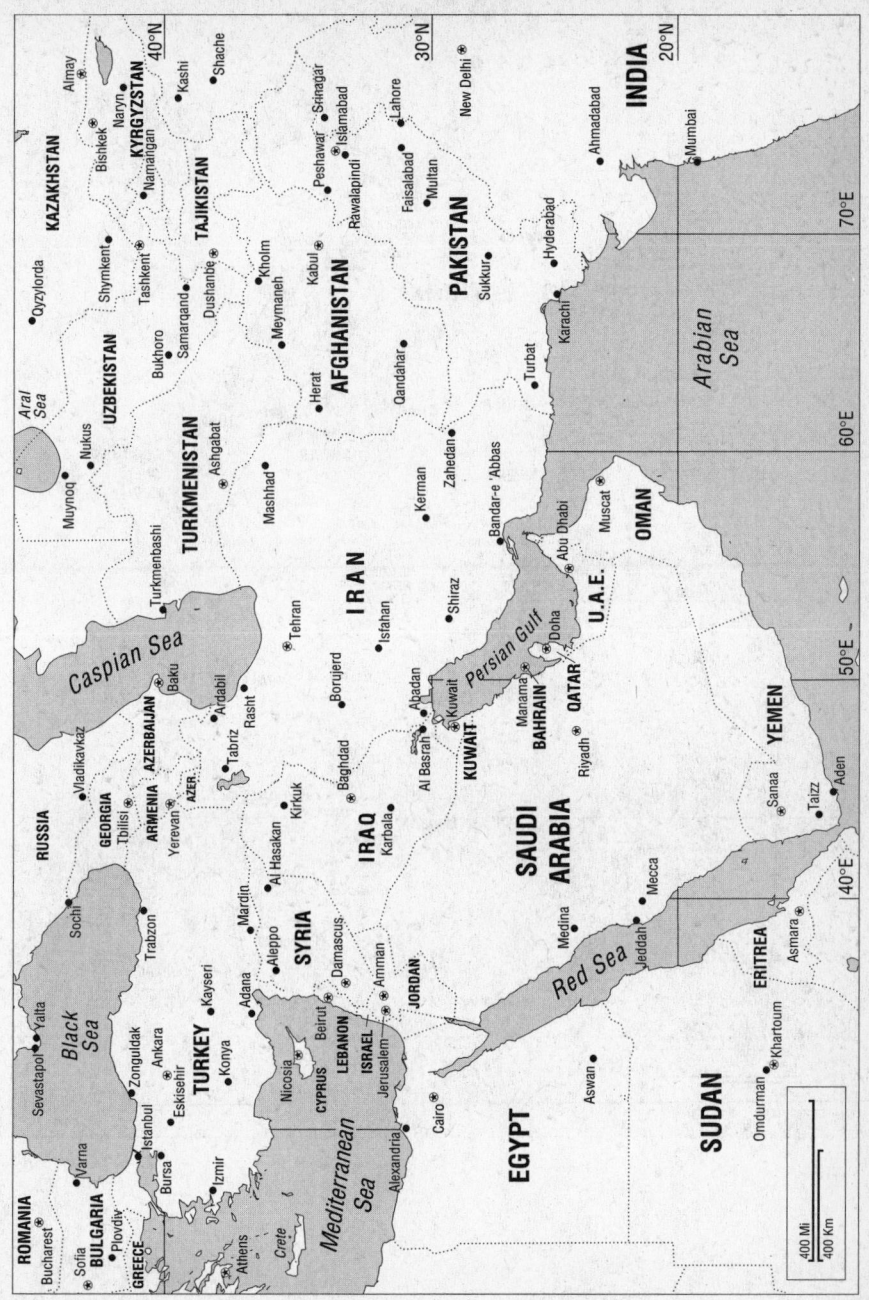

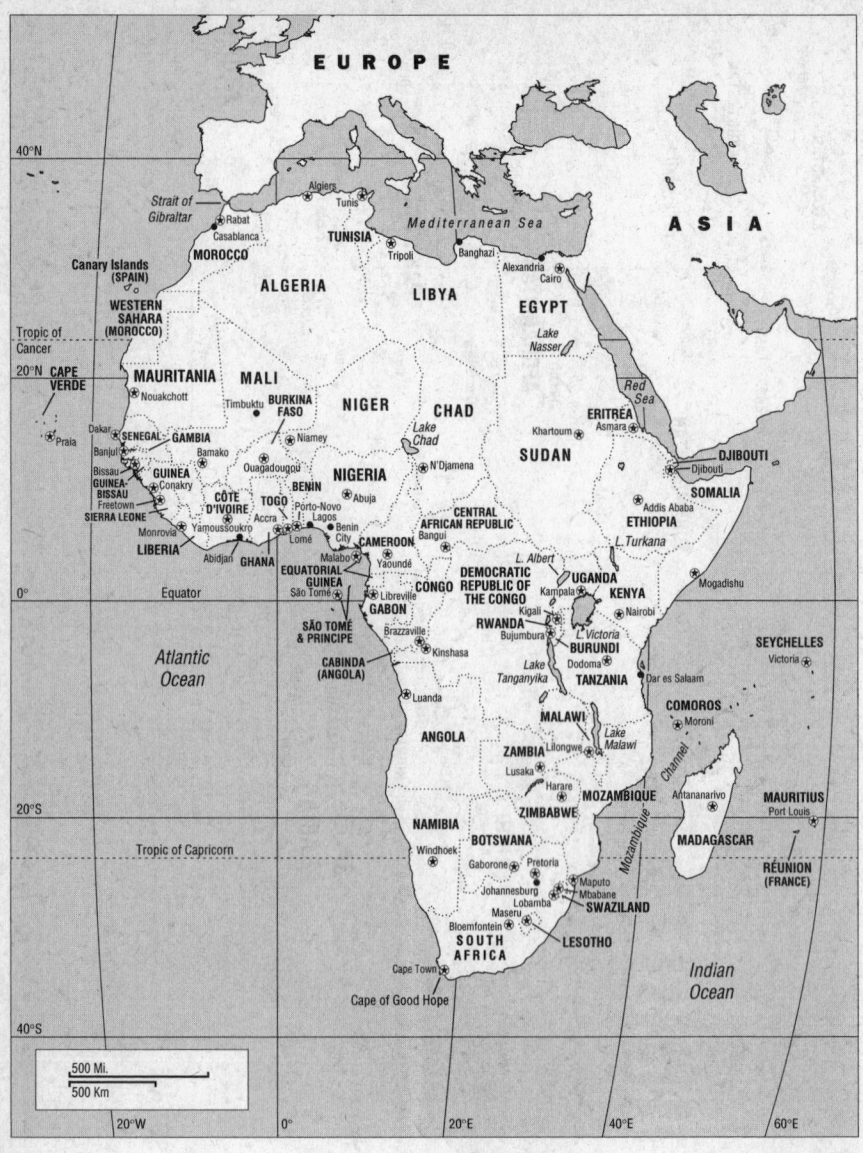

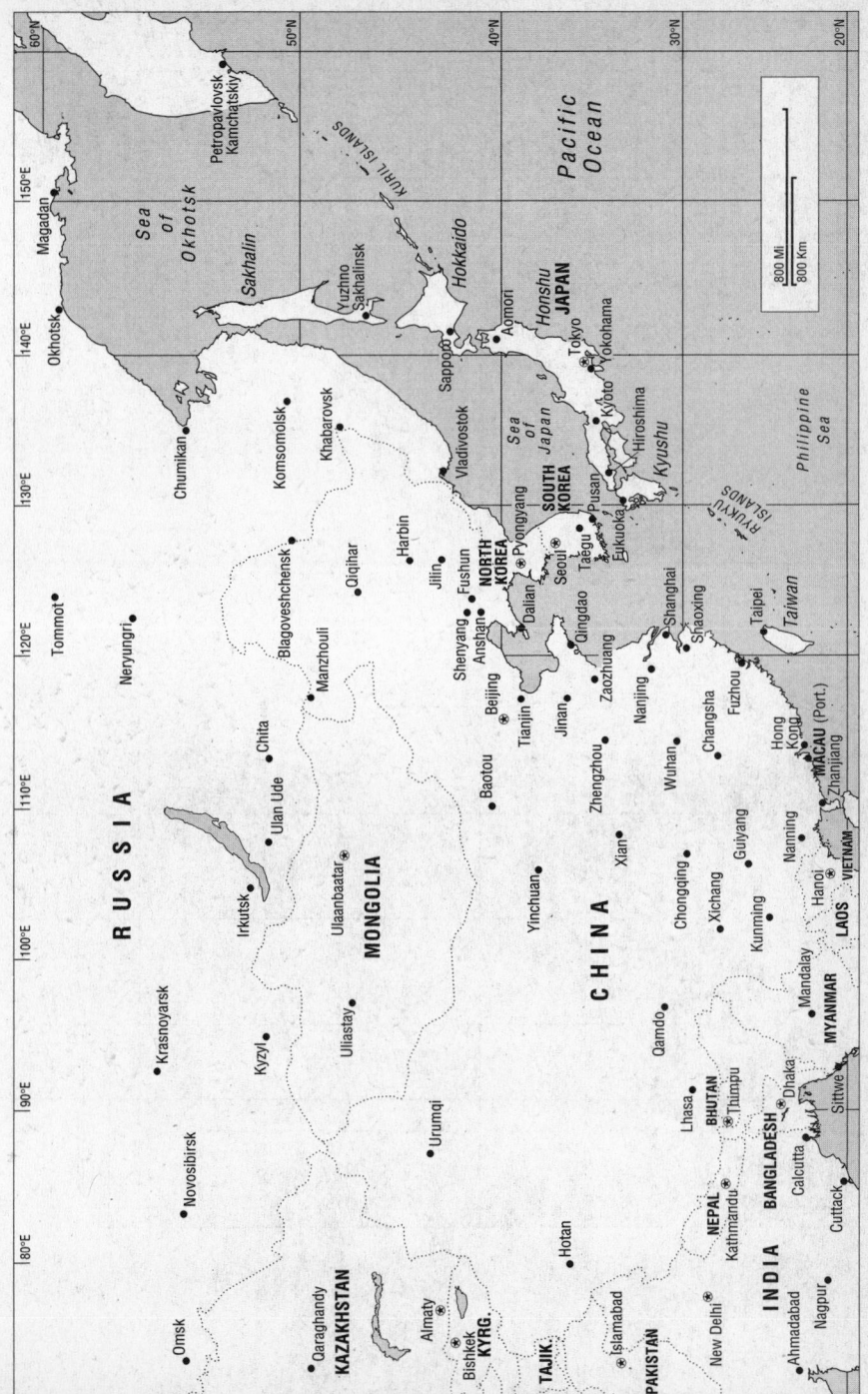

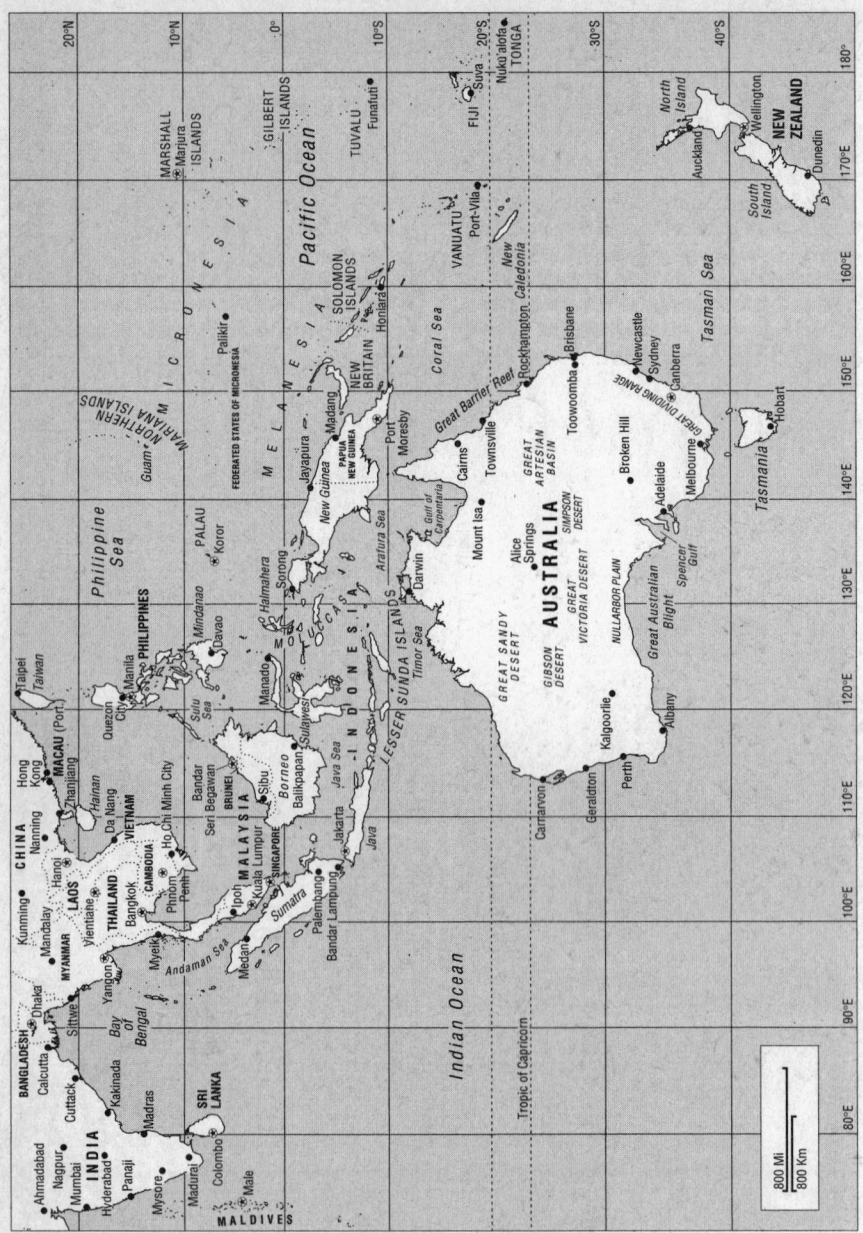

THE UNITED NATIONS

The United Nations is an organization of sovereign nations, not a world government. It provides the machinery to help find solutions to disputes or problems, and to deal with virtually any matter of concern to humanity.

The U.N. has six main organs, listed below. All are based at U.N. Headquarters in New York, except the International Court of Justice, which is located at The Hague, Netherlands.

The General Assembly

The General Assembly, sometimes called the nearest thing to a world parliament, is the main deliberative body. All 185 member states are represented in it, and each has one vote. Decisions on ordinary matters are taken by simple majority. Important questions require a two-thirds majority.

The Assembly holds its regular sessions from mid-September to mid-December; special or emergency sessions are held when necessary. When the Assembly is not in session, its work goes on in special committees and bodies.

The Assembly has the right to discuss and make recommendations on all matters within the scope of the U.N. Charter. It has no power to compel action by any state, but its recommendations carry the weight of world opinion. The Assembly also sets policies and determines programs for the U.N. Secretariat, directs activities for development and approves the U.N. budget, including peace-keeping operations. Occupying a central position in the U.N., the Assembly receives reports from other organs, admits new members and appoints the U.N. Secretary-General.

The Security Council

The *U.N. Charter*, an international treaty, obligates states to settle their international disputes by peaceful means. They are to refrain from the threat or use of force against other states, and may bring any dispute before the Security Council.

The Council is the organ to which the Charter gives primary responsibility for maintaining peace and security. It can be convened at any time, whenever peace is threatened. Member states are obligated to carry out its decisions.

The Council has 15 members. Five of these—China, France, the Russian Federation, the United Kingdom and the United States—are permanent members. The other 10 are elected by the Assembly for two-year terms. Decisions require nine votes; except in votes on procedural questions, a decision cannot be taken if there is a negative vote by a permanent member (known as the "veto").

When a threat to international peace is brought before the Council, it usually first asks the parties to reach agreement by peaceful means. The Council may undertake mediation or set forth principles for a settlement. It may deploy peace-keepers to prevent the outbreak of conflict. If fighting breaks out, the Council tries to secure a cease-fire. It may send peace-keeping missions to troubled areas, with the consent of the parties involved, to reduce tension and keep opposing forces apart. It has the power to enforce its decisions by imposing economic sanctions and by ordering collective military action.

The Council also makes recommendations to the Assembly on a candidate for Secretary-General and on the admission of new members to the U.N.

The Economic and Social Council

Working under the authority of the General Assembly, the Economic and Social Council coordinates the economic and social work of the U.N. and its specialized agencies and institutions. The Council has 54 members.

The Trusteeship Council

The Trusteeship Council was established to ensure that governments responsible for administering trust territories take adequate steps to prepare them for self-government or independence. The task of the Trusteeship System was completed in 1994, when the Security Council terminated the Trusteeship Agreement for the last of the original 11 U.N. Trusteeships—the Trust Territory of the Pacific Islands (Palau), administered by the United States. All trust territories have attained self-government or independence, either as separate states or by joining neighboring independent countries. The trusteeship Council, by amending its rules of procedure, will now meet as and where occasion may require.

The International Court of Justice

The International Court of Justice (also known as the World Court) is the main judicial organ of the U.N. It consists of 15 judges elected by the General Assembly and the Security Council. Only countries may be parties in cases brought before the Court. If a country does not wish to take part in a proceeding it does not have to do so (unless required by special treaty provisions), but if it accepts, it is obligated to comply with the Court's decision.

The Secretariat

The Secretariat works for all the other organs of the U.N. and administers their programs. With a staff of some 9,000, working at headquarters and all over the world, it carries out the day-to-day work of the U.N. At its head is the Secretary-General. Staff members are drawn from some 170 countries.

The Specialized Agencies

Fourteen specialized agencies work for development and international cooperation in their areas of expertise:
1. *International Labour Organization* (ILO)
2. *Food and Agriculture Organization of the U.N.* (FAO)
3. *U.N. Educational, Scientific and Cultural Organization* (UNESCO)
4. *World Health Organization* (WHO)
5. *World Bank*
6. *International Monetary Fund* (IMF)
7. *International Civil Aviation Organization* (ICAO)
8. *Universal Postal Union* (UPU)
9. *International Telecommunication Union* (ITU)
10. *World Meteorological Organization* (WMO)
11. *International Maritime Organization* (IMO)
12. *World Intellectual Property Organization* (WIPO)
13. *International Fund for Agricultural Development* (IFAD)
14. *U.N. Industrial Development Organization* (UNIDO)

Although not a specialized agency, the *International Atomic Energy Agency* (IAEA) is an autonomous intergovernmental organization under the aegis of the U.N. The *World Trade Organization* (WTO) cooperates with some U.N. bodies, although it does not have the formal status of a specialized agency.

Budget

The U.N. regular budget ($1.3 billion) is paid through assessed contributions from member states. But most of its assistance programs are funded through voluntary contributions.

Selected Countries

AFGHANISTAN

GEOGRAPHY:
Location: Southern Asia
Area:
total area: 647,500 sq km
land area: 647,500 sq km
Capital city: Kabul
Natural Resources: Natural gas, petroleum, coal, copper, talc, barites, sulfur, lead, zinc, iron ore, salt, precious and semi-precious stones
PEOPLE:
Population: 24,792,375

Age structure:
0–14 years: 43%
15–64 years: 54%
65 years & over: 3%
Literacy rate: *(age 15 and over can read and write)* 31.5% of total population, *(males:* 47.2%, *females:* 15%)
Languages: Pastu, Afghan Persian (*Dari*), Turk languages (*primarily Uzbek and Turkmen*), 30 minor languages (*primarily Balochi and Pashai*)
Religions: 84%- Sunni Muslim, 15%-Shi'a Muslim, 1%-Other

VITAL STATISTICS:
Birth rate: 42.72 *(per 1,000 population)* (1997)
Death rate: 17.78 *(per 1,000 population)*
Infant mortality rate: 146.7 *(deaths per 1,000 live births)*

Fertility rate: 6.07 *(per woman)*
Life expectancy at birth:
total population: 46.34
(males: 46.89, *females:* 45.76)

GOVERNMENT:
Type of government: Transitional Government
Independence: August 19, 1919 *(from UK)*
Leaders:
Afghanistan has no functioning government at this time, and the country remains divided among fighting factions.

ECONOMY:
GDP: purchasing power parity - $18.1 billion (1996)
GDP real growth rate: NA%
GDP per capita: $800
Inflation Rate (consumer prices): 240% (1996)
National budget:
revenues: $NA
expenditures: $NA
External debt: $2.3 billion
Currency: 1 Afghani = 100 puls
Labor Force: 7.1 million (1980)
Unemployment rate: 8% (1995)
Agriculture: Wheat, fruit, nuts, karakul pelts; wool, mutton
Industries: Small-scale production of textiles, soap, furniture, shoes, fertilizer, cement; handwoven carpets; natural gas, oil, coal, copper
Exports: $80 million
commodities: Fruits and nuts, hand-woven carpets, wool, cotton, hides and pelts, precious and semiprecious gems
Imports: $150 million
commodities: Food and petroleum products; most consumer goods

DEFENSE:
Defense expenditures: $NA, NA% of GDP

ALBANIA

GEOGRAPHY:
Location: Southeastern Europe
Area:
total area: 28,750 sq km
land area: 27,400 sq km
Capital city: Tirana
Natural Resources: Petroleum, natural gas, coal, chromium, copper, timber, nickel

PEOPLE:
Population: 3,330,754
Age structure:
0–14 years: 34%
15–64 years: 60%
65 years & over: 6%
Literacy rate: 72% *of total population,*
(males: 80%, *females:* 63%)
Languages: Albanian *(Tosk is the official dialect),*
Greek

Religions: 70%-Muslim, 20%-Albanian Orthodox, 10%-Roman Catholic

VITAL STATISTICS:
Birth rate: 21.96 *(per 1,000 population)* (1997)
Death rate: 7.54 *(per 1,000 population)*
Infant mortality rate: 47.1 *(deaths per 1,000 live births*
Fertility rate: 2.64 *(per woman)*
Life expectancy at birth:
total population: 62.28
(males: 65.24, *females:* 71.55)

GOVERNMENT:
Type of government: Emerging Democracy
Independence: November 28, 1912 *(from Ottoman Empire)*
Leaders:
chief of state: President of the Republic Rexhep Mejdani
head of government: Former Prime Minister of the Council of Ministers Fatos Nano announced his resignation in September 1998. No replacement has been named.

ECONOMY:
GDP: purchasing power parity - $4.4 billion (1996)
GDP real growth rate: 5%
GDP per capita: $1,290
Inflation Rate *(consumer prices):* 17.4% (1996)
National budget:
revenues: $624 million
expenditures: $996 million
External debt: $500 million
Currency: 1 lek = 100 qintars
Labor Force: 1.692 million
Unemployment rate: 13%
Agriculture: Wide range of temperate-zone crops, livestock
Industries: Food processing, textiles and clothing; lumber, oil, cement, chemicals, mining, basic metals, hydropower
Exports: $205 million
commodities: Asphalt, metals and metallic ores, electricity, crude oil, vegetables, fruits, tobacco
Imports: $680 million
commodities: Machinery, consumer goods, grains

DEFENSE:
Defense expenditures: *exchange rate conversion -* $42 *million,* 1.5% *of GDP*

ALGERIA

GEOGRAPHY:
Location: Northern Africa
Area:
total area: 2,381,740 sq km
land area: 2,381,740 sq km
Capital city: Algiers
Natural Resources: Petroleum, natural gas, iron ore, phosphates, uranium, lead, zinc

PEOPLE:
Population: 30,480,793

Age structure:
0–14 years: 39%
15–64 years: 57%
65 years & over: 4%
Literacy rate: 61.6% *of total population,*
(males: 73.9%, *females:* 49%)
Languages: Arabic *(official),* French, Berber dialects
Religions: 99%- Sunni Muslim *(state religion),* 1%-
Christian and Jewish

VITAL STATISTICS:
Birth rate: 28.01 *(per 1,000 population)* (1997)
Death rate: 5.76 *(per 1,000 population)*
Infant mortality rate: 47.1 *(deaths per 1,000 live births*
Fertility rate: 3.48 *(per woman)*
Life expectancy at birth:
total population: 68.62
(males: 67.5, *females:* 69.79)

GOVERNMENT:
Type of government: Republic
Independence: July 5, 1962 *(from France)*
Leaders:
chief of state: President General Liamine Zeroual
head of government: Prime Minister Ahmed Ouyahia

ECONOMY:
GDP: purchasing power parity - $115.9 billion (1996)
GDP real growth rate: 4%
GDP per capita: $4,000
Inflation Rate *(consumer prices):* 19.8% (1996)
National budget:
revenues: $14.3 billion
expenditures: $17.9 billion
External debt: $32 billion
Currency: 1 Algerian dinar = 100 centimes
Labor Force: 7.8 million (1996)
Unemployment rate: 28% (1996)
Agriculture: Wheat, barley, oats, grapes, olives, citrus,
fruits; cattle, sheep
Industries: Petroleum, light industries, natural gas,
mining, electrical, petrochemical, food processing
Exports: $11 billion
commodities: Petroleum and natural gas
Imports: $10.5 billion
commodities: Capital goods, food and beverages,
consumer goods

DEFENSE:
Defense expenditures: *exchange rate conversion -*
$1.3 *billion,* 2.7% *of GDP*

ANGOLA

GEOGRAPHY:
Location: Southern Africa
Area:
total area: 1,246,700 sq km
land area: 1,246,700 sq km
Capital city: Luanda
Natural Resources: Petroleum, diamonds, iron ore,
phosphates, copper, feldspar, gold, bauxite,
uranium

PEOPLE:
Population: 10,864,512
Age structure:
0–14 years: 45%
15–64 years: 52%
65 years & over: 3%
Literacy rate: 42% *of total population,*
(males: 56%, *females:* 28%)
Languages: Portuguese *(official),* Bantu and other
African Languages
Religions: 47%- indigenous beliefs, 38%-Roman
Catholic, 15%-Protestant

VITAL STATISTICS:
Birth rate: 44.11 *(per 1,000 population)* (1997)
Death rate: 17.24 *(per 1,000 population)*
Infant mortality rate: 135.7 *(deaths per 1,000 live*
births)
Fertility rate: 6.27 *(per woman)*
Life expectancy at birth:
total population: 47.32
(males: 45.12, *females:* 49.64)

GOVERNMENT:
Type of government: Transitional government nominally a multiparty democracy with strong presidential system
Independence: November 11, 1975
(from Portugal)
Leaders:
chief of state: President José Eduardo Dos Santos
head of government: Prime Minister M. Fernando
José de Franca Dias Van-Dunem

ECONOMY:
GDP: purchasing power parity - $8.3 billion (1996)
GDP real growth rate: 9%
GDP per capita: $700
Inflation Rate *(consumer prices):* 1,700% (1996)
National budget: .
revenues: $928 million
expenditures: $2.5 billion
External debt: $12.5 billion
Currency: 1 new kwanza = 100 lwei
Labor Force: 2.783 million
Unemployment rate: *(extensive unemployment and*
underemployment affecting more than half the
population) (1994)
Agriculture: Bananas, sugarcane, coffee, sisal, corn,
cotton, manioc *(tapioca),* tobacco, vegetables, plantains; livestock; forest products; fish
Industries: Petroleum; diamonds, iron ore, phosphates, feldspar, bauxite, uranium, and gold; fish
processing; food processing; brewing; tobacco;
sugar; textiles; cement; basic metal products
Exports: $4 billion
commodities: Oil, diamonds, refined petroleum
products, gas, coffee, sisal, fish and fish products, timber, cotton
Imports: $1.7 billion
commodities: Capital equipment *(machinery and*
elecrical equipment), food, vehicles and spare

parts, textiles and clothing, medicines, substantial military deliveries

DEFENSE:
Defense expenditures: *exchange rate conversion -* $1.1 *billion*, 31% *of GDP*

ARGENTINA

GEOGRAPHY:
Location: Southern South America
Area:
total area: 2,766,890 sq km
land area: 2,736,690 sq km
Capital city: Buenos Aires
Natural Resources: Fertile plains of the pampas, lead, zinc, tin, copper, iron ore, manganese, petroleum, uranium

PEOPLE:
Population: 36,265,463
Age structure:
0–14 years: 28%
15–64 years: 62%
65 years & over: 10%
Literacy rate: 96.2% *of total population,*
(males: 96.2%, *females:* 96.2%)
Languages: Spanish *(official)*, English, Italian, German, French
Religions: 90%-Roman Catholic *(less than* 20% *practicing)*, 2%- Protestant, 2%-Jewish, 6%- other

VITAL STATISTICS:
Birth rate: 20.01 *(per 1,000 population)* (1997)
Death rate: 7.68 *(per 1,000 population)*
Infant mortality rate: 28.3 *(deaths per 1,000 live births)*
Fertility rate: 2.69 *(per woman)*
Life expectancy at birth:
total population: 74.31
(males: 70.67, *females:* 78.12)

GOVERNMENT:
Type of government: Republic
Independence: July 9, 1816 *(from Spain)*
Leaders:
chief of state & head of government: President Carlos Saul Menem

ECONOMY:
GDP: purchasing power parity - $296.9 billion (1996)
GDP real growth rate: 4.4%
GDP per capita: $8,600
Inflation Rate *(consumer prices):* 0.1% (1996)
National budget:
revenues: $50.3 billion
expenditures: $51.7 billion
External debt: $95 billion
Currency: 1 nuevo peso Argentino = 100 centavos
Labor Force: 14.5 million (1995)
Unemployment rate: 17.3% (1996)
Agriculture: Wheat, corn, sorghum, soybeans, sugar beets; livestock
Industries: Food processing, motor vehicles, consumer

durables, textiles, chemicals and petrochemicals, printing, metallurgy, steel
Exports: $23.8 billion
commodities: Meat, wheat, corn, oilseed, manufactured goods
Imports: $23.7 billion
commodities: Machinery and equipment, chemicals, metals, fuels and lubricants, agricultural products

DEFENSE:
Defense expenditures: *exchange rate conversion -* $4.6 *billion*, 1.6% *of GDP*

ARMENIA

GEOGRAPHY:
Location: Southwestern Asia
Area:
total area: 29,800 sq km
land area: 28,400 sq km
Capital city: Yerevan
Natural Resources: Small deposits of gold, copper, molybdenum, zinc, alumina

PEOPLE:
Population: 3,421,775
Age structure:
0–14 years: 27%
15–64 years: 65%
65 years & over: 8%
Literacy rate: 99% *of total population,*
(males: 99%, *females:* 98%)
Languages: Armenian, Russian, other
Religions: 94%- Armenian Orthodox

VITAL STATISTICS:
Birth rate: 13.59 *(per 1,000 population)* (1997)
Death rate: 8.6 *(per 1,000 population)*
Infant mortality rate: 40.4 *(deaths per 1,000 live births)*
Fertility rate: 1.71 *(per woman)*
Life expectancy at birth:
total population: 66.9
(males: 62.69, *females:* 71.32)

GOVERNMENT:
Type of government: Republic
Independence: May 28, 1918 *(from First Armenian Republic)* September 23, 1991 *(from Soviet Union)*
Leaders:
chief of state: President Robert Kocharian
head of government: Prime Minister Armen Darbinyan

ECONOMY:
GDP: purchasing power parity - $9.7 billion (1996)
GDP real growth rate: 4%
GDP per capita: $2,800
Inflation Rate *(consumer prices):* 5.7%
National budget:
revenues: $NA
expenditures: $NA
External debt: $850 million
Currency: 1 dram = 100 luma

Labor Force: 1.6 million (1996)
Unemployment rate: 7.4% *(officially registered unemployed, large numbers of underemployed)* (1996)
Agriculture: Fruit *(especially grapes)*, vegetables; brandy, liqueurs; minor livestock sector
Industries: Much of industry is shut down; metal-cutting machine tools, forging-pressing machines, electric motors, tires, knitted wear, hoisery, shoes, silk fabric, washing machines, chemicals, trucks, watches, instruments, microelectronics
Exports: $273 million
commodities: Gold and jewelry, aluminum, transport equipment, electrical equipment, scrap metal
Imports: $830 million
commodities: Grain, other foods, fuel, other energy

DEFENSE:
Defense expenditures: *exchange rate conversion* - $75 million, NA% of GDP

AUSTRALIA

GEOGRAPHY:
Location: Oceania
Area:
total area: 7,686,850 sq km
land area: 7,617,930 sq km
Capital city: Canberra
Natural Resources: Bauxite, coal, iron ore, copper, tin, silver, uranium, nickel, tungsten, mineral sands, lead, zinc, diamonds, natural gas, petroleum

PEOPLE:
Population: 18,613,087
Age structure:
0–14 years: 22%
15–64 years: 66%
65 years & over: 12%
Literacy rate: 100% *of total population*
Languages: English, Native Languages
Religions: 26.1%- Anglican, 26%-Roman Catholic, 24.3%-Other Christian

VITAL STATISTICS:
Birth rate: 13.73 *(per 1,000 population)* (1997)
Death rate: 6.89 *(per 1,000 population)*
Infant mortality rate: 5.4 *(deaths per 1,000 live births)*
Fertility rate: 1.83 *(per woman)*
Life expectancy at birth:
total population: 79.64
(males: 76.69, *females:* 82.74)

GOVERNMENT:
Type of government: Federal Parliamentary State
Independence: January 1, 1901 *(federation of UK colonies)*
Leaders:
chief of state: Queen Elizabeth II, represented by Governor General Sir William Deane

head of government: Prime Minister John Winston Howard

ECONOMY:
GDP: purchasing power parity - $430.5 billion (1996)
GDP real growth rate: 3.6%
GDP per capita: $23,600
Inflation Rate *(consumer prices):* 3.1%
National budget:
revenues: $95.69 billion
expenditures: $95.15 billion
External debt: $134 billion
Currency: 1 Australian dollar = 100 cents
Labor Force: 8.4 million (1996)
Unemployment rate: 8.5% (1996)
Agriculture: Wheat, barley, sugarcane, fruits; cattle sheep, poultry
Industries: Mining, industrial and transportation equipment, food processing, chemicals, steel
Exports: $59.5 billion
commodities: Coal, gold, meat, wool, alumina, wheat, machinery and transport equipment
Imports: $59.7 billion
commodities: Machinery and transport equipment, computers and office machines, crude oil and petroleum products

DEFENSE:
Defense expenditures: *exchange rate conversion* - 7.9 billion, 1.9% of GDP

AUSTRIA

GEOGRAPHY:
Location: Central Europe
Area:
total area: 83,850 sq km
land area: 82,730 sq km
Capital city: Vienna
Natural Resources: Iron ore, oil, timber, magnesite, lead, coal, lignite, copper, hydropower

PEOPLE:
Population: 8,133,611
Age structure:
0–14 years: 17%
15–64 years: 68%
65 years & over: 15%
Literacy rate: 99% *of total population*
Languages: German
Religions: 85%-Roman Catholic, 6%- Protestant, 9%- other

VITAL STATISTICS:
Birth rate: 10.17 *(per 1,000 population)* (1997)
Death rate: 10.05 *(per 1,000 population)*
Infant mortality rate: 5.2 *(deaths per 1,000 live births)*
Fertility rate: 1.37 *(per woman)*
Life expectancy at birth:
total population: 77.15
(males: 73.96, *females:* 80.51)

GOVERNMENT:
Type of government: Federal Republic
Independence: November 12, 1918 *(from Austro-Hungarian Empire)*
Leaders:
chief of state: President Thomas Klestil
head of government: Chancellor Viktor Klima

ECONOMY:
GDP: purchasing power parity - $157.6 billion (1996)
GDP real growth rate: 1.1%
GDP per capita: $19,700
Inflation Rate *(consumer prices):* 1.8% (1996)
National budget:
revenues: $61.2 billion
expenditures: $71 billion
External debt: $30.2 billion
Currency: 1 Austrian schilling = 100 groschen
Labor Force: 3.648 million (1996)
Unemployment rate: 6.2% (1996)
Agriculture: Grains, fruits, potatoes, sugar beets; cattle, pigs, poultry; sawn wood
Industries: Food, iron and steel, machines, textiles, chemicals, electrical, paper and pulp, tourism, mining, motor vehicles
Exports: $55.5 billion
commodities: Machinery and equipment, iron and steel, lumber, textiles, paper products, chemicals
Imports: $65.8 billion
commodities: Petroleum, foodstuffs, machinery and equipment, vehicles, chemicals, textiles and clothing, pharmaceuticals

DEFENSE:
Defense expenditures: *exchange rate conversion -* $2.1 billion, 1.0% of GDP

AZERBAIJAN

GEOGRAPHY:
Location: Southwestern Asia
Area:
total area: 86,600 sq km
land area: 86,100 sq km
Capital city: Baku (Baki)
Natural Resources: Petroleum, natural gas, iron ore, nonferrous metals, alumina

PEOPLE:
Population: 7,855,576
Age structure:
0–14 years: 33%
15–64 years: 61%
65 years & over: 6%
Literacy rate: 97%, *of total population*
(males: 99%, *females:* 96%)
Languages: Azeri, Russian, Armenian, other
Religions: 93.4%-Muslim, 2.5%-Russian Orthodox, 2.3%-Armenian Orthodox, 1.8%-other *(note— religious affiliation is still nominal in Azerbaijan; actual practicing adherents are much lower)*

VITAL STATISTICS
Birth rate: 22.89 *(per 1,000 population)*
Death rate: 9.32 *(per 1,000 population)*
Infant mortality rate: 80.7 *(deaths per 1,000 live births)*
Fertility rate: 2.77 *(per woman)*
Life expectancy at birth:
total population: 63.52,
(males: 59.27, *females:* 67.99)

GOVERNMENT:
Type of government: Republic
Independence: August 30, 1991 *(from Soviet Union)*
Leaders:
chief of state: President Heydar Aliyev
head of government: Prime Minister Artur Razizade

ECONOMY:
GDP: purchasing power parity-$11.9 billion (1996)
GDP real growth rate: 1.2%
GDP per capita: $1,550
Inflation Rate *(consumer prices):* 20%
National budget:
revenues: $565 million
expenditures: $682 million
External debt: $100 million
Currency: 1 manat = 100 gopik
Labor Force: 2.789 million
Unemployment rate: 1.1% *(registered unemployed);* *(large numbers of unregistered unemployed and underemployed workers)*
Agriculture: Cotton, grain, rice, grapes, fruit, vegetables, tea, tobacco; cattle, pigs, sheep, goats
Industries: Petroleum and natural gas, petroleum products, oil field equipment; steel, iron ore, cement; chemicals and petrochemicals; textiles
Exports: $700 million
commodities: Oil and gas, chemicals, oil field equipment, textiles, cotton
Imports: $900 million
commodities: Machinery and parts, consumer durables, foodstuffs, textiles

DEFENSE:
Defense expenditures: 33.5 *billion manats,* NA% *of GDP; (note—conversion of defense expenditures into US dollars using the current exchange rate could produce misleading results)*

BAHRAIN

GEOGRAPHY:
Location: Middle East
Area:
total area: 620 sq km
land area: 620 sq km
Capital city: Manama
Natural Resources: Oil, associated and nonassociated natural gas, fish

PEOPLE:
Population: 616,342

Age structure:
0–14 years: 31%
15–64 years: 66%
65 years & over: 3%
Literacy rate: 85.2%, *of total population,*
(males: 89.1%, *females:* 79.4%)
Languages: Arabic, English, Farsi, Urdu
Religions: 75%-Shi'a Muslim, 25%-Sunni Muslim

VITAL STATISTICS:
Birth rate: 23.01 *(per 1,000 population)* (1997)
Death rate: 3.27 *(per 1,000 population)*
Infant mortality rate: 16.4 *(deaths per 1,000 live births)*
Fertility rate: 3.08 *(per woman)*
Life expectancy at birth:
total population: 74.63,
(males: 72.1, *females:* 77.24)

GOVERNMENT:
Type of government: Traditional Monarchy
Independence: August 15, 1971 *(from UK)*
Leaders:
chief of state: Amir Isa bin Salman Al Khalifa
head of government: Prime Minister Khalifa bin Salman Al Khalifa

ECONOMY:
GDP: purchasing power parity-$7.7 billion (1996)
GDP real growth rate: 3%
GDP per capita: $13,000
Inflation Rate *(consumer prices):* 0%
National budget:
revenues: $1.49 billion
expenditures: $1.67 billion
External debt: $3.2 billion
Currency: 1 Bahraini dinar = 1,000 fils
Labor Force: 140,000
Unemployment rate: 15%
Agriculture: Fruit, vegetables; poultry, dairy products; shrimp, fish
Industries: Petroleum processing and refining, aluminum smelting, offshore banking, ship repairing
Exports: $4.2 billion
commodities: Petroleum and petroleum products, aluminum
Imports: $3.5 billion
commodities: Crude oil

DEFENSE:
Defense expenditures: *exchange rate conversion*-$256 million, 6.4% *of GDP*

BANGLADESH

GEOGRAPHY:
Location: Southern Asia
Area:
total area: 144,000 sq km
land area: 133,910 sq km
Capital city: Dhaka
Natural Resources: Natural gas, arable land, timber

PEOPLE:
Population: 127,567,002
Age structure:
0–14 years: 38%
15–64 years: 59%
65 years & over: 3%
Literacy rate: 38.1% *of total population,*
(males: 49.4%, *females:* 26.1%)
Languages: Bangla *(official),* English
Religions: 88.3%- Muslim, 10.5%-Hindu, 1.2%-other

VITAL STATISTICS:
Birth rate: 29.8 *(per 1,000 population)*
Death rate: 10.9 *(per 1,000 population)*
Infant mortality rate: 100 *(deaths per 1,000 live births)*
Fertility rate: 3.45 *(per woman)*
Life expectancy at birth:
total population: 56.26
(males: 56.35, *females:* 56.16)

GOVERNMENT:
Type of government: Republic
Independence: December 16, 1971 *(from Pakistan)*
Leaders:
chief of state: President Shahabuddin Ahmed
head of government: Prime Minister Skeikh Hasina

ECONOMY:
GDP: purchasing power parity - $155.1 billion
GDP real growth rate: 4.7%
GDP per capita: $1,260
Inflation Rate *(consumer prices):* 4%
National budget:
revenues: $4 billion
expenditures: $6 billion
External debt: $17.1 billion
Currency: 1 taka = 100 poiska
Labor Force: 50.1 million
Unemployment rate: 35.9%
Agriculture: Jute, rice, wheat, tea, sugarcane, potatoes; beef, milk, poultry
Industries: Jute manufacturing, cotton textiles, food processing, steel, fertilizer
Exports: $3.9 billion
commodities: Garments, jute and jute goods, leather, frozen fish, seafood
Imports: $6.8 billion
commodities: Capital goods, petroleum, food, textiles

DEFENSE:
Defense expenditures: *exchange rate conversion -*
$481 *million,* 1.7% *of GDP*

BELARUS

GEOGRAPHY:
Location: Eastern Europe
Area:
total area: 207,600 sq km
land area: 207,600 sq km
Capital city: Minsk
Natural Resources: Forests, peat deposits, small quantities of oil and natural gas

PEOPLE:
Population: 10,409,050
Age structure:
0–14 years: 21%
15–64 years: 66%
65 years & over: 13%
Literacy rate: 98% *of total population,*
(*males:* 99%, *females:* 97%)
Languages: Byelorussian, Russian, other
Religions: 80%- Eastern Orthodox, 20%-other *(Including Roman Catholic, Muslim, Protestant, Jewish)*

VITAL STATISTICS:
Birth rate: 9.75 *(per 1,000 population)*
Death rate: 13.25 *(per 1,000 population)*
Infant mortality rate: 13.9 *(deaths per 1,000 live births)*
Fertility rate: 1.35 *(per woman)*
Life expectancy at birth:
total population: 68.4
(*males:* 62.48, *females:* 74.61)

GOVERNMENT:
Type of government: Republic
Independence: August 25, 1991 *(from Soviet Union);* the Belarussian Supreme Soviet issued a proclamation of independence; on July 17, 1990 Belarus issued a declaration of sovereignty
Leaders:
chief of state: President Aleksandr Lukashenko
head of government: Prime Minister Syargei Ling

ECONOMY:
GDP: purchasing power parity - $51.9 billion
GDP real growth rate: 3%
GDP per capita: $5,000
Inflation Rate *(consumer prices)*: 33%
National budget:
revenues: NA
expenditures: NA
External debt: $2 billion
Currency: Belarussian ruble
Labor Force: 4.731 million
Unemployment rate: 3.1% *(large number of underemployed workers)*
Agriculture: Grain, potatoes, vegetables; meat, milk
Industries: Tractors, metal-cutting machine tools, off-

highway dump trucks, wheel-type earthmovers for construction and mining, eight-wheel-drive, high-flotation trucks for use in tundra and roadless areas, equipment for animal husbandry and livestock feeding, motorcycles, television sets, chemical fibers, fertilizer, linen fabric, wool fabric, radios, refrigerators, other consumer goods
Exports: $5.2 billion
commodities: Machinery and transport equipment, chemicals, foodstuffs
Imports: $6.8 billion
commodities: Fuel, natural gas, industrial raw materials, textiles, sugar
DEFENSE:
Defense expenditures: 2.4 *trillion rubles, NA% of GDP (note-Conversion of defense expenditures into US dollars could produce misleading results)*

BELGIUM

GEOGRAPHY:
Location: Western Europe
Area:
total area: 30,510 sq km
land area: 30,230 sq km
Capital city: Brussels
Natural Resources: Coal, natural gas

PEOPLE:
Population: 10,174,922
Age structure:
0–14 years: 17%
15–64 years: 66%
65 years & over: 17%
Literacy rate: 99% *of total population*
Languages: Dutch, French, German
Religions: 75%-Roman Catholic, 25%-Protestant and other

VITAL STATISTICS:
Birth rate: 10.43 *(per 1,000 population)* (1997)
Death rate: 10.41 *(per 1,000 population)*
Infant mortality rate: 6.4 *(deaths per 1,000 live births)*
Fertility rate: 1.5 *(per woman)*
Life expectancy at birth:
total population: 77.19
(*males:* 73.95, *females:* 80.59)

GOVERNMENT:
Type of government: Constitutional Monarchy
Independence: October 4, 1830 *(from the Netherlands)*
Leaders:
chief of state: King Albert II
head of government: Prime Minister Jean-Luc Dehaene

ECONOMY:
GDP: purchasing power parity - $204.8 billion (1996)
GDP real growth rate: 1.4%
GDP per capita: $20,300
Inflation Rate *(consumer prices)*: 1.6%

National budget:
revenues: $NA
expenditures: $NA
External debt: $31.3 billion
Currency: 1 Belgian franc = 100 centimes
Labor Force: 4.126 million
Unemployment rate: 14%
Agriculture: Sugar beets, fresh vegetables, fruits, grain, tobacco; beef, veal, pork, milk
Industries: Engineering and metal products, motor vehicle assembly, processed food and beverages, chemicals, basic metals, textiles, glass, petroleum, coal
Exports: $108 billion
commodities: Iron and steel, transportation equipment, tractors, diamonds, petroleum products
Imports: $140 billion
commodities: Fuels, grains, chemicals, foodstuffs

DEFENSE:
Defense expenditures: *exchange rate conversion -* $4.6 *billion*, 1.7% *of GDP*

BOLIVIA

GEOGRAPHY:
Location: Central South America
Area:
total area: 1,098,580 sq km
land area: 1,084,390 sq km
Capital city: Sucre *(judicial)*, La Paz *(administrative)*
Natural Resources: Tin, natural gas, petroleum, zinc, tungsten, antimony, silver, iron, lead, gold, timber

PEOPLE:
Population: 7,826,352
Age structure:
0–14 years: 40%
15–64 years: 56%
65 years & over: 4%
Literacy rate: 83.1% *of total population,* (*males:* 90.5%, *females:* 76%)
Languages: Spanish*(official)*, Quechua*(official)*, Aymara*(official)*
Religions: 95%- Roman Catholic; Protestant*(Evangelical Methodist)*

VITAL STATISTICS:
Birth rate: 32.14 *(per 1,000 population)* (1997)
Death rate: 10.18 *(per 1,000 population)*
Infant mortality rate: 65.7 *(deaths per 1,000 live births)*
Fertility rate: 4.25 *(per woman)*
Life expectancy at birth:
total population: 60.34
(*males:* 57.49, *females:* 63.38)

GOVERNMENT:
Type of government: Republic
Independence: August 6, 1825 *(from Spain)*
Leaders:
chief of state & head of government: President Hugo Banzer

ECONOMY:
GDP: purchasing power parity - $21.5 billion (1996)
GDP real growth rate: 3.9%
GDP per capita: $3,000
Inflation Rate *(consumer prices)*: 8%
National budget:
revenues: $3.75 billion
expenditures: $3.75 billion
External debt: $4.4 billion
Currency: 1 boliviano = 100 centavos
Labor Force: 2.3 million
Unemployment rate: 18.8% (1995)
Agriculture: Coffee, coca, cotton, corn, sugarcane, rice, potatoes; timber
Industries: Mining, smelting, petroleum, food and beverages, tobacco, handicrafts, clothing
Exports: $1.1 billion
commodities: Metals, natural gas, soybeans, jewelry, wood
Imports: $1.4 billion
commodities: Capital goods, chemicals, petroleum, food

DEFENSE:
Defense expenditures: *exchange rate conversion -* $145 *million*, 1.9% *of GDP*

BOSNIA AND HERZEGOVINA

GEOGRAPHY:
Location: Southeastern Europe
Area:
total area: 51,233 sq km
land area: 51,233 sq km
Capital city: Sarajevo
Natural Resources: Coal, iron, bauxite, manganese, forests, copper, chromium, lead, zinc

PEOPLE:
Population: 3,365,727 *(note: All data dealing with population are subject to considerable error because of the dislocation caused by military action and ethnic fighting)*
Age structure:
0–14 years: 18%
15–64 years: 70%
65 years & over: 12%
Literacy rate: NA%
Languages: Serbo-Croatian (often called Bosnian)
Religions: 40%-Muslim, 31%- Orthodox, 15%- Catholic, 4%- Protestant, 10%-other

VITAL STATISTICS:
Birth rate: 8.29 *(per 1,000 population)* (1997)
Death rate: 13.88 *(per 1,000 population)*
Infant mortality rate: 37 *(deaths per 1,000 live births)*
Fertility rate: 1.09 *(per woman)*
Life expectancy at birth:
 total population: 59.42
 (males: 54.58, *females:* 64.59)

GOVERNMENT:
Type of government: Emerging Democracy
Independence: April 1992 *(from Yugoslavia)*
Leaders:
 chief of state: President Alija Izetbegovic
 head of government: Prime Minister Moncilo Krajisnik
  Prime Minister Kresimir Zubak

ECONOMY:
GDP: purchasing power parity - $1.9 billion (1995)
 GDP real growth rate: NA%
 GDP per capita: $600
Inflation Rate *(consumer prices):* NA%
National budget:
 revenues: $NA
 expenditures: $NA
External debt: $NA
Currency: 1 dinar = 100 para *(note-Croatian luna used in Croat-held area; old & new Serbian dinars used in Serb-held area; the deutsche mark [DM] has supplanted local currencies throughout Bosnia)*
Labor Force: 1,026,254
Unemployment rate: (officially about 70% but probably much lower, perhaps 40%-50%)
Agriculture: Wheat, corn, fruits, vegetables; livestock
Industries: Steel, coal, iron ore, lead, zinc, manganese, bauxite, vehicle assembly, textiles, tobacco products, wooden furniture, tank and aircraft assembly, domestic appliances, oil refining; much of capacity damaged or shut down
Exports: $152 million
 commodities: NA
Imports: $1.1 billion
 commodities: NA

DEFENSE:
Defense expenditures: $NA, NA% of GDP

B R A Z I L

GEOGRAPHY:
Location: Eastern South America
Area:
 total area: 8,511,965 sq km
 land area: 8,456,510 sq km
Capital city: Brasilia
Natural Resources: Bauxite, gold, iron ore, manganese, nickel, phosphate, platinum, tin, uranium, petroleum, hydropower timber

PEOPLE:
Population: 169,806,557

Age structure:
 0–14 years: 30%
 15–64 years: 65%
 65 years & over: 5%
Literacy rate: 83.3% *of total population,*
 (males: 83.3%, *females:* 83.2%)
Languages: Portuguese*(official)*, Spanish, English, French
Religions: 70%-Roman Catholic *(nominal)*

VITAL STATISTICS:
Birth rate: 20.43 *(per 1,000 population)*
Death rate: 9.42 *(per 1,000 population)*
Infant mortality rate: 53.4 *(deaths per 1,000 live births)*
Fertility rate: 2.29 *(per woman)*
Life expectancy at birth:
 total population: 61.42
 (males: 56.78, *females:* 66.3)

GOVERNMENT:
Type of government: Federal Republic
Independence: September 7, 1822 *(from Portugal)*
Leaders:
 chief of state & head of government:
  President Fernando Henrique Cardoso

ECONOMY:
GDP: purchasing power parity - $1.022 trillion (1996)
 GDP real growth rate: 2.9%
 GDP per capita: $6,300
Inflation Rate *(consumer prices):* 10%
National budget:
 revenues: $86 billion
 expenditures: $90 billion
External debt: $176 billion
Currency: 1 real = 100 centavos
Labor Force: 57 million (1989)
Unemployment rate: 5.2%
Agriculture: Coffee, soybeans, wheat, rice, corn, sugarcane, cocoa, citrus; beef
Industries: Textiles, shoes, chemicals, cement, lumber, iron ore, tin, steel, aircraft, motor vehicles and parts, other machinery and equipment
Exports: $47.7 billion
 commodities: Iron ore, soybean bran, orange juice, footwear, coffee, motor vehicle parts
Imports: $53.3 billion
 commodities: Crude oil, capital goods, chemical products, foodstuffs, coal

DEFENSE:
Defense expenditures: *exchange rate conversion -* $6.736 *billion*, 1.1% *of GDP*

B R U N E I

GEOGRAPHY:
Location: Southeastern Asia
Area:
 total area: 5,770 sq km
 land area: 5,270 sq km
Capital city: Bandar Seri Begawan
Natural Resources: Petroleum, natural gas, timber

PEOPLE:
Population: 315,292
Age structure:
0–14 years: 33%
15–64 years: 63%
65 years & over: 4%
Literacy rate: 88.2%, *of total population,*
(males: 92.6%, *females:* 83.4%)
Languages: Malay *(official),* English, Chinese
Religions: 63%-Muslim *(official),* 14%-Buddhism,
8%-Christian, 15%-indigenous beliefs and other

VITAL STATISTICS:
Birth rate: 25.2 *(per 1,000 population)*
Death rate: 5.13 *(per 1,000 population)*
Infant mortality rate: 23.8 *(deaths per 1,000 live births)*
Fertility rate: 3.37 *(per woman)*
Life expectancy at birth:
total population: 71.54
(males: 70, *females:* 73.16)

GOVERNMENT:
Type of government: Constitutional Sultanate
Independence: January 1, 1984 *(from UK)*
Leaders:
chief of state & head of government: Sultan Haji
Hassanal Bolkiah

ECONOMY:
GDP: purchasing power parity-$4.6 billion
GDP real growth rate: 2%
GDP per capita: $15,800
Inflation Rate *(consumer prices):* 2.5%
National budget:
revenues: $2.5 billion
expenditures: $2.6 billion
External debt: $0
Currency: 1 Bruneian dollar = 100 cents
Labor Force: 119,000 includes members of the Army
(1993)
Unemployment rate: 4.8% (1994)
Agriculture: Rice, cassava *(tapioca),* bananas; water
buffalo, pigs
Industries: Petroleum, petroleum refining, liquefied
natural gas, construction
Exports: $2.7 billion
commodities: Crude oil, liquefied natural gas, petroleum products
Imports: $2 billion
commodities: Machinery and transport
equipment, manufactured goods, food,
chemicals

DEFENSE:
Defense expenditures: *exchange rate conversion-*$312
million, 6.2% *of GDP*

BULGARIA

GEOGRAPHY:
Location: Southeastern Europe
Area:
total area: 110,910 sq km
land area: 110,550 sq km
Capital city: Sofia
Natural Resources: Bauxite, copper, lead, zinc, coal,
timber, arable land

PEOPLE:
Population: 8,240,426
Age structure:
0–14 years: 17%
15–64 years: 67%
65 years & over: 16%
Literacy rate: 98% *of total population,*
(males: 99%, *females:* 97%)
Languages: Bulgarian
Religions: 85%- Bulgarian Orthodox, 13% - Muslim,
0.8%-Jewish, 0.5%-Roman Catholic, 0.2%-uniate
Catholic

VITAL STATISTICS:
Birth rate: 8.05 *(per 1,000 population)*
Death rate: 13.38 *(per 1,000 population)*
Infant mortality rate: 13.2 *(deaths per 1,000 live births)*
Fertility rate: 1.14 *(per woman)*
Life expectancy at birth:
total population: 71.65
(males: 68.06, *females:* 75.44)

GOVERNMENT:
Type of government: Emerging Democracy
Independence: September 22, 1908 *(from Ottoman
Empire)*
Leaders:
chief of state: President Petar Stoyanov
head of government: Chairman of the Council of
Ministers (Prime Minister) Ivan Kostov

ECONOMY:
GDP: purchasing power parity - $39.9 billion (1996)
GDP real growth rate: 10%
GDP per capita: $4,630
Inflation Rate *(consumer prices):* 311% (1996)
National Budget:
revenues: $3 billion
expenditures: $4 billion
External debt: $10.4 billion
Currency: 1 lev = 100 stotinki
Labor Force: 3.57 million (1996)
Unemployment rate: 12.5% (1996)
Agriculture: Grain, oilseed, vegetables, fruits, tobacco;
livestock
Industries: Machine building and metal working, food
processing, chemicals, textiles, construction materi-
als, ferrous and nonferrous metals
Exports: $4.2 billion

commodities: Machinery and equipment, agriculture and food, textiles and apparel, metals and ores, chemicals, minerals and fuels
Imports: $4.1 billion
commodities: Fuels, minerals, raw materials, machinery and equipment, textiles and apparel, agricultural products, metals and ores, chemicals

DEFENSE:
Defense expenditures: exchange rate conversion - $418.6 million, 2.0% of GDP

CAMBODIA

GEOGRAPHY:
Location: Southeastern Asia
Area:
total area: 181,040 sq km
land area: 176,520 sq km
Capital city: Phnom Penh
Natural Resources: Timber, gemstones, some iron ore, manganese, phosphates, hydropower potential

PEOPLE:
Population: 11,339,562
Age structure:
0–14 years: 45%
15–64 years: 52%
65 years & over: 3%
Literacy rate: 35% of total population, (males: 48%, females: 22%)
Languages: Khmer (official), French
Religions: 95%- Theravada Buddhism, 5%-other

VITAL STATISTICS:
Birth rate: 42.63 (per 1,000 population) (1997)
Death rate: 15.39 (per 1,000 population)
Infant mortality rate: 106 (deaths per 1,000 live births)
Fertility rate: 5.81 (per woman)
Life expectancy at birth:
total population: 50.25
(males: 48.79, females: 51.79)

GOVERNMENT:
Type of government: Multiparty liberal democracy under a constitutional monarchy established in September 1993
Independence: November 9, 1949 (from France)
Leaders:
chief of state: King Norodom Sihanouk
head of government: (Shared Power) First Prime Minister Norodom Ranariddh and Second Prime Minister Hun Sen

ECONOMY:
GDP: purchasing parity - $7.7 billion (1996)
GDP real growth rate: 7.4%
GDP per capita: $710
Inflation Rate (consumer prices): 5% (1996)
National budget:
revenues: $261 million

expenditures: $496 million
External debt: $1.9 million
Currency: 1 new riel = 100 sen
Labor Force: 2.5–3 million (1996)
Unemployment rate: NA%
Agriculture: Rice, rubber, corn, vegetables
Industries: Rice milling, fishing, wood and wood products, rubber, cement, gem mining
Exports: $464 million
commodities: Timber, rubber, soybeans, sesame
Imports: $1.4 billion
commodities: Cigarettes, construction materials, petroleum products, machinery, motor vehicles

DEFENSE:
Defense expenditures: exchange rate conversion - $160 million, NA% of GDP

CANADA

GEOGRAPHY:
Location: Northern North America
Area:
total area: 9,976,140 sq km
land area: 9,220,970 sq km
Capital city: Ottawa
Natural Resources: Nickel, zinc, copper, gold, lead, molybdenum, potash, silver, fish, timber, wildlife, coal, petroleum, natural gas

PEOPLE:
Population: 30,675,398
Age structure:
0–14 years: 21%
15–64 years: 67%
65 years & over: 12%
Literacy rate: 97% of total population
Languages: English (official), French (official)
Religions: 45%-Roman Catholic, 12%-United Church, 8%-Anglican, 35%-other

VITAL STATISTICS:
Birth rate: 12.4 (per 1,000 population) (1997)
Death rate: 7.23 (per 1,000 population) (1997)
Infant mortality rate: 5.7 (deaths per 1,000 live births)
Fertility rate: 1.81 (per woman)
Life expectancy at birth:
total population: 78.96
(males: 75.61, females: 82.48)

GOVERNMENT:
Type of government: Confederation with parliamentary democracy
Independence: July 1, 1867 (from UK)
Leaders:
chief of state: Queen Elizabeth II represented by Governor General Romeo Le Blanc
head of government: Prime Minister Jean Chrétien

ECONOMY:
GDP: purchasing power parity - $721 billion (1996)
GDP real growth rate: 1.4%

GDP per capita: $25,000
Inflation Rate *(consumer prices):* 1.4% (1996)
National budget:
  revenues: $94.3 billion
  expenditures: $115.2 billion
External debt: $253 billion
Currency: 1 Canadian dollar = 100 cents
Labor Force: 15.1 million (1996)
Unemployment rate: 9.7% (1996)
Agriculture: Wheat, barley, oilseed, tobacco, fruits, vegetables; dairy products; forest products, commercial fisheries *(provide annual catch of 1.5 million metric tons)*
Industries: Processed and unprocessed minerals, food products, wood and paper products, transportation equipment, chemicals, fish products, petroleum and natural gas
Exports: $195.4 billion
  commodities: Newsprint, wood pulp, timber, crude petroleum, machinery, natural gas, aluminum, motor vehicles and parts; telecommunications equipment
Imports: $169.5 billion
  commodities: Crude oil, chemicals, motor vehicles and parts, durable consumer goods, electronic computers; telecommunications equipment and parts

DEFENSE:
Defense expenditures: *exchange rate conversion -* $9 *billion,* 1.6% *of GDP*

CHILE

GEOGRAPHY:
Location: Southern South America
Area:
  total area: 756,950 sq km
  land area: 748,800 sq km
Capital city: Santiago
Natural Resources: Copper, timber, iron ore, nitrates, precious metals, molybdenum

PEOPLE:
Population: 14,787,781
Age structure:
  0–14 years: 28%
  15–64 years: 65%
  65 years & over: 7%
Literacy rate: 95.2% *of total population,* (*males:* 95.4%, *females:* 95%)
Languages: Spanish
Religions: 89%-Roman Catholic, 11%-Protestant, Jewish

VITAL STATISTICS:
Birth rate: 17.53 *(per 1,000 population)* (1997)
Death rate: 5.68 *(per 1,000 population)*
Infant mortality rate: 13.2 *(deaths per 1,000 live births)*
Fertility rate: 2.17 *(per woman)*

Life expectancy at birth:
  total population: 74.73
    (*males:* 71.5, *females:* 77.95)

GOVERNMENT:
Type of government: Republic
Independence: September 18, 1810 *(from Spain)*
Leaders:
  chief of state & head of government: President Eduardo Frei Ruiz-Tagle

ECONOMY:
GDP: purchasing power parity - $120.6 billion (1996)
  GDP real growth rate: 6.5%
  GDP per capita: $8,400
Inflation Rate *(consumer prices):* 6.7% (1996)
National budget:
  revenues: $17 billion
  expenditures: $17 billion
External debt: $21.1 billion
Currency: 1 Chilean peso = 100 centavos
Labor Force: 5.5 million
Unemployment rate: 6.5% (1996)
Agriculture: Wheat, corn, grapes, beans, sugar beets, potatoes, fruit; beef, poultry, wool; timber; fish *(catch of 6.6 million metric tons)*
Industries: Copper, other minerals, foodstuffs, fish processing, iron and steel, wood and wood products, transport equipment, cement, textiles
Exports: $15.2 billion
  commodities: Copper, other metals and minerals, wood products, fish and fishmeal, fruits
Imports: $16.5 billion
commodities: Capital goods, spare parts, raw materials, petroleum, foodstuffs

DEFENSE:
Defense expenditures: *exchange rate conversion -* $2.8 *million,* 3.5% *of GDP (note-Includes earnings from CODELCO Company; may exclude costs of pensions and internal security)*

CHINA

GEOGRAPHY:
Location: Eastern Asia
Area:
  total area: 9,596,960 sq km
  land area: 9,326,410 sq km
Capital city: Beijing
Natural Resources: Coal, iron ore, petroleum, mercury, tin, tungsten, antimony, manganese, molybdenum, vanadium, magnetite, aluminum, lead, zinc, uranium, hydropower potential *(world's largest)*

PEOPLE:
Population: 1,243,621,623
Age structure:
  0–14 years: 26%
  15–64 years: 68%
  65 years & over: 6%
Literacy rate: 81.5% *of total population,* (*males:* 89.9%, *females:* 72.7%)

Languages: Standard Chinese or Mandarin *(putonghua, based on the Beijing dialect),* Yue *(Cantonese),* Wu *(Shanghaise),* Minbei *(Fuzhou),* Minnan *(Hokkien-Taiwanese),* Xiang, Gan, Hakka dialects

Religions: Daoism (Taoism), Buddhism; 2%-3%-Muslim, 1%-Christian

VITAL STATISTICS:
Birth rate: 16.52 *(per 1,000 population)* (1997)
Death rate: 6.87 *(per 1,000 population)*
Infant mortality rate: 39.6 *(deaths per 1,000 live births)*
Fertility rate: 1.81 *(per woman)*
Life expectancy at birth:
total population: 81.5
 (males: 69.9, *females:* 72.7)

GOVERNMENT:
Type of government: Communist State
Independence: 221 BC *(unification under the Qin or Ch'in Dynasty 221 BC; Qing or Ch'ing Dynasty replaced by the Republic on February 12, 1912; People's Republic established October 1, 1949)*
Leaders:
 chief of state: President Jiang Zemin
 head of government: Premier Zhu Rongji

ECONOMY:
GDP: purchasing power parity - $3.39 trillion (1996 estimate as extrapolated from World Bank estimate for 1995 with use of official Chinese growth figure for 1996; the result may overstate China's GDP by as much as 25%)
 GDP real growth rate: 9.7%
 GDP per capita: $2,800
Inflation Rate *(consumer prices):* 10% (1996)
National budget:
 revenues: $NA
 expenditures: $NA
External debt: $92 billion
Currency: 1 yuan = 10 jiao
Labor Force: 614.7 million (1994)
Unemployment rate: 3% *(substantial underemployment)*
Agriculture: Rice, potatoes, sorghum, peanuts, tea, millet, barley, cotton, other fibers, oilseed; pork and other livestock products; fish
Industries: Steel, coal, machine building, armaments, textiles and apparel, petroleum, cement, chemicals, fertilizers, consumer durables, food processing, autos, consumer electronics, telecommunications
Exports: $151.07 billion
 commodities: Garments, textiles, footwear, toys, machinery and equipment
Imports: $138.83 billion
 commodities: Industrial machinery, textiles, plastics, telecommunications equipment, steel bars, aircraft

DEFENSE:
Defense expenditures: *The officially announced but suspect figures are:* 70.2 *billion yuan,* NA% *of GDP. (note-Conversion of defense budget into dollars*

using the current exchange rate could produce misleading results)

COLOMBIA

GEOGRAPHY:
Location: Northern South America
Area:
 total area: 1,138,910 sq km
 land area: 1,038,700 sq km
Capital city: Bogota
Natural Resources: Petroleum, natural gas, coal, iron ore, nickel, gold, copper, emeralds

PEOPLE:
Population: 38,580,949
Age structure:
 0–14 years: 31%
 15–64 years: 64%
 65 years & over: 5%
Literacy rate: 91.3% *of total population,*
 (males: 91.2%, *females:* 91.4%)
Languages: Spanish
Religions: 95%-Roman Catholic

VITAL STATISTICS:
Birth rate: 20.78 *(per 1,000 population)* (1997)
Death rate: 4.62 *(per 1,000 population)*
Infant mortality rate: 24.7 *(deaths per 1,000 live births)*
Fertility rate: 2.31 *(per woman)*
Life expectancy at birth:
 total population: 73.14
 (males: 70.28, *females:* 76.09)

GOVERNMENT:
Type of government: Republic; executive branch dominates government stucture
Independence: July 20, 1810 *(Spain)*
Leaders:
 chief of state & head of government: President Andres Pastrana

ECONOMY:
GDP: purchasing power parity - $201.4 billion (1996)
 GDP real growth rate: 2.1%
 GDP per capita: $5,400
Inflation Rate *(consumer prices):* 21.6%
National budget:
 revenues: $27
 expenditures: $30 billion
External debt: $16.5 billion
Currency: 1 Colombian peso = 100 centavos
Labor Force: 12 million (1990)
Unemployment rate: 11.5% (1996)
Agriculture: Coffee, cut flowers, bananas, rice, tobacco, corn, sugarcane, cocoa beans, oilseed, vegetables; forest products, shrimp farming
Industries: Textiles, food processing, oil, clothing and footwear, beverages, chemicals, cement; gold, coal, emeralds
Exports: $10.3 billion
 commodities: Petroleum, coffee, coal, bananas,

fresh cut flowers
Imports: $12.4 billion
commodities: Industrial equipment, transportation equipment, consumer goods, chemicals, paper products

DEFENSE:
Defense expenditures: *exchange rate conversion* - $2 billion, 2.8% of GDP

COSTA RICA

GEOGRAPHY:
Location: Central America
Area:
total area: 51,100 sq km
land area: 50,660 sq km
Capital city: San José
Natural Resources: Hydropower potential

PEOPLE:
Population: 3,604,642
Age structure:
0–14 years: 34%
15–64 years: 61%
65 years & over: 5%
Literacy rate: 94.8% *of total population,*
(males: 94.7%, *females:* 95%)
Languages: Spanish *(official),* English spoken around Puerto Limon
Religions: 95%-Roman Catholic

VITAL STATISTICS:
Birth rate: 23.35 *(per 1,000 population)* (1997)
Death rate: 4.15 *(per 1,000 population)*
Infant mortality rate: 13.3 *(deaths per 1,000 live births)*
Fertility rate: 2.85 *(per woman)*
Life expectancy at birth:
total population: 75.82
(males: 73.41, *females:* 78.36)

GOVERNMENT:
Type of government: Democratic Republic
Independence: September 15, 1821 *(from Spain)*
Leaders:
chief of state & head of government: President Miguel Angel Rodriguez

ECONOMY:
GDP: purchasing power parity- $19 billion (1996)
GDP real growth rate: -0.9%
GDP per capita: $5,500
Inflation Rate *(consumer prices):* 13.9% (1996)
National budget:
revenues: $1.1 billion
expenditures: $1.34 billion
External debt: $3.2 billion
Currency: 1 Costa Rican colon = 100 centimos
Labor Force: 868,300 (1995)
Unemployment rate: 5.5% (1996) *(much underemployment)*
Agriculture: Coffee, bananas, sugar, corn, rice, beans,

potatoes; beef; timber *(depletion of forest resources has resulted in declining timber output)*
Industries: Food processing, textiles and clothing, construction materials, fertilizer, plastic products
Exports: $3.82 billion
commodities: Coffee, bananas, textiles, sugar
Imports: $3.857 billion
commodities: Raw materials, consumer goods, capital equipment, petroleum

DEFENSE:
Defense expenditures: *exchange rate conversion -* $55 million, 2.0% of GDP

CÔTE D'IVOIRE

GEOGRAPHY:
Location: Western Africa
Area:
total area: 322,460 sq km
land area: 318,000 sq km
Capital city: Yamoussoukro
Natural Resources: Petroleum, diamonds, manganese, iron ore, cobalt, bauxite, copper

PEOPLE:
Population: 15,446,231
Age structure:
0–14 years: 47%
15–64 years: 51%
65 years & over: 2%
Literacy rate: 40.1% *of total population,*
(males: 49.9%, *females:* 30%)
Languages: French *(official),* 60 native dialects with Dioula the most widely spoken
Religions: 60%-Muslim, 25%-indigenous, 12%-Christian

VITAL STATISTICS:
Birth rate: 42.43 *(per 1,000 population)*
Death rate: 17.11 *(per 1,000 population)*
Infant mortality rate: 99.7 *(deaths per 1,000 live births)*
Fertility rate: 6.06 *(per woman)*
Life expectancy at birth:
total population: 44.81
(males: 43.63, *females:* 46.03)

GOVERNMENT:
Type of government: Republic; multiparty presidential regime established 1960
Independence: August 7, 1960 *(from France)*
Leaders:
chief of state: President Henri Konan Bedie
head of government: Prime Minister Daniel Kablan Duncan

ECONOMY:
GDP: purchasing power parity-$23.9 billion (1996)
GDP real growth rate: 6.5%
GDP per capita: $1,620
Inflation Rate *(consumer prices):* 8% (1996)
National budget:
revenues: $1.9 billion

expenditures: $3.4 billion
External debt: $16.7 billion
Currency: 1 Communaute Financière Africaine
franc = 100 centimes
Labor Force: NA
Unemployment rate: NA%
Agriculture: Coffee, cocoa beans, bananas, palm kernels, corn, rice, manioc, sweet potatoes, sugar; cotton, rubber; timber
Industries: Foodstuffs, beverages; wood products, oil refining, automobile assembly, textiles, fertilizer, construction materials, electricity
Exports: $3.7 billion
commodities: Cocoa, coffee, tropical woods, petroleum, cotton, bananas, pineapples, palm oil; fish
Imports: $2.4 billion
commodities: Food, capital gods, consumer goods, fuel

DEFENSE:
Defense expenditures: *exchange rate conversion -*
$140 *million,* 1.4% *of GDP*

CROATIA

GEOGRAPHY:
Location: Southeastern Europe
Area:
total area: 56,538 sq km
land area: 56,410 sq km
Capital city: Zagreb
Natural Resources: Oil, some coal, bauxite, low-grade iron ore, calcium, natural asphalt, silica, mica, clays, salt

PEOPLE:
Population: 4,671,584
Age structure:
0–14 years: 18%
15–64 years: 68%
65 years & over: 14%
Literacy rate: 97% *of total population,*
(*males:* 99%, *females:* 95%)
Languages: Serbo-Croatian and other
Religions: 76.5%-Catholic, 11.1%-Orthodox, 1.2% Slavic Muslim, 0.4%-Protestant, 10.8%- others and unknown

VITAL STATISTICS:
Birth rate: 10.63 *(per 1,000 population)* (1997)
Death rate: 11.2 *(per 1,000 population)*
Infant mortality rate: 8.2 *(deaths per 1,000 live births)*
Fertility rate: 1.56 *(per woman)*
Life expectancy at birth:
total population: 73.49
(*males:* 70.16, *females:* 77.03)

GOVERNMENT:
Type of government: Parlimentary Democracy
Independence: June 25, 1991 *(from Yugoslavia)*
Leaders:
chief of state: President Franjo Tudjman
head of government: Prime Minister Zlatko Matesa

ECONOMY:
GDP: purchasing power parity - $21.4 billion (1996)
GDP real growth rate: 4%
GDP per capita: $4,300
Inflation Rate *(consumer prices):* 4%
National budget:
revenues: $3.86 billion
expenditures: $3.72 billion
External debt: $3.15 billion
Currency: 1 Croatian kuna = 100 paras
Labor Force: 1.444 million (1995)
Unemployment rate: 13% (1996)
Agriculture: Wheat, corn, sugar beets, sunflower seed, alfalfa, clover, olives, citrus, grapes, vegetables; livestock breeding, dairy farming
Industries: Chemicals and plastic, machine tools, fabricated metals, electronics, pig iron and rolled steel products, aluminum, paper, wood products, construction materials, textiles, shipbuilding, petroleum and petroleum refining, food and beverages
Exports: $4.6 billion
commodities: Machinery and transport equipment, miscellaneous manufactures, chemicals, food and live animals, raw materials, fuels and lubricants, beverages and tobacco
Imports: $7.6 billion
commodities: Machinery and transport equipment, fuels and lubricants, food and live animals, chemicals, miscellaneous manufactured articles, raw materials, beverages and tobacco

DEFENSE:
Defense expenditures: *exchange rate conversion-*1.56 billion, 10% of GDP.

CUBA

GEOGRAPHY:
Location: Caribbean
Area:
total area: 110,860 sq km
land area: 110,860 sq km
Capital city: Havana
Natural Resources: Cobalt, nickel, iron ore, copper, manganese, salt, timber, silica, petroleum

PEOPLE:
Population: 11,050,729
Age structure:
0–14 years: 22%
15–64 years: 68%
65 years & over: 10%
Literacy rate: 95.7% *of total population,*
(*males:* 96.2%, *females:* 95.3%)
Languages: Spanish
Religions: 85%-Roman Catholic *(prior to Castro's assuming power),* Protestant, Jehovah's Witnesses, Jews and Santeria are also represented

VITAL STATISTICS:
Birth rate: 13.37 *(per 1,000 population)*
Death rate: 7.39 *(per 1,000 population)*

Infant mortality rate: 9 *(deaths per 1,000 live births)*
Fertility rate: 1.52 *(per woman)*
Life expectancy at birth:
total population: 75.05
(males: 72.71, *females:* 77.54)

GOVERNMENT:
Type of government: Communist State
Independence: May 20, 1902 *(from Spain December 10, 1898; administered by the US from 1898 to 1902)*
Leaders:
chief of state & head of government: President of the Council of State and President of the Council of Ministers Fidel Castro

ECONOMY:
GDP: purchasing power parity - $14.7 billion
GDP real growth rate: 2.5%
GDP per capita: $1,300
Inflation Rate *(consumer prices):* NA%
National budget:
revenues: $NA
expenditures: $NA
External debt: $9.1 billion
Currency: 1 Cuban peso = 100 centavos
Labor Force: 4.71 million
Unemployment rate: NA%
Agriculture: Sugarcane, tobacco, citrus, coffee, rice, potatoes, and other tubers, beans; livestock
Industries: Sugar, petroleum, food, tobacco, textiles, chemicals, paper and wood products, metals *(particularly nickel)*, cement, fertilizer, consumer goods, agricultural machinery
Exports: $1.6 billion
commodities: Sugar, nickel, shellfish, tobacco, medical products, citrus, coffee
Imports: $2.4 billion
commodities: Petroleum, food, machinery, chemicals

DEFENSE:
Defense expenditures: *exchange rate conversion - $NA, 4% of GDP roughly (note-Moscow, for decades the key military supporter and supplier of Cuba, cut off almost all military aid by 1993)*

C Y P R U S

GEOGRAPHY:
Location: Middle East
Area:
total area: 9,250 sq km
land area: 9,240 sq km
Capital city: Nicosia
Natural Resources: Copper, pyrites, asbestos, gypsum, timber, salt, marble, clay earth pigment

PEOPLE:
Population: 748,982
Age structure:
0–14 years: 25%

15–64 years: 65%
65 years & over: 10%
Literacy rate: 94% *of total population,*
(males: 98%, *females:* 91%)
Languages: Greek, Turkish, English
Religions: 78%-Greek Orthodox, 18%-Muslim, 4%-Maronite, Armenian Apostolic and other

VITAL STATISTICS:
Birth rate: 15.04 *(per 1,000 population)* (1997)
Death rate: 7.58 *(per 1,000 population)*
Infant mortality rate: 8.2 *(deaths per 1,000 live births)*
Fertility rate: 2.17 *(per woman)*
Life expectancy at birth:
total population: 76.54
(males: 74.38, *females:* 78.81)

GOVERNMENT:
Type of government: Republic
Independence: August 16, 1960 *(from UK)*
(note - Turkish area proclaimed self-rule in February 1975 from Republic of Cyprus)
Leaders:
chief of state & head of government: President Glafcos Clerides

ECONOMY:
GDP: purchasing power parity: $8.8 billion (1996)
Greek area: $8.3 billion
Turkish area: $536 million
GDP real growth rate: 3.4%
Greek area: 4%
Turkish area: 0.5%
GDP per capita: $11,800
Greek area: $13,700
Turkish area: $3,950
Inflation Rate *(consumer prices):*
Greek area: 33%
Turkish area: 86%
National budget:
revenues:
Greek area: $2.9 billion
Turkish area: $149 million
expenditures:
Greek area: $3.3 billion
Turkish area: $304 million
External debt:
Greek area: $1.8 billion
Currency: 1 Cypriot pound = 100 cents
1 Turkish lira = 100 kurus
Labor Force: (1995)
Greek area: 299,700
Turkish area: 76,500
Unemployment rate: (1996)
Greek area: 3.3%
Turkish area: 8.6%
Agriculture: Potatoes, vegetables, barley, grapes, olives, citrus
Industries: Food, beverages, textiles, chemicals, metal products, tourism, wood products
Exports:
Greek area: $1.4 billion

commodities: Citrus, potatoes, grapes, wine, cement, clothing and shoes

Turkish area: $71 million
  commodities: Citrus, potatoes, textiles

Imports:
  Greek area: $4 billion
    commodities: Consumer goods, petroleum and lubricants, food and feed grains, machinery
  Turkish area: $330 million
    commodities: food, minerals, chemicals, machinery

DEFENSE:
Defense expenditures: *exchange rate conversion -* $405 *million,* 5.4% *of GDP*

CZECH REPUBLIC

GEOGRAPHY:
Location: Central Europe
Area:
  total area: 78,703 sq km
  land area: 78,645 sq km
Capital city: Prague
Natural Resources: Hard coal, soft coal, kaolin, clay, graphite

PEOPLE:
Population: 10,286,470
Age structure:
  0–14 years: 18%
  15–64 years: 69%
  65 years & over: 13%
Literacy rate: 99% *of total population*
Languages: Czech, Slovak
Religions: 39.8%-atheist, 39.2%-Roman Catholic, 4.6%-Protestant, 3%-Orthodox, 13.4%-other

VITAL STATISTICS:
Birth rate: 8.84 *(per 1,000 population)* (1997)
Death rate: 11.02 *(per 1,000 population)*
Infant mortality rate: 6.9 *(deaths per 1,000 live births)*
Fertility rate: 1.17 *(per woman)*
Life expectancy at birth:
  total population: 73.86
    (males: 70.49, *females:* 77.42)

GOVERNMENT:
Type of government: Parlimentary Democracy
Independence: January 1, 1993 *(from Czechoslovakia)*
Leaders:
  chief of state: President Vaclav Havel
  head of government: Prime Minister Milos Zeman

ECONOMY:
GDP: purchasing power parity - $114.3 billion (1996)
  GDP real growth rate: 5%
  GDP per capita: $11,100
Inflation Rate *(consumer prices):* 8.7% (1996)
National budget:
  revenues: $18.4 billion
  expenditures: $18.4 billion
External debt: $17.1 billion

Currency: 1 koruna = 100 haleru
Labor Force: 5.107 million
Unemployment rate: 3.3% (1996)
Agriculture: Grains, potatoes, sugar beets, hops, fruit; pigs, cattle, poultry; forest products
Industries: Fuels, ferrous metallurgy, machinery and equipment, coal, motor vehicles, glass, armaments
Exports: $21.9 billion
  commodities: Manufactured goods, machinery and transport equipment, chemicals, fuels, minerals, metals, agricultural products
Imports: $27.8 billion
  commodities: Machinery and transport equipment, manufactured goods, chemicals, fuels and lubricants, raw materials, agricultural products

DEFENSE:
Defense expenditures: *exchange rate conversion -* $1.22 *billion,* 2.2% *of GDP*

DEMOCRATIC REPUBLIC OF CONGO
(formerly Zaire)

GEOGRAPHY:
Location: Central Africa
Area:
  total area: 2,345,410 sq km
  land area: 2,267,600 sq km
Capital city: Kinshasa
Natural Resources: Cobalt, copper, cadmium, petroleum, industrial and gem diamonds, gold, silver, zinc, manganese, tin, germanium, uranium, radium, bauxite, iron ore, coal, hydropower potential

PEOPLE:
Population: 49,000,511
Age structure:
  0–14 years: 48%
  15–64 years: 49%
  65 years & over: 3%
Literacy rate: 77.3% *of total population,*
    (males: 86.6%, *females:* 67.7%)
Languages: French *(official),* Lingala *(a lingua franca trade language),* Kingwana *(a dialect of Kiswahili or Swahili),* Kikongo, Tshiluba
Religions: 50%-Roman Catholic, 20%-Protestant, 10%-Kimbanguist, 10%-Muslim, 10%-other syncretic sects and traditional beliefs

VITAL STATISTICS:
Birth rate: 48.1 *(per 1,000 population)*
Death rate: 16.9 *(per 1,000 population)*
Infant mortality rate: 108 *(deaths per 1,000 live births)*
Fertility rate: 6.64 *(per woman)*
Life expectancy at birth:
  total population: 46.7
    (males: 44.97, *females:* 48.47)

GOVERNMENT:
Type of government: Transitional government—Civil

war
Independence: June 30, 1960 *(from Belgium)*
Leaders:
chief of state & head of government: Laurent Kabila

ECONOMY:
GDP: purchasing power parity - $16.5 billion
GDP real growth rate: -7.4%
GDP per capita: $400
Inflation Rate *(consumer prices):* 12%
National budget:
revenues: $479 million
expenditures: $479 million
External debt: $11.3 billion
Currency: 1 zaire = 100 makuta
Labor Force: 14.51 million
Unemployment rate: NA%
Agriculture: Coffee, sugar, palm oil, rubber, tea, qui-
nine, cassava *(tapioca)*, palm oil, bananas, root
crops, corn, fruits; wood products
Industries: Mining, mineral processing, consumer
products *(including textiles, footwear, cigarettes,
processed foods and beverages)*, cement,
diamonds
Exports: $419 million
commodities: Copper, coffee, diamonds, cobalt,
crude oil
Imports: $382 million
commodities: Consumer goods, foodstuffs, mining
and other machinery, transport equipment, fuels

DEFENSE:
Defense expenditures: *exchange rate conversion -*
$46 *million*, 1.5% *of GDP*

DENMARK

GEOGRAPHY:
Location: Northern Europe
Area:
total area: 43,094 sq km
land area: 42,394 sq km
Capital city: Copenhagen
Natural Resources: Petroleum, natural gas, fish, salt,
limestone, stone, gravel and sand

PEOPLE:
Population: 5,333,617
Age structure:
0–14 years: 18%
15–64 years: 67%
65 years & over: 15%
Literacy rate: 99% *of total population*
Languages: Danish, Faroese, Greenlandic *(an Eskimo
dialect)*, German *(small minority)*
Religions: 91%-Evangelical Lutheran, 2%-Protestant
and Roman Catholic, 7%-other

VITAL STATISTICS:
Birth rate: 12.78 *(per 1,000 population)* (1997)
Death rate: 11.22 *(per 1,000 population)*
Infant mortality rate: 4.8 *(deaths per 1,000 live births)*

Fertility rate: 1.75 *(per woman)*
Life expectancy at birth:
total population: 76.1
(males: 73.44, *females:* 78.9)

GOVERNMENT:
Type of government: Constitutional Monarchy
Independence: 10th century first organized as a
unified state; in 1849 became a constitutional
monarchy
Leaders:
chief of state: Queen Margrethe II
head of government: Prime Minister Poul Nyrup
Rasmussen

ECONOMY:
GDP: purchasing power parity - $118.2 billion (1996)
GDP real growth rate: 2%
GDP per capita: $22,700
Inflation Rate *(consumer prices):* 2.1% (1996)
National budget:
revenues: $62.1 billion
expenditures: $66.4 billion
External debt: $44 billion
Currency: 1 Danish krone = 100 oere
Labor Force: 2,895,950 (1995)
Unemployment rate: 8.2% (1996)
Agriculture: Grain, potatoes, rape, sugar beets; meat,
dairy products; fish
Industries: Food processing, machinery and equip-
ment, textiles and clothing, chemical products, electronics, construction, furniture, and other wood
products, shipbuilding
Exports: $47.6 billion
commodities: Meat and meat products, dairy products, transport equipment (shipbuilding), fish,
chemicals, industrial machinery
Imports: $42.4 billion
commodities: Petroleum, machinery and equipment,
chemicals, grain and foodstuffs, textiles, paper

DEFENSE:
Defense expenditures: *exchange rate conversion -*
$2.9 *billion*, 1.6% *of GDP*

DOMINICAN REPUBLIC

GEOGRAPHY:
Location: Caribbean
Area:
total area: 48,730 sq km
land area: 48,380 sq km
Capital city: Santo Domingo
Natural Resources: Nickel, bauxite, gold, silver

PEOPLE:
Population: 7,998,766
Age structure:
0–14 years: 36%
15–64 years: 60%
65 years & over: 4%
Literacy rate: 82.1% *of total population,*
(males: 82%, *females:* 82.2%)

Languages: Spanish
Religions: 95%-Roman Catholic

VITAL STATISTICS:
Birth rate: 26.87 *(per 1,000 population)* (1997)
Death rate: 5.81 *(per 1,000 population)*
Infant mortality rate: 46 *(deaths per 1,000 live births)*
Fertility rate: 3.1 *(per woman)*
Life expectancy at birth:
   total population: 69.39
      (males: 67.21, *females:* 71.69)

GOVERNMENT:
Type of government: Republic
Independence: February 27, 1844 *(from Haiti)*
Leaders:
   chief of state & head of government: President Leonel Fernandez

ECONOMY:
GDP: purchasing power parity - $29.8 billion (1996)
   GDP real growth rate: 7.3%
   GDP per capita: $3,670
Inflation Rate *(consumer prices)*: 12.5% (1995)
National budget:
   revenues: $1.8 billion
   expenditures: $2.2 billion
External debt: $3.6 billion
Currency: 1 Dominican peso = 100 centavos
Labor Force: 2.3–2.6 million (1991)
Unemployment rate: 30% (1996)
Agriculture: Sugarcane, coffee, cotton, cocoa, tobacco, rice, beans, potatoes, corn, bananas; cattle, pigs, dairy products, meat, eggs
Industries: Tourism, sugar processing, ferronickel and gold mining, textiles, cement, tobacco
Exports: $3.1 billion
   commodities: Ferronickel, sugar, gold, coffee, cocoa
Imports: $5.3 billion
   commodities: Foodstuffs, petroleum, cotton and fabrics, chemicals and pharmaceuticals

DEFENSE:
Defense expenditures: *exchange rate conversion -* $116 *million,* 1.4% *of GDP*

E C U A D O R

GEOGRAPHY:
Location: Western South America
Area:
   total area: 283,560 sq km
   land area: 276,840 sq km
Capital city: Quito
Natural Resources: Petroleum, fish, timber

PEOPLE:
Population: 12,336,572
Age structure:
   0–14 years: 37%
   15–64 years: 59%
   65 years & over: 4%

Literacy rate: 90.1% *of total population,*
   (males: 92% *and females:* 88.2%)
Languages: Spanish *(official),* Amerindian languages *(especially Quechua)*
Religions: 95%-Roman Catholic

VITAL STATISTICS:
Birth rate: 24.04 *(per 1,000 population)* (1997)
Death rate: 5.28 *(per 1,000 population)*
Infant mortality rate: 33.4 *(deaths per 1,000 live births)*
Fertility rate: 2.87 *(per woman)*
Life expectancy at birth:
   total population: 71.44
      (males: 68.83, *females:* 74.17)

GOVERNMENT:
Type of government: Republic
Independence: May 24, 1822 *(from Spain)*
Leaders:
   chief of state & head of government: President Jamil Mahuad

ECONOMY:
GDP: purchasing power parity - $47 billion (1996)
   GDP real growth rate: 2%
   GDP per capita: $4,100
Inflation Rate *(consumer prices)*: 26% (1996)
National budget:
   revenues: $3.6 billion
   expenditures: $3.6 billion
External debt: $12.6 billion
Currency: 1 sucre = 100 centavos
Labor Force: 3.4 million (1990)
Unemployment rate: 8.5% *(note: With widespread underemployment)* (1996)
Agriculture: Bananas, coffee, cocoa, rice, potatoes, manioc, plantains, sugarcane, cattle, sheep, pigs, beef, pork, dairy products; balsa wood; fish, shrimp
Industries: Petroleum, food processing, textiles, metal work, paper products, wood products, chemicals, plastics, fishing, lumber
Exports: $4.9 billion
   commodities: Petroleum, bananas, shrimp, cocoa, coffee
Imports: $3.7 billion
   commodities: Transport equipment, consumer goods, vehicles, machinery, chemicals

DEFENSE:
Defense expenditures: *exchange rate conversion -* $390.2 *million,* 2.1 % *of GDP*

E G Y P T

GEOGRAPHY:
Location: Northern Africa
Area:
   total area: 1,001,450 sq km
   land area: 995,450 sq km
Capital city: Cairo
Natural Resources: Petroleum, natural gas, iron ore,

phosphates, maganese, limestone, gypsum, talc, asbestos, lead, zinc

PEOPLE:
Population: 66,050,004
Age structure:
0–14 years: 36%
15–64 years: 60%
65 years & over: 4%
Literacy rate: 51.4% *of total population,*
(males: 63.6%, *females:* 38.8%)
Languages: Arabic *(official),* English and French
(widely understood by educated classes)
Religions: 94%-Muslim *(mostly Sunni),* 6%-Coptic
Christian and other *(official estimates)*

VITAL STATISTICS:
Birth rate: 27.82 *(per 1,000 population)* (1997)
Death rate: 8.56 *(per 1,000 population)*
Infant mortality rate: 71 *(deaths per 1,000 live births)*
Fertility rate: 3.5 *(per woman)*
Life expectancy at birth:
total population: 61.75
(males: 59.8, *females:* 63.8)

GOVERNMENT:
Type of government: Republic
Independence: February 28, 1922 *(from UK)*
Leaders:
chief of state: President Mohammed Hosni Mubarak
head of government: Prime Minister Kamal
Ganzouri

ECONOMY:
GDP: purchasing power parity - $183.9 billion (1996)
GDP real growth rate: 4.9%
GDP per capita: $2,900
Inflation Rate *(consumer prices):* 7.3% (1996)
National budget:
revenues: $17.4 billion
expenditures: $18.8 billion
External debt: $31 billion
Currency: 1 Egyptian pound = 100 piasters
Labor Force: 17.4 million (1996)
Unemployment rate: 9.4% *(1995-96 official estimate)*
Agriculture: Cotton, rice, corn, wheat, beans, fruits,
vegetables; cattle, water buffalo, sheep, goats; fish
(annual catch about 14,000 metric tons)
Industries: Textiles, food processing,tourism, chemicals, petroleum, construction, cement, metals
Exports: $4.6 billion
commodities: Crude oil and petroleum products,
cotton yarn, raw cotton, textiles, metal products,
chemicals
Imports: $13.8 billion
commodities: Machinery and equipment, foods, fertilizers, wood products, durable consumer goods,
capital goods

DEFENSE:
Defense expenditures: *exchange rate conversion -*
$3.28 *billion,* 8.2% *of GDP*

EL SALVADOR

GEOGRAPHY:
Location: Central America
Area:
total area: 21,040 sq km
land area: 20,720 sq km
Capital city: San Salvador
Natural Resources: Hydropower, geothermal power,
petroleum

PEOPLE:
Population: 5,752,067
Age structure:
0–14 years: 38%
15–64 years: 57%
65 years & over: 5%
Literacy rate: 71.5% *of total population,*
(males: 73.5%, *females:* 69.8 %)
Languages: Spanish, Nahua *(among some Amerindians)*
Religions: 75%-Roman Catholic

VITAL STATISTICS:
Birth rate: 27.22 *(per 1,000 population)* (1997)
Death rate: 6.44 *(per 1,000 population)*
Infant mortality rate: 30.3 *(deaths per 1,000 live births)*
Fertility rate: 3.3 *(per woman)*
Life expectancy at birth:
total population: 69.27
(males: 65.89, *females:* 72.81)

GOVERNMENT:
Type of government: Republic
Independence: September 15, 1821 *(from Spain)*
Leaders:
chief of state & head of government: President Armando Calderon Sol

ECONOMY:
GDP: purchasing power parity - $12.2 billion (1996)
GDP real growth rate: 3%
GDP per capita: $2,080
Inflation Rate *(consumer prices):* 7.4% (1996)
National budget:
revenues: $1.75 billion
expenditures: $1.82 billion
External debt: $2.54 billion
Currency: 1 Salvadoran colones = 100 centavos
Labor Force: 2.2 milion (1996)
Unemployment rate: 7.6% (1996)
Agriculture: Coffee, sugarcane, corn, rice, beans,
oilseed; beef, dairy products; shrimp
Industries: Food processing, beverages, petroleum, tobacco, chemicals, textiles, furniture
Exports: $1.8 billion
commodities: Coffee, sugarcane, shrimp
Imports: $3.2 billion
commodities: Raw materials, consumer goods, capital goods

DEFENSE:
Defense expenditures: *exchange rate conversion -* $101 *million,* 0.9% *of GDP*

E S T O N I A

GEOGRAPHY:
Location: Eastern Europe
Area:
total area: 45,226 sq km
land area: 43,211 sq km
Capital city: Tallinn
Natural Resources: Shale oil, peat, phosphorite, amber, Cambrian blue clay

PEOPLE:
Population: 1,421,335
Age structure:
0–14 years: 19%
15–64 years: 67%
65 years & over: 14%
Literacy rate: 100% *of total population*
Languages: Estonian *(official)*, Latvian, Lithuanian, Russian, other
Religions: Evangelical Lutheran, others include Baptist, Methodist, 7th Day Adventist, Roman Catholic, Pentecostal, Word of Life, 7th Day Baptist, Judaism

VITAL STATISTICS:
Birth rate: 9.04 *(per 1,000 population)* (1997)
Death rate: 14.08 *(per 1,000 population)*
Infant mortality rate: 14.1 *(deaths per 1,000 live births)*
Fertility rate: 1.29 *(per woman)*
Life expectancy at birth:
total population: 68.38
(males: 62.39, *females:* 74.67)

GOVERNMENT:
Type of government: Republic
Independence: September 6, 1991 *(from Soviet Union)*
Leaders:
chief of state: President Lennart Meri
head of government: Prime Minister Mart Siimann

ECONOMY:
GDP: purchasing power parity - $8.1 billion (1996)
GDP real growth rate: 3%
GDP per capita: $5,560
Inflation Rate *(consumer prices):* 23% (1996)
National budget:
revenues: $620 million
expenditures: $582 million
External debt: $270 million
Currency: 1 Estonian kroon = 100 cents *(introduced in August 1992)*
Labor Force: 750,000 (1992)
Unemployment rate: 5% (1996)
Agriculture: Potatoes, fruits, vegetables; livestock and dairy products; fish
Industries: Oil shale, shipbuilding, phosphates, electric motors, excavators, cement, furniture, clothing, textiles, paper, shoes, apparel

Exports: $2 billion
commodities: Textiles, food products, vehicles, metals
Imports: $3.1 billion
commodities: Machinery, fuels, vehicles, textiles
DEFENSE:
Defense expenditures: *exchange rate conversion* - $35 *million,* 1.5% *of GDP*

E T H I O P I A

GEOGRAPHY:
Location: Eastern Africa
Area:
total area: 1,127,127 sq km
land area: 1,119,683 sq km
Capital city: Addis Ababa
Natural Resources: Small reserves of gold, platinum, copper, potash

PEOPLE:
Population: 58,390,351
Age structure:
0–14 years: 46%
15–64 years: 51%
65 years & over: 3%
Literacy rate: 35.5% *of total population,* *(males:* 45.5%, *females:* 25.3%)
Languages: Amharic *(official)*, Tigrinya, Orominga, Guaraginga, Somali, Arabic, English *(major foreign language taught in schools)*
Religions: 45–50%-Muslim, 35–40%-Ethiopian Orthodox, 12%-animist, 3%-8%-other

VITAL STATISTICS:
Birth rate: 45.59 *(per 1,000 population)* (1997)
Death rate: 17.56 *(per 1,000 population)*
Infant mortality rate: 121.5 *(deaths per 1,000 live births)*
Fertility rate: 6.94 *(per woman)*
Life expectancy at birth:
total population: 46.62
(males: 45.48, *females:* 47.8)

GOVERNMENT:
Type of government: Federal Republic
Independence: Oldest independent country in Africa and one of the oldest in the world - at least 2,000 years
Leaders:
chief of state: President Negasso Ghidada
head of government: Prime Minister Meles Zenawi

ECONOMY:
GDP: purchasing power parity - $24.8 billion
GDP real growth rate: 7.7%
GDP per capita: $430
Inflation Rate *(consumer prices):* 10%
National budget:
revenues: $1 billion
expenditures: $1.48 billion
External debt: $4.3 billion
Currency: 1 birr = 100 cents

Labor Force: 18 million
Unemployment rate: NA%
Agriculture: Cereals, pulses, coffee, oilseed, sugarcane, potatoes, other vegetables; hides, cattle, sheep, goats
Industries: Food processing, beverages, textiles, chemicals, metals processing, cement
Exports: $423 million
  commodities: Coffee, leather products, gold
Imports: $1.15 billion
  commodities: Capital goods, consumer goods, fuel

DEFENSE:
Defense expenditures: *exchange rate conversion -* $110 *million,* NA% *of GDP*

F I J I

GEOGRAPHY:
Location: Oceania
Area:
  total area: 18,270 sq km
  land area: 18,270 sq km
Capital city: Suva
Natural Resources: Timber, fish, gold, copper, offshore oil potential

PEOPLE:
Population: 802,611
Age structure:
  0–14 years: 35%
  15–64 years: 62%
  65 years & over: 3%
Literacy rate: 91.6% *of total population,* (*males:* 93.8%, *females:* 89.3%)
Languages: English *(official)*, Fijian, Hindustani
Religions: 52%-Christian, (37%-*Methodist*, 9%-*Roman Catholic*), 38%-Hindu, 8%-Muslim, 2%-other

VITAL STATISTICS:
Birth rate: 23.12 *(per 1,000 population)* (1997)
Death rate: 6.3 *(per 1,000 population)*
Infant mortality rate: 17.4 *(deaths per 1,000 live births)*
Fertility rate: 2.78 *(per woman)*
Life expectancy at birth:
  total population: 66
  (*males:* 63.66, *females:* 68.46)

GOVERNMENT:
Type of government: Republic
Independence: October 10, 1970 *(from UK)*
Leaders:
  chief of state: President Ratu Sir Kamisese Mara
  head of government: Prime Minister Sitiveni Ligamamada Rabuka

ECONOMY:
GDP: purchasing power parity - $5.1 billion (1996)
  GDP real growth rate: 5%
  GDP per capita: $6,500
Inflation Rate *(consumer prices):* 3%

National budget:
  revenues: $540.64 million
  expenditures: $742.65 million
External debt: $670 million
Currency: 1 Fijian dollar = 100 cents
Labor Force: 235,000 (1987)
Unemployment rate: 6%
Agriculture: Sugarcane, coconuts, cassava *(tapioca),* rice, sweet potatoes, bananas; cattle, pigs, horses, goats; fish *(annual catch nearly 13,796 metric tons)*
Industries: Sugar, tourism, copra, gold, silver, clothing, lumber, small cottage industries
Exports: $670 million
  commodities: Sugar, clothing, gold, processed fish, lumber
Imports: $864 million
  commodities: Machinery and transport equipment, petroleum products, food, consumer goods, chemicals

DEFENSE:
Defense expenditures: *exchange rate conversion -* $32 *million,* 5% *of GDP*

F I N L A N D

GEOGRAPHY:
Location: Northern Europe
Area:
  total area: 337,030 sq km
  land area: 305,470 sq km
Capital city: Helsinki
Natural Resources: Timber, copper, zinc, iron ore, silver

PEOPLE:
Population: 5,149,242
Age structure:
  0–14 years: 19%
  15–64 years: 67%
  65 years & over: 14%
Literacy rate: 100% *of total population*
Languages: Finnish *(official)*, Swedish *(official)*, small Lapp- and Russian-speaking minorities
Religions: 89%-Evangelical Lutheran, 1%-Greek Orthodox, 9%-none, and 1%-other

VITAL STATISTICS:
Birth rate: 11.75 *(per 1,000 population)* (1996)
Death rate: 9.62 *(per 1,000 population)*
Infant mortality rate: 3.8 *(deaths per 1,000 live births)*
Fertility rate: 1.78 *(per woman)*
Life expectancy at birth:
  total population: 76.97
  (*males:* 73.41, *females:* 80.68)

GOVERNMENT:
Type of government: Republic
Independence: December 6, 1917 *(from Soviet Union)*
Leaders:
  chief of state: President Martti Ahtisaari
  head of government: Prime Minister Paavo Tapio Lipponen

ECONOMY:
GDP: purchasing power parity - $97.1 billion (1996)
  GDP real growth rate: 2.5%
  GDP per capita: -$19,000
Inflation Rate *(consumer prices)*: 0.7%
National budget:
  revenues: $25.9 billion
  expenditures: $35 billion
External debt: $30 billion
Currency: 1 markka or finmark = 100 pennia
Labor Force: 2.533 million
Unemployment rate: 16.6%
Agriculture: Cereals, sugar beets, potatoes; dairy cattle; fish *(annual catch about 160,000 metric tons)*
Industries: Metal products, shipbuilding, pulp and paper, copper refining, foodstuffs, chemicals, textiles, clothing
Exports: $29.7 billion
  commodities: Paper and pulp, machinery, chemicals, metals, timber
Imports: $23.2 billion
  commodities: Foodstuffs, petroleum and petroleum products, chemicals, transport equipment, iron and steel, machinery, textile yarn and fabrics, fodder grains

DEFENSE:
Defense expenditures: *exchange rate conversion -* $1.9 *billion,* 1.6% *of GDP*

FRANCE

GEOGRAPHY:
Location: Western Europe
Area:
  total area: 547,030 sq km
  land area: 545,630 sq km
Capital city: Paris
Natural Resources: Coal, iron ore, bauxite, fish, timber, zinc, potash

PEOPLE:
Population: 58,804,944
Age structure:
  0–14 years: 19%
  15–64 years: 65%
  65 years & over: 16%
Literacy rate: 99% *of total population*
Languages: French 100%, rapidly declining regional dialects and languages *(Provençal, Breton, Alsatian, Corsican, Catalan, Basque, Flemish)*
Religions: 90%-Roman Catholic, 2%-Protestant, 1%-Jewish, 1%-Muslim *(North African workers),* and 6%-unaffiliated

VITAL STATISTICS:
Birth rate: 11.98 *(per 1,000 population)* (1997)
Death rate: 9.08 *(per 1,000 population)*
Infant mortality rate: 5.3 *(deaths per 1,000 live births)*
Fertility rate: 6.6 *(per woman)*
Life expectancy at birth:
  total population: 78.38
    (males: 74.44, *females:* 82.53)

GOVERNMENT:
Type of government: Republic
Independence: 486 *(unified by Clovis)*
Leaders:
  chief of state: President Jacques Chirac
  head of government: Prime Minister Lionel Jospin

ECONOMY:
GDP: purchasing power parity - $1.22 trillion (1996)
  GDP real growth rate: 1.3%
  GDP per capita: $20,900
Inflation Rate *(consumer prices)*: 1.7%
National budget:
  revenues: $250 billion
  expenditures: $300 billion
External debt: $117.6 billion
Currency: 1 French franc = 100 centimes
Labor Force: 25.5 million (1995)
Unemployment rate: 12.7% (1996)
Agriculture: Wheat, cereals, sugar beets, potatoes, wine grapes; beef, dairy products; fish *(annual catch of 850,000 metric tons ranks among world's top 20 countries and is all used domestically)*
Industries: Machinery, chemicals, automobiles, metallurgy, aircraft, electronics, mining, textiles, food processing, tourism
Exports: $275 billion
  commodities: Machinery and transportation equipment, chemicals, foodstuffs, agricultural products, iron and steel products, textiles and clothing
Imports: $255.5 billion
  commodities: Crude oil, machinery and equipment, agricultural products, chemicals, iron and steel products

DEFENSE:
Defense expenditures: *exchange rate conversion -* $47.7 *billion,* 2.5% *of GDP*

GERMANY

GEOGRAPHY:
Location: Central Europe
Area:
  total area: 356,910 sq km
  land area: 349,520 sq km
Capital city: Berlin
Natural Resources: Iron ore, coal, potash, timber, lignite, uranium, copper, natural gas, salt, nickel

PEOPLE:
Population: 82,079,454
Age structure:
  0–14 years: 16%
  15–64 years: 68%
  65 years & over: 16%
Literacy rate: 99% *of total population*
Languages: German
Religions: 38%- Protestant, 34%-Roman Catholic, 1.7%-Muslim, 26.3%-unaffiliated or other

VITAL STATISTICS:
Birth rate: 8.98 *(per 1,000 population)* (1997)
Death rate: 10.82 *(per 1,000 population)*
Infant mortality rate: 5.3 *(deaths per 1,000 live births)*
Fertility rate: 1.24 *(per woman)*
Life expectancy at birth:
  total population: 76.81
    (*males:* 73.64, *females:* 80.16)

GOVERNMENT:
Type of government: Federal Republic
Independence: January 18, 1871 *(German Empire uni-
fication)*; divided into four zones of occupation *(UK,
US, USSR, and later, France)* in 1945 following
WWII; Federal Republic of Germany *(FRG or West
Germany)* proclaimed May 23, 1949 and included
the former UK, US and French zones; German
Democratic Republic *(GDR or East Germany)* pro-
claimed October 7, 1949 and included the former
USSR zone; unification of West Germany and East
Germany took place October 3, 1990; all four power
rights formally relinquished March 15, 1991
Leaders:
  chief of state: President Roman Herzog
  head of government: Chancellor Helmut Kohl

ECONOMY:
GDP: purchasing power parity -
  (Germany) $1.7 trillion
  (western) $1.56 trillion
  (eastern) $142 billion (1996)
  GDP real growth rate:
  (Germany) 1.4%
  (western) 1.3%
  (eastern) 2.0%
  GDP per capita:
  (Germany) $20,400
  (western) $23,000
  (eastern) $9,000
Inflation Rate *(consumer prices):* 1.5%
  National budget;
  revenues: $755 billion
  expenditures: $832.1 billion
External debt: $NA
Currency: 1 deutsche mark = 100 pfennige
Labor Force: 38.7 million
Unemployment rate: 10.8%
  (western) 9.6%
  (eastern) 15.9%
Agriculture:
  (western)- Potatoes, wheat, barley, sugar beets,
    fruit, cabbage; cattle, pigs, poultry
  (eastern)- Wheat, rye, barley, potatoes, sugar beets,
    fruit; pork, beef, chicken, milk, hides
Industries:
  (western:)- Among the world's largest and most
    technologically advanced producers of iron, steel,
    coal, cement, chemicals, machinery, vehicles,
    machine tools, electronics, food and beverages
  (eastern)- Metal fabrication, chemicals. brown coal,
    shipbuilding, machine building, food and bever-
    ages, textiles, petroleum refining

Exports: $501.3 billion
  commodities: Manufactured goods *(including ma-
    chines and machine tools, chemicals, motor ve-
    hicles, iron and steel products)*, agricultural
    products, raw materials, fuels
Imports: $430.7 billion
  commodities: Manufactured goods, agricultural
    products, fuels, raw materials

DEFENSE:
Defense expenditures: *exchange rate conversion -*
  $42.8 *billion*, 1.5% *of GDP*

GHANA

GEOGRAPHY:
Location: Western Africa
Area:
  total area: 238,540 sq km
  land area: 230,020 sq km
Capital city: Accra
Natural Resources: Gold, timber, industrial diamonds,
  bauxite, manganese, fish, rubber

PEOPLE:
Population: 18,497,206
Age structure:
  0–14 years: 43%
  15–64 years: 54%
  65 years & over: 3%
Literacy rate: 64.5%, *of total population,*
  (*males:* 75.9%, *females:* 53.5%)
Languages: English *(official)*, African languages *(including Akan, Moshi-Dagomba, Ewe, and Ga)*
Religions: 38%-indigenous beliefs, 30%-Muslim,
  24%-Christian, 8%-other

VITAL STATISTICS:
Birth rate: 33.88 *(per 1,000 population)* (1997)
Death rate: 10.37 *(per 1,000 population)*
Infant mortality rate: 78.9 *(deaths per 1,000 live
  births)*
Fertility rate: 4.43 *(per woman)*
Life expectancy at birth:
  total population: 56.49
    (*males:* 54.47, *females:* 57)

GOVERNMENT:
Type of government: Constitutional Democracy
Independence: March 6, 1957 *(from UK)*
Leaders:
  chief of state & head of government: President Jerry
    John Rawlings

ECONOMY:
GDP: purchasing power parity - $27 billion (1996)
  GDP real growth rate: 5%
  GDP per capita: $1,530
Inflation Rate *(consumer prices):* 36%
National budget:
  revenues: $1.05 billion
  expenditures: $1.2 billion
External debt: $5.2 billion
Currency: 1 new cedi = 100 pesewas

Labor Force: 3.7 million
Unemployment rate: 10% (1993)
Agriculture: Cocoa, rice, coffee, cassava *(tapioca)*, peanuts, corn, shea nuts, bananas; timber
Industries: mining, lumbering, light manufacturing, aluminum, food processing
Exports: $1.43 billion
commodities: Cocoa, gold, timber, tuna, bauxite, aluminum, manganese ore, diamonds
Imports: $1.84 billion
commodities: Petroleum, consumer goods, intermediate goods, capital equipment

DEFENSE:
Defense expenditures: *exchange rate conversion* - $30 million, 0.8% of GDP

GREECE

GEOGRAPHY:
Location: Southern Europe
Area:
total area: 131,940 sq km
land area: 130,800 sq km
Capital city: Athens
Natural Resources: Bauxite, lignite, magnesite, petroleum, marble

PEOPLE:
Population: 10,662,138
Age structure:
0–14 years: 17%
15–64 years: 67%
65 years & over: 16%
Literacy rate: 95% *of total population,* (*males:* 98%, *females:* 93%)
Languages: Greek *(official)*, English, French
Religions: 98%-Greek Orthodox, 1.3%-Muslim, 0.7%-other

VITAL STATISTICS:
Birth rate: 9.75 *(per 1,000 population)* (1997)
Death rate: 9.32 *(per 1,000 population)*
Infant mortality rate: 7.4 *(deaths per 1,000 live births)*
Fertility rate 1.33 *(per woman)*
Life expectancy at birth:
total population: 78.17
(*males:* 75.64, *females:* 80.89)

GOVERNMENT:
Type of government: Parlimentary republic; monarchy rejected by referendum December 8, 1974
Independence: 1829 *(from the Ottoman Empire)*
Leaders:
chief of state: President Constantinos (Kostis) Stephanopoulos
head of government: Prime Minister Konstantine Simitis

ECONOMY:
GDP: purchasing power parity - $106.9 billion (1996)
GDP real growth rate: 2.2%
GDP per capita: $10,000
Inflation Rate *(consumer prices):* 8.6%

National budget:
revenues: $33 billion
expenditures: $45 billion
External debt: $34.2 billion
Currency: 1 drachma = 100 lepta
Labor Force: 4.21 million
Unemployment rate: 10%
Agriculture: Wheat, corn, barley, sugar beets, olives, tomatoes, wine, tobacco, potatoes; meat, dairy products
Industries: Tourism; food and tobacco processing, textiles; chemicals, metal products, mining, petroleum
Exports: $5.9 billion
commodities: Manufactured goods, foodstuffs, fuels
Imports: $20.3 billion
commodities: Manufactured goods, foodstuffs, fuels

DEFENSE:
Defense expenditures: *exchange rate conversion* - $4.9 *billion,* 4.6% *of GDP*

GREENLAND

GEOGRAPHY:
Location: Northern North America
Area:
total area: 2,175,600 sq km
land area: 2,175,600 sq km *(341,600 sq km ice-free, 1,834,000 sq km ice-covered)*
Capital city: Nuuk (Godthab)
Natural Resources: Zinc, lead, iron ore, coal, molybdenum, gold, platinum, uranium, fish, seals, whales

PEOPLE:
Population: 59,309
Age structure:
0–14 years: 27%
15–64 years: 68%
65 years & over: 5%
Literacy rate: NA *(similar to Denmark Proper)*
Languages: Eskimo dialects, Danish, Greenlandic *(an Inuit dialect)*
Religions: Evangelical Lutheran

VITAL STATISTICS:
Birth rate: 16.39 *(per 1,000 population)* (1997)
Death rate: 6.99 *(per 1,000 population)*
Infant mortality rate: 22.6 *(deaths per 1,000 live births)*
Fertility rate: 2.19 *(per woman)*
Life expectancy at birth:
total population: 68.84
(*males:* 64.62, *females:* 73.08)

GOVERNMENT:
Type of government: Part of the Danish realm; self-governing overseas administrative division
Independence: None
Leaders:
chief of state: Queen Margrethe II, represented by High Commissioner Gunnar Martens
head of government: Premier Jonathan Motzfeldt

ECONOMY:
GDP: purchasing power parity - $892 million (1995)
  GDP real growth rate: NA%
  GDP per capita: $15,500
Inflation Rate: *(consumer prices)* 1.8%
National budget:
  revenues: $703 million
  expenditures: $697 million
External debt: $243 million
Currency: 1 Danish krone = 100 oere
Labor Force: 24,500
Unemployment rate: 10.5%
Agriculture: Forage crops, small garden vegetables; sheep; fish
Industries: Fish processing *(mainly shrimp)*, furs, handicrafts, small shipyards
Exports: $363.4 million
  commodities: Fish and fish products
Imports: $421 million
  commodities: Manufactured goods, machinery and transport equipment, food and live animals, petroleum products

DEFENSE:
Defense expenditures: *Defense is the responsibility of Denmark*

GUATEMALA

GEOGRAPHY:
Location: Central America
Area:
  total area: 108,890 sq km
  land area: 108,430 sq km
Capital city: Guatemala City
Natural Resources: Petroleum, nickel, rare wood, fish, chicle

PEOPLE:
Population: 12,007,580
Age structure:
  0–14 years: 43%
  15–64 years: 53%
  65 years & over: 4%
Literacy rate: 55.6% *of total population,* (*males:* 62.5%, *females:* 48.6%)
Languages: Spanish, Amerindian language *(23 Amerindian languages, including Quiche, Cakchiquel, Kekchi)*
Religions: Roman Catholic, Protestant, traditional Mayan

VITAL STATISTICS:
Birth rate: 36.45 *(per 1,000 population)* (1997)
Death rate: 7.13 *(per 1,000 population)*
Infant mortality rate: 49.2 *(deaths per 1,000 live births)*
Fertility rate: 4.89 *(per woman)*
Life expectancy at birth:
  total population: 65.64
    (*males:* 63.02, *females:* 68.39)

GOVERNMENT:

Type of government: Republic
Independence: September 15, 1821 *(from Spain)*
Leaders:
  chief of state & head of government: President Alvaro Enrique Arzu Irigoyen

ECONOMY:
GDP: purchasing power parity - $39 billion (1996)
  GDP real growth rate: 3%
  GDP per capita: $3,460
Inflation Rate *(consumer prices)*: 10.9%
National budget:
  revenues: $1.25 billion
  expenditures: $1.35 billion
External debt: $3.1 billion
Currency: 1 quetzal = 100 centavos
Labor Force: 3.1 million
Unemployment rate: 4.9% *(Underemployment 30–40%)* (1994)
Agriculture: Sugarcane, corn, bananas, coffee, beans, cardamom; cattle, sheep, pigs, chickens
Industries: Sugar, textiles and clothing, furniture, chemicals, petroleum, metals, rubber, tourism
Exports: $1.81 billion
  commodities: Coffee, sugar, bananas, cardamom, beef
Imports: $3.11 billion
  commodities: Fuel and petroleum products, machinery, grain, fertilizers, motor vehicles

DEFENSE:
Defense expenditures: *exchange rate conversion -* $128.3 *million,* 0.8% *of GDP*

HAITI

GEOGRAPHY:
Location: Caribbean
Area:
  total area: 27,750 sq km
  land area: 27,560 sq km
Capital city: Port-au-Prince
Natural Resources: Bauxite

PEOPLE:
Population: 6,780,501
Age structure:
  0–14 years: 43%
  15–64 years: 53%
  65 years & over: 4%
Literacy rate: 45% *of total population,* (*males:* 48%, *females:* 42.2%)
Languages: French *(official)*, Creole
Religions: 80%-Roman Catholic *(of which an overwhelming majority also practice Voodoo)*, 16%-Protestant (*10%-Baptist, 4%- Pentecostal, 1%-Adventist, and 1%- other*), 1%-none, 3%-other

VITAL STATISTICS:
Birth rate: 33.12 *(per 1,000 population)* (1997)
Death rate: 15.25 *(per 1,000 population)*

Infant mortality rate: 103.8 *(deaths per 1,000 live births)*
Fertility rate: 4.76 *(per woman)*
Life expectancy at birth:
total population: 49.49
(males: 47.45, *females:* 51.63)

GOVERNMENT:
Type of government: Republic
Independence: January 1, 1804 *(from France)*
Leaders:
chief of state: President Rene Garcia Préval
head of government: Prime Minister (vacant)

ECONOMY:
GDP: purchasing power parity - $6.8 billion
GDP real growth rate: 2%
GDP per capita: $1,000
Inflation Rate *(consumer prices):* 18%
National budget:
revenues: $240 million
expenditures: $250 million
External debt: $827 million
Currency: 1 gourde = 100 centimes
Labor Force: 2.3 million
Unemployment rate: 60%
Agriculture: Coffee, mangoes, sugarcane, rice, corn, sorghum; wood
Industries: Sugar refining, flour milling, textiles, cement, tourism, light assembly industries based on imported parts
Exports: $123 million
commodities: Light manufactured goods, coffee, other agriculture
Imports: $666 million
commodities: Machines and manufactured goods, food and beverages, petroleum products, chemicals, fats and oils

DEFENSE:
Defense expenditures: $NA, NA% of GDP

HONDURAS

GEOGRAPHY:
Location: Central America
Area:
total area: 112,090 sq km
land area: 111,890 sq km
Capital city: Tegucigalpa
Natural Resources: Timber, gold, silver, copper, lead, zinc, iron ore, antimony, coal, fish

PEOPLE:
Population: 5,861,955
Age structure:
0–14 years: 42%
15–64 years: 54%
65 years & over: 4%
Literacy rate: 72.7%, *of total population,*
(males: 72.6%, *females:* 72.7%)

Languages: Spanish, Amerindian dialects
Religions: 97%-Roman Catholic, Protestant minority

VITAL STATISTICS:
Birth rate: 32.63 *(per 1,000 population)* (1997)
Death rate: 5.66 *(per 1,000 population)*
Infant mortality rate: 40.2 *(deaths per 1,000 live births)*
Fertility rate: 4.41 *(per woman)*
Life expectancy at birth:
total population: 68.81
(males: 66.38, *females:* 71.37)

GOVERNMENT:
Type of government: Republic
Independence: September 15, 1821 *(from Spain)*
Leaders:
chief of state & head of government: President Carlos Flores Facusse

ECONOMY:
GDP: purchasing power parity - $11.5 billion
GDP real growth rate: 3%
GDP per capita: $2,000
Inflation Rate *(consumer prices):* 25.4%
National budget:
revenues: $655 million
expenditures: $850 million
External debt: $4.6 billion
Currency: 1 lempira = 100 centavos
Labor Force: 1.3 million
Unemployment rate: 15% *(Underemployed about 40%)*
Agriculture: Bananas, coffee, citrus; beef; timber; shrimp
Industries: Sugar, coffee, textiles, clothing, wood products
Exports: $2.401 billion
commodities: Bananas, coffee, shrimp, lobster, minerals, meat, lumber
Imports: $3.133 billion
commodities: Machinery and transport equipment, chemical products, manufactured goods, fuel and oil, foodstuffs

DEFENSE:
Defense expenditures: *exchange rate conversion -* $42.5 *million,* 1.5% *of GDP*

HUNGARY

GEOGRAPHY:
Location: Central Europe
Area:
total area: 93,030 sq km
land area: 92,340 sq km
Capital city: Budapest
Natural Resources: Bauxite, coal, natural gas, fertile soils

PEOPLE:
Population: 10,208,127
Age structure:

0–14 years: 18%
15–64 years: 68%
65 years & over: 14%
Literacy rate: 99% *of total population,*
(*males:* 99%, *females:* 98%)
Languages: Hungarian, other
Religions: 67.5%-Roman Catholic, 20%-Calvinist, 5%-
Lutheran, 7.5%-atheist and other

VITAL STATISTICS:
Birth rate: 10.73 *(per 1,000 population)* (1997)
Death rate: 13.67 *(per 1,000 population)*
Infant mortality rate: 10 *(deaths per 1,000 live births)*
Fertility rate: 1.47 *(per woman)*
Life expectancy at birth:
total population: 70.48
(*males:* 66.06, *females:* 75.13)

GOVERNMENT:
Type of government: Republic
Independence: 1001 *(unification by King Stephen I)*
Leaders:
chief of state: President Arpad Goncz
head of government: Prime Minister Viktor Orban

ECONOMY:
GDP: purchasing power parity - $74.7 billion (1996)
GDP real growth rate: 0.5%
GDP per capita: $7,500
Inflation Rate*(consumer prices):* 20%
National budget:
revenues: $10.2 billion
expenditures: $11 billion
External debt: 27.5 billion
Currency: 1 forint = 100 filler
Labor Force: 6.2 million
Unemployment rate: 11%
Agriculture: Wheat, corn, sunflower seed, potatoes,
sugar beets; pigs, cattle, poultry, dairy products
Industries: Mining, metallurgy, construction materials,
processed foods, textiles, chemicals *(especially
pharmaceuticals)*, motor vehicles
Exports: $14.2 billion
commodities: Raw material and semi-finished
goods, consumer goods, food and agriculture,
capital goods, fuels and energy
Imports: $16.8 billion
commodities: Fuel and energy, raw materials and
semi-finished goods, capital goods, consumer
goods, food and agriculture

DEFENSE:
Defense expenditures: *exchange rate conversion -*
$550 *million*, 1.5% *of GDP*

I C E L A N D

GEOGRAPHY:
Location: Northern Europe
Area:
total area: 103,000 sq km
land area: 100,250 sq km
Capital city: Reykjavik

Natural Resources: Fish, hydropower, geothermal
power, diatomite

PEOPLE:
Population: 271,033
Age structure:
0–14 years: 24%
15–64 years: 64%
65 years & over: 12%
Literacy rate: 100% *of total population*
Languages: Icelandic
Religions: 96%- Evangelical Lutheran, 3%-other
Protestant and Roman Catholic, and 1%-none

VITAL STATISTICS:
Birth rate: 15.35 *(per 1,000 population)* (1997)
Death rate: 6.93 *(per 1,000 population)*
Infant mortality rate: 5.3 *(deaths per 1,000 live births)*
Fertility rate: 2.05 *(per woman)*
Life expectancy at birth:
total population: 78.73
(*males:* 76.68, *females:* 80.9)

GOVERNMENT:
Type of government: Republic
Independence: June 17, 1944 *(from Denmark)*
Leaders:
chief of state: President Olafur Ragnar Grimsson
head of government: Prime Minister David Oddsson

ECONOMY:
GDP: purchasing power parity - $5.3 billion (1996)
GDP real growth rate: 3.3%
GDP per capita: $19,800
Inflation Rate *(consumer prices):* 2.5%
National budget:
revenues: $1.9 billion
expenditures: $2.1 billion
External debt: $2.5 billion
Currency: 1 Icelandic krona = 100 aurar
Labor Force: 145,000 (1994)
Unemployment rate: 5% (1996)
Agriculture: Potatoes, turnips; cattle, sheep; fish
(catch of about 1.1 million metric tons in 1992)
Industries: Fish processing, aluminum smelting, fer-
rosilicon production, geothermal power
Exports: $1.67 billion
commodities: Fish and fish products, animal prod-
ucts, aluminum, ferrosilicon, diatomite
Imports: $1.62 billion
commodities: Machinery and transportation equipment, petroleum products, food stuffs, textiles

DEFENSE:
Defense expenditures: $NA, NA% of GDP

I N D I A

GEOGRAPHY:
Location: Southern Asia
Area:
total area: 3,287,590 sq km
land area: 2,973,190 sq km
Capital city: New Delhi

Natural Resources: Coal, iron ore, manganese, mica, bauxite, titanium ore, chromite, natural gas, diamonds, petroleum, limestone

PEOPLE:
Population: 984,003,683
Age structure:
0–14 years: 35%
15–64 years: 61%
65 years & over: 4%
Literacy rate: 52% *of total population,*
(*males:* 65.5%, *females:* 37.7%)
Languages: English enjoys associate status but is the most important language for national, political, and commercial communication, Hindi the national language and primary tongue of 30% of the people, Bengali*(official),* Telugu *(official),* Marathi *(official),* Tamil *(official),* Urdu *(official),* Gujarati *(official),* Malayalam *(official),* Kannada *(official),* Oriya *(official),* Punjabi *(official),* Assamese *(official),* Kashmiri *(official),* Sindhi *(official),* Sanskrit *(official),* Hindustani, a popular variant of Hindu/Urdu, is spoken widely throughout northern India; *(note-24 languages each spoken by a million or more persons; numerous other languages and dialects, for the most part mutually unintelligible)*
Religions: 80%-Hindu, 14%-Muslim, 2.4%-Christian, 2%-Sikh, 0.7%-Buddhist, 0.5%-Jains, 0.4%-other

VITAL STATISTICS:
Birth rate: 26.19 *(per 1,000 population)* (1997)
Death rate: 8.87 *(per 1,000 population)*
Infant mortality rate: 65.5 *(deaths per 1,000 live births)*
Fertility rate: 3.29 *(per woman)*
Life expectancy at birth:
total population: 52
(*males:* 65.5, *females:* 37.7)

GOVERNMENT:
Type of government: Federal Republic
Independence: August 15, 1947 *(from the UK)*
Leaders:
Chief of State: President K. R. Narayanan
Head of government: Prime Minister Atal Bihari Vajpayee
ECONOMY:
GDP: purchasing power parity - $1.538 trillion (1996)
GDP real growth rate: 6.5%
GDP per capita: $1,600
Inflation Rate *(consumer prices):* 10.3% (1995)
National budget:
revenues: $34 billion
expenditures: $52.3 billion
External debt: $97.9 billion
Currency: Indian rupee = 100 paise
Labor Force: 370 million (1995)
Unemployment rate: NA
Agriculture: Rice, wheat, oilseed, cotton, jute, tea, sug-

arcane, potatoes; cattle, water buffalo, sheep, goats, poultry; fish *(annual catch of about 3 million metric tons ranks India among the world's top 10 fishing nations)*
Industries: Textiles, chemicals, food processing, steel, transportation equipment, cement, mining, petroleum, machinery
Exports: $30.5 billion
commodities: Clothing, gems and jewelry, engineering goods, chemicals, leather manufactures, cotton yarn, fabric
Imports: $34.5 billion
commodities: Crude oil and petroleum products, machinery, gems, fertilizers, chemicals

DEFENSE:
Defense expenditures: *exchange rate conversion -* $8 billion, 2.7% *of GDP*

INDONESIA

GEOGRAPHY:
Location: Southeastern Asia
Area:
total area: 1,919,440 sq km
land area: 1,826,440 sq km
Capital city: Jakarta
Natural Resources: Petroleum, tin, natural gas, nickel, timber, bauxite, copper, fertile soils, coal, gold, silver

PEOPLE:
Population: 212,941,810
Age structure:
0–14 years: 31%
15–64 years: 65%
65 years & over: 4%
Literacy rate: 83.8% *of total population,*
(*males:* 89.6%, *females:* 78%)
Languages: Bahasa Indonesian, *(official, modified form of Malay),* English, Dutch, local dialects the most widely spoken of which is Javanese
Religions: 87%-Muslim, 6%-Protestant, 3%-Roman Catholic, 2%-Hindu, 1%-Buddhist, 1%-other

VITAL STATISTICS:
Birth rate: 23.39 *(per 1,000 population)* (1997)
Death rate: 8.3 *(per 1,000 population)*
Infant mortality rate: 61.2 *(deaths per 1,000 live births)*
Fertility rate: 2.66 *(per woman)*
Life expectancy at birth:
total population: 62.06
(*males:* 59.89, *females:* 64.34)

GOVERNMENT:
Type of government: Republic
Independence: August 17, 1945 *(proclaimed independence; on December 27, 1949, Indonesia became legally independent from the Netherlands)*
Leaders:
Chief of State and head of government: President

Bacharuddin Jusuf Habibie

ECONOMY:
GDP: purchasing power parity - $779.7 billion (1996)
  GDP real growth rate: 7%
  GDP per capita: $3,770
Inflation Rate(consumer prices): 7%
National budget:
  revenues: $41.5 billion
  expenditures: $41.5 billion
External debt: $110 billion
Currency: Inonesian rupiah
Labor Force: 67 million (1985)
Unemployment rate: 3% official rate; Underemployment 40% (1994)
Agriculture: Rice, cassava *(tapioca)*, peanuts, rubber, cocoa, coffee, palm oil, copra, other tropical products; poultry, beef, pork, eggs
Industries: Petroleum and natural gas, textiles, mining, cement, chemical fertilizers, plywood, food, rubber
Exports: $49.8 billion
  commodities: Manufactured goods, fuels, foodstuffs, raw materials
Imports: $42.9 billion
  commodities: Manufactured goods, raw materials, foodstuffs, fuels

DEFENSE:
Defense expenditures: *exchange rate conversion -* $3.3 billion, 1.3% *of GNP*

I R A N

GEOGRAPHY:
Location: Middle East
Area:
  total area: 1.648 million sq km
  land area: 1.636 million sq km
Capital city: Tehran
Natural Resources: Petroleum, natural gas, coal, chromium, copper, iron ore, lead, manganese, zinc, sulfur

PEOPLE:
Population: 68,959,931
Age structure:
  0–14 years: 44%
  15–64 years: 52%
  65 years & over: 4%
Literacy rate: 72.1% *of total population,*
  (*males:* 78.4%, *females:* 65.8%)
Languages: Persian and Persian dialects, Turkic and Turkic dialects, Kurdish, Arabic, Turkish
Religions: 89%-Shi'a Muslim, 10%-Sunni Muslim, 1%-Zoroastrian, Jewish, Christian and Baha'i

VITAL STATISTICS:
Birth rate: 32.51 *(per 1,000 population)* (1997)
Death rate: 6.39 *(per 1,000 population)*
Infant mortality rate: 50.8 *(deaths per 1,000 live births)*
Fertility rate: 4.52 *(per woman)*
Life expectancy at birth:

  total population: 67.82
    (*males:* 66.47, *females:* 69.23)

GOVERNMENT:
Type of government: Theocratic Republic
Independence: April 1, 1979 *(Islamic Republic of Iran proclaimed)*
Leaders:
  chief of state & head of government: President Mohammed Khatami

ECONOMY:
GDP: purchasing power parity - $343.5 billion (1996)
  GDP real growth rate: 3.6%
  GDP per capita: $5,200
Inflation Rate *(consumer prices):* 23%
National budget:
  revenues: $NA
  expenditures: $NA
External debt: $30 billion
Currency: 10 Iranian rials = 1 toman
Labor Force: 15.4 million (1997)
Unemployment rate: over 30% (1995)
Agriculture: Wheat, rice, other grains, sugar beets, fruits, nuts, cotton; dairy products, wool; caviar
Industries: Petroleum, petrochemicals, textiles, cement and other construction materials, food processing*(particularly sugar refining and vegetable oil production)*, metal fabrication, armaments
Exports: $21.3 billion
  commodities: Petroleum, carpets, fruits, nuts, hides, iron, steel
Imports: $13.3 billion
  commodities: Machinery, military supplies, metal works, foodstuffs, pharmaceuticals, technical services, refined oil products

DEFENSE:
Defense expenditures: *According to official Iranian data, Iran in 1994 budgeted 8,283.9 billion rials and in 1993 spent 2,182 billion rials, including $850 million in hard currency (note- conversion of defense expenditures into US dollars using current exchange rates could produce misleading results)*

I R A Q

GEOGRAPHY:
Location: Middle East
Area:
  total area: 437,072 sq km
  land area: 432,162 sq km
Capital city: Baghdad
Natural Resources: Petroleum, natural gas, phosphates, sulfur

PEOPLE:
Population: 21,722,287
Age structure:
  0–14 years: 47%
  15–64 years: 50%
  65 years & over: 3%
Literacy rate: 58% *of total population,*

(*males:* 70.7%, *females:* 45%)
Languages: Arabic, Kurdish *(official in Kurdish regions)*, Assyrian, Armenian
Religions: 97%-Muslim *(60–65% -Shi'a, 32–37%-Sunni)*, 3%-Christian or other

VITAL STATISTICS:
Birth rate: 42.52 *(per 1,000 population)* (1997)
Death rate: 6.33 *(per 1,000 population)*
Infant mortality rate: 57.5 *(deaths per 1,000 live births)*
Fertility rate: 6.26 *(per woman)*
Life expectancy at birth:
total population: 67.38
(*males:* 66.31, *females:* 68.5)

GOVERNMENT:
Type of government: Republic
Independence: October 3, 1932 *(from League of Nations mandate under British administration)*
Leaders:
chief of state & head of government: President Saddam Hussein

ECONOMY:
GDP: purchasing power parity - $42 billion (1996)
GDP real growth rate: 0%
GDP per capita: $2,000
Inflation Rate *(consumer prices):* NA%
National budget:
revenues: $NA
expenditures: $NA
External debt: very heavy relative to GDP but amount unknown (1996)
Currency: 1 Iraqi dinar = 1,000 fils
Labor Force: 4.4 million (1989)
Unemployment rate: NA%
Agriculture: Wheat, barley, rice, vegetables, dates, other fruit, cotton; cattle, sheep
Industries: Petroleum. chemicals, textiles, construction materials, food processing
Exports: $NA
commodities: Crude oil and refined products, fertilizer, sulfur
Imports: $NA
commodities: Manufactured goods, food

DEFENSE:
Defense expenditures: $NA, NA% of GDP

I R E L A N D

GEOGRAPHY:
Location: Western Europe
Area:
total area: 70,280 sq km
land area: 68,890 sq km
Capital city: Dublin
Natural Resources: Zinc, lead, natural gas, petroleum, barite, copper, gypsum, limestone, dolomite, peat, silver

PEOPLE:
Population: 3,619,480
Age structure:
0–14 years: 23%
15–64 years: 66%
65 years & over: 11%
Literacy rate: 98% *of total population*
Languages: Irish *(Gaelic)*, spoken mainly in areas located along the western seaboard, English is the language generally used
Religions: 93%-Roman Catholic, 3%-Anglican, 1%-none, 2%-unknown, 1%-other

VITAL STATISTICS:
Birth rate: 13.43 *(per 1,000 population)* (1997)
Death rate: 8.6 *(per 1,000 population)*
Infant mortality rate: 6.1 *(deaths per 1,000 live births)*
Fertility rate: 1.83 *(per woman)*
Life expectancy at birth:
total population: 75.98
(*males:* 73.24, *females:* 78.89)

GOVERNMENT:
Type of government: Republic
Independence: December 6, 1921 *(from UK)*
Leaders:
chief of state: President Mary McAleese
head of government: Prime Minister Bertie Ahern

ECONOMY:
GDP: purchasing power parity - $59.9 billion (1996)
GDP real growth rate: 7%
GDP per capita: $16,800
Inflation Rate: *(consumer prices)* 1.8% (1996)
National budget:
revenues: $22.6 billion
expenditures: $23.6 billion
External debt: $17.5 billion
Currency: 1 Irish pound = 100 pence
Labor Force: 1.474 million
Unemployment rate: 11.9%
Agriculture: Turnips, barley, potatoes, sugar beets, wheat; meat and dairy products
Industries: Food products, brewing, textiles, clothing, chemicals, pharmaceuticals, machinery, transportation equipment, glass and crystal
Exports: $43.4 billion
commodities: Chemicals, data processing equipment, industrial machinery, live animals, animal products
Imports: $32.7 billion
commodities: Food, animal feed, data processing equipment, pertroleum and petroleum products, machinery, textiles, clothing

DEFENSE:
Defense expenditures: *exchange rate conversion -* $618 *million,* 1.3% *of GDP*

ISRAEL

GEOGRAPHY:
Location: Middle East
Area:
total area: 20,770 sq km
land area: 20,330 sq km
Capital city: Jerusalem
Natural Resources: Copper, phosphates, bromide, potash, clay, sand, sulfur, asphalt, manganese, small amounts of natural gas and crude oil

PEOPLE:
Population: 5,643,966
Age structure:
0–14 years: 28%
15–64 years: 62%
65 years & over: 10%
Literacy rate: 95% *of total population,*
(*males:* 97%, *females:* 93%)
Languages: Hebrew *(official),* Arabic used officially for Arab minority, English most commonly used foreign language
Religions: 82%-Judaism, 14%-Islam *(mostly Sunni Muslim),* 2%-Christian, 2%-Druze and other

VITAL STATISTICS:
Birth rate: 20.16 *(per 1,000 population)* (1997)
Death rate: 6.22 *(per 1,000 population)*
Infant mortality rate: 8.3 *(deaths per 1,000 live births)*
Fertility rate: 2.74 *(per woman)*
Life expectancy at birth:
total population: 78.21
(*males:* 76.34, *females:* 80.18)

GOVERNMENT:
Type of government: Republic
Independence: May 14, 1948 *(from League of Nations mandate under British administration)*
Leaders:
chief of state: President Ezer Weizman
head of government: Prime Minister Benjamin Netanyahu

ECONOMY:
GDP: purchasing power parity - $85.7 billion (1996)
GDP real growth rate: 4.6%
GDP per capita: $16,400
Inflation Rate *(consumer prices):* 11.3% (1996)
National budget:
revenues: $41 billion
expenditures: $53 billion
External debt: $25.7 billion
Currency: 1 new Israeli shekel = 100 new agorot
Labor Force: 2.2 million (1996)
Unemployment rate: 6.5% (1996)
Agriculture: Citrus and other fruits, vegetables, cotton; beef, poultry, dairy products
Industries: Food processing, diamond cutting and polishing, textiles and apparel, chemicals, metal products, military equipment, transport equipment, electrical equipment, potash mining, high-technology, electronics, tourism

Exports: $20.3 billion
commodities: Machinery and equipment, cut diamonds, chemicals, textiles and apparel, agricultural products
Imports: $28.3 billion
commodities: Military equipment, investment goods, rough diamonds, oil, other productive inputs, consumer goods

DEFENSE:
Defense expenditures: *exchange rate conversion -* $9.2 *billion,* 9.8% *of GDP*

ITALY

GEOGRAPHY:
Location: Southern Europe
Area:
total area: 301,230 sq km
land area: 294,020 sq km
Capital city: Rome
Natural Resources: Mercury, potash, marble, sulfur, dwindling natural gas and crude oil reserves, fish, coal

PEOPLE:
Population: 56,782,748
Age structure:
0–14 years: 15%
15–64 years: 68%
65 years & over: 17%
Literacy rate: 97% *of total population,*
(*males:* 98%, *females:* 96%)
Languages: Italian, German *(parts of Trentino-Alto Adige region are predominantly German-speaking),* French *(small French-speaking minority in Valle d'Aosta region),* Slovene *(Slovene-speaking minority in the Trieste-Gorizia area)*
Religions: 98%-Roman Catholic, 2%-other

VITAL STATISTICS:
Birth rate: 8.96 *(per 1,000 population)* (1997)
Death rate: 10.07 *(per 1,000 population)*
Infant mortality rate: 6.5 *(deaths per 1,000 live births)*
Fertility rate: 1.16 *(per woman)*
Life expectancy at birth:
total population: 78.25
(*males:* 75.13, *females:* 81.58)

GOVERNMENT:
Type of government: Republic
Independence: March 17, 1861 *(Kingdom of Italy proclaimed)*
Leaders:
chief of state: President Oscar Luigi Scalfaro
head of government: Prime Minister *(referred to in Italy as the President of the Council of Ministers)* Romano Prodi *(announced resignation October 1997)*

ECONOMY:
GDP: purchasing power parity - $1.12 trillion (1996)
GDP real growth rate: 0.8%
GDP per capita: $19,600

Inflation Rate *(consumer prices):* 4%
National budget:
revenues: $416 billion
expenditures: $506 billion
External debt: $45 billion
Currency: 1 Italian lira = 100 centesimi
Labor Force: 22.851 million (1996)
Unemployment rate: 12% (1996)
Agriculture: Fruits, vegetables, grapes, potatoes, sugar beets, soybeans, grains, olives; meats and dairy products, fish *(annual catch of 525,000 metric tons)*
Industries: Tourism, machinery, iron and steel, food processing, textiles, motor vehicles, clothing, footwear, ceramics
Exports: $250 billion
commodities: Metals, textiles and clothing, production machinery, motor vehicles, transportation equipment, chemicals
Imports: $205 billion
commodities: Industrial machinery, chemicals, transport equipment, petroleum, metals, food, agricultural products

DEFENSE:
Defense expenditures: *exchange rate conversion -* $20.4 *billion,* 1.9% *of GDP*

JAMAICA

GEOGRAPHY:
Location: Caribbean
Area:
total area: 10,990 sq km
land area: 10,830 sq km
Capital city: Kingston
Natural Resources: Bauxite, gypsum, limestone

PEOPLE:
Population: 2,634,678
Age structure:
0–14 years: 32%
15–64 years: 61%
65 years & over: 7%
Literacy rate: 85% *of total population,* *(males:* 80.8%, *females:* 89.1%)
Languages: English, Creole
Religions: 55.9%-Protestant *(18.4%-Church of God, 10%-Baptist, 7.1%-Anglican, 6.9%-Seventh-Day Adventist, 5.2%-Pentecostal, 3.1%-Methodist, 2.7%-United Church, 2.5%-other),* 5%-Roman Catholic, 39.1%-other, including spiritual cults

VITAL STATISTICS:
Birth rate: 21.56 *(per 1,000 population)* (1997)
Death rate: 5.5 *(per 1,000 population)*
Infant mortality rate: 15 *(deaths per 1,000 live births)*
Fertility rate: 2.39 *(per woman)*
Life expectancy at birth:
total population: 75.12
(males: 72.8, *females:* 77.56)

GOVERNMENT:
Type of government: Parliamentary Democracy
Independence: August 6, 1962 *(from UK)*
Leaders:
chief of state: Queen Elizabeth II, represented by Sir Howard Cooke
head of government: Prime Minister Percival James Patterson

ECONOMY:
GDP: purchasing power parity - $8.4 billion (1996)
GDP real growth rate: 0.5%
GDP per capita: $3,260
Inflation Rate *(consumer prices):* 17% (1996)
National budget:
revenues: $1.45 billion
expenditures: $2 billion
External debt: $4.2 billion
Currency: 1 Jamaican dollar = 100 cents
Labor Force: 1,062,100 (1989)
Unemployment rate: 15.4% (1994)
Agriculture: Sugarcane, bananas, coffee, citrus, potatoes, vegetables; poultry, goats, milk
Industries: Bauxite, tourism, textiles, food processing, light manufactures
Exports: $1.4 billion
commodities: Alumina, bauxite, sugar, bananas, rum
Imports: $2.8 billion
commodities: Machinery and transport equipment, construction materials, fuel, food, chemicals

DEFENSE:
Defense expenditures: *exchange rate conversion -* $30 *million,* NA% *of GDP*

JAPAN

GEOGRAPHY:
Location: Eastern Asia
Area:
total area: 377,835 sq km
land area: 374,744 sq km
Capital city: Tokyo
Natural Resources: Negligible mineral resources, fish

PEOPLE:
Population: 125,931,533
Age structure:
0–14 years: 15%
15–64 years: 69%
65 years & over: 16%
Literacy rate: 99% *of total population*
Languages: Japanese
Religions: 84%-observe both Shinto and Buddhist, 16%-other *(including 0.7%-Christian)*

VITAL STATISTICS:
Birth rate: 10.01 *(per 1,000 population)* (1997)
Death rate: 7.39 *(per 1,000 population)*
Infant mortality rate: 4 *(deaths per 1,000 live births)*
Fertility rate: 1.44 *(per woman)*

Life expectancy at birth:
total population: 80.45
(*males:* 77.4, *females:* 83.65)

GOVERNMENT:
Type of government: Constitutional Monarchy
Independence: 660 BC *(traditional founding by Emperor Jimmu)*
Leaders:
chief of state: Emperor Akihito
head of government: Prime Minister Keizo Obuchi

ECONOMY:
GDP: purchasing power parity - $2.85 trillion (1996)
GDP real growth rate: 3.6%
GDP per capita: $22,700
Inflation Rate *(consumer prices):* 0.3% (1996)
National budget:
revenues: $528 billion
expenditures: $673 billion
External debt: $NA
Currency: Yen
Labor Force: 67.23 million (1997)
Unemployment rate: 3.4% (1996)
Agriculture: Rice, sugar beets, vegetables, fruit; pork, poultry, dairy products, eggs; fish *(annual catch of 10 million metric tons)*
Industries: Among world's largest and technologically advanced producers of steel and nonferrous metallurgy, heavy electrical equipment, construction and mining equipment, motor vehicles and parts, electronic and telecommunication equipment, machine tools, automated production systems, locomotives and railroad rolling stock, ships, chemicals; textiles, processed foods
Exports: $385 billion
commodities: Manufactured goods *(including machinery, motor vehicles, consumer electronics)*
Imports: $329 billion
commodities: Manufactured goods, fossil fuels, foodstuffs and raw materials

DEFENSE:
Defense expenditures: *exchange rate conversion -* $48.5 *billion,* 1% *of GDP*

JORDAN

GEOGRAPHY:
Location: Middle East
Area:
total area: 89,213 sq km
land area: 88,884 sq km
Capital city: Amman
Natural Resources: phosphates, potash, shale oil

PEOPLE:
Population: 4,434,978
Age structure:
0–14 years: 44%
15–64 years: 53%
65 years & over: 3%
Literacy rate: 86.6% *of total population,*

(*males:* 93.4%, *females:* 79.4%)
Languages: Arabic *(official),* English widely understood among upper and middle classes
Religions: 92%-Sunni Muslim, 8%-Christian

VITAL STATISTICS:
Birth rate: 35.95 *(per 1,000 population)* (1997)
Death rate: 3.88 *(per 1,000 population)*
Infant mortality rate: 30.7 *(deaths per 1,000 live births)*
Fertility rate: 4.94 *(per woman)*
Life expectancy at birth:
total population: 72.69
(*males:* 70.81, *females:* 74.68)

GOVERNMENT:
Type of government: Constitutional Monarchy
Independence: May 25, 1946 *(from League of Nations mandate under British administration)*
Leaders:
chief of state: King Hussein
head of government: Prime Minister Fayiz al-Tarawinah

ECONOMY:
GDP: purchasing power parity - $20.9 billion (1996)
GDP real growth rate: 5.9%
GDP per capita: $5,000
Inflation Rate *(consumer prices):* 4.5% (1996)
National budget:
revenues: $2.7 billion
expenditures: $2.8 billion
External debt: $7.3 billion
Currency: 1 Jordanian dinars = 1,000 fils
Labor Force: 600,000 (1992)
Unemployment rate: 16% (1994)
Industries: Phosphate mining, petroleum refining, cement, potash, light manufacturing
Agriculture: Wheat, barley, citrus, tomatoes, melons, olives; sheep, goats, poultry
Exports: $1.7 billion
commodities: Phosphates, fertilizers, potash, agricultural products, manufactured goods
Imports: $3.8 billion
commodities: Crude oil, machinery, transport equipment, food, live animals, manufactured goods

DEFENSE:
Defense expenditures: *exchange rate conversion -* $589 *million,* 8.2% *of GDP*

KAZAKSTAN

GEOGRAPHY:
Location: Central Asia
Area:
total area: 2,717,300 sq km
land area: 2,669,800 sq km
Capital city: Almaty
Natural Resources: Major deposits of petroleum, coal, iron ore, manganese, chrome ore, nickel, cobalt, copper, molybdenum, lead, zinc, bauxite, gold, uranium

PEOPLE:
Population: 16,846,808
Age structure:
0–14 years: 30%
15–64 years: 63%
65 years & over: 7%
Literacy rate: 98% *of total population,*
(*males:* 99%, *females:* 96%)
Languages: Kazak *(Qazaqz) (official language spoken by over 40% of the population),* Russian *(language of interethnic communication spoken by two-thirds of population and used in everyday business)*
Religions: 47%-Muslim, 44%-Russian Orthodox, 2%-Protestant, 7%-other

VITAL STATISTICS:
Birth rate: 17.36 *(per 1,000 population)* (1997)
Death rate: 9.97 *(per 1,000 population)*
Infant mortality rate: 57.7 *(deaths per 1,000 live births)*
Fertility rate: 2.14 *(per woman)*
Life expectancy at birth:
total population: 63.79
(*males:* 58.32, *females:* 69.53)

GOVERNMENT:
Type of government: Republic
Independence: December 16, 1991 *(from the Soviet Union)*
Leaders:
chief of state: President Nursultan A. Nazarbayev
head of government: Prime Minister Nurlan Balgimbayev

ECONOMY:
GDP: purchasing power parity - $48.6 billion (1996)
GDP real growth rate: 1.1%
GDP per capita: $2,880
Inflation Rate *(consumer prices):* 28.7% (1996)
National budget:
revenues: $NA
expenditures: $NA
External debt: $3.5 billion
Currency: Tenge
Labor Force: 6.9 million (1996)
Unemployment rate: 2.6% (1996); *(large number of underemployed workers)*
Agriculture: Grain, mostly spring wheat, cotton; wool, meat
Industries: Oil, coal, iron ore, manganese, chromite, lead, zinc, copper, titanium, bauxite, gold, silver, phosphates, sulfur, iron and steel, nonferrous metal, tractors and other agricultural machinery, electric motors, construction materials; much of industrial capacity is shut down and/or is in need of repair
Exports: $5.7 billion
commodities: Oil, ferrous and nonferrous metals, chemicals, grain, wool, meat, coal
Imports: $6 billion
commodities: Machinery and parts, industrial materials, oil and gas

DEFENSE:
Defense expenditures: $18.9 billion tenges, NA% of GDP *(note - conversion of defense expenditures into US dollars using the current exchange rate could produce misleading results)*

KENYA

GEOGRAPHY:
Location: Eastern Africa
Area:
total area: 582,650 sq km
land area: 569,250 sq km
Capital city: Nairobi
Natural Resources: Gold, limestone, soda ash, salt barytes, rubies, fluorspar, garnets, wildlife

PEOPLE:
Population: 28,337,071
Age structure:
0–14 years: 44%
15–64 years: 53%
65 years & over: 3%
Literacy rate: 78.1% *of total population*
(*males:* 86.3% *females:* 70%)
Languages: English *(official)*, Swahili *(official)*, numerous indigenous languages
Religions: 38%-Protestant *(including Anglican)*, 28%-Roman Catholic, 26%-indigenous beliefs, 8%-other

VITAL STATISTICS:
Birth rate: 32.44 *(per 1,000 population)* (1997)
Death rate: 10.83 *(per 1,000 population)*
Infant mortality rate: 55.2 *(deaths per 1,000 live births)*
Fertility rate: 4.26 *(per woman)*
Life expectancy at birth:
total population: 54.39
(*males:* 54.21, *females:* 54.59)

GOVERNMENT:
Type of government: Republic
Independence: December 12, 1963 *(from UK)*
Leaders:
chief of state & head of government: President Daniel Toroitich arap Moi

ECONOMY:
GDP: purchasing power parity - $39.2 billion (1996)
GDP real growth rate: 4%
GDP per capita: $1,400
Inflation Rate *(consumer prices):* 1.6% (1995)
National budget:
revenues: $2.7 billion
expenditures: $2.7 billion
External debt: $7 billion
Currency: 1 Kenyan shilling = 100 cents
Labor Force: 8.78 million (1993)
Unemployment rate: 35% urban (1994)
Agriculture: Coffee, tea, corn, wheat, sugarcane, fruit, vegetables; dairy products, beef, pork, poultry, eggs
Industries: Small-scale consumer goods *(plastic, fur-*

niture, batteries, textiles, soap, cigarettes, flour), agricultural processing; oil refining, cement; tourism

Exports: $1.9 billion

commodities: Tea, coffee, petroleum products

Imports: $2.6 billion

commodities: Machinery and transportation equipment, petroleum and petroleum products, iron and steel, raw materials, food and consumer goods

DEFENSE:

Defense expenditures: *exchange rate conversion -* $134 *million, 3.9% of GDP*

NORTH KOREA

GEOGRAPHY:

Location: Eastern Asia

Area:

total area: 120,540 sq km

land area: 120,410 sq km

Capital city: Pyongyang

Natural Resources: Coal, lead, tungsten, zinc, graphite, magnesite, iron ore, copper, gold, pyrites, salt, fluorspar, hydropower

PEOPLE:

Population: 21,234,387

Age structure:

0–14 years: 30%

15–64 years: 66%

65 years & over: 4%

Literacy rate: 99% *of total population,* (*males:* 99%, *females:* 99%)

Languages: Korean

Religions: Buddism and Confucianism, some Christianity and syncretic Chondogyo *(note: Autonomous religious activities now almost nonexistant; government-sponsored religious groups exist to provide illusion of religious freedom)*

VITAL STATISTICS:

Birth rate: 22.27 *(per 1,000 population)* (1997)

Death rate: 5.43 *(per 1,000 population)*

Infant mortality rate: 25 *(deaths per 1,000 live births)*

Fertility rate: 2.29 *(per woman)*

Life expectancy at birth:

total population: 70.6

(*males:* 67.5, *females:* 73.85)

GOVERNMENT:

Type of government: Communist State; Stalinist dictatorship

Independence: September 9, 1948

Leader:

chief of state: Kim Jong Il

ECONOMY:

GDP: purchasing power parity - $20.9 billion (1996)

GDP real growth rate: -5%

GDP per capita: $900

Inflation Rate *(consumer prices):* NA%

National budget:

revenues: $19.3 billion

expenditures: $19.3 billion

External debt: $8 billion

Currency: 1 North Korean won = 100 chon

Labor Force: 9.615 million

Unemployment rate: NA%

Agriculture: Rice, corn, potatoes, soybeans, pulses; cattle, pigs, pork, eggs

Industries: Military products; machine building, electric power, chemicals; mining *(coal, iron ore, magnesite, graphite, copper, zinc, lead, and precious metals),* metallurgy; textiles, food processing

Exports: $805 million

commodities: Minerals, metallurgical products, agricultural and fishery products, manufactured goods *(including armaments)*

Imports: $1.24 billion

commodities: Petroleum, grain, coking coal, machinery and equipment, consumer goods

DEFENSE:

Defense expenditures: *exchange rate conversion -* $5 *billion-$7 billion, 25% of GDP*

SOUTH KOREA

GEOGRAPHY:

Location: Eastern Asia

Area:

total area: 98,480 sq km

land area: 98,190 sq km

Capital city: Seoul

Natural Resources: Coal, tungsten, graphite, molybdenum, lead, hydropower

PEOPLE:

Population: 46,416,796

Age structure:

0–14 years: 23%

15–64 years: 71%

65 years & over: 6%

Literacy rate: 98% *of total population,* (*male:* 99.3%, *female:* 96.7%)

Languages: Korean, English widely taught in high school

Religions: 48.6%-Christianity, 47.4%-Buddhism, 3%-Confucianism, pervasive folk religion *(shamanism),* 0.2%-Chondogyo *(religion of the Heavenly Way)*

VITAL STATISTICS:

Birth rate: 16.17 *(per 1,000 population)* (1997)

Death rate: 5.66 *(per 1,000 population)*

Infant mortality rate: 8 *(deaths per 1,000 live births)*

Fertility rate: 1.78 *(per woman)*

Life expectancy at birth:

total population: 73.6

(*males:* 70.01, *females:* 77.69)

GOVERNMENT:

Type of government: Republic

Independence: August 15, 1948

Leaders:

chief of state: President Kim Dae-jung

head of government: Prime Minister Kim Jong-pil

ECONOMY:
GDP: purchasing power parity - $647.2 billion (1996)
GDP real growth rate: 6.9%
GDP per capita: $14,200
Inflation Rate *(consumer prices):* 5% (1996)
National budget:
revenues: $69 billion
expenditures: $67 billion
External debt: $93 billion
Currency: 1 South Korean won = 100 chun (theoretical)
Labor Force: 20 million (1991)
Unemployment rate: 1.9% (1996)
Agriculture: Rice, root crops, barley, vegetables, fruit; cattle, pigs, chickens, milk, eggs; fish *(annual catch of 2.9 million metric tons, seventh largest in the world)*
Industries: Electronics, automobile production, chemicals, shipbuilding, steel, textiles, clothing, footwear, food processing
Exports: $130.9 billion
commodities: Electronics and electrical equipment, machinery, steel, automobiles, ships; textiles, clothing, footwear; fish
Imports: $150.2 billion
commodities: Machinery, electronics and electrical equipment, oil, steel, transport equipment, textiles, organic chemicals, grains

DEFENSE:
Defense expenditures: *exchange rate conversion -* $17.4 *billion,* 3.3% *of GDP*

K U W A I T

GEOGRAPHY:
Location: Middle East
Area:
total area: 17,820 sq km
land area: 17,820 sq km
Capital city: Kuwait
Natural Resources: Petroleum, fish, shrimp, natural gas

PEOPLE:
Population: 1,913,285
Age structure:
0–14 years: 33%
15–64 years: 65%
65 years & over: 2%
Literacy rate: 78.6% *of total population,* (*males:* 82.2%, *females:* 74.9%)
Languages: Arabic *(official),* English widely spoken
Religions: 85%-Muslim (30%-*Shi'a,* 45%-*Sunni,* 10%-*other*), 15%-Christian, Hindu, Parsi, other

VITAL STATISTICS:
Birth rate: 21.54 *(per 1,000 population)* (1997)
Death rate: 21.54 *(per 1,000 population)*
Infant mortality rate: 11.2 *(deaths per 1,000 live births)*

Fertility rate: 3.54 *(per woman)*
Life expectancy at birth:
total population: 76.44
(*males:* 74.43, *females:* 78.56)

GOVERNMENT:
Type of government: Nominal Constitutional Monarchy
Independence: June 19, 1961 *(from UK)*
Leaders:
chief of state: Amir Sheikh Jabar
head of government: Acting Prime Minister and Crown Prince Sheikh Al-Abdullah Al-Sabah

ECONOMY:
GDP: purchasing power parity - $32.5 billion (1996)
GDP real growth rate: 3%
GDP per capita: $16,700
Inflation Rate *(consumer prices):* 4.5% (1996)
National budget:
revenues: $10 billion
expenditures: $14 billion
External debt: $8 billion
Currency: 1 Kuwaiti dinar = 1,000 fils
Labor Force: 1 million (1994)
Unemployment rate: 18% (1996)
Agriculture: Practically no crops; extensive fishing in territorial waters
Industries: Petroleum, petrochemicals, desalination, food processing, construction materials, salt, construction
Exports: $13.6 billion
commodities: Oil
Imports: $8.4 billion
commodities: Food, construction materials, vehicles and parts, clothing

DEFENSE:
Defense expenditures: *exchange rate conversion -* $3.5 *billion,* 12.8% *of GDP*

K Y R G Y Z S T A N

GEOGRAPHY:
Location: Central Asia
Area:
total area: 198,500 sq km
land area: 191,300 sq km
Capital city: Bishkek
Natural Resources: Abundant hydroelectric potential; significant deposits of gold and rare earth metals; ocally exploitable coal, oil, and natural gas; other deposits of nepheline, mercury, bismuth, lead, zinc

PEOPLE:
Population: 4,522,281
Age structure:
0–14 years: 36%
15–64 years: 58%
65 years & over: 6%
Literacy rate: 97%, *of total population,* (*males:* 99%, *females:* 96%)

Languages: Kirghiz *(Kyrgyz) (official)*, Russian *(official) (note—In March 1996, the Kyrgyz legislature amended the constitution to make Russian an official language, along with Kyrgyz, in territories and work places where Russian-speaking citizens predominate)*
Religions: Muslim, Russian Orthodox

VITAL STATISTICS:
Birth rate: 22.27 *(per 1,000 population)* (1997)
Death rate: 8.59 *(per 1,000 population)*
Infant mortality rate: 73.6 *(deaths per 1,000 live births)*
Fertility rate: 2.73 *(per woman)*
Life expectancy at birth:
total population: 63.97
(males: 59.65, *females:* 68.49)

GOVERNMENT:
Type of government: Republic
Independence: August 31, 1991 *(from Soviet Union)*
Leaders:
chief of state: President Askar Akayev
head of government: Prime Minister Kubanychbeck Jumaliyev

ECONOMY:
GDP: purchasing power parity - $5.8 billion (1996)
GDP real growth rate: 5.6%
GDP per capita: $1,290
Inflation Rate *(consumer prices):* 32% (1996)
National budget:
revenues: $NA
expenditures: $NA
External debt: $584 million
Currency: introduced national currency, the som *(May 10, 1993)*
Labor Force: 1.7 million (1995)
Unemployment rate: 4.8% *(large number of underemployed)* (1996)
Agriculture: Wool, tobacco, cotton, potatoes, vegetables, grapes, fruits and berries; sheep, goats, cattle
Industries: Small machinery, textiles, food processing, cement, shoes, sawn logs, refrigerators, furniture, electric motors, gold, rare earth metals
Exports: $506 million
commodities: Cotton, wool, meat, tobacco; gold, mercury, uranium, hydropower; machinery; shoes
Imports: $890 million
commodities: Grain, lumber, industrial products, ferrous metals, fuel, machinery, textiles, footwear
DEFENSE:
Defense expenditures: 151 million soms, NA% of GDP *(note - Conversion of defense expenditures into US dollars using the current exchange rate could produce misleading results)*

LAOS

GEOGRAPHY:
Location: Southeastern Asia

Area:
total area: 236,800 sq km
land area: 230,800 sq km
Capital city: Vientiane
Natural Resources: Timber, hydropower, gypsum, tin, gold, gemstones

PEOPLE:
Population: 5,260,842
Age structure:
0–14 years: 45%
15–64 years: 52%
65 years & over: 3%
Literacy rate: 56.6% *of total population,*
(males: 69.4%, *females:* 44.4%)
Languages: Lao *(official)*, French, English, and various ethnic languages
Religions: 60%-Buddhist, 40%-animist and other

VITAL STATISTICS:
Birth rate: 41.25 *(per 1,000 population)* (1997)
Death rate: 13.4 *(per 1,000 population)*
Infant mortality rate: 94.3 *(deaths per 1,000 live births)*
Fertility rate: 5.67 *(per woman)*
Life expectancy at birth:
total population: 53.19
(males: 51.63, *females:* 54.83)

GOVERNMENT:
Type of government: Communist State
Independence: July 19, 1949 *(from France)*
Leaders:
chief of state: President Khamtay Siphandone
head of government: Prime Minister General Sisavat Keobounphan

ECONOMY:
GDP: purchasing power parity - $5.7 billion (1996)
GDP real growth rate: 7.5%
GDP per capita: $1,150
Inflation Rate *(consumer prices):* 15% (1996)
National budget:
revenues: $218 million
expenditures: $379 million
External debt: $2 billion
Currency: 1 new kip = 100 at
Labor Force: 1–1.5 million (1992)
Unemployment rate: 5.6% (1994)
Agriculture: Sweet potatoes, vegetables, corn, coffee, sugarcane, cotton; water buffalo, pigs, cattle, poultry
Industries: Tin and gypsum mining, timber, electric power, agricultural processing, construction
Exports: $240 million
commodities: electricity, wood products, coffee, tin, garments
Imports: $570 million
commodities: Food, fuel oil, consumer goods, manufactured goods

DEFENSE:
Defense expenditures: *exchange rate conversion -*
$105 *million*, 8.1% *of GDP*

LATVIA

GEOGRAPHY:
Location: Eastern Europe
Area:
total area: 64,100 sq km
land area: 64,100 sq km
Capital city: Riga
Natural Resources: Minimal; amber, peat, limestone,
dolomite

PEOPLE:
Population: 2,385,396
Age structure:
0-14 years: 19%
15-64 years: 66%
65 years & over: 15%
Literacy rate: 100% *of total population,*
(*males:* 100%, *females:* 99%)
Languages: Lettish*(official)*, Lithuanian, Russian, other
Religions: Lutheran, Roman Catholic, Russian Orthodox

VITAL STATISTICS:
Birth rate: 8.21 *(per 1,000 population)* (1997)
Death rate: 15.72 *(per 1,000 population)*
Infant mortality rate: 17.7 *(deaths per 1,000 live*
births)
Fertility rate: 1.21 *(per woman)*
Life expectancy at birth:
total population: 66.91
(*males:* 60.8, *females:* 73.33)

GOVERNMENT:
Type of government: Republic
Independence: September 6, 1991 *(from Soviet*
Union)
Leaders:
chief of state: President Guntis Ulmanis
head of government: Prime Minister Guntars Krasts

ECONOMY:
GDP: purchasing power parity - $9.4 billion (1996)
GDP real growth rate: -2.5%
GDP per capita: $3,800
Inflation Rate *(consumer prices):* 13.2% (1996)
National budget:
revenues: $NA
expenditures: $NA
External debt: $NA
Currency: 1 lat = 100 cents *(introduced March*
1993)
Labor Force: 1.268 million (1995)
Unemployment rate: 7.5% (1996)
Agriculture: Grain, sugar beets, potatoes, vegetables;
meat, milk, eggs; fish
Industries: Buses, vans, street and railroad cars, syn-
thetic fibers, agricultural machinery, fertilizers,

washing machines, radios, electronics, pharmaceuticals, processed foods, textiles; dependent on imports for energy, raw materials, and intermediate
products
Exports: $1.6 billion
commodities: Timber, textiles, dairy products
Imports: $2.4 billion
commodities: Fuels, cars, chemicals

DEFENSE:
Defense expenditures: 176 million rubles, 3% to 5%
of the GDP *(note-Conversion of defense expendi-*
tures into US dollars using prevailing exchange rate
could produce misleading results)

LEBANON

GEOGRAPHY:
Location: Middle East
Area:
total area: 10,400 sq km
land area: 10,230 sq km
Capital city: Beirut
Natural Resources: Limestone, iron ore, salt, water-
surplus state in a water-deficit region

PEOPLE:
Population: 3,505,794
Age structure:
0–14 years: 30%
15–64 years: 64%
65 years & over: 6%
Literacy rate: 92.4% *of total population,*
(*males:* 94.7%, *females:* 90.3%)
Languages: Arabic *(official)*, French *(official)*, Armenian, English
Religions: 70%-Islam *(5 legally recognized Islamic*
groups-Alawite or Nusayri, Druze, Isma'ilite, Shi'a,
Sunni), 30%-Christian *(11 legally recognized Christ-*
ian groups-4 Orthodox Christian, 6 Catholic, 1
Protestant), Judaism

VITAL STATISTICS:
Birth rate: 22.74 *(per 1,000 population)* (1997)
Death rate: 6.56 *(per 1,000 population)*
Infant mortality rate: 32.8 *(deaths per 1,000 live*
births)
Fertility rate: 2.32 *(per woman)*
Life expectancy at birth:
total population: 70.35
(*males:* 67.82, *females:* 73)

GOVERNMENT:
Type of government: Republic
Independence: November 22, 1943 *(from the League*
of Nations mandate under French administration)
Leaders:
chief of state: President Elias Hrawi
head of government: Prime Minister Rafiq
Hariri

ECONOMY:
GDP: purchasing power parity - $13 billion (1996)

GDP real growth rate: 3.5%
GDP per capita: $3,400
Inflation Rate *(consumer prices):* 10% (1996)
National budget:
  revenues: $1.9 billion
  expenditures: $3.9 billion
External debt: $3 billion
Currency: 1 Lebanese pound = 100 piasters
Labor Force: 1 million *(plus as many as 1 million foreign workers)*
Unemployment rate: 20% (1996)
Agriculture: Citrus, vegetable, potatoes, olives, tobacco, hemp *(hashish);* sheep, goats
Industries: Banking, food processing, textiles, cement, oil refining, chemicals, jewelry, some metal fabricating
Exports: $1 billion
  commodities: Agricultural products, chemicals, textiles, precious and semiprecious metals and jewelry, metals and metal products
Imports: $7 billion
  commodities: Consumer goods, machinery and transport equipment, petroleum products

DEFENSE:
Defense expenditures: *exchange rate conversion -* $278 *million,* 5.5% *of GDP*

LIBERIA

GEOGRAPHY:
Location: Western Africa
Area:
  total area: 111,370 sq km
  land area: 96,320 sq km
Capital city: Monrovia
Natural Resources: Iron ore, timber, diamonds, gold

PEOPLE:
Population: 2,771,901
Age structure:
  0–14 years: 45%
  15–64 years: 52%
  65 years & over: 3%
Literacy rate: 38.3% *of total population,*
  (males: 53.9%, *females:* 22.4%)
Languages: English *(official),* Niger-Congo language group, about 20 local languages come from this group
Religions: 70%- traditional, 20%-Muslim, 10%- Christian

VITAL STATISTICS:
Birth rate: 42.3 *(per 1,000 population)* (1997)
Death rate: 11.53 *(per 1,000 population)*
Infant mortality rate: 105.6 *(deaths per 1,000 live births)*
Fertility rate: 6.16 *(per woman)*
Life expectancy at birth:
  total population: 59.02
  (males: 56.43, *females:* 61.69)

GOVERNMENT:
Type of government: Republic
Independence: July 26, 1847
Leaders:
  chief of state & head of government: President Charles G. Taylor

ECONOMY:
GDP: purchasing power parity - $2.4 billion (1995)
  GDP real growth rate: 0%
  GDP per capita: $1,100
Inflation Rate *(consumer prices):* 50% (1994)
National budget:
  revenues: $225 million
  expenditures: $285 million
External debt: $1.9 billion
Currency: 1 Liberian dollar = 100 cents
Labor Force: 510,000 *(including 220,000 in the monetary economy)*
Unemployment rate: NA%
Agriculture: Rubber, coffee, cocoa, rice, cassava*(tapioca),* palm oil, sugarcane, bananas; sheep, goats; timber
Industries: Rubber processing, food processing, construction materials, furniture, palm oil processing, iron ore, diamonds
Exports: $667 million
  commodities: Iron ore, rubber, timber, coffee
Imports: $5.8 billion
  commodities: Mineral fuels, chemicals, machinery, transporation equipment, manufactured goods; rice and other foodstuffs

DEFENSE:
Defense expenditures: *exchange rate conversion -* $14 *million,* 2.9% *of GDP*

LIBYA

GEOGRAPHY:
Location: Northern Africa
Area:
  total area: 1,759,540 sq km
  land area: 1,759,540 sq km
Capital city: Tripoli
Natural Resources: Petroleum, natural gas, gypsum

PEOPLE:
Population: 5,690,727
Age structure:
  0–14 years: 48%
  15–64 years: 49%
  65 years & over: 3%
Literacy rate: 76.2% *of total population,*
  (males: 87.9%, *females:* 63%)
Languages: Arabic, Italian, English, all are widely understood in the major cities
Religions: 97%-Sunni Muslim

VITAL STATISTICS:
Birth rate: 43.94 *(per 1,000 population)* (1997)

Death rate: 7.49 *(per 1,000 population)*
Infant mortality rate: 57.7 *(deaths per 1,000 live births)*
Fertility rate: 6.19 *(per woman)*
Life expectancy at birth:
  total population: 65.05
    (*males:* 62.84, *females:* 67.37)

GOVERNMENT:

Type of government: Jamahiriya *(a state of the masses)* in theory, governed by the populace through local councils; in fact, a military dictatorship
Independence: December 24, 1951 *(from Italy)*
Leaders:
  chief of state: Revolutionary Leader Col. Muammar Gadhafi
  head of government: Secretary of the General People's Committee *(Premier)* Ahmad Muhammad al-Manqush

ECONOMY:

GDP: purchasing power parity - $34.5 billion (1995)
  GDP real growth rate: 2.2%
  GDP per capita: $6,570
Inflation Rate *(consumer prices):* 25% (1996)
National budget:
  revenues: $13 billion
  expenditures: $14.9 billion
External debt: $2.6 billion
Currency: 1 Libyan dinar = 100 dirhams
Labor Force: 1 million (1997)
Unemployment rate: NA
Agriculture: Wheat, barley, olives, dates, citrus, vegetables, peanuts; meat, eggs
Industries: Petroleum, food processing, textiles, handicrafts, cement
Exports: $8.4 billion
  commodities: Crude oil, refined petroleum products, natural gas
Imports: $7.3 billion
  commodities: Machinery, transport equipment, food, manufactured goods

DEFENSE:

Defense expenditures: *exchange rate conversion -* $1.4 billion, 6.1% of GDP

LIECHTENSTEIN

GEOGRAPHY:

Location: Central Europe
Area:
  total area: 160 sq km
  land area: 160 sq km
Capital city: Vaduz
Natural Resources: Hydroelectric potential

PEOPLE:

Population: 31,717
Age structure:
  0–14 years: 19%
  15–64 years: 70%
  65 years & over: 11%
Literacy rate: 100% *of total population*

Languages: German*(official)*, Alemannic dialect
Religions: 80%- Roman Catholic, 6.9%- Protestant, 5.6%-unknown, 7.5%-other

VITAL STATISTICS:

Birth rate: 13.03 *(per 1,000 population)* (1997)
Death rate: 7.33 *(per 1,000 population)*
Infant mortality rate: 5.3 *(deaths per 1,000 live births)*
Fertility rate: 1.62 *(per woman)*
Life expectancy at birth:
  total population: 77.82
    (*males:* 75.38, *females:* 80.36)

GOVERNMENT:

Type of government: Hereditary Constitutional Monarchy
Independence: January 23, 1719 *(Imperial Principality of Liechtenstein established)*
Leaders:
  chief of state: Prince Hans Adam II
  head of government: Mario Frick

ECONOMY:

GDP: purchasing power parity - $713 million (1996)
  GDP real growth rate: NA%
  GDP per capita: $23,000
Inflation Rate *(consumer prices):* 0.8% (1996)
National budget:
  revenues: $455 million
  expenditures: $435 million
External debt: $NA
Currency: 1 Swiss franc, franken, or franco = 100 centimes, rappen, or centesimi
Labor Force: 22,187 (1995)
Unemployment rate: 1.1% (1996)
Agriculture: Vegetables, corn, wheat, potatoes, grapes, livestock
Industries: Electronics, metal manufacturing, textiles, ceramics, pharmaceuticals, food products, precision instruments
Exports: $2.14 billion
  commodities: Small specialty machinery, dental products, stamps, hardware, pottery
Imports: $852.3 million
  commodities: Machinery, metal goods, textiles, foodstuffs, motor vehicles

DEFENSE:

Defense expenditures: *defense is the responsibility of Switzerland*

LITHUANIA

GEOGRAPHY:

Location: Eastern Europe
Area:
  total area: 65,200 sq km
  land area: 65,200 sq km
Capital city: Vilnius
Natural Resources: Peat

PEOPLE:

Population: 3,600,158

Age structure:
0–14 years: 21%
15–64 years: 66%
65 years & over: 13%
Literacy rate: 98% *of total population,*
(*males:* 99%, *females:* 98%)
Languages: Lithuanian *(official)*, Polish, Russian
Religions: Roman Catholic, Lutheran, other

VITAL STATISTICS:
Birth rate: 10.64 *(per 1,000 population)* (1997)
Death rate: 12.96 *(per 1,000 population)*
Infant mortality rate: 14.8 *(deaths per 1,000 live
births)*
Fertility rate: 1.47 *(per woman)*
Life expectancy at birth:
total population: 68.7
(*males:* 62.61, *females:* 75.11)

GOVERNMENT:
Type of government: Republic
Independence: March 11, 1990 *(from Soviet Union)*
Leaders:
chief of state: President Valdas Adamkus
head of government: Prime Minister Gediminas
Vagnorius

ECONOMY:
GDP: purchasing power parity - $14.1 billion (1996)
GDP real growth rate: 3.4%
GDP per capita: $3,870
Inflation Rate *(consumer prices)*: 13.1% (1996)
National budget:
revenues: $1.4 billion
expenditures: $1.5 billion
External debt: $895 million
Currency: 1 Lithuanian litas = 100 centas
Labor Force: 1.836 million (1990)
Unemployment rate: 8% (1997)
Agriculture: Grain, potatoes, sugar beets, vegetables;
meat, milk, eggs; fish
Industries: Metal-cutting machine tools, electric mo-
tors, television sets, refrigerators and freezers, pe-
troleum refining, shipbuilding *(small ships)*,
furniture making, textiles, food processing, fertilizers, agricultural machinery, optical equipment, electronic components, computers, amber
Exports: $3.3 billion
commodities: Electronics, food, chemicals, petroleum products
Imports: $4.56 billion
commodities: Oil, machinery, chemicals, grain
DEFENSE:
Defense expenditures: *exchange rate conversion -*
$31.7 *million*, 1% *of GDP*

LUXEMBOURG

GEOGRAPHY:
Location: Western Europe
Area:
total area: 2,586 sq km
land area: 2,586 sq km
Capital city: Luxembourg
Natural Resources: Iron ore *(no longer exploited)*

PEOPLE:
Population: 425,017
Age structure:
0–14 years: 18%
15–64 years: 67%
65 years & over: 15%
Literacy rate: 100% *of total population*
Languages: Luxembourgisch, German, French, English
Religions: 97%-Roman Catholic, 3%-Protestant and
Jewish

VITAL STATISTICS:
Birth rate: 11.92 *(per 1,000 population)* (1997)
Death rate: 9.29 *(per 1,000 population)*
Infant mortality rate: 5.1 *(deaths per 1,000 live births)*
Fertility rate: 1.7 *(per woman)*
Life expectancy at birth:
total population: 77.33
(*males:* 74.24, *females:* 80.52)

GOVERNMENT:
Type of government: Constitutional Monarchy
Independence: 1839
Leaders:
chief of state: Grand Duke Jean
head of government: Prime Minister Jean-Claude
Juncker

ECONOMY:
GDP: purchasing power parity - $10 billion (1995)
GDP real growth rate: 3.7%
GDP per capita: $24,500
Inflation Rate *(consumer prices)*: 2.3% (1995)
National budget:
revenues: $5.46 billion
expenditures: $5.44 billion
External debt: $NA
Currency: 1 Luxembourg franc = 100 centimes
Labor Force: 213,100 (1995)
Unemployment rate: 3% (1995)
Agriculture: Barley, oats, potatoes, wheat, fruits, wine
grapes; livestock products
Industries: Banking, iron and steel, food processing,
chemicals, metal products, engineering, tires, glass,
aluminum
Exports: $7.3 million
commodities: Finished steel products, chemicals,
rubber products, glass, aluminum, other indus-

trial products
Imports: $9.1 million
commodities: Minerals, metals, foodstuffs, quality consumer goods

DEFENSE:
Defense expenditures: *exchange rate conversion -* $142 *million,* 0.8% *of GDP*

MALAYSIA

GEOGRAPHY:
Location: Southeastern Asia
Area:
total area: 329,750 sq km
land area: 328,550 sq km
Capital city: Kuala Lumpur
Natural Resources: Tin, petroleum, timber, copper, iron ore, natural gas, bauxite

PEOPLE:
Population: 20,932,901
Age structure:
0–14 years: 36%
15–64 years: 60%
65 years & over: 4%
Literacy rate: 83.5% *of total population,* (*males:* 89.1%, *females:* 78.1%)
Languages: *Peninsular Malaysia:* Maylay *(official),* English, Chinese dialects, Tamil
Sabah: English, Malay, numerous tribal dialects, Chinese *(Mandarin and Hakka dialects predominate)*
Sarawak: English, Malay, Mandarin, numerous tribal languages
Religions:
Peninsular Malaysia: Muslim (*Malays*), Buddhist (*Chinese*), Hindu *(Indians)*
Sabah: 38%-Muslim, 17%-Christian, 45%-other
Sarawak: 35%-Tribal Religion, 24%-Buddhist and Confucianist, 20%-Muslim, 16%-Christian, 5%-other

VITAL STATISTICS:
Birth rate: 26.94 *(per 1,000 population)* (1997)
Death rate: 5.43 *(per 1,000 population)*
Infant mortality rate: 23.2 *(deaths per 1,000 live births)*
Fertility rate: 3.4 *(per woman)*
Life expectancy at birth:
total population: 70.06
(*males:* 67.08, *females:* 73.22)

GOVERNMENT:
Type of government: Constitutional Monarchy
Independence: August 31, 1957 *(from UK)*
Leaders:
chief of state: Paramount Ruler Tuanku Ja'afar
head of government: Prime Minister Mahathir Mohamad

ECONOMY:
GDP: purchasing power parity - $214.7 billion (1996)

GDP real growth rate: 8.2%
GDP per capita: $10,750
Inflation Rate *(consumer prices):* 3.5% (1996)
National budget:
revenues: $22.6 billion
expenditures: $22 billion
External debt: $27.5 million
Currency: 1 ringgit = 100 sen
Labor Force: 8.398 million (1996)
Unemployment rate: 2.6% (1996)
Agriculture:
Peninsular: Natural rubber, palm oil, rice
Sabah: Subsistence crops, rubber, timber, coconut, rice
Sarawak: Rubber, pepper; timber
Industries:
Peninsular: Rubber and oil palm processing and manufacturing, light manufacturing industry, electronics, tin, mining and smelting, logging and processing timber
Sabah: Logging, petroleum production
Sarawak: Agriculture processing, petroleum production and refining, logging
Exports: $84.6 billion
commodities: Electronic equipment, petroleum and petroleum products, palm oil, wood and wood products, rubber, textiles
Imports: $83.2 billion
commodities: Machinery and equipment, chemicals, food, petroleum products

DEFENSE:
Defense expenditures: *exchange rate conversion -* $2.5 billion, 2.6% of GDP

MALTA

GEOGRAPHY:
Location: Southern Europe
Area:
total area: 320 sq km
land area: 320 sq km
Capital city: Valletta
Natural Resources: Limestone, salt

PEOPLE:
Population: 379,563
Age structure:
0–14 years: 21%
15–64 years: 67%
65 years & over: 12%
Literacy rate: 84% *of total population,* (*males:* 86%, *females:* 82%)
Languages: Maltese *(official),* English *(official)*
Religions: 98%-Roman Catholic

VITAL STATISTICS:
Birth rate: 12.47 *(per 1,000 population)* (1997)
Death rate: 7.34 *(per 1,000 population)*
Infant mortality rate: 7.7 *(deaths per 1,000 live births)*
Fertility rate: 1.84 *(per woman)*
Life expectancy at birth:

total population: 77.44
   (*males:* 75.16, *females:* 79.87)

GOVERNMENT:
Type of government: Parliamentary Democracy
Independence: September 21, 1964 (*from UK*)
Leaders:
   chief of state: President Ugo Mifsud Bonnici
   head of government: Prime Minister Eddie Fenech
   Adami

ECONOMY:
GDP: purchasing power parity - $4.7 billion (1996)
   GDP real growth rate: 4%
   GDP per capita: $12,600
Inflation Rate (*consumer prices*): 3% (1996)
National budget:
   revenues: $1.66 billion
   expenditures: $1.69 billion
External debt: $134 million
Currency: 1 Maltese lira = 100 cents
Labor Force: 148,085 (1996)
Unemployment rate: 3.7% (1996)
Agriculture: Potatoes, cauliflower, grapes, wheat, bar-
   ley, tomatoes, citrus, cut flowers, green peppers;
   pork, milk, poultry, eggs
Industries: Tourism, electronics, ship repair yard, construction, food manufacturing, textiles, footwear,
   clothing, beverages, tobacco
Exports: $1.9 billion
   commodities: Machinery and transport equipment,
   clothing and footwear, printed matter
Imports: $3 billion
   commodities: Food, petroleum, machinery, semi-
   manufactured goods

DEFENSE:
Defense expenditures: *exchange rate conversion -*
   $65.5 *million,* 2.7% *of GDP*

M E X I C O

GEOGRAPHY:
Location: Central America
Area:
   total area: 1,972,550 sq km
   land area: 1,923,040 sq km
Capital city: Mexico City
Natural Resources: Petroleum, silver, copper, gold,
   lead, zinc, natural gas, timber

PEOPLE:
Population: 98,552,776
Age structure:
   0–14 years: 36%
   15–64 years: 60%
   65 years & over: 4%
Literacy rate: 89.6% *of total population,*
   (*males:* 91.8%, *females:* 87.4%)
Languages: Spanish, various Mayan dialects
Religions: 89%-Roman Catholic, 6%-Protestant

VITAL STATISTICS:
Birth rate: 25.8 (*per 1,000 population*) (1997)

Death rate: 4.52 (*per 1,000 population*)
Infant mortality rate: 23.9 (*deaths per 1,000 live
births*)
Fertility rate: 2.97 (*per woman*)
Life expectancy at birth:
   total population: 74
   (*males:* 70.39, *females:* 77.78)

GOVERNMENT:
Type of government: Federal Republic operating under
   centralized government
Independence: September 16, 1810 (*from Spain*)
Leaders:
   chief of state & head of government: President
   Ernesto Zedillo

ECONOMY:
GDP: purchasing power parity - $777.3 billion (1996)
   GDP real growth rate: 5.1%
   GDP per capita: $8,100
Inflation Rate (*consumer prices*): 28% (1996)
National budget:
   revenues: $73.8 billion
   expenditures: $74 billion
External debt: $170 billion
Currency: 1 New Mexican peso = 100 centavos
Labor Force: 36.3 million (1996)
Unemployment rate: 10% (1996)
Agriculture: Corn, wheat, soybeans, rice, beans, cot-
   ton, coffee, fruit, tomatoes; beef, poultry, dairy products; wool
Industries: Food and beverages, tobacco, chemicals,
   iron and steel, petroleum, mining, textiles, clothing,
   motor vehicles, consumer durables, tourism
Exports: $95 billion
   commodities: Crude oil, oil products, coffee, silver,
   engines, motor vehicles, cotton, consumer electronics
Imports: $88.5 billion
   commodities: Metal-working machines, steel mill
   products, agricultural machinery, electrical equipment, car parts for assembly, repair parts for motor vehicles, aircraft, and aircraft parts

DEFENSE:
Defense expenditures: *exchange rate conversion -*
   $1.56 *billion,* 1.5% *of GDP*

M O N A C O

GEOGRAPHY:
Location: Western Europe
Area:
   total area: 1.9 sq km
   land area: 1.9 sq km
Capital city: Monaco
Natural Resources: None

PEOPLE:
Population: 32,035
Age structure:
   0–14 years: 17%
   15–64 years: 63%

65 years & over: 20%
Literacy rate: NA%
Languages: French *(official)*, English, Italian, Monegasque
Religions: 95%-Roman Catholic

VITAL STATISTICS:
Birth rate: 10.66 *(per 1,000 population)* (1997)
Death rate: 12.01 *(per 1,000 population)*
Infant mortality rate: 6.7 *(deaths per 1,000 live births)*
Fertility rate: 1.7 *(per woman)*
Life expectancy at birth:
total population: 78.24
(males: 74.59, *females:* 82.07)

GOVERNMENT:
Type of government: Constitutional Monarchy
Independence: 1419 *(rule by the House of Grimaldi)*
Leaders:
chief of state: Prince Rainier III
head of government: Minister of State Michel Leveque

ECONOMY:
GDP: purchasing power parity - $800 million (1996)
GDP real growth rate: NA%
GDP per capita: $25,000
Inflation Rate *(consumer prices):* NA%
National budget:
revenues: $570.4 million
expenditures: $570.1 million
External debt: NA%
Currency: 1 French franc = 100 centimes
Labor Force: NA
Unemployment rate: 3.1% (1994)
Agriculture: None
Industries: None
Exports: $NA; full customs integration with France, which collects and rebates Monacan trade duties; also participating in EU market system through customs union with France
Imports: $NA; full customs integration with France, which collects and rebates Monacan trade duties; also participating in EU market system through customs union with France

DEFENSE:
Defense expenditures: *defense is the responsibility of France*

MONGOLIA

GEOGRAPHY:
Location: Northern Asia
Area:
total area: 1.565 million sq km
land area: 1.565 million sq km
Capital city: Ulaanbaatar
Natural Resources: Oil, coal, copper, molybdenum, tungsten, phosphates, tin, nickel, zinc, wolfram, fluorspar, gold

PEOPLE:
Population: 2,578,530

Age structure:
0–14 years: 38%
15–64 years: 58%
65 years & over: 4%
Literacy rate: 82.9% *of total population,*
(males: 88.6%, *females:* 77.2%)
Languages: Khalkha Mongol, Turkic, Russian, Chinese
Religions: Tibetan Buddhist, 4%-Muslim

VITAL STATISTICS:
Birth rate: 24.57 *(per 1,000 population)* (1997)
Death rate: 8.41 *(per 1,000 population)*
Infant mortality rate: 68 *(deaths per 1,000 live births)*
Fertility rate: 2.89 *(per woman)*
Life expectancy at birth:
total population: 61.1
(males: 59.1, *females:* 63.2)

GOVERNMENT:
Type of government: Republic
Independence: March 13, 1921 *(from China)*
Leaders:
chief of state: President Natsagiin Bagabandi
head of government: Prime Minister Tsakhiagiin Elbegdori

ECONOMY:
GDP: purchasing power parity - $5.1 billion (1996)
GDP real growth rate: 3%
GDP per capita: $2,060
Inflation Rate *(consumer prices):* 53%
National budget:
revenues: $1.5 billion
expenditures: $1.3 billion
External debt: $500 million
Currency: 1 tughrik = 100 mongos
Labor Force: 1.115 million (1993)
Unemployment rate: 6% (1995)
Agriculture: Wheat, barley, potatoes, forage crops; sheep, goats, cattle, camels, horses
Industries: Copper, construction material, mining *(particularly coal)*, food and beverages, processing of animal products
Exports: $400 million
commodities: Copper, livestock, animal products, cashmere, wool, hides, fluorspar, other nonferrous metals
Imports: $473 million
commodities: Machinery and equipment, fuels, food products, industrial consumer goods, chemicals, building materials, sugar, tea

DEFENSE:
Defense expenditures: *exchange rate conversion -* $22.8 *million,* 1% *of GDP*

MOROCCO

GEOGRAPHY:
Location: Northern Africa
Area:
total area: 446,550 sq km
land area: 446,300 sq km

Capital city: Rabat
Natural Resources: phosphates, iron ore, manganese, lead, zinc, fish, salt

PEOPLE:
Population: 29,114,497
Age structure:
0–14 years: 37%
15–64 years: 59%
65 years & over: 4%
Literacy rate: 43.7% *of total population,*
(males: 56.6%, *females:* 31%)
Languages: Arabic *(official),* Berber dialects, French the language of business, government, and diplomacy
Religions: 98.7%- Muslim, 1.1%-Christian, 0.2%-Jewish

VITAL STATISTICS:
Birth rate: 26.83 *(per 1,000 population)*
Death rate: 5.58 *(per 1,000 population)*
Infant mortality rate: 40.7 *(deaths per 1,000 live births)*
Fertility rate: 3.47 *(per woman)*
Life expectancy at birth:
total population: 70.08
(males: 68.04, *females:* 72.21)

GOVERNMENT:
Type of government: Constitutional Monarchy
Independence: March 2, 1956 *(from France)*
Leaders:
chief of state: King Hassan II
head of government: Prime Minister Abderrahmane Youssoufi

ECONOMY:
GDP: purchasing power parity - $97.6 billion (1996)
GDP real growth rate: 9%
GDP per capita: $3,000
Inflation Rate *(consumer prices):* 5%
National budget:
revenues: $10.4 billion
expenditures: $10.75 billion
External debt: $23.4 billion
Currency: 1 Moroccan dirham = 100 centimes
Labor Force: 7.4 million (1995)
Unemployment rate: 20% (1995)
Agriculture: Barley, wheat, citrus, wine, vegetables, olives; livestock
Industries: Phosphate rock mining and processing, food processing, leather goods, textiles, construction, tourism
Exports: $7.7 billion
commodities: Food and beverages, semiprocessed foods, consumer goods, phospates
Imports: $9.8 billion
commodities: Capital goods, semiprocessed goods, raw materials, fuel and lubricants, food and beverages, consumer goods

DEFENSE:
Defense expenditures: *exchange rate conversions -* $1.38 *billion,* 4.1% *of GDP*

MYANMAR

GEOGRAPHY:
Location: Southeastern Asia
Area:
total area: 678,500 sq km
land area: 657,740 sq km
Capital city: Rangoon *(regime refers to the capital as* Yangon*)*
Natural Resources: Petroleum, timber, tin, copper, antimony, zinc, tungsten, lead, coal, some marble, limestone, precious stones, natural gas

PEOPLE:
Population: 47,305,319
Age structure:
0–14 years: 37%
15–64 years: 59%
65 years & over: 4%
Literacy rate: 83.1% *of total population,*
(males: 88.7%, *females:* 77.7%)
Languages: Burmese, minority ethnic groups have their own languages
Religions: 89%- Buddhist, 4% -Christian (3%-Baptist, 1%-Roman Catholic), 4%-Muslim, 1%- animist beliefs, 2%-other

VITAL STATISTICS:
Birth rate: 29.54 *(per 1,000 population)*
Death rate: 11.41 *(per 1,000 population)*
Infant mortality rate: 78.5 *(deaths per 1,000 live births)*
Fertility rate: 3.76 *(per woman)*
Life expectancy at birth:
total population: 56.62
(males: 58.89, *females:* 58.45)

GOVERNMENT:
Type of government: Military Regime
Independence: January 4, 1948 *(from UK)*
Leaders:
chief of state & head of government: Prime Minister and Chairman of the State Law and Order Restoration Council General Than Shwe
State Law and Order Restoration Council: Military junta which assumed power September 18, 1988

ECONOMY:
GDP: purchasing power parity - $51.5 billion (1996)
GDP real growth rate: 7%
GDP per capita: $1,120
Inflation Rate *(consumer prices):* 30%-40% (1996)
National budget:
revenues: $5.3 billion
expenditures: $10 billion
External debt: $5.5 billion
Currency: 1 kyat = 100 pyas
Labor Force: 16.007 million
Unemployment rate: NA%
Agriculture: Paddy rice, corn, oilseed, sugarcane, pulses; hardwood
Industries: Agricultural processing; textiles and footwear; wood and wood products; petroleum

refining; copper, tin, tungsten, iron; construction materials; pharmeceuticals; fertilizer

Exports: $1 billion

commodities: Rice, pulses and beans, teak, hardwood

Imports: $2 billion

commodities: Machinery, transport equipment, construction materials, food products, consumer goods

DEFENSE:

Defense expenditures: *exchange rate conversion -* $135 *million,* NA% *of GDP*

NEPAL

GEOGRAPHY:

Location: Southern Asia

Area:

total area: 140,800 sq km

land area: 136,800 sq km

Capital city: Katmandu

Natural Resources: Quartz, water, timber, hydropower potential, scenic beauty, small deposits of lignite, copper, cobalt, iron ore

PEOPLE:

Population: 23,698,421

Age structure:

0–14 years: 42%

15–64 years: 55%

65 years & over: 3%

Literacy rate: 27.5% *of total population,* (*males:* 40.9%, *females:* 14%)

Languages: Nepali *(official),* 20 other languages divided into numerous dialects

Religions: 90%- Hindu, 5%-Buddhist, 3%-Muslim, and 2%-other

VITAL STATISTICS:

Birth rate: 35.99 *(per 1,000 population)* (1997)

Death rate: 10.71 *(per 1,000 population)*

Infant mortality rate: 78.4 *(deaths per 1,000 live births)*

Fertility rate: 4.96 *(per woman)*

Life expectancy at birth:

total population: 57.38

(*males:* 57.61, *females:* 57.13)

GOVERNMENT:

Type of government: Parliamentary Democracy as of May 12, 1991

Independence: 1768 *(unified by Prithvi Narayan Shan)*

Leaders:

chief of state: King Birendra Bir Bikram Shah Debv

head of government: Prime Minister Girija Prasad Koirala

ECONOMY:

GDP: purchasing power parity - $26.5 billion (1996)

GDP real growth rate: 2.9%

GDP per capita: $1200

Inflation Rate *(consumer prices):* 9.2%

National budget:

revenues: $645 million

expenditures: $1.05 billion

External debt: $2.85 billion

Currency: 1 Nepalese rupee = 100 paisa

Labor Force: 9.2 million (1996)

Unemployment rate: NA%

Agriculture: Rice, corn, wheat, sugarcane, root crops; milk, water buffalo meat

Industries: Tourism, carpets, textiles; small rice, jute, sugar, and oilseed mills; cigarette; cement, brick production

Exports: $343 million

commodities: Carpets, clothing, leather goods, jute goods, grain

Imports: $1.3 billion

commodities: Petroleum products, fertilizer, machinery

DEFENSE:

Defense expenditures: *exchange rate conversion -* $36 *million,* 1.2% *of GDP*

NETHERLANDS

GEOGRAPHY:

Location: Western Europe

Area:

total area: 37,330 sq km

land area: 33,920 sq km

Capital city: Amsterdam; The Hague is the seat of government

Natural Resources: Natural gas, petroleum, fertile soil

PEOPLE:

Population: 15,731,112

Age structure:

0–14 years: 18%

15–64 years: 68%

65 years & over: 14%

Literacy rate: 99% *of total population*

Languages: Dutch

Religions: 34%- Roman Catholic, 25%-Protestant, 3%-Muslim, 2%-other, 36%-unaffiliated

VITAL STATISTICS:

Birth rate: 11.84 *(per 1,000 population)* (1997)

Death rate: 8.69 *(per 1,000 population)*

Infant mortality rate: 5.2 *(deaths per 1,000 live births)*

Fertility rate: 1.5 *(per woman)*

Life expectancy at birth:

total population: 77.87

(*males:* 75, *females:* 80.88)

GOVERNMENT:

Type of government: Constitutional Monarchy

Independence: 1579 *(from Spain)*

Leaders:

chief of state: Queen Beatrix, Queen of the Netherlands

head of government: Prime Minister Wim Kok

ECONOMY:
GDP: purchasing power parity - $317.8 billion (1996)
GDP real growth rate: 2.7%
GDP per capita: $20,500
Inflation Rate *(consumer prices):* 2% (1996)
National budget:
revenues: $107.2 billion
expenditures: $118.9 billion
External debt: $0
Currency: 1 Netherlands guilder, gulden, or florin = 100 cents
Labor Force: 6.4 million (1993)
Unemployment rate: 6.5% (1996)
Agriculture: Grains, potatoes, sugar beets, fruits, vegetables; livestock
Industries: Agroindustries, metal and engineering products, electrical machinery and equipment, chemicals, petroleum, fishing, construction, microelectronics
Exports: $176.2 billion
commodities: Metal products, chemicals, processed food and tobacco, agricultural products
Imports: $159.7 billion
commodities: Raw materials and semifinished products, consumer goods, transportation equipment, crude oil, food products

DEFENSE:
Defense expenditures: *exchange rate conversion -* $8.2 *billion,* 2.1% *of GDP*

NEW ZEALAND

GEOGRAPHY:
Location: Oceania
Area:
total area: 268,680 sq km
land area: 268,670 sq km
Capital city: Wellington
Natural Resources: Natural gas, iron ore, sand, timber, hydropower, gold, limestone

PEOPLE:
Population: 3,625,388
Age structure:
0–14 years: 23%
15–64 years: 65%
65 years & over: 12%
Literacy rate: 99% *of total population*
Languages: English *(official),* Maori
Religions: 24%-Anglican, 18%-Presbyterian, 15%-Roman Catholic, 5%-Methodist, 2%-Baptist, and 3%-other Protestant, 33%-unspecified or none

VITAL STATISTICS:
Birth rate: 15.35 *(per 1,000 population)* (1997)
Death rate: 7.67 *(per 1,000 population)*
Infant mortality rate: 6.5 *(deaths per 1,000 live births)*
Fertility rate: 1.96 *(per woman)*

Life expectancy at birth:
total population: 77.27
(males: 74.16, *females:* 80.56)

GOVERNMENT:
Type of government: Parlimentary Democracy
Independence: September 26, 1907 *(from UK)*
Leaders:
chief of state: Queen Elizabeth II, represented by Sir Michael Hardie-Boys
head of government: Prime Minister Jenny Shipley

ECONOMY:
GDP: purchasing power parity - $65.6 billion (1996)
GDP real growth rate: 2.8%
GDP per capita: $18,500
Inflation Rate *(consumer prices):* 2.8% (1996)
National budget:
revenues: $22.18 billion
expenditures: $20.28 billion
External debt: $38.5 billion
Currency: 1 New Zealand dollar = 100 cents
Labor Force: 1,634,500 (1995)
Unemployment rate: 5.9% (1996)
Agriculture: Wheat, barley, potatoes, pulses, fruits, vegetables; wool, meat, dairy products; fish *(catch reached a record 503,000 metric tons in 1988)*
Industries: Food processing, wool and paper products, textiles, machinery, transportation equipment, banking and insurance, tourism, mining
Exports: $13.7 billion
commodities: Wool, lamb, mutton, beef, fish, vegetables, cheese, chemicals, forestry products, fruits and vegetables, manufactured goods
Imports: $14 billion
commodities: Machinery and equipment, vehicles and aircraft, petroleum, consumer goods

DEFENSE:
Defense expenditures: *exchange rate conversion -* $677 *million,* 1.1% *of GDP*

NICARAGUA

GEOGRAPHY:
Location: Central America
Area:
total area: 129,494 sq km
land area: 120,254 sq km
Capital city: Managua
Natural Resources: Gold, silver, copper, tungsten, lead, zinc, timber, fish

PEOPLE:
Population: 4,583,379
Age structure:
0–14 years: 43%
15–64 years: 53%
65 years & over: 4%

Literacy rate: 65.7% *of total population,*
(*males:* 64.6%, *females:* 66.6%)
Languages: Spanish *(official)*
Religions: 95%-Roman Catholic, 5%-Protestant

VITAL STATISTICS:
Birth rate: 33.01 *(per 1,000 population)* (1997)
Death rate: 5.83 *(per 1,000 population)*
Infant mortality rate: 44.1 *(deaths per 1,000 live
births)*
Fertility rate: 3.9 *(per woman)*
Life expectancy at birth:
total population: 66.17
(*males:* 63.83, *females:* 68.6)

GOVERNMENT:
Type of government: Republic
Independence: September 15, 1821 *(from Spain)*
Leaders:
chief of state & head of government: President
Arnoldo Aleman

ECONOMY:
GDP: purchasing power parity - $7.7 billion (1996)
GDP real growth rate: 5.5%
GDP per capita: $1,800
Inflation Rate *(consumer prices):* 11% (1996)
National budget:
revenues: $389 million
expenditures: $551 million
External debt: $6 billion
Currency: 1 gold cordoba = 100 centavos
Labor Force: 1.086 million (1986)
Unemployment rate: 16%; underemployment 36%
(1996)
Agriculture: Coffee, bananas, sugarcane, cotton, rice,
corn, cassava *(tapioca),* citrus, beans; beef, veal,
pork, poultry, dairy products
Industries: Food processing, chemicals, metal products, textiles, clothing, petroleum refining and distribution, beverages, footwear
Exports: $670 million
commodities: Meat, coffee, cotton, sugar, seafood,
gold, bananas
Imports: $1.188 billion
commodities: Consumer goods, machinery and
equipment, petroleum products

DEFENSE:
Defense expenditures: *exchange rate conversion -*
$27.48 *million,* 1.35% *of GDP*

NIGERIA

GEOGRAPHY:
Location: Western Africa
Area:
total area: 923,770 sq km
land area: 910,770 sq km
Capital city: Abuja

Natural Resources: Petroleum, tin, columbite, iron ore,
coal, limestone, lead, zinc, natural gas

PEOPLE:
Population: 110,532,242
Age structure:
0–14 years: 45%
15–64 years: 52%
65 years & over: 3%
Literacy rate: 57.1% *of total population,*
(*males:* 67.3%, *females:* 47.3%)
Languages: English *(official),* Hausa, Yoruba, Ibo, Fu-
lani
Religions: 50%- Muslim, 40%-Christian, 10%-indige-
nous beliefs

VITAL STATISTICS:
Birth rate: 42.58 *(per 1,000 population)* (1997)
Death rate: 12.45 *(per 1,000 population)*
Infant mortality rate: 70.2 *(deaths per 1,000 live
births)*
Fertility rate: 6.17 *(per woman)*
Life expectancy at birth:
total population: 54.65
(*males:* 53.32, *females:* 56.03)

GOVERNMENT:
Type of government: Military government; Nigeria has
been ruled by one military regime after another since
December 31, 1983; on October 1, 1995, the present
military government announced it will turn power
over to democratically elected civilian authorities in
October 1998
Independence: October 1, 1960 *(from UK)*
Leaders:
chief of state & head of government: Chairman of
the Provisional Ruling Council and Commander in
Chief of Armed Forces and Defense Minister Gen.
Abdulsalami Abubakar

ECONOMY:
GDP: purchasing power parity - $143.5 billion (1996)
GDP real growth rate: 3%
GDP per capita: $1,380
Inflation Rate *(consumer prices):* 57%
National budget:
revenues: $16.1 billion
expenditures: $16 billion
External debt: $34 billion
Currency: 1 naira = 100 kobo
Labor Force: 42.844 million (1992)
Unemployment rate: 28% (1992)
Agriculture: Cocoa, peanuts, palm oil, rubber, corn,
rice, sorghum, millet, cassava *(tapioca),* yams; cat-
tle, sheep, goat, pigs; fishing and forest resources
extensively exploited
Industries: Crude oil, coal, tin, columbite, palm oil,
peanuts, cotton, rubber, wood, hides and skins, textiles, cement and other construction materials, food
products, footwear, chemicals, ceramics, fertilizer,
steel
Exports: $11.6 billion
commodities: Oil, cocoa, rubber

Imports: $10 billion
commodities: Machinery, transportation equipment, manufactured goods, chemicals, food and animals

DEFENSE:
Defense expenditures: *exchange rate conversion -* $243 *million,* 1% *of GDP*

N O R W A Y

GEOGRAPHY:
Location: Northern Europe
Area:
total area: 324,220 sq km
land area: 307,860 sq km
Capital city: Oslo
Natural Resources: Petroleum, copper, natural gas, pyrites, nickel, iron ore, zinc, lead, fish, timber, hydropower

PEOPLE:
Population: 4,419,955
Age structure:
0-14 years: 19%
15-64 years: 65%
65 years & over: 16%
Literacy rate: 99% *of total population*
Languages: Norwegian *(official)*
Religions: 87.8%-Evangelical Lutheran *(state church),* 3.8%-other Protestant and Roman Catholic, 3.2%-none

VITAL STATISTICS:
Birth rate: 13.25 *(per 1,000 population)* (1997)
Death rate: 10.22 *(per 1,000 population)*
Infant mortality rate: 5.1 *(deaths per 1,000 live births)*
Fertility rate: 1.83 *(per woman)*
Life expectancy at birth:
total population: 78.09
(males: 75.29, *females:* 81.07)

GOVERNMENT:
Type of government: Constitutional Monarchy
Independence: October 26, 1905 *(from Sweden)*
Leaders:
chief of state: King Harald V
head of government: Prime Minister Kjell Magne Bondevik

ECONOMY:
GDP: purchasing power parity - $114.1 billion (1996)
GDP real growth rate: 4.8%
GDP per capita: $26,200
Inflation Rate *(consumer prices):* 1.2%
National budget:
revenues: $48.6 billion
expenditures: $53 billion
External debt: $NA
Currency: 1 Norwegian krone = 100 oere
Labor Force: 2.13 million (1993)
Unemployment rate: 4.5% (1996)
Agriculture: Oats, other grains; beef, milk; livestock output exceeds value of crop; fish *(among the*

world's top 10 fishing nations, fish catch of 1.76 million metric tons in 1989)
Industries: Petroleum and gas, food processing, shipbuilding, pulp and paper products, metal, chemicals, timber, mining, textiles, fishing
Exports: $41.7 billion
commodities: Petroleum and petroleum products, metals and products, foodstuffs *(mostly fish),* chemicals and raw materials, natural gas, ships
Imports: $32.7 billion
commodities: Machinery and equipment and manufactured consumer goods, chemicals and other industrial inputs, foodstuffs

DEFENSE:
Defense expenditures: *exchange rate conversion -* $3.7 *billion,* 2.9% *of GDP*

O M A N

GEOGRAPHY:
Location: Middle East
Area:
total area: 212,460 sq km
land area: 212,460 sq km
Capital city: Muscat
Natural Resources: Petroleum, copper, asbestos, some marble, limestone, chromium, gypsum, natural gas

PEOPLE:
Population: 2,363,591
Age structure:
0–14 years: 46%
15–64 years: 51%
65 years & over: 3%
Literacy rate: NA%
Languages: Arabic *(official),* English, Baluchi, Urdu, Indian dialects
Religions: 75%- Ibadhi Muslim, Sunni Muslim, Shi'a Muslim, Hindu

VITAL STATISTICS:
Birth rate: 37.85 *(per 1,000 population)* (1997)
Death rate: 4.39 *(per 1,000 population)*
Infant mortality rate: 26.4 *(deaths per 1,000 live births)*
Fertility rate: 6.02 *(per woman)*
Life expectancy at birth:
total population: 70.8
(males: 68.84, *females:* 72.85)

GOVERNMENT:
Type of government: Monarchy
Independence: 1650 *(expulsion of the Portuguese)*
Leaders:
chief of state & head of government: Sultan Qaboos

ECONOMY:
GDP: purchasing power parity - $20.8 billion (1996)
GDP real growth rate: 6.5%
GDP per capita: $9,500
Inflation Rate *(consumer prices):* 0.5% (1996)

National budget:
   revenues: $5.3 billion
   expenditures: $6 billion
External debt: $2.7 billion
Currency: 1 Omani rial = 1000 baiza
Labor Force: 454,000 (1993)
Unemployment rate: NA%
Agriculture: Dates, limes, bananas, alfalfa, vegetables; camels, cattle; fish *(annual fish catch averages 100,000 metric tons)*
Industries: Crude oil production and refining, natural gas production, construction, cement, copper
Exports: $7.2 billion
   commodities: Petroleum, fish, processed copper, textiles
Imports: $5.5 billion
   commodities: Machinery and transportation equipment, manufactured goods, food, livestock, lubricants

DEFENSE:
Defense expenditures: *exchange rate conversion -* $1.82 *billion*, 13.7% *of GDP*

PAKISTAN

GEOGRAPHY:
Location: Southern Asia
Area:
   total area: 803,940 sq km
   land area: 778,720 sq km
Capital city: Islamabad
Natural Resources: Land, extensive natural gas reserves, limited petroleum, poor quality coal, iron ore, copper, salt, limestone

PEOPLE:
Population: 135,135,195
Age structure:
   0–14 years: 42%
   15–64 years: 54%
   65 years & over: 4%
Literacy rate: 37.8% *of total population,* (*males:* 50%, *females:* 24.4%)
Languages: Punjabi, Sindhi, Siraiki *(a Punjabi variant),* Pashtu, Urdu, Balochi, Hindko, Brahui, English *(official and lingua franca of Pakistani elite and most government ministries),* Burushaski, other
Religions: 97%- Muslim *(77%-Sunni, 20%-Shi'a),* Christian, Hindu, and 3%-other

VITAL STATISTICS:
Birth rate: 35.26 *(per 1,000 population)* (1997)
Death rate: 10.95 *(per 1,000 population)*
Infant mortality rate: 95.1 *(deaths per 1,000 live births)*
Fertility rate: 5.08 *(per woman)*
Life expectancy at birth:
   total population: 58.77
   (*males:* 57.97, *females:* 59.61)

GOVERNMENT:
Type of government: Republic
Independence: August 14, 1947 *(from UK)*

Leaders:
   chief of state: President Mohammad Rafiq Tarar
   head of government: Prime Minister Mohammad Nawaz Sharif

ECONOMY:
GDP: purchasing power parity - $296.5 billion (1996)
   GDP real growth rate: 5.5%
   GDP per capita: $2,300
Inflation Rate *(consumer prices):* 10.8% (95/96)
National budget:
   revenues: $12.5 billion
   expenditures: $14 billion
External debt: $28.6 billion
Currency: 1 Pakistani rupee = 100 paisa
Labor Force: 36.7 million (1997)
Unemployment rate: NA%
Agriculture: Cotton, wheat, rice sugarcane, fruits vegetables; milk, beef, mutton, eggs
Industries: Textiles, food processing, beverages, construction materials, clothing, paper products, shrimp
Exports: $8.3 billion
   commodities: Cotton, textiles, clothing, rice, leather, carpets
Imports: $12 billion
   commodities: Petroleum and petroleum products, machinery and transportation equipment, vegetable oils, animal fats, chemicals

DEFENSE:
Defense expenditures: *exchange rate conversion -* $3.3 *billion*, 5.3% *of GDP*

PANAMA

GEOGRAPHY:
Location: Central America
Area:
   total area: 78,200 sq km
   land area: 75,990 sq km
Capital city: Panama City
Natural Resources: Copper, mahogany forests, shrimp

PEOPLE:
Population: 2,735,943
Age structure:
   0–14 years: 32%
   15–64 years: 62%
   65 years & over: 6%
Literacy rate: 90.8% *of total population,* (*males:* 91.4%, *females:* 90.2%)
Languages: Spanish *(official),* English
Religions: 85%- Roman Catholic, 15% Protestant

VITAL STATISTICS:
Birth rate: 22.27 *(per 1,000 population)* (1997)
Death rate: 5.15 *(per 1,000 population)*
Infant mortality rate: 24.6 *(deaths per 1,000 live births)*
Fertility rate: 2.6 *(per woman)*
Life expectancy at birth:
   total population: 74.28
   (*males:* 71.55, *females:* 77.1)

GOVERNMENT:
Type of government: Constitutional Republic
Independence: November 3, 1903 *(from Colombia)*; November 28, 1821 *(from Spain)*
Leaders:
  chief of state & head of government: President Ernesto Perez Balladares

ECONOMY:
GDP: purchasing power parity - $14 billion (1996)
  GDP real growth rate: 1.5%
  GDP per capita: $5,300
Inflation Rate *(consumer prices):* 1.3% (1996)
National budget:
  revenues: $1.86 billion
  expenditures: $1.86 billion
External debt: $5.63 billion
Currency: 1 balboa = 100 centesimos
Labor Force: 1.015 million (1996)
Unemployment rate: 14% (1996)
Agriculture: Bananas, rice, corn, coffee, sugarcane, vegetables; livestock, fishing *(shrimp)*
Industries: Construction, petroleum refining, brewing, cement and other construction materials, sugar milling
Exports: $570 million
  commodities: Bananas, shrimp, sugar, clothing, coffee
Imports: $2.512 billion
  commodities: Capital goods, crude oil, foodstuffs, consumer goods, chemicals

DEFENSE:
Defense expenditures: *exchange rate conversions -* $78 *million,* NA% *of GDP*

PAPUA NEW GUINEA

GEOGRAPHY:
Location: Southeastern Asia
Area:
  total area: 462,840 sq km
  land area: 452,860 sq km
Capital city: Port Moresby
Natural Resources: Gold, silver, copper, natural gas, timber, oil potential

PEOPLE:
Population: 4,599,785
Age structure:
  0–14 years: 40%
  15–64 years: 57%
  65 years & over: 3%
Literacy rate: 72.2% *of total population,* (*males:* 81%, *females:* 62.7%)
Languages: English, pidgin English, Motu, 715 indigenous languages
Religions: 22%- Roman Catholic, 16%-Lutheran, 8%-Presbyterian/Methodist/London Missionary Society, 5%-Anglican, 4%-Evangelican Alliance, 1%-Seventh-Day Adventist, 10%-other Protestant sects, 34%-indigenous beliefs

VITAL STATISTICS:
Birth rate: 32.65 *(per 1,000 population)* (1997)
Death rate: 9.83 *(per 1,000 population)*
Infant mortality rate: 58.6 *(deaths per 1,000 live births)*
Fertility rate: 4.36 *(per woman)*
Life expectancy at birth:
  total population: 57.65
    (*males:* 56.78, *females:* 58.56)

GOVERNMENT:
Type of government: Parliamentary Democracy
Independence: September 16, 1975 *(from the Australian-administered UN trusteeship)*
Leaders:
  chief of state: Queen Elizabeth II represented by Governor General Silas Atopare
  head of government: Prime Minister Bill Skates

ECONOMY:
GDP: purchasing power parity - $10.7 billion (1996)
  GDP real growth rate: 2.3%
  GDP per capita: $2,400
Inflation Rate *(consumer prices):* 6% (1996)
National budget:
  revenues: $1.5 billion
  expenditures: $1.35 billion
External debt: $3.2 billion
Currency: 1 kina = 100 toea
Labor Force: 1.941 million
Unemployment rate: NA%
Agriculture: Coffee, cocoa, coconuts, palm kernels, tea, rubber, sweet potatoes, fruit, vegetables; poultry, pork
Industries: Copra crushing, palm oil processing, plywood production, wood chip production; mining of gold, silver, copper; construction, tourism
Exports: $2.7 billion
  commodities: Gold, copper ore, oil, logs, palm oil, coffee, cocoa, lobster
Imports: $1.3 billion
  commodities: Machinery and transport equipment, manufactured goods, food, fuels, chemicals

DEFENSE:
Defense expenditures: *Exchange rate conversion -* $63 *million,* NA% *of GDP*

PARAGUAY

GEOGRAPHY:
Location: Central South America
Area:
  total area: 406,750 sq km
  land area: 397,300 sq km
Capital city: Asunción
Natural Resources: Hydropower, timber, iron ore, manganese, limestone

PEOPLE:
Population: 5,291,020
Age structure:
  0–14 years: 40%

15–64 years: 56%
65 years & over: 4%
Literacy rate: 92.1% of total population,
(males: 93.5%, females: 90.6%)
Languages: Spanish (official), Guarani
Religions: 90%- Roman Catholic, Mennonite and other
Protestant denominations

VITAL STATISTICS:
Birth rate: 30.47 (per 1,000 population) (1997)
Death rate: 4.24 (per 1,000 population)
Infant mortality rate: 22.3 (deaths per 1,000 live
births)
Fertility rate: 4.08 (per woman)
Life expectancy at birth:
total population: 74.1
(males: 72.6, females: 75.68)

GOVERNMENT:
Type of government: Republic
Independence: May 14, 1811 (from Spain)
Leaders:
chief of state & head of government: President Juan
Carlos Wasmosy

ECONOMY:
GDP: purchasing power parity - $17.7 billion (1996)
GDP real growth rate: 1.5%
GDP per capita: $3,200
Inflation Rate (consumer prices): 8.2%
National budget:
revenues: $1.25 billion
expenditures: $1.66 billion
External debt: $1.3 billion
Currency: 1 guarani = 100 centimos
Labor Force: 1.8 million (1995)
Unemployment rate: 5.3%
Agriculture: Cotton, sugarcane, soybeans, corn, wheat,
tobacco, cassava (tapioca), fruits, vegetables; beef,
pork, eggs, milk; timber
Industries: Meatpacking, oilseed crushing, milling,
brewing, textiles, other light consumer goods, cement, construction
Exports: $819.5 million
commodities: Cotton, soybeans, timber, vegetable
oils, meatpacking, coffee, tung oil
Imports: $2.871 billion
commodities: Capital goods, foodstuffs, consumer
goods, raw materials, fuels

DEFENSE:
Defense expenditures: exchange rate conversion - $94
million, 0.6% of GDP

PERU

GEOGRAPHY:
Location: Western South America
Area:
total area: 1,285,220 sq km
land area: 1,280,000 sq km
Capital city: Lima

Natural Resources: Copper, silver, gold, petroleum,
timber, fish, iron ore, coal, phosphate, potash

PEOPLE:
Population: 26,111,110
Age structure:
0–14 years: 36%
15–64 years: 59%
65 years & over: 5%
Literacy rate: 88.7% of total population,
(males: 94.5%, females: 83%)
Languages: Spanish (official), Quechua (official), Aymara
Religions: Roman Catholic

VITAL STATISTICS:
Birth rate: 27.26 (per 1,000 population) (1997)
Death rate: 6.14 (per 1,000 population)
Infant mortality rate: 50 (deaths per 1,000 live births)
Fertility rate: 3.4 (per woman)
Life expectancy at birth:
total population: 69.55
(males: 67.38, females: 71.82)

GOVERNMENT:
Type of government: Republic
Independence: July 28, 1821 (from Spain)
Leaders:
chief of state & head government: President Alberto
Kenyo Fujimori

ECONOMY:
GDP: purchasing power parity - $92 billion (1996)
GDP real growth rate: 2.8%
GDP per capita: $3,800
Inflation Rate (consumer prices): 11.5% (1996)
National budget:
revenues: $8.5 billion
expenditures: $9.3 billion
External debt: $23.4 billion
Currency: 1 nuevo sol = 100 centimos
Labor Force: 7.6 million (1996)
Unemployment rate: 8.2% (1996)
Agriculture: Coffee, cotton, sugarcane, rice, wheat,
potatoes, plantains, cocoa; poultry, red meats, dairy
products, wool; fish (annual catch of 6.9 million
metric tons in 1990)
Industries: Mining of metals, petroleum, fishing, textiles, clothing, food processing, cement, auto assembly, steel, shipbuilding, metal fabrication
Exports: $6 billion
commodities: Copper, zinc, fishmeal, crude petroleum and byproducts, lead, refined silver, coffee,
cotton
Imports: $7.5 billion
commodities: Machinery, transport equipment,
foodstuffs, petroleum, iron and steel, chemicals,
pharmaceuticals

DEFENSE:
Defense expenditures: exchange rate conversion -
$998 million, 1.9% of GDP

PHILIPPINES

GEOGRAPHY:
Location: Southeastern Asia
Area:
total area: 300,000 sq km
land area: 298,170 sq km
Capital city: Manila
Natural Resources: Timber, petroleum, nickel, cobalt, silver, gold, salt, copper

PEOPLE:
Population: 77,725,862
Age structure:
0–14 years: 38%
15–64 years: 59%
65 years & over: 3%
Literacy rate: 94.6% *of total population,*
(*males:* 95%, *females:* 94.3%)
Languages: Philipino *(official, based on Tagalog),* English *(official)*
Religions: 83%-Roman Catholic, 9%-Protestant, 5%-Muslim, 3%-Buddhist and other

VITAL STATISTICS:
Birth rate: 28.97 *(per 1,000 population)* (1997)
Death rate: 6.59 *(per 1,000 population)*
Infant mortality rate: 35.2 *(deaths per 1,000 live births)*
Fertility rate: 3.62 *(per woman)*
Life expectancy at birth:
total population: 66.13
(*males:* 63.35, *females:* 69.05)

GOVERNMENT:
Type of government: Republic
Independence: July 4, 1946 *(from US)*
Leaders:
chief of state & head of government: President Joseph Estrada

ECONOMY:
GDP: purchasing power parity - $194.2 billion (1996)
GDP real growth rate: 5.5%
GDP per capita: $2,600
Inflation Rate *(consumer prices)*: 8.4% (1996)
National budget:
revenues: $18.4 billion
expenditures: $16.5 billion
External debt: $42.7 billion
Currency: 1 Philippine peso = 100 centavos
Labor Force: 29.13 million (1996)
Unemployment rate: 8.6% (1996)
Agriculture: Rice, coconuts, corn, sugarcane, bananas, pineapples, mangoes; pork, eggs, beef; fish *(catch of 2 million metric tons annually)*
Industries: Textiles, pharmaceuticals, chemicals, wood products, food processing, electronics assembly, petroleum refining, fishing
Exports: $20.5 billion
commodities: Electronics, textiles, coconut products, copper, fish

Imports: $33.3 billion
commodities: Raw materials, capital goods, petroleum products

DEFENSE:
Defense expenditures: *exchange rate conversion -* $1.3 *billion,* 0.7% *of GDP*

POLAND

GEOGRAPHY:
Location: Central Europe
Area:
total area: 312,683 sq km
land area: 304,510 sq km
Capital city: Warsaw
Natural Resources: Coal, sulfur, copper, natural gas, silver, lead, salt

PEOPLE:
Population: 38,606,922
Age structure:
0–14 years: 21%
15–64 years: 67%
65 years & over: 12%
Literacy rate: 99% *of total population,*
(*males:* 99%, *females:* 98%)
Languages: Polish
Religions: 95%-Roman Catholic *(about 75% practicing),* 5%-Eastern Orthodox, Protestant and other

VITAL STATISTICS:
Birth rate: 10.18 *(per 1,000 population)* (1997)
Death rate: 9.82 *(per 1,000 population)*
Infant mortality rate: 13.6 *(deaths per 1,000 live births)*
Fertility rate: 1.43 *(per woman)*
Life expectancy at birth:
total population: 72.47
(*males:* 68.27, *females:* 76.91)

GOVERNMENT:
Type of government: Democratic State
Independence: November 11, 1918 *(independent republic proclaimed)*
Leaders:
chief of state: President Aleksander Kwasniewski
head of government: Prime Minister Jerzy Buzek

ECONOMY:
GDP: purchasing power parity - $246.3 billion (1996)
GDP real growth rate: 6%
GDP per capita: $6,400
Inflation Rate *(consumer prices)*: 18.8% (1996)
National budget:
revenues: $37.1 billion
expenditures: $40.8 billion
External debt: $45.8 billion
Currency: 1 zloty = 100 groszy

Labor Force: 17.662 million (1996)
Unemployment rate: 13.3% (1996)
Agriculture: Potatoes, milk, fruits, vegetables, wheat; poultry, eggs, pork, beef
Industries: Machine building, iron and steel, coal mining, chemicals, shipbuilding, food processing, glass, beverages, textiles
Exports: $30.9 billion
  commodities: Intermediate goods, machinery and transport equipment, miscellaneous manufactured goods
Imports: $34.6 billion
  commodities: Machinery and transport equipment, intermediate goods, chemicals, fuels, miscellaneous manufactured goods

DEFENSE:
Defense expenditures: *exchange rate conversion -* $3.46 *billion,* 2.3% *of GDP*

PORTUGAL

GEOGRAPHY:
Location: Southwestern Europe
Area:
  total area: 92,391 sq km
  land area: 91,951 sq km
Capital city: Lisbon
Natural Resources: Fish, forest (cork), tungsten, iron ore, uranium ore, marble

PEOPLE:
Population: 9,927,556
Age structure:
  0–14 years: 18%
  15–64 years: 68%
  65 years & over: 14%
Literacy rate: 85% *of total population,* (*males:* 89%, *females:* 82%)
Languages: Portuguese
Religions: 97%-Roman Catholic, 1%-Protestant denominations, 2%- other

VITAL STATISTICS:
Birth rate: 10.75 *(per 1,000 population)* (1997)
Death rate: 10.3 *(per 1,000 population)*
Infant mortality rate: 7 *(deaths per 1,000 live births)*
Fertility rate: 1.36 *(per woman)*
Life expectancy at birth:
  total population: 75.42
  (*males:* 72.02, *females:* 79.04)

GOVERNMENT:
Type of government: Republic
Independence: 1140 *(independent republic proclaimed October 5, 1910)*
Leaders:
  chief of state: President Jorge Sampaio
  head of government: Prime Minister Antonio Guterres

ECONOMY:
GDP: purchasing power parity - $122.1 billion (1996)
  GDP real growth rate: 2.5%
  GDP per capita: $12,400
Inflation Rate *(consumer prices):* 3.4% (1996)
National budget:
  revenues: $48 billion
  expenditures: $52 billion
External debt: $13.6 billion
Currency: 1 Portuguese escudo = 100 centavos
Labor Force: 4.53 million (1992)
Unemployment rate: 7% (1996)
Agriculture: Grain, potatoes, olives, grapes; sheep, cattle, goats, poultry, meat, dairy products
Industries: Textiles and footwear; wood pulp, paper and cork; metalworking; oil refining; chemicals; fish canning; wine; tourism
Exports: $25.8 billion
  commodities: Clothing and footwear, machinery, cork and paper products, hides
Imports: $34.2 billion
  commodities: Machinery and transport equipment, agricultural products, chemicals, petroleum, textiles

DEFENSE:
Defense expenditures: *exchange rate conversion -* $2.07 *billion,* 1.9% *of GDP*

ROMANIA

GEOGRAPHY:
Location: Southeastern Europe
Area:
  total area: 237,500 sq km
  land area: 230,340 sq km
Capital city: Bucharest
Natural Resources: Petroleum, timber, natural gas, coal, iron ore, salt

PEOPLE:
Population: 22,395,848
Age Structure:
  0-14 years: 19%
  15-64 years: 68%
  65 years & over: 13%
Literacy rate: 97% *of total population,* (*males:* 98%, *females:* 95%)
Languages: Romanian, Hungarian, German
Religions: 70%-Romanian Orthodox, 6%-Roman Catholic *(of which 3% are Uniate),* 6%-Protestant, 18%-unaffiliated

VITAL STATISTICS:
Birth rate: 9.8 *(per 1,000 population)*
Death rate: 11.75 *(per 1,000 population)*
Infant mortality rate: 19.6 *(deaths per 1,000 live births)*
Fertility rate: 1.23 *(per woman)*
Life expectancy at birth:
  total population: 70.11

(*males:* 66.28, *females:* 74.13)

GOVERNMENT:
Type of government: Republic
Independence: 1881 *(from Turkey; republic proclaimed December 30, 1947)*
Leaders:
chief of state: President Emil Constantinescu
head of government: Prime Minister Radu Vasile

ECONOMY:
GDP: purchasing power parity - $113.2 billion (1996)
GDP real growth rate: 4.1%
GDP per capita: $5,200
Inflation Rate *(consumer prices)*: 56.9% (1996)
National budget:
revenues: $6 billion
expenditures: $7.3 billion
External debt: $4.7 billion
Currency: 1 leu = 100 bani
Labor Force: 10.1 million (1996)
Unemployment rate: 6.1% (1996)
Agriculture: Wheat, corn, sugar beets, sunflower seed, potatoes, grapes; milk, eggs, meat
Industries: Mining, timber, construction materials, metallurgy, chemicals, machine building, food processing, petroleum production and refining
Exports: $7.7 billion
commodities: Textiles and footwear, metals and metal products, fuels and mineral products, machinery and transport equipment, chemicals, food and agricultural goods
Imports: $93.8 billion
commodities: Fuels and minerals, machinery and transport equipment, textiles and footwear, food and agricultural goods, chemicals

DEFENSE:
Defense expenditures: *exchange rate conversion -* $650 *million*, 2.5% *of GDP*

RUSSIA

GEOGRAPHY:
Location: Northern Asia
Area:
total area: 17,075,200 sq km
land area: 16,995,800 sq km
Capital city: Moscow
Natural Resources: Wide natural resource base including major deposits of oil, natural gas, coal, and many strategic minerals, timber

PEOPLE:
Population: 146,861,022
Age structure:
0-14 years: 20%
15-64 years: 67%
65 years & over: 13%
Literacy rate: 98% *of total population,*
(*males:* 100%, *females:* 97%)
Languages: Russian, other
Religions: Russian Orthodox, Muslim, other

VITAL STATISTICS:
Birth rate: 9.52 *(per 1,000 population)* (1997)
Death rate: 14.84 *(per 1,000 population)*
Infant mortality rate: 23.5 *(deaths per 1,000 live births)*
Fertility rate: 1.35 *(per woman)*
Life expectancy at birth:
total population: 64.81
(*males:* 58.39, *females:* 71.56)

GOVERNMENT:
Type of government: Federation
Independence: August 24, 1991 *(from Soviet Union)*
Leaders:
chief of state: President Boris Yeltsin
head of government: Prime Minister Yevgeny Primakov

ECONOMY:
GDP: purchasing power parity - $767 billion (1996)
GDP real growth rate: -6%
GDP per capita: $5,200
Inflation Rate *(consumer prices):* 22% (1996)
National budget:
revenues: $NA
expenditures: $NA
External debt: $130 billion
Currency: 1 ruble = 100 kopeks
Labor Force: 73 million (1996)
Unemployment rate: 9.3% *(with considerable additional underemployment)* (1996)
Agriculture: Grain, sugar beets, sunflower seed, vegetables, fruits; meat, milk
Industries: Complete range of mining and extractive industries producing coal, oil, gas, chemicals, and metals; all forms of machine building from rolling mills to high-performance aircraft and space vehicles; shipbuilding; road and rail transportation equipment; communication equipment; agricultural machinery, tractors, and construction equipment; electric power generating and transmitting equipment; medical and scientific instruments; consumer durables, textiles, foodstuffs, handicrafts
Exports: $88.3 billion
commodities: Petroleum and petroleum products, natural gas, wood and wood products, metal, chemicals, and a wide variety of civilian military manufactured goods
Imports: $59.8 billion
commodities: Machinery and equipment, consumer goods, medicines, meat, grain, sugar, semifinished metal products

DEFENSE:
Defense expenditures: $NA, NA % *of GDP (note - The Intelligence Community estimates that defense spending in Russia fell by 20% in real terms in 1995, reducing Russian defense outlays to about one-fifth of peak Soviet levels in the late 1980s)*

R W A N D A

GEOGRAPHY:
Location: Central Africa
Area:
total area: 26,340 sq km
land area: 24,950 sq km
Capital city: Kigali
Natural Resources: Gold, cassiterite *(tin ore)*, wolframite *(tungsten ore)*, natural gas, hydropower

PEOPLE:
Population: 7,956,172
Age structure:
0-14 years: 45%
15-64 years: 52%
65 years & over: 3%
Literacy rate: 60.5% *of total population,*
(males: 69.8%, *females:* 51.6%)
Languages: Kinyarwanda *(official)*, French *(official)*, Kiswahili *(Swahili)* used in commercial centers
Religions: 65%-Roman Catholic, 9%-Protestant, 1%-Muslim, 25%-indigenous beliefs and other

VITAL STATISTICS:
Birth rate: 38.73 *(per 1,000 population)* (1997)
Death rate: 21.06 *(per 1,000 population)*
Infant mortality rate: 118.8 *(deaths per 1,000 live births)*
Fertility rate: 5.93 *(per woman)*
Life expectancy at birth:
total population: 39.11
(males: 38.64, *females:* 39.6)

GOVERNMENT:
Type of government: Republic; presidential system
Independence: July 1, 1962 *(from Belgium-administered UN trusteeship)*
Leaders:
chief of state: President Pasteur Bizimungu
head of government: Prime Minister Pierre Celestine Rwigema

ECONOMY:
GDP: purchasing power parity - $3.8 billion (1995)
GDP real growth rate: NA%
GDP per capita: $400
Inflation Rate *(consumer prices):* 22% (1995)
National budget:
revenues: $NA
expenditures: $NA
External debt: $873 million
Currency: 1 Rwandan franc = 100 centimes
Labor Force: 3.6 million
Unemployment rate: NA%
Agriculture: Coffee, tea, pyrethrum *(insecticide made from chrysanthemums)*, bananas, beans, sorghum, potatoes; livestock
Industries: Mining of cassiterite *(tin ore)*, and wolframite *(tungsten ore)*, tin, cement, agricultural processing, small-scale beverage production, soap, furniture, shoes, plastic goods, textiles, cigarettes

Exports: $51.2 million
commodities: Coffee, tea, cassiterite, wolframite, pyrethrum
Imports: $237.3 million
commodities: Textiles, foodstuffs, machines and equipment, capital goods, steel, petroleum products, cement and construction material

DEFENSE:
Defense expenditures: *exchange rate conversion -* $112.5 *million,* 7% of GDP

S A U D I   A R A B I A

GEOGRAPHY:
Location: Middle East
Area:
total area: 1,960,582 sq km
land area: 1,960,582 sq km
Capital city: Riyadh
Natural Resources: Petroleum, natural gas, iron ore, gold, copper

PEOPLE:
Population: 20,785,955
Age structure:
0-14 years: 43%
15-64 years: 55%
65 years & over: 2%
Literacy rate: 62.8% *of total population,*
(males: 71.5%, *females:* 50.2%)
Languages: Arabic
Religions: 100%-Muslim

VITAL STATISTICS:
Birth rate: 37.94 *(per 1,000 population)* (1997)
Death rate: 5.18 *(per 1,000 population)*
Infant mortality rate: 43.9 *(deaths per 1,000 live births)*
Fertility rate: 6.41 *(per woman)*
Life expectancy at birth:
total population: 69.51
(males: 67.72, *females:* 71.4)

GOVERNMENT:
Type of government: Monarchy
Independence: September 23, 1932 *(unification)*
Leaders:
chief of state & head of government: King Fahd

ECONOMY:
GDP: purchasing power parity - $205.6 billion (1996)
GDP real growth rate: 6%
GDP per capita: $10,600
Inflation Rate *(consumer prices):* 1% (1996)
National budget:
revenues: $43.7 billion
expenditures: $48.3 billion
External debt: $NA
Currency: 1 Saudi riyal = 100 halalah
Labor Force: 6 million - 7 million (1997)
Unemployment rate: 6.5% (1992)
Agriculture: Wheat, barley, tomatoes, melons, dates, citrus; mutton, chickens, eggs, milk

Industries: Crude oil production, petroleum refining, basic petrochemicals, cement, two small steel-rolling mills, construction, fertilizer, plastics
Exports: $53.1 billion
commodities: Petroleum and petroleum products
Imports: $25.5 billion
commodities: Machinery and equipment, chemicals, foodstuffs, motor vehicles, textiles

DEFENSE:
Defense expenditures: *exchange rate conversion -* $13.3 *billion,* 10% *of GDP*

SERBIA AND MONTENEGRO

GEOGRAPHY:
Location: Southeastern Europe
Area:
total area: 102,350 sq km
land area: 102,136 sq km
Capital city: Belgrade
Natural Resources: Oil, gas, coal, antimony, copper, lead, zinc, nickel, gold, pyrite, chrome

PEOPLE:
Population:
Total: 11,206,039
Montenegro: 679,904
Serbia: 10,526,135
Age structure:
Montenegro: 0-14 years: 22%
Montenegro: 15-64 years: 68%
Montenegro: 65 years & over: 10%
Serbia: 0-14 years: 21%
Serbia: 15-64 years: 67%
Serbia: 65 years & over: 12%
Literacy rate: NA%
Languages: Serbo-Croatian, Albanian
Religions: 65%-Orthodox, 19%-Muslim, 4%-Roman Catholic, 1%-Protestant, 11%-other

VITAL STATISTICS:
Birth rate:
Montenegro: 13.93 *(per 1,000 population)* (1997)
Serbia: 12.68 *(per 1,000 population)*
Death rate:
Montenegro: 7.33 *(per 1,000 population)*
Serbia: 9.64 *(per 1,000 population)*
Infant mortality rate:
Montenegro: 11.50 *(deaths per 1,000 live births)*
Serbia: 17.8 *(deaths per 1,000 live births)*
Fertility rate:
Montenegro: 1.80 *(per woman)*
Serbia: 1.76 *(per woman)*
Life expectancy at birth:
Montenegro: total population: 75.96
(*males:* 72.48, *females:* 79.76)
Serbia: total population: 72.9
(*males:* 70.51, *females:* 75.47)

GOVERNMENT:
Type of government: Republic

Independence: April 11, 1992 *(Federal Republic of Yugoslavia formed as self-proclaimed successor to the Socialist Federal Republic of Yugoslavia—SFRY)*
Leaders:
chief of state: President Slobodan Milosevic
head of government: Prime Minister Momir Bulatovic

ECONOMY:
GDP: purchasing power parity - $21 billion (1995)
GDP real growth rate: 6%
GDP per capita: $1,900
Inflation Rate *(consumer prices):* 79% (1995)
National budget:
revenues: $NA
expenditures: $NA
External debt: $11.2 billion
Currency: 1 Yugoslav New Dinar = 100 paras
Labor Force: 2.178 million (1994)
Unemployment rate: more than 35% (1995)
Agriculture: Cereals, fruits, vegetables, tobacco, olives; cattle, sheep, goats
Industries: Machine building *(aircraft, trucks, and automobiles; armored vehicles and weapons; electrical equipment; agricultural machinery),* metallurgy *(steel, aluminum, copper, lead, zinc, chromium, antimony, bismuth, cadmium),* mining *(coal, bauxite, nonferrous ore, iron ore, limestone),* consumer goods *(textiles, footwear, foodstuffs, appliances),* electronics, petroleum products, chemicals, pharmaceuticals
Exports: $1.4 billion
commodities: prior to the breakup of the federation, Yugoslavia exported machinery and transport equipment, manufactured goods, chemicals, food and live animals, raw materials
Imports: $2.4 billion
commodities: prior to the breakup of the federation, Yugoslavia imported machinery and transport equipment, fuels, and lubricants, manufactured goods, chemicals, food and live animals, raw materials including coking coal for the steel industry

DEFENSE:
Defense expenditures: 6.5 billion dinars, 24% of GDP *(note - Conversion of defense expenditures into US dollars using current exchange rate could produce misleading results)*

SINGAPORE

GEOGRAPHY:
Location: Southeastern Asia
Area:
total area: 647.5 sq km
land area: 637.5 sq km
Capital city: Singapore
Natural Resources: Fish, deepwater ports

PEOPLE:
Population: 3,490,356

Age structure:
0-14 years: 21%
15-64 years: 72%
65 years & over: 7%
Literacy rate: 91.1% *of total population,*
(males: 95.9%, *females:* 86.3%)
Languages: Chinese *(official),* Malay, *(official and national),* Tamil *(official),* English *(official)*
Religions: Buddhist *(Chinese),* Muslim *(Malays),* Christian, Hindu, Sikh, Taoist, Confucianist

VITAL STATISTICS:
Birth rate: 14.13 *(per 1,000 population)* (1997)
Death rate: 4.68 *(per 1,000 population)*
Infant mortality rate: 3.9 *(deaths per 1,000 live births)*
Fertility rate: 1.46 *(per woman)*
Life expectancy at birth:
total population: 78.15
(males: 75.14, *females:* 81.4)

GOVERNMENT:
Type of government: Republic within Commonwealth
Independence: August 9, 1965 *(from Malaysia)*
Leaders:
chief of state: President Ong Teng Cheong
head of government: Prime Minister Goh Chok Tong

ECONOMY:
GDP: purchasing power parity - $72.2 billion (1996)
GDP real growth rate: 6.5%
GDP per capita: $21,200
Inflation Rate *(consumer prices):* 1.3% (1996)
National budget:
revenues: $18.5 billion
expenditures: $13.5 billion
External debt: $NA
Currency: 1 Singapore dollar = 100 cents
Labor Force: 1.801 million (1996)
Unemployment rate: 2.7% (1996)
Agriculture: Rubber, copra, fruit, vegetables; poultry
Industries: Petroleum refining, electronics, oil drilling equipment, rubber processing and rubber products, processed food and beverages, ship repair, entrepôt trade, financial services, biotechnology
Exports: $144.8 billion
commodities: Computer equipment, rubber and rubber products, petroleum products, telecommunications equipment
Imports: $151.1 billion
commodities: Aircraft, petroleum, chemicals, foodstuffs

DEFENSE:
Defense expenditures: *exchange rate conversion -* $3.64 *billion,* 5.2% *of GDP*

S L O V A K I A

GEOGRAPHY:
Location: Central Europe
Area:
total area: 48,845 sq km
land area: 48,800 sq km
Capital city: Bratislava
Natural Resources: Brown coal and lignite; small amounts of iron ore, copper and manganese ore; salt

PEOPLE:
Population: 5,392,982
Age structure:
0-14 years: 21%
15-64 years: 68%
65 years & over: 11%
Literacy rate: NA
Languages: Slovak *(official),* Hungarian
Religions: 60.3%-Roman Catholic, 9.7%-atheist, 8.4%-Protestant, 4.1%-Orthodox, 17.5%-other

VITAL STATISTICS:
Birth rate: 10.37 *(per 1,000 population)*
Death rate: 9.58 *(per 1,000 population)*
Infant mortality rate: 10 *(deaths per 1,000 live births)*
Fertility rate: 1.34 *(per woman)*
Life expectancy at birth:
total population: 72.91
(males: 69.11, *females:* 76.9)

GOVERNMENT:
Type of government: Parliamentary Democracy
Independence: January 1, 1993 *(from Czechoslovakia)*
Leaders:
chief of state: President Michal Kovic resigned March 2, 1998. As of September 1998, a successor had not been elected.
head of government: Prime Minister Vladimir Meciar

ECONOMY:
GDP: purchasing power parity - $42.8 billion (1996)
GDP real growth rate: 7%
GDP per capita: $8,000
Inflation Rate *(consumer prices):* 5.5% (1996)
National budget:
revenues: $5.3 billion
expenditures: $5.6 billion
External debt: $4.6 billion *(hard currency indebtedness)*
Currency: 1 koruna = 100 halierov
Labor Force: 2.538 million (1994)
Unemployment rate: 12% (1996)
Agriculture: Grains, potatoes, sugar beets, hops, fruits; hogs, cattle, poultry; forest products
Industries: Metal and metal products; food and beverages; electricity, gas, coke, oil, nuclear fuel; chemicals and manmade fibers; machinery; paper and printing; earthenware and ceramics; transport vehicles; textiles; electrical and optical apparatus; rubber products
Exports: $8.1 billion
commodities: Machinery and transport equipment; chemicals; fuels, minerals, metals; agricultural products
Imports: $9.6 billion
commodities: Machinery and transport equipment, fuels and lubricants; manufactured goods; raw materials; chemicals; agricultural products

DEFENSE:
Defense expenditures: *exchange rate conversion* -
$423 *billion,* 2.7% *of GDP*

SLOVENIA

GEOGRAPHY:
Location: Southeastern Europe
Area:
total area: 20,256 sq km
land area: 20,256 sq km
Capital city: Ljubljana
Natural Resources: Lignite, coal, lead, zinc, mercury,
uranium, silver

PEOPLE:
Population: 1,971,739
Age structure:
0-14 years: 17%
15-64 years: 70%
65 years & over: 13%
Literacy rate: NA%
Languages: Slovenian, Serbo-Croatian, other
Religions: 96%-Roman Catholic *(including 2%-
uniate)*, 1%-Muslim, 3%-other

VITAL STATISTICS:
Birth rate: 8.91 *(per 1,000 population)* (1997)
Death rate: 9.54 *(per 1,000 population)*
Infant mortality rate: 5.4 *(deaths per 1,000 live births)*
Fertility rate: 1.22 *(per woman)*
Life expectancy at birth:
total population: 74.93
(males: 71.24, *females:* 78.84)

GOVERNMENT:
Type of government: Emerging Democracy
Independence: June 25, 1991 *(from Yugoslavia)*
Leaders:
chief of state: President Milan Kucan
head of government: Prime Minister Janez Drnovsek

ECONOMY:
GDP: purchasing power parity - $24 billion (1996)
GDP real growth rate: 3%
GDP per capita: $12,300
Inflation Rate *(consumer prices):*8.8%
National budget:
revenues: $8.48 billion
expenditures: $8.53 billion
External debt: $4.3 billion
Currency: 1 tolar = 100 stotins
Labor Force: 857,400
Unemployment rate: 13% (1996)
Agriculture: Potatoes, hops, wheat, sugar beets, corn,
grapes; cattle, sheep, poultry
Industries: Ferrous metallurgy and rolling mill prod-
ucts, aluminum reduction and rolled products, lead
and zinc smelting, electronics *(including military
electronics)*, trucks, electric power equipment, wood
products, textiles, chemicals, machine tools
Exports: $8.3 billion

commodities: Machinery and transport equipment;
intermediate manufactured goods, chemicals;
food, raw materials, consumer goods
Imports: $9.5 billion
commodities: Machinery and transport equipment,
intermediate manufactured goods, chemicals, raw
materials, fuels and lubricants, food

DEFENSE:
Defense expenditures: *exchange rate conversion*-$298
million 1.5-1.7% *of GDP*

SOMALIA

GEOGRAPHY:
Location: Eastern Africa
Area:
total area: 637,660 sq km
land area: 627,340 sq km
Capital city: Mogadishu
Natural Resources: Uranium and largely unexploited
reserves of iron ore, tin, gypsum, bauxite, copper,
salt

PEOPLE:
Population: 6,841,695
Age structure:
0–14 years: 44%
15–64 years: 53%
65 years & over: 3%
Literacy rate: 24% *of total population,*
(males: 36%, *females:* 14%)
Languages: Somali *(official)*, Arabic, Italian, English
Religions: Sunni Muslim

VITAL STATISTICS:
Birth rate: 45.49 *(per 1,000 population)*
Death rate: 18.34 *(per 1,000 population)*
Infant mortality rate: 125.8 deaths *(per 1,000 live births)*
Fertility rate: 6.76 *(per woman)*
Life expectancy at birth:
total population: 46.23
(males: 44.66, *females:* 47.85)

GOVERNMENT:
Type of government: None
Independence: July 1, 1960 *(from a merger of British
Somaliland, which became independent from the
UK on June 26, 1960, and Italian Somaliland, which
became independent from the Italian-administered
UN trusteeship on July 1, 1960, to form the Somali
Republic)*
Leaders:
*Somalia has no functioning government; the United
Somali Congress (USC) ousted the regime of Ma-
jor General Mohamed Siad Barre on January 27,
1991; the present political situation is one of an-
archy, marked by interclan fighting and random
banditry*

ECONOMY:
GDP: purchasing power parity - $3.6 billion (1995)
GDP real growth rate: 2%
GDP per capita: $500
Inflation Rate *(consumer prices):* NA%
National budget:
revenues: $NA
expenditures: $NA
External debt: $2.6 billion
Currency: 1 Somali shilling = 100 cents
Labor Force: 3.7 million *(very few are skilled laborers)* (1993)
Unemployment rate: NA%
Agriculture: Bananas, sorghum, corn, mangoes, sugarcane; cattle, sheep, goats; fishing potential largely unexploited
Industries: A few small industries, including sugar refining, textiles, petroleum refining *(mostly shut down)*
Exports: $130 million
commodities: Bananas, live animals, fish, hides
Imports: $269 million
commodities: Petroleum products, foodstuffs, construction materials

DEFENSE:
Defense expenditures: $NA, NA% *of GDP*

SOUTH AFRICA

GEOGRAPHY:
Location: Southern Africa
Area:
total area: 1,219,912 sq km
land area: 1,219,912 sq km
Capital city: Pretoria *(administrative)*; Cape Town *(legislative)*; Bloemfontein *(judicial)*
Natural Resources: Gold, chromium, antimony, coal, iron ore, manganese, nickel, phosphates, tin, uranium, gems, diamonds, platinum, copper, vanadium, salt, natural gas

PEOPLE:
Population: 42,834,520
Age structure:
0-14 years: 35%
15-64 years: 61%
65 years & over: 4%
Literacy rate: 81.8% *of total population,*
(males: 81.9%, *females:* 81.7%)
Languages: 11 official languages, including Afrikaans, English, Ndebele, Pedi, Sotho, Swazi, Tsonga, Tswana, Venda, Xhosa, Zulu
Religions: Christians *(most whites and coloreds and about 60% of blacks)*, Hindu *(60% of Indians)*, 2%-Muslim

VITAL STATISTICS:
Birth rate: 26.89 *(per 1,000 population)* (1997)
Death rate: 11.89 *(per 1,000 population)*

Infant mortality rate: 53.2 *(deaths per 1,000 live births)*
Fertility rate: 3.22 *(per woman)*
Life expectancy at birth:
total population: 56.29
(males: 54.4, *females:* 58.23)

GOVERNMENT:
Type of government: Republic
Independence: May 31, 1910 *(from UK)*
Leaders:
chief of state & head of government: President Nelson R. Mandela

ECONOMY:
GDP: purchasing power parity - $227 billion (1996)
GDP real growth rate: 3%
GDP per capita: $5,400
Inflation Rate *(consumer prices):* 9% (1996)
National budget:
revenues: $30.5 billion
expenditures: $38 billion
External debt: $30 billion
Currency: 1 rand = 100 cents
Labor Force: 14.2 million (1996)
Unemployment rate: 34% *(an additional 11% underemployment)* (1996)
Agriculture: Corn, wheat, sugarcane, fruits, vegetables; cattle, poultry, sheep, wool, milk, beef
Industries: Mining *(world's largest producer of platinum, gold, chromium)*, automobile assembly, metalworking, machinery, textiles, iron and steel, chemicals, fertilizer, foodstuffs
Exports: $29.2 billion
commodities: Gold, other minerals and metals, food, chemicals
Imports: $26.9 billion
commodities: Machinery, transport equipment, chemicals, oil, textiles, scientific instruments

DEFENSE:
Defense expenditures: *exchange rate conversion -* $2.9 *billion,* 2.2% *of GDP*

SPAIN

GEOGRAPHY:
Location: Southwestern Europe
Area:
total area: 504,750 sq km
land area: 499,400 sq km
Capital city: Madrid
Natural Resources: Coal, lignite, iron ore, uranium, mercury, pyrites, fluorspar, gypsum, zinc, lead, tungsten, copper, kaolin, potash, hydropower

PEOPLE:
Population: 39,133,996
Age structure:
0-14 years: 15%
15-64 years: 69%
65 years & over: 16%
Literacy rate: 96% *of total population,*

(males: 98%, *females:* 94%)
Languages: Castilian Spanish, Catalan, Galician, Basque
Religions: 99%-Roman Catholic, 1%-other sects

VITAL STATISTICS:
Birth rate: 9.94 *(per 1,000 population)* (1997)
Death rate: 9.54 *(per 1,000 population)*
Infant mortality rate: 6.6 *(deaths per 1,000 live births)*
Fertility rate: 1.18 (per woman)
Life expectancy at birth:
  total population: 77.39
    (males: 73.59, *females:* 81.46)

GOVERNMENT:
Type of government: Parliamentary Monarchy
Independence: 1492 *(expulsion of the Moors and unification)*
Leaders:
  chief of state: King Juan Carlos I
  head of government: Prime Minister José Maria Aznar

ECONOMY:
GDP: purchasing power parity - $593 billion (1996)
  GDP real growth rate: 2.4%
  GDP per capita: $15,300
Inflation Rate *(consumer prices)*: 3.7% (1996)
National budget:
  revenues: $113 billion
  expenditures: $139 billion
External debt: $90 billion
Currency: 1 peseta = 100 centimos
Labor Force: 12.475 million (1996)
Unemployment rate: 22% (1996)
Agriculture: Grain, vegetables, olives, wine grapes, sugar beets, citrus; beef, pork, poultry, dairy products; fish *(annual catch of 1.4 million metric tons is among top 20 nations)*
Industries: Textiles and apparel *(including footwear)*, food and beverages, metals and metal manufactures, chemicals, shipbuilding, automobiles, machine tools, tourism
Exports: $94.5 billion
  commodities: Cars and trucks, semifinished manufactured goods, foodstuffs, machinery
Imports: $118.3 billion
  commodities: Machinery, transport equipment fuels, semifinished goods, foodstuffs, consumer goods, chemicals

DEFENSE:
Defense expenditures: *exchange rate conversion -* $6.3 *billion,* 1.4% *of GDP*

SRI LANKA

GEOGRAPHY:
Location: Southern Asia
Area:
  total area: 65,610 sq km
  land area: 64,740 sq km
Capital city: Colombo

Natural Resources: Limestone, graphite, mineral sands, gems, phosphates, clay

PEOPLE:
Population: 18,933,558
Age structure:
  0-14 years: 28%
  15-64 years: 66%
  65 years & over: 6%
Literacy rate: 90.2% *of total population,*
  (males: 93.4%, *females:* 87.2%)
Languages: Sinhala *(official and national language),* Tamil *(national language),* English *(commonly used in government and spoken by 10% of population)*
Religions: 69%-Buddhist, 15%-Hindu, 8%-Christian, 8%-Muslim

VITAL STATISTICS:
Birth rate: 18.64 *(per 1,000 population)* (1997)
Death rate: 5.9 *(per 1,000 population)*
Infant mortality rate: 20.8 *(deaths per 1,000 live births)*
Fertility rate: 2.15 *(per woman)*
Life expectancy at birth:
  total population: 72.42
    (males: 69.75, *females:* 75.23)

GOVERNMENT:
Type of government: Republic
Independence: February 4, 1948 *(from UK)*
Leaders:
  chief of state & head of government: President Chandrika Bandaranaike Kumaratunga

ECONOMY:
GDP: purchasing power parity - $69.7 billion (1996)
  GDP real growth rate: 3.7%
  GDP per capita: $3,760
Inflation Rate *(consumer prices)*: 15.9% (1996)
National budget:
  revenues: $3 billion
  expenditures: $4.2 billion
External debt: $9.6 billion
Currency: 1 Sri Lankan rupee = 100 cents
Labor Force: 6.2 million (1994)
Unemployment rate: 13.1% (1994)
Agriculture: Rice, sugarcane, grains, pulses, oilseed, roots, spices, tea, rubber, coconuts; milk, eggs, hides, meat
Industries: Processing of rubber, tea, coconuts, and other agricultural commodities; clothing, cement, petroleum refining, textiles, tobacco
Exports: $4 billion
  commodities: Garments and textiles, teas, diamonds, other gems, petroleum products, rubber products, other agricultural products, marine products, graphite
Imports: $5 billion
  commodities: Textiles and textile materials, machinery and equipment, transport equipment, food, petroleum, building material

DEFENSE:
Defense expenditures: *exchange rate conversion -* $736 *million, 5.7% of GDP*

S U D A N

GEOGRAPHY:
Location: Northern Africa
Area:
total area: 2,505,810 sq km
land area: 2,376,000 sq km
Capital city: Khartoum
Natural Resources: Petroleum; small reserves of iron ore, copper, chromium ore, zinc, tungsten, mica, silver, gold

PEOPLE:
Population: 33,550,552
Age structure:
0–14 years: 46%
15–64 years: 52%
65 years & over: 2%
Literacy rate: 46.1% *of total population,*
(*males:* 57.7%,*females:* 34.6%)
Languages: Arabic*(official)*, Nubian, Ta Bedawie, diverse dialects of Nilotic, Nilo-Hamitic, Sudanic languages, English
Religions: 70%-Sunni Muslim*(in North)*, 25%-indigenous beliefs, 5%- Christian*(mostly in the south and Khartoum)*

VITAL STATISTICS:
Birth rate: 40.54 *(per 1,000 population)* (1997)
Death rate: 11.16 *(per 1,000 population)*
Infant mortality rate: 74.3 *(deaths per 1,000 live births)*
Fertility rate: 5.79 *(per woman)*
Life expectancy at birth:
total population: 55.54
(*males:* 54.6, *females:* 56.53)

GOVERNMENT:
Type of government: Transitional- previously ruling military junta; presidential and National Assembly elections held in March 1996; new constitution to be drafted by the National Assembly
Independence: January 1, 1956 *(from Egypt and UK)*
Leaders:
chief of state and head of government: President Lt. General Omar Hassan Ahmed el-Bashir

ECONOMY:
GDP: purchasing power parity - $26.6 billion (1996)
GDP real growth rate: 4%
GDP per capita: $860
Inflation Rate *(consumer prices):* 133% (1996)
National budget:
revenues: $382 million
expenditures: $1.06 billion
External debt: $18.5 billion
Currency: 1 Sudanese pound = 100 piastres
Labor Force: 11 million (1996)
Unemployment rate: 30% (1992/93)
Agriculture: Cotton, oilseed, sorghum, millet, wheat, gum arabic; sheep
Industries: Cotton ginning, textiles, cement, edible oils, sugar, soap distilling, shoes, petroleum refining
Exports: $500 million
commodities: Cotton, livestock/meat, gum arabic
Imports: $1 billion
commodities: Foodstuffs, petroleum products, manufactured goods, machinery and equipment, medicines and chemicals, textiles

DEFENSE:
Defense expenditures: $NA, NA% *of GDP*

S W E D E N

GEOGRAPHY:
Location: Northern Europe
Area:
total area: 449,964 sq km
land area: 410,928 sq km
Capital city: Stockholm
Natural Resources: Zinc, iron ore, lead, copper, silver, timber, uranium, hydropower potential

PEOPLE:
Population: 8,886,738
Age structure:
0-14 years: 19%
15-64 years: 64%
65 years & over: 17%
Literacy rate: 99% *of total population*
Languages: Swedish
Religions: 94%-Evangelical Lutheran, 1.5%-Roman Catholic, 1%-Pentecostal, 3.5%-other

VITAL STATISTICS:
Birth rate: 11.37 *(per 1,000 population)* (1997)
Death rate: 10.78 *(per 1,000 population)*
Infant mortality rate: 3.9 *(deaths per 1,000 live births)*
Fertility rate: 1.7 *(per woman)*
Life expectancy at birth:
total population: 79.08
(*males:* 76.42, *females:* 81.89)

GOVERNMENT:
Type of government: Constitutional Monarchy
Independence: June 6, 1523 *(Gustav Vasa was elected king);* June 6, 1809 *(a constitutional monarchy was established)*
Leaders:
chief of state: King Carl XVI Gustaf
head of government: Prime Minister Goeran Persson

ECONOMY:
GDP: purchasing power parity - $184.3 billion (1996)
GDP real growth rate: 1.4%
GDP per capita: $20,800
Inflation Rate *(consumer prices):* 0.2% (1996)
National budget:
revenues: $109.4 billion
expenditures: $146.1 billion
External debt: $66.5 billion
Currency: 1 Swedish krona = 100 oere

Labor Force: 4.552 million (1992)
Unemployment rate: 8% *(plus about 6% in training programs)* (1996)
Agriculture: Grains, sugar beets, potatoes; meat, milk
Industries: Iron and steel, precision equipment *(bearings, radio and telephone parts, armaments)*, wood pulp and paper products, processed food, motor vehicles
Exports: $79.9 billion
  commodities: Machinery, motor vehicles, paper products, pulp and wood, iron and steel products, chemicals, petroleum and petroleum products
Imports: $64.4 billion
  commodities: Machinery, petroleum and petroleum products, chemicals, motor vehicles, foodstuffs, iron and steel, clothing

DEFENSE:
Defense expenditures: *exchange rate conversion -* $5.8 billion, 2.5% *of GDP*

SWITZERLAND

GEOGRAPHY:
Location: Central Europe
Area:
  total area: 41,290 sq km
  land area: 39,770 sq km
Capital city: Bern
Natural Resources: Hydropower potential, timber, salt

PEOPLE:
Population: 7,260,357
Age structure:
  0-14 years: 17%
  15-64 years: 68%
  65 years & over: 15%
Literacy rate: 99% *of total population*
Languages: German, French, Italian, Romansch, other
Religions: 47.6%-Roman Catholic, 44.3%-Protestant, 8.1%-other

VITAL STATISTICS:
Birth rate: 11.05 *(per 1,000 population)* (1997)
Death rate: 9 *(per 1,000 population)*
Infant mortality rate: 5 *(deaths per 1,000 live births)*
Fertility rate: 1.45 *(per woman)*
Life expectancy at birth:
  total population: 78.77
    (males: 75.59, *females:* 82.11)

GOVERNMENT:
Type of government: Federal Republic
Independence: August 1, 1291
Leaders:
  chief of state & head of government: President Flavio Cotti

ECONOMY:
GDP: purchasing power parity - $161.3 billion (1996)
  GDP real growth rate: 0.8%
  GDP per capita: $22,600
Inflation Rate *(consumer prices):* 0.8% (1996)
National budget:
  revenues: $31 billion
  expenditures: $36.9 billion
External debt: $NA
Currency: 1 Swiss franc, franken, or franco = 100 centimes, rappen, or centesimi
Labor Force: 3.776 million *(900,000 foreign workers, mostly Italian)* (1994)
Unemployment rate: 5.3% (1996)
Agriculture: Grains, fruits, vegetables; meat, eggs
Industries: Machinery, chemicals, watches, textiles, precision instruments
Exports: $81.35 billion
  commodities: Machinery and equipment, precision instruments, metal products, foodstuffs, textiles and clothing
Imports: $80.05 billion
  commodities: Agricultural products, machinery and transportation equipment, chemicals, textiles, construction materials

DEFENSE:
Defense expenditures: *exchange rate conversion -* $3.74 *billion,* 1.4% *of GDP*

SYRIA

GEOGRAPHY:
Location: Middle East
Area:
  total area: 185,180 sq km
  land area: 184,050 sq km
Capital city: Damascus
Natural Resources: Petroleum, phosphates, chrome and manganese ores, asphalt, iron ore, rock salt, marble, gypsum

PEOPLE:
Population: 16,673,282
Age structure:
  0-14 years: 46%
  15-64 years: 51%
  65 years & over: 3%
Literacy rate: 70.8% *of total population,*
  (males: 85.7%, *females:* 55.8%)
Languages: Arabic *(official)*, Kurdish, Armenian, Aramaic, Circassian, French widely understood
Religions: 74%-Sunni Muslim, 16%-Alawite, Druze, and other Muslim sects, 10%-Christian (various sects), Jewish

VITAL STATISTICS:
Birth rate: 38.7 *(per 1,000 population)* (1997)
Death rate: 5.7 *(per 1,000 population)*
Infant mortality rate: 38.8 *(deaths per 1,000 live births)*
Fertility rate: 5.73 *(per woman)*

Dow Jones Indexes *Special Offer*:

25% DISCOUNT ON THE
1999 DOW JONES GUIDE TO
THE GLOBAL STOCK MARKET

If you are looking for comprehensive general, business and investment information, **The Wall Street Journal Almanac** is a good start. But to have financial performance data including revenues, earnings, dividends, stock prices and financial ratios for more than 2,900 companies in 34 countries at your fingertips, you need the 1999 edition of the **Dow Jones Guide to the Global Stock Market.**

This three-volume set provides you with a concise yet comprehensive profile of every country and company in the Dow Jones Global Index family (DJGI) and China -- an invaluable tool for virtually anyone with global business interests. The guide is regularly priced at $34.95, but through this special offer you can receive it for only $26.20 *(plus tax and $6.00 shipping).* Quantities are limited. Call today to take advantage of this special offer (800) 975-2209.

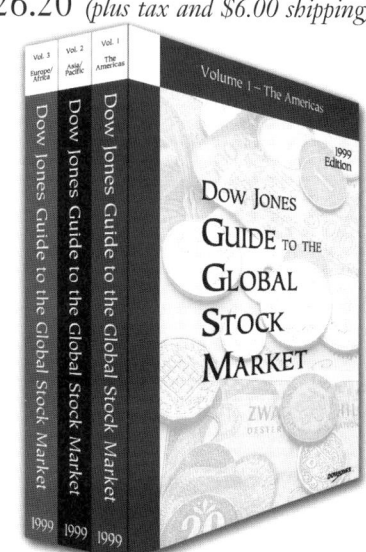

For more information on Dow Jones Indexes, please visit us at *http://indexes.dowjones.com* or email *dji@wsj.dowjones.com*.

Dow Jones Indexes

DOWJONES

Life expectancy at birth:
total population: 67.44
(*males:* 66.21, *females:* 68.74)

GOVERNMENT:
Type of government: Republic under military regime since March 1963
Independence: April 17, 1946 *(from League of Nations mandate under French administration)*
Leaders:
chief of state: President Hafez al-Assad
head of government: Prime Minister Mahmoud Zoubi

ECONOMY:
GDP: purchasing power parity - $98.3 billion (1996)
GDP real growth rate: 5.2%
GDP per capita: $6,300
Inflation Rate *(consumer prices)*: 20%
National budget:
revenues: $3 billion
expenditures: $3.7 billion
External debt: $22 billion
Currency: 1 Syrian pound = 100 piastres
Labor Force: 4.7 million
Unemployment rate: 9%
Agriculture: Wheat, barley, cotton, lentils, chickpeas; beef, lamb, eggs, poultry, milk
Industries: Textiles, food processing, beverages, tobacco, phosphate rock mining, petroleum
Exports: $4.4 billion
commodities: Petroleum, cotton, fruits and vegetables, textiles, animal products, industrial products
Imports: $5.2 billion
commodities: Machinery, metal products, transport equipment, foodstuffs, textiles

DEFENSE:
Defense expenditures: *exchange rate conversion - $875 million, 8% of GDP (note-Based on official budget data that understate actual spending)*

TAIWAN

GEOGRAPHY:
Location: Eastern Asia
Area:
total area: 35,980 sq km
land area: 32,260 sq km
Capital city: Taipei
Natural Resources: Small deposits of coal, natural gas, limestone, marble, asbestos

PEOPLE:
Population: 21,908,135
Age structure:
0-14 years: 23%
15-64 years: 69%
65 years & over: 8%
Literacy rate: 86% *of total population*, (*males:* 93%, *females:* 79%)
Languages: Mandarin Chinese *(official)*, Taiwanese

(Min), Hakka dialects
Religions: 93%-Mixture of Buddhist, Confucianist, and Taoist, 4.5%-Christian, 2.5%-other

VITAL STATISTICS:
Birth rate: 14.97 *(per 1,000 population)* (1997)
Death rate: 5.45 *(per 1,000 population)*
Infant mortality rate: 7 *(deaths per 1,000 live births)*
Fertility rate: 1.77 *(per woman)*
Life expectancy at birth:
total population: 77.04
(*males:* 73.81, *females:* 80.52)

GOVERNMENT:
Type of government: Multiparty democratic regime; opposition political parties legalized in March 1989
Leaders:
chief of state: President Lee Teng-hui
head of government: Premier Vincent Siew

ECONOMY:
GDP: purchasing power parity - $315 billion
GDP real growth rate: 5.7%
GDP per capita: $14,700
Inflation Rate *(consumer prices)*: 3.1%
National budget:
revenues: $57.6 billion
expenditures: $79.5 billion
External debt: $600 million
Currency: 1 new Taiwan dollar = 100 cents
Labor Force: 9.31 million (1996)
Unemployment rate: 2.6% (1996)
Agriculture: Rice, wheat, corn, soybeans, vegetables, fruit, tea; pigs, poultry, beef, milk; fish *(annual catch increasing, reached 1.4 million metric tons)*
Industries: Electronics, textiles, chemicals, clothing, food processing, plywood, sugar milling, cement, shipbuilding, petroleum refining
Exports: $116 billion
commodities: Electrical machinery, electronic products, textiles, footwear, foodstuffs, plywood and wood products
Imports: $102.4 billion
commodities: Machinery and equipment, electronic products, chemicals, iron and steel, crude oil, foodstuffs

DEFENSE:
Defense expenditures: *exchange rate conversion - $11.5 billion, and 3.6% of GDP*

TAJIKISTAN

GEOGRAPHY:
Location: Central Asia
Area:
total area: 143,100 sq km
land area: 142,700 sq km
Capital city: Dushanbe
Natural Resources: Significant hydropower potential, some petroleum, uranium, mercury, brown coal, lead, zinc, antimony, tungsten

PEOPLE:
Population: 6,020,095
Age structure:
  0–14 years: 42%
  15–64 years: 53%
  65 years & over: 5%
Literacy rate: 98% *of total population,*
  (*males:* 99%, *females:* 97%)
Languages: Tajik *(official),* Russian widely used in government and business
Religions: 80%-Sunni Muslim, 5%-Shi'a Muslim

VITAL STATISTICS:
Birth rate: 27.93 *(per 1,000 population)*
Death rate: 7.74 *(per 1,000 population)*
Infant mortality rate: 109.5 *(deaths per 1,000 live births)*
Fertility rate: 3.58 *(per woman)*
Life expectancy at birth:
  total population: 64.68
    (*males:* 61.55, *females:* 67.97)

GOVERNMENT:
Type of government: Republic
Independence: September 9, 1991 *(from Soviet Union)*
Leaders:
  chief of state: President Emomali Rakhmonov
  head of government: Prime Minister Yahyo Azimov

ECONOMY:
GDP: purchasing power parity - $5.4 billion (1996)
  GDP real growth rate: -17%
  GDP per capita: $920
Inflation Rate *(consumer prices):* 65%
National budget:
  revenues: $NA
  expenditures: $NA
External debt: $635 million
Currency: introduced its own currency, the Tajik ruble, in May 1995
Labor Force: 1.9 million (1996)
Unemployment rate: 2.4% *(includes only officially registered unemployed; large number of underemployed and unregistered unemployed)* (1996)
Agriculture: Cotton, grain, fruits, grapes, vegetables; cattle, sheep, goats
Industries: Aluminum, zinc, lead, chemicals and fertilizers, cement, vegetable oil, metal-cutting machine tools, refrigerators and freezers
Exports: $768 million
  commodities: Cotton, aluminum, fruits, vegetable oil, textiles
Imports: $657 million
  commodities: Fuel, chemicals, machinery and transport equipment, textiles, foodstuffs

DEFENSE:
Defense expenditures: 180 *billion rubles,* 3.4% *of GDP (note - Conversion of defense expenditures into US dollars could produce misleading results)*

TANZANIA

GEOGRAPHY:
Location: Eastern Africa
Area:
  total area: 945,090 sq km
  land area: 886,040 sq km
Capital city: Dar es Salaam
Natural Resources: Hydropower potential, tin, phosphates, iron ore, coal, diamonds, gemstones, gold, natural gas, nickel

PEOPLE:
Population: 30,608,769
Age structure:
  0–14 years: 45%
  15–64 years: 52%
  65 years & over: 3%
Literacy rate: 67.8% *of total population,*
  (*males:* 79.4%, *females:* 56.8%) *(note-Age 15 and over can read and write Kiswahili [Swahili], English, or Arabic)*
Languages: Kiswahili or Swahili *(official),* Kiunguju *(name for Swahili in Zanzibar),* English *(official, primary language of commerce, administration, and higher education),* Arabic *(widely spoken in Zanzibar),* many local languages *(note-Kiswahili [Swahili] is the mother tongue of Bantu people living in Zanzibar and nearby coastal Tanzania; although Kiswahili is Bantu in structure and origin, its vocabulary draws on a variety of sources, including Arabic and English, and it has become the lingua franca of central and eastern Africa; the first language of most people is one of the local languages)*
Religions:
  -Mainland: 45%-Christian, 35%-Muslim, 20%-indigenous beliefs
  -Zanzibar: 99%-Muslim

VITAL STATISTICS:
Birth rate: 40.92 *(per 1,000 population)*
Death rate: 19.84 *(per 1,000 population)*
Infant mortality rate: 105.9 *(deaths per 1,000 live births)*
Fertility rate: 5.58 *(per woman)*
Life expectancy at birth:
  total population: 41.71
    (*male:* 40.34, *female:* 43.13)

GOVERNMENT:
Type of government: Republic
Independence: April 26, 1964; Tanganyika became independent December 9, 1961 *(from UK-administered UN trusteeship);* Zanzibar became independent December 19, 1963 *(from UK);* Tanganyika united with Zanzibar April 26, 1964 to form the United Republic of Tanganyika and Zanzibar; renamed United Republic of Tanzania October 29, 1964
Leaders:
  chief of state: President Benjamin William Mkapa
  head of government: Prime Minister Frederick Sumaye

ECONOMY:
GDP: purchasing power parity - $18.9 billion (1995)
GDP real growth rate: 3.5%
GDP per capita: $650
Inflation Rate *(consumer prices):* 30% (1995)
National budget:
revenues: $495 million
expenditures: $631 million
External debt: $7.4 billion
Currency: 1 Tanzanian shilling = 100 cents
Labor Force: 13.495 million (1995)
Unemployment rate: NA%
Agriculture: Coffee, sisal, tea, cotton, pyrethrum *(insecticide made from chrysanthemums)*, cashews, tobacco, cloves *(Zanzibar),* corn, wheat, cassava *(tapioca)*, bananas, fruits, vegetables; cattle, sheep, goats
Industries: Primarily agricultural processing *(sugar, beer, cigarettes, sisal twine)*, diamond and gold mining, oil refining, shoes, cement, textiles, wood products, fertilizer
Exports: $679 million
commodities: Coffee, cotton, tobacco, tea, cashew nuts, sisal
Imports: $1.69 billion
commodities: Manufactured goods, machinery and transporation equipment, cotton piece goods, crude oil, foodstuffs

DEFENSE:
Defense expenditures: *exchange rate conversion -* $69 *million,* NA% *of GDP*

THAILAND

GEOGRAPHY:
Location: Southeastern Asia
Area:
total area: 514,000 sq km
land area: 511,770 sq km
Capital city: Bangkok
Natural Resources: Tin, rubber, natural gas, tungsten, tantalum, timber, lead, fish, gypsum, lignite, fluorite

PEOPLE:
Population: 60,037,366
Age structure:
0-14 years: 25%
15-64 years: 69%
65 years & over: 6%
Literacy rate: 93.8% *of total population,*
(males: 96%, *females:* 91.6%)
Languages: Thai, English the secondary language of the elite, ethnic and regional dialects
Religions: 95%-Buddhism, 3.8%-Muslim, 0.5%-Christianity, 0.1%-Hinduism, 0.6%-other

VITAL STATISTICS:
Birth Rate: 17.03 *(per 1,000 population)*

Death rate: 7.05 *(per 1,000 population)*
Infant mortality rate: 32.1 *(deaths per 1,000 live births)*
Fertility rate: 1.86 *(per woman)*
Life expectancy at birth:
total population: 68.8
(males: 65.12, *females:* 72.66)

GOVERNMENT:
Type of government: Constitutional Monarchy
Independence: 1238 *(traditional founding date; never colonized)*
Leaders:
chief of state: King Bhumibol Adulyadej
head of government: Prime Minister Chuan Leekpai

ECONOMY:
GDP: purchasing power parity - $455.7 billion (1996)
GDP real growth rate: 6.7%
GDP per capita: $7,700
Inflation Rate *(consumer prices):* 5.9% (1996)
National budget:
revenues: $28.4 billion
expenditures: $28.4 billion
External debt: $61.6 billion
Currency: 1 baht = 100 satang
Labor Force: 34.03 million (1996)
Unemployment rate: 2.6% (1996)
Agriculture: Rice, cassava *(tapioca)*, rubber, corn, sugarcane, coconuts, soybeans
Industries: Tourism; textiles and garments, agricultural processing, beverages, tobacco, cement, light manufacturing (such as jewelry); electric appliances and components, integrated circuits, furniture, plastics; world's second-largest tungsten producer and third-largest tin producer
Exports: $57.3 billion
commodities: Manufactured goods, agricultural products and fisheries, raw materials, fuels
Imports: $72.4 billion
commodities: Manufactured goods, fuels, raw materials, foodstuffs

DEFENSE:
Defense expenditures: *exchange rate conversion -* $4.0 *billion, and* 2.5% *of GDP*

TUNISIA

GEOGRAPHY:
Location: Northern Africa
Area:
total area: 163,610 sq km
land area: 155,360 sq km
Capital city: Tunis
Natural Resources: Petroleum, phosphates, iron ore, lead, zinc, salt

PEOPLE:
Population: 9,380,404

Age structure:
0–14 years: 32%
15–64 years: 62%
65 years & over: 6%
Literacy rate: 66.7% *of total population,*
(males: 78.6%, *females:* 54.6%)
Languages: Arabic *(official and one of the languages of commerce),* French *(commerce)*
Religions: 98%-Muslim, 1%-Christian, 1%-Jewish

VITAL STATISTICS:
Birth rate: 20.56 *(per 1,000 population)*
Death rate: 5.08 *(per 1,000 population)*
Infant mortality rate: 33.9 *(deaths per 1,000 live births)*
Fertility rate: 2.52 *(per woman)*
Life expectancy at birth:
total population: 72.85
(males: 71.5, *females:* 74.3)

GOVERNMENT:
Type of government: Republic
Independence: March 20, 1956 *(from France)*
Leaders:
chief of state: President Zine El Abidine Ben Ali
head of government: Prime Minister Hamed Karoui

ECONOMY:
GDP: purchasing power parity - $43.3 billion (1996)
GDP real growth rate: 7.1%
GDP per capita: $4,800
Inflation Rate *(consumer prices):* 6%
National budget:
revenues: $5.2 billion
expenditures: $7.2 billion
External debt: $9.6 billion
Currency: 1 Tunisian dinar = 1,000 millimes
Labor Force: 2.917 million (1995)
Unemployment rate: 16% (1995)
Agriculture: Olives, dates, oranges, almonds, grain, sugar beets, grapes; poultry, beef, dairy products
Industries: Petroleum, mining *(particularly phosphate and iron ore),* tourism, textiles, footwear, food, beverages
Exports: $5.7 billion
commodities: Hydrocarbons, agricultural products, phosphates and chemicals
Imports: $7.7 billion
commodities: Industrial goods and equipment, hydrocarbons, food, consumer goods

DEFENSE:
Defense expenditures: *exchange rate conversion -* $535 *million,* 2.8% *of GDP*

T U R K E Y

GEOGRAPHY:
Location: Southwestern Asia
Area:
total area: 780,580 sq km
land area: 770,760 sq km
Capital city: Ankara
Natural Resources: Antimony, coal, chromium, mercury, copper, borate, sulfur, iron ore

PEOPLE:
Population: 64,566,511
Age structure:
0-14 years: 31%
15-64 years: 63%
65 years & over: 6%
Literacy rate: 82.3% *of total population,*
(males: 91.7%, *females:* 72.4%)
Languages: Turkish *(official),* Kurdish, Arabic
Religions: 99.8%-Muslim *(mostly Sunni),* 0.2%-other *(Christians and Jews)*

VITAL STATISTICS:
Birth rate: 21.83 *(per 1,000 population)*
Death rate: 5.43 *(per 1,000 population)*
Infant mortality rate: 43.2 *(deaths per 1,000 live births)*
Fertility rate: 2.52 *(per woman)*
Life expectancy at birth:
total population: 72.37
(males: 69.95, *females:* 74.91)

GOVERNMENT:
Type of government: Republican Parliamentary Democracy
Independence: October 29, 1923 *(successor state to the Ottoman Empire)*
Leaders:
chief of state: President Suleyman Demirel
head of government: Prime Minister A. Mesut Yilmaz

ECONOMY:
GDP: purchasing power parity - $379.1 billion (1996)
GDP real growth rate: 7%
GDP per capita: $6,100
Inflation Rate: *(consumer prices):* 80% (1996)
National budget:
revenues: $32.9 billion
expenditures: $50.8 billion
External debt: $78.8 billion
Currency: Turkish lira
Labor Force: 21.3 million (1994)
Unemployment rate: 6.3% *(63% officially considered underemployed)* (1996)
Agriculture: Tobacco, cotton, grain, olives, sugar beets, pulses, citrus; livestock
Industries: Textiles, food processing, mining *(coal, chromite, copper, boron),* steel, petroleum, con-

struction, lumber, paper
Exports: $22 billion
  commodities: Textiles and apparel, steel products,
    fruits and vegetables
Imports: $42 billion
  commodities: Machinery, fuels, raw materials, food-
    stuffs

DEFENSE:
Defense expenditures: *exchange rate conversion -
$4.3 billion, and 35% of GDP (note - Figures do not
include about $7 billion for the government's
counterinsurgency effort against the separatist Kur-
distan Workers' Party [PKK]) .*

TURKMENISTAN

GEOGRAPHY:
Location: Central Asia
Area:
  total area: 488,100 sq km
  land area: 488,100 sq km
Capital city: Ashgabat
Natural Resources: Petroleum, natural gas, coal, sul-
fur, salt

PEOPLE:
Population: 4,297,629
Age structure:
  0–14 years: 39%
  15–64 years: 57%
  65 years & over: 4%
Literacy rate: 98% *of total population,*
  (males: 99%, *females:* 97%)
Languages: Turkmen, Russian, Uzbek, other
Religions: 87%-Muslim, 11%-Eastern Orthodox, 2%-
unknown

VITAL STATISTICS:
Birth rate: 26.61 *(per 1,000 population)*
Death rate: 8.65 *(per 1,000 population)*
Infant mortality rate: 72.7 *(deaths per 1,000 live
births)*
Fertility rate: 3.31 *(per woman)*
Life expectancy at birth:
  total population: 61.51
    (males: 57.88, *females:* 65.31)

GOVERNMENT:
Type of government: Republic
Independence: October 27, 1991 *(from the Soviet
Union)*
Leaders:
  chief of state and head of government: President
    and Prime Minister Saparmyrat Niyazov

ECONOMY:
GDP: purchasing power parity - $11.8 billion (1996)
  GDP real growth rate: 0.1%
  GDP per capita: $2,840
Inflation Rate *(consumer prices):* 600% (1996)
National budget:
  revenues: $NA
  expenditures: $NA

External debt: $400 million
Currency: 1 Tukmen manat = 100 tenesi *(introduced
November 1993)*
Labor Force: 1.68 million
Unemployment rate: NA%
Agriculture: Cotton, grain; livestock
Industries: Natural gas, oil, petroleum products, tex-
tiles, food processing
Exports: $1.8 billion
  commodities: Natural gas, cotton, petroleum prod-
    ucts, electricity, textiles, carpets
Imports: $1.3 billion
  commodities: Machinery and parts, grain and food,
    plastics and rubber, consumer durables, textiles

DEFENSE:
Defense expenditures: 4.5 billion manats, 3% of GDP
*(note-Conversion of defense expenditures into US
dollars using current exchange rate could produce
misleading results)*

UGANDA

GEOGRAPHY:
Location: Eastern Africa
Area:
  total area: 236,040 sq km
  land area: 199,710 sq km
Capital city: Kampala
Natural Resources: Copper, cobalt, limestone, salt

PEOPLE:
Population: 22,167,195
Age structure:
  0-14 years: 50%
  15-64 years: 48%
  65 years & over: 2%
Literacy rate: 61.8% *of total population,*
  (males: 73.7%, females: 50.2%)
Languages: English *(official),* Luganda, Swahili, Bantu
  languages, Nilotic languages
Religions: 33%-Roman Catholic, 33%-Protestant,
  16%-Muslim, 18%-indigenous beliefs

VITAL STATISTICS:
Birth rate: 45.08 *(per 1,000 population)* (1997)
Death rate: 20.98 *(per 1,000 population)*
Infant mortality rate: 98.4 *(deaths per 1,000 live
births)*
Fertility rate: 6.52 *(per woman)*
Life expectancy at birth:
  total population: 39.69
    (males: 39.3, *females:* 40.1)

GOVERNMENT:
Type of government: Republic
Independence: October 9, 1962 *(from UK)*
Leaders:
  chief of state: President Lt. General Yoweri Kaguta
    Museveni
  head of government: Prime Minister Kintu Musoke

ECONOMY:
GDP: purchasing power parity - $16.8 billion (1995)

GDP real growth rate: 7.1%
GDP per capita: $900
Inflation Rate *(consumer prices):* 7.3% (1996)
National budget:
revenues: $766.5 million
expenditures: $894.3 million
External debt: $3.4 billion
Currency: 1 Ugandan shilling = 100 cents
Labor Force: 8.361 million (1993)
Unemployment rate: NA%
Agriculture: Coffee, tea, cotton, tobacco, cassava *(tapioca)*, potatoes, corn, millet, pulses; beef, goat meat, milk, poultry
Industries: Sugar, brewing, tobacco, cotton textiles, cement
Exports: $555 million
commodities: Coffee, cotton, tea
Imports: $1.18 billion
commodities: Petroleum products, machinery, cotton piece goods, metals, transportation equipment, food

DEFENSE:
Defense expenditure: *exchange rate conversion* - $56 million, 1.7% *of budget*

UKRAINE

GEOGRAPHY:
Location: Eastern Europe
Area:
total area: 603,700 sq km
land area: 603,700 sq km
Capital city: Kiev
Natural Resources: Iron ore, coal, manganese, natural gas, oil, salt, graphite, titanium, magnesium, kaolin, nickel, mercury, timber

PEOPLE:
Population: 50,125,108
Age structure:
0-14 years: 19%
15-64 years: 67%
65 years & over: 14%
Literacy rate: 98% *of total population,* (*males:* 100%, *females:* 97%)
Languages: Ukrainian, Russian, Romanian, Polish, Hungarian
Religions: Ukranian Orthodox-Moscow Patriarchate, Ukrainian Orthodox-Kiev Patriarchate, Ukrainian Autocephalous Orthodox, Ukrainian Catholic *(Uniate),* Protestant, Jewish

VITAL STATISTICS:
Birth rate: 9.55 *(per 1,000 population)* (1997)
Death rate: 16.26 *(per 1,000 population)*
Infant mortality rate: 21.9 *(deaths per 1,000 live births)*
Fertility rate: 1.36 *(per woman)*
Life expectancy at birth:
total population: 65.77
(*males:* 59.93, *females:* 71.91)

GOVERNMENT:
Type of government: Republic
Independence: December 1, 1991 *(from Soviet Union)*
Leaders:
chief of state: President Leonid D. Kuchma
head of government: Prime Minister Valery Pustovoitenko

ECONOMY:
GDP: purchasing power parity - $161.1 billion (1996)
GDP real growth rate: -10%
GDP per capita: $3,170
Inflation Rate *(consumer prices):* 40%
National budget:
revenues: $NA
expenditures: $NA
External debt: $8.8 billion
Currency: hryvnis = 100 hryvni
Labor Force: 23 million (1996)
Unemployment rate: 1% *(officially registered; large numbers of underemployed)*
Agriculture: Grain, sugar beets, vegetables; meat, milk
Industries: Coal, electric power, ferrous and nonferrous metals, machinery and transport equipment, chemicals, food-processing *(especially sugar)*
Exports: $18.6 billion
commodities: Coal, electric power, ferrous and nonferrous metals, chemicals, machinery and transport equipment, grain, meat
Imports: $19.4 billion
commodities: Energy, machinery and parts, transportation equipment, chemicals, textiles

DEFENSE:
Defense expenditures: 1.35 billion hryvnis, less than 2% of GDP *(Ukrainian government's forecast for 1996) (note-Conversion of defense expenditures into US dollars using the current exchange rate could produce misleading results)*

UNITED ARAB EMIRATES

GEOGRAPHY:
Location: Middle East
Area:
total area: 82,880 sq km
land area: 82,880 sq km
Capital city: Abu Dhabi
Natural Resources: Petroleum, natural gas

PEOPLE:
Population: 2,303,088
Age structure:
0-14 years: 32%
15-64 years: 66%
65 years & over: 2%
Literacy rate: 79.2% *of total population,* (*males:* 78.9%, *females:* 79.8%)
Languages: Arabic *(official),* Persian, English, Hindu, Urdu

Religions: 96%-Muslim *(Shi'a-16%)*, 4%-Christian, Hindu, other

VITAL STATISTICS:
Birth rate: 18.46 *(per 1,000 population)* (1997)
Death rate: 3.01 *(per 1,000 population)*
Infant mortality rate: 15.5 *(deaths per 1,000 live births)*
Fertility rate: 3.62 *(per woman)*
Life expectancy at birth:
   total population: 74.64
      (males: 73.18, *females:* 76.17)

GOVERNMENT:
Type of government: Federation with specified powers delegated to the UAE central government and other powers reserved to member emirates
Independence: December 2, 1971 *(from UK)*
Leaders:
   chief of state: Sheik Zayed bin Sultan Al-Nahyan
   head of government: Prime Minister Maktoum bin Rashid Al-Maktoum

ECONOMY:
GDP: purchasing power parity - $72.9 billion (1996)
   GDP real growth rate: 1.4%
   GDP per capita: $23,800
Inflation Rate *(consumer prices):* 5.2%
National budget:
   revenues: $5.1 billion
   expenditures: $5.4 billion
External debt: $14 billion
Currency: 1 Emirian dirham = 100 fils
Labor Force: 794,400 (1994)
Unemployment rate: NA%
Agriculture: Dates, vegetables, watermelons; poultry, eggs, dairy products; fish
Industries: Petroleum, fishing, petrochemicals, construction materials, some boat building, handicrafts, pearling
Exports: $31.3 billion
   commodities: Crude oil, natural gas, re-exports, dried fish, dates
Imports: $22.3 billion
   commodities: Manufactured goods, machinery and transport equipment, food

DEFENSE:
Defense expenditures: *exchange rate conversion -* $1.59 *billion,* 4.3% *of GDP*

UNITED KINGDOM

GEOGRAPHY:
Location: Western Europe
Area:
   total area: 244,820 sq km
   land area: 241,590 sq km
Capital city: London
Natural Resources: Coal, petroleum, natural gas, tin, limestone, iron ore, salt, clay, chalk, gypsum, lead, silica

PEOPLE:
Population: 58,970,119

Age structure:
   0-14 years: 19%
   15-64 years: 65%
   65 years & over: 16%
Literacy rate: 99% *of total population*
Languages: English, Welsh *(about 26% of the population of Wales),* Scottish form of Gaelic *(about 60,000 in Scotland)*
Religions: 27 million-Anglican, 9 million-Roman Catholic, 1 million-Muslim, 800,000-Presbyterian, 760,000-Methodist, 400,000-Sikh, 350,000-Hindu, 300,000-Jewish

VITAL STATISTICS:
Birth rate: 11.83 *(per 1,000 population)* (1997)
Death rate: 11.83 *(per 1,000 population)*
Infant mortality rate: 6 *(deaths per 1,000 live births)*
Fertility rate: 1.65 *(per woman)*
Life expectancy at birth:
   total population: 77.25
      (males: 74.67, *females:* 79.96)

GOVERNMENT:
Type of government: Constitutional Monarchy
Independence: January 1, 1801 *(United Kingdom established)*
Leaders:
   chief of state: Queen Elizabeth II
   head of government: Prime Minister Tony Blair

ECONOMY:
GDP: purchasing power parity - $1.19 trillion (1996)
   GDP real growth rate: 2.4%
   GDP per capita: $20,400
Inflation Rate *(consumer prices):* 2.6%
National budget:
   revenues: $421.5 billion
   expenditures: 474.9 billion
External debt: $16.2 billion
Currency: 1 British pound = 100 pence
Labor Force: 28.1 million (1992)
Unemployment rate: 6.7% (1996)
Agriculture: Cereals, oilseed, potatoes, vegetables; cattle, sheep, poultry, fish
Industries: Production machinery including machine tools, electric power equipment, automation equipment, railroad equipment, shipbuilding, aircraft, motor vehicles and parts, electronics and communication equipment, metals, chemicals, coal, petroleum, paper and paper products, food processing, textiles, clothing and other consumer goods
Exports: $240.4 billion
   commodities: Manufactured goods, machinery, fuels, chemicals, semifinished goods, transportation equipment
Imports: $258.8 billion
   commodities: Manufactured goods, machinery, semifinished goods, foodstuffs, consumer goods

DEFENSE:
Defense expenditures: *exchange rate conversion -* $35.1 *billion,* 3.1% *of GDP*

UNITED STATES

GEOGRAPHY:
Location: North America
Area:
total area: 9,629,091 sq km
land area: 9,158,960 sq km
Capital city: Washington D.C.
Natural Resources: Coal, copper, lead, molybdenum, phosphates, uranium, bauxite, gold, iron, mercury, nickel, potash, silver, tungsten, zinc, petroleum, natural gas, timber

PEOPLE:
Population: 268,922,000
Age structure:
0-14 years: 22%
15-64 years: 65%
65 years & over: 13%
Literacy rate: 97% *of total population,*
(males: 97%, *females:* 97%)
Languages: English, Spanish *(spoken by a sizable minority)*
Religions: 58%-Protestant, 26%-Roman Catholic, 1%-Jewish, 9%-other, 6%-none

VITAL STATISTICS:
Birth rate: 14.5 *(per 1,000 population)*
Death rate: 8.6 *(per 1,000 population)*
Infant mortality rate: 7.0 *(deaths per 1,000 live births)*
Fertility rate: 2.06 *(per woman)*
Life expectancy at birth:
total population: 76.1
(males: 73.1, *females:* 79.1)

GOVERNMENT:
Type of government: Federal Republic; strong democratic tradition
Independence: July 4, 1776 *(from England)*
Leaders:
chief of state & head of government: President Bill Clinton

ECONOMY:
GDP: purchasing power parity - $7.61 trillion (1996)
GDP real growth rate: 2.4%
GDP per capita: $28,600
Inflation Rate *(consumer prices):* 1.7% (1997)
National budget:
revenues: $1.704 trillion (1998)
expenditures: $1.665 trillion
Currency: 1 United States dollar = 100 cents
Labor Force: 136,297,000 *(includes unemployed)* (1997)
Unemployment rate: 4.9% (1997)
Agriculture: Wheat, other grains, corn, fruits, vegetables, cotton; beef, pork, poultry, dairy products; forest products; fish
Industries: Leading industrial power in the world, highly diversified and technologically advanced; petroleum, steel, motor vehicles, aerospace, telecommunications, chemicals, electronics, food processing, consumer goods, lumber, mining
Exports: $678.2 billion (goods) and $253.2 billion (services)
commodities: Capital goods, automobiles, industrial supplies and raw materials, consumer goods, agricultural products
Imports: $877.1 billion (goods) and $167.9 billion (services)
commodities: Crude oil and refined petroleum products, machinery, automobiles, consumer goods, industrial raw materials, food and beverages

DEFENSE:
Defense expenditures: *exchange rate conversion -* $267.2 *billion,* 3.4% *of GDP*

URUGUAY

GEOGRAPHY:
Location: Southern South America
Area:
total area: 176,220 sq km
land area: 173,620 sq km
Capital city: Montevideo
Natural Resources: Fertile soil, hydropower potential, minor minerals

PEOPLE:
Population: 3,284,841
Age structure:
0-14 years: 24%
15-64 years: 63%
65 years & over: 13%
Literacy rate: 97.3% *of total population,*
(males: 96.9%, *females:* 97.7%)
Languages: Spanish, Brazilero *(Portuguese-Spanish mix on the Brazilian frontier)*
Religions: 66%-Roman Catholic *(less than one-half of the adult population attends church regularly),* 2%-Protestant, 2%-Jewish, 30%-nonprofessing or other

VITAL STATISTICS:
Birth rate: 16.98 *(per 1,000 population)* (1997)
Death rate: 8.97 *(per 1,000 population)*
Infant mortality rate: 14.7 *(deaths per 1,000 live births)*
Fertility rate: 2.3 *(per woman)*
Life expectancy at birth:
total population: 75.23
(males: 72.09, *females:* 78.55)

GOVERNMENT:
Type of government: Republic
Independence: August 25, 1828 *(from Brazil)*
Leaders:
chief of state & head of government: President Julio Maria Sanguinetti

ECONOMY:
GDP: purchasing power parity - $26 billion (1996)
GDP real growth rate: 4.9%
GDP per capita: $8,000

Inflation Rate *(consumer prices)*: 24.4% (1996)
National budget:
revenues: $3.03 billion
expenditures: $3.37 billion
External debt: $4.95 billion
Currency: 1 Uruguayan peso = 100 centesimos
Labor Force: 1.436 million (1996)
Unemployment rate: 12% (1996)
Agriculture: Wheat, rice, corn, sorghum; livestock; fishing
Industries: Meat processing, wool and hides, sugar, textiles, footwear, leather apparel, tires, cement, petroleum refining, wine
Exports: $2.4 billion
commodities: Wool and textiles, manufactured goods, beef and other animal products, leather, rice
Imports: $3.3 billion
commodities: Machinery and equipment, vehicles, chemicals, minerals, plastics

DEFENSE:
Defense expenditures: *exchange rate conversion -* $256 *million*, 1.5% *of GDP*

UZBEKISTAN

GEOGRAPHY:
Location: Central Asia
Area:
total area: 447,400 sq km
land area: 425,400 sq km
Capital city: Tashkent
Natural Resources: Natural gas, petroleum, coal, gold, uranium, silver, copper, lead and zinc, tungsten, molybdenum

PEOPLE:
Population: 23,784,321
Age structure:
0-14 years: 39%
15-64 years: 57%
65 years & over: 4%
Literacy rate: 97%, *of total population*, *(males:* 98%, *females:* 96%)
Languages: Uzbek, Russian, Tajik, other
Religions: 88%-Muslim *(mostly Sunnis)*, 9%-Eastern Orthodox, 3%-other

VITAL STATISTICS:
Birth rate: 24.02 *(per 1,000 population)* (1997)
Death rate: 7.63 *(per 1,000 population)*
Infant mortality rate: 70.5 *(deaths per 1,000 live births)*
Fertility rate: 2.92 *(per woman)*
Life expectancy at birth:
total population: 64.31
(males: 60.69, *females:* 68.11)

GOVERNMENT:
Type of government: Republic
Independence: August 31, 1991 *(from Soviet Union)*
Leaders:

chief of state: President Islam A. Karimov
head of government: Prime Minister Otkir T. Sultanov

ECONOMY:
GDP: purchasing power parity - $57 billion (1996)
GDP real growth rate: 1.6%
GDP per capita: $2,430
Inflation Rate *(consumer prices):* 55% (1996)
National budget:
revenues: $NA
expenditures: $NA
External debt: $1.285 billion
Currency: introduced provisional som-coupons November 10, 1993 which circulated parallel to the Russian rubles; became the sole legal currency January 31, 1994; was replaced in July 1994 by the som currency
Labor Force: 8.2 million (1995)
Unemployment rate: 0.3% *(includes only officially registered unemployed; large numbers of underemployed workers)* (1996)
Agriculture: Cotton, vegetable, fruits, grains; livestock
Industries: Textiles, food processing, machine building, metallurgy, natural gas
Exports: $3.2 billion
commodities: Cotton, gold, natural gas, mineral fertilizers, ferrous metals, textiles, food products
Imports: $3.2 billion
commodities: Grain, machinery and parts, consumer durables, other foods

DEFENSE:
Defense expenditures: 164 *million soms*, 3.7% *of GDP (note - conversion of defense expenditures into US dollars using the current exchange rate could produce misleading results)*

VENEZUELA

GEOGRAPHY:
Location: Northern South America
Area:
total area: 912,050 sq km
land area: 882,050 sq km
Capital city: Caracas
Natural Resources: Petroleum, natural gas, iron ore, gold, bauxite, other minerals, hydropower, diamonds

PEOPLE:
Population: 22,803,409
Age structure:
0-14 years: 34%
15-64 years: 61%
65 years & over: 5%
Literacy rate: 91.1% *of total population,* *(males:* 91.8%, *females:* 90.3%)
Languages: Spanish *(official)*, native dialects spoken by about 200,000 Amerindians in the remote interior
Religions: 96%-Roman Catholic *(nominally)*, 2%-

Protestant

VITAL STATISTICS:
Birth rate: 23.67 *(per 1,000 population)* (1997)
Death rate: 5.03 *(per 1,000 population)*
Infant mortality rate: 28.5 *(deaths per 1,000 live births)*
Fertility rate: 2.78 *(per woman)*
Life expectancy at birth:
total population: 72.37
(males: 69.4, *females:* 75.58)

GOVERNMENT:
Type of government: Republic
Independence: July 5, 1811 *(from Spain)*
Leaders:
chief of state & head of government: President Rafael Caldera

ECONOMY:
GDP: purchasing power parity - $197 billion (1996)
GDP real growth rate: -1.6%
GDP per capita: $9,000
Inflation Rate *(consumer prices):* 103% (1993)
National budget:
revenues: $11.99 billion
expenditures: $11.48 billion
External debt: $26.5 billion
Currency: 1 bolivar = 100 centimos
Labor Force: 8.8 million (1993)
Unemployment rate: 13% (1996)
Agriculture: Corn, sorghum, sugarcane, rice, bananas, vegetables, coffee; beef, pork, milk, eggs; fish
Industries: Petroleum, iron ore mining, construction materials, food processing, textiles, steel, aluminum, motor vehicle assembly
Exports: $22.8 billion
commodities: Petroleum, bauxite and aluminum, steel, chemicals, agricultural products, basic manufactured goods
Imports: $10.2 billion
commodities: Raw materials, machinery and equipment, transport equipment, construction materials

DEFENSE:
Defense expenditures: *exchange rate conversion -* $902 *million,* 1.4% *of GDP*

VIETNAM

GEOGRAPHY:
Location: Southeastern Asia
Area:
total area: 329,560 sq km
land area: 325,360 sq km
Capital city: Hanoi
Natural Resources: Phosphates, coal, manganese, bauxite, chromate, offshore oil deposits, forests

PEOPLE:
Population: 76,236,259
Age structure:
0-14 years: 36%

15-64 years: 59%
65 years & over: 5%
Literacy rate: 93.7% *of total population,* *(males:* 96.5%, *females:* 91.2%)
Languages: Vietnamese *(official),* French, Chinese, English, Khmer, tribal language *(Mon-Khmer and Malayo-Polynesian)*
Religions: Buddhist, Taoist, Roman Catholic, indigenous beliefs, Islam, Protestant

VITAL STATISTICS:
Birth rate: 22.3 *(per 1,000 population)* (1997)
Death rate: 6.8 *(per 1,000 population)*
Infant mortality rate: 37.2 *(deaths per 1,000 live births)*
Fertility rate: 2.6 *(per woman)*
Life expectancy at birth:
total population: 67.38
(males: 65.03, *females:* 69.86)

GOVERNMENT:
Type of government: Communist State
Independence: September 2, 1945 *(from France)*
Leaders:
chief of state: President Tran Duc Luong
head of government: Prime Minister Phan Van Khai

ECONOMY:
GDP: purchasing power parity - $108.7 billion (1996)
GDP real growth rate: 9.4%
GDP per capita: $1,470
Inflation Rate *(consumer prices):* 4.5% (1996)
National budget:
revenues: $4.67 billion
expenditures: $5 billion
External debt: $7.3 billion
Currency: 1 new dong = 100 xu
Labor Force: 32.7 million (1990)
Unemployment rate: 25% (1995)
Agriculture: Paddy rice, corn, potatoes, rubber, soybeans, coffee, tea, bananas; poultry, pigs; fish *(annual catch of 943,100 metric tons)*
Industries: Food processing, textiles, machine building, mining, cement, chemical fertilizer, glass, tires, oil
Exports: $7.1 billion
commodities: Crude oil, rice, marine products, coffee, rubber, tea; garments
Imports: $11.1 billion
commodities: Petroleum products, machinery and equipment, steel products, fertilizer, raw cotton, grain

DEFENSE:
Defense expenditures: *exchange rate conversions -* $544 *million,* 2.7% *of GDP*

YEMEN

GEOGRAPHY:
Location: Middle East
Area:
total area: 527,970 sq km

land area: 527,970 sq km
Capital city: San'a
Natural Resources: Petroleum, fish, rock salt, marble, small deposits of coal, gold, lead, nickel, copper, fertile soil in west

PEOPLE:
Population: 16,387,963
Age structure:
0–14 years: 48%
15–64 years: 49%
65 years & over: 3%
Literacy rate: 38% *of total population,*
(*males:* 53%, *females:* 26%)
Languages: Arabic
Religions: Muslim including Sha'fi *(Sunni)* and Zaydi *(Shi'a),* small numbers of Jewish, Christian, and Hindu

VITAL STATISTICS:
Birth rate: 44.83 *(per 1,000 population)* (1997)
Death rate: 9.17 *(per 1,000 population)*
Infant mortality rate: 68.1 *(deaths per 1,000 live births)*
Fertility rate: 7.18 *(per woman)*
Life expectancy at birth:
total population: 60.31
(*males:* 58.9, *females:* 61.78)

GOVERNMENT:
Type of government: Republic
Independence: May 22, 1990 Republic of Yemen was established with the merger of the Yemen Arab Republic {Yemen *(San'a)* or North Yemen} and the Marxist-dominated People's Democratic Republic of Yemen {Yemen *(Aden)* or South Yemen}; previously North Yemen had become independent in November 1918 *(from the Ottoman Empire)* and South Yemen had become independent on November 30, 1967 *(from the UK)*
Leaders:
chief of state: President Lt. Gen. Ali Abdallah Salih
head of government: Prime Minister Dr. Abd al-Karim Iryani

ECONOMY:
GDP: purchasing power parity - $39.1 billion (1996)
GDP real growth rate: 2.8%
GDP per capita: $2,900
Inflation Rate *(consumer prices):* 85% (1996)
National budget:
revenues: $3 billion
expenditures: $3.1 billion
External debt: $8 billion
Currency: Yameni rial *(new currency)*
Labor Force: *(no reliable estimates exist)*
Unemployment rate: 30% (1995)
Agriculture: Grain, fruits, vegetables, qat*(mildly narcotic shrub),* coffee, cotton; dairy products, poultry, meat; fish
Industries: Crude oil production and petroleum refining; small-scale production of cotton textiles and leather goods; food processing; handicrafts; small aluminum products factory; cement

Exports: $2.5 billion
commodities: Crude oil, cotton, coffee, hides, vegetables, dried and salted fish
Imports: $2.2 billion
commodities: Textiles and other manufactured consumer goods, petroleum products, sugar, grain, flour, other foodstuffs, cement, machinery, chemicals

DEFENSE:
Defense expenditures: $NA, NA% of GDP

ZAMBIA

GEOGRAPHY:
Location: Southern Africa
Area:
total area: 752,610 sq km
land area: 740,720 sq km
Capital city: Lusaka
Natural Resources: Copper, cobalt, zinc, lead, coal, emeralds, gold, silver, uranium, hydropower potential

PEOPLE:
Population: 9,460,736
Age structure:
0–14 years: 49%
15–64 years: 48%
65 years & over: 3%
Literacy rate: 78.2% *of total population,*
(*males:* 85.6%, *females:* 71.3%)
Languages: English*(official),* major vernaculars- Bemba, Kaonda, Lozi, Lunda, Luvale, Nyanja, Tonga, and about 70 other indigenous languages
Religions: 50%–75%-Christian, 24%–49%-Muslim and Hindu, 1%-indigenous beliefs

VITAL STATISTICS:
Birth rate: 44.37 *(per 1,000 population)* (1997)
Death rate: 24.18 *(per 1,000 population)*
Infant mortality rate: 96.5 *(deaths per 1,000 live births)*
Fertility rate: 6.48 *(per woman)*
Life expectancy at birth:
total population: 35.58
(*males:* 35.58, *females:* 35.59)

GOVERNMENT:
Type of government: Republic
Independence: October 24, 1964 *(from UK)*
Leaders:
chief of state & head of government: President Frederick Chiluba

ECONOMY:
GDP: purchasing power parity - $9.7 billion (1996)
GDP real growth rate: 6.4%
GDP per capita: $1,060
Inflation Rate *(consumer prices):* 34% (1995)
National budget:
revenues: $888 million
expenditures: $835 million
External debt: $7.2 billion

Currency: 1 Zambian kwacha = 100 ngwee
Labor Force: 3.4 million
Unemployment rate: 22%
Agriculture: Corn, sorghum, rice, peanuts, sunflower seed, tobacco, cotton, sugarcane, cassava *(tapioca)*; cattle, goats, beef, eggs
Industries: Copper mining and processing, construction, foodstuffs, beverages, chemicals, textiles, fertilizer
Exports: $975 billion
commodities: Copper, zinc, cobalt, lead, tobacco
Imports: $990 million
commodities: Machinery, transportation equipment, foodstuffs, fuels, manufactures

DEFENSE:
Defense expenditures: *exchange rate conversion* -$96 million, 2.7% of GDP

ZIMBABWE

GEOGRAPHY:
Location: Southern Africa
Area:
total area: 390,580 sq km
land area: 386,670 sq km
Capital city: Harare
Natural Resources: Coal, chromium ore, asbestos, gold, nickel, copper, iron ore, vanadium, lithium, tin, platinum group metals

PEOPLE:
Population: 11,044,147
Age structure:
0-14 years: 43%
15-64 years: 54%
65 years & over: 3%
Literacy rate: 85% *of total population*, *(males:* 90%, *females:* 80%)
Languages: English *(official)*, Shona, Sindebele *(the language of the Ndebele, sometimes called Ndebele)*, numerous but minor tribal dialects
Religions: 50%-syncretic *(part Christan, part indigenous beliefs)*, 25%-Christian, 24%-indigenous beliefs, 1%-Muslim and other

VITAL STATISTICS:
Birth rate: 31.65 *(per 1,000 population)* (1997)

Death rate: 31.65 *(per 1,000 population)*
Infant mortality rate: 72.6 *(deaths per 1,000 live births)*
Fertility rate: 3.94 *(per woman)*
Life expectancy at birth:
total population: 40.84
(males: 40.85, *females:* 40.85)

GOVERNMENT:
Type of government: Parliamentary Democracy
Independence: April 18, 1980 *(from UK)*
Leaders:
chief of state & head of government: Executive President Robert Gabriel Mugabe

ECONOMY:
GDP: purchasing power parity - $26.4 billion (1996)
GDP real growth rate: 5.5%
GDP per captia: $2,340
Inflation Rate *(consumer prices):* 21.7% (1996)
National budget:
revenues: $2.5 billion
expenditures: $2.9 billion
External debt: $4.4 billion
Currency: 1 Zimbabwean dollar = 100 cents
Labor Force: 4.228 million (1993)
Unemployment rate: at least 45% (1994)
Agriculture: Corn, cotton, tobacco, wheat, coffee, sugarcane, peanuts; cattle, sheep, goats, pigs
Industries: Mining, steel, clothing and footwear, chemicals, foodstuffs, fertilizer, beverages, transportation equipment, wood products
Exports: $2.4 billion
commodities: Agricultural *(tobacco and other)*, manufactured goods, gold, ferrochrome, textiles
Imports: $2.2 billion
commodities: Machinery and transportation equipment, other manufactured goods, chemicals, fuels

DEFENSE:
Defense expenditures: *exchange rate conversion -* $236 *million*, 3.4% *of GDP*

Sources: CIA World Factbook, *U.S. Census Bureau and the U.S. embassies of the countries.*

Compiled by Suzanne Vranica

GLOBAL ECONOMY

Top 20 Economies Ranked by Real 1997 GDP (Billions of 1995 U.S. $)

	1997
United States	$7,815.77
Japan	$5,390.59
Germany	$2,502.85
France	$1,595.26
United Kingdom	$1,172.53
Italy	$1,111.69
China	$828.02
Brazil	$778.90
Canada	$611.27
Spain	$591.65
Korea	$515.53
Netherlands	$424.30
Australia	$377.81
India	$364.45
Russia	$340.50
Mexico	$322.63
Argentina	$318.13
Switzerland	$309.71
Taiwan	$293.57
Belgium	$285.37

Top 20 Economies Ranked by Real 1997 GDP per Capita (1995 U.S. $)

	1997
Switzerland	$43,479.93
Japan	$42,736.09
Denmark	$36,656.21
Norway	$36,206.64
Singapore	$31,600.89
Germany	$30,493.78
Austria	$29,485.56
United States	$29,142.63
Belgium	$28,002.34
France	$27,228.94
Netherlands	$27,179.38
Sweden	$26,941.52
Finland	$26,894.44
Hong Kong	$23,955.67
Australia	$20,380.37
Ireland	$20,304.91
Canada	$20,121.92
United Kingdom	$19,893.68
Italy	$19,378.54
Israel	$16,754.10

Top 20 Economies Ranked by Real GDP % Growth in 1997

	1997
Georgia	10.6%
Kyrgyzstan	10.4%
Belarus	10.0%
Ireland	9.8%
Estonia	9.5%
China	8.8%
Yugoslavia	8.8%
Malaysia	7.8%
Singapore	7.8%
Argentina	7.3%
Peru	7.2%
Turkey	7.2%
Chile	7.1%
Mexico	7.0%
Latvia	7.0%
Poland	6.9%
Taiwan	6.8%
Croatia	6.5%
Slovakia	6.5%
Finland	6.0%

Top 20 Economies Ranked by Real GDP per Capita % Growth in 1997

	1997
Georgia	10.5%
Estonia	10.3%
Belarus	10.3%
Ireland	8.8%
Yugoslavia	8.4%
Latvia	8.2%
Kyrgyzstan	8.1%
China	7.6%
Turkey	7.4%
Poland	6.9%
Slovakia	6.3%
Lithuania	6.1%
Argentina	5.9%
Chile	5.8%
Taiwan	5.7%
Singapore	5.7%
Croatia	5.7%
Finland	5.7%
Malaysia	5.3%
Peru	5.1%

20 Countries with Largest 1997 Trade Deficit (billions of current U.S. dollars)

	1997
United States	$-197.95
United Kingdom	$-21.25
Hong Kong	$-20.50
Greece	$-18.26
Turkey	$-15.10
Spain	$-13.42
India	$-11.71
Poland	$-11.27
Philippines	$-10.07
Portugal	$-9.77
Egypt	$-8.99
Brazil	$-8.48
Austria	$-7.40
Israel	$-7.33
Croatia	$-4.93
Thailand	$-4.90
Czech	$-4.44
Ukraine	$-4.10
Korea	$-3.87
Argentina	$-3.43

20 Countries with Largest 1997 Trade Surplus (billions of current U.S. dollars)

	1997
Japan	$102.26
Germany	$70.18
Italy	$47.11
China	$40.40
France	$27.89
Saudi Arabia	$25.38
Russia	$19.80
Sweden	$18.14
Ireland	$16.79
Canada	$16.75
Taiwan	$13.99
Netherlands	$12.82
Indonesia	$11.48
Norway	$10.79
Finland	$9.94
Venezuela	$9.78
Kuwait	$6.13
Belgium	$5.22
Nigeria	$4.72
Denmark	$4.69

Source: Standard & Poor's DRI

Riskiest Countries with Which to Do Business:

- Democratic Republic of the Congo
- Albania
- Myanmar (Burma)
- Yugoslavia
- Belarus
- Tajikistan
- Ukraine
- Nigeria
- Sierra Leone
- Nicaragua

Least Risky Countries with Which to Do Business:

- United States
- Denmark
- Luxembourg
- France
- Germany
- United Kingdom
- Canada
- Netherlands
- Austria
- Switzerland

Source: International Risk and Payment Review, Dun & Bradstreet UK Ltd.

Top Countries for Tourism

World's Top 25 Tourism Destinations, 1997
International tourist arrivals (excluding same-day visitors)
(Thousands of arrivals)

	Country	Arrivals 1997	% change 1997/96	% of total 1997		Country	Arrivals 1997	% change 1997/96	% of total 1997
1	France	66,864	7.1%	10.9%	14	Russian Federation	15,350	5.2%	2.5%
2	United States	48,409	4.1	7.9	15	Switzerland	11,077	4.5	1.8
3	Spain	43,378	7.0	7.1	16	Hong Kong	10,406	-11.1	1.7
4	Italy	34,087	3.8	5.6	17	Greece	10,246	11.0	1.7
5	United Kingdom	25,960	2.6	4.2	18	Portugal	10,100	3.8	1.7
6	China	23,770	4.4	3.9	19	Turkey	9,040	13.5	1.5
7	Poland	19,514	0.5	3.2	20	Thailand	7,263	1.0	1.2
8	Mexico	19,351	-9.6	3.2	21	Netherlands	6,674	1.4	1.1
9	Canada	17,610	1.6	2.9	22	Singapore	6,542	-1.0	1.1
10	Czech Republic	17,400	2.4	2.8	23	Malaysia	6,211	-13.0	1.0
11	Hungary	17,248	-16.6	2.8	24	Belgium	5,875	0.8	1.0
12	Austria	16,646	-2.6	2.7	25	Ireland	5,540	4.9	0.9
13	Germany	15,837	4.2	2.6					

World's Top 25 Tourism Earners, 1997
International tourism receipts (excluding transport)
(US$ million)

	Country	Receipts 1997	% change 1997/96	% of total 1997		Country	Receipts 1997	% change 1997/96	% of total 1997
1	United States	$75,056	7.4%	16.9%	13	Singapore	$7,993	0.4%	1.8%
2	Italy	30,000	-0.1	6.8	14	Switzerland	7,960	-10.5	1.8
3	France	28,316	-0.1	6.4	15	Mexico	7,593	9.5	1.7
4	Spain	26,595	-3.9	6.0	16	Turkey	7,000	17.4	1.6
5	United Kingdom	20,569	6.6	4.6	17	Russian Federation	6,669	-3.0	1.5
6	Germany	16,418	-6.5	3.7	18	Netherlands	6,597	5.5	1.5
7	Austria	12,393	-11.4	2.8	19	Indonesia	6,589	8.2	1.5
8	China	12,074	18.4	2.7	20	Belgium	5,997	1.8	1.4
9	Australia	9,324	5.8	2.1	21	Korea Republic	5,200	-4.2	1.2
10	Hong Kong	9,242	-14.7	2.1	22	Argentina	5,069	10.9	1.1
11	Canada	8,928	0.7	2.0	23	Japan	4,322	6.0	1.0
12	Thailand	8,700	0.4	2.0	24	Portugal	4,264	0.0	1.0
12	Poland	8,700	3.6	2.0	25	Malaysia	3,850	-1.9	0.9

Source: World Tourism Organization

World Geography: Earth's Extremes

The Earth

Mass:	5,974,000,000,000,000,000,000 metric tons
Area:	510,066,000 sq km
Land:	148,429,000 sq km (29.1%)
Water:	361,637,000 sq km (70.9%)

The Continents

	Area (sq km)	Percent of Earth's Land
Asia	44,579,000	30.0
Africa	30,065,000	20.3
North America	24,256,000	16.3
South America	17,819,000	12.0
Antarctica	13,209,000	8.9
Europe	9,938,000	6.7
Australia	7,687,000	5.2

Highest Point on Each Continent

		Meters
1	Everest, *Asia*	8,848
2	Aconcagua, *South America*	6,960
3	McKinley (Denali), *North America*	6,194
4	Kilimanjaro, *Africa*	5,895
5	El'brus, *Europe*	5,642
6	Vinson Massif, *Antarctica*	4,897
7	Kosciusko, *Australia*	2,228

Lowest Surface Point on Each Continent

			Meters
1	Dead Sea, *Asia*		-408
2	Lake Assal, *Africa*		-156
3	Death Valley, *North America*		-86
4	Valdés Peninsula, *South America*		-40
5	Caspian Sea, *Europe*		-28
6	Lake Eyre, *Australia*		-16
7	Antarctica	(Ice covered)	-2,538

The Oceans

	Area (sq km)	Percent of Earth's Water Area
Pacific	166,241,000	46.0
Atlantic	86,557,000	23.9
Indian	73,427,000	20.3
Arctic	9,485,000	2.6

Deepest Point in Each Ocean

		Meters
1	Challenger Deep, Mariana Trench, *Pacific*	10,920
2	Puerto Rico Trench, *Atlantic*	8,605
3	Java Trench, *Indian*	7,125
4	Eurasia Basin, *Arctic*	5,122

Major Seas

		Area (sq km)	Average Depth (meters)
1	South China	2,974,600	1,464
2	Caribbean	2,515,900	2,575
3	Mediterranean	2,510,000	1,501
4	Bering	2,261,100	1,491
5	Gulf of Mexico	1,507,600	1,615
6	Sea of Okhotsk	1,392,100	973
7	Sea of Japan	1,012,900	1,667
8	Hudson Bay	730,100	93
9	East China	664,600	189
10	Andaman	564,900	1,118
11	Black	507,900	1,191
12	Red	453,000	538

Major Islands

		Area (sq km)
1	Greenland	2,175,600
2	New Guinea	792,500
3	Borneo	725,500
4	Madagascar	587,000
5	Baffin	507,500
6	Sumatra	427,300
7	Honshu	227,400
8	Great Britain	218,100
9	Victoria	217,300
10	Ellesmere	196,200
11	Celebes	178,700
12	South (New Zealand)	151,000
13	Java	126,700
14	North (New Zealand)	114,000
15	Newfoundland	108,900

Major Lakes

		Area (sq km)	Greatest Depth (meters)
1	Caspian Sea, *Europe-Asia*	371,000	1,025
2	Superior, *North America*	82,100	406
3	Victoria, *Africa*	69,500	82
4	Huron, *North America*	59,600	229
5	Michigan, *North America*	57,800	281
6	Tanganyika, *Africa*	32,900	1,470
7	Baikal, *Asia*	31,500	1,637
8	Great Bear, *North America*	31,300	446
9	Aral Sea, *Asia*	30,700	51
10	Malawi, *Africa*	28,900	695

Other Superlatives

Highest Waterfall: Angel, Venezuela; 979 m

Largest Canyon: Grand Canyon, Colorado River, Arizona; 446 km long along river, 549m to 29 km wide, about 1.6 km deep

Most Predictable Geyser: Old Faithful, Wyoming; annual average interval 60 to 79 minutes

Longest Reef: Great Barrier Reef, Australia; 2,012 km

Greatest Tides: Bay of Fundy, Nova Scotia; 16m

Largest Desert: Sahara, Africa; 9,000,000 sq km

Biggest Cave: Mammoth-Flint Ridge cave system, Kentucky; more than 531 km of passageways

Longest Rivers

		Length (km)
1	Nile, *Africa*	6,825
2	Amazon, *South America*	6,437
3	Chang Jiang (Yangtze), *Asia*	6,380
4	Mississippi-Missouri, *North America*	5,971
5	Yenisey-Angara, *Asia*	5,536
6	Huang (Yellow), *Asia*	5,464
7	Ob-Irtysh, *Asia*	5,410
8	Amur, *Asia*	4,416
9	Lena, *Asia*	4,400
10	Congo (Zaire), *Africa*	4,370
11	MacKenzie-Peace, *North America*	4,241
12	Mekong, *Asia*	4,184
13	Niger, *Africa*	4,170

Source: National Geographic Society

LIVING IN AMERICA

Calvin Klein's advertisements have long reflected the darker side of American life, but he has never seemed more on target than with his latest campaign.

This time Mr. Klein has tapped into people's feelings of alienation at the turn of the millennium. His stark black-and-white ads show fashion models together in body—but hardly in spirit. They resemble statues as they pose stiffly with arms at their sides and gaze coldly away from each other. "There's a decided disconnect being communicated in the ads, reflecting the times," says Carol Moog, a psychologist in suburban Philadelphia. "The models have a vacant look. And unlike Calvin Klein's past ads, these men and women don't even have a narcissistic glow to them."

Call it America the Aloof. At a time when communications technology is at its peak, Americans are feeling less connected than ever. According to most social barometers, people have grown increasingly distant from one another during the 1990s, accelerating a trend that began in the 1950s. We are no longer a nation of joiners, whether it be a labor union, fraternal organization or volunteer group. We don't bother getting to know our neighbors well, quickly moving on to the next cul-de-sac. We do our banking at ATMs and shop on-line, never dealing with real live tellers and salesclerks. We spend much of our time alone in cars and devote most of our leisure time to the television or computer. And when we do engage in other pastimes, they tend to be of a solitary nature—reading, gardening, fishing.

"More and more households are totally abandoned during the day," says Tom W.

Smith, director of the General Social Survey at the National Opinion Research Center at the University of Chicago. "It used to be that stay-at-home wives got to know other stay-at-home wives during the day, and then they would get together as couples in the evening." But he notes that only 20 percent of people said they frequently spent social evenings with a neighbor in 1996, down from nearly a third in 1974.

People have partly replaced neighborhood socializing with more interaction with co-workers. The General Social Survey found that the percentage of people who say they socialize often with workplace colleagues increased to 24 percent in 1996 from 22 percent in 1974, reflecting the growing number of working women.

Beyond their neighborhoods, Americans also feel alienated from the larger society and its institutions. Membership in religious congregations has remained relatively low through most of the 1990s—about two-thirds of the adult population, compared with more than 70 percent in past decades. And forget citizenship. Voting is fast going out of fashion, with less than half of eligible Americans casting ballots in the last presidential election.

The annual Harris Poll's Alienation Index hit its highest level ever—67—in 1995 and stood at 62 in December 1997. The 1990s average of 64 compares with averages of 57 in the 1980s, 52 in the 1970s and 34 in the 1960s. Among replies to specific poll questions in 1997: 78 percent of the public said they think "the rich get richer and the poor get poorer," 43 percent felt "left out of things going on around them," 63 percent believed that "what you think doesn't count very much anymore," and 76 percent declared that "the people in Washington are out of touch with the rest of the country." Certainly, President Clinton's loss of credibility over the Monica Lewinsky affair will only increase the distrust and disinterest in government.

Even so, "it is remarkable that public alienation remains so high when the economy is strong, crime rates have fallen dramatically and no American troops are being killed," says Humphrey Taylor, chairman and chief executive officer of Louis Harris & Associates Inc. "If peace and prosperity is what counts, we seem to have it."

Because of the approach of the new millennium, psychologists believe more people are taking stock of their lives and realizing something is missing. "It's as if America itself is experiencing a midlife crisis; people are facing the millennium and seeing that the money they're making isn't doing it for them," says Dr. Moog, the psychologist. "Adults don't have extended families and support systems and are feeling empty, with no sense of community. Kids feel lonely and less connected, too, with their parents gone so much of the time." Young people also aren't joining social organizations as much. For example, the Boy Scouts of America's youth membership has fallen to 4,205,849 from 4,859,580 in 1990 and the peak of 6,169,213 in 1972.

Some psychologists and social workers blame feelings of alienation for the recent rash of schoolyard shootings. The number of school-associated violent deaths jumped to 42 in 1997–98 from 25 the year before, and rejection by peers and adults often figures into such incidents.

"Many of the young people who are responsible for killings in schools are experiencing isolation and are angry about that," says Marjorie Walsleben of the National School Safety Center in Westlake Village, California. "These are marginalized kids who are barely on the fringe of acceptance, if they're accepted at all by peers." She notes that 14-year-old Michael Carneal, who killed three classmates and wounded five others in Kentucky in December 1997, had been teased for years by other kids and complained that

people didn't pay attention to him and take him seriously.

It isn't surprising that so many people feel lonely today given the way we live. The share of U.S. households with a single person increased to 25 percent in 1997 from 17 percent in 1970. What's more, only a quarter of households included married couples with children, compared with 40 percent in 1970. Even more Americans are expected to live alone in the twenty-first century largely because of the aging of the baby-boom generation and the resulting increase in the number of widows and widowers. Elderly people today tend to be more isolated because their children have left the neighborhood and scattered to other states or even other countries. In the past, aging parents often just packed up and moved down the street into their children's homes.

Television has traditionally received much of the blame for the loss of community feeling in America. And for good reason: Households devote an average of more than 50 hours a week to watching the tube. People also are renting films on video more, instead of going out with friends to the movie theater.

Now, a new culprit has emerged—the Internet. A widely publicized study in 1998 by researchers at Carnegie Mellon University in Pittsburgh concluded that being on-line is a downer. They found that greater use of the Internet was associated with declines in social involvement and increases in loneliness and depression. The study casts doubt on the conventional wisdom that chat rooms and electronic mail make computer users feel more connected to others. The study's authors believe people are sacrificing time with family and friends to go on-line, where interaction with others tends to be impersonal and short-lived. Words on a computer screen, it seems, are no match for the human voice and touch.

"Talking on the Net takes time and attention away from your real life," says Sara Kiesler, professor of social and decision sciences at Carnegie Mellon. "Think of the teenager avidly typing away in his room instead of playing a pick-up game of softball with his friends and avoiding that party where he doesn't know anyone. Friends in real life are sometimes more troublesome, but they are the people who play a bigger role in one's life—the people who know you as a person and who are there to give the most all-around social support."

There are a few signs that Americans are trying to become friendlier and less remote. Some neighborhoods have actually revived "block parties" so folks get together at least once a year. Urban planners, meanwhile, are hoping that a new type of suburb, with a town center, wide sidewalks, civic buildings and open green spaces, can spark more community spirit. One such town is Seaside, Florida, which was the picturesque setting for the 1998 movie *The Truman Show*.

"The goal is to bring the human scale back into urban planning," says Rob Steuteville, publisher and editor of *New Urban News*, a newsletter. "We want to get people walking again and encourage the kind of social interaction we had with older cities and towns." He says some 200 "new urbanist" developments are in the planning or construction stage in America.

But some experts on urban design are skeptical about whether the "new urbanism" can really make people feel more rooted and secure. "We feel a loss of simplicity in the late 1990s and miss villages with Main Streets, but we're looking through rose-colored glasses when we try to find intimacy in sentimental ways," says Alex Krieger, a professor of urban design at Harvard University. "We need to form communities of shared interests, not just communities of spatial closeness."

Ronald J. Alsop,
Editor of *The Wall Street Journal Almanac 1999*

Growth Chart

States Ranked by Percentage Population Change Between 1990 and 1997

State	% change	State	% change
Nevada	39.5%	Kentucky	6.0%
Arizona	24.3	Indiana	5.8
Idaho	20.2	Wyoming	5.8
Utah	19.5	New Hampshire	5.7
Colorado	18.2	Wisconsin	5.7
Georgia	15.6	Missouri	5.6
Washington	15.3	Oklahoma	5.5
Texas	14.4	Michigan	5.1
New Mexico	14.2	Nebraska	5.0
Oregon	14.1	Kansas	4.7
Florida	13.3	Vermont	4.7
North Carolina	12.0	Illinois	4.1
Alaska	10.8	New Jersey	3.9
Tennessee	10.1	Ohio	3.1
Montana	10.0	Louisiana	3.1
Delaware	9.8	Iowa	2.7
Virginia	8.8	Massachusetts	1.7
California	8.3	West Virginia	1.2
South Carolina	7.9	Pennsylvania	1.2
Arkansas	7.3	Maine	1.2
Minnesota	7.1	New York	0.8
Hawaii	7.1	North Dakota	0.3
Alabama	6.9	Connecticut	-0.5
Maryland	6.6	Rhode Island	-1.6
South Dakota	6.0	District of Columbia	-12.8
Mississippi	6.0		

Source: U.S. Census Bureau

Regional and State Population (In thousands)

U.S. region, state	Population, April 1, 1990 (Census)	Population, July 1, 1996 (Estimate)	Population, July 1, 1997 (Estimate)
Northeast	50,828	51,502	51,588
New England	13,207	13,326	13,379
Middle Atlantic	37,621	38,176	38,210
Midwest	59,669	62,182	62,460
East North Central	42,009	43,713	43,890
West North Central	17,660	18,468	18,571
South	85,456	93,010	94,187
South Atlantic	43,571	47,589	48,230
East South Central	15,180	16,187	16,326
West South Central	26,704	29,234	29,631
West	52,812	58,486	59,400
Mountain	13,659	16,124	16,482
Pacific	39,153	42,361	42,918
Alabama	4,040	4,287	4,319
Alaska	550	605	609
Arizona	3,665	4,434	4,555
Arkansas	2,351	2,506	2,523
California	29,786	31,858	32,268
Colorado	3,294	3,816	3,893
Connecticut	3,287	3,267	3,270
Delaware	666	723	732
District of Columbia	607	539	529
Florida	12,938	14,419	14,654
Georgia	6,478	7,334	7,486
Hawaii	1,108	1,183	1,187
Idaho	1,007	1,188	1,210
Illinois	11,431	11,845	11,896
Indiana	5,544	5,828	5,864
Iowa	2,777	2,848	2,852
Kansas	2,478	2,579	2,595
Kentucky	3,687	3,882	3,908
Louisiana	4,222	4,341	4,352
Maine	1,228	1,239	1,242
Maryland	4,781	5,060	5,094
Massachusetts	6,016	6,085	6,118
Michigan	9,295	9,731	9,774
Minnesota	4,376	4,649	4,686
Mississippi	2,575	2,711	2,731
Missouri	5,117	5,364	5,402
Montana	799	877	879
Nebraska	1,578	1,649	1,657
Nevada	1,202	1,601	1,677
New Hampshire	1,109	1,160	1,173
New Jersey	7,748	8,002	8,053
New Mexico	1,515	1,711	1,730
New York	17,991	18,134	18,137
North Carolina	6,632	7,309	7,425
North Dakota	639	643	641
Ohio	10,847	11,163	11,186
Oklahoma	3,146	3,295	3,317
Oregon	2,842	3,196	3,243
Pennsylvania	11,883	12,040	12,020
Rhode Island	1,003	988	987
South Carolina	3,486	3,717	3,760
South Dakota	696	738	738
Tennessee	4,877	5,307	5,368
Texas	16,986	19,091	19,439
Utah	1,723	2,018	2,059
Vermont	563	586	589
Virginia	6,189	6,666	6,734
Washington	4,867	5,520	5,610
West Virginia	1,793	1,820	1,816
Wisconsin	4,892	5,146	5,170
Wyoming	454	480	480

Source: U.S. Census Bureau

State Population Projections (Numbers in thousands)

State	2000	2010	2015	2020	2025
New England					
Maine	1,259	1,323	1,362	1,396	1,423
New Hampshire	1,224	1,329	1,372	1,410	1,439
Vermont	617	651	662	671	678
Massachusetts	6,199	6,431	6,574	6,734	6,902
Rhode Island	998	1,038	1,070	1,105	1,141
Connecticut	3,284	3,400	3,506	3,621	3,739
Middle Atlantic					
New York	18,146	18,530	18,916	19,359	19,830
New Jersey	8,178	8,638	8,924	9,238	9,558
Pennsylvania	12,202	12,352	12,449	12,567	12,683
East North Central					
Ohio	11,319	11,505	11,588	11,671	11,744
Indiana	6,045	6,318	6,404	6,481	6,546
Illinois	12,051	12,515	12,808	13,121	13,440
Michigan	9,679	9,836	9,917	10,002	10,078
Wisconsin	5,326	5,590	5,693	5,788	5,867
West North Central					
Minnesota	4,830	5,147	5,283	5,406	5,510
Iowa	2,900	2,968	2,994	3,019	3,040
Missouri	5,540	5,864	6,005	6,137	6,250
North Dakota	662	690	704	717	729
South Dakota	777	826	840	853	866
Nebraska	1,705	1,806	1,850	1,892	1,930
Kansas	2,668	2,849	2,939	3,026	3,108
South Atlantic					
Delaware	768	817	832	847	861
Maryland	5,275	5,657	5,862	6,071	6,274
District of Columbhia	523	560	594	625	655
Virginia	6,997	7,627	7,921	8,204	8,466
West Virginia	1,841	1,851	1,851	1,850	1,845
North Carolina	7,777	8,552	8,840	9,111	9,349
South Carolina	3,858	4,205	4,369	4,517	4,645
Georgia	7,875	8,824	9,200	9,552	9,869
Florida	15,233	17,363	18,497	19,634	20,710
East South Central					
Kentucky	3,995	4,170	4,231	4,281	4,314
Tennessee	5,657	6,180	6,365	6,529	6,665
Alabama	4,451	4,798	4,956	5,100	5,224
Mississippi	2,816	2,974	3,035	3,093	3,142
West South Central					
Arkansas	2,631	2,840	2,922	2,997	3,055
Louisiana	4,425	4,683	4,840	4,991	5,133
Oklahoma	3,373	3,639	3,789	3,930	4,057
Texas	20,119	22,857	24,280	25,729	27,183
Mountain					
Montana	950	1,040	1,069	1,097	1,121
Idaho	1,347	1,557	1,622	1,683	1,739
Wyoming	525	607	641	670	694
Colorado	4,168	4,658	4,833	5,012	5,188
New Mexico	1,860	2,155	2,300	2,454	2,612
Arizona	4,798	5,522	5,808	6,111	6,412
Utah	2,207	2,551	2,670	2,781	2,883
Nevada	1,871	2,131	2,179	2,241	2,312
Pacific					
Washington	5,858	6,658	7,058	7,446	7,808
Oregon	3,397	3,803	3,992	4,177	4,349
California	32,521	37,644	41,373	45,278	49,285
Alaska	653	745	791	838	885
Hawaii	1,257	1,440	1,553	1,677	1,812

Source: U.S. Census Bureau

Changing State Demographics

Percent of Total Population 65 Years and Over

Region, division, and state	Persons 65 and over				Region, division, and state	Persons 65 and over			
	1990	2000	2010	2020		1990	2000	2010	2020
United States	12.5%	12.6%	13.2%	16.5%					
Northeast	13.7	14.1	14.3	16.9	South Atlantic	13.3%	14.3%	15.5%	19.2%
New England	13.3	14.0	14.4	17.5	Delaware	12.1	13.1	13.8	16.7
Middle Atlantic	13.8	14.1	14.2	16.7	Maryland	10.8	11.3	12.1	14.8
Midwest	12.9	13.1	13.4	16.2	District of Columbia	12.7	13.5	12.5	13.7
East North Central	12.6	12.8	13.2	15.9	Virginia	10.7	11.4	12.5	15.7
West North Central	13.8	13.7	14.0	17.1	West Virginia	14.9	15.1	15.2	18.5
South	12.5	13.1	14.0	17.5	North Carolina	12.1	13.1	14.4	18.1
South Atlantic	13.3	14.3	15.5	19.2	South Carolina	11.3	12.3	13.3	16.8
East South Central	12.7	12.9	13.7	17.0	Georgia	10.0	10.5	11.7	15.0
West South Central	11.0	11.2	11.8	14.9	Florida	18.2	19.6	21.0	25.6
West	10.9	10.9	11.6	14.6	East South Central	12.7	12.9	13.7	17.0
Mountain	11.1	11.4	12.4	16.0	Kentucky	12.6	12.8	13.5	16.9
Pacific	10.8	10.8	11.4	14.1	Tennessee	12.6	12.9	14.0	17.6
New England	13.3	14.0	14.4	17.5	Alabama	12.9	13.2	13.8	16.7
Maine	13.3	14.2	14.6	18.3	Mississippi	12.4	12.7	13.4	16.6
Vermont	11.7	12.2	13.1	16.8	West South Central	11.0	11.2	11.8	14.9
New Hampshire	11.2	12.1	13.0	16.9	Arkansas	14.8	14.9	15.7	19.3
Massachusetts	13.5	14.1	14.5	17.4	Louisiana	11.1	11.5	11.8	14.3
Rhode Island	14.9	15.1	14.8	17.9	Oklahoma	13.4	13.4	13.6	16.5
Connecticut	13.5	14.4	14.8	2.6	Texas	10.1	10.3	11.1	14.2
Middle Atlantic	13.8	14.1	14.2	16.7	Mountain	11.1	11.4	12.4	16.0
New York	13.0	13.3	13.6	15.8	Montana	13.3	12.8	13.0	16.2
New Jersey	13.3	13.7	13.9	16.3	Idaho	12.0	11.1	11.9	15.4
Pennsylvania	15.3	15.6	15.3	18.2	Wyoming	10.4	9.7	9.0	11.2
East North Central	12.6	12.8	13.2	15.9	Colorado	10.0	10.2	11.4	15.3
Ohio	12.9	13.5	13.9	2.3	New Mexico	10.7	11.2	11.9	15.0
Indiana	12.5	12.8	13.3	16.2	Arizona	13.0	14.0	15.4	19.6
Illinois	12.5	12.4	12.6	14.8	Utah	8.7	8.7	9.3	12.1
Michigan	11.9	12.4	12.7	15.2	Nevada	10.5	10.8	12.0	15.5
Wisconsin	13.3	13.2	13.8	17.3	Pacific	10.8	10.8	11.4	14.1
West North Central	13.8	13.7	14.0	17.1	Washington	11.8	11.1	11.9	15.6
Minnesota	12.5	12.5	13.3	16.9	Oregon	13.7	12.7	13.0	16.6
Iowa	15.3	15.0	15.0	18.0	California	10.5	10.6	11.2	13.8
Missouri	14.0	14.1	14.5	17.5	Alaska	4.0	4.4	4.8	6.2
North Dakota	14.2	14.5	13.7	16.2	Hawaii	11.2	11.9	12.3	14.4
South Dakota	14.7	14.0	13.6	16.4					
Nebraska	14.1	13.8	13.9	16.8					
Kansas	13.8	13.5	13.5	16.5					

Source: U.S. Census Bureau

Top Five States with the Largest Population, Ranked by Race and Hispanic Origin: 1995 and 2025 (In thousands)

YEAR AND RANK	WHITE		NON-HISPANIC BLACK		AMERICAN INDIAN		ASIAN		HISPANIC ORIGIN*	
	State	Pop.	State	Pop.	State	Pop.	State.	Pop.	State.	Pop.
1995										
1	California	16,630	New York	2,635	Oklahoma	257	California	3,380	California	9,206
2	New York	12,082	Texas	2,189	Arizona	217	New York	825	Texas	5,173
3	Texas	10,891	California	2,184	California	189	Hawaii	704	New York	2,541
4	Pennsylvania	10,474	Georgia	2,004	New Mexico	140	Texas	412	Florida	1,955
5	Florida	10,010	Florida	1,964	Arkansas	90	New Jersey	357	Illinois	1,090
2025										
1	California	16,626	Texas	3,466	Oklahoma	363	California	8,564	California	21,232
2	Texas	12,501	Georgia	3,292	Arizona	292	New York	1,807	Texas	10,230
3	Florida	12,196	Florida	3,067	New Mexico	257	Hawaii	1,179	Florida	4,944
4	New York	10,585	New York	3,065	California	183	New Jersey	960	New York	4,309
5	Pennsylvania	10,181	California	2,680	Washington	136	Texas	911	Illinois	2,275

*Persons of Hispanic origin may be of any race.

Source: U.S. Census Bureau

States of the Union

ALABAMA

GEOGRAPHY:
Area:
  total area: 52,237 sq mi
  land area: 50,750 sq mi
Capital: Montgomery, (population: 195,471)
Statehood: December 14, 1819 (22nd state)
Postal abbreviation: AL
State symbols:
  State motto: Audemus jura nostra defendere (We dare defend our rights)
  State song: "Alabama"
  State bird: Yellowhammer
  State flower: Camellia
  State tree: Southern Pine

PEOPLE:
Population: 4,319,000
Change since 1990: 5.8%
Population density: 83.8 per sq mi
% population 65 years and over: 13.0 (1996)

VITAL STATISTICS:
Birth rate: 14.4 *(per 1,000 population)*
Death rate: 996.1 *(per 100,000 population)*
Infant mortality rate: 10.1 *(deaths per 1,000 live births)*

GOVERNMENT:
Governor: Fob James, Jr. (Republican)
  Regular term: 4 years
  Current term began: January 1995
  Salary: $81,151
Lt. Governor: Don Siegelman (Democrat)

STATE ECONOMY:
Gross state product: $88.661 billion
State budget: *(in thousands)*
  State revenues: $14,007,883
  Total expenditures: $12,944,867
  Debt at end of fiscal year: $3,780,493
  Cash and security holdings: $21,639,230
Chief products:
  Agriculture: Poultry, beef cattle, soybeans, eggs, peanuts, hogs, corn, cotton, forest products
  Fishing Industry: Shrimp and oysters

Manufacturing: Primary metals, paper products, chemicals, textiles, fabricated metal products, clothing, food products, rubber and plastics products

Minerals: Coal, petroleum, natural gas, stone, iron-ore, steel, limestone

PERSONAL FINANCES:
Per capita personal income: $20,842
Median household income: $28,530
Average annual pay: $25,180
Percent of persons in poverty: 17.1%
Homeownership rate: 71.3%

EMPLOYMENT:
Labor force: 2,174,000
Unemployment rate: 5.1%
Total number of businesses: 227,119
Total number of women owned businesses: 71,466
Total number of minority owned businesses: 17,432

CRIME:
Crime rate: 4,820.1 (per 100,000 people)
Violent crime: 565.4 (per 100,000)
Property crime: 4,254.7 (per 100,000)
Total prisoners in custody: 21,424
Prison capacity occupied: 98.5%

HEALTH CARE:
Persons without health insurance coverage: 12.9%
Low income uninsured children: 12.7%
Occupancy rate in community hospitals: 60.7%

EDUCATION:
Current high school completion rate: 86.8%
High school drop out rate: 6.2%
Educational Attainment-High school graduate: 77.6%
Bachelor degree: 19.3%
Estimated public elementary and secondary school finances (in millions):
Revenues: $3,364,055
Expenditures: $3,353,363

ALASKA

GEOGRAPHY:
Area:
total area: 615,230 sq mi
land area: 507,374 sq mi
Capital: Juneau, (population: 26,751)
Statehood: January 3, 1959 (49th state)
Postal abbreviation: AK
State symbols:
State motto: North to the future
State song: "Alaska's Flag"
State bird: Willow Ptarmigan
State flower: Forget-Me-Not
State tree: Sitka Spruce

PEOPLE:
Population: 609,000
Change since 1990: 10.4%
Population density: 1.1 per sq mi
% population 65 years and over: 5.2 (1996)

VITAL STATISTICS:
Birth rate: 16.7 (per 1,000 population)
Death rate: 423.0 (per 100,000 population)
Infant mortality rate: 7.6 (deaths per 1,000 live births)

GOVERNMENT:
Governor: Tony Knowles (Democrat)
Regular term: 4 years
Current term began: December 1994
Salary: $81,648
Lt. Governor: Fran Ulmer (Democrat)

STATE ECONOMY:
Gross state product: $22.720 billion
State budget: (in thousands)
State revenues: $9,438,512
Total expenditures: $5,722,455
Debt at end of fiscal year: $3,290,599
Cash and security holdings: $34,320,002
Chief products:
Agriculture: Greenhouse products, dairy products, potatoes, poultry, cattle, barley
Fishing Industry: Salmon, crab, shrimp, groundfish
Manufacturing: Food products, petroleum, coal products, lumber and wood products, areospace industries
Minerals: Petroleum, natural gas, sand and gravel, gold, silver, lead, zinc, coal

PERSONAL FINANCES:
Per capita personal income: $25.305
Median household income: $51,074
Average annual pay: $32,461
Percent of persons in poverty: 7.7%
Homeownership rate: 67.2%

EMPLOYMENT:
Labor force: 316,000
Unemployment rate: 7.9%
Total number of businesses: 58,898
Total number of women owned businesses: 19,380
Total number of minority owned businesses: 5,382

CRIME:
Crime rate: 5,450.4 (per 100,000 people)
Violent crime: 727.7 (per 100,000)
Property crime: 4,722.7 (per 100,000)
Total prisoners in custody: 2,968
Prison capacity occupied: 104.6%

HEALTH CARE:
Persons without health insurance coverage: 13.5%
Low income uninsured children: 4.5%
Occupancy rate in community hospitals: 52.8%

EDUCATION:
Current high school completion rate: 87.8%
High school drop out rate: 4.9%
Educational Attainment-High school graduate: 92.1%
Bachelor degree: 27.5%
Estimated public elementary and secondary school finances (in millions):
Revenues: $1,117,068
Expenditures: $1,203,817

ARIZONA

GEOGRAPHY:
Area:
  total area: 114,006 sq mi
  land area: 113,642 sq mi
Capital: Phoenix, (population: 1,048,949)
Statehood: February 14, 1912 (48th state)
Postal abbreviation: AZ
State symbols:
  State motto: Ditat Deus (God enriches)
  State songs: "Arizona March Song" and "Arizona"
  State bird: Cactus Wren
  State flower: Saguaro Cactus Blossom
  State tree: Palo Verde

PEOPLE:
Population: 4,555,000
Change since 1990: 20.8%
Population density: 37.1 per sq mi
% population 65 years and over: 13.2 (1996)

VITAL STATISTICS:
Birth rate: 18.0 *(per 1,000 population)*
Death rate: 837.9 *(per 100,000 population)*
Infant mortality rate: 7.8 *(deaths per 1,000 live births)*

GOVERNMENT:
Governor: Jane Dee Hull (Republican)*
  Regular term: 4 years
  Current term began: September 1997
  Salary: $75,000 to $95,000
Lt. Governor: (vacant)

STATE ECONOMY:
Gross State Product: $94.093 billion
State budget: *(in thousands)*
  State revenues: $13,692,375
  Total expenditures: $12,418,681
  Debt at end of fiscal year: $2,741,940
  Cash and security holdings: $25,614,579
Chief products:
  Agriculture: Wheat, cotton, soybeans, cattle, poultry, hogs
  Manufacturing: Transportation equipment, aerospace, electronics, printers and publishers, communications
  Mineral products: Coal, copper ore

PERSONAL FINANCES:
Per capita personal income: $22,364
Median household income: $31,706
Average annual pay: $22,294
Percent of persons in poverty: 18.3%
Homeownership rate: 63.0%

EMPLOYMENT:
Labor Force: 2,165,000
Unemployment Rate: 4.6%
Total number of businesses: 248,337
  Total number of women owned businesses: 93,300
  Total number of minority owned businesses: 26,185

CRIME:
Crime rate: 7,067.0 *(per 100,000 people)*
  Violent crime: 631.5 *(per 100,000)*
  Property crime: 6,435.5 *(per 100,000)*
Total prisoners in custody: 22,493
Prison capacity occupied: 105.9%

HEALTH CARE:
Persons without health insurance coverage: 24.1%
Low income uninsured children: 15.2%
Occupancy rate in community hospitals: 57.1%

EDUCATION:
Current high school completion rate: 85.8%
High school drop out rate: N.A.
Educational Attainment-High school graduate: 82.6%
                                   Bachelor degree: 19.5%
Estimated public elementary and secondary school finances *(in millions)*:
  Revenues: $3,790,614
  Expenditures: $4,021,566

---

*Assumed governorship in September 1997, due to resignation of Fife Symington.

ARKANSAS

GEOGRAPHY:
Area:
  total area: 53,182 sq mi
  land area: 52,075 sq mi
Capital: Little Rock, (population: 178,136)
Statehood: June 15, 1836 (25th state)
Postal abbreviation: AR
State symbols:
  State motto: Regnat Populus (The people rule)
  State songs: "Arkansas (You Run Deep in Me)" "Oh, Arkansas"
  State bird: Mockingbird
  State flower: Apple Blossom
  State tree: Pine

PEOPLE:
Population: 2,523,000
Change since 1990: 6.8%
Population density: 47.7 per sq mi
% population 65 years and over: 14.4 (1996)

VITAL STATISTICS:
Birth rate: 14.5 *(per 1,000 population)*
Death rate: 1,075.1 *(per 100,000 population)*
Infant mortality rate: 9.2 *(deaths per 1,000 live births)*

GOVERNMENT:
Governor: Mike Huckabee* (Republican)
  Regular term: 4 years
  Current term began: July 1996
  Salary: $65,182
Lt. Governor: Winthrop Rockefeller (Republican)

STATE ECONOMY:
Gross state product: $50.575 billion

State budget: *(in thousands)*
State revenues: $8,843,946
Total expenditures: $7,684,652
Debt at end of fiscal year: $2,247,810
Cash and security holdings: $11,898,594

Chief products:
Agriculture: Wheat, barley, cotton, hay, vegetables, cattle, poultry
Manufacturing: Consumer goods, food products, paper products, textiles, fabricated metal products, clothing, rubber and plastics products, lumber, electrical and nonelectrical machinery
Minerals: Bauxite (aluminum ore) coal, petroleum, natural gas, stone

PERSONAL FINANCES:
Per capita personal income: $19,585
Median household income: $26,850
Average annual pay: $22,294
Percent of persons in poverty: 16.1%
Homeownership rate: 66.7%

EMPLOYMENT:
Labor force: 1,211,000
Unemployment rate: 5.3%
Total number of businesses: 159,820
Total number of women owned businesses: 50,440
Total number of minority owned businesses: 7,594

CRIME:
Crime rate: 4,699.2 *(per 100,000 people)*
Violent crime: 524.3 *(per 100,000)*
Property crime: 4,174.9 *(per 100,000)*
Total prisoners in custody: 8,675
Prison capacity occupied: 109.5%

HEALTH CARE:
Persons without health insurance coverage: 21.7%
Low income uninsured children: 13.4%
Occupancy rate in community hospitals: 58.3%

EDUCATION:
Current high school completion rate: 86.7%
High school drop out rate: NA
Educational Attainment-High school graduate: 76.9%
Bachelor degree: 14.6%
Estimated public elementary and secondary school finances *(in millions)*:
Revenues: $2,040,749
Expenditures: $2,132,382

---

*Governor Huckabee, as lieutenant governor, became governor after Governor Jim Guy Tucker resigned. After Mr. Huckabee completes his term, he is eligible to serve two more terms.

CALIFORNIA

GEOGRAPHY:
Area:
total area: 158,869 sq mi
land area: 155,973 sq mi
Capital: Sacramento, (population: 373,964)
Statehood: September 9, 1850 (31st state)
Postal abbreviation: CA
State symbols:
State motto: Eureka (I have found it)
State song: "I Love You California"
State bird: California Valley Quail
State flower: Golden Poppy
State tree: California Redwood

PEOPLE:
Population: 32,268,000
Change since 1990: 7.1%
Population density: 202.5 per sq mi
% population 65 years and over: 11.0 (1996)

VITAL STATISTICS:
Birth rate: 16.9 *(per 1,000 population)*
Death rate: 709.8 *(per 100,000 population)*
Infant mortality rate: 7.0 *(deaths per 1,000 live births)*

GOVERNMENT:
Governor: Pete Wilson (Republican)
Regular term: 4 years
Current term began: January 1995
Salary: $114,286*
Lt. Governor: Gray Davis (Democrat)

STATE ECONOMY:
Gross state product: $875.697 billion
State budget: *(in thousands)*
State revenues: $131,348,880
Total expenditures: $117,643,273
Debt at end of fiscal year: $45,336,911
Cash and security holdings: $226,142,025

Chief products:
Agriculture: Dairy products, grapes, almonds, artichokes, dates, figs, kiwi, olives, oranges, pistachios, prunes, raisins, walnuts, cattle, livestock, hogs
Manufacturing: Aerospace-defense, electric and electronic equipment, transportation equipment, machinery, processed food
Minerals: Petroleum, natural gas, boron, cement, sand, gravel

PERSONAL FINANCES:
Per capita personal income: $26,570
Median household income: $38,457
Average annual pay: $31,773
Percent of persons in poverty: 16.8%
Homeownership rate: 55.7%

EMPLOYMENT:
Labor force: 15,972,000
Unemployment rate: 6.3%
Total number of businesses: 2,259,327
Total number of women owned businesses: 801,487

Total number of minority owned businesses:
541,414

CRIME:
Crime rate: 5,207.8 *(per 100,000 people)*
 Violent crime: 862.7 *(per 100,000)*
 Property crime: 4,345.1 *(per 100,000)*
Total prisoners in custody: 145,565
Prison capacity occupied: 175.3%

HEALTH CARE:
Persons without health insurance coverage: 20.1%
Low income uninsured children: 13.4%
Occupancy rate in community hospitals: 61.1%

EDUCATION:
Current high school completion rate: 78.6%
High school drop out rate: 4.4%
Educational Attainment-High school graduate: 80.7%
                                   Bachelor degree: 27.5%
Estimated public elementary and secondary school fi-
 nances *(in millions)*:
 Revenues: $29,297,146
 Expenditures: $30,073,436

---

*Governor has taken a voluntary 5% cut in statatory salary

COLORADO

GEOGRAPHY:
Area:
 total area: 104,100 sq mi
 land area: 103,729 sq mi
Capital: Denver, (population: 493,559)
Statehood: August 1, 1876 (38th state)
Postal abbreviation: CO
State symbols:
 State motto: Nil Sine Numine
  (Nothing without the deity)
 State song: "Where the Columbines Grow"
 State bird: Lark Bunting
 State flower: White and Lavender Columbine
 State tree: Colorado Blue Spruce

PEOPLE:
Population: 3,893,000
Change since 1990: 16.0%
Population density: 36.1 per sq mi
% population 65 years and over: 10.1 (1996)

VITAL STATISTICS:
Birth rate: 14.6 *(per 1,000 population)*
Death rate: 667.6 *(per 100,000 population)*
Infant mortality rate: 7.0 *(deaths per 1,000 live births)*

GOVERNMENT:
Governor: Roy Romer (Democrat)
 Regular term: 4 years
 Current term began: January 1995
 Salary: $70,000
Lt. Governor: Gail Schoettler (Democrat)

STATE ECONOMY:
Gross state product: $99.767 billion
State budget: *(in thousands)*

State revenues: $12,779,639
Total expenditures: $10,861,228
Debt at end of fiscal year: $3,402,235
Cash and security holdings: $23,591,436
Chief products:
 Agriculture: Alfalfa, wheat, corn, cattle, sheep, live-
  stock, sorghum
 Manufacturing: Food products, military ordnance,
  machinery equipment
 Minerals: Molybdenum, petroleum, coal

PERSONAL FINANCES:
Per capita personal income: $27,051
Median household income: $41,429
Average annual pay: $28,520
Percent of persons in poverty: 9.7%
Homeownership rate: 64.1%

EMPLOYMENT:
Labor force: 2,158,000
Unemployment rate: 3.3%
Total number of businesses: 323,147
 Total number of women owned businesses: 121,659
 Total number of minority owned businesses: 23,463

CRIME:
Crime rate: 5,118.5 *(per 100,000 people)*
 Violent crime: 404.5 *(per 100,000)*
 Property crime: 4,714.0 *(per 100,000)*
Total prisoners in custody: 10,302
Prison capacity occupied: 101.0%

HEALTH CARE:
Persons without health insurance coverage: 16.6%
Low income uninsured children: 7.0%
Occupancy rate in community hospitals: 58.6%

EDUCATION:
Current high school completion rate: 87.9%
High school drop out rate: NA
High school graduate: 87.6%
Educational Attainment-High school graduate: 87.6%
                                   Bachelor degree: 28.9%
Estimated public elementary and secondary school fi-
 nances *(in millions)*:
 Revenues: $3,705,495
 Expenditures: $3,802,908

---

*Includes off-grounds inmates

CONNECTICUT

GEOGRAPHY:
Area:
 total area: 5,544 sq mi
 land area: 4,845 sq mi
Capital: Hartford, (population: 124,196)
Statehood: January 9, 1788 (5th state)
Postal abbreviation: CT
State symbols:
 State motto: Qui Transtulit Sustinet
  (He who transplanted still sustains)
 State song: "Yankee Doodle"
 State bird: American Robin

State flower: Mountain Laurel
State tree: White Oak

PEOPLE:
Population: 3,270,000
Change since 1990: -0.4%
Population density: 675.9 per sq mi
% population 65 years and over: 14.3 (1996)

VITAL STATISTICS:
Birth rate: 13.5 (per 1,000 population)
Death rate: 899.5 (per 100,000 population)
Infant mortality rate: 7.9 (deaths per 1,000 live births)

GOVERNMENT:
Governor: John G. Rowland (Republican)
  Regular term: 4 years
  Current term began: January 1995
  Salary: $78,000
Lt. Governor: M. Jodi Rell (Republican)

STATE ECONOMY:
Gross state product: $110.449 billion
State budget: (in thousands)
  State revenues: $14,519,780
  Total expenditures: $13,826,021
  Debt at end of fiscal year: $17,050,816
  Cash and security holdings: $22,887,339
Chief products:
  Agriculture: Dairy products, tobacco, livestock
  Fishing Industry: Oysters
  Manufacturing: Transportation equipment, helicopters, submarines, aircraft engines, guns and ammunition, chemicals
  Minerals: Sand, gravel, stone, limestone, feldspar, clay, mica

PERSONAL FINANCES:
Per capita personal income: $36,263
Median household income: $41,775
Average annual pay: $36,579
Percent of persons in poverty: 10.7%
Homeownership rate: 68.1%

EMPLOYMENT:
Labor force: 1,723,000
Unemployment rate: 5.1%
Total number of businesses: 237,705
  Total number of women owned businesses: 79,931
  Total number of minority owned businesses: 13,435

CRIME:
Crime rate: 4,227.7 (per 100,000 people)
  Violent crime: 412.0 (per 100,000)
  Property crime: 3,815.6 (per 100,000)
Total prisoners in custody: 14,997
Prison capacity occupied: 90.6%

HEALTH CARE:
Persons without health insurance coverage: 8.8%
Low income uninsured children: 6.2%
Occupancy rate in community hospitals: 74.5%

EDUCATION:
Current high school completion rate: 96.1%
High school drop out rate: 4.9%
Educational Attainment-High school graduate: 84.0%
                              Bachelor degree: 30.3%
Estimated public elementary and secondary school finances (in millions):
  Revenues: $4,331,851
  Expenditures: $4,144,819

DELAWARE

GEOGRAPHY:
Area:
  total area: 2,396 sq mi
  land area: 1,955 sq mi
Capital: Dover, (population: 27,630)
Statehood: December 7, 1787, (1st state)
Postal abbreviation: DE
State symbols:
  State motto: Liberty and Independence
  State song: "Our Delaware"
  State bird: Blue Hen Chicken
  State flower: Peach Blossom
  State tree: American Holly

PEOPLE:
Population: 732,000
Change since 1990: 8.8%
Population density: 366.9 per sq mi
% population 65 years and over: 12.8 (1996)

VITAL STATISTICS:
Birth rate: 14.1 (per 1,000 population)
Death rate: 875.9 (per 100,000 population)
Infant mortality rate: 6.8 (deaths per 1,000 live births)

GOVERNMENT:
Governor: Thomas R. Carper (Democrat)
  Regular term: 4 years
  Current term began: January 1997
  Salary: $107,000
Lt. Governor: Ruth Ann Minner (Democrat)

STATE ECONOMY:
Gross state product: $26.697 billion
State budget: (in thousands)
  State revenues: $4,210,673
  Total expenditures: $3,403,619
  Debt at end of fiscal year: $3,434,196
  Cash and security holdings: $7,510,105
Chief products:
  Agriculture: Broilers, soybeans, corn, milk
  Fishing Industry: Crabs and clams
  Manufacturing: Chemicals, food products, paper and rubber products, primary metals, printed materials
  Mining: Sand, gravel, magnesium compounds

PERSONAL FINANCES:
Per capita personal income: $29,022

Median household income: $37,634
Average annual pay: $30,711
Percent of persons in poverty: 9.5%
Homeownership rate: 69.2%

EMPLOYMENT:
Labor force: 380,000
Unemployment rate: 4.0%
Total number of businesses: 42,228
  Total number of women owned businesses:
  14,904
  Total number of minority owned businesses:
  3,301

CRIME:
Crime rate: 4,894.9 *(per 100,000 people)*
  Violent crime: 668.3 *(per 100,000)*
  Property crime: 4,226.6 *(per 100,000)*
Total prisoners in custody: 5,107
Prison capacity occupied: 145.1%

HEALTH CARE:
Persons without health insurance coverage: 13.4%
Low income uninsured children: 7.3%
Occupancy rate in community hospitals: 70.9%

EDUCATION:
Current high school completion rate: 88.8%
High school drop out rate: NA
Educational Attainment-High school graduate: 84.4%
                Bachelor degree: 26.8%
Estimated public elementary and secondary school fi-
  nances *(in millions)*:
  Revenues: $782,705
  Expenditures: $756,478

DISTRICT OF COLUMBIA

GEOGRAPHY:
Area:
  total area: 68 sq mi
  land area: 61 sq mi
Postal abbreviation: DC
Symbols:
  Motto: Justitia omnibus (Justice for all)
  Bird: Wood Thrush
  Flower: American Beauty Rose
  Tree: Scarlet Oak

PEOPLE:
Population: 592,000
Change since 1990: -10.5%
Population density: 9,086.2 per sq mi
% population 65 years and over: 13.9 (1996)

VITAL STATISTICS:
Birth rate: 15.3 *(per 1,000 population)*
Death rate: 1,244.2 *(per 100,000 population)*
Infant mortality rate: 18.2 *(deaths per 1,000 live*
  births)

GOVERNMENT:
Mayor: Marion Barry (Democrat)

  Regular term: 4 years
  Salary: $90,705

ECONOMY:
Gross product: $48.028 billion
Chief products:
  Manufacturing: Printing and publishing, food prod-
  ucts, stone and glass products

PERSONAL FINANCES:
Per capita personal income: $35,852
Median household income: $31,811
Average annual pay: $44,458
Percent of persons in poverty: 23.2%
Homeownership rate: 42.5%

EMPLOYMENT:
Labor force: 270,000
Unemployment rate: 7.9%
Total number of businesses: 35,344
  Total number of women owned businesses: 14,599
  Total number of minority owned businesses: 12,669

CRIME:
Crime rate: 11,896.7 *(per 100,000 people)*
  Violent crime: 2,469.8 *(per 100,000)*
  Property crime: 9,426.9 *(per 100,000)*
Total prisoners in custody: 8,819
Prison capacity occupied: 95.8%

HEALTH CARE:
Persons without health insurance coverage: 14.8%
Low income uninsured children: 11.2%
Occupancy rate in community hospitals: 73.2%

EDUCATION:
Current high school completion rate: 87.8%
High school drop out rate: 10.6%
Educational Attainment-High school graduate: 80.3%
                Bachelor degree: 33.7%
Estimated public elementary and secondary school fi-
  nances *(in millions)*:
  Revenues: $700,111
  Expenditures: $708,224

FLORIDA

GEOGRAPHY:
Area:
  total area: 59,928 sq mi
  land area: 53,937 sq mi
Capital: Tallahassee, (population: 133,718)
Statehood: March 3, 1845 (27th state)
Postal abbreviation: FL
State symbols:
  State motto: "In God We Trust"
  State song: "The Swanee River"
  State bird: Mockingbird
  State flower: Orange Blossom
  State tree: Sabal Palm

PEOPLE:
Population: 14,654,000
Change since 1990: 11.3%
Population density: 262.3 per sq mi

% population 65 years and over: 18.5 (1996)

VITAL STATISTICS:
Birth rate: 13.2 *(per 1,000 population)*
Death rate: 1,081.3 *(per 100,000 population)*
Infant mortality rate: 8.1 *(deaths per 1,000 live births)*

GOVERNMENT:
Governor: Lawton Chiles (Democrat)
  Regular term: 4 years
  Current term began: January 1995
  Salary: $97,850
Lt. Governor: Buddy MacKay (Democrat)

STATE ECONOMY:
Gross state product: $317.829 billion
State budget: *(in thousands)*
  State revenues: $37,359,429
  Total expenditures: $34,749,505
  Debt at end of fiscal year: $15,369,609
  Cash and security holdings: $52,464,253
Chief products:
  Agriculture: Citrus fruit, nuts, berries, vegetables, livestock
  Manufacturing: Electronics, aerospace, food products, chemicals, rubber and plastic
  Minerals: Phosphate, titanium, zircon, petroleum

PERSONAL FINANCES:
Per capita personal income: $25,255
Median household income: $30,632
Average annual pay: $25,640
Percent of persons in poverty: 15.2%
Homeownership rate: 66.9%

EMPLOYMENT:
Labor force: 7,106,000
Unemployment rate: 4.8%
Total number of businesses: 1,000,542
  Total number of women owned businesses: 352,048
  Total number of minority owned businesses: 173,287

CRIME:
Crime rate: 7,497.4 *(per 100,000 people)*
  Violent crime: 1,051.0 *(per 100,000)*
  Property crime: 6,446.3 *(per 100,000)*
Total prisoners in custody: 63,763
Prison capacity occupied: 99.2%

HEALTH CARE:
Persons without health insurance coverage: 18.9%
Low income uninsured children: 11.9%
Occupancy rate in community hospitals: 60.2%

EDUCATION:
Current high school completion rate: 80.1%
High school drop out rate: NA
Educational Attainment-High school graduate: 81.4%
                    Bachelor degree: 21.7%
Estimated public elementary and secondary school finances *(in millions)*:
  Revenues: $13,242,457
  Expenditures: $13,473,977

GEORGIA

GEOGRAPHY:
Area:
  total area: 58,977 sq mi
  land area: 57,919 sq mi
Capital: Atlanta, (population: 396,052)
Statehood: January 2, 1788 (4th state)
Postal abbreviation: GA
State symbols:
  State motto: "Wisdom, Justice, and Moderation."
  State song: "Georgia On My Mind"
  State bird: Brown Thrasher
  State flower: Cherokee Rose
  State tree: Live Oak

PEOPLE:
Population: 7,486,000
Change since 1990: 13.5%
Population density: 124.3 per sq mi
% population 65 years and over: 9.9 (1996)

VITAL STATISTICS:
Birth rate: 15.6 *(per 1,000 population)*
Death rate: 810.8 *(per 100,000 population)*
Infant mortality rate: 10.2 *(deaths per 1,000 live births)*

GOVERNMENT:
Governor: Zell Miller (Democrat)
  Regular term: 4 years
  Current term began: January 1995
  Salary: $107,200
Lt. Governor: Pierre Howard (Democrat)

STATE ECONOMY:
Gross state product: $183.042 billion
State budget: *(in thousands)*
  State revenues: $24,028,450
  Total expenditures: $21,975,372
  Debt at end of fiscal year: $6,185,586
  Cash and security holdings: $36,319,938
Chief products:
  Agriculture: Peanuts, cotton, wheat, tobacco, soybeans, poultry, cattle, pigs
  Manufacturing: Textiles, airplane and automobile assembly, mobile homes, chemicals, food processing, lumber
  Minerals: Marble, granite, kaolin

PERSONAL FINANCES:
Per capita personal income: $24,061
Median household income: $33,801
Average annual pay: $27,488
Percent of persons in poverty: 13.5%
Homeownership rate: 70.9%

EMPLOYMENT:
Labor force: 3,907,000
Unemployment rate: 4.5%
Total number of businesses: 425,118
  Total number of women owned businesses: 143,045
  Total number of minority owned businesses: 52,131

CRIME:
Crime rate: 6,309.7 *(per 100,000 people)*
  Violent crime: 638.7 *(per 100,000)*
  Property crime: 5,671.0 *(per 100,000)*
Total prisoners in custody: 35,139
Prison capacity occupied: 101.4%

HEALTH CARE:
Persons without health insurance coverage: 17.8%
Low income uninsured children: 10.7%
Occupancy rate in community hospitals: 63.4%

EDUCATION:
Current high school completion rate: 81.3%
High school drop out rate: 9.0%
Educational Attainment-High school graduate: 78.8%
                          Bachelor degree: 22.3%
Estimated public elementary and secondary school finances (*in millions*):
  Revenues: $7,020,195
  Expenditures: $7,282,499

HAWAII

GEOGRAPHY:
Area:
  total area: 6,459 sq mi
  land area: 6,423 sq mi
Capital: Honolulu, (population: 385,881)
Statehood: August 21, 1959 (50th state)
Postal abbreviation: HI
State symbols:
  State motto: Ua mau ke ea o ka aina i ka pono (The life of the land is perpetuated in righteousness.)
  State song: "Hawaii Ponoi"
  State bird: Nene (Hawaiian Goose)
  State flower: Yellow Hibiscus
  State-tree: KuKui (Candlenut)

PEOPLE:
Population: 1,187,000
Change since 1990: 6.8%
Population density: 184.8 per sq mi
% Population 65 years and over: 12.9 (1996)

VITAL STATISTICS:
Birth rate: 15.5 *(per 1,000 population)*
Death rate: 643.1 *(per 100,000 population)*
Infant mortality rate: 6.7 *(deaths per 1,000 live births)*

GOVERNMENT:
Governor: Benjamin J. Cayetano (Democrat)
  Regular term: 4 years
  Current term began: December 1994
  Salary: $94,780
Lt. Governor: Mazie Hirono (Democrat)

STATE ECONOMY:
Gross state product: $36.718 billion
State budget: *(in thousands)*
  State revenues: $6,700,545
  Total expenditures: $6,093,375
  Debt at end of fiscal year: $5,252,711
  Cash and security holdings: $10,842,971

Chief products:
  Agriculture: Sugarcane, sorghum, corn, pineapple, macadamia nuts
  Manufacturing: Sugar, canned pineapple, oilrefining, steelmilling, printing and publishing
  Minerals: Stone, cement, sand, gravel

PERSONAL FINANCES:
Per capita personal income: $26,034
Median household income: $42,944
Average annual pay: $27,363
Percent of persons in poverty: 11.2%
Homeownership rate: 50.2%

EMPLOYMENT:
Labor force: 592,000
Unemployment rate: 6.4%
Total number of businesses: 79,050
  Total number of women owned businesses: 29,743
  Total number of minority owned businesses: 41,111

CRIME:
Crime rate: 6,584.5 *(per 100,000 people)*
  Violent crime: 280.6 *(per 100,000)*
  Property crime: 6,304.0 *(per 100,000)*
Total prisoners in custody: 3,309
Prison capacity occupied: 171.5%

HEALTH CARE:
Persons without health insurance coverage: 8.6%
Low income uninsured children: 4.5%
Occupancy rate in community hospitals: 82.6%

EDUCATION:
Current high school completion rate: 92.6%
High school drop out rate: 4.9%
Educational Attainment-High school graduate: 83.7%
                          Bachelor degree: 22.5%
Estimated public elementary and secondary school finances (*in millions*):
  Revenues: $1,173,579
  Expenditures: $1,157,159

IDAHO

GEOGRAPHY:
Area:
  total area: 83,574 sq mi
  land area: 82,751 sq mi
Capital: Boise, (population: 145,987)
Statehood: July 3, 1890 (43rd state)
Postal abbreviation: ID
State symbols:
  State motto: Esto Perpetua (It is perpetual)
  State song: "Here We Have Idaho"
  State bird: Mountain Bluebird
  State flower: Syringa
  State tree: Western White Pine

PEOPLE:
Population: 1,210,000
Change since 1990: 18.1%
Population density: 14.1 per sq mi
% Population 65 years and over: 11.4 (1996)

VITAL STATISTICS:
Birth rate: 16.0 *(per 1,000 population)*
Death rate: 732.1 *(per 100,000 population)*
Infant mortality rate: 6.9 *(deaths per 1,000 live births)*

GOVERNMENT:
Governor: Philip E. Batt (Republican)
Regular term: 4 years
Current term began: January 1995
Salary: $85,000
Lt. Governor: C.L. "Butch" Otter (Republican)

STATE ECONOMY:
Gross state product: $24.185 billion
State budget: *(in thousands)*
State revenues: $4,289,173
Total expenditures: $3,674,210
Debt at end of fiscal year: $1,598,125
Cash and security holdings: $7,294,362
Chief products:
Agriculture: Potatoes, wheat, sugar beets, cattle, livestock, sheep, forestry
Manufacturing: Food processing, machinery, electronic equipment, chemicals
Minerals: Silver, lead, antimony, molybdenum, semiprecious stones

PERSONAL FINANCES:
Per capita personal income: $20,478
Median household income: $34,175
Average annual pay: $23,353
Percent of persons in poverty: 13.2%
Homeownership rate: 72.3%

EMPLOYMENT:
Labor force: 634,000
Unemployment rate: 5.3%
Total number of businesses: 88,712
Total number of women owned businesses: 29,946
Total number of minority owned businesses: 2,747

CRIME:
Crime rate: 4,012.5 *(per 100,000 people)*
Violent crime: 267.2 *(per 100,000)*
Property crime: 3,745.3 *(per 100,00)*
Total prisoners in custody: 3,257
Prison capacity occupied: 106.3%

HEALTH CARE:
Persons without health insurance coverage: 16.5%
Low income uninsured children: 8.6%
Occupancy rate in community hospitals: 55.5%

EDUCATION:
Current high school completion rate: 85.2%
High school drop out rate: NA
Educational Attainment-High school graduate: 85.7%
Bachelor degree: 19.4%
Estimated public elementary and secondary school finances *(in millions)*:
Revenues: $1,082,353
Expenditures: $1,108,075

ILLINOIS

GEOGRAPHY:
Area:
total area: 57,918 sq mi
land area: 55,593 sq mi
Capital: Springfield, (population: 105,938)
Statehood: December 3, 1818 (21st state)
Postal abbreviation: IL
State symbols:
State motto: State Sovereignty, National Union
State song: "Illinois"
State bird: Cardinal
State flower: Violet
State tree: White oak

PEOPLE:
Population: 11,896,000
Change since 1990: 3.6%
Population density: 212.8 per sq mi
% population 65 years and over: 12.5 (1996)

VITAL STATISTICS:
Birth rate: 15.6 *(per 1,000 population)*
Death rate: 916.9 *(per 100,000 population)*
Infant mortality rate: 9.3 *(deaths per 1,000 live births)*

GOVERNMENT:
Governor: Jim Edgar (Republican)
Regular term: 4 years
Current term began: January 1995
Salary: $126,500
Lt. Governor: vacancy

STATE ECONOMY:
Gross state product: $332.853 billion
State budget: *(in thousands)*
State revenues: $39,038,066
Total expenditures: $35,301,874
Debt at end of fiscal year: $23,800,807
Cash and security holdings: $59,776,435
Chief products:
Agriculture: Soybean, wheat, corn, pork, dairy products, beef
Manufacturing: Fabricated metals, food products, rubber products, electrical and nonelectrical machinery, chemicals
Minerals: Fluorite, coal, sulfur, lead, zinc, limestone, silica, florite

PERSONAL FINANCES:
Per capita personal income: $28,202
Median household income: $39,375
Average annual pay: $31,285
Percent of persons in poverty: 12.3%
Homeownership rate: 68.1%

EMPLOYMENT:
Labor force: 6,130,000
Unemployment rate: 4.7%
Total number of businesses: 726,974
Total number of women owned businesses: 250,613
Total number of minority owned businesses: 67,603

CRIME:
Crime rate: 5,315.8 *(per 100,000)*
  Violent crime: 886.2 *(per 100,000)*
  Property crime: 4,429.6 *(per 100,000)*
Total prisoners in custody: 38,852
Prison capacity occupied: 138.5%

HEALTH CARE:
Persons without health insurance coverage: 11.3%
Low income uninsured children: 6.4%
Occupancy rate in community hospitals: 63.5%

EDUCATION:
Current high school completion rate: 89.3%
High school drop out rate: NA
Educational Attainment-High school graduate: 84.4%
  Bachelor degree: 25.0%
Estimated public elementary and secondary school finances *(in millions)*:
  Revenues: $12,169,540
  Expenditures: $11,528,302

I N D I A N A

GEOGRAPHY:
Area:
  total area: 36,420 sq mi
  land area: 35,870 sq mi
Capital: Indianapolis, (population: 752,279)
Statehood: December 11, 1816 (19th state)
Postal abbreviation: IN
State symbols:
  State motto: The Crossroads of America
  State song: "On the Banks of the Wabash, Far Away"
  State bird: Cardinal
  State flower: Peony
  State tree: Tulip Tree

PEOPLE:
Population: 5,864,000
Change since 1990: 5.3%
Population density: 161.8 per sq mi
% Population 65 years and over: 12.6 (1996)

VITAL STATISTICS:
Birth rate: 14.3 *(per 1,000 population)*
Death rate: 918.2 *(per 100,000 population)*
Infant mortality rate: 8.8 *(deaths per 1,000 live births)*

GOVERNMENT:
Governor: Frank O'Bannon (Democrat)
  Regular term: 4 years
  Current term began: January 1997
  Salary: $77,200
Lt. Governor: Joe Kernan (Democrat)

STATE ECONOMY:
Gross state product: $138.190 billion
State budget: *(in thousands)*
  State revenues: $17,536,856
  Total expenditures: $16,370,436
  Debt at end of fiscal year: $6,140,051
  Cash and security holdings: $23,268,867

Chief products:
  Agriculture: Corn, soybeans, wheat, tomatoes, cattle, hogs
  Manufacturing: Transportation equipment, steel, musical instruments, diamond cutting tools, chemicals
  Minerals: Coal, quarry stone

PERSONAL FINANCES:
Per capita personal income: $23,604
Median household income: $34,759
Average annual pay: $26,477
Percent of persons in poverty: 8.6%
Homeownership rate: 74.1%

EMPLOYMENT:
Labor force: 3,094,000
Unemployment rate: 3.5%
Total number of businesses: 364,253
  Total number of women owned businesses: 125,411
  Total number of minority owned businesses: 13,865

CRIME:
Crime rate: 4,498.2 *(per 100,000 people)*
  Violent crime: 537.0 *(per 100,000)*
  Property crime: 3,961.2 *(per 100,000)*
Total prisoners in custody: 15,766
Prison capacity occupied: 114.6%

HEALTH CARE:
Persons without health insurance coverage: 10.6%
Low income uninsured children: 7.9%
Occupancy rate in community hospitals: 58.7%

EDUCATION:
Current high school completion rate: 88.3%
High school drop out rate: 4.6%
Educational Attainment-High school graduate: 81.9%
  Bachelor degree: 16.2%
Estimated public elementary and secondary school finances *(in millions)*:
  Revenues: $6,347,970
  Expenditures: $6,208,110

---

*Accepts $66,000

I O W A

GEOGRAPHY:
Area:
  total area: 56,276 sq mi
  land area: 55,875 sq mi
Capital: Des Moines, (population: 194,965)
Statehood: December 28, 1846 (29th state)
Postal abbreviation: IA
State symbols:
  State motto: Our Liberties We Prize, Our Rights We Will Maintain
  State song: "Song of Iowa"
  State bird: Eastern Goldfinch
  State flower: Wild Rose
  State tree: Oak

PEOPLE:
Population: 2,852,000
Change since 1990: 2.7%
Population density: 50.9 per sq mi
% population 65 years and over: 15.2 (1996)

VITAL STATISTICS:
Birth rate: 13.0 *(per 1,000 population)*
Death rate: 986.0 *(per 100,000 population)*
Infant mortality rate: 7.5 *(deaths per 1,000 live births)*

GOVERNMENT:
Governor: Terry E. Branstad (Republican)
Regular term: 4 years
Current term began: January 1995
Salary: $101,312
Lt. Governor: Joy Corning (Republican)

STATE ECONOMY:
Gross state product: $68.298 billion
State budget: *(in thousands)*
State revenues: $9,509,064
Total expenditures: $9,347,768
Debt at end of fiscal year: $2,013,891
Cash and security holdings: $18,888,500
Chief Products:
Agriculture: Corn, soybean,oats, grain, beef, pork
Manufacturing: Food processing, agricultural machinery, refrigeration equipment
Minerals: Cement and gypsum

PERSONAL FINANCES:
Per capita personal income: $23,102
Median household income: $34,888
Average annual pay: $23,679
Percent of persons in poverty: 10.9%
Homeownership rate: 72.7%

EMPLOYMENT:
Labor force: 1,577,000
Unemployment rate: 3.3%
Total number of businesses: 206,840
Total number of women owned businesses: 71,040
Total number of minority owned businesses: 2,939

CRIME:
Crime rate: 3,648.9 *(per 100,000 people)*
Violent crime: 272.5 *(per 100,000)*
Property crime: 3,376.4 *(per 100,000)*
Total prisoners in custody: 6,342
Prison capacity occupied: 117.6%

HEALTH CARE:
Persons without health insurance coverage: 11.6%
Low income uninsured children: 8.1%
Occupancy rate in community hospitals: 57.9%

EDUCATION:
Current high school completion rate: 91.6%
High school drop out rate: 3.4%

Educational Attainment-High school graduate: 86.7%
Bachelor degree: 21.7%
Estimated public elementary and secondary school finances *(in millions)*:
Revenues: $2,855,058
Expenditures: $2,856,447

KANSAS

GEOGRAPHY:
Area:
total area: 82,282 sq mi
land area: 81,823 sq mi
Capital: Topeka, (population: 120,646)
Statehood: January 29, 1861 (34th state)
Postal abbreviation: KS
State symbols:
State motto: Ad Astra Per Aspera
(To the stars through difficulties)
State song: "Home on the Range"
State bird: Western Meadowlark
State flower: Wild Native Sunflower
State tree: Cottonwood

PEOPLE:
Population: 2,595,000
Change since 1990: 3.8%
Population density: 31.4 per sq mi
% population 65 years and over: 13.7 (1996)

VITAL STATISTICS:
Birth rate: 15.4 *(per 1,000 population)*
Death rate: 933.0 *(per 100,000 population)*
Infant mortality rate: 7.7 *(deaths per 1,000 live births)*

GOVERNMENT:
Governor: Bill Graves (Republican)
Regular term: 4 years
Current term began: January 1995
Salary: $85,000
Lt. Governor: Gary Sherrer (Republican)

STATE ECONOMY:
Gross state product: $61.758 billion
State budget: *(in thousands)*
State revenues: $7,949,762
Total expenditures: $7,496,081
Debt at end of fiscal year: $1,211,295
Cash and security holdings: $8,825,615
Chief products:
Agriculture: Wheat, corn, sorghum, tobacco, soybeans, beef, veal, hogs
Manufacturing: Meat-packing, grain-milling, aviation aircraft, the assembly of machinery, printing and publishing
Minerals: Petroleum and natural gas

PERSONAL FINANCES:
Per capita personal income: $24,379
Median household income: $31,911
Average annual pay: $24,609
Percent of persons in poverty: 11.0%
Homeownership rate: 66.5%

EMPLOYMENT:
Labor force: 1,366,000
Unemployment rate: 3.8%
Total number of businesses: 191,262
  Total number of women owned businesses: 66,429
  Total number of minority owned businesses: 7,244

CRIME:
Crime rate: 4,681.7 *(per 100,000 people)*
  Violent crime: 413.8 *(per 100,000)*
  Property crime: 4,268.0 *(per 100,000)*
Total prisoners in custody: 7,755
Prison capacity occupied: 94.7%

HEALTH CARE:
Persons without health insurance coverage: 11.4%
Low income uninsured children: 8.1%
Occupancy rate in community hospitals: 54.5%

EDUCATION:
Current high school completion rate: 91.6%
High school drop out rate: 5.0%
Educational Attainment-High school graduate: 88.1%
                       Bachelor degree: 27.5%
Estimated public elementary and secondary school finances *(in millions)*
  Revenues: $2,807,787
  Expenditures: $2,715,601

K E N T U C K Y

GEOGRAPHY:
Area:
  total area: 40,411 sq mi
  land area: 39,732 sq mi
Capital: Frankfort, (population: 41,302)
Statehood: June 1, 1792 (15th state)
Postal abbreviation: KY
State symbols:
  State motto: United We Stand, Divided We Fall
  State song: "My Old Kentucky Home, Good Night!"
  State bird: Cardinal
  State flower: Goldenrod
  State tree: Tulip poplar

PEOPLE:
Population: 3,908,000
Change since 1990: 5.3%
Population density: 97.2 per sq mi
% population 65 years and over: 12.6 (1996)

VITAL STATISTICS:
Birth rate: 13.6 *(per 1,000 population)*
Death rate: 963.7 *(per 100,000 population)*
Infant mortality rate: 7.8 *(deaths per 1,000 live births)*

GOVERNMENT:
Governor: Paul E. Patton (Democrat)
  Regular term: 4 years
  Current term began: December 1995
  Salary: $86,352

Lt. Governor: Stephen Henry, M.D. (Democrat)

STATE ECONOMY:
Gross state product: $86.485 billion
State budget: *(in thousands)*
  State revenues: $15,032,508
  Total expenditures: $12,949,018
  Debt at end of fiscal year: $7,120,354
  Cash and security holdings: $24,059,347
Chief products:
  Agriculture: Tobacco farming, wheat, soybeans, corn, hogs, livestock, cattle
  Manufacturing: Bourbon whiskey, thoroughbred horses, transportation equipment, chemicals
  Minerals: Bituminous coal, coal, natural gas, petroleum, asphalt, iron ore

PERSONAL FINANCES:
Per capita personal income: $20,657
Median household income: $31,552
Average annual pay: $24,462
Percent of persons in poverty: 15.9%
Homeownership rate: 75.0%

EMPLOYMENT:
Labor force: 1,928,000
Unemployment rate: 5.4%
Total number of businesses: 236,525
  Total number of women owned businesses: 74,280
  Total number of minority owned businesses: 7,421

CRIME:
Crime rate: 3,166.3 *(per 100,000 people)*
  Violent crime: 320.5 *(per 100,000)*
  Property crime: 2,845.8 *(per 100,000)*
Total prisoners in custody: 10,148
Prison capacity occupied: 99.2%

HEALTH CARE:
Persons without health insurance coverage: 15.4%
Low income uninsured children: 8.9%
Occupancy rate in community hospitals: 62.2%

EDUCATION:
Current high school completion rate: 82.2%
High school drop out rate: NA
Educational Attainment-High school graduate: 75.4%
                       Bachelor degree: 17.6%
Estimated public elementary and secondary school finances *(in millions)*:
  Revenues: $3,389,904
  Expenditures: $3,226,769

L O U I S I A N A

GEOGRAPHY:
Area:
  total area: 49,651 sq mi
  land area: 43,566 sq mi
Capital: Baton Rouge, (population: 227,482)
Statehood: April 30, 1812 (18th state)

Postal abbreviation: LA
State symbols:
State motto: Union, Justice, Confidence
State song: "Give Me Louisiana" and "You Are My Sunshine"
State bird: Eastern Brown Pelican
State flower: Magnolia
State tree: Bald Cypress

PEOPLE:
Population: 4,352,000
Change since 1990: 3.1%
Population density: 99.7 per sq mi
% population 65 years and over: 11.4 (1996)

VITAL STATISTICS:
Birth rate: 15.2 *(per 1,000 population)*
Death rate: 914.4 *(per 100,000 population)*
Infant mortality rate: 10.6 *(deaths per 1,000 live births)*

GOVERNMENT:
Governor: Mike Foster (Republican)
Regular term: 4 years
Current term began: January 1996
Salary: $95,000
Lt. Governor: Kathleen Blanco (Democrat)

STATE ECONOMY:
Gross state product: $101.101 billion
State budget: *(in thousands)*
State revenues: $15,928,979
Total expenditures: $14,285,704
Debt at end of fiscal year: $7,030,252
Cash and security holdings: $26,721,914
Chief products:
Agriculture: Soybeans, cotton, beef cattle, poultry, dairy products, tree-farming, sugarcane
Fishing Industry: Shrimp
Manufacturing: Chemicals, refined petroleum, paper, transportation equipment, processed food
Minerals: Natural gas, petroleum, sulfur, salt

PERSONAL FINANCES:
Per capita personal income: $20,680
Median household income: $29,518
Average annual pay: $24,528
Percent of persons in poverty: 20.1%
Homeownership rate: 66.5%

EMPLOYMENT:
Labor Force: 2,024,000
Unemployment rate: 6.1%
Total number of businesses: 236,589
Total number of women owned businesses: 76,849
Total number of minority owned businesses: 29,784

CRIME:
Crime rate: 6,838.8 *(per 100,000 people)*
Violent crime: 929.1 *(per 100,000)*
Property crime: 5,909.7 *(per 100,000)*

Total prisoners in custody: 17,664
Prison capacity occupied: 97.4%

HEALTH CARE:
Persons without health insurance coverage: 20.9%
Low income uninsured children: 14.9%
Occupancy rate in community hospitals: 57.0%

EDUCATION:
Current high school completion rate: 82.2%
High school drop out rate: 3.5%
Educational Attainment-High school graduate: 75.7%
Bachelor degree: 18.1%
Estimated public elementary and secondary school finances *(in millions)*:
Revenues: $3,790,184
Expenditures: $3,732,880

MAINE

GEOGRAPHY:
Area:
total area: 33,741 sq mi
land area: 30,865 sq mi
Capital: Augusta,(population: 21,325)
Statehood: March 15, 1820 (23rd state)
Postal abbreviation: ME
State symbols:
State motto: Dirigo (I lead)
State song: "State of Maine Song"
State bird: Chickadee
State flower: White Pine Cone and Tassel
State tree: White Pine

PEOPLE:
Population: 1,242,000
Change since 1990: 1.3%
Population density: 40.2 per sq mi
% population 65 years and over: 13.9 (1996)

VITAL STATISTICS:
Birth rate: 11.1 *(per 1,000 population)*
Death rate: 946.8 *(per 100,000 population)*
Infant mortality rate: 6.2 *(deaths per 1,000 live births)*

GOVERNMENT:
Governor: Angus S. King, Jr. (Independent)
Regular term: 4 years
Current term began: January 1995
Salary: $70,000
Senate President: Mark Lawrence (Democrat)

STATE ECONOMY:
Gross state product: $26.069 billion
State budget: *(in thousands)*
State revenues: $5,215,004
Total expenditures: $4,441,284
Debt at end of fiscal year: $3,202,599
Cash and security holdings: $6,399,966
Chief products:
Agriculture: Potatoes, oats, apples, blueberries,

poultry, dairy products
Fishing Industry: Shellfish
Manufacturing: Paper and pulp products
Minerals: Sand, gravel, limestone, building stone

PERSONAL FINANCES:
Per capita personal income: $22,078
Median household income: $34,777
Average annual pay: $23,850
Percent of persons in poverty: 11.2%
Homeownership rate: 74.9%

EMPLOYMENT:
Labor force: 659,000
Unemployment rate: 5.4%
Total number of businesses: 109,360
  Total number of women owned businesses: 35,260
  Total number of minority owned businesses: 1,099

CRIME:
Crime rate: 3,394.1 *(per 100,000 people)*
  Violent crime: 124.9 *(per 100,000)*
  Property crime: 3,269.2 *(per 100,000)*
Total prisoners in custody: 1,476
Prison capacity occupied: 85.4%

HEALTH CARE:
Persons without health insurance coverage: 12.1%
Low income uninsured children: 7.4%
Occupancy rate in community hospitals: 68.0%

EDUCATION:
Current high school completion rate: 91.8%
High school drop out rate: 3.3%
Educational Attainment-High school graduate: 85.8%
               Bachelor degree: 20.0%
Estimated public elementary and secondary school finances *(in millions)*:
  Revenues: $1,394,492
  Expenditures: $1,391,570

MARYLAND

GEOGRAPHY:
Area:
  total area: 12,297 sq mi
  land area: 9,775 sq mi
Capital: Annapolis, (population: 33,187)
Statehood: April 28, 1788 (7th state)
Postal abbreviation: MD
State symbols:
  State motto: Fatti Mashii, Parole Femine
    (Manly deeds, womanly words)
  State song: "Maryland, My Maryland"
  State bird: Baltimore Oriole
  State flower: Black-Eyed Susan
  State tree: White Oak

PEOPLE:
Population: 5,094,000
Change since 1990: 6.1%

Population density: 515.9 per sq mi
% population 65 years and over: 11.4 (1996)

VITAL STATISTICS:
Birth rate: 13.7 *(per 1,000 population)*
Death rate: 829.8 *(per 100,000 population)*
Infant mortality rate: 9.0 *(deaths per 1,000 live births)*

GOVERNMENT:
Governor: Parris N. Glendening (Democrat)
  Regular term: 4 years
  Current term began: January 1995
  Salary: $120,000
Lt. Governor: Kathleen Kennedy Townsend
  (Democrat)

STATE ECONOMY:
Gross state product: $132.703 billion
State budget: *(in thousands)*
  State revenues: $20,128,472
  Total expenditures: $16,199,545
  Debt at end of fiscal year: $9,873,357
  Cash and security holdings: $40,443,157
Chief products:
  Agriculture: Chicken, corn, soybeans,
    tobacco
  Fishing Industry: Crab and finfish
  Manufacturing: Primary metals, electronic and electrical equipment, food products, transportation equipment
  Minerals: Sand, gravel, bituminous coal

PERSONAL FINANCES:
Per capita personal income: $28,969
Median household income: $43,123
Average annual pay: $30,293
Percent of persons in poverty: 10.2%
Homeownership rate: 70.5%

EMPLOYMENT:
Labor force: 2,798,000
Unemployment rate: 5.1%
Total number of businesses: 328,403
  Total number of women owned businesses: 121,777
  Total number of minority owned businesses: 55,587

CRIME:
Crime rate: 6,061.9 *(per 100,000 people)*
  Violent crime: 931.2 *(per 100,000)*
  Property crime: 5,130.7 *(per 100,000)*
Total prisoners in custody: 21,729
Prison capacity occupied: 164.7%

HEALTH CARE:
Persons without health insurance coverage: 11.4%
Low income inunsured children: 7.6%
Occupancy rate in community hospitals: 75.2%

EDUCATION:
Current high school completion rate: 93.4%
High school drop out rate: NA
Educational Attainment-High school graduate: 84.7%
               Bachelor degree: 32.2%

Estimated public elementary and secondary school finances (*in millions*):
Revenues: $5,574,700
Expenditures: $5,598,151

MASSACHUSETTS

GEOGRAPHY:
Area:
total area: 9,241 sq mi
land area: 7,838 sq mi
Capital: Boston, (population: 547,725)
Statehood: February 6, 1788, (6th state)
Postal abbreviation: MA
State symbols:
State motto: Ense Petit Placidam Sub Libertate Quietem (By the sword we seek peace, but peace only under liberty)
State song: "All Hail to Massachusetts"
State bird: Chickadee
State flower: Mayflower
State tree: American Elm

PEOPLE:
Population: 6,119,000
Change since 1990: 1.3%
Population density: 774.9 per sq mi
% population 65 years and over: 14.1 (1996)

VITAL STATISTICS:
Birth rate: 13.2 *(per 1,000 population)*
Death rate: 913.4 *(per 100,000 population)*
Infant mortality rate: 6.0 *(deaths per 1,000 live births)*

GOVERNMENT:
Governor: Argeo Paul Cellucci* (Republican)
Regular term: 4 years
Current term began: January 1995
Salary: $90,000
Lt. Governor: (vacant)

STATE ECONOMY:
Gross state product: $186.199 billion
State budget: *(in thousands)*
State revenues: $25,537,977
Total expenditures: $25,790,660
Debt at end of fiscal year: $29,386,049
Cash and security holdings: $35,435,241
Chief products:
Agriculture: Cranberries, greenhouse and nursery products, potatoes, dairy products
Manufacturing: Electronic and electrical equipment, watches, cutlery, guns, leather goods
Minerals: Babingtonite

PERSONAL FINANCES:
Per capita personal income: $31,524
Median household income: $39,604
Average annual pay: $33,940
Percent of persons in poverty: 10.6%
Homeownership rate: 62.3%

EMPLOYMENT:
Labor force: 3,260,000
Unemployment rate: 4.0%
Total number of businesses: 442,848
Total number of women owned businesses: 147,572
Total number of minority owned businesses: 20,749

CRIME:
Crime rate: 3,837.1 *(per 100,000 people)*
Violent crime: 642.2 *(per 100,000)*
Property crime: 3,194.9 *(per 100,000)*
Total prisoners in custody: 10,803
Prison capacity occupied: %

HEALTH CARE:
Persons without health insurance coverage: 12.4%
Low income uninsured children: 4.5%
Occupancy rate in community hospitals: 71.5%

EDUCATION:
Current high school completion rate: 92.0%
High school drop out rate: 3.5%
Educational Attainment-High school graduate: 85.9%
 Bachelor degree: 33.5%
Estimated public elementary and secondary school finances (*in millions*):
Revenues: $6,491,815
Expenditures: $6,090,534

---

*Formerly Lt. Governor, Mr. Cellucci became governor on July 29, 1997, when William Weld resigned the post. He is eligible to serve two more terms.

MICHIGAN

GEOGRAPHY:
Area:
total area: 96,705 sq mi
land area: 56,809 sq mi
Capital: Lansing, (population: 119,590)
Statehood: January 26, 1837 (26th state)
Postal abbreviation: MI
State symbols:
State motto: Si Quaeris Peninsulam Amoenam Circumspice (If you seek a pleasant peninsula, look about you)
State song: "Michigan, My Michigan"
State bird: Robin
State flower: Apple Blossom
State tree: White Pine

PEOPLE:
Population: 9,774,000
Change since 1990: 3.2%
Population density: 168.1 per sq mi
% Population 65 years and over: 12.4 (1996)

VITAL STATISTICS:
Birth rate: 14.3 *(per 1,000 population)*
Death rate: 876.1 *(per 100,000 population)*
Infant mortality rate: 8.6 *(deaths per 1,000 live births)*

GOVERNMENT:
Governor: John Engler (Republican)
  Regular term: 4 years
  Current term began: January 1995
  Salary: $127,300
Lt. Governor: Connie Binsfeld (Republican)

STATE ECONOMY:
Gross state product: $240.390 billion
State budget: *(in thousands)*
  State revenues: $45,509,221
  Total expenditures: $36,092,175
  Debt at end of fiscal year: $14,431,375
  Cash and security holdings: $60,166,323
Chief products:
  Agriculture: Dairy products, grains, potatoes, fruit, corn
  Manufacturing: Automobiles, machinery, fabricated metals, rubber and plastic products, chemicals
  Minerals: Copper and iron ore

PERSONAL FINANCES:
Per capita personal income: $25,560
Median household income: $38,364
Average annual pay: $31,522
Percent of persons in poverty: 11.7%
Homeownership rate: 73.3%

EMPLOYMENT:
Labor force: 4,986,000
Unemployment rate: 4.2%
Total number of businesses: 551,091
  Total number of women owned businesses: 193,820
  Total number of minority owned businesses: 31,740

CRIME:
Crime rate: 5,117.5 *(per 100,000 people)*
  Violent crime: 635.3 *(per 100,000)*
  Property crime: 4,482.2 *(per 100,000)*
Total prisoners in custody: 42,349
Prison capacity occupied: 104.5%

HEALTH CARE:
Persons without health insurance coverage: 8.9%
Low income uninsured children: 5.6%
Occupancy rate in community hospitals: 64.6%

EDUCATION:
Current high school completion rate: 89.1%
High school drop out rate: NA
Educational Attainment-High school graduate: 86.0%
              Bachelor degree: 21.0%
Estimated public elementary and secondary school finances *(in millions)*:
  Revenues: $12,100,525
  Expenditures: $12,049,700

MINNESOTA

GEOGRAPHY:
Area:
  total area: 86,943 sq mi
  land area: 79,617 sq mi
Capital: St. Paul, (population: 262,071)
Statehood: May 11, 1858 (32th state)
Postal abbreviation: MN
State symbols:
  State motto: L'Etoile du Nord
    (The star of the north)
  State song: "Hail! Minnesota"
  State bird: Common Loon
  State flower: Pink & White Lady Slipper
  State tree: Norway Pine

PEOPLE:
Population: 4,686,000
Change since 1990: 6.4%
Population density: 57.9 per sq mi
% Population 65 years and over: 12.4 (1996)

VITAL STATISTICS:
Birth rate: 13.7 *(per 1,000 population)*
Death rate: 813.7 *(per 100,000 population)*
Infant mortality rate: 7.0 *(deaths per 1,000 live births)*

GOVERNMENT:
Governor: Arne H. Carlson (Republican)
  Regular term: 4 years
  Current term began: January 1995
  Salary: $109.053
Lt. Governor: Joanne Benson (Republican)

STATE ECONOMY:
Gross state product: $124.641 billion
State budget: *(in thousands)*
  State revenues: $22,881,630
  Total expenditures: $18,443,264
  Debt at end of fiscal year: $4,862,084
  Cash and security holdings: $36,924,899
Chief products:
  Agriculture: Dairy products, grain, cattle, livestock
  Manufacturing: Processed food, pulp and paper products, electrical and electronic equipment
  Minerals: Iron ore, taconite, granite, limestone

PERSONAL FINANCES:
Per capita personal income: $26,797
Median household income: $40,022
Average annual pay: $28,869
Percent of persons in poverty: 9.5%
Homeownership rate: 75.4%

EMPLOYMENT:
Labor force: 2,625,000
Unemployment rate: 3.3%
Total number of businesses: 358,921

Total number of women owned businesses: 124,143
Total number of minority owned businesses: 7,449

CRIME:
Crime rate: 4,463.1 *(per 100,000 people)*
  Violent crime: 338.8 *(per 100,000)*
  Property crime: 4,124.3 *(per 100,000)*
Total prisoners in custody: 4,804
Prison capacity occupied: 108.3%

HEALTH CARE:
Persons without health insurance coverage: 10.2%
Low income uninsured children: 3.9%
Occupancy rate in community hospitals: 65.9%

EDUCATION:
Current high school completion rate: 95.3%
High school drop out rate: 5.2%
Educational Attainment-High school graduate: 87.9%
                    Bachelor degree: 28.3%
Estimated public elementary and secondary school finances *(in millions)*:
  Revenues: $5,581,958
  Expenditures: $6,028,765

MISSISSIPPI

GEOGRAPHY:
Area:
  total area: 48,286 sq mi
  land area: 46,914 sq mi
Capital: Jackson, (population: 193,097)
Statehood: December 10, 1817 (20th state)
Postal abbreviation: MS
State symbols:
  State motto: "*Virtute et Armis*" By Valor & Arms
  State song: "Go Mississippi"
  State bird: Northern Mockingbird
  State flower: Southern Magnolia
  State tree: Southern Magnolia

PEOPLE:
Population: 2,731,000
Change since 1990: 5.5%
Population density: 57.5 per sq mi
% population 65 years and over: 12.3 (1996)

VITAL STATISTICS:
Birth rate: 15.3 *(per 1,000 population)*
Death rate: 1,002.0 *(per 100,000 population)*
Infant mortality rate: 11.0 *(deaths per 1,000 live births)*

GOVERNMENT:
Governor: Kirk Fordice (Republican)
  Regular term: 4 years
  Current term began: January 1996
  Salary: $83,160
Lt. Governor: Ronnie Musgrove (Democrat)

STATE ECONOMY:
Gross state product: $50.587 billion

State budget: *(in thousands)*
  State revenues: $9,400,400
  Total expenditures: $9,005,740
  Debt at end of fiscal year: $2,454,627
  Cash and security holdings: $14,574,295
Chief products:
  Agriculture: Cotton, Soybeans, wheat, rice, corn, poultry, cattle
  Manufacturing: Processed food, pulp and paper products, primary metals, electrical equipment, apparel and textiles, lumber and wood products
  Minerals: Petroleum, natural gas, iron ore, bauxite

PERSONAL FINANCES:
Per capita personal income: $18,272
Median household income: $27,000
Average annual pay: $21,822
Percent of persons in poverty: 22.1%
Homeownership rate: 73.7%

EMPLOYMENT:
Labor force: 1,265,000
Unemployment rate: 5.7%
Total number of businesses: 135,497
  Total number of women owned businesses: 40,879
  Total number of minority owned businesses: 16,386

CRIME:
Crime rate: 4,522.9 *(per 100,000 people)*
  Violent crime: 488.3 *(per 100,000)*
  Property crime: 4,034.6 *(per 100,000)*
Total prisoners in custody: 10,030
Prison capacity occupied: 100.7%

HEALTH CARE:
Persons without health insurance coverage: 18.5%
Low income uninsured children: 14.1%
Occupancy rate in community hospitals: 59.0%

EDUCATION:
Current high school completion rate: 83.9%
High school drop out rate: 6.4%
Educational Attainment-High school graduate: 77.5%
                    Bachelor degree: 20.9%
Estimated public elementary and secondary school finances *(in millions)*:
  Revenues: $2,115,268
  Expenditures: $2,160,068

MISSOURI

GEOGRAPHY:
Area:
  total area: 69,709 sq mi
  land area: 68,898 sq mi
Capital: Jefferson City, (population: 35,481)
Statehood: August 10, 1821 (24th state)
Postal abbreviation: MO
State symbols:
  State motto: Salus populi Suprema lex esto (Let the good of the people be the Supreme Law)

State song: "Missouri Waltz"
State bird: Bluebird
State flower: Blossom of the Hawthorn
State tree: Dogwood

PEOPLE:
Population: 5,402,000
Change since 1990: 4.7%
Population density: 77.3 per sq mi
% Population 65 years and over: 13.8 (1996)

VITAL STATISTICS:
Birth rate: 13.8 *(per 1,000 population)*
Death rate: 1,021.9 *(per 100,000 population)*
Infant mortality rate: 8.1 *(deaths per 1,000 live births)*

GOVERNMENT:
Governor: Mel Carnahan (Democrat)
Regular term: 4 years
Current term began: January 1997
Salary: $107,329
Lt. Governor: Roger B. Wilson (Democrat)

STATE ECONOMY:
Gross state product: $128.216 billion
State budget: *(in thousands)*
State revenues: $16,600,626
Total expenditures: $14,229,714
Debt at end of fiscal year: $7,579,129
Cash and security holdings: $32,266,896
Chief products:
Agriculture: Soybeans, corn, wheat, cattle, sheep
Manufacturing: Processed food, aerospace and
transportation equipment, rubber, chemicals
Minerals: Lead, iron ore, limestone

PERSONAL FINANCES:
Per capita personal income: $24,001
Median household income: $35,059
Average annual pay: $26,608
Percent of persons in poverty: 9.5%
Homeownership rate: 70.5%

EMPLOYMENT:
Labor force: 2,888,000
Unemployment rate: 4.2%
Total number of businesses: 348,978
Total number of women owned businesses: 117,885
Total number of minority owned businesses: 15,437

CRIME:
Crime rate: 5,084.0 *(per 100,000 people)*
Violent crime: 590.9 *(per 100,000)*
Property crime: 4,493.0 *(per 100,000)*
Total prisoners in custody: 22,018
Prison capacity occupied: 95.4%

HEALTH CARE:
Persons without health insurance coverage: 13.2%
Low income uninsured children: 7.3%
Occupancy rate in community hospitals: 58.7%

EDUCATION:
Current high school completion rate: 88.0%
High school drop out rate: 7.1%
Educational Attainment-High school graduate: 80.1%
Bachelor degree: 22.9%

Estimated public elementary and secondary school finances *(in millions)*:
Revenues: $4,817,215
Expenditures: $4,915,424

MONTANA

GEOGRAPHY:
Area:
total area: 147,046 sq mi
land area: 145,556 sq mi
Capital: Helena, (population: 24,569)
Statehood: November 8, 1889 (41st state)
Postal abbreviation: MT
State symbols:
State motto: Oro y Plata (Gold and Silver)
State song: "Montana"
State bird: Western Meadowlark
State flower: Bitterroot
State tree: Ponderosa Pine

PEOPLE:
Population: 879,000
Change since 1990: 10.1%
Population density: 6.0 per sq mi
% population 65 years and over: 13.2 (1996)

VITAL STATISTICS:
Birth rate: 12.2 *(per 1,000 population)*
Death rate: 876.6 *(per 100,000 population)*
Infant mortality rate: 7.4 *(deaths per 1,000 live births)*

GOVERNMENT:
Governor: Marc Racicot (Republican)
Regular term: 4 years
Current term began: January 1997
Salary: $78,245
Lt Governor: Judy Martz (Republican)

STATE ECONOMY:
Gross state product: $16.862 billion
State budget: *(in thousands)*
State revenues: $3,523,812
Total expenditures: $3,203,897
Debt at end of fiscal year: $2,055,644
Cash and security holdings: $6,727,293
Chief products:
Agriculture: Oats, barley, wheat, sugar beets, live-
stock, cattle
Manufacturing: Lumber and wood products, petro-
leum, food products
Minerals: Coal, petroleum, natural gas, copper,
phosphates, vermiculite, bentonite, sand, gravel,
gypsum

PERSONAL FINANCES:
Per capita personal income: $20,046
Median household income: $28,631
Average annual pay: $21,146
Percent of persons in poverty: 16.2%
Homeownership rate: 67.5%

EMPLOYMENT:
Labor force: 454,000
Unemployment rate: 5.4%
Total number of businesses: 76,331
  Total number of women owned businesses: 25,310
  Total number of minority owned businesses:
    1,498

CRIME:
Crime rate: 4,493.6 *(per 100,000 people)*
  Violent crime: 161.0 *(per 100,000)*
  Property crime: 4,332.7 *(per 100,000)*
Total prisoners in custody: 1,590
Percent of prison capacity occupied: 182.4%

HEALTH CARE:
Persons without health insurance coverage: 13.6%
Low income uninsured children: 8.4%
Occupancy rate in community hospitals: 64.1%

EDUCATION:
Current high school completion rate: 89.8%
High school drop out rate: NA
Educational Attainment-High school graduate: 88.6%
                              Bachelor degree: 25.2%
Estimated public elementary and secondary school finances *(in millions)*:
  Revenues: $908,403
  Expenditures: $898,698

*Crime data for Montana are estimated.

NEBRASKA

GEOGRAPHY:
Area:
  total area: 77,358 sq mi
  land area: 76,878 sq mi
Capital: Lincoln, (population: 203,076)
Statehood: March 1, 1867 (37th state)
Postal abbreviation: NE
State symbols:
  State motto: Equality Before the Law
  State song: "Beautiful Nebraska"
  State bird: Western Meadowlark
  State flower: Goldenrod
  State tree: Cottonwood

PEOPLE:
Population: 1,657,000
Change since 1990: 4.7%
Population density: 21.3 per sq mi
% population 65 years and over: 13.8 (1996)

VITAL STATISTICS:
Birth rate: 14.1 *(per 1,000 population)*
Death rate: 932.6 *(per 100,000 population)*
Infant mortality rate: 7.7 *(deaths per 1,000 live births)*

GOVERNMENT:
Governor: E. Benjamin Nelson (Democrat)

  Regular term: 4 years
  Current term began: January 1995
  Salary: $65,000
Lt. Governor: Kim Robak (Democrat)

STATE ECONOMY:
Gross state product: $41.357 billion
State budget: *(in thousands)*
  State *revenues:* $5,537,331
  Total expenditures: $4,801,745
  Debt at end of fiscal year: $1,494,425
  Cash and security holdings: $6,895,323
Chief products:
  Agriculture: Corn, hay, wheat, sorghum, soybeans, sugar beets, cattle, hogs
  Manufacturing: Food processing, machinery, chemicals, printing and publishing, electronic, transportation equipment, metals
  Minerals: Petroleum

PERSONAL FINANCES:
Per capita personal income: $23,803
Median household income: $33,958
Average annual pay: $23,291
Persons below poverty level: 9.9%
Homeownership rate: 66.7%

EMPLOYMENT:
Labor force: 906,000
Unemployment rate: 2.6%
Total number of businesses: 124,212
  Total number of women owned businesses: 43,637
  Total number of minority owned businesses: 3,138

CRIME:
Crime rate: 4,436.6 *(per 100,000 people)*
  Violent crime: 434.7 *(per 100,000)*
  Property crime: 4,001.8 *(per 100,000)*
Total prisoners in custody: 3,216
Prison capacity occupied: 127.7%

HEALTH CARE:
Persons without health insurance coverage: 11.4%
Low income uninsured children: 6.0%
Occupancy rate in community hospitals: 55.2%

EDUCATION:
Current high school completion rate: 93.3%
High school drop out rate: 4.5%
Educational Attainment-High school graduate: 86.0%
                              Bachelor degree: 21.3%
Estimated public elementary and secondary school finances *(in millions)*:
  Revenues: $1,789,089
  Expenditures: $1,849,414

NEVADA

GEOGRAPHY:
Area:
  total area: 110,567 sq mi

land area: 109,806 sq mi
Capital: Carson City, (population: 40,443)
Statehood: October 31, 1864 (36th state)
Postal abbreviation: NV
State symbols:
 State motto: All For Our Country
 State song: "Home Means Nevada"
 State bird: Mountain Bluebird
 State flower: Sagebrush
 State tree: Pinon Pine and Bristlecone Pine

PEOPLE:
Population: 1,677,000
Change since 1990: 33.4%
Population density: 13.9 per sq mi
% population 65 years and over: 11.4 (1996)

VITAL STATISTICS:
Birth rate: 16.2 *(per 1,000 population)*
Death rate: 818.6 *(per 100,000 population)*
Infant mortality rate: 6.5 *(deaths per 1,000 live births)*

GOVERNMENT:
Governor: Bob Miller (Democrat)
 Regular term: 4 years
 Current term began: January 1995
 Salary: $90,000
Lt. Governor: Lonnie Hammargren, M.D.
 (Republican)

STATE ECONOMY:
Gross state product: $43.958 billion
State budget: *(in thousands)*
 State revenues: $6,494,347
 Total expenditures: $5,129,625
 Debt at end of fiscal year: $2,769,136
 Cash and security holdings: $12,360,253
Chief products:
 Agriculture: Hay, dairy products, potatoes, onions,
 cattle
 Manufacturing: Gaming devices, printing and pub-
 lishing
 Minerals: Gold, silver, barite, mercury

PERSONAL FINANCES:
Per capita personal income: $26,791
Median household income: $37,845
Average annual pay: $27,788
Percent of persons in poverty: 9.6%
Homeownership rate: 61.2%

EMPLOYMENT:
Labor force: 883,000
Unemployment rate: 4.1%
Total number of businesses: 87,786
 Total number of women owned businesses: 32,430
 Total number of minority owned businesses: 8,223

CRIME:
Crime rate: 5,992.0 *(per 100,000 people)*
 Violent crime: 811.3 *(per 100,000)*
 Property crime: 5,180.7 *(per 100,000)*

Total prisoners in custody: 8,081
Prison capacity occupied: 107.0%

HEALTH CARE:
Persons without health insurance coverage: 15.6%
Low income uninsured children: 10.8%
Occupancy rate in community hospitals: 67.8%

EDUCATION:
Current high school completion rate: 81.4%
High school drop out rate: 10.3%
Educational Attainment-High school graduate: 85.4%
 Bachelor degree: 19.9%
**Estimated public elementary and secondary school fi-
 nances** *(in millions):*
 Revenues: $1,364,259
 Expenditures: $1,381,200

NEW HAMPSHIRE

GEOGRAPHY:
Area:
 total area: 9,283 sq mi
 land area: 8,969 sq mi
Capital: Concord, (population: 36,006)
Statehood: June 21, 1788 (9th state)
Postal abbreviation: NH
State symbols:
 State motto: Live Free or Die
 State song: "Old New Hampshire."
 State bird: Purple Finch
 State flower: Purple Lilac
 State tree: White Birch

PEOPLE:
Population: 1,173,000
Change since 1990: 4.8%
Population density: 128.0 per sq mi
% population 65 years and over: 12.0 (1996)

VITAL STATISTICS:
Birth rate: 12.5 *(per 1,000 population)*
Death rate: 803.6 *(per 100,000 population)*
Infant mortality rate: 6.2 *(deaths per 1,000 live births)*

GOVERNMENT:
Governor: Jeanne Shaheen (Democrat)
 Regular term: 2 years
 Current term began: January 1997
 Salary: $86,235
Senate President: Joseph Delahunty (Republican)

STATE ECONOMY:
Gross state product $29.393 billion
State budget: *(in thousands)*
 State revenues: 3,560,750
 Total expenditures: $3,323,538
 Debt at end of fiscal year: $5,848,446
 Cash and security holdings: $9,089,544
Chief products:
 Agriculture: Dairy products, sugar, fruits, and vegta-

bles, maple syrup and sugar
Manufacturing: Lumber, paper, pulp, maple syrup, electrical and electric goods
Minerals: Granite

PERSONAL FINANCES:
Per capita personal income: $28,047
Median household income: $39,868
Average annual pay: $27,691
Persons below poverty level: 5.9%
Homeownership rate: 66.8%

EMPLOYMENT:
Labor force: 645,000
Unemployment rate: 3.1%
Total number of businesses: 97,772
Total number of women owned businesses: 31,492
Total number of minority owned businesses: 1,463

CRIME:
Crime rate: 2,823.5 *(per 100,000 people)*
Violent crime: 118.2 *(per 100,000)*
Property crime: 2,705.3 *(per 100,000)*
Total prisoners in custody: 2,037
Prison capacity occupied: 115.6%

HEALTH CARE:
Persons without health insurance coverage: 9.5%
Low income uninsured children: 6.6%
Occupancy rate in community hospitals: 63.7%

EDUCATION:
Current high school completion rate: 87.7%
High school drop out rate: NA
Educational Attainment-High school graduate: 85.1%
Bachelor degree: 27.0%
Estimated public elementary and secondary school finances (*in millions*):
Revenues: $1,148,024
Expenditures: $1,170,750

*Governor refuses a pay raise and has given 10 percent of his salary back to the state. Actual salary is $71,587

NEW JERSEY

GEOGRAPHY:
Area:
total area: 8,215 sq mi
land area: 7,419 sq mi
Capital: Trenton, (population: 88,675)
Statehood: December 18, 1787 (3rd state)
Postal abbreviation: NJ
State symbols:
State motto: Liberty & Prosperity
State song: "New Jersey Loyalty" (unofficial)
State bird: Eastern Goldfinch
State flower: Purple Violet
State tree: Red Oak

PEOPLE:
Population: 8,053,000
Change since 1990: 3.3%
Population density: 1,070.9 per sq mi
% population 65 years and over: 13.8 (1996)

VITAL STATISTICS:
Birth rate: 14.3 *(per 1,000 population)*
Death rate: 932.5 *(per 100,000 population)*
Infant mortality rate: 7.7 *(deaths per 1,000 live births)*

GOVERNMENT:
Governor: Christine T. Whitman (Republican)
Regular term: 4 years
Current term began: January 1998
Salary: $85,000
Senate President: Donald T. DiFrancesco (Republican)

STATE ECONOMY:
Gross state product: $254.945 billion
State budget: *(in thousands)*
State revenues: $36,086,757
Total expenditures: $29,429,586
Debt at end of fiscal year: $26,590,636
Cash and security holdings: $63,138,073
Chief products:
Agriculture: Fruits and vegtables, nursery and greenhouse products
Manufacturing: Chemicals, electronic and electrical equipment, clothing, toys, sporting goods, glass and stone products
Minerals: Stone, glass, clay

PERSONAL FINANCES:
Per capita personal income: $32,654
Median household income: $46,345
Average annual pay: $35,928
Percent of persons in poverty: 8.5%
Homeownership rate: 63.1%

EMPLOYMENT:
Labor force: 4,194,000
Unemployment rate: 5.1%
Total number of businesses: 517,204
Total number of women owned businesses: 164,798
Total number of minority owned businesses: 64,074

CRIME:
Crime rate: 4,332.9 *(per 100,000 people)*
Violent crime: 531.5 *(per 100,000)*
Property crime: 3,801.4 *(per 100,000)*
Total prisoners in custody: 23,123
Prison capacity occupied: 138.7%

HEALTH CARE:
Persons without health insurance coverage: 16.7%
Low income uninsured children: 6.4%
Occupancy rate in community hospitals: 77.0%

EDUCATION:
Current high school completion rate: 87.0%
High school drop out rate: NA

Educational Attainment-High school graduate: 84.8%

Bachelor degree: 28.5%

Estimated public elementary and secondary school finances (*in millions*):

Revenues: $11,629,218

Expenditures: $11,633,557

---

*Governor accepts only $85,000

NEW MEXICO

GEOGRAPHY:

Area:

total area: 121,598 sq mi

land area: 121,364 sq mi

Capital: Santa Fe, (population: 55,859)

Statehood: January 6, 1912 (47th state)

Postal abbreviation: NM

State symbols:

State motto: Crescit Eundo (It grows as it goes)

State song: "O, Fair New Mexico"

State bird: Roadrunner

State flower: Yucca

State tree: Pine

PEOPLE:

Population: 1,730,000

Change since 1990: 13.1%

Population density: 13.9 per sq mi

% population 65 years and over: 11.0 (1996)

VITAL STATISTICS:

Birth rate: 15.9 *(per 1,000 population)*

Death rate: 744.3 *(per 100,000 population)*

Infant mortality rate: 8.3 *(deaths per 1,000 live births)*

GOVERNMENT:

Governor: Gary E. Johnson (Republican)

Regular term: 4 years

Current term began: January 1995

Salary: $90,000

Lt. Governor: Walter Bradley (Republican)

STATE ECONOMY:

Gross state product: $37.832 billion

State budget: *(in thousands)*

State revenues: $8,188,172

Total expenditures: $7,058,693

Debt at end of fiscal year: $2,458,248

Cash and security holdings: $18,665,255

Chief products:

Agriculture: Beef, milk, hay

Manufacturing: Food processing, petroleum refining, smelting, construction materials, electronics, precision instruments

Minerals: Oil, natural gas, potash, uranium, coal

PERSONAL FINANCES:

Per capita personal income: $19,587

Median household income: $25,922

Average annual pay: $23,716

Percent of persons in poverty: 25.4%

Homeownership rate: 69.6%

EMPLOYMENT:

Labor force: 820,000

Unemployment rate: 6.2%

Total number of businesses: 107,377

Total number of women owned businesses: 40,636

Total number of minority owned businesses: 26,729

CRIME:

Crime rate: 6,602.3 *(per 100,000 people)*

Violent crime: 840.6 *(per 100,000)*

Property crime: 5,761.7 *(per 100,000)*

Total prisoners in custody: 4,733

Prison capacity occupied: 95.2%

HEALTH CARE:

Persons without health insurance coverage: 22.3%

Low income uninsured children: 19.5%

Occupancy rate in community hospitals: 53.8%

EDUCATION:

Current high school completion rate: 82.7%

High school drop out rate: 8.5%

Educational Attainment-High school graduate: 78.0%

Bachelor degree: 23.6%

Estimated public elementary and secondary school finances *(in millions)*:

Revenues: $1,646,244

Expenditures: $1,540,683

NEW YORK

GEOGRAPHY:

Area:

total area: 53,989 sq mi

land area: 47,224 sq mi

Capital: Albany, (population: 104,828)

Statehood: July 26, 1788, (11th state)

Postal abbreviation: NY

State symbols:

State motto: Excelsior (Ever Upward)

State song: "I Love New York"

State bird: Red-breasted Bluebird

State flower: Rose

State tree: Sugar Maple

PEOPLE:

Population: 18,137,000

Change since 1990: 1.1%

Population density: 384.0 per sq mi

% population that is 65 years and over: 13.4 (1996)

VITAL STATISTICS:

Birth rate: 14.9 *(per 1,000 population)*

Death rate: 928.4 *(per 100,000 population)*

Infant mortality rate: 7.8 *(deaths per 1,000 live births)*

GOVERNMENT:

Governor: George E. Pataki (Republican)

Regular term: 4 years

Current term began: January 1995
Salary: $130,000
Lt. Governor: Betsy McCaughey Ross
(Republican)

STATE ECONOMY:
Gross state product: $570.994 billion
State budget: *(in thousands)*
State revenues: $95,442,410
Total expenditures: $83,243,290
Debt at end of fiscal year: $74,078,490
Cash and security holdings: $153,765,511
Chief products:
Agriculture: Dairy Products, cattle, hay, corn, apples, potatoes
Manufacturing: Photographic and optical equipment, primary metals, machinery, paper products
Minerals: Stone, sand, gravel, zinc, salt

PERSONAL FINANCES:
Per capita personal income: $30,752
Median household income: $34,707
Average Annual Pay: $36,831
Percent of persons in poverty: 16.6%
Homeownership rate: 52.6%

EMPLOYMENT:
Labor Force: 8,807,000
Unemployment rate: 6.4%
Total number of businesses: 1,159,700
Total number of women owned businesses: 395,944
Total number of minority owned businesses: 160,751

CRIME:
Crime rate: 4,132.3 *(per 100,000 people)*
Violent crime: 727.0 *(per 100,000)*
Property crime: 3,405.3 *(per 100,000)*
Total prisoners in custody: 69,709
Prison capacity occupied: 130.8%

HEALTH CARE:
Persons without health insurance coverage: 17.0%
Low income uninsured children: 8.4%
Occupancy rate in community hospitals: 82.8%

EDUCATION:
Current high school completion rate: 90.9%
High school drop out rate: 4.1%
Educational Attainment-High school graduate: 80.0%
Bachelor degree: 25.8%
Estimated public elementary and secondary school finances (*in millions*):
Revenues: $24,859,923
Expenditures: $25,912,977

NORTH CAROLINA

GEOGRAPHY:
Area:
total area: 52,672 sq mi
land area: 48,718 sq mi
Capital: Raleigh, (population: 236,707)
Statehood: November 21, 1789 (12th state)
Postal abbreviation: NC
State symbols:
State motto: Esse Quam Videri
(To be rather than to seem)
State song: "The Old North State"
State bird: Cardinal
State flower: Dogwood
State tree: Pine

PEOPLE:
Population: 7,425,000
Change since 1990: 10.4%
Population density: 147.7 per sq mi
% population 65 years and over: 12.5 (1996)

VITAL STATISTICS:
Birth rate: 14.4 *(per 1,000 population)*
Death rate: 902.2 *(per 100,000 population)*
Infant mortality rate: 10.0 *(deaths per 1,000 live births)*

GOVERNMENT:
Governor: James B. Hunt, Jr. (Democrat)
Regular term: 4 years
Current term began: January 1997
Salary: $107,132
Lt. Governor: Dennis A. Wicker (Democrat)

STATE ECONOMY:
Gross state product: $181.521 billion
State budget: *(in thousands)*
State revenues: $25,526,697
Total expenditures: $22,864,451
Debt at end of fiscal year: $4,547,541
Cash and security holdings: $35,305,857
Chief products:
Agriculture: Tobacco, corn, soybeans, sweet potatoes, peanuts
Manufacturing: Textiles, tobacco, furniture, pulp and paper products, chemicals, metal working, plastics, food processing
Minerals: Phosphate, kaolin, mica, feldspar, granite, copper, limestone, marl

PERSONAL FINANCES:
Per capita personal income: $20,755
Median household income: $34,262
Average annual pay: $25,408
Percent of persons in poverty: 12.4%
Homeownership rate: 70.2%

EMPLOYMENT:
Labor force: 3,844,000
Unemployment rate: 4.5%
Total number of businesses: 439,301
Total number of women owned businesses: 142,516
Total number of minority owned businesses: 37,670

CRIME:
Crime rate: 5,526.2 *(per 100,000 people)*
 Violent crime: 588.1 *(per 100,000)*
 Property crime: 4,938.1 *(per 100,000)*
Total prisoners in custody: 28,756
Prison capacity occupied: 103.1%

HEALTH CARE:
Persons without health insurance coverage: 16.0%
Low income uninsured children: 8.3%
Occupancy rate in community hospitals: 69.5%

EDUCATION:
Current high school completion rate: 87.2%
High school drop out rate: NA
Educational Attainment-High school graduate: 78.4%
 Bachelor degree: 22.6%
Estimated public elementary and secondary school finances (*in millions*):
 Revenues: $6,075,778
 Expenditures: $6,217,951

NORTH DAKOTA

GEOGRAPHY:
Area:
 total area: 70,704 sq mi
 land area: 68,994 sq mi
Capital: Bismarck, (population: 49,256)
Statehood: November 2, 1889 (39th state)
Postal abbreviation: ND
State symbols:
 State motto: "Liberty and Union Now and Forever, One and Inseparable"
 State song: North Dakota Hymn
 State bird: Western Meadowlark
 State flower: Wild Prairie Rose
 State tree: American Elm

PEOPLE:
Population: 641,000
Change since 1990: 0.7%
Population density: 9.3 per sq mi
% population 65 years and over: 14.5 (1996)

VITAL STATISTICS:
Birth rate: 13.0 *(per 1,000 population)*
Death rate: 931.6 *(per 100,000 population)*
Infant mortality rate: 7.2 *(deaths per 1,000 live births)*

GOVERNMENT:
Governor: Edward T. Schafer (Republican)
 Regular term: 4 years
 Current term began: December 1996
 Salary: $73,176
Lt. Governor: Rosemarie Myrdal (Republican)

STATE ECONOMY:
Gross state product: $13.494 billion
State budget: *(in thousands)*
 State revenues: $2,817,603

 Total expenditures: $2,425,660
 Debt at end of fiscal year: $900,079
 Cash and security holdings: $4,561,710
Chief products:
 Agriculture: Wheat, cattle, grains, sunflower, seeds, flaxseed, rye, potatoes
 Manufacturing: Farm equipment, processed food
 Minerals: Oil, lignite coal, natural gas

PERSONAL FINANCES:
Per capita personal income: $20,271
Median household income: $30,709
Average annual pay: $21,242
Percent of persons in poverty: 11.5%
Homeownership rate: 68.1%

EMPLOYMENT:
Labor force: 348,000
Unemployment rate: 2.5%
Total number of businesses: 48,368
 Total number of woman owned businesses: 15,355
 Total number of minority owned businesses: 613

CRIME:
Crime rate: 2,669.1 *(per 100,000 people)*
 Violent crime: 84.0 *(per 100,000)*
 Property crime: 2,585.1 *(per 100,000)*
Total prisoners in custody: 765
Prison capacity occupied: 87.7%

HEALTH CARE:
Persons without health insurance coverage: 9.8%
Low income uninsured children: 5.4%
Occupancy rate in community hospitals: 64.2%

EDUCATION:
Current high school completion rate: 93.0%
High school drop out rate: 2.5%
Educational Attainment-High school graduate: 82.6%
 Bachelor degree: 20.5%
Estimated public elementary and secondary school finances (*in millions*):
 Revenues: $599,668
 Expenditures: $586,123

OHIO

GEOGRAPHY:
Area:
 total area: 44,828 sq mi
 land area: 40,953 sq mi
Capital: Columbus, (population: 635,913)
Statehood: March 1, 1803 (17th state)
Postal abbreviation: OH
State symbols:
 State motto: With God, All Things Are Possible
 State song: "Beautiful Ohio"
 State bird: Cardinal

State flower: Scarlet Carnation
State tree: Buckeye Tree

PEOPLE:

Population: 11,186,000
Change since 1990: 3.0%
Population density: 272.3 per sq mi
% population 65 years and over: 13.4 (1996)

VITAL STATISTICS:

Birth rate: 13.7 *(per 1,000 population)*
Death rate: 950.1 *(per 100,000 population)*
Infant mortality rate: 8.7 *(deaths per 1,000 live births)*

GOVERNMENT:

Governor: George V. Voinovich (Republican)
   Regular term: 4 years
   Current term began: January 1995
   Salary: $115,752
Lt. Governor: Nancy Hollister (Republican)

STATE ECONOMY:

Gross state product: $274.844 billion
State budget: *(in thousands)*
   State revenues: $45,249,896
   Total expenditures: $37,406,884
   Debt at end of fiscal year: $13,437,403
   Cash and security holdings: $113,511,439
Chief products:
   Agriculture: Corn, soybeans, wheat, oats, fruit, feed,
      livestock, poultry
   Manufacturing: Rubber products, porcelain, electri-
      cal machinery and apparatus, pumps and plumb-
      ing equipment
   Minerals: Coal, petroleum, natural gas, limestone,
      sandstone, clays, shales, gypsum, peat, salt

PERSONAL FINANCES:

Per capita personal income: $24,661
Median household income: $35,022
Average annual pay: $27,775
Percent of persons in poverty: 12.1%
Homeownership rate: 69.0%

EMPLOYMENT:

Labor force: 5,710,000
Unemployment rate: 4.6%
Total number of businesses: 666,183
   Total number of women owned businesses: 224,693
   Total number of minority owned businesses: 33,844

CRIME:

Crime rate: 4,455.7 *(per 100,000 people)*
   Violent crime: 428.7 *(per 100,000)*
   Property crime: 4,027.0 *(per 100,000)*
Total prisoners in custody: 45,968
Prison capacity occupied: 170.1%

HEALTH CARE:

Persons without health insurance coverage: 11.5%
Low income uninsured children: 6.3%
Occupancy rate in community hospitals: 60.5%

EDUCATION:

Current high school completion rate: 87.7%
High school drop out rate: 5.3%
Educational Attainment-High school graduate: 86.2%
                                    Bachelor degree: 21.5%
**Estimated public elementary and secondary school fi-
nances** *(in millions)*:
   Revenues: $11,301,147
   Expenditures: $11,308,735

OKLAHOMA

GEOGRAPHY:

Area:
   total area: 69,903 sq mi
   land area: 68,679 sq mi
Capital: Oklahoma City, (population: 463,201)
Statehood: November 16, 1907 (46th state)
Postal abbreviation: OK
State symbols:
   State motto: Labor Omnia Vincit
      (Labor Conquers All Things)
   State song: "Oklahoma"
   State bird: Scissor-tailed Flycatcher
   State flower: Mistletoe
   State tree: Redbud

PEOPLE:

Population: 3,317,000
Change since 1990: 4.9%
Population density: 47.7 per sq mi
% population 65 years and over: 13.5 (1996)

VITAL STATISTICS:

Birth rate: 14.0 *(per 1,000 population)*
Death rate: 1,002.3 *(per 100,000 population)*
Infant mortality rate: 8.5 *(deaths per 1,000 live births)*

GOVERNMENT:

Governor: Frank Keating (Republican)
   Regular term: 4 years
   Current terms began: January 1995
   Salary: $70,000 to $101,040
Lt. Governor: Mary Fallin (Republican)

STATE ECONOMY:

Gross state product: $66.189 billion
State budget: *(in thousands)*
   State revenues: $11,327,842
   Total expenditures: $9,592,711
   Debt at end of fiscal year: $3,795,206
   Cash and security holdings: $16,868,732
Chief products:
   Agriculture: Livestock, cattle, wheat, hay, sorghum,
      peanuts
   Manufacturing: Transportation equipment, machin-
      ery, fabricated metal products, rubber, and plastic
      products
   Minerals: Natural gas, coal, petroleum, stone, timber

PERSONAL FINANCES:

Per capita personal income: $20,556

Median household income: $27,263
Average annual pay: $23,329
Percent of persons in poverty: 16.9%
Homeownership rate: 68.5%

EMPLOYMENT:
Labor force: 1,600,000
Unemployment rate: 4.1%
Total number of businesses: 246,936
  Total number of women owned businesses: 82,894
  Total number of minority owned businesses: 12,865

CRIME:
Crime rate: 5,652.9 *(per 100,000 people)*
  Violent crime: 597.1 *(per 100,000)*
  Property crime: 5,055.8 *(per 100,000)*
Total prisoners in custody: 15,130
Prison capacity occupied: 106.4%

HEALTH CARE:
Persons without health insurance coverage: 17.0%
Low income uninsured children: 16.9%
Occupancy rate in community hospitals: 54.3%

EDUCATION:
Current high school completion rate: 87.0%
High school drop out rate: NA
Educational Attainment-High school graduate: 85.2%
                                        Bachelor degree: 20.5%
Estimated public elementary and secondary school finances (*in millions*):
  Revenues: $3,135,075
  Expenditures: $3,173,322

OREGON

GEOGRAPHY:
Area:
  total area: 97,132 sq mi
  land area: 96,002 sq mi
Capital: Salem, (population: 115,912)
Statehood: February 14, 1859 (33rd state)
Postal abbreviation: OR
State symbols:
  State motto: She Flies With Her Own Wings
  State song: "Oregon, My Oregon"
  State bird: Western Meadowlark
  State Flower: Oregon Grape
  State tree: Douglas Fir

PEOPLE:
Population: 3,243,000
Change since 1990: 12.7%
Population density: 32.7 per sq mi
% population 65 years and over: 13.4 (1996)

VITAL STATISTICS:
Birth rate: 13.6 *(per 1,000 population)*
Death rate: 898.4 *(per 100,000 population)*
Infant mortality rate: 7.1 *(deaths per 1,000 live births)*

GOVERNMENT:
Governor: John A. Kitzhaber (Democrat)
  Regular term: 4 years
  Current term began: January 1995
  Salary: $80,000
Secretary of State: Phil Keisling (Democrat)

STATE ECONOMY:
Gross state product: $74.366 billion
State budget: *(in thousands)*
  State revenues: $15,004,426
  Total expenditures: $12,388,248
  Debt at end of fiscal year: $5,840,879
  Cash and security holdings: $24,103,019
Chief products:
Agriculture: Livestock, cattle, wheat, barley, vegetables, fruit
Manufacturing: Lumber, plywood and hardwood, pulp and paper, metals related industries, aluminum
Fishing Industry: Salmon and shellfish
Minerals: Nickel, sand, gravel, cement, pumice

PERSONAL FINANCES:
Per capita personal income: $24,393
Median household income: $36,470
Average annual pay: $27,027
Percent of persons in poverty: 11.5%
Homeownership rate: 61.0%

EMPLOYMENT:
Labor force: 1,732,000
Unemployment rate: 5.8%
Total number of businesses: 238,967
  Total number of women owned businesses: 87,970
  Total number of minority owned businesses: 10,160

CRIME:
Crime rate: 5,996.6 *(per 100,000 people)*
  Violent crime: 463.1 *(per 100,000)*
  Property crime: 5,533.6 *(per 100,000)*
Total prisoners in custody: 8,457
Prison capacity occupied: 102.5%

HEALTH CARE:
Persons without health insurance coverage: 15.3%
Low income uninsured children: 7.8%
Occupancy rate in community hospitals: 54.6%

EDUCATION:
Current high school completion rate: 81.1%
High school drop out rate: 7.1%
Educational Attainment-High school graduate: 84.7%
                                        Bachelor degree: 24.3%
Estimated public elementary and secondary school finances (*in millions*):
  Revenues: $3,251,750
  Expenditures: $3,240,116

PENNSYLVANIA

GEOGRAPHY:
Area:
total area: 46,058 sq mi
land area: 44,820 sq mi
Capital: Harrisburg, (population: 52,376)
Statehood: December 12, 1787 (2nd state)
Postal abbreviation: PA
State symbols:
State motto: Virtue, Liberty, and Independence
State song: "Pennsylvania"
State bird: Ruffed Grouse
State flower: Mountain Laurel
State tree: Hemlock

PEOPLE:
Population: 12,020,000
Change since 1990: 1.5%
Population density: 269.3 per sq mi
% population 65 years and over: 15.9 (1996)

VITAL STATISTICS:
Birth rate: 12.4 *(per 1,000 population)*
Death rate: 1,059.2 *(per 100,000 population)*
Infant mortality rate: 8.2 *(deaths per 1,000 live births)*

GOVERNMENT:
Governor: Tom Ridge (Republican)
Regular term: 4 years
Current term began: January 1995
Salary: $105,000
Lt. Governor: Mark Schweiker (Republican)

STATE ECONOMY:
Gross state product: $294.431 billion
State budget: *(in thousands)*
State revenues: $49,317,529
Total expenditures: $39,296,244
Debt at end of fiscal year: $15,367,631
Cash and security holdings: $77,928,916
Chief products:
Agriculture: Dairy products, oats, mushrooms, corn, hay, apples, grapes, poultry
Manufacturing: Steel, food processing, chemicals, machinery, electrical and electronic equipment
Minerals: Coal, natural gas, iron ore, limestone, silver, gold, copper, cobalt, zinc, salt

PERSONAL FINANCES:
Per capita personal income: $26,058
Median household income: $35,221
Average annual pay: $28,973
Percent of persons in poverty: 11.9%
Homeownership rate: 73.3%

EMPLOYMENT:
Labor force: 5,984,000
Unemployment rate: 5.2%
Total number of businesses: 728,063
Total number of women owned businesses: 227,500

Total number of minority owned businesses: 32,712

CRIME:
Crime rate: 3,392.5 *(per 100,000 people)*
Violent crime: 432.5 *(per 100,000)*
Property crime: 2,960.1 *(per 100,000)*
Total prisoners in custody: 34,476
Percent of prison capacity occupied: 121.7%

HEALTH CARE:
Persons without health insurance coverage: 9.9%
Low income uninsured children: 6.3%
Occupancy rate in community hospitals: 72.6%

EDUCATION:
Current high school completion rate: 89.6%
High school drop out rate: 4.1%
Educational Attainment-High school graduate: 82.4%
        Bachelor degree: 22.9%
Estimated public elementary and secondary school finances *(in millions)*:
Revenues: $13,515,928
Expenditures: $13,059,303

PUERTO RICO

GEOGRAPHY:
Area:
total area: 3,508 sq mi
land area: 3,427 sq mi
Capital city: San Juan, (population 437,745)

PEOPLE:
Population: 3,819,023
Population growth rate: 0.18%

VITAL STATISTICS:
Birth rate: 16.7 *(rate per 1,000 population)*
Death rate: NA
Infant mortality rate: 12.4 *(deaths per 1,000 live births)*
Life expectancy: 73.9

GOVERNMENT:
Type of government: Commonwealth associated with the U.S.
Governor: Governor Pedro Rossello (Democrat and New Progressive Party)
Regular term: 4 years
Current term began: January 1997
Salary: $70,000
Secretary of State: Norma Burgos (New Progressive Party)

ECONOMY:
GDP: $29.7 billion
GDP real growth rate: 4.3%
GDP per capita: $7,800
Inflation Rate *(consumer prices):* 2.9%
National budget:
revenues: $5.1 billion
expenditures: $5.1 billion

Chief Products:
Agriculture: Sugarcane, coffee, pineapples, plantains, bananas; cattle, chickens
Industries: Pharmaceuticals, electronics, apparel, food products, instruments, tourism

PERSONAL FINANCES:
Per capita personal income: $7,296
Average family income: $24,337

EMPLOYMENT:
Labor force: 1,308,000
Unemployment rate: 13.5%

RHODE ISLAND

GEOGRAPHY:
Area:
total area: 1,231 sq mi
land area: 1,045 sq mi
Capital: Providence, (population: 150,639)
Statehood: May 29, 1790 (13th state)
Postal abbreviation: RI
State symbols:
State motto: Hope
State song: "Rhode Island"
State bird: Rhode Island Red
State flower: Violet
State tree: Red Maple

PEOPLE:
Population: 987,000
Change since 1990: -1.3%
Population density: 947.2 per sq mi
% population 65 years and over: 15.8 (1996)

VITAL STATISTICS:
Birth rate: 12.6 *(per 1,000 population)*
Death rate: 975.7 *(per 100,000 population)*
Infant mortality rate: 5.0 *(deaths per 1,000 live births)*

GOVERNMENT:
Governor: Lincoln Almond (Republican)
Regular term: 4 years
Current term began: January 1995
Salary: $69,900
Lt. Governor: Bernard Jackvony (Republican)

STATE ECONOMY:
Gross state product: $23.867 billion
State budget: *(in thousands)*
State revenues: $4,229,308
Total expenditures: $4,001,776
Debt at end of fiscal year: $5,301,681
Cash and security holdings: $9,586,571
Chief products:
Agriculture: Nursery and greenhouse products, potatoes, dairy products, poultry
Manufacturing: Jewelry and silverware, textile and clothing, electrical machinery and electronics, ships

Fishing Industry: Shellfish and finfish
Minerals: Granite, limestone, sand, gravel; cumberlandite, bowenite

PERSONAL FINANCES:
Per capita personal income: $25,760
Median household income: $36,695
Average annual pay: $27,194
Percent of persons in poverty: 10.8%
Homeownership rate: 58.7%

EMPLOYMENT:
Labor force: 505,000
Unemployment rate: 5.3%
Total number of businesses: 67, 641
Total number of women owned businesses: 21,353
Total number of minority owned businesses: 3,047

CRIME:
Crime rate: 3,993.5 *(per 100,000 people)*
Violent crime: 347.2 *(per 100,000)*
Property crime: 3,646.4 *(per 100,000)*
Total prisoners in custody: 3,233
Prison capacity occupied: 110.7%

HEALTH CARE:
Persons without health insurance coverage: 9.9%
Low income uninsured children: 7.8%
Occupancy rate in community hospitals: 73.3%

EDUCATION:
Current high school completion rate: 87.5%
High school drop out rate: 4.6%
Educational Attainment-High school graduate: 77.5%
Bachelor degree: 25.7%
Estimated public elementary and secondary school finances (*in millions*):
Revenues: $1,082,655
Expenditures: $1,049,425

SOUTH CAROLINA

GEOGRAPHY:
Area:
total area: 31,189 sq mi
land area: 30,111 sq mi
Capital: Columbia, (population: 104,104)
Statehood: May 23, 1788 (8th state)
Postal abbreviation: SC
State symbols:
State mottos: Animis Opibusque Parati (Ready In Soul & Resource) *Dum Spiro Spero* (While I Breathe I Hope)
State songs: "Carolina" and "South Carolina on My Mind"
State bird: Carolina Wren
State flower: Carolina Yellow Jessamine
State tree: Palmetto

PEOPLE:
Population: 3,760,000

Change since 1990: 6.1%
Population density: 122.0 per sq mi
% population 65 years and over: 12.1 (1996)

VITAL STATISTICS:
Birth rate: 13.7 *(per 1,000 population)*
Death rate: 912.7 *(per 100,000 population)*
Infant mortality rate: 9.3 *(deaths per 1,000 live births)*

GOVERNMENT:
Governor: David M. Beasley (Republican)
  Regular term: 4 years
  Current term began: January 1995
  Salary: $106,078
Lt. Governor: Bob Peeler (Republican)

STATE ECONOMY:
Gross state product: $79.925 billion
State budget: *(in thousands)*
  State revenues: $13,804,751
  Total expenditures: $12,847,221
  Debt at end of fiscal year: $5,349,807
  Cash and security holdings: $20,139,801
Chief products:
  Agriculture: Tobacco, soybeans, peaches, wheat,
    peanuts, watermelon, poultry, cattle
  Manufacturing: Textiles, chemicals, apparel
  Fishing Industries: Shrimp, crabs, oysters
  Minerals: Clay, cement, stone, gravel

PERSONAL FINANCES:
Per capita personal income: $20,755
Median household income: $32,297
Average annual pay: $24,039
Percent of persons in poverty: 16.5%
Homeownership rate: 74.1%

EMPLOYMENT:
Labor force: 1,913,000
Unemployment rate: 4.5%
Total number of businesses: 197,330
  Total number of women owned businesses: 64,812
  Total number of minority owned businesses: 21,127

CRIME:
Crime rate: 6,214.1 *(per 100,000 people)*
  Violent crime: 996.9 *(per 100,000)*
  Property crime: 5,217.2 *(per 100,000)*
Total prisoners in custody: 19,860
Prison capacity occupied: 106.4%

HEALTH CARE:
Persons without health insurance coverage: 17.1%
Low income uninsured children: 10.6%
Occupancy rate in community hospitals: 67.3%

EDUCATION:
Current high school completion rate: 88.4%
High school drop out rate: NA
Educational Attainment-High school graduate: 77.3%
                         Bachelor degree: 19.2%
Estimated public elementary and secondary school finances *(in millions)*:

Revenues: $3,381,747
Expenditures: $3,282,344

SOUTH DAKOTA

GEOGRAPHY:
Area:
  total area: 77,121 sq mi
  land area: 75,896 sq mi
Capital: Pierre, (population: 12,906)
Statehood: November 2, 1889 (40th state)
Postal abbreviation: SD
State symbols:
  State motto: Under God the People Rule
  State song: "Hail, South Dakota"
  State bird: Chinese Ring-Neck Pheasant
  State flower: Pasque
  State tree: Black Hills Spruce

PEOPLE:
Population: 738,000
Change since 1990: 5.2%
Population density: 9.6 per sq mi
% population 65 years and over: 14.4 (1996)

VITAL STATISTICS:
Birth rate: 14.3 *(per 1,000 population)*
Death rate: 948.5 *(per 100,000 population)*
Infant mortality rate: 9.6 *(deaths per 1,000 live births)*

GOVERNMENT:
Governor: Edward T. Schafer (Republican)
  Regular term: 4 years
  Current term began: January 1995
  Salary: $82,271
Lt. Governor: Carole Hillard (Republican)

STATE ECONOMY:
Gross state product: $17.250 billion
State budget: *(in thousands)*
  State revenues: $2,315,652
  Total expenditures: $2,070,482
  Debt at end of fiscal year: $1,840,686
  Cash and security holdings: $5,896,695
Chief products:
  Agriculture: Grains, sunflower seed, livestock, cattle,
    hogs
  Manufacturing: Meat processing, industrial machinery
  Minerals: Rose quartz, gold

PERSONAL FINANCES:
Per capita personal income: $21,447
Median household income: $29,989
Average annual pay: $20,724
Percent of persons in poverty: 13.2%
Homeownership rate: 67.6%

EMPLOYMENT:
Labor force: 393,000
Unemployment rate: 3.1%

Total number of businesses: 57,084
Total number of women owned businesses: 18,215
Total number of minority owned businesses: 891

CRIME:
Crime rate: 2,969.9 *(per 100,000 people)*
Violent crime: 177.2 *(per 100,000)*
Property crime: 2,792.8 *(per 100,000)*
Total prisoners in custody: 2,063
Prison capacity occupied: 109.6%

HEALTH CARE:
Persons without health insurance coverage: 9.5%
Low income uninsured children: 6.4%
Occupancy rate in community hospitals: 60.7%

EDUCATION:
Current high school completion rate: 89.6%
High school drop out rate: NA
Educational Attainment-High school graduate: 85.6%
                              Bachelor degree: 20.1%
Estimated public elementary and secondary school finances *(in millions)*:
Revenues: $680,171
Expenditures: $690,189

TENNESSEE

GEOGRAPHY:
Area:
total area: 42,146 sq mi
land area: 41,219 sq mi
Capital: Nashville, (population: 504,505)
Statehood: June 1, 1796 (16th state)
Postal abbreviation: TN
State symbols:
State motto: Agriculture and Commerce
State song: "The Tennessee Waltz"
State bird: Mockingbird
State flower: Iris
State tree: Tulip Popular

PEOPLE:
Population: 5,368,000
Change since 1990: 9.1%
Population density: 127.5 per sq mi
% population that is 65 years and over: 12.5 (1996)

VITAL STATISTICS:
Birth rate: 13.9 *(per 1,000 population)*
Death rate: 976.1 *(per 100,000 population)*
Infant mortality rate: 8.9 *(deaths per 1,000 live births)*

GOVERNMENT:
Governor: Don Sundquist (Republican)
Regular term: 4 years
Current term began: January 1995
Salary: $85,000
Lt. Governor: John S. Wilder (Democrat)

STATE ECONOMY:

Gross state product: $126.539 billion
State budget: *(in thousands)*
State revenues: $15,696,299
Total expenditures: $14,284,301
Debt at end of fiscal year: $3,314,928
Cash and security holdings: $22,631,753
Chief products:
Agriculture: Cotton, tobacco, poultry, fruits and vegetables, hogs, pigs, soybeans, corn
Manufacturing: Chemicals, food processing, transportation equipment, lumber
Minerals: Zinc

PERSONAL FINANCES:
Per capita personal income: $23,018
Median household income: $30,331
Average annual pay: $25,963
Percent of persons in poverty: 15.7%
Homeownership rate: 70.2%

EMPLOYMENT:
Labor force: 2,708,000
Unemployment rate: 5.4%
Total number of businesses: 325,371
Total number of women owned businesses: 101,134
Total number of minority owned businesses: 19,382

CRIME:
Crime rate: 5,449.3 *(per 100,000 people)*
Violent crime: 774.0 *(per 100,000)*
Property crime: 4,675.4 *(per 100,000)*
Total prisoners in custody: 13,565
Prison capacity occupied: 95.6%

HEALTH CARE:
Persons without health insurance coverage: 15.2%
Low income uninsured children: 7.9%
Occupancy rate in community hospitals: 60.7%

EDUCATION:
Current high school completion rate: 83.3%
High school drop out rate: NA
Educational Attainment-High school graduate: 76.1%
                              Bachelor degree: 17.1%
Estimated public elementary and secondary school finances *(in millions)*:
Revenues: $3,850,382
Expenditures: $3,958,733

TEXAS

GEOGRAPHY:
Area:
total area: 267,277 sq mi
land area: 261,914 sq mi
Capital: Austin, (population: 514,013)
Statehood: December 29, 1845 (28th state)
Postal abbreviation: TX
State symbols:
State motto: Friendship
State song: "Texas, Our Texas"

State bird: Mockingbird
State flower: Bluebonnet
State tree: Pecan

PEOPLE:
Population: 19,439,000
Change since 1990: 12.6%
Population density: 71.5 per sq mi
% population 65 years and over: 10.2 (1996)

VITAL STATISTICS:
Birth rate: 17.1 *(per 1,000 population)*
Death rate: 736.1 *(per 100,000 population)*
Infant mortality rate: 7.1 *(deaths per 1,000 live births)*

GOVERNMENT:
Governor: George W. Bush, Jr. (Republican)
Regular term: 4 years
Current term began: January 1995
Salary: $115,345
Lt. Governor: Bob Bullock (Democrat)

STATE ECONOMY:
Gross state product: $479.774 billion
State budget: *(in thousands)*
State revenues: $63,864,034
Total expenditures: $48,887,370
Debt at end of fiscal year: $12,461,867
Cash and security holdings: $121,587,189
Chief products:
Agriculture: Cotton, sorghum, grains, beef cattle, sheep
Manufacturing: Petroleum, sulfur, petrochemicals, electronic and electrical machinery
Minerals: Oil, natural gas

PERSONAL FINANCES:
Per capita personal income: $23,656
Median household income: $33,029
Average annual pay: $28,129
Percent of persons in poverty: 17.0%
Homeownership rate: 61.5%

EMPLOYMENT:
Labor force: 9,881,000
Unemployment rate: 5.4%
Total number of businesses: 1,256,121
Total number of women owned busineses: 414,179
Total number of minority owned businesses: 241,334

CRIME:
Crime rate: 5,708.9 *(per 100,000 people)*
Violent crime: 644.4 *(per 100,000)*
Property crime: 5,064.5 *(per 100,000)*
Total prisoners in custody: 132,383
Prison capacity occupied: 94.6%

HEALTH CARE:
Persons without health insurance coverage: 24.3%
Low income uninsured children: 17.9%
Occupancy rate in community hospitals: 55.1%

EDUCATION:
Current high school completion rate: 79.3%
High school drop out rate: 2.7%
Educational Attainment-High school graduate: 78.5%
                          Bachelor degree: 22.4%
Estimated public elementary and secondary school finances *(in millions)*:
Revenues: $20,475,338
Expenditures: $20,179,361

U T A H

GEOGRAPHY:
Area:
total area: 84,904 sq mi
land area: 82,168 sq mi
Capital: Salt Lake City, (population: 171,849)
Statehood: January 4, 1896 (45th state)
Postal abbreviation: UT
State symbols:
State motto: Industry
State song: "Utah, We Love Thee"
State bird: California Gull (Seagull)
State flower: Sego Lily
State tree: Blue Spruce

PEOPLE:
Population: 2,059,000
Change since 1990: 16.1%
Population density: 23.7 per sq mi
% population 65 years and over: 8.8 (1996)

VITAL STATISTICS:
Birth rate: 20.7 *(per 1,000 population)*
Death rate: 560.6 *(per 100,000 population)*
Infant mortality rate: 6.2 *(deaths per 1,000 live births)*

GOVERNMENT:
Governor: Michael O. Leavitt (Republican)
Regular term: 4 years
Current term began: January 1997
Salary: $87,600
Lt. Governor: Olene S. Walker (Republican)

STATE ECONOMY:
Gross state product: $41.657 billion
State budget: *(in thousands)*
State revenues: $7,723,664
Total expenditures: $6,817,750
Debt at end of fiscal year: $2,450,730
Cash and security holdings: $12,537,573
Chief products:
Agriculture: Livestock, hay, wheat, barley, corn
Manufacturing: Printing and publishing, food processing, rocket engines, fabricated metals, petroleum refining, transportation equipment, computer software and hardware
Minerals: Cooper, beryllium, gold, silver, lead, uranium, coal, petroleum, molybdenum

PERSONAL FINANCES:
Per capita personal income: $20,432
Median household income: $37,298
Average annual pay: $24,572
Percent of persons in poverty: 8.1%
Homeownership rate: 72.5%

EMPLOYMENT:
Labor force: 1,040,000
Unemployment rate: 3.1%
Total number of businesses: 129,202
   Total number of women owned businesses: 45,626
   Total number of minority owned businesses: 4,352

CRIME:
Crime rate: 5,985.9 *(per 100,000 people)*
   Violent crime: 331.9 *(per 100,000)*
   Property crime: 5,654.0 *(per 100,000)*
Total prisoners in custody: 4,560
Prison capacity occupied: 99.8%

HEALTH CARE:
Persons without health insurance coverage: 12.0%
Low income uninsured children: 6.4%
Occupancy rate in community hospitals: 53.4%

EDUCATION:
Current high school completion rate: 91.3%
High school drop out rate: 3.5%
Educational Attainment-High school graduate: 89.5%
               Bachelor degree: 26.7%
Estimated public elementary and secondary school finances (*in millions*):
   Revenues: $1,952,436
   Expenditures: $2,045,331

VERMONT

GEOGRAPHY:
Area:
   total area: 9,615 sq mi
   land area: 9,249 sq mi
Capital: Montpelier, (population: 8,392)
Statehood: March 4, 1791, (14th state)
Postal abbreviation: VT
State symbols:
   State motto: Freedom and Unity
   State song: "Hail, Vermont"
   State bird: Hermit Thrush
   State flower: Red Clover
   State tree: Sugar Maple

PEOPLE:
Population: 589,000
Change since 1990: 4.6%
Population density: 63.2 per sq mi
% population 65 years and over: 12.1 (1996)

VITAL STATISTICS:
Birth rate: 11.5 *(per 1,000 population)*
Death rate: 846.7 *(per 100,000 population)*

Infant mortality rate: 7.5 *(deaths per 1,000 live births)*

GOVERNMENT:
Governor: Howard Dean, M.D. (Democrat)
   Regular term: 2 years
   Current term began: January 1997
   Salary: $80,724
Lt. Governor: Douglas Racine (Democrat)

STATE ECONOMY:
Gross state product: $13.282 billion
State budget: *(in thousands)*
   State revenues: $2,369,972
   Total expenditures: $2,123,269
   Debt at end of fiscal year: $2,037,435
   Cash and security holdings: $2,584,566
Chief products:
   Agriculture: Dairy products, corn
   Manufacturing: Wood and paper products, printing
   Minerals: Marble, granite, and slate

PERSONAL FINANCES:
Per capita personal income: $23,401
Median household income: $33,591
Average Annual Pay: $24,480
Percent of persons in poverty: 11.5%
Homeownership rate: 69.1%

EMPLOYMENT:
Labor force: 326,000
Unemployment rate: 4.0%
Total number of businesses: 58,924
   Total number of women owned businesses: 21,033
   Total number of minority owned businesses:
   747

CRIME:
Crime rate: 3,002.9 *(per 100,000 people)*
   Violent crime: 121.2 *(per 100,000)*
   Property crime: 2,881.7 *(per 100,000)*
Total prisoners in custody: 1,119
Prison capacity occupied: 99.1%

HEALTH CARE:
Persons without health insurance coverage: 13.2%
Low income uninsured children: 4.4%
Occupancy rate in community hospitals: 64.3%

EDUCATION:
Current high school completion rate: 87.0%
High school drop out rate: NA
Educational Attainment-High school graduate: 84.4%
               Bachelor degree: 23.7%
Estimated public elementary and secondary school finances (*in millions*):
   Revenues: $732,118
   Expenditures: $691,716

VIRGINIA

GEOGRAPHY:
Area:
total area: 42,326 sq mi
land area: 39,589 sq mi
Capital: Richmond, (population: 201,108)
Statehood: June 25, 1788 (10th state)
Postal abbreviation: VA
State symbols:
State motto: Sic Semper Tyrannis
(Thus Always to Tyrants)
State song: "Carry Me Back to Old Virginia"
State bird: Cardinal
State flower: Dogwood
State tree: Dogwood

PEOPLE:
Population: 6,734,000
Change since 1990: 7.9%
Population density: 167.1 per sq mi
% population 65 years and over: 11.2 (1996)

VITAL STATISTICS:
Birth rate: 13.8 *(per 1,000 population)*
Death rate: 799.9 *(per 100,000 population)*
Infant mortality rate: 8.3 *(deaths per 1,000 live births)*

GOVERNMENT:
Governor: James S. Gilmore III (Republican)
Regular term: 4 years
Current term began: January 1998
Salary: $110,000*
Lt. Governor: John H. Hager (Republican)

STATE ECONOMY:
Gross state product: $177.708 billion
State budget: *(in thousands)*
State revenues: $24,322,031
Total expenditures: $19,286,506
Debt at end of fiscal year: $9,940,870
Cash and security holdings: $42,854,897
Chief products:
Agriculture: Tobacco, dairy products, vegetables, apples, peaches
Manufacturing: Food processing, tobacco products, textiles, apparel, chemicals, pine timber
Minerals: Coal, stone, clay, sand, gravel

PERSONAL FINANCES:
Per capita personal income: $26,438
Median household income: $38,252
Average annual pay: $28,001
Percent of persons in poverty: 11.3%
Homeownership rate: 68.4%

EMPLOYMENT:
Labor force: 3,405,000
Unemployment rate: 4.0%
Total number of businesses: 391,451
Total number of women owned businesses: 138,494
Total number of minority owned businesses: 46,666

CRIME:
Crime rate: 3,968.3 *(per 100,000 people)*
Violent crime: 341.3 *(per 100,000)*
Property crime: 3,627.0 *(per 100,000)*
Total prisoners in custody: 25,149
Percent of prison capacity occupied: 139.8%

HEALTH CARE:
Persons without health insurance coverage: 12.5%
Low income uninsured children: 6.9%
Occupancy rate in community hospitals: 64.2%

EDUCATION:
Current high school completion rate: 86.6%
High school drop out rate: %
Educational Attainment-High school graduate: 81.3%
Bachelor degree: 28.0%
Estimated public elementary and secondary school finances (*in millions*):
Revenues: $6,266,343
Expenditures: $6,506,168

---

*Governor returns 10 percent of his salary.

WASHINGTON

GEOGRAPHY:
Area:
total area: 70,637 sq mi
land area: 66,581 sq mi
Capital: Olympia, (population: 15,003)
Statehood: November 11, 1889 (42nd state)
Postal abbreviation: WA
State symbols:
State motto: Alki (Bye and bye)
State song: "Washington, My Home"
State bird: Willow Goldfinch
State flower: Western Rhododendron
State tree: Western Hemlock

PEOPLE:
Population: 5,610,000
Change since 1990: 13.7%
Population density: 81.6 per sq mi
% population 65 years and over: 11.6 (1996)

VITAL STATISTICS:
Birth rate: 14.5 *(per 1,000 population)*
Death rate: 751.0 *(per 100,000 population)*
Infant mortality rate: 6.2 *(deaths per 1,000 live births)*

GOVERNMENT:
Governor: Gary Locke (Democrat)
Regular term: 4 years
Current term began: January 1997
Salary: $121,000
Lt. Governor: Brad Owen (Democrat)

STATE ECONOMY:

Gross state product: $143.867 billion
State budget: *(in thousands)*
  State revenues: $26,841,468
  Total expenditures: $22,206,885
  Debt at end of fiscal year: $9,493,472
  Cash and security holdings: $47,229,933
Chief products:
  Agriculture: Wheat, timber, apples, potatoes
  Manufacturing: Aircraft and aircraft parts, lumber
    and wood products, processed food, paper and
    allied products, primary metals (aluminum), non-
    electrical machinery
  Fishing industry: Shrimp, oysters, clams, tuna, hal-
    ibut, red snapper
  Minerals: Lead, zinc, magnesium, gold, coal, sand,
    gravel

PERSONAL FINANCES:

Per capita personal income: $26,718
Median household income: $36,647
Average annual pay: $28,881
Percent of persons in poverty: 12.2%
Homeownership rate: 62.9%

EMPLOYMENT:

Labor force: 2,988,000
Unemployment rate: 4.8%
Total number of businesses: 372,975
  Total number of women owned businesses:
    136,377
  Total number of minority owned businesses:
    25,935

CRIME:

Crime rate: 5,909.4 *(per 100,000 people)*
  Violent crime: 431.2 *(per 100,000)*
  Property crime: 5,478.2 *(per 100,000)*
Total prisoners in custody: 12,588
Prison capacity occupied: 134.4%

HEALTH CARE:

Persons without health insurance coverage:
  13.5%
Low income uninsured children: 6.0%
Occupancy rate in community hospitals:
  57.6%

EDUCATION:

Current high school completion rate: 86.8%
High school drop out rate: NA
Educational Attainment-High school graduate: 88.8%
  Bachelor degree: 26.1%
**Estimated public elementary and secondary school fi-
  nances** *(in millions)*:
  Revenues: $5,948,181
  Expenditures: $6,189,792

WEST VIRGINIA

GEOGRAPHY:

Area:
  total area: 24,231 sq mi
  land area: 24,087 sq mi
Capital: Charleston, (population: 57,256)
Statehood: June 20, 1863 (35th state)
Postal abbreviation: WV
State symbols:
  State motto: Montani Semper Liberi
    (Mountaineers are always free)
  State songs: "West Virginia, My Home Sweet
    Home," "The West Virginia Hills," and "This Is My
    West Virginia"
  State bird: Cardinal
  State flower: Big Rhododendron
  State tree: Sugar Maple

PEOPLE:

Population: 1,816,000
Change since 1990: 1.8%
Population density: 75.9 per sq mi
% population 65 years and over: 15.2 (1996)

VITAL STATISTICS:

Birth rate: 11.3 *(per 1,000 population)*
Death rate: 1,107.0 *(per 100,000 population)*
Infant mortality rate: 6.7 *(deaths per 1,000 live births)*

GOVERNMENT:

Governor: Cecil H. Underwood (Republican)
  Regular term: 4 years
  Current term began: January 1997
  Salary: $90,000
Senate President: Earl Ray Tomblin (Democrat)

STATE ECONOMY:

Gross state product: $34.654 billion
State budget: *(in thousands)*
  State revenues: $7,466,718
  Total expenditures: $7,145,479
  Debt at end of fiscal year: $3,039,506
  Cash and security holdings: $7,478,216
Chief products:
  Agriculture: Greenhouse products, cattle, poultry
  Manufacturing: Chemicals, primary and fabricated
    metals, transportation equipment
  Minerals: Bituminous coal, natural gas, petroleum,
    limestone, rock-salt

PERSONAL FINANCES:

Per capita personal income: $18,957
Median household income: $25,431
Average annual pay: $24,075
Percent of persons in poverty: 17.6%
Homeownership rate: 74.6%

EMPLOYMENT:

Labor force: 805,000
Unemployment rate: 6.9%

Total number of businesses: 94,912
   Total number of women owned businesses: 30,644
   Total number of minority owned businesses: 2,070

CRIME:
Crime rate: 2,483.4 *(per 100,000 people)*
   Violent crime: 210.1 *(per 100,000)*
   Property crime: 2,273.3 *(per 100,000)*
Total prisoners in custody: 2,468
Prison capacity occupied: 88.8%

HEALTH CARE:
Persons without health insurance coverage:
15.3%
Low income uninsured children: 10.5%
Occupancy rate in community hospitals: 62.0%

EDUCATION:
Current high school completion rate: 89.3%
High school drop out rate: %
Educational Attainment-High school graduate: 77.3%
                      Bachelor degree: 14.7%
Estimated public elementary and secondary school finances *(in millions)*:
   Revenues: $1,915,412
   Expenditures: $1,922,939

WISCONSIN

GEOGRAPHY:
Area:
   total area: 65,499 sq mi
   land area: 54,314 sq mi
Capital: Madison, (population: 194,586)
Statehood: May 29, 1848 (30th state)
Postal abbreviation: WI
State symbols:
   State motto: Forward
   State song: "On, Wisconsin!"
   State bird: Robin
   State flower: Wood Violet
   State tree: Sugar Maple

PEOPLE:
Population: 5,170,000
Change since 1990: 5.5%
Population density: 94.3 per sq mi
% population 65 years and over: 13.3 (1996)

VITAL STATISTICS:
Birth rate: 13.0 *(per 1,000 population)*
Death rate: 880.1 *(per 100,000 population)*
Infant mortality rate: 7.9 *(deaths per 1,000 live births)*

GOVERNMENT:
Governor: Tommy G. Thompson (Republican)
   Regular term: 4 years
   Current term began: January 1995
   Salary: $101,861
Lt. Governor: Scott McCallum (Republican)

STATE ECONOMY:
Gross state product: $125.321 billion
State budget: *(in thousands)*
   State revenues: $23,591,564
   Total expenditures: $18,199,533
   Debt at end of fiscal year: $9,831,858
   Cash and security holdings: $53,025,998
Chief products:
   Agriculture: Dairy products, livestock
   Manufacturing: Food products, industrial machinery and equipment, paper products, printing and publishing
   Minerals: Stone, sand/gravel, lime

PERSONAL FINANCES:
Per capita personal income: $24,475
Median household income: $41,082
Average annual pay: $26,021
Percent of persons in poverty: 8.7%
Homeownership rate: 68.3%

EMPLOYMENT:
Labor force: 2,928,000
Unemployment rate: 3.7%
Total number of businesses: 300,348
   Total number of women owned businesses: 99,357
   Total number of minority owned businesses: 7,619

CRIME:
Crime rate: 3,821.4 *(per 100,000 people)*
   Violent crime: 252.7 *(per 100,000)*
   Property crime: 3,568.7 *(per 100,000)*
Total prisoners in custody: 12,530
Prison capacity occupied: 147.8%

HEALTH CARE:
Persons without health insurance coverage: 8.4%
Low income uninsured children: 4.8%
Occupancy rate in community hospitals:
63.4%

EDUCATION:
Current high school completion rate: 92.5%
Educational Attainment-High school graduate: 87.1%
                      Bachelor degree: 22.4%
Estimated public elementary and secondary school finances *(in millions)*:
   Revenues: $5,959,541
   Expenditures: $6,026,582

WYOMING

GEOGRAPHY:
Area:
   total area: 97,818 sq mi
   land area: 97,105 sq mi
Capital: Cheyenne, (population: 5,839)
Statehood: July 10, 1890 (44th state)
Postal abbreviation: WY
State symbols:
   State motto: Equal Rights

State song: "Wyoming"
State bird: Meadowlark
State flower: Indian Paintbrush
State tree: Plains Cottonwood

PEOPLE:
Population: 480,000
Change since 1990: 6.1%
Population density: 4.9 per sq mi
% population 65 years and over: 11.2 (1996)

VITAL STATISTICS:
Birth rate: 13.1 *(per 1,000 population)*
Death rate: 774.7 *(per 100,000 population)*
Infant mortality rate: 6.7 *(deaths per 1,000 live births)*

GOVERNMENT:
Governor: Jim Geringer (Republican)
  Regular term: 4 years
  Current term began: January 1995
  Salary: $92,000
Secretary of State: Diana Ohman (Republican)

STATE ECONOMY:
Gross state product: $15.660 billion
State budget: *(in thousands)*
  State revenues: $2,559,063
  Total expenditures: $2,126,805
  Debt at end of fiscal year: $871,948
  Cash and security holdings: $6,955,103
Chief products:
  Agriculture: Barley, wheat, corn, hay, oats, sugar
    beets, dry beans, potatoes
  Manufacturing: Wool, petroleum refining,
    chemicals, fertilizer, glass, electrical energy
  Minerals: Coal, petroleum, natural-gas, uranium,
    bentonite, trona, iron-ore

PERSONAL FINANCES:
Per capita personal income: $22,648
Median household income: $31,707
Average annual pay: $22,870

Percent of persons in poverty: 12.1%
Homeownership rate: 67.6%

EMPLOYMENT:
Labor force: 251,000
Unemployment rate: 5.1%
Total number of businesses: 40,696
  Total number of women owned businesses: 14,617
  Total number of minority owned businesses: 1,195

CRIME:
Crime rate: 4,254.1 *(per 100,000 people)*
  Violent crime: 249.7 *(per 100,000)*
  Property crime: 4,004.4 *(per 100,000)*
Total prisoners in custody: 1,327
Prison capacity occupied: 106.2%

HEALTH CARE:
Persons without health insurance coverage:
  13.5%
Low income uninsured children: 9.9%
Occupancy rate in community hospitals:
  48.5%

EDUCATION:
Current high school completion rate: 89.4%
High school drop out rate: 6.7%
Educational Attainment-High school graduate: 91.3%
                    Bachelor degree: 22.2%
Estimated public elementary and secondary school finances (*in millions*):
  Revenues: $632,430
  Expenditures: $637,417

Sources: U.S. Census Bureau, U.S. Bureau of Economic Analysis. National Center for Health Statistics, Council of State Governments, Bureau of Justice Statistics, National Governors' Association and individual states

Compiled by Suzanne Vranica

Population of U.S. Metropolitan Areas

Resident Population and Change for Metropolitan Areas in the U.S. April 1, 1990 to July 1, 1996

Metropolitan area	April 1, 1990 census	July 1, 1996 estimate	Numerical population change 1990–1996	Percent population change 1990–1996
Abilene, TX MSA	119,655	122,130	2,475	2.1%
Albany, GA MSA	112,571	117,286	4,715	4.2
Albany-Schenectady-Troy, NY MSA	861,623	878,527	16,904	2.0
Albuquerque, NM MSA	589,131	670,092	80,961	13.7
Alexandria, LA MSA	131,556	126,290	-5,266	-4.0
Allentown-Bethlehem-Easton, PA MSA	595,081	614,304	19,223	3.2
Altoona, PA MSA	130,542	131,450	908	0.7
Amarillo, TX MSA	187,514	206,015	18,501	9.9
Anchorage, AK MSA	226,338	250,505	24,167	10.7
Anniston, AL MSA	116,032	113,511	-2,521	-2.2
Appleton-Oshkosh-Neenah, WI MSA	315,121	340,564	25,443	8.1
Asheville, NC MSA	191,772	210,042	18,270	9.5
Athens, GA MSA	126,262	137,204	10,942	8.7
Atlanta, GA MSA	2,959,500	3,541,230	581,730	19.7
Augusta-Aiken, GA-SC MSA	415,220	453,612	38,392	9.2
Austin-San Marcos, TX MSA	846,227	1,041,330	195,103	23.1
Bakersfield, CA MSA	544,981	622,729	77,748	14.3
Bangor, ME MSA	91,629	89,364	-2,265	-2.5
Barnstable-Yarmouth, MA MSA	134,954	145,867	10,913	8.1
Baton Rouge, LA MSA	528,261	567,388	39,127	7.4
Beaumont-Port Arthur, TX MSA	361,218	375,795	14,577	4.0
Bellingham, WA MSA	127,780	152,512	24,732	19.4
Benton Harbor, MI MSA	161,378	161,434	56	0.0
Billings, MT MSA	113,419	125,966	12,547	11.1
Biloxi-Gulfport-Pascagoula, MS MSA	312,368	343,184	30,816	9.9
Binghamton, NY MSA	264,497	254,053	-10,444	-3.9
Birmingham, AL MSA	839,942	894,702	54,760	6.5
Bismarck, ND MSA	83,831	90,103	6,272	7.5
Bloomington, IN MSA	108,978	116,176	7,198	6.6
Bloomington-Normal, IL MSA	129,180	139,133	9,953	7.7
Boise City, ID MSA	295,851	372,587	76,736	25.9
Boston-Worcester-Lawrence, MA-NH-ME-CT CMSA	5,455,403	5,563,475	108,072	2.0
Boston, MA-NH MSA	3,227,707	3,263,060	35,353	1.1
Brockton, MA PMSA	236,409	246,082	9,673	4.1
Fitchburg-Leominster, MA PMSA	138,165	139,435	1,270	0.9
Lawrence, MA-NH PMSA	353,232	372,693	19,461	5.5

Metropolitan area	April 1, 1990 census	July 1, 1996 estimate	Numerical population change 1990–1996	Percent population change 1990–1996
Lowell, MA-NH PMSA	280,578	290,753	10,175	3.6%
Manchester, NH PMSA	173,783	182,173	8,390	4.8
Nashua, NH PMSA	168,233	178,335	10,102	6.0
New Bedford, MA PMSA	175,641	175,090	-551	-0.3
Portsmouth-Rochester, NH-ME PMSA	223,271	230,625	7,354	3.3
Worcester, MA-CT PMSA	478,384	485,229	6,845	1.4
Brownsville-Harlingen-San Benito, TX MSA	260,120	315,015	54,895	21.1
Bryan-College Station, TX MSA	121,862	131,904	10,042	8.2
Buffalo-Niagara Falls, NY MSA	1,189,340	1,175,240	-14,100	-1.2
Burlington, VT MSA	151,506	162,776	11,270	7.4
Canton-Massillon, OH MSA	394,106	402,928	8,822	2.2
Casper, WY MSA	61,226	63,875	2,649	4.3
Cedar Rapids, IA MSA	168,767	179,411	10,644	6.3
Champaign-Urbana, IL MSA	173,025	167,392	-5,633	-3.3
Charleston-North Charleston, SC MSA	506,877	495,143	-11,734	-2.3
Charleston, WV MSA	250,454	254,575	4,121	1.6
Charlotte-Gastonia-Rock Hill, NC-SC MSA	1,162,140	1,321,068	158,928	13.7
Charlottesville, VA MSA	131,373	144,815	13,442	10.2
Chattanooga, TN-GA MSA	424,347	446,096	21,749	5.1
Cheyenne, WY	73,142	79,175	6,033	8.2
Chicago-Gary-Kenosha, IL-IN-WI CMSA	8,239,820	8,599,774	359,954	4.4
Chicago, IL PMSA	7,410,858	7,733,876	323,018	4.4
Gary, IN PMSA	604,526	622,303	17,777	2.9
Kankakee, IL PMSA	96,255	101,949	5,694	5.9
Kenosha, WI PMSA	128,181	141,646	13,465	10.5
Chico-Paradise, CA MSA	182,120	192,507	10,387	5.7
Cincinnati-Hamilton, OH-KY-IN CMSA	1,817,569	1,920,931	103,362	5.7
Cincinnati, OH-KY-IN PMSA	1,526,090	1,597,352	71,262	4.7
Hamilton-Middletown, OH PMSA	291,479	323,579	32,100	11.0
Clarksville-Hopkinsville, TN-KY MSA	169,439	186,368	16,929	10.0
Cleveland-Akron, OH CMSA	2,859,644	2,913,430	53,786	1.9
Akron, OH PMSA	657,575	680,142	22,567	3.4
Cleveland-Lorain-Elyria, OH PMSA	2,202,069	2,233,288	31,219	1.4
Colorado Springs, CO MSA	397,014	472,924	75,910	19.1
Columbia, MO MSA	112,379	125,676	13,297	11.8
Columbia, SC MSA	453,932	488,207	34,275	7.6

Metropolitan area	April 1, 1990 census	July 1, 1996 estimate	Numerical population change 1990–1996	Percent population change 1990–1996
Columbus, GA-AL MSA	260,862	272,273	11,411	4.4%
Columbus, OH MSA	1,345,450	1,447,646	102,196	7.6
Corpus Christi, TX MSA	349,894	384,056	34,162	9.8
Cumberland, MD-WV MSA	101,643	100,600	-1,043	-1.0
Dallas-Fort Worth, TX CMSA	4,037,282	4,574,561	537,279	13.3
Dallas, TX PMSA	2,676,248	3,047,983	371,735	13.9
Fort Worth-Arlington, TX PMSA	1,361,034	1,526,578	165,544	12.2
Danville, VA MSA	108,728	109,246	518	0.5
Davenport-Moline-Rock Island, IA-IL MSA	350,855	357,800	6,945	2.0
Dayton-Springfield, OH MSA	951,270	950,661	-609	-0.1
Daytona Beach, FL MSA	399,438	456,464	57,026	14.3
Decatur, AL MSA	131,556	139,979	8,423	6.4
Decatur, IL MSA	117,206	115,416	-1,790	-1.5
Denver-Boulder-Greeley, CO CMSA	1,980,140	2,277,401	297,261	15.0
Boulder-Langmont, CO PMSA	225,339	258,234	32,895	14.6
Denver, CO PMSA	1,622,980	1,866,978	243,998	15.0
Greeley, CO PMSA	131,821	152,189	20,368	15.5
Des Moines, IA	392,928	427,436	34,508	8.8
Detroit-Ann Arbor-Flint, MI CMSA	5,187,171	5,284,171	97,000	1.9
Ann Arbor, MI PMSA	490,058	529,898	39,840	8.1
Detroit, MI PMSA	4,266,654	4,318,145	51,491	1.2
Flint, MI PMSA	430,459	436,128	5,669	1.3
Dothan, AL MSA	130,964	132,945	1,981	1.5
Dover, DE MSA	110,993	122,244	11,251	10.1
Dubuque, IA MSA	86,403	88,201	1,798	2.1
Duluth-Superior, MN-WI MSA	239,971	239,465	-506	-0.2
Eau Claire, WI MSA	137,543	143,245	5,702	4.1
El Paso, TX MSA	591,610	684,446	92,836	15.7
Elkhart-Goshen, IN MSA	156,198	168,941	12,743	8.2
Elmira, NY MSA	95,195	93,282	-1,913	-2.0
Enid, OK MSA	56,735	57,312	577	1.0
Erie, PA MSA	275,572	280,570	4,998	1.8
Eugene-Springfield, OR MSA	282,912	306,862	23,950	8.5
Evansville-Henderson, IN-KY MSA	278,990	288,735	9,745	3.5
Fargo-Moorhead, ND-MN MSA	153,296	165,191	11,895	7.8
Fayetteville, NC MSA	274,713	284,800	10,087	3.7
Fayetteville-Springdale-Rogers, AR MSA	210,908	260,940	50,032	23.7
Flagstaff, AZ-UT MSA	101,760	118,011	16,251	16.0
Florence, AL MSA	131,327	136,083	4,756	3.6

Metropolitan area	April 1, 1990 census	July 1, 1996 estimate	Numerical population change 1990–1996	Percent population change 1990–1996
Florence, SC MSA	114,344	123,365	9,021	7.9%
Fort Collins-Loveland, CO MSA	186,136	221,725	35,589	19.1
Fort Myers-Cape Coral, FL MSA	335,113	380,001	44,888	13.4
Fort Pierce-Port St. Lucie, FL MSA	251,071	287,255	36,184	14.4
Fort Smith, AR-OK MSA	175,911	191,482	15,571	8.9
Fort Walton Beach, FL MSA	143,777	165,873	22,096	15.4
Fort Wayne, IN MSA	456,281	475,299	19,018	4.2
Fresno, CA MSA	755,580	861,753	106,173	14.1
Gadsden, AL MSA	99,840	102,129	2,289	2.3
Gainesville, FL MSA	181,596	196,525	14,929	8.2
Glens Falls, NY MSA	118,539	122,267	3,728	3.1
Goldsboro, NC MSA	104,666	111,581	6,915	6.6
Grand Forks, ND-MN MSA	103,272	103,883	611	0.6
Grand Junction, CO MSA	93,145	108,371	15,226	16.3
Grand Rapids-Muskegon-Holland, MI MSA	937,891	1,015,099	77,208	8.2
Great Falls, MT MSA	77,691	81,087	3,396	4.4
Green Bay, WI MSA	194,594	213,072	18,478	9.5
Greensboro-Winston-Salem-High Point, NC MSA	1,050,304	1,141,238	90,934	8.7
Greenville, NC MSA	108,480	119,064	10,584	9.8
Greenville-Spartanburg-Anderson, SC MSA	830,539	896,679	66,140	8.0
Harrisburg-Lebanon-Carlisle, PA MSA	587,986	614,755	26,769	4.6
Hartford, CT MSA	1,157,585	1,144,574	-13,011	-1.1
Hattiesburg, MS MSA	98,738	107,897	9,159	9.3
Hickory-Morganton-Lenoir, NC MSA	292,405	314,965	22,560	7.7
Honolulu, HI MSA	836,231	871,766	35,535	4.2
Houma, LA MSA	182,842	189,869	7,027	3.8
Houston-Galveston-Brazoria, TX CMSA	3,731,029	4,253,428	522,399	14.0
Brazoria, TX PMSA	191,707	220,854	29,147	15.2
Galveston-Texas City, TX PMSA	217,396	240,653	23,257	10.7
Houston, TX PMSA	3,321,926	3,791,921	469,995	14.1
Huntington-Ashland, WV-KY-OH MSA	312,529	316,641	4,112	1.3
Huntsville, AL MSA	293,047	330,153	37,106	12.7
Indianapolis, IN MSA	1,380,491	1,492,297	111,806	8.1
Iowa City, IA MSA	96,119	101,609	5,490	5.7
Jackson, MI MSA	149,756	154,563	4,807	3.2
Jackson, MS MSA	395,396	421,068	25,672	6.5
Jackson, TN MSA	90,801	98,489	7,688	8.5
Jacksonville, FL MSA	906,727	1,008,633	101,906	11.2
Jacksonville, NC MSA	149,838	144,533	-5,305	-3.5

Metropolitan area	April 1, 1990 census	July 1, 1996 estimate	Numerical population change 1990–1996	Percent population change 1990–1996
Jamestown, NY MSA	141,895	140,800	-1,095	-0.8%
Janesville-Beloit, WI MSA	139,510	150,584	11,074	7.9
Johnson City-Kingsport-Bristol, TN-VA MSA	436,047	458,229	22,182	5.1
Johnstown, PA MSA	241,280	239,017	-2,263	-0.9
Jonesboro, AR MSA	68,956	76,155	7,199	10.4
Joplin, MO MSA	134,910	145,716	10,806	8.0
Kalamazoo-Battle Creek, MI MSA	429,453	444,428	14,975	3.5
Kansas City, MO-KS MSA	1,582,874	1,690,343	107,469	6.8
Killeen-Temple, TX MSA	255,299	296,896	41,597	16.3
Knoxville, TN MSA	585,960	649,277	63,317	10.8
Kokomo, IN MSA	96,946	100,579	3,633	3.7
La Crosse, WI-MN MSA	116,401	121,544	5,143	4.4
Lafayette, LA MSA	345,053	368,635	23,582	6.8
Lafayette, IN MSA	161,572	171,200	9,628	6.0
Lake Charles, LA MSA	168,134	178,881	10,747	6.4
Lakeland-Winter Haven, FL MSA	405,382	440,954	35,572	8.8
Lancaster, PA MSA	422,822	450,834	28,012	6.6
Lansing-East Lansing, MI MSA	432,684	447,538	14,854	3.4
Laredo, TX MSA	133,239	176,792	43,553	32.7
Las Cruces, NM MSA	135,510	163,849	28,339	20.9
Las Vegas, NV-AZ MSA	852,646	1,201,073	348,427	40.9
Lawrence, KS MSA	81,798	89,899	8,101	9.9
Lawton, OK MSA	111,486	111,171	-315	-0.3
Lewiston-Auburn, ME MSA	93,679	89,893	-3,786	-4.0
Lexington, KY MSA	405,936	441,073	35,137	8.7
Lima, OH MSA	154,340	155,499	1,159	0.8
Lincoln, NE MSA	213,641	231,765	18,124	8.5
Little Rock-North Little Rock, AR MSA	513,026	548,352	35,326	6.9
Longview-Marshall, TX MSA	193,801	206,732	12,931	6.7
Los Angeles-Riverside-Orange County, CA CMSA	14,531,529	15,495,155	963,626	6.6
Los Angeles-Long Beach, CA PMSA	8,863,052	9,127,751	264,699	3.0
Orange County, CA PMSA	2,410,668	2,636,888	226,220	9.4
Riverside-San Bernardino, CA PMSA	2,588,793	3,015,783	426,990	16.5
Ventura, CA PMSA	669,016	714,733	45,717	6.8
Louisville, KY-IN MSA	949,012	991,765	42,753	4.5
Lubbock, TX MSA	222,636	232,035	9,399	4.2
Lynchburg, VA MSA	193,928	205,559	11,631	6.0
Macon, GA MSA	291,079	312,689	21,610	7.4
Madison, WI MSA	367,085	395,366	28,281	7.7
Mansfield, OH MSA	174,007	175,441	1,434	0.8
McAllen-Edinburg-Mission, TX MSA	383,545	495,594	112,049	29.2

Metropolitan area	April 1, 1990 census	July 1, 1996 estimate	Numerical population change 1990–1996	Percent population change 1990–1996
Medford-Ashland, OR MSA	146,387	168,609	22,222	15.2%
Melbourne-Titusville-Palm Bay, FL MSA	398,978	453,998	55,020	13.8
Memphis, TN-AR-MS MSA	1,007,306	1,078,151	70,845	7.0
Merced, CA MSA	178,403	192,311	13,908	7.8
Miami-Fort Lauderdale, FL CMSA	3,192,725	3,514,403	321,678	10.1
Fort Lauderdale, FL PMSA	1,255,531	1,438,228	182,697	14.6
Miami, FL PMSA	1,937,194	2,076,175	138,981	7.2
Milwaukee-Racine, WI CMSA	1,607,183	1,642,658	35,475	2.2
Milwaukee-Waukesha, WI PMSA	1,432,149	1,457,655	25,506	1.8
Racine, WI PMSA	175,034	185,003	9,969	5.7
Minneapolis-St. Paul, MN-WI MSA	2,538,776	2,765,116	226,340	8.9
Mobile, AL MSA	476,923	518,975	42,052	8.8
Modesto, CA MSA	370,522	415,786	45,264	12.2
Monroe, LA MSA	142,191	147,302	5,111	3.6
Montgomery, AL MSA	292,517	314,955	22,438	7.7
Muncie, IN MSA	119,659	118,600	-1,059	-0.9
Myrtle Beach, SC MSA	144,053	163,856	19,803	13.7
Naples, FL MSA	152,099	188,187	36,088	23.7
Nashville, TN MSA	985,026	1,117,178	132,152	13.4
New London-Norwich, CT-RI MSA	290,734	286,719	-4,015	-1.4
New Orleans, LA MSA	1,285,262	1,312,890	27,628	2.1
New York-Northern New Jersey-Long Island, NY-NJ-CT-PA CMSA	19,549,649	19,938,492	388,843	2.0
Bergen-Passaic, NJ PMSA	1,278,682	1,311,331	32,649	2.6
Bridgeport, CT PMSA	443,722	443,637	-85	-0.0
Danbury, CT PMSA	193,597	199,315	5,718	3.0
Dutchess County, NY PMSA	259,462	262,675	3,213	1.2
Jersey City, NJ PMSA	553,099	550,789	-2,310	-0.4
Middlesex-Somerset-Hunterdon, NJ PMSA	1,019,858	1,091,097	71,239	7.0
Monmouth-Ocean, NJ PMSA	986,296	1,065,284	78,988	8.0
Nassau-Suffolk, NY PMSA	2,609,212	2,660,285	51,073	2.0
New Haven-Meriden, CT PMSA	530,180	523,724	-6,456	-1.2
New York, NY PMSA	8,546,846	8,643,437	96,591	1.1
Newark, NJ PMSA	1,915,694	1,940,470	24,776	1.3
Newburgh, NY-PA PMSA	335,613	362,561	26,948	8.0
Stamford-Norwalk, CT PMSA	329,935	331,767	1,832	0.6
Trenton, NJ PMSA	325,824	330,226	4,402	1.4
Waterbury, CT PMS	221,629	221,894	265	0.1
Norfolk-Virginia Beach-Newport News, VA-NC MSA	1,444,710	1,540,252	95,542	6.6
Ocala, FL MSA	194,835	230,068	35,233	18.1
Odessa-Midland, TX MSA	225,545	239,414	13,869	6.1
Oklahoma City, OK MSA	958,839	1,026,657	67,818	7.1
Omaha, NE-IA MSA	639,580	681,698	42,118	6.6
Orlando, FL MSA	1,224,844	1,417,291	192,447	15.7

Metropolitan area	April 1, 1990 census	July 1, 1996 estimate	Numerical population change 1990–1996	Percent population change 1990–1996
Owensboro, KY MSA	87,189	90,818	3,629	4.2%
Panama City, FL MSA	126,994	144,637	17,643	13.9
Parkersburg-Marietta, WV-OH MSA	149,169	151,597	2,428	1.6
Pensacola, FL MSA	344,406	385,820	41,414	12.0
Peoria-Pekin, IL MSA	339,172	346,501	7,329	2.2
Philadelphia-Wilmington-Atlantic City, PA-NJ-DE-MD CMSA	5,893,019	5,973,463	80,444	1.4
Atlantic City-Cape May, NJ PMSA	319,416	333,699	14,283	4.5
Philadelphia, PA-NJ PMSA	4,922,257	4,952,929	30,672	0.6
Vineland-Millville-Bridgeton, NJ PMSA	138,053	135,943	-2,110	-1.5
Wilmington-Newark, DE-MD PMSA	513,293	550,892	37,599	7.3
Phoenix-Mesa, AZ MSA	2,238,498	2,746,703	508,205	22.7
Pine Bluff, AR MSA	85,487	83,007	-2,480	-2.9
Pittsburgh, PA MSA	2,394,811	2,379,411	-15,400	-0.6
Pittsfield, MA MSA	88,695	85,342	-3,353	-3.8
Pocatello, ID MSA	66,026	73,608	7,582	11.5
Portland, ME MSA	221,095	228,916	7,821	3.5
Portland-Salem, OR-WA CMSA	1,793,476	2,078,357	284,881	15.9
Portland-Vancouver, OR-WA PMSA	1,515,452	1,758,937	243,485	16.1
Salem, OR PMSA	278,024	319,420	41,396	14.9
Providence-Fall River-Warwick, RI-MA MSA	1,134,350	1,124,044	-10,306	-0.9
Provo-Orem, UT MSA	263,590	319,694	56,104	21.3
Pueblo, CO MSA	123,051	131,217	8,166	6.6
Punta Gorda, FL MSA	110,975	130,426	19,451	17.5
Raleigh-Durham-Chapel Hill, NC MSA	858,485	1,025,253	166,768	19.4
Rapid City, SD MSA	81,343	87,145	5,802	7.1
Reading, PA MSA	336,523	352,353	15,830	4.7
Redding, CA MSA	147,036	161,740	14,704	10.0
Reno, NV MSA	254,667	298,787	44,120	17.3
Richland-Kennewick-Pasco, WA MSA	150,033	179,949	29,916	19.9
Richmond-Petersburg, VA MSA	865,640	935,174	69,534	8.0
Roanoke, VA MSA	224,592	229,105	4,513	2.0
Rochester, MN MSA	106,470	113,182	6,712	6.3
Rochester, NY MSA	1,062,470	1,088,037	25,567	2.4
Rockford, IL MSA	329,676	352,369	22,693	6.9
Rocky Mount, NC MSA	133,369	144,157	10,788	8.1
Sacramento-Yolo, CA CMSA	1,481,220	1,632,133	150,913	10.2
Sacramento, CA PMSA	1,340,010	1,482,208	142,198	10.6
Yolo, CA PMSA	141,210	149,925	8,715	6.2
Saginaw-Bay City-Midland, MI MSA	399,320	403,301	3,981	1.0
Salinas, CA MSA	355,660	339,047	-16,613	-4.7
Salt Lake City-Ogden, UT MSA	1,072,227	1,217,842	145,615	13.6

Metropolitan area	April 1, 1990 census	July 1, 1996 estimate	Numerical population change 1990–1996	Percent population change 1990–1996
San Angelo, TX MSA	98,458	102,580	4,122	4.2%
San Antonio, TX MSA	1,324,749	1,490,111	165,362	12.5
San Diego, CA MSA	2,498,016	2,655,463	157,447	6.3
San Francisco-Oakland-San Jose, CA CMSA	6,249,881	6,605,428	355,547	5.7
Oakland, CA PMSA	2,080,434	2,209,629	129,195	6.2
San Francisco, CA PSMA	1,603,678	1,655,454	51,776	3.2
San Jose, CA PMSA	1,497,577	1,599,604	102,027	6.8
Santa Cruz-Watsonville, CA PMSA	229,734	237,821	8,087	3.5
Santa Rosa, CA PMSA	388,222	420,872	32,650	8.4
Vallejo-Fairfield-Napa, CA PMSA	450,236	482,048	31,812	7.1
San Luis Obispo-Atascadero-Paso Robles, CA MSA	217,162	229,437	12,275	5.7
Santa Barbara-Santa Maria-Lompoc, CA MSA	369,608	385,573	15,965	4.3
Santa Fe, NM MSA	117,043	137,223	20,180	17.2
Sarasota-Bradenton, FL MSA	489,483	528,803	39,320	8.0
Savannah, GA MSA	257,899	282,610	24,711	9.6
Scranton–Wilkes-Barre–Hazleton, PA MSA	638,524	628,073	-10,451	-1.6
Seattle-Tacoma-Bremerton, WA CMSA	2,970,300	3,320,829	350,529	11.8
Bremerton, WA PMSA	189,731	231,741	42,010	22.1
Olympia, WA PMSA	161,238	197,109	35,871	22.2
Seattle-Bellevue-Everett, WA PMSA	2,033,128	2,234,707	201,579	9.9
Tacoma, WA PMSA	586,203	657,272	71,069	12.1
Sharon, PA MSA	121,003	122,155	1,152	1.0
Sheboygan, WI MSA	103,877	109,705	5,828	5.6
Sherman-Denison, TX MSA	95,019	100,589	5,570	5.9
Shreveport-Bossier City, LA MSA	376,330	379,596	3,266	0.9
Sioux City, IA-NE MSA	115,018	121,108	6,090	5.3
Sioux Falls, SD MSA	139,236	156,598	17,362	12.5
South Bend, IN MSA	247,052	257,740	10,688	4.3
Spokane, WA MSA	361,333	404,920	43,587	12.1
Springfield, IL MSA	189,550	204,130	14,580	7.7
Springfield, MO MSA	264,346	296,345	31,999	12.1
Springfield, MA MSA	587,884	576,561	-11,323	-1.9
St. Cloud, MN MSA	149,509	160,326	10,817	7.2
St. Joseph, MO MSA	97,715	97,336	-379	-0.4
St. Louis, MO-IL MSA	2,492,348	2,548,238	55,890	2.2
State College, PA MSA	124,812	131,489	6,677	5.3
Steubenville-Weirton, OH-WV MSA	142,523	138,315	-4,208	-3.0
Stockton-Lodi, CA MSA	480,628	533,392	52,764	11.0
Sumter, SC MSA	101,276	107,161	5,885	5.8
Syracuse, NY MSA	742,237	745,691	3,454	0.5

Metropolitan area	April 1, 1990 census	July 1, 1996 estimate	Numerical population change 1990–1996	Percent population change 1990–1996
Tallahassee, FL MSA	233,609	259,380	25,771	11.0%
Tampa-St. Petersburg-Clearwater, FL MSA	2,067,959	2,199,231	131,272	6.3
Terre Haute, IN MSA	147,585	149,671	2,086	1.4
Texarkana, TX-Texarkana, AR MSA	120,132	123,919	3,787	3.2
Toledo, OH MSA	614,128	611,417	-2,711	-0.4
Topeka, KS MSA	160,976	164,938	3,962	2.5
Tucson, AZ MSA	666,957	767,873	100,916	15.1
Tulsa, OK MSA	708,954	756,493	47,539	6.7
Tuscaloosa, AL MSA	150,522	158,779	8,257	5.5
Tyler, TX MSA	151,309	165,002	13,693	9.0
Utica-Rome, NY MSA	316,645	302,405	-14,240	-4.5
Victoria, TX MSA	74,361	81,541	7,180	9.7
Visalia-Tulare-Porterville, CA MSA	311,921	349,922	38,001	12.2
Waco, TX MSA	189,123	201,775	12,652	6.7
Washington-Baltimore, DC-MD-VA-WV CMSA	6,726,395	7,164,519	438,124	6.5
Baltimore, MD PMSA	2,382,172	2,474,118	91,946	3.9
Hagerstown, MD PMSA	121,393	127,278	5,885	4.8
Washington, DC-MD-VA-WV PMSA	4,222,830	4,563,123	340,293	8.1
Waterloo-Cedar Falls, IA MSA	123,798	122,806	-992	-0.8
Wausau, WI MSA	115,400	121,791	6,391	5.5
West Palm Beach-Boca Raton, FL MSA	863,503	992,840	129,337	15.0
Wheeling, WV-OH MSA	159,301	155,808	-3,493	-2.2
Wichita, KS MSA	485,270	512,965	27,695	5.7
Wichita Falls, TX MSA	130,351	136,311	5,960	4.6
Williamsport, PA MSA	118,710	119,083	373	0.3
Wilmington, NC MSA	171,269	206,738	35,469	20.7
Yakima, WA MSA	188,823	216,234	27,411	14.5
York, PA MSA	339,574	368,332	28,758	8.5
Youngstown-Warren, OH MSA	600,895	598,582	-2,313	-0.4
Yuba City, CA MSA	122,643	136,555	13,912	11.3
Yuma, AZ MSA	106,895	125,142	18,247	17.1

Note: Areas defined by Office of Management and Budget, June 30, 1996. Primary MSAs (PMSAs) appear under their consolidated MSA (CMSA)).
Source: U.S. Census Bureau

Population of U.S. Cities

Resident Population for Cities with 1996 Population Greater Than 100,000

City	April 1, 1990 census	July 1, 1996	Numerical change	% change	Rank 4/90 pop.	Rank 7/96 pop.
New York, NY	7,322,564	7,380,906	58,342	0.8%	1	1
Los Angeles, CA	3,485,557	3,553,638	68,081	2.0	2	2
Chicago, IL	2,783,726	2,721,547	-62,179	-2.2	3	3
Houston, TX	1,637,859	1,744,058	106,199	6.5	4	4
Philadelphia, PA	1,585,577	1,478,002	-107,575	-6.8	5	5
San Diego, CA	1,110,623	1,171,121	60,498	5.4	6	6
Phoenix, AZ	984,310	1,159,014	174,704	17.7	9	7
San Antonio, TX	959,295	1,067,816	108,521	11.3	10	8
Dallas, TX	1,007,618	1,053,292	45,674	4.5	8	9
Detroit, MI	1,027,974	1,000,272	-27,702	-2.7	7	10
San Jose, CA	782,224	838,744	56,520	7.2	11	11
Indianapolis, IN	731,278	746,737	15,459	2.1	13	12
San Francisco, CA	723,959	735,315	11,356	1.6	14	13
Jacksonville, FL	635,230	679,792	44,562	7.0	15	14
Baltimore, MD	736,014	675,401	-60,613	-8.2	12	15
Columbus, OH	632,945	657,053	24,108	3.8	16	16
El Paso, TX	515,342	599,865	84,523	16.4	22	17
Memphis, TN	618,652	596,725	-21,927	-3.5	18	18
Milwaukee, WI	628,088	590,503	-37,585	-6.0	17	19
Boston, MA	574,283	558,394	-15,889	-2.8	20	20
Washington, DC	606,900	543,213	-63,687	-10.5	19	21
Austin, TX	472,020	541,278	69,258	14.7	26	22
Seattle, WA	516,259	524,704	8,445	1.6	21	23
Nashville-Davidson, TN	488,366	511,263	22,897	4.7	25	24
Cleveland, OH	505,616	498,246	-7,370	-1.5	23	25
Denver, CO	467,610	497,840	30,230	6.5	27	26
Portland, OR	463,634	480,824	17,190	3.7	28	27
Fort Worth, TX	447,619	479,716	32,097	7.2	29	28
New Orleans, LA	496,938	476,625	-20,313	-4.1	24	29
Oklahoma City, OK	444,724	469,852	25,128	5.7	30	30
Tucson, AZ	411,480	449,002	37,522	9.1	34	31
Charlotte, NC	419,539	441,297	21,758	5.2	33	32
Kansas City, MO	434,829	441,259	6,430	1.5	31	33
Virginia Beach, VA	393,089	430,385	37,296	9.5	37	34
Honolulu, HI	377,059	423,475	46,416	12.3	39	35
Long Beach, CA	429,321	421,904	-7,417	-1.7	32	36
Albuquerque, NM	384,915	419,681	34,766	9.0	38	37
Atlanta, GA	393,929	401,907	7,978	2.0	36	38
Fresno, CA	354,091	396,011	41,920	11.8	47	39
Tulsa, OK	367,302	378,491	11,189	3.0	44	40
Las Vegas, NV	258,204	376,906	118,702	46.0	63	41
Sacramento, CA	369,365	376,243	6,878	1.9	42	42
Oakland, CA	372,242	367,230	-5,012	-1.3	40	43
Miami, FL	358,648	365,127	6,479	1.8	46	44
Omaha, NE	342,862	364,253	21,391	6.2	48	45
Minneapolis, MN	368,383	358,785	-9,598	-2.6	43	46
St. Louis, MO	396,685	351,565	-45,120	-11.4	35	47
Pittsburgh, PA	369,879	350,363	-19,516	-5.3	41	48
Cincinnati, OH	364,114	345,818	-18,296	-5.0	45	49
Colorado Springs, CO	280,430	345,127	64,697	23.1	54	50
Mesa, AZ	289,199	344,764	55,565	19.2	53	51
Wichita, KS	304,017	320,395	16,378	5.4	51	52
Toledo, OH	332,943	317,606	-15,337	-4.6	49	53
Buffalo, NY	328,175	310,548	-17,627	-5.4	50	54

City	April 1, 1990 census	July 1, 1996	Numerical change	% change	Rank 4/90 pop.	Rank 7/96 pop.
Santa Ana, CA	293,827	302,419	8,592	2.9%	52	55
Arlington, TX	261,717	294,816	33,099	12.6	61	56
Anaheim, CA	266,406	288,945	22,539	8.5	59	57
Tampa, FL	280,015	285,206	5,191	1.9	55	58
Corpus Christi, TX	257,453	280,260	22,807	8.9	64	59
Newark, NJ	275,221	268,510	-6,711	-2.4	56	60
Louisville, KY	269,555	260,689	-8,866	-3.3	58	61
St. Paul, MN	272,235	259,606	-12,629	-4.6	57	62
Birmingham, AL	265,347	258,543	-6,804	-2.6	60	63
Riverside, CA	226,546	255,069	28,523	12.6	68	64
Aurora, CO	222,103	252,341	30,238	13.6	72	65
Anchorage, AK	226,338	250,505	24,167	10.7	69	66
Raleigh, NC	212,092	243,835	31,743	15.0	74	67
Lexington-Fayette, KY	225,366	239,942	14,576	6.5	70	68
St. Petersburg, FL	240,318	235,988	-4,330	-1.8	65	69
Norfolk, VA	261,250	233,430	-27,820	-10.6	62	70
Stockton, CA	210,943	232,660	21,717	10.3	75	71
Jersey City, NJ	228,517	229,039	522	0.2	67	72
Rochester, NY	230,356	221,594	-8,762	-3.8	66	73
Akron, OH	223,019	216,882	-6,137	-2.8	71	74
Baton Rouge, LA	219,531	215,882	-3,649	-1.7	73	75
Lincoln, NE	191,972	209,192	17,220	9.0	81	76
Bakersfield, CA	176,264	205,508	29,244	16.6	97	77
Hialeah, FL	188,008	204,684	16,676	8.9	87	78
Mobile, AL	196,263	202,581	6,318	3.2	79	79
Richmond, VA	202,798	198,267	-4,531	-2.2	76	80
Madison, WI	190,766	197,630	6,864	3.6	83	81
Montgomery, AL	190,350	196,363	6,013	3.2	84	82
Greensboro, NC	183,894	195,426	11,532	6.3	89	83
Lubbock, TX	186,206	193,565	7,359	4.0	88	84
Des Moines, IA	193,189	193,422	233	0.1	80	85
Jackson, MS	202,062	192,923	-9,139	-4.5	77	86
Chesapeake, VA	151,982	192,342	40,360	26.6	115	87
Plano, TX	127,885	192,280	64,395	50.4	142	88
Shreveport, LA	198,525	191,558	-6,967	-3.5	78	89
Huntington Beach, CA	181,519	190,751	9,232	5.1	91	90
Yonkers, NY	188,082	190,316	2,234	1.2	86	91
Garland, TX	180,635	190,055	9,420	5.2	92	92
Grand Rapids, MI	189,126	188,242	-884	-0.5	85	93
Fremont, CA	173,339	187,800	14,461	8.3	99	94
Spokane, WA	177,165	186,562	9,397	5.3	95	95
Fort Wayne, IN	191,839	184,783	-7,056	-3.7	82	96
Glendale, CA	180,038	184,321	4,283	2.4	93	97
San Bernardino, CA	170,036	183,474	13,438	7.9	102	98
Columbus, GA	178,683	182,828	4,145	2.3	94	99
Glendale, AZ	147,864	182,219	34,355	23.2	119	100
Tacoma, WA	176,664	179,114	2,450	1.4	96	101
Scottsdale, AZ	130,075	179,012	48,937	37.6	140	102
Modesto, CA	164,746	178,559	13,813	8.4	105	103
Irving, TX	155,037	176,993	21,956	14.2	113	104
Newport News, VA	171,439	176,122	4,683	2.7	100	105
Little Rock, AR	175,727	175,752	25	0.0	98	106
Arlington, VA	170,897	175,334	4,437	2.6	101	107
Orlando, FL	164,674	173,902	9,228	5.6	106	108
Dayton, OH	182,005	172,947	-9,058	-5.0	90	109
Salt Lake City, UT	159,928	172,575	12,647	7.9	109	110

City	April 1, 1990 census	July 1, 1996	Numerical change	% change	Rank 4/90 pop.	Rank 7/96 pop.
Huntsville, AL	159,880	170,424	10,544	6.6%	110	111
Amarillo, TX	157,571	169,588	12,017	7.6	111	112
Knoxville, TN	169,761	167,535	-2,226	-1.3	103	113
Worcester, MA	169,759	166,350	-3,409	-2.0	104	114
Laredo, TX	122,899	164,899	42,000	34.2	148	115
Tempe, AZ	141,993	162,701	20,708	14.6	123	116
Syracuse, NY	163,860	155,865	-7,995	-4.9	107	117
Reno, NV	133,850	155,499	21,649	16.2	133	118
Winston-Salem, NC	150,958	153,541	2,583	1.7	117	119
Boise City, ID	126,685	152,737	26,052	20.6	144	120
Providence, RI	160,728	152,558	-8,170	-5.1	108	121
Chula Vista, CA	135,160	151,963	16,803	12.4	132	122
Fort Lauderdale, FL	149,238	151,805	2,567	1.7	118	123
Oxnard, CA	142,560	151,009	8,449	5.9	122	124
Chattanooga, TN	152,393	150,425	-1,968	-1.3	114	125
Paterson, NJ	140,891	150,270	9,379	6.7	127	126
Springfield, MA	156,983	149,948	-7,035	-4.5	112	127
Durham, NC	138,894	149,799	10,905	7.9	130	128
Garden Grove, CA	142,965	149,208	6,243	4.4	121	129
Oceanside, CA	128,090	145,941	17,851	13.9	141	130
Ontario, CA	133,179	144,854	11,675	8.8	135	131
Rockford, IL	141,787	143,531	1,744	1.2	124	132
Springfield, MO	140,494	143,407	2,913	2.1	128	133
Chandler, AZ	89,862	142,918	53,056	59.0	210	134
Kansas City, KS	151,521	142,654	-8,867	-5.9	116	135
Moreno Valley, CA	118,779	140,932	22,153	18.7	153	136
Hampton, VA	133,811	138,757	4,946	3.7	134	137
Warren, MI	144,864	138,078	-6,786	-4.7	120	138
Bridgeport, CT	141,686	137,990	-3,696	-2.6	125	139
Tallahassee, FL	124,773	136,812	12,039	9.6	147	140
Savannah, GA	137,812	136,262	-1,550	-1.1	131	141
Torrance, CA	133,107	136,183	3,076	2.3	136	142
Lakewood, CO	126,475	134,999	8,524	6.7	145	143
Flint, MI	140,925	134,881	-6,044	-4.3	126	144
Pomona, CA	131,700	134,706	3,006	2.3	137	145
Pasadena, CA	131,586	134,116	2,530	1.9	138	146
Hartford, CT	139,739	133,086	-6,653	-4.8	129	147
Brownsville, TX	107,027	132,091	25,064	23.4	182	148
Pasadena, TX	119,604	131,620	12,016	10.0	152	149
Overland Park, KS	111,790	131,053	19,263	17.2	164	150
Hollywood, FL	121,720	127,894	6,174	5.1	149	151
Irvine, CA	110,330	127,873	17,543	15.9	169	152
Lansing, MI	127,321	125,736	-1,585	-1.2	143	153
Sunnyvale, CA	117,324	125,156	7,832	6.7	155	154
Santa Clarita, CA	120,050	125,153	5,103	4.3	150	155
New Haven, CT	130,474	124,665	-5,809	-4.5	139	156
Eugene, OR	112,733	123,718	10,985	9.7	162	157
Evansville, IN	126,272	123,456	-2,816	-2.2	146	158
Salem, OR	107,793	122,566	14,773	13.7	180	159
Henderson, NV	64,948	122,339	57,391	88.4	219	160
Santa Rosa, CA	113,261	121,879	8,618	7.6	161	161
Hayward, CA	114,705	121,631	6,926	6.0	157	162
Fullerton, CA	114,144	120,188	6,044	5.3	159	163
Orange, CA	110,658	119,890	9,232	8.3	168	164
Topeka, KS	119,883	119,658	-225	-0.2	151	165
Sterling Heights, MI	117,810	118,698	888	0.8	154	166

City	April 1, 1990 census	July 1, 1996	Numerical change	% change	Rank 4/90 pop.	Rank 7/96 pop.
Alexandria, VA	111,182	117,586	6,404	5.8%	166	167
Rancho Cucamonga, CA	101,409	116,613	15,204	15.0	195	168
Aurora, IL	99,672	116,405	16,733	16.8	200	169
Escondido, CA	108,648	116,184	7,536	6.9	178	170
Lancaster, CA	97,300	115,675	18,375	18.9	204	171
Concord, CA	111,308	114,850	3,542	3.2	165	172
Cedar Rapids, IA	108,772	113,482	4,710	4.3	176	173
Thousand Oaks, CA	104,381	113,368	8,987	8.6	188	174
Macon, GA	107,365	113,352	5,987	5.6	181	175
Sioux Falls, SD	100,836	113,223	12,387	12.3	197	176
Springfield, IL	105,417	112,921	7,504	7.1	186	177
Columbia, SC	110,734	112,773	2,039	1.8	167	178
Peoria, IL	113,513	112,306	-1,207	-1.1	160	179
Mesquite, TX	101,484	111,947	10,463	10.3	194	180
Salinas, CA	108,777	111,757	2,980	2.7	175	181
Beaumont, TX	114,323	111,224	-3,099	-2.7	158	182
Inglewood, CA	109,602	111,040	1,438	1.3	172	183
Gary, IN	116,646	110,975	-5,671	-4.9	156	184
Independence, MO	112,301	110,303	-1,998	-1.8	163	185
Elizabeth, NJ	110,002	110,149	147	0.1	170	186
Stamford, CT	108,056	110,056	2,000	1.9	179	187
El Monte, CA	106,162	110,026	3,864	3.6	184	188
Vallejo, CA	109,199	109,593	394	0.4	173	189
Grand Prairie, TX	99,606	109,231	9,625	9.7	201	190
Ann Arbor, MI	109,608	108,758	-850	-0.8	171	191
Abilene, TX	106,707	108,476	1,769	1.7	183	192
Waco, TX	103,590	108,412	4,822	4.7	190	193
Naperville, IL	85,806	107,001	21,195	24.7	213	194
Simi Valley, CA	100,218	106,974	6,756	6.7	198	195
Palmdale, CA	70,262	106,540	36,278	51.6	217	196
Waterbury, CT	108,961	106,412	-2,549	-2.3	174	197
Coral Springs, FL	78,864	105,275	26,411	33.5	215	198
Erie, PA	108,718	105,270	-3,448	-3.2	177	199
Livonia, MI	100,850	105,099	4,249	4.2	196	200
Lafayette, LA	101,852	104,899	3,047	3.0	193	201
Fort Collins, CO	87,491	104,196	16,705	19.1	212	202
Fontana, CA	87,535	104,124	16,589	19.0	211	203
Albany, NY	100,031	103,564	3,533	3.5	199	204
McAllen, TX	84,021	103,352	19,331	23.0	214	205
Berkeley, CA	102,724	103,243	519	0.5	192	206
Allentown, PA	105,301	102,211	-3,090	-2.9	187	207
South Bend, IN	105,511	102,100	-3,411	-3.2	185	208
Green Bay, WI	96,466	102,076	5,610	5.8	205	209
West Covina, CA	96,226	101,526	5,300	5.5	208	210
Portsmouth, VA	103,910	101,308	-2,602	-2.5	189	211
Lowell, MA	103,439	100,973	-2,466	-2.4	191	212
Manchester, NH	99,332	100,967	1,635	1.6	202	213
Costa Mesa, CA	96,357	100,938	4,581	4.8	206	214
Pembroke Pines, FL	65,566	100,662	35,096	53.5	218	215
Norwalk, CA	94,279	100,209	5,930	6.3	209	216
Corona, CA	75,943	100,208	24,265	32.0	216	217
Wichita Falls, TX	96,259	100,138	3,879	4.0	207	218
Clearwater, FL	98,669	100,132	1,463	1.5	203	219

Source: U.S. Census Bureau

Mayors of Major U.S. Cities

CITY	NAME	SALARY	CITY	NAME	SALARY
New York City, NY	Rudolph Giuliani	$165,000	Jacksonville, FL	John A. Delaney	$127,230
Los Angeles, CA	Richard Riordan	$1	Columbus, OH	Gregory S. Lashutka	$107,087
Chicago, IL	Richard M. Daley	$170,000	Milwaukee, WI	John O. Norquist	$115,851
Houston, TX	Lee P. Brown	$160,500	Memphis, TN	Willie W. Herenton	$110,000
Philadelphia, PA	Edward Rendell	$110,000	El Paso, TX	Carlos Ramirez	$27,562
San Diego, CA	Susan Golding	$71,992	Washington, DC	Marion Barry, Jr.	$90,705
Phoenix. AZ	Skip Rimsza	$37,500	Boston, MA	Thomas Menino	$125,000
Detroit, MI	Dennis W. Archer	$157,300	Seattle, WA	Paul Schell	$112,731
Dallas, TX	Ronald Kirk	$2,400	Austin, TX	Kirk Watson	$35,000
San Antonio, TX	Howard Peak	$2,400	Nashville, TN	Philip N. Bredesen	$75,000
San Jose, CA	Susan Hammer	$90,000	Denver, CO	Wellington E. Webb	$103,056
Indianapolis, IN	Stephen Goldsmith	$90,000			
San Francisco, CA	Willie L. Brown, Jr.	$146,891			
Baltimore, MD	Kurt Schmoke	$95,000			

Source: U.S. Conference of Mayors

Where Most Minorities Live

Number of Minorities and Their Share of the Total 1990 Population in Cities of 200,000 or More People

Cities with the Most Blacks

Rank	City	Black population	%	Rank	City	Black population	%
1	New York, NY	2,102,512	28.7	11	Dallas, TX	296,994	29.5
2	Chicago, IL	1,087,711	39.1	12	Atlanta, GA	264,262	67.1
3	Detroit, MI	777,916	75.7	13	Cleveland, OH	235,405	46.6
4	Philadelphia, PA	631,936	39.9	14	Milwaukee, WI	191,255	30.5
5	Los Angeles, CA	487,674	14.0	15	St. Louis, MO	188,408	47.5
6	Houston, TX	457,990	28.1	16	Birmingham, AL	168,277	63.3
7	Baltimore, MD	435,768	59.2	17	Indianapolis, IN	165,570	22.6
8	Washington, DC	399,604	65.8	18	Oakland, CA	163,335	43.9
9	Memphis, TN	334,737	54.8	19	Newark, NJ	160,885	58.5
10	New Orleans, LA	307,728	61.9	20	Jacksonville, FL	160,283	25.2

Cities with the Most Hispanics

Rank	City	Hispanic population	%	Rank	City	Hispanic population	%
1	New York, NY	1,783,511	24.4	11	Phoenix, AZ	197,103	20.0
2	Los Angeles, CA	1,391,411	39.9	12	Santa Ana, CA	191,383	65.2
3	Chicago, IL	545,852	19.6	13	Albuquerque, NM	132,706	34.5
4	San Antonio, TX	520,282	55.6	14	Corpus Christi, TX	129,708	50.4
5	Houston, TX	450,483	27.6	15	Tucson, AZ	118,595	29.3
6	El Paso, TX	355,669	69.0	16	Denver, CO	107,382	23.0
7	San Diego, CA	229,519	20.7	17	Austin, TX	106,868	23.0
8	Miami, FL	223,964	62.5	18	Fresno, CA	105,787	29.9
9	Dallas, TX	210,240	20.9	19	Long Beach, CA	101,419	23.6
10	San Jose, CA	208,388	26.6	20	San Francisco, CA	100,717	13.9

Cities with the Most Asians or Pacific Islanders

Rank	City	Asian or Pacific Islander population	%	Rank	City	Asian or Pacific Islander population	%
1	New York, NY	512,719	7.0	11	Sacramento, CA	55,426	15.0
2	Los Angeles, CA	341,807	9.8	12	Oakland, CA	54,931	14.8
3	Honolulu, HI	257,552	70.5	13	Stockton, CA	48,087	22.8
4	San Francisco, CA	210,876	29.1	14	Fresno, CA	44,358	12.5
5	San Jose, CA	152,815	19.5	15	Philadelphia, PA	43,522	2.7
6	San Diego, CA	130,945	11.8	16	Boston, MA	30,388	5.3
7	Chicago, IL	104,118	3.7	17	Santa Ana, CA	28,585	9.7
8	Houston, TX	67,113	4.1	18	Jersey City, NJ	25,959	11.4
9	Seattle, WA	60,819	11.8	19	Anaheim, CA	25,018	9.4
10	Long Beach, CA	58,266	13.6	20	Portland, OR	23,185	5.3

Source: U.S. Census Bureau

Metropolitan Area Job Growth

(Total employment and job gain are in thousands)

Rank % change 1Q '97–'98	Metro area	Total employment 1Q '98	Job gain 1Q '97–'98	% change 1Q '97–'98	Rank job gain 1Q '97–'98
1	Sarasota, FL	263.7	20.5	8.44%	44
2	McAllen-Edinburg-Mission, TX	141.9	9.0	6.74	64
3	Phoenix, AZ	1,438.8	80.5	5.92	5
4	Dallas, TX	1,806.0	100.8	5.91	2
5	Seattle, WA	1,320.9	69.0	5.51	7
6	Raleigh-Durham, NC	629.9	32.8	5.49	22
7	Orlando, FL	819.7	41.9	5.39	15
8	Charleston, SC	226.7	11.4	5.28	58
9	San Jose, CA	946.9	47.3	5.25	14
10	Jacksonville, FL	531.6	26.1	5.16	30
11	Austin, TX	580.4	28.4	5.14	27
12	Houston, TX	1,939.4	92.6	5.01	3
13	West Palm Beach-Boca Raton, FL	456.3	21.7	5.00	42
14	Riverside-San Bernardino, CA	867.5	40.8	4.93	17
15	Orange County, CA	1,256.6	58.0	4.84	9
16	Tampa-St. Petersburg, FL	1,099.6	49.8	4.75	11
17	Las Vegas, NV	646.8	29.3	4.74	26
18	Middlesex-Somerset-Hunterdon, NJ	618.6	26.8	4.50	29
19	Omaha, NE-IA	404.6	17.1	4.41	52
20	Kansas City, KS/MO	933.6	39.3	4.39	18
21	Atlanta, GA	1,999.9	84.1	4.39	4
22	Boise City, ID	195.5	8.2	4.38	68
23	Santa Rosa-Petaluma, CA	166.9	7.0	4.36	72
24	Fort Worth-Arlington, TX	716.3	29.9	4.36	25
25	Wilmington, DE-NJ-MD	305.8	12.6	4.31	56
26	Tulsa, OK	379.5	14.8	4.06	54
27	Portland, OR	930.0	35.9	4.02	21
28	San Antonio, TX	672.7	24.9	3.84	33
29	San Diego, CA	1,065.2	39.0	3.80	19

Rank % change 1Q '97–'98	Metro area	Total employment 1Q '98	Job gain 1Q '97–'98	% change 1Q '97–'98	Rank job gain 1Q '97–'98
30	Salt Lake City-Ogden, UT	678.7	24.8	3.80%	32
31	Denver, CO	1,065.5	38.5	3.75	20
32	Fort Lauderdale-Hollywood, FL	643.8	23.1	3.73	39
33	Ventura, CA	246.6	8.6	3.60	66
34	Oakland, CA	961.0	32.6	3.61	23
35	Richmond-Petersburg, VA	532.8	17.7	3.44	51
36	Grand Rapids, MI	556.8	18.5	3.43	47
37	Charlotte-Gastonia-Rock Hill, NC-SC	765.7	25.3	3.41	31
38	Louisville, KY-IN	554.4	18.1	3.37	49
39	Sacramento, CA	630.4	20.3	3.33	45
40	Baton Rouge, LA	286.0	9.0	3.25	63
41	Tucson, AZ	321.0	9.7	3.10	61
42	Columbus, OH	820.2	24.7	3.10	35
43	Indianapolis, IN	834.9	24.7	3.05	34
44	Nashville, TN	632.4	18.4	3.00	48
45	Springfield, MA	253.4	7.4	2.99	69
46	Milwaukee, WI	832.5	23.8	2.94	38
47	San Francisco, CA	990.2	28.3	2.94	28
48	El Paso, TX	244.7	6.8	2.87	73
49	Los Angeles-Long Beach, CA	3,926.0	107.6	2.82	1
50	Cincinnati, OH-KY-IN	846.9	23.1	2.80	40
51	Boston, MA	1,922.6	51.5	2.75	10
52	Cleveland, OH	1,138.9	30.2	2.73	24
53	Madison, WI	267.9	7.0	2.67	71
54	Minneapolis-St. Paul, MN-WI	1,613.4	40.8	2.59	16
55	Mobile, AL	221.0	5.5	2.57	81
56	Bakersfield, CA	181.4	4.5	2.54	85
57	Greenville-Spartanburg, SC	463.5	11.4	2.52	57
58	Bergen-Passaic, NJ	639.1	15.7	2.51	53
59	Newark, NJ	953.4	22.8	2.45	41
60	Detroit, MI	2,098.5	49.2	2.40	13
61	Fresno, CA	273.1	6.4	2.39	78
62	Birmingham, AL	468.1	10.0	2.19	59
63	Baltimore, MD	1,162.9	24.4	2.14	36
64	Little Rock-North Little Rock, AR	303.3	6.3	2.11	77
65	Greensboro-Winston-Salem, NC	636.7	12.8	2.05	55
66	Fort Myers, FL	154.8	3.1	2.04	89
67	Washington, DC-MD-VA	2,483.6	49.3	2.02	12
68	Nassau-Suffolk, NY	1,111.4	21.5	1.98	43
69	Miami-Hialeah, FL	974.8	18.5	1.94	48
70	Chicago, IL	4,016.5	75.5	1.91	6
71	Albuquerque, NM	332.0	6.1	1.86	79
72	Monmouth-Ocean, NJ	352.4	6.4	1.86	75
73	Akron, OH	321.3	5.8	1.85	80
74	Oklahoma City, OK	501.3	8.9	1.81	65
75	New York, NY	3,922.1	67.6	1.75	8
76	Providence, RI	502.3	8.6	1.74	87
77	New Orleans, LA	615.7	9.9	1.83	60
78	Colorado Springs, CO	214.1	3.4	1.61	87
79	Harrisburg-Lebanon-Carlisle, PA	350.4	5.5	1.60	82
80	Knoxville, TN	313.3	4.9	1.60	84
81	Des Moines, IA	268.1	3.8	1.45	86
82	Norfolk-Virginia Beach-Newport News, VA	661.3	9.4	1.45	82

Rank % change 1Q '97–'98	Metro area	Total employment 1Q '98	Job gain 1Q '97–'98	% change 1Q '97–'98	Rank job gain 1Q '97–'98
83	Dayton-Springfield, OH	474.4	6.7	1.43%	74
84	St. Louis, MO-IL	1,285.6	17.8	1.40	50
85	Memphis, TN-AR-MS	556.4	6.2	1.12	78
86	Philadelphia, PA-NJ	2,245.4	24.3	1.09	37
87	Hartford, CT	594.5	5.1	0.86	83
88	Albany-Schenectady- Troy, NY	425.8	3.3	0.77	88
89	Scranton–Wilkes-Barre, PA	272.2	2.0	0.74	92
90	Toledo, OH	314.5	2.2	0.72	90
91	Pittsburgh, PA	1,061.0	7.0	0.66	70
92	Gary-Hammond, IN	261.5	1.7	0.64	95
93	Syracuse, NY	331.0	2.0	0.82	91
94	Buffalo, NY	534.5	1.9	0.38	93
95	Rochester, NY	519.5	1.7	0.33	94

Source: M/PF Research Inc.

Major Metro Area Incomes

Metropolitan area	Income per capita	
	1997	2007*
Los Angeles-Long Beach, CA PMSA	$26,193.7	$41,161.9
New York, NY PMSA	35,775.0	57,468.7
Chicago, IL PMSA	31,158.5	50,197.2
Boston, MA-NH-ME-CT NECMA	32,218.6	56,575.9
Philadelphia, PA-NJ-DE-MD PMSA	29,485.7	47,199.3
Washington, DC-MD-VA-WV PMSA	34,482.1	52,448.8
Detroit, MI PMSA	28,260.0	45,469.3
Houston, TX PMSA	28,495.0	44,819.7
Atlanta, GA MSA	27,931.2	43,583.8
Dallas, TX PMSA	30,319.8	45,599.8
Riverside-San Bernardino, CA PMSA	20,331.2	33,059.9
Phoenix-Mesa, AZ MSA	24,259.7	37,723.5
Minneapolis-St. Paul, MN-WI MSA	30,353.6	46,897.1
San Diego, CA MSA	24,865.6	40,150.5
Orange County, CA MSA	29,966.9	48,854.0
Nassau-Suffolk, NY PMSA	33,772.4	54,821.6
St. Louis, MO-IL MSA	27,488.8	44,223.3
Baltimore, MD PMSA	27,785.0	42,568.3
Pittsburgh, PA PMSA	26,275.3	42,797.6
Oakland, CA PMSA	30,798.4	50,877.4
Seattle-Bellevue-Everett, WA PMSA	33,379.6	55,324.1
Tampa-St. Petersburg-Clearwater, FL MSA	24,862.8	39,998.1
Cleveland-Lorain-Elyria, OH PMSA	27,873.3	44,545.2
Miami, FL PMSA	23,931.6	35,088.0
Newark, NJ PMSA	34,938.2	54,979.0
Denver, CO PMSA	29,956.0	44,773.1
Portland-Vancouver, OR-WA PMSA	27,389.5	39,766.7
Kansas City, MO-KS MSA	27,072.4	42,275.0
San Francisco, CA PMSA	40,776.7	66,717.8
New Haven-Bridgeport-Stamford-Danbury-Waterbury, CT NECMA	39,452.2	66,623.7
San Jose, CA PMSA	36,145.1	59,056.3

Metropolitan area	Income per capita	
	1997	2007*
Cincinnati, OH-KY-IN PMSA	26,497.0	40,646.8
Fort Worth-Arlington, TX PMSA	24,569.8	38,501.7
Norfolk-Virginia Beach-Newport News, VA-NC MSA	23,129.0	34,656.9
San Antonio, TX MSA	22,573.3	32,671.2
Indianapolis, IN MSA	26,760.5	42,284.4
Sacramento, CA PMSA	25,389.9	43,528.2
Fort Lauderdale, FL PMSA	28,204.8	40,613.0
Orlando, FL MSA	23,037.7	35,848.2
Columbus, OH MSA	26,418.3	41,208.2
Milwaukee-Waukesha, WI PMSA	28,689.6	46,046.4
Charlotte-Gastonia-Rock Hill, NC-SC MSA	26,702.3	40,584.7
Bergen-Passaic, NJ PMSA	36,234.0	58,383.3
New Orleans, LA MSA	23,200.9	36,291.3
Las Vegas, NV-AZ MSA	25,100.9	40,124.6
Salt Lake City-Ogden, UT MSA	22,359.0	36,560.6
Buffalo-Niagara Falls, NY MSA	24,732.5	41,197.8
Greensboro–Winston-Salem–High Point, NC MSA	25,800.6	40,924.9
Nashville, TN MSA	27,122.8	40,108.2
Middlesex-Somerset-Hunterdon, NJ PMSA	36,107.7	57,597.3

*Projected.
Source: Regional Financial Associates

City Cost Comparisons

Cost of Living Values in Selected U.S. Locations, 1998

Location	Total annual cost	Index
San Francisco, CA	$80,863	134.8
New York, NY	73,438	122.4
Boston, MA	72,867	121.4
Washington, DC	68,216	113.7
Chicago, IL	66,630	111.1
Los Angeles, CA	66,481	110.8
Milwaukee, WI	62,368	103.9
Atlanta, GA	62,214	103.7
Standard City, USA	**60,000**	**100.0**
Miami, FL	59,775	99.6
St. Louis, MO	59,284	98.8
Phoenix, AZ	59,139	98.6
Raleigh, NC	58,121	96.9
Indianapolis, IN	56,837	94.7
Dallas, TX	56,734	94.6

NOTE: The table above is based on a family of four with a $60,000 annual income residing in a 2,200 sq. ft., 8-room, 4-bedroom, 2.5-bath home. They own two vehicles, a late-model car and a 4-year-old vehicle.
Source: Runzheimer International

The Smartest Towns

The towns with the highest percentage of adults with college degrees, based on an analysis of 1990 U.S. census results.

Rank	Place	Population aged 25 and older	Percent with Bachelor's degree or higher
1	Stanford. CA	6,090	90.9%
2	Chevy Chase, MD (town)	1,879	80.2
3	Winnetka, IL	8,030	79.2
4	Scarsdale, NY	10,969	74.7
5	Portola Valley, CA	3,203	74.1
6	Mission Hills, KS	2,487	73.7
7	Princeton, NJ (township)	9,585	73.6
8	University Heights, VA	1,204	73.1
9	Hanover, NH	4,072	73.0
10	University Park, TX	13,334	72.9
11	Kensington, CA	3,957	72.6
12	Bunker Hill Village, TX	2,370	72.3
13	Glencoe, IL	5,821	72.1
14	Fox Chapel, PA	3,604	71.5
	Mountain Lakes, NJ	2,480	71.5
16	Chapel Hill, NC	19,230	71.2
	East Lansing, MI	16,425	71.2
	Piedmont, CA	7,263	71.2
19	Ann Arbor, MI (township)	2,784	70.3
20	Potomac, MD	30,406	70.2
21	Bloomfield Hills, MI	3,118	69.8
22	Cherry Hills Village, CO	3,455	69.6
23	Bronxville, NY	4,018	69.5
	Ottawa Hills, OH	3,066	69.5
25	Kingston, RI	922	69.4

Source: American Demographics

Normal Daily Maximum and Minimum Temperatures for 50 Major U.S. Cities (°F)

City	January Max.	January Min.	February Max.	February Min.	March Max.	March Min.	April Max.	April Min.	May Max.	May Min.	June Max.	June Min.
New York, NY	37.6	25.3	40.3	26.9	50.0	34.8	61.2	43.8	71.1	53.7	80.1	63.0
Los Angeles, CA	65.7	47.8	65.9	49.3	65.5	50.5	67.4	52.8	69.0	56.3	71.9	59.5
Chicago, IL	29.0	12.9	33.5	17.2	45.8	28.5	58.6	38.6	70.1	47.7	79.6	57.5
Houston, TX	61.0	39.7	65.3	42.6	71.1	50.0	78.4	58.1	84.6	64.4	90.1	70.6
Philadelphia, PA	37.9	22.8	41.0	24.8	51.6	33.2	62.6	42.1	73.1	52.7	81.7	61.8
San Diego, CA	65.9	48.9	66.5	50.7	66.3	52.8	68.4	55.6	69.1	59.1	71.6	61.9
Phoenix, AZ	65.9	41.2	70.7	44.7	75.5	48.8	84.5	55.3	93.6	63.9	103.5	72.9
Dallas, TX	54.1	32.7	58.9	36.9	67.8	45.6	76.3	54.7	82.9	62.6	91.9	70.0
San Antonio, TX	60.8	37.9	65.7	41.3	73.5	49.7	80.3	58.4	85.3	65.7	91.8	72.6
Detroit, MI	30.3	15.6	33.3	17.6	44.4	27.0	57.7	36.8	69.6	47.1	78.9	56.3
San Jose, CA	58.2	40.6	62.5	43.9	65.3	45.4	70.0	47.1	74.6	50.9	79.6	54.6
Indianapolis, IN	33.7	17.2	38.3	20.9	50.9	31.9	63.3	41.5	73.8	51.7	82.7	61.0
San Francisco, CA	55.6	41.8	59.4	45.0	60.8	45.8	63.9	47.2	66.5	49.7	70.3	52.6
Baltimore, MD	40.2	23.4	43.7	25.9	54.0	34.1	64.3	42.5	74.2	52.6	83.2	61.8
Jacksonville, FL	64.2	40.5	67.0	43.3	73.0	49.2	79.1	54.9	84.7	62.1	89.3	69.1
Columbus, OH	34.1	18.5	38.0	21.2	50.5	31.2	62.0	40.0	72.3	50.1	80.4	58.0
Milwaukee, WI	26.1	11.6	30.1	15.9	40.4	26.2	52.9	35.8	64.3	44.8	74.9	55.0
Memphis, TN	48.5	30.9	53.5	34.8	63.2	43.0	73.3	52.4	81.0	61.2	89.3	68.9
El Paso, TX	56.1	29.4	62.2	33.9	69.9	40.2	78.7	48.0	87.1	56.5	96.5	64.3
Washington, DC	42.3	26.8	45.9	29.1	56.5	37.7	66.7	46.4	76.2	56.6	84.7	66.5
Boston, MA	35.7	21.6	37.5	23.0	45.8	31.3	55.9	40.2	66.6	49.8	76.3	59.1
Seattle, WA	45.0	35.2	49.5	37.4	52.7	38.5	57.2	41.2	63.9	46.3	69.9	51.9
Austin, TX	58.9	38.6	63.4	42.1	71.9	51.1	79.4	59.8	84.7	66.5	91.1	71.5
Nashville-Davidson, TN	45.9	26.5	50.8	29.9	61.2	39.1	70.8	47.5	78.8	56.6	86.5	64.7
Denver, CO	43.2	16.1	46.6	20.2	52.2	25.8	61.8	34.5	70.8	43.6	81.4	52.4
Cleveland, OH	31.9	17.6	35.0	19.3	46.3	28.2	57.9	37.3	68.6	47.3	78.3	56.8
New Orleans, LA	60.8	41.8	64.1	44.4	71.6	51.6	78.5	58.4	84.4	65.2	89.2	70.8
Oklahoma City, OK	46.7	25.2	52.1	29.6	62.0	38.5	71.9	48.8	79.1	57.7	87.3	66.1
Fort Worth, TX	54.1	32.7	58.9	36.9	67.8	45.6	76.3	54.7	82.9	62.6	91.9	70.0
Portland, OR	45.4	33.7	51.0	36.1	56.0	38.6	60.6	41.3	67.1	47.0	74.0	52.9
Kansas City, MO	34.7	16.7	40.6	21.8	52.8	32.6	65.1	43.8	74.3	53.9	83.3	63.1
Charlotte, NC	49.0	29.6	53.0	31.9	62.3	39.4	71.2	47.5	78.3	56.4	85.8	65.6
Tucson, AZ	63.9	38.6	67.8	41.0	72.8	44.6	81.2	50.4	89.9	58.0	99.6	67.9
Long Beach, CA	66.8	44.9	67.7	46.9	68.0	49.0	71.5	51.8	73.3	56.3	77.0	59.8
Albuquerque, NM	46.8	21.7	53.5	26.4	61.4	32.2	70.8	39.6	79.7	48.6	90.0	58.3
Atlanta, GA	50.4	31.5	55.0	34.5	64.3	42.5	72.7	50.2	79.6	58.7	85.8	66.2
Fresno, CA	54.1	37.4	61.7	40.5	66.6	43.4	75.1	47.3	84.2	53.7	92.7	60.4
Honolulu, HI	80.1	65.6	80.5	65.4	81.6	67.2	82.8	68.7	84.7	70.3	86.5	72.2
Tulsa, OK	45.4	24.9	51.0	29.5	62.1	39.1	73.0	49.9	79.7	58.8	87.7	67.7
Sacramento, CA	52.7	37.7	60.0	41.1	64.0	43.2	71.1	45.5	80.3	50.3	87.8	55.3
Miami, FL	75.2	59.2	76.5	60.4	79.1	64.2	82.4	67.8	85.3	72.1	87.6	75.1
St. Louis, MO	37.7	20.8	42.6	25.1	54.6	35.5	66.9	46.4	76.1	56.0	85.2	65.7
Pittsburgh, PA	33.7	18.5	36.9	20.3	49.0	29.8	60.3	38.8	70.6	48.4	78.9	56.9
Minneapolis, MN	20.7	2.8	26.6	9.2	39.2	22.7	56.5	36.2	69.4	47.6	78.8	57.6
Omaha, NE	31.3	10.9	37.1	16.7	49.4	27.7	63.8	39.9	74.0	50.9	83.7	60.4
Las Vegas, NV	57.3	33.6	63.3	38.8	68.8	43.8	77.5	50.7	87.8	60.2	100.3	69.4
Toledo, OH	30.2	14.9	33.4	17.0	45.5	26.8	58.8	36.4	70.5	46.7	79.8	56.0
Colorado Springs, CO	41.1	16.1	44.6	19.3	50.0	24.6	59.8	33.0	68.7	42.1	79.0	51.1
Buffalo, NY	30.2	17.0	31.6	17.4	41.7	25.9	54.2	36.2	66.1	47.0	75.3	56.5
Wichita, KS	39.8	19.2	45.9	23.7	57.2	33.6	68.3	44.5	76.9	54.3	86.8	64.6

City	July Max.	Min.	August Max.	Min.	September Max.	Min.	October Max.	Min.	November Max.	Min.	December Max.	Min.
New York, NY	85.2	68.4	83.7	67.3	76.2	60.1	65.3	49.7	54.0	41.1	42.5	30.7
Los Angeles, CA	75.3	62.8	76.6	64.2	76.6	63.2	74.4	59.2	70.3	52.8	65.9	47.9
Chicago, IL	83.7	62.6	81.8	61.6	74.8	53.9	63.3	42.2	48.4	31.6	34.0	19.1
Houston, TX	92.7	72.4	92.5	72.0	88.4	67.9	81.6	57.6	72.4	49.6	64.7	42.2
Philadelphia, PA	86.1	67.2	84.6	66.3	77.6	58.7	66.3	46.4	55.1	37.6	43.4	28.1
San Diego, CA	76.2	65.7	77.8	67.3	77.1	65.6	74.6	60.9	69.9	53.9	66.1	48.8
Phoenix, AZ	105.9	81.0	103.7	79.2	98.3	72.8	88.1	60.8	74.9	48.9	66.2	41.8
Dallas, TX	96.5	74.1	96.2	73.6	87.8	66.9	78.5	55.8	66.8	45.4	57.5	36.3
San Antonio, TX	95.0	75.0	95.3	74.5	89.3	69.2	81.7	58.8	71.9	48.8	63.5	40.8
Detroit, MI	83.3	61.3	81.3	59.6	73.9	52.5	61.5	40.9	48.1	32.2	35.2	21.4
San Jose, CA	82.4	56.6	82.0	56.6	80.6	55.8	74.5	51.6	64.4	45.5	57.5	40.7
Indianapolis, IN	85.5	65.2	83.6	62.8	77.6	55.6	65.8	43.5	51.9	34.1	38.5	23.2
San Francisco, CA	71.6	53.9	72.3	55.0	73.6	55.2	70.1	51.8	62.4	47.1	56.1	42.7
Baltimore, MD	87.2	66.8	85.4	65.7	78.5	58.4	67.3	45.9	56.4	37.1	45.2	28.2
Jacksonville, FL	91.4	71.9	90.7	71.8	87.2	69.0	80.2	59.3	73.6	50.2	66.8	43.4
Columbus, OH	83.7	62.7	82.1	60.8	76.2	54.8	64.5	42.9	51.4	34.3	39.2	24.6
Milwaukee, WI	79.9	62.0	77.8	60.8	70.6	52.8	58.7	41.8	44.7	30.7	31.2	17.5
Memphis, TN	92.3	72.9	90.8	71.1	83.9	64.5	74.3	51.9	62.3	42.7	52.5	34.8
El Paso, TX	96.1	68.4	93.5	66.6	87.1	61.6	78.4	49.6	66.4	38.4	57.5	30.7
Washington, DC	88.5	71.4	86.9	70.0	80.1	62.5	69.1	50.3	58.3	41.1	47.0	31.7
Boston, MA	81.8	65.1	79.8	64.0	72.8	56.8	62.7	46.9	52.2	38.3	40.4	26.7
Seattle, WA	75.2	55.2	75.2	55.7	69.3	51.9	59.7	45.8	50.5	40.1	45.1	35.8
Austin, TX	95.0	73.9	95.5	73.9	90.5	69.8	82.1	60.0	71.8	49.9	62.0	41.2
Nashville-Davidson, TN	89.5	68.9	88.4	67.7	82.5	61.1	72.5	48.3	60.4	39.6	50.2	30.9
Denver, CO	88.2	58.6	85.8	56.9	76.9	47.6	66.3	36.4	52.5	25.4	44.5	17.4
Cleveland, OH	82.4	61.4	80.5	60.3	73.6	54.2	62.1	43.5	50.0	35.0	37.4	24.5
New Orleans, LA	90.6	73.1	90.2	72.8	86.6	69.5	79.4	58.7	71.1	51.1	64.3	44.8
Oklahoma City, OK	93.4	70.6	92.5	69.6	83.8	62.2	73.6	50.4	60.4	38.6	49.9	28.6
Fort Worth, TX	96.5	74.1	96.2	73.6	87.8	66.9	78.5	55.8	66.8	45.4	57.5	36.3
Portland, OR	79.9	56.5	80.3	56.9	74.6	52.0	64.0	44.9	52.6	39.5	45.6	34.8
Kansas City, MO	88.7	68.2	86.4	65.7	78.1	56.9	67.5	45.7	52.6	33.6	38.8	21.9
Charlotte, NC	88.9	69.6	87.7	68.9	81.9	62.9	72.0	50.6	62.6	41.5	52.3	32.8
Tucson, AZ	99.4	73.6	96.8	72.1	93.3	67.5	84.3	56.6	72.7	45.6	64.3	39.8
Long Beach, CA	82.7	63.4	84.0	64.8	82.1	62.7	78.4	57.8	72.1	50.4	67.0	45.0
Albuquerque, NM	92.5	64.4	89.0	62.6	81.9	55.2	71.0	43.0	57.3	31.2	47.5	23.1
Atlanta, GA	88.0	69.5	87.1	69.0	81.8	63.5	72.7	51.9	63.4	42.8	54.0	35.0
Fresno, CA	98.6	65.1	96.7	63.8	90.1	58.8	79.7	50.7	64.7	42.5	53.7	37.1
Honolulu, HI	87.5	73.5	88.7	74.2	88.5	73.5	86.9	72.3	84.1	70.3	81.2	67.0
Tulsa, OK	93.7	72.8	92.5	70.6	83.6	63.0	73.8	50.7	60.3	39.5	48.8	28.9
Sacramento, CA	93.2	58.1	92.1	58.0	87.3	55.7	77.9	50.4	63.1	43.4	52.7	37.8
Miami, FL	89.0	76.2	89.0	76.7	87.8	75.9	84.5	72.1	80.4	66.7	76.7	61.5
St. Louis, MO	89.3	70.4	87.3	67.9	79.9	60.5	68.5	48.3	54.7	37.7	41.7	26.0
Pittsburgh, PA	82.6	61.6	80.8	60.2	74.3	53.5	62.5	42.3	50.4	34.1	38.6	24.4
Minneapolis, MN	84.0	63.1	80.7	60.3	70.7	50.3	58.8	38.8	41.0	25.2	25.5	10.2
Omaha, NE	87.9	65.9	85.2	62.9	76.5	53.6	65.6	41.2	49.3	28.7	34.6	15.6
Las Vegas, NV	105.9	76.2	103.2	74.2	94.7	66.2	82.1	54.3	67.4	42.6	57.5	33.9
Toledo, OH	83.4	60.6	81.3	58.4	74.4	51.5	62.4	40.0	48.5	31.5	35.2	20.5
Colorado Springs, CO	84.4	57.1	81.3	55.2	73.6	47.1	63.5	36.3	50.7	24.9	42.2	17.4
Buffalo, NY	80.2	61.9	77.9	60.1	70.8	53.0	59.4	42.7	47.1	33.9	35.3	22.9
Wichita, KS	92.8	69.9	90.7	67.9	81.4	59.2	70.6	46.6	55.3	33.9	43.0	23.0

Source: National Oceanic and Atmospheric Administration

Weather Report

The record-setting cities in different weather categories in the 48 contiguous states:

10 Hottest Cities (Mean temp °F)

1	Key West, FL	77.8
2	Miami, FL	75.9
3	West Palm Beach, FL	74.7
4	Fort Myers, FL	74.4
5	Yuma, AZ	74.2
6	Brownsville, TX	73.8
7	Phoenix, AZ	72.6
8	Vero Beach, FL	72.4
9	Orlando, FL	72.3
9	Tampa, FL	72.3

10 Coldest Cities (Mean temp °F)

1	International Falls, MN	36.8
2	Duluth, MN	38.5
3	Caribou, ME	38.8
4	Marquette, MI	39.1
5	Sault Ste. Marie, MI	39.7
6	Fargo, ND	41.0
7	Alamosa, CO	41.1
8	St. Cloud, MN	41.5
8	Williston, ND	41.5
10	Bismarck, ND	41.6

10 Driest Cities (Precip. in inches)

1	Yuma, AZ	3.17
2	Las Vegas, NV	4.13
3	Bishop, CA	5.37
4	Bakersfield, CA	5.72
5	Reno, NV	7.53
6	Alamosa, CO	7.57
7	Phoenix, AZ	7.66
8	Yakima, WA	7.97
9	Winslow, AZ	8.04
10	Winnemucca, NV	8.23

10 Wettest Cities (Precip. in inches)

1	Quillayute, WA	105.18
2	Astoria, OR	66.40
3	Tallahassee, FL	65.71
4	Mobile, AL	63.96
5	Pensacola, FL	62.25
6	New Orleans, LA	61.88
7	Baton Rouge, LA	60.89
8	West Palm Beach, FL	60.75
9	Meridian, MS	56.71
10	Tupelo, MS	55.87

10 Windiest Cities (Mean speed mph)

1	Blue Hill, MA	15.4
2	Dodge City, KS	13.9
3	Amarillo, TX	13.5
4	Rochester, MN	13.1
5	Cheyenne, WY	12.9
6	Casper, WY	12.8
7	Great Falls, MT	12.6
8	Goodland, KS	12.5
8	Boston, MA	12.5
10	Lubbock, TX	12.4

10 Snowiest Cities (Snowfall in inches)

1	Marquette, MI	130.6
2	Sault Ste, Marie, MI	117.1
3	Syracuse, NY	114.7
4	Caribou, ME	110.7
5	Lander, WY	102.2
6	Flagstaff, AZ	100.3
7	Muskegon, MI	97.9
8	Buffalo, NY	91.8
9	Rochester, NY	90.3
10	Erie, PA	86.5

10 Sunniest Cities (% of possible)

1	Yuma, AZ	90
2	Redding, CA	88
3	Phoenix, AZ	86
4	Tucson, AZ	85
5	Las Vegas, NV	85
6	El Paso, TX	84
7	Fresno, CA	79
7	Reno, NV	79
9	Flagstaff, AZ	78
9	Sacramento, CA	78

10 Cloudiest Cities (No. of cloudy days)

1	Quillayute, WA	239
1	Astoria, OR	239
3	Olympia, WA	228
4	Seattle, WA	226
5	Portland. OR	222
6	Kalispell, MT	214
7	Binghamton, NY	212
7	Elkins, WV	212
9	Beckley, WV	210
10	Eugene, OR	209

Source: National Oceanic and Atmospheric Administration

The 10 Most Costly U.S. Civil Disorders

Date	Location	Estimated insured losses
April 29-May 4, 1992	Los Angeles	$775,000,000
Aug. 11-17, 1965	Los Angeles	44,000,000
July 23, 1967	Detroit	41,500,000
May 17-19, 1980	Miami	65,250,000
April 4-9, 1968	Washington, D.C.	24,000,000
July 13-14, 1977	New York City	28,000,000
July 12, 1967	Newark	15,000,000
April 6-9, 1968	Baltimore	14,000,000
April 4-11, 1968	Chicago	13,000,000
April 4-11, 1968	New York City	4,200,000

Sources: Property Claim Services division of American Insurance Services Group, and Insurance Information Institute

People Patterns

Grandparents are spoiling their grandkids more than ever—to the delight of marketers of everything from toys to fast-food.

For years, makers of toys, clothing and other products for children focused their marketing exclusively on parents, who traditionally did the bulk of the buying. But that's changing as more companies tap into the increasingly lucrative target market of grandparents. While grandparents have long had a reputation for lavishing their grandchildren with gifts, today's elders often have more frequent contact with their grandchildren, live longer and, most significantly, have more disposable income than past generations.

There are roughly 60 million grandparents in the Unites States today, and their numbers are expected to swell to 72 million by 2005 and to 80 million by 2010, according to Roper Starch Worldwide, a research company that tracks social and marketing trends. The oldest members of the baby-boom generation began turning 50 in 1996, and the aging of this huge demographic group will drive the growth of the grandparent market.

Today, about eight of 10 American adults who are 60 or older are grandparents. More than half in this group have at least five grandchildren. Nearly half of adults from 45 to 59 are grandparents, most with fewer than five grandchildren.

More grandchildren also are living with their grandparents. According to Census Bureau data, about 3.9 million children in the United States live in households maintained by grandparents, compared with about 2.2 million in 1970. But such households generally have less disposable income and are less attractive to companies selling gifts and services aimed at grandparents.

Marketers have found that grandparents buy gifts for their grandchildren much more often than in the past when presents typically were reserved for holidays. Today, grandparents spend a median of $505 annually on their grandchildren, more than double the $250 in 1988. And more people are spending large sums: 23 percent of grandparents spend more than $800 a year, compared with 14 percent a decade ago, according to Roper Starch.

Genesis Direct Inc., a Secaucus, New Jersey, catalog retailer, has homed in on the grandparent market with "Gifts for Grandkids," a catalog featuring toys, clothing, educational materials and craft supplies. For example, the section with gifts for kids five to seven includes a camera, binoculars, luggage and other travel-related items. Text on the page suggests that grandparents plan trips with grandchildren and include the gifts to make the experience more fun. Another section includes toys grandparents should keep on hand when grandchildren visit their homes.

"During holiday periods, this is a catalog that has been getting a lot of attention from customers," says Helene Fink, a spokeswoman for Genesis Direct. "Grandparents still want to spoil their grandchildren." The company also publishes a newsletter called *Grand News*.

Another beneficiary of the growing grandparent population is the telecommunications industry. Nearly 60 percent of grandparents say in surveys that they have talked to a grandchild on the phone in the last month. Several special-rate packages offered by phone companies, including MCI Communications Corp.'s Friends and Family program, are at least in part aimed at grandparents.

Restaurants, too, are getting more business from grandparents and kids. The traditional trip to grandma's house for a big dinner has declined in frequency, with about 46 percent of grandparents saying they have had grandchildren visit their home for dinner in the last month, down from 52 percent in 1988, according to the Roper Starch survey. At the same time, a growing number of grandparents—40 percent currently compared with 29 percent in 1988—say they have taken grandchildren out to a restaurant during the last month.

And grandparents have boosted the greeting-card industry, with nearly half saying they have sent a card to a grandchild during the last month, according to the Roper Starch survey. "We have a growing number of prod-uct lines designed to appeal to grandparents," says Rachel Bolton, a spokeswoman for greeting-card giant Hallmark Cards Inc. In 1998, the company introduced "Isn't Life Grandchildren," a line of cards specifically for grandchildren and great-grandchildren. Hallmark also began selling "Shoestrings," a group of cards within its line of humorous Shoebox greetings, in response to consumer requests for more cards aimed at teens and preteens.

"With a grandkid like you, what more could a grandparent need?" says one Hallmark card, "other than some fancy-schmancy electronic doohickey to keep up with your busy schedule." Some cards include detachable postcards on which the child can list recent activities and accomplishments. They urge youngsters to keep in regular contact with grandparents who might live far away.

Ms. Bolton says company research shows that there are more grandparents in the market today than at any time before and that they "are quite different than they once were." Not only are they younger, with many in their 40s, she says, but they also don't tend to regard themselves as "old" and don't want others to view them that way.

Jonathan Welsh

Demographic Trends

U.S. Population: 1790–1998

Year	Number	% increase over preceding census	Year	Number	% increase over preceding census
1790	3,929,214	–	1900	75,994,575	20.7
1800	5,308,483	35.1	1910	91,972,266	21.0
1810	7,239,881	36.4	1920	105,710,620	14.9
1820	9,638,453	33.1	1930	122,775,046	16.1
1830	12,866,020	33.5	1940	131,669,275	7.2
1840	17,069,453	32.7	1950	150,697,361	14.5
1850	23,191,876	35.9	1960	179,323,175	18.5
1860	31,443,321	35.6	1970	203,302,031	13.5
1870	39,818,449	26.6	1980	226,546,000	11.4
1880	50,155,783	26.0	1990	249,398,000	10.1
1890	62,947,714	25.5	1998	268,922,000	7.8

U.S. Population Projections: 2000–2050

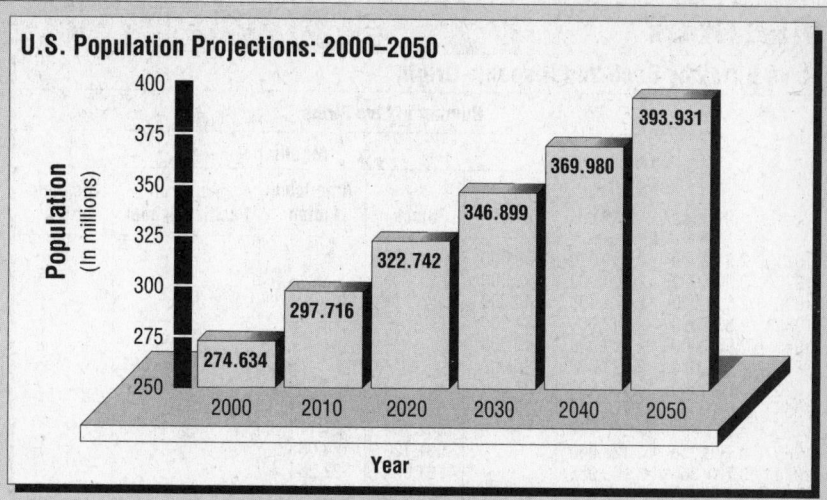

Percent Distribution of the U.S. Population By Age: 1995–2050

Year	Total	Under 5 years	5–13 years	14–17 years	18–24 years	25–34 years	35–44 years	45–64 years	65 years and over	85 years and over	100 years and over
1995	100.0	7.4	13.0	5.6	9.6	15.5	16.2	19.9	12.8	1.4	0.0
2000	100.0	6.9	13.1	5.7	9.6	13.6	16.3	22.2	12.6	1.6	0.0
2005	100.0	6.7	12.5	5.9	9.9	12.7	14.7	24.9	12.6	1.7	0.0
2010	100.0	6.7	12.0	5.7	10.1	12.9	12.9	26.5	13.2	1.9	0.0
2020	100.0	6.8	12.0	5.3	9.3	13.3	12.3	24.6	16.5	2.0	0.1
2030	100.0	6.6	12.0	5.4	9.2	12.3	12.8	21.7	20.0	2.4	0.1
2040	100.0	6.8	11.9	5.4	9.3	12.4	11.9	22.0	20.3	3.7	0.1
2050	100.0	6.9	12.1	5.4	9.2	12.5	12.0	21.8	20.0	4.6	0.2

Source: U.S. Census Bureau

Vital Stats

Birth Rate Per 1,000*

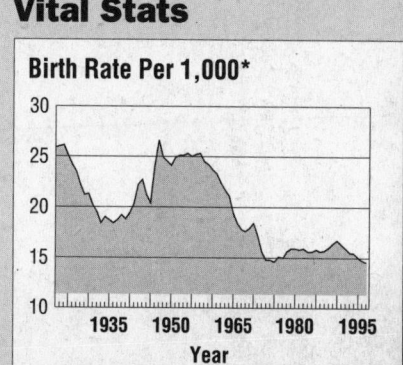

Fertility Rate Per 1,000*

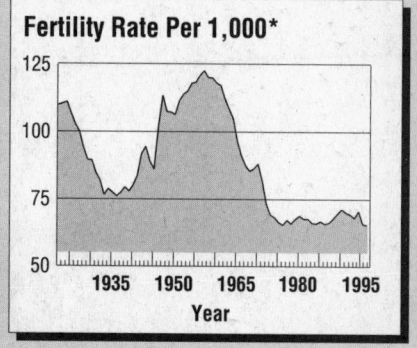

*Birth rates are live births per 1,000 population. Fertility rates are live births per 1,000 women aged 15-44 years.
Source: National Center for Health Statistics

Vital Stats

Live Births by Race and Hispanic Origin

Year	All races	White	Number of Live Births				
			All other				
			Total	Black	American Indian	Asian or Pacific Islander	Hispanic origin[†]
1923	2,910,000	2,531,000	380,000	–	–	–	–
1925	2,909,000	2,506,000	403,000	–	–	–	–
1930	2,618,000	2,274,000	344,000	–	–	–	–
1935	2,377,000	2,042,000	334,000	–	–	–	–
1940	2,559,000	2,199,000	360,000	–	–	–	–
1945	2,858,000	2,471,000	388,000	–	–	–	–
1950	3,632,000	3,108,000	524,000	–	–	–	–
1955	4,097,000	3,485,000	613,000	–	–	–	–
1960	4,257,850	3,600,744	–	602,264	21,114	–	–
1965	3,760,358	3,123,860	–	581,126	24,066	–	–
1970	3,731,386	3,109,956	–	561,992	22,264	–	–
1975	3,144,198	2,576,818	–	496,829	22,690	–	–
1980	3,612,258	2,936,351	–	568,080	29,389	74,355	307,163
1981	3,629,238	2,947,679	–	564,955	29,688	84,553	321,954
1982	3,680,537	2,984,817	–	568,506	32,436	93,193	337,390
1983	3,638,933	2,946,468	–	562,624	32,881	95,713	336,833
1984	3,669,141	2,967,100	–	568,138	33,256	98,926	346,986
1985	3,760,561	3,037,913	–	581,824	34,037	104,606	372,814
1986	3,756,547	3,019,175	–	592,910	34,169	107,797	389,048
1987	3,809,394	3,043,828	–	611,173	35,322	116,560	406,153
1988	3,909,510	3,102,083	–	638,562	37,088	129,035	449,604
1989	4,040,958	3,192,355	–	673,124	39,478	133,075	532,249
1990	4,158,212	3,290,273	–	684,336	39,051	141,635	595,073
1991	4,110,907	3,241,273	–	682,602	38,841	145,372	623,085
1992	4,065,014	3,201,678	–	673,633	39,453	150,250	643,271
1993	4,000,240	3,149,833	–	658,875	38,732	152,800	654,418
1994	3,952,767	3,121,004	–	636,391	37,740	157,632	665,026
1995	3,899,589	3,098,885	–	603,139	37,278	160,287	679,768
1996	3,891,494	3,093,057	–	594,781	37,880	165,776	701,339
1997*	3,882,000	–	–	–	–	–	–

[†]Persons of Hispanic origin may be of any race.
*Preliminary

Birth Rates by Race and Hispanic Origin

Year	All races	White	Birth Rate*				
			All other				
			Total	Black	American Indian	Asian or Pacific Islander	Hispanic origin
1923	26.0	25.2	33.2	–	–	–	–
1925	25.1	24.1	34.2	–	–	–	–
1930	21.3	20.6	27.5	–	–	–	–
1935	18.7	17.9	25.8	–	–	–	–
1940	19.4	18.6	26.7	–	–	–	–
1945	20.4	19.7	26.5	–	–	–	–
1950	24.1	23.0	33.3	–	–	–	–
1955	25.0	23.8	34.5	–	–	–	–
1960	23.7	22.7	–	31.9	–	–	–
1965	19.4	18.3	–	27.7	–	–	–
1970	18.4	17.4	–	25.3	–	–	–
1975	14.6	13.6	–	20.7	–	–	–
1980	15.9	15.1	–	21.3	20.7	19.9	23.5
1981	15.8	15.0	–	20.8	20.0	20.1	24.1
1982	15.9	15.1	–	20.7	21.1	20.3	23.9
1983	15.6	14.8	–	20.2	20.6	19.5	22.8
1984	15.6	14.8	–	20.1	20.1	18.8	22.7
1985	15.8	15.0	–	20.4	19.8	18.7	23.3
1986	15.6	14.8	–	20.5	19.2	18.0	23.3
1987	15.7	14.9	–	20.8	19.1	.18.4	23.3
1988	16.0	15.0	–	21.5	19.3	19.2	24.1
1989	16.4	15.4	–	22.3	19.7	18.7	26.2
1990	16.7	15.8	–	22.4	18.9	19.0	26.7
1991	16.3	15.4	–	21.9	18.3	18.2	26.7
1992	15.9	15.0	–	21.3	18.4	18.0	26.5
1993	15.5	14.7	–	20.5	17.8	17.7	26.0
1994	15.2	14.4	–	19.5	17.1	17.5	25.5
1995	14.8	14.2	–	18.2	16.6	17.3	25.2
1996	14.7	14.1	–	17.8	16.6	17.0	24.8
1997**	14.5	–	–	–	–	–	–

*Birth rates are live births per 1,000 population in specified groups.
**Preliminary.

Fertility Rates by Race and Hispanic Origin

Year	All races	White	Fertility rate* All other				
			Total	Black	American Indian	Asian or Pacific Islander	Hispanic origin
1923	110.5	108.0	130.5	–	–	–	–
1925	106.6	103.3	134.0	–	–	–	–
1930	89.2	87.1	105.9	–	–	–	–
1935	77.2	74.5	98.4	–	–	–	–
1940	79.9	77.1	102.4	–	–	–	–
1945	85.9	83.4	106.0	–	–	–	–
1950	106.2	102.3	137.3	–	–	–	–
1955	118.3	113.7	154.3	–	–	–	–
1960	118.0	113.2	–	153.5	–	–	–
1965	96.3	91.3	–	133.2	–	–	–
1970	87.9	84.1	–	115.4	–	–	–
1975	66.0	62.5	–	87.9	–	–	–
1980	68.4	65.6	–	84.7	82.7	73.2	95.4
1981	67.3	64.8	–	82.0	79.6	73.7	97.5
1982	67.3	64.8	–	80.9	83.6	74.8	96.1
1983	65.7	63.4	–	78.7	81.8	71.7	91.8
1984	65.5	63.2	–	78.2	79.8	69.2	91.5
1985	66.3	64.1	–	78.8	78.6	68.4	94.0
1986	65.4	63.1	–	78.9	75.9	66.0	93.9
1987	65.8	63.3	–	80.1	75.6	67.1	93.0
1988	67.3	64.5	–	82.6	76.8	70.2	96.4
1989	69.2	66.4	–	86.2	79.0	68.2	104.9
1990	70.9	68.3	–	86.8	76.2	69.6	107.7
1991	69.6	67.0	–	85.2	75.1	67.6	108.1
1992	68.9	66.5	–	83.2	75.4	67.2	108.6
1993	67.6	65.4	–	80.5	73.4	66.7	106.9
1994	66.7	64.9	–	76.9	70.9	66.8	105.6
1995	65.6	64.4	–	72.3	69.1	66.4	105.0
1996	65.4	64.3	–	70.7	68.7	65.9	104.9
1997**	65.0	–	–	–	–	–	–

*Fertility rates are live births per 1,000 women aged 15-44 years in specified group.
**Preliminary.
Source: National Center for Health Statistics

Marriage Rates Per 1,000 Population Over 15 Years of Age by Sex

Marriages and Marriage Rates

| Year | Number | Rate per 1,000 population | | |
		Total population	Men 15 years of age and over	Women 15 years of age and over
1920	1,274,476	12.0	34.2	36.0
1925	1,188,334	10.3	29.2	30.3
1930	1,126,856	9.2	25.6	26.2
1935	1,327,000	10.4	28.4	28.8
1940	1,595,879	12.1	32.3	32.3
1945	1,612,992	12.2	35.8	30.5
1950	1,667,231	11.1	30.7	29.8
1955	1,531,000	9.3	27.2	25.8
1960	1,523,000	8.5	25.4	24.0
1965	1,800,000	9.3	27.9	26.0
1970	2,158,802	10.6	31.1	28.4
1975	2,152,662	10.0	27.9	25.6
1980	2,390,252	10.6	28.5	26.1
1985	2,412,625	10.1	27.0	24.9
1986	2,407,099	10.0	26.6	24.5
1987	2,403,378	9.9	26.3	24.3
1988	2,395,926	9.8	26.0	24.0
1989	2,403,268	9.7	25.8	23.9
1990	2,443,489	9.8	26.0	24.1
1991	2,371,000	9.4	–	–
1992	2,362,000	9.3	–	–
1993	2,334,000	9.0	–	–
1994	2,362,000	9.1	–	–
1995	2,336,000	8.9	–	–
1996	2,344,000	8.8	–	–
1997	2,384,000	8.9	–	–

Source: National Center for Health Statistics

Divorce and Annulment Rate Per 1,000 Population

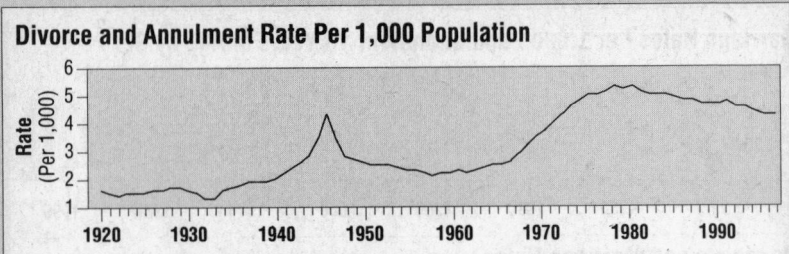

Divorces and Annulments and Rates Per 1,000 Population

Year	Divorces and annulments	Rate per 1,000 population	Year	Divorces and annulments	Rate per 1,000 population
1920	170,505	1.6	1983	1,158,000	5.0
1925	175,449	1.5	1984	1,169,000	5.0
1930	195,961	1.6	1985	1,190,000	5.0
1935	218,000	1.7	1986	1,178,000	4.9
1940	264,000	2.0	1987	1,166,000	4.8
1945	485,000	3.5	1988	1,167,000	4.8
1950	385,000	2.6	1989	1,157,000	4.7
1955	377,000	2.3	1990	1,175,000	4.7
1960	393,000	2.2	1991	1,187,000	4.7
1965	479,000	2.5	1992	1,215,000	4.8
1970	708,000	3.5	1993	1,187,000	4.6
1975	1,036,000	4.8	1994	1,191,000	4.6
1980	1,189,000	5.2	1995	1,169,000	4.4
1981	1,213,000	5.3	1996	1,150,000	4.3
1982	1,170,000	5.1	1997	1,163,000	4.3

Source: National Center for Health Statistics

Death Rates Per 1,000 Population

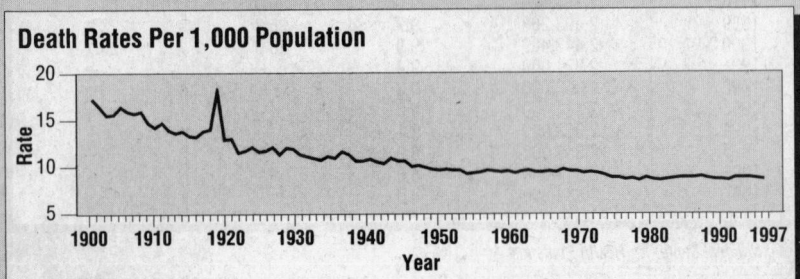

Death Rates*
(Per 1,000 population)

Year	Rate	Total deaths	Year	Rate	Total deaths
1940	10.8	1,417,269	1991	8.6	2,169,518
1950	9.6	1,452,454	1992	8.5	2,175,613
1960	9.5	1,711,982	1993	8.8	2,268,553
1970	9.5	1,921,031	1994	8.8	2,278,994
1980	8.8	1,989,841	1995	8.8	2,312,132
1985	8.8	2,086,440	1996	8.7	2,314,690
1990	8.6	2,148,463	1997*	8.6	2,294,000

*Preliminary.
Source: National Center for Health Statistics

Infant Mortality Rate, 1915–1997*
(Per 1,000 live births)

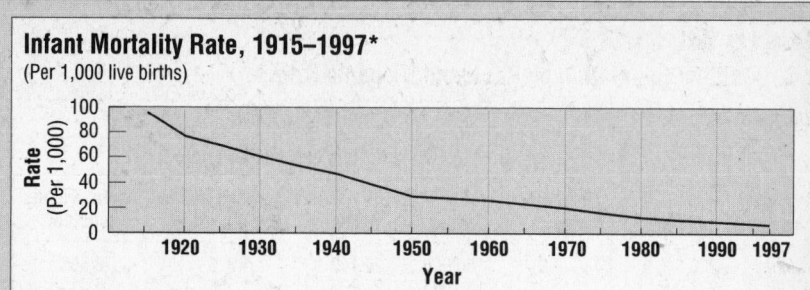

Infant Mortality Rates*
(Per 1,000 live births)

	Infant Mortality Rate											
	All races			White			All other					
							Total			Black		
Year	Both sexes	Male	Female	Both sexes	Male	Female	Both sexes	Male	Female	Both sexes	Male	Female
1915-19	95.7	–	–	92.8	–	–	149.7	–	–	150.4	–	–
1920-24	76.7	–	–	73.3	–	–	115.3	–	–	117.4	–	–
1925-29	69.0	–	–	65.0	–	–	105.4	–	–	105.3	–	–
1930-34	60.4	–	–	55.2	–	–	98.6	–	–	90.5	–	–
1935-39	53.2	–	–	49.2	–	–	81.3	–	–	80.1	–	–
1940	47.0	52.5	41.3	43.2	48.3	37.8	73.8	82.2	65.2	72.9	81.1	64.6
1950	29.2	32.8	25.5	26.8	30.2	23.1	44.5	48.9	39.9	43.9	48.3	39.4
1960	26.0	29.3	22.6	22.9	26.0	19.6	43.2	47.9	38.5	44.3	49.1	39.4
1970	20.0	22.4	17.5	17.8	20.0	15.4	30.9	34.2	27.5	32.6	36.2	29.0
1975	16.1	17.9	14.2	14.2	15.9	12.3	24.2	26.2	22.2	26.2	28.3	24.0
1980	12.6	13.9	11.2	10.9	12.1	9.5	20.2	21.9	18.4	22.2	24.2	20.2
1985	10.6	11.9	9.3	9.2	10.4	7.9	16.8	18.3	15.3	19.0	20.8	17.2
1986	10.4	11.5	9.1	8.8	9.9	7.7	16.7	18.5	14.9	18.9	20.9	16.8
1987	10.1	11.2	8.9	8.5	9.5	7.5	16.5	18.1	14.8	18.8	20.6	16.8
1988	10.0	11.0	8.9	8.4	9.4	7.3	16.1	17.3	14.8	18.5	20.0	17.0
1989	9.8	10.8	8.8	8.1	9.0	7.1	16.3	17.6	15.0	18.6	20.0	17.2
1990	9.2	10.3	8.1	7.6	8.5	6.6	15.5	17.0	14.0	18.0	19.6	16.2
1991	8.9	10.0	7.8	7.3	8.3	6.3	15.1	16.5	13.6	17.6	19.4	15.7
1992	8.5	9.4	7.6	6.9	7.7	6.1	14.4	15.7	13.1	16.8	18.4	15.3
1993	8.4	9.3	7.4	6.8	7.6	6.0	14.1	15.6	12.5	16.5	18.3	14.7
1994	8.0	8.8	7.2	6.6	7.2	5.9	13.5	14.8	12.1	15.8	17.5	14.1
1995	7.6	8.3	6.8	6.3	7.0	5.6	12.6	13.5	11.6	15.1	16.3	13.9
1996	7.3	–	–	6.1	–	–	–	–	–	14.7	–	–
1997**	7.0	–	–	–	–	–	–	–	–	–	–	–

*Rates are infant (under 1 year) deaths per 1,000 live births in specified group. Beginning in 1980, race for live births is tabulated according to race of mother.
**Preliminary.
Source: National Center for Health Statistics

White Minority?

U.S. Resident Population by Race and Hispanic Origin

(In thousands)

Year	Total number	Hispanic origin*	Not of Hispanic origin			
			White	Black	American Indian, Eskimo, Aleut	Asian, Pacific Islander
1980	226,546	14,609	180,906	26,142	1,326	3,563
1985	237,924	18,368	184,945	27,738	1,558	5,315
1990	249,398	22,558	188,583	29,374	1,802	7,080
1995	262,890	27,277	193,281	31,565	1,931	8,836
1996	265,284	28,269	193,978	31,912	1,954	9,171
2000	274,634	31,366	197,061	33,568	2,054	10,584
2010	297,716	41,139	202,390	37,466	2,320	14,402
2020	322,742	52,652	207,393	41,538	2,601	18,557
2030	346,899	65,570	209,998	45,448	2,891	22,993
2040	369,980	80,164	209,621	49,379	3,203	27,614
2050	393,931	96,508	207,901	53,555	3,534	32,432

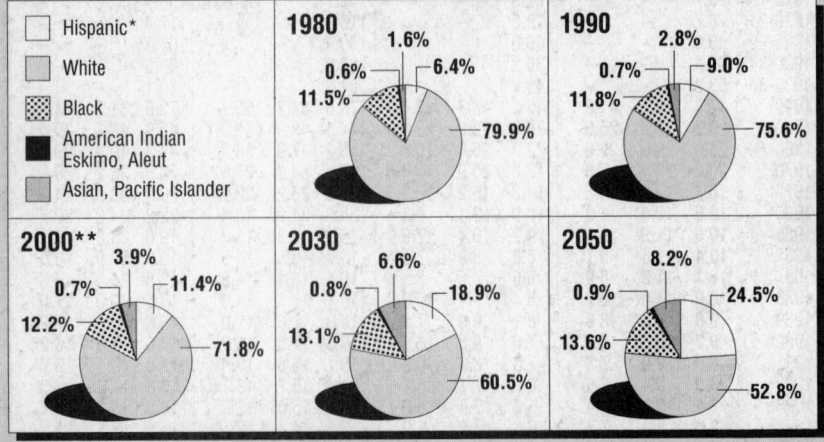

Legend:
- Hispanic*
- White
- Black
- American Indian Eskimo, Aleut
- Asian, Pacific Islander

1980
- 1.6%
- 0.6%
- 6.4%
- 11.5%
- 79.9%

1990
- 2.8%
- 0.7%
- 9.0%
- 11.8%
- 75.6%

2000**
- 3.9%
- 0.7%
- 11.4%
- 12.2%
- 71.8%

2030
- 6.6%
- 0.8%
- 18.9%
- 13.1%
- 60.5%

2050
- 8.2%
- 0.9%
- 24.5%
- 13.6%
- 52.8%

*Persons of Hispanic origin can be of any race.
**Data for years 1995 and beyond are estimates.
Source: U.S. Census Bureau

Minority Mothers

A growing percentage of births in the 21st century will be to minority women.

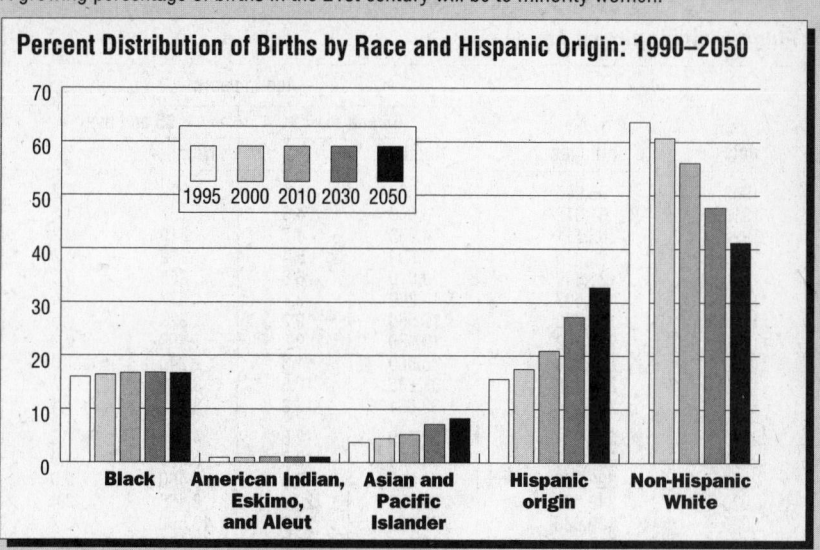

Percent Distribution of Births by Race and Hispanic Origin: 1990–2050

Legend: 1995 2000 2010 2030 2050

Source: U.S. Census Bureau

An Aging America

The elderly will represent a growing share of the population well into the 21st century.

Elderly Population by Age (In thousands)

Census date	Total, all ages	Age in years			
		65 and over		85 and over	
		Number	%	Number	%
1900	75,995	3,080	4.1	122	0.2
1910	91,972	3,949	4.3	167	0.2
1920	105,711	4,933	4.7	210	0.2
1930	122,775	6,634	5.4	272	0.2
1940	131,669	9,019	6.8	365	0.3
1950	150,697	12,269	8.1	577	0.4
1960	179,323	16,560	9.2	929	0.5
1970	203,302	19,980	9.8	1,409	0.7
1980	226,546	25,550	11.3	2,240	1.0
1990	249,398	31,235	12.5	3,059	1.2
1996*	265,284	33,861	12.8	3,762	1.4
2000	274,634	34,709	12.6	4,259	1.6
2010	297,716	39,408	13.2	5,671	1.9
2020	322,742	53,220	16.5	6,460	2.0
2030	346,899	69,379	20.0	8,455	2.4
2040	369,980	75,233	20.3	13,552	3.7
2050	393,931	78,859	20.0	18,223	4.6

Elderly Population by Age

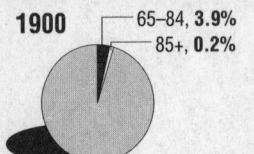

1900 — 65–84, **3.9%** / 85+, **0.2%**

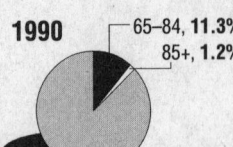

1990 — 65–84, **11.3%** / 85+, **1.2%**

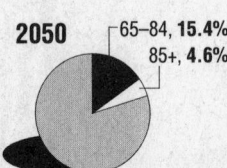

2050 — 65–84, **15.4%** / 85+, **4.6%**

Projected Population for Top 20 Countries With Largest Elderly Population
(In thousands)

Country/area	Rank		Population aged 65 years and over		Country/area	Rank		Population aged 65 years and over	
	1997	2020	1997	2020		1997	2020	1997	2020
China	1	1	77,891	169.925	Brazil	11	8	7,895	17,702
India	2	2	40,063	88,140	Ukraine	12	18	7,210	7,773
United States	**3**	**3**	**34,097**	**53,220**	Spain	13	16	6,298	8,243
Japan	4	4	19,385	32,226	Pakistan	14	13	5,338	9,439
Russia	5	5	18,019	21,582	Poland	15	22	4,455	6,573
Germany	6	7	12,908	18,532	Mexico	16	12	4,352	10,625
Italy	7	10	9,764	12,846	Bangladesh	17	14	4,051	8,731
United Kingdom	8	11	9,226	11,667	Vietnam	18	21	3,920	6,643
France	9	9	9,144	13,121	Canada	19	23	3,655	6,537
Indonesia	10	6	8,041	19,476	Argentina	20	25	3,589	5,591

*Estimate for 1996 and beyond.
Source: U.S. Census Bureau

America's Generations

Age Range of Selected Birth Cohorts, 1998–2010

Year	GI generation pre-1930	Depression generation 1930–39	War babies 1940–45	Baby boom 1946–64	Baby bust 1965–76	Baby boomlet 1977–94	Echo bust 1995–?
1998	69+	59-68	53-58	34-52	22-33	4-21	0-3
2000	71+	61-70	55-60	36-54	24-35	6-23	0-5
2005	76+	66-75	60-65	41-59	29-40	11-28	0-10
2010	81+	71-80	65-70	46-64	34-45	16-33	0-15

Source: American Demographics

Baby Boomers and Their Babies

The baby-boom generation, born between 1946 and 1964, produced their own smaller boom between 1977 and 1994.

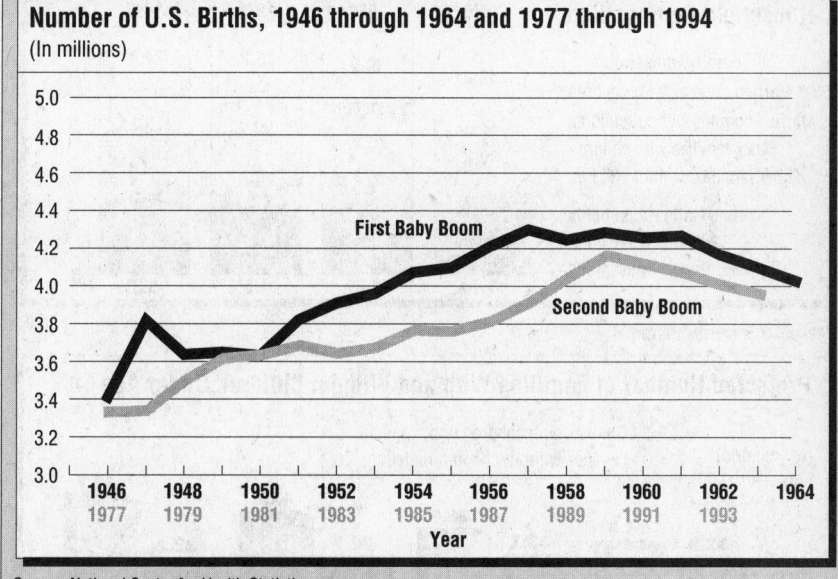

Number of U.S. Births, 1946 through 1964 and 1977 through 1994
(In millions)

First Baby Boom

Second Baby Boom

Source: National Center for Health Statistics

Small and Solitary Households

Households by Size
(Percent of total households)

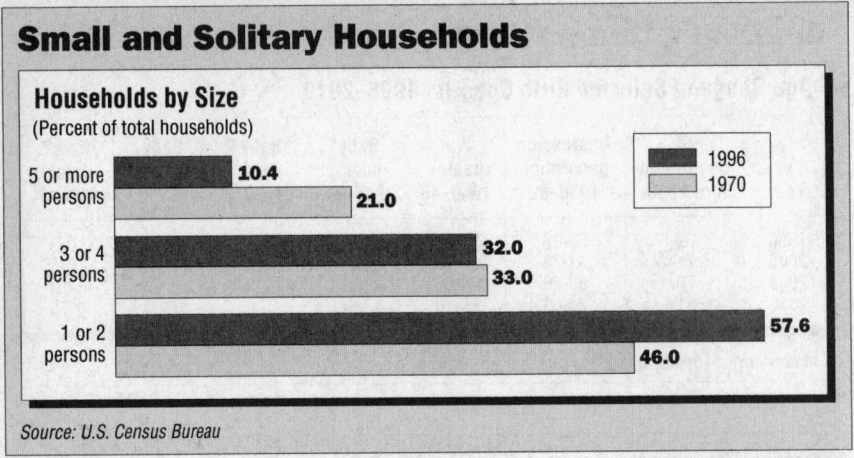

	1996	1970
5 or more persons	10.4	21.0
3 or 4 persons	32.0	33.0
1 or 2 persons	57.6	46.0

Source: U.S. Census Bureau

Fewer Traditional Families

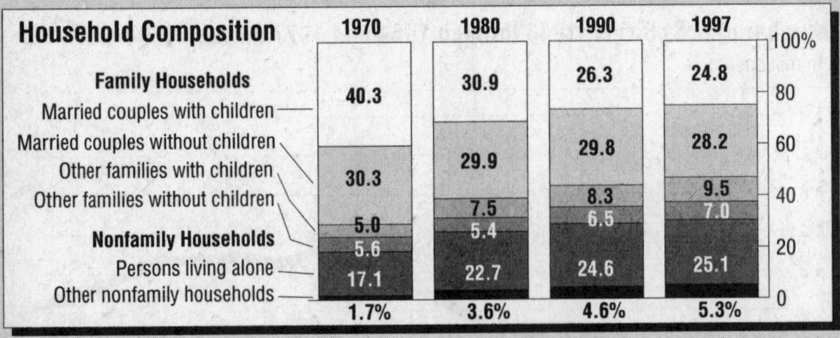

Household Composition

	1970	1980	1990	1997
Family Households				
Married couples with children	40.3	30.9	26.3	24.8
Married couples without children	30.3	29.9	29.8	28.2
Other families with children			8.3	9.5
Other families without children	5.0	7.5	6.5	7.0
Nonfamily Households	5.6	5.4		
Persons living alone	17.1	22.7	24.6	25.1
Other nonfamily households	1.7%	3.6%	4.6%	5.3%

Source: U.S. Census Bureau

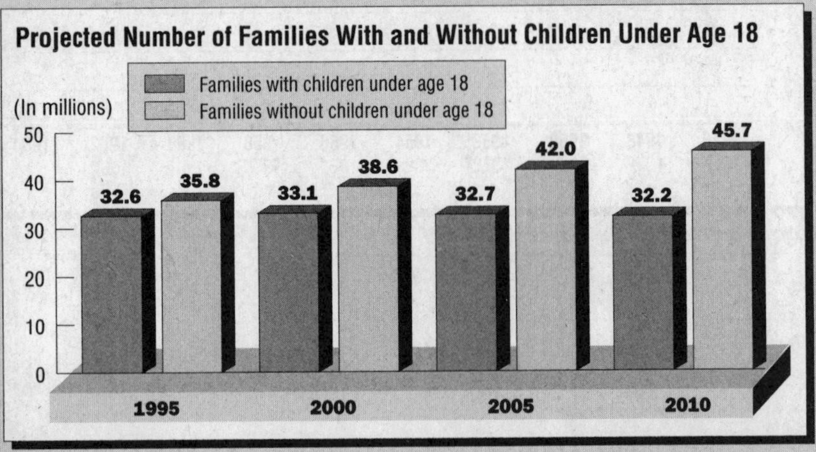

Projected Number of Families With and Without Children Under Age 18

(In millions)

- Families with children under age 18
- Families without children under age 18

	1995	2000	2005	2010
Families with children under age 18	32.6	33.1	32.7	32.2
Families without children under age 18	35.8	38.6	42.0	45.7

Source: U.S. Census Bureau

The State of Matrimony

Marital Status of Persons 18 Years and Over, by Race and Hispanic Origin

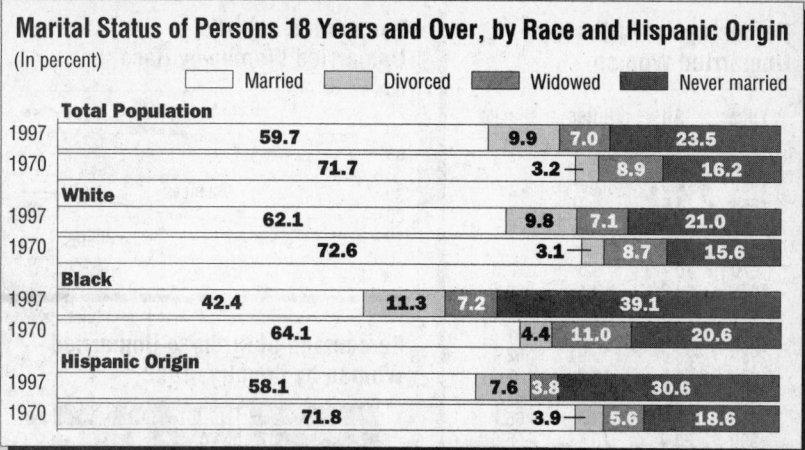

(In percent)

Legend: Married | Divorced | Widowed | Never married

Total Population
- 1997: 59.7 | 9.9 | 7.0 | 23.5
- 1970: 71.7 | 3.2 | 8.9 | 16.2

White
- 1997: 62.1 | 9.8 | 7.1 | 21.0
- 1970: 72.6 | 3.1 | 8.7 | 15.6

Black
- 1997: 42.4 | 11.3 | 7.2 | 39.1
- 1970: 64.1 | 4.4 | 11.0 | 20.6

Hispanic Origin
- 1997: 58.1 | 7.6 | 3.8 | 30.6
- 1970: 71.8 | 3.9 | 5.6 | 18.6

Median Age at First Marriage, by Sex

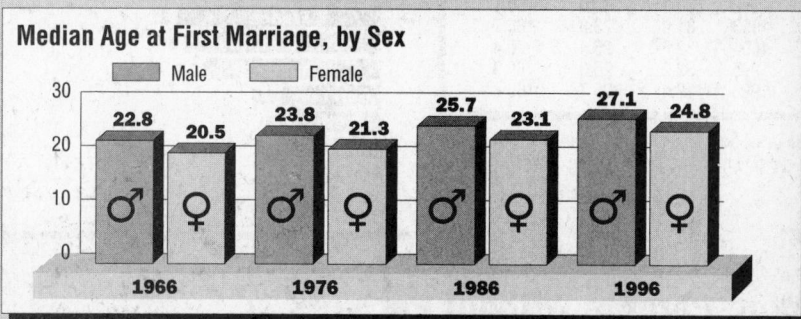

Legend: Male | Female

Year	Male	Female
1966	22.8	20.5
1976	23.8	21.3
1986	25.7	23.1
1996	27.1	24.8

Interracial Married Couples

(Numbers in thousands. Includes all interracial married couples with at least one spouse of White or Black race.)

Year	Total married couples	Interracial married couples				
		Total	Black husband White wife	White husband Black wife	White/Other race*	Black/Other race*
1996	54,664	1,260	220	117	884	39
1995	54,937	1,392	206	122	988	76
1994	54,251	1,283	196	100	909	78
1993	54,199	1,195	182	60	920	33
1992	53,512	1,161	163	83	883	32
1991	53,227	994	156	75	720	43
1990	53,256	964	150	61	720	33
1985	51,114	792	117	47	599	29
1980	49,714	651	122	45	450	34

*Any race other than White or Black, such as American Indian, Japanese, Chinese, etc.
Source: U.S. Census Bureau

Single Mothers

Percentage of Births to Unmarried Women

Year	All	Whites	Blacks
1940	3.8	–	–
1950	4.0	–	–
1955	4.5	–	–
1960	5.3	–	–
1965	7.7	–	–
1970	10.7	5.5	37.5
1975	14.3	7.1	49.5
1980	18.4	11.2	56.1
1985	22.0	14.7	61.2
1986	23.4	15.9	62.4
1987	24.5	16.9	63.4
1988	25.7	18.0	64.7
1989	27.1	19.2	65.7
1990	28.0	20.4	66.5
1991	29.5	21.8	67.9
1992	30.1	22.6	68.1
1993	31.0	23.6	68.7
1994	32.6	25.4	70.4
1995	32.2	25.3	69.9
1996	32.4	25.7	69.8

Sources: National Center for Health Statistics and Department of Health and Human Services

Percentage of Births to Unmarried Women by Race

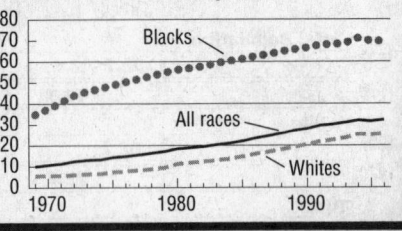

Percentage of Births to Unmarried Women by Country, 1992

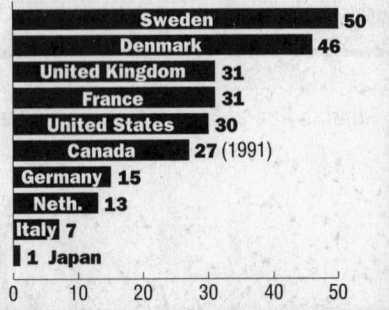

More Parents Without Partners

Children by Presence of Parents
(In percent)

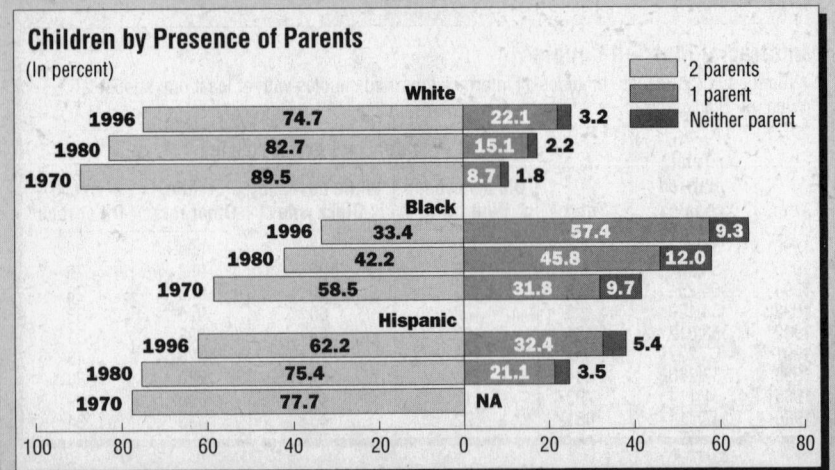

Source: U.S. Census Bureau

Homeless People in Shelters and on the Streets

Count of Persons in Selected Locations Where Homeless Persons Are Found:1990 Census of Population*

Shelter and Street Enumeration

State	Emergency shelters		Shelters for runaway, neglected and homeless youth		Visible in street locations		Shelters for abused women	
	Number	Percent	Number	Percent	Number	Percent	Number	Percent
United States	168,309	100.0	10,329	100.0	49,734	100.0	11,768	100.0
Alabama	1,367	0.8	163	1.6	364	0.7	127	1.1
Alaska	402	0.2	45	0.4	79	0.2	157	1.3
Arizona	2,600	1.5	135	1.3	1,697	3.6	279	2.4
Arkansas	398	0.2	91	0.9	62	0.1	105	0.9
California	29,930	17.7	976	9.4	18,081	36.4	1,257	10.7
Colorado	2,444	1.5	110	1.1	393	0.8	167	1.4
Connecticut	3,965	2.4	229	2.2	221	0.4	155	1.3
Delaware	302	0.2	11	0.1	19	0.0	36	0.3
District of Columbia	4,419	2.6	263	2.5	131	0.3	49	0.4
Florida	6,275	3.7	835	8.1	3,189	6.4	601	5.1
Georgia	3,697	2.2	233	2.3	450	0.9	192	1.6
Hawaii	773	0.5	81	0.8	1,071	2.2	73	0.6
Idaho	390	0.2	71	0.7	19	0.0	78	0.7
Illinois	7,002	4.2	479	4.6	1,755	3.5	536	4.6
Indiana	1,902	1.1	349	3.4	268	0.5	279	2.4
Iowa	780	0.5	209	2.0	148	0.3	164	1.4
Kansas	797	0.5	143	1.4	158	0.3	60	0.5
Kentucky	1,127	0.7	157	1.5	118	0.2	190	1.6
Louisiana	1,321	0.8	238	2.3	184	0.4	244	2.1
Maine	389	0.2	30	0.3	7	0.0	43	0.4
Maryland	2,365	1.4	142	1.4	523	1.1	199	1.7
Massachusetts	5,948	3.5	259	2.5	674	1.4	269	2.3
Michigan	3,442	2.0	342	3.3	262	0.5	506	4.3
Minnesota	2,152	1.3	101	1.0	138	0.3	230	2.0
Mississippi	223	0.1	160	1.5	83	0.2	125	1.1
Missouri	2,154	1.3	122	1.2	215	0.4	117	1.0
Montana	419	0.2	26	0.3	17	0.0	49	0.4
Nebraska	719	0.4	45	0.4	20	0.0	41	0.3
Nevada	978	0.6	35	0.3	436	0.9	49	0.4
New Hampshire	334	0.2	43	0.4	8	0.0	27	0.2
New Jersey	7,299	4.3	171	1.7	1,639	3.3	255	2.2
New Mexico	642	0.4	25	0.2	164	0.3	108	0.9
New York	31,436	18.7	1,036	10.0	10,732	21.6	756	6.4
North Carolina	2,453	1.5	184	1.8	259	0.5	315	2.7
North Dakota	279	0.2	0	0.0	30	0.1	36	0.3
Ohio	3,814	2.3	463	4.5	188	0.4	496	4.2
Oklahoma	2,025	1.2	197	1.9	340	0.7	113	1.0
Oregon	3,170	1.9	84	0.8	564	1.1	251	2.1
Pennsylvania	7,815	4.6	422	4.1	1,312	2.6	603	5.1
Rhode Island	433	0.3	36	0.3	44	0.1	33	0.3
South Carolina	814	0.5	159	1.5	102	0.2	87	0.7
South Dakota	329	0.2	67	0.6	71	0.1	41	0.3
Tennessee	1,644	1.0	220	2.1	357	0.7	230	2.0
Texas	7,082	4.2	734	7.1	1,442	2.9	1,049	8.9
Utah	894	0.5	31	0.3	276	0.6	49	0.4
Vermont	232	0.1	0	0.0	16	0.0	29	0.2
Virginia	2,544	1.5	113	1.1	319	0.6	185	1.6
Washington	4,493	2.7	72	0.7	772	1.6	297	2.5
West Virginia	404	0.2	47	0.5	33	0.1	128	1.1
Wisconsin	1,464	0.9	91	0.9	71	0.1	258	2.2
Wyoming	129	0.1	54	0.5	13	0.0	45	0.4

*Includes persons counted the evening of March 20th in sites listed as shelters for the homeless; women and children counted the evening of March 20th in shelters and safe houses for abused women; persons counted during the early morning hours of March 21st at pre-identified street sites, abandoned buildings and open public locations where homeless persons were likely to congregate.

Source: U.S. Census Bureau

How Americans Eat

Eating Out

Annual Meals (Including Snacks) Purchased at Commercial Restaurants Per Person

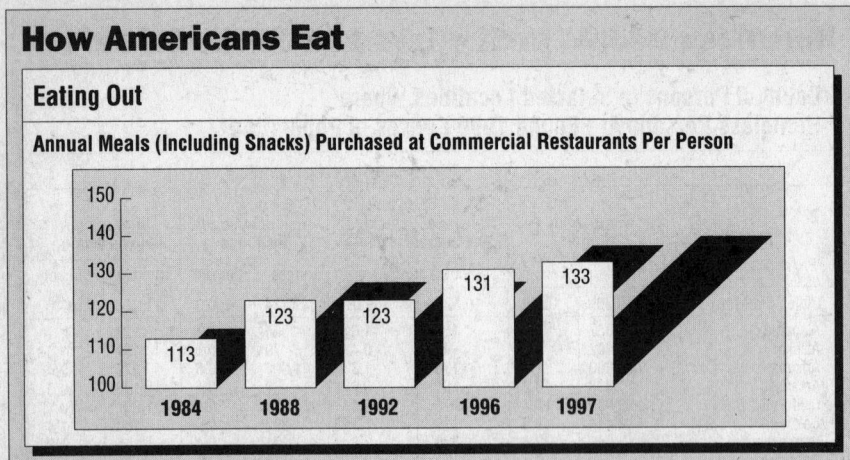

Source: NPD Group's CREST service

Take-Out Takes Off

Number of Take-Out and On-premise Meals Purchased at Commercial Restaurants Per Person Annually

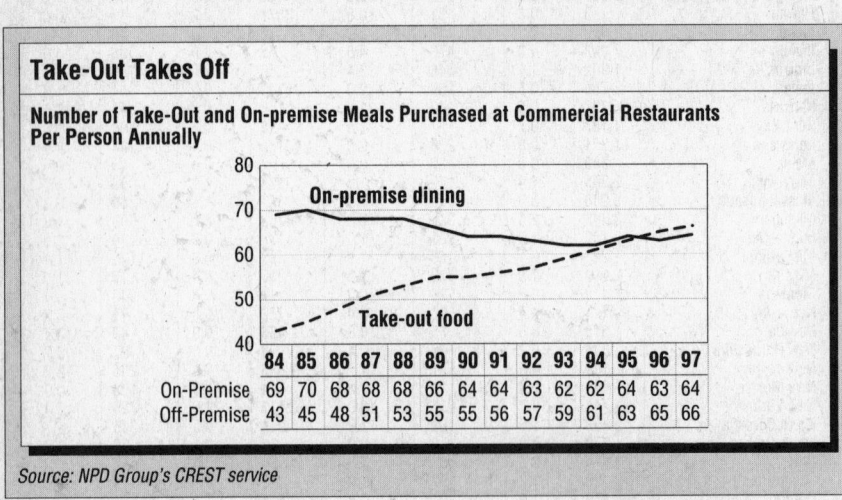

	84	85	86	87	88	89	90	91	92	93	94	95	96	97
On-Premise	69	70	68	68	68	66	64	64	63	62	62	64	63	64
Off-Premise	43	45	48	51	53	55	55	56	57	59	61	63	65	66

Source: NPD Group's CREST service

Changing Tastes

Changes in U.S. Per Capita Consumption, 1970–96

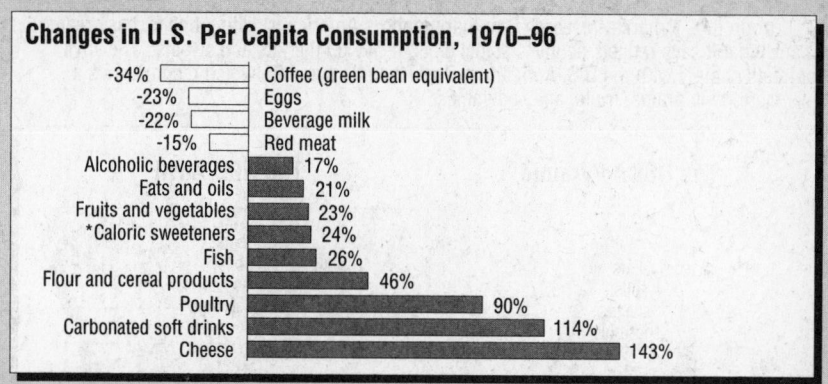

- -34% Coffee (green bean equivalent)
- -23% Eggs
- -22% Beverage milk
- -15% Red meat
- Alcoholic beverages 17%
- Fats and oils 21%
- Fruits and vegetables 23%
- *Caloric sweeteners 24%
- Fish 26%
- Flour and cereal products 46%
- Poultry 90%
- Carbonated soft drinks 114%
- Cheese 143%

*Includes caloric sweeteners used in soft drinks.

Per Capita Beverage Consumption, Gallons in 1996

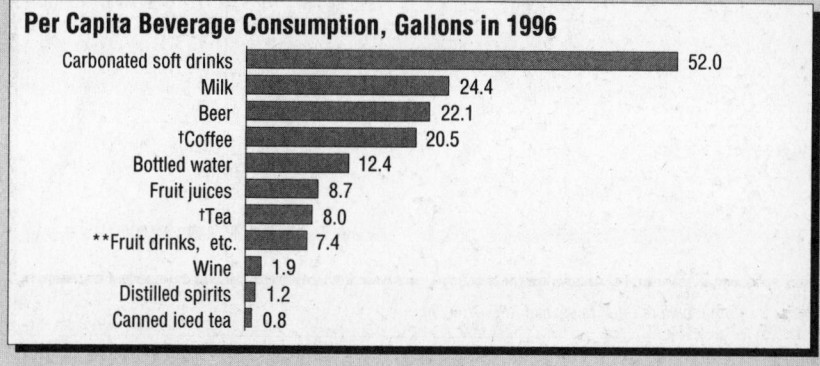

- Carbonated soft drinks 52.0
- Milk 24.4
- Beer 22.1
- †Coffee 20.5
- Bottled water 12.4
- Fruit juices 8.7
- †Tea 8.0
- **Fruit drinks, etc. 7.4
- Wine 1.9
- Distilled spirits 1.2
- Canned iced tea 0.8

**Includes fruit cocktails and ades.
†1995 data
Source: U.S. Agriculture Department

Reality Check

NPD Group Inc., a market-research firm that monitors Americans' eating habits, has created an anvil that it says reflects people's actual diets, heavy on the fats and sweets. The anvil contrasts sharply with the U.S. Agriculture Department's pyramid, which recommends a daily diet rich in grains, fruits, and vegetables.

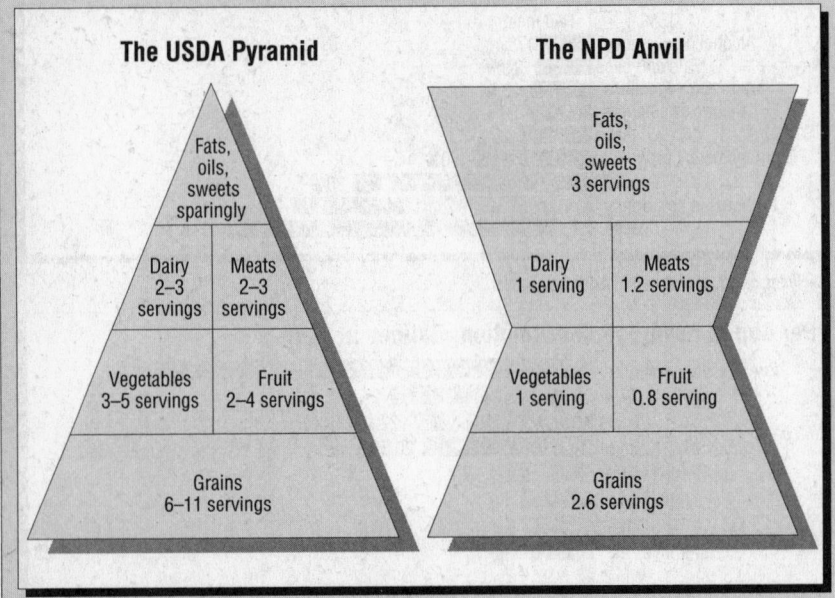

The USDA Pyramid

Fats,
oils,
sweets
sparingly

Dairy
2–3
servings

Meats
2–3
servings

Vegetables
3–5 servings

Fruit
2–4 servings

Grains
6–11 servings

The NPD Anvil

Fats,
oils,
sweets
3 servings

Dairy
1 serving

Meats
1.2 servings

Vegetables
1 serving

Fruit
0.8 serving

Grains
2.6 servings

Sources: U.S. Agriculture Department and NPD Group Inc.

Belief in God

Percentage of Americans who believe in God or a universal spirit according to a December 1994 Gallup Poll

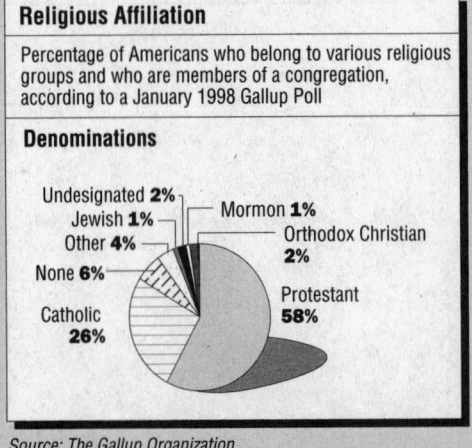

No 3%
No opinion 1%
Yes 96%

Membership in a Congregation

No 33%
Yes 67%

Religious Affiliation

Percentage of Americans who belong to various religious groups and who are members of a congregation, according to a January 1998 Gallup Poll

Denominations

Undesignated 2%
Jewish 1%
Other 4%
None 6%
Catholic 26%
Mormon 1%
Orthodox Christian 2%
Protestant 58%

Source: The Gallup Organization

U.S. Christian Church Membership

Ranking of the largest denominations that reported membership data.

Denomination	Membership	Percent of total reported
Roman Catholic Church	61,207,914	38.38%
Southern Baptist Convention	15,691,964	9.84
United Methodist Church	8,495,378	5.33
National Baptist Convention, U.S.A., Inc.	8,200,000	5.14
Church of God in Christ	5,499,875	3.45
Evangelical Lutheran Church in America	5,180,910	3.25
Church of Jesus Christ of Latter-day Saints	4,800,000	3.01
Presbyterian Church (U.S.A.)	3,637,375	2.28
African Methodist Episcopal Church	3,500,000	2.19
National Baptist Convention of America, Inc.	3,500,000	2.19
Lutheran Church - Missouri Synod	2,601,144	1.63
Episcopal Church	2,536,550	1.59
National Missionary Baptist Convention of America	2,500,000	1.57
Progressive National Baptist Convention, Inc.	2,500,000	1.57
Assemblies of God	2,467,588	1.55
Churches of Christ	2,250,000	1.41
Orthodox Church in America	2,000,000	1.25
Greek Orthodox Archdiocese of North and South America	1,950,000	1.22
American Baptist Churches in the U.S.A.	1,503,267	0.94
Baptist Bible Fellowship International	1,500,000	0.94
United Church of Christ	1,452,565	0.91
African Methodist Episcopal Zion Church	1,252,369	0.79
Christian Churches and Churches of Christ	1,071,616	0.67
Pentecostal Assemblies of the World	1,000,000	0.63
Jehovah's Witnesses	975,829	0.61
Christian Church (Disciples of Christ)	910,297	0.57
Seventh-day Adventists	809,159	0.51
Church of God (Cleveland, Tennessee)	753,230	0.47
Christian Methodist Episcopal Church	718,922	0.45
Church of the Nazarene	608,008	0.38
Salvation Army	453,150	0.28

Source: National Council of the Churches of Christ in the U.S.A.

Pet Population

Americans love their pets: Market Statistics Inc. of New York estimates that people spend more than $21 billion a year on their animals. Here are the estimated number of pets and percentages of households with different types of pets:

	Pet population (In millions)		Percent of households	
	1991	1998	1991	1998
Cats	57.0	61.1	30.9%	31.4%
Dogs	52.5	53.6	36.5	34.3
Birds	11.7	–	5.7	–
Horses	4.9	–	2.0	–

Source: American Veterinary Medical Association

Health and Medicine

In the movie *As Good as It Gets*, actress Helen Hunt delivers an expletive-filled tirade against an HMO for refusing to pay for her son's asthma treatment. Never mind that better asthma care is one of the managed care industry's notable success stories. Her rant was greeted with rousing ovations in theaters across the United States.

Indeed, the scene resonated so powerfully among consumers, says Leonard D. Schaeffer, chief executive officer of WellPoint Health Networks, Inc., a big California managed-care company, that "the 'Hillary Effect' has now been replaced by the 'Helen Hunt Effect.'"

That is just one sign of the challenges facing an industry that rose to prominence in the 1990s as the private sector cure for runaway health costs in the wake of the failure of President and Hillary Rodham Clinton's plan to overall the health-care system. Indeed, HMOs are so riddled with maladies that they now need a cure of their own.

That the HMO industry is in trouble seems at odds with what it has accomplished. For the past five years, it has enabled U.S. employers to hold annual percentage growth in their health costs, on average, to low single digits, ending several consecutive years of rises as high as 18 percent. U.S. health expenditures have held steady at 13.6 percent of gross domestic product for four consecutive years, defying predictions of the early 1990s that they would be in the high teens by the turn of the century.

Along the way, managed health-care plans have evolved in less than a decade from a cost-containment experiment to the nation's dominant form of financing medical care: A stunning 85 percent of the insured American workforce is now covered by some kind of managed care. Government Medicare and Medicaid programs have also enlisted HMOs to help them control costs.

But evidence of turmoil abounds:

- Oxford Health Plans Inc., which soared to prominence in the metropolitan New York market with a popular provider network and consumer friendly benefits, crashed late in 1997 amid a disastrous computer system conversion. Cleaning up the mess exposed management lapses and led to a string of losses that in total dwarf the company's seven-year cumulative profit as a public company. The company doesn't expect profits to return until the second half of 1999.
- United HealthCare Corp., another bellwether HMO company, posted a whopping loss of $900 million in its 1998 second quarter, reflecting, among other things, a restructuring of its Medicare operations where costs soared out of control.
- Kaiser Permanente, the big nonprofit HMO that is one of the models of the genre, disclosed early this year it had lost $270 million in 1997, partly because it couldn't control costs for out-of-network care it had sanctioned to meet consumer demands.

These industry leaders have plenty of company: Some 75 percent of the nation's health plans lost money on their health-care operations in 1997, according to Interstudy, a managed-care research firm. To return to financial health, many plans are asking employer customers for rate increases from 6 to 9 percent—or even higher—raising the specter of a reignition of medical cost inflation.

In the mid-1990s, a surprisingly effective weapon in the war on health costs turned out to be the Hillary Effect—a significant slowdown in medical cost growth that just happened to coincide with the debate over the Clinton health reform plan. Doctors, hospitals, and drug companies acted with exceptional restraint during those years, hoping that good behavior on the cost front would undermine the case for aggressive regulation.

HMOs benefited, but they added plenty of cost-cutting strategies of their own. They prospered by cutting inpatient hospital stays, demanding lower fees for doctors and restricting access of their members to specialist physicians. Meanwhile, they bid aggressively for customers in the belief that competitive rates were crucial to gaining the market share needed to maintain their leverage over doctors and hospitals.

Now, much of that is unraveling. New technology and soaring use of new prescription drugs are buckling managed-care companies, some of whom missed the upturn in costs and use of medical services and underpriced their products in the bidding war for customers. HMO medicine's own efforts to expand prevention programs is fueling an increase in doctor visits. Medicare and Medicaid patients, whose medical needs are much different than the typical HMO member, turn out to be more costly to care for than managed-care companies thought.

Underlying all of this is growing consumer resistance to managed-care tactics. HMOs have made unwelcome headlines for denying coverage of experimental treatments for dying cancer patients or for shooing mastectomy patients out of hospitals within 24 hours of their surgery. But more troubling for the vast majority of patients are annoying hassles just getting routine care: limited choice of physicians, repeated trips to the family doctor for referral slips to see the cardiologist, separate lab visits for blood tests that could be done in a doctor's office.

Managed-care companies are responding to this frustration. Much of their recent growth has come from members who signed up for less restrictive point-of-service plans that allow them to see doctors outside of an established provider network. But these plans are difficult to administer and hamper cost-control efforts.

In any event, as the Helen Hunt Effect suggests, HMO rules have caused distrust among consumers, many of whom believe that managed care means a loss of control over their health-care decisions. Now, as health plans address their financial predicament, they face a daunting challenge: how to chart the very narrow course between lackluster performance and further alienation of their constituents.

Oxford is a case in point. It found out the hard way that delivering consumer-friendly health care isn't cheap. Now, it is seeking 9 percent rate hikes from customers, restructuring or jettisoning Medicare and Medicaid business lines, negotiating lower doctor fees and strengthening cost-containment strategies that could annoy patients. Other plans are taking similar steps even as political initiatives for "patients rights" protection

More Doctors on Call

Total Number of U.S. Physicians

Year	Total physicians	Physicians per 100,000 population
1950	219,997	142
1955	241,711	144
1960	260,484	142
1965	292,088	148
1970	334,028	161
1975	393,742	180
1980	467,679	202
1985	552,716	228
1990	615,421	244
1994	684,414	263
1995	720,325	274
1996	737,764	278

States with Largest Number of Private Physicians

State	Total private physicians	Private physicians per 100,000 population
1980		
California	58,368	248
New York	49,105	280
Pennsylvania	23,347	197
Texas	22,571	159
Illinois	21,740	191
Florida	20,374	208
Ohio	18,342	170
Massachusetts	16,342	285
Michigan	15,347	166
New Jersey	14,799	201
1996		
California	87,593	276
New York	71,718	395
Florida	39,715	277
Texas	39,556	208
Pennsylvania	36,477	303
Illinois	31,994	271
Ohio	27,457	246
Massachusetts	25,950	426
New Jersey	24,409	306
Michigan	22,778	237

Source: American Medical Association

Physicians' Financial Health

Median Fees for Selected Surgical Procedures, for Private Physicians, 1995
(In dollars)

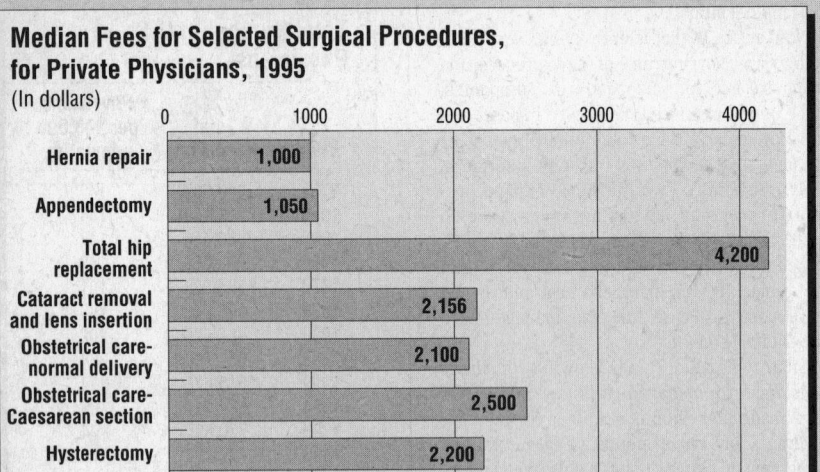

Hernia repair	1,000
Appendectomy	1,050
Total hip replacement	4,200
Cataract removal and lens insertion	2,156
Obstetrical care– normal delivery	2,100
Obstetrical care– Caesarean section	2,500
Hysterectomy	2,200

Median Physician Income after Expenses, before Taxes
(In thousands of dollars)

Specialty	1985	1996
All physicians	94	166
General/Family practice	70	130
Internal medicine	90	150
Surgery	129	230
Pediatrics	70	125
Obstetrics/Gynecology	120	200
Radiology	135	240
Psychiatry	80	122
Anesthesiology	133	215
Pathology	115	190

Average Annual Percentage Change in Median Income after Expenses before Taxes, for Private Physicians, for Selected Specialties, 1986–1996

Specialty	Change
All physicians	5.2
General/Family practice	5.7
Internal medicine	4.7
Surgery	5.0
Pediatrics	5.2
Obstetrics/Gynecology	4.6
Radiology	4.5
Psychiatry	4.1
Anesthesiology	3.7
Pathology	4.7

Source: American Medical Association

against managed care are debated in Congress and in nearly every state.

A potential winning strategy for HMOs is to develop more programs that truly manage care—like the ones they use to attack asthma. Harvard Pilgrim Health Care in Boston, for instance, works aggressively to help children control asthma symptoms to avoid medical crises. It has slashed emergency-room visits, reduced days absent from school and improved lives for parents and children alike. It also has saved more than $1 million a year in emergency-room and hospital costs.

Managed care now must deliver on its long-stated promise to make similar inroads in other diseases. The problem is, consumers remain skeptical that anything that cuts costs also improves quality. Just ask Helen Hunt.

Ron Winslow

Doctor's Fees

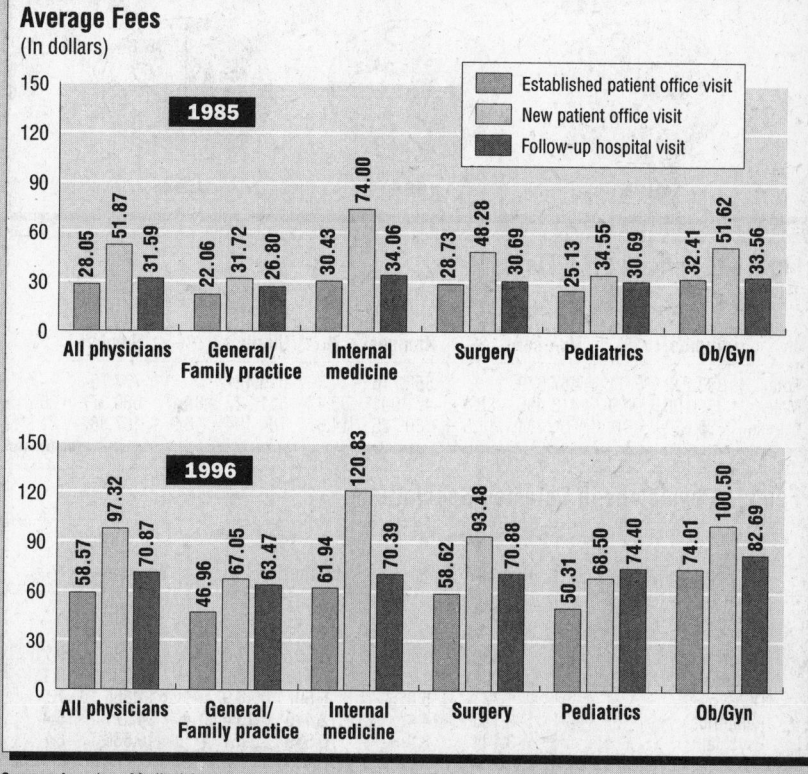

Percentage Change in Average Fees for Selected Types of Visits for All Physicians, 1985–1996

- Established patient office visit
- New patient office visit
- Follow-up hospital visit
- Inflation

Period	Established	New	Follow-up
1985–86	7.3	7.5	4.9
1988–89	9.4	7.9	5.6
1989–90	7.5	9.2	8.9
1990–91	5.5	11.0	8.8
1991–92	10.3	6.2	12.1
1992–93	14.0	4.1	9.9
1993–94	6.3	5.9	5.3
1994–95	5.6	5.8	9.8
1995–96	-1.4	-5.3	5.7

Average Fees (In dollars)

- Established patient office visit
- New patient office visit
- Follow-up hospital visit

1985

	Established	New	Follow-up
All physicians	28.05	51.87	31.59
General/Family practice	22.06	31.72	26.80
Internal medicine	30.43	74.00	34.06
Surgery	28.73	48.28	30.69
Pediatrics	25.13	34.55	30.69
Ob/Gyn	32.41	51.62	33.56

1996

	Established	New	Follow-up
All physicians	58.57	97.32	70.87
General/Family practice	46.96	67.05	63.47
Internal medicine	61.94	120.83	70.39
Surgery	58.62	93.48	70.88
Pediatrics	50.31	68.50	74.40
Ob/Gyn	74.01	100.50	82.69

Source: American Medical Association

Fields of Medicine

Number of Physicians in Selected Specialties

Specialty	1975 Number	1975 %	1985 Number	1985 %	1996 Number	1996 %
Total	393,742		552,716		737,764	
Anesthesiology	12,861	3.3	22,021	4.0	33,318	4.5
Family practice	12,183	3.1	40,021	7.2	62,301	8.4
General practice	42,374	10.8	27,030	4.9	16,895	2.3
General surgery	31,562	8.0	38,169	6.9	37,943	5.1
Ob/Gyn	21,731	5.5	30,867	5.6	38,424	5.2
Pediatrics	22,192	5.6	36,026	6.5	53,369	7.2
Psychiatry	23,922	6.1	32,255	5.8	38,417	5.2

Source: American Medical Association

Women in Medicine

Physicians Under 35, by Sex
(In percent)

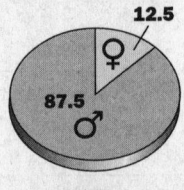

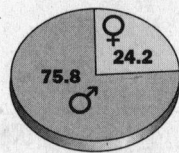
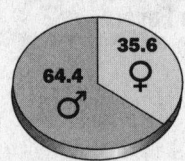

Male and Female Physicians

	1975 Number	1975 %	1980 Number	1980 %	1985 Number	1985 %	1990 Number	1990 %	1996 Number	1996 %
Total	393,742		467,679		552,716		615,421		737,764	
Male	358,106	90.9	413,395	88.4	471,991	85.4	511,227	83.1	580,377	78.7
Female	35,636	9.1	54,284	11.6	80,725	14.6	104,194	16.9	157,387	21.3

Female Physicians in Selected Specialties

Specialty	1975 Number	1975 %	1985 Number	1985 %	1996 Number	1996 %
Total	35,636		80,725		157,387	
Family practice	590	1.7	5,657	7.0	15,337	9.7
Internal medicine	4,006	11.2	14,716	18.2	30,087	19.1
Ob/Gyn	1,777	5.0	5,597	6.9	11,865	7.5
Pediatrics	5,135	14.4	12,440	15.4	24,271	15.4
Psychiatry	3,144	8.8	6,539	8.1	10,586	6.7

Source: American Medical Association

Health Care and the Economy

Health Care as a Percent of U.S. Gross Domestic Product

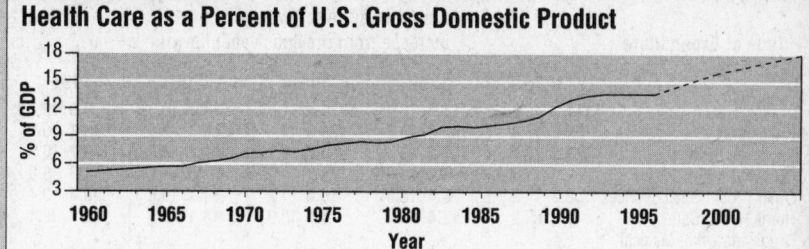

National Health Expenditures

Year	Amount (In billions)	% GDP	Amount Per Capita	Year	Amount (In billions)	% GDP	Amount Per Capita
1960	$26.9	5.1	$141	1990	$699.5	12.2	$2,691
1965	41.1	5.7	202	1991	766.8	13.0	2,920
1970	73.2	7.1	341	1992	836.6	13.4	3,154
1975	130.7	8.0	582	1993	895.1	13.6	3,341
				1994	945.7	13.6	3,497
1980	247.3	8.9	1,052	1995	991.4	13.6	3,633
1985	428.2	10.2	1,733	1996	1,035.1	13.6	3,759
1986	460.9	10.4	1,847				
1987	500.1	10.7	1,984	2000*	1,481.7	15.9	5,198
1988	559.6	11.1	2,198	2005*	2,173.7	17.9	7,352
1989	622.0	11.4	2,418				

*Projections
Source: U.S. Health Care Financing Administration

Annual Spending for Different Types of Health Care

Type of Expenditure	Amount in billions (average annual % increase from previous year shown)				
	1975	**1980**	**1985**	**1990**	**1991**
Personal Health Care	$114.5 12.4%*	$217.0 13.6%	$376.4 11.6%	$614.7 10.3%	$679.6 10.6%
Hospital Care	52.6 13.4	102.7 14.3	168.3 10.4	256.4 8.8	282.3 10.1
Physician Services	23.9 12.0	45.2 13.6	83.6 13.1	146.3 11.8	162.2 10.8
Dental Services	8.0 11.2	13.3 10.9	21.7 10.2	31.6 7.8	33.3 5.6
Other Professional Services	2.7 14.2	6.4 18.4	16.6 21.2	34.7 15.8	38.3 10.4
Home Health Care	0.6 23.2	2.4 30.7	5.6 18.9	13.1 18.4	16.1 22.4
Drugs and Other Medical Non-Durables	13.0 8.1	21.6 10.7	37.1 11.4	59.9 10.1	65.6 9.4
Vision Products and Other Medical Durables	2.5 9.5	3.8 8.1	6.7 12.4	10.5 9.2	11.2 7.0
Nursing Home Care	8.7 15.5	17.6 15.3	30.7 11.7	50.9 10.7	57.2 12.2
Other Personal Health Care	2.5 13.8	4.0 10.2	6.1 8.8	11.2 12.9	13.6 20.7
	1992	**1993**	**1994**	**1995**	**1996**
Personal Health Care	$740.7 9.0%	$787.0 6.2%	$828.5 5.3%	$869.0 4.9%	$907.2 4.4%
Hospital Care	305.3 8.2	323.0 5.8	335.7 3.9	346.7 3.3	358.5 3.4
Physician Services	175.9 8.5	183.6 4.4	190.4 3.7	196.4 3.1	202.1 2.9
Dental Services	37.0 11.0	39.1 5.6	41.7 6.6	44.7 7.3	47.6 6.4
Other Professional Services	42.1 10.0	46.3 9.9	50.3 8.8	54.3 7.9	58.0 6.8
Home Health Care	19.6 22.3	22.9 16.5	25.6 12.2	28.4 10.9	30.2 6.2
Drugs and Other Medical Non-Durables	71.2 8.6	75.6 6.2	79.5 5.2	84.9 6.8	91.4 7.7
Vision Products and Other Medical Durables	11.9 6.3	12.3 3.4	12.5 1.5	13.1 4.9	13.3 1.4
Nursing Home Care	62.3 9.0	66.3 6.5	70.9 6.8	75.2 6.2	78.5 4.3
Other Personal Health Care	15.4 13.3	18.0 17.0	21.9 21.8	25.3 15.4	27.6 9.4

*Average annual percent change since 1970.
Source: U.S. Health Care Financing Administration

Health Benefit Costs

Health benefit costs moderated in the mid-1990s, after years of much larger increases.

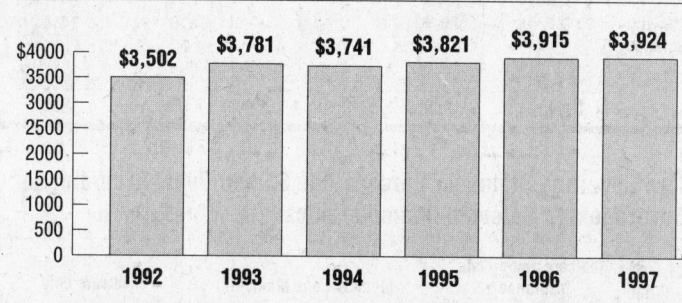

Total Health Benefit Cost Per Employee for Active and Retired Workers, 1992–1997

1992: $3,502
1993: $3,781
1994: $3,741
1995: $3,821
1996: $3,915
1997: $3,924

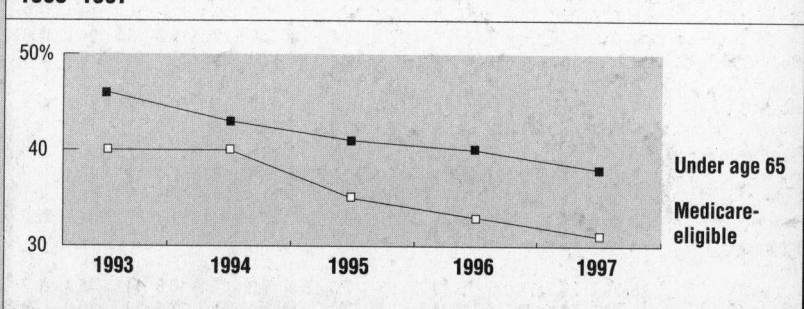

Decline in Percentage of Employers Offering Retiree Medical Coverage, 1993–1997

Under age 65
Medicare-eligible

Source: Foster Higgins

Health-Care Safety Net

Insurance Status of People Under Age 65

	1984	1989	1994	1995	1996*
% not covered	14.5	15.6	17.7	16.2	16.7
% under Medicaid	6.8	7.2	10.6	11.0	10.8
% with private insurance	76.8	75.9	70.3	71.6	71.4

Health-Care Coverage Status for Persons Age 65 and Over, According to Type of Coverage and Selected Characteristics (Percent of each group)

Characteristic	Medicare and private insurance					Medicare and Medicaid					Medicare only				
	'84	'89	'94	'95	'96*	'84	'89	'94	'95	'96*	'84	'89	'94	'95	'96*
Total	73.3	76.5	77.3	74.8	72.0	7.0	7.0	7.9	9.2	8.5	17.9	15.4	13.2	14.8	18.1
Age															
65–74 years	76.5	78.2	78.4	75.3	72.4	6.0	6.3	6.8	8.3	7.5	15.2	13.8	12.3	14.4	18.0
75 years and over	68.1	73.9	75.8	74.2	71.3	8.5	8.2	9.6	10.4	9.9	22.3	17.8	14.5	15.2	18.2
75–84 years	70.8	75.9	77.9	76.0	73.3	7.7	7.9	8.4	9.5	9.0	20.6	16.2	13.3	14.1	16.8
85 years and over	56.8	65.5	67.9	67.8	63.9	11.7	9.7	14.2	13.7	13.0	29.8	24.9	19.1	19.3	23.4
Sex															
Male	74.3	77.5	78.9	76.5	73.6	4.5	5.0	4.7	5.6	5.5	17.4	14.6	12.9	14.4	17.1
Female	72.9	76.2	76.5	73.9	71.0	8.6	8.4	10.0	11.5	10.4	18.1	15.6	13.3	14.9	18.7
Race/Ethnic origin															
White	76.8	80.3	81.2	78.6	75.3	5.0	5.4	6.0	6.9	6.6	16.5	13.4	11.6	13.4	16.9
Black	42.3	43.0	44.7	41.9	44.0	24.9	20.4	21.7	26.8	21.8	30.7	34.5	28.7	28.6	30.1
Hispanic	40.5	44.6	51.2	40.9	38.6	24.9	25.6	26.5	31.1	28.9	28.5	21.6	18.7	24.5	29.0
Geographic region															
Northeast	76.8	76.7	78.3	76.0	72.9	5.3	5.4	7.3	8.9	7.3	17.1	16.8	14.0	15.4	20.3
Midwest	79.6	82.3	84.6	82.5	80.8	4.2	3.6	3.7	5.6	5.1	15.2	13.4	10.7	10.9	12.8
South	68.0	73.5	71.2	71.6	67.2	9.5	9.1	10.3	10.8	9.9	19.8	16.3	16.0	15.8	19.7
West	70.8	75.1	78.2	69.3	69.0	7.9	9.3	9.4	10.8	10.8	18.4	13.8	10.3	17.3	18.6

*Preliminary.
Source: Centers for Disease Control and Prevention, National Center for Health Statistics

Hospital Industry's Vital Signs

Total Number of Hospital Admissions and Outpatient Visits, 1965–1996
(In millions)

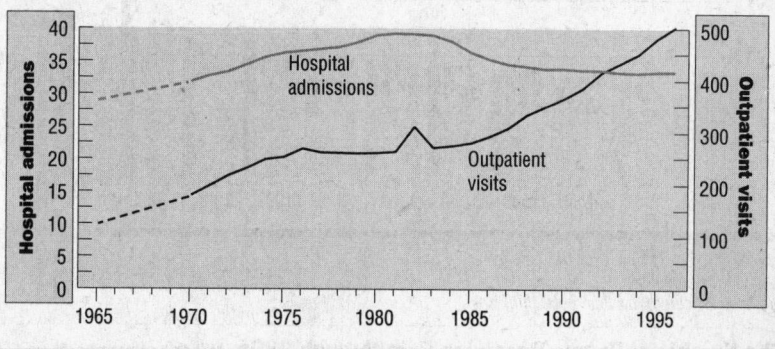

Number of Hospitals, Beds, Admissions, and Outpatient Visits, and Total Expenses in the U.S.

Year	Hospitals	Beds (In thousands)	Admissions (In thousands)	Outpatient Visits (In thousands)	Total Expenses (In millions)
1946	6,125	1,436	15,675	–	$ 1,963
1950	6,788	1,456	18,483	–	3,651
1955	6,956	1,604	21,073	–	5,594
1960	6,876	1,658	25,027	–	8,421
1965	7,123	1,704	28,812	125,793	12,948
1970	7,123	1,616	31,759	181,370	25,556
1975	7,156	1,466	36,157	254,844	48,706
1980	6,965	1,365	38,892	262,951	91,886
1985	6,872	1,318	36,304	282,140	153,327
1986	6,841	1,290	35,219	294,634	165,194
1987	6,821	1,267	34,439	310,707	178,662
1988	6,780	1,248	34,107	336,208	196,704
1989	6,720	1,226	33,742	352,248	214,886
1990	6,649	1,213	33,774	368,184	234,870
1991	6,634	1,202	33,567	387,675	258,508
1992	6,539	1,178	33,536	417,874	282,531
1993	6,467	1,163	33,201	435,619	301,538
1994	6,374	1,128	33,125	453,584	310,834
1995	6,291	1,081	33,282	483,195	320,252
1996	6,201	1,062	33,307	505,455	330,531

Source: American Hospital Association

The Move to Managed Care

The Number of People Receiving Care in HMOs*

(Millions of members)

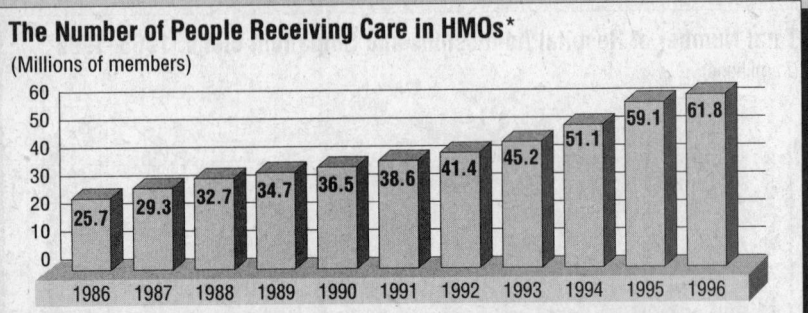

*Includes POS enrollment, excludes employer
self-insured enrollment.
Source: American Association of Health Plans

The Number of People Receiving Care through PPOs (Millions of members)

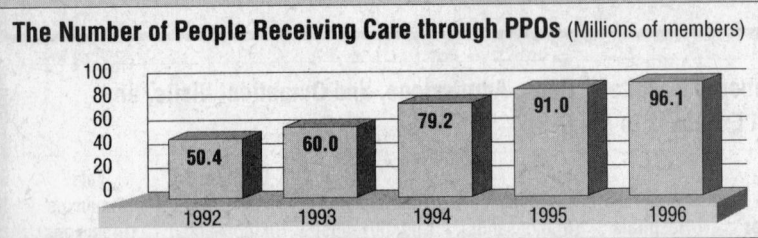

Source: American Association of Health Plans

Average Cost Per Employee

Traditional Indemnity / -5.8%
3,739
3,521

PPO / +0.9%
3,293
3,321

POS / -0.4%
3,494
3,481

HMO / -0.6%
3,185
3,165

■ 1996 ☐ 1997

Source: Mercer/Foster Higgins

Type of Health Plan

Traditional indemnity plan
Fee-for-service health insurance. Plan
participants or providers are reimbursed
following submission of a claim. Participants
have no restrictions on which hospitals or
doctors they may use.

Preferred provider plan (PPO)
An indemnity plan in which a group of health-
care providers offer their services under defined
financial arrangements. Plan participants
usually have incentives to use the "preferred
provider" network. A participant's access to
specialists in the network is *not* controlled by
a primary care physician.

Point-of-service plan (POS)
A "managed care" plan in which a participant's
access to a provider network (usually an HMO)
is controlled by a primary care physician.
Participants retain the option to seek care
outside the network, but at reduced coverage
levels. Includes open-ended HMOs.

Health Maintenance Organization (HMO)
A prepaid health plan in which participants may
obtain care only from a specified list of
providers. No benefits are available outside
the HMO network. Includes Exclusive Provider
Organizations (EPOs).

Top HMO Marketers

National Managed Care Firms Ranked by Total HMO Enrollment, July 1, 1997

National managed care firm	Number of plans	Reported total enrollment
1 The Blue Cross and Blue Shield System	85	13,317,160
2 Kaiser Foundation Health Plans, Inc.	12	8,054,722
3 United HealthCare Corporation	38	4,680,685
4 Aetna U.S. Healthcare, Inc.	27	4,201,608
5 PacifiCare Health Systems, Inc.	12	4,027,065
6 Foundation Health Systems	19	3,507,096
7 CIGNA Health Plans, Inc.	47	3,292,842
8 Prudential Health Care Plan, Inc.	33	2,435,410
9 Oxford Health Plans, Inc.	5	1,736,300
10 Humana, Inc.	13	1,677,521
11 NYLCare Health Plans, Inc.	10	1,265,992
12 Health Insurance Plan of Greater New York	4	1,110,696
13 Group Health Cooperative of Puget Sound	2	888,780
14 Principal Health Care, Inc.	18	866,715
15 Coventry Corporation	8	666,420
16 Physician Corporation of America	3	603,317
17 Maxicare Health Plans, Inc.	6	510,237
18 Henry Ford Health Care Corporation	2	497,012
19 PHS, Inc.	3	410,775
20 Mid-Atlantic Medical Services, Inc.	3	348,685

Source: InterStudy Publications

Pharmaceutical Prices

The Weighed Average Price Change for Pharmaceuticals

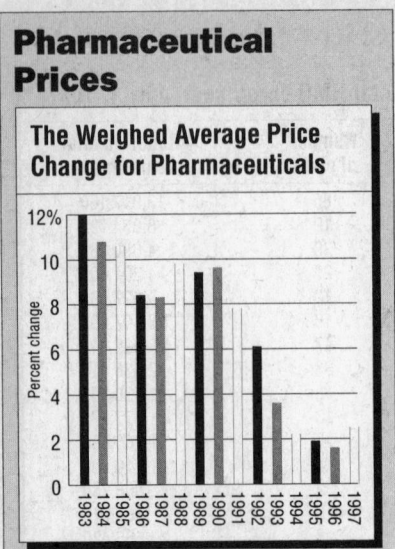

Source: IMS America

World's Largest Pharmaceutical Companies

Worldwide Pharmaceutical Sales and Market Share

Corporations	1997 US $ millions	market share % 1996	1997
Merck & Co.	11,296	4.2 %	4.6 %
Glaxo Wellcome	10,870	4.6	4.5
Novartis	10,537	4.4	4.3
Bristol-Myers Squibb	9,048	3.5	3.7
Johnson & Johnson	8,557	3.4	3.5
Pfizer	8,333	3.2	3.4
American Home	8,117	3.3	3.3
SmithKline Beecham	7,227	2.8	3.0
Hoechst	6,861	3.2	2.8
Lilly	6,363	2.3	2.6
Leading 10 corporations	**87,209**	**34.8**	**35.8**
Roche	6,232	2.6	2.6
Abbott	5,988	2.3	2.5
Schering Plough	5,524	2.1	2.3
Bayer	5,278	2.2	2.2
Astra	5,163	2.1	2.1
Warner-Lambert	4,503	1.5	1.9
Rhone Poulenc	4,393	1.9	1.8
Pharmacia & Upjohn	4,391	1.8	1.8
Boehringer Ingelheim	3,553	1.5	1.5
Takeda	3,516	1.5	1.4
Leading 20 corporations	**135,750**	**54.1**	**55.7**

Source: IMS International

Pharmaceutical Companies, Ranked by 1997 U.S. Sales

Rank	Company	Total sales (Thousands)	Percent change vs. 1996
1	Bristol-Myers Squibb	$ 5,696,998	13%
2	Johnson & Johnson	5,659,224	8
3	Merck & Co.	5,647,145	14
4	Glaxo Wellcome	5,536,504	-3
5	American Home Products	5,329,789	3
6	Pfizer	4,949,872	11
7	Lilly	4,390,951	23
8	SmithKline Beecham	4,015,666	14
9	Novartis	3,987,844	7
10	Schering Plough	3,810,682	18
11	Abbott	3,672,544	5
12	Astra Merck	2,398,986	33
13	Warner-Lambert	2,214,258	87
14	Hoffman-LaRoche	2,202,351	-1
15	Bayer	2,149,420	11
16	Hoechst-Marion-Roussel	2,029,145	-16
17	Amgen	1,891,036	3
18	Pharmacia & Upjohn	1,828,470	14
19	Zeneca	1,517,438	19
20	TAP	1,448,711	39
	Total all companies	**93,974,476**	**11.4**

Source: IMS America

Top 20 Prescription Drugs, Based on 1997 U.S. Sales

Rank	Drug	Total sales (Thousands)	Percent change vs. 1996
1	Prilosec (ulcer medicine)	$ 2,281,782	33
2	Prozac (antidepressant)	1,942,001	14
3	Zocor (cholesterol drug)	1,379,289	38
4	Epogen (anemia)	1,200,765	2
5	Zoloft (antidepressant)	1,195,863	11
6	Zantac (ulcer medicine)	1,097,233	-37
7	Paxil (antidepressant)	949,341	39
8	Norvasc (blood pressure drug)	914,800	28
9	Claritin (antihistamine)	907,672	40
10	Vasotec (blood pressure drug)	843,361	-1
11	Premarin (estrogen)	807,454	7
12	Augmentin (antibiotic)	804,802	21
13	Imitrex (migraine headache drug)	791,533	38
14	Procardia XL (blood pressure drug)	784,780	-17
15	Pravachol (cholesterol drug)	768,324	38
16	Biaxin (antibiotic)	743,695	-1
17	Lupron Depot (prostate cancer treatment)	711,953	-1
18	Cipro (antibiotic)	709,727	5
19	Cardizem CD (blood pressure drug)	698,806	-3
20	Pepcid (ulcer medicine)	698,208	9
	Total all products	**93,974,476**	**11.4**

Source: IMS America

Top 20 Drugs, Based on Number of Prescriptions Dispensed in U.S. in 1997

Rank	Drug	Total prescriptions (Thousands)	Percent change vs. 1996
1	Premarin (estrogen)	45,106	1%
2	Synthroid (thyroid treatment)	36,194	8
3	Trimox (antibiotic)	34,504	-2
4	Lanoxin (cardiac treatment)	25,282	-2
5	Hydrocodone (analgesic)	25,021	33
6	Prozac (antidepressant)	22,776	10
7	Albuterol (asthma treatment)	21,847	41
8	Prilosec (ulcer medicine)	21,130	31
9	Vasotec (blood pressure drug)	20,274	-6
10	Norvasc (blood pressure drug)	19,683	26
11	Coumadin Sodium (anticoagulant)	19,103	9
12	Zoloft (antidepressant)	18,552	8
13	Claritin (antihistamine)	18,302	36
14	Zocor (cholesterol drug)	17,526	31
15	Paxil (antidepressant)	15,859	32
16	Procardia XL (blood pressure drug)	15,283	-19
17	Zantac (ulcer medicine)	15,077	-35
18	Zestril (blood pressure drug)	15,019	11
19	Furosemide (diuretic)	14,912	21
20	Cardizem CD (blood pressure drug)	14,652	-6
	Total all products	**2,523,304**	**5**

Source: IMS America

Health News of 1998
The Good News

An enzyme that inhibits cell aging has been found by researchers who say the work may lead to treatments that, while not prolonging life, could keep people healthier longer.

Researchers identified a hair-loss gene, a finding that may lead to better treatments for male-pattern baldness. The gene plays a role in a rare form of hair loss affecting infants, but could provide insights about hair growth in general.

High intake of two B vitamins, folate and B-6, may reduce women's risk of heart disease by nearly half. The study included only women, but researchers said the results would probably apply to men as well. The B vitamins are found in such foods as spinach, bananas and chicken.

AZT can cut transmission of the AIDS virus from mother to child in half even when taken for less than a month at the end of pregnancy, the Centers for Disease Control and Prevention said. The short treatment could be given for $80.

German heart researchers succeeded in using genetic-engineering techniques to grow new blood vessels around blockages in coronary arteries. The accomplishment represents a milestone in the effort to replace or at least complement traditional bypass surgery.

New U.S. cancer cases dropped for the first time ever from 1990 to 1995. The report by government agencies and the American Cancer Society charts an average drop of 0.5% a year for the period, the first decline since data began to be collected in the 1930s. Public health officials cite numerous factors, including a reduction in smoking, lifestyle changes, heightened use of more sensitive detection methods and better treatments.

Vitamin E reduced the risk of prostate cancer by one-third and cut the death rate for the disease by 41%, according to a study of Finnish smokers in the Journal of the National Cancer Institute. Other researchers cautioned that more study is needed to confirm the findings.

Seat belts and bike helmets have helped cut the number of children killed in accidents 26%

over the past decade, according to the National Safe Kids Campaign. The group also found, however, that the number of children's sports injuries is rising.

A nasal-spray flu vaccine showed promise in fighting the viruses and ear infections that often accompany them in children. The study's findings, announced by the National Institutes of Health and Aviron, the drug's maker, indicate the spray could cut rampant use of antibiotics.

A hepatitis C treatment was approved by the FDA, which recommended it be used for chronic patients who have relapsed after trying other therapies. The treatment consists of two Schering-Plough drugs, one taken orally and the other injected. It isn't a cure, but it was found to reduce virus levels in 45% of patients.

A major new study shows that aggressive treatment to reduce blood pressure among people with hypertension significantly reduces chances of a heart attack.

Human nerve cells were transplanted in the brain of a patient by doctors at the University of Pittsburgh Medical Center in a bid to reverse the effects of paralysis and other damage from a stroke. If the technique is successful, doctors say it could be used to treat other neurological disorders, such as spinal-cord injuries.

Thalidomide was approved for the first time in the U.S. for treatment of skin lesions caused by leprosy. The FDA said the drug, which is manufactured by Celgene and notorious for causing severe birth defects, will become the nation's most tightly regulated compound.

A Lyme-disease vaccine appears to be 76% to 92% effective in preventing infections in adults, two studies found. They focused on two versions of essentially the same vaccine, one by SmithKline Beecham, the other by a Rhone Poulenc unit.

Cocaine addiction may be treated with an epilepsy drug widely used in Europe. New York scientists found Hoechst's Sabril blocked cocaine's effects by nearly 50% in rats. It also appears to work on nicotine.

An FDA advisory panel urged approval of tamoxifen, a breast-cancer treatment, for use by women who are healthy but at risk of developing the disease. The panel added, however, that the

benefits of Zeneca's Nolvadex as a preventative haven't been proved over the long term.

A new type of depression drug tested effectively without side effects produced by current medications, Merck researchers said. The experimental drug MK-869 represents the first new class of antidepressants in at least 10 years.

The Bad News

Researchers found strong evidence that a past smoking habit or exposure to secondhand smoke can irreversibly damage arteries. The large study indicates that the damage to arteries from environmental smoke exposure lingers and may be much greater than previously realized.

AIDS cases have risen faster among people over 50—22 percent from 1991 through 1996—than among young adults, the Centers for Disease Control and Prevention said. The agency cited rising transmission among heterosexuals and intravenous drug users.

People who are socially ill at ease and insecure may be at higher risk for heart attacks. Researchers studied men who had suffered heart attacks and found that those who were socially inhibited and anxious—dubbed "Type D" personalities—were more likely to have second attacks.

A report on pesticides in food said more than one million children are exposed each day to potentially unsafe doses. Many health officials worry about the possible effects of long-term, low-level exposure to neurotoxic chemicals, particularly on children's intellectual development. The Environmental Working Group's study drew denunciations from food and pesticide makers.

An unacceptable risk of stroke was found among as many as 15,000 of the 130,000 Americans who undergo a procedure each year to clear blocked carotid arteries. The study found the risk exceeded benefits among those with stroke symptoms whose blockages are under 50 percent.

A study of AIDS patients at two New England hospitals found 78 percent of women and 52 percent of men told their sexual partners they were HIV-positive, and most reported irregular condom use.

A review of cancer studies appeared to challenge the widely held belief that sunscreens lower the risk of melanoma skin cancer. But some dermatologists disagreed with the findings.

Long-term cigar smoking nearly doubles the risk of dying from cancer or heart disease, according to a study by Kaiser Permanente. Cigar consumption in the U.S. has jumped 68% since 1993 after a steady decline for 30 years.

Diesel exhaust fumes may pose a significant cancer risk even in low-level exposure, according to a draft EPA report. The agency cautioned that data are sketchy, but the report could affect a drive toward development of engines with higher fuel efficiency.

Bad reactions to medicines kill 100,000 Americans a year, a study argues. The figure, if accurate, would make the problem the fourth leading cause of death. Millions more suffer injuries such as heart irregularities and internal bleeding as a result of complications from drugs often prescribed by doctors, the controversial study, published in the AMA Journal, asserts. Statistics are even higher when they include cases in which patients got the wrong drug or dose.

False-positive mammogram results are common, according to a New England Journal of Medicine study, which says a woman who is tested once a year for a decade runs a 50-50 chance of a false breast-cancer alarm. Researchers said findings shouldn't turn women away from the test, but that they should be made aware of its limitations.

Some AIDS patients are developing a syndrome of disfiguring fat deposits on parts of their bodies as their faces and limbs shrink. Doctors say these are possible side effects from lifesaving drugs called protease inhibitors. The FDA says some patients also are developing risks for heart disease.

Black smokers inhale significantly more nicotine per cigarette than whites, two studies in the AMA Journal say. The research may explain why blacks are 30% more likely than whites to develop lung cancer, and have more trouble quitting the habit than most other ethnic groups.

New AIDS strains resist combination therapies, researchers are convinced. Several presentations at the big AIDS conference in Geneva showed strains of HIV found in recently infected people are able to resist treatment with the drug combinations that have revolutionized the AIDS battle in the past two years.

Men who have suffered clinical depression are more than twice as likely to develop heart disease as those who haven't, according to Johns Hopkins University researchers.

Women heart patients are more likely to die after bypass surgery than men, according to a study by a University of Florida surgeon in the Annals of Thoracic Surgery. His review of records on 344,000 patients from 1994 to 1996 found 4.5% of women died after surgery, compared with 2.6% of men.

A strain of resistant bacteria may be generated by triclosan, a germ-killing agent in many consumer products, a Tufts University study found. Wide resistance would make it harder to keep environments sterile when necessary.

Estrogen therapy may not help postmenopausal women cut their risk of heart attack as is widely believed, a four-year study of 2,763 women indicates. While the study tracked only women who had already had an attack or heart disease, the findings add uncertainty to the decision facing all women weighing therapy.

Smoking marijuana or cocaine can cause molecular abnormalities that indicate an increased cancer risk, California researchers found. The study also indicates smoking both cigarettes and drugs brings more risk than tobacco alone.

Implants of radioactive pellets don't work as well as prostate-removal surgery for patients at risk of their cancer spreading, a study by Brigham and Women's Hospital found. The study of 1,872 men contradicts earlier findings that showed the implants to be just as effective.

The Changing Face of Death

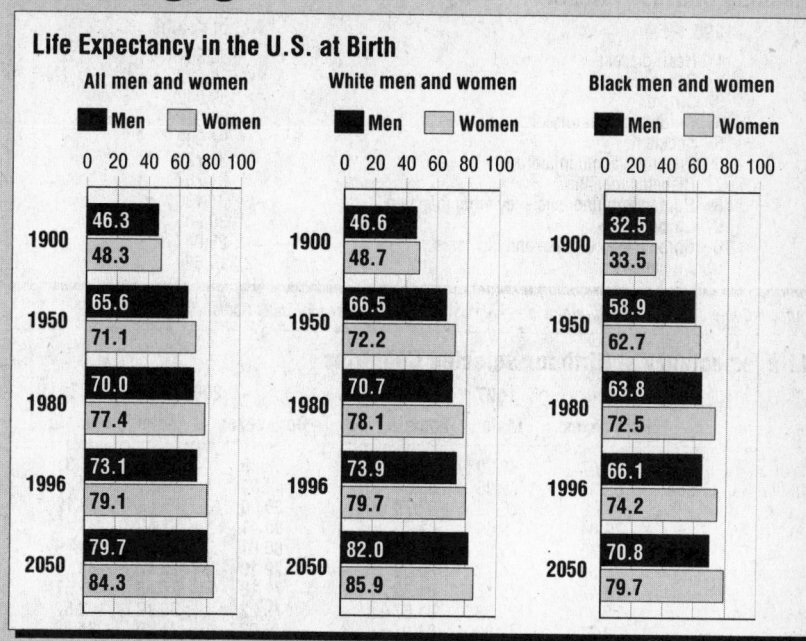

Life Expectancy in the U.S. at Birth

All men and women — Men / Women
White men and women — Men / Women
Black men and women — Men / Women

Year	All Men	All Women	White Men	White Women	Black Men	Black Women
1900	46.3	48.3	46.6	48.7	32.5	33.5
1950	65.6	71.1	66.5	72.2	58.9	62.7
1980	70.0	77.4	70.7	78.1	63.8	72.5
1996	73.1	79.1	73.9	79.7	66.1	74.2
2050	79.7	84.3	82.0	85.9	70.8	79.7

Source: National Center for Health Statistics, U.S. Census Bureau

Leading Causes of Death

1900
No. of deaths
1. Pneumonia and influenza — 40,362
2. Tuberculosis — 38,820
3. Diarrhea, enteritis, and ulceration of the intestines — 28,491
4. Heart disease — 27,427
5. Stroke — 21,353
6. Nephritis — 17,699
7. All accidents — 14,429
8. Cancer — 12,769
9. Senility — 10,015
10. Diphtheria — 8,056
All causes — 343,217

1940
1. Heart disease — 385,191
2. Cancer — 158,335
3. Stroke — 119,753
4. Nephritis — 107,351
5. Pneumonia and influenza — 92,525
6. Accidents, excluding motor-vehicle — 62,384
7. Tuberculosis — 60,428
8. Diabetes mellitus — 35,015
9. Motor-vehicle accidents — 34,501
10. Premature birth — 32,346
All causes — 1,417,269

Leading Causes of Death

1996		No. of deaths
1	Heart disease	733,361
2	Cancer	539,533
3	Stroke	159,942
4	Chronic respiratory diseases	106,027
5	Accidents	94,948
6	Pneumonia and influenza	83,727
7	Diabetes mellitus	61,767
8	Human immunodeficiency virus infection	31,130
9	Suicide	30,903
10	Chronic liver disease and cirrhosis	25,047
	All causes	**2,314,690**

Sources: Centers for Disease Control and Prevention, National Center for Health Statistics

Life Expectancy at Birth for Selected Countries

	1997			2000 projected		
	Both sexes	Male	Female	Both sexes	Male	Female
World	62.67	61.00	64.43	63.39	61.57	65.31
China, Hong Kong	82.35	79.06	85.84	82.84	79.61	86.25
Japan	79.66	76.68	82.79	80.00	77.03	83.12
Australia	79.64	76.69	82.74	80.41	77.49	83.48
Canada	79.30	75.92	82.86	80.01	76.69	83.49
France	78.56	74.72	82.62	79.19	75.47	83.11
Spain	78.47	75.17	81.99	79.10	75.86	82.57
Singapore	78.40	75.33	81.67	79.22	76.12	82.52
Greece	78.31	75.80	81.01	78.97	76.40	81.73
Israel	78.21	76.34	80.18	78.82	76.89	80.84
Italy	78.20	75.00	81.60	78.64	75.49	81.99
Sweden	78.18	75.74	80.74	78.54	76.12	81.08
Netherlands	77.85	75.05	80.79	78.23	75.47	81.13
Switzerland	77.75	74.72	80.93	78.14	75.16	81.26
United Kingdom	76.58	73.96	79.34	77.13	74.52	79.87
China, Taiwan	76.33	73.72	79.14	77.27	74.62	80.14
Germany	76.13	73.00	79.44	76.70	73.62	79.96
Ireland	75.74	73.06	78.61	76.24	73.60	79.05
Cuba	75.20	72.83	77.71	75.64	73.21	78.22
Chile	74.73	71.50	77.95	75.45	72.25	78.65
Mexico	74.00	70.39	77.78	75.02	71.39	78.83
Czech Republic	73.87	70.18	77.78	74.21	70.48	78.16
South Korea	73.60	70.01	77.69	74.66	71.13	78.65
Colombia	73.14	70.28	76.09	74.15	71.20	77.20
Turkey	72.37	69.95	74.91	73.75	71.25	76.38
Poland	72.22	68.14	76.55	72.61	68.49	76.99
China, Mainland	69.98	68.61	71.50	71.08	69.48	72.85
Saudi Arabia	69.51	67.72	71.40	71.09	69.16	73.11
Thailand	68.80	65.12	72.66	69.41	65.81	73.19
Iran	67.82	66.47	69.23	69.12	67.55	70.78
Vietnam	67.38	65.03	69.86	68.47	66.06	71.03
Philippines	66.13	63.35	69.05	66.80	64.01	69.73
Russia	63.77	57.20	70.68	65.36	59.37	71.65
Indonesia	62.06	59.89	64.34	63.36	61.06	65.77
Egypt	61.75	59.80	63.80	62.71	60.69	64.83
Brazil	61.42	56.78	66.30	60.87	57.09	64.84
India	60.15	59.52	60.81	61.51	60.73	62.32
South Africa	58.88	56.64	61.19	57.17	54.98	59.43
Pakistan	58.77	57.97	59.61	59.67	58.75	60.64
Nigeria	54.65	53.32	56.03	55.61	54.10	57.17

Source: U.S. Census Bureau

Cancer Targets

Leading Sites of New Cancer Cases and Deaths — 1998 Estimates*

Cancer cases by site and sex		Cancer deaths by site and sex	
Male	**Female**	**Male**	**Female**
Prostate 184,500	Breast 178,700	Lung 93,100	Lung 67,000
Lung 91,400	Lung 80,100	Prostate 39,200	Breast 43,500
Colon & rectum 64,600	Colon & rectum 67,000	Colon & rectum 27,900	Colon & rectum 28,600
Urinary bladder 39,500	Endometrium (uterus) 36,100	Pancreas 14,000	Pancreas 14,900
Non-Hodgkin's lymphoma 31,100	Ovary 25,400	Non-Hodgkin's lymphoma 13,000	Ovary 14,500
Melanoma of the skin 24,300	Non-Hodgkin's lymphoma 24,300	Leukemia 12,000	Non-Hodgkin's lymphoma 11,900
Oral cavity 20,600	Melanoma of the skin 17,300	Esophagus 9,100	Leukemia 9,600
Kidney 17,600	Urinary bladder 14,900	Urinary bladder 8,400	Endometrium (uterus) 6,300
Leukemia 16,100	Pancreas 14,900	Stomach 8,100	Brain 6,000
Stomach 14,300	Cervix (uterus) 13,700	Liver 7,900	Stomach 5,600
All sites 627,900	All sites 600,700	All sites 294,200	All sites 270,600

*Excluding basal and squamous cell skin cancer and in situ carcinomas except urinary bladder.
Source: American Cancer Society

Percentage of Population (Probability) Developing Invasive Cancers at Certain Ages, 1992–1994

		Birth to 39	40–59	60–79	Birth to death
All sites*	Male	1.68 (1 in 60)	8.23 (1 in 12)	36.69 (1 in 3)	46.64 (1 in 2)
	Female	1.94 (1 in 52)	9.05 (1 in 11)	22.21 (1 in 5)	38.00 (1 in 3)
Breast	Female	0.44 (1 in 227)	3.94 (1 in 25)	6.89 (1 in 15)	12.52 (1 in 8)
Colon & rectum	Male	0.06 (1 in 1,667)	0.88 (1 in 114)	4.19 (1 in 24)	5.88 (1 in 17)
	Female	0.05 (1 in 2,000)	0.68 (1 in 147)	3.18 (1 in 31)	5.72 (1 in 17)
Lung & bronchus	Male	0.04 (1 in 2,500)	1.39 (1 in 72)	6.69 (1 in 15)	8.43 (1 in 12)
	Female	0.03 (1 in 3,333)	1.00 (1 in 100)	3.88 (1 in 26)	5.55 (1 in 18)
Prostate	Male	Less than 1 in 10,000	1.74 (1 in 57)	16.40 (1 in 6)	18.85 (1 in 5)

*Excludes basal and squamous cell skin cancers and in situ carcinomas except urinary bladder.
Sources: American Cancer Society, National Cancer Institute

20 Year Trends in Cancer Death Rates* per 100,000 Population, 1972–1974 to 1992–1994

Sites	Sex	Rates in 1972–74	Rates in 1992–94	% changes	Number of deaths 1974	Number of deaths 1994
All sites	Male	206.2	217.3	5%	195,873	280,465
	Female	132.1	141.8	7%	163,088	253,845
Brain	Male	4.7	5.1	9%	4,740	6,702
	Female	3.2	3.5	9%	3,659	5,611
Breast	Male	0.3	0.3	0%	292	364
	Female	26.9	25.9	-4%	32,132	43,644
Cervix	Female	5.3	2.9	-45%	5,963	4,602
Colon & rectum	Male	25.4	22.1	-13%	23,853	28,471
	Female	19.8	14.9	-25%	25,440	28,936
Endometrium	Female	4.6	3.4	-26%	5,603	6,163
Esophagus	Male	5.1	6.3	24%	4,917	8,191
	Female	1.4	1.5	7%	1,735	2,626
Hodgkin's disease	Male	1.7	0.6	-65%	1,588	773
	Female	1.0	0.4	-60%	1,087	667
Kidney	Male	4.4	5.1	16%	4,204	6,522
	Female	1.9	2.3	21%	2,449	4,228
Larynx	Male	2.9	2.5	-14%	2,826	3,127
	Female	0.4	0.5	25%	436	820
Leukemia	Male	8.8	8.4	-5%	8,231	10,948
	Female	5.2	4.9	-6%	6,344	8,885
Liver	Male	3.3	4.8	45%	3,113	6,388
	Female	1.8	2.1	17%	2,166	4,039
Lung	Male	62.9	72.3	15%	61,507	91,825
	Female	13.5	33.4	147%	17,213	57,535
Melanoma	Male	2.1	3.1	48%	2,201	4,117
	Female	1.3	1.5	15%	1,534	2,563
Multiple myeloma	Male	2.8	3.8	36%	2,690	5,137
	Female	1.9	2.6	37%	2,430	4,843
Non-Hodgkin's lymphoma	Male	5.8	8.2	41%	5,686	11,280
	Female	4.0	5.4	35%	4,933	10,528
Oral cavity	Male	5.9	4.3	-27%	5,686	5,227
	Female	1.9	1.5	-21%	2,282	2,688
Ovary	Female	8.5	7.7	-9%	10,203	13,500
Pancreas	Male	11.0	10.0	-9%	10,208	12,920
	Female	6.7	7.3	9%	8,688	13,914
Prostate	Male	21.6	26.6	23%	19,184	34,902
Stomach	Male	10.1	6.3	-38%	9,159	8,039
	Female	4.8	2.9	-40%	6,012	5,531
Testis	Male	0.7	0.2	-71%	755	349
Thyroid	Male	0.4	0.3	-25%	316	402
	Female	0.5	0.4	-20%	663	660
Urinary bladder	Male	7.3	5.7	-22%	6,651	7,457
	Female	2.2	1.7	-23%	2,926	3,713

*Adjusted to the age distribution of the 1970 U.S. census population.
Note: Even though death rates declined or remained stable, the number of deaths increased because the population over 65 has become larger and older.
Source: American Cancer Society

AIDS in America

AIDS Cases, Case-Fatality Rates, and Deaths, by Half-Year and Age Group, Through December 1997*

Half-year	Adults/adolescents			Children under 13 years old		
	Cases diagnosed during interval	Case-fatality rate**	Deaths occurring during interval	Cases diagnosed during interval	Case-fatality rate**	Deaths occurring during interval
Before 1981	85	91.8	30	8	75.0	1
1981 Jan.–June	108	88.9	37	10	80.0	2
July–Dec.	208	93.8	83	6	100.0	6
1982 Jan.–June	440	93.2	151	14	92.9	10
July–Dec.	730	92.3	298	17	82.4	4
1983 Jan.–June	1,349	94.3	528	33	100.0	14
July–Dec.	1,719	94.2	950	44	93.2	16
1984 Jan.–June	2,700	93.6	1,427	53	88.7	27
July–Dec.	3,516	94.2	2,027	66	87.9	24
1985 Jan.–June	5,185	92.9	2,875	111	82.9	47
July–Dec.	6,555	93.5	3,979	139	87.8	71
1986 Jan.–June	8,713	92.4	5,208	144	85.4	70
July–Dec.	10,264	93.0	6,734	198	80.8	98
1987 Jan.–June	13,579	91.9	7,824	230	81.7	122
July–Dec.	14,920	90.7	8,294	270	77.4	172
1988 Jan.–June	17,436	88.9	9,724	265	70.2	140
July–Dec.	17,907	89.1	11,076	349	71.3	179
1989 Jan.–June	21,071	86.5	12,756	363	70.5	175
July–Dec.	21,382	85.9	14,667	352	71.0	193
1990 Jan.–June	24,484	83.7	15,073	394	66.5	195
July–Dec.	23,802	82.6	16,072	409	60.9	198
1991 Jan.–June	28,608	80.1	17,151	408	62.0	174
July–Dec.	30,710	78.1	19,069	398	57.8	222
1992 Jan.–June	37,604	72.8	19,709	487	56.3	195
July–Dec.	40,513	69.9	20,965	450	57.6	225
1993 Jan.–June	42,664	61.0	21,464	439	53.1	257
July–Dec.	35,500	56.7	22,644	446	53.8	271
1994 Jan.–June	37,132	49.2	23,543	422	49.3	298
July–Dec.	33,299	42.2	24,567	356	45.5	255
1995 Jan.–June	35,324	33.7	24,082	317	33.8	270
July–Dec.	30,290	26.4	23,776	302	27.2	243
1996 Jan.–June	30,125	19.4	20,012	243	22.6	218
July–Dec.	24,112	14.7	14,545	176	14.2	172
1997 Jan.–June	21,255	10.2	10,045	139	15.8	112
July–Dec.	9,731	5.6	4,140	28	7.1	41
Total***	633,000	61.0	385,968	8,086	58.4	4,724

*Recent year data are incomplete because of a long lag in reporting cases and deaths.
**Case-fatality rates are calculated for each half-year by date of diagnosis. Each 6-month case-fatality rate
is the number of deaths ever reported among cases diagnosed in that period (regardless of the year of death),
divided by the number of total cases diagnosed in that period, multiplied by 100. For example, during the interval
January through June 1982, AIDS was diagnosed in 440 adults/adolescents. Through December 1997, 410 of
these 440 were reported as dead. Therefore, the case fatality rate is 93.2 (410 divided by 440, multiplied by 100).
The case-fatality rates shown here may be underestimates because of incomplete reporting of deaths. Reported
deaths are not necessarily caused by HIV-related disease.
***Death totals include 443 adults/adolescents and 7 children known to have died, but whose dates of death
are unknown.
Source: Centers for Disease Control and Prevention

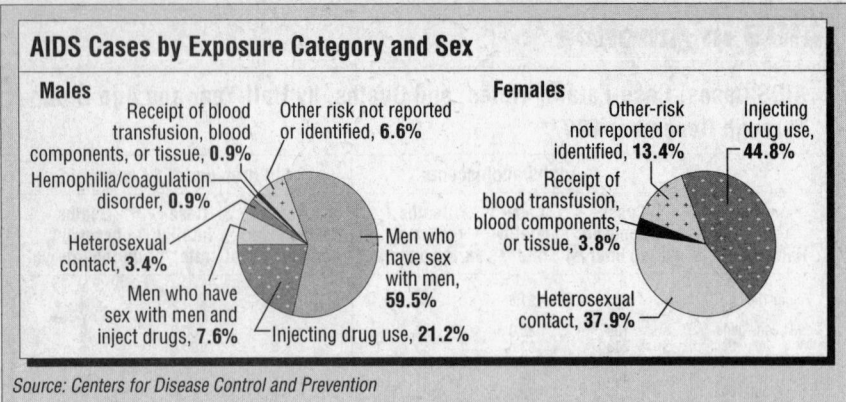

AIDS Cases by Exposure Category and Sex

Males
- Receipt of blood transfusion, blood components, or tissue, **0.9%**
- Hemophilia/coagulation disorder, **0.9%**
- Heterosexual contact, **3.4%**
- Men who have sex with men and inject drugs, **7.6%**
- Injecting drug use, **21.2%**
- Men who have sex with men, **59.5%**
- Other risk not reported or identified, **6.6%**

Females
- Other-risk not reported or identified, **13.4%**
- Injecting drug use, **44.8%**
- Receipt of blood transfusion, blood components, or tissue, **3.8%**
- Heterosexual contact, **37.9%**

Source: Centers for Disease Control and Prevention

The Global HIV/AIDS Pandemic

The Joint United Nations Programme on HIV/AIDS estimates that 30.6 million people are infected with human immunodeficiency virus (HIV) throughout the world, including those who have AIDS and those who have not yet developed AIDS.

Prevalence of HIV, by region of the world:

Sub-Saharan Africa: 20.8 million
Asia and Pacific: 6.5 million
Latin America and the Caribbean: 1.6 million
North America: 860,000
Western Europe: 530,000
North Africa and the Middle East: 210,000
Eastern Europe and Central Asia: 150,000

Cumulative AIDS Deaths by Region Through 1997

Sub-Saharan Africa	9.7 million
Asia and Pacific	759,100
Latin America and the Caribbean	580,000
North America	420,000
Western Europe	190,000
North Africa and the Middle East	42,000
Eastern Europe and Central Asia	4,500

MALADIES OF THE 1990S

A look at some of the diseases and other ailments that have received increased attention in the 1990s.

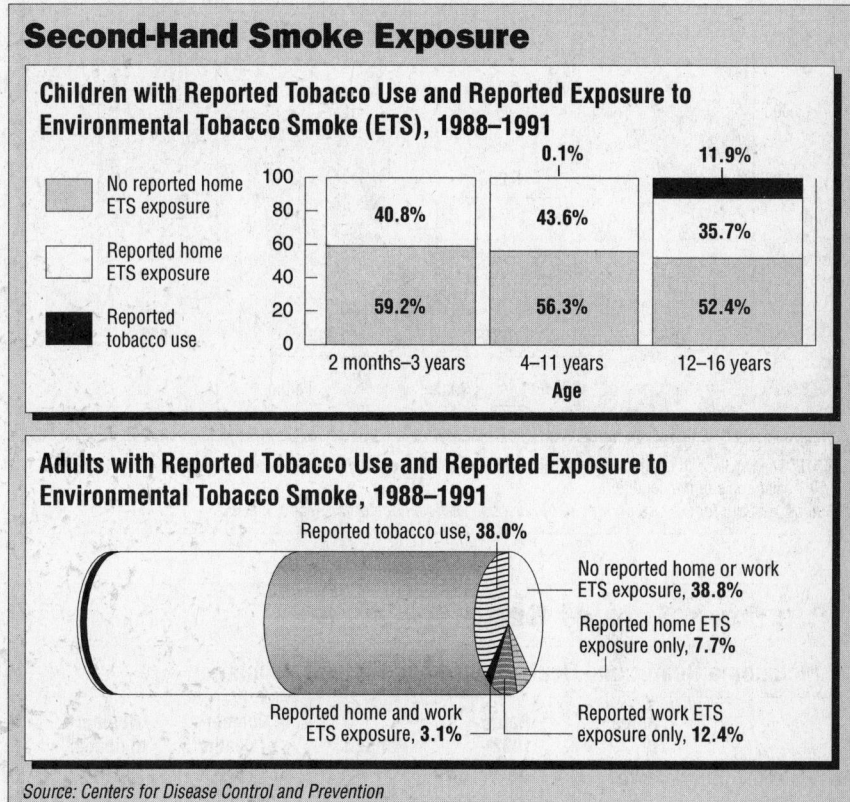

Second-Hand Smoke Exposure

Children with Reported Tobacco Use and Reported Exposure to Environmental Tobacco Smoke (ETS), 1988–1991

Legend:
- No reported home ETS exposure
- Reported home ETS exposure
- Reported tobacco use

Age	2 months–3 years	4–11 years	12–16 years
Reported tobacco use		0.1%	11.9%
Reported home ETS exposure	40.8%	43.6%	35.7%
No reported home ETS exposure	59.2%	56.3%	52.4%

Adults with Reported Tobacco Use and Reported Exposure to Environmental Tobacco Smoke, 1988–1991

Reported tobacco use, **38.0%**

No reported home or work ETS exposure, **38.8%**

Reported home ETS exposure only, **7.7%**

Reported home and work ETS exposure, **3.1%**

Reported work ETS exposure only, **12.4%**

Source: Centers for Disease Control and Prevention

Alzheimer's Disease

Number of Deaths from Alzheimer's

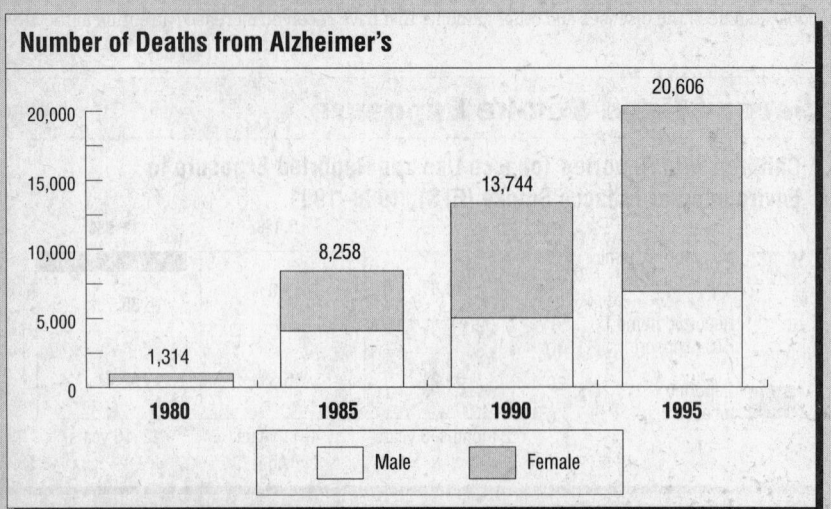

NOTE: The increase in deaths from Alzheimer's disease at least partly reflects improvements in reporting and diagnosis of the condition.
Source: Centers for Disease Control and Prevention, National Center for Health Statistics

The Dark Side of Sun Exposure

Melanoma Deaths and Death Rates* per 100,000 Population

Sex	Rates 1972–1974	Rates 1992–1994	Percent changes	Number of deaths 1974	Number of deaths 1994
Male	2.1	3.1	48%	2,201	4,117
Female	1.3	1.5	15	1,534	2,563

*Adjusted to the age distribution of the 1970 U.S. census population.
Source: American Cancer Society

Incidence and Cost of Uncured Disease in the U.S.

Uncured disease	Approximate 1995 incidence	Approximate 1995 economic cost (Billions)
Heart disease	60,340,000	$128
Cancer	1,359,000	104
Alzheimer's Disease	4,000,000	100
Diabetes	16,000,000	92
Arthritis	37,000,000	65
Depression	26,000,000*	44
Stroke	550,000	30
Osteoporosis	25,000,000	10

*Extrapolation based on 10.3 percent active prevalence of major depression in U.S. population.
Source: Pharmaceutical Research and Manufacturers of America

Slowing the Spread of Disease

Selected Disease Rates in the U.S.

Disease	1950	1960	1970	1980	1990	1991	1992	1993	1994	1995	1996
	Cases per 100,000 population										
Diphtheria	3.83	0.51	0.21	0.00	0.00	0.00	0.00	–	0.00	–	0.01
Hepatitis A	–	–	27.87	12.84	12.64	9.67	9.06	9.40	10.29	12.13	11.70
Hepatitis B	–	–	4.08	8.39	8.48	7.14	6.32	5.18	4.81	4.19	4.01
Mumps	–	–	55.55	3.86	2.17	1.72	1.03	0.66	0.60	0.35	0.29
Pertussis (whooping cough)	79.82	8.23	2.08	0.76	1.84	1.08	1.60	2.55	1.77	1.97	2.94
Poliomyelitis, total	22.02	1.77	0.02	0.00	0.00	0.00	0.00	0.00	0.00	0.00	0.01
Paralytic	–	1.40	0.02	0.00	0.00	0.00	0.00	0.00	0.00	0.00	0.01
Rubella (German measles)	–	–	27.75	1.72	0.45	0.56	0.06	0.07	0.09	0.05	0.10
Rubeola (measles)	211.01	245.42	23.23	5.96	11.17	3.82	0.88	0.12	0.37	0.12	0.20
Salmonellosis, excluding typhoid fever	–	3.85	10.84	14.88	19.54	19.10	16.04	16.15	16.64	17.66	17.15
Shigellosis	15.45	6.94	6.79	8.41	10.89	9.34	9.38	12.48	11.44	12.32	9.80
Tuberculosis	80.45	30.83	18.28	12.25	10.33	10.42	10.46	9.82	9.36	8.70	8.04
Sexually transmitted diseases											
Syphilis	146.02	68.78	45.26	30.51	54.30	51.00	44.20	39.30	31.40	26.40	20.20
Gonorrhea	192.50	145.40	297.22	445.10	278.00	247.10	196.70	172.00	165.10	149.40	124.00

Disease	1950	1960	1970	1980	1990	1991	1992	1993	1994	1995	1996
	Number of cases										
Diphtheria	5,796	918	435	3	4	5	4	–	2	–	2
Hepatitis A	–	–	56,797	29,087	31,441	24,378	23,112	24,238	29,796	31,582	31,032
Hepatitis B	–	–	8,310	19,015	21,102	18,003	16,126	13,361	12,517	10,805	10,637
Mumps	–	–	104,953	8,576	5,292	4,264	2,572	1,692	1,537	906	751
Pertussis (whooping cough)	120,718	14,809	4,249	1,730	4,570	2,719	4,083	6,586	4,617	5,137	7,796
Poliomyelitis, total	33,300	3,190	33	9	6	9	6	4	8	6	5
Paralytic	–	2,525	31	8	6	9	6	4	8	6	5
Rubella (German measles)	–	–	56,552	3,904	1,125	1,401	160	192	227	128	238
Rubeola (measles)	319,124	441,703	47,351	13,506	27,786	9,643	2,237	312	963	281	508
Salmonellosis, excluding typhoid fever	–	6,929	22,096	33,715	48,603	48,154	40,912	41,641	43,323	45,970	45,471
Shigellosis	23,367	12,487	13,845	19,041	27,077	23,548	23,931	32,198	29,769	32,080	25,978
Tuberculosis	121,742	55,494	37,137	27,749	25,701	26,283	26,673	25,287	24,361	22,860	21,337
Sexually transmitted diseases											
Syphilis	217,558	122,538	91,382	68,832	135,043	128,637	112,816	101,335	81,696	69,320	52,995
Gonorrhea	286,746	258,933	600,072	1,004,029	691,368	623,009	501,777	443,278	418,068	392,622	325,883

Source: Centers for Disease Control and Prevention

Selected Major Infectious Diseases Identified, 1975–1994

Year	Agent	Disease
1976	Cryptosporidium parvum	Acute enterocolitis
1977	Ebola virus	Ebola hemorrhagic fever
1977	Legionella pneumophila	Legionnaire's disease
1977	Hantaan virus	Hemorrhagic fever with renal syndrome (HFRS)
1980	Human T-cell lymphotropic virus	T-cell lymphoma leukemia
1981	Staphylococcus toxin	Toxic shock syndrome associated with tampon use
1982	Escherichia coli O157:H7	Hemorrhagic colitis; hemolytic uremic syndrome
1982	HTLV II	Hairy cell leukemia
1982	Borrelia burgdorferi	Lyme disease
1983	Human immunodeficiency virus (HIV)	Acquired immunodeficiency syndrome (AIDS)
1989	Ehrlichia chaffeensis	Human ehrlichiosis
1989	Hepatitis C	Parenterally transmitted non-A, non-B hepatitis
1991	Guanarito virus	Venezuelan hemorrhagic fever
1992	Bartonella	Cat-scratch disease; bacillary angiomatosis
1993	Hantavirus	Hantavirus pulmonary syndrome
1994	Sabia virus	Brazilian hemorrhagic fever

Source: Centers for Disease Control and Prevention

The State of Mental Health in America

Number of U.S. Adults With Mental Disorders, 1990*

Disorders	In a one-month period		In a one-year period	
	Number (millions)	Percent	Number (millions)	Percent
Any mental disorder and substance use disorder covered in survey	28.7	15.7%	51.3	28.1%
Any mental disorder except substance use disorders	23.7	13.0	40.4	22.1
Schizophrenia/schizophreniform disorders	1.3	0.7	2.0	1.1
Depressive (affective) disorders	9.5	5.2	17.4	9.5
Manic-depressive illness (Bipolar disorder)	1.1	0.6	2.2	1.2
Major depression	3.3	1.8	9.1	5.0
Dysthymia	6.0	3.3	9.9	5.4
Anxiety disorders	13.3	7.3	23.0	12.6
Phobia	11.5	6.3	19.9	10.9
Panic disorder	0.9	0.5	2.4	1.3
Obsessive-compulsive disorder	2.4	1.3	3.8	2.1
Somatization disorder**	0.2	0.1	0.4	0.2
Antisocial personality disorder	0.9	0.5	2.7	1.5
Severe cognitive impairment	3.1	1.7	4.9	2.7
Substance use disorders	6.9	3.8	17.3	9.5
Alcohol abuse/dependence	5.1	2.8	13.5	7.4
Drug abuse/dependence	2.4	1.3	5.7	3.1

*Number of affected adults is based on estimates of the U.S. resident population from the 1990 census of 182.6 million persons aged 18 and over. Some people have more than one mental disorder. Therefore, the numbers for each type of disorder, if added together, will be more than the total number for all individuals with mental disorders.

**Somatization disorder is a chronic psychiatric condition characterized by multiple physical complaints for which there is no apparent physical cause.

Source: National Institute of Mental Health

Accidental Deaths

Someone dies from an unintentional injury every six minutes, according to the National Safety Council. Here are the major types of accidents and the number of deaths in 1996:

Type of accident	Number of deaths	Percent change since 1995
Motor-vehicle accidents	43,300	–
Falls	14,100	4 %
Poisoning by solids and liquids	9,800	4
Drowning	3,900	-9
Fires, burns and deaths associated with fires	3,200	-16
Suffocation by ingested object	3,000	3
Firearms	1,400	17
Poisoning by gases and vapors	600	–
Other	14,100	–
Total	93,400	–

Source: National Safety Council

Household Hazards

The estimated number of deaths and injuries treated at hospital emergency rooms that were associated with the use of these consumer products.

Product group	Total injuries Oct. 1, 1996– Sept. 30, 1997	Total deaths Oct. 1, 1995– Sept. 30, 1996
Sports and recreational activities and equipment	3,853,295	1,286
Home structures and construction materials	3,083,776	395
Home furnishings and fixtures	1,903,978	878
Housewares	753,844	22
Personal use items	389,268	240
Packaging and containers for household products	327,621	82
Home workshop apparatus, tools and attachments	318,907	101
Yard and garden equipment	219,024	358
Miscellaneous	201,104	47
Toys	137,151	11
General household appliances	134,137	44
Space heating, cooling and ventilating appliances	125,531	155
Home and family maintenance products	115,734	48
Home communication, entertainment and hobby equipment	103,143	24
Child nursery equipment and supplies	86,428	53

Source: U.S. Consumer Product Safety Commission

Tipping the Scales

These are the weights at which people should enjoy the greatest longevity.

Height and Weight Tables for Men and Women According to Frame, Ages 25–59
(Weight in pounds, in indoor clothing*)

Height (in shoes)		Small frame	Medium frame	Large frame
Feet	Inches			
		Men		
5	2	128–134	131–141	138–150
5	3	130–136	133–143	140–153
5	4	132–138	135–145	142–156
5	5	134–140	137–148	144–160
5	6	136–142	139–151	146–164
5	7	138–145	142–154	149–168
5	8	140–148	145–157	152–172
5	9	142–151	148–160	155–176
5	10	144–154	151–163	158–180
5	11	146–157	154–166	161–184
6	0	149–160	157–170	164–188
6	1	152–164	160–174	168–192
6	2	155–168	164–178	172–197
6	3	158–172	167–182	176–202
6	4	162–176	171–187	181–207
		Women		
4	10	102–111	109–121	118–131
4	11	103–113	111–123	120–134
5	0	104–115	113–126	122–137
5	1	106–118	115–129	125–140
5	2	108–121	118–132	128–143
5	3	111–124	121–135	131–147
5	4	114–127	124–138	134–151
5	5	117–130	127–141	137–155
5	6	120–133	130–144	140–159
5	7	123–136	133–147	143–163
5	8	126–139	136–150	146–167
5	9	129–142	139–153	149–170
5	10	132–145	142–156	152–173
5	11	135–148	145–159	155–176
6	0	138–151	148–162	158–179

*Indoor clothing weighing 5 pounds for men and 3 pounds for women. Shoes with 1-inch heels.
Source: Metropolitan Life Insurance Co.

A More Ample America

Percentage of Adults Who Are Overweight

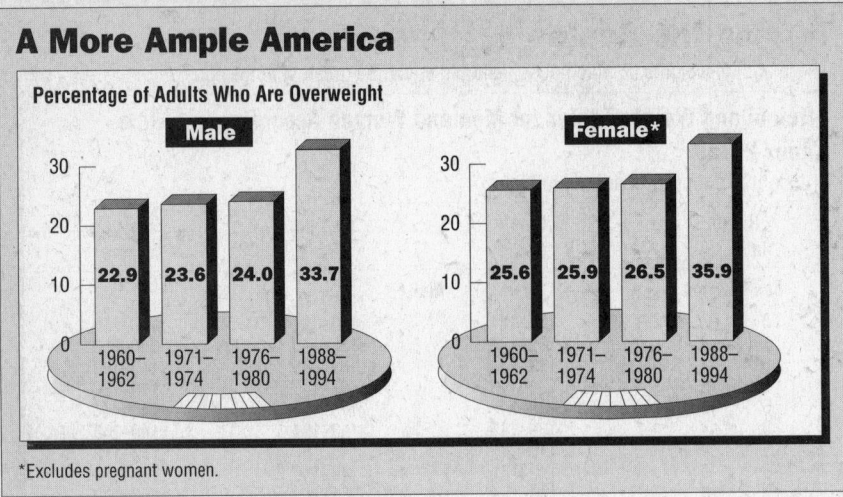

*Excludes pregnant women.

Fat City

Metropolitan Areas Ranked by Percentage of Adults Who Are Overweight

	City	Total %		City	Total %
1	New Orleans	37.55%	16	Portland	27.15%
2	Norfolk	33.94	17	Chicago	27.13
3	San Antonio	32.96	18	New York	27.05
4	Kansas City	31.66	19	Miami	26.95
5	Cleveland	31.50	20	Baltimore	26.43
6	Detroit	31.01	21	Boston	26.17
7	Columbus	30.75	22	Seattle	25.87
8	Cincinnati	30.71	23	Indianapolis	25.77
9	Pittsburgh	29.99	24	Atlanta	25.49
10	Houston	29.19	25	Los Angeles	25.22
11	Philadelphia	29.05	26	San Francisco	25.16
12	Milwaukee	28.79	27	Tampa	24.91
13	Buffalo	28.43	28	St. Louis	24.78
14	Sacramento	28.15	29	Phoenix	24.36
15	Dallas-Ft. Worth	27.46	30	Washington, DC	23.84

Source: Centers for Disease Control and Prevention, and Coalition for Excess Weight Risk Education

Cholesterol Count

Serum Cholesterol Levels Among Adults

	% of population with high serum cholesterol*				Mean serum cholesterol level, mg/dL			
	1960–1962	1971–1974	1976–1980	1988–1994	1960–1962	1971–1974	1976–1980	1988–1994
Male								
20–34 years	15.1	12.4	11.9	8.2	198	194	192	186
35–44 years	33.9	31.8	27.9	19.4	227	221	217	206
45–54 years	39.2	37.5	36.9	26.6	231	229	227	216
55–64 years	41.6	36.2	36.8	28.0	233	229	229	216
65–74 years	38.0	34.7	31.7	21.9	230	226	221	212
75 years and over	–	–	–	20.4	–	–	–	205
Female								
20–34 years	12.4	10.9	9.8	7.3	194	191	189	184
35–44 years	23.1	19.3	20.7	12.3	214	207	207	195
45–54 years	46.9	38.7	40.5	26.7	237	232	232	217
55–64 years	70.1	53.1	52.9	40.9	262	245	249	235
65–74 years	68.5	57.7	51.6	41.3	266	250	246	233
75 years and over	–	–	–	38.2	–	–	–	229

*High serum cholesterol is defined as greater than or equal to 240 mg/dL.
Source: Centers for Disease Control and Prevention, National Center for Health Statistics

Fitness Activities

Adults Reporting Participation in Selected Common Physical Activities in the Prior 2 Weeks, by Sex and Age

(Percentage)

Activity category	Males	Females	Activity category	Males	Females
Walking for exercise	39.4	48.3	Bowling	4.7	3.6
Gardening or yard work	34.2	25.1	Golf	8.2	1.8
Stretching exercises	25.0	26.0	Baseball or softball	5.8	1.4
Weight lifting or other exercise to increase muscle strength	20.0	8.8	Handball, racquetball, or squash	2.7	0.5
			Skiing	0.9	0.5
Jogging or running	12.8	5.7	Cross-country skiing	0.4	0.4
Aerobics or aerobic dance	2.8	11.1	Water skiing	0.7	0.4
Riding a bicycle or exercise bike	16.2	14.6	Basketball	10.5	1.5
			Volleyball	3.1	1.8
Stair climbing	9.9	11.6	Soccer	1.4	0.4
Swimming for exercise	6.9	6.2	Football	2.7	0.3
Tennis	3.5	2.0	Other sports	7.3	4.1

Young People Reporting Participation in Selected Physical Activities in the Prior Week

(Percentage)

Activity	Males	Females
Aerobics or dancing	22.6	53.9
Baseball, softball, or Frisbee	27.2	17.5
Basketball, football, or soccer	61.7	29.7
Housecleaning or yardwork (30 minutes or more)	78.1	87.5
Running, jogging, or swimming	57.6	53.0
Skating, skiing, or skateboarding	15.9	10.6
Tennis, racquetball, or squash	11.7	9.3

Source: Centers for Disease Control and Prevention, National Center for Health Statistics

America's Addictions

Percentage of People Age 12 and Older Reporting Past Month Use of Alcohol or Any Illicit Drug, by Race and Sex, 1997

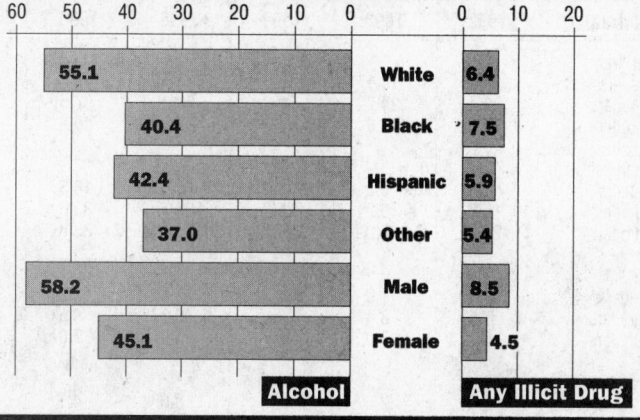

	Alcohol	Any Illicit Drug
White	55.1	6.4
Black	40.4	7.5
Hispanic	42.4	5.9
Other	37.0	5.4
Male	58.2	8.5
Female	45.1	4.5

Estimated Past-Year Users of Illicit Drugs and Alcohol in the U.S. Age 12 and Older and Their Percentage of the Population

(Numbers in thousands)

Drug	1985 No.	1985 %	1990 No.	1990 %	1995 No.	1995 %	1996 No.	1996 %	1997 No.	1997 %
Any illicit drug*	31,488	16.3	23,449	11.7	22,662	10.7	23,182	10.8	24,189	11.2
Marijuana and hashish	26,145	13.6	18,931	9.4	17,755	8.4	18,398	8.6	19,446	9.0
Cocaine	9,839	5.1	5,442	2.7	3,664	1.7	4,033	1.9	4,169	1.9
Crack	–	–	1,463	0.7	1,018	0.5	1,375	0.6	1,375	0.6
Inhalants	2,657	1.4	2,212	1.1	2,308	1.1	2,427	1.1	2,329	1.1
Hallucinogens	3,198	1.7	2,350	1.2	3,416	1.6	3,602	1.7	4,063	1.9
PCP	455	0.2	136	0.1	322	0.2	382	0.2	369	0.2
LSD	–	–	–	–	2,108	1.0	2,104	1.0	1,956	0.9
Heroin	347	0.2	443	0.2	428	0.2	455	0.2	597	0.3
Nonmedical use of any psychotherapeutic**	11,988	6.2	6,878	3.4	6,166	2.9	6,652	3.1	6,112	2.8
Stimulants	5,637	2.9	2,319	1.2	1,656	0.8	1,896	0.9	1,687	0.8
Sedatives	2,209	1.1	991	0.5	666	0.3	678	0.3	638	0.3
Tranquilizers	6,181	3.2	2,376	1.2	2,210	1.0	2,430	1.1	2,122	1.0
Analgesics	6,921	3.6	4,986	2.5	4,102	1.9	4,510	2.1	4,210	1.9
Alcohol	140,394	72.9	132,859	66.0	138,314	65.4	138,912	64.9	138,500	64.1

*Any illicit drug indicates use at least once of marijuana or hashish, cocaine (including crack), inhalants, hallucinogens (including PCP and LSD), heroin, or any prescription-type psychotherapeutic used nonmedically.
**Nonmedical use of any prescription-type stimulant, sedative, tranquilizer, or analgesic; does not include over-the-counter drugs.
Source: Substance Abuse and Mental Health Services Administration

Youth and Addictive Substances

Percentages of Eighth, Tenth, and Twelfth Graders Who Used Drugs or Consumed Alcohol in the Past Year

Type of drug	1992	1993	1994	1995	1996	1997
Any illicit drug						
8th graders	12.9	15.1	18.5	21.4	23.6	22.1
10th graders	20.4	24.7	30.0	33.3	37.5	38.5
12th graders	27.1	31.0	35.8	39.0	40.2	42.4
Marijuana/hashish						
8th graders	7.2	9.2	13.0	15.8	18.3	17.7
10th graders	15.2	19.2	25.2	28.7	33.6	34.8
12th graders	21.9	26.0	30.7	34.7	35.8	38.5
Inhalants						
8th graders	9.5	11.0	11.7	12.8	12.2	11.8
10th graders	7.5	8.4	9.1	9.6	9.5	8.7
12th graders	6.2	7.0	7.7	8.0	7.6	6.7
Hallucinogens						
8th graders	2.5	2.6	2.7	3.6	4.1	3.7
10th graders	4.3	4.7	5.8	7.2	7.8	7.6
12th graders	5.9	7.4	7.6	9.3	10.1	9.8
Cocaine						
8th graders	1.5	1.7	2.1	2.6	3.0	2.8
10th graders	1.9	2.1	2.8	3.5	4.2	4.7
12th graders	3.1	3.3	3.6	4.0	4.9	5.5
Heroin						
8th graders	0.7	0.7	1.2	1.4	1.6	1.3
10th graders	0.6	0.7	0.9	1.1	1.2	1.4
12th graders	0.6	0.5	0.6	1.1	1.0	1.2
Stimulants						
8th graders	6.5	7.2	7.9	8.7	9.1	8.1
10th graders	8.2	9.6	10.2	11.9	12.4	12.1
12th graders	7.1	8.4	9.4	9.3	9.5	10.2
Alcohol*						
8th graders	53.7	45.4	46.8	45.3	46.5	45.5
10th graders	70.2	63.4	63.9	63.5	65.0	65.2
12th graders	76.8	72.7	73.0	73.7	72.5	74.8
Been drunk						
8th graders	18.3	18.2	18.2	18.4	19.8	18.4
10th graders	37.0	37.8	38.0	38.5	40.1	40.7
12th graders	50.3	49.6	51.7	52.5	51.9	53.2

Note: Two of the major sources of data on drug and alcohol abuse conduct different types of surveys and produce results that are not comparable. The University of Michigan's Monitoring the Future Study focuses on eighth, tenth, and twelfth graders, while the Substance Abuse and Mental Health Services Administration's National Household Survey on Drug Abuse includes a sample of all Americans, age twelve and older.

*In 1993, the survey was changed to indicate that a "drink" meant "more than a few sips."

Source: The Monitoring the Future Study, University of Michigan

Drugs and Drinking on the Job

Businesses and Professions with the Highest and Lowest Rates of Illicit Drug Use, Full-time Workers, Ages 18–49, 1991–1993

Ten Highest Rates of Illicit Drug Use

Rank	Industry	Percentage of workers reporting drug use
1	Eating and Drinking Places	16.3
2	Furniture and Appliance Retail Sales	14.4
3	Entertainment and Recreation	13.7
4	Advertising, Business Management, and Consulting	13.1
5	Telegraph and Miscellaneous Communications	12.3
6	Construction	12.2
7	Automotive Service and Repair	12.0
8	Other Business and Repair Services	11.9
9	Printing and Publishing	11.7
10	Auto Supply and Gas Stations	11.2

Ten Lowest Rates of Illicit Drug Use

Rank	Industry	Percentage of workers reporting drug use
1	Child-Care Services	1.3
2	Physicians, Dentists, Chiropractors Offices	1.5
3	Administration of Programs	1.8
4	Elementary and Secondary Schools	2.2
5	Justice and Public Order	2.2
6	Rubber and Plastic Products	2.5
7	Air Transportation	3.2
8	National Security	3.4
9	Telephone	3.4
10	Agricultural	3.6
	Chemical Products	3.6
	Colleges and Universities	3.6

Businesses and Professions with the Highest and Lowest Rates of Heavy Alcohol Use, Full-time Workers, Ages 18–49, 1991–1993

Ten Highest Rates of Heavy Alcohol Use

Rank	Industry	Percentage of workers reporting heavy alcohol use
1	Computer and Data Processing	16.2
2	Eating and Drinking Places	15.4
3	Construction	13.4
4	Auto Supply and Gas Stations	13.2
5	Lumber and Wood Products	12.0
6	Automotive Service and Repair	11.4
7	Horticultural	10.8
8	Electrical Machinery	10.0
9	Wholesale Grocery	9.8
10	Hotel and Motel	9.6

Ten Lowest Rates of Heavy Alcohol Use

Rank	Industry	Percentage of workers reporting heavy alcohol use
1	Physicians, Dentists, Chiropractors Offices	0.1
2	Professional and Related Services, miscellaneous	0.6
3	Child-Care Services	0.9
4	Apparel and Shoe Stores	1.5
5	Hospitals	2.1
6	Accounting and Bookkeeping	2.3
7	Electrical Machinery	2.7
8	Elementary and Secondary Schools	2.7
9	Private Household	2.8
10	Legal Services	3.0

Source: Substance Abuse and Mental Health Services Administration

Smoker Profile

Percentage of People Over Age 18 Who Smoke Cigarettes, by Race and Sex

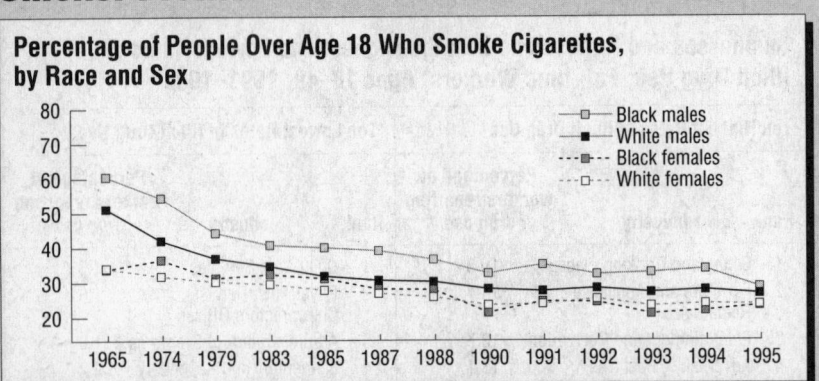

Percentage of People Over Age 18 Who Smoke, by Age and Sex

	1965	1974	1983	1985	1988	1990	1991	1992	1993	1994	1995
All persons											
18 years and older	42.4	37.1	32.1	30.1	28.1	25.5	25.6	26.5	25.0	25.5	24.7
Males											
18 years and older	51.9	43.1	35.1	32.6	30.8	28.4	28.1	28.6	27.7	28.2	27.0
18–24 years	54.1	42.1	32.9	28.0	25.5	26.6	23.5	28.0	28.8	29.8	27.8
25–34 years	60.7	50.5	38.8	38.2	36.2	31.6	32.8	32.8	30.2	31.4	29.5
35–44 years	58.2	51.0	41.0	37.6	36.5	34.5	33.1	32.9	32.0	33.2	31.5
45–64 years	51.9	42.6	35.9	33.4	31.3	29.3	29.3	28.6	29.2	28.3	27.1
65 years and older	28.5	24.8	22.0	19.6	18.0	14.6	15.1	16.1	13.5	13.2	14.9
Females											
18 years and older	33.9	32.1	29.5	27.9	25.7	22.8	23.5	24.6	22.5	23.1	22.6
18–24 years	38.1	34.1	35.5	30.4	26.3	22.5	22.4	24.9	22.9	25.2	21.8
25–34 years	43.7	38.8	32.6	32.0	31.3	28.2	28.4	30.1	27.3	28.8	26.4
35–44 years	43.7	39.8	33.8	31.5	27.8	24.8	27.6	27.3	27.4	26.8	27.1
45–64 years	32.0	33.4	31.0	29.9	27.7	24.8	24.6	26.1	23.0	22.8	24.0
65 years and older	9.6	12.0	13.1	13.5	12.8	11.5	12.0	12.4	10.5	11.1	11.5

Percentage of People Age 25 and Over Who Smoke, by Level of Education

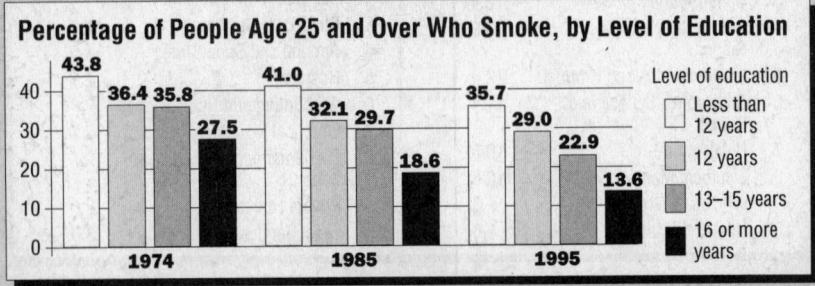

Note: Data for 1992 and beyond are not strictly comparable with data for earlier years.
Sources: Centers for Disease Control and Prevention, National Center for Health Statistics

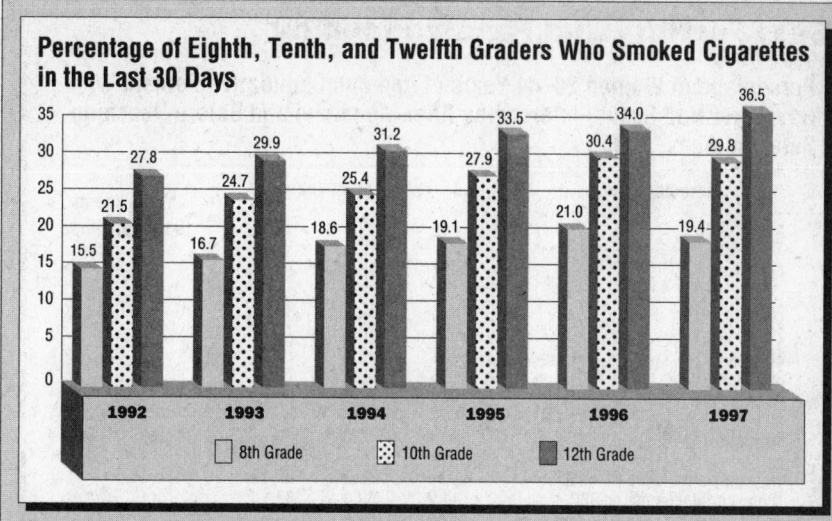

Percentage of Eighth, Tenth, and Twelfth Graders Who Smoked Cigarettes in the Last 30 Days

Source: The Monitoring the Future Study, University of Michigan

Look, Ma, No Cavities!

Not quite, but more people are getting preventive dental care, such as cleanings and fluoride treatments, and a smaller percentage need fillings and tooth extractions.

Percentage of Patients Receiving Selected Dental Services from Private Practitioners

Procedure	1959	1969	1979	1990
Oral examination	20.1%	27.8%	30.1%	42.8%
X-rays	18.1	23.9	21.0	25.3
Prophylaxis (teeth cleaning)	19.9	25.5	24.9	38.6
Fluoride treatment	0.9	4.0	6.8	9.8
Amalgam, 1 surface (filling)	20.1	15.9	8.5	5.3
Amalgam, 2 surface (filling)	20.6	16.4	9.6	7.2
Crown	1.6	2.9	5.2	5.3
Root canal	1.7	2.9	3.2	2.6
Extraction	13.0	9.8	5.4	4.9
Periodontal treatment	3.2	2.5	3.3	4.1
Orthodontic treatment	3.7	6.5	6.8	3.6

Source: American Dental Association

Sex, Fertility and Family Planning

Percentage of Women 20–44 Years of Age and Cumulative Percent Who Have Ever Had Sexual Intercourse After Menarche and Before Reaching Selected Ages, 1995

Characteristic	Exact age in years			Mean age at first intercourse
Age	**15**	**18**	**20**	
All women	9.2%	52.3%	75.0%	17.3
20–24 years	13.6	62.2	80.2	16.6
25–29 years	10.9	54.9	75.0	17.5
30–34 years	10.1	53.1	75.8	17.8
35–39 years	7.6	52.2	75.2	18.0
40–44 years	4.6	40.6	69.2	18.6
Education				
No high school diploma or GED	20.4%	73.0%	87.1%	16.5
High school diploma or GED	11.2	59.8	83.1	17.3
Some college, no Bachelor's degree	7.0	49.5	73.6	17.9
Bachelor's degree or higher	2.2	31.7	56.6	19.3
Race and Hispanic origin				
Hispanic	7.6%	42.2%	66.7%	18.4
Non-Hispanic white	8.3	52.8	76.0	17.7
Non-Hispanic black	16.1	65.9	85.6	16.8
Non-Hispanic other	8.1	28.4	48.1	20.0

Source: Centers for Disease Control and Prevention, National Center for Health Statistics

Number of Currently Married Women 15–44 Years of Age and Percent Distribution by Infertility Status, According to Selected Characteristics, 1995

Characteristic	Surgically sterile	Infertile	Fecund
		Percent distribution	
All women	41.0%	7.1%	52.0%
Age			
15–24 years	6.2	4.4	89.4
25–34 years	27.3	6.6	66.1
35–44 years	59.1	8.0	32.9
0 births			
15–44 years	13.1	17.1	69.8
15–24 years	2.5	6.0	91.6
25–34 years	6.5	13.5	80.0
35–44 years	31.1	30.3	38.6
1 or more births			
15–44 years	47.6	4.7	47.7
15–24 years	8.8	3.3	87.8
25–34 years	33.5	4.5	62.0
35–44 years	62.9	5.0	32.2

Number of Women 15–44 Years of Age, Percent Who Have Received Any Infertility Services, and Percent Who Have Ever Received the Specified Infertility Services, by Selected Characteristics, 1995

Characteristic	Any services[4]	Advice	Tests on woman or man	Ovulation drugs	Surgery or treatment for blocked tubes	Assisted reproductive technology[5]
All women	15.4%	6.4%	4.2%	3.0%	1.5%	1.0%
Age						
15–24 years	4.4	1.1	0.2	0.3	0.1	0.0
25–34 years	17.1	6.3	3.7	3.1	1.2	0.8
35–44 years	22.9	10.9	8.1	5.2	2.9	2.1
0 births	6.4	4.6	3.7	2.2	1.1	1.2
15–24 years	1.2	0.5	0.2	0.2	0.1	0.1
25–34 years	8.7	6.5	4.6	3.0	1.0	1.1
35–44 years	20.7	15.5	14.5	8.0	4.8	5.3
1 or more births	21.8	7.7	4.6	3.6	1.8	0.9
15–24 years	16.1	3.3	0.3	0.6	0.5	–
25–34 years	21.5	6.2	3.1	3.1	1.3	0.6
35–44 years	23.4	9.8	6.7	4.6	2.4	1.4

[1]Mean ages are based only on women who ever had intercourse after menarche.
[2]Limited to women 22–44 years of age at time of interview.
[3]GED is general equivalency dilpoma.
[4]Includes services to help get pregnant as well as to prevent miscarriages.
[5]Includes artificial insemination, in vitro fertilization (IVF), gamete intrafallopian transfer (GIFT), and other techniques not shown separately.
Source: Centers for Disease Control and Prevention, National Center for Health Statistics

Infertility Treatment

The number of live deliveries through assisted reproductive technology, such as in-vitro fertilization, has grown steadily in the 1990s.

Year	Number of live deliveries
1989	3,472
1990	3,951
1991	5,699
1992	7,355
1993	8,741
1994	9,573
1995	11,631

Source: American Society for Reproductive Medicine

Multiple Births

The number of babies born as twins, triplets, and other multiples has increased rapidly both because more women are having children after they reach the age of 30, when chances of such births increase, and because more are using fertility drugs.

Year	Twins	Triplets	Quads	Quintuplets and larger multiples
1989	90,118	2,529	229	40
1990	93,865	2,830	185	13
1991	94,779	3,121	203	22
1992	95,372	3,547	310	26
1993	96,445	3,834	277	57
1994	97,064	4,233	315	46
1995	96,736	4,551	365	57
1996	100,750	5,298	560	81

Source: National Center for Health Statistics

Birth Control

Nearly 65% of women 15 to 44 years of age used contraception in 1995, up from about 56% in 1982. Here are the percentages of women using contraception who choose these methods:

	1982	1988	1990	1995
Female sterilization	23.2	27.5	29.5	27.7
Male sterilization	10.9	11.7	12.6	10.9
Birth control pill	28.0	30.7	28.5	26.9
Intrauterine device	7.1	2.0	1.4	0.8
Diaphragm	8.1	5.7	2.8	1.9
Condom	12.0	14.6	17.7	20.4

Source: National Center for Health Statistics

Number of Reported Abortions, Rate per 1,000 Women Aged 15–44 and Ratio of Abortions per 100 Pregnancies Ending in Abortions or Live Births

Year	Abortions (in 000s)	Rate	Ratio	Year	Abortions (in 000s)	Rate	Ratio
1973	744.6	16.3	19.3	1985	1,588.6	28.0	29.7
1974	898.6	19.3	22.0	1986	(1,574.0)	(27.4)	(29.4)
1975	1,034.2	21.7	24.9	1987	1,559.1	26.9	28.8
1976	1,179.3	24.2	26.5	1988	1,590.8	27.3	28.6
1977	1,316.7	26.4	28.6	1989	(1,566.9)	(26.8)	(27.5)
1978	1,409.6	27.7	29.2	1990	(1,608.6)	(27.4)	(28.0)
1979	1,497.7	28.8	29.6	1991	1,556.5	26.3	27.4
1980	1,553.9	29.3	30.0	1992	1,528.9	25.9	27.5
1981	1,577.3	29.3	30.1	1993*	1,500.0	25.4	27.4
1982	1,573.9	28.8	30.0	1994*	1,430.0	24.1	26.7
1983	(1,575.0)	(28.5)	(30.4)	1995	1,363.7	22.9	26.0
1984	1,577.2	28.1	29.7				

Note: Figures in parentheses are estimated by interpolation of numbers of abortions.
*Estimate.
Source: Alan Guttmacher Institute

When Women Have Abortions (In weeks)

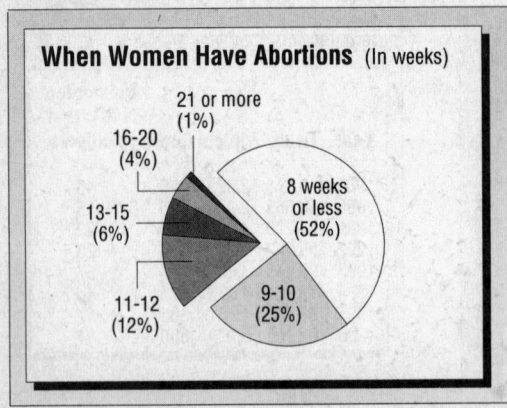

21 or more (1%)
16-20 (4%)
13-15 (6%)
11-12 (12%)
9-10 (25%)
8 weeks or less (52%)

Education

Competition results in better-running cars and lower airfares. Could it work the same magic on America's imploding public schools?

With public-school funding soaring and performance woeful, competition in the form of school vouchers is getting a hard look. Congress passed its first-ever voucher plan in 1998, a small program in the Washington D.C. schools that President Clinton quickly vetoed. Voucher bills were introduced in 10 state legislatures. The Supreme Court is widely expected to hear a voucher case during its 1998-1999 session, with a ruling likely to decide whether the idea withers or spreads. And perhaps most tellingly, opinion polls for the first time show a majority of the public in favor of some sort of vouchers.

The idea of vouchers, sort of a government-issued ticket good for a year's education, has been around since the economist Milton Friedman proposed it in 1955. Let parents choose where they want to send their children, the theory goes, and the good schools will flourish; the others will close for lack of business—and deservedly so.

Voucher opponents, most notably the teachers' unions, say vouchers would bleed the public schools of money and the best students, just when they're most in need of both. Public education would become more segregated, a last refuge instead of a common experience, they contend.

Voucher proponents counter that public-school spending has doubled in the past decade, to an average $5,400 per child nationwide, and meanwhile, student performance by almost every measure remains woeful. "Maybe we'll make some mistakes, but if we don't try something new, we won't make much headway," says Paul Peterson, a Harvard University professor and voucher proponent.

Only Milwaukee and Cleveland have ever proposed using public funds for vouchers, taking money they would have spent educating a child in their public schools and using it instead to pay tuition at a private school or a public school in a better-performing district. Both of those projects have been in court since they were announced, with opponents contending that they violate the Constitu-

tional separation of church and state by including religious schools. A Wisconsin Supreme Court decision in June cleared Milwaukee's plan, but both sides in the argument have asked the Supreme Court to finally decide the matter.

Meanwhile, about 60 privately funded voucher plans have sprung up around the country, most funded by a loose national organization called the Children's Educational Opportunity Foundation, or CEO, which says it has awarded over $50 million in vouchers since 1991. James Leininger, a San Antonio physician-turned-entrepreneur, says he got involved with CEO when he realized that most of the people asking for jobs with his company (it makes high-tech hospital beds) couldn't read well enough to fill out the application blank. Now he's putting up much of the money for a 10-year, $50 million experiment that alone in the United States is offering vouchers to almost every child in an entire district. "I heard about vouchers and I said, 'that is the answer,'" he remembers.

Whether vouchers really are the answer is a long way from settled. Only the eight-year-old Milwaukee project has been around long enough to compare the test results of children who got vouchers and those who didn't. But three studies, conducted by researchers using the same test data, came to three different conclusions. "You can argue that vouchers work and that vouchers don't work," says Isabel Sawhill, a fellow at the Brookings Institution. "We just don't know for sure."

That's where Mr. Leininger's San Antonio project comes in. Six years ago, he and a group of other Texas businessmen began offering scholarships to low-income families that felt trapped in their low performing public schools. But the scholarships were too scattered to have much impact on even one school, much less to test whether vouchers could leverage change in a whole school district.

So, the Leininger group singled out the Edgewood Independent School District, one of 17 districts in San Antonio, and offered a voucher to every low-income family. With a 93 percent poverty rate, and an average family income of just $16,000, that means almost every family in a 14.2 square mile neighborhood is eligible.

Overwhelmingly Hispanic, wedged between a freeway and an air force base on the western edge of town, Edgewood is a neighborhood of tiny houses, rattly cars, shuttered storefronts and gritty businesses. By many measures, the schools are as woeful as the neighborhood. Last year, only a third of the eighth graders passed all five standardized tests that Texas requires its public school students take. SAT college-entrance scores were a limp 839 out of 1,600—154 points

below the state average. Dropout rates were more than double the state average. And for this, the district spent $5,852 per student.

The CEO offer rocked Edgewood. Eleven percent of the district's 14,000 students applied; 700 eventually left for 53 other schools. Five new private schools opened. But Edgewood is a district on the way up, which makes the voucher offer more complicated. Five years ago, Edgewood set about turning itself around. It opened math and technology magnet schools, and launched advanced-placement classes. Schools were rebuilt, curricu-

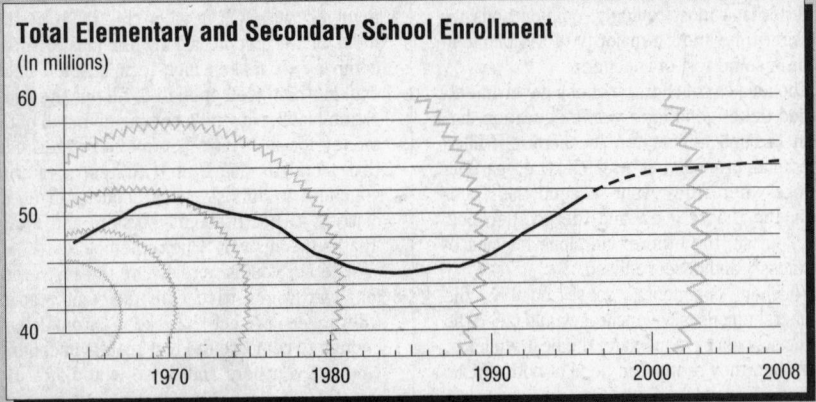

Baby Boom Echo

The baby-boom generation's children have caused a resurgence in elementary and secondary school enrollment that will continue into the 21st century.

Total Elementary and Secondary School Enrollment
(In millions)

Elementary and Secondary School Enrollment
(In thousands)

Year	Total	Public	Private*	Year	Total	Public	Private*
1964	47,716	41,416	6,300	1990	46,448	41,217	5,232
1966	49,239	43,039	6,200	1992	48,198	42,823	5,375
1968	50,744	44,944	5,800	1993	48,936	43,465	5,471
1970	51,257	45,894	5,363	1994	49,707	44,111	5,596
1972	50,726	45,726	5,000	1995	50,540	44,840	5,700
1974	50,073	45,073	5,000		Projected		
1976	49,478	44,311	5,167				
1978	47,637	42,551	5,086	1996	51,413	45,630	5,783
1980	46,208	40,877	5,331	1997	52,175	46,308	5,867
1982	45,166	39,566	5,600	1998	52,718	46,792	5,927
1984	44,908	39,208	5,700	1999	53,112	47,143	5,970
1986	45,205	39,753	5,452	2000	53,445	47,439	6,006
1988	45,430	40,189	5,241	2008	54,268	48,201	6,067

*Beginning in fall 1980, data include estimates for an expanded universe of private schools.
Source: U.S. Education Department

School Enrollment Growth

Fifteen States with the Largest Projected Enrollment Increases in Public Elementary and Secondary Schools: Fall 1998 to Fall 2008

State	Projected enrollment (In thousands)		Number of additional students, 1998 to 2008
	1998	2008	
California	5,961	6,854	893
Texas	3,967	4,343	376
Georgia	1,395	1,505	110
Arizona	828	928	100
Virginia	1,128	1,190	62
Utah	489	544	55
New Mexico	351	393	42
North Carolina	1,268	1,310	42
Tennessee	938	978	40
Colorado	696	724	28
Alabama	761	789	28
Hawaii	204	231	27
Idaho	256	282	26
South Carolina	664	688	24
Washington	998	1,021	23

Fifteen States with the Largest Projected Percent Increases in Public Elementary and Secondary Enrollment: Fall 1998 to Fall 2008

State	Projected enrollment (In thousands)		Percent change, 1998 to 2008
	1998	2008	
California	5,961	6,854	15.0
Hawaii	204	231	13.2
Arizona	828	928	12.1
New Mexico	351	393	12.0
Utah	489	544	11.2
Alaska	132	146	10.6
Idaho	256	282	10.2
Texas	3,967	4,343	9.5
Wyoming	98	106	8.2
Georgia	1,395	1,505	7.9
Virginia	1,128	1,190	5.5
Delaware	114	119	4.4
Tennessee	938	978	4.3
Colorado	696	724	4.0
Alabama	761	789	3.7

Source: U.S. Education Department

lums rewritten, teachers retrained. Edgewood still lags the rest of the state, but 2 1/2 times as many eighth-graders passed their math exams last year as in 1993. Dropout rates have been cut in half; SATs are up 134 points. And perhaps in consequence, parent participation, a key to how well children do in school, is soaring.

Edgewood's superintendent, Dolores Munoz, says all that headway is threatened by the vouchers, though. That's because Edgewood gets most of its money from state coffers, not local taxes, and Texas funding depends on how many students enroll. Between the voucher students and the down-sizing at nearby Kelly

Taking Attendance in Catholic Schools

Enrollment in Catholic schools reversed course in the 1990s, ending about 25 years of decline. At the same time, non-Catholics account for a growing share of the students.

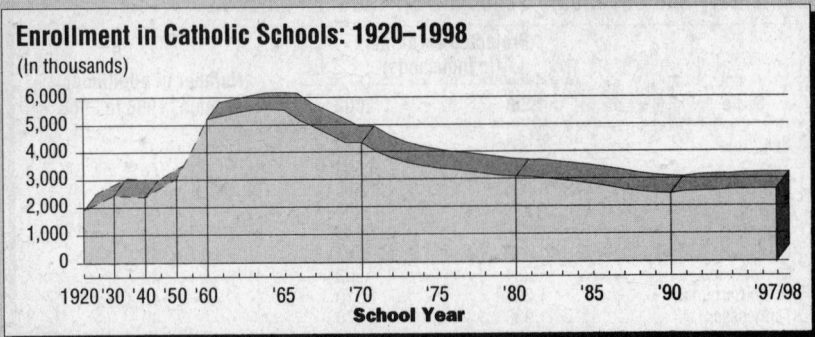

Enrollment in Catholic Schools: 1920–1998
(In thousands)

Enrollment in Catholic Schools

School year	Total enrollment	School year	Total enrollment	School year	Total enrollment
1920	1,926,000	1970–1971	4,363,000	1992–1993	2,567,630
1930	2,465,000	1975–1976	3,415,000	1993–1994	2,576,845
1940	2,396,000	1980–1981	3,106,000	1994–1995	2,618,567
1950	3,067,000	1985–1986	2,821,000	1995–1996	2,635,218
1960	5,253,000	1990–1991	2,475,439	1996–1997	2,645,462
1965	5,574,000	1991–1992	2,550,863	1997–1998	2,648,859

Source: National Catholic Educational Association

Air Force Base, Dr. Munoz expects to lose $5.5 million from her $83 million budget.

That means a plan to extend pre-kindergarten to all three-year-olds will be dropped, computer purchases may be cut, and advanced-placement classes may end, she says. CEO's "intent wasn't to break our district, but it may be looking like that's what it does," she says. Mr. Leininger counters that if Edgewood "responds the same way as a business" to the competition, "the schools will be stronger and better."

That's a challenge that extends to San Antonio's 100 or so private schools as well. The private schools already were full when CEO made its offer, and classes in some Catholic schools have as many as 35 children—half again as many students as Texas allows in its public schools. CEO's scholarships pay up to $4,000 per child in tuition—more than enough to cover the costs at most private schools, but only half what San Antonio's best schools charge. Moreover, private schools can pick and choose their students, refusing children who perform badly on entrance exams or who have physical and learning disabilities.

So, of the 900 Edgewood children who eventually qualified for CEO scholarships—that is, they lived in the district and met federal poverty definitions—200 still hadn't enrolled in private schools a month after classes began. CEO concedes that many of them just couldn't get in.

To meet the growing demand, new schools sprang up. As part of its urban outreach program, for example, a church in San Antonio's northern suburbs is opening the Family Faith Academy with spaces for about 45 children in a converted roadside bar. Family Faith says it may use Texas' standardized tests to measure student performance, but that its curriculum will be its own—Christian and Bible based.

Texas requires that its public schools

Public-School Teacher Salaries

Average Salaries of Public-School Teachers, 1996–97

State	Salary	State	Salary	State	Salary
Alaska	$50,647	Minnesota	$38,281	Missouri	$33,143
Connecticut	50,426	Washington	37,860	Texas	33,038
New Jersey	49,349	Nevada	37,340	South Carolina	32,830
Michigan	48,238	Vermont	37,200	Alabama	32,549
New York	48,000	Colorado	36,271	Idaho	31,818
Pennsylvania	47,147	New Hampshire	36,029	Nebraska	31,768
District of Columbia	45,012	Hawaii	35,842	Utah	31,750
Massachusetts	43,806	Virginia	35,837	Wyoming	31,721
California	43,474	Kansas	35,802	North Carolina	31,286
Rhode Island	43,019	Georgia	35,596	Oklahoma	30,369
Illinois	42,125	Tennessee	34,222	Arkansas	30,319
Delaware	41,436	Florida	33,889	Montana	29,958
Maryland	41,148	Kentucky	33,797	New Mexico	29,685
Oregon	40,960	Maine	33,676	Louisiana	28,347
Wisconsin	39,057	Arizona	33,350	Mississippi	27,720
Indiana	38,876	Iowa	33,272	North Dakota	27,711
Ohio	38,831	West Virginia	33,257	South Dakota	26,764

Source: National Education Association

follow a statewide outline to teach math, science, English and social studies. It also short lists textbooks, certifies teachers and rates schools. But Texas exempts its 2,700 private schools from all regulations, and doesn't even require that they be accredited. So, also among the start-ups is Sword of the Lord Christian Academy, which notified CEO it will begin taking students mid-year. But at the address CEO gives for Sword of the Lord, there's only a tumbledown cottage with trash cans in the front yard, old cars in the back, and a poster reading "Property of Jesus Christ" across the door.

CEO only says that it will be up to parents to sort out the worthy schools from the weak, and indeed, its chief backer, Mr. Leininger, uses the language of business to talk about the schools. He speaks of parents as consumers, enrollment as market share, curriculum as a product, competition as an incentive to improve.

Certainly, competition already is showing results in the public schools. To stanch its enrollment decline, Edgewood opened a fine-arts academy that it hopes will attract students from other school districts, and is telling parents from other neighborhoods that it will accept transfers.

Harvard's Mr. Peterson will track the changes in Edgewood's public and private schools as the experiment moves ahead—everything from how clean the schools are to how happy the parents are. But he says it will be at least three years before he can reliably measure any differences. Whether the market works as powerfully on schools as its proponents say it will, is still far from clear.

June Kronholz

Classroom Costs

As School Revenues Climb...
Revenues for Public Elementary and Secondary Schools
(In billions)

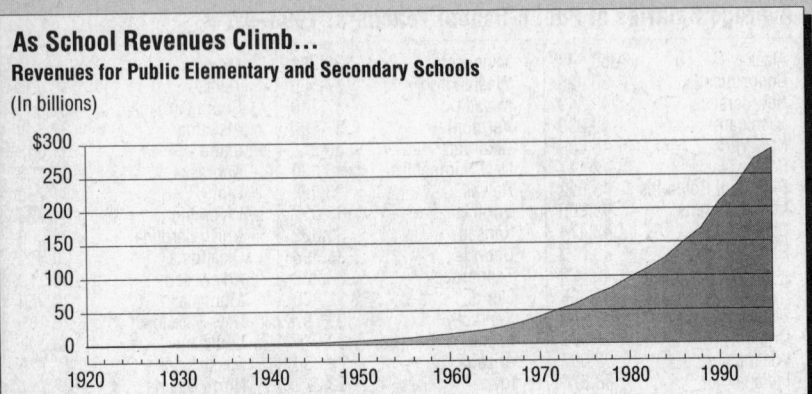

School Year

...the State Share Is Rising
Percent Distribution of Revenues

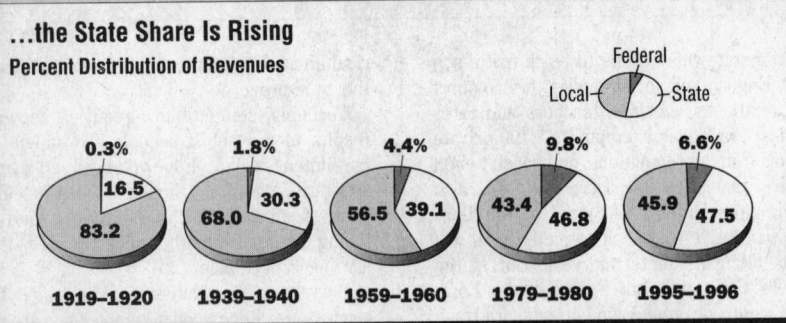

Total Expenditures for Public Elementary and Secondary Education
(In thousands)

School year	Total expenditures	Expenditure per pupil	
		Current $	Constant 1997–98 $
1919–20	$ 1,036,151	$64	$ 543
1929–30	2,316,790	108	1,025
1939–40	2,344,049	106	1,224
1949–50	5,837,643	260	1,778
1959–60	15,613,255	471	2,593
1969–70	40,683,429	955	4,089
1979–80	95,961,561	2,491	5,189
1989–90	212,473,108	5,550	7,070
1990–91	229,429,715	5,885	7,108
1991–92	241,062,373	6,074	7,109
1992–93	252,934,872	6,281	7,120
1993–94	265,306,634	6,492	7,181
1994–95	279,000,318	6,725	7,232
1995–96	293,610,849	6,961	7,287

Source: U.S. Education Department

Growth of Special Education

The number of students in special-education programs has increased significantly, largely because more are being classified as learning disabled.

Children in Federally Supported Programs for the Disabled
(In thousands)

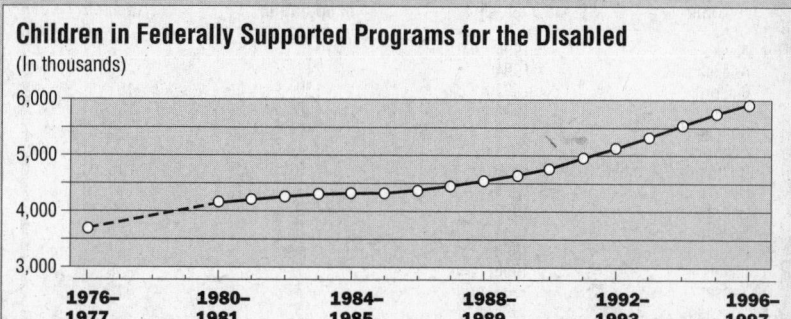

Number of disabled children (In thousands)

Type of disability	1976–1977	1980–1981	1985–1986	1990–1991	1991–1992	1995–1996	1996–1997
All disabilities	3,692	4,142	4,317	4,762	4,949	5,745	5,920
Specific learning disabilities	796	1,462	1,862	2,130	2,234	2,579	2,651
Speech or language impairments	1,302	1,168	1,125	985	997	1,022	1,045
Mental retardation	959	829	660	534	538	570	579
Serious emotional disturbance	283	346	375	390	399	438	446
Hearing impairments	87	79	66	58	60	67	68
Orthopedic impairments	87	58	57	49	51	63	66
Other health impairments	141	98	57	55	58	133	160
Visual impairments	38	31	27	23	24	25	25
Multiple disabilities	–	68	86	96	97	93	98
Deaf-blindness	–	3	2	1	1	1	1
Autism and other	–	–	–	–	5	38	45
Preschool disabled	–	–	–	441	484	717	737

Number served as a percent of total enrollment

Type of disability	1976–1977	1980–1981	1985–1986	1990–1991	1991–1992	1995–1996	1996–1997
All disabilities	8.33%	10.13%	10.95%	11.55%	11.77%	12.81%	12.98%
Specific learning disabilities	1.80	3.58	4.72	5.17	5.31	5.75	5.81
Speech or language impairments	2.94	2.86	2.85	2.39	2.37	2.28	2.29
Mental retardation	2.16	2.03	1.68	1.30	1.28	1.27	1.27
Serious emotional disturbance	0.64	0.85	0.95	0.95	0.95	0.98	0.98
Hearing impairments	0.20	0.19	0.17	0.14	0.14	0.15	0.15
Orthopedic impairments	0.20	0.14	0.14	0.12	0.12	0.14	0.14
Other health impairments	0.32	0.24	0.14	0.13	0.14	0.30	0.35
Visual impairments	0.09	0.08	0.07	0.06	0.06	0.06	0.06
Multiple disabilities	–	0.17	0.22	0.23	0.23	0.21	0.21
Deaf-blindness	–	0.01	0.01	0.00	0.00	0.00	0.00
Autism and other	–	–	–	–	0.01	0.09	0.10
Preschool disabled	–	–	–	1.07	1.15	1.60	1.62

Source: U.S. Education Department

Charter Schools Operating or Approved to Open, August 1998

State	Year charter school law adopted	Schools in operation	Schools approved to open
Alaska	1995	15	3
Arizona	1994	241	27
California	1992	130	151
Colorado	1993	50	10
Connecticut	1996	12	5
Delaware	1995	1	7
District of Columbia	1996	3	16
Florida	1996	33	51
Georgia	1993	20	6
Hawaii	1994	2	-
Idaho	1998	-	1
Illinois	1996	7	9
Kansas	1994	3	12
Louisiana	1995	6	7
Massachusetts	1993	24	13
Michigan	1993	108	25
Minnesota	1991	27	10
Mississippi	1997	-	1
New Hampshire	1995	-	-
New Jersey	1996	13	26
New Mexico	1993	5	-
North Carolina	1996	33	33
Ohio	1997	-	13
Pennsylvania	1997	6	29
Rhode Island	1995	1	1
South Carolina	1996	3	3
Texas	1995	20	41
Utah	1998	-	2
Wisconsin	1993	18	3
28 states and D.C.		**781**	**505**

Source: Center for Education Reform

Number of Children Home Educated in the U.S. (Estimated)

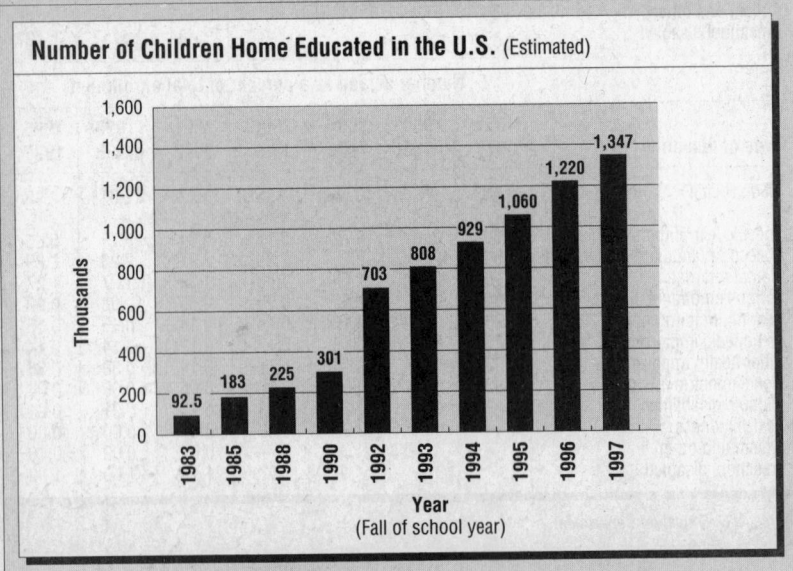

Source: National Home Education Research Institute, Salem, OR

Computers in the Schools

The ratio of students per computer has dropped from 125:1 in 1983-84 to 7.8:1 in 1996-97.

Public School
Students Per Computer (Average)

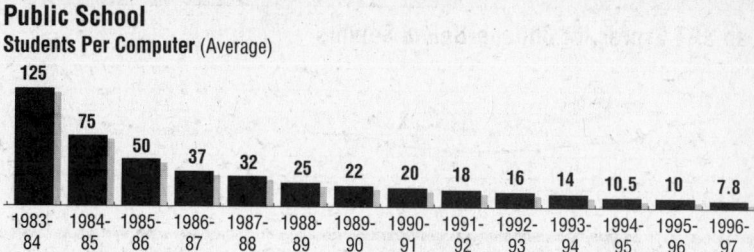

1983-84	1984-85	1985-86	1986-87	1987-88	1988-89	1989-90	1990-91	1991-92	1992-93	1993-94	1994-95	1995-96	1996-97
125	75	50	37	32	25	22	20	18	16	14	10.5	10	7.8

School year

Public School
Students Per Computer by Grade Level (Average)

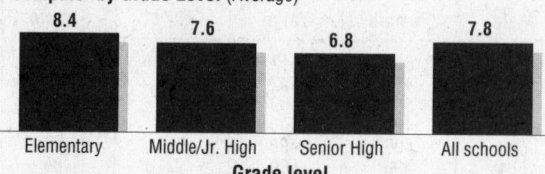

Elementary	Middle/Jr. High	Senior High	All schools
8.4	7.6	6.8	7.8

Grade level

Public School
Students Per Multimedia Capable Computer (Average)

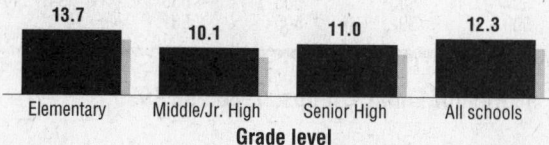

Elementary	Middle/Jr. High	Senior High	All schools
13.7	10.1	11.0	12.3

Grade level

Public Schools with CD-ROM
(Percent of schools)

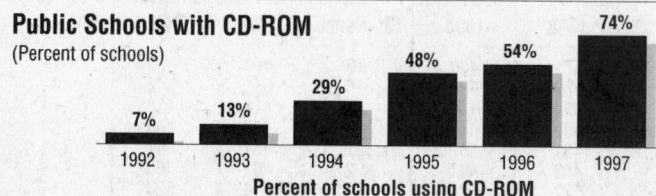

1992	1993	1994	1995	1996	1997
7%	13%	29%	48%	54%	74%

Percent of schools using CD-ROM

Public Schools with Online Access by Grade Level
(Percent of schools)

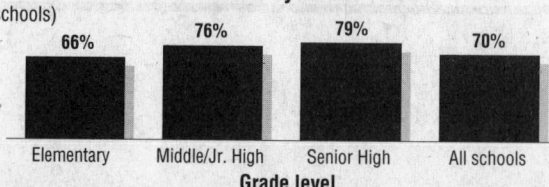

Elementary	Middle/Jr. High	Senior High	All schools
66%	76%	79%	70%

Grade level

Source: Quality Education Data

SAT Scorecard

Past SAT scores have been recalculated to reflect revisions in the test's 200–800 scoring scale.

Mean SAT Scores for College-Bound Seniors

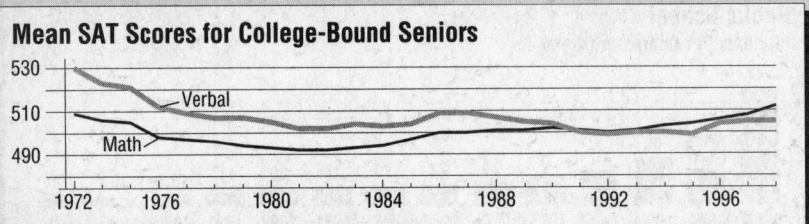

Mean SAT Scores for Males and Females

Year	Verbal			Math		
	Male	Female	Total	Male	Female	Total
1975	515	509	512	518	479	498
1980	506	498	502	515	473	492
1985	514	503	509	522	480	500
1990	505	496	500	521	483	501
1991	503	495	499	520	482	500
1992	504	496	500	521	484	501
1993	504	497	500	524	484	503
1994	501	497	499	523	487	504
1995	505	502	504	525	490	506
1996	507	503	505	527	492	508
1997	507	503	505	530	494	511
1998	509	502	505	531	496	512

Average SAT Scores for Ethnic Groups, 1988 and 1998

Ethnic group	Verbal			Math		
	1988	1998	Difference	1988	1998	Difference
American Indian	471	480	+9	466	483	+17
Asian American	482	498	+16	541	562	+21
Black	429	434	+5	418	426	+8
Mexican American	459	453	-6	460	460	0
Puerto Rican	431	452	+21	434	447	+13
Other Hispanic	463	461	-2	463	466	+3
White	522	526	+4	514	528	+14
Other	485	511	+26	487	514	+27
All Students	505	505	0	501	512	+11

Source: College Board

Making the Grade

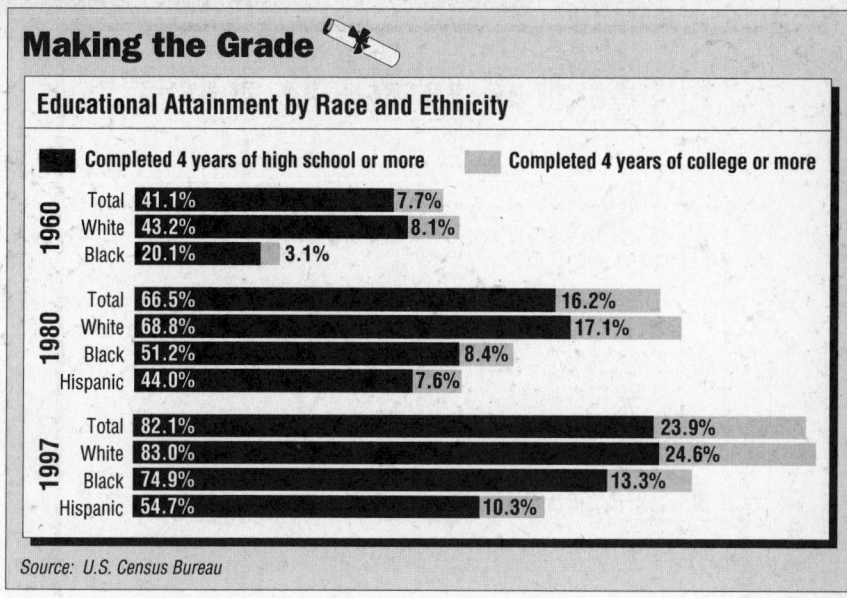

Educational Attainment by Race and Ethnicity

■ Completed 4 years of high school or more **▨ Completed 4 years of college or more**

1960
- Total: 41.1% | 7.7%
- White: 43.2% | 8.1%
- Black: 20.1% | 3.1%

1980
- Total: 66.5% | 16.2%
- White: 68.8% | 17.1%
- Black: 51.2% | 8.4%
- Hispanic: 44.0% | 7.6%

1997
- Total: 82.1% | 23.9%
- White: 83.0% | 24.6%
- Black: 74.9% | 13.3%
- Hispanic: 54.7% | 10.3%

Source: U.S. Census Bureau

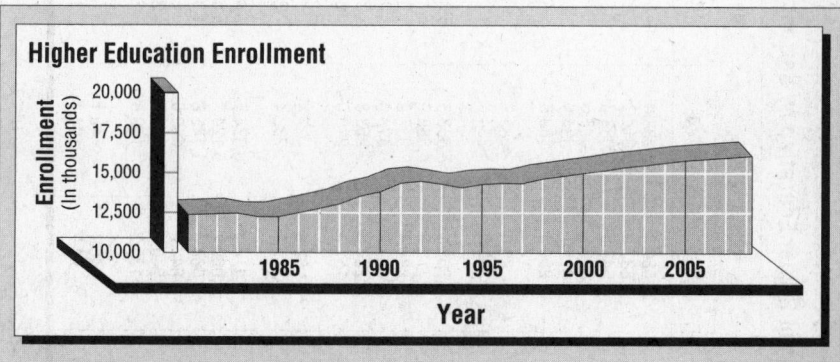

Higher Education Enrollment

Higher Education Enrollment

(In thousands)

Year	Total	Year	Projected Total*
1985	12,247	1997	14,350
1990	13,819	1998	14,590
1995	14,262	2000	14,889
1996	14,334	2008	16,083

*Projections are based on data through 1994.
Source: U.S. Education Department

Total Fall Enrollment in Institutions of Higher Education by Sex and Race/Ethnic Origin

Number (In thousands)

Sex and race/ethnicity of student	1976	1980	1984	1988	1990	1994	1995	1996
Total	10,985.6	12,086.8	12,233.0	13,043.1	13,818.6	14,278.8	14,261.8	14,300.3
White, non-Hispanic	9,076.1	9,833.0	9,814.7	10,283.2	10,722.5	10,427.0	10,311.2	10,226.0
Total minority	1,690.8	1,948.8	2,083.8	2,398.8	2,704.7	3,395.9	3,496.2	3,609.3
Black, non-Hispanic	1,033.0	1,106.8	1,075.8	1,129.6	1,247.0	1,448.6	1,473.7	1,499.4
Hispanic	383.8	471.7	534.9	680.0	782.4	1,045.6	1,093.8	1,152.2
Asian or Pacific Islander	197.9	286.4	389.5	496.7	572.4	774.3	797.4	823.6
American Indian/ Alaskan Native	76.1	83.9	83.6	92.5	102.8	127.4	131.3	134.0
Nonresident alien	218.7	305.0	334.6	361.2	391.5	455.9	454.4	464.9
Men	5,794.4	5,868.1	5,858.3	5,998.2	6,283.9	6,371.9	6,342.5	6,344.0
White, non-Hispanic	4,813.7	4,772.9	4,689.9	4,711.6	4,861.0	4,650.7	4,594.1	4,553.0
Total minority	826.6	884.4	937.9	1,051.3	1,176.6	1,451.7	1,484.2	1,524.3
Black, non-Hispanic	469.9	463.7	436.8	442.7	484.7	549.7	555.9	563.6
Hispanic	209.7	231.6	253.8	310.3	353.9	464.0	480.2	501.3
Asian or Pacific Islander	108.4	151.3	210.0	259.2	294.9	385.0	393.3	403.6
American Indian/ Alaskan Native	38.5	37.8	37.4	39.1	43.1	53.0	54.8	55.7
Nonresident alien	154.1	210.8	230.4	235.3	246.3	269.5	264.3	266.7
Women	5,191.2	6,218.7	6,374.7	7,044.9	7,534.7	7,906.9	7,919.2	7,956.3
White, non-Hispanic	4,262.4	5,060.1	5,124.7	5,571.6	5,861.5	5,776.3	5,717.2	5,673.1
Total minority	864.2	1,064.4	1,145.8	1,347.4	1,528.1	1,944.2	2,012.0	2,085.0
Black, non-Hispanic	563.1	643.0	639.0	686.9	762.3	898.9	917.8	935.8
Hispanic	174.1	240.1	281.2	369.6	428.5	581.6	613.7	650.9
Asian or Pacific Islander	89.4	135.2	179.5	237.5	277.5	389.3	404.1	420.0
American Indian/ Alaskan Native	37.6	46.1	46.1	53.4	59.7	74.4	76.5	78.2
Nonresident alien	64.6	94.2	104.1	125.9	145.2	186.4	190.1	198.2

Source: U.S. Education Department

Higher Prices for Higher Education
Average Undergraduate Tuition and Fees and Room and Board Rates

Year and control of institution	Total tuition, room, and board					Tuition and required fees (in-state)				
	All institutions	4-year institutions			2-year	All institutions	4-year institutions			2-year
		All 4-year	Universities	Other 4-year			All 4-year	Universities	Other 4-year	
All institutions										
1979–80	$2,809	$3,167	$3,223	$3,124	$1,979	$1,163	$1,513	$1,484	$1,530	$451
1984–85	4,563	5,160	5,236	5,107	3,179	1,985	2,567	2,539	2,583	821
1989–90	6,207	7,212	7,347	7,120	3,705	2,839	3,800	3,765	3,819	978
1994–95	8,306	9,728	9,863	9,646	4,633	4,044	5,391	5,287	5,441	1,488
1995–96	8,800	10,330	10,560	10,195	4,725	4,338	5,786	5,733	5,812	1,522
1996–97*	9,206	10,841	11,033	10,726	4,895	4,564	6,118	6,055	6,150	1,543
Public institutions										
1979–80	$2,165	$2,327	$2,487	$2,198	$1,822	$583	$738	$840	$662	$355
1984–85	3,408	3,682	3,899	3,518	2,807	971	1,228	1,386	1,117	584
1989–90	4,504	4,975	5,324	4,723	3,299	1,356	1,780	2,035	1,608	756
1994–95	5,965	6,670	7,077	6,409	4,137	2,057	2,681	2,977	2,499	1,192
1995–96	6,256	7,014	7,448	6,730	4,217	2,179	2,868	3,151	2,660	1,239
1996–97*	6,530	7,334	7,792	7,035	4,404	2,271	2,987	3,323	2,778	1,276
Private institutions										
1979–80	$4,912	$5,013	$5,891	$4,700	$3,751	$3,130	$3,225	$3,811	$3,020	$2,062
1984–85	8,202	8,451	10,243	7,849	6,203	5,315	5,556	6,843	5,135	3,485
1989–90	12,018	12,284	15,098	11,374	8,670	8,147	8,396	10,348	7,778	5,196
1994–95	16,207	16,602	21,041	15,363	11,170	11,111	11,481	14,537	10,653	6,914
1995–96	17,208	17,612	22,502	16,198	11,563	11,864	12,243	15,605	11,297	7,094
1996–97*	18,039	18,442	23,520	16,994	11,954	12,498	12,881	16,552	11,871	7,236

Year and control of institution	Dormitory rooms					Board (7-day basis)				
	All insti-tutions	4-year institutions			2-year	All insti-tutions	4-year institutions			2-year
		All 4-year	Univer-sities	Other 4-year			All 4-year	Univer-sities	Other 4-year	
All institutions										
1979–80	$751	$759	$803	$729	$628	$895	$895	$936	$865	$900
1984–85	1,267	1,282	1,343	1,242	1,058	1,310	1,311	1,353	1,282	1,301
1989–90	1,638	1,675	1,732	1,638	1,105	1,730	1,737	1,850	1,663	1,622
1994–95	2,145	2,200	2,281	2,155	1,396	2,116	2,138	2,295	2,049	1,750
1995–96	2,264	2,318	2,423	2,260	1,473	2,199	2,226	2,404	2,123	1,730
1996–97*	2,365	2,422	2,518	2,368	1,522	2,276	2,301	2,460	2,208	1,830
Public institutions										
1979–80	$715	$725	$750	$703	$574	$867	$865	$898	$833	$893
1984–85	1,196	1,217	1,237	1,200	921	1,241	1,237	1,276	1,201	1,302
1989–90	1,513	1,557	1,561	1,554	962	1,635	1,638	1,728	1,561	1,581
1994–95	1,959	2,023	1,992	2,044	1,232	1,949	1,967	2,108	1,866	1,712
1995–96	2,057	2,121	2,104	2,133	1,297	2,020	2,045	2,192	1,937	1,681
1996–97*	2,148	2,214	2,187	2,232	1,339	2,111	2,133	2,282	2,025	1,789
Private institutions										
1979–80	$827	$831	$1,001	$768	$766	$955	$957	$1,078	$912	$923
1984–85	1,426	1,426	1,753	1,309	1,424	1,462	1,469	1,647	1,405	1,294
1989–90	1,923	1,935	2,411	1,774	1,663	1,948	1,953	2,339	1,823	1,811
1994–95	2,587	2,601	3,469	2,347	2,233	2,509	2,520	3,035	2,362	2,023
1995–96	2,738	2,751	3,680	2,472	2,371	2,606	2,617	3,218	2,429	2,098
1996–97*	2,878	2,889	3,826	2,602	2,537	2,663	2,672	3,142	2,520	2,181

*Preliminary data.
Source: U.S. Education Department

Academic Aid

Total financial aid for college students continues to increase, but the federal share has shifted more to loans in recent years.

Aid Awarded to Postsecondary Students in Constant 1996 Dollars (In millions)

	Academic Year							
	1963–1964	1970–1971	1975–1976	1980–1981	1985–1986	1990–1991	1995–1996	1996–1997
Total Federal Aid	1,176	13,277	24,562	26,010	22,967	24,855	38,178	39,941
State Grant Programs	285	932	1,386	1,450	1,890	2,177	3,045	3,149
Non-Federal loans	—	—	—	—	—	—	1,252	1,492
Institutional and Other Grants	1,371	3,304	3,305	2,941	4,270	6,743	9,712	10,432
Total Federal, State, and Institutional Aid	2,832	17,513	29,252	30,402	29,127	33,775	52,188	55,014

Source: The College Board

100 Largest Four-Year Colleges, Ranked by Undergraduate and Graduate Student Enrollment

Name and campus	State	Total 1996 enrollment	1997-98 undergrad tuition and fees
University of Texas, Austin	Texas	47,476	$2,866
Ohio State University, Columbus	Ohio	45,462	3,687
Texas A&M University	Texas	44,271	2,715
Michigan State University	Michigan	40,150	4,796
Arizona State University	Arizona	38,664	2,058
Penn State University, University Park	Pennsylvania	37,718	5,832
University of Florida	Florida	37,483	1,926
University of Illinois, Urbana	Illinois	36,439	4,340
University of Wisconsin, Madison	Wisconsin	36,022	3,242
University of Minnesota, Twin Cities	Minnesota	34,553	4,268
Purdue University	Indiana	33,673	3,352
University of Michigan	Michigan	33,400	5,878
University of California, Los Angeles	California	33,256	4,050
University of Washington	Washington	32,972	3,366
Indiana University, Bloomington	Indiana	32,351	3,929
University of Maryland, College Park	Maryland	31,471	4,460
University of Arizona	Arizona	31,341	2,058
New York University	New York	31,282	21,730
Brigham Young University	Utah	30,850	2,630
University of South Florida	Florida	30,552	2,086
University of California, Berkeley	California	30,584	4,354
San Diego State University	California	29,331	1,902
Wayne State University	Michigan	28,530	3,358
Florida State University	Florida	28,285	1,988
University of Georgia	Georgia	28,056	2,838
University of Houston	Texas	27,962	2,389
University of Southern California	California	27,874	20,480
San Francisco State University	California	27,420	1,982
California State University, Northridge	California	27,189	1,970
University of Central Florida	Florida	26,350	2,024
Western Michigan University	Michigan	25,699	3,552
California State University, Long Beach	California	25,591	1,836
San Jose State University	California	25,517	2,017
Florida International University	Florida	25,042	2,035
University of Iowa	Iowa	25,022	2,760
University of Colorado, Boulder	Colorado	24,622	2,974
Virginia Tech	Virginia	24,481	4,147
Louisiana State University A&M	Louisiana	24,394	2,711
Temple University	Pennsylvania	24,390	6,150
Iowa State University	Iowa	24,341	2,766
California State University, Fullerton	California	24,308	1,948
University of Utah	Utah	24,155	2,602
North Carolina State University	North Carolina	24,141	2,232
Texas Tech University	Texas	24,075	2,414
Georgia State University	Georgia	24,069	2,673
University of North Texas	Texas	24,060	2,128
University of Kansas	Kansas	23,922	2,385
Fashion Institute of Technology	New York	23,452	2,710
University of Tennessee, Knoxville	Tennessee	23,412	2,576
Boston University	Massachusetts	23,345	22,278
University of Massachusetts, Amherst	Massachusetts	23,334	5,330
University of Akron	Ohio	23,309	3,661
Central Michigan University	Michigan	23,095	3,447
Eastern Michigan University	Michigan	23,083	3,338

Name and campus	State	Total 1996 enrollment	1997-98 undergrad tuition and fees
University of South Carolina	South Carolina	22,836	$3,534
University of Nebraska, Lincoln	Nebraska	22,393	2,769
University of Pittsburgh	Pennsylvania	22,209	6,164
Indiana University/Purdue University, Indianapolis	Indiana	22,144	3,440
Colorado State University	Colorado	21,970	2,933
University of Wisconsin, Milwaukee	Wisconsin	21,877	3,328
California State University, Sacramento	California	21,838	1,982
University of California, Davis	California	21,747	4,332
University of Illinois, Chicago	Illinois	21,645	4,364
Auburn University	Alabama	21,498	2,610
SUNY, Buffalo	New York	21,409	4,340
Southern Illinois University, Carbondale	Illinois	21,151	3,694
University of Kentucky	Kentucky	20,924	2,736
George Mason University	Virginia	20,900	4,296
University of Missouri, Columbia	Missouri	20,891	4,280
University of North Carolina, Chapel Hill	North Carolina	20,800	2,173
University of Texas, Arlington	Texas	20,548	2,507
University of Cincinnati	Ohio	20,464	4,359
Kansas State University	Kansas	20,325	2,467
University of New Mexico	New Mexico	20,235	2,165
Northern Illinois University	Illinois	20,027	4,318
Southwest Texas State University	Texas	20,018	2,641
University of Toledo	Ohio	20,000	4,745
University of Puerto Rico, Rio Piedras	Puerto Rico	19,995	1,270
Kent State University	Ohio	19,947	4,460
University of Oklahoma	Oklahoma	19,886	2,311
Washington State University	Washington	19,429	3,266
Utah State University	Utah	19,429	2,175
University of Memphis	Tennessee	19,271	2,412
West Virginia University	West Virginia	19,136	2,336
Illinois State University	Illinois	19,060	3,970
California State University, Los Angeles	California	18,849	1,757
Ball State University	Indiana	18,730	3,414
University of California, Santa Barbara	California	18,531	4,098
Ohio University	Ohio	18,517	4,275
Northern Arizona University	Arizona	18,358	2,060
Oklahoma State University	Oklahoma	18,198	2,167
University of Alabama	Alabama	18,098	2,694
University of Nevada, Las Vegas	Nevada	18,007	2,041
Cornell University	New York	18,001	21,914
University of Delaware	Delaware	17,932	4,574
University of California, Irvine	California	17,775	4,065
Middle Tennessee State University	Tennessee	17,710	2,196
University of Texas, San Antonio	Texas	17,547	3,060
University of Louisville	Kentucky	17,408	2,630
University of Alaska, Anchorage	Alaska	17,090	2,294

Source: College Entrance Examination Board

The Value of Education

Median Weekly Earnings of Full-time Wage and Salary Workers 25 Years and Over, by Educational Attainment

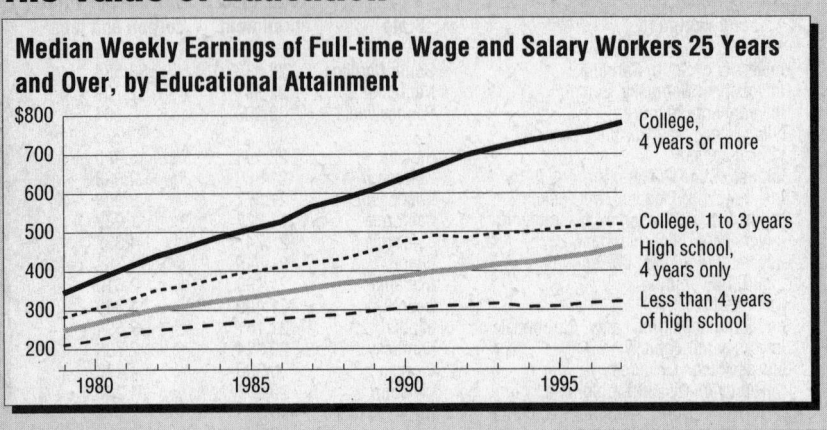

Year	Less than 4 years of high school*	High school, 4 years only*	College, 1 to 3 years*	College, 4 years or more*
1980	$222	$266	$304	$376
1982	248	302	351	438
1984	263	323	382	486
1986	278	344	409	525
1988	288	368	430	585
1990	304	386	476	639
1992	312	404	485	697
1994	307	421	499	733
1995	309	432	508	747
1996	317	443	518	758
1997	321	461	518	779

*Since 1992, data on educational attainment have been based on the "highest diploma or degree received" rather than the "number of years of school completed." Data for 1994 and beyond are not directly comparable with data from earlier years.

Source: U.S. Bureau of Labor Statistics

THE JUSTICE SYSTEM

The question for the tobacco industry in 1997 was one of fine points—not whether it was going to have to change the way it sells cigarettes in the United States but by how much.

Facing a barrage of class-action suits and billions of dollars in state recoupment claims for treating sick smokers, cigarette companies had abandoned their traditional legal defenses and were scrambling to negotiate the terms of their survival.

In exchange for congressional immunity from big-ticket lawsuits suits like the state claims and class actions, the industry would pay $368.5 billion over 25 years and overhaul the way it sells cigarettes. Gone would be billboard advertising, cigarette vending machines, sports promotions pushing cigarette brands and ads with human figures and cartoon characters. The Food and Drug Administration would get limited authority to regulate tobacco as a drug and the companies would print bold black and white labels on all cigarette packs warning: "Cigarettes Cause Lung Cancer" and "Smoking Can Kill You."

But what a difference a year makes.

The global deal collapsed in June 1998, after Congress unexpectedly upped its price tag to $516 billion and killed the proposed liability protections. Tobacco companies brashly abandoned the talks in April, and Congress, unable to pass a tobacco law on its own, let the opportunity pass.

Meanwhile, the huge wave of lawsuits threatening to swamp the industry showed early signs of receding. "The overall litigation tide has clearly turned in favor of the industry," says tobacco analyst David Adelman, at Morgan, Stanley, Dean Witter.

In April, the Iowa Supreme Court rejected the theory that states can sue the tobacco industry directly to recover Medicaid expenditures related to smoking. The court found that Iowa's alleged losses derived from injuries to individual smokers, forcing the state to proceed case by case and guaranteeing an insurmountable backlog of individual suits. Lower courts in other states had reached similar conclusions, but Iowa's high court was the first to embrace it.

Indiana went a step farther in July. A state judge threw out that state's suit entirely, including more attenuated claims left standing in Iowa and elsewhere that allowed recovery of damages for alleged violations of state antitrust and consumer protection laws.

At the same time, a new line of suits by union health funds seeking to recover their payouts to members with smoking-related illnesses also hit a wall. Judges in Maryland, Oregon, Florida and California rejected those claims as too remote for the unions to collect damages. And, one by one, class-action suits on behalf of millions of addicted smokers nationwide were tossed out by influential federal courts in Kansas, Puerto Rico and Pennsylvania. In New York, a state court appeals panel reviewing a lower court ruling allowing a tobacco class-action in that state threw it out, citing the Pennsylvania federal court decision. Damages in these suits, too, most courts have ruled this year, could be won only case by case.

Suits by individuals also fared poorly. In March, a six-member jury found that the nation's six largest cigarette makers should not be held liable in a suit brought by the widower of a non-smoking nurse exposed to secondhand smoke on the job who died of lung cancer. And two major victories against the industry won by individual smokers at trial suffered big setbacks on appeal. In June, a Florida appeals panel reversed the landmark $750,000 verdict against Brown & Williamson Tobacco Co. won two years ago by Grady Carter, a former air-traffic controller from Jacksonville, Florida, with lung cancer. The court relied largely on the narrow ground that Mr. Carter filed his suit too late, but it also cited reasons that could affect other cases. Among them: Mr. Carter's lawyers should not have been allowed to argue that warning labels on cigarette packs are inadequate.

Then in August, the same appeals panel threw into question a $1 million verdict won this year by the family of a deceased smoker in Jacksonville. That case, which resulted in the first punitive damage award ever against a tobacco company, was tried in the wrong county, the appeals judges ruled.

And capping its success against liability suits, the industry won two major decisions against federal regulators. In July, a federal judge declared that a 1993 Environmental Protection Agency study relied upon to enact many local government and workplace bans on indoor smoking overstated the proven link between secondhand smoke and cancer. And in August, a federal appeals court overturned a landmark lower court ruling and found that the Food and Drug Administration did not have a congressional mandate to regulate tobacco companies.

Despite the industry's many victories, the courtroom battles aren't over. Just before closing arguments by Minnesota in its Medicaid recoupment suit were to begin in May, the industry agreed to fork over $6.1 billion, 50 percent more than Minnesota was entitled to under the 1997 proposed global deal. While the industry had mounted strong defenses, the risk of losing still struck the companies as too high. A major uncertainty was how millions of embarrassing industry documents made public during the 15-week trial would play with the jury. They included extensive evidence that tobacco companies have targeted teens as future smokers for decades while mounting a disingenuous public relations campaign to play down the health risks of lighting up.

The industry had settled similar suits in Mississippi, Florida and Texas for a total of more than $30 billion, citing plaintiff-friendly state statutes there or early court rulings against them. Their overriding concern then had been achieving a global peace in Congress. And even though tobacco companies abandoned talks in April, a global settlement was still viewed as preferable to endless lawsuits. To that end, tobacco companies pursued settlement talks with eight state attorneys general in hopes of ridding themselves of the more than two dozen similar Medicaid recoupment suits pending.

But when they sat at a negotiating table this time, tobacco companies were on far firmer legal footing than the year before—and far more willing to fight it out in court if need be.

Milo Geyelin

The Cost of Crime

Justice System Expenditures in the U.S.
(In billions of dollars)

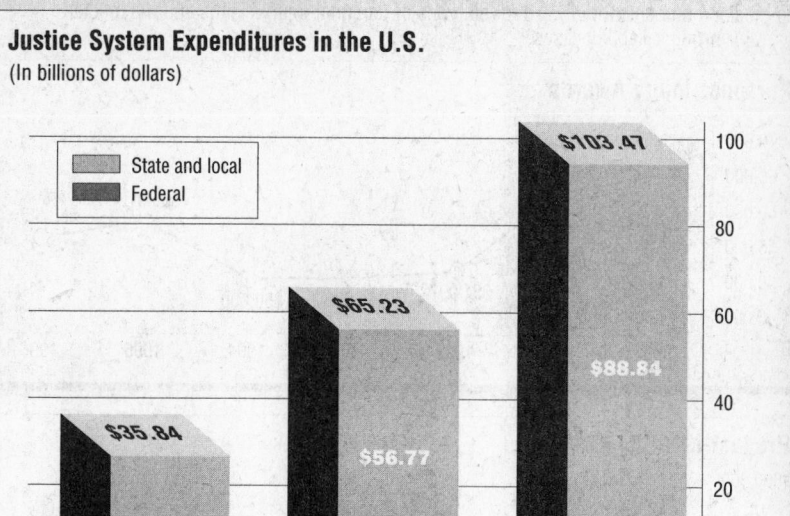

Justice System Expenditures by Level of Government and Type of Activity
(In millions of dollars)

Fiscal year	Total justice system	Level of government*		Type of activity		
		Federal	State and local	Police protection	Judicial and legal	Corrections
1982	$35,842	$4,269	$31,573	$19,022	$7,771	$9,049
1983	39,680	4,844	34,836	20,648	8,621	10,411
1984	43,943	5,787	38,156	22,686	9,463	11,794
1985	48,563	6,279	42,284	24,399	10,629	13,535
1986	53,500	6,430	47,070	26,255	11,485	15,759
1987	58,871	7,231	51,640	28,768	12,555	17,549
1988	65,231	8,464	56,767	30,961	13,971	20,299
1989	70,949	9,204	61,745	32,794	15,589	22,567
1990	79,434	10,219	69,215	35,923	17,357	26,154
1991	87,567	12,106	75,461	38,971	19,298	29,297
1992	93,777	13,529	80,248	41,327	20,989	31,461
1993	97,556	14,429	83,127	44,007	21,575	31,974
1994	103,471	14,626	88,845	46,005	22,602	34,864

*Data show direct expenditures by level of government and do not include duplicated intergovernmental expenditures.
Source: U.S. Justice Department

Personal-Injury Verdicts

The median compensatory award for all types of personal-injury claims and the median award for product-liability cases:

Personal-Injury Awards

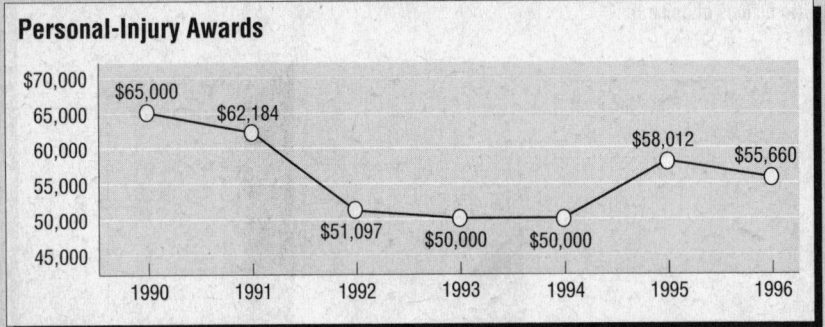

Product-Liability Awards

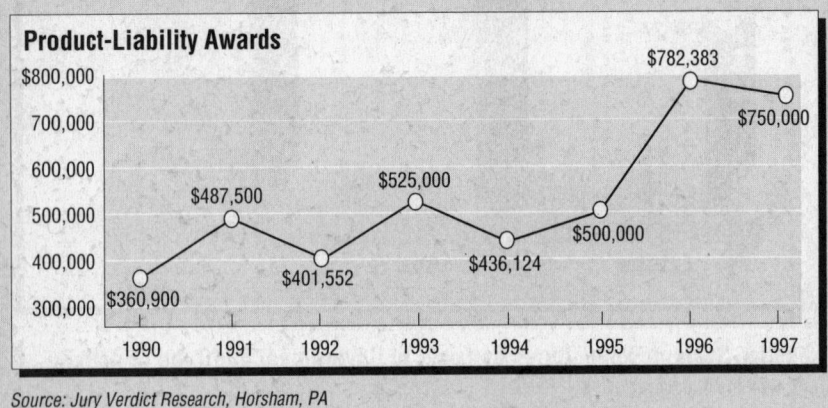

Source: Jury Verdict Research, Horsham, PA

Crime in America

Estimated Rate (per 100,000 Inhabitants) of Offenses Known to Police

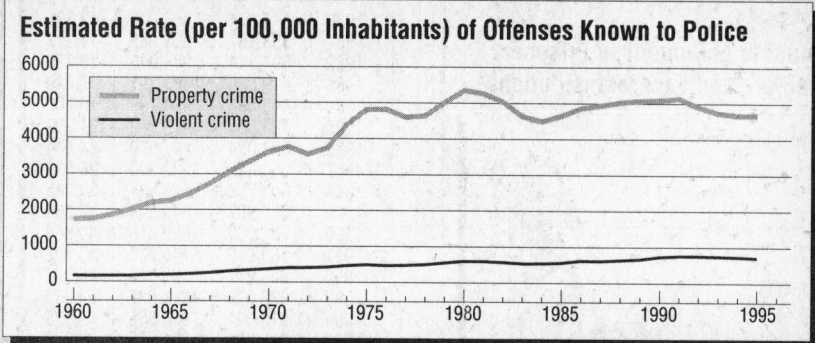

Year	Total crime index	Violent crime	Property crime	Murder and non-negligent man-slaughter	Forcible rape	Robbery	Aggravated assault	Burglary	Larceny-theft	Motor vehicle theft
				Rate per 100,000 inhabitants						
1960	1,887.2	160.9	1,726.3	5.1	9.6	60.1	86.1	508.6	1,034.7	183.0
1965	2,449.0	200.2	2,248.8	5.1	12.1	71.7	111.3	662.7	1,329.3	256.8
1970	3,984.5	363.5	3,621.0	7.9	18.7	172.1	164.8	1,084.9	2,079.3	456.8
1975	5,298.5	487.8	4,810.7	9.6	26.3	220.8	231.1	1,532.1	2,804.8	473.7
1980	5,950.0	596.6	5,353.3	10.2	36.8	251.1	298.5	1,684.1	3,167.0	502.2
1985	5,207.1	556.6	4,650.5	7.9	37.1	208.5	302.9	1,287.3	2,901.2	462.0
1986	5,480.4	617.7	4,862.6	8.6	37.9	225.1	346.1	1,344.6	3,010.3	507.8
1987	5,550.0	609.7	4,940.3	8.3	37.4	212.7	351.3	1,329.6	3,081.3	529.4
1988	5,664.2	637.2	5,027.1	8.4	37.6	220.9	370.2	1,309.2	3,134.9	582.9
1989	5,741.0	663.7	5,077.9	8.7	38.1	233.0	383.4	1,276.3	3,171.3	630.4
1990	5,820.3	731.8	5,088.5	9.4	41.2	257.0	424.1	1,235.9	3,194.8	657.8
1991	5,897.8	758.1	5,139.7	9.8	42.3	272.7	433.3	1,252.0	3,228.8	659.0
1992	5,660.2	757.5	4,902.7	9.3	42.8	263.6	441.8	1,168.2	3,103.0	631.5
1993	5,484.4	746.8	4,737.6	9.5	41.1	255.9	440.3	1,099.2	3,032.4	606.1
1994	5,373.5	713.6	4,660.0	9.0	39.3	237.7	427.6	1,042.0	3,026.7	591.3
1995	5,275.9	684.6	4,591.3	8.2	37.1	220.9	418.3	987.1	3,043.8	560.4
1996	5,078.9	634.1	4,444.8	7.4	36.1	202.4	388.2	943.0	2,975.9	525.9
				Number of offenses						
1960	3,384,200	288,460	3,095,700	9,110	17,190	107,840	154,320	912,100	1,855,400	328,200
1965	4,739,400	387,390	4,352,000	9,960	23,410	138,690	215,330	1,282,500	2,572,600	496,900
1970	8,098,000	738,820	7,359,200	16,000	37,990	349,860	334,970	2,205,000	4,225,800	928,400
1975	11,292,400	1,039,710	10,252,700	20,510	56,090	470,500	492,620	3,265,300	5,977,700	1,009,600
1980	13,408,300	1,344,520	12,063,700	23,040	82,990	565,840	672,650	3,795,200	7,136,900	1,131,700
1985	12,431,400	1,328,800	11,102,600	18,980	88,670	497,870	723,250	3,073,300	6,926,400	1,102,900
1986	13,211,900	1,489,170	11,722,700	20,610	91,460	542,780	834,320	3,241,400	7,257,200	1,224,100
1987	13,508,700	1,484,000	12,024,700	20,100	91,110	517,700	855,090	3,236,200	7,499,900	1,288,700
1988	13,923,100	1,566,220	12,356,900	20,680	92,490	542,970	910,090	3,218,100	7,705,900	1,432,900
1989	14,251,400	1,646,040	12,605,400	21,500	94,500	578,330	951,710	3,168,200	7,872,400	1,564,800
1990	14,475,600	1,820,130	12,655,500	23,440	102,560	639,270	1,054,860	3,073,900	7,945,700	1,635,900
1991	14,872,900	1,911,770	12,961,100	24,700	106,590	687,730	1,092,740	3,157,200	8,142,200	1,661,700
1992	14,438,200	1,932,270	12,505,900	23,760	109,060	672,480	1,126,970	2,979,900	7,915,200	1,610,800
1993	14,144,800	1,926,020	12,218,800	24,530	106,010	659,870	1,135,610	2,834,800	7,820,900	1,563,100
1994	13,989,500	1,857,670	12,131,900	23,330	102,220	618,950	1,113,180	2,712,800	7,879,800	1,539,300
1995	13,862,700	1,798,790	12,063,900	21,610	97,470	580,510	1,099,210	2,593,800	7,997,700	1,472,400
1996	13,473,600	1,682,280	11,791,300	19,650	95,770	537,050	1,029,810	2,501,500	7,894,600	1,395,200

Source: U.S. Justice Department, Federal Bureau of Investigation

Prison Population Surge

Number of Sentenced Prisoners in State and Federal Institutions

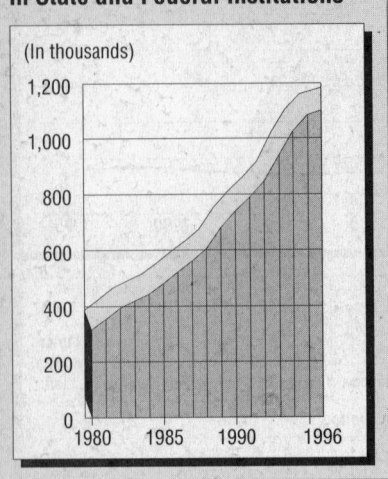

(In thousands)

Year	Total	Male	Female
1980	315,974	303,643	12,331
1981	353,167	338,940	14,227
1982	394,374	378,045	16,329
1983	419,820	402,391	17,429
1984	443,398	424,193	19,205
1985	480,568	458,972	21,296
1986	522,084	497,540	24,544
1987	560,812	533,990	26,822
1988	603,732	573,587	30,145
1989	680,907	643,643	37,264
1990	739,980	699,416	40,564
1991	789,610	745,808	43,802
1992	846,277	799,776	46,501
1993	932,074	878,037	54,037
1994	1,016,691	956,566	60,125
1995	1,085,022	1,021,059	63,963
1996	1,138,984	1,069,257	69,727
1997	1,197,590	1,123,478	74,112

Source: U.S. Justice Department

Crowding on Death Row

Prisoners Executed, by Race

Year	Under sentence of death on Dec. 31	Executions Total	White	Black	Other	Year	Under sentence of death on Dec. 31	Executions Total	White	Black	Other
1968	517	0	0	0	0	1983	1,209	5	4	1	0
1969	575	0	0	0	0	1984	1,405	21	13	8	0
1970	631	0	0	0	0	1985	1,591	18	11	7	0
1971	642	0	0	0	0	1986	1,781	18	11	7	0
1972	334	0	0	0	0	1987	1,984	25	13	12	0
1973	134	0	0	0	0	1988	2,124	11	6	5	0
1974	244	0	0	0	0	1989	2,250	16	8	8	0
1975	488	0	0	0	0	1990	2,356	23	16	7	0
1976	420	0	0	0	0	1991	2,482	14	7	7	0
1977	423	1	1	0	0	1992	2,575	31	19	11	1
1978	482	0	0	0	0	1993	2,716	38	23	14	1
1979	593	2	2	0	0	1994	2,890	31	20	11	0
1980	691	0	0	0	0	1995	3,064	56	33	22	1
1981	856	1	1	0	0	1996	3,219	45	31	14	0
1982	1,050	2	1	1	0						

Source: U.S. Justice Department

Energy and Environment

Plunging crude oil prices held the energy patch in thrall for most of 1998, as robust production and crumbling demand provided a stark reminder that the price of any commodity is inexorably linked to the amount of product available.

In sharp contrast to the previous year, 1998 opened with a steady and ultimately dramatic decline in oil prices. Prices for gasoline and heating oil also moved south, spurred by a stubborn supply glut. The glut, blamed on a warm winter and cooling economies, primarily in Asia, was especially apparent in the summer, when a barrel of crude dipped to less than $12, the lowest price for the commodity in more than a decade. The drop stood in sharp contrast to 1997, when a barrel of oil hit a high of $26.62 a barrel.

While oil prices stabilized somewhat in the ensuing months and into the fall, edging into a range that oil companies consider marginally profitable, the market for petroleum products could hardly be termed robust. Even as the U.S. government was releasing figures showing that oil stocks were dropping modestly, the spot price of West Texas Intermediate languished at about $14.50 a barrel. This lack of enthusiasm was in large part due to traders' doubts that the Organization of Petroleum Exporting Countries, which produces about 40 percent of the world's supply of crude, would be able to sop up the oversupply. OPEC ratcheted up production in 1997 and spent most of 1998 trying to reverse that move.

The upshot: Even though OPEC struggled mightily through the summer of 1998 to shut off the spigots, the efforts proved to be too little, too late. By the early fall, world demand for oil was down not only in Asia, but also in Europe and North America, and inventories, while falling, remained bloated. In late August, for example, the U.S. Department of Energy said the nation's crude inventories stood at 337.4 million barrels—about 11 percent higher than they were a year before.

Commodities traders reacted with a pessimism that few had predicted earlier in the year. While many analysts and oil executives said in early 1998 that oil prices would rebound late in the year, the idea never caught on. Some analysts glumly predicted at summer's end that the world will be awash in oil for some time to come. "In the long term, you're looking at $15-a-barrel oil," said Benjamin Rice Jr., of Brown Brothers Harriman in New York. "I don't see a good oil price for years."

The generally accepted benchmark of a "good" oil price, one that keeps oil company exploration budgets steady, if not growing, is $18 a barrel. Mr. Rice said that even if OPEC is able to stem the flow of oil, technological advances and new discoveries, such as those off the coast of Africa and in the deepwater Gulf of Mexico, will make it increasingly difficult to keep world supplies in check.

Too much product for too few customers also played havoc with oil products, notably gasoline and heating oil. For heating oil, the world's oversupply was blamed in part on El Niño, the Pacific Ocean weather phenomenon credited with producing the mild winter of 1997-1998. The supply of distillates, which include heating oil and diesel, were even more pronounced than that of oil in late 1998. Heating oil prices for delivery late in the year stood at about 41 cents a gallon, down from about 58 cents a gallon going into the mild winter. Like oil, distillates hit lows in 1998 that hadn't been seen in a decade.

Some traders held out hope that an unusually cold winter in 1998-1999 could help absorb the glut. While demand-side uncertainties will likely depress oil prices for some time to come, heating oil could rebound nicely on the tail of a few northeastern blizzards, said John Saucer, first vice president and energy analyst for Solomon Smith Barney in Houston. "Winter can make a huge difference. We need to see some cold weather." On the other hand, back-to-back mild winters could leave heating oil stocks at record highs come spring.

Retail prices for gasoline marched in lockstep with oil throughout 1998 and if anything were even more sensitive to oversupply and slack demand. In January 1998, gasoline fell to just shy of $1 a gallon at the pump and bumped around in that range for most of the year. An anticipated increase in demand for the summer driving season never materialized; spot prices for gasoline hovered around 40 cents a gallon through the fall. This was good news for consumers, who had not seen gasoline below a buck since 1990. Indeed, according to Exxon Corp., inflation-adjusted prices for gasoline in 1998 were the lowest they had been in 50 years.

Christopher Cooper

Energy Levels
U.S. energy consumption, production, imports, and exports

Energy Overview (Quadrillion BTUs)

	Production	Consumption*	Imports	Exports
1973	62.060	74.282	14.731	2.051
1975	59.860	70.546	14.111	2.359
1980	64.761	75.955	15.971	3.723
1985	64.871	73.981	12.103	4.231
1990	70.780	84.120	18.990	4.910
1991	70.450	84.030	18.590	5.220
1992	69.980	85.550	19.660	5.017
1993	68.340	87.370	21.540	4.350
1994	70.710	89.250	22.710	4.130
1995	71.040	90.860	22.480	4.580
1996	72.320	93.870	23.970	4.710
1997	72.320	94.210	24.960	4.570

*The sum of domestic energy production and net imports of energy does not equal domestic energy consumption. The difference is attributed to stock changes; losses and gains in conversion, transportation, and distribution; the addition of blending compounds; shipments of anthracite to U.S. Armed Forces in Europe; and adjustments to account for discrepancies between reporting systems.

Energy Production by Source

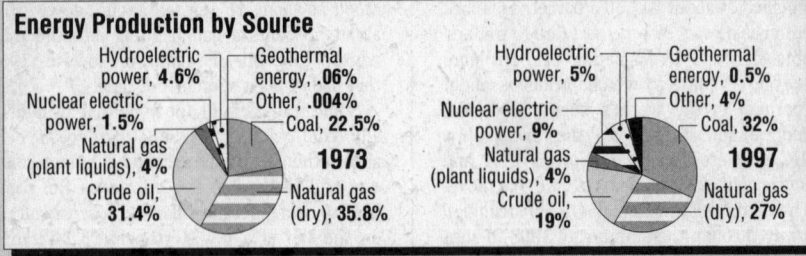

1973
- Hydroelectric power, **4.6%**
- Geothermal energy, **.06%**
- Nuclear electric power, **1.5%**
- Other, **.004%**
- Natural gas (plant liquids), **4%**
- Coal, **22.5%**
- Crude oil, **31.4%**
- Natural gas (dry), **35.8%**

1997
- Hydroelectric power, **5%**
- Geothermal energy, **0.5%**
- Nuclear electric power, **9%**
- Other, **4%**
- Natural gas (plant liquids), **4%**
- Coal, **32%**
- Crude oil, **19%**
- Natural gas (dry), **27%**

Source: U.S. Energy Department

Energy Powers

World's Major Producers of Primary Energy,* 1996 (Quadrillion Btu)

1	United States	72.32	14	United Arab Emirates	6.43
2	Russia	39.68	15	Germany	5.53
3	China	37.41	16	Algeria	5.37
4	Saudi Arabia	20.39	17	France	4.97
5	Canada	17.29	18	Brazil	4.96
6	United Kingdom	11.49	19	Nigeria	4.96
7	Iran	9.60	20	South Africa	4.87
8	India	9.33	21	Kuwait	4.82
9	Norway	9.28	22	Japan	4.05
10	Venezuela	8.84	23	Poland	3.76
11	Mexico	8.59	24	Ukraine	3.28
12	Australia	7.58	25	Libya	3.28
13	Indonesia	7.50		**World Total**	**375.11**

World's Major Consumers of Primary Energy,* 1996 (Quadrillion Btu)

1	United States	93.87	14	Mexico	5.62
2	China	37.04	15	Spain	4.50
3	Russia	25.98	16	South Africa	4.26
4	Japan	21.37	17	Australia	4.08
5	Germany	14.44	18	Saudi Arabia	4.03
6	Canada	12.20	19	Iran	4.03
7	India	11.55	20	Poland	3.77
8	United Kingdom	10.05	21	Netherlands	3.76
9	France	9.87	22	Indonesia	3.51
10	Italy	7.63	23	Taiwan	3.11
11	Brazil	7.24	24	Turkey	2.67
12	South Korea	7.16	25	Argentina	2.60
13	Ukraine	6.25		**World Total**	**375.58**

*Primary energy production and consumption include petroleum, natural gas, coal, and net hydroelectric, nuclear, geothermal, solar and wind electric power. Data for the U.S. also include electricity generated from wood and waste.
Source: U.S. Energy Department

U.S. Petroleum Supply

(Million barrels per day)

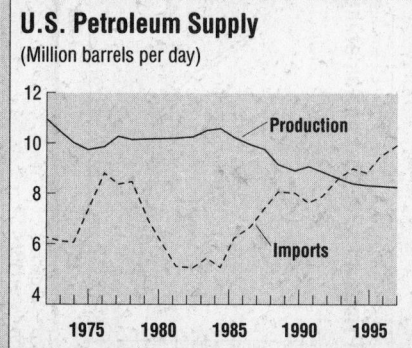

Source: U.S. Energy Department

U.S. Production vs. Imports

(Million barrels per day)

	Production	Imports
1973	10.95	6.26
1975	10.01	6.06
1978	10.27	8.36
1980	10.17	6.91
1982	10.20	5.11
1984	10.51	5.44
1986	10.23	6.22
1988	9.76	7.40
1990	8.91	8.02
1991	9.08	7.63
1992	8.87	7.89
1993	8.58	8.62
1994	8.39	9.00
1995	8.32	8.83
1996	8.29	9.48
1997	8.25	9.91

Outside Sources of Petroleum

Petroleum Imports by Country of Origin (Thousand barrels per day)

Year	Persian Gulf nations	Selected OPEC countries					Selected non-OPEC countries					Total imports	Imports from Persian Gulf nations as share of total imports	Imports from OPEC as share of total imports
		Algeria	Nigeria	Saudi Arabia	Venezuela	Total OPEC	Canada	Mexico	United Kingdom	Virgin Islands and Puerto Rico	Total non-OPEC			
1960	NA	NA	0	84	911	1,314	120	16	–	36	500	1,815	NA	72.4%
1965	NA	NA	15	158	994	1,476	323	48	-	47	992	2,468	NA	59.8
1970	NA	NA	50	30	989	1,343	766	42	11	271	2,076	3,419	NA	39.3
1975	1,165	282	762	715	702	3,601	846	71	14	496	2,454	6,056	19.2%	59.5
1980	1,519	488	857	1,261	481	4,300	455	533	176	476	2,609	6,909	22.0	62.2
1985	312	187	293	168	605	1,830	770	816	310	275	3,237	5,067	6.1	36.1
1990	1,966	280	800	1,339	1,025	4,296	934	755	189	315	3,721	8,018	24.5	53.6
1995	1,573	234	627	1,344	1,480	4,002	1,332	1,068	383	293	4,833	8,835	17.8	45.3
1997*	1,737	285	678	1,391	1,729	4,487	1,473	1,366	224	316	5,420	9,907	17.5	45.3

* Preliminary.
Source: U.S. Energy Department

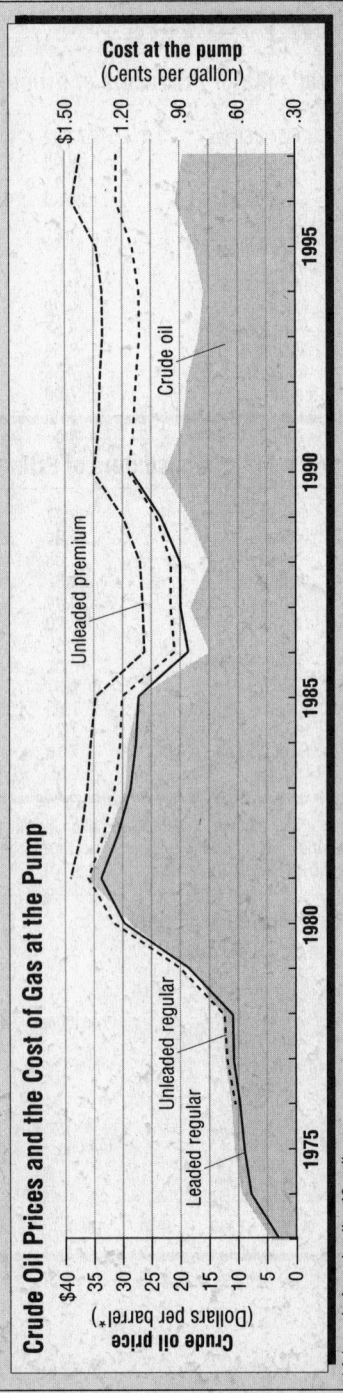

Crude Oil Prices and the Cost of Gas at the Pump

Cost at the pump (Cents per gallon)

Crude oil price (Dollars per barrel*)

* A barrel of crude oil = 42 gallons.
Source: U.S. Energy Department

WORLD'S LARGEST ENERGY COMPANIES

Largest Producers of Crude Oil and Other Liquids in 1996

Rank	Company	Ownership Status	Production (1,000 barrels per day)
1.	Saudi Arabian Oil Co.	State-owned	8,797
2.	National Iranian Oil Co.	State-owned	3,781
3.	Petroleos Mexicanos (Pemex)	State-owned	3,277
4.	Petroleos de Venezuela	State-owned	2,967
5.	China National Petroleum Corp.	State-owned	2,828
6.	Royal Dutch/Shell	Private	2,305
7.	Kuwait Petroleum Corp.	State-owned	2,100
8.	Exxon	Private	1,615
9.	Sonatrach	State-owned (Algeria)	1,345
10.	Nigerian National Petroleum Corp.	State-owned	1,335
11.	Libya National Oil Co.	State-owned	1,291
12.	British Petroleum	Private	1,241
13.	Abu Dhabi National Oil Co.	State-owned	1,226
14.	Lukoil	45% state-owned (Russia)	1,163
15.	Chevron	Private	1,044
16.	Pertamina	State-owned (Indonesia)	1,039
17.	Mobil	Private	854
18.	Petrobras	51% state-owned (Brazil)	809
19.	Texaco	Private	787
20.	Elf Aquitaine	Private	779

Companies With Largest Worldwide Reserves of Crude Oil and Other Liquids, 1996

Rank	Company	Ownership Status	Reserves (millions of barrels)
1.	Saudi Arabian Oil Co.	State-owned	261,444
2.	Iraq National Oil Co.	State-owned	112,000
3.	Kuwait Petroleum Corp.	State-owned	96,500
4.	National Iranian Oil Co.	State-owned	92,600
5.	Petroleos de Venezuela	State-owned	72,574
6.	Abu Dhabi National Oil Co.	State-owned	63,570
7.	Petroleos Mexicanos (Pemex)	State-owned	48,472
8.	Libya National Oil Co.	State-owned	26,550
9.	China National Petroleum Corp.	State-owned	21,000
10.	Nigerian National Petroleum Corp.	State-owned	12,500
11.	Lukoil	45% state-owned (Russia)	10,702
12.	Sonatrach	State-owned (Algeria)	9,979
13.	Royal Dutch/Shell	Private	9,049
14.	Yukos	51% state-owned (Russia)	7,150
15.	Gazprom	40% state-owned (Russia)	7,000
16.	Sidanco	49% state-owned (Russia)	6,935
17.	Exxon	Private	6,782
18.	British Petroleum	Private	6,771
19.	Rosneft	State-owned (Russia)	6,570
20.	Oil & Natural Gas Commission	State-owned (India)	5,500

Largest Producers of Natural Gas in 1996

Rank	Company	Ownership status	Production (million cubic feet per day)
1.	Gazprom	40% state-owned (Russia)	54,000
2.	Royal Dutch/Shell	Private	8,354
3.	Exxon	Private	6,577
4.	Sonatrach	State-owned (Algeria)	6,495
5.	Pertamina	State-owned (Indonesia)	5,366
6.	Mobil	Private	4,587
7.	Amoco	Private	4,382
8.	Petroleos Mexicanos (Pemex)	State-owned	4,195
9.	Saudi Arabian Oil Co.	State-owned	3,989
10.	National Iranian Oil Co.	State-owned	3,918
11.	Petroleos de Venezuela	State-owned	3,710
12.	Abu Dhabi National Oil Co.	State-owned	3,400
13.	Chevron	Private	2,459
14.	Ente Nazionale Idrocarburi	State-owned (Italy)	2,087
15.	Texaco	Private	2,057
16.	Unocal	Private	1,812
17.	Arco	Private	1,774
18.	Petronas	State-owned (Malaysia)	1,712
19.	Oil & Natural Gas Commission	State-owned (India)	1,659
20.	China National Petroleum Corp.	State-owned	1,586

Companies With Largest Worldwide Reserves of Natural Gas, 1996

Rank	Company	Ownership status	Reserves (billion cubic feet)
1.	Gazprom	40% state-owned (Russia)	1,179,000
2.	National Iranian Oil Co.	State-owned	815,430
3.	Qatar General Petroleum Corp.	State-owned	300,050
4.	Abu Dhabi National Oil Co.	State-owned	220,378
5.	Saudi Arabian Oil Co.	State-owned	200,962
6.	Petroleos de Venezuela	State-owned	142,976
7.	Sonatrach	State-owned (Algeria)	130,610
8.	Iraq National Oil Co.	State-owned	118,608
9.	Nigerian National Petroleum Corp.	State-owned	73,622
10.	Petroleos Mexicanos (Pemex)	State-owned	69,721
11.	Pertamina	State-owned (Indonesia)	63,364
12.	Surgutneftegaz	51% state-owned (Russia)	57,537
13.	Sidanco	49% state-owned (Russia)	54,828
14.	Kuwait Petroleum Corp.	State-owned	52,562
15.	Royal Dutch/Shell	Private	47,477
16.	Libya National Oil Co.	State-owned	46,349
17.	Petronas	State-owned (Malaysia)	44,900
18.	Exxon	Private	41,500
19.	China National Petroleum Corp.	State-owned	39,652
20.	Rosneft	State-owned (Russia)	35,300

Companies With the Largest Oil Refining Capacity, 1996

Rank	Company	Ownership status	Capacity (1,000 barrels per day)
1.	Exxon	Private	4,273
2.	Royal Dutch/Shell	Private	3,791
3.	China Petrochemical Corp.	State-owned (China)	2,867
4.	Petroleos de Venezuela	State-owned	2,437
5.	Mobil	Private	2,297
6.	Saudi Arabian Oil Co.	State-owned	1,970
7.	British Petroleum	Private	1,965
8.	Chevron	Private	1,661
9.	Petrobras	51% state-owned	1,540
10.	Texaco	Private	1,532
11.	Petroleos Mexicanos (Pemex)	State-owned	1,520
12.	National Iranian Oil Co.	State-owned	1,092
13.	Amoco	Private	1,009
14.	Pertamina	State-owned (Indonesia)	990
15.	Kuwait Petroleum Corp.	State-owned	932
16.	Elf Aquitaine	Private	924
17.	Idemitsu	Private	910
18.	Ente Nazionale Idrocarburi	State-owned	897
19.	Total	Private	886
20.	Nippon Oil	Private	872

Source: Petroleum Intelligence Weekly

America's Nuclear Generation

The nuclear industry's share of America's electricity generation rose steadily in the 1980s, then leveled off at about 20% in the 1990s. But the amount of nuclear power is expected to drop considerably in the early part of the next century, according to the U.S. Energy Department.

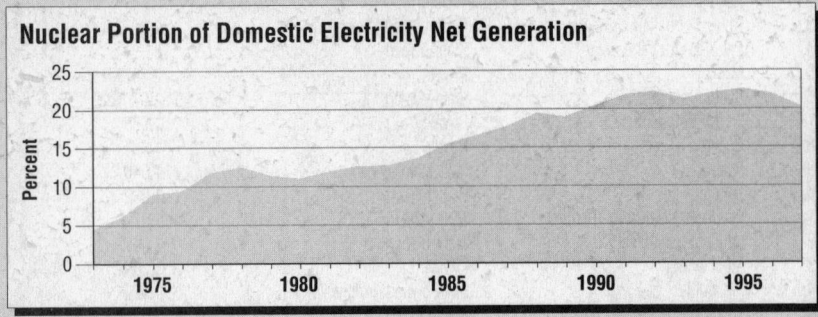

Nuclear Portion of Domestic Electricity Net Generation

Nuclear Power Plant Operations

	Operable units (Number)	Nuclear electricity net generation (Million kilowatt-hours)	Nuclear portion of domestic electricity net generation (Percent)
1973	39	83,479	4.5
1975	54	172,505	9.0
1980	70	251,116	11.0
1985	95	383,691	15.5
1990	111	576,862	20.5
1991	111	612,565	21.7
1992	109	618,776	22.1
1993	109	610,291	21.2
1994	109	640,440	22.0
1995	109	673,402	22.5
1996	109	674,729	21.9
1997	107	629,400	20.1

Source: U.S. Energy Department, Nuclear Regulatory Commission

Global Nuclear Energy Rankings

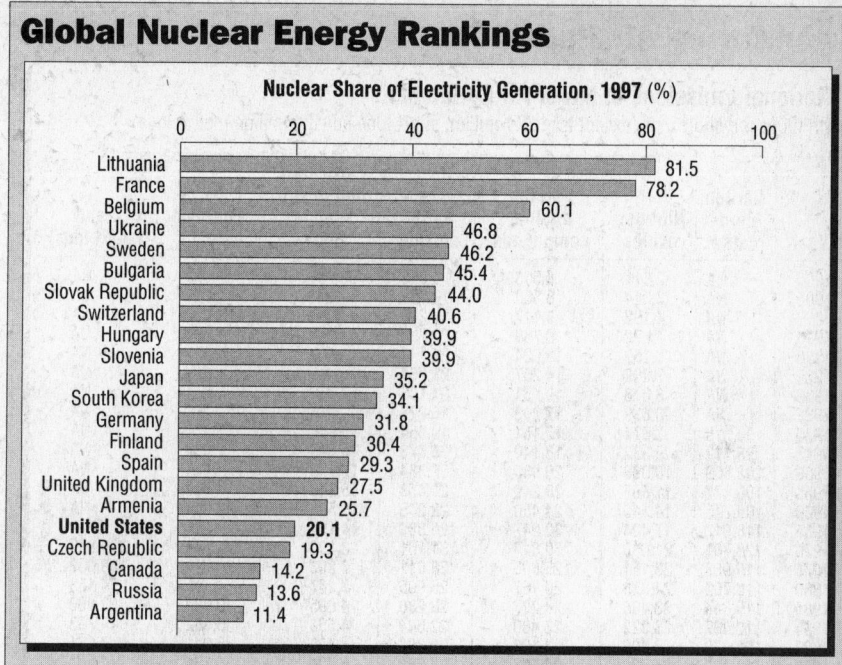

Nuclear Share of Electricity Generation, 1997 (%)

Country	%
Lithuania	81.5
France	78.2
Belgium	60.1
Ukraine	46.8
Sweden	46.2
Bulgaria	45.4
Slovak Republic	44.0
Switzerland	40.6
Hungary	39.9
Slovenia	39.9
Japan	35.2
South Korea	34.1
Germany	31.8
Finland	30.4
Spain	29.3
United Kingdom	27.5
Armenia	25.7
United States	**20.1**
Czech Republic	19.3
Canada	14.2
Russia	13.6
Argentina	11.4

Source: *International Atomic Energy Agency*

Monitoring Air Pollution

National Emissions of Major Air Pollutants
(In thousand short tons, except lead; 1.1 million short tons equal 1 million metric tons)

Year	Carbon monoxide	Nitrogen oxides	Volatile organic compounds	Sulfur dioxide	Particulate matter w/o fugitve dust	Fugitive dust	Lead (short tons)
1900	NA	2,611	8,503	9,988	NA	NA	NA
1905	NA	3,314	8,850	13,959	NA	NA	NA
1910	NA	4,102	9,117	17,275	NA	NA	NA
1915	NA	4,672	9,769	20,290	NA	NA	NA
1920	NA	5,159	10,004	21,144	NA	NA	NA
1925	NA	7,302	14,257	23,264	NA	NA	NA
1930	NA	8,018	19,451	21,106	NA	NA	NA
1935	NA	6,639	17,208	16,978	NA	NA	NA
1940	93,615	7,374	17,161	19,954	15,956	NA	NA
1945	98,112	9,332	18,140	26,373	16,545	NA	NA
1950	102,609	10,093	20,936	22,384	17,133	NA	NA
1955	106,177	11,667	23,249	21,453	16,346	NA	NA
1960	109,745	14,140	24,459	22,245	15,558	NA	NA
1965	118,912	17,424	30,247	26,380	14,198	NA	NA
1970	128,761	21,639	30,817	31,161	13,190	NA	220,869
1975	115,968	23,151	25,895	28,011	7,803	NA	159,659
1980	116,702	24,875	26,167	25,905	7,287	NA	74,153
1985	115,644	23,488	24,227	23,230	4,695	40,889	22,890
1986	110,437	23,329	23,480	22,544	4,553	46,582	14,763
1987	108,879	22,806	23,193	22,308	4,492	38,041	7,681
1988	117,169	24,526	24,167	22,767	5,424	55,851	7,053
1989	104,447	24,057	22,383	22,907	4,590	48,650	5,468
1990	96,535	23,792	20,985	23,136	4,639	25,308	4,975
1991	98,461	23,772	21,100	22,496	4,299	25,258	4,168
1992	95,123	24,137	20,695	22,240	4,198	25,308	3,808
1993	95,291	24,482	20,895	21,879	4,086	23,937	3,911
1994	99,677	24,892	21,546	21,262	4,353	26,572	4,043
1995	89,721	23,935	20,586	18,552	4,068	22,820	3,943
1996	88,822	23,393	19,086	19,113	4,068	27,233	3,869
2000**	79,805	21,596	16,139	16,860	29,574***	-	*
2005**	77,068	21,146	15,097	17,279	30,760***	-	*
2010**	78,651	21,099	15,342	16,929	31,809***	-	*

Carbon Monoxide (CO) Two-thirds of all emissions of carbon monoxide, a colorless, odorless, poisonous gas, are caused by motor-vehicle exhaust. In cities, automobiles account for almost 95 percent of emissions. Exposure to high levels of CO can lead to eyesight problems, poor learning ability, reduced manual dexterity, and difficulty in performing complex tasks.

Lead (Pb) Lead in the air is caused primarily by smelters and battery plants. Lead can also be found in food, paint, water, soil, or dust. Exposure to lead can cause anemia, kidney disease, and reproductive and neurological problems.

Nitrogen Oxides Motor-vehicle exhaust and the byproducts of electric utilities and industrial boilers are the primary sources of nitrogen oxides. Nitrogen dioxide (NO_2) can cause respiratory problems.

Ozone (O_3) Ozone is the major component of smog. It is formed by sunlight acting on NO and VOC (Volatile Organic Compounds), gasses that can be emitted from gas stations, factories, and dry cleaners, among other sources. Exposure to ozone can cause respiratory problems.

Particulate Matter (PM-10) Particulate matter consists of solid or liquid airborne particles that can originate from any number of sources, including power plants and diesel trucks. Exposure can cause respiratory problems and cancer.

Sulfur Dioxide (SO_2) Sulfur dioxide is formed when sulfur-containing fuels are burned. Exposure can cause respiratory problems and exacerbate heart disease.

*Lead levels are expected to diminish at such a rate that they will be minimal by the year 2000.
**Projections.
***Includes fugitive dust.

Source: U.S Environmental Protection Agency

Water Quality in Lakes and Rivers

The following charts illustrate water quality in the nation's rivers, lakes, and the Great Lakes, which, according to the EPA, contain one-fifth of the world's fresh surface water. A good rating describes bodies of water that have attained the water quality standards of states and other jurisdictions. Those with a bad rating have fallen short of those standards.

Impaired River Miles

Rivers surveyed = 693,905 miles
19% of total rivers (3.6 million miles)

Total Good =
444,099 miles

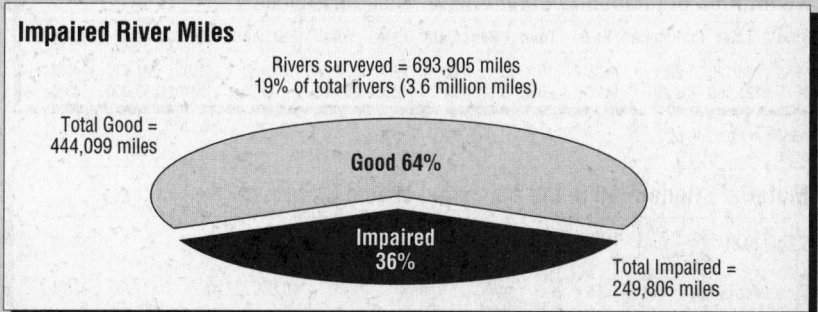

Good 64%

Impaired
36%

Total Impaired =
249,806 miles

Impaired Lake Acres

Lakes surveyed = 17 million acres
40% of total lakes (42 million acres)

Total Good =
10.4 million acres

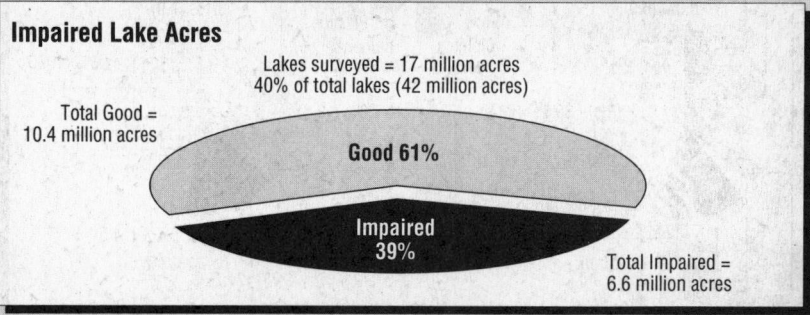

Good 61%

Impaired
39%

Total Impaired =
6.6 million acres

Impaired Great Lakes Shoreline

Shoreline surveyed = 5,186 miles
94% of total shoreline (5,521 miles)

Good 3%

Total Good =
156 miles

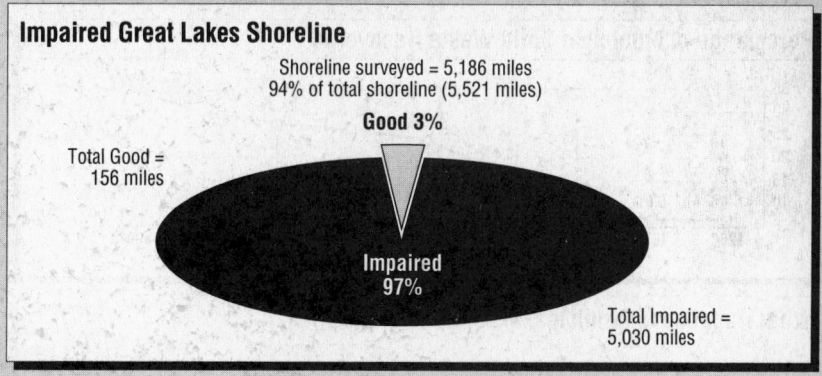

Impaired
97%

Total Impaired =
5,030 miles

Source: U.S. Environmental Protection Agency

Municipal Waste

Municipal solid waste includes materials such as containers and packaging, food scraps, yard trimmings, and durable and nondurable goods (including appliances, automobile tires, and newspapers).

Generation of Municipal Solid Waste (Thousands of tons)

Year	Total	Per capita*	Year	Total	Per capita*	Year	Total	Per capita*	Year	Total	Per capita*
1960	88,120	2.68	1980	151,640	3.66	1994	214,700	4.51	2000	221,670	4.42
1970	121,060	3.25	1990	205,210	4.51	1996	209,660	4.33	2010	253,000	4.66

*Pounds per person per day.

Materials Generated in the Municipal Waste Stream (Millions of tons)

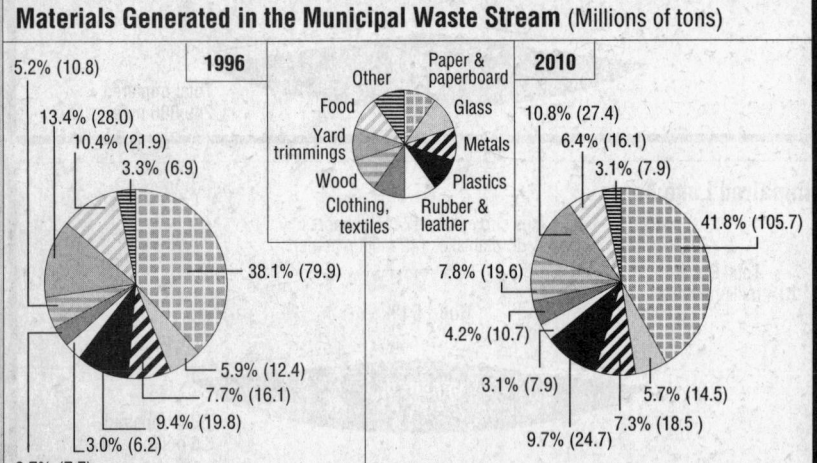

1996

5.2% (10.8)
13.4% (28.0)
10.4% (21.9)
3.3% (6.9)
38.1% (79.9)
5.9% (12.4)
7.7% (16.1)
9.4% (19.8)
3.0% (6.2)
3.7% (7.7)

Other
Food
Yard trimmings
Wood
Clothing, textiles
Paper & paperboard
Glass
Metals
Plastics
Rubber & leather

2010

10.8% (27.4)
6.4% (16.1)
3.1% (7.9)
41.8% (105.7)
7.8% (19.6)
4.2% (10.7)
3.1% (7.9)
9.7% (24.7)
7.3% (18.5)
5.7% (14.5)

Percentage of Municipal Solid Waste Recovered

Year	1960	1970	1980	1990	1994	1995	1996	2000	2010
	6.4%	6.6%	9.6%	16.4%	23.8%	26.1%	27.3%	30.0%	35.0%

What Happens to Municipal Waste?

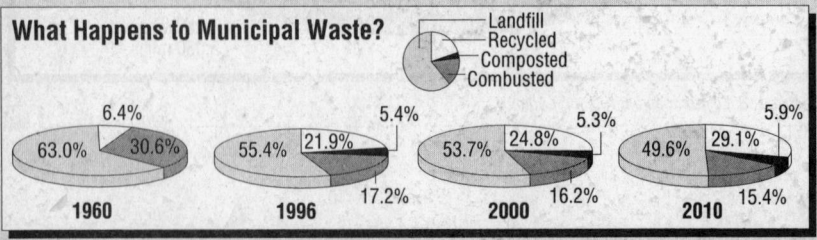

Landfill
Recycled
Composted
Combusted

1960: 63.0%, 30.6%, 6.4%
1996: 55.4%, 21.9%, 5.4%, 17.2%
2000: 53.7%, 24.8%, 5.3%, 16.2%
2010: 49.6%, 29.1%, 5.9%, 15.4%

Source: U.S. Environmental Protection Agency

States, Ranked by Total Release of Toxic Chemicals, 1996

State	Total on- and off-site releases (Pounds)	State	Total on- and off-site releases (Pounds)
Texas	267,440,786	Kansas	26,576,384
Louisiana	184,537,787	Oklahoma	26,421,809
Ohio	145,139,835	Minnesota	20,970,579
Pennsylvania	122,423,185	New Mexico	19,963,709
Indiana	108,988,034	New Jersey	18,076,905
Illinois	107,663,656	Idaho	15,152,687
Tennessee	103,874,399	Maryland	13,098,751
Alabama	102,922,534	Nebraska	13,022,778
Michigan	90,158,602	Massachusetts	9,977,171
North Carolina	85,174,574	Wyoming	9,664,368
Utah	82,889,834	Maine	9,351,265
Florida	80,957,682	Puerto Rico	8,548,778
Missouri	59,794,580	Connecticut	8,185,179
Georgia	58,831,731	Alaska	6,908,783
South Carolina	56,668,160	Colorado	5,711,491
Virginia	56,092,193	South Dakota	5,196,074
Mississippi	54,846,362	Nevada	3,766,636
California	50,082,638	Delaware	3,660,020
Montana	48,477,642	Rhode Island	2,601,984
Arizona	47,964,210	New Hampshire	2,468,237
Kentucky	47,366,863	North Dakota	2,325,120
Wisconsin	47,023,091	Virgin Islands	1,506,139
New York	35,654,003	Hawaii	540,267
Arkansas	34,032,075	Vermont	462,849
Iowa	33,308,409	American Samoa	10,500
Oregon	29,735,693	District of Columbia	9,460
West Virginia	28,837,730	Guam	3,000
Washington	28,439,371		
		Total	2,433,506,582

Source: U.S. Environmental Protection Agency

Industries With Largest Total Release of Toxic Chemicals, 1996

Industry	Total release (Pounds)
Chemicals	785,178,163
Primary metals	564,535,183
Paper	227,563,372
Plastics	116,409,291
Transportation equipment	111,352,769
Fabricated metals	90,254,367
Food	83,303,395
Petroleum	68,887,258
Electrical equipment	41,765,377

Parent Companies With the Largest Releases of Toxic Chemicals, 1996

Industry	Total air emissions (Pounds)	Surface water discharges (Pounds)	Underground injection (Pounds)	Releases to land (Pounds)	Total on-site releases (Pounds)
Renco Group Inc.	65,833,745	600	0	7,645,248	73,479,593
ASARCO Inc.	2,134,717	6,183	251,535	62,956,452	65,348,887
Du Pont Co.	24,945,688	3,060,907	36,718,368	26,323	64,751,286
Potash Corp. of Saskatchewan	15,799,831	21,616,044	0	16,304,477	53,720,352
Monsanto Co.	1,524,283	491,471	37,329,363	70,565	39,415,682
International Paper Co.	35,613,763	1,024,801	0	76,198	36,714,762
General Motors Corp.	19,317,331	92,174	0	15,649,871	35,059,376
Cyprus Amax Minerals Co.	4,694,536	6,266	0	25,536,191	30,236,993
Courtaulds United States Inc.	29,605,596	35,620	0	454,300	30,095,516
Cytec Industries Inc.	1,487,359	712,070	23,748,075	123,827	26,071,331

20 Facilities With the Largest Total Release of Toxic Chemicals, 1996

Facility name	City	State	Total on- and off-site releases (Pounds)
Magnesium Corp. of America	Rowley	UT	65,311,364
ASARCO Inc.	East Helena	MT	44,470,126
Courtaulds Fibers Inc.	Axis	AL	28,182,560
Cyprus Miami Mining Co.	Claypool	AZ	25,838,430
Cytec Industries Inc.	Westwego	LA	24,075,620
Du Pont	Victoria	TX	23,832,658
Zinc Corp. of America	Monaca	PA	23,472,626
PCS Nitrogen Fertilizer L.P.	Geismar	LA	23,193,735
Monsanto Co.	Gonzalez	FL	22,372,928
Lenzing Fibers Corp.	Lowland	TN	18,448,320
Elkem Metals Co.	Marietta	OH	17,050,768
Nucor Steel	Crawfordsville	IN	16,899,416
BASF Corp.	Freeport	TX	16,473,532
National Steel Corp.	Ecorse	MI	15,322,532
Northwestern Steel & Wire Co.	Sterling	IL	14,484,220
General Motors Powertrain	Defiance	OH	14,362,843
PCS Phosphate Co. Inc.	Aurora	NC	13,202,617
Rouge Steel Co.	Dearborn	MI	13,143,855
BP Chemicals Inc.	Lima	OH	13,130,245
IMC-Agrico Co.	Saint James	LA	12,794,917

Source: U.S. Environmental Protection Agency

Hazardous-Waste Sites

States Ranked by Final and Proposed Hazardous-Waste Sites for the National Priorities List

These are uncontrolled hazardous-waste sites that warrant further investigation to determine if long-term cleanup and other remedial action are needed under the Superfund program.

State	Total	State	Total
New Jersey	110	Connecticut	14
Pennsylvania	100	Alabama	13
California	96	Maine	12
New York	80	Rhode Island	12
Michigan	74	Arkansas	11
Florida	55	Kansas	11
Washington	47	Oklahoma	11
Illinois	41	Oregon	11
Wisconsin	39	Arizona	10
Ohio	37	Nebraska	10
Massachusetts	31	New Mexico	10
Indiana	30	Puerto Rico	10
Texas	30	Idaho	9
Minnesota	28	Montana	9
South Carolina	26	Vermont	8
Virginia	26	Alaska	7
North Carolina	23	West Virginia	7
Missouri	22	Hawaii	4
New Hampshire	18	Mississippi	3
Colorado	17	Wyoming	3
Delaware	17	Guam	2
Georgia	17	South Dakota	2
Iowa	17	Virgin Islands	2
Kentucky	16	District of Columbia	1
Louisiana	16	Nevada	1
Maryland	16	North Dakota	0
Utah	16		
Tennessee	15	**Total**	**1,251**

Source: U.S. Environmental Protection Agency

Cleaning Up

A large environmental services industry has developed in the U.S., but its growth rate has slowed during the 1990s.

Growth Rate of U.S. Environmental Services Industry

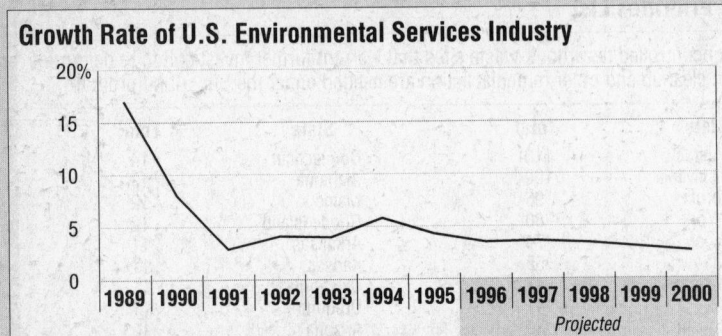

1989 | 1990 | 1991 | 1992 | 1993 | 1994 | 1995 | 1996 | 1997 | 1998 | 1999 | 2000

Projected

U.S. Environmental Industry Breakdown

Industry Segment	Revenues ($ billions)		
	1990	1996	2000*
Services			
Analytical Services	1.5	1.2	1.2
Wastewater Treatment Works	19.8	24.0	27.8
Solid Waste Management	26.1	33.9	37.4
Hazardous Waste Management	6.3	6.0	5.1
Remediation/Industrial Services	8.5	8.6	8.8
Consulting and Engineering	12.5	15.2	15.8
Equipment			
Water Equipment and Chemicals	13.5	17.5	20.4
Instruments and Information Systems	2.0	3.1	3.7
Air Pollution Control Equipment	10.7	15.7	16.5
Waste Management Equipment	10.4	12.0	12.5
Process and Prevention Technology	0.4	0.8	1.3
Resources			
Water Utilities	19.8	26.4	29.9
Resource Recovery	13.1	14.3	16.6
Environmental Energy Sources	1.8	2.4	3.1
Total Industry:	**146.4**	**181.0**	**200.1**

*Projected.
Source: Environmental Business International, Inc.

America's Deadliest Disasters*

Type and Location	No. of deaths	Date
Floods:		
Galveston tidal wave	6,000	Sept. 8, 1900
Johnstown, PA	2,209	May 31, 1889
Ohio and Indiana	732	Mar. 28, 1913
St. Francis, CA, dam burst	450	Mar. 13, 1928
Ohio and Mississippi River valleys	380	Jan. 22, 1937
Hurricanes:		
Florida	1,833	Sept. 16–17, 1928
New England	657	Sept. 21, 1938
Louisiana	500	Sept. 29, 1915
Florida	409	Sept. 1–2, 1935
Louisiana and Texas	395	June 27–28, 1957
Tornadoes:		
Illinois	606	Mar. 18, 1925
Mississippi, Alabama, Georgia	402	Apr. 2-7, 1936
Southern and Midwestern states	307	Apr. 3, 1974
Indiana, Ohio, Michigan, Illinois, Wisconsin	272	April 11, 1965
Arkansas, Tennessee, Missouri, Mississippi, Alabama	229	Mar. 21–22, 1952
Earthquakes:		
San Francisco earthquake and fire	452	Apr. 18, 1906
Alaskan earthquake-tsunami hit Hawaii, California	173	Apr. 1, 1946
Long Beach, CA, earthquake	120	Mar. 10, 1933
Alaskan earthquake and tsunami	117	Mar. 27, 1964
San Fernando–Los Angeles, CA, earthquake	64	Feb. 9, 1971
Marine:		
Sultana exploded - Mississippi River	1,547	Apr. 27, 1865
General Slocum burned - East River	1,030	June 15, 1904
Empress of Ireland ship collision - St. Lawrence River	1,024	May 29, 1914
Eastland capsized - Chicago River	812	July 24, 1915
Morro-Castle burned - off New Jersey coast	135	Sept. 8, 1934
Aircraft:		
Crash of scheduled plane near O'Hare Airport, Chicago	273	May 25, 1979
Explosion and crash of scheduled plane off Long Island, NY	230	July 17, 1996
Crash of scheduled plane, Detroit, MI	156	Aug. 16, 1987
Crash of scheduled plane in Kenner, LA	154	July 9, 1982
Two-plane collision over San Diego, CA	144	Sept. 25, 1978
Railroad:		
Two-train collision near Nashville, TN	101	July 9, 1918
Two-train collision, Eden, CO	96	Aug. 7, 1904
Avalanche hit two trains near Wellington, WA	96	Mar. 1, 1910
Bridge collapse under train, Ashtabula, OH	92	Dec. 29, 1876
Rapid transit train derailment, Brooklyn, NY	92	Nov. 1, 1918
Fires:		
Peshtigo, WI, and surrounding area, forest fire	1,152	Oct. 9, 1871
Iroquois Theatre, Chicago	603	Dec. 30, 1903
Northeastern Minnesota, forest fire	559	Oct. 12, 1918
Cocoanut Grove nightclub, Boston	492	Nov. 28, 1942
North German Lloyd Steamships, Hoboken, NJ	326	June 30, 1900
Explosions:		
Texas City, TX, ship explosion	552	Apr. 16, 1947
Port Chicago, CA, ship explosion	322	July 18, 1944
New London, TX, school explosion	294	Mar. 18, 1937
Oakdale, PA, munitions plant explosion	158	May 18, 1918
Eddystone, PA, munitions plant explosion	133	Apr. 10, 1917
Mines:		
Monongha, WV, coal mine explosion	361	Dec. 6, 1907
Dawson, NM, coal mine fire	263	Oct. 22, 1913
Cherry, IL, coal mine fire	259	Nov. 13, 1909
Jacobs Creek, PA, coal mine explosion	239	Dec. 19, 1907
Scofield, UT, coal mine explosion	200	May 1, 1900

*Based on unintentional accidents or disasters.
Source: National Safety Council

Costliest Catastrophes

Total Insured Losses for U.S. Catastrophes (In millions)

Year	Estimated loss payment	No. of catastrophes	Year	Estimated loss payment	No. of catastrophes
1985	$2,816	34	1991	$4,723	36
1986	872	26	1992	22,970	36
1987	905	24	1993	5,705	36
1988	1,409	32	1994	17,010	38
1989	7,642	34	1995	8,310	34
1990	2,825	32	1996	7,375	41

The 10 Most Costly Insured U.S. Catastrophes

Month/Year	Catastrophe	Estimated insured loss
Aug. 1992	Hurricane Andrew	$15,500,000,000
Jan. 1994	Northridge, CA earthquake, fire	12,500,000,000
Sept. 1989	Hurricane Hugo	4,195,000,000
Oct. 1995	Hurricane Opal	2,100,000,000
March 1993	Multi-state winter storm	1,750,000,000
Oct. 1991	Oakland, CA fire	1,700,000,000
Sept. 1992	Hurricane Iniki	1,600,000,000
Sept. 1996	Hurricane Fran	1,600,000,000
May 1995	Texas and New Mexico: wind, hail, flooding	1,135,000,000
Oct. 1989	Loma Prieta, CA earthquake	960,000,000

Sources: Property Claim Services division of American Insurance Services Group and Insurance Information Institute

The 10 Most Costly U.S. Earthquakes*

Year	Locality	Estimated property damage
1994	Northridge, CA	$13–20,000,000,000
1989	San Francisco Bay area (Loma Prieta quake)	7,000,000,000
1971	San Fernando, CA	553,000,000
1964	Alaska and west coast of United States (tsunami damage from earthquake near Anchorage, AK)	500,000,000
1987	Southern California; primarily in Los Angeles-Pasadena-Whittier area	358,000,000
1992	Southern California; Landers, Joshua Tree, Big Bear	92,000,000
1992	Northern California coast; Petrolia, Eureka	66,000,000
1952	Kern County, CA	60,000,000
1933	Long Beach, CA	40,000,000
1983	Central California (Coalinga)	31,000,000

*One of history's most catastrophic occurrences, the San Francisco earthquake-fire of 1906 caused direct quake losses of some $24 million, plus fire losses of $350 million to $500 million, for a total loss in current dollars of nearly $6.0 billion.
Sources: National Geophysical Data Center, National Oceanic and Atmospheric Administration, and Insurance Information Institute

The 10 Most Costly Insured Hurricanes

Dates	Place	Hurricane	Estimated insured loss
Aug. 1992	FL, LA, MS	Andrew	$15,500,000,000
Sept. 1989	U.S. Virgin Islands, PR, GA, SC, NC, VA	Hugo	4,195,000,000
Oct. 1995	FL, AL, GA, SC, NC, TN	Opal	2,100,000,000
Sept. 1992	Kauai and Oahu, HI	Iniki	1,600,000,000
Sept. 1996	NC, SC, VA, MD, WV, PA, OH	Fran	1,600,000,000
Sept. 1995	U.S. Virgin Islands, PR	Marilyn	875,000,000
Sept. 1979	MS, AL, FL, LA, TN, KY, WV, OH, PA, NY	Frederic	752,510,000
Aug. 1983	TX	Alicia	675,520,000
Aug. 1991	NC, NY, CT, RI, MA, ME	Bob	620,000,000
Aug. 1985	FL, AL, MS, LA	Elena	543,300,000

Sources: Property Claim Services division of American Insurance Services Group and Insurance Information Institute

Travel and Transportation

Outwardly, cars have changed so dramatically over this century that Henry Ford probably would hardly recognize the latest models from the company that bears his name. But under the hood, the mechanisms that turn gasoline into energy to make the wheels turn are fundamentally the same now as on a model T.

That could be about to change.

Auto makers around the world are scrambling for the lead in the race to develop the first really new approaches to what engineers call powertrain since the internal-combustion engine appeared over a century ago. And while hundreds of thousands of vehicles on America's roads already run on natural gas, alcohol and other alternative fuels, more radical technologies are closer to the mainstream than ever before.

"We now have a higher probability of a dramatic shift of vehicle powertrains than at any time in the last 100 years," says David Cole, director of the University of Michigan's Center for the Study of Automotive Transportation.

Most major auto makers already offer elec-

tric cars that run on batteries, although few can travel much more than 100 miles on a charge. Heading for showrooms soon are so-called hybrids, which combine electric power with gasoline or diesel engines to sharply increase fuel economy and cut emissions. And the holy grail of alternative technologies, the fuel cell, which produces none of the noxious emissions current cars do, is said to be at least a decade away from economical production.

So far, governments have been driving much of the innovation by requiring auto makers to reduce emissions and improve mileage in an effort to control air pollution and reduce oil consumption. In the United States, California has taken the lead, demanding that by 2003, 10 percent of the vehicles auto makers sell produce no emissions at all. Overseas, where gasoline prices usually are several times what they are in the United States, demand for better mileage has pushed auto makers toward the new technologies.

"No car company is going to survive on just internal-combustion engines," says Bill Ball, director of strategic planning for advanced-technology vehicles at General Motors Corp. "As we look at 25 years down the road, this will be regarded as the gestation and birth period of a set of new technologies that will be firmly in the portfolio by that time."

Some already are out. Toyota Motor Corp. introduced its Prius sedan in Japan in late 1997 and sold 10,000 of them in the first nine months. In Japan's stop-and-go urban traffic, Toyota says the Prius gets 66 miles per gallon, about double what most traditional cars do, and cuts emissions in half. Toyota plans to sell the Prius in the United States starting in 2000, making it the first hybrid on the market here. Toyota first must adjust the design to improve performance and fuel economy at the highway speeds popular in the United States, plus reduce emissions further to meet California's tight standards.

The Prius uses a combination of a small gasoline engine and an electric motor to power the car. Because of the shared power system, the Prius doesn't use a traditional transmission. The gasoline engine runs mostly at a constant speed and is shut off when it would normally idle, enhancing efficiency and reducing wear. The Prius doesn't need to be recharged because it automatically charges the batteries, using the on-board generator as a brake or diverting engine power to it as needed.

Toyota expects Prius's price tag in the United States to be $15,000 to $20,000 when it's introduced. Officials concede that it's still a money-loser, but they say the public awareness and market experience it provides are critical.

"Initially, it's an investment in our future," says Mark Amstock, Toyota's U.S. manager for alternative-fuel vehicles. "Through volume, we'll be able to make this car profitable."

Other auto makers seem to agree, and virtually all have plans to sell some kind of hybrid in the United States in the next few years. Some use more efficient diesel engines instead of gasoline, and the ways they balance electric and engine power vary. Though they are of many different shapes and sizes, all offer far better mileage than traditional cars and reduced emissions. Major advances improving performance and reducing weight and cost will be needed to make them truly attractive to consumers, however.

Nonetheless, many industry analysts say hybrids could be more promising than all-electric cars, a few test models of which are in showrooms already. Though they can't touch electrics' green credentials—battery-powered cars produce no exhaust at all—hybrids offer much longer range and don't need hours of recharging every night.

"The hybrid will be the attractive vehicle," says Thad Melash, an analyst at J.D. Power and Associates, a California automotive consulting firm. Mr. Cole of the University of Michigan says some in the industry expect hybrids to take as much as 5 percent of the U.S. vehicle market in the next 10 years, meaning annual sales of as many as 750,000 units. So far, auto makers are talking about figures in the tens of thousands, however.

Mr. Melash believes diesel engines could soon approach hybrids' mileage and cleanliness, provided that improvements to fuel now in the works prove successful. Already, major auto makers are investing in new diesel technologies they hope will remove the problems of noise, poor performance and noxious odors that now limit diesel penetration in the United States to about 1 percent of the market.

Mr. Melash notes that his firm's surveys of consumers show Americans aren't willing to pay much of a premium for cleaner, more efficient cars, particularly if they have to give up the versatility of traditional automobiles. But auto makers say they will continue to bring new technologies to market, both to meet regulatory requirements and to build experience in the marketplace. Both electric vehicles and hybrids are critical test beds for the drive systems that will be used in what most expect to be the next generation of alternative vehicles—the fuel cell. This technology uses hydrogen as fuel to generate electricity, but produces only carbon dioxide and water as exhaust. Most in the industry say fuel cells won't be ready for the market for at least 10 years, although Mercedes is planning to offer one around 2004. Among the biggest obstacles are high cost and the lack of a way to store hydrogen safely and efficiently.

The different technologies are expected to battle it out in the marketplace, starting in niches. Electric vehicles, for example, are well suited to corporate and government fleets, where range isn't a major issue. Hybrids might take off in Europe and Japan, where high fuel prices put a premium on their efficiency. And tax and other incentives in energy-producing areas might stimulate the use of natural gas or alcohol as fuels in those regions.

"There's nothing that looks like a clear winner at this point," says Tom Moore, Chrysler Corp.'s advanced-technology chief.

And the gasoline engine isn't headed for extinction, either. Honda Motor Co., for example, is developing one that produces virtually no significant emissions. "The gasoline engine is far from dead," says Mr. Melash of J.D. Power. "It'll continue to push the other technologies. It will be the benchmark."

Gregory L. White

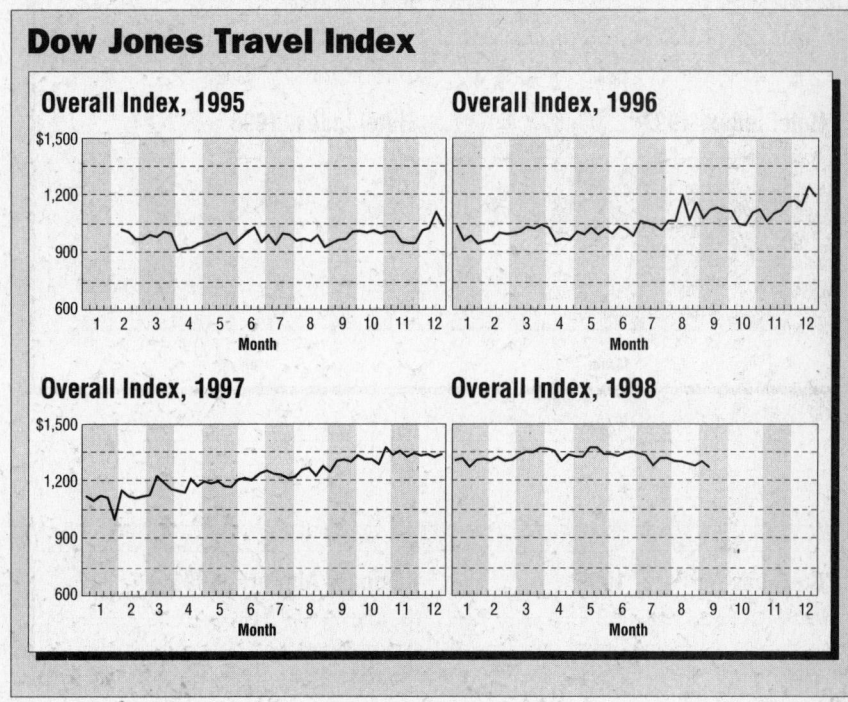

Dow Jones Travel Index

Overall Index, 1995

Overall Index, 1996

Overall Index, 1997

Overall Index, 1998

Hotel Index, 1995

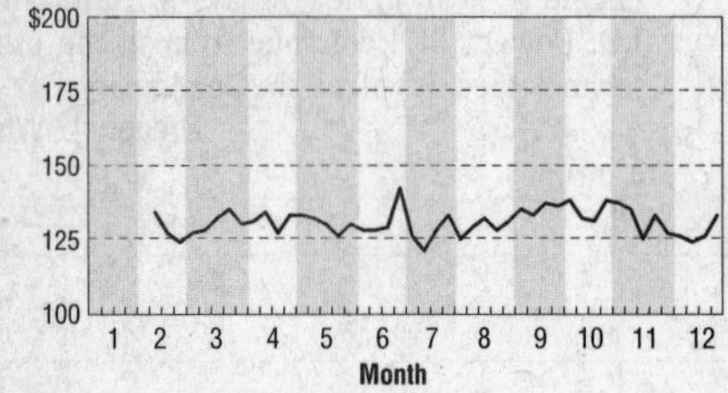

Hotel Index, 1996

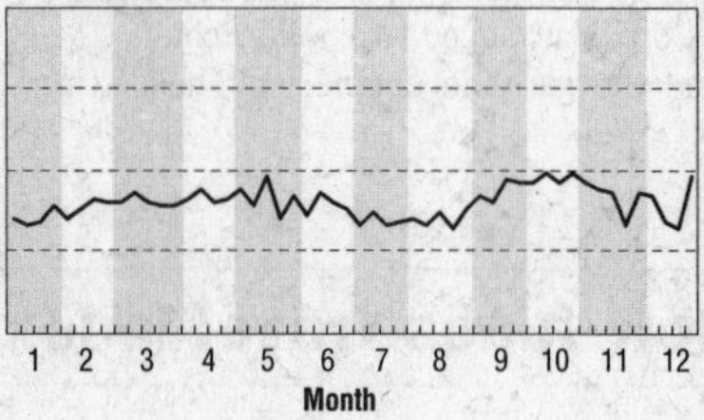

Hotel Index, 1997

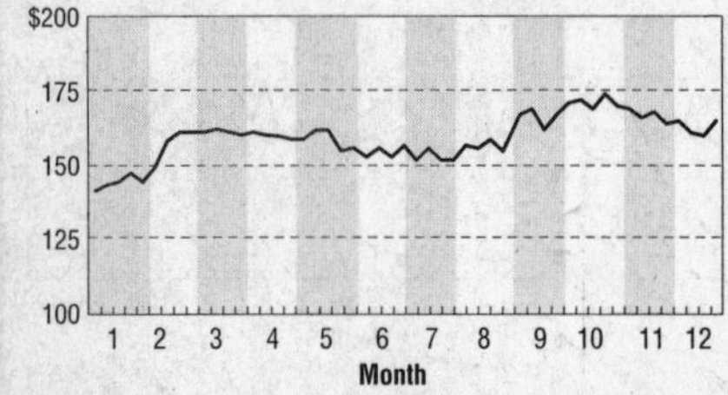

Hotel Index, 1998

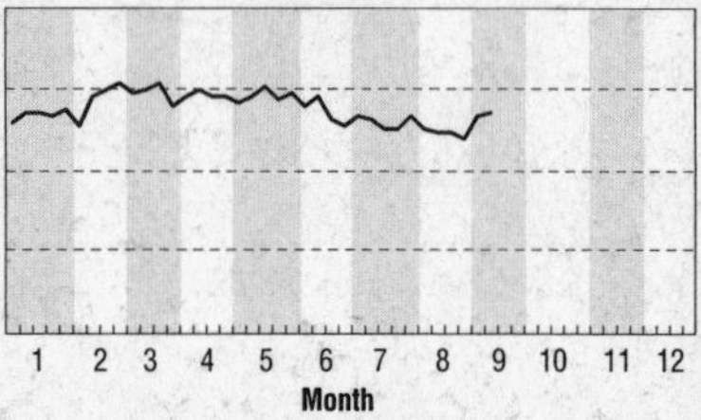

Business Air Fare, 1995

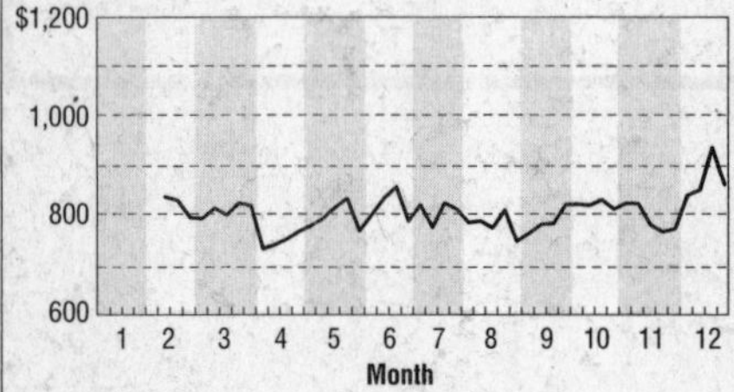

Business Air Fare, 1996

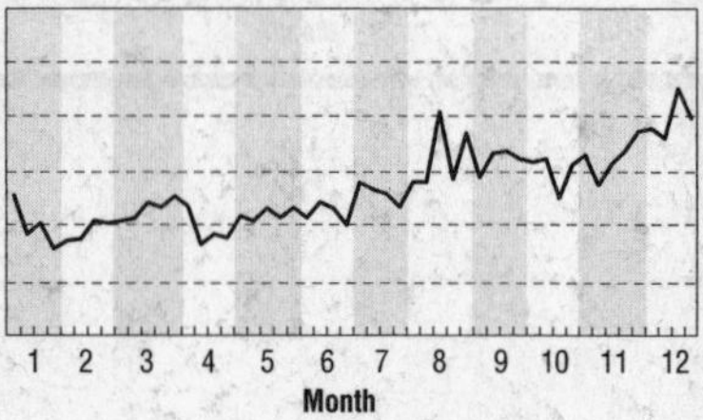

Business Air Fare, 1997

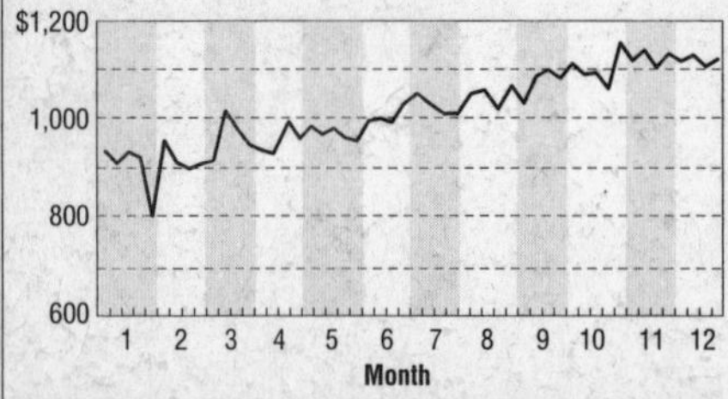

Business Air Fare, 1998

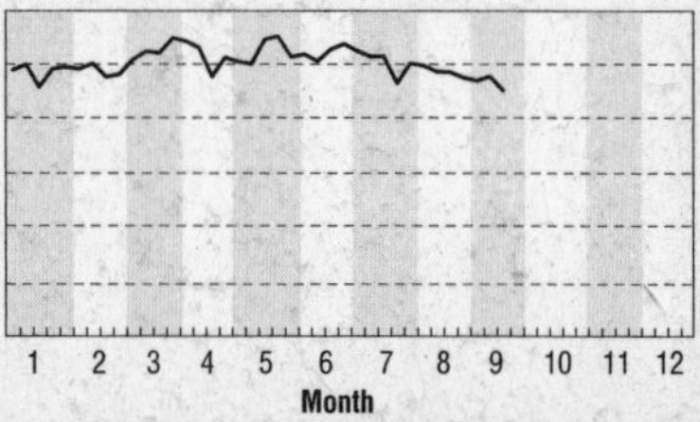

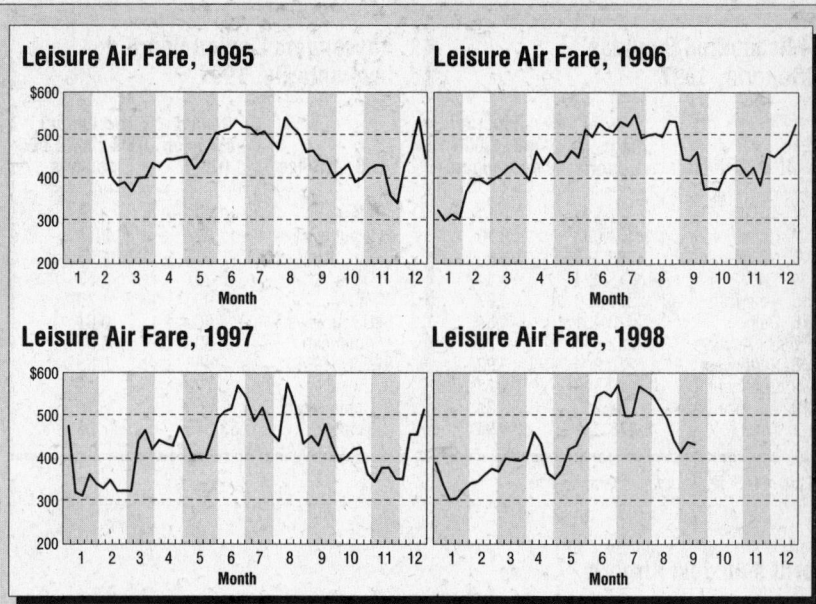

Leisure Air Fare, 1995

Leisure Air Fare, 1996

Leisure Air Fare, 1997

Leisure Air Fare, 1998

Note: The overall index——reflecting the average cost of an overnight business trip— tracks the cost of business fares on 20 major routes plus hotel and car-rental rates in 20 cities. Hotel data based on daily rates from 10 leading hotel chains. Business fares based on refundable fares on 20 major routes. Leisure fares based on advance-purchase-fares on the same routes.

Airline Performance Rankings

Percentage of Reported Flights Arriving on Time

U.S. Airlines	1997 %	Sept. 87– Dec. 97 %
1 Southwest	81.9%	84.4%
2 TWA	80.2	77.5
3 US Airways	80.1	79.2
4 American	79.1	80.0
5 Continental	78.2	78.6
6 America West	77.5	81.9
7 United	75.9	77.2
8 Alaska	74.9	78.7
9 Northwest	74.7	80.9
10 Delta	74.1	77.3
Total	**77.7**	**79.3**

Air Travel Consumer Complaint Report, 1997

U.S. Airlines	Complaints	Complaints per 100,000 passengers
1 America West	277	1.51
2 Northwest	763	1.39
3 American	859	1.06
4 United	802	0.95
5 TWA	195	0.83
6 US Airways	457	0.78
7 Continental	300	0.77
8 Delta	661	0.64
9 Alaska	77	0.63
10 Southwest	159	0.28
Total	**4,550**	**0.86**

Mishandled Baggage Reports, 1997

U.S. Airlines	Total baggage reports	Reports per 1,000 passengers
1 Alaska	77,904	7.19
2 United	471,092	6.70
3 Northwest	263,783	6.05
4 TWA	115,424	5.44
5 American	300,760	4.87
6 Delta	423,451	4.54
7 US Airways	232,814	4.24
8 Southwest	210,924	3.92
9 Continental	124,406	3.78
10 America West	58,283	3.39
Total	**2,278,841**	**4.96**

Passengers Denied Boarding Involuntarily, 1997

U.S. Airlines	Denied boardings (DB's)	Involuntary DB's per 10,000 persons
1 Alaska	3,409	2.78
2 Southwest	12,074	2.16
3 America West	3,771	1.98
4 Delta	15,297	1.53
5 TWA	2,930	1.30
6 US Airways	4,662	0.81
7 American	4,596	0.63
8 Northwest	2,655	0.53
9 United	3,792	0.49
10 Continental	360	0.10
Total	**53,546**	**1.06**

Source: U.S. Transportation Department

World's Busiest Airports

RANK	CITY (AIRPORT)	1997 TOTAL PASSENGERS
1	Chicago (O'Hare Int'l)	70,294,601
2	Atlanta (Hartsfield Atlanta Int'l)	68,205,769
3	Dallas/Ft. Worth Airport, (Dallas/Fort Worth Int'l)	60,488,713
4	Los Angeles (Los Angeles Int'l)	60,142,588
5	London (Heathrow)	57,974,931
6	Tokyo (Haneda)	49,302,268
7	San Francisco (San Francisco Int'l)	40,499,947
8	Frankfurt/Main (Rheim/Main)	40,262,691
9	Seoul (Kimpo Int'l)	36,757,280
10	Paris (Charles de Gaulle)	35,293,661
11	Denver (Denver Int'l)	34,972,936
12	Miami (Miami Int'l)	34,533,268
13	Amsterdam (Schiphol)	31,569,977
14	Detroit (Metro Wayne County)	31,520,656
15	New York (J.F. Kennedy Int'l)	31,228,956
16	Newark (Newark Int'l)	30,866,374
17	Phoenix (Sky Harbor Int'l)	30,536,061
18	Las Vegas (McCarran Int'l)	30,305,553
19	Minneapolis/St. Paul (Minneapolis/St. Paul Int'l)	29,070,480
20	Hong Kong (Hong Kong Int'l)	29,020,369
21	Houston (Intercontinental)	28,701,092
22	St. Louis (Lambert-St. Louis Int'l)	27,657,026
23	Orlando (Orlando Int'l)	27,305,249
24	London (Gatwick)	26,961,453
25	Toronto (Lester B. Pearson Int'l)	26,082,713

Source: Airports Council International

Top 30 Domestic Airline Markets*

			Number of Passengers (outbound plus inbound) (in thousands)
1	New York	Los Angeles	3,725
2	New York	Miami	3,093
3	New York	Chicago	2,980
4	New York	Boston	2,689
5	Honolulu	Kahului, Maui	2,620
6	New York	San Francisco	2,609
7	New York	Orlando	2,454
8	New York	Washington	2,398
9	Dallas/Ft. Worth	Houston	2,219
10	Los Angeles	Las Vegas	2,111
11	Los Angeles	San Francisco	2,021
12	New York	Atlanta	2,016
13	New York	San Juan	1,834
14	New York	Ft. Lauderdale	1,823
15	Honolulu	Lihue, Kauai	1,696
16	Chicago	Los Angeles	1,581
17	New York	West Palm Beach	1,530
18	Honolulu	Kona, Hawaii	1,493
19	Los Angeles	Oakland	1,462
20	Chicago	Detroit	1,433
21	New York	Dallas/Ft. Worth	1,429
22	Los Angeles	Honolulu	1,423
23	Chicago	Atlanta	1,359
24	Los Angeles	Phoenix	1,340
25	Chicago	Minneapolis/St. Paul	1,303
26	Honolulu	Hilo, Hawaii	1,250
27	Chicago	Dallas/Ft. Worth	1,206
28	Chicago	San Francisco	1,194
29	Boston	Washington	1,182
30	Chicago	Orlando	1,153

*Twelve months ended December 1997. Includes all commercial airports in a metropolitan area. Does not include connecting passengers.

Sources: Air Transport Association, U.S. Transportation Department

The Soaring Airline Industry

The U.S. airline industry achieved record profits in 1997 of $5.2 billion. Passenger traffic increased 4.6% to 605 billion revenue passenger miles, while cargo traffic rose 15.5% to 20.5 billion revenue ton miles.

Individual Airlines, 1997

Airline	Number of aircraft	Employees	Aircraft departures	Passengers (Thousands)	Revenue passenger miles (Millions)	Passenger revenues (Millions)	Cargo revenues (Millions)	Total operating revenues (Millions)	Operating profit/ (loss) (Millions)	Net profit/ (loss) (Millions)
Airborne Express	105	4,626	73,055	–	–	–	$890	$894	$98	$97
Alaska	78	8,016	159,146	12,245	10,362	$1,256	82	1,457	133	76
Aloha	17	1,901	76,617	5,191	721	195	30	233	6	4
America West	103	10,195	211,577	18,294	16,171	1,753	51	1,887	163	75
American	641	80,321	796,167	81,083	106,936	14,284	678	15,856	1,447	766
American Trans Air	45	4,349	30,691	3,157	4,534	369	–	746	10	0
Atlas Air*	19	592	25	–	–	–	80	401	56	23
Continental	388	31,705	446,642	38,756	44,072	5,686	205	6,361	645	385
Delta	559	62,934	968,893	103,133	99,624	12,773	588	14,204	1,621	934
DHL Airways	27	8,564	72,261	–	–	–	664	1,226	77	(13)
Emery Worldwide*	77	967	51,584	–	–	–	256	262	39	25
Evergreen International*	20	429	10,062	–	–	–	208	256	32	21
Federal Express	581	105,649	328,591	–	–	–	5,360	12,730	901	458
Hawaiian	22	2,357	49,827	4,938	3,134	332	20	404	2	(1)
Midwest Express	24	1,689	38,378	1,651	1,409	273	11	310	38	24
Northwest	405	46,753	584,324	54,650	71,998	8,722	788	9,984	1,203	604
Polar Air Cargo	16	481	6,545	–	–	–	288	344	6	(2)
Reeve Aleutian	5	312	3,859	62	38	14	8	30	(3)	(3)
Southwest	261	23,749	786,096	55,946	28,359	3,639	95	3,817	524	318
Trans World	184	22,930	279,886	23,370	25,099	2,924	119	3,328	(29)	(111)
United	571	83,324	798,131	84,203	121,350	15,069	891	17,335	1,226	932
United Parcel Service*	214	4,349	121,855	–	–	–	404	1,863	56	15
US Airways	376	39,734	734,971	58,659	41,578	7,112	177	8,501	586	1,052
Associate Members										
Aeromexico	58	5,930	106,551	7,520	5,418	1,009	19	1,087	101	95
Air Canada	155	21,215	NA	14,000	22,788	4,533	387	5,572	368	427
Canadian	76	15,706	NA	8,595	16,022	2,629	243	3,076	97	5
KLM-Royal Dutch**	116	26,923	NA	NA	34,904	3,956	956	6,495	394	1,071
Mexicana	51	6,324	91,027	7,138	6,195	875	18	960	110	118

*Includes nonscheduled service. **KLM data are for the 12 months ended March 31, 1998, at a rate of 48.6 cents per guilder.
Source: Air Transport Association

Total U.S. Scheduled Airlines

	1986	1987	1988	1989	1990	1991	1992	1993	1994	1995	1996	1997
Traffic–Scheduled Service												
Revenue passengers enplaned (Millions)	418.9	447.7	454.6	453.7	465.6	452.3	475.1	488.5	528.8	547.8	581.2	598.9
Revenue passenger miles (Millions)	366,545.9	404,471.5	423,301.6	432,714.3	457,926.3	447,954.8	478,553.7	489,684.4	519,381.7	540,656.2	578,663.0	605,434.0
Available seat miles (Millions)	607,435.8	648,720.9	676,802.3	684,375.9	733,374.9	715,199.1	752,772.4	771,640.6	784,330.9	807,077.8	835,071.0	860,564.0
Revenue passenger load factor (%)	60.3	62.3	62.5	63.2	62.4	62.6	63.6	63.5	66.2	67.0	69.3	70.4
Average passenger trip length (Miles)	875	903	931	954	984	990	1,007	1,002	982	987	996	1,011
Freight and express ton miles (Millions)	7,344.1	8,260.3	9,632.2	10,275.0	10,546.3	10,225.2	11,129.7	11,943.6	13,792.2	14,577.5	15,301.0	17,959.0
Aircraft departures (Thousands)	6,427.0	6,581.3	6,699.6	6,622.1	6,923.6	6,782.8	7,050.6	7,245.4	7,531.0	8,061.5	8,230.0	8,157.0
Financial												
Passenger revenues ($ millions)	40,056.1	44,940.4	50,295.7	53,802.1	58,453.2	57,091.7	59,828.5	63,945.2	65,421.5	69,594.4	75,286.0	79,469.0
Freight and express revenues ($ millions)	5,628.0	6,398.2	7,477.7	6,892.8	5,431.6	5,508.6	5,915.7	6,662.4	7,283.9	8,616.2	9,679.0	10,464.0
Mail revenues ($ millions)	838.3	923.0	971.8	955.4	970.5	957.1	1,184.2	1,211.6	1,183.3	1,265.5	1,279.0	1,360.0
Charter revenues ($ millions)	1,268.9	1,611.7	1,697.8	2,051.9	2,876.6	3,717.4	2,801.2	3,082.0	3,548.4	3,484.6	3,447.0	3,553.0
Total operating revenues ($ millions)	50,524.9	56,985.7	63,748.9	69,315.9	76,141.7	75,158.5	78,140.2	84,559.2	88,313.4	94,577.7	101,938.0	109,535.0
Total operating expenses ($ millions)	49,201.8	54,516.8	60,312.4	67,504.6	78,054.1	76,943.2	80,584.7	83,121.0	85,600.0	88,718.1	95,729.0	100,924.0
Operating profit ($ millions)	1,323.1	2,468.9	3,436.5	1,811.3	(1,912.4)	(1,784.7)	(2,444.5)	1,438.2	2,713.5	5,859.5	6,209.0	8,611.0
Interest expense ($ millions)	1,692.5	1,695.4	1,845.8	1,944.4	1,978.2	1,777.0	1,742.6	2,026.8	2,347.5	2,423.9	1,981.0	1,749.0
Net profit ($ millions)	(234.9)	593.4	1,685.6	127.9	(3,921.0)	(1,940.2)	(4,791.3)	(2,135.6)	(344.1)	2,313.6	2,804.0	5,195.0
Revenue per passenger mile (Cents)	10.9	11.1	11.9	12.4	12.8	12.7	12.5	13.1	12.6	12.9	13.0	13.1
Rate of return on investment (%)	4.9	7.2	10.8	6.3	(6.0)	(0.5)	(9.3)	(0.4)	5.2	11.9	11.5	14.9
Operating profit margin (%)	2.6	4.3	5.4	2.6	(2.5)	(2.4)	(3.1)	1.7	3.1	6.2	6.1	7.9
Net profit margin (%)	(0.5)	1.0	2.6	0.2	(5.1)	(2.6)	(6.1)	(2.5)	(0.4)	2.4	2.8	4.7
Employees	421,686	457,349	480,553	506,728	545,809	533,565	540,413	537,111	539,759	546,987	564,425	586,509

U.S. Aviation Accidents

	Year	Accidents		Fatalities		Accident rates per 100,000 aircraft hours	
		Total	Fatal	Total	Aboard	Total	Fatal
Large Commercial Carriers	1985	17	4	197	196	0.206	0.048
	1986	21	2	5	4	0.211	0.011
	1987	32	4	231	229	0.306	0.030
	1988	28	3	285	274	0.257	0.019
	1989	24	8	131	130	0.226	0.075
	1990	22	6	39	12	0.191	0.052
	1991	25	4	62*	49	0.224	0.036
	1992	16	4	33	31	0.136	0.034
	1993	22	1	1	0	0.184	0.008
	1994	19	4	239	237	0.146	0.033
	1995	34	2	166	160	0.266	0.016
	1996	32	3	342	342	0.243	0.023
	1997	42	3	3	2	0.290	0.021
Commuter Carriers	1985	21	7	37	36	1.209	0.403
	1986	15	2	4	4	0.870	0.116
	1987	33	10	59	57	1.695	0.514
	1988	19	2	21	21	0.908	0.096
	1989	19	5	31	31	0.848	0.223
	1990	16	4	7	5	0.683	0.171
	1991	22	8	99*	77	0.960	0.349
	1992	23	7	21	21	0.942	0.300
	1993	16	4	24	23	0.606	0.152
	1994	10	3	25	25	0.359	0.108
	1995	11	2	9	9	0.419	0.076
	1996	11	1	14	12	0.433	0.039
	1997	16	5	46	46	1.429	0.446
Unscheduled Air Taxis	1985	154	35	76	75	5.99	1.36
	1986	117	31	65	61	4.35	1.15
	1987	96	30	65	63	3.61	1.13
	1988	101	28	59	55	3.84	1.06
	1989	110	25	83	81	3.64	0.83
	1990	106	28	50	48	4.71	1.24
	1991	87	27	70	66	3.88	1.20
	1992	76	24	68	65	3.80	1.20
	1993	69	19	42	42	4.06	1.12
	1994	85	26	63	62	4.47	1.37
	1995	75	24	52	52	4.31	1.38
	1996	90	29	63	63	4.50	1.45
	1997	82	16	40	40	4.14	0.81
General Aviation**	1985	2,739	498	956	945	9.66	1.75
	1986	2,582	474	967	879	9.54	1.75
	1987	2,495	447	838	823	9.25	1.65
	1988	2,387	460	800	792	8.69	1.68
	1989	2,233	431	768	765	7.98	1.53
	1990	2,215	443	765	762	7.77	1.55
	1991	2,176	434	794	780	7.98	1.59
	1992	2,073	446	857	855	8.35	1.79
	1993	2,038	398	736	732	8.93	1.74
	1994	1,995	404	730	723	8.96	1.81
	1995	2,055	412	734	727	8.57	1.71
	1996	1,905	359	631	614	7.90	1.49
	1997	1,854	350	646	640	7.51	1.42

*Includes 12 persons killed aboard a Skywest commuter plane and 22 persons killed aboard a US Airways plane when the aircraft collided.

**Private planes.

Source: National Transportation Safety Board

Amtrak's Shaky Ride

Financial Results (In millions of dollars)

Fiscal year	Revenue	Expenses	Operating loss	Federal subsidies	Net loss
1990	$1,308	$2,012	-$703	$520	-$183
1991	1,359	2,081	-722	488	-234
1992	1,325	2,037	-712	481	-231
1993	1,403	2,134	-731	498	-233
1994	1,413	2,490	-834	502	-332
1995	1,497	2,305	-808	542	-266
1996	1,555	2,318	-764	441	-322
1997	1,674	2,436	-762	444	-318

Ridership (In millions of passenger trips)

Fiscal year	Northeast corridor	Intercity*	Amtrak West	Total
1990	11.2	11.0	–	22.2
1991	10.9	11.1	–	22.0
1992	10.1	11.2	–	21.3
1993	10.3	11.8	–	22.1
1994	11.7	6.3	3.1	21.2
1995	11.6	6.1	3.0	20.7
1996	11.0	5.4	3.3	19.7
1997	11.1	5.4	3.7	20.2

*For years 1990-1993, this number includes Amtrak West Ridership.
Source: Amtrak

Top Summer Travel Destinations

1995

1. Disneyland/Walt Disney World
2. Las Vegas
3. Europe
4. Caribbean
5. Florida
6. Mexico
7. Other
8. Hawaii
9. California
10. Alaska

1998

1. Walt Disney World
2. Florida
3. Las Vegas
4. Caribbean
5. Europe
6. Mexico
7. Hawaii
8. Alaska
9. California
10. Canada

Source: Carlson Wagonlit Travel

Checking In

The top 25 hotel markets in the U.S. and their average occupancy rates and room rates for 1997.

Largest U.S. Hotel Markets Based on Room Count 1997 Year End

Rank	Market	Number of hotels	Rooms	Occupancy percent	Average room rate
1	Las Vegas, NV	256	106,100	78.5 %	$ 74.76
2	Orlando, FL	327	92,200	78.7	80.99
3	Los Angeles-Long Beach, CA	640	80,000	68.7	82.48
4	Atlanta, GA	512	73,100	63.9	76.50
5	Chicago, IL	405	71,000	71.7	101.76
6	Washington, DC-Metro Area	366	68,700	70.8	100.25
7	New York, NY	245	66,600	80.5	169.19
8	Dallas, TX	316	48,500	66.9	78.74
9	San Diego, CA	393	47,200	71.5	86.50
10	Anaheim-Santa Ana, CA	353	44,600	68.1	76.43
11	San Francisco, CA	303	42,900	79.9	118.60
12	Houston, TX	274	42,700	64.1	70.05
13	Miami-Hialeah, FL	256	41,300	71.9	91.77
14	Phoenix, AZ	263	40,400	69.5	99.18
15	Oahu Island, HI	113	35,800	77.5	111.99
16	Tampa-St. Petersburg, FL	297	35,300	65.4	72.98
17	Boston, MA	222	35,100	74.3	116.58
18	Norfolk-Virginia Beach, VA	310	33,200	57.7	64.93
19	Detroit, MI	255	31,900	66.1	70.25
20	Riverside-San Bernardino, CA	345	30,700	58.0	74.33
21	Philadelphia, PA	206	29,700	70.7	90.49
22	Nashville, TN	226	28,300	66.8	73.20
23	Minneapolis-St.Paul, MN	206	27,000	69.0	76.84
24	Seattle, WA	236	27,000	72.4	89.82
25	St. Louis, MO	195	26,900	63.1	68.80
	New Orleans, LA	141	26,900	69.0	104.96

Source: Smith Travel Research

Where America Sleeps

Average U.S. Hotel Occupancy and Daily Room Rates

Year	Occupancy rate	Room rate	Year	Occupancy rate	Room rate
1987	63.2 %	$ 52.58	1993	63.5 %	$ 60.53
1988	63.5	54.47	1994	64.7	62.86
1989	64.3	56.35	1995	65.1	65.81
1990	63.5	57.96	1996	65.0	70.81
1991	61.8	58.08	1997	64.5	75.16
1992	62.6	58.91			

Source: Smith Travel Research

The Largest Hotel and Motel Chains in the U.S., Ranked by Total Number of Rooms, January 1998

Chain	Number of rooms	Number of properties	Chain	Number of rooms	Number of properties
1. Holiday Inn	209,765	1,119	6. Super 8	97,007	1,583
2. Best Western	186,410	2,072	7. Comfort Inn	94,738	1,168
3. Days Inn	156,376	1,749	8. Motel 6	83,276	747
4. Ramada	109,205	725	9. Hampton Inn	77,519	726
5. Marriott	101,628	230	10. Sheraton Hotel	60,454	153

Source: Smith Travel Research

Top Car-Rental Companies In 1997

Company	U.S. cars in service (average) 1997	# U.S. locations	U.S. rental revenue* ($ millions) 1996	1997 (est.)
Enterprise**	355,000	3,100	$ 3,100**	$ 3,570 **
Hertz	250,000	1,150	2,700	3,000
Avis	200,000	1,000	1,800	2,000
National	145,000	968	1,350	1,750
Alamo	130,000	175	1,300	1,300
Budget	125,000	955	1,500	1,600
Dollar	62,000	229	597	707
FRCS (Ford)	53,150	1,462	309	325
Thrifty	34,000	488	349	363
Republic Replacement Group	32,000	315	171	230
DRAC (Chrysler)	27,000	1,400	165	170
U-Save	12,000	450	95	115
Rent-A-Wreck	12,000	470	82	90
Payless	12,000	70	52	57
Advantage	9,000	100	67	80
Total market	**1,607,850**	**21,252**	**14,670**	**16,400**

*Revenue comes from car rental operations only, including ancillary counter sales. Revenue represents the entire system, including corporate and franchise revenue.
**Rental revenue includes some leasing revenue.
Source: Auto Rental News

How I Spent My Summer Vacation

Top Travel Activities (Percentage of trips that included the activity)

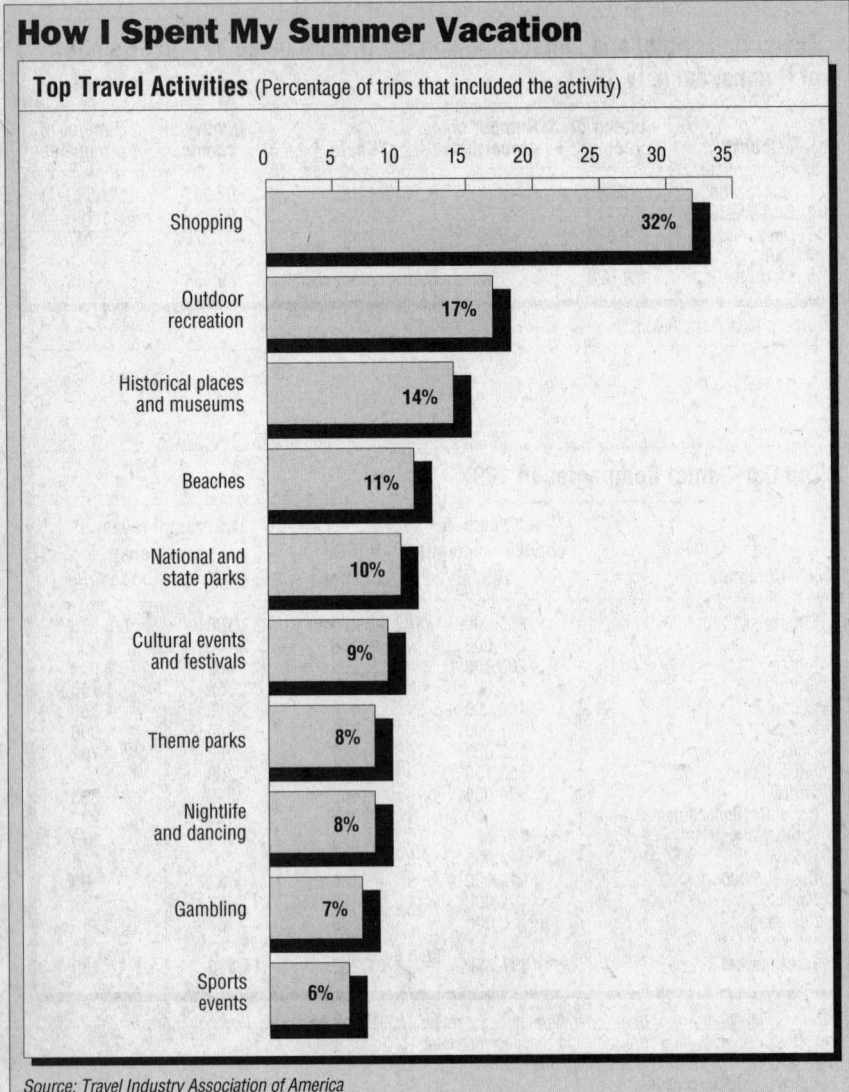

Activity	Percentage
Shopping	32%
Outdoor recreation	17%
Historical places and museums	14%
Beaches	11%
National and state parks	10%
Cultural events and festivals	9%
Theme parks	8%
Nightlife and dancing	8%
Gambling	7%
Sports events	6%

Source: Travel Industry Association of America

Animals, Aquariums and Amusements

Annual Attendance Figures

Year	Zoos	Aquariums	Amusement Parks
1990	80,385,123	24,520,550	253,000,000
1991	75,598,685	24,750,410	260,000,000
1992	77,917,025	30,734,641	267,000,000
1993	79,850,529	35,485,101	275,000,000
1994	81,415,327	34,289,580	267,000,000
1995	85,045,542	34,770,315	280,000,000
1996	85,504,189	34,738,589	290,000,000
1997	86,588,369	35,781,485	300,000,000

Sources: American Zoo and Aquarium Association and
    International Association of Amusement Parks and Attractions

Attendance at Top 10 Amusement/Theme Parks in the U.S.* (in millions)

Name	1994	1995	1996	1997
The Magic Kingdom at Walt Disney World Lake Buena Vista, FL	11.2	12.9	13.8	17.0
Disneyland Anaheim, CA	10.3	14.1	15.0	14.3
Epcot at Walt Disney World Lake Buena Vista, FL	9.7	10.7	11.2	11.8
Disney-MGM Studios at Walt Disney World Lake Buena Vista, FL	8.0	9.5	10.0	10.5
Universal Studios Florida Orlando, FL	7.7	8.0	8.4	8.9
Universal Studios Hollywood Universal City, CA	4.6	4.7	5.4	5.4
Sea World of Florida Orlando, FL	4.6	5.0	5.1	4.9
Busch Gardens Tampa Tampa, FL	3.7	3.8	4.2	4.2
Sea World of California San Diego, CA	3.7	3.75	3.9	4.0
Six Flags Great Adventure Jackson, NJ	3.2	4.0	4.0	3.7

*Top 10 designation derived from 1997 attendance ranking.
Source: Amusement Business

On the Go

Total Number of Trips Taken by Americans
(In millions)

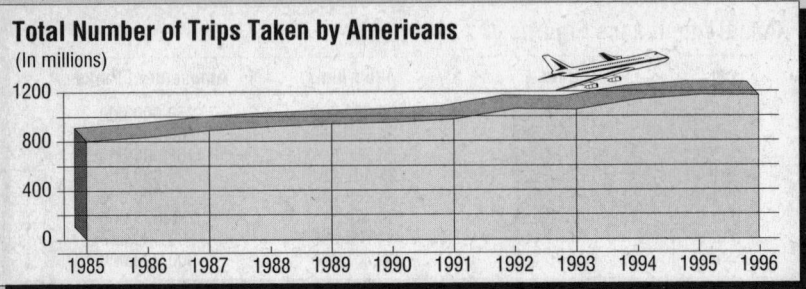

Type of Trip (In millions)

Year	Pleasure	Business	Total*
1985	540	196	808
1986	576	200	841
1987	603	218	894
1988	621	224	925
1989	633	246	945
1990	649	222	956
1991	667	224	980
1992	736	278	1,063
1993	740	275	1,058
1994	781	247	1,139
1995	810	275	1,173
1996	808	251	1,161

*Includes other types of trips, such as for funerals or other personal reasons.
Source: Travel Industry Association of America

1998 Vacation Cost Survey

Average Daily Meal Costs* and Nightly Lodging Rate** For a Family of Two Adults and Two Children

Most Expensive States		Least Expensive States	
Hawaii	$409	North Dakota	$131
New York	330	South Dakota	138
Massachusetts	300	Kansas	152
Louisiana	284	Nebraska	155
New Jersey	268	Iowa	155

*Excludes beverages, taxes and gratuity.
**2 persons/2 beds rate plus $12 for two children.
Source: American Automobile Association

Tourist Dollars

Growth in Travel Receipts Over the Past Decade

Year	Expenditures (billions)	
	Domestic	International
1986	$216	$26
1987	235	31
1988	258	38
1989	273	47
1990	291	58
1991	296	64
1992	308	71
1993	322	75
1994	339	78
1995	360	80
1996	383	90

Economic Impact of Travel and Tourism in the United States in 1997

Expenditures: $473 billion   Payroll: $121.6 billion   Jobs: 6.8 million   Tax revenue: $67 billion

Source: Travel Industry Association of America

Foreign Invasion

International Travel to the United States

YEAR	FOREIGN VISITORS (MILLIONS)	TRADE SURPLUS (BILLIONS)
1986	26.0	$-6.5
1987	29.5	-6.0
1988	34.1	-1.4
1989	36.6	5.2
1990	39.5	10.4
1991	43.0	18.9
1992	47.3	22.2
1993	45.7	21.9
1994	45.5	18.8
1995	44.0	22.0
1996	46.3	26.0
1997	48.9	26.2

Source: Travel Industry Association of America

International Travelers to the U.S.

RANK IN 1996	1996	1997	% CHANGE 97/96
Canada	15,301,000	15,127,000	-1.1%
Mexico	8,530,000	8,445,000	-1.0%
Japan	5,182,555	5,367,578	3.6%
United Kingdom	3,246,237	3,720,979	14.6%
Germany	1,996,824	1,994,296	-0.1%
France	987,126	978,327	-0.9%
Brazil	848,453	940,698	10.9%
South Korea	749,474	746,550	-0.4%
Italy	525,246	580,261	10.5%
Argentina	412,581	503,393	22.0%
Australia	463,177	500,615	8.1%
Venezuela	447,276	487,981	9.1%
Netherlands	440,243	473,420	7.5%
Taiwan	414,541	442,780	6.8%
Switzerland	417,064	410,209	-1.6%

Source: Tourism Industries, International Trade Administration

America Keeps on Truckin'

Americans are buying more sport-utility vehicles and other types of trucks, reducing passenger cars' share of the total vehicle market.

Passenger Car and Truck Retail Sales, 1987 and 1997
(Percentage)

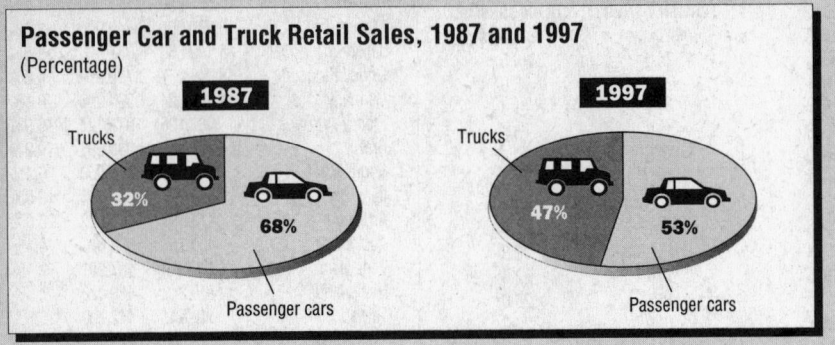

1987 — Trucks 32%, Passenger cars 68%

1997 — Trucks 47%, Passenger cars 53%

Annual U.S. Motor Vehicle Retail Sales
(In thousands)

Year	Passenger cars Domestic	Import	Total	Trucks Domestic	Import	Total	Motor vehicles Domestic	Import	Total
1931	1,903	NA	1,903	328	NA	328	2,231	NA	2,231
1941	3,763	NA	3,763	902	NA	902	4,665	NA	4,665
1951	5,143	21	5,164	1,111	NA	1,111	6,254	21	6,275
1961	5,556	379	5,935	908	29	937	6,464	408	6,872
1971	8,681	1,561	10,242	2,011	85	2,096	10,693	1,646	12,338
1981	6,209	2,327	8,536	1,809	451	2,260	8,018	2,778	10,796
1982	5,759	2,224	7,982	2,146	414	2,560	7,905	2,637	10,542
1983	6,795	2,387	9,182	2,658	471	3,129	9,454	2,858	12,312
1984	7,952	2,439	10,390	3,475	618	4,093	11,427	3,057	14,484
1985	8,205	2,838	11,042	3,902	779	4,682	12,107	3,617	15,724
1986	8,215	3,245	11,460	3,921	941	4,863	12,136	4,186	16,322
1987	7,081	3,196	10,277	4,055	858	4,912	11,136	4,053	15,189
1988	7,526	3,004	10,530	4,508	641	5,149	12,034	3,645	15,679
1989	7,073	2,699	9,772	4,403	538	4,941	11,476	3,237	14,713
1990	6,897	2,403	9,300	4,215	631	4,846	11,112	3,034	14,146
1991	6,137	2,038	8,175	3,813	551	4,365	9,950	2,589	12,539
1992	6,277	1,937	8,213	4,481	422	4,903	10,758	2,359	13,116
1993	6,742	1,776	8,518	5,287	394	5,681	12,029	2,170	14,199
1994	7,255	1,735	8,991	5,995	426	6,421	13,251	2,161	15,411
1995	7,129	1,506	8,635	6,064	417	6,481	13,193	1,923	15,116
1996	7,254	1,273	8,527	6,478	452	6,930	13,731	1,725	15,456
1997	6,917	1,355	8,272	6,633	593	7,226	13,550	1,948	15,498

Source: American Automobile Manufacturers Association

U.S. Auto Market

U.S. Retail Sales of Passenger Cars

	Domestic sales					
	1992	**1993**	**1994**	**1995**	**1996**	**1997**
Chrysler	617,412	766,144	782,975	771,357	827,941	736,530
Ford	1,731,250	1,836,508	1,899,156	1,732,034	1,699,893	1,575,919
General Motors	2,749,943	2,851,818	3,052,686	2,930,568	2,755,995	2,635,255
BMW	–	–	–	6,194	20,508	20,584
Honda	475,718	417,928	464,622	511,044	665,511	665,311
Hyundai Sonata	16,985	15,420	1,190	7	–	–
Mazda	79,267	100,441	109,165	105,852	85,904	79,346
Mitsubishi	64,592	75,980	117,485	101,033	125,634	101,157
Nissan	144,588	249,844	313,058	299,884	308,891	292,983
Subaru Legacy	55,116	49,395	55,938	74,151	94,950	92,913
Suzuki Swift	188	2,960	2,907	4,126	3,379	1,615
Toyota	341,498	368,053	384,048	498,635	555,746	593,932
Volkswagen	–	7,176	72,073	93,822	110,205	121,224
Total	6,276,557	6,741,667	7,255,303	7,128,707	7,254,557	6,916,769

	Import sales					
	1992	**1993**	**1994**	**1995**	**1996**	**1997**
Chrysler	62,174	67,988	28,849	14,823	4,692	–
Ford	46,385	41,641	39,685	59,191	37,359	33,243
General Motors	93,917	56,871	5,186	51	1,676	25,411
Alfa Romeo	2,828	1,325	565	414	–	–
BMW	65,693	78,010	84,501	87,115	85,253	101,916
Daihatsu	5,030	–	–	–	–	–
Honda	293,127	298,512	297,620	229,443	120,643	164,069
Hyundai	91,564	93,376	124,905	107,371	108,468	113,186
Isuzu	7,823	1,762	109	16	1	–
Jaguar	8,681	12,734	15,195	18,085	17,878	19,501
Mazda	169,007	159,449	173,634	117,859	95,071	89,194
Mercedes-Benz	63,315	61,899	73,002	76,752	90,844	107,696
Mitsubishi	90,980	92,222	83,518	74,234	45,549	49,225
Nissan	273,382	232,802	224,170	220,374	191,486	174,517
Porsche	4,133	3,714	5,824	5,771	7,152	12,976
Saab	26,451	18,784	21,679	25,592	28,439	28,453
Subaru	49,698	54,784	44,627	26,256	25,798	24,882
Suzuki	6,098	3,648	4,229	4,385	7,009	6,969
Toyota	418,661	373,773	381,095	295,339	237,846	228,650
Volkswagen/Audi	87,949	49,251	32,870	37,956	52,086	49,029
Volvo	67,916	72,955	81,788	88,505	88,581	90,894
Other imports	1,743	692	12,163	16,725	25,366	35,494
Total	1,936,555	1,776,192	1,735,214	1,506,257	1,271,197	1,355,305
Total passenger car sales	8,213,112	8,517,859	8,990,517	8,634,964	8,525,754	8,272,074

Top 20 Selling Passenger Cars in the U.S.

	1995			1996			1997	
1	Ford Taurus	366,266	1	Ford Taurus	401,049	1	Toyota Camry	397,156
2	Honda Accord	341,384	2	Honda Accord	382,298	2	Honda Accord	384,609
3	Toyota Camry	328,595	3	Toyota Camry	359,433	3	Ford Taurus	357,162
4	Honda Civic	289,435	4	Honda Civic	286,350	4	Honda Civic	315,546
5	Saturn	285,674	5	Ford Escort	284,644	5	Chevrolet Cavalier	302,161
6	Ford Escort	285,570	6	Saturn	278,574	6	Ford Escort	283,898
7	Dodge/Plymouth Neon	240,189	7	Chevrolet Cavalier	277,222	7	Saturn	250,810
8	Pontiac Grand Am	234,226	8	Chevrolet Lumina	237,973	8	Chevrolet Lumina	228,451
9	Chevrolet Lumina	214,595	9	Pontiac Grand Am	222,477	9	Toyota Corolla	218,461
10	Toyota Corolla	213,636	10	Toyota Corolla	209,048	10	Pontiac Grand Am	204,078
11	Chevrolet Cavalier	212,767	11	Ford Contour	174,187	11	Chevrolet Malibu	164,654
12	Chevrolet Corsica/ Beretta	192,361	12	Chevrolet Corsica/ Beretta	149,117	12	Ford Contour	151,060
13	Ford Contour	174,214	13	Nissan Altima	147,910	13	Buick LeSabre	150,744
14	Nissan Altima	148,172	14	Dodge Intrepid	145,402	14	Nissan Altima	144,483
15	Dodge Intrepid	147,576	15	Dodge Neon	139,831	15	Pontiac Grand Prix	142,018
16	Buick LeSabre	141,410	16	Buick LeSabre	131,316	16	Nissan Maxima	123,215
17	Ford Mustang	136,962	17	Nissan Sentra	129,596	17	Nissan Sentra	122,468
18	Nissan Sentra	134,854	18	Nissan Maxima	128,395	18	Dodge Neon	121,854
19	Pontiac Grand Prix	131,747	19	Ford Mustang	122,674	19	Dodge Intrepid	118,537
20	Oldsmobile Ciera	128,860	20	Mercury Sable	114,164	20	Ford Mustang	116,610

Sources: American Automobile Manufacturers Association and Ward's Automotive Reports

Top 10 Selling Trucks in the U.S.

	1995			1996			1997	
1	Ford F Series	691,452	1	Ford F Series	780,838	1	Ford F Series	746,111
2	Chevrolet C/K	536,901	2	Chevrolet C/K	549,167	2	Chevrolet C/K	553,729
3	Ford Explorer	395,227	3	Ford Explorer	402,663	3	Ford Explorer	383,852
4	Ford Ranger	309,085	4	Dodge Ram Pickup	383,960	4	Dodge Ram Pickup	350,257
5	Dodge Ram Pickup	271,501	5	Dodge Caravan	300,117	5	Ford Ranger	298,796
6	Dodge Caravan	264,937	6	Ford Ranger	288,393	6	Dodge Caravan	285,736
7	Jeep Grand Cherokee	252,186	7	Jeep Grand Cherokee	279,195	7	Jeep Grand Cherokee	260,875
8	Ford Windstar	222,147	8	Chevrolet Blazer	246,307	8	Chevrolet S10 Blazer	221,400
9	Chevrolet Blazer	214,661	9	Ford Windstar	209,033	9	Ford Expedition	214,524
10	Chevrolet S10 Pickup	207,193	10	Chevrolet S10 Pickup	190,178	10	Ford Windstar	205,356

Automotive Paint Color Popularity for Full-Size/Intermediate Cars, 1997 Model Year

Color	Percent	Color	Percent
Medium/dark green	17.5	Dark red	5.2
White	17.0	Silver	4.8
Light brown	14.4	Bright red	4.0
Black	8.0	Medium blue	3.9
Medium red	7.4	Other	11.2
Medium gray	6.6		

Sources: DuPont Automotive Products and American Automobile Manufacturers Association

Global Car Market

World Motor Vehicle Production
(In thousands)

Year	United States	Canada	Europe	Japan	Other	World total	U.S. as percent of world total
1950	8,006	388	1,991	32	160	10,577	75.7
1960	7,905	398	6,837	482	866	16,488	47.9
1970	8,284	1,160	13,049	5,289	1,637	29,419	28.2
1980	8,010	1,324	15,496	11,043	2,692	38,565	20.8
1990	9,783	1,928	18,866	13,487	4,496	48,554	20.1
1991	8,811	1,888	17,804	13,245	5,180	46,928	18.8
1992	9,729	1,961	17,628	12,499	6,269	48,088	20.2
1993	10,898	2,246	15,208	11,228	7,205	46,785	23.3
1994	12,263	2,321	16,195	10,554	8,167	49,500	24.8
1995	11,985	2,420	17,001	10,196	8,405	50,008	24.0
1996	11,799	2,397	17,728	10,346	9,244	51,513	22.9

New Car Ratings Top Three Vehicles Per Segment In Initial Quality

Car Segments

Compact Car
BEST: FORD ESCORT
Mercury Tracer
Honda Civic (tie)
Saturn SL Sedan (tie)

Entry Midsize Car
BEST: CHRYSLER CIRRUS
Nissan Altima
Ford Contour

Premium Midsize Car
BEST: CHRYSLER CONCORDE
Chevrolet Lumina
Mercury Sable

Sporty Car
BEST: HONDA PRELUDE
Acura Integra
BMW 318Ti

Entry Luxury Car
BEST: LEXUS ES300
BMW 3-Series
Acura TL

Premium Luxury Car
BEST: LEXUS LS400
Acura RL
BMW 5-Series

Sports Car
BEST: MERCEDES-BENZ SLK
PORSCHE BOXSTER (tie)
PORSCHE 911 (tie)

Truck Segments

Compact Pickup
BEST: NISSAN FRONTIER
Toyota Tacoma
Mazda B-Series

Full-Size Pickup
BEST: TOYOTA T100
Ford F-Series
Chevrolet C/K

Compact Van
BEST: HONDA ODYSSEY
Dodge Caravan
Toyota Sienna

Compact Sport Utility Vehicle
BEST: HONDA CR-V
Nissan Pathfinder
Toyota 4Runner

Full-Size Sport Utility Vehicle
BEST: FORD EXPEDITION
Chevrolet Suburban
GMC Yukon

Luxury Sport Utility Vehicle
BEST: INFINITI QX4 (tie)
BEST: LINCOLN NAVIGATOR (tie)
Land Rover Range Rover

Note: Rankings are based on surveys of new-vehicle owners about any problems during the first 90 days of ownership.

Source: J.D. Power and Associates 1998 Initial Quality Study

J.D. Power's 1998 Customer Satisfaction Study

Customer Satisfaction Index Performance
(Rankings reflect customers' experience with vehicle reliability after one year and the quality of treatment during dealer service or repair visits)

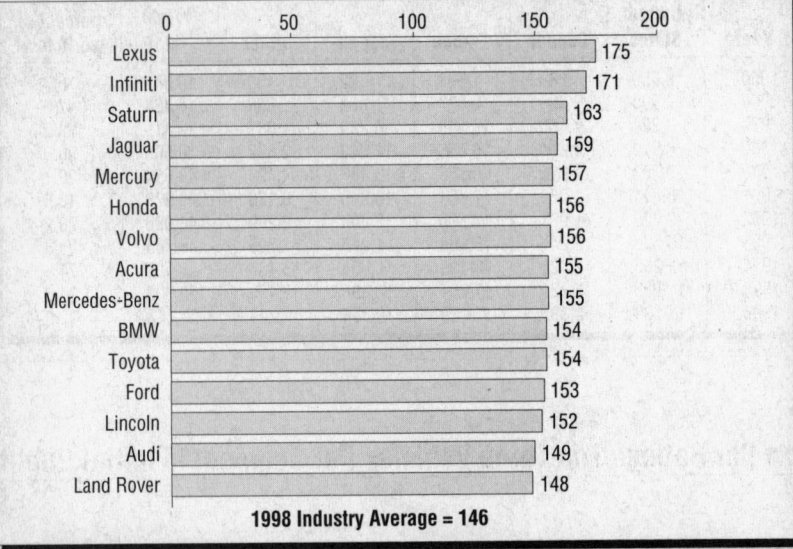

Lexus	175
Infiniti	171
Saturn	163
Jaguar	159
Mercury	157
Honda	156
Volvo	156
Acura	155
Mercedes-Benz	155
BMW	154
Toyota	154
Ford	153
Lincoln	152
Audi	149
Land Rover	148

1998 Industry Average = 146

Note: Finishing below industry average, in alphabetical order, are: Buick, Cadillac, Chevrolet, Chrysler, Dodge, Eagle, Geo, GMC, Hyundai, Isuzu, Jeep, Kia, Mazda, Mitsubishi, Nissan, Oldsmobile, Plymouth, Pontiac, Porsche, Saab, Subaru, Suzuki and Volkswagen.
Source: J.D. Power & Associates

Largest Auto Recalls

MANUFACTURER	Number of Vehicles	RECALL	SUBJECT
Ford	7,900,000	6-1-96	Ignition switch
General Motors	6,682,084	12-10-71	Engine mounts
General Motors	5,821,160	2-20-81	Single axle-rear control arm
Chrysler	4,300,000	3-27-95	Minivan latches
Ford	4,072,000	6-28-72	Shoulder belts
General Motors	3,707,064	1-19-73	Power brake booster shield
Volkswagen	3,700,000	10-12-72	Windshield wiper arm
Honda	3,700,000	4-16-95	Seat belts
Ford	3,600,000	9-01-87	Fuel line coupling
General Motors	3,100,000	12-17-84	Axle shaft separation
General Motors	2.,966,979	3-25-69	Throttle linkage
Nissan	2,730,462	4-16-95	Seat belts
General Motors	2,570,914	3-25-69	Exhaust system
General Motors	2,216,325	9-11-95	Seat belt anchorage
General Motors	2,200,000	4-28-77	Hydraulic power assist

Source: National Highway Traffic Safety Administration

Private Passenger Automobile Insurance State Average Expenditures, 1996

State	Average expenditure	Rank
Alabama	$577.86	33
Alaska	750.91	16
Arizona	785.05	12
Arkansas	557.70	34
California	790.70	11
Colorado	751.25	15
Connecticut	899.27	5
Delaware	806.05	8
District of Columbia	993.07	2
Florida	783.23	13
Georgia	627.47	25
Hawaii	958.69	4
Idaho	464.59	47
Illinois	637.98	24
Indiana	548.06	38
Iowa	445.39	50
Kansas	495.26	43
Kentucky	581.05	31
Louisiana	802.17	10
Maine	470.18	46
Maryland	759.44	14
Massachusetts	832.83	7
Michigan	697.38	18
Minnesota	653.98	23

State	Average expenditure	Rank
Mississippi	$604.17	27
Missouri	599.35	29
Montana	478.96	44
Nebraska	475.13	45
Nevada	802.50	9
New Hampshire	612.44	26
New Jersey	1,099.07	1
New Mexico	659.80	22
New York	959.83	3
North Carolina	518.28	41
North Dakota	401.55	51
Ohio	553.27	36
Oklahoma	545.42	39
Oregon	584.76	30
Pennsylvania	687.43	19
Rhode Island	869.50	6
South Carolina	601.97	28
South Dakota	448.33	49
Tennessee	556.90	35
Texas	726.03	17
Utah	580.72	32
Vermont	514.17	42
Virginia	549.67	37
Washington	665.88	21
West Virginia	671.25	20
Wisconsin	533.49	40
Wyoming	451.62	48
U.S. Average	**690.56**	

Source: National Association of Insurance Commissioners

Hot Cars

The 25 Vehicles Stolen Most Often in 1997

Rank	Model year	Make	Model name	Rank	Model year	Make	Model name
1	'89	Toyota	Camry	14	'91	Acura	Legend
2	'94	Honda	Accord EX	15	'87	Oldsmobile	Cutlass Supreme
3	'90	Toyota	Camry	16	'91	Honda	Accord EX
4	'95	Honda	Accord EX	17	'89	Chevrolet	Caprice
5	'88	Toyota	Camry	18	'96	Toyota	Corolla
6	'88	Honda	Accord LX	19	'96	Honda	Accord EX
7	'90	Honda	Accord EX	20	'92	Honda	Accord LX
8	'91	Toyota	Camry	21	'87	Chevrolet	Caprice
9	'92	Honda	Accord EX	22	'95	Toyota	Camry LE
10	'95	Ford	Mustang	23	'97	Ford	F150 4X2
11	'96	Honda	Accord LX	24	'96	Toyota	Camry LE
12	'89	Honda	Accord LX	25	'94	Honda	Accord LX
13	'90	Honda	Accord LX				

Source: CCC Information Services Inc.

Highway Death Toll

Number of Fatal Crashes

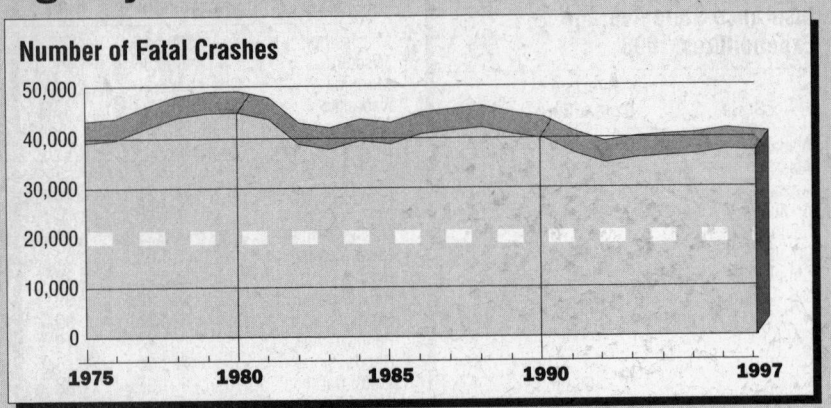

Automobile Fatalities

Year	Number of persons killed	Fatality rate per 100,000 population	Year	Number of persons killed	Fatality rate per 100,000 population	Year	Number of persons killed	Fatality rate per 100,000 population
1966	50,894	26.02	1977	47,878	21.79	1988	47,087	19.26
1967	50,724	25.69	1978	50,331	22.66	1989	45,582	18.47
1968	52,725	26.44	1979	51,093	22.75	1990	44,599	17.88
1969	53,543	26.59	1980	51,091	22.48	1991	41,508	16.46
1970	52,627	25.80	1981	49,301	21.49	1992	39,250	15.39
1971	52,542	25.40	1982	43,945	18.97	1993	40,150	15.57
1972	54,589	26.08	1983	42,589	18.22	1994	40,716	15.64
1973	54,052	25.57	1984	44,257	18.77	1995	41,817	15.91
1974	45,196	21.18	1985	43,825	18.42	1996	42,065	15.86
1975	44,525	20.66	1986	46,087	19.19	1997	41,967	15.68
1976	45,523	20.92	1987	46,390	19.15			

Source: National Highway Traffic Safety Administration

Traffic Deaths Linked to Alcohol

Number of Persons Killed, by Highest Blood Alcohol Concentration (BAC) in the Crash

Year	BAC = 0.00 Number	%	BAC = 0.01–0.09 Number	%	BAC = 0.10+ Number	%	Total fatalities in alcohol-related crashes Number	%
1982	18,780	42.7	4,809	10.9	20,356	46.3	25,165	57.3
1984	20,499	46.3	4,766	10.8	18,992	42.9	23,758	53.7
1986	22,042	47.8	5,109	11.1	18,936	41.1	24,045	52.2
1988	23,461	49.8	4,895	10.4	18,731	39.8	23,626	50.2
1990	22,515	50.5	4,434	9.9	17,650	39.6	22,084	49.5
1991	21,621	52.1	3,957	9.5	15,930	38.4	19,887	47.9
1992	21,392	54.5	3,625	9.2	14,234	36.3	17,859	45.5
1993	22,677	56.5	3,496	8.7	13,977	34.8	17,473	43.5
1994	24,136	59.3	3,480	8.5	13,100	32.2	16,580	40.7
1995	24,570	58.8	3,746	9.0	13,501	32.3	17,247	41.2
1996	24,847	59.1	3,774	9.0	13,444	32.0	17,218	40.9
1997	25,778	61.4	3,485	8.3	12,704	30.3	16,189	38.6

Total Fatalities in Alcohol-Related Crashes

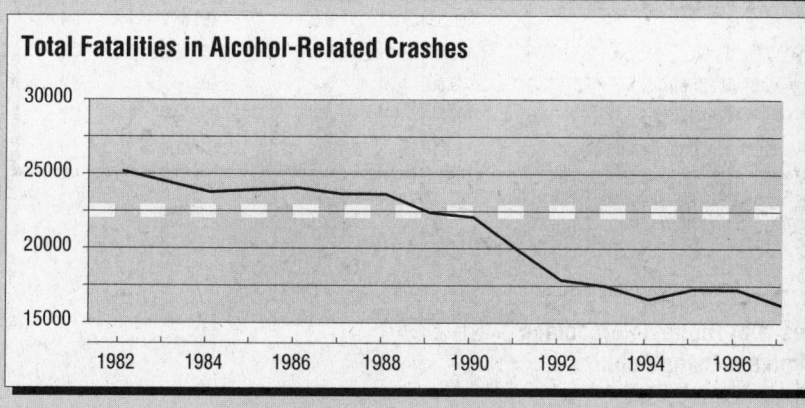

Source: National Highway Traffic Safety Administration

Journey to Work

Commuters are doing less to help the environment and conserve energy, according to the latest government data. People in car pools, riders of public transportation, bicyclists, and pedestrians make up a smaller share of the work force, as more Americans drive to work alone. One positive sign for gasoline conservation: more people working from home.

Means of Transportation	1980		1990	
	Number	Percent	Number	Percent
Total workers	96,617,296	100.0%	115,070,274	100.0%
⇨ Private vehicle	81,258,496	84.1	99,592,932	86.5
Drove alone	62,193,449	64.4	84,215,298	73.2
Carpooled	19,065,047	19.7	15,377,634	13.4
⇨ Public transportation	6,175,061	6.4	6,069,589	5.3
Bus or trolley bus*	3,924,787	4.1	3,445,000	3.0
Streetcar or trolley car*	NA	NA	78,130	0.1
Subway or elevated	1,528,852	1.6	1,755,476	1.5
Railroad	554,089	0.6	574,052	0.5
Ferryboat	NA	NA	37,497	0.0
Taxicab	167,133	0.2	179,434	0.2
⇨ Motorcycle	419,007	0.4	237,404	0.2
⇨ Bicycle	468,348	0.5	466,856	0.4
⇨ Walked only	5,413,248	5.6	4,488,886	3.9
⇨ Worked at home	2,179,863	2.3	3,406,025	3.0
⇨ All other means	703,273	0.7	808,582	0.7
Average travel time (minutes)	21.7		22.4	

*This category was "Bus or streetcar" in 1980.
Source: U.S. Census Bureau

Cities with Highest Percentage of Workers Using Public Transportation, 1990

CITY	PERCENT USING PUBLIC TRANSPORTATION	CITY	PERCENT USING PUBLIC TRANSPORTATION
New York, NY	53.4	Evanston, IL	20.9
Hoboken, NJ	51.0	Atlanta, GA	20.0
Jersey City, NJ	36.7	White Plains, NY	19.1
Washington, DC	36.6	Camden, NJ	18.1
San Francisco, CA	33.5	Oakland, CA	17.9
Boston, MA	31.5	Hartford, CT	17.1
Chicago, IL	29.7	New Orleans, LA	16.9
Philadelphia, PA	28.7	Idaho Falls, ID	16.5
Atlantic City, NJ	26.2	Minneapolis, MN	16.0
Arlington, VA	25.4	Seattle, WA	15.9
Newark, NJ	24.6	Berkeley, CA	15.2
Cambridge, MA	23.5	Albany, NY	15.1
Pittsburgh, PA	22.2		
Baltimore, MD	22.0		

Source: U.S. Census Bureau

Transit Ridership Trend

From 1900 to 1929, transit ridership grew steadily; first due to technical innovation and investment opportunities during the early development of street railways and then due to the economic boom of World War I and the post-war period. The Great Depression caused a steep decline in ridership between 1929 and 1939 as people made fewer work trips and often could not afford to take pleasure trips. World War II caused motor fuel rationing and an economic boom that led to a new rapid growth cycle in transit ridership. Ridership quickly declined from artificially high war levels as people fled to suburbs. In 1973, the ridership cycle reversed again and transit showed modest growth.

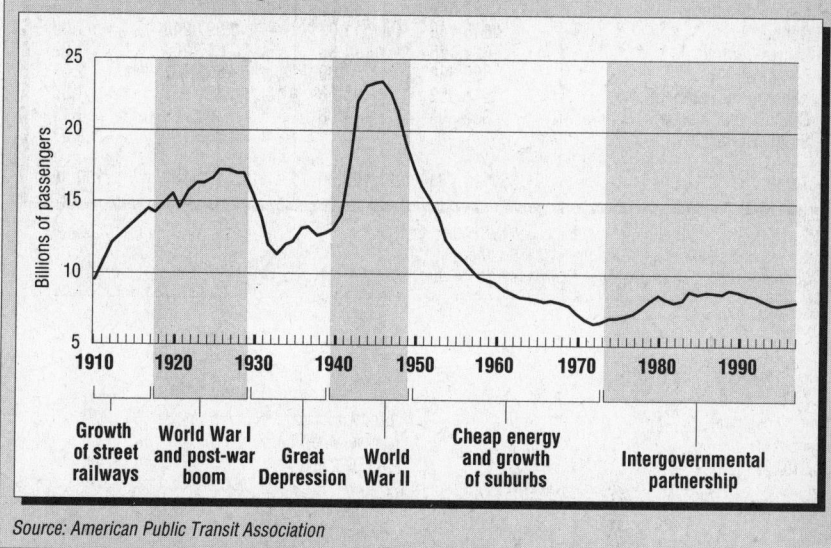

Source: American Public Transit Association

TOP TRUCKERS

25 Largest U.S. Motor Carriers by 1997 Revenue

United Parcel Service
Atlanta, GA
$15,730,318,252

Roadway Express
Akron, OH
$2,577,328,172

Schneider National, Inc.
Green Bay, WI
$2,512,000,000

Yellow Freight System
Shawnee Mission, KS
$2,509,537,231

Consolidated Freightways Corp.
Menlo Park, CA
$2,187,801,128

RPS, Inc.
Pittsburgh, PA
$1,581,754,000

Con-Way Transportation Svcs.
Menlo Park, CA
$1,359,549,513

J.B. Hunt Transport, Inc.
Lowell, AR
$1,351,007,445

Ryder Integrated Logistics
Miami, FL
$1,298,407,690

ABF Freight System
Fort Smith, AR
$1,136,402,336

Overnite Transportation Co.
Richmond, VA
$945,968,043

Freight Railroads

	1997		1996	
Railroad	Operating revenue (Thousands)	Percent of Total	Operating revenue (Thousands)	Percent of Total
Union Pacific*	$ 9,800,688	29.59	$ 6,728,470	20.58
Burlington Northern Santa Fe	8,408,503	25.39	8,186,986	25.04
CSX	4,989,450	15.07	4,909,073	15.02
Norfolk Southern	4,222,649	12.75	4,101,038	12.54
Conrail**	3,646,148	11.01	3,597,248	11.00
Illinois Central	622,475	1.88	617,264	1.89
Soo Line	559,668	1.69	668,961	2.05
Kansas City Southern	516,052	1.56	491,635	1.50
Grand Trunk Western	352,398	1.06	361,769	1.11
Southern Pacific*			3,030,194	9.27
Total	**33,118,031**	**100.00**	**32,692,638**	**100.00**

*Union Pacific and Southern Pacific merged in September 1996.
**Conrail was acquired by CSX and Norfolk Southern in 1998.
Source: Association of American Railroads

American Freightways
Harrison, AR
$870,318,662

Werner Enterprises
Omaha, NE
$772,094,529

United Van Lines
Fenton, MO
$730,261,166

Swift Transportation Co.
Phoenix, AZ
$713,638,000

USF Holland Motor Express
Holland, MI
$711,137,026

Watkins Motor Lines
Lakeland, FL
$650,895,683

North American Van Lines
Fort Wayne, IN
$642,052,000

Allied Van Lines
Naperville, IL
$486,222,000

Landstar Ranger
Jacksonville, FL
$456,322,000

Preston Trucking Co.
Preston, MD
$447,289,623

M.S. Carriers
Memphis, TN
$415,932,825

Estes Express Lines
Richmond, VA
$404,614,615

Landstar Inway, Inc.
Rockford, IL
$386,940,114

U.S. Xpress, Inc.
Chattanooga, TN
371,029,752

Source: American Trucking Associations

9

MEDIA & ENTERTAINMENT

Will the media giants be nibbled to death by goldfish?
Perhaps no companies have as much at stake in the digital revolution as the current leaders of the $318 billion communications industry—Time Warner Inc., Walt Disney Co., Viacom Inc., the broadcast networks and other mainstream media.

While the explosion of activity on the Internet will certainly create lucrative new opportunities for big companies skilled in producing movies, magazines and television shows, there also is an immense risk that brash newcomers will siphon away advertisers, audiences and profits from the current ruling class. What's more, the established media companies are facing new competition from well-financed high-technology giants like Microsoft Corp., which is reverse engineering itself into a media company and trying to use its head start in personal computers to muscle its way into a key position in the interactive world.

Already, "new media" companies have more buzz and sex appeal and are trading at higher stock-price multiples than the traditional media. These newcomers are betting that a small toehold now will lead to a massive market share lead in the future. Which is why pioneers like Internet bookseller Amazon.com are investing heavily in the face of ongoing financial losses. "People want to lock in the habits of new users coming on-line," says Bill Bass, an analyst at Forrester Research Inc., who expects the population of adult Internet users to double in the next five years to 100 million and on-line advertising to reach $15 billion by 2003, up from a scrawny $1.3 billion in 1998.

So, like Gulliver ensnared by swarming Lilliputians, the major media companies are now scrambling to try to catch up with the upstart electronic-media companies. After largely sitting on the sidelines or making costly missteps, the big media firms have started spending hundreds of millions to buy digital businesses or redirect parts of their empire to focus on digital opportunities. For example, Walt Disney, after years of disdaining the digital world, has sharply reversed course and is investing heavily in Web sites like Disney Blast. In one multimillion dollar investment in 1998, Disney acquired a stake in Infoseek Corp., an Internet search and directory service, signaling that it is really embracing the Web.

"If you don't participate, you risk being marginalized," says Thomas Rogers, president of cable and business development for General Electric Co.'s NBC television unit. Mr. Rogers says the big media companies have no choice but to remake themselves in response to the rapidly changing environment. "If we don't, the viability of what we are as a company would be highly suspect."

In 1996, NBC struck a deal with Microsoft Corp. to jointly fund the MSNBC cable news channel, which has a robust news Web site. NBC also has invested in CNET Inc., with plans to take control of its Snap directory service and become the first broadcast network to have a stake in a critical "portal" site, the screen that consumers click on first when they log onto the Internet. That will help NBC steer viewers to its various sites—broadcast, Internet and cable networks—and hang on to its audience as consumers hop from TV to the

Internet. A recent study by Nielsen Media Research for America Online Inc. reports that households with Internet or on-line access watch 15 percent less television than nonwired homes. And those households are among the most desirable to advertisers because they're better educated and more affluent.

Even as they venture into the brave new digital world, however, many media executives face significant obstacles. One is generational. The top management of many companies isn't very comfortable with interactive computer technology. The executives didn't grow up playing computer games or surfing the Web. For the younger generation, "digital is cooler than live action," says Bing Gordon, chief creative officer of Electronic Arts Inc., an electronic-games company. Among consumers younger than 25, says Mr. Gordon, "Lara Croft is cooler than Madonna and probably more human." (Translation for readers over 25: Lara Croft is the sultry, hugely popular global superstar featured in the Tomb Raider computer games.)

Some media executives also fear cannibalization or other damage to their traditional media operations. Newspaper publishers, for instance, are at best ambivalent about establishing electronic classified sections that are certain to siphon sales away from their lucrative print classified sections. "It's always difficult to cannibalize your own business," says Olaf Olafsson, the executive who helped make Sony Corp.'s PlayStation electronic-games business into one of Sony's most important profit centers. When developing the PlayStation, Mr. Olafsson says, other Sony executives were concerned that the machine would steal customers away from the company's core television and CD players. "I heard the argument that we were competing with ourselves, but if we weren't going to do it, somebody else would," he says.

Some media companies even disassociated themselves from their initial on-line ventures, according to Mr. Bass of Forrester Research. ESPN called its site Sportszone, while Time Warner put its various sites under the Pathfinder moniker. The reason, says Mr. Bass, is that "if they were a disaster, they didn't want any collateral damage to the core brands."

Media executives also are struggling to understand that what sells on-line isn't the same as what sells on the newsstand. Time Warner has invested tens of millions of dollars attempting to convert *People, Sports Illustrated* and *Money* into lucrative Web sites, but

results have been mixed. Time Inc. is skilled at producing magazines with hot cover stories, good photographs and top writers that attract loyal readers. But "content has not been successful on-line," says Mr. Bass. Online, the way to gather big audiences is with tools, such as search engines and e-mail. "These notions are completely foreign to traditional media companies," says Mr. Bass. "That is why you see the big winners on-line being nontraditional media companies."

Adapting to the new electronic age also can totally disrupt the competitive landscape that exists in the print world, making it all the more confusing for the established players. In a highly unsettling case study for publishers, the encyclopedia business has been completely turned on its head. Encyclopaedia Brittanica dominated print sales for years, with Compton's as an also-ran. But reference books are ideally suited to the quick searches that digital CD-ROMs allow and Compton's was quicker to jump into CD-ROM than its rivals. The results, according to PC Data, for the first half of 1998, Compton's disks outsell Encyclopaedia Britannica disks by a margin of two to one.

Meanwhile, Encyclopaedia Britannica has belatedly entered the race, curtailing its famous door-to-door operation in 1996, aggressively promoting its CD-ROMs and making a big push to establish an Internet business. The company has established E Blast, a search engine taking advantage of the company's rich heritage as a source for research. "What's really important is having a serious position as an Internet player," says a spokesman for the 230-year-old company.

Record labels face perhaps the greatest emerging threat from the Internet. Scores of sites are springing up that allow fans to download songs. "The music business has a lot to worry about," says Michael J. Wolf, a senior partner at Booz Allen & Hamilton Inc., a management-consulting firm. "The bleakest scenario is rampant piracy."

For record companies, there is an increasing number of irksome examples of new music filtering out on the Web and getting copied ahead of schedule. In 1997, the management of Sony Music artist Oasis moved to halt the unauthorized use of photos and music from the popular British band that were being distributed by more than 100 Web-based fan sites.

Even if people pay for the music downloaded from the Web, major artists could bypass labels and distribute their new music directly to fans. Does U2 or Madonna really need a record label? David Bowie has already established his own Web site. Also, the technology will allow listeners to selectively order just one or two cuts from an album. "Unbundling singles from an album will hurt the value equation," says Mr. Wolf.

Compounding the threat is the fact that teen-age music buyers are extremely adept at surfing the Web and employing the latest technologies. Also, for years teenagers have been cheating record companies the old-fashioned way by ordering records from record clubs and not paying for them. Says Mr. Wolf, "There is not a well-established sense among teenagers that they should pay for music."

Eben Shapiro,
staff reporter for
The Wall Street Journal
in New York

HOLLYWOOD'S SUMMER OF SURPRISES

Conventional wisdom took a beating in Hollywood during 1998. Just ask the near-unanimous chorus of executives and pundits who began the year declaring that *Titanic* was sure to be a financial disaster for the studios that made it, News Corp.'s 20th Century Fox and Viacom Inc.'s Paramount Pictures.

The reasoning behind such dire predictions seemed sound. *Titanic* was, after all, the most expensive movie ever, costing $200 million to produce and tens of millions more to market. To have even a prayer of breaking even, it would need to top box-office titans such as *Star Wars*, which grossed more than $322 million in the United States during its initial theatrical run. And after its opening weekend in December 1997, *Titanic* was having a hard time staying ahead of the latest James Bond movie, much less keeping pace with Luke Skywalker.

Yet in the end, it was the arm-chair studio heads who took a dive, not *Titanic*. While the expensive, innovative effects were the film's focus before it opened, *Titanic* was propelled instead by the love story at its heart. That attracted a demographic powerhouse few in Hollywood saw coming—the teenage children of baby boomers—and helped *Titanic* gross more than $600 million in the United States and an astonishing $1.8 billion worldwide. Rather than sending the executives who greenlit *Titanic* into early retirement, the film instead anchored a banner year for both Fox and Paramount.

Titanic indeed set the tone for a year in which Hollywood came to expect the unexpected and saw some of its mainstay operating principles upended. Yet on its face, it was yet another "record breaking" year of the type Hollywood loves to hype. For the year through September 7, domestic box office receipts totaled $4.9 billion, up more than 8 percent from the year-earlier period. During the crucial Memorial Day-Labor Day summer season, movies rang up $2.58 billion at the box office, up nearly 16 percent from the same period in 1997. But because Labor Day

Favorite Leisure Pursuits

Percentage of people in 1998 who consider these activities their favorite ways to spend leisure time:

Activity	All adults	Men	Women
Reading	30%	19%	40%
TV watching	21	20	22
Gardening	14	11	17
Spending time with family/kids	13	13	12
Fishing	11	21	3
Team sports	9	14	4
Going to movies	8	7	8
Sewing/crocheting	8	–	15
Walking	7	4	10
Swimming	7	5	9
Golf	6	11	1
Entertaining	5	5	6
Hunting	4	9	–
Listening to music	4	5	4
Traveling	4	5	3

Source: Louis Harris & Associates

fell late, the summer of 1998 included an extra week; without it, the summer 1998 total was $2.44 billion, for a more modest increase of about 6 percent.

But box-office numbers are always deceiving—it's rising ticket prices, not extra admissions, that usually account for increases. And in any case, the revenue film companies take in both at the box-office and from ancillary sources such as home video are not keeping pace with the cost of making and marketing motion pictures, which continues to skyrocket.

The Motion Picture Association of America estimated that the average cost of a major studio release in 1997 was $53.4 million, up a staggering 34 percent from 1996. Marketing costs for each film leaped 12 percent to $22.3 million. The situation prompted long-time MPAA president Jack Valenti to cry, "Costs remain a great shaggy beast prowling the movie forest, a fiscal Godzilla slouching toward our future."

It was, in fact, Sony Corp.'s $120 million *Godzilla* that became the standard bearer for

At the Movies

The Cost of Making Movies
(In thousands)

Year	Average production costs	Average marketing costs
1980	$9,383	$4,329
1981	11,336	4,407
1982	11,850	4,936
1983	11,885	5,205
1984	14,413	6,651
1985	16,779	6,454
1986	17,455	6,673
1987	20,051	8,257
1988	18,061	8,509
1989	23,454	9,248
1990	26,783	11,967
1991	26,136	12,064
1992	28,858	13,456
1993	29,910	14,066
1994	34,288	16,060
1995	36,370	17,737
1996	39,836	19,838
1997	53,416	22,260

NOTE: These figures are for MPAA members which include Disney, Paramount, Universal, Warner Brothers, MGM, Fox, Sony, and Turner.

Movie Admission Prices
(Average price of ticket)

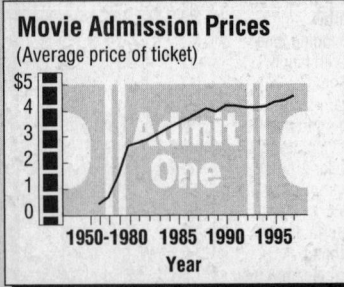

Note: 1989–1997 based on National Association of Theater Owners Average Ticket Prices. 1980–1988 based on CPI-W Index.

Movie Box-Office Gross
(In millions)

Source: Motion Picture Association of America

Movie Box-Office Gross and Attendance (In millions)

Year	Box office gross	Attendance/ admissions
1950	$1,379.0	3,017.5
1960	984.4	1,304.5
1970	1,429.2	920.6
1980	2,748.5	1,021.5
1981	2,965.6	1,067.0
1982	3,452.7	1,175.4
1983	3,766.0	1,196.9
1984	4,030.6	1,199.1
1985	3,749.4	1,056.1
1986	3,778.0	1,017.2
1987	4,252.9	1,088.5
1988	4,458.4	1,084.8
1989	5,033.4	1,262.8
1990	5,021.8	1,188.6
1991	4,803.2	1,140.6
1992	4,871.0	1,173.2
1993	5,154.2	1,244.0
1994	5,396.2	1,291.7
1995	5,493.5	1,262.6
1996	5,911.5	1,338.6
1997	6,365.9	1,387.7

one of 1998's biggest surprises—the inability of the industry's traditional array of summer "popcorn" movies to pop as expected. That left the door open for untraditional offerings like DreamWorks SKG's *Saving Private Ryan* to draw substantial crowds during the industry's biggest season. Even small dramas like the Sandra Bullock film *Hope Floats* found larger audiences than expected.

The lesson some studios divined is that a lot of people want to go to the movies during the summer, and the industry needs to provide more than just action epics to get crowds through the door. So, as studios think up their summer 1999 releases, many are planning more diverse fare that will go beyond the usual lineup of "event" movies.

While the industry touted a record number of summer films grossing more than $100 million—historically the gold standard for a Hollywood blockbuster—the studios were dismayed to find that even some of those were considered unsuccessful because they had been so costly to produce.

Lethal Weapon 4 was considered a dud by everyone except Warner Bros., which produced the film. It took in more than $125 million domestically, but cost about $180 million to produce and market. In the end, *Lethal* was no better than a break-even proposition for the studio, if that.

Another surprise: When films did work, it was often because they were patronized by an audience the industry has historically ignored—teenage girls. Hollywood has always believed that pushy young boys decided which movies to see in most households. But Girl Power began to take root late in 1997, when it pushed films as diverse as *Scream 2*

and *Good Will Hunting* to unexpected heights. And girls saw *Titanic* over and over again, drawn in by heartthrob Leonardo DiCaprio.

By the time summer arrived, studios were bending their marketing campaigns in all sorts of ways to capture the hit-making girls. That's how Walt Disney Co.'s *Armageddon*— one of the most action-intensive films of the year—wound up with a slew of TV ads pushing a romantic subplot between young stars Ben Affleck and Liv Tyler.

Despite the apparent shift away from expensive action-adventure movies, however, no one expects Hollywood to stop blowing things up any time soon. The negative publicity attached to *Titanic*'s $200 million budget caused most studios to shy away from films that might get too bogged down in expensive special effects. But slowly, the industry is delving again into effects-driven fare. The biggest film of 1999 is expected to be the long-anticipated *Star Wars* prequel. "You still have to bet big to win big," says Paul Dergarabedian of Exhibitor Relations Co., which tracks box-office results.

The next frontier for big-event films will be artificial, computer-created environments. Seagram Co.'s Universal Pictures is planning *Frankenstein vs. the Wolfman* in that vein, and Warner Bros. is developing a largely computer-animated remake of the 1960s Don Knotts film *The Incredible Mr. Limpet*, with Jim Carrey in the starring role.

Whether Hollywood can succeed in keeping costs in check for such films is an open question. But historically, the industry has never been able to control costs during periods of major innovation in special effects.

Bruce Orwall

THE SILVER SCREEN

Top Movies that Opened in 1997, ranked by total box-office receipts.

	Title	Distributor	Gross	Opened
1.*	Titanic	Paramount	$600,649,457	12/22/97
2.	Men in Black	Sony	$250,147,615	7/2/97
3.	The Lost World: Jurassic Park	Universal	$229,074,525	5/23/97
4.	Liar Liar	Universal	$181,395,380	3/21/97
5.	Air Force One	Sony	$171,880,017	7/25/97
6.	As Good As It Gets	Sony	$147,540,545	12/23/97
7.	Good Will Hunting	Miramax	$138,339,411	12/5/97
8.	Star Wars: Special Edition	Fox	$138,247,327	1/31/97
9.	My Best Friend's Wedding	Sony	$126,805,112	6/20/97
10.	Tomorrow Never Dies	MGM	$125,210,295	12/22/97
11.	Face/Off	Paramount	$112,273,211	6/27/97
12.	Batman and Robin	Warner Bros.	$107,285,004	6/6/97
13.	George of the Jungle	Buena Vista	$105,263,257	7/18/97
14.	Con Air	Buena Vista	$100,927,613	6/13/97
15.	Contact	Warner Bros.	$100,769,177	7/11/97
16.	Hercules	Disney/Buena Vista	$99,111,505	6/13/97
17.	Scream 2	Miramax	$96,297,177	12/12/97
18.	Flubber	Buena Vista	$92,969,824	11/26/97
19.	Conspiracy Theory	Warner Bros.	$75,912,202	8/8/97
20.	I Know What You Did Last Summer	Sony	$72,219,395	10/17/97

*Indicates a movie is still being tracked.

Source: Exhibitor Relations Co.

Top Movies that Opened in 1998, ranked by total box-office receipts.

(As of September 7, 1998)

	Title	Distributor	Gross	Opened
1.*	Armageddon	Buena Vista	$192,140,665	7/1/98
2.*	Saving Private Ryan	DreamWorks	$167,071,590	7/24/98
3.*	Deep Impact	Paramount	$140,387,792	5/8/98
4.*	Doctor Dolittle	Fox	$139,485,308	6/26/98
5.*	Godzilla	Sony	$135,888,409	5/20/98
6.*	There's Something About Mary	Fox	$130,268,038	7/15/98
7.*	Lethal Weapon 4	Warner Bros.	$126,166,385	7/10/98
8.*	The Truman Show	Paramount	$124,867,391	6/5/98
9.*	Mulan	Disney/Buena Vista	$117,725,653	6/16/98
10.*	The Mask of Zorro	Sony	$87,940,321	7/17/98
11.*	The X-Files	Fox	$83,413,927	6/19/98
12.	The Wedding Singer	New Line	$80,224,502	2/13/98
13.	City of Angels	Warner Bros.	$78,647,175	4/10/98
14.*	The Horse Whisperer	Buena Vista	$74,956,940	5/15/98
15.*	Six Days Seven Nights	Buena Vista	$72,503,351	6/12/98
16.	Lost in Space	New Line	$69,102,910	4/3/98
17.*	A Perfect Murder	Warner Bros.	$67,604,425	6/5/98

	Title	Distributor	Gross	Opened
18.*	The Parent Trap	Buena Vista	$60,443,951	7/29/98
19.*	Hope Floats	Fox	$59,217,290	5/29/98
20.	U.S. Marshals	Warner Bros.	$57,254,590	3/6/98

*Indicates a movie is still being tracked.
Source: Exhibitor Relations Co.

THE REAL BOX-OFFICE CHAMPS

Top 20 Films of All-Time (adjusted for inflation)*

RANK	TITLE AND DISTRIBUTOR	ADMISSIONS	OPENED	GROSS	ADJUSTED GROSS
1	Gone With the Wind (MGM)**	199,170,927	12/15/39	$173,153,142	$914,431,997
2	Star Wars (Fox)**	178,119,595	5/25/77	$460,987,469	$817,568,941
3	The Sound of Music (Fox)**	142,415,376	3/2/65	$158,671,368	$653,686,576
4	E.T. (Universal)**	135,987,938	6/11/82	$399,804,539	$624,184,637
5	The Ten Commandments (Paramount)	131,000,000	11/9/56	$65,500,000	$601,290,000
6	Titanic (Paramount)	130,860,448	12/19/97	$600,649,457	$600,649,457
7	Jaws (Universal)**	128,078,818	6/20/75	$260,000,000	$587,881,773
8	Snow White (RKO/Buena Vista)**	109,000,000	12/21/37	$184,925,486	$500,310,000
9	101 Dalmations (Buena Vista)**	105,207,663	1/25/61	$152,551,111	$482,903,172
10	The Empire Strikes Back, (Fox)**	98,106,044	5/21/80	$290,268,568	$450,306,742
11	Ben-Hur (MGM)**	98,000,000	11/19/59	$74,000,000	$449,820,000
12	The Exorcist (Warner Bros.)	94,285,714	12/26/73	$165,000,000	$432,771,429
13	Return of the Jedi (Fox)**	94,026,245	5/25/83	$309,161,884	$431,580,465
14	The Sting (Universal)	91,209,330	12/25/73	$159,616,327	$418,650,823
15	Raiders of the Lost Ark (Paramount)**	87,185,055	6/12/81	$242,374,454	$400,179,404
16	Jurassic Park (Universal)	86,193,170	6/11/93	$356,839,725	$395,626,652
17	Fantasia (Walt Disney/ Buena Vista)**	83,043,478	11/13/40	$75,400,000	$381,169,565
18	The Godfather (Paramount)	79,353,089	3/15/72	$134,900,252	$364,230,680
19	Forrest Gump (Paramount)	78,873,439	7/6/94	$329,690,974	$362,029,084
20	Mary Poppins (Buena Vista)	78,181,818	8/29/64	$86,000,000	$358,854,545

*Grosses through 7/5/98; includes reissues

**Indicates reissues

Source: Exhibitor Relations Co.

Top 20 Films of All-Time
(in current dollars)

RANK	FILM	DOMESTIC GROSS	OPENED
1	Titanic	$600,649,457	12/19/97
2	Star Wars	460,987,469	5/25/77
3	E.T.	399,804,539	6/11/82
4	Jurassic Park	356,839,725	6/11/93
5	Forrest Gump	329,690,974	7/6/94
6	The Lion King	312,855,561	6/15/94
7	Return of the Jedi	309,161,884	5/25/83
8	Independence Day	306,169,255	7/3/96
9	The Empire Strikes Back	290,268,568	5/21/80
10	Home Alone	285,016,000	11/16/90
11	Jaws	260,000,000	6/20/75

RANK	FILM	DOMESTIC GROSS	OPENED
12	Batman	$251,188,924	6/23/89
13	Men in Black	250,147,615	7/2/97
14	Raiders of the Lost Ark	245,034,358	6/12/81
15	Twister	241,708,908	5/10/96
16	Beverly Hills Cop	234,760,478	12/5/84
17	The Lost World: Jurassic Park	229,074,524	5/23/97
18	Ghostbusters	220,858,490	7/8/84
19	Mrs. Doubtfire	219,194,773	11/24/93
20	Ghost	217,631,306	7/13/90

*Grosses through 9/7/98; includes reissues

Source: Exhibitor Relations Co.

Entertainment Favorites

Television shows, performers (excluding soap opera actors), and cartoon characters that received the highest Q scores in recent studies by Marketing Evaluations Inc.

Television Program Q Scores

	Familiarity	Score		Familiarity	Score
E.R.	60%	50	Law & Order	47%	35
The X-Files	50	42	America's Most Wanted:		
Touched by an Angel	56	41	America Fights Back	51	34
Seinfeld	66	41	Diagnosis Murder	36	34
Home Improvement	83	39	Party of Five	30	34
Friends	51	37	Walker, Texas Ranger	60	34
Dawson's Creek	20	36	Cops	54	33
Promised Land	33	36	The Simpsons	59	33

Performer Q Scores

	Familiarity	Score		Familiarity	Score
Robin Williams	90%	57	Whoopi Goldberg	90%	39
Tim Allen	93	46	David Duchovny	58	38
Bill Cosby	88	44	Noah Wyle	49	38
Michael Richards	70	42	John Lithgow	63	37
Richard Karn	78	40	Helen Hunt	66	37
Della Reese	72	40	George Clooney	71	37
Scott Hamilton	68	39	Danny Glover	77	36
Michael Jordan	87	39			

Cartoon Character Q Scores

	Familiarity	Score		Familiarity	Score
Bugs Bunny	95%	50	Tigger	88%	40
Mickey Mouse	95	42	Minnie Mouse	94	39
Winnie the Pooh	90	42	Tweety Bird	94	38
Wile E. Coyote	84	42	Snoopy as "Joe Cool"	78	37
Snoopy	90	41	Looney Tunes	91	36
Road Runner	91	41	Speedy Gonzales	72	36
Tasmanian Devil	84	41	Scooby Doo	88	35
Tommy (from Rugrats)	52	40			

Q Score is based on the number of people who are familiar with program, performer or character and rate it "One of My Favorites."

Source: Marketing Evaluations Inc.

BAD TV RECEPTION

Never has there been a worse time to be in the network television business.

The four networks' combined share of the prime-time audience fell to 59 percent last season, down four percentage points from the previous year. That translates to 2.3 million fewer viewers for ABC, NBC, CBS and Fox, with most of those viewers bailing to cable or to a handful of new broadcasting upstarts.

The decline in viewership was evident on nearly every front. CBS's broadcast of the Winter Olympics in Nagano, Japan, for instance, was among the lowest-rated Olympics in memory, and ABC's *Monday Night Football* last season hit a new low. Of the 26 new entertainment series that debuted on the three biggest networks last fall, only four survived cancellation.

The result is that the network business is in serious financial trouble. Of the four big players, only NBC is expected to make money this year. CBS and ABC are in the middle of serious job-cutting, and analysts are whispering that at least two of the networks could be on the sale block.

"We're bound by an economic model of yesterday which no longer works," said ABC Inc. President Robert Iger, in an unusually downbeat speech to an industry trade group. "If we continue to ignore the change, or attempt to conduct business as usual, we won't be conducting much business at all."

Network executives are casting about for ways to stem the ratings declines—and to find new ways of making money. All of them have revamped their relationships with their affiliates, changing the way they work with the local stations that show network programs. CBS, for instance, has shifted about $50 million away from its affiliates to help defray the cost of showing professional football. In exchange, the local stations get slightly more advertising time on the network, plus the added advantage of once again having the NFL on Sunday afternoon.

NBC, meantime, spent $26.2 million for a stake in the on-line news company CNET Inc., hoping to develop a money-making presence on the Web, and all the networks are looking to the advent of digital television in 1999 as a possible solution. One plan under consideration is for the networks to charge

Broadcast Television Networks' Average Prime-Time Audience Ratings

	1996–97 TV SEASON	1997–98 TV SEASON
ABC	9.2%	8.4%
CBS	9.6	9.6
NBC	10.5	10.2
FOX	7.7	7.1
WB	2.6	3.1
UPN	3.2	2.8

Note: The audience rating is the percentage of all 98 million U.S. households with TV sets.

Source: Nielsen Media Research

subscription fees for some of their digital channels, in addition to the free, analog channels that they currently show.

At one point, the entertainment executives of the four major networks even pledged to stop sniping at each other—a traditional industry blood sport—and unite against cable, their common enemy. That truce, though, lasted less than two months, before panic set in over how much advertising each of the networks would be able to sell. Within two weeks, NBC and ABC were taking out full-page newspaper ads trying to convince advertisers to snub their broadcast competition.

They were right to be worried. Ad sales during the May "upfront" selling season—when most prime-time advertising space is purchased—were flat for the big networks in 1998, at about $6 billion. In 1997, upfront ad sales rose about 6 percent.

TV execs also have taken aim at Nielsen Media Research, the New York-based company that measures the size of the TV audience. Convinced that the 50-year-old ratings system is flawed—anybody who watches TV in a hotel or bar, for instance, isn't counted—the four big networks have agreed to chip in more than $60 million to launch a rival service. The networks, which each pay about $10 million a year for Nielsen's data, have been joined in the initiative by advertisers and media buyers and have vowed to have a new service off the ground by the end of 1999.

Nielsen officials, though, suspect sour grapes, and say the networks are simply looking for someone to blame for their lousy performance and that the new service will face the same kind of people-counting problems that has plagued Nielsen. "I've seen nothing to suggest that they would be able to offer anything that even matches what we have," said John Dimling, Nielsen's chief executive.

The central problem for the networks is that even as their viewership and ad base is slipping, their programming costs are sky-rocketing. The proliferation of cable channels has turned the TV production business into a sellers' market, meaning that there's huge demand for anything that resembles a hit. As a result, NBC in January agreed to pay $13 million an hour to renew its hit drama, *ER*, and the other networks ponied up a combined $17.6 billion for rights to show the National Football League. "The kinds of TV fees we used to see have basically been blown out of the water," said Christopher Dixon, a media analyst at PaineWebber Inc. in New York.

The irony of all the big spending is that the networks seem to be getting very little bang for their programming buck. Much of the excitement, at least on the screen, seems now to be generated by what were once considered the "upstart" networks. Fox had the only clear hit of the last TV season, *Ally McBeal*, and the new WB market has zoomed out of nowhere to all but control the teen audience. With teen-oriented hits like *Dawson's Creek* and *Buffy, the Vampire Slayer*, the WB was the only broadcast to increase its audience last season, jumping by 25 percent even as the other broadcast networks are slumping.

On the screen, the woes of the TV networks translated to fewer choices. The three big networks loaded up their schedules either with newsmagazines—which are easy to move around and relatively cheap to produce—or with shows that they own. The hope is that if the shows turn into a *Seinfeld*-size megahit, the networks will be able to make millions in syndication—and help pay for the dozens of other duds that don't work.

In Hollywood, many producers have begun to fret that the focus on owning programs has influenced what makes it on to the tube. They note that the majority of shows that debuted in the last TV season were canceled, and that viewers increasingly are complaining about the poor quality of network fare. During the prime-time Emmy Awards in September, cable's Home Box Office for the first time received as many awards as CBS and Fox combined. "I wish that the networks were thinking more about the audience," said Tom Werner, the veteran producer behind *Cosby*.

But given the slip in audience, the networks for now seem focused mostly on surviving.

Kyle Pope

Tuned In

The percentage of homes with television sets grew quickly, from 10% in 1950 to 67% in 1955 to 87% by 1960. The ownership rate reached 98% in 1980 and has held steady since then.

Percentage of U.S. Households with Various Products and Services

Year	Multiple sets	Color	Cable	VCR	Remote control	Pay cable
1955	4	–	–	–	–	–
1960	12	–	–	–	–	–
1965	22	7	–	–	–	–
1970	35	41	7	–	–	–
1975	43	74	12	–	–	–
1980	50	83	20	–	–	–
1985	57	91	43	14	29	26
1990	65	98	56	66	77	29
1998	74	99	74	84	93	40

Source: Nielsen Media Research

Average Weekly Hours and Minutes of Viewing per TV Household

0 10 20 30 40 50 60

Year	Hours:Minutes
1971	42:04
1980	46:06
1990	48:29
1994	50:50
1997	50:24

Changing Channels

Shifting Share of the Television Audience as More Homes Receive Cable Programming*

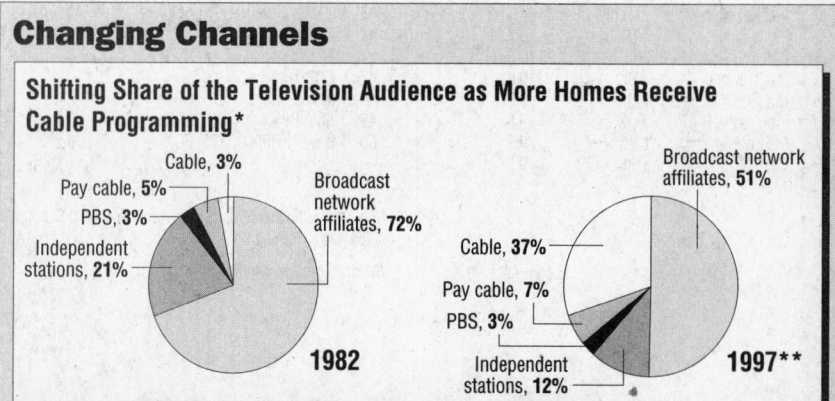

1982
- Cable, **3%**
- Pay cable, **5%**
- PBS, **3%**
- Independent stations, **21%**
- Broadcast network affiliates, **72%**

1997**
- Broadcast network affiliates, **51%**
- Cable, **37%**
- Pay cable, **7%**
- PBS, **3%**
- Independent stations, **12%**

*Shares don't add to 100% because of viewing of multiple TV sets in some households.
**Independent stations include all superstations except TBS; broadcast network affiliates include Fox; cable includes TBS.
Source: Nielsen Media Research

Top Rated Network Television Shows, 1997-1998 TV Season

RANK	PROGRAM NAME	NETWORK	AVERAGE AUDIENCE RATING	RANK	PROGRAM NAME	NETWORK	AVERAGE AUDIENCE RATING
1	Seinfeld	NBC	22.0	28	Dateline NBC-Fri	NBC	9.5
2	E.R.	NBC	20.7	28	Dharma & Greg	ABC	9.5
3	Veronica's Closet	NBC	16.8	28	NBC Sunday Night Movie	NBC	9.5
4	Friends	NBC	16.4	32	Hiller and Diller	ABC	9.3
5	NFL Monday Night Football	ABC	15.0	32	Simpsons	FOX	9.3
6	Touched by an Angel	CBS	14.4	32	Walker, Texas Ranger	CBS	9.3
7	60 Minutes	CBS	13.9	35	Dateline NBC Sunday	NBC	9.2
8	Union Square	NBC	13.6	35	Everybody Loves Raymond	CBS	9.2
9	CBS Sunday Movie	CBS	13.3	37	Soul Man	ABC	9.1
10	Frasier	NBC	12.0	38	Lateline	NBC	9.0
10	Home Improvement	ABC	12.0	39	Chicago Hope	CBS	8.9
10	Just Shoot Me	NBC	12.0	39	JAG	CBS	8.9
13	Dateline NBC-Tue	NBC	11.5	39	Promised Land	CBS	8.9
13	NFL Monday Showcase	ABC	11.5	42	Ellen	ABC	8.8
15	Dateline NBC-Mon	NBC	11.4	42	Two Guys, Girl & Pizza Place	ABC	8.8
16	Drew Carey Show	ABC	11.1	44	ABC Sunday Night Movie	ABC	8.5
16	Fox NFL Sunday-Post Game I	FOX	11.1	44	3rd Rock From The Sun	NBC	8.5
18	20/20	ABC	10.9	44	20/20-Thurs	ABC	8.5
19	NYPD Blue	ABC	10.8	47	Caroline In The City	NBC	8.4
19	Primetime Live	ABC	10.8	47	CBS Tuesday Movie	CBS	8.4
19	X-Files	FOX	10.8	47	Spin City	ABC	8.4
22	Fox NFL Sun-Post Game II	FOX	10.7	50	Beverly Hills 90210	FOX	8.3
23	Law and Order	NBC	10.2				
24	20/20-Mon	ABC	10.0				
25	Diagnosis Murder	CBS	9.8				
25	King of the Hill	FOX	9.8				
27	Mad About You	NBC	9.7				
28	Cosby	CBS	9.5				

Note: The audience rating is the percentage of all U.S. households with TV sets

Source: Nielsen Media Research

Top Ranking Network Series Programs (Sept-April)

Season	Program	Network	Rating*
1950-51	Texaco Star Theatre	NBC	61.6
1951-52	Godfrey's Talent Scouts	CBS	53.8
1952-53	I Love Lucy	CBS	67.3
1953-54	I Love Lucy	CBS	58.8
1954-55	I Love Lucy	CBS	49.3
1955-56	$64,000 Question	CBS	47.5
1956-57	I Love Lucy	CBS	43.7
1957-58	Gunsmoke	CBS	43.1
1958-59	Gunsmoke	CBS	39.6
1959-60	Gunsmoke	CBS	40.3
1960-61	Gunsmoke	CBS	37.3
1961-62	Wagon Train	NBC	32.1
1962-63	Beverly Hillbillies	CBS	36.0
1963-64	Beverly Hillbillies	CBS	39.1
1964-65	Bonanza	NBC	36.3
1965-66	Bonanza	NBC	31.8
1966-67	Bonanza	NBC	29.1
1967-68	Andy Griffith	CBS	27.6
1968-69	Rowan & Martin Laugh-In	NBC	31.8
1969-70	Rowan & Martin Laugh-In	NBC	26.3
1970-71	Marcus Welby, MD	ABC	29.6
1971-72	All In The Family	CBS	34.0
1972-73	All In The Family	CBS	33.3
1973-74	All In The Family	CBS	31.2
1974-75	All In The Family	CBS	30.2
1975-76	All In The Family	CBS	30.1
1976-77	Happy Days	ABC	31.5
1977-78	Laverne & Shirley	ABC	31.6
1978-79	Laverne & Shirley	ABC	30.5
1979-80	60 Minutes	CBS	28.2
1980-81	Dallas	CBS	31.2
1981-82	Dallas	CBS	28.4
1982-83	60 Minutes	CBS	25.5
1983-84	Dallas	CBS	25.7
1984-85	Dynasty	ABC	25.0
1985-86	Bill Cosby Show	NBC	33.8
1986-87	Bill Cosby Show	NBC	34.9
1987-88	Bill Cosby Show	NBC	27.8
1988-89	Roseanne	ABC	25.5
1989-90	Roseanne	ABC	23.4
1990-91	Cheers	NBC	21.6
1991-92	60 Minutes	CBS	21.7
1992-93	60 Minutes	CBS	21.6
1993-94	Home Improvement	ABC	21.9
1994-95	Seinfeld	NBC	20.5
1995-96	E.R.	NBC	22.0
1996-97	E.R.	NBC	21.2
1997-98	Seinfeld	NBC	22.0

*Each rating point represents 1% of all U.S. households with television sets.
Source: Nielsen Media Research

TV Programs With the Largest Audience Ratings of All Time

Rank	Program	Telecast date	Network	Average audience rating (%)	Share (%)	Average audience (in thousands)
1	M*A*S*H Special	Feb. 28, 1983	CBS	60.2	77	50,150
2	Dallas	Nov. 21, 1980	CBS	53.3	76	41,470
3	Roots Pt. VIII	Jan. 30, 1977	ABC	51.1	71	36,380
4	Super Bowl XVI Game	Jan. 24, 1982	CBS	49.1	73	40,020
5	Super Bowl XVII Game	Jan. 30, 1983	NBC	48.6	69	40,480
6	XVII Winter Olympics	Feb. 23, 1994	CBS	48.5	64	45,690
7	Super Bowl XX Game	Jan. 26, 1986	NBC	48.3	70	41,490
8	Gone with the Wind Pt. 1 (Big Event - Pt.1)	Nov. 7, 1976	NBC	47.7	65	33,960
9	Gone with the Wind Pt. 2 (NBC Monday Movie)	Nov. 8, 1976	NBC	47.4	64	33,750
10	Super Bowl XII Game	Jan. 15, 1978	CBS	47.2	67	34,410
11	Super Bowl XIII Game	Jan. 21, 1979	NBC	47.1	74	35,090
12	Bob Hope Christmas Show	Jan. 15, 1970	NBC	46.6	64	27,260
13	Super Bowl XVIII Game	Jan. 22, 1984	CBS	46.4	71	38,800
13	Super Bowl XIX Game	Jan. 20, 1985	ABC	46.4	63	39,390
15	Super Bowl XIV Game	Jan. 20, 1980	CBS	46.3	67	35,330
16	Super Bowl XXX Game	Jan. 28, 1996	NBC	46.0	68	44,150
16	ABC Theater (The Day After)	Nov. 20, 1983	ABC	46.0	62	38,550
18	Roots Pt. VI	Jan. 28, 1977	ABC	45.9	66	32,680
18	The Fugitive	Aug. 29, 1967	ABC	45.9	72	25,700
20	Super Bowl XXI Game	Jan. 25, 1987	CBS	45.8	66	40,030
21	Roots Pt. V	Jan. 27, 1977	ABC	45.7	71	32,540
22	Super Bowl XXVIII Game	Jan. 29, 1994	NBC	45.5	66	42,860
22	Cheers	May 20, 1993	NBC	45.5	64	42,360
24	Ed Sullivan	Feb. 9, 1964	CBS	45.3	60	23,240
25	Super Bowl XXVII	Jan. 31, 1993	NBC	45.1	66	41,990
26	Bob Hope Christmas Show	Jan. 14, 1971	NBC	45.0	61	27,050
27	Roots Pt. III	Jan. 25, 1977	ABC	44.8	68	31,900
28	Super Bowl XXXII Game	Jan. 25, 1998	NBC	44.6	67	43,630
29	Super Bowl XI Game	Jan. 9, 1977	NBC	44.4	73	31,610
29	Super Bowl XV Game	Jan. 25, 1981	NBC	44.4	63	34,540
31	Super Bowl VI Game	Jan. 16, 1972	CBS	44.2	74	27,450
32	XVII Winter Olympics	Feb. 25, 1994	CBS	44.1	64	41,540
32	Roots Pt. II	Jan. 24, 1977	ABC	44.1	62	31,400
34	Beverly Hillbillies	Jan. 8, 1964	CBS	44.0	65	22,570
35	Roots Pt. IV	Jan. 26, 1977	ABC	43.8	66	31,190
35	Ed Sullivan	Feb. 16, 1964	CBS	43.8	60	22,445
37	Super Bowl XXIII Game	Jan. 22, 1989	NBC	43.5	68	39,320
38	Academy Awards	Apr. 7, 1970	ABC	43.4	78	25,390
39	Super Bowl XXXI Game	Jan. 26, 1997	Fox	43.3	65	42,000
40	Thorn Birds Pt. III	Mar. 29, 1983	ABC	43.2	62	35,990
41	Thorn Birds Pt. IV	Mar. 30, 1983	ABC	43.1	62	35,900
42	CBS NFC Championship Game	Jan. 10, 1982	CBS	42.9	62	34,960
43	Beverly Hillbillies	Jan. 15, 1964	CBS	42.8	62	21,960
44	Super Bowl VII Game	Jan. 14, 1973	NBC	42.7	72	27,670
45	Thorn Birds Pt. II	Mar. 28, 1983	ABC	42.5	59	35,400
46	Super Bowl IX Game	Jan. 12, 1975	NBC	42.4	72	29,040
46	Beverly Hillbillies	Feb. 26, 1964	CBS	42.4	60	21,750
48	Super Bowl X Game	Jan. 18, 1976	CBS	42.3	78	29,440
48	Airport (Movie Specials)	Nov. 11, 1973	ABC	42.3	63	28,000
48	Love Story (Sun. Night Mov.)	Oct. 1, 1972	ABC	42.3	62	27,410
48	Cinderella	Feb. 22, 1965	CBS	42.3	59	22,250
48	Roots Pt. VII	Jan. 29, 1977	ABC	42.3	65	30,120

Note: The rating is the percentage of all TV households; the share is the percentage of all TVs in use at the time.
Source: Nielsen Media Research

Top Cable Networks by Number of Subscribers

The cable-television networks that reached the largest number of subscribers.

1. ESPN	71,000,000
2. CNN	71,000,000
3. TNT	70,549,000
4. TBS	69,920,000
5. C-SPAN	69,700,000
6. USA Network	69,677,000
7. Discovery Channel	69,499,000
8. TNN: The Nashville Network	68,875,000
9. LIfetime Television	67,000,000
10. The Family Channel	66,900,000
11. A&E Television Network	66,880,000
12. MTV: Music Television	66,700,000
13. Nickelodeon/Nick at Nite	66,000,000
14. The Weather Channel	66,000,000
15. Headline News	64,200,000
16. AMC (American Movie Classics)	61,500,000
17. CNBC	60,000,000
18. QVC	58,174,602
19. VH1 (Music First)	56,328,000
20. The Learning Channel	55,000,000

Source: National Cable Television Association

Rising Cable-TV Rates

Average Monthly Cable Rates

YEAR	BASIC RATE
1980	$7.69
1981	7.99
1982	8.30
1983	8.61
1984	8.98
1985	9.73
1986	10.67
1987	12.18
1988	13.86
1989	15.21
1990	16.78
1991	18.10
1992	19.08
1993	19.39
1994	21.62
1995	23.07
1996	24.41
1997	26.48

Note: As of year-end 1994, the basic and expanded basic rates are combined as regulated basics.

Source: Paul Kagan Associates, Inc.

Home Video: A Buyer's Market

Growth of the home-video industry is slowing, and in a major shift, video buyers are starting to generate more revenue than renters.

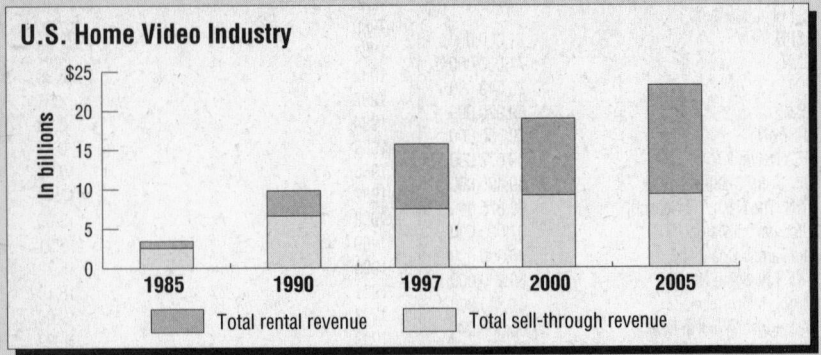

U.S. Home Video Industry

In billions

■ Total rental revenue   □ Total sell-through revenue

Year	Total rental revenue* (In billions)	Total sell-through revenue* (In billions)	Total revenue* (In billions)
1985	$2.55	$0.86	$3.41
1990	6.63	3.18	9.81
1997	7.46	8.24	15.70
2000	9.18	9.76	18.94
2005	9.26	13.90	23.16

*Includes digital videodisks (DVDs).
Source: Paul Kagan Associates Inc.

Top Video Rentals for 1997

Rank	Title	Video label	Turns (In millions)	Revenues (In millions)
1	Jerry Maguire	Columbia TriStar	22.55	$60.19
2	Liar Liar	Universal	20.91	57.41
3	A Time to Kill	Warner	18.77	50.71
4	The First Wives Club	Paramount	17.82	47.84
5	Ransom	BV/Touchstone	17.39	46.78
6	Phenomenon	BV/Touchstone	17.26	46.24
7	Scream	BV/Dimension	16.50	44.91
8	Michael	Warner	15.82	42.51
9	The Long Kiss Goodnight	New Line	15.53	41.35
10	Sleepers	Warner	15.16	41.02
11	The Ghost and the Darkness	Paramount	15.06	40.34
12	Absolute Power	Warner	14.23	38.28
13	The Rock	BV/Hollywood	13.88	37.59
14	Kingpin	MGM	13.95	37.54
15	Men in Black	Columbia TriStar	13.64	37.46
16	The Devil's Own	Columbia TriStar	13.27	36.23
17	Tin Cup	Warner	12.93	34.90
18	The Glimmer Man	Warner	12.78	34.05
19	Jack	BV/Hollywood	12.47	33.54
20	Jungle 2 Jungle	Buena Vista	12.00	31.86

Source: Video Software Dealers Association

Top Selling Videos in 1997

	Title	Studio	Units Sold
1	*101 Dalmatians*	Disney	15,000,000
2	*Men in Black*	Columbia	14,000,000
3	*Hunchback of Notre Dame*	Disney	12,500,000
4	*Lost World*	Universal	12,000,000
5	*Empire Strikes Back*	Fox	10,000,000
6	*Return of the Jedi*	Fox	10,000,000
7	*Star Wars*	Fox	10,000,000
8	*Liar, Liar*	Universal	9,000,000
9	*Space Jam*	Warner	8,500,000
10	*George of the Jungle*	Disney	7,200,000

Source: Paul Kagan Associates, Inc.

Home Video's Greatest Hits: Top 10 Selling Videos of All Time

	Title	Studio	Date	Units Sold (in millions)
1	*The Lion King*	Disney	03/95	30.0
2	*Snow White*	Disney	10/94	28.0
3	*Aladdin*	Disney	10/93	24.0
4	*Jurassic Park*	Universal	10/92	24.0
5	*Beauty & the Beast*	Disney	10/92	22.0
6	*Independence Day*	Fox	11/96	22.0
7	*Toy Story*	Disney	10/96	21.0
8	*Pocahontas*	Disney	02/96	17.0
9	*Forrest Gump*	Paramount	04/95	16.0
10	*101 Dalmatians*	Disney	04/97	15.0

Source: Paul Kagan Associates, Inc.

Top Video-Game Players

Top 25 Publishers Ranked by Interactive Entertainment Software Units Sold, 1997

		Publisher's sales mix		
		Percent of entertainment software units sold		
Rank	Publisher	Video game console	vs.	Computer
1	Nintendo of America	100%		0%
2	Electronic Arts	62		38
3	Sony	97		3
4	Cendant Software	1		99
5	GT Interactive	12		88
6	Acclaim	93		7
7	Sega of America	93		7
8	Midway Home Entertainment	100		0
9	Hasbro Interactive	39		61
10	Virgin Interactive	41		59
11	Namco	100		0
12	Mindscape	34		66
13	Microsoft	0		100
14	THQ	99		1
15	Activision	27		73
16	Interplay	31		69
17	Eidos	70		30
18	LucasArts Entertainment	18		82
19	Broderbund	0		100
20	Capcom	99		1
21	Microprose	12		88
22	Learning Co.	0		100
23	Gametek	65		35
24	Accolade	52		48
25	Konami	100		0

Source: NPD Interactive Entertainment Software Service

Sour Note

Sales of recorded music declined in 1997 in both unit shipments and dollar value.

Record Manufacturers' Unit Shipments and Dollar Value
(In millions, net after returns)

	1988	1989	1990	1991	1992	1993	1994	1995	1996	% change 1995–1996	1997	% change 1996–1997
(Units shipped) CD	149.7	207.2	286.5	333.3	407.5	495.4	662.1	722.9	778.9	7.7%	753.1	-3.3%
(Dollar value) CD	$2,089.9	$2,587.7	$3,451.6	$4,337.7	$5,326.5	$6,511.4	$8,464.5	$9,377.4	$9,934.7	5.9	$9,915.1	-0.2
CD single	1.6	-0.1	1.1	5.7	7.3	7.8	9.3	21.5	43.2	100.9	66.7	54.4
	9.8	-0.7	6.0	35.1	45.1	45.8	56.1	110.9	184.1	66.0	272.7	48.1
Cassette	450.1	446.2	442.2	360.1	366.4	339.5	345.4	272.6	225.3	-17.4	172.6	-23.4
	3,385.1	3,345.8	3,472.4	3,019.6	3,116.3	2,915.8	2,976.4	2,303.6	1,905.3	-17.3	1,522.7	-20.1
Cassette single	22.5	76.2	87.4	69.0	84.6	85.6	81.1	70.7	59.9	-15.3	42.2	-29.5
	57.3	194.6	257.9	230.4	298.8	298.5	274.9	236.3	189.3	-19.9	133.5	-29.5
LP/EP	72.4	34.6	11.7	4.8	2.3	1.2	1.9	2.2	2.9	31.8	2.7	-6.9
	532.2	220.3	86.5	29.4	13.5	10.6	17.8	25.1	36.8	46.6	33.3	-9.5
Vinyl single	65.6	36.6	27.6	22.0	19.8	15.1	11.7	10.2	10.1	-1.0	7.5	-25.7
	180.4	116.4	94.4	63.9	66.4	51.2	47.2	46.7	47.5	1.7	35.6	-25.1
Music video	–	6.1	9.2	6.1	7.6	11.0	11.2	12.6	16.9	34.1	18.6	10.1
	–	115.4	172.3	118.1	157.4	213.3	231.1	220.3	236.1	7.2	323.9	37.2
Total units	761.9	806.7	865.7	801.0	895.5	955.6	1,122.7	1,112.7	1,137.2	2.2	1,063.4	-6.5
Total value	$6,254.8	$6,579.4	$7,541.1	$7,834.2	$9,024.0	$10,046.6	$12,068.0	$12,320.3	$12,533.8	1.7	$12,236.8	-2.4

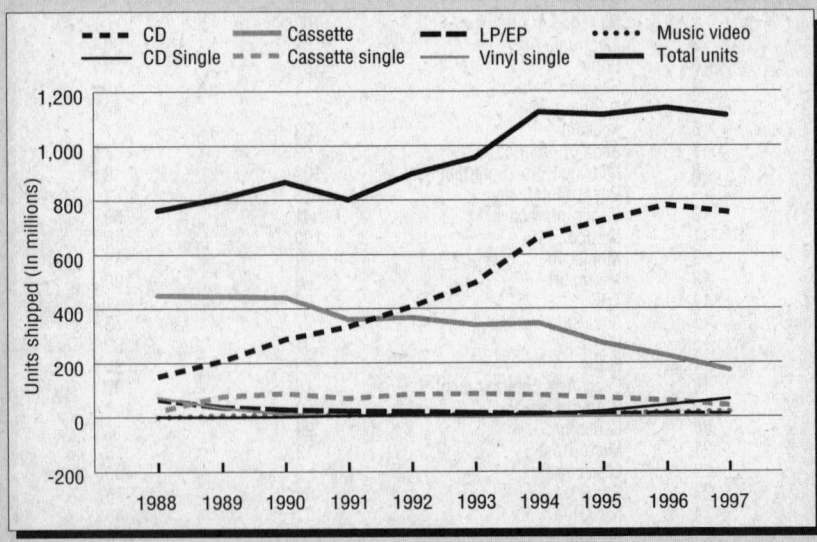

Source: Recording Industry Association of America

Changing the Tune

Market shares of different types of recorded music in 1987 and 1997 show America's changing musical tastes.

	1987	1997
Rock	45.5%	32.5%
Country	10.6	14.4
R&B	9.0	11.2
Pop	13.5	10.1
Rap	3.8	9.4
Gospel	2.9	4.5
Classical	3.9	2.8
Jazz	3.8	2.8
Oldies	0.7	0.8
Soundtracks	0.2	1.2
New Age	NA	0.8
Children's	0.5	0.9
Other	4.8	5.7

Source: Recording Industry Association of America.

Top 40 Singles of 1997

1. Candle in the Wind 1997/Something About the Way You Look Tonight—*Elton John—Rocket/A&M*
2. You Were Meant for Me/Foolish Games—*Jewel—Atlantic*
3. I'll Be Missing You—*Puff Daddy & Faith Evans (Featuring 112)—Bad Boy/Arista*
4. Un-Break My Heart—*Toni Braxton—LaFace/Arista*
5. Can't Nobody Hold Me Down—*Puff Daddy (Featuring Mase)—Bad Boy/Arista*
6. I Believe I Can Fly (From "Space Jam")—*R. Kelly—Warner Sunset/Atlantic/Jive*
7. Don't Let Go (Love) (From "Set It Off")—*En Vogue—EastWest/EEG*
8. Return of the Mack—*Mark Morrison—Atlantic*
9. How Do I Live—*LeAnn Rimes—Curb*
10. Wannabe—*Spice Girls—Virgin*
11. Quit Playing Games (with My Heart)—*Backstreet Boys—Jive*
12. MMMBOP—*Hanson—Mercury*
13. For You I Will (From "Space Jam")—*Monica—Rowdy/Warner Sunset/Atlantic*
14. You Make Me Wanna—*Usher—LaFace/Arista*
15. Bitch—*Meredith Brooks—Capitol*
16. Nobody—*Keith Sweat Featuring Athena Cage—Elektra/EEG*
17. Semi-Charmed Life—*Third Eye Blind—Elektra/EEG*
18. Barely Breathing—*Duncan Sheik—Atlantic*
19. Hard to Say I'm Sorry—*Az Yet Featuring Peter Cetera—LaFace/Arista*
20. Mo Money Mo Problems—*The Notorious B.I.G. (Featuring Puff Daddy & Mase)—Bad Boy/Arista*
21. The Freshmen—*The Verve Pipe—RCA*
22. I Want You—*Savage Garden—Columbia*
23. No Diggity—*BLACKstreet (Featuring Dr. Dre)—Interscope*
24. I Belong To You (Every Time I See Your Face)—*Rome—Grand Jury/RCA*
25. Hypnotize—*The Notorious B.I.G.—Bad Boy/Arista*
26. Every Time I Close My Eyes—*Babyface—Epic*
27. In My Bed—*Dru Hill—Island*
28. Say You'll Be There—*Spice Girls—Virgin*
29. Do You Know (What It Takes)—*Robyn—RCA*
30. 4 Seasons of Loneliness—*Boyz II Men—Motown*
31. G.H.E.T.T.O.U.T—*Changing Faces—Big Beat/Atlantic*
32. Honey—*Mariah Carey—Columbia*
33. I Believe In You and Me (From "The Preacher's Wife")—*Whitney Houston—Arista*
34. Da' Dip—*FreakNasty—Hard Hood/Power/Triad*
35. 2 Become 1—*Spice Girls—Virgin*
36. All For You—*Sister Hazel—Universal*
37. Cupid—*112—Bad Boy/Arista*
38. Where Have All the Cowboys Gone?—*Paula Cole—Imago/Warner Bros.*
39. Sunny Came Home—*Shawn Colvin—Columbia*
40. It's Your Love—*Tim McGraw (With Faith Hill)—Curb*

Source: Billboard Hot 100 Singles Chart for 1997, which is based on amount of radio air play and sales data.

Top-Selling Music Albums of 1997

1. Spice Girls, *Spice*	5,300,000
2. Jewel, *Pieces of You*	4,300,000
3. Puff Daddy, *No Way Out*	3,400,000
4. Garth Brooks, *Sevens*	3,400,000
5. Hanson, *Middle of Nowhere*	3,200,000
6. Notorious B.I.G., *Life After Death*	3,200,000
7. Wallflowers, *Bringing Down the Horse*	3,100,000
8. Celine Dion, *Falling Into You*	3,000,000
9. *Space Jam*, Soundtrack	3,000,000
10. LeAnn Rimes, *You Light Up My Life*	3,000,000
11. Matchbox 20, *Yourself or Someone Like You*	2,800,000
12. LeAnn Rimes, *Blue*	2,700,000
13. No Doubt, *Tragic Kingdom*	2,700,000
14. *Men In Black*, Soundtrack	2,600,000
15. Celine Dion, *Let's Talk About Love*	2,500,000
16. Fleetwood Mac, *Dance*	2,200,000
17. Mariah Carey, *Butterfly*	2,200,000
18. Barbra Streisand, *Higher Ground*	2,100,000
19. Sublime, *Sublime*	2,100,000
20. Erykah Badu, *Baduizm*	2,000,000

Source: SoundScan Inc.

Top-Selling Music Albums of All Time

25,000,000
TITLE: *Thriller*
ARTIST: Michael Jackson
LABEL: Epic

24,000,000
TITLE: *Eagles—Their Greatest Hits 1971–1975*
ARTIST: Eagles
LABEL: Elektra

22,000,000
TITLE: *The Wall*
ARTIST: Pink Floyd
LABEL: Columbia

18,000,000
TITLE: *Rumours*
ARTIST: Fleetwood Mac
LABEL: Warner Bros.

TITLE: *Greatest Hits, Volume I & II*
ARTIST: Billy Joel
LABEL: Columbia

17,000,000
TITLE: *Led Zeppelin IV*
ARTIST: Led Zeppelin
LABEL: Swan Song

16,000,000
TITLE: *Back In Black*
ARTIST: AC/DC
LABEL: ATCO

TITLE: *The Beatles*
ARTIST: The Beatles
LABEL: Capitol

TITLE: *Boston*
ARTIST: Boston
LABEL: Epic

TITLE: *The Bodyguard* (Soundtrack)
ARTIST: Whitney Houston, et al.
LABEL: Arista

TITLE: *Jagged Little Pill*
ARTIST: Alanis Morissette
LABEL: Maverick

TITLE: *No Fences*
ARTIST: Garth Brooks
LABEL: Capitol Nashville

15,000,000
TITLE: *Born in the U.S.A.*
ARTIST: Bruce Springsteen
LABEL: Columbia

TITLE: *Cracked Rear View*
ARTIST: Hootie & The Blowfish
LABEL: Atlantic

TITLE: *Appetite for Destruction*
ARTIST: Guns 'N Roses
LABEL: Geffen

TITLE: *Greatest Hits*
ARTIST: Elton John
LABEL: Rocket

TITLE: *The Dark Side of the Moon*
ARTIST: Pink Floyd
LABEL: Capitol

14,000,000
TITLE: *The Beatles 1967–1970*
ARTIST: The Beatles
LABEL: Capitol

TITLE: *Hotel California*
ARTIST: Eagles
LABEL: Elektra

13,000,000
TITLE: *The Beatles 1962–1966*
ARTIST: The Beatles
LABEL: Capitol

TITLE: *Purple Rain* (Soundtrack)
ARTIST: Prince & The Revolution
LABEL: Warner Bros.

TITLE: *Bat Out of Hell*
ARTIST: Meat Loaf
LABEL: Epic

TITLE: *Ropin' the Wind*
ARTIST: Garth Brooks
LABEL: Liberty

12,000,000
TITLE: *Slippery When Wet*
ARTIST: Bon Jovi
LABEL: Mercury

TITLE: *II*
ARTIST: Boyz II Men
LABEL: Motown

TITLE: *Whitney Houston*
ARTIST: Whitney Houston
LABEL: Arista

TITLE: *Bruce Springsteen & E Street Band Live 1975–'85*
ARTIST: Bruce Springsteen
LABEL: Columbia

TITLE: *Kenny Rogers' Greatest Hits*
ARTIST: Kenny Rogers
LABEL: Capitol Nashville

TITLE: *Hysteria*
ARTIST: Def Leppard
LABEL: Mercury

TITLE: *Breathless*
ARTIST: Kenny G
LABEL: Arista

11,000,000

TITLE: *Saturday Night Fever* (Soundtrack)
ARTIST: Bee Gees
LABEL: RSO

TITLE: *Dirty Dancing*
ARTIST: Soundtrack
LABEL: RCA

TITLE: *James Taylor's Greatest Hits*
ARTIST: James Taylor
LABEL: Warner Bros.

TITLE: *Abbey Road*
ARTIST: The Beatles
LABEL: Capitol

TITLE: *Sgt. Pepper's Lonely Hearts Club Band*
ARTIST: The Beatles
LABEL: Capitol

10,000,000

TITLE: *Unplugged*
ARTIST: Eric Clapton
LABEL: Reprise

TITLE: *Best of the Doobies*
ARTIST: Doobie Brothers
LABEL: Warner Bros.

TITLE: *Please Hammer Don't Hurt 'em*
ARTIST: Hammer
LABEL: Capitol

TITLE: *Tapestry*
ARTIST: Carole King
LABEL: Ode

TITLE: *Music Box*
ARTIST: Mariah Carey
LABEL: Columbia

TITLE: *Like a Virgin*
ARTIST: Madonna
LABEL: Sire

TITLE: *Metallica*
ARTIST: Metallica
LABEL: Elektra

TITLE: *The Woman In Me*
ARTIST: Shania Twain
LABEL: Mercury Nashville

TITLE: *Falling Into You*
ARTIST: Celine Dion
LABEL: 550 Music

TITLE: *Titanic*
ARTIST: Soundtrack
LABEL: Sony Classical

TITLE: *Can't Slow Down*
ARTIST: Lionel Richie
LABEL: Motown

TITLE: *The Lion King*
ARTIST: Soundtrack
LABEL: Walt Disney

TITLE: *Crazy, Sexy, Cool*
ARTIST: TLC
LABEL: LaFace

TITLE: *The Joshua Tree*
ARTIST: U2
LABEL: Island

TITLE: *Van Halen*
ARTIST: Van Halen
LABEL: Warner Bros.

TITLE: *Eliminator*
ARTIST: ZZ Top
LABEL: Warner Bros.

TITLE: *Ten*
ARTIST: Pearl Jam
LABEL: Epic

TITLE: *Faith*
ARTIST: George Michael
LABEL: Columbia

Source: Recording Industry Association of America

Making Music—and Money

Major Concert Ticket Sales in North America

Top Concert Tours of All Time

Rank	Performer	Year	Gross revenues
1	Rolling Stones	1994	$121,200,000
2	Pink Floyd	1994	103,500,000
3	Rolling Stones	1989	98,000,000
4	Rolling Stones	1997	89,300,000
5	U2	1997	79,900,000
6	Eagles	1994	79,400,000
7	New Kids On The Block	1990	74,100,000
8	U2	1992	67,000,000
9	Eagles	1995	63,300,000
10	Barbra Streisand	1994	58,900,000

Source: Pollstar

1997 Concert Tours with the Largest Ticket Revenues (In millions)

Rank	Gross	Artist
1	$89.3	The Rolling Stones
2	79.9	U2
3	36.3	Fleetwood Mac
4	34.1	Metallica
5	33.0	Brooks & Dunn/Reba McEntire
6	26.9	Garth Brooks
7	24.8	Tina Turner
8	24.6	The Artist (fka Prince)
9	24.4	Jimmy Buffett
10	22.3	Aerosmith
11	21.3	Phish
12	17.6	Phil Collins
13	16.6	Alan Jackson
14	16.5	ZZ Top
15	16.5	Bush
16	16.4	"Lilith Fair"
17	16.1	Barry Manilow
18	15.8	Kenny G/Toni Braxton
19	14.7	Puff Daddy & The Family
20	14.2	Vince Gill
21	13.1	"Ozzfest"
22	12.4	Elton John
23	12.2	KISS
24	12.2	Counting Crows/The Wallflowers
25	12.1	No Doubt

Source: Pollstar

Radio Industry Consolidation

The radio industry has experienced major consolidation since federal legislation allowed companies to own as many stations as they want nationwide and as many as eight stations in a single market. The new law spurred a shopping spree in 1996 and 1997. Since then, advertising rates and revenues have risen, sparking concern among marketers and their ad agencies that some radio markets now will be controlled by only two companies.

Radio Station Transaction Volume

Year	No. of stations sold	Value of transactions (In millions)
1987	1,021	$2,254
1988	1,082	3,315
1989	1,205	2,248
1990	1,059	773
1991	1,009	807
1992	1,194	1,412
1993	1,410	2,829
1994	1,255	2,650
1995	1,259	5,371
1996	2,157	14,336
1997	2,250	18,046

Note: Based on dates announced, not approved.

20 Largest Radio Groups in 1997

Owner rank	Owner	Total stations	Revenues (In $000)	Owner rank	Owner	Total stations	Revenues (In $000)
1	CBS Corp.	166	$1,541,230	11	Susquehanna Radio Corp.	20	$141,400
2	Chancellor Media Corp.	99	917,000	12	Entercom	27	115,900
3	Capstar Broadcasting Partners	317	603,970	13	Citadel Communications Corp.	88	112,530
4	Jacor Communications Inc.	183	596,230	14	Bonneville Intl. Corp.	14	109,600
5	Clear Channel Communications	175	436,870	15	Greater Media	14	103,200
6	ABC Radio Inc.	28	310,350	16	Jefferson-Pilot	17	92,300
7	Cox Radio Inc.	50	234,550	17	Beasley Broadcast Group	29	79,250
8	Sinclair Communications	62	158,350	18	Spanish Broadcasting System	10	74,000
9	Emmis Broadcasting Corp.	13	154,600	19	Saga Communications Inc.	37	64,690
10	Heftel Broadcasting Corp.	34	143,800	20	Radio One Inc.	13	56,800

Note: Proforma revenues for entire year based on all stations owned or under contract at the end of the year.
Source: BIA Research Inc.

On the Radio Dial

Number of Radio Stations by Format, 1997

	Primary Format	AM	%		Primary Format	FM	%
1	News, Talk	1,073	22.6	1	Country	1,632	21.6
2	Country	873	18.4	2	Adult Contemporary	690	9.1
3	Adult Standards	476	10.0	3	News, Talk	494	6.5
4	Religion (Teaching, Variety)	360	7.6	4	Oldies	466	6.2
5	Spanish	303	6.4	5	Top-40 (CHR)	390	5.2
6	Oldies	294	6.2	6	Religion (Teaching, Variety)	379	5.0
7	Adult Contemporary	227	4.8	7	Variety	372	4.9
8	Sports	212	4.5	8	Alternative Rock	359	4.7
9	Southern Gospel	203	4.3	9	Contemporary Christian	322	4.3
10	Black Gospel	185	3.9	10	Soft Adult Contemporary	277	3.7
11	Soft Adult Contemporary	72	1.5	11	Rock	258	3.4
12	Contemporary Christian	67	1.4	12	Adult Hits, Hot AC	249	3.3
13	Ethnic	61	1.3	13	Classic Rock	232	3.1
14	Variety	54	1.1	14	Spanish	213	2.8
15	Urban, R&B	45	0.9	15	Classic Hits	169	2.2
16	Urban AC	39	0.8	16	Classical, Fine Arts	154	2.0
17	Pre-Teen	39	0.8	17	Urban, R&B	151	2.0
18	Gospel	34	0.7	18	Jazz	150	2.0
19	R&B Oldies	33	0.7	19	New Rock, Modern Rock	133	1.8
20	Rock	16	0.3	20	Urban AC	95	1.3
21	Adult Hits, Hot AC	13	0.3	21	Adult Standards	82	1.1
22	Easy Listening	13	0.3	22	Southern Gospel	82	1.1
23	Top-40 (CHR)	11	0.2	23	Modern AC	69	0.9
24	Jazz	11	0.2	24	Easy Listening	44	0.6
25	Classic Rock	10	0.2	25	Black Gospel	33	0.4
26	Alternative Rock	7	0.1	26	Gospel	26	0.3
27	Classical, Fine Arts	7	0.1	27	Ethnic	21	0.3
28	Classic Hits	4	0.1	28	R&B Oldies	13	0.2
29	New Rock, Modern Rock	4	0.1	29	Sports	8	0.1
30	Modern AC	1	0.0	30	Pre-Teen	1	0.0
	not available or changing	0	0.0		not available or changing	4	0.1
	Total Operating Stations	**4,747**	**100**		**Total Operating Stations**	**7,566**	**100**

Source: M Street Corp.

On Broadway

Box Office Gross and Attendance on Broadway

Season	Gross	Attendance
1957-58	$38 million	7.2 million
1960-61	44 million	7.7 million
1965-66	54 million	9.6 million
1970-71	55 million	7.4 million
1975-76	71 million	7.3 million
1980-81	197 million	11.0 million
1985-86	189,517,166	6,511,591
1990-91	266,823,321	7,316,095
1991-92	293,014,578	7,379,506
1992-93	327,740,483	7,856,793
1993-94	356,065,697	8,102,927
1994-95	406,121,744	9,038,977
1995-96	436,000,000	9,455,284
1996-97	499,000,000	10,600,000
1997-98	558,000,000	11,500,000

Longest Running Broadway Shows

Show	Opening date	Closing date
Cats	9/23/82	currently running
A Chorus Line	7/25/75	4/28/90
Oh Calcutta	9/24/76	8/06/89
Les Miserables	2/28/87	currently running
Phantom of the Opera	1/09/88	currently running
42nd Street	8/25/80	1/08/89
Grease	2/14/72	4/13/80
Fiddler on the Roof	9/22/64	7/01/72
Life With Father	11/08/39	7/12/47
Miss Saigon	4/11/91	currently running

Broadway Road Tours

Season	Box office gross	Number of shows
1992-93	$626.0 million	52
1993-94	705.0 million	42
1994-95	702.0 million	44
1995-96	810.0 million	47
1996-97	781.8 million	46
1997-98	721.0 million	34

Average Top Ticket Prices on Broadway

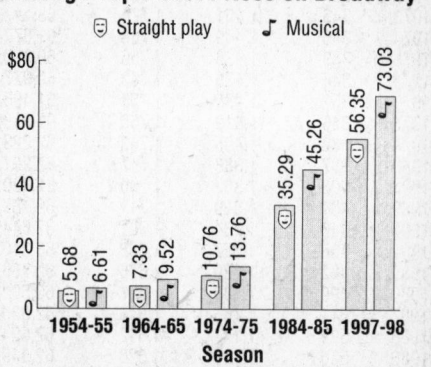

Straight play   Musical

Season	Straight play	Musical
1954-55	5.68	6.61
1964-65	7.33	9.52
1974-75	10.76	13.76
1984-85	35.29	45.26
1997-98	56.35	73.03

Broadway Box Office Gross

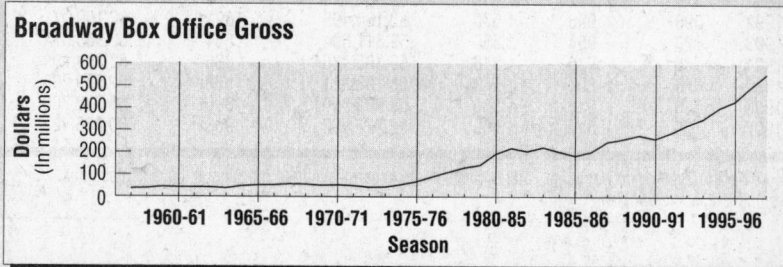

Dollars (In millions) — Season: 1960-61, 1965-66, 1970-71, 1975-76, 1980-85, 1985-86, 1990-91, 1995-96

Source: League of American Theatres and Producers

The Printed Word

Fewer Dailies, Fewer Readers

Number of Newspapers and Their Circulation

Year	Morning	Evening	Total*	Total circulation	Sunday	Sunday circulation
1920	437	1,605	2,042	27,790,656	522	17,083,604
1930	388	1,554	1,942	39,589,172	521	26,413,047
1940	380	1,498	1,878	41,131,611	525	32,371,092
1950	322	1,450	1,772	53,829,072	549	46,582,348
1960	312	1,459	1,763	58,881,746	563	47,698,651
1970	334	1,429	1,748	62,107,527	586	49,216,602
1971	339	1,425	1,749	62,231,258	590	49,747,308
1972	337	1,441	1,761	62,510,242	605	50,000,669
1973	343	1,451	1,774	63,147,280	634	51,717,465
1974	340	1,449	1,768	61,877,197	645	51,678,726
1975	339	1,436	1,756	60,955,011	639	51,096,323
1976	346	1,435	1,762	60,977,011	650	51,565,334
1977	352	1,435	1,753	61,495,140	668	52,429,234
1978	355	1,419	1,756	61,989,997	696	53,990,033
1979	382	1,405	1,763	62,223,040	720	54,379,923
1980	387	1,388	1,747	62,201,840	736	54,676,173
1981	408	1,352	1,730	61,430,745	755	55,180,004
1982	434	1,310	1,711	62,487,177	768	56,260,764
1983	446	1,284	1,701	62,644,603	772	56,747,436
1984	458	1,257	1,688	63,340,320	783	57,573,979
1985	482	1,220	1,676	62,766,232	798	58,825,978
1986	499	1,188	1,657	62,502,036	802	58,924,518
1987	511	1,166	1,645	62,826,273	820	60,111,863
1988	529	1,141	1,642	62,694,816	840	61,474,189
1989	530	1,125	1,626	62,649,213	849	62,008,154
1990	559	1,084	1,611	62,327,962	863	62,634,512
1991	571	1,042	1,586	60,687,125	875	66,093,415
1992	596	996	1,570	60,164,499	891	62,159,971
1993	623	954	1,556	59,811,594	884	62,565,574
1994	635	935	1,548	59,305,436	886	62,294,799
1995	656	891	1,533	58,193,391	888	61,529,296
1996	686	846	1,520	56,983,290	890	63,732,708
1997	705	816	1,509	56,727,902	903	60,486,463

*Morning and Evening do not equal Total because some papers have both morning and evening editions.
Source: Editor & Publisher

Top 50 Daily Newspapers in the U.S. According to Circulation
(Sept. 30,1997)

New York (NY) *Wall Street Journal*	(m)	1,774,880
Arlington (VA) *USA Today*	(m)	1,629,665
New York (NY) *Times*	(m)	1,074,741
Los Angeles (CA) *Times*	(m)	1,050,176
Washington (DC) *Post*	(m)	775,894
New York (NY) *Daily News*	(m)	721,256
Chicago (IL) *Tribune*	(m)	653,554
Long Island (NY) *Newsday*	(m)	568,914
Houston (TX) *Chronicle*	(m)	549,101
Chicago (IL) *Sun-Times*	(m)	484,379
San Francisco (CA) *Chronicle*	(m)	484,218
Dallas (TX) *Morning News*	(m)	481,032
Boston (MA) *Globe*	(m)	476,966
Phoenix (AZ) *Arizona Republic*	(m)	437,118
New York (NY) *Post*	(m)	436,226
Philadelphia (PA) *Inquirer*	(m)	428,233
Newark (NJ) *Star-Ledger*	(m)	406,010
Minneapolis (MN) *Star Tribune*	(m)	387,412
Detroit (MI) *Free Press*	(m)	384,624
Cleveland (OH) *Plain Dealer*	(m)	383,586
San Diego (CA) *Union-Tribune*	(all day)	375,598
Miami (FL) *Herald*	(m)	356,803
Orange County (CA) *Register*	(m)	356,520
Portland (OR) *Oregonian*	(all day)	342,454
St. Petersburg (FL) *Times*	(m)	342,189
Denver (CO) *Post*	(m)	337,372
St. Louis (MO) *Post-Dispatch*	(m)	313,594
Baltimore (MD) *Sun*	(m)	312,826
Denver (CO) *Rocky Mountain News*	(m)	302,953
Atlanta (GA) *Constitution*	(m)	296,669
San Jose (CA) *Mercury News*	(m)	290,811
Milwaukee (WI) *Journal Sentinel*	(m)	288,173
Sacramento (CA) *Bee*	(m)	281,471
Boston (MA) *Herald*	(m)	277,106
Kansas City (MO) *Star*	(m)	276,349
Buffalo (NY) *News*	(all day)	262,085
New Orleans (LA) *Times-Picayune*	(m)	260,552
Orlando (FL) *Sentinel*	(all day)	258,037
Fort Lauderdale (FL) *Sun-Sentinel*	(m)	257,118
Detroit (MI) *News*	(e)	246,638
Columbus (OH) *Dispatch*	(m)	246,095
Pittsburgh (PA) *Post-Gazette*	(m)	243,024
Tampa (FL) *Tribune*	(m)	240,990
Charlotte (NC) *Observer*	(m)	239,016
Los Angeles (CA) *Investor's Business Daily*	(m)	234,596
Fort Worth (TX) *Star-Telegram*	(m)	229,701
Louisville (KY) *Courier-Journal*	(m)	228,185
Seattle (WA) *Times*	(e)	227,162
Omaha (NE) *World-Herald*	(all day)	225,761
Indianapolis (IN) *Star*	(m)	224,372

Top 50 Sunday Newspapers in the U.S. According to Circulation
(Sept. 30,1997)

New York (NY) *Times*	1,658,718
Los Angeles (CA) *Times*	1,361,748
Washington (DC) *Post*	1,102,329
Chicago (IL) *Tribune*	1,023,736
Philadelphia (PA) *Inquirer*	878,660
Detroit (MI) *News and Free Press*	829,178
New York (NY) *Daily News*	807,788
Dallas (TX) *Morning News*	789,004
Boston (MA) *Sunday Globe*	758,843
Houston (TX) *Chronicle*	748,036
Atlanta (GA) *Journal and Constitution*	674,240
Minneapolis (MN) *Star Tribune*	668,466
Long Island (NY) *Newsday*	664,988
San Francisco (CA) *Examiner and Chronicle*	625,106
Newark (NJ) *Star-Ledger*	606,007
Phoenix (AZ) *Arizona Republic*	560,031
St. Louis (MO) *Post-Dispatch*	521,809
Cleveland (OH) *Plain Dealer*	508,787
Seattle (WA) *Times/Post-Intelligencer*	505,808
Baltimore (MD) *Sunday Sun*	479,811
Miami (FL) *Herald*	477,969
Denver (CO) *Post*	471,180
Milwaukee (WI) *Journal Sentinel*	462,473
San Diego (CA) *Union-Tribune*	454,085
Portland (OR) *Oregonian*	437,508
St. Petersburg (FL) *Times*	436,806
Pittsburgh (PA) *Post-Gazette*	424,431
Chicago (IL) *Sun-Times*	423,685
Denver (CO) *Rocky Mountain News*	415,708
Orange County (CA) *Register*	415,638
Kansas City (MO) *Star*	408,135
Indianapolis (IN) *Star*	392,823
Fairfax (VA) *Journal Newspapers*	386,000
Columbus (OH) *Dispatch*	383,829
Orlando (FL) *Sentinel*	381,234
Fort Lauderdale (FL) *Sun-Sentinel*	372,745
San Antonio (TX) *Express-News*	371,831
Buffalo (NY) *News*	347,090
Sacramento (CA) *Bee*	346,117
San Jose (CA) *Mercury News*	342,902
Fort Worth (TX) *Star-Telegram*	340,935
Tampa (FL) *Tribune*	338,221
Cincinnati (OH) *Enquirer*	329,692
New York (NY) *Post*	326,087
Louisville (KY) *Courier-Journal*	314,538
Hartford (CT) *Courant*	302,859
Charlotte (NC) *Observer*	302,188
New Orleans (LA) *Times-Picayune*	301,631
Oklahoma City (OK) *Sunday Oklahoman*	297,758
Omaha (NE) *World-Herald*	283,939

Source: Editor and Publisher Yearbook

Leading U.S. Magazines Ranked by Advertising Revenue in 1997

Rank	Publication	Advertising revenue 1997*	% change from 1996	1997 Ad pages	% change from 1996
1	People Weekly	$588,503,553	12.0	3,998.89	7.8
2	Sports Illustrated	548,616,906	5.0	2,905.21	1.2
3	Time	533,197,540	21.3	2,781.11	16.2
4	TV Guide	469,254,735	16.4	3,305.05	8.8
5	Newsweek	408,510,127	6.4	2,647.21	4.5
6	Better Homes & Gardens	377,450,890	12.5	1,925.26	6.4
7	PC Magazine	333,512,719	4.9	6,061.37	-0.1
8	Business Week	329,674,885	10.3	4,114.39	5.9
9	Forbes	243,780,227	9.6	4,662.84	2.5
10	U.S. News & World Report	239,219,264	5.1	2,124.42	2.0
11	Woman's Day	228,424,924	5.3	1,810.38	8.7
12	Fortune	225,896,103	13.6	3,599.77	7.9
13	Good Housekeeping	219,189,364	18.6	1,346.76	15.5
14	Reader's Digest	212,321,538	5.3	1,086.59	1.4
15	Family Circle	205,875,264	17.4	1,427.02	6.4
16	Cosmopolitan	188,503,005	20.6	1,893.13	12.2
17	Ladies' Home Journal	183,921,716	15.3	1,472.73	1.4
18	Vogue	148,980,330	12.1	2,782.45	9.3
19	Entertainment Weekly	145,995,795	17.2	1,937.43	4.8
20	Glamour	137,374,775	17.7	1,940.62	16.3
21	Money	132,643,791	13.1	1,362.32	4.5
22	Rolling Stone	121,571,578	13.1	1,861.99	2.0
23	Southern Living	120,783,213	7.0	1,537.42	0.9
24	Golf Digest	120,189,465	18.7	1,400.04	11.8
25	McCall's	118,335,170	14.9	1,052.96	5.2
26	Redbook	113,190,210	13.4	1,215.57	7.5
27	Martha Stewart Living	110,974,634	69.2	1,199.59	40.2
28	PC Computing	110,447,642	11.9	2,818.67	5.8
29	Car and Driver	108,069,510	10.3	1,441.73	4.3
30	Elle	100,400,826	19.4	2,114.81	14.9
31	Parents	97,627,049	8.8	1,399.68	0.6
32	Vanity Fair	95,537,356	13.1	1,696.96	11.9
33	New Yorker	94,053,304	11.1	2,141.96	5.1
34	Inc.	90,295,606	16.2	1,471.71	6.7
35	Country Living	89,000,775	17.9	1,184.40	10.7
36	Bride's	83,353,893	10.6	3,106.28	1.4
37	Golf Magazine	78,732,847	10.9	1,171.96	3.6
38	Windows Magazine	77,717,408	10.0	2,713.44	-2.7
39	W	77,366,627	22.2	1,892.24	19.3
40	Travel & Leisure	76,728,350	16.2	1,417.86	10.8
41	Gentlemen's Quarterly	75,850,443	23.1	1,830.97	17.5
42	Seventeen	75,335,345	22.5	1,311.37	7.5
43	Modern Bride	75,001,956	18.6	3,018.98	10.8
44	Road & Track	73,842,898	20.4	1,438.60	9.5
45	Harper's Bazaar	73,530,546	3.4	1,525.07	1.7
46	Parenting	69,825,627	14.4	1,252.61	6.9
47	Self	69,399,710	19.2	1,355.34	17.3
48	National Geographic	66,945,392	10.3	418.58	11.7
49	Mademoiselle	63,082,319	11.0	1,317.71	7.7
50	House Beautiful	62,690,805	14.5	936.03	3.8

*Based on the published ad rates provided by each magazine.
Sources: Publishers Information Bureau

50 Leading Magazines by Average Total Paid Circulation Per Issue For Second Six Months of 1997

Rank	Publication name	Avg. total circ. for July-Dec. 1997	Avg. total circ. for July-Dec. 1996	Percent change
1	NRTA/AARP Bulletin	20,415,981	20,567,352	-0.74 %
2	Modern Maturity	20,390,755	20,528,786	-0.67
3	Reader's Digest	15,038,708	15,072,260	-0.22
4	TV Guide	13,103,187	13,013,938	0.69
5	National Geographic	9,012,074	9,025,003	-0.14
6	Better Homes and Gardens	7,605,187	7,605,325	0.00
7	Family Circle	5,107,477	5,239,074	-2.51
8	Good Housekeeping	4,739,592	4,951,240	-4.27
9	Ladies' Home Journal	4,590,155	4,544,416	1.01
10	Woman's Day	4,461,023	4,317,604	3.32
11	McCall's	4,216,145	4,290,216	-1.73
12	Time	4,155,806	4,102,168	1.31
13	People Weekly	3,608,111	3,449,852	4.59
14	Prevention	3,310,278	3,311,244	-0.03
15	Sports Illustrated	3,223,810	3,173,639	1.58
16	Newsweek	3,177,407	3,194,769	-0.54
17	Playboy	3,169,697	3,236,517	-2.06
18	Redbook	2,889,466	2,926,702	-1.27
19	Home & Away	2,759,565	2,719,931	1.46
20	The American Legion Magazine	2,734,318	2,777,351	-1.55
21	Cosmopolitan	2,701,916	2,486,393	8.67
22	Seventeen	2,567,613	2,442,090	5.14
23	Southern Living	2,474,463	2,490,542	-0.65
24	Martha Stewart Living	2,339,799	2,025,182	15.54
25	National Enquirer	2,324,678	2,480,349	-6.28
26	U.S. News & World Report	2,224,003	2,260,857	-1.63
27	YM	2,221,937	2,153,815	3.16
28	Glamour	2,115,642	2,115,488	0.01
29	Smithsonian	2,065,432	2,095,819	-1.45
30	Star	1,948,247	2,220,711	-12.27
31	V.F.W. Magazine	1,935,807	1,980,947	-2.28
32	Money	1,935,402	1,993,119	-2.90
33	Teen	1,842,186	1,327,893	38.73
34	Ebony	1,819,431	1,803,566	0.88
35	Field & Stream	1,751,772	1,750,180	0.09
36	Parents	1,745,292	1,737,249	0.46
37	Country Living	1,697,742	1,674,925	1.36
38	Life	1,568,565	1,601,069	-2.03
39	Popular Science	1,558,655	1,793,192	-13.08
40	Golf Digest	1,529,671	1,515,829	0.91
41	Men's Health	1,511,345	1,373,817	10.01
42	Woman's World	1,505,637	1,504,067	0.10
43	Sunset	1,471,825	1,431,549	2.81
44	Popular Mechanics	1,425,692	1,428,356	-0.19
45	First For Women	1,408,419	1,331,399	5.78
46	Cooking Light	1,387,037	1,379,055	0.58
47	Outdoor Life	1,377,139	1,353,061	1.78
48	American Rifleman	1,341,176	1,545,242	-13.21
49	Golf Magazine	1,339,970	1,292,980	3.63
50	Entertainment Weekly	1,315,550	1,280,230	2.76
	Total for top 50 magazines	**192,160,785**	**191,916,358**	**0.13**

Source: Audit Bureau of Circulations and Magazine Publishers of America

Getting a Reading on Book Sales

Book Publishers' Net Dollar Sales and Net Unit Sales*

$30,000
25,000
20,000
15,000
10,000
5,000
0
Sales (In millions)
$Sales
Units
30,000
25,000
20,000
15,000
10,000
5,000
0
Units (In millions)
1993 1994 1995 1996 1997 1998 1999 2000 2001 2002 2003
Projections

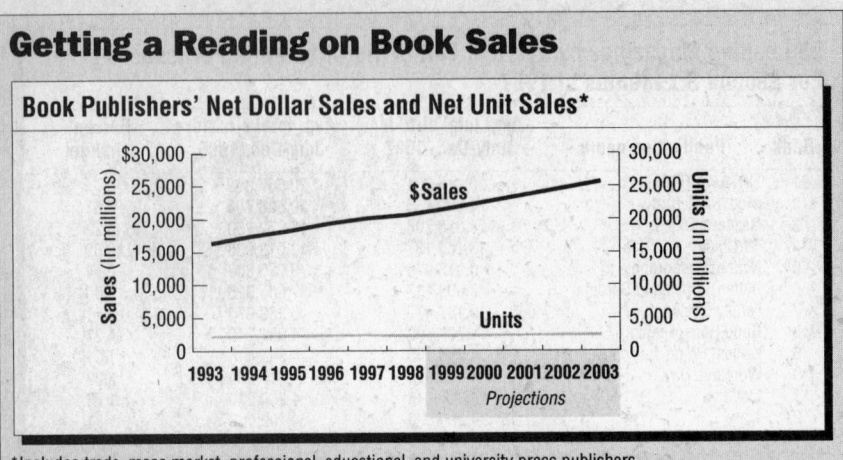

*Includes trade, mass market, professional, educational, and university press publishers.
Source: Book Industry Study Group

What People Are Reading

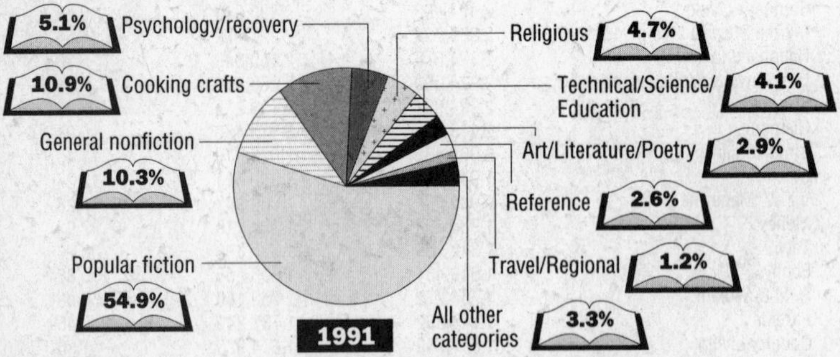

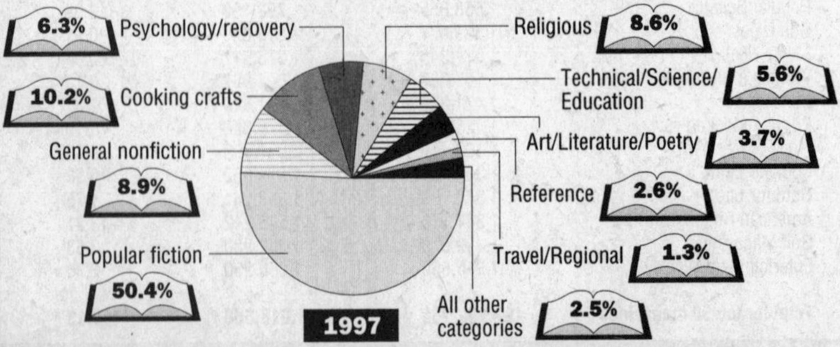

5.1% Psychology/recovery
10.9% Cooking crafts
General nonfiction 10.3%
Popular fiction 54.9%
Religious 4.7%
Technical/Science/ Education 4.1%
Art/Literature/Poetry 2.9%
Reference 2.6%
Travel/Regional 1.2%
All other categories 3.3%
1991

6.3% Psychology/recovery
10.2% Cooking crafts
General nonfiction 8.9%
Popular fiction 50.4%
Religious 8.6%
Technical/Science/ Education 5.6%
Art/Literature/Poetry 3.7%
Reference 2.6%
Travel/Regional 1.3%
All other categories 2.5%
1997

Source: Book Industry Study Group

Where Book Buyers Shop

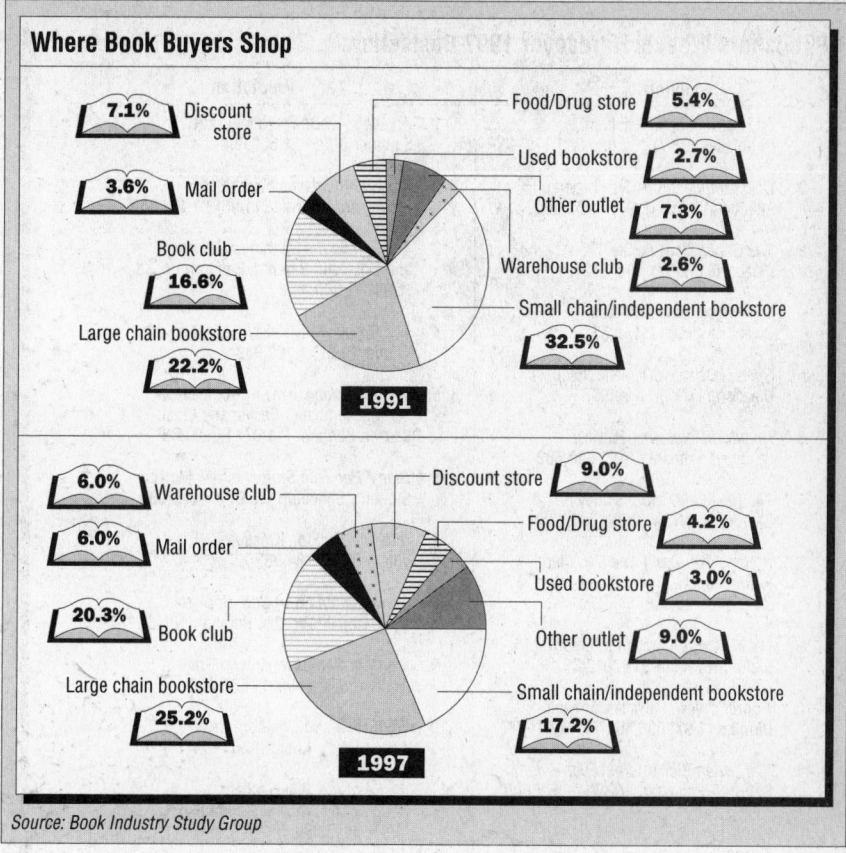

1991

- 7.1% Discount store
- 3.6% Mail order
- 16.6% Book club
- 22.2% Large chain bookstore
- 5.4% Food/Drug store
- 2.7% Used bookstore
- 7.3% Other outlet
- 2.6% Warehouse club
- 32.5% Small chain/independent bookstore

1997

- 6.0% Warehouse club
- 6.0% Mail order
- 20.3% Book club
- 25.2% Large chain bookstore
- 9.0% Discount store
- 4.2% Food/Drug store
- 3.0% Used bookstore
- 9.0% Other outlet
- 17.2% Small chain/independent bookstore

Source: Book Industry Study Group

Publishers Weekly Hardcover 1997 Bestsellers

Fiction	Nonfiction
1 *The Partner*. John Grisham. Doubleday (3/97) **2,625,000	1 *Angela's Ashes*. Frank McCourt. Scribner (9/96) *1,650,000
2 *Cold Mountain*. Charles Frazier. Atlantic Monthly (6/97) 1,458,280	2 *Simple Abundance*. Sarah Ban Breathnach. Warner (11/95) *1,462,663
3 *The Ghost*. Danielle Steel. Delacorte (12/97) 1,161,121	3 *Midnight in the Garden of Good and Evil*. John Berendt. Random House (1/94) *1,300,799
4 *The Ranch*. Danielle Steel. Delacorte (5/97) 1,158,631	4 *The Royals*. Kitty Kelley. Warner (9/97) 1,120,943
5 *Special Delivery*. Danielle Steel. Delacorte (7/97) 1,152,937	5 *Joy of Cooking*. Irma S. Rombauer, Marion Rombauer Becker and Ethan Becker. Scribner (11/97) 1,000,000
6 *Unnatural Exposure*. Patricia Cornwell. Putnam (7/97) 869,682	6 *Diana: Her True Story*. Andrew Morton. Simon & Schuster. (10/97) **825,000
7 *The Best Laid Plans*. Sidney Sheldon. Morrow (9/97) 730,755	7 *Into Thin Air*. Jon Krakauer. Villard (5/97) 784,969
8 *Pretend You Don't See Her*. Mary Higgins Clark. Simon & Schuster (4/97) **725,000	8 *Conversations with God, Book I*. Neale Donald Walsch. Putnam (10/96) *749,001
9 *Cat & Mouse*. James Patterson. Little, Brown (11/97) 701,237	9 *Men Are from Mars...* John Gray. HarperCollins (4/93) *687,267
10 *Hornet's Nest*. Patricia Cornwell. Putnam (1/97) 636,400	10 *Eight Weeks to Optimum Health*. Andrew Weil. Knopf (3/97) 674,117
11 *The Letter*. Richard Paul Evans. Simon & Schuster (10/97) **575,000	11 *Just As I Am*. Billy Graham. Harper San Francisco/Zondervan (4/97) 647,008
12 *Flood Tide*. Clive Cussler. Simon & Schuster (9/97) **550,000	12 *The Man Who Listens to Horses*. Monty Roberts. Random House (8/97) 593,165
13 *Violin*. Anne Rice. Knopf (10/97) 501,702	13 *The Millionaire Next Door*. Thomas J. Stanley and William D. Danko. Longstreet (10/96) *585,924
14 *The Matarese Countdown*. Robert Ludlum. Bantam (11/97) **500,000	14 *The Perfect Storm*. Sebastian Junger. Norton (5/97) **550,000
15 *Plum Island*. Nelson DeMille. Warner (5/97) 474,848	15 *Kids Are Punny*. Rosie O'Donnell. Warner (4/97) 558,880

Note: Rankings are determined by sales figures provided by publishers; the numbers generally reflect reports of copies "shipped and billed" in calendar year 1997 and publishers were instructed to adjust sales figures to include returns through Feb., 10, 1998. Publishers did not at that time know what their total returns would be—indeed, the majority of returns occur later in the year. So none of these figures should be regarded as final net sales. (Dates in parentheses indicate month and year of publication.)
*Sales figures reflect only books sold in calendar year 1997.
**Sales figures were submitted to *PW* in confidence, for use in placing titles on the lists. Numbers shown are rounded down to the nearest 25,000 to indicate relationship to sales figures of other titles.
Source: Publishers Weekly

Trade Paperbacks

1 *Don't Sweat the Small Stuff and It's All Small Stuff.* Richard Carlson. Orig. Hyperion (4,506,683)

2 *Chicken Soup for the Woman's Soul.* Jack Canfield, Mark Victor Hansen et al. Orig. Health Communications (2,228,000)

3 *She's Come Undone.* Wally Lamb. Rep. Pocket/Washington Square.

4 *Chicken Soup for the Mother's Soul.* Jack Canfield, Mark Victor Hansen et al. Orig. Health Communications (1,406,739)

5 *Wizard and Glass.* Stephen King. Orig. Plume (1,298,664)

6 *Stones from the River.* Ursula Hegi. Rep. Scribner (1,285,000)

7 *Prescription for Nutritional Healing.* James F. & Phyllis A. Balch. Orig. Avery (1,275,000)

8 *Windows 95 for Dummies, 2nd ed.* Andy Rathbone. Orig. IDG (1,148,107)

9 *Chicken Soup for the Christian Soul.* Jack Canfield, Mark Victor Hansen et al. Orig. Health Communications (1,263,328)

10 *Songs in Ordinary Time.* Mary McGarry Morris. Rep. Penguin (1,120,000)

11 *A 4th Course of Chicken Soup for the Soul.* Jack Canfield, Mark Victor Hansen et al. Orig. Health Communications (1,088,952)

12 *Rapture of Canaan.* Sheri Reynolds. Rep. Berkley (1,000,000)

13 *Heart of a Woman.* Maya Angelou. Rep. Bantam

14 *Petals on the River.* Kathleen E. Woodiwiss. Orig. Avon

15 *Undaunted Courage.* Stephen E. Ambrose. Rep. Touchstone (589,000)

Mass Market Paperbacks

1 *The Runaway Jury.* John Grisham. Rep. Dell/Island (4,995,438)

2 *Five Days in Paris.* Danielle Steel. Rep. Dell (2,932,226)

3 *Malice.* Danielle Steel. Rep. Dell (2,930,012)

4 *Silent Honor.* Danielle Steel. Rep. Dell (2,821,930)

5 *Executive Orders.* Tom Clancy. Rep. Berkley (2,400,000)

6 *Moonlight Becomes You.* Mary Higgins Clark. Rep. Pocket

7 *Desperation.* Stephen King. Rep. Signet (2,088,269)

8 *My Gal Sunday.* Mary Higgins Clark. Rep. Pocket

9 *Airframe.* Michael Crichton. Rep. Ballantine (2,002,049)

10 *Cause of Death.* Patricia Cornwell. Rep. Berkley (2,000,000)

11 *The Deep End of the Ocean.* Jacquelyn Mitchard. Rep. Signet (1,904,414)

12 *Ticktock.* Dean Koontz. Orig. Ballantine (1,817,299)

13 *The Regulators.* Richard Bachman. Rep. Signet (1,813,788)

14 *The Lost World.* Michael Crichton. Movie tie-in. Ballantine (1,689,113)

15 *The Hornet's Nest.* Patricia Cornwell. Rep. Berkley (1,600,000)

Source: Publishers Weekly

Children's Hardcover Frontlist

1 *Hercules (Classic)*. Disney/Mouse Works (558,992)

2 *Anastasia (Little Golden Book)*. Golden (396,360)

3 *Disney: Pooh's Grand Adventure*. Golden (376,950)

4 *Disney: Pooh and the Dragon*. Golden (364,610)

5 *Sesame Street: Tickle Me: My Name is Elmo*. Golden (349,400)

6 *Disney's Hercules*. Golden (314,800)

7 *The Children's Book of Heroes*. Edited by William J. Bennett, illus. by Michael Hague. S&S

8 *Disney's Pooh: Eyeore, Be Happy!* Golden (307,070)

9 *Disney's Pooh: Happy Easter*. Golden (301,810)

10 *Disney's 101 Dalmations*. Golden (295,260)

11 *Dr. Seuss' ABC (board book)*. Dr. Seuss. Random House (264,047)

12 *Mr. Brown Can Moo: Can You? (board book)*. Dr. Seuss. Random House (258,504)

13 *Seussisms*. Dr. Seuss. Random House (256,693)

14 *Disney's Bambi*. Golden (255,860)

15 *Sesame Street: Shake a Leg!* Golden (254,550)

Children's Hardcover Backlist

1 *Disney's Pooh: Thank You, Pooh!* Golden, 1996 (598,820)

2 *Disney's Pooh: A Grand and Wonderful Day*. Golden, 1996 (494,300)

3 *Guess How Much I Love You (board book)*. Sam McBratney, illus. by Anita Jeram. Candlewick, 1995 (481,488)

4 *Goodnight Moon (board book)*. Margaret Wise Brown, illus. by Clement Hurd. HarperFestival, 1991 (468,240)

5 *Disney's 101 Dalmations*. Golden, 1996 (448,930)

6 *Brown Bear, Brown Bear, What Do You See? (board book)*. Bill Martin Jr., illus. by Eric Carle. Holt, 1996 (441,709)

7 *Disney's Pooh: The Sweetest Christmas*. Golden. 1996 (433,130)

8 *Oh, the Places You'll Go!* Dr. Seuss. Random House, 1990 (408,779)

9 *Arthur Goes to School*. Marc Brown. Random House, 1995 (394,880)

10 *The Scholastic Children's Dictionary*. Scholastic, 1996 (368,000)

11 *Disney's Pooh: Winnie the Pooh and the Honey Tree*. Golden, 1994 (351,960)

12 *Barney: Sharing is Caring*. Golden, 1996 (348,060)

13 *Green Eggs and Ham*. Dr. Seuss. Random House, 1966 (333,318)

14 *Disney's The Lion King: Way to Go Simba*. Golden, 1996 (332,300)

15 *Sesame Street: Count to Ten*. Golden, 1993 (328,980)

Source: Publishers Weekly

Gambling Fever

Americans are gambling more of their money than ever, as revenue-hungry states have legalized more types of wagering and Indians have opened more casinos. But the industry's revenue growth rate has slowed from the heated pace of the early 1990s.

Gross Gambling Revenues (Dollars in millions)

	1982 gross revenues	1996 gross revenues	1997 gross revenues	1982-97 increase/ decrease in gross revenues (Dollars)	(Percent)	Average annual rate 1982-1997 (Percent)
Horses	$2,250.0	$3,181.4	$3,251.4	$1,001.42	44.5%	2.0%
Greyhounds	430.0	538.8	509.4	79.44	18.5	1.0
Jai Alai	112.0	61.4	50.1	(61.91)	(55.3)	-5.2
Lotteries	2,170.0	16,201.8	16,566.8	14,396.84	663.4	14.5
Casinos	4,200.0	19,144.5	20,527.6	16,327.63	388.8	11.2
Legal Bookmaking	25.8	86.5	96.3	70.50	273.7	9.2
Card Rooms	50.0	684.3	700.2	650.16	1300.3	19.2
Charitable Bingo	780.0	959.1	956.9	176.86	22.7	1.4
Charitable Games	396.0	1,471.0	1,562.2	1,166.18	294.5	9.6
Indian Reservations	–	5,605.1	6,678.5	6,678.5	–	–
Grand Total	**$10,413.8**	**$47,933.9**	**$50,899.3**	**$40,485.6**	**388.8**	**11.2**

Sources: International Gaming & Wagering Business and Christiansen/Cummings Associates

More Players Sharing the Pot

With increased competition from riverboat and Indian casinos, both Las Vegas and Atlantic City have experienced a slowdown in the growth of gambling revenues.

Atlantic City	Casino gambling revenues	Number of visitors	Las Vegas and the rest of Clark County	Casino gambling revenues	Number of Las Vegas visitors
1990	$ 2,951,580,214	31,812,733	1990	$ 4,104,001,000	20,954,420
1991	2,991,561,232	30,788,400	1991	4,152,407,000	21,315,116
1992	3,215,968,867	30,705,332	1992	4,381,710,000	21,886,865
1993	3,301,365,943	30,224,968	1993	4,727,424,000	23,522,593
1994	3,422,615,117	31,321,500	1994	5,430,651,000	28,214,362
1995	3,726,581,413	33,271,808	1995	5,717,567,000	29,002,122
1996	3,789,350,761	34,041,548	1996	5,783,735,000	29,636,631
1997	3,879,650,762	34,070,587	1997	6,152,415,000	30,500,000

Sources: New Jersey Casino Control Commission and South Jersey Transportation Authority; Las Vegas Convention and Visitors Authority

Awards

Nobel Laureates

Alfred Nobel, a nineteenth-century Swedish industrialist and the inventor of dynamite, created the Nobel Prizes to recognize and reward outstanding achievements in physics, chemistry, physiology or medicine, literature, and the peace process. His will stipulated that the bulk of his estate, more than 31 million Swedish kronor, should be invested, with the income awarded to "those who during the preceding year shall have conferred the greatest benefit on mankind." The prize in economics was established in 1968 by the Bank of Sweden.

Physics

1901 Röntgen, Wilhelm Conrad (Germany)	1933* Schrödinger, Erwin (Austria)
1902* Lorentz, Hendrik Antoon (The Netherlands)	Dirac, Paul Adrien Maurice (Great Britain)
Zeeman, Pieter (The Netherlands)	1934[†] –
1903** Becquerel, Antoine Henri (France)	1935 Chadwick, Sir James (Great Britain)
Curie, Pierre (France) and	1936** Hess, Victor Franz (Austria)
Curie, Marie (France)*	Anderson, Carl David (USA)
1904 Rayleigh, Lord (John William Strutt)	1937* Davisson, Clinton Joseph (USA)
(Great Britain)	Thomson, Sir George Paget
1905 Lenard, Philipp Eduard Anton (Germany)	(Great Britain)
1906 Thomson, Sir Joseph John (Great Britain)	1938 Fermi, Enrico (Italy)
1907 Michelson, Albert Abraham (USA)	1939 Lawrence, Ernest Orlando (USA)
1908 Lippmann, Gabriel (France)	1940–42[†] –
1909* Marconi, Guglielmo (Italy)	1943[‡] Stern, Otto (USA)
Braun, Carl Ferdinand (Germany)	1944 Rabi, Isidor Isaac (USA)
1910 Van Der Waals, Johannes Diderik	1945 Pauli, Wolfgang (Austria)
(The Netherlands)	1946 Bridgman, Percy Williams (USA)
1911 Wien, Wilhelm (Germany)	1947 Appleton, Sir Edward Victor
1912 Dalén, Nils Gustaf (Sweden)	(Great Britain)
1913 Kamerlingh-Onnes, Heike (The Netherlands)	1948 Blackett, Lord Patrick Maynard Stuart
1914 Von Laue, Max (Germany)	(Great Britain)
1915* Bragg, Sir William Henry (Great Britain)	1949 Yukawa, Hideki (Japan)
Bragg, Sir William Lawrence (Great Britain)	1950 Powell, Cecil Frank (Great Britain)
1916[†] –	1951* Cockcroft, Sir John Douglas
1917[‡] Barkla, Charles Glover (Great Britain)	(Great Britain)
1918[‡] Planck, Max Karl Ernst Ludwig (Germany)	Walton, Ernest Thomas Sinton
1919 Stark, Johannes (Germany)	(Ireland)
1920 Guillaume, Charles Edouard (Switzerland)	1952* Bloch, Felix (USA)
1921[‡] Einstein, Albert (Germany and Switzerland)	Purcell, Edward Mills (USA)
1922 Bohr, Niels (Denmark)	1953 Zernike, Frits (Frederik)
1923 Millikan, Robert Andrews (USA)	(The Netherlands)
1924[‡] Siegbahn, Karl Manne Georg (Sweden)	1954** Born, Max (Great Britain)
1925[‡]* Franck, James (Germany)	Bothe, Walther (Germany)
Hertz, Gustav (Germany)	1955** Lamb, Willis Eugene (USA)
1926 Perrin, Jean Baptiste (France)	Kusch, Polykarp (USA)
1927** Compton, Arthur Holly (USA)	1956* Shockley, William (USA)
Wilson, Charles Thomson Rees	Bardeen, John (USA)
(Great Britain)	Brattain, Walter Houser (USA)
1928[‡] Richardson, Sir Owen Willans	1957* Yang, Chen Ning (China)
(Great Britain)	Lee, Tsung-Dao (China)
1929 De Broglie, Prince Louis-Victor (France)	1958* Cherenkov, Pavel Alekseyevich (USSR)
1930 Raman, Sir Chandrasekhara Venkata	Frank, Il'ja Mikhailovich (USSR)
(India)	Tamm, Igor Yevgenyevich (USSR)
1931[†] –	1959* Segré, Emilio Gino (USA)
1932[‡] Heisenberg, Werner (Germany)	Chamberlain, Owen (USA)

Physics

1960	Glaser, Donald A. (USA)
1961**	Hofstadter, Robert (USA)
	Mössbauer, Rudolf Ludwig (Germany)
1962	Landau, Lev Davidovich (USSR)
1963**	Wigner, Eugene P. (USA)
	Goeppert-Mayer, Maria (USA) and
	Jensen, J. Hans D. (Germany)*
1964**	Townes, Charles H. (USA)
	Basov, Nicolay Gennadiyevich
	(USSR) and
	Prokhorov, Aleksandr Mikhailovich
	(USSR)*
1965*	Tomonaga, Sin-Itiro (Japan)
	Schwinger, Julian (USA)
	Feynman, Richard P. (USA)
1966	Kastler, Alfred (France)
1967	Bethe, Hans Albrecht (USA)
1968	Alvarez, Luis W. (USA)
1969	Gell-Mann, Murray (USA)
1970**	Alfvén, Hannes (Sweden)
	Néel, Louis (France)
1971	Gabor, Dennis (Great Britain)
1972*	Bardeen, John (USA)
	Cooper, Leon N. (USA)
	Schrieffer, J. Robert (USA)
1973**	Esaki, Leo (Japan) and
	Giaever, Ivar (USA)
	Josephson, Brian D. (Great Britain)
1974*	Ryle, Sir Martin (Great Britain)
	Hewish, Antony (Great Britain)
1975*	Bohr, Aage (Denmark)
	Mottelson, Ben (Denmark)
	Rainwater, James (USA)
1976**	Richter, Burton (USA)
	Ting, Samuel C. C. (USA)
1977**	Anderson, Philip W. (USA)
	Mott, Sir Nevill F. (Great Britain)
	Van Vleck, John H. (USA)
1978**	Kapitsa, Pyotr Leonidovich (USSR)
	Penzias, Arno A. (USA) and
	Wilson, Robert W. (USA)
1979**	Glashow, Sheldon L. (USA)
	Salam, Abdus (Pakistan)
	Weinberg, Steven (USA)
1980**	Cronin, James, W. (USA)
	Fitch, Val L. (USA)
1981**	Bloembergen, Nicolaas (USA) and
	Schawlow, Arthur L. (USA)
	Siegbahn, Kai M. (Sweden)
1982	Wilson, Kenneth G. (USA)
1983**	Chandrasekhar, Subramanyan (USA)
	Fowler, William A. (USA)
1984*	Rubbia, Carlo (Italy)
	Van Der Meer, Simon (The Netherlands)
1985	Von Klitzing, Klaus
	(Federal Republic of Germany)
1986**	Ruska, Ernst
	(Federal Republic of Germany)
	Binnig, Gerd and
	(Federal Republic of Germany)
	Rohrer, Heinrich (Switzerland)*

1987*	Bednorz, J. Georg
	(Federal Republic of Germany)
	Müller, K. Alexander (Switzerland)
1988*	Lederman, Leon M. (USA)
	Schwartz, Melvin (USA)
	Steinberger, Jack (USA)
1989**	Ramsey, Norman F. (USA)
	Dehmelt, Hans G. (USA) and
	Paul, Wolfgang
	(Federal Republic of Germany)
1990*	Friedman, Jerome I. (USA)
	Kendall, Henry W. (USA)
	Taylor, Richard E. (Canada)
1991	de Gennes, Pierre-Gilles (France)
1992	Charpak, Georges (France)
1993*	Hulse, Russell A. (USA)
	Taylor Jr., Joseph H. (USA)
1994**	Brockhouse, Bertram N. (Canada)
	Shull, Clifford G. (USA)
1995**	Perl, Martin L. (USA)
	Reines, Frederick (USA)
1996*	Lee, David M. (USA)
	Osheroff, Douglas D. (USA) and
	Richardson, Robert C. (USA)
1997*	Chu, Steven (USA)
	Cohen-Tannoudji, Claude (France) and
	Phillips, William D. (USA)

Chemistry

1901	Van't Hoff, Jacobus Henricus
	(The Netherlands)
1902	Fischer, Hermann Emil (Germany)
1903	Arrhenius, Svante August (Sweden)
1904	Ramsay, Sir William (Great Britain)
1905	Von Baeyer, Johann Friedrich
	Wilhelm, Adolf (Germany)
1906	Moissan, Henri (France)
1907	Buchner, Eduard (Germany)
1908	Rutherford, Lord Ernest (Great Britain)
1909	Ostwald, Wilhelm (Germany)
1910	Wallach, Otto (Germany)
1911	Curie, Marie (France)
1912**	Grignard, Victor (France)
	Sabatier, Paul (France)
1913	Werner, Alfred (Switzerland)
1914‡	Richards, Theodore William (USA)
1915	Willstätter, Richard Martin (Germany)
1916†	–
1917†	–
1918‡	Haber, Fritz (Germany)
1919†	–
1920‡	Nernst, Walther Hermann (Germany)
1921‡	Soddy, Frederick (Great Britain)
1922	Aston, Francis William (Great Britain)
1923	Pregl, Fritz (Austria)
1924†	–
1925‡	Zsigmondy, Richard Adolf (Germany)
1926	Svedberg, The (Theodor) (Sweden)
1927‡	Wieland, Heinrich Otto (Germany)
1928	Windaus, Adolf Otto Reinhold
	(Germany)

Chemistry

1929**	Harden, Sir Arthur (Great Britain)
	Von Euler-Chelpin, Hans Karl August Simon (Sweden)
1930	Fischer, Hans (Germany)
1931*	Bösch, Carl (Germany)
	Bergius, Friedrich (Germany)
1932	Langmuir, Irving (USA)
1933†	–
1934	Urey, Harold Clayton (USA)
1935*	Joliot, Frédéric (France)
	Joliot-Curie, Irene (France)
1936	Debye, Petrus (Peter) Josephus Wilhelmus (The Netherlands)
1937**	Haworth, Sir Walter Norman (Great Britain)
	Karrer, Paul (Switzerland)
1938‡	Kuhn, Richard (Germany)
1939**	Butenandt, Adolf Friedrich Johann (Germany)
	Ruzicka, Leopold (Switzerland)
1940–42†	–
1943‡	De Hevesy, George (Hungary)
1944‡	Hahn, Otto (Germany)
1945	Virtanen, Artturi Ilmari (Finland)
1946**	Sumner, James Batcheller (USA)
	Northrop, John Howard (USA) and
	Stanley, Wendell Meredith (USA)
1947	Robinson, Sir Robert (Great Britain)
1948	Tiselius, Arne Wilhelm Kaurin (Sweden)
1949	Giauque, William Francis (USA)
1950*	Diels, Otto Paul Hermann (Germany)
	Alder, Kurt (Germany)
1951*	McMillan, Edwin Mattison (USA)
	Seaborg, Glenn Theodore (USA)
1952*	Martin, Archer John Porter (Great Britain)
	Synge, Richard Laurence Millington (Great Britain)
1953	Staudinger, Hermann (Germany)
1954	Pauling, Linus Carl (USA)
1955	Du Vigneaud, Vincent (USA)
1956*	Hinshelwood, Sir Cyril Norman (Great Britain)
	Semenov, Nikolay Nikolaevich (USSR)
1957	Todd, Lord Alexander R. (Great Britain)
1958	Sanger, Frederick (Great Britain)
1959	Heyrovsky, Jaroslav (Czechoslovakia)
1960	Libby, Willard Frank (USA)
1961	Calvin, Melvin (USA)
1962**	Perutz, Max Ferdinand (Great Britain)
	Kendrew, Sir John Cowdery (Great Britain)
1963**	Ziegler, Karl (Germany)
	Natta, Giulio (Italy)
1964	Hodgkin, Dorothy Crowfoot (Great Britain)
1965	Wooward, Robert Burns (USA)
1966	Mulliken, Robert S. (USA)
1967**	Eigen, Manfred (Federal Republic of Germany)
	Norrish, Ronald George Wreyford (Great Britain) and
	Porter, Lord (George) (Great Britain)
1968	Onsager, Lars (USA)
1969**	Barton, Sir Derek H. R. (Great Britain)
	Hassel, Odd (Norway)
1970	Leloir, Luis F. (Argentina)
1971	Herzberg, Gerhard (Canada)
1972**	Anfinsen, Christian B. (USA)
	Moore, Stanford (USA)
	Stein, William (USA)
1973**	Fischer, Ernst Otto (Federal Republic of Germany)
	Wilkinson, Sir Geoffrey (Great Britain)
1974	Flory, Paul J. (USA)
1975**	Cornforth, Sir John Warcup (Australia and Great Britain)
	Prelog, Vladimir (Switzerland)
1976	Lipscomb, William N. (USA)
1977	Prigogine, Ilya (Belgium)
1978	Mitchell, Peter D. (Great Britain)
1979**	Brown, Herbert C. (USA)
	Wittig, Georg (Federal Republic of Germany)
1980**	Berg, Paul (USA)
	Gilbert, Walter (USA) and
	Sanger, Frederick (Great Britain)
1981*	Fukui, Kenichi (Japan)
	Hoffmann, Roald (USA)
1982	Klug, Sir Aaron (Great Britain)
1983	Taube, Henry (USA)
1984	Merrifield, Robert Bruce (USA)
1985*	Hauptman, Herbert A. (USA)
	Karle, Jerome (USA)
1986*	Herschbach, Dudley R. (USA)
	Lee, Yuan T. (USA)
	Polanyi, John C. (Canada)
1987*	Cram, Donald J. (USA)
	Lehn, Jean-Marie (France)
	Pedersen, Charles J. (USA)
1988*	Deisenhofer, Johann (Federal Republic of Germany)
	Huber, Robert (Federal Republic of Germany)
	Michel, Hartmut (Federal Republic of Germany)
1989*	Altman, Sidney (USA)
	Cech, Thomas R. (USA)
1990	Corey, Elias James (USA)
1991	Ernst, Richard R. (Switzerland)
1992	Marcus, Rudolph A. (USA)
1993**	Mullis, Kary B. (USA)
	Smith, Michael (Canada)
1994	Olah, George A. (USA)
1995*	Rowland, F. Sherwood (USA)
	Molina, Mario (USA)
	Crutzen, Paul (The Netherlands)
1996*	Curl, Robert F., Jr. (USA)
	Kroto, Sir Harold W. (Great Britain)
	Smalley, Richard E. (USA)
1997**	Boyer, Paul D. (USA) and
	Walker, John E. (Great Britain), and
	Skou, Jens C. (Denmark)

Physiology or Medicine

1901	Von Behring, Emil Adolf (Germany)
1902	Ross, Sir Ronald (Great Britain)
1903	Finsen, Niels Ryberg (Denmark)
1904	Pavlov, Ivan Petrovich (Russia)
1905	Koch, Robert (Germany)
1906*	Golgi, Camillo (Italy)
	Ramon y Cajal, Santiago (Spain)
1907	Laveran, Charles Louis Alphonse (France)
1908*	Mechnikov, Ilya Ilyich (Russia)
	Ehrlich, Paul (Germany)
1909	Kocher, Emil Theodor (Switzerland)
1910	Kossel, Albrecht (Germany)
1911	Gullstrand, Allvar (Sweden)
1912	Carrel, Alexis (France)
1913	Richet, Charles Robert (France)
1914	Bárány, Robert (Austria)
1915–1918†	–
1919‡	Bordet, Jules (Belgium)
1920	Krogh, Schack August Steenberger (Denmark)
1921†	–
1922‡**	Hill, Sir Archibald Vivian
	Meyerhof, Otto Fritz (Germany)
1923*	Banting, Sir Frederick Grant (Canada)
	Macleod, John James Richard (Canada)
1924	Einthoven, Willem (The Netherlands)
1925†	–
1926‡	Fibiger, Johannes Andreas Grib (Denmark)
1927	Wagner-Jauregg, Julius (Austria)
1928	Nicolle, Charles Jules Henri (France)
1929**	Eijkman, Christiaan (The Netherlands)
	Hopkins, Sir Frederick Gowland (Great Britain)
1930	Landsteiner, Karl (Austria)
1931	Warburg, Otto Heinrich (Germany)
1932*	Sherrington, Sir Charles Scott (Great Britain)
	Adrian, Lord (Edgar Douglas) (Great Britain)
1933	Morgan, Thomas Hunt (USA)
1934*	Whipple, George Hoyt (USA)
	Minot, George Richards (USA)
	Murphy, William Parry (USA)
1935	Spemann, Hans (Germany)
1936*	Dale, Sir Henry Hallett (Great Britain)
	Loewi, Otto (Austria)
1937	Szent-Györgyi Von Nagyrapolt, Albert (Hungary)
1938‡	Heymans, Corneille Jean François (Belgium)
1939	Domagk, Gerhard (Germany)
1940–1942†	–
1943‡**	Dam, Henrik Carl Peter (Denmark)
	Doisy, Edward Adelbert (USA)
1944*	Erlanger, Joseph (USA)
	Gasser, Herbert Spencer (USA)
1945*	Fleming, Sir Alexander (Great Britain)

	Chain, Sir Ernst Boris (Great Britain)
	Florey, Lord (Howard Walter) (Great Britain)
1946	Muller, Hermann Joseph (USA)
1947**	Cori, Carl Ferdinand (USA) and
	Cori, Gerty Theresa (USA)*
	Houssay, Bernardo Alberto (Argentina)
1948	Müller, Paul Hermann (Switzerland)
1949**	Hess, Walter Rudolf (Switzerland)
	Moniz, Antonio Caetano de Abreu Freire Egas (Portugal)
1950*	Kendall, Edward Calvin (USA)
	Reichstein, Tadeus (Switzerland)
	Hench, Philip Showalter (USA)
1951	Theiler, Max (Union of South Africa)
1952	Waksman, Selman Abraham (USA)
1953**	Krebs, Sir Hans Adolf (Great Britain)
	Lipmann, Fritz Albert (USA)
1954*	Enders, John Franklin (USA)
	Weller, Thomas Huckle (USA)
	Robbins, Frederick Chapman (USA)
1955	Theorell, Axel Hugo Theodor (Sweden)
1956*	Cournand, André Frédéric (USA)
	Forssmann, Werner (Germany)
	Richards, Dickinson W. (USA)
1957	Bovet, Daniel (Italy)
1958**	Beadle, George Wells (USA) and
	Tatum, Edward Lawrie (USA)
	Lederberg, Joshua (USA)
1959*	Ochoa, Severo (USA)
	Kornberg, Arthur (USA)
1960*	Burnet, Sir Frank MacFarlane (Australia)
	Medawar, Sir Peter Brian (Great Britain)
1961	Von Békésy, Georg (USA)
1962*	Crick, Francis Harry Compton (Great Britain)
	Watson, James Dewey (USA)
	Wilkins, Maurice Hugh Frederick (Great Britain)
1963*	Eccles, Sir John Carew (Australia)
	Hodgkin, Sir Alan Lloyd (Great Britain)
	Huxley, Sir Andrew Fielding (Great Britain)
1964*	Bloch, Konrad (USA)
	Lynen, Feodor (Germany)
1965*	Jacob, François (France)
	Lwoff, André (France)
	Monod, Jacques (France)
1966**	Rous, Peyton (USA)
	Huggins, Charles Brenton (USA)
1967*	Granit, Ragnar (Sweden)
	Hartline, Haldan Keffer (USA)
	Wald, George (USA)
1968*	Holley, Robert W. (USA)
	Khorana, Har Gobind (USA)
	Nirenberg, Marshall W. (USA)
1969*	Delbrück, Max (USA)
	Hershey, Alfred D. (USA)

Physiology or Medicine

Luria, Salvador E. (USA)
1970* Katz, Sir Bernard (Great Britain)
Von Euler, Ulf (Sweden)
Axelrod, Julius (USA)
1971 Sutherland, Earl W., Jr. (USA)
1972* Edelman, Gerald M. (USA)
Porter, Rodney R. (Great Britain)
1973* Von Frisch, Karl (Federal Republic
of Germany)
Lorenz, Konrad (Austria)
Tinbergen, Nikolaas (Great Britain)
1974* Claude, Albert (Belgium)
De Duve, Christian (Belgium)
1975* Palade, George E. (USA)
Baltimore, David (USA)
Dulbecco, Renato (USA)
1976* Temin, Howard Martin (USA)
Blumberg, Baruch S. (USA)
1977** Gajdusek, D. Carleton (USA)
Guillemin, Roger (USA) and
Schally, Andrew V. (USA)
1978* Yalow, Rosalyn (USA)
Arber, Werner (Switzerland)
Nathans, Daniel (USA)
1979* Smith, Hamilton O. (USA)
Cormack, Alan M. (USA)
Hounsfield, Sir Godfrey N.
(Great Britain)
1980* Benacerraf, Baruj (USA)
Dausset, Jean (France)
1981** Snell, George D. (USA)
Sperry, Roger W. (USA) and
Hubel, David H. (USA)
1982* Wiesel, Torsten N. (Sweden)
Bergström, Sune K. (Sweden)
Samuelsson, Bengt I. (Sweden)
1983 Vane, Sir John R. (Great Britain)
1984* McClintock, Barbara (USA)
Jerne, Niels K. (Denmark)
Köhler, Georges J. F. (Federal Republic
of Germany)
Milstein, César (Great Britain and
Argentina)
1985* Brown, Michael S. (USA)
1986* Goldstein, Joseph L. (USA)
Cohen, Stanley (USA)
1987 Levi-Montalcini, Rita (Italy and USA)
1988* Tonegawa, Susumu (Japan)
Black, Sir James W. (Great Britain)
Elion, Gertrude B. (USA)
1989* Hitchings, George H. (USA)
Bishop, J. Michael (USA)
1990* Varmus, Harold E. (USA)
Murray, Joseph E. (USA)
1991* Thomas, E. Donnall (USA)
Neher, Erwin (Germany)
1992* Sakmann, Bert (Germany)
Fischer, Edmond H. (USA)
1993* Krebs, Edwin G. (USA)
Roberts, Richard J. (England)
Sharp, Phillip A. (USA)

1994* Gilman, Alfred G. (USA) and
Rodbell, Martin (USA)
1995* Wieschaus, Eric F. (USA)
Lewis, Edward B. (USA)
Nuesslein-Volhard, Christiane (Germany)
1996* Doherty, Peter C. (Australia)
Zinkernagel, Rolf M. (Switzerland)
Prudhomme, René François Armand
(France)
1997 Prusiner, Stanley B. (USA)

Literature

1901 Sully, Prudhomme (France)
1902 Mommsen, Christian Matthias Theodor
(Germany)
1903 Bjørnson, Bjørnstjerne Martinus
(Norway)
1904** Mistral, Frédéric (France)
Echegaray y Eizaguirre, José (Spain)
1905 Sienkiewicz, Henryk (Poland)
1906 Carducci, Giosuè (Italy)
1907 Kipling, Rudyard (Great Britain)
1908 Eucken, Rudolf Christoph (Germany)
1909 Lagerlöf, Selma Ottilia Lovisa (Sweden)
1910 Heyse, Paul Johann Ludwig (Germany)
1911 Maeterlinck, Count, Maurice (Mooris)
Polidore Marie Bernhard (Belgium)
1912 Hauptmann, Gerhart Johann Robert
(Germany)
1913 Tagore, Rabindranath (India)
1914† –
1915‡ Rolland, Romain (France)
1916 Von Heidenstam, Carl Gustaf Verner
(Sweden)
1917** Gjellerup, Karl Adolph (Denmark)
Pontoppidan, Henrik (Denmark)
1918† –
1919‡ Spitteler, Carl Friedrich Georg
(Switzerland)
1920 Hamsun, Knut Pedersen (Norway)
1921 Anatole France (pen-name of Thibault,
Jacques Anatole) (France)
1922 Benavente, Jacinto (Spain)
1923 Yeats, William Butler (Ireland)
1924 Reymont, (pen-name of Reyment),
Wladyslaw Stanislaw (Poland)
1925‡ Shaw, George Bernard (Great Britain)
1926‡ Grazia Deledda (pen-name of
Madesani, Grazia) (Italy)
1927‡ Bergson, Henri (France)
1928 Undset, Sigrid (Norway)
1929 Mann, Thomas (Germany)
1930 Lewis, Sinclair (USA)
1931 Karlfeldt, Erik Axel (Sweden)
1932 Galsworthy, John (Great Britain)
1933 Bunin, Ivan Alekseyevich (stateless
domicile in France)
1934 Pirandello, Luigi (Italy)
1935† –
1936 O'Neill, Eugene Gladstone (USA)

Literature

Year	Laureate
1937	Martin du Gard, Roger (France)
1938	Pearl Buck (pen-name of Walsh, Pearl) (USA)
1939	Sillanpää, Frans Eemil (Finland)
1940–43[†]	–
1944	Jensen, Johannes Vilhelm (Denmark)
1945	Gabriela Mistral (pen-name of Godoy y Alcayaga, Lucila) (Chile)
1946	Hesse, Hermann (Switzerland)
1947	Gide, André Paul Guillaume (France)
1948	Eliot, Thomas Stearns (Great Britain)
1949[‡]	Faulkner, William (USA)
1950	Russell, Earl (Bertrand Arthur William) (Great Britain)
1951	Lagerkvist, Pär Fabian (Sweden)
1952	Mauriac, François (France)
1953	Churchill, Sir Winston Leonard Spencer (Great Britain)
1954	Hemingway, Ernest Miller (USA)
1955	Laxness, Halldór Kiljan (Iceland)
1956	Jiménez, Juan Ramón (Spain)
1957	Camus, Albert (France)
1958	Pasternak, Boris Leonidovich (USSR)
1959	Quasimodo, Salvatore (Italy)
1960	Saint-John Perse (pen-name of Léger, Alexis) (France)
1961	Andríc, Ívo (Yugoslavia)
1962	Steinbeck, John (USA)
1963	Seferis, Giorgos (pen-name of Seferiadis, Giorgos) (Greece)
1964	Sartre, Jean-Paul (France) (declined the prize)
1965	Sholokhov, Michail Aleksandrovich (USSR)
1966**	Agnon, Shmuel Yosef (Israel) Sachs, Nelly (Sweden)
1967	Asturias, Miguel Angel (Guatemala)
1968	Kawabata, Yasunari (Japan)
1969	Beckett, Samuel (Ireland)
1970	Solzhenitsyn, Aleksandr Isaevich (USSR)
1971	Neruda, Pablo (Chile)
1972	Böll, Heinrich (Federal Republic of Germany)
1973	White, Patrick (Australia)
1974**	Johnson, Eyvind (Sweden) Martinson, Harry (Sweden)
1975	Montale, Eugenio (Italy)
1976	Bellow, Saul (USA)
1977	Aleixandre, Vicente (Spain)
1978	Singer, Isaac Bashevis (USA)
1979	Elytis Odysseus (pen-name of Alepoudhelis, Odysseus) (Greece)
1980	Milosz, Czeslaw (USA and Poland)
1981	Canetti, Elias (Great Britain)
1982	García Márquez, Gabriel (Colombia)
1983	Golding, Sir William (Great Britain)
1984	Seifert, Jaroslav (Czechoslovakia)
1985	Simon, Claude (France)
1986	Soyinka, Wole (Nigeria)
1987	Brodsky, Joseph (USA)
1988	Mahfouz, Naguib (Egypt)
1989	Cela, Camilo José (Spain)
1990	Paz, Octavio (Mexico)
1991	Gordimer, Nadine (South Africa)
1992	Walcott, Derek (Saint Lucia)
1993	Morrison, Toni (USA)
1994	Oe, Kenzaburo (Japan)
1995	Seamus, Heaney (Ireland)
1996	Szymborska, Wislawa (Poland)
1997	Fo, Dario (Italy)

Peace

1901**	Dunant, Jean Henri (Switzerland) Passy, Frédéric (France)
1902**	Ducommun, Élie (Switzerland) Gobat, Charles Albert (Switzerland)
1903	Cremer, Sir William Randal (Great Britain)
1904	Institut de Droit International (Institute of International Law) (Ghent)
1905	Von Suttner, Baroness Bertha Sophie Felicita (Austria)
1906	Roosevelt, Theodore (USA)
1907**	Moneta, Ernesto Teodoro (Italy) Renault, Louis (France)
1908**	Arnoldson, Klas Pontus (Sweden) Bajer, Fredrik (Denmark)
1909**	Beernaert, Auguste Marie François (Belgium) D'Estournelles de Constant, Paul Henri Benjamin Balluet, Baron de Constant de Rebecque (France)
1910	Bureau International Permanent de la Paix (Permanent International Peace Bureau) (Berne)
1911**	Asser, Tobias Michael Carel (The Netherlands) Fried, Alfred Hermann (Austria)
1912	Root, Elihu (USA)
1913	La Fontaine, Henri (Belgium)
1914–16[†]	–
1917	Comité International de la Croix-Rouge (International Committee of the Red Cross) (Geneva)
1918[†]	–
1919[‡]	Wilson, Thomas Woodrow (USA)
1920	Bourgeois, Léon Victor Auguste (France)
1921**	Branting, Karl Hjalmar (Sweden) Lange, Christian Lous (Norway)
1922	Nansen, Fridtjof (Norway)
1923[†]	–
1924[†]	–
1925[‡]**	Chamberlain, Sir Austen (Great Britain) Dawes, Charles Gates (USA)
1926*	Briand, Aristide (France) Stresemann, Gustav (Germany)
1927**	Buisson, Ferdinand (France) Quidde, Ludwig (Germany)

Peace

1928[+]	–
1929[‡]	Kellogg, Frank Billings (USA)
1930	Söderblom, Lars Olof Nathan (Jonathan) (Sweden)
1931**	Addams, Jane (USA)
	Butler, Nicholas Murray (USA)
1932[†]	–
1933[‡]	Angell (Ralph Lane), Sir Norman (Great Britain)
1934	Henderson, Arthur (Great Britain)
1935[‡]	Von Ossietzky, Carl (Germany)
1936	Saavedra Lamas, Carlos (Argentina)
1937	Cecil of Chelwood, Viscount, (Lord Edgar Algernon Robert Gascoyne Cecil) (Great Britain)
1938	Office International Nansen pour les Réfugiés (Nansen International Office for Refugees) (Geneva)
1939–43[†]	–
1944[‡]	Comité International de la Croix-Rouge (International Committee of the Red Cross) (Geneva)
1945[‡]	Hull, Cordell (USA)
1946**	Balch, Emily Greene (USA)
	Mott, John Raleigh (USA)
1947*	The Friends Service Council (The Quakers) (London)
	The American Friends Service Committee (The Quakers) (Washington)
1948[†]	–
1949	Boyd Orr of Brechin, Lord (John) (Great Britain)
1950	Bunche, Ralph (USA)
1951	Jouhaux, Léon (France)
1952[‡]	Schweitzer, Albert (France)
1953	Marshall, George Catlett (USA)
1954[‡]	Office of the United Nations High Commissioner for Refugees (Geneva)
1955[†]	–
1956[†]	–
1957	Pearson, Lester Bowles (Canada)
1958	Pire, Georges (Belgium)
1959	Noel-Baker, Philip J. (Great Britain)
1960[‡]	Lutuli, Albert John (South Africa)
1961	Hammarskjöld, Dag Hjalmar Agne Carl (Sweden)
1962[‡]	Pauling, Linus Carl (USA)
1963**	Comité International de la Croix-Rouge (International Committee of the Red Cross) (Geneva)
	Ligue des Sociétés de la Croix-Rouge (League of Red Cross Societies) (Geneva)
1964	King Jr., Martin Luther (USA)
1965	United Nations Children's Fund (UNICEF) (New York)
1966[†]	–
1967[†]	–
1968	Cassin, René (France)
1969	International Labour Organization (I.L.O.) (Geneva)
1970	Borlaug, Norman (USA)

1971	Brandt, Willy (Federal Republic of Germany)
1972[†]	–
1973*	Kissinger, Henry A. (USA)
	Le Duc Tho (Democratic Republic of Viet Nam) (declined the prize)
1974**	Mac Bride, Seán (Ireland)
	Sato, Eisaku (Japan)
1975	Sakharov, Andrei Dmitrievich (USSR)
1976[‡]	Williams, Betty (Northern Ireland)
1977	Corrigan, Mairead (Northern Ireland)
	Amnesty International (Great Britain)
1978**	El Sadat, Mohamed Anwar (Egypt)
	Begin, Menachem (Israel)
1979	Mother Teresa (India)
1980	Perez Esquivel, Adolfo (Argentina)
1981	Office of the United Nations High Commissioner for Refugees (Geneva)
1982*	Myrdal, Alva (Sweden)
	García Robles, Alfonso (Mexico)
1983	Walesa, Lech (Poland)
1984	Tutu, Desmond Mpilo (South Africa)
1985	International Physicians for the Prevention of Nuclear War, Inc. (USA)
1986	Wiesel, Elie (USA)
1987	Arias Sanchez, Oscar (Costa Rica)
1988	The United Nations Peace-Keeping Forces, New York USA)
1989	The 14th Dalai Lama (Tenzin Gyatso) (Tibet)
1990	Gorbachev, Mikhail Sergeyevich (USSR)
1991	Aung San Suu Kyi (Burma)
1992	Menchu Tum, Rigoberta (Guatemala)
1993*	Mandela, Nelson (South Africa)
	de Klerk, Fredrik Willem (South Africa)
1994*	Arafat, Yasser (Palestine)
	Peres, Shimon (Israel)
	Rabin, Yitzhak (Israel)
1995	Rotblat, Joseph (Great Britain)
	Pugwash Conferences on Science and World Affairs (Canada)
1996**	Belo, Carlos Filipe Ximenes (East Timor)
	Ramos Horta, José (East Timor)
1997**	International Campaign to Ban Landmines (USA) and Williams, Jody (USA)

Economic Sciences

1969*	Frisch, Ragnar (Norway)
	Tinbergen, Jan (The Netherlands)
1970	Samuelson, Paul A. (USA)
1971	Kuznets, Simon (USA)
1972*	Hicks, Sir John R. (Great Britain)
	Arrow, Kenneth J. (USA)
1973	Leontief, Wassily (USA)
1974**	Myrdal, Gunnar (Sweden)
	Von Hayek, Friedrich August (Great Britain)
1975*	Kantorovich, Leonid Vitaliyevich (USSR)
	Koopmans, Tjalling C. (USA)

Economic Sciences

1976	Friedman, Milton (USA)	1989	Haavelmo, Trygve (Norway)
1977**	Ohlin, Bertil (Sweden) and	1990**	Markowitz, Harry M. (USA)
	Meade, James E. (Great Britain)		Miller, Merton M. (USA)
1978	Simon, Herbert A. (USA)		Sharpe, William F. (USA)
1979**	Shultz, Theodore W. (USA)	1991	Coase, Ronald H. (Great Britain)
	Lewis, Sir Arthur (United Kingdom)	1992	Becker, Gary S. (USA)
1980	Klein, Lawrence R. (USA)	1993*	Fogel, Robert W. (USA)
1981	Tobin, James (USA)		North, Douglass C. (USA)
1982	Stigler, George J. (USA)	1994*	Harsanyi, John C. (USA)
1983	Debreu, Gerard (USA)		Nash, John F. (USA)
1984	Stone, Sir Richard (Great Britain)		Selten, Reinhard (Germany)
1985	Modigliani, Franco (USA)	1995	Lucas, Robert E. (USA)
1986	Buchanan, Jr., James M. (USA)	1996*	Mirrlees, James A. (Great Britain)
1987	Solow, Robert M. (USA)		Vickrey, William (USA)
1988	Allais, Maurice (France)	1997*	Merton, Robert C. (USA) and
			Scholes, Myron S. (USA)

*Awarded jointly.
**Award divided.
†Award reserved.
‡Award reserved and awarded the following year.
Source: Nobel Foundation

Pulitzer Prize Awards, 1998

Prizes in Journalism

Public Service
Grand Forks (N.D.) Herald, for its sustained and informative coverage, vividly illustrated with photographs, that helped hold its community together in the wake of flooding, a blizzard and fire that devastated much of the city, including the newspaper plant itself.

Breaking News Reporting
Los Angeles Times staff for its comprehensive coverage of a botched bank robbery and subsequent police shoot-out in North Hollywood.

Investigative Reporting
Gary Cohn and Will Englund of *The Baltimore Sun* for their compelling series on the international shipbreaking industry that revealed the dangers posed to workers and the environment when discarded ships are dismantled.

Explanatory Reporting
Paul Salopek of the *Chicago Tribune* for his enlightening profile of the Human Genome Diversity Project, which seeks to chart the genetic relationship among all people.

Beat Reporting
Linda Greenhouse of *The New York Times* for her consistently illuminating coverage of the United States Supreme Court.

National Reporting
Russell Carollo and Jeff Nesmith of the *Dayton Daily News* for their reporting that disclosed dangerous flaws and mismanagement in the military health care system and prompted reforms.

International Reporting
The New York Times staff for its revealing series that profiled the corrosive effects of drug corruption in Mexico.

Feature Writing
Thomas French of the *St. Petersburg Times* for his detailed and compassionate narrative portrait of a mother and two daughters slain on a Florida vacation, and the three-year investigation into their murders.

Commentary
Mike McAlary of the *Daily News*, New York, N.Y., for his coverage of the brutalization of a Haitian immigrant by police officers at a Brooklyn stationhouse.

Criticism
Michiko Kakutani of *The New York Times* for her passionate, intelligent writing on books and contemporary literature.

Editorial Writing
Bernard L. Stein of *The Riverdale (N.Y.) Press*, a weekly, for his gracefully written editorials on politics and other issues affecting New York City residents.

Editorial Cartooning
Stephen P. Breen of the *Asbury Park Press*, Neptune, N.J.

Spot News Photography
Martha Rial of the *Pittsburgh Post-Gazette* for her life-affirming portraits of survivors of the conflicts of Rwanda and Burundi.

Feature Photography
Clarence Williams of the *Los Angeles Times* for his powerful images documenting the plight of young children with parents addicted to alcohol and drugs.

Letters and Drama Prizes

Fiction
American Pastoral by Philip Roth

Drama
How I Learned to Drive by Paula Vogel.

History
Summer for the Gods: The Scopes Trial and America's Continuing Debate Over Science and Religion by Edward J. Larson

Biography
Personal History by Katharine Graham

Poetry
Black Zodiac by Charles Wright

General Non-Fiction
Guns, Germs, and Steel: The Fates of Human Societies, by Jared Diamond

Prize in Music
"String Quartet No. 2 (musica instrumentalis)" by Aaron Jay Kernis, premiered on January 10, 1998, at Merkin Concert Hall, New York City, by The Lark Quartet.

Special Citation
Bestowed posthumously on George Gershwin, commemorating the centennial year of his birth, for his distinguished and enduring contributions to American music.

Pulitzer Prizes, 1917–1997

Journalism

Meritorious Public Service

1917	–
1918	*The New York Times*
1919	*Milwaukee Journal*
1920	–
1921	*Boston Post*
1922	*New York World*
1923	*Memphis Commercial Appeal*
1924	*New York World*
1925	–
1926	*Columbus* (GA) *Enquirer Sun*
1927	*Canton* (OH) *Daily News*
1928	*Indianapolis Times*
1929	*New York Evening World*
1930	–
1931	*Atlanta Constitution*
1932	*Indianapolis News*
1933	*New York World-Telegram*
1934	*Medford* (OR) *Mail Tribune*
1935	*The Sacramento* (CA) *Bee*
1936	*The Cedar Rapids* (IA) *Gazette*
1937	*St. Louis Post-Dispatch*
1938	*The Bismarck* (ND) *Tribune*
1939	*The Miami Daily News*
1940	*Waterbury* (CT) *Republican & American*
1941	*St. Louis Post-Dispatch*
1942	*Los Angeles Times*
1943	*Omaha* (NE) *World-Herald*
1944	*The New York Times*
1945	*The Detroit Free Press*
1946	*Scranton Times*
1947	*Baltimore Sun*
1948	*St. Louis Post-Dispatch*
1949	*Nebraska State Journal*
1950	*Chicago Daily News* and *St. Louis Post-Dispatch*
1951	*The Miami Herald* and *Brooklyn Eagle*
1952	*St. Louis Post-Dispatch*
1953	*Whiteville* (NC) *News Reporter* and *Tabor City* (NC) *Tribune*
1954	*Newsday* (Garden City, NY)
1955	*Columbus* (GA) *Ledger* and *Sunday Ledger-Enquirer*
1956	*Watsonville* (CA) *Register-Pajaronian*
1957	*Chicago Daily News*
1958	*Arkansas Gazette*
1959	*Utica* (NY) *Observer-Dispatch* and *The Utica Daily Press*
1960	*Los Angeles Times*
1961	*Amarillo* (TX) *Globe-Times*
1962	*Panama City* (FL) *News-Herald*
1963	*Chicago Daily News*
1964	*St. Petersburg* (FL) *Times*
1965	*Hutchinson* (KS) *News*
1966	*The Boston Globe*
1967	*The Louisville Courier-Journal* *The Milwaukee Journal*
1968	*The Riverside* (CA) *Press-Enterprise*
1969	*Los Angeles Times*
1970	*Newsday* (Garden City, NY)
1971	*The Winston-Salem* (NC) *Journal and Sentinel*
1972	*The New York Times*
1973	*The Washington Post*
1974	*Newsday* (Garden City, NY)
1975	*The Boston Globe*
1976	*Anchorage Daily News*
1977	*The Lufkin* (TX) *News*
1978	*The Philadelphia Inquirer*
1979	*Point Reyes* (CA) *Light*
1980	*Gannett News Service*
1981	*Charlotte* (NC) *Observer*
1982	*The Detroit News*
1983	*The Jackson* (MS) *Clarion-Ledger*
1984	*Los Angeles Times*
1985	*The Fort Worth* (TX) *Star-Telegram*
1986	*The Denver Post*
1987	*The Pittsburgh Press*
1988	*The Charlotte Observer*
1989	*Anchorage Daily News*
1990	*The Philadelphia Inquirer* *The Washington* (NC) *Daily News*
1991	*The Des Moines Register*
1992	*The Sacramento* (CA) *Bee*
1993	*The Miami Herald*
1994	*Akron Beacon Journal*
1995	*The Virgin Islands Daily News* (St. Thomas)
1996	*The News & Observer* (Raleigh, NC)
1997	*The Times- Picayune* (New Orleans)

Reporting

1917 Herbert Bayard Swope, *New York World*
1918 Harold A. Littledale, *New York Evening Post*
1919 –
1920 John J. Leary, Jr., *New York World*
1921 Louis Seibold, *New York World*
1922 Kirke L. Simpson, Associated Press
1923 Alva Johnston, *The New York Times*
1924 Magner White, *San Diego Sun*
1925 James W. Mulroy and Alvin H. Goldstein, *Chicago Daily News*
1926 William Burke Miller, *Louisville Courier-Journal*
1927 John T. Rogers, *St. Louis Post-Dispatch*
1928 –
1929 Paul Y. Anderson, *St. Louis Post-Dispatch*
1930 Russell D. Owen, *The New York Times*
1931 A. B. MacDonald, *Kansas City* (MO) *Star*
1932 W. C. Richards, D. D. Martin, J. S. Pooler, F. D. Webb, and J. N. W. Sloan, *Detroit Free Press*
1933 Francis A. Jamieson, Associated Press
1934 Royce Brier, *San Francisco Chronicle*
1935 William H. Taylor, *New York Herald Tribune*
1936 Lauren D. Lyman, *The New York Times*
1937 John J. O'Neill, *New York Herald Tribune*; William L. Laurence, *The New York Times*; Howard W. Blakeslee, AP; Gobind Behari Lal, Universal Service; and David Dietz, Scripps-Howard
1938 Raymond Sprigle, *Pittsburgh Post-Gazette*
1939 Thomas Lunsford Stokes, Scripps-Howard Newspaper Alliance
1940 S. Burton Heath, *New York World-Telegram*
1941 Westbrook Pegler, *New York World-Telegram*
1942 Stanton Delaplane, *San Francisco Chronicle*
1943 George Weller, *Chicago Daily News*
1944 Paul Schoenstein and associates, *New York Journal-American*
1945 Jack S. McDowell, *San Francisco Call-Bulletin*
1946 William Leonard Laurence, *The New York Times*
1947 Frederick Woltman, *New York World-Telegram*

Local Reporting

1948 George E. Goodwin, *Atlanta Journal*
1949 Malcolm Johnson, *New York Sun*
1950 Meyer Berger, *The New York Times*
1951 Edward S. Montgomery, *San Francisco Examiner*
1952 George De Carvalho, *San Francisco Chronicle*

Local Reporting, Edition Time

1953 *Providence* (RI) *Journal* and *Evening Bulletin*
1954 *Vicksburg* (MS) *Sunday Post-Herald*
1955 Mrs. Caro Brown, *Alice* (TX) *Daily Echo*
1956 Lee Hills, *Detroit Free Press*
1957 *Salt Lake* (UT) *Tribune*
1958 *Fargo* (ND) *Forum*
1959 Miss Mary Lou Werner, *The Evening Star* (Washington, DC)
1960 Jack Nelson, *Atlanta Constitution*
1961 Sanche De Gramont, *New York Herald Tribune*
1962 Robert D. Mullins, *Deseret News* (Salt Lake City)
1963 Sylvan Fox, Anthony Shannon, and William Longgood, *New York World-Telegram and Sun*

Local General Spot News Reporting

1964 Norman C. Miller, Jr., *The Wall Street Journal*
1965 Melvin H. Ruder, *The Hungry Horse News* (Columbia Falls, MT)
1966 *Los Angeles Times* staff
1967 Robert V. Cox, *Chambersburg* (PA) *Public Opinion*
1968 *The Detroit Free Press*
1969 John Fetterman, *Louisville Times* and *Courier-Journal*
1970 Thomas Fitzpatrick, *Chicago Sun-Times*
1971 The staff of the *Akron* (OH) *Beacon Journal*
1972 Richard Cooper and John Machacek, *Rochester* (NY) *Times-Union*
1973 *Chicago Tribune*
1974 Arthur M. Petacque and Hugh F. Hough, *Chicago Sun-Times*
1975 The staff of the *Xenia* (OH) *Daily Gazette*
1976 Gene Miller, *The Miami Herald*
1977 Margo Huston, *The Milwaukee Journal*
1978 Richard Whitt, *The Louisville Courier-Journal*
1979 *The San Diego* (CA) *Evening Tribune*
1980 The staff of *The Philadelphia Inquirer*
1981 *The Longview* (WA) *Daily News* staff
1982 *The Kansas City Star* and *The Kansas City Times*
1983 *The Fort Wayne* (IN) *News-Sentinel* editorial staff
1984 *Newsday* (Long Island, NY) team of reporters

General News Reporting

1985 Thomas Turcol, *The Virginian-Pilot and Ledger-Star* (Norfolk, VA)
1986 Edna Buchanan, *The Miami Herald*
1987 *Akron Beacon Journal* staff
1988 The staff of *The Alabama Journal* (Montgomery, AL)
    Lawrence (MA) *Eagle-Tribune* staff
1989 *The Louisville Courier-Journal* staff
1990 *San Jose* (CA) *Mercury News* staff

Spot News Reporting

1991 *The Miami Herald* staff
1992 *New York Newsday* staff
1993 *Los Angeles Times* staff
1994 *The New York Times* staff
1995 *Los Angeles Times* staff
1996 Robert D. McFadden, *The New York Times*
1997 *Newsday* staff (Long Island, NY)

Local Reporting, No Edition Time

1953 Edward J. Mowery, *New York World-Telegram & Sun*
1954 Alvin Scott McCoy, *Kansas City* (MO) *Star*
1955 Roland Kenneth Towery, *Cuero* (TX) *Record*

1956 Arthur Daley, *The New York Times*
1957 Wallace Turner and William Lambert, *Portland Oregonian*
1958 George Beveridge, *The Evening Star* (Washington, DC)
1959 John Harold Brislin, *Scranton* (PA) *Tribune* and *The Scrantonian*
1960 Miriam Ottenberg, *The Evening Star* (Washington, DC)
1961 Edgar May, *Buffalo* (NY) *Evening News*
1962 George Bliss, *Chicago Tribune*
1963 Oscar Griffin, Jr., *Pecos* (TX) *Independent and Enterprise*

Local Investigative Specialized Reporting

1964 James V. Magee, Albert V. Gaudiosi, and Frederick A. Meyer, *Philadelphia Bulletin*
1965 Gene Goltz, *The Houston Post*
1966 John Anthony Frasca, *Tampa* (FL) *Tribune*
1967 Gene Miller, *The Miami Herald*
1968 J. Anthony Lukas, *The New York Times*
1969 Albert L. Delugach and Denny Walsh, *St. Louis Globe-Democrat*
1970 Harold Eugene Martin, *Montgomery Advertiser* and *Alabama Journal*
1971 William Jones, *Chicago Tribune*
1972 Timothy Leland, Gerard M. O'Neill, Stephen A. Kurkjian, and Ann Desantis, *The Boston Globe*
1973 Sun Newspapers of Omaha
1974 William Sherman, *New York Daily News*
1975 *Indianapolis Star*
1976 *Chicago Tribune* staff members
1977 Acel Moore and Wendell Rawls Jr., *The Philadephia Inquirer*
1978 Anthony R. Dolan, *Stamford* (CT) *Advocate*
1979 Gilbert M. Gaul and Elliot G. Jaspin, *Pottsville* (PA) *Republican*
1980 Stephen A. Kurkjian, Alexander B. Hawes Jr., Nils Bruzelius, Joan Vennochi, and Robert M. Porterfield, *The Boston Globe Spotlight* team
1981 Clark Hallas and Robert B. Lowe, *Arizona Daily Star*
1982 Paul Henderson, *The Seattle Times*
1983 Loretta Tofani, *The Washington Post*
1984 Kenneth Cooper, Joan Fitz Gerald, Jonathan Kaufman, Norman Lockman, Gary McMillan, Kirk Scharfenberg, and David Wessel, *The Boston Globe*

Investigative Reporting

1985 William K. Marimow, *The Philadelphia Inquirer*; Lucy Morgan and Jack Reed, *St. Petersburg* (FL) *Times*
1986 Jeffrey A. Marx and Michael M. York, *Lexington* (KY) *Herald-Leader*
1987 Daniel R. Biddle, H. G. Bissinger, and Frederic N. Tulsky, *The Philadelphia Inquirer*; John Woestendiek, *The Philadelphia Inquirer*
1988 Dean Baquet, William Gaines, and Ann Marie Lipinski, *Chicago Tribune*

1989 Bill Dedman, *Atlanta Journal and Constitution*
1990 Lou Kilzer and Chris Ison, *Star Tribune* (Minneapolis-St. Paul, MN)
1991 Joseph T. Hallinan and Susan M. Headden, *The Indianapolis Star*
1992 Lorraine Adams and Dan Malone, *The Dallas Morning News*
1993 Jeff Brazil and Steve Berry, *The Orlando Sentinel*
1994 *The Providence Journal-Bulletin*
1995 Brian Donovan and Stephanie Saul, *Newsday* (Long Island, NY)
1996 *Orange County Register* (Santa Ana, CA)
1997 Eric Nalder, Deborah Nelson and Alex Tizon, *The Seattle Times*

Explanatory Journalism

1985 Jon Franklin, *The Baltimore Evening Sun*
1986 *The New York Times* staff
1987 Jeff Lyon and Peter Gorner, *Chicago Tribune*
1988 Daniel Hertzberg and James B. Stewart, *The Wall Street Journal*
1989 David Hanners, William Snyder, and Karen Blessen, *The Dallas Morning Star*
1990 David A. Vise and Steve Coll, *The Washington Post*
1991 Susan C. Faludi, *The Wall Street Journal*
1992 Robert S. Capers and Eric Lipton, *The Hartford* (CT) *Courant*
1993 Mike Toner, *The Atlanta Journal-Constitution*
1994 Ronald Kotulak, *Chicago Tribune*
1995 Leon Dash and Lucian Perkins, *The Washington Post*
1996 Laurie Garrett, *Newsday* (Long Island, NY)
1997 Michael Vitez, April Saul and Ron Cortes, *The Philadelphia Inquirer*

Specialized Reporting

1985 Randall Savage and Jackie Crosby, *Macon* (GA) *Telegraph and News*
1986 Andrew Schneider and Mary Pat Flaherty, *The Pittsburgh Press*
1987 Alex S. Jones, *The New York Times*
1988 Walt Bogdanich, *The Wall Street Journal*
1989 Edward Humes, *The Orange County Register*
1990 Tamar Stieber, *Albuquerque Journal*

Beat Reporting

1991 Natalie Angier, *The New York Times*
1992 Deborah Blum, *The Sacramento Bee*
1993 Paul Ingrassia and Joseph B. White, *The Wall Street Journal*
1994 Eric Freedman and Jim Mitzelfeld, *The Detroit News*
1995 David Shribman, *The Boston Globe*
1996 Bob Keeler, *Newsday* (Long Island, NY)
1997 Byron Acohido, *The Seattle Times*

Correspondence

1929 Paul Scott Mowrer, *Chicago Daily News*
1930 Leland Stowe, *New York Herald Tribune*
1931 H. R. Knickerbocker, *Philadelphia Public Ledger* and *New York Evening Post*
1932 Walter Duranty, *The New York Times*; Charles G. Ross, *St. Louis Post-Dispatch*

1933 Edgar Ansel Mowrer, *Chicago Daily News*
1934 Frederick T. Birchall, *The New York Times*
1935 Arthur Krock, *The New York Times*
1936 Wilfed C. Barber, *Chicago Tribune*
1937 Anne O'Hare McCormick, *The New York Times*
1938 Arthur Krock, *The New York Times*
1939 Louis P. Lochner, Associated Press
1940 Otto D. Tolischus, *The New York Times*
1941 Group Award—American news reporters in the war zones of Europe, Asia, and Africa.
1942 Carlos P. Romulo, *Philippines Herald*
1943 Hanson W. Baldwin, *The New York Times*
1944 Ernest Taylor Pyle, Scripps-Howard Newspaper Alliance
1945 Harold V. (Hal) Boyle, Associated Press
1946 Arnaldo Cortesi, *The New York Times*
1947 Brooks Atkinson, *The New York Times*

Telegraphic Reporting (National)

1942 Louis Stark, *The New York Times*
1943 –
1944 Dewey L. Fleming, *The Baltimore Sun*
1945 James B. Reston, *The New York Times*
1946 Edward A. Harris, *St. Louis Post-Dispatch*
1947 Edward T. Folliard, *The Washington Post*

National Reporting

1948 Bert Andrews, *New York Herald Tribune*
      Nat S. Finney, *Minneapolis Tribune*
1949 C. P. Trussel, *The New York Times*
1950 Edwin O. Guthman, *Seattle Times*
1951 –
1952 Anthony Leviero, *The New York Times*
1953 Don Whitehead, Associated Press
1954 Richard Wilson, *Des Moines Register & Tribune*
1955 Anthony Lewis, *Washington Daily News*
1956 Charles L. Bartlett, *Chattanooga Times*
1957 James Reston, *The New York Times*
1958 Relman Morin, Associated Press
      Clark Mollenhoff, *Des Moines Register and Tribune*
1959 Howard Van Smith, *Miami* (FL) *News*
1960 Vance Trimble, Scripps-Howard Newspaper Alliance
1961 Edward R. Cony, *The Wall Street Journal*
1962 Nathan G. Caldwell and Gene S. Graham, *Nashville Tennessean*
1963 Anthony Lewis, *The New York Times*
1964 Merriman Smith, United Press International
1965 Louis M. Kohlmeier, *The Wall Street Journal*
1966 Haynes Johnson, *Washington Evening Star*
1967 Stanley Penn and Monroe Karmin, *The Wall Street Journal*
1968 Howard James, *Christian Science Monitor*
      Nathan K. (Nick) Kotz, *The Des Moines Register* and *Minneapolis Tribune*
1969 Robert Cahn, *Christian Science Monitor*
1970 William J. Eaton, *Chicago Daily News*
1971 Lucinda Franks and Thomas Powers, United Press International
1972 Jack Anderson, syndicated columnist

1973 Robert Boyd and Clark Hoyt, the Knight Newspapers
1974 James R. Polk, *Washington Star-News*
      Jack White, *Providence* (RI) *Journal and Evening Bulletin*
1975 Donald L. Barlett and James B. Steele, *The Philadelphia Inquirer*
1976 James Risser, *The Des Moines Register*
1977 Walter Mears, Associated Press
1978 Gaylord D. Shaw, *Los Angeles Times*
1979 James Risser, *The Des Moines Register*
1980 Bette Swenson Orsini and Charles Stafford, *St. Petersburg* (FL) *Times*
1981 John M. Crewdson, *The New York Times*
1982 Rick Atkinson, *The Kansas City Times*
1983 *The Boston Globe*
1984 John Noble Wilford, *The New York Times*
1985 Thomas J. Knudson, *The Des Moines Register*
1986 Arthur Howe, *The Philadelphia Inquirer*
      Craig Flournoy and George Rodrigue, *The Dallas Morning News*
1987 *The Miami Herald* staff
      The New York Times staff
1988 Tim Weiner, *The Philadelphia Inquirer*
1989 Donald L. Barlett and James B. Steele, *The Philadelphia Inquirer*
1990 Ross Anderson, Bill Dietrich, Mary Ann Gwinn and Eric Nalder, *The Seattle Times*
1991 Marjie Lundstrom and Rochelle Sharpe, Gannett News Service
1992 Jeff Taylor and Mike McGraw, *The Kansas City Star*
1993 David Maraniss, *The Washington Post*
1994 Eileen Welsome, *The Albuquerque Tribune*
1995 Tony Horwitz, *The Wall Street Journal*
1996 Alix M. Freedman, *The Wall Street Journal*
1997 *The Wall Street Journal* staff

Telegraphic Reporting (International)

1942 Laurence Edmund Allen, Associated Press
1943 Ira Wolfert, North American Newspaper Alliance Inc.
1944 Daniel De Luce, Associated Press
1945 Mark S. Watson, *Baltimore Sun*
1946 Homer William Bigart, *New York Herald Tribune*
1947 Eddy Gilmore, Associated Press

International Reporting

1948 Paul W. Ward, *Baltimore Sun*
1949 Price Day, *Baltimore Sun*
1950 Edmund Stevens, *Christian Science Monitor*
1951 Keyes Beech, *Chicago Daily News*; Homer Bigart, *New York Herald Tribune*; Marguerite Higgins, *New York Herald Tribune*; Relman Morin, Associated Press; Fred Sparks, *Chicago Daily News*; and Don Whitehead, Associated Press

1952 John M. Hightower, Associated Press
1953 Austin Wehrwein, *Milwaukee Journal*
1954 Jim G. Lucas, Scripps-Howard Newspapers
1955 Harrison E. Salisbury, *The New York Times*
1956 William Randolph Hearst Jr., J. Kingsbury-
       Smith, and Frank Conniff, International
       News Service
1957 Russell Jones, United Press
1958 *The New York Times*
1959 Joseph Martin and Philip Santora,
       The New York Daily News
1960 A. M. Rosenthal, *The New York Times*
1961 Lynn Heinzerling, Associated Press
1962 Walter Lippmann, *New York Herald Tribune*
       Syndicate
1963 Hal Hendrix, *Miami* (FL) *News*
1964 Malcolm W. Browne, Associated Press,
       David Halberstam, *The New York Times*
1965 J. A. Livingston, *Philadelphia Bulletin*
1966 Peter Arnett, Associated Press
1967 R. John Hughes, *Christian Science Monitor*
1968 Alfred Friendly, *The Washington Post*
1969 William Tuohy, *Los Angeles Times*
1970 Seymour M. Hersh, Dispatch News Service
       (Washington, DC)
1971 Jimmie Lee Hoagland, *The Washington Post*
1972 Peter R. Kann, *The Wall Street Journal*
1973 Max Frankel, *The New York Times*
1974 Hedrick Smith, *The New York Times*
1975 William Mullen and Ovie Carter, *Chicago
       Tribune*
1976 Sydney H. Schanberg, *The New York Times*
1977 –
1978 Henry Kamm, *The New York Times*
1979 Richard Ben Cramer, *The Philadelphia Inquirer*
1980 Joel Brinkley and Jay Mather, *The Louisville
       Courier-Journal*
1981 Shirley Christian, *The Miami Herald*
1982 John Darnton, *The New York Times*
1983 Thomas L. Friedman, *The New York Times*
       and Loren Jenkins, *The Washington Post*
1984 Karen Elliott House, *The Wall Street Journal*
1985 Josh Friedman and Dennis Bell, and Ozier
       Muhammad, *Newsday* (Long Island, NY)
1986 Lewis M. Simons, Pete Carey and Katherine
       Ellison, *San Jose* (CA) *Mercury News*
1987 Michael Parks, *Los Angeles Times*
1988 Thomas L. Friedman, *The New York Times*
1989 Glenn Frankel, *The Washington Post*
       Bill Keller, *The New York Times*
1990 Nicholas D. Kristof and Sheryl Wu Dunn,
       The New York Times
1991 Caryle Murphy, *The Washington Post*
       Serge Schmemann, *The New York Times*
1992 Patrick J. Sloyan, *Newsday* (Long Island, NY)
1993 John F. Burns, *The New York Times* and
       Roy Gutman, *Newsday* (Long Island, NY)
1994 *The Dallas Morning News* team
1995 Mark Fritz, Associated Press
1996 David Rohde, *Christian Science Monitor*
1997 John F. Burns, *The New York Times*

Feature Writing

1979 Jon D. Franklin, *The Baltimore Evening Sun*
1980 Madeleine Blais, *The Miami Herald*
1981 Teresa Carpenter, *The Village Voice*
1982 Saul Pett, Associated Press
1983 Nan Robertson, *The New York Times*
1984 Peter Mark Rinearson, *The Seattle Times*
1985 Alice Steinbach, *The Baltimore Sun*
1986 John Camp, *St. Paul Pioneer Press
       and Dispatch*
1987 Steve Twomey, *The Philadelphia Inquirer*
1988 Jacqui Banaszynski, *St. Paul Pioneer
       Press Dispatch*
1989 David Zucchino, *The Philadelphia Inquirer*
1990 Dave Curtin, *Colorado Springs Gazette
       Telegraph*
1991 Sheryl James, *St. Petersburg* (FL) *Times*
1992 Howell Raines, *The New York Times*
1993 George Lardner Jr., *The Washington Post*
1994 Isabel Wilkerson, *The New York Times*
1995 Ron Suskind, *The Wall Street Journal*
1996 Rick Bragg, *The New York Times*
1997 Lisa Pollak, *The Baltimore Sun*

Commentary

1970 Marquis W. Childs, *St. Louis Post-Dispatch*
1971 William A. Caldwell, *The Record*
       (Hackensack, NJ)
1972 Mike Royko, *Chicago Daily News*
1973 David S. Broder, *The Washington Post*
1974 Edwin A. Roberts Jr., *National Observer*
1975 Mary McGrory, *Washington Star*
1976 Walter Wellesley (Red) Smith, *The
       New York Times*
1977 George F. Will, *Washington Post*
       Writer's Group
1978 William Safire, *The New York Times*
1979 Russell Baker, *The New York Times*
1980 Ellen H. Goodman, *The Boston Globe*
1981 Dave Anderson, *The New York Times*
1982 Art Buchwald, *Los Angeles Times Syndicate*
1983 Claude Sitton, *Raleigh* (NC) *News & Observer*
1984 Vermont Royster, *The Wall Street Journal*
1985 Murray Kempton, *Newsday* (Long Island, NY)
1986 Jimmy Breslin, *New York Daily News*
1987 Charles Krauthammer, *Washington Post*
       Writer's Group
1988 Dave Barry, *The Miami Herald*
1989 Clarence Page, *Chicago Tribune*
1990 Jim Murray, *Los Angeles Times*
1991 Jim Hoagland, *The Washington Post*
1992 Anna Quindlen, *The New York Times*
1993 Liz Balmaseda, *The Miami Herald*
1994 William Raspberry, *The Washington Post*
1995 Jim Dwyer, *Newsday* (Long Island, NY)
1996 E. R. Shipp, *New York Daily News*
1997 Eileen McNamara, *The Boston Globe*

Criticism

1970 Ada Louise Huxtable, *The New York Times*
1971 Harold C. Schonberg, *The New York Times*
1972 Frank Peters Jr., *St. Louis Post-Dispatch*
1973 Ronald Powers, *Chicago Sun-Times*

1974 Emily Genauer, *Newsday* Syndicate
1975 Roger Ebert, *Chicago Sun-Times*
1976 Alan M. Kriegsman, *The Washington Post*
1977 William McPherson, *The Washington Post*
1978 Walter Kerr, *The New York Times*
1979 Paul Gapp, *Chicago Tribune*
1980 William A. Henry III, *The Boston Globe*
1981 Jonathan Yardley, *The Washington Star*
1982 Martin Bernheimer, *Los Angeles Times*
1983 Manuela Hoelterhoff, *The Wall Street Journal*
1984 Paul Goldberger, *The New York Times*
1985 Howard Rosenberg, *Los Angeles Times*
1986 Donal Henahan, *The New York Times*
1987 Richard Eder, *Los Angeles Times*
1988 Tom Shales, *The Washington Post*
1989 Michael Skube, *The News and Observer*
    (Raleigh, NC)
1990 Allan Temko, *San Francisco Chronicle*
1991 David Shaw, *Los Angeles Times*
1992 –
1993 Michael Dirda, *The Washington Post*
1994 Lloyd Schwartz, *The Boston Phoenix*
1995 Margo Jefferson, *The New York Times*
1996 Robert Campbell, *The Boston Globe*
1997 Tim Page, *The Washington Post*

Editorial Writing

1917 *New York Tribune*
1918 *Louisville Courier Journal*
1919 –
1920 Harvey E. Newbranch, *Evening World Herald*
    (Omaha, NE)
1921 –
1922 Frank M. O'Brien, *New York Herald*
1923 William Allen White, *Emporia* (KS) *Gazette*
1924 *Boston Herald*
1925 *Charleston* (SC) *News and Courier*
1926 Edward M. Kingsbury, *The New York Times*
1927 F. Lauriston Bullard, *Boston Herald*
1928 Grover Cleveland Hall, *Montgomery* (AL)
    Advertiser
1929 Louis Isaac Jaffe, *Norfolk Virginian-Pilot*
1930 –
1931 Charles S. Ryckman, *Fremont* (NE) *Tribune*
1932 –
1933 *Kansas City* (MO) *Star*
1934 E. P. Chase, *Atlantic* (IA) *News -Telegraph*
1935 –
1936 Felix Morley, *The Washington Post*, and
    George B. Parker, Scripps-Howard
    Newspapers
1937 John W. Owens, *The Baltimore Sun*
1938 William Wesley Waymack, *The Register &
    Tribune* (Des Moines, IA)
1939 Ronald G. Callvert, *The Oregonian*
1940 Bart Howard, *St. Louis Post-Dispatch*
1941 Reuben Maury, *New York Daily News*
1942 Geoffrey Parsons, *New York Herald Tribune*
1943 Forrest W. Seymour, *Register & Tribune*
    (Des Moines, IA)
1944 Henry J. Haskell, *Kansas City* (MO) *Star*
1945 George W. Potter, *Providence* (RI)
    Journal-Bulletin

1946 Hodding Carter, *Delta Democrat-Times*
    (Greenville, MS)
1947 William H. Grimes, *The Wall Street Journal*
1948 Virginius Dabney, *Richmond Times-Dispatch*
1949 John H. Crider, *Boston Herald*, and
    Herbert Elliston, *The Washington Post*
1950 Carl M. Saunders, *Jackson* (MI)
    Citizen Patriot
1951 William Harry Fitzpatrick, *New Orleans States*
1952 Louis LaCoss, *St. Louis Globe Democrat*
1953 Vermont Connecticut Royster, *The Wall
    Street Journal*
1954 *Boston Herald*, Don Murray
1955 *Detroit Free Press*, Royce Howes
1956 Lauren K. Soth, *Register and Tribune*
    (Des Moines, IA)
1957 Buford Boone, *Tuscaloosa* (AL) *News*
1958 Harry S. Ashmore, *Arkansas Gazette*
1959 Ralph McGill, *Atlanta* (GA) *Constitution*
1960 Lenoir Chambers, *Norfolk Virginian-Pilot*
1961 William J. Dorvillier, *San Juan* (PR) *Star*
1962 Thomas M. Storke, *Santa Barbara* (CA)
    News-Press
1963 Ira B. Harkey Jr., *Pascagoula* (MS) *Chronicle*
1964 Hazel Brannon Smith, *Lexington* (MS)
    Advertiser
1965 John R. Harrison, *Gainesville* (FL) *Sun*
1966 Robert Lasch, *St. Louis Post-Dispatch*
1967 Eugene Patterson, *Atlanta Constitution*
1968 John S. Knight, Knight Newspapers
1969 Paul Greenberg, *Pine Bluff* (AR) *Commercial*
1970 Philip L. Geyelin, *The Washington Post*
1971 Horance G. Davis Jr., *Gainesville* (FL) *Sun*
1972 John Strohmeyer, *Bethlehem* (PA)
    Globe-Times
1973 Roger B. Linscott, *Berkshire Eagle*
    (Pittsfield, MA)
1974 F. Gilman Spencer, *Trentonian* (Trenton, NJ)
1975 John Daniell Maurice, *Charleston* (WV)
    Daily Mail
1976 Philip P. Kerby, *Los Angeles Times*
1977 Warren L. Lerude, Foster Church, and
    Norman F. Cardoza, *Reno* (NV) *Evening
    Gazette* and *Nevada State Journal*
1978 Meg Greenfield, *The Washington Post*
1979 Edwin M. Yoder Jr., *The Washington Star*
1980 Robert L. Bartley, *The Wall Street Journal*
1981 –
1982 Jack Rosenthal, *The New York Times*
1983 *The Miami Herald* editorial board
1984 Albert Scardino, *The Georgia Gazette*
    (Savannah)
1985 Richard Aregood, *The Philadelphia
    Daily News*
1986 Jack Fuller, *Chicago Tribune*
1987 Jonathan Freedman, *The Tribune*
    (San Diego, CA)
1988 Jane Healy, *The Orlando Sentinel*
1989 Lois Wille, *Chicago Tribune*
1990 Thomas J. Hylton, *The Pottstown* (PA)
    Mercury
1991 Ron Casey, Harold Jackson, and Joey
    Kennedy, *The Birmingham* (AL) *News*

1992 Maria Henson, *Lexington* (KY) *Herald-Leader*
1993 –
1994 R. Bruce Dold, *Chicago Tribune*
1995 Jeffrey Good, *St. Petersburg* (FL) *Times*
1996 Robert B. Semple Jr., *The New York Times*
1997 Michael Gartner, *The Daily Tribune* (Ames, IA)

Cartoons

1922 Rollin Kirby, *New York World*
1923 –
1924 Jay Norwood Darling, *Des Moines Reigister & Tribune*
1925 Rollin Kirby, *The New York World*
1926 D. R. Fitzpatrick, *St. Louis Post-Dispatch*
1927 Nelson Harding, *Brooklyn Daily Eagle*
1928 Nelson Harding, *Brooklyn Daily Eagle*
1929 Rollin Kirby, *The New York World*
1930 Charles R. Macauley, *Brooklyn Daily Eagle*
1931 Edmund Duffy, *The Baltimore Sun*
1932 John T. McCutcheon, *Chicago Tribune*
1933 H. M. Talburt, *Washington Daily News*
1934 Edmund Duffy, *The Baltimore Sun*
1935 Ross A. Lewis, *Milwaukee Journal*
1936 –
1937 C. D. Batchelor, *New York Daily News*
1938 Vaughn Shoemaker, *Chicago Daily News*
1939 Charles G. Werner, *Daily Oklahoman*
1940 Edmund Duffy, *The Baltimore Sun*
1941 Jacob Burck, *Chicago Times*
1942 Herbert Lawrence Block (Herblock), NEA Service
1943 Jay Norwood Darling, *Des Moines Register & Tribune*
1944 Clifford K. Berryman, *The Evening Star* (Washington, DC)
1945 Sergeant Bill Mauldin, United Feature Syndicate, Inc.
1946 Bruce Alexander Russell, *Los Angeles Times*
1947 Vaughn Shoemaker, *Chicago Daily News*
1948 Reuben L. Goldberg, *New York Sun*
1949 Lute Pease, *Newark Evening News*
1950 James T. Berryman, *The Evening Star* (Washington, DC)
1951 Reg (Reginald W.) Manning, *Arizona Republic*
1952 Fred L. Packer, *New York Mirror*
1953 Edward D. Kuekes, *Cleveland Plain Dealer*
1954 Herbert L. Block (Herblock), *Washington Post & Times-Herald*
1955 Daniel R. Fitzpatrick, *St. Louis Post-Dispatch*
1956 Robert York, *Louisville* (KY) *Times*
1957 Tom Little, *Nashville Tennessean*
1958 Bruce M. Shanks, *Buffalo* (NY) *Evening News*
1959 William H. (Bill) Mauldin, *St. Louis Post-Dispatch*
1960 –
1961 Carey Orr, *Chicago Tribune*
1962 Edmund S. Valtman, *Hartford Times*
1963 Frank Miller, *The Des Moines Register*
1964 Paul Conrad, *The Denver Post*
1965 –
1966 Don Wright, *Miami News*
1967 Patrick B. Oliphant, *Denver Post*
1968 Eugene Gray Payne, *Charlotte Observer*

1969 John Fischetti, *Chicago Daily News*
1970 Thomas F. Darcy, *Newsday* (Garden City, NY)
1971 Paul Conrad, *Los Angeles Times*
1972 Jeffrey K. MacNelly, *Richmond News-Leader*
1973 –
1974 Paul Szep, *The Boston Globe*
1975 Garry Trudeau
1976 Tony Auth, *The Philadelphia Inquirer*
1977 Paul Szep, *The Boston Globe*
1978 Jeffrey K. MacNelly, *The Richmond News-Leader*
1979 Herbert L. Block, *The Washington Post*
1980 Don Wright, *The Miami News*
1981 Mike Peters, *Dayton* (OH) *Daily News*
1982 Ben Sargent, *The Austin* (TX) *American-Statesman*
1983 Richard Locher, *Chicago Tribune*
1984 Paul Conrad, *Los Angeles Times*
1985 Jeff MacNelly, *Chicago Tribune*
1986 Jules Feiffer, *The Village Voice* (New York, NY)
1987 Berke Breathed, *The Washington Post* Writers Group
1988 Doug Marlette, *The Atlanta Constitution* and *The Charlotte Observer*
1989 Jack Higgins, *Chicago Sun-Times*
1990 Tom Toles, *The Buffalo News*
1991 Jim Borgman, *The Cincinnati Enquirer*
1992 Signe Wilkinson, *Philadelphia Daily News*
1993 Stephen R. Benson, *The Arizona Republic*
1994 Michael P. Ramirez, *The Commercial Appeal* (Memphis, TN)
1995 Mike Luckovich, *The Atlanta Constitution*
1996 Jim Morin, *The Miami Herald*
1997 Walt Handelsman, *The Times-Picayune* (New Orleans)

Photography

1942 Milton Brooks, *Detroit News*
1943 Frank Noel, Associated Press
1944 Frank Filan, Associated Press
      Earle L. Bunker, *World-Herald* (Omaha, NE)
1945 Joe Rosenthal, Associated Press
1946 –
1947 Arnold Hardy
1948 Frank Cushing, *Boston Traveler*
1949 Nathaniel Fein, *New York Herald-Tribune*
1950 Bill Crouch, *Oakland* (CA) *Tribune*
1951 Max Desfor, Associated Press
1952 John Robinson and Don Ultang, *Des Moines Register and Tribune*
1953 William M. Gallagher, *Flint* (MI) *Journal*
1954 Mrs. Walter M. Schau
1955 John L. Gaunt Jr., *Los Angeles Times*
1956 *New York Daily News*
1957 Harry A. Trask, *Boston Traveler*
1958 William C. Beall, *Washington* (DC) *Daily News*
1959 William Seaman, *Minneapolis Star*
1960 Andrew Lopez, United Press International
1961 Yasushi Nagao, *Mainichi* (Tokyo)
1962 Paul Vathis, Associated Press
1963 Hector Rondon, *La Republica* (Caracas, Venezuela)

1964 Robert H. Jackson, *Dallas Times-Herald*
1965 Horst Faas, Associated Press
1966 Kyoichi Sawada, United Press International
1967 Jack R. Thornell, Associated Press

Spot News Photography

1968 Rocco Morabito, *Jacksonville* (FL) *Journal*
1969 Edward T. Adams, Associated Press
1970 Steve Starr, Associated Press
1971 John Paul Filo, *Valley Daily News and Daily Dispatch* (Tarentum and New Kensington, PA)
1972 Horst Faas and Michel Laurent, Associated Press
1973 Huynh Cong Ut, Associated Press
1974 Anthony K. Roberts, freelance photographer (Beverly Hills, CA)
1975 Gerald H. Gay, *The Seattle Times*
1976 Stanley Forman, *Boston Herald American*
1977 Neal Ulevich, Associated Press
     Stanley Forman, *Boston Herald American*
1978 John H. Blair, United Press International
1979 Thomas J. Kelly III, *The Pottstown* (PA) *Mercury*
1980 An unnamed photographer, United Press International
1981 Larry C. Price, *Fort Worth* (TX) *Star-Telegram*
1982 Ron Edmonds, Associated Press
1983 Bill Foley, Associated Press
1984 Stan Grossfeld, *The Boston Globe*
1985 The photo staff of *The Register* (Santa Ana, CA)
1986 Carol Guzy and Michel duCille, *The Miami Herald*
1987 Kim Komenich, *San Francisco Examiner*
1988 Scott Shaw, *The Odessa* (TX) *American*
1989 Ron Olshwanger, freelance photographer
1990 The photo staff of *The Tribune* (Oakland, CA)
1991 Greg Marinovich, Associated Press
1992 The Associated Press staff
1993 Ken Geiger and William Snyder, *The Dallas Morning News*
1994 Paul Watson, *The Toronto Star*
1995 Carol Guzy, *The Washington Post*
1996 Charles Porter IV, freelance photographer
1997 Annie Wells, *The Press Democrat* (Santa Rosa, CA)

Feature Photography

1968 Toshio Sakai, United Press International
1969 Moneta Sleet Jr., *Ebony*
1970 Dallas Kinney, *Palm Beach Post*
1971 Jack Dykinga, *Chicago Sun-Times*
1972 Dave Kennerly, United Press International
1973 Brian Lanker, *Topeka Capital-Journal*
1974 Slava Veder, Associated Press

1975 Matthew Lewis, *The Washington Post*
1976 *The Louisville Courier-Journal and Times* photo staff
1977 Robin Hood, *Chattanooga News-Free Press*
1978 J. Ross Baughman, Associated Press
1979 Staff photographers of *The Boston Herald American*
1980 Erwin H. Hagler, *Dallas Times Herald*
1981 Taro M. Yamasaki, *Detroit Free Press*
1982 John H. White, *Chicago Sun-Times*
1983 James B. Dickman, *Dallas Times Herald*
1984 Anthony Suau, *The Denver Post*
1985 Stan Grossfeld, *The Boston Globe*
     Larry C. Price, *The Philadelphia Inquirer*
1986 Tom Gralish, *The Philadelphia Inquirer*
1987 David Peterson, *The Des Moines Register*
1988 Michel duCille, *The Miami Herald*
1989 Manny Crisostomo, *Detroit Free Press*
1990 David C. Turnley, *Detroit Free Press*
1991 William Snyder, *The Dallas Morning News*
1992 John Kaplan, Block Newspapers (Toledo, OH)
1993 The Associated Press staff
1994 Kevin Carter, freelance photographer
1995 The Associated Press staff
1996 Stephanie Welsh, freelance photographer
1997 Alexander Zemlianichenko, Associated Press

Newspaper History Award

1918 Minna Lewinson and Henry Beetle Hough

Special Awards and Citations

1930 William O. Dapping, *The Auburn* (NY) *Citizen*
1938 *Edmonton* (Alberta) *Journal*
1941 *The New York Times*
1944 Byron Price
     Mrs. William Allen White
1945 The cartographers of the American press
1947 (Pulitzer centennial year) Columbia University and the Graduate School of Journalism
1948 Dr. Frank Diehl Fackenthal
1951 Cyrus L. Sulzberger, *The New York Times*
1952 Max Kase, *New York Journal-American*
     Kansas City (MO) *Star*
1953 *The New York Times*
1958 Walter Lippmann, *The New York Herald Tribune*
1964 Gannett Newspapers
1976 Professor John Hohenberg
1978 Richard Lee Strout
1987 Joseph Pulitzer Jr.
1996 Herb Caen, *San Francisco Chronicle*

Letters

Fiction

1917 –
1918 *His Family*, Ernest Poole
1919 *The Magnificent Ambersons*, Booth Tarkington
1920 –
1921 *The Age of Innocence*, Edith Wharton
1922 *Alice Adams*, Booth Tarkington
1923 *One of Ours*, Willa Cather
1924 *The Able McLaughlins*, Margaret Wilson
1925 *So Big*, Edna Ferber
1926 *Arrowsmith*, Sinclair Lewis
1927 *Early Autumn*, Louis Bromfield
1928 *The Bridge of San Luis Rey*, Thornton Wilder
1929 *Scarlet Sister Mary*, Julia Peterkin
1930 *Laughing Boy*, Oliver LaFarge
1931 *Years of Grace*, Margaret Ayer Barnes
1932 *The Good Earth*, Pearl S. Buck
1933 *The Store*, T. S. Stribling
1934 *Lamb in His Bosom*, Caroline Miller
1935 *Now in November*, Josephine Winslow Johnson
1936 *Honey in the Horn*, Harold L. Davis
1937 *Gone With the Wind*, Margaret Mitchell
1938 *The Late George Apley*, John Phillips Marquand
1939 *The Yearling*, Marjorie Kinnan Rawlings
1940 *The Grapes of Wrath*, John Steinbeck
1941 –
1942 *In This Our Life*, Ellen Glasgow
1943 *Dragon's Teeth*, Upton Sinclair
1944 *Journey in the Dark*, Martin Flavin
1945 *A Bell for Adano*, John Hersey
1946 –
1947 *All the King's Men*, Robert Penn Warren
1948 *Tales of the South Pacific*, James A. Michener
1949 *Guard of Honor*, James Gould Cozzens
1950 *The Way West*, A. B. Guthrie Jr.
1951 *The Town*, Conrad Richter
1952 *The Caine Mutiny*, Herman Wouk
1953 *The Old Man and the Sea*, Ernest Hemingway
1954 –
1955 *A Fable*, William Faulkner
1956 *Andersonville*, MacKinlay Kantor
1957 –
1958 *A Death in the Family*, James Agee
1959 *The Travels of Jaimie McPheeters*, Robert Lewis Taylor
1960 *Advise and Consent*, Allen Drury
1961 *To Kill a Mockingbird*, Harper Lee
1962 *The Edge of Sadness*, Edwin O'Connor
1963 *The Reivers*, William Faulkner
1964 –
1965 *The Keepers of the House*, Shirley Ann Grau
1966 *Collected Stories*, Katherine Anne Porter
1967 *The Fixer*, Bernard Malamud
1968 *The Confessions of Nat Turner*, William Styron
1969 *House Made of Dawn*, N. Scott Momaday
1970 *Collected Stories*, Jean Stafford
1971 –

1972 *Angle of Repose*, Wallace Stegner
1973 *The Optimist's Daughter*, Eudora Welty
1974 –
1975 *The Killer Angels*, Michael Shaara
1976 *Humboldt's Gift*, Saul Bellow
1977 –
1978 *Elbow Room*, James Alan McPherson
1979 *The Stories of John Cheever*, John Cheever
1980 *The Executioner's Song*, Norman Mailer
1981 *A Confederacy of Dunces*, John Kennedy Toole
1982 *Rabbit Is Rich*, John Updike
1983 *The Color Purple*, Alice Walker
1984 *Ironweed*, William Kennedy
1985 *Foreign Affairs*, Alison Lurie
1986 *Lonesome Dove*, Larry McMurtry
1987 *A Summons to Memphis*, Peter Taylor
1988 *Beloved*, Toni Morrison
1989 *Breathing Lessons*, Anne Tyler
1990 *The Mambo Kings Play Songs of Love*, Oscar Hijuelos
1991 *Rabbit at Rest*, John Updike
1992 *A Thousand Acres*, Jane Smiley
1993 *A Good Scent from a Strange Mountain*, Robert Olen Butler
1994 *The Shipping News*, E. Annie Proulx
1995 *The Stone Diaries*, Carol Shields
1996 *Independence Day*, Richard Ford
1997 *Martin Dressler: The Tale of an American Dreamer*, Steven Millhauser

Drama

1917 –
1918 *Why Marry?*, Jesse Lynch Williams
1919 –
1920 *Beyond the Horizon*, Eugene O'Neill
1921 *Miss Lulu Bett*, Zona Gale
1922 *Anna Christie*, Eugene O'Neill
1923 *Icebound*, Owen Davis
1924 *Hell-Bent fer Heaven*, Hatcher Hughes
1925 *They Knew What They Wanted*, Sidney Howard
1926 *Craig's Wife*, George Kelly
1927 *In Abraham's Bosom*, Paul Green
1928 *Strange Interlude*, Eugene O'Neill
1929 *Street Scene*, Elmer L. Rice
1930 *The Green Pastures*, Marc Connelly
1931 *Alison's House*, Susan Glaspell
1932 *Of Thee I Sing*, George S. Kaufman, Morrie Ryskind, and Ira Gershwin
1933 *Both Your Houses*, Maxwell Anderson
1934 *Men in White*, Sidney Kingsley
1935 *The Old Maid*, Zoe Akins
1936 *Idiot's Delight*, Robert E. Sherwood
1937 *You Can't Take It With You*, Moss Hart and George S. Kaufman
1938 *Our Town*, Thornton Wilder
1939 *Abe Lincoln in Illinois*, Robert E. Sherwood
1940 *The Time of Your Life*, William Saroyan
1941 *There Shall Be No Night*, Robert E. Sherwood
1942 –
1943 *The Skin of Our Teeth*, Thornton Wilder
1944 –
1945 *Harvey*, Mary Chase

1946 *State of the Union*, Russel Crouse and Howard Lindsay
1947 –
1948 *A Streetcar Named Desire*, Tennessee Williams
1949 *Death of a Salesman*, Arthur Miller
1950 *South Pacific*, Richard Rodgers, Oscar Hammerstein II, and Joshua Logan
1951 –
1952 *The Shrike*, Joseph Kramm
1953 *Picnic*, William Inge
1954 *The Teahouse of the August Moon*, John Patrick
1955 *Cat on a Hot Tin Roof*, Tennessee Williams
1956 *Diary of Anne Frank*, Albert Hackett and Frances Goodrich
1957 *Long Day's Journey Into Night*, Eugene O'Neill
1958 *Look Homeward, Angel*, Ketti Frings
1959 *J. B.*, Archibald MacLeish
1960 *Fiorello!*, book by Jerome Weidman and George Abbott, music by Jerry Bock, and lyrics by Sheldon Harnick
1961 *All the Way Home*, Tad Mosel
1962 *How To Succeed In Business Without Really Trying*, Frank Loesser and Abe Burrows
1963 –
1964 –
1965 *The Subject Was Roses*, Frank D. Gilroy
1966 –
1967 *A Delicate Balance*, Edward Albee
1968 –
1969 *The Great White Hope*, Howard Sackler
1970 *No Place to Be Somebody*, Charles Gordone
1971 *The Effect of Gamma Rays on Man-in-the-Moon Marigolds*, Paul Zindel
1972 –
1973 *That Championship Season*, Jason Miller
1974 –
1975 *Seascape*, Edward Albee
1976 *A Chorus Line*, conceived, choreographed and directed by Michael Bennett, with book by James Kirkwood and Nicholas Dante, music by Marvin Hamlisch, and lyrics by Edward Kleban
1977 *The Shadow Box*, Michael Cristofer
1978 *The Gin Game*, Donald L. Coburn
1979 *Buried Child*, Sam Shepard
1980 *Talley's Folly*, Lanford Wilson
1981 *Crimes of the Heart*, Beth Henley
1982 *A Soldier's Play*, Charles Fuller
1983 *'Night, Mother*, Marsha Norman
1984 *Glengarry Glen Ross*, David Mamet
1985 *Sunday in the Park With George*, music and lyrics by Stephen Sondheim
1986 –
1987 *Fences*, August Wilson
1988 *Driving Miss Daisy*, Alfred Uhry
1989 *The Heidi Chronicles*, Wendy Wasserstein
1990 *The Piano Lesson*, August Wilson
1991 *Lost in Yonkers*, Neil Simon
1992 *The Kentucky Cycle*, Robert Schenkkan

1993 *Angels in America: Millennium Approaches*, Tony Kushner
1994 *Three Tall Women*, Edward Albee
1995 *The Young Man From Atlanta*, Horton Foote
1996 *Rent*, Jonathan Larson
1997 –

History

1917 *With Americams of Past and Present Days*, His Excellency J. J. Jusserand
1918 *A History of the Civil War, 1861-1865*, James Ford Rhodes
1919 –
1920 *The War with Mexico*, 2 vols., Justin H. Smith
1921 *The Victory at Sea*, William Sowden Sims in collaboration with Burton J. Hendrick
1922 *The Founding of New England*, James Truslow Adams
1923 *The Supreme Court in United States History*, Charles Warren
1924 *The American Revolution—A Constitutional Interpretation*, Charles Howard McIlwain
1925 *History of the American Frontier*, Frederic L. Paxson
1926 *A History of the United States*, Edward Channing
1927 *Pinckney's Treaty*, Samuel Flagg Bemis
1928 *Main Currents in American Thought*, 2 vols., Vernon Louis Parrington
1929 *The Organization and Administration of the Union Army, 1861-1865*, Fred Albert Shannon
1930 *The War of Independence*, Claude H. Van Tyne
1931 *The Coming of the War 1914*, Bernadotte E. Schmitt
1932 *My Experiences in the World War*, John J. Pershing
1933 *The Significance of Sections in American History*, Frederick J. Turner
1934 *The People's Choice*, Herbert Agar
1935 *The Colonial Period of American History*, Charles McLean Andrews
1936 *A Constitutional History of the United States*, Andrew C. McLaughlin
1937 *The Flowering of New England 1815-1865*, Van Wyck Brooks
1938 *The Road to Reunion, 1865-1900*, Paul Herman Buck
1939 *A History of American Magazines*, Frank Luther Mott
1940 *Abraham Lincoln: The War Years*, Carl Sandburg
1941 *The Atlantic Migration, 1607-1860*, Marcus Lee Hansen
1942 *Reveille in Washington, 1860-1865*, Margaret Leech
1943 *Paul Revere and the World He Lived In*, Esther Forbes
1944 *The Growth of American Thought*, Merle Curti
1945 *Unfinished Business*, Stephen Bonsal
1946 *The Age of Jackson*, Arthur Meier Schlesinger Jr.

1947 *Scientists Against Time*, James Phinney Baxter 3rd
1948 *Across the Wide Missouri*, Bernard DeVoto
1949 *The Disruption of American Democracy*, Roy Franklin Nichols
1950 *Art and Life in America*, Oliver W. Larkin
1951 *The Old Northwest, Pioneer Period 1815-1840*, R. Carlyle Buley
1952 *The Uprooted*, Oscar Handlin
1953 *The Era of Good Feelings*, George Dangerfield
1954 *A Stillness at Appomattox*, Bruce Catton
1955 *Great River: The Rio Grande in North American History*, Paul Horgan
1956 *The Age of Reform*, Richard Hofstadter
1957 *Russia Leaves the War: Soviet-American Relations, 1917-1920*, George F. Kennan
1958 *Banks and Politics in America*, Bray Hammond
1959 *The Republican Era: 1869-1901*, Leonard D. White, with the assistance of Miss Jean Schneider
1960 *In the Days of McKinley*, Margaret Leech
1961 *Between War and Peace: The Potsdam Conference*, Herbert Feis
1962 *The Triumphant Empire: Thunder-Clouds Gather in the West 1763-1766*, Lawrence H. Gipson
1963 *Washington, Village and Capital, 1800-1878*, Constance McLaughlin Green
1964 *Puritan Village: The Formation of a New England Town*, Sumner Chilton Powell
1965 *The Greenback Era*, Irwin Unger
1966 *The Life of the Mind in America*, Perry Miller
1967 *Exploration and Empire: The Explorer and the Scientist in the Winning of the American West*, William H. Goetzmann
1968 *The Ideological Origins of the American Revolution*, Bernard Bailyn
1969 *Origins of the Fifth Amendment*, Leonard W. Levy
1970 *Present at the Creation: My Years in the State Department*, Dean Acheson
1971 *Roosevelt: The Soldier of Freedom*, James MacGregor Burns
1972 *Neither Black Nor White*, Carl N. Degler
1973 *People of Paradox: An Inquiry Concerning the Origins of American Civilization*, Michael Kammen
1974 *The Americans: The Democratic Experience*, Daniel J. Boorstin
1975 *Jefferson and His Time*, vols. I-V, Dumas Malone
1976 *Lamy of Santa Fe*, Paul Horgan
1977 *The Impending Crisis, 1841-1861*, David M. Potter, manuscript finished by Don E. Fehrenbacher
1978 *The Visible Hand: The Managerial Revolution in American Business*, Alfred D. Chandler, Jr.
1979 *The Dred Scott Case*, Don E. Fehrenbacher
1980 *Been in the Storm So Long*, Leon F. Litwack
1981 *American Education: The National Experince, 1783-1876*, Lawrence A. Cremin

1982 *Mary Chesnut's Civil War*, edited by C. Vann Woodward
1983 *The Transformation of Virginia, 1740-1790*, Rhys L. Isaac
1984 –
1985 *Prophets of Regulation*, Thomas K. McCraw
1986 *...the Heavens and the Earth*, Walter A. McDougall
1987 *Voyagers to the West*, Bernard Bailyn
1988 *The Launching of Modern American Science 1846-1876*, Robert V. Bruce
1989 *Parting the Waters*, Taylor Branch
   Battle Cry of Freedom, James M. McPherson
1990 *In Our Image*, Stanley Karnow
1991 *A Midwife's Tale*, Laurel Thatcher Ulrich
1992 *The Fate of Liberty: Abraham Lincoln and Civil Liberties*, Mark E. Neely, Jr.
1993 *The Radicalism of the American Revolution*, Gordon S. Wood
1994 –
1995 *No Ordinary Time: Franklin and Eleanor Roosevelt: The Home Front in World War II*, Doris Kearns Goodwin
1996 *William Cooper's Town: Power and Persuasion on the Frontier of the Early American Republic*, Alan Taylor
1997 *Original Meanings: Politics and Ideas in the Making of the Constitution*, Jack N. Rakove

Biography or Autobiography

1917 *Julia Ward Howe*, Laura E. Richards and Maude Howe Elliott, assisted by Florence Howe Hall
1918 *Benjamin Franklin, Self-Revealed*, William Cabell Bruce
1919 *The Education of Henry Adams*, Henry Adams
1920 *The Life of John Marshall*, 4 vols., Albert J. Beveridge
1921 *The Americanization of Edward Bok*, Edward Bok
1922 *A Daughter of the Middle Border*, Hamlin Garland
1923 *The Life and Letters of Walter H. Page*, Burton J. Hendrick
1924 *From Immigrant to Inventor*, Michael Idvorsky Pupin
1925 *Barrett Wendell and His Letters*, M. A. DeWolfe Howe
1926 *The Life of Sir William Osler*, 2 vols., Harvey Cushing
1927 *Whitman*, Emory Holloway
1928 *The American Orchestra and Theodore Thomas*, Charles Edward Russell
1929 *The Training of an American. The Earlier Life and Letters of Walter H. Page*, Burton J. Hendrick
1930 *The Raven*, Marquis James
1931 *Charles W. Eliot*, Henry James
1932 *Theodore Roosevelt*, Henry F. Pringle
1933 *Grover Cleveland*, Allan Nevins
1934 *John Hay*, Tyler Dennett
1935 *R. E. Lee*, Douglas S. Freeman

1936 *The Thought and Character of William James*, Ralph Barton Perry
1937 *Hamilton Fish*, Allan Nevins
1938 *Pedlar's Progress*, Odell Shepard
      Andrew Jackson, 2 vols., Marquis James
1939 *Benjamin Franklin*, Carl Van Doren
1940 *Woodrow Wilson, Life and Letters*, vols. VII and VIII, Ray Stannard Baker
1941 *Jonathan Edwards*, Ola Elizebeth Winslow
1942 *Crusader in Crinoline*, Forrest Wilson
1943 *Admiral of the Ocean Sea*, Samuel Eliot Morison
1944 *The American Leonardo: The Life of Samuel F. B. Morse*, Carleton Mabee
1945 *George Bancroft: Brahmin Rebel*, Russell Blaine Nye
1946 *Son of the Wilderness*, Linnie Marsh Wolfe
1947 *The Autobiography of William Allen White*
1948 *Forgotten First Citizen: John Bigelow*, Margaret Clapp
1949 *Roosevelt and Hopkins*, Robert E. Sherwood
1950 *John Quincy Adams and the Foundations of American Foreign Policy*, Samuel Flagg Bemis
1951 *John C. Calhoun: American Portrait*, Margaret Louise Coit
1952 *Charles Evans Hughes*, Merlo J. Pusey
1953 *Edmund Pendleton 1721-1803*, David J. Mays
1954 *The Spirit of St. Louis*, Charles A. Lindbergh
1955 *The Taft Story*, William S. White
1956 *Benjamin Henry Latrobe*, Talbot Faulkner Hamlin
1957 *Profiles in Courage*, John F. Kennedy
1958 *George Washington*, vols. I-VI, Douglas Southall Freeman, and vol. VII, written by John Alexander Carroll and Mary Wells Ashworth after Dr. Freeman's death in 1953
1959 *Woodrow Wilson, American Prophet*, Arthur Walworth
1960 *John Paul Jones*, Samuel Eliot Morison
1961 *Charles Sumner and the Coming of the Civil War*, David Donald
1962 –
1963 *Henry James*, Leon Edel
1964 *John Keats*, Walter Jackson Bate
1965 *Henry Adams*, 3 vols., Ernest Samuels
1966 *A Thousand Days*, Arthur M. Schlesinger, Jr.
1967 *Mr. Clemens and Mark Twain*, Justin Kaplan
1968 *Memoirs*, George F. Kennan
1969 *The Man From New York: John Quinn and His Friends*, Benjamin Lawrence Reid
1970 *Huey Long*, T. Harry Williams
1971 *Robert Frost: The Years of Triumph, 1915-1938*, Lawrance Thompson
1972 *Eleanor and Franklin*, Joseph P. Lash
1973 *Luce and His Empire*, W. A. Swanberg
1974 *O'Neill, Son and Artist*, Louis Sheaffer
1975 *The Power Broker: Robert Moses and the Fall of New York*, Robert Caro
1976 *Edith Wharton: A Biography*, R. W. B. Lewis
1977 *A Prince of Our Disorder, The Life of T. E. Lawrence*, John E. Mack
1978 *Samuel Johnson*, Walter Jackson Bate

1979 *Days of Sorrow and Pain: Leo Baeck and the Berlin Jews*, Leonard Baker
1980 *The Rise of Theodore Roosevelt*, Edmund Morris
1981 *Peter the Great: His Life and World*, Robert K. Massie
1982 *Grant: A Biography*, William McFeely
1983 *Growing Up*, Russell Baker
1984 *Booker T. Washington*, Louis R. Harlan
1985 *The Life and Times of Cotton Mather*, Kenneth Silverman
1986 *Louise Bogan: A Portrait*, Elizabeth Frank
1987 *Bearing the Cross*, David J. Garrow
1988 *Look Homeward: A Life of Thomas Wolfe*, David Herbert Donald
1989 *Oscar Wilde*, Richard Ellmann
1990 *Machiavelli in Hell*, Sebastian de Grazia
1991 *Jackson Pollock*, Steven Naifeh and Gregory White Smith
1992 *Fortunate Son: The Healing of a Vietnam Vet*, Lewis B. Puller, Jr.
1993 *Truman*, David McCullough
1994 *W. E. B. Du Bois: Biography of a Race 1868-1919*, David Levering Lewis
1995 *Harriet Beecher Stowe: A Life*, Joan D. Hedrick
1996 *God: A Biography*, Jack Miles
1997 *Angela's Ashes: A Memoir*, Frank McCourt

Poetry*

1918* *Love Songs*, Sara Teasdale
1919* *Old Road to Paradise*, Margaret Widdemer
      Corn Huskers, Carl Sandburg
1922 *Collected Poems*, Edwin Arlington Robinson
1923 *The Ballad of the Harp-Weaver; A Few Figs from Thistles; Eight Sonnets in American Poetry, 1922, A Miscellany*, Edna St. Vincent Millay
1924 *New Hampshire: A Poem with Notes and Grace Notes*, Robert Frost
1925 *The Man Who Died Twice*, Edwin Arlington Robinson
1926 *What's O'Clock*, Amy Lowell
1927 *Fiddler's Farwell*, Leonora Speyer
1928 *Tristram*, Edwin Arlington Robinson
1929 *John Brown's Body*, Stephen Vincent Benét
1930 *Selected Poems*, Conrad Aiken
1931 *Collected Poems*, Robert Frost
1932 *The Flowering Stone*, George Dillon
1933 *Conquistador*, Archibald MacLeish
1934 *Collected Verse*, Robert Hillyer
1935 *Bright Ambush*, Audrey Wurdemann
1936 *Strange Holiness*, Robert P. Tristram Coffin
1937 *A Further Range*, Robert Frost
1938 *Cold Morning Sky*, Marya Zaturenska
1939 *Selected Poems*, John Gould Fletcher
1940 *Collected Poems*, Mark Van Doren
1941 *Sunderland Capture*, Leonard Bacon
1942 *The Dust Which Is God*, William Rose Benét

*Previous to the establishment of this prize in 1922, these awards had been made from gifts provided by the Poetry Society.

1943 *A Witness Tree*, Robert Frost
1944 *Western Star*, Stephen Vincent Benét
1945 *V-Letter and Other Poems*, Karl Shapiro
1946 –
1947 *Lord Weary's Castle*, Robert Lowell
1948 *The Age of Anxiety*, W. H. Auden
1949 *Terror and Decorum*, Peter Viereck
1950 *Annie Allen*, Gwendolyn Brooks
1951 *Complete Poems*, Carl Sandburg
1952 *Collected Poems*, Marianne Moore
1953 *Collected Poems 1917-1952*,
        Archibald MacLeish
1954 *The Waking*, Theodore Roethke
1955 *Collected Poems*, Wallace Stevens
1956 *Poems—North & South*, Elizabeth Bishop
1957 *Things of This World*, Richard Wilbur
1958 *Promises: Poems 1954-1956*, Robert
        Penn Warren
1959 *Selected Poems 1928-1958*, Stanley Kunitz
1960 *Heart's Needle*, W. D. Snodgrass
1961 *Times Three: Selected Verse From Three
        Decades*, Phyllis McGinley
1962 *Poems*, Alan Dugan
1963 *Pictures from Breughel*, William
        Carlos Williams
1964 *At the End of the Open Road*, Louis Simpson
1965 *77 Dream Songs*, John Berryman
1966 *Selected Poems*, Richard Eberhart
1967 *Live or Die*, Anne Sexton
1968 *The Hard Hours*, Anthony Hecht
1969 *Of Being Numerous*, George Oppen
1970 *Untitled Subjects*, Richard Howard
1971 *The Carrier of Ladders*, William S. Merwin
1972 *Collected Poems*, James Wright
1973 *Up Country*, Maxine Kumin
1974 *The Dolphin*, Robert Lowell
1975 *Turtle Island*, Gary Snyder
1976 *Self-Portrait in a Convex Mirror*,
        John Ashbery
1977 *Divine Comedies*, James Merrill
1978 *Collected Poems*, Howard Nemerov
1979 *Now and Then*, Robert Penn Warren
1980 *Selected Poems*, Donald Justice
1981 *The Morning of the Poem*, James Schuyler
1982 *The Collected Poems*, Sylvia Plath
1983 *Selected Poems*, Galway Kinnell
1984 *American Primitive*, Mary Oliver
1985 *Yin*, Carolyn Kizer
1986 *The Flying Change*, Henry Taylor
1987 *Thomas and Beulah*, Rita Dove
1988 *Partial Accounts*, William Meredith
1989 *New and Collected Poems*, Richard Wilbur
1990 *The World Doesn't End*, Charles Simic
1991 *Near Changes*, Mona Van Duyn
1992 *Selected Poems*, James Tate
1993 *The Wild Iris*, Louise Glück
1994 *Neon Vernacular: New and Selected
        Poems*, Yusef Komunyakaa
1995 *The Simple Truth*, Philip Levine
1996 *The Dream of the Unified Field*,
        Jorie Graham
1997 *Alive Together: New and Selected Poems*,
        Lisel Mueller

General Non-Fiction

1962 *The Making of the President 1960*,
        Theodore H. White
1963 *The Guns of August*, Barbara W. Tuchman
1964 *Anti-Intellectualism in American Life*,
        Richard Hofstadter
1965 *O Strange New World*, Howard
        Mumford Jones
1966 *Wandering Through Winter*, Edwin Way Teale
1967 *The Problem of Slavery in Western Culture*,
        David Brion Davis
1968 *Rousseau and Revolution*, the tenth and
        concluding volume of *The Story of
        Civilization*, Will and Ariel Durant
1969 *So Human an Animal*, René Jules Dubos
        The Armies of the Night, Norman Mailer
1970 *Gandhi's Truth*, Erik K. Erikson
1971 *The Rising Sun*, John Toland
1972 *Stilwell and the American Experience in China,
        1911-1945*, Barbara W. Tuchman
1973 *Children of Crisis*, vols. II and III, Robert Coles
        *Fire in the Lake: The Vietnamese and the
        Americans in Vietnam*, Frances FitzGerald
1974 *The Denial of Death*, Ernest Becker
1975 *Pilgrim at Tinker Creek*, Annie Dillard
1976 *Why Survive? Being Old in America*,
        Robert N. Butler
1977 *Beautiful Swimmers*, William W. Warner
1978 *The Dragons of Eden*, Carl Sagan
1979 *On Human Nature*, Edward O. Wilson
1980 *Gödel, Escher, Bach: an Eternal Golden Braid*,
        Douglas R. Hofstadter
1981 *Fin-de Siécle Vienna: Politics and Culture*,
        Carl E. Schorske
1982 *The Soul of a New Machine*, Tracy Kidder
1983 *Is There No Place on Earth for Me?*
        Susan Sheehan
1984 *The Social Transformation of American
        Medicine*, Paul Starr
1985 *The Good War*, Studs Terkel
1986 *Move Your Shadow*, Joseph Lelyveld
        Common Ground, J. Anthony Lukas
1987 *Arab and Jew*, David K. Shipler
1988 *The Making of the Atomic Bomb*,
        Richard Rhodes
1989 *A Bright Shining Lie*, Neil Sheehan
1990 *And Their Children After Them*, Dale Maharidge
        and Michael Williamson
1991 *The Ants*, Bert Hölldobler and Edward O. Wilson
1992 *The Prize: The Epic Quest for Oil, Money
        & Power*, Daniel Yergin
1993 *Lincoln at Gettysburg: The Words that
        Remade America*, Garry Wills
1994 *Lenin's Tomb: The Last Days of the Soviet
        Empire*, David Remnick
1995 *The Beak of the Finch: A Story of Evolution
        in Our Time*, Jonathan Weiner
1996 *The Haunted Land: Facing Europe's Ghosts
        After Communism*, Tina Rosenberg
1997 *Ashes to Ashes: America's Hundred-Year
        Cigarette War, the Public Health, and the
        Unabashed Triumph of Philip Morris*
        Richard Kluger

Music

1943 William Schuman for his *Secular Cantata No. 2, A Free Song*
1944 Howard Hanson, *Symphony No. 4, Opus 34*
1945 Aaron Copland, *Appalachian Spring*
1946 Leo Sowerby, *The Canticle of the Sun*
1947 Charles Ives, *Symphony No. 3*
1948 Walter Piston, *Symphony No. 3*
1949 Virgil Thomson, music for the film *Louisiana Story*
1950 Gian-Carlo Menotti, music in *The Consul*
1951 Douglas S. Moore, music in *Giants in the Earth*
1952 Gail Kubik, *Symphony Concertante*
1953 –
1954 Quincy Porter, *Concerto for Two Pianos and Orchestra*
1955 Gian-Carlo Menotti, *The Saint of Bleecker Street*
1956 Ernst Toch, *Symphony No. 3*
1957 Norman Dello Joio, *Meditations on Ecclesiastes*
1958 Samuel Barber, *Vanessa*, an opera in four acts, Libretto by Gian-Carlo Menotti
1959 John LaMontaine, *Concerto for Piano and Orchestra*
1960 Elliott Carter, *Second String Quartet*
1961 Walter Piston, *Symphony No. 7*
1962 Robert Ward, *The Crucible*, an opera in three acts, Libretto by Bernard Stambler, based on the play by Arthur Miller
1963 Samuel Barber, *Piano Concerto No. 1*
1964 –
1965 –
1966 Leslie Bassett, *Variations for Orchestra*
1967 Leon Kirchner, *Quartet No. 3*
1968 George Crumb, orchestral suite, *Echoes of Time and the River*
1969 Karel Husa, *String Quartet No. 3*
1970 Charles Wuorinen, *Time's Encomium*
1971 Mario Davidovsky, *Synchronisms No. 6 for Piano and Electronic Sound (1970)*
1972 Jacob Druckman, *Windows*
1973 Elliott Carter, *Spring Quartet No. 3*
1974 Donald Martino, *Notturno*
1975 Dominick Argento, *From the Diary of Virginia Woolf*, for medium voice and piano
1976 Ned Rorem, *Air Music* (Ten Etudes for Orchestra)
1977 Richard Wernick, *Visions of Terror and Wonder* for mezzo-soprano and orchestra
1978 Michael Colgrass, *Deja Vu for Percussion Quartet and Orchestra*
1979 Joseph Schwantner, *Aftertones of Infinity*
1980 David Del Tredici, *In Memory of a Summer Day*, a work for soprano solo and orchestra
1981 –
1982 Roger Sessions, *Concerto for Orchestra*
1983 Ellen Taaffe Zwilich, *Symphony No. 1* (Three Movements for Orchestra)
1984 Bernard Rands, *"Canti del Sole"* for Tenor and Orchestra
1985 Stephen Albert for *Symphony, RiverRun*
1986 George Perle, *Wind Quintet IV*
1987 John Harbison, *The Flight Into Egypt*
1988 William Bolcom, *12 New Etudes for Piano*
1989 Roger Reynolds, *Whispers Out of Time*
1990 Mel Powell, *"Duplicates": A Concerto for Two Pianos and Orchestra*
1991 Shulamit Ran, *Symphony*
1992 Wayne Peterson, *The Face of the Night, The Heart of the Dark*
1993 Christopher Rouse, *Trombone Concerto*
1994 Gunther Schuller, *Of Reminiscences and Reflections*
1995 Morton Gould, *Stringmusic*
1996 George Walker, *Lilacs*
1997 Wynton Marsalis, *Blood on the Fields*

Special Awards and Citations

1974 A special citation to Roger Sessions for his life's work as a distinguished American composer.
1976 A special award bestowed posthumously on Scott Joplin for his contributions to American music.
1982 A special citation to Milton Babbitt for his life's work as a distinguished and seminal American composer.
1985 A special citation to William Schuman for more than half a century of contribution to American music as composer and educational leader.

Source: Columbia University

Academy Award Winners

Awards No. year	Date awarded	Best picture	Actor in a leading role*	Actress in a leading role**	Actor in a supporting role	Actress in a supporting role	Directing
1 1927–1928	May 16, 1929	Wings	Emil Jannings, *The Way of All Flesh*	Janet Gaynor *7th Heaven*	–	–	**Comedy Picture:** Lewis Milestone, *Two Arabian Knights* **Dramatic Picture:** Frank Borzage, *7th Heaven*
2 1928–1929	April 3, 1930	*The Broadway Melody*	Warner Baxter, *In Old Arizona*	Mary Pickford, *Coquette*	–	–	Frank Lloyd, *The Divine Lady*
3 1929–1930	Nov. 5, 1930	*All Quiet on the Western Front*	George Arliss, *Disraeli*	Norma Shearer, *The Divorcée*	–	–	Lewis Milestone, *All Quiet on the Western Front*
4 1930–1931	Nov. 10, 1931	*Cimarron*	Lionel Barrymore, *A Free Soul*	Marie Dressler, *Min and Bill*	–	–	Norman Taurog, *Skippy*
5 1931–1932	Nov. 18, 1932	*Grand Hotel*	†Fredric March, *Dr. Jeckyll and Mr. Hyde* †Wallace Beery, *The Champ*	Helen Hayes, *The Sin of Madelon Claudet*	–	–	Frank Borzage, *Bad Girl*
6 1932–1933	March 16, 1934	*Cavalcade*	Charles Laughton, *The Private Life of Henry VIII*	Katharine Hepburn, *Morning Glory*	–	–	Frank Lloyd, *Cavalcade*
7 1934	Feb. 27, 1935	*It Happened One Night*	Clark Gable, *It Happened One Night*	Claudette Colbert, *It Happened One Night*	–	–	Frank Capra, *It Happened One Night*
8 1935	March 5, 1936	*Mutiny on the Bounty*	Victor McLaglen, *The Informer*	Bette Davis, *Dangerous*	–	–	John Ford, *The Informer*
9 1936	March 4, 1937	*The Great Ziegfeld*	Paul Muni, *The Story of Louis Pasteur*	Luise Rainer, *The Great Ziegfeld*	Walter Brennan, *Come and Get It*	Gale Sondergaard, *Anthony Adverse*	Frank Capra, *Mr. Deeds Goes to Town*
10 1937	March 10, 1938	*The Life of Emile Zola*	Spencer Tracy, *Captains Courageous*	Luise Rainer, *The Good Earth*	Joseph Schildkraut, *The Life of Emile Zola*	Alice Brady, *In Old Chicago*	Leo McCarey, *The Awful Truth*
11 1938	Feb. 23, 1939	*You Can't Take It With You*	Spencer Tracy, *Boys Town*	Bette Davis, *Jezebel*	Walter Brennan, *Kentucky*	Fay Bainter, *Jezebel*	Frank Capra, *You Can't Take it With You*
12 1939	Feb. 29, 1940	*Gone With the Wind*	Robert Donat, *Goodbye, Mr. Chips*	Vivien Leigh, *Gone With the Wind*	Thomas Mitchell, *Stagecoach*	Hattie McDaniel, *Gone With the Wind*	Victor Fleming, *Gone With the Wind*

*Prior to the 1976 (49th) Awards, this category was known as "Actor."
**Prior to the 1976 (49th) Awards, this category was known as "Actress."
†Tie

Awards No. year	Date awarded	Best picture	Actor in a leading role*	Actress in a leading role**	Actor in a supporting role	Actress in a supporting role	Directing
13 1940	Feb. 27, 1941	Rebecca	James Stewart, The Philadelphia Story	Ginger Rogers, Kitty Foyle	Walter Brennan, The Westerner	Jane Darwell, The Grapes of Wrath	John Ford, The Grapes of Wrath
14 1941	Feb. 26, 1942	How Green Was My Valley	Gary Cooper, Sergeant York	Joan Fontaine, Suspicion	Donald Crisp, How Green Was My Valley	Mary Astor, The Great Lie	John Ford, How Green Was My Valley
15 1942	March 4, 1943	Mrs. Miniver	James Cagney, Yankee Doodle Dandy	Greer Garson, Mrs. Miniver	Van Heflin, Johnny Eager	Teresa Wright, Mrs. Miniver	William Wyler, Mrs. Miniver
16 1943	March 2, 1944	Casablanca	Paul Lukas, Watch on the Rhine	Jennifer Jones, The Song of Bernadette	Charles Coburn, The More the Merrier	Katina Paxinou, For Whom the Bell Tolls	Michael Curtiz, Casablanca
17 1944	March 15, 1945	Going My Way	Bing Crosby, Going My Way	Ingrid Bergman, Gaslight	Barry Fitzgerald, Going My Way	Ethel Barrymore, None But the Lonely Heart	Leo McCarey, Going My Way
18 1945	March 7, 1946	The Lost Weekend	Ray Milland, The Lost Weekend	Joan Crawford, Mildred Pierce	James Dunn, A Tree Grows in Brooklyn	Anne Revere, National Velvet	Billy Wilder, The Lost Weekend
19 1946	March 13, 1947	The Best Years of Our Lives	Fredric March, The Best Years of Our Lives	Olivia de Havilland, To Each His Own	Harold Russell, The Best Years of Our Lives	Anne Baxter, The Razor's Edge	William Wyler, The Best Years of Our Lives
20 1947	March 20, 1948	Gentleman's Agreement	Ronald Colman, A Double Life	Loretta Young, The Farmer's Daughter	Edmund Gwenn, Miracle on 34th Street	Celeste Holm, Gentleman's Agreement	Elia Kazan, Gentleman's Agreement
21 1948	March 24, 1949	Hamlet	Laurence Olivier, Hamlet	Jane Wyman, Johnny Belinda	Walter Huston, The Treasure of the Sierra Madre	Claire Trevor, Key Largo	John Huston, The Treasure of the Sierra Madre
22 1949	March 23, 1950	All the King's Men	Broderick Crawford, All The King's Men	Olivia de Havilland, The Heiress	Dean Jagger, Twelve O'Clock High	Mercedes McCambridge, All the King's Men	Joseph L. Mankiewicz, A Letter to Three Wives
23 1950	March 29, 1951	All About Eve	José Ferrer, Cyrano de Bergerac	Judy Holliday, Born Yesterday	George Sanders, All About Eve	Josephine Hull, Harvey	Joseph L. Mankiewicz, All About Eve
24 1951	March 20, 1952	An American in Paris	Humphrey Bogart, The African Queen	Vivien Leigh, A Streetcar Named Desire	Karl Malden, A Streetcar Named Desire	Kim Hunter, A Streetcar Named Desire	George Stevens, A Place in the Sun
25 1952	March 19, 1953	The Greatest Show on Earth	Gary Cooper, High Noon	Shirley Booth, Come Back, Little Sheba	Anthony Quinn, Viva Zapata!	Gloria Grahame, The Bad and the Beautiful	John Ford, The Quiet Man
26 1953	March 25, 1954	From Here to Eternity	William Holden, Stalag 17	Audrey Hepburn, Roman Holiday	Frank Sinatra, From Here to Eternity	Donna Reed, From Here to Eternity	Fred Zinnemann, From Here to Eternity

*Prior to the 1976 (49th) Awards, this category was known as "Actor."

**Prior to the 1976 (49th) Awards, this category was known as "Actress."

Awards No. / year	Date awarded	Best picture	Actor in a leading role*	Actress in a leading role**	Actor in a supporting role	Actress in a supporting role	Directing
27 1954	March 30, 1955	On the Waterfront	Marlon Brando, On the Waterfront	Grace Kelly, The Country Girl	Edmond O'Brien, The Barefoot Contessa	Eva Marie Saint, On the Waterfront	Elia Kazan, On the Waterfront
28 1955	March 21, 1956	Marty	Ernest Borgnine, Marty	Anna Magnani, The Rose Tattoo	Jack Lemmon, Mister Roberts	Jo Van Fleet, East of Eden	Delbert Mann, Marty
29 1956	March 27, 1957	Around the World in 80 Days	Yul Brynner, The King and I	Ingrid Bergman, Anastasia	Anthony Quinn, Lust for Life	Dorothy Malone, Written on the Wind	George Stevens, Giant
30 1957	March 26, 1958	The Bridge on the River Kwai	Alec Guinness, The Bridge on the River Kwai	Joanne Woodward, The Three Faces of Eve	Red Buttons, Sayonara	Miyoshi Umeki, Sayonara	David Lean, The Bridge on the River Kwai
31 1958	April 6, 1959	Gigi	David Niven, Separate Tables	Susan Hayward, I Want to Live!	Burl Ives, The Big Country	Wendy Hiller, Separate Tables	Vincente Minnelli, Gigi
32 1959	April 4, 1960	Ben-Hur	Charlton Heston, Ben-Hur	Simone Signoret, Room at the Top	Hugh Griffith, Ben-Hur	Shelley Winters, The Diary of Anne Frank	William Wyler, Ben-Hur
33 1960	April 17, 1961	The Apartment	Burt Lancaster, Elmer Gantry	Elizabeth Taylor, Butterfield 8	Peter Ustinov, Spartacus	Shirley Jones, Elmer Gantry	Billy Wilder, The Apartment
34 1961	April 9, 1962	West Side Story	Maximilian Schell, Judgment at Nuremberg	Sophia Loren, Two Women	George Chakiris, West Side Story	Rita Moreno, West Side Story	Robert Wise, Jerome Robbins, West Side Story
35 1962	April 8, 1963	Lawrence of Arabia	Gregory Peck, To Kill a Mockingbird	Anne Bancroft, The Miracle Worker	Ed Begley, Sweet Bird of Youth	Patty Duke, The Miracle Worker	David Lean, Lawrence of Arabia
36 1963	April 13, 1964	Tom Jones	Sidney Poitier, Lilies of the Field	Patricia Neal, Hud	Melvyn Douglas, Hud	Margaret Rutherford, The V.I.P.s	Tony Richardson, Tom Jones
37 1964	April 5, 1965	My Fair Lady	Rex Harrison, My Fair Lady	Julie Andrews, Mary Poppins	Peter Ustinov, Topkapi	Lila Kedrova, Zorba the Greek	George Cukor, My Fair Lady
38 1965	April 18, 1966	The Sound of Music	Lee Marvin, Cat Ballou	Julie Christie, Darling	Martin Balsam, A Thousand Clowns	Shelley Winters, A Patch of Blue	Robert Wise, The Sound of Music
39 1966	April 10, 1967	A Man for All Seasons	Paul Scofield, A Man for All Seasons	Elizabeth Taylor, Who's Afraid of Virginia Woolf?	Walter Matthau, The Fortune Cookie	Sandy Dennis, Who's Afraid of Virginia Woolf?	Fred Zinnemann, A Man for All Seasons
40 1967	April 10, 1968	In the Heat of the Night	Rod Steiger, In the Heat of the Night	Katharine Hepburn, Guess Who's Coming to Dinner?	George Kennedy, Cool Hand Luke	Estelle Parsons, Bonnie and Clyde	Mike Nichols, The Graduate
41 1968	April 14, 1969	Oliver!	Cliff Robertson, Charly	†Katharine Hepburn, The Lion in Winter †Barbra Streisand, Funny Girl	Jack Albertson, The Subject Was Roses	Ruth Gordon, Rosemary's Baby	Carol Reed, Oliver!

*Prior to the 1976 (49th) Awards, this category was known as "Actor."
**Prior to the 1976 (49th) Awards, this category was known as "Actress."
†Tie

Awards No.	year	Date awarded	Best picture	Actor in a leading role*	Actress in a leading role**	Actor in a supporting role	Actress in a supporting role	Directing
42	1969	April 7, 1970	Midnight Cowboy	John Wayne, True Grit	Maggie Smith, The Prime of Miss Jean Brodie	Gig Young, They Shoot Horses, Don't They?	Goldie Hawn, Cactus Flower	John Schlesinger, Midnight Cowboy
43	1970	April 15, 1971	Patton	George C. Scott, Patton	Glenda Jackson, Women in Love	John Mills, Ryan's Daughter	Helen Hayes, Airport	Franklin J. Schaffner, Patton
44	1971	April 10, 1972	The French Connection	Gene Hackman, The French Connection	Jane Fonda, Klute	Ben Johnson, The Last Picture Show	Cloris Leachman, The Last Picture Show	William Friedkin, The French Connection
45	1972	March 27, 1973	The Godfather	Marlon Brando, The Godfather	Liza Minnelli, Cabaret	Joel Grey, Cabaret	Eileen Heckart, Butterflies Are Free	Bob Fosse, Cabaret
46	1973	April 2, 1974	The Sting	Jack Lemmon, Save the Tiger	Glenda Jackson, A Touch of Class	John Houseman, The Paper Chase	Tatum O'Neal, Paper Moon	George Roy Hill, The Sting
47	1974	April 8, 1975	The Godfather Part II	Art Carney, Harry and Tonto	Ellen Burstyn, Alice Doesn't Live Here Anymore	Robert De Niro, The Godfather Part II	Ingrid Bergman, Murder on the Orient Express	Francis Ford Coppola, The Godfather Part II
48	1975	March 29, 1976	One Flew Over the Cuckoo's Nest	Jack Nicholson, One Flew Over the Cuckoo's Nest	Louise Fletcher, One Flew Over the Cuckoo's Nest	George Burns, The Sunshine Boys	Lee Grant, Shampoo	Milos Forman, One Flew Over the Cuckoo's Nest
49	1976	March 28, 1977	Rocky	Peter Finch, Network	Faye Dunaway, Network	Jason Robards, All the President's Men	Beatrice Straight, Network	John G. Avildsen, Rocky
50	1977	April 3, 1978	Annie Hall	Richard Dreyfuss, The Goodbye Girl	Diane Keaton, Annie Hall	Jason Robards, Julia	Vanessa Redgrave, Julia	Woody Allen, Annie Hall
51	1978	April 9, 1979	The Deer Hunter	Jon Voight, Coming Home	Jane Fonda, Coming Home	Christopher Walken, The Deer Hunter	Maggie Smith, California Suite	Michael Cimino, The Deer Hunter
52	1979	April 14, 1980	Kramer vs. Kramer	Dustin Hoffman, Kramer vs. Kramer	Sally Field, Norma Rae	Melvyn Douglas, Being There	Meryl Streep, Kramer vs. Kramer	Robert Benton, Kramer vs. Kramer
53	1980	March 31, 1981	Ordinary People	Robert De Niro, Raging Bull	Sissy Spacek, Coal Miner's Daughter	Timothy Hutton, Ordinary People	Mary Steenburgen, Melvin and Howard	Robert Redford, Ordinary People
54	1981	March 29, 1982	Chariots of Fire	Henry Fonda, On Golden Pond	Katherine Hepburn, On Golden Pond	John Gielgud, Arthur	Maureen Stapleton, Reds	Warren Beatty, Reds

*Prior to the 1976 (49th) Awards, this category was known as "Actor."

**Prior to the 1976 (49th) Awards, this category was known as "Actress."

Awards No.	year	Date awarded	Best picture	Actor in a leading role	Actress in a leading role	Actor in a supporting role	Actress in a supporting role	Directing
55	1982	April 11, 1983	Gandhi	Ben Kingsley, Gandhi	Meryl Streep, Sophie's Choice	Louis Gossett, Jr., An Officer and a Gentleman	Jessica Lange, Tootsie	Richard Attenborough, Gandhi
56	1983	April 9, 1984	Terms of Endearment	Robert Duvall, Tender Mercies	Shirley MacLaine, Terms of Endearment	Jack Nicholson, Terms of Endearment	Linda Hunt, The Year of Living Dangerously	James L. Brooks, Terms of Endearment
57	1984	March 25, 1985	Amadeus	F. Murray Abraham, Amadeus	Sally Field, Places in the Heart	Haing S. Ngor, The Killing Fields	Peggy Ashcroft, A Passage to India	Milos Forman, Amadeus
58	1985	March 24, 1986	Out of Africa	William Hurt, Kiss of the Spider Woman	Geraldine Page, The Trip to Bountiful	Don Ameche, Cocoon	Anjelica Huston, Prizzi's Honor	Sydney Pollack, Out of Africa
59	1986	March 30, 1987	Platoon	Paul Newman, The Color of Money	Marlee Matlin, Children of a Lesser God	Michael Caine, Hannah and Her Sisters	Dianne Wiest, Hannah and Her Sisters	Oliver Stone, Platoon
60	1987	April 11, 1988	The Last Emperor	Michael Douglas, Wall Street	Cher, Moonstruck	Sean Connery, The Untouchables	Olympia Dukakis, Moonstruck	Bernardo Bertolucci, The Last Emperor
61	1988	March 29, 1989	Rain Man	Dustin Hoffman, Rain Man	Jodie Foster, The Accused	Kevin Kline, A Fish Called Wanda	Geena Davis, The Accidental Tourist	Barry Levinson, Rain Man
62	1989	March 26, 1990	Driving Miss Daisy	Daniel Day Lewis, My Left Foot	Jessica Tandy, Driving Miss Daisy	Denzel Washington, Glory	Brenda Fricker, My Left Foot	Oliver Stone, Born on the Fourth of July
63	1990	March 25, 1991	Dances With Wolves	Jeremy Irons, Reversal of Fortune	Kathy Bates, Misery	Joe Pesci, Goodfellas	Whoopi Goldberg, Ghost	Kevin Costner, Dances With Wolves
64	1991	March 30, 1992	The Silence of the Lambs	Anthony Hopkins, The Silence of the Lambs	Jodie Foster, The Silence of the Lambs	Jack Palance, City Slickers	Mercedes Ruehl, The Fisher King	Jonathan Demme, The Silence of the Lambs
65	1992	March 29, 1993	Unforgiven	Al Pacino, Scent of a Woman	Emma Thompson, Howards End	Gene Hackman, Unforgiven	Marisa Tomei, My Cousin Vinny	Clint Eastwood, Unforgiven
66	1993	March 21, 1994	Schindler's List	Tom Hanks, Philadelphia	Holly Hunter, The Piano	Tommy Lee Jones, The Fugitive	Anna Paquin, The Piano	Steven Spielberg, Schindler's List
67	1994	March 27, 1995	Forrest Gump	Tom Hanks, Forrest Gump	Jessica Lange, Blue Sky	Martin Landau, Ed Wood	Dianne Wiest, Bullets Over Broadway	Robert Zemeckis, Forrest Gump
68	1995	March 25, 1996	Braveheart	Nicolas Cage, Leaving Las Vegas	Susan Sarandon, Dead Man Walking	Kevin Spacey, The Usual Suspects	Mira Sorvino, Mighty Aphrodite	Mel Gibson, Braveheart
69	1996	March 24, 1997	The English Patient	Geoffrey Rush, Shine	Frances McDormand, Fargo	Cuba Gooding, Jr., Jerry Maguire	Juliette Binoche, The English Patient	Anthony Minghella, The English Patient
70	1997	March 23, 1998	Titanic	Jack Nicholson, As Good as It Gets	Helen Hunt, As Good as It Gets	Robin Williams, Good Will Hunting	Kim Basinger, L.A. Confidential	James Cameron, Titanic

Source: Academy of Motion Picture Arts and Sciences

Emmy Awards

1948
Most Popular Television Program
Pantomime Quiz. KTLA.
Best Film Made for Television
The Necklace (*Your Show Time* series), Marshall Grant-Realm Productions.

1949
Best Live Show
The Ed Wynn Show. KTTV (CBS).
Best Kinescope Show
Texaco Star Theater. KNBH (NBC).

1950
Best Dramatic Show
Pulitzer Prize Playhouse. KECA-TV (ABC).
Best Variety Show
The Alan Young Show. KTTV (CBS).

1951
Best Dramatic Show
Studio One. CBS
Best Comedy Show
Red Skelton Show. NBC.

1952
Best Dramatic Program
Robert Montgomery Presents. NBC.
Best Situation Comedy
I Love Lucy. CBS.

1953
Best Dramatic Program
U.S. Steel Hour. ABC.
Best Situation Comedy
I Love Lucy. CBS.

1954
Best Dramatic Series
U.S. Steel Hour. ABC.
Best Situation Comedy Series
Make Room for Daddy. ABC.

1955
Best Dramatic Series
Producers' Showcase. NBC.
Best Comedy Series
The Phil Silvers Show. CBS.

1.956
Best Series—One Hour or More
Caesar's Hour. NBC.
Best Series—Half Hour or Less
The Phil Silvers Show. CBS.

1957
Best Dramatic Series with Continuing Characters
Gunsmoke. CBS
Best Comedy Series
The Phil Silvers Show. CBS.

1958–59
Best Dramatic Series—One Hour or Longer
Playhouse 90. CBS.
Best Dramatic Series—Less Than One Hour
The Alcoa Hour/Goodyear Playhouse. NBC.
Best Comedy Series
The Jack Benny Show. CBS.

1959–60
Outstanding Program Achievement in the Field of Drama
Playhouse 90. CBS.
Outstanding Program Achievement in the Field of Humor
Art Carney Special. NBC.

1960–61
Outstanding Program Achievement in the Field of Drama
Macbeth, Hallmark Hall of Fame. NBC.
Outstanding Program Achievement in the Field of Humor
The Jack Benny Show. CBS.

1961–62
Outstanding Program Achievement in the Field of Drama
The Defenders. CBS.
Outstanding Program Achievement in the Field of Humor
The Bob Newhart Show. NBC.

1962–63
Outstanding Program Achievement in the Field of Drama
The Defenders. CBS.
Outstanding Program Achievement in the Field of Humor
The Dick Van Dyke Show. CBS.

1963–64
Outstanding Program Achievement in the Field of Drama
The Defenders. CBS.

**Outstanding Program Achievement
in the Field of Comedy**
The Dick Van Dyke Show. CBS.

**1964–65
Outstanding Program Achievements
in Entertainment**
The Dick Van Dyke Show. CBS.
The Magnificent Yankee, Hallmark Hall of Fame. NBC.
My Name is Barbra. CBS.
"What is Sonata Form?," *New York Philharmonic Young People's Concerts with Leonard Bernstein.* CBS.

**1965–66
Outstanding Dramatic Series**
The Fugitive. ABC.
Outstanding Comedy Series
The Dick Van Dyke Show. CBS.

**1966–67
Outstanding Dramatic Series**
Mission: Impossible. CBS.
Outstanding Comedy Series
The Monkees. NBC.

**1967–68
Outstanding Dramatic Series**
Mission: Impossible. CBS.
Outstanding Comedy Series
Get Smart. NBC.

**1968–69
Outstanding Dramatic Series**
NET Playhouse. NET.
Outstanding Comedy Series
Get Smart. NBC.

**1969–70
Outstanding Dramatic Series**
Marcus Welby, M.D. ABC.
Outstanding Comedy Series
My World and Welcome To It. NBC.

**1970–71
Outstanding Series—Drama**
The Senator, The Bold Ones. NBC.
Outstanding Series—Comedy
All in the Family. CBS.

**1971–72
Outstanding Series—Drama**
Elizabeth R, Masterpiece Theatre. PBS.
Outstanding Series—Comedy
All in the Family. CBS.

**1972–73
Outstanding Drama Series**
The Waltons. CBS.

Outstanding Comedy Series
All in the Family. CBS.

**1973–74
Outstanding Drama Series**
Upstairs, Downstairs, Masterpiece Theatre. PBS.
Outstanding Comedy Series
M*A*S*H. CBS.

**1974–75
Outstanding Drama Series**
Upstairs, Downstairs, Masterpiece Theatre. PBS.
Outstanding Comedy Series
The Mary Tyler Moore Show. CBS.

**1975–76
Outstanding Drama Series**
Police Story. NBC.
Outstanding Comedy Series
The Mary Tyler Moore Show. CBS.

**1976–77
Outstanding Drama Series**
Upstairs, Downstairs, Masterpiece Theatre. PBS.
Outstanding Comedy Series
The Mary Tyler Moore Show. CBS.

**1977–78
Outstanding Drama Series**
The Rockford Files. NBC.
Outstanding Comedy Series
All in the Family. CBS.

**1978–79
Outstanding Drama Series**
Lou Grant. CBS.
Outstanding Comedy Series
Taxi. ABC.

**1979–80
Outstanding Drama Series**
Lou Grant. CBS.
Outstanding Comedy Series
Taxi. ABC.

**1980–81
Outstanding Drama Series**
Hill Street Blues. NBC.
Outstanding Comedy Series
Taxi. ABC.

**1981–82
Outstanding Drama Series**
Hill Street Blues. NBC.
Outstanding Comedy Series
Barney Miller. ABC.

1982–83
Outstanding Drama Series
Hill Street Blues. NBC.
Outstanding Comedy Series
Cheers. NBC.

1983–84
Outstanding Drama Series
Hill Street Blues. NBC.
Outstanding Comedy Series
Cheers. NBC.

1984–85
Outstanding Drama Series
Cagney & Lacey. CBS.
Outstanding Comedy Series
The Cosby Show. NBC.

1985–86
Outstanding Drama Series
Cagney & Lacey. CBS.
Outstanding Comedy Series
The Golden Girls. NBC.

1986–87
Outstanding Drama Series
L.A. Law. NBC.
Outstanding Comedy Series
The Golden Girls. NBC.

1987–88
Outstanding Drama Series
thirtysomething. ABC.
Outstanding Comedy Series
The Wonder Years. ABC.

1988–89
Outstanding Drama Series
L.A. Law. NBC.
Outstanding Comedy Series
Cheers. NBC.

1989–90
Outstanding Drama Series
L.A. Law. NBC.
Outstanding Comedy Series
Murphy Brown. CBS.

1990–91
Outstanding Drama Series
L.A. Law. NBC.

Outstanding Comedy Series
Cheers. NBC.

1991–92
Outstanding Drama Series
Northern Exposure. CBS.
Outstanding Comedy Series
Murphy Brown. CBS.

1992–93
Outstanding Drama Series
Picket Fences. CBS.
Outstanding Comedy Series
Seinfeld. NBC.

1993–94
Outstanding Drama Series
Picket Fences. CBS.
Outstanding Comedy Series
Frasier. NBC.

1994–95
Outstanding Drama Series
NYPD Blue. ABC.
Outstanding Comedy Series
Frasier. NBC.

1995–96
Outstanding Drama Series
E.R. NBC.
Outstanding Comedy Series
Frasier. NBC.

1996–97
Outstanding Drama Series
Law and Order. NBC.
Outstanding Comedy Series
Frasier. NBC.

1997–98
Outstanding Drama Series
The Practice. ABC.
Outstanding Comedy Series
Frasier. NBC.

Source: Academy of Television Art and Sciences

Grammy Award Winners

Year	Record of the year	Album of the year	Song of the year
1958	*Nel Blu Dipinto Di Blu (Volare)* Domenico Modugno	*The Music from Peter Gunn* Henry Mancini	*Nel Blu Dipinto Di Blu (Volare)* Domenico Modugno
1959	*Mack the Knife* Bobby Darin	*Come Dance with Me* Frank Sinatra	*The Battle of New Orleans* Composer: Jimmy Driftwood
1960	*Theme from A Summer Place* Percy Faith	*Button Down Mind* Bob Newhart	*Theme from Exodus* Composer: Ernest Gold
1961	*Moon River* Henry Mancini	*Judy at Carnegie Hall* Judy Garland	*Moon River* Comps: Henry Mancini and Johnny Mercer
1962	*I Left My Heart in San Francisco* Tony Bennett	*The First Family* Vaughn Meader	*What Kind of Fool Am I* Comps: Leslie Bricusse and Anthony Newley
1963	*The Days of Wine and Roses* Henry Mancini	*The Barbra Streisand Album* Barbra Streisand	*The Days of Wine and Roses* Comps: Henry Mancini and Johnny Mercer
1964	*The Girl from Ipanema* Stan Getz, Astrud Gilberto	*Getz/Gilberto* Stan Getz, Joao Gilberto	*Hello, Dolly!* Composer: Jerry Herman
1965	*A Taste of Honey* Herb Albert & the Tijuana Brass	*September of My Years* Frank Sinatra	*The Shadow of Your Smile (Love Theme from The Sandpiper)* Comps: Paul Francis Webster and Johnny Mandel
1966	*Strangers in the Night* Frank Sinatra	*Sinatra: a Man & His Music* Frank Sinatra	*Michelle* Songwriters: John Lennon and Paul McCartney
1967	*Up, Up and Away* 5th Dimension	*Sgt. Pepper's Lonely Hearts Club Band* The Beatles	*Up, Up and Away* Songwriter: Jimmy L. Webb
1968	*Mrs. Robinson* Simon & Garfunkel	*By the Time I Get to Phoenix* Glen Campbell	*Little Green Apples* Songwriter: Bobby Russell
1969	*Aquarius/Let the Sunshine In* 5th Dimension	*Blood, Sweat & Tears* Blood, Sweat & Tears	*Games People Play* Songwriter: Joe South
1970	*Bridge Over Troubled Water* Simon & Garfunkel	*Bridge Over Troubled Water* Simon & Garfunkel	*Bridge Over Troubled Water* Songwriter: Paul Simon
1971	*It's Too Late* Carole King	*Tapestry* Carole King	*You've Got a Friend* Songwriter: Carole King
1972	*The First Time Ever I Saw Your Face* Roberta Flack	*The Concert for Bangladesh* Various artists	*The First Time Ever I Saw Your Face* Songwriter: Ewan MacColl
1973	*Killing Me Softly with His Song* Roberta Flack	*Innervisions* Stevie Wonder	*Killing Me Softly with His Song* Songwriters: Norman Gimbel and Charles Fox

Year	Record of the year	Album of the year	Song of the year
1974	*I Honestly Love You* Olivia Newton-John	*Fulfillingness' First Finale* Stevie Wonder	*The Way We Were* Songwriters: Marylyn and Alan Bergman, Marvin Hamlisch
1975	*Love Will Keep Us Together* Captain & Tennille	*Still Crazy After All* *These Years* Paul Simon	*Send in the Clowns* Songwriter: Stephen Sondheim
1976	*This Masquerade* George Benson	*Songs in the Key of Life* Stevie Wonder	*I Write the Songs* Songwriter: Bruce Johnston
1977	*Hotel California* Eagles	*Rumours* Fleetwood Mac	*Love Theme from* *A Star Is Born (Evergreen)* * Songwriters: Barbra Streisand and Paul Williams *You Light Up My Life* * Songwriter: Joe Brooks
1978	*Just the Way You Are* Billy Joel	*Saturday Night Fever* Various artists	*Just the Way You Are* Songwriter: Billy Joel
1979	*What a Fool Believes* The Doobie Brothers	*52nd Street* Billy Joel	*What a Fool Believes* Songwriters: Kenny Loggins and Michael McDonald
1980	*Sailing* Christopher Cross	*Christopher Cross* Christopher Cross	*Sailing* Songwriter: Christopher Cross
1981	*Bette Davis Eyes* Kim Carnes	*Double Fantasy* John Lennon/Yoko Ono	*Bette Davis Eyes* Songwriters: Donna Weiss and Jackie DeShannon
1982	*Rosanna* Toto	*Toto IV* Toto	*Always on My Mind* Songwriters: Johnny Christopher, Mark James, and Wayne Carson
1983	*Beat It* Michael Jackson	*Thriller* Michael Jackson	*Every Breath You Take* Songwriter: Sting
1984	*What's Love Got to Do with It* Tina Turner	*Can't Slow Down* Lionel Richie	*What's Love Got to Do with It* Songwriters: Graham Lyle and Terry Britten
1985	*We Are the World* USA for Africa	*No Jacket Required* Phil Collins	*We Are the World* Songwriters: Michael Jackson and Lionel Richie
1986	*Higher Love* Steve Winwood	*Graceland* Paul Simon	*That's What Friends Are For* Songwriters: Burt Bacharach and Carole Bayer Sager
1987	*Graceland* Paul Simon	*Joshua Tree* U2	*Somewhere Out There* Songwriters: James Horner, Barry Mann, Cynthia Weil

*Tie

Year	Record of the year	Album of the year	Song of the year
1988	*Don't Worry Be Happy* Bobby McFerrin	*Faith* George Michael	*Don't Worry Be Happy* Songwriter: Bobby McFerrin
1989	*Wind Beneath My Wings* Bette Midler	*Nick of Time* Bonnie Raitt	*Wind Beneath My Wings* Songwriters: Larry Henley and Jeff Silbar
1990	*Another Day in Paradise* Phil Collins	*Back on the Block* Quincy Jones	*From a Distance* Songwriter: Julie Gold
1991	*Unforgettable* Natalie Cole (with Nat King Cole)	*Unforgettable* Natalie Cole	*Unforgettable* Songwriter: Irving Gordon
1992	*Tears in Heaven* Eric Clapton	*Unplugged* Eric Clapton	*Tears in Heaven* Songwriters: Eric Clapton and Will Jennings
1993	*I Will Always Love You* Whitney Houston	*The Bodyguard - Original Soundtrack Album* Various artists	*A Whole New World (Aladdin's Theme)* Songwriters: Alan Menken and Tim Rice
1994	*All I Wanna Do* Sheryl Crow	*MTV Unplugged: Tony Bennett* Tony Bennett	*Streets of Philadelphia* Songwriter: Bruce Springsteen
1995	*Kiss from a Rose* Seal	*Jagged Little Pill* Alanis Morissette	*Kiss from a Rose* Songwriter: Seal
1996	*Change the World* Eric Clapton	*Falling Into You* Celine Dion	*Change the World* Songwriters: Gordon Kennedy, Wayne Kirkpatrick, and Tommy Sims
1997	*Sunny Came Home* Shawn Colvin	*Time Out of Mind* Bob Dylan	*Sunny Came Home* Songwriters: Shawn Colvin and John Leventhal

Source: National Academy of Recording Arts and Sciences

Tony Award Winners

Year	Best Play	Best Musical
1949	Death of a Salesman	Kiss Me Kate
1950	The Cocktail Party	South Pacific
1951	The Rose Tattoo	Guys and Dolls
1952	The Fourposter	The King & I
1953	The Crucible	Wonderful Town
1954	The Teahouse of the August Moon	Kismet
1955	The Desperate Hours	The Pajama Game
1956	The Diary of Ann Frank	Damn Yankees
1957	Long Day's Journey Into Night	My Fair Lady
1958	Sunrise at Campobello	The Music Man
1959	J.B.	Redhead
1960	The Miracle Worker	The Sound of Music; Fiorello!
1961	Becket	Bye, Bye Birdie
1962	A Man for All Seasons	How to Succeed in Business Without Really Trying
1963	Who's Afraid of Virginia Woolf?	A Funny Thing Happened on the Way to the Forum
1964	Luther	Hello, Dolly!
1965	The Subject Was Roses	Fiddler on the Roof
1966	Marat/Sade	Man of La Mancha
1967	The Homecoming	Cabaret
1968	Rosencrantz and Guildenstern Are Dead	Hallelujah, Baby!
1969	The Great White Hope	1776
1970	Borstal Boy	Applause
1971	Sleuth	Company
1972	Sticks and Bones	Two Gentlemen of Verona
1973	That Championship Season	A Little Night Music
1974	The River Niger	Raisin
1975	Equus	The Wiz
1976	Travesties	A Chorus Line
1977	The Shadow Box	Annie
1978	Da	Ain't Misbehavin'
1979	The Elephant Man	Sweeney Todd
1980	Children of a Lesser God	Evita
1981	Amadeus	42nd Street
1982	The Life and Adventures of Nicholas Nickleby	Nine
1983	Torch Song Trilogy	Cats
1984	The Real Thing	La Cage aux Folles
1985	Biloxi Blues	Big River
1986	I'm Not Rappaport	The Mystery of Edwin Drood
1987	Fences	Les Miserables
1988	M. Butterfly	The Phantom of the Opera
1989	The Heidi Chronicles	Jerome Robbins' Broadway
1990	The Grapes of Wrath	City of Angels
1991	Lost in Yonkers	The Will Rogers Follies
1992	Dancing at Lughnasa	Crazy for You
1993	Angels in America: Millennium Approaches	Kiss of the Spider Woman
1994	Angels in America: Perestroika	Passion
1995	Love! Valour! Compassion!	Sunset Boulevard
1996	Master Class	Rent
1997	The Last Night of Ballyhoo	Titanic
1998	Art	The Lion King

Sources: The League of American Theatres and Producers and the American Theatre Wing

1998 National Magazine Awards

(Sponsored by the American Society of Magazine Editors and administered by the Graduate School of Journalism, Columbia University)

PUBLIC INTEREST
The Atlantic Monthly

SPECIAL INTERESTS
Entertainment Weekly

FEATURE WRITING
Harper's Magazine

REPORTING
Rolling Stone

GENERAL EXCELLENCE IN NEW MEDIA
The Sporting News Online

ESSAYS & CRITICISM
The New Yorker

PERSONAL SERVICE
Men's Journal

PHOTOGRAPHY
W

DESIGN
Entertainment Weekly

FICTION
The New Yorker

SINGLE TOPIC ISSUE
The Sciences

GENERAL EXCELLENCE
(under 100,000 circulation)
DoubleTake

GENERAL EXCELLENCE
(100,000 to 400,000 circulation)
Preservation

GENERAL EXCELLENCE
(400,000 to 100,000,000 circulation)
Outside

GENERAL EXCELLENCE
(over 1,000,000 circulation)
Rolling Stone

National Book Award Winners

Year	Fiction	Nonfiction
1984	Ellen Gilchrist, *Victory Over Japan: A Book of Stories*	Robert V. Remini, *Andrew Jackson & the Course of American Democracy, 1833–1845*
1985	Don DeLillo, *White Noise*	J. Anthony Lukas, *Common Ground: A Turbulent Decade in the Lives of Three American Families*
1986	E.L. Doctorow, *World's Fair*	Barry Lopez, *Arctic Dreams*
1987	Larry Heinemann, *Paco's Story*	Richard Rhodes, *The Making of the Atom Bomb*
1988	Pete Dexter, *Paris Trout*	Neil Sheehan, *A Bright Shining Lie: John Paul Vann and America in Vietnam*
1989	John Casey, *Spartina*	Thomas L. Friedman, *From Beruit to Jerusalem*
1990	Charles Johnson, *Middle Passage*	Ron Chernow, *The House of Morgan: An American Banking Dynasty and the Rise of Modern Finance*

Year	Fiction	Nonfiction	Poetry
1991	Norman Rush, *Mating*	Orlando Patterson, *Freedom*	Philip Levin, *What Work Is*
1992	Cormac McCarthy, *All the Pretty Horses*	Paul Monette, *Becoming a Man: Half a Life Story*	Mary Oliver, *New & Selected Poems*
1993	E. Annie Proulx, *The Shipping News*	Gore Vidal, *United States: Essays 1952–1992*	A.R. Ammons, *Garbage*
1994	William Gaddis, *A Frolic of His Own*	Sherwin B. Nuland, *How We Die: Reflections on Life's Final Chapter*	James Tate, *A Worshipful Company of Fletchers*
1995	Philip Roth, *Sabbath's Theater*	Tina Rosenberg, *The Haunted Land: Facing Europe's Ghosts After Communism*	Stanley Kunitz, *Passing Through: The Later Poems, New & Selected*
1996	Andrea Barrett, *Ship Fever and Other Stories*	James Carroll, *An American Requiem: God, My Father, and the War that Came Between Us*	Hayden Carruth, *Scrambled Eggs and Whiskey, Poems 1991–1995*
1997	Charles Frazier, *Cold Mountain*	Joseph J. Ellis, *American Sphinx: The Character of Thomas Jefferson*	William Meredith, *Effort at Speech: New & Selected Poems*

Source: National Book Foundation

The National Book Critics Circle Awards

1976

FICTION: John Gardner, *October Light*
GENERAL NONFICTION: Maxine Hong Kingston, *The Woman Warrior: Memoirs of a Girlhood Among Ghosts*
POETRY: Elizabeth Bishop, *Geography III*
CRITICISM: Bruno Bettelheim, *The Uses of Enchantment: The Meaning and Importance of Fairy Tales*

1977

FICTION: Toni Morrison, *Song of Solomon*
GENERAL NONFICTION: Walter Jackson Bate, *Samuel Johnson*
POETRY: Robert Lowell, *Day by Day*
CRITICISM: Susan Sontag, *On Photography*

1978

FICTION: John Cheever, *The Stories of John Cheever*
GENERAL NONFICTION: Maureen Howard, *Facts of Life*
POETRY: (Edited by Peter Davison), *Hello, Darkness: The Collected Poems of L.E. Sissman*
CRITICISM: Meyer Schapiro, *Modern Art: 19th & 20th Centuries, Selected Papers*

1979

FICTION: Thomas Flanagan, *The Year of the French*
GENERAL NONFICTION: Telford Taylor, *Munich: The Price of Peace*
POETRY: Philip Levine, *Ashes* and *7 Years from Somewhere*
CRITICISM: Elaine Pagels, *The Gnostic Gospels*
IVAN SANDROF/BOARD AWARD: Flannery O'Connor

1980

FICTION: Shirley Hazzard, *The Transit of Venus*
GENERAL NONFICTION: Ronald Steel, *Walter Lippmann and the American Century*
POETRY: Frederick Seidel, *Sunrise*
CRITICISM: Helen Vendler, *Part of Nature, Part of Us: Modern American Poets*

1981

FICTION: John Updike, *Rabbit is Rich*
GENERAL NONFICTION: Stephen Jay Gould, *The Mismeasure of Man*
POETRY: A.R. Ammons, *A Coast of Trees*
CRITICISM: Virgil Thomson, *A Virgil Thomson Reader*

1982

FICTION: Stanley Elkin, *George Mills*
GENERAL NONFICTION: Robert A. Caro, *The Path of Power: The Years of Lyndon Johnson*
POETRY: Katha Pollitt, *Antarctic Traveler*
CRITICISM: Gore Vidal, *The Second American Revolution and Other Essays, 1976–82*
IVAN SANDROF/BOARD AWARD: Leslie A. Marchand

1983

FICTION: William Kennedy, *Ironweed*
GENERAL NONFICTION: Seymour M. Hersh, *The Price of Power: Kissinger in the Nixon White House*
BIOGRAPHY/AUTOBIOGRAPHY: Joyce Johnson, *Minor Characters*
POETRY: James Merrill, *The Changing Light at Sandover*

CRITICISM: John Updike, *Hugging the Shore: Essays and Criticism*

1984

FICTION: Louise Erdrich, *Love Medicine*
GENERAL NONFICTION: Freeman Dyson, *Weapons and Hope*
BIOGRAPHY/AUTOBIOGRAPHY: Joseph Frank, *Dostoevsky: The Years of Ordeal, 1850–1859*
POETRY: Sharon Olds, *The Dead and the Living*
CRITICISM: Robert Hass, *Twentieth Century Pleasures: Prose on Poetry*
IVAN SANDROF/BOARD AWARD: The Library of America

1985

FICTION: Anne Tyler, *The Accidental Tourist*
GENERAL NONFICTION: J. Anthony Lukas, *Common Ground: A Turbulent Decade in the Lives of Three American Families*
BIOGRAPHY/AUTOBIOGRAPHY: Leon Edel, *Henry James: A Life*
POETRY: Louise Gluck, *The Triumph of Achilles*
CRITICISM: William H. Gass, *Habitations of the Word: Essays*

1986

FICTION: Reynolds Price, *Kate Vaiden*
GENERAL NONFICTION: John W. Dower, *War Without Mercy: Race and Power in the Pacific War*
BIOGRAPHY/AUTOBIOGRAPHY: Theodore Rosengarten, *Tombee: Portrait of a Cotton Planter*
POETRY: Edward Hirsch, *Wild Gratitude*
CRITICISM: Joseph Brodsky, *Less Than One: Selected Essays*

1987

FICTION: Philip Roth, *The Counterlife*
GENERAL NONFICTION: Richard Rhodes, *The Making of the Atomic Bomb*
BIOGRAPHY/AUTOBIOGRAPHY: Donald R. Howard, *Chaucer: His Life, His Works, His World*
POETRY: C.K. Williams, *Flesh and Blood*
CRITICISM: Edwin Denby, (Edited by Robert Cornfield and William MacKay), *Dance Writings*
IVAN SANDROF/BOARD AWARD: Robert Giroux

1988

FICTION: Bharati Mukherjee, *The Middleman and Other Stories*
GENERAL NONFICTION: Taylor Branch, *Parting the Waters: America in the King Years, 1954–63*
BIOGRAPHY/AUTOBIOGRAPHY: Richard Ellman, *Oscar Wilde*
POETRY: Donald Hall, *The One Day*
CRITICISM: Clifford Geertz, *Works and Lives: The Anthropologist as Author*

1989

FICTION: E. L. Doctorow, *Billy Bathgate*
GENERAL NONFICTION: Michael Dorris, *The Broken Cord*
BIOGRAPHY/AUTOBIOGRAPHY: Geoffrey C. Ward, *A First-Class Temperament: The Emergence of Franklin Roosevelt*
POETRY: Rodney Jones, *Transparent Gestures*
CRITICISM: John Clive, *Not by Fact Alone: Essays on the Writing and Reading of History*
IVAN SANDROF/BOARD AWARD: James Laughlin

1990

FICTION: John Updike, *Rabbit at Rest*
GENERAL NONFICTION: Shelby Steele, *The Content of Our Character: A New Vision of Race in America*
BIOGRAPHY/AUTOBIOGRAPHY: Robert A. Caro, *Means of Ascent: The Years of Lyndon Johnson, Vol. II*
POETRY: Amy Gerstler, *Bitter Angel*
CRITICISM: Arthur C. Danto, *Encounters and Reflections: Art in the Historical Present*
IVAN SANDROF/BOARD AWARD: Donald Keene

1991

FICTION: Jane Smiley, *A Thousand Acres*
GENERAL NONFICTION: Susan Faludi, *Backlash: The Undeclared War Against American Women*
BIOGRAPHY/AUTOBIOGRAPHY: Philip Roth, *Patrimony: A True Story*
POETRY: Albert Goldbarth, *Heaven and Earth: A Cosmology*
CRITICISM: Lawrence L. Langer, *Holocaust Testimonies: The Ruins of Memory*
NONA BALAKIAN EXCELLENCE IN REVIEWING AWARD: George Scialabba

1992

FICTION: Cormac McCarthy, *All the Pretty Horses*
GENERAL NONFICTION: Norman Maclean, *Young Men and Fire*
BIOGRAPHY/AUTOBIOGRAPHY: Carol Brightman, *Writing Dangerously: Mary McCarthy and Her World*
POETRY: Hayden Carruth, *Collected Shorter Poems 1946–1991*
CRITICISM: Garry Wills, *Lincoln at Gettysburg: The Words That Remade America*
IVAN SANDROF/BOARD AWARD: Gregory Rabassa
NONA BALAKIAN EXCELLENCE IN REVIEWING AWARD: Elizabeth Ward

1993

FICTION: Ernest J. Gaines, *A Lesson Before Dying*
GENERAL NONFICTION: Alan Lomax, *The Land Where the Blues Began*
BIOGRAPHY/AUTOBIOGRAPHY: Edmund White, *Genet*
POETRY: Mark Doty, *My Alexandria*
CRITICISM: John Dizikes, *Opera in America: A Cultural History*
NONA BALAKIAN EXCELLENCE IN REVIEWING AWARD: Brigitte Frase

1994

FICTION: Carol Shields, *The Stone Diaries*
GENERAL NONFICTION: Lynn H. Nicholas, *The Rape of*

Europa: The Fate of Europe's Treasures in the Third Reich and the Second World War

BIOGRAPHY/AUTOBIOGRAPHY: Mikal Gilmore, *Shot in the Heart*

POETRY: Mark Rudman, *Rider*

CRITICISM: Gerald Early, *The Culture of Bruising: Essays on Prizefighting, Literature and Modern American Culture*

NONA BALAKIAN EXCELLENCE IN REVIEWING AWARD: JoAnn C. Gutin, Berkeley, CA

IVAN SANDROF AWARD FOR LIFETIME ACHIEVEMENT IN PUBLISHING: William Maxwell

1995

FICTION: Stanley Elkin, *Mrs. Ted Bliss*

GENERAL NONFICTION: Jonathan Harr, *A Civil Action*

BIOGRAPHY/AUTOBIOGRAPHY: Robert Polito, *Savage Art: A Biography of Jim Thompson*

POETRY: William Matthews, *Time & Money*

CRITICISM: Robert Darnton, *The Forbidden Bestsellers of Pre-Revolutionary France*

1996

FICTION: Gina Berriault, *Women in Their Beds*

GENERAL NONFICTION: Jonathan Raban, *Bad Land*

BIOGRAPHY/AUTOBIOGRAPHY: Frank McCourt, *Angela's Ashes*

POETRY: Robert Hass, *Sun Under Wood*

CRITICISM: William Gass, *Finding a Form*

1997

FICTION: Penelope Fitzgerald, *The Blue Flower*

GENERAL NONFICTION: Anne Fadiman, *The Spirit Catches You and You Fall Down*

BIOGRAPHY/AUTOBIOGRAPHY: James Tobin, *Ernie Pyle's War: America's Eyewitness to World War II*

POETRY: Charles Wright, *Black Zodiac*

CRITICISM: Mario Vargas Llosa, *Making Waves*

Source: The National Book Critics Circle Journal

Booker Prize Winners

1969: P.H. Newby, *Something to Answer For*
1970: Bernice Rubens, *The Elected Member*
1971: V.S. Naipaul, *In a Free State*
1972: John Berger, *G*
1973: J.G. Farrell, *The Seige of Krishnapur*
1974: *Nadine Gordimer, *The Conservationist*
　　　Stanley Middleton, *Holiday*
1975: Ruth Prawer Jhabvala, *Heat and Dust*
1976: David Storey, *Saville*
1977: Paul Scott, *Staying On*
1978: Irish Murdoch, *The Sea, The Sea*
1979: Penelope Fitzgerald, *Offshore*
1980: William Golding, *Rites of Passage*
1981: Salman Rushdie, *Midnight's Children*
1982: Thomas Keneally, *Schindler's Ark*
1983: J.M. Coetzee, *Life & Times of Michael K*
1984: Anita Brookner, *Hotel du Lac*

1985: Keri Hulme, *The Bone People*
1986: Kingsley Amis, *The Old Devils*
1987: Penelope Lively, *Moon Tiger*
1988: Peter Carey, *Oscar and Lucinda*
1989: Kazuo Ishiguro, *The Remains of the Day*
1990: A.S. Byatt, *Possession*
1991: Ben Okri, *The Famished Road*
1992:* Michael Ondaatje, *The English Patient*
　　　Barry Unsworth, *Sacred Hunger*
1993: Roddy Doyle, *Paddy Clarke Ha Ha Ha*
1994: James Kelman, *How Late it Was, How Late*
1995: Pat Barker, *The Ghost Road*
1996: Graham Swift, *The Last Orders*
1997: Arundhati Roy, *The God of Small Things*

―――――
*Joint winners.

10

SPORTS

Mark McGwire. Sammy Sosa.

In 1998, two athletes helped fans forget that the sports business was business first, sports second. As they shattered the most revered record in any game, few seemed to care how much Mr. Sosa was earning (for the record, $8 million, tied for No. 8 in the major leagues) or even that Mr. McGwire ($8.3 million, No. 5) was swallowing a steroid supplement known as androstenedione. Fans who caught the historic balls were returning them to the players for nothing more than an autographed bat, a jersey and some tickets, passing up thousands of dollars from memorabilia dealers. For once, the playing was the thing.

Mr. McGwire wound up with 70 homers to Mr. Sosa's 66—far more than the fallen record of 61 by Roger Maris in 1961. But even if fans were momentarily distracted, the rest of the industry took its cue from the sluggers. More, more, more was the slogan for the sports business in 1998. More home runs. More media attention. More money. Television contracts hit 11 digits. A football team went for $530 million. When that seemed like a lot, along came the sale of a British soccer team for a cool $1 billion.

It was all about TV programming. Don't tell Messrs. McGwire and Sosa, but they demonstrated the growing nexus of sports on television. Networks need to fill time. Sports draw an in-demand male audience. In the fragmented TV worlds, ratings for sports have been dropping—only baseball, thanks to you know who, posted increases in 1998—but the price keeps going up. The National Basketball Association wrangled a new deal worth $2.6 billion over four years. The struggling National Hockey League commanded $600 million over five years. And the National Football League staged a frantic bidding war that alienated plenty of network executives, but in the end produced an eight-year, $17.6 billion contract with Walt Disney Co.'s ABC and ESPN, News Corp.'s Fox Sports and, after a four-year absence, CBS Inc.

League broadcast rights were only part of it. Rather than pay up to show local teams, companies are figuring out that it might be cheaper just to buy them. (Or start their own league. After losing out in the NFL bidding, Time Warner Inc.'s Turner Sports and General Electric Co.'s NBC announced plans to form a rival league.) Indeed, by the end of 1998, nearly 60 publicly traded U.S. companies had ownership interest in U.S. sports teams, two-thirds of them with media as their primary or secondary businesses. News Corp.'s $311 million acquisition of the Dodgers in 1998 was the most prominent media-company deal, but there were others below the radar. Gaylord Entertainment Co., for instance, grabbed a piece of the Nashville Predators, an NHL expansion franchise. "The teams and the entertainment companies are realizing that if they don't pick their teams now they may be left out later on," says Paul Much, a sports investment banker with Houlihan Lokey Howard & Zukin in Chicago.

One deal that wasn't consummated but which began looking likely: the sale of the New York Yankees to Cablevision Systems Corp., the Long Island-based cable operator run by cable mogul Charles Dolan. Like News Corp.'s acquisition of the Dodgers, the sale of the hallowed Yankees is predicated on two factors: estate taxes and programming, not necessarily in that order. The Yankees' principal owner, George Steinbrenner, who bought the team in 1973 for $10 million, turned 68 years old. If his son Hal and his son-in-law Steve Swindal want to run the team, they will face gargantuan estate taxes. And no one around the team thought they had the same desire to be the boss as The Boss.

Enter Cablevision. The company's broadcast rights to the Yankees, for which it paid $486 million for 12 years—the deal was mocked at the time—expire in 2000. So what would they be worth now for another dozen seasons? $700 million? $1 billion? Rather than fork that over, Cablevision, which already owns stakes in basketball's New York Knicks and hockey's New York Rangers, would be wise to just buy the franchise. And a billion for the Yankees didn't seem far-fetched, especially if Mr. Steinbrenner was able to coax a new Manhattan stadium from city officials.

But until that time, the king of sports remained Rupert Murdoch. After Fox snagged the Dodgers, Mr. Murdoch's Sky Broadcasting PLC, a satellite television company, bought Britain's Manchester United soccer team for $1 billion. The price represented a 50% premium over the team's stock market value, but so what? Harvey Schiller, president of Time Warner Inc.'s Turner Sports, figured that if 50 million Europeans were willing to pay $1 a month for Manchester United games, "that's $600 million a year, and you haven't sold a ticket or a T-shirt yet," he told *Barrons* magazine. Nor have you capitalized on soccer's global popularity—the goal of any sports franchise owner in a world where Japanese pitchers strike out Dominican hitters and French children play soccer in Michael Jordan T-shirts.

Still, reports of the death of individual rich guys with fat wallets were greatly exaggerated. The NFL remained the holdout to allowing corporations to own teams, so the bidding for the Cleveland Browns expansion franchise (replacing the team spirited away to Baltimore by Art Modell) was a battle of fat cats. The winner was Al Lerner, who made his riches—

Most Valuable Players

Sports stars with the largest estimated income from endorsements, from June 1998 to May 1999.

1	Michael Jordan	$42 million
2	Tiger Woods	30 million
3	Shaquille O'Neal	28 million
4	Arnold Palmer	23 million
5	Jack Nicklaus	19 million
6	Grant Hill	15 million
7	Cal Ripken Jr.	9.75 million
8	Dale Earnhardt	8.5 million
9	Ken Griffey Jr.	6.5 million
10	Jeff Gordon	5.5 million

Source: Sports Marketing Letter, Southport, CT

he has an estimated net worth of $2.5 billion—as chairman of MBNA Credit Corp., the giant credit-card company. Mr. Lerner agreed to pay $530 million. Compare that to the $140 million paid for the last two NFL expansion franchises, Carolina and Jacksonville, in 1993. "It's an outstanding deal, both for the owner and the city of Cleveland," Dallas Cowboys owner Jerry Jones says. Not to mention the NFL's 30 other owners, who share the expansion fee.

Still, franchises that aren't attractive to a tentacled media company or a wealthy individual—and there will be plenty—will need to find alternative buyers in the coming years. Major League Baseball in 1998 recognized that not every one of its 30 clubs is in the same class as the Yankees and Dodgers. So the lords of baseball for the first time allowed owners to go public. The Cleveland Indians were the first to take advantage—if that's the right word. The Indians, put on the market by an owner, real-estate mogul Richard Jacobs, concerned about his own estate taxes, debuted at $15 a share, which valued the team at around $224 million. By the time one of baseball's most successful and profitable franchises had qualified yet again for the playoffs, its stock was looking like a washed-up pitcher: At around $6 a share, the Indians suddenly were valued at $90 million.

"Sports teams as pure plays continue to be poor investment vehicles," Mr. Much says. "The way value is being captured is through a strategic alliance. More and more owners are realizing that."

Take Me Out to the Ball Game

The cost of attending professional sporting events has been outpacing the national inflation rate in recent years.

Professional sports league average ticket prices and Fan Cost Index*

MLB Season	Average ticket price	Ticket % change	FCI	FCI % change
1991	$ 8.64	–	$ 77.40	–
1992	9.30	7.6%	86.24	11.4%
1993	9.60	3.2	90.84	5.3
1994	10.45	8.9	95.80	5.5
1995	10.55	1.0	96.83	1.1
1996	11.19	6.1	102.58	5.9
1997	12.36	10.5	107.13	4.4
1998	13.60	10.0	114.82	7.2

NFL Season	Average ticket price	Ticket % change	FCI	FCI % change
1991	$25.21	–	$151.55	–
1992	27.19	7.8%	163.19	7.6%
1993	28.68	5.5	173.33	6.2
1994	30.56	6.6	182.72	5.4
1995	33.52	9.7	199.09	9.0
1996	35.58	6.1	207.80	4.4
1997	38.09	7.1	221.17	6.4

NHL Season‡	Average ticket price	Ticket % change	FCI	FCI % change
1994-95	$32.75	–	$193.10	–
1995-96	34.75	6.1%	203.46	5.4%
1996-97	38.34	10.3	220.72	8.5
1997-98	40.64	6.0	228.39	3.5

NBA Season	Average ticket price	Ticket % change	FCI	FCI % change
1991-92	$23.24	–	$144.10	–
1992-93	25.16	8.3%	158.17	9.8%
1993-94	27.12	7.8	168.68	6.6
1994-95	28.63	5.6	177.12	5.0
1995-96	31.56	10.2	191.31	8.0
1996-97	33.77	7.0	202.14	5.7
1997-98	36.32	7.6	214.28	6.0

*The Fan Cost Index (FCI) includes the cost of four average-price tickets, four small soft drinks, two small beers, four hot dogs, parking for one car, two game programs and two souvenir caps.
‡No NHL surveys were conducted prior to 1994-95.
Source: Team Marketing Report, Chicago

But the era of complex franchise ownership structures and growing league revenues was complicating sports at the same time it was aiding it. Take the NBA lockout. The worst labor crisis in the league's 52 years erupted after (but not because) the Chicago Bulls in June won their sixth championship. At its core: a dispute over how to divvy up the NBA's spoils. Under the collective-bargaining agreement, the players were entitled to nearly half of what's known as "basketball-related income," which included a portion of luxury-box income, in-stadium signs (though not income from arena naming rights) and the sale of seat licenses. But in the 1997-98 season, the league spent around 57 percent of that money on salaries. Too much, said the owners, who exercised an option to renegotiate the labor deal. When talks failed, the owners locked out the players.

The gambit was due to owners' paying ever-increasing sums—around $1 billion in the NBA—to players. The league said it was losing money, a notion disputed by the players union, which maintained the league wasn't sharing all its revenue. (The league denied the charge.) And franchises that own their own arenas and TV stations, for instance, can shield income in other ways. As sports become more global, Smith College sports economist Andrew Zimbalist notes, defining whether new sources of income are directly related to the games played is as complicated as an NBA offense.

The NBA's woes were among the cautionary flags in the sports industry. Even before the lockout, sneaker and apparel companies were reporting slumping sales as fashion trends moved away from high-top basketball sneakers and team-themed merchandise. Nike Inc., for one, laid off 1,600 employees, reported its first quarterly loss in 13 years and even announced it was de-emphasizing its ubiquitous swoosh logo.

On televison, the new NFL broadcasters had difficulty selling all their ad time at inflated rates, and ratings at the start of the 1998 season were down. Despite baseball's thrilling story line, fans displayed disgust with poor teams in small markets that lacked the money to compete on the field. More than half of the sport's teams (excluding the two first-year expansion franchises) reported attendance drops. And in Minneapolis and Montreal, legislators and fans nixed proposed new stadiums.

In Los Angeles, some fans expressed their opinion of Fox's takeover from the O'Malley family. Fox pledged not to tamper with the baseball operation, but that lasted as long as Mr. Steinbrenner's promise not to meddle when he bought his team 25 years earlier. Fox executives traded beloved catcher Mike Piazza (a free-agent-to-be who was demanding $100 million) and fired the team's manager and general manager. "Thanks Fox," one fan wrote to the *Los Angeles Times* in June. "In two and a half months you have managed to destroy what was one of the last classy organizations in sports."

In 1998, the home-run derby helped obscure deeper fault lines that bedevil baseball, as well as other sports. But media moguls and other sports titans might do well to beware. They can't count on once-in-a-lifetime athletic achievements to carry the business. They need, well, more, more, more.

**Stefan Fatsis,
a sports reporter for
*The Wall Street Journal***

TOP SPORTS PERSONALITIES OF 1998

John Elway. John Elway won the Super Bowl. Say it again! John Elway and the Denver Broncos finally, *finally* won the Super Bowl. Playing behind what was surely the best of the four teams he had quarterbacked to the National Football League's title game, Mr. Elway completed just 12 of 22 passes, but he unquestionably led the Broncos to a 31–24 win over the defending champion Green Bay Packers in Super Bowl XXXII on January 25. One play in the third quarter told the entire tale of Mr. Elway's 14-year, career-long desire, need, *want* for a Super Bowl ring. At third and six at the Packers' 12, Mr. Elway scrambled, then helicoptered through the air over a tackler to secure a much-needed first down. A TV closeup caught all the intensity in Mr. Elway's eyes. With the trophy finally in Mr. Elway's grasp, he smiled that trademark toothy grin. The rest of the country, it seemed, smiled with him.

Dominik Hasek. "The Terminator" from the Czech Republic led his country to its first-ever gold medal in Olympic Ice Hockey with a 1–0 victory over, poetically, Russia, a team the old Czechoslovakia had lost to countless times when Russia was known as the Soviet Union. The Nagano, Japan, Olympics featured for the first time U.S. National Hockey League players on six "Dream Team" sides. The United States lost early, and Canada failed to take home a medal. But the Czech Republic, with the indomitable Hasek in goal, was simply not to be denied its moment of destiny.

Michael Jordan. Again. You know this story, if not the particulars, then at least the general theme. It's Michael Jordan and the rest of the Chicago Bulls in the National Basketball Association finals against somebody, and "Air" does something and the Bulls win, again. In 1998 the Bulls played the Utah Jazz for the second year in a row. It's in game six, in Salt Lake City, with the Bulls down one with 18 seconds to go. Chicago needs a basket. Guess who? Jordan at the top of the key. He fakes Howard Eisley of the Jazz nearly into the Great Salt Lake and launches an 18-footer with 5.2 seconds left. It is good, of course, and Chicago wins, 87–86, for its sixth title in eight years. All season, speculation had run wild that this was Jordan's last time around the league. Who knew for sure? But after netting the game winner, Mr. Jordan stood in place, arm extended above his head in follow-through for a long second. And it looked for all the world like a final curtain call, a sweet good-bye from the best player on the planet.

Hermann Maier. His was, perhaps the signature moment of the 1998 Winter Olympics in Nagano, Japan. Attempting to negotiate a left turn in the men's downhill ski race at about 70 miles an hour, Mr. Maier took off into the air like a crippled jet off an aircraft carrier. He crashed to earth some 80 feet later in a bouncing, tumbling, cartwheeling jumble of legs and arms and skis, finally coming to a stop in a snow bank after breaking through two retaining fences. And it was all captured live on TV. But incredibly, he was unhurt. He roused himself, stood up and waved at the camera. A few days later he took to the mountain again, winning the super giant slalom on much the same course.

Nikki McCray. The 1997–98 Most Valuable Player of the little-known and unheralded American Basketball League jumped to the Women's National Basketball Association, the circuit bankrolled by the men's NBA. But give her credit for honesty. It is generally conceded that the ABL has the better players farther down the bench than the WNBA, which relies on the star power of a few big names. But despite playing the better brand of basketball, the ABL is hard pressed to compete with the marketing muscle of the WNBA. An athlete's life is short-lived, and Ms. McCray admitted as much when she said she moved into the WNBA camp and the Washington Mystics looking to score some marketing dollars while she still had the legs.

Mark McGwire and Sammy Sosa. In the greatest home-run race in major-league history, Mark McGwire of the St. Louis Cardinals and Sammy Sosa of the Chicago Cubs entered the final weekend of the season tied for the four-sack lead with an improbable 65 each. It was only fitting. Their exploits over the summer had long since inextricably bound them together forever. McGwire had entered the campaign as America's designated New Babe Ruth, surely destined in this expansion year to break Roger Maris's record of 61 in 1961. And he didn't disappoint, turning the summer into the Mark McGwire Home Runs Across America Tour. It was Slammin' Sammy Sosa who was the unexpected delight. With 20 homers in June, he injected himself four-square into the homer race, and he never faded, though everyone fully expected that he would. The two made for a wonderful Only-in-America pairing: McGwire the blue-eyed Paul Bunyan, Sosa the dark-skinned Dominican from a Caribbean island overflowing with baseball players. It was McGwire who surpassed Maris's mark first, on Sept. 8 in St. Louis against Sosa's Cubs. Sosa, who had perfected the role of gracious, self-deprecating second-banana, embraced his rival at home plate in what was perhaps the sports picture of the year. And then there was that final weekend. Sosa hit number 66, his last one, on Friday, September 25, to take the lead—for about 45 minutes. That's when McGwire started a five homer tear in 11 at bats in three games to end the season with a totally impossible 70 home runs. Ruth-Gehrig. Maris-Mantle. *McGwire-Sosa.* For baseball fans, it was the good old days all over again.

Jana Novotna. The Duchess of Kent was right, the third time *was* the charm. In 1993 against Steffi Graf in the Wimbledon final, Ms. Novotna blew a 4–1 lead in the third set and then cried unabashedly on the duchess's shoulder. In 1997, she reached the Wimbledon final and lost once more—leaving her with the double identity as the best player on the women's tour never to have won a major and, worse, a drop-dead choke artist. But in one of 1998's better feel-good sports stories, Ms. Novotna beat defending champion Martina Hingis in the Wimbledon semifinal and then dispatched Nathalie Tauziat in the final, (6–4, 7–6, 7–2). The duchess was there again, and this time the two shared a warm, happy embrace.

Mark O'Meara. Cue the music: "Fanfare for the Common Man." Mark O'Meara gave hope to all not-real-tall, not-real-thin, not-real-handsome male-golfers-who-are-going-a-little-bald when he won not one, but two of golf's majors—the Masters and the British Open. And he took both in much the same fashion: by simply refusing to go away. The Masters was Fred Couples's to win for the better part of four days and 70 of 72 holes. But O'Meara went birdie-birdie on the final two holes that ended with a 20-foot putt to snatch the green jacket for himself. At Royal Birkdale in

England, Mr. O'Meara got his hands around the Auld Claret Jug by staring down the resolve of an even "commoner" man, Bryan Watts, who plays most of his golf on the Japan Tour. The two needed the extra holes of a four-hole aggregate playoff, but in the end it was Mr. O'Meara, an unlikely looking candidate to be the year's best-looking golfer.

Se Ri Pak. Same story, next year. A young golfer with ties to Asia and an overbearing father turns the golfing establishment on its ear. In 1997, it was Tiger Woods on the men's side. In 1998, it was Se Ri Pak on the women's. But Ms. Pak was no Tiger Woods. She was better. Midway through the summer, the 20-year-old Pak had already won two majors, the McDonald's LPGA Championship and the U.S. Women's Open, and she backed up her win in the Open with a victory the very next week in the Jamie Farr Kroger Classic, where she crushed the course and the competition with an 18-under-par victory. Her Open win was doubly impressive for having weathered an 18-hole play-off followed by two sudden holes before besting Jenny Chuasiriporn, a 20-year-old Duke undergrad. Ms. Pak's idol is Nancy Lopez, who in 1978 blitzed the golf world with 11 victories, including five straight. She chooses her idols well.

Mike Piazza. The All-Star catcher became the poster boy of modern baseball when in the space of a week he was traded by the Los Angeles Dodgers to the Florida Marlins and by the Marlins to the New York Mets. The reason? Money. A free agent at the end of the current season, the hard-hitting Piazza turned down an $85 million multiyear contract with the Dodgers, asking instead for $100 million. Whereupon the Dodgers' new owners, the Fox division of Rupert Murdoch's News Corp., traded him to the Marlins with scant consultation with the Dodgers' "baseball" people. The Marlins, meanwhile, were more than happy to take him on because that meant they could unload four high-priced players who had helped the Marlins to the World Series title in 1997. Owner Wayne Hiuzenga no longer wanted them in his efforts to slash costs so he could sell the team. No one expected Mr. Piazza to stay very long with the Marlins, but one week? Once in New York, Mr. Piazza settled in well enough and had a particularly good September, but $100 million for his future services was starting to look a little steep. Chances were at least reasonable that by the start of the 1999 season, he would be in his fourth baseball uniform in 10 months.

Zinedine Zedane. Ronaldo who? The Frenchman from the tough streets of Marseille with the parents from Algeria played the game of his life in the match of his life to lead unheralded France to soccer's World Cup title with a 3–0 victory over vaunted Brazil. "Zuzou" used his head to score two explosive goals off corner kicks and stun the defending champions and Brazil's 21-year-old Ronaldo, acknowledged as the world's best player. The 26-year-old Zedane, with parents from Algeria, also symbolized the emergence of the "new" France: Six of his 10 teammates in the title game hailed from outside France's traditional European borders.

Gordy Sheer and Chris Thorpe, and Mark Grimmette and Brian Martin. They didn't exactly become household names for doing it, but these four U.S. Winter Olympians went where no other U.S. athletes had ever gone: to the medals stand of the luge competition. In almost storybook fashion, Grimmette and Martin slid down "The Spiral" at the Nagano, Japan, luge venue and into a certain medal. They were followed down the hill by Sheer and Thorpe, who slid right past them into second place. After having gone 0-for-the-Olympics, suddenly USA Luge found itself awash in medals. If only the luge wasn't taken so un-seriously by the United States, this quartet could legitimately be considered for a group award as the U.S. athletes of the year.

Steve McKee

Most Popular Sports Personalities

	Familiarity	Q score*
Michael Jordan	90%	61%
Harlem Globetrotters	87	54
Joe Montana	89	47
Jerry Rice	75	46
Cal Ripken Jr.	79	45
Tiger Woods	88	45
Nolan Ryan	79	45
Ken Griffey Jr.	79	45
Walter Payton	74	44
John Madden	78	44
Barry Sanders	75	42
Magic Johnson	90	41
Scott Hamilton	81	40
Wayne Gretzky	82	40
George Foreman	83	40

*Q score is based on the number of people who
are familiar with personality and rate
"One of My Favorites."
Source: Marketing Evaluations Inc.

10 Highest-Paid Athletes by Sport

National Football League (1998 season)
(Average over life of contract)

1. Steve Young, San Francisco 49ers, $8.2 million
2. Peyton Manning, Indianapolis Colts, $7.1 million
3. Andre Wadsworth, Arizona Cardinals, $7 million
4. Brett Favre, Green Bay Packers, $6.75 million
5. Sean Gilbert, Carolina Panthers, $6.7 million
6. John Randle, Minnesota Vikings, $6.5 million
7. Troy Aikman, Dallas Cowboys, $6.4 million
8. Ryan Leaf, San Diego Chargers, $6.25 million
9. Terrell Davis, Denver Broncos, $6.2 million
10. Rob Johnson, Buffalo Bills, $6.16 million

Major League Baseball (1998 season)

1. Albert Belle, Chicago White Sox, $10 million
   Gary Sheffield, Los Angeles Dodgers, $10 million
3. Greg Maddux, Atlanta Braves, $9.6 million
4. Barry Bonds, San Francisco Giants, $8.9 million
5. Mark McGwire, St. Louis Cardinals, $8.3 million
6. Roger Clemens, Toronto Blue Jays, $8.25 million
   Bernie Williams, New York Yankees, $8.25 million
8. Andres Galarraga, Atlanta Braves, $8 million
   Mike Piazza, New York Mets, $8 million
   Sammy Sosa, Chicago Cubs, $8 million

National Basketball Association
(1997–98 season)

1. Michael Jordan, Chicago Bulls, $33.1 million
2. Patrick Ewing, New York Knicks, $20.5 million
3. Horace Grant, Orlando Magic, $14.3 million
4. Shaquille O'Neal, Los Angeles Lakers, $12.9 million
5. David Robinson, San Antonio Spurs, $12.4 million
6. Alonzo Mourning, Miami Heat, $11.26 million
7. Juwan Howard, Washington Wizards, $11.25 million
8. Hakeem Olajuwon, Houston Rockets, $11.16 million
9. Gary Payton, Seattle Supersonics, $10.5 million
10. Dikembe Mutumbo, Atlanta Hawks, $9.6 million

National Hockey League (1998–99 season)

1. Sergei Fedorov, Detroit Red Wings, $14 million
2. Paul Kariya, Anaheim Mighty Ducks, $8.5 million
   Eric Lindros, Philadelphia Flyers, $8.5 million
4. Dominik Hasek, Buffalo Sabres, $8 million
5. Mats Sundin, Toronto Maple Leafs, $6.3 million
6. Peter Forsberg, Colorado Avalanche, $6 million
   Doug Gilmour, Chicago Blackhawks, $6 million
   Wayne Gretzky, New York Rangers, $6 million
   Mark Messier, Vancouver Canucks, $6 million
10. Curtis Joseph, Toronto Maple Leafs, $5.5 million

Average Major-League Player Salaries

Major League Baseball Salaries

Year	Minimum Salary	Average Salary
1980	$ 30,000	$ 143,756
1981	32,500	185,651
1982	33,500	241,497
1983	35,000	289,194
1984	40,000	329,408
1985	60,000	371,157
1986	60,000	412,520
1987	62,500	412,454
1988	62,500	438,729
1989	68,000	497,254
1990	100,000	597,537
1991	100,000	851,492
1992	109,000	1,028,667
1993	109,000	1,076,089
1994	109,000	1,168,263
1995	109,000	1,110,766
1996	109,000	1,119,981
1997	150,000	1,336,609

Source: Major League Baseball Players Association

National Hockey League Average Salaries

1970	$ 25,000
1975	74,000
1976	86,000
1977	96,000
1978	92,000
1979	101,000
1980	108,000
1981–82	120,000
1982–83	110,000*
1983–84	118,000*
1984–85	120,000*
1985–86	144,000
1986–87	158,000
1987–88	172,000
1988–89	188,000
1989–90	211,000
1990–91	271,000
1991–92	368,000
1992–93	467,000
1993–94	562,000
1994–95	733,000
1995–96	892,000
1996–97	984,500
1997–98	1,167,713

*These figures represent not the average salary, but the median salary.
Source: National Hockey League Players Association

National Football League Average Salaries (In thousands of dollars)

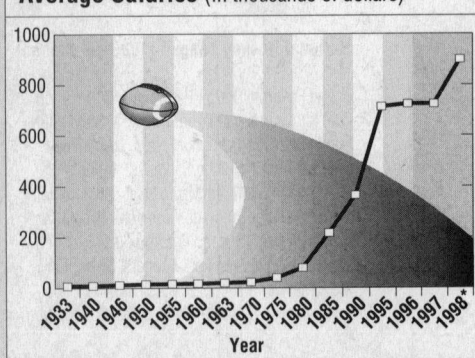

Year

*Estimated

Average Salary for NFL Quarterbacks

Year	Salary	Year	Salary
1990	$ 660,000	1994	$ 1,138,000
1991	803,000	1995	1,307,000
1992	911,000	1996	1,336,000
1993	1,523,000	1997	1,346,000

Source: NFL Players Association

NBA Average Salaries and Salary Caps

Season	Average salary (per player)	Salary cap (per team)
1976–77	$ 130,000	
1977–78	139,000	
1978–79	148,000	
1979–80	170,000	
1980–81	171,000	
1981–82	212,000	
1982–83	249,000	
1983–84	275,000	
1984–85	325,000	$ 3,600,000
1985–86	375,000	4,233,000
1986–87	440,000	4,945,000
1987–88	510,000	6,164,000
1988–89	600,000	7,232,000
1989–90	750,000	9,802,000
1990–91	900,000	11,871,000
1991–92	1,100,000	12,500,000
1992–93	1,300,000	14,000,000
1993–94	1,700,000	15,125,000
1994–95	1,900,000	15,900,000
1995–96	2,000,000	23,000,000
1996–97	2,200,000	24,400,000
1997-98	—	26,900,000
1998-99	—	27,700,000*
1999-00	—	30,000,000*
2000-01	—	32,500,000*

* Projections
Source: National Basketball Association

FOOTBALL

Any recap of the National Football Season that ended on January 25, 1998, at Super Bowl XXXII must begin at that game in San Diego. Because John Elway and the Denver Broncos finally, *finally* won a Super Bowl, beating the defending champion Green Bay Packers 31–24. Sometimes, it's the fourth time that's the charm.

Running back Terrell Davis scored a record-setting three touchdowns and was selected the game's Most Valuable Player, rushing for 157 yards on 30 carries. But the game belonged squarely to John Elway, the 37-year-old quarterback who had taken three other Bronco teams to the Big Game only to leave humiliated each time.

Mr. Elway was only 12 of 22 passing for the game, with no touchdowns and one interception. It didn't matter. He put his stamp on the game for good in the third quarter. Needing a first down on a third and six play at the Packers' 12-yard line, Mr. Elway scrambled to the right, then took to the air—his body carrying the ball, not his arm throwing it—in a desperate attempt to gain the necessary yards. Diving over two Packers, he took a hit from safety Leroy Butler that sent the quarterback to the ground, with the first down. It was the game's defining moment, perhaps also the defining moment of Mr. Elway's long, storied career.

But if Mr. Elway's story was the final—and, perhaps, best—story to emerge from the 1997 NFL season, it surely wasn't the only one.

A few of the highlights:

Barry Sanders of the Detroit Lions proved as elusive as ever, rushing for 2,053 yards to become only the third player to break the 2,000-yard barrier. He also tallied 14 100-yard games, a record.

The Broncos' Terrell Davis ran his way to 1,750 yards and passed the 4,000-yard career mark in only his forty-first game to put him behind just Eric Dickerson (33), Jim Brown (38) and Earl Campbell (39).

Quarterback Brett Favre of the Packers threw 35 touchdown passes, becoming the first quarterback in history to throw for 30 or more TDs four years in a row.

Warren Moon—make that the 41-year-old Warren Moon—did old guys proud everywhere when he became the first 40-plus NFL player ever to score a touchdown, a one-yard run against Indianapolis, as well as the only 40-year-old to throw for more than 400 yards (409, to be exact) in a game.

And Jerry Rice, hurt in the first game of the season with a knee injury, did the injured weekend warriors proud by returning against all odds to score a touchdown against the Denver Broncos in December. Unfortunately, in doing so he broke his kneecap, raising much debate as to the advisability of players rushing back onto the field of battle.

On the sidelines there were a number of coaches who made a story for themselves.

Tony Dungy took the forever-hapless Tampa Bay Buccaneers to a 10–6 record and the playoffs in just his second year as the head coach.

Steve Mariucci, the rookie coach of the San Francisco 49ers, proved that transitions can be easy when done correctly. The Niners lost to the Bucs in their opener, but they ran off 11 straight during the season (an NFL record for a rookie coach), finished 13–3 and didn't bow out until the NFC championship game.

Pete Carroll also did the successful transition shuffle, with the New England Patriots, stepping in for the larger-than-life Bill Parcells and steering the Pats to a 10–6 record and a second-straight AFC East crown.

The aforementioned Mr. Parcells arrived in New York to helm the Jets amid much fanfare and not a little controversy. (The Jets were accused of tampering and were forced to give the Patriots compensatory draft picks.) But ask any Jet fan and he'll tell you it was worth it. Mr. Parcells turned a 1–15 laughingstock into a 9–7 team that was in the playoff hunt until the last game of the season.

Jim Fassell, the professorial-looking coach of the New York Giants, worked all season long in the Parcells shadow but finished at 10–6, with an NFC East title and went undefeated (7-0-1) in division play.

Finally, in the highlight division (at least to those football fans outside the state of Texas), the Dallas Cowboys finished 6–10 amid much rancor, disorganization and accusations of rape and drug use. The swirl of it all cost Barry Switzer his job as head coach.

Final 1997 NFL Regular-Season Standings

American Football Conference	W	L	T	Pct.	Pts.	OP	National Football Conference	W	L	T	Pct.	Pts.	OP
Eastern Division							**Eastern Division**						
New England	10	6	0	.625	369	289	New York Giants	10	5	1	.656	307	265
Miami*	9	7	0	.563	339	327	Washington	8	7	1	.531	327	289
New York Jets	9	7	0	.563	348	287	Philadelphia	6	9	1	.406	317	372
Buffalo	6	10	0	.375	255	367	Dallas	6	10	0	.375	304	314
Indianapolis	3	13	0	.188	313	401	Arizona	4	12	0	.250	283	379
Central Division							**Central Division**						
Pittsburgh	11	5	0	.688	372	307	Green Bay	13	3	0	.813	422	282
Jacksonville*	11	5	0	.688	394	318	Tampa Bay*	10	6	0	.625	299	263
Tennessee	8	8	0	.500	333	310	Detroit*	9	7	0	.563	379	306
Cincinnati	7	9	0	.438	355	405	Minnesota*	9	7	0	.563	354	359
Baltimore	6	9	1	.406	326	345	Chicago	4	12	0	.250	263	421
Western Division							**Western Division**						
Kansas City	13	3	0	.813	375	232	San Francisco	13	3	0	.813	375	265
Denver*	12	4	0	.750	472	287	Carolina	7	9	0	.438	265	314
Seattle	8	8	0	.500	365	362	Atlanta	7	9	0	.438	320	361
Oakland	4	12	0	.250	324	419	New Orleans	6	10	0	.375	237	327
San Diego	4	12	0	.250	266	425	St. Louis	5	11	0	.313	299	359

*Wild Card qualifier for playoffs.

NFL Post Season   Home team in CAPS.

Wild Card Playoffs

American Football Conference
DENVER 42, Jacksonville 17
NEW ENGLAND 17, Miami 3

National Football Conference
Minnesota 23, NEW YORK GIANTS 22
TAMPA BAY 20, Detroit 10

Divisional Playoffs

American Football Conference
PITTSBURGH 7, New England 6
Denver 14, KANSAS CITY 10

National Football Conference
SAN FRANCISCO 38, Minnesota 22
GREEN BAY 21, Tampa Bay 7

Championship Games

American Football Conference
Denver 24, PITTSBURGH 21

National Football Conference
Green Bay 23, SAN FRANCISCO 10

Super Bowl XXXI

Denver (AFC) 31, Green Bay (NFC) 24, at Qualcomm Stadium, San Diego, CA

AFC-NFC Pro Bowl

AFC 29, NFC 24, at Aloha Stadium, Honolulu, HI

Source: National Football League

Super Bowl Results

Season	Date	Winner	Loser	Score	Site	Attendance
I	Jan. 15,1967	Green Bay	Kansas City	35-10	Los Angeles, CA	61,946
II	Jan. 14,1968	Green Bay	Oakland	33-14	Miami, FL	75,546
III	Jan. 12,1969	N.Y. Jets	Baltimore	16-7	Miami, FL	75,389
IV	Jan. 11,1970	Kansas City	Minnesota	23-7	New Orleans, LA	80,562
V	Jan. 17,1971	Baltimore	Dallas	16-13	Miami, FL	79,204
VI	Jan. 16,1972	Dallas	Miami	24-3	New Orleans, LA	81,023
VII	Jan. 14,1973	Miami	Washington	14-7	Los Angeles, CA	90,182
VIII	Jan. 13,1974	Miami	Minnesota	24-7	Houston, TX	71,882
IX	Jan. 12,1975	Pittsburgh	Minnesota	16-6	New Orleans, LA	80,997
X	Jan. 18,1976	Pittsburgh	Dallas	21-17	Miami, FL	80,187
XI	Jan. 09,1977	Oakland	Minnesota	32-14	Pasadena, CA	103,438
XII	Jan. 15,1978	Dallas	Denver	27-10	New Orleans, LA	75,583
XIII	Jan. 21,1979	Pittsburgh	Dallas	35-31	Miami, FL	79,484
XIV	Jan. 20,1980	Pittsburgh	Los Angeles	31-19	Pasadena, CA	103,985
XV	Jan. 25,1981	Oakland	Philadelphia	27-10	New Orleans, LA	76,135
XVI	Jan. 24,1982	San Francisco	Cincinnati	26-21	Pontiac, MI	81,270
XVII	Jan. 30,1983	Washington	Miami	27-17	Pasadena, CA	103,667
XVIII	Jan. 22,1984	L.A. Raiders	Washington	38-9	Tampa, FL	72,920
XIX	Jan. 20,1985	San Francisco	Miami	38-16	Stanford, CA	84,059
XX	Jan. 26,1986	Chicago	New England	46-10	New Orleans, LA	73,818
XXI	Jan. 25,1987	N.Y. Giants	Denver	39-20	Pasadena, CA	101,063
XXII	Jan. 31,1988	Washington	Denver	42-10	San Diego, CA	73,302
XXIII	Jan. 22,1989	San Francisco	Cincinnati	20-16	Miami, FL	75,129
XXIV	Jan. 28,1990	San Francisco	Denver	55-10	New Orleans, LA	72,919
XXV	Jan. 27,1991	N.Y. Giants	Buffalo	20-19	Tampa, FL	73,813
XXVI	Jan. 26,1992	Washington	Buffalo	37-24	Minneapolis, MN	63,130
XXVII	Jan. 31,1993	Dallas	Buffalo	52-17	Pasadena, CA	98,374
XXVIII	Jan. 30,1994	Dallas	Buffalo	30-13	Atlanta, GA	72,817
XXIX	Jan. 29,1995	San Francisco	San Diego	49-26	Miami, FL	74,107
XXX	Jan. 28,1996	Dallas	Pittsburgh	27-17	Tempe, AZ	76,347
XXXI	Jan. 26, 1997	Green Bay	New England	35-21	New Orleans, LA	72,301
XXXII	Jan. 25, 1998	Denver	Green Bay	31-24	San Diego, CA	68,912

Source: National Football League

Super Bowl Composite Standings

Team	W	L	Pct.	Pts.	OP	Team	W	L	Pct.	Pts.	OP
San Francisco 49ers	5	0	1.000	188	89	Kansas City Chiefs	1	1	.500	33	42
New York Giants	2	0	1.000	59	39	Miami Dolphins	2	3	.400	74	103
Chicago Bears	1	0	1.000	46	10	Denver Broncos	1	4	.200	81	187
New York Jets	1	0	1.000	16	7	Los Angeles Rams	0	1	.000	19	31
Pittsburgh Steelers	4	1	.800	120	100	Philadelphia Eagles	0	1	.000	10	27
Green Bay Packers	3	1	.750	127	76	San Diego Chargers	0	1	.000	26	49
Oakland/L.A. Raiders	3	1	.750	111	66	Cincinnati Bengals	0	2	.000	37	46
Dallas Cowboys	5	3	.625	221	132	New England Patriots	0	2	.000	31	81
Washington Redskins	3	2	.600	122	103	Buffalo Bills	0	4	.000	73	139
Baltimore Colts	1	1	.500	23	29	Minnesota Vikings	0	4	.000	34	95

Source: National Football League

In the play-offs' Wildcard Weekend, the Minnesota Vikings beat the Giants 23–22, the Broncos avenged a crushing loss to the Jacksonville Jaguars the year before with a 42–17 victory, the Patriots beat the Dolphins 17–3, and Tampa Bay bested Detroit 20–10.

The second week of the play-offs provided one surprise and one squeaker. The surprise

Super Bowl Most Valuable Player

Super Bowl I	— QB Bart Starr, Green Bay	Super Bowl XVII	— RB John Riggins, Washington
Super Bowl II	— QB Bart Starr, Green Bay	Super Bowl XVIII	— RB Marcus Allen, L.A. Raiders
Super Bowl III	— QB Joe Namath, N.Y. Jets	Super Bowl XIX	— QB Joe Montana, San Francisco
Super Bowl IV	— QB Len Dawson. Kansas City	Super Bowl XX	— DE Richard Dent, Chicago
Super Bowl V	— LB Chuck Howley, Dallas	Super Bowl XXI	— QB Phil Simms, N.Y. Giants
Super Bowl VI	— QB Roger Staubach, Dallas	Super Bowl XXII	— QB Doug Williams, Washington
Super Bowl VII	— S Jake Scott, Miami	Super Bowl XXIII	— WR Jerry Rice, San Francisco
Super Bowl VIII	— RB Larry Csonka, Miami	Super Bowl XXIV	— QB Joe Montana, San Francisco
Super Bowl IX	— RB Franco Harris, Pittsburgh	Super Bowl XXV	— RB Ottis Anderson, N.Y. Giants
Super Bowl X	— WR Lynn Swann, Pittsburgh	Super Bowl XXVI	— QB Mark Rypien, Washington
Super Bowl XI	— WR Fred Biletnikoff, Oakland	Super Bowl XXVII	— QB Troy Aikman, Dallas
Super Bowl XII	— DT Randy White and	Super Bowl XXVIII	— RB Emmitt Smith, Dallas
	DE Harvey Martin, Dallas	Super Bowl XXIX	— QB Steve Young, San Francisco
Super Bowl XIII	— QB Terry Bradshaw, Pittsburgh	Super Bowl XXX	— CB Larry Brown, Dallas
Super Bowl XIV	— QB Terry Bradshaw, Pittsburgh	Super Bowl XXXI	— KR-PR Desmond Howard, Green Bay
Super Bowl XV	— QB Jim Plunkett, Oakland	Super Bowl XXXII	— RB Terrell Davis, Denver
Super Bowl XVI	— QB Joe Montana, San Francisco		

Source: National Football League

The Super Bowl of Selling

The cost of 30 seconds of advertising time has soared on the annual Super Bowl telecast, which has become a showcase for marketers' splashiest commercials.

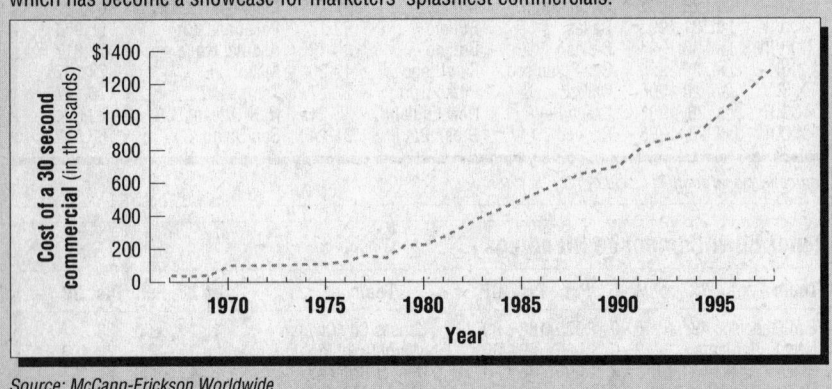

Source: McCann-Erickson Worldwide

was Denver's 14–10 victory over the 13–3 regular-season Kansas City Chiefs, whom many had picked to win the Super Bowl. Once again Kansas City coach Marty Shottenheimer was forced to watch as John Elway handed him yet another playoff defeat. The squeaker was the Pittsburgh Steelers' 7–6 win over the Pats.

In the other two second-week games, the Battle of the Bays ended with Green beating Tamps, 21–7, and San Francisco defeated Minnesota 38–22.

That set up two meetings between four of the NFL's more storied franchises: Denver vs. Pittsburgh for the AFC title and San Francisco vs. Green Bay for the NFC crown. It was Denver 24, Pittsburgh 21; Green Bay 23, San Francisco 10.

And so we're back at the beginning: the end of the season, Super Bowl XXXII. The John Elway Lifetime Achievement Award.

Steve McKee

Super Bowl TV Ratings

While advertisers pay more each year for commercial time on the Super Bowl, television ratings have been erratic.

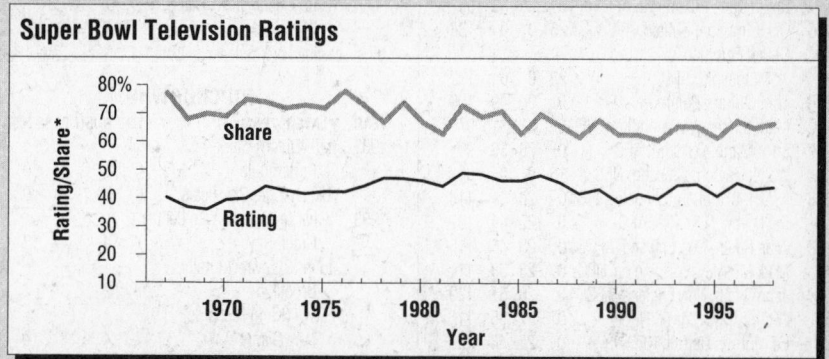

Super Bowl Television Ratings

*The rating represents the percentage of all U.S. households with television sets watching the program. The share represents the percentage of all television sets in use at the time that were tuned to the program.
Source: Nielsen Media Research

From the NFL Records Book
ANNUAL STATISTICAL LEADERS

SCORING

YEAR	PLAYER, TEAM	TD	FG	PAT	TP
1932	Earl (Dutch) Clark, Portsmouth	6	3	10	55
1933	Ken Strong, N.Y. Giants	6	5	13	64
	Glenn Presnell, Portsmouth	6	6	10	64
1934	Jack Manders, Chi. Bears	3	10	31	79
1935	Earl (Dutch) Clark, Detroit	6	1	16	55
1936	Earl (Dutch) Clark, Detroit	7	4	19	73
1937	Jack Manders, Chi. Bears	5	8	15	69
1938	Clarke Hinkle, Green Bay	7	3	7	58
1939	Andy Farkas, Washington	11	0	2	68
1940	Don Hutson, Green Bay	7	0	15	57
1941	Don Hutson, Green Bay	12	1	20	95
1942	Don Hutson, Green Bay	17	1	33	138
1943	Don Hutson, Green Bay	12	3	36	117
1944	Don Hutson, Green Bay	9	0	31	85
1945	Steve Van Buren, Philadelphia	18	0	2	110
1946	Ted Fritsch, Green Bay	10	9	13	100
1947	Pat Harder, Chi. Cardinals	7	7	39	102
1948	Pat Harder, Chi. Cardinals	6	7	53	110
1949	Pat Harder, Chi. Cardinals	8	3	45	102
	Gene Roberts, N.Y. Giants	17	0	0	102
1950	*Doak Walker, Detroit	11	8	38	128
1951	Elroy (Crazylegs) Hirsch, Los Angeles	17	0	0	102
1952	Gordy Soltau, San Francisco	7	6	34	94
1953	Gordy Soltau, San Francisco	6	10	48	114
1954	Bobby Walston, Philadelphia	11	4	36	114
1955	Doak Walker, Detroit	7	9	27	96
1956	Bobby Layne, Detroit	5	12	33	99
1957	Sam Baker, Washington	1	14	29	77
	Lou Groza, Cleveland	0	15	32	77
1958	Jim Brown, Cleveland	18	0	0	108
1959	Paul Hornung, Green Bay	7	7	31	94
1960	Paul Honung, Green Bay, NFL	15	15	41	176
	*Gene Mingo, Denver, AFL	6	18	33	123
1961	Gino Cappelletti, Boston, AFL	8	17	48	147
	Paul Hornung, Green Bay, NFL	10	15	41	146
1962	Gene Mingo, Denver, AFL	4	27	32	137
	Jim Taylor, Green Bay, NFL	19	0	0	114
1963	Gino Cappelletti, Boston, AFL	2	22	35	113
	Don Chandler, N.Y. Giants, NFL	0	18	52	106
1964	Gino Cappelletti, Boston, AFL	7	25	36	155
	Lenny Moore, Baltimore, NFL	20	0	0	120
1965	*Gale Sayers, Chicago, NFL	22	0	0	132
	Gino Cappelletti, Boston, AFL	9	17	27	132
1966	Gino Cappelletti, Boston, AFL	6	16	35	119
	Bruce Gossett, Los Angeles, NFL	0	28	29	113
1967	Jim Bakken, St. Louis, NFL	0	27	36	117
	George Blanda, Oakland, AFL	0	20	56	116
1968	Jim Turner, N.Y. Jets, AFL	0	34	43	145
	Leroy Kelly, Cleveland, NFL	20	0	0	120
1969	Jim Turner, N.Y. Jets, AFL	0	32	33	129
	Fred Cox, Minnesota, NFL	0	26	43	121
1970	Fred Cox, Minnesota, NFC	0	30	35	125
	Jan Stenerud, Kansas City, AFC	0	30	26	116
1971	Garo Yepremian, Miami, AFC	0	28	33	117
	Curt Knight, Washington, NFC	0	29	27	114
1972	*Chester Marcol, Green Bay, NFC	0	33	29	128

	Bobby Howfield, N.Y. Jets, AFC	0	27 40	121
1973	David Ray, Los Angeles, NFC	0	30 40	130
	Roy Gerela, Pittsburgh, AFC	0	29 36	123
1974	Chester Marcol, Green Bay, NFC	0	25 19	94
	Roy Gerela, Pittsburgh, AFC	0	20 33	93
1975	O.J. Simpson, Buffalo, AFC	23	0 0	138
	Chuck Foreman, Minnesota, NFC	22	0 0	132
1976	Toni Linhart, Baltimore, AFC	0	20 49	109
	Mark Moseley, Washington, NFC	0	22 31	97
1977	Errol Mann, Oakland, AFC	0	20 39	99
	Walter Payton, Chicago, NFC	16	0 0	96
1978	*Frank Corral, Los Angeles, NFC	0	29 31	118
	Pat Leahy, N.Y. Jets, AFC	0	22 41	107
1979	John Smith, New England, AFC	0	23 46	115
	Mark Moseley, Washington, NFC	0	25 39	114
1980	John Smith, New England, AFC	0	26 51	129
	*Ed Murray, Detroit, NFC	0	27 35	116
1981	Ed Murray, Detroit, NFC	0	25 46	121
	Rafael Septien, Dallas, NFC	0	27 40	121
	Jim Breech, Cincinnati, AFC	0	22 49	115
	Nick Lowery, Kansas City, AFC	0	26 37	115
1982	*Marcus Allen, L.A. Raiders, AFC	14	0 0	84
	Wendell Tyler, L.A. Rams, NFC	13	0 0	78
1983	Mark Moseley, Washington, NFC	0	33 62	161
	Gary Anderson, Pittsburgh, AFC	0	27 38	119
1984	Ray Wersching, San Francisco, NFC	0	25 56	131
	Gary Anderson, Pittsburgh, AFC	0	24 45	117
1985	*Kevin Butler, Chicago, NFC	0	31 51	144
	Gary Anderson, Pittsburgh, AFC	0	33 40	139
1986	Tony Franklin, New England, AFC	0	32 44	140
	Kevin Butler, Chicago, NFC	0	28 36	120
1987	Jerry Rice, San Francisco, NFC	23	0 0	138
	Jim Breech, Cincinnati, AFC	0	24 25	97
1988	Scott Norwood, Buffalo, AFC	0	32 33	129
	Mike Cofer, San Francisco, NFC	0	27 40	121
1989	Mike Cofer, San Francisco, NFC	0	29 49	136
	*David Treadwell, Denver, AFC	0	27 39	120
1990	Nick Lowery, Kansas City, AFC	0	34 37	139
	Chip Lohmiller, Washington, NFC	0	30 41	131
1991	Chip Lohmiller, Washington, NFC	0	31 56	149
	Pete Stoyanovich, Miami, AFC	0	31 28	121
1992	Pete Stoyanovich, Miami, AFC	0	30 34	124
	Morten Andersen, New Orleans, NFC	0	29 33	120
	Chip Lohmiller, Washington, NFC	0	30 30	120
1993	Jeff Jaeger, L.A. Raiders, AFC	0	35 27	132
	Jason Hanson, Detroit, NFC	0	34 28	130
1994	John Carney, San Diego, AFC	0	34 33	135
	Fuad Reveiz, Minnesota, NFC	0	34 30	132
1995	Emmitt Smith, Dallas, NFC	25	0 0	150
	Norm Johnson, Pittsburgh, AFC	0	34 39	141
1996	John Kasay, Carolina, NFC	0	37 34	145
	Cary Blanchard, Indianapolis, AFC	0	36 27	135
1997	Mike Hollis, Jacksonville, AFC	0	31 41	134
	Richie Cunningham, Dallas, NFC	0	34 24	126

*First season of professional football.

TOUCHDOWNS

YEAR	PLAYER, TEAM	TD	RUSH	PASS	RET.
1932	Earl (Dutch) Clark, Portsmouth	6	3	3	0
	Red Grange, Chi. Bears	6	3	3	0
1933	*Charlie (Buckets) Goldenberg, Green Bay	7	4	1	2
	John (Shipwreck) Kelly, Brooklyn	7	2	3	2
	*Elvin (Kink) Richards, N.Y. Giants	7	4	3	0
1934	*Beattie Feathers, Chi. Bears	9	8	1	0
1935	*Don Hutson, Green Bay	7	0	6	1
1936	Don Hutson, Green Bay	9	0	8	1
1937	Cliff Battles, Washington	7	5	1	1
	Clarke Hinkle, Green Bay	7	5	2	0
	Don Hutson, Green Bay	7	0	7	0
1938	Don Hutson, Green Bay	9	0	9	0
1939	Andrew Farkas, Washington	11	5	5	1
1940	John Drake, Cleveland	9	9	0	0
	Richard Todd, Washington	9	4	4	1
1941	Don Hutson, Green Bay	12	2	10	0
	George McAfee, Chi. Bears	12	6	3	3
1942	Don Hutson, Green Bay	17	0	17	0
1943	Don Hutson, Green Bay	12	0	11	1
	*Bill Paschal, N.Y. Giants	12	10	2	0
1944	Don Hutson, Green Bay	9	0	9	0
	Bill Paschal, N.Y. Giants	9	9	0	0
1945	Steve Van Buren, Philadelphia	18	15	2	1
1946	Ted Fritsch, Green Bay	10	9	1	0
1947	Steve Van Buren, Philadelphia	14	13	0	1
1948	Mal Kutner, Chi. Cardinals	15	1	14	0
1949	Gene Roberts, N.Y. Giants	17	9	8	0
1950	Bob Shaw, Chi. Cardinals	12	0	12	0
1951	Elroy (Crazylegs) Hirsch, Los Angeles	17	0	17	0
1952	Cloyce Box, Detroit	15	0	15	0
1953	Joseph Perry, San Francisco	13	10	3	0
1954	*Harlon Hill, Chi. Bears	12	0	12	0
1955	*Alan Ameche, Baltimore	9	9	0	0
	Harlon Hill, Chi. Bears	9	0	9	0
1956	Rick Casares, Chi. Bears	14	12	2	0
1957	Lenny Moore, Baltimore	11	3	7	1
1958	Jim Brown, Cleveland	18	17	1	0
1959	Raymond Berry, Baltimore	14	0	14	0
	Jim Brown, Cleveland	14	14	0	0
1960	Paul Hornung, Green Bay, NFL	15	13	2	0

Year	Player	Total	Rush	Rec	Ret
	Sonny Randle, St. Louis, NFL	15	0	15	0
	Art Powell, N.Y. Titans, AFL	14	0	14	0
1961	Bill Groman, Houston, AFL	18	1	17	0
	Jim Taylor, Green Bay, NFL	16	15	1	0
1962	Abner Haynes, Dallas, AFL	19	13	6	0
	Jim Taylor, Green Bay, NFL	19	19	0	0
1963	Art Powell, Oakland, AFL	16	0	16	0
	Jim Brown, Cleveland, NFL	15	12	3	0
1964	Lenny Moore, Baltimore, NFL	20	16	3	1
	Lance Alworth, San Diego, AFL	15	2	13	0
1965	*Gale Sayers, Chicago, NFL	22	14	6	2
	Lance Alworth, San Diego, AFL	14	0	14	0
	Don Maynard, N.Y. Jets, AFL	14	0	14	0
1966	Leroy Kelly, Cleveland, NFL	16	15	1	0
	Dan Reeves, Dallas, NFL	16	8	8	0
	Lance Alworth, San Diego, AFL	13	0	13	0
1967	Homer Jones, N.Y. Giants, NFL	14	1	13	0
	Emerson Boozer, N.Y. Jets, AFL	13	10	3	0
1968	Leroy Kelly, Cleveland, NFL	20	16	4	0
	Warren Wells, Oakland, AFL	12	1	11	0
1969	Warren Wells, Oakland, AFL	14	0	14	0
	Tom Matte, Baltimore, NFL	13	11	2	0
	Lance Rentzel, Dallas, NFL	13	0	12	1
1970	Dick Gordon, Chicago, NFC	13	0	13	0
	MacArthur Lane, St. Louis, NFC	13	11	2	0
	Gary Garrison, San Diego, AFC	12	0	12	0
1971	Duane Thomas, Dallas, NFC	13	11	2	0
	Leroy Kelly, Cleveland, AFC	12	10	2	0
1972	Emerson Boozer, N.Y. Jets, AFC	14	11	3	0
	Ron Johnson, N.Y. Giants, NFC	14	9	5	0
1973	Larry Brown, Washington, NFC	14	8	6	0
	Floyd Little, Denver, AFC	13	12	1	0
1974	Chuck Foreman, Minnesota, NFC	15	9	6	0
	Cliff Branch, Oakland, AFC	13	0	13	0
1975	O.J. Simpson, Buffalo, AFC	23	16	7	0
	Chuck Foreman, Minnesota, NFC	22	13	9	0
1976	Chuck Foreman, Minnesota, NFC	14	13	1	0
	Franco Harris, Pittsburgh, AFC	14	14	0	0
1977	Walter Payton, Chicago, NFC	16	14	2	0
	Nat Moore, Miami, AFC	13	1	12	0
1978	David Sims, Seattle, AFC	15	14	1	0
	Terdell Middleton, Green Bay, NFC	12	11	1	0
1979	Earl Campbell, Houston, AFC	19	19	0	0
	Walter Payton, Chicago, NFC	16	14	2	0
1980	*Billy Sims, Detroit, NFC	16	13	3	0
	Earl Campbell, Houston, AFC	13	13	0	0
	Curtis Dickey, Baltimore, AFC	13	11	2	0
	John Jefferson, San Diego, AFC	13	0	13	0
1981	Chuck Muncie, San Diego, AFC	19	19	0	0
	Wendell Tyler, Los Angeles, NFC	17	12	5	0
1982	*Marcus Allen, L.A. Raiders, AFC	14	11	3	0
	Wendell Tyler, L.A. Rams, NFC	13	9	4	0
1983	John Riggins, Washington, NFC	24	24	0	0
	Pete Johnson, Cincinnati, AFC	14	14	0	0
	*Curt Warner, Seattle, AFC	14	13	1	0
1984	Marcus Allen, L.A. Raiders, AFC	18	13	5	0
	Mark Clayton, Miami, AFC	18	0	18	0
	Eric Dickerson, L.A. Rams, NFC	14	14	0	0
	John Riggins, Washington, NFC	14	14	0	0
1985	Joe Morris, N.Y. Giants, NFC	21	21	0	0
	Louis Lipps, Pittsburgh, AFC	15	1	12	2
1986	George Rogers, Washington, NFC	18	18	0	0
	Sammy Winder, Denver, AFC	14	9	5	0
1987	Jerry Rice, San Francisco, NFC	23	1	22	0
	Johnny Hector, N.Y. Jets, AFC	11	11	0	0
1988	Greg Bell, L.A. Rams, NFC	18	16	2	0
	Eric Dickerson, Indianapolis, AFC	15	14	1	0
	*Ickey Woods, Cincinnati, AFC	15	15	0	0
1989	Dalton Hilliard, New Orleans, NFC	18	13	5	0
	Christian Okoye, Kansas City, AFC	12	12	0	0
	Thurman Thomas, Buffalo, AFC	12	6	6	0
1990	Barry Sanders, Detroit, NFC	16	13	3	0

	Derrick Fenner, Seattle, AFC	15	14	1	0
1991	Barry Sanders, Detroit, NFC	17	16	1	0
	Mark Clayton, Miami, AFC	12	0	12	0
	Thurman Thomas, Buffalo, AFC	12	7	5	0
1992	Emmitt Smith, Dallas, NFC	19	18	1	0
	Thurman Thomas, Buffalo, AFC	12	9	3	0
1993	Jerry Rice, San Francisco, NFC	16	1	15	0
	Marcus Allen, Kansas City, AFC	15	12	3	0
1994	Emmitt Smith, Dallas, NFC	22	21	1	0
	*Marshall Faulk, Indianapolis, AFC	12	11	1	0
	Natrone Means, San Diego, AFC	12	12	0	0
1995	Emmitt Smith, Dallas, NFC	25	25	0	0
	Carl Pickens, Cincinnati, AFC	17	0	17	0
1996	Terry Allen, Washington, NFC	21	21	0	0
	Curtis Martin, New England, AFC	17	14	3	0
1997	Karim Abdul-Jabbar, Miami, AFC	16	15	1	0
	Barry Sanders, Detroit, NFC	14	11	3	0

*First season of professional football.

MOST FIELD GOALS MADE

YEAR	PLAYER, TEAM	ATT.	MADE	PCT.
1932	Earl (Dutch) Clark, Portsmouth		3	
1933	*Jack Manders, Chi. Bears		6	
	Glenn Presnell, Portsmouth		6	
1934	Jack Manders, Chi. Bears		10	
1935	Armand Niccolai, Pittsburgh		6	
	Bill Smith, Chi. Cardinals		6	
1936	Jack Manders, Chi. Bears		7	
	Armand Niccolai, Pittsburgh		7	
1937	Jack Manders, Chi. Bears		8	
1938	Ward Cuff, N.Y. Giants	9	5	55.6
	Ralph Kercheval, Brooklyn	13	5	38.5
1939	Ward Cuff, N.Y. Giants	16	7	43.8
1940	Clarke Hinkle, Green Bay	14	9	64.3
1941	Clarke Hinkle, Green Bay	14	6	42.9
1942	Bill Daddio, Chi. Cardinals	10	5	50.0
1943	Ward Cuff, N.Y. Giants	9	3	33.3
	Don Hutson, Green Bay	5	3	60.0
1944	Ken Strong, N.Y. Giants	12	6	50.0
1945	Joe Aguirre, Washington	13	7	53.8
1946	Ted Fritsch, Green Bay	17	9	52.9
1947	Ward Cuff, Green Bay	16	7	43.8
	Pat Harder, Chi. Cardinals	10	7	70.0
	Bob Waterfield, Los Angeles	16	7	43.8
1948	Cliff Patton, Philadelphia	12	8	66.7
1949	Cliff Patton, Philadelphia	18	9	50.0
	Bob Waterfield, Los Angeles	16	9	56.3
1950	Lou Groza, Cleveland	19	13	68.4
1951	Bob Waterfield, Los Angeles	23	13	56.5
1952	Lou Groza, Cleveland	33	19	57.6
1953	Lou Groza, Cleveland	26	23	88.5
1954	Lou Groza, Cleveland	24	16	66.7
1955	Fred Cone, Green Bay	24	16	66.7
1956	Sam Baker, Washington	25	17	68.0
1957	Lou Groza, Cleveland	22	15	68.2
1958	Paige Cothren, Los Angeles	25	14	56.0
	*Tom Miner, Pittsburgh	28	14	50.0
1959	Pat Summerall, N.Y. Giants	29	20	69.0
1960	Tommy Davis, San Francisco, NFL	32	19	59.4
	*Gene Mingo, Denver, AFL	28	18	64.3
1961	Steve Myhra, Baltimore, NFL	39	21	53.8
	Gino Cappelletti, Boston, AFL	32	17	53.1
1962	Gene Mingo, Denver, AFL	39	27	69.2
	Lou Michaels, Pittsburgh, NFL	42	26	61.9
1963	Jim Martin, Baltimore, NFL	39	24	61.5
	Gino Cappelletti, Boston, AFL	38	22	57.9
1964	Jim Bakken, St. Louis, NFL	38	25	65.8
	Gino Cappelletti, Boston, AFL	39	25	64.1
1965	Pete Gogolak, Buffalo, AFL	46	28	60.9
	Fred Cox, Minnesota, NFL	35	23	65.7
1966	Bruce Gossett, Los Angeles, NFL	49	28	57.1
	Mike Mercer, Oakland-Kansas City, AFL	30	21	70.0
1967	Jim Bakken, St. Louis, NFL	39	27	69.2
	Jan Stenerud, Kansas City, AFL	36	21	58.3
1968	Jim Turner, N.Y. Jets, AFL	46	34	73.9
	Mac Percival, Chicago, NFL	36	25	69.4
1969	Jim Turner, N.Y. Jets, AFL	47	32	68.1
	Fred Cox, Minnesota, NFL	37	26	70.3
1970	Jan Stenerud, Kansas City, AFC	42	30	71.4
	Fred Cox, Minnesota, NFC	46	30	65.2
1971	Curt Knight, Washington, NFC	49	29	59.2
	Garo Yepremian, Miami, AFC	40	28	70.0
1972	*Chester Marcol, Green Bay, NFC	48	33	68.8
	Roy Gerela, Pittsburgh, AFC	41	28	68.3
1973	David Ray, Los Angeles, NFC	47	30	63.8
	Roy Gerela, Pittsburgh, AFC	43	29	67.4
1974	Chester Marcol, Green Bay, NFC	39	25	64.1
	Roy Gerela, Pittsburgh, AFC	29	20	69.0
1975	Jan Stenerud, Kansas City, AFC	32	22	68.8
	Toni Fritsch, Dallas, NFC	35	22	62.9
1976	Mark Moseley, Washington, NFC	34	22	64.7
	Jan Stenerud, Kansas City, AFC	38	21	55.3
1977	Mark Moseley, Washington, NFC	37	21	56.8
	Errol Mann, Oakland, AFC	28	20	71.4
1978	*Frank Corral, Los Angeles, NFC	43	29	67.4
	Pat Leahy, N.Y. Jets, AFC	30	22	73.3
1979	Mark Moseley, Washington, NFC	33	25	75.8
	John Smith, New England, AFC	33	23	69.7
1980	*Ed Murray, Detroit, NFC	42	27	64.3
	John Smith, New England, AFC	34	26	76.5
	Fred Steinfort, Denver, AFC	34	26	76.5
1981	Rafael Septien, Dallas, NFC	35	27	77.1
	Nick Lowery, Kansas City, AFC	36	26	72.2
1982	Mark Moseley, Washington, NFC	21	20	95.2
	Nick Lowery, Kansas City, AFC	24	19	79.2

1983	*Ali-Haji-Sheikh,			
	N.Y. Giants, NFC	42	35	83.3
	*Raul Allegre, Baltimore, AFC	35	30	85.7
1984	*Paul McFadden,			
	Philadelphia, NFC	37	30	81.1
	Gary Anderson, Pittsburgh, AFC	32	24	75.0
	Matt Bahr, Cleveland, AFC	32	24	75.0
1985	Gary Anderson, Pittsburgh, AFC	42	33	78.6
	Morten Andersen,			
	New Orleans, NFC	35	31	88.6
	*Kevin Butler, Chicago, NFC	37	31	83.8
1986	Tony Franklin, New England, AFC	41	32	78.0
	Kevin Butler, Chicago, NFC	41	28	68.3
1987	Morten Andersen,			
	New Orleans, NFC	36	28	77.8
	Dean Biasucci, Indianapolis, AFC	27	24	88.9
	Jim Breech, Cincinnati, AFC	30	24	80.0
1988	Scott Norwood, Buffalo, AFC	37	32	86.5
	Mike Cofer, San Francisco, NFC	38	27	71.1
1989	Rich Karlis, Minnesota, NFC	39	31	79.5
	*David Treadwell, Denver, AFC	33	27	81.8
1990	Nick Lowery, Kansas City, AFC	37	34	91.9
	Chip Lohmiller, Washington, NFC	40	30	75.0
1991	Pete Stoyanovich, Miami, AFC	37	31	83.8
	Chip Lohmiller, Washington, NFC	43	31	72.1
1992	Pete Stoyanovich, Miami, AFC	37	30	81.1
	Chip Lohmiller, Washington, NFC	40	30	75.0
1993	Jeff Jaeger, L.A. Raiders, AFC	44	35	79.5
	Jason Hanson, Detroit, NFC	43	34	79.1
1994	John Carney, San Diego, AFC	38	34	89.5
	Fuad Reveiz, Minnesota, NFC	39	34	87.2
1995	Norm Johnson, Pittsburgh, AFC	41	34	82.9
	Morten Andersen, Atlanta, NFC	37	31	83.8
1996	John Kasay, Carolina, NFC	45	37	82.2
	Cary Blanchard, Indianapolis, AFC	40	36	90.0
1997	Richie Cunningham, Dallas, NFC	37	34	91.9
	Cary Blanchard, Indianapolis, AFC	41	32	78.0

*First season of professional football.

RUSHING

YEAR	PLAYER, TEAM	ATT.	YARDS	AVG.	TD
1932	*Cliff Battles, Boston	148	576	3.9	3
1933	Jim Musick, Boston	173	809	4.7	5
1934	*Beattie Feathers, Chi. Bears	119	1,004	8.4	8
1935	Doug Russell,				
	Chi. Cardinals	140	499	3.6	0
1936	*Alphonse (Tuffy) Leemans,				
	N.Y. Giants	206	830	4.0	2
1937	Cliff Battles, Washington	216	874	4.0	5
1938	*Byron (Whizzer) White,				
	Pittsburgh	152	567	3.7	4
1939	*Bill Osmanski, Chicago	121	699	5.8	7
1940	Byron (Whizzer) White,				
	Detroit	146	514	3.5	5
1941	Clarence (Pug) Manders,				
	Brooklyn	111	486	4.4	5
1942	*Bill Dudley, Pittsburgh	162	696	4.3	5
1943	*Bill Paschal, N.Y. Giants	147	572	3.9	10

1944	Bill Paschal, N.Y. Giants	196	737	3.8	9
1945	Steve Van Buren,				
	Philadelphia	143	832	5.8	15
1946	Bill Dudley, Pittsburgh	146	604	4.1	3
1947	Steve Van Buren,				
	Philadelphia	217	1,008	4.6	13
1948	Steve Van Buren,				
	Philadelphia	201	945	4.7	10
1949	Steve Van Buren,				
	Philadelphia	263	1,146	4.4	11
1950	Marion Motley, Cleveland	140	810	5.8	3
1951	Eddie Price, N.Y. Giants	271	971	3.6	7
1952	Dan Towler, Los Angeles	156	894	5.7	10
1953	Joe Perry, San Francisco	192	1,018	5.3	10
1954	Joe Perry, San Francisco	173	1,049	6.1	8
1955	*Alan Ameche, Baltimore	213	961	4.5	9
1956	Rick Casares, Chi. Bears	234	1,126	4.8	12
1957	*Jim Brown, Cleveland	202	942	4.7	9
1958	Jim Brown, Cleveland	257	1,527	5.9	17
1959	Jim Brown, Cleveland	290	1,329	4.6	14
1960	Jim Brown,				
	Cleveland, NFL	215	1,257	5.8	9
	*Abner Haynes,				
	Dall. Texans, AFL	156	875	5.6	9
1961	Jim Brown,				
	Cleveland, NFL	305	1,408	4.6	8
	Billy Cannon, Houston, AFL	200	948	4.7	6
1962	Jim Taylor, Green Bay, NFL	272	1,474	5.4	19
	Cookie Gilchrist,				
	Buffalo, AFL	214	1,096	5.1	13
1963	Jim Brown, Cleveland, NFL	291	1,863	6.4	12
	Clem Daniels,				
	Oakland, AFL	215	1,099	5.1	3
1964	Jim Brown, Cleveland, NFL	280	1,446	5.2	7
	Cookie Gilchrist,				
	Buffalo, AFL	230	981	4.3	6
1965	Jim Brown,				
	Cleveland, NFL	289	1,544	5.3	17
	Paul Lowe, San Diego, AFL	222	1,121	5.0	7
1966	Jim Nance, Boston, AFL	299	1,458	4.9	11
	Gale Sayers, Chicago, NFL	229	1,231	5.4	8
1967	Jim Nance, Boston, AFL	269	1,216	4.5	7
	Leroy Kelly,				
	Cleveland, NFL	235	1,205	5.1	11
1968	Leroy Kelly,				
	Cleveland, NFL	248	1,239	5.0	16
	*Paul Robinson,				
	Cincinnati, AFL	238	1,023	4.3	8
1969	Gale Sayers, Chicago, NFL	236	1,032	4.4	8
	Dickie Post,				
	San Diego, AFL	182	873	4.8	6
1970	Larry Brown,				
	Washington, NFC	237	1,125	4.7	5
	Floyd Little, Denver, AFC	209	901	4.3	3
1971	Floyd Little, Denver, AFC	284	1,133	4.0	6
	*John Brockington,				
	Green Bay, NFC	216	1,105	5.1	4
1972	O.J. Simpson, Buffalo, AFC	292	1,251	4.3	6

	Larry Brown,				
	Washington, NFC	285	1,216	4.3	8
1973	O.J. Simpson, Buffalo, AFC	332	2,003	6.0	12
	John Brockington,				
	Green Bay, NFC	265	1,144	4.3	3
1974	Otis Armstrong,				
	Denver, AFC	263	1,407	5.3	9
	Lawrence McCutcheon,				
	Los Angeles, NFC	236	1,109	4.7	3
1975	O.J. Simpson, Buffalo, AFC	329	1,817	5.5	16
	Jim Otis, St. Louis, NFC	269	1,076	4.0	5
1976	O.J. Simpson, Buffalo, AFC	290	1,503	5.2	8
	Walter Payton,				
	Chicago, NFC	311	1,390	4.5	13
1977	Walter Payton,				
	Chicago, NFC	339	1,852	5.5	14
	Mark van Eeghen,				
	Oakland, AFC	324	1,273	3.9	7
1978	*Earl Campbell,				
	Houston, AFC	302	1,450	4.8	13
	Walter Payton,				
	Chicago, NFC	333	1,395	4.2	11
1979	Earl Campbell,				
	Houston, AFC	368	1,697	4.6	19
	Walter Payton,				
	Chicago, NFC	369	1,610	4.4	14
1980	Earl Campbell,				
	Houston, AFC	373	1,934	5.2	13
	Walter Payton,				
	Chicago, NFC	317	1,460	4.6	6
1981	*George Rogers,				
	New Orleans, NFC	378	1,674	4.4	13
	Earl Campbell,				
	Houston, AFC	361	1,376	3.8	10
1982	Freeman McNeil,				
	N.Y. Jets, AFC	151	786	5.2	6
	Tony Dorsett, Dallas, NFC	177	745	4.2	5
1983	*Eric Dickerson,				
	L.A. Rams, NFC	390	1,808	4.6	18
	*Curt Warner, Seattle, AFC	335	1,449	4.3	13
1984	Eric Dickerson,				
	L.A. Rams, NFC	379	2,105	5.6	14
	Earnest Jackson,				
	San Diego, AFC	296	1,179	4.0	8
1985	Marcus Allen,				
	L.A. Raiders, AFC	380	1,759	4.6	11
	Gerald Riggs, Atlanta, NFC	397	1,719	4.3	10
1986	Eric Dickerson,				
	L.A. Rams, NFC	404	1,821	4.5	11
	Curt Warner, Seattle, AFC	319	1,481	4.6	13
1987	Charles White,				
	L.A. Rams, NFC	324	1,374	4.2	11
	Eric Dickerson,				
	Indianapolis, AFC	223	1,011	4.5	5
1988	Eric Dickerson,				
	Indianapolis, AFC	388	1,659	4.3	14
	Herschel Walker,				
	Dallas, NFC	361	1,514	4.2	5

1989	Christian Okoye,				
	Kansas City, AFC	370	1,480	4.0	12
	*Barry Sanders,				
	Detroit, NFC	280	1,470	5.3	14
1990	Barry Sanders,				
	Detroit, NFC	255	1,304	5.1	13
	Thurman Thomas,				
	Buffalo, AFC	271	1,297	4.8	11
1991	Emmitt Smith,				
	Dallas, NFC	365	1,563	4.3	12
	Thurman Thomas,				
	Buffalo, AFC	288	1,407	4.9	7
1992	Emmitt Smith,				
	Dallas, NFC	373	1,713	4.6	18
	Barry Foster,				
	Pittsburgh, AFC	390	1,690	4.3	11
1993	Emmitt Smith,				
	Dallas, NFC	283	1,486	5.3	9
	Thurman Thomas,				
	Buffalo, AFC	355	1,315	3.7	6
1994	Barry Sanders,				
	Detroit, NFC	331	1,883	5.7	7
	Chris Warren, Seattle, AFC	333	1,545	4.6	9
1995	Emmitt Smith,				
	Dallas, NFC	377	1,773	4.7	25
	Curtis Martin,				
	New England, AFC	368	1,487	4.0	14
1996	Barry Sanders,				
	Detroit, NFC	307	1,553	5.1	11
	Terrell Davis, Denver, AFC	345	1,538	4.5	13
1997	Barry Sanders,				
	Detroit, NFC	335	2,053	6.1	11
	Terrell Davis, Denver, AFC	369	1,750	4.7	15

*First season of professional football.

PASSING

(Current rating system implemented in 1973)

YEAR PLAYER, TEAM	ATT.	COMP.	YARDS	TD	INT.	RATING
1932 Arnie Herber,						
Green Bay	101	37	639	9	9	
1933 *Harry Newman,						
N.Y. Giants	136	53	973	11	17	
1934 Arnie Herber,						
Green Bay	115	42	799	8	12	
1935 Ed Danowski,						
N.Y. Giants	113	57	794	10	9	
1936 Arnie Herber,						
Green Bay	173	77	1,239	11	13	
1937 *Sammy Baugh,						
Washington	171	81	1,127	8	14	
1938 Ed Danowski,						
N.Y. Giants	129	70	848	7	8	
1939 *Parker Hall,						
Cleveland	208	106	1,227	9	13	
1940 Sammy Baugh,						
Washington	177	111	1,367	12	10	
1941 Cecil Isbell,						
Green Bay	206	117	1,479	15	11	

1942 Cecil Isbell,
Green Bay 268 146 2,021 24 14
1943 Sammy Baugh,
Washington 239 133 1,754 23 19
1944 Frank Filchock,
Washington 147 84 1,139 13 9
1945 Sammy Baugh,
Washington 182 128 1,669 11 4
Sid Luckman,
Chi. Bears 217 117 1,725 14 10
1946 Bob Waterfield,
Los Angeles 251 127 1,747 18 17
1947 Sammy Baugh,
Washington 354 210 2,938 25 15
1948 Tommy Thompson,
Philadelphia 246 141 1,965 25 11
1949 Sammy Baugh,
Washington 255 145 1,903 18 14
1950 Norm Van Brocklin,
Los Angeles 233 127 2,061 18 14
1951 Bob Waterfield,
Los Angeles 176 88 1,566 13 10
1952 Norm Van Brocklin,
Los Angeles 205 113 1,736 14 17
1953 Otto Graham,
Cleveland 258 167 2,722 11 9
1954 Norm Van Brocklin,
Los Angeles 260 139 2,637 13 21
1955 Otto Graham,
Cleveland 185 98 1,721 15 8
1956 Ed Brown,
Chi. Bears 168 96 1,667 11 12
1957 Tommy O'Connell,
Cleveland 110 63 1,229 9 8
1958 Eddie LeBaron,
Washington 145 79 1,365 11 10
1959 Charlie Conerly,
N.Y. Giants 194 113 1,706 14 4
1960 Milt Plum,
Cleveland, NFL 250 151 2,297 21 5
Jack Kemp,
L.A. Chargers, AFL 406 211 3,018 20 25
1961 George Blanda,
Houston, AFL 362 187 3,330 36 22
Milt Plum,
Cleveland, NFL 302 177 2,416 18 10
1962 Len Dawson,
Dall. Texans, AFL 310 189 2,759 29 17
Bart Starr,
Green Bay, NFL 285 178 2,438 12 9
1963 Y.A. Tittle,
N.Y. Giants, NFL 367 221 3,145 36 14
Tobin Rote,
San Diego, AFL 286 170 2,510 20 17
1964 Len Dawson,
Kansas City, AFL 354 199 2,879 30 18
Bart Starr,
Green Bay, NFL 272 163 2,144 15 4

1965 Rudy Bukich,
Chicago, NFL 312 176 2,641 20 9
John Hadl,
San Diego, AFL 348 174 2,798 20 21
1966 Bart Starr,
Green Bay, NFL 251 156 2,257 14 3
Len Dawson,
Kansas City, AFL 284 159 2,527 26 10
1967 Sonny Jurgensen,
Washington, NFL 508 288 3,747 31 16
Daryle Lamonica,
Oakland, AFL 425 220 3,228 30 20
1968 Len Dawson,
Kansas City, AFL 224 131 2,109 17 9
Earl Morrall,
Baltimore, NFL 317 182 2,909 26 17
1969 Sonny Jurgensen,
Washington, NFL 442 274 3,102 22 15
*Greg Cook,
Cincinnati, AFL 197 106 1,854 15 11
1970 John Brodie, San
Francisco, NFC 378 223 2,941 24 10
Daryle Lamonica,
Oakland, AFC 356 179 2,516 22 15
1971 Roger Staubach,
Dallas, NFC 211 126 1,882 15 4
Bob Griese,
Miami, AFC 263 145 2,089 19 9
1972 Norm Snead, N.Y.
Giants, NFC 325 196 2,307 17 12
Earl Morrall,
Miami, AFC 150 83 1,360 11 7
1973 Roger Staubach,
Dallas, NFC 286 179 2,428 23 15 94.6
Ken Stabler,
Oakland, AFC 260 163 1,997 14 10 88.5
1974 Ken Anderson,
Cincinnati, AFC 328 213 2,667 18 10 95.9
Sonny Jurgensen,
Washington, NFC 167 107 1,185 11 5 94.6
1975 Ken Anderson,
Cincinnati, AFC 377 228 3,169 21 11 94.1
Fran Tarkenton,
Minnesota, NFC 425 273 2,994 25 13 91.7
1976 Ken Stabler,
Oakland, AFC 291 194 2,737 27 17 103.4
James Harris,
Los Angeles, NFC 158 91 1,460 8 6 89.8
1977 Bob Griese,
Miami, AFC 307 180 2,252 22 13 88.0
Roger Staubach,
Dallas, NFC 361 210 2,620 18 9 87.1
1978 Roger Staubach,
Dallas, NFC 413 231 3,190 25 16 84.9
Terry Bradshaw,
Pittsburgh, AFC 368 207 2,915 28 20 84.8
1979 Roger Staubach,
Dallas, NFC 461 267 3,586 27 11 92.4

Dan Fouts,
San Diego, AFC 530 332 4,082 24 24 82.6
1980 Brian Sipe,
Cleveland, AFC 554 337 4,132 30 14 91.4
Ron Jaworski,
Philadelphia, NFC 451 257 3,529 27 12 90.9
1981 Ken Anderson,
Cincinnati, AFC 479 300 3,754 29 10 98.5
Joe Montana, San
Francisco, NFC 488 311 3,565 19 12 88.2
1982 Ken Anderson,
Cincinnati, AFC 309 218 2,495 12 9 95.5
Joe Theismann,
Washington, NFC 252 161 2,033 13 9 91.3
1983 Steve Bartkowski,
Atlanta, NFC 432 274 3,167 22 5 97.6
*Dan Marino,
Miami, AFC 296 173 2,210 20 6 96.0
1984 Dan Marino,
Miami, AFC 564 362 5,084 48 17 108.9
Joe Montana, San
Francisco, NFC 432 279 3,630 28 10 102.9
1985 Ken O'Brien,
N.Y. Jets, AFC 488 297 3,888 25 8 96.2
Joe Montana, San
Francisco, NFC 494 303 3,653 27 13 91.3
1986 Tommy Kramer,
Minnesota, NFC 372 208 3,000 24 10 92.6
Dan Marino,
Miami, AFC 623 378 4,746 44 23 92.5
1987 Joe Montana, San
Francisco, NFC 398 266 3,054 31 13 102.1
Bernie Kosar,
Cleveland, AFC 389 241 3,033 22 9 95.4
1988 Boomer Esiason,
Cincinnati, AFC 388 223 3,572 28 14 97.4
Wade Wilson,
Minnesota, NFC 332 204 2,746 15 9 91.5
1989 Joe Montana, San
Francisco, NFC 386 271 3,521 26 8 112.4
Boomer Esiason,
Cincinnati, AFC 455 258 3,525 28 11 92.1
1990 Jim Kelly,
Buffalo, AFC 346 219 2,829 24 9 101.2
Phil Simms, N.Y.
Giants, NFC 311 184 2,284 15 4 92.7
1991 Steve Young, San
Francisco, NFC 279 180 2,517 17 8 101.8
Jim Kelly,
Buffalo, AFC 474 304 3,844 33 17 97.6
1992 Steve Young, San
Francisco, NFC 402 268 3,465 25 7 107.0
Warren Moon,
Houston, AFC 346 224 2,521 18 12 89.3
1993 Steve Young, San
Francisco, NFC 462 314 4,023 29 16 101.5
John Elway,
Denver, AFC 551 348 4,030 25 10 92.8

1994 Steve Young, San
Francisco, NFC 461 324 3,969 35 10 112.8
Dan Marino,
Miami, AFC 615 385 4,453 30 17 89.2
1995 Jim Harbaugh,
Indianapolis, AFC 314 200 2,575 17 5 100.7
Brett Favre,
Green Bay, NFC 570 359 4,413 38 13 99.5
1996 Steve Young, San
Francisco, NFC 316 214 2,410 14 6 97.2
John Elway,
Denver, AFC 466 287 3,328 26 14 89.2
1997 Steve Young, San
Francisco, NFC 356 241 3,029 19 6 104.7
Mark Brunell,
Jacksonville, AFC 435 264 3,281 18 7 91.2

*First season of professional football.

NFL ALL-TIME RECORDS

POINTS

MOST POINTS, CAREER
2,002 George Blanda, Chi. Bears, 1949, 1950–58; Baltimore, 1950; Houston, 1960–66; Oakland, 1967–75 (9-td, 943-pat, 335-fg)
1,711 Nick Lowery, New England, 1978; Kansas City, 1980–93; N.Y. Jets, 1994–96 (562-pat, 383-fg)
1,699 Jan Stenerud, Kansas City, 1967–79; Green Bay, 1980–83; Minnesota, 1984–85 (580-pat, 373-fg)

MOST POINTS, SEASON
176 Paul Hornung, Green Bay, 1960 (15-td, 41-pat, 15-fg)
161 Mark Moseley, Washington, 1983 (62-pat, 33-fg)
155 Gino Cappelletti, Boston, 1964 (7-td, 38-pat, 25-fg)

TOUCHDOWNS

MOST TOUCHDOWNS, CAREER
166 Jerry Rice, San Francisco, 1985–97 (10-r, 155-p, 1 ret)
145 Marcus Allen, L.A. Raiders, 1982–92; Kansas City, 1993–97 (123-r, 21-p, 1-ret)
126 Jim Brown, Cleveland, 1957–65 (106-r, 20-p)

MOST TOUCHDOWNS, SEASON
25 Emmitt Smith, Dallas, 1995 (25-r)
24 John Riggins, Washington, 1983 (24-r)
23 O.J. Simpson, Buffalo, 1975 (16-r, 7-p)
Jerry Rice, San Francisco, 1987 (1-r, 22-p)

FIELD GOALS

MOST FIELD GOALS, CAREER
385 Gary Anderson, Pittsburgh, 1982–94; Philadelphia, 1995–96, San Francisco, 1997
383 Nick Lowery, New England, 1978; Kansas City, 1980–93; N.Y. Jets, 1994–96
378 Morten Andersen, New Orleans, 1982–94; Atlanta, 1995–97

MOST FIELD GOALS, SEASON
37   John Kasay, Carolina, 1996
36   Cary Blanchard, Indianapolis, 1996
35   Ali Haji-Sheikh, N.Y. Giants, 1983
     Jeff Jaeger, L.A. Raiders, 1993

RUSHING
MOST YARDS GAINED, CAREER
16,726   Walter Payton, Chicago, 1975–87
13,778   Barry Sanders, Detroit, 1989–97
13,259   Eric Dickerson, L.A. Rams, 1983–87; India-
         napolis, 1987–91; L.A. Raiders, 1992;
         Atlanta, 1993
MOST YARDS GAINED, SEASON
2,105   Eric Dickerson, L.A. Rams, 1984
2,053   Barry Sanders, Detroit, 1997
2,003   O.J. Simpson, Buffalo, 1973

PASSING
MOST PASSES COMPLETED, CAREER
4,453 Dan Marino, Miami, 1983–97

3,913   John Elway, Denver 1983–97
3,827   Warren Moon, Houston, 1984–93;
        Minnesota 1994–96; Seattle, 1997

MOST PASSES COMPLETED, SEASON
404   Warren Moon, Houston, 1991
400   Drew Bledsoe, New England, 1994
385   Dan Marino, Miami, 1994

MOST TOUCHDOWN PASSES, CAREER
385   Dan Marino, Miami, 1983–97
342   Fran Tarkenton, Minnesota, 1961–66, 1972–78;
      N.Y. Giants, 1967–71
290   Johnny Unitas, Baltimore, 1956–72; San Diego,
      1973

MOST TOUCHDOWN PASSES, SEASON
48 Dan Marino, Miami, 1984
44 Dan Marino, Miami, 1986
39 Brett Favre, Green Bay, 1996

Basketball

The 1997–1998 National Basketball Association season started where pro hoops always seems to start these days: in the summer, with talk of money. But the wrinkle in the game plan this time was that the money talk involved coaches, not players.

Rick Pitino, late of the University of Kentucky and a national championship the year before, signed with the Boston Celtics as the coach for $5 million a year. Larry Brown, late of the Indiana Pacers, moved over to the Philadelphia 76ers as the coach for $5 million a year. They were both following in the large footsteps of Pat Riley, who the year before had bolted the New York Knicks for the Miami Heat as the coach for $3 million a year. Welcome to the era of the NBA coach as the 800-pound gorilla.

And then Larry Bird—yes, *that* Larry Bird—went back home to Indiana as the head coach of the Pacers for $4.5 million a year. Sure, he was a legend, but a coach? Messrs. Riley, Pitino and Brown were card-carrying bench guys. Mr. Bird? Just another superstar who would never cut it as a coach.

As for the 82-game NBA season, it became the Pure Speculation Michael Jordan Retire-

ment Tour. The defending champion Chicago Bulls, owned by Jerry Reinsdorf, managed by Jerry Krause, coached by Phil Jackson and starring Mr. Jordan, Scottie Pippen and Dennis Rodman seemed intent all year on self-destruction. Mr. Krause made no secret of his desire to hire Iowa State's coach, Tim Floyd, as the Bulls' new coach. Mr. Jackson declared this to be his last season on the bench. Mr. Jordan promised he would never play for any coach but Mr. Jackson. Scottie Pippen, injured and out much of the early going and long slighted by his relatively meager contract, proclaimed he would never (never!) play for the Bulls again. Mr. Rodman kept changing the color of his hair but otherwise by comparison was the very center of sanity.

Speaking of which, there appeared to be very little of it in evidence in December when Latrell Sprewell of the Golden State Warriors twice assaulted head coach P. J. Carelsimo at practice. Mr. Sprewell was immediately dropped by the team and his contract voided. The NBA then declared Mr. Sprewell banned from the league. Much hand-wringing ensued as to what The Incident really meant. Even more wringing would ensue when a judge later declared the NBA had acted too harshly and reinstated the remainder of Mr. Sprewell's contract, minus the '97–'98 portion, and ruled he could return to the league in '98–'99.

Basketball was also played.

In the Western Conference, two venerable old guys, John Stockton (36) and Karl Malone (34), returned from their six-game elimination in the '97 NBA finals against the Bulls to lead the Utah Jazz to the league's best record at 62–20.

The Los Angeles Lakers, sometimes too talented for their own good (Shaquille O'Neal, Kobe Bryant, Nick Van Exel, et al.), gave coach Del Harris even more white hair but somehow still managed to win 61 games.

After missing most of the previous season, "The Admiral" David Robinson, returned to the San Antonio Spurs and combined with Tim Duncan, the eventual Rookie of the Year award winner, and Will Purdue, of all people, to create the "Triple Towers." The trio led the Spurs to a 56–26 record.

In the Eastern Conference, a season-ending wrist injury to Patrick Ewing of the New York Knicks radically altered the familiar power structure. The Bulls remained atop the heap, of course, but it was the Indiana Pacers who rushed into the void left by the Knicks' absence.

Pat Riley did his usual job of flogging an undermanned Miami Heat team to heights (55–27) it had no right to imagine. Even the New Jersey Nets made some noise. Coached by John Calipari, another coach/general manager/gorilla with a hefty contract, the Nets finished the season at 43–39 and made it into the first round of the play-offs where they lost to the Bulls, 3–0. With stars-in-the-making Kerry Kittles and rookie Keith Van Horn, the Nets served notice that there was finally something at the Meadowlands beside swamp gas.

Now, about Larry Bird. The self-proclaimed "Hick from French Lick" confounded the conventional wisdom that a superstar can't coach. He demonstrated *enormous* patience with the players who were less talented than he had been (which meant everybody on the Pacers), asking only that they practice hard for two hours and play hard for the 25-or-so minutes he would require of them in games. "What's so hard about that?" the Legend seemed to ask with a shrug.

On the sidelines he was absolutely implacable. About the most excitement he exhibited was to stand up and put his hands in his pockets. His main responsibility appeared to be to provide his team with the confidence that there was no court situation he hadn't already confronted and conquered.

Of course, it always looks easier than it is. And in truth, though the team he inherited from Larry Brown had gone only 39–43 the year before, the Pacers were better than the record indicated. And having 7-foot-four-inch Rik Smits healthy for an entire year didn't hurt, either.

But what Mr. Bird did more than anything was seemingly to reinvent the art of coaching an NBA team. He hired only two assistants, Dick Harter for defense and Rick Carlisle for offense, then had the nerve to get out of their way and let them actually coach. And not just in practice but in games, too, even during time-outs, when everyone could see him standing in the huddle not saying anything.

Whatever, it worked. The Pacers finished 58–24, their best record since entering the NBA in 1976. In the play-offs the Pacers took the Bulls to the seventh game of the Eastern Conference finals before succumbing.

There were other intriguing subplots in the play-offs as well. For one, the Bulls were supposed to be old and vulnerable. (A healthy Scottie Pippen, by the way, returned to the Bulls in February.) The Los Angeles Lakers looked like world beaters when they removed the Seattle Supersonics in the second round of the Western Conference, four games to one. Miami and New York came to blows for the second straight year, resulting in suspensions to both teams (Alonzo Mourning, Miami; Larry Johnson, New York) that materially affected the outcome, won by New York this time, 3–2. And the Utah Jazz completely dismantled the Lakers in the Western Conference final in four straight games. With the home court advantage and with the Bulls pressed to the limit by Indiana, the stage appeared set for a rested Stockton and Malone to finally claim an NBA title.

And so it came to another game-six confrontation between the Bulls and Jazz. Mr. Jordan's 18-footer with 5.2 seconds remaining sealed the victory, 87–86, this time, giving the Bulls their sixth title in eight years, a "three-peat repeat." Mr. Jordan stood with his arm extended for a long moment after the ball dropped through the hoop. All season long he

1997-98 NBA Regular Season Statistics

Eastern Conference

Atlantic Division

	W	L	Pct.	GB	Home	Road	Last-10	Streak	
Miami	55	27	.671	–	30-11	25-16	4-6	Lost	3
New York	43	39	.524	12	28-13	15-26	3-7	Lost	1
New Jersey	43	39	.524	12	26-15	17-24	6-4	Won	1
Washington	42	40	.512	13	24-17	18-23	6-4	Won	4
Orlando	41	41	.500	14	24-17	17-24	4-6	Lost	1
Boston	36	46	.439	19	24-17	12-29	5-5	Lost	1
Philadelphia	31	51	.378	24	19-22	12-29	5-5	Won	1

Central Division

	W	L	Pct.	GB	Home	Road	Last-10	Streak	
Chicago	62	20	.756	–	37-4	25-16	7-3	Won	2
Indiana	58	24	.707	4	32-9	26-15	8-2	Lost	1
Charlotte	51	31	.622	11	32-9	19-22	5-5	Won	1
Atlanta	50	32	.610	12	29-12	21-20	7-3	Won	2
Cleveland	47	35	.573	15	27-14	20-21	6-4	Won	1
Detroit	37	45	.451	25	25-16	12-29	3-7	Lost	1
Milwaukee	36	46	.439	26	21-20	15-26	5-5	Lost	2
Toronto	16	66	.195	46	9-32	7-34	1-9	Lost	3

Western Conference

Midwest Division

	W	L	Pct.	GB	Home	Road	Last-10	Streak	
Utah	62	20	.756	–	36-5	26-15	8-2	Lost	1
San Antonio	56	26	.683	6	31-10	25-16	7-3	Won	3
Minnesota	45	37	.549	17	26-15	19-22	7-3	Won	2
Houston	41	41	.500	21	24-17	17-24	4-6	Lost	2
Dallas	20	62	.244	42	13-28	7-34	2-8	Lost	3
Vancouver	19	63	.232	43	14-27	5-36	3-7	Won	1
Denver	11	71	.134	51	9-32	2-39	2-8	Lost	1

Pacific Division

	W	L	Pct.	GB	Home	Road	Last-10	Streak	
Seattle	61	21	.744	–	35-6	26-15	7-3	Won	1
LA Lakers	61	21	.744	–	33-8	28-13	9-1	Won	5
Phoenix	56	26	.683	5	30-11	26-15	9-1	Won	1
Portland	46	36	.561	15	26-15	20-21	6-4	Lost	2
Sacramento	27	55	.329	34	21-20	6-35	1-9	Lost	7
Golden State	19	63	.232	42	12-29	7-34	4-6	Won	3
LA Clippers	17	65	.207	44	11-30	6-35	1-9	Won	1

had been asked if he was going to retire. His answers had always been evasive. But his final pose of the 1997–1998 season certainly looked to many to be a final curtain call.

And with that the summer hoop season began again. Phil Jackson quit as coach of the Bulls; at least he said he did. Jerry Krause hired Tim Floyd to work for the Bulls, but, he said, only as the coach if Mr. Jackson had really quit. Michael Jordan restated, sort of, that he would play only for Mr. Jackson . . . maybe.

The owners, exercising their contractual right, reopened the collective bargaining agreement and locked the players out on July 1. The NBA players selected to the latest "Dream Team" for the World Championships in Greece hinted they might not go, and USA Basketball picked an entirely different team of minor-

1998 NBA Playoffs

First Round - Eastern Conference

Chicago vs. New Jersey

April 24	New Jersey	93	at	Chicago	96 OT
April 26	New Jersey	91	at	Chicago	96
April 29	Chicago	116	at	New Jersey	101

(Bulls won series 3-0)

Indiana vs. Cleveland

April 23	Cleveland	77	at	Indiana	106
April 25	Cleveland	86	at	Indiana	92
April 27	Indiana	77	at	Cleveland	86
April 30	Indiana	80	at	Cleveland	74

(Pacers won series 3-1)

Miami vs. New York

April 24	New York	79	at	Miami	94
April 26	New York	96	at	Miami	86
April 28	Miami	91	at	New York	85
April 30	Miami	85	at	New York	90
May 3	New York	98	at	Miami	81

(Knicks won series 3-2)

Charlotte vs. Atlanta

April 23	Atlanta	87	at	Charlotte	97
April 25	Atlanta	85	at	Charlotte	92
April 28	Charlotte	64	at	Atlanta	96
May 1	Charlotte	91	at	Atlanta	82

(Hornets won series 3-1)

First Round - Western Conference

Utah vs. Houston

April 23	Houston	103	at	Utah	90
April 25	Houston	90	at	Utah	105
April 29	Utah	85	at	Houston	89
May 1	Utah	93	at	Houston	71
May 3	Houston	70	at	Utah	84

(Jazz won series 3-2)

LA Lakers vs. Portland

April 24	Portland	102	at	LA Lakers	104
April 26	Portland	99	at	LA Lakers	108
April 28	LA Lakers	94	at	Portland	99
April 30	LA Lakers	110	at	Portland	99

(LA Lakers won series 3-1)

Seattle vs. Minnesota

April 24	Minnesota	83	at	Seattle	108
April 26	Minnesota	98	at	Seattle	93
April 28	Seattle	90	at	Minnesota	98
April 30	Seattle	92	at	Minnesota	88
May 2	Minnesota	84	at	Seattle	97

(SuperSonics won series 3-2)

Phoenix vs. San Antonio

April 23	San Antonio	102	at	Phoenix	96
April 25	San Antonio	101	at	Phoenix	108
April 27	Phoenix	88	at	San Antonio	100
April 29	Phoenix	80	at	San Antonio	99

(Spurs won series 3-1)

league and European-based players. Both sides agreed this latest round of labor unrest was going to get real ugly. Regular season games, they predicted, would be lost for the first time.

Just another summer in the NBA.

Steve McKee

Conference Semifinals - Eastern Conference

Chicago vs. Charlotte

May 3	Charlotte	70	at	Chicago	83
May 6	Charlotte	78	at	Chicago	76
May 8	Chicago	103	at	Charlotte	89
May 10	Chicago	94	at	Charlotte	80
May 13	Charlotte	84	at	Chicago	93

(Bulls won series 4-1)

Indiana vs. New York

May 5	New York	83	at	Indiana	93	
May 7	New York	77	at	Indiana	85	
May 9	Indiana	76	at	New York	83	
May 10	Indiana	118	at	New York	107	OT
May 13	New York	88	at	Indiana	99	

(Pacers won series 4-1)

Conference Semifinals - Western Conference

Utah vs. San Antonio

May 5	San Antonio	82	at	Utah	83	
May 7	San Antonio	106	at	Utah	109	OT
May 9	Utah	64	at	San Antonio	86	
May 10	Utah	82	at	San Antonio	73	
May 12	San Antonio	77	at	Utah	87	

(Jazz won series 4-1)

Seattle vs. LA Lakers

May 4	LA Lakers	92	at	Seattle	106
May 6	LA Lakers	92	at	Seattle	68
May 8	Seattle	103	at	LA Lakers	119
May 10	Seattle	100	at	LA Lakers	112
May 12	LA Lakers	110	at	Seattle	95

(LA Lakers won series 4-1)

Conference Finals - Eastern Conference

Chicago vs. Indiana

May 17	Indiana	79	at	Chicago	85
May 19	Indiana	98	at	Chicago	104
May 23	Chicago	105	at	Indiana	107
May 25	Chicago	94	at	Indiana	96
May 27	Indiana	87	at	Chicago	106
May 29	Chicago	89	at	Indiana	92
May 31	Indiana	83	at	Chicago	88

(Bulls won series 4-3)

Conference Finals - Western Conference

Utah vs. LA Lakers

May 16	LA Lakers	77	at	Utah	112
May 18	LA Lakers	95	at	Utah	99
May 22	Utah	109	at	LA Lakers	98
May 24	Utah	96	at	LA Lakers	92

(Jazz won series 4-0)

NBA Finals

Utah vs. Chicago

June 3	Chicago	85	at	Utah	88	OT
June 5	Chicago	93	at	Utah	88	
June 7	Utah	54	at	Chicago	96	
June 10	Utah	82	at	Chicago	86	
June 12	Utah	83	at	Chicago	81	
June 14	Chicago	87	at	Utah	86	

(Bulls won series 4-2)

National Basketball Association Champions

Season	Champion	Eastern Div./Conf. (W-L)	Western Div./Conf. (W-L)
1946-47	Philadelphia	Philadelphia (35-25)	Chicago (39-22)
1947-48	Baltimore	Philadelphia (27-21)	Baltimore (28-20)
1948-49	Minneapolis	Washington (38-22)	Minneapolis (44-16)
1949-50	Minneapolis	Syracuse (51-13)	Minneapolis (51-17)
1950-51	Rochester	New York (36-30)	Rochester (41-27)
1951-52	Minneapolis	New York (37-29)	Minneapolis (40-26)
1952-53	Minneapolis	New York (47-23)	Minneapolis (48-22)
1953-54	Minneapolis	Syracuse (42-30)	Minneapolis (46-26)
1954-55	Syracuse	Syracuse (43-29)	Fort Wayne (43-29)
1955-56	Philadelphia	Philadelphia (45-27)	Fort Wayne (37-35)
1956-57	Boston	Boston (44-28)	St. Louis (34-38)
1957-58	St. Louis	Boston (49-23)	St. Louis (41-31)
1958-59	Boston	Boston (52-20)	Minneapolis (33-39)
1959-60	Boston	Boston (59-16)	St. Louis (46-29)
1960-61	Boston	Boston (57-22)	St. Louis (51-28)
1961-62	Boston	Boston (60-20)	Los Angeles (54-26)
1962-63	Boston	Boston (58-22)	Los Angeles (53-27)
1963-64	Boston	Boston (59-21)	San Francisco (48-32)
1964-65	Boston	Boston (62-18)	Los Angeles (49-31)
1965-66	Boston	Boston (54-26)	Los Angeles (45-35)
1966-67	Philadelphia	Philadelphia (68-13)	San Francisco (44-37)
1967-68	Boston	Boston (54-28)	Los Angeles (52-30)
1968-69	Boston	Boston (48-34)	Los Angeles (55-27)
1969-70	New York	New York (60-22)	Los Angeles (46-36)
1970-71	Milwaukee	Baltimore (42-40)	Milwaukee (66-16)
1971-72	Los Angeles	New York (48-34)	Los Angeles (69-13)
1972-73	New York	New York (57-25)	Los Angeles (60-22)
1973-74	Boston	Boston (56-26)	Milwaukee (59-23)
1974-75	Golden State	Washington (60-22)	Golden State (48-34)
1975-76	Boston	Boston (54-28)	Phoenix (42-40)
1976-77	Portland	Philadelphia (50-32)	Portland (49-33)
1977-78	Washington	Washington (44-38)	Seattle (47-35)
1978-79	Seattle	Washington (54-28)	Seattle (52-30)
1979-80	Los Angeles	Philadelphia (59-23)	Los Angeles (60-22)
1980-81	Boston	Boston (62-20)	Houston (40-42)
1981-82	Los Angeles	Philadelphia (58-24)	Los Angeles (57-25)
1982-83	Philadelphia	Philadelphia (65-17)	Los Angeles (58-24)
1983-84	Boston	Boston (62-20)	Los Angeles (54-28)
1984-85	L.A. Lakers	Boston (63-19)	L.A. Lakers (62-20)
1985-86	Boston	Boston (67-15)	Houston (51-31)
1986-87	L.A. Lakers	Boston (59-23)	L.A. Lakers (65-17)
1987-88	L.A. Lakers	Detroit (54-28)	L.A. Lakers (62-20)
1988-89	Detroit	Detroit (63-19)	L.A. Lakers (57-25)
1989-90	Detroit	Detroit (59-23)	Portland (59-23)
1990-91	Chicago	Chicago (61-21)	L.A.Lakers (58-24)
1991-92	Chicago	Chicago (67-15)	Portland (57-25)
1992-93	Chicago	Chicago (57-25)	Phoenix (62-20)
1993-94	Houston	New York (57-25)	Houston (58-24)
1994-95	Houston	Orlando (57-25)	Houston (47-35)
1995-96	Chicago	Chicago (72-10)	Seattle (64-18)
1996-97	Chicago	Chicago (69-13)	Utah (64-18)
1997-98	Chicago	Chicago (62-20)	Utah (62-20)

Source: National Basketball Association

From the NBA Records Book

NBA Most Valuable Player*

1955-56	Bob Pettit, St. Louis	1976-77	Kareem Abdul-Jabbar, Los Angeles
1956-57	Bob Cousy, Boston	1977-78	Bill Walton, Portland
1957-58	Bill Russell, Boston	1978-79	Moses Malone, Houston
1958-59	Bob Pettit, St. Louis	1979-80	Kareem Abdul-Jabbar, Los Angeles
1959-60	Wilt Chamberlain, Philadelphia	1980-81	Julius Erving, Philadelphia
1960-61	Bill Russell, Boston	1981-82	Moses Malone, Houston
1961-62	Bill Russell, Boston	1982-83	Moses Malone, Philadelphia
1962-63	Bill Russell, Boston	1983-84	Larry Bird, Boston
1963-64	Oscar Robertson, Cincinnati	1984-85	Larry Bird, Boston
1964-65	Bill Russell, Boston	1985-86	Larry Bird, Boston
1965-66	Wilt Chamberlain, Philadelphia	1986-87	Magic Johnson, L.A. Lakers
1966-67	Wilt Chamberlain, Philadelphia	1987-88	Michael Jordan, Chicago
1967-68	Wilt Chamberlain, Philadelphia	1988-89	Magic Johnson, L.A. Lakers
1968-69	Wes Unseld, Baltimore	1989-90	Magic Johnson, L.A. Lakers
1969-70	Willis Reed, New York	1990-91	Michael Jordan, Chicago
1970-71	Kareem Abdul-Jabbar, Milwaukee	1991-92	Michael Jordan, Chicago
1971-72	Kareem Abdul-Jabbar, Milwaukee	1992-93	Charles Barkley, Phoenix
1972-73	Dave Cowens, Boston	1993-94	Hakeem Olajuwon, Houston
1973-74	Kareem Abdul-Jabbar, Milwaukee	1994-95	David Robinson, San Antonio
1974-75	Bob McAdoo, Buffalo	1995-96	Michael Jordan, Chicago
1975-76	Kareem Abdul-Jabbar, Los Angeles	1996-97	Karl Malone, Utah
		1997-98	Michael Jordan, Chicago

NBA Yearly Scoring Leaders in Regular Season Play

Season	Pts.	Scoring	Season	Pts.	Scoring
1946-47	1,389	Joe Fulks, Philadelphia	1979-80	33.1[†]	George Gervin, San Antonio
1947-48	1,007	Max Zaslofsky, Chicago	1980-81	30.7[†]	Adrian Dantley, Utah
1948-49	1,698	George Mikan, Minneapolis	1981-82	32.3[†]	George Gervin, San Antonio
1949-50	1,865	George Mikan, Minneapolis	1982-83	28.4[†]	Alex English, Denver
1950-51	1,932	George Mikan, Minneapolis	1983-84	30.6[†]	Adrian Dantley, Utah
1951-52	1,674	Paul Arizin, Philadelphia	1984-85	32.9[†]	Bernard King, New York
1952-53	1,564	Neil Johnston, Philadelphia	1985-86	30.3[†]	Dominique Wilkins, Atlanta
1953-54	1,759	Neil Johnston, Philadelphia	1986-87	37.1[†]	Michael Jordan, Chicago
1954-55	1,631	Neil Johnston, Philadelphia	1987-88	35.0[†]	Michael Jordan, Chicago
1955-56	1,849	Bob Pettit, St. Louis	1988-89	32.5[†]	Michael Jordan, Chicago
1956-57	1,817	Paul Arizin, Philadelphia	1989-90	33.6[†]	Michael Jordan, Chicago
1957-58	2,001	George Yardley, Detroit	1990-91	31.5[†]	Michael Jordan, Chicago
1958-59	2,105	Bob Pettit, St. Louis	1991-92	30.1[†]	Michael Jordan, Chicago
1959-60	2,707	Wilt Chamberlain, Philadelphia	1992-93	32.6[†]	Michael Jordan, Chicago
1960-61	3,033	Wilt Chamberlain, Philadelphia	1993-94	29.8[†]	David Robinson, San Antonio
1961-62	4,029	Wilt Chamberlain, Philadelphia	1994-95	29.3[†]	Shaquille O'Neal, Orlando
1962-63	3,586	Wilt Chamberlain, San Francisco	1995-96	30.4[†]	Michael Jordan, Chicago
1963-64	2,948	Wilt Chamberlain, San Francisco	1996-97	29.6[†]	Michael Jordan, Chicago
1964-65	2,534	Wilt Chamberlain, S.F.-Phi.	1997-98	28.7[†]	Michael Jordan, Chicago
1965-66	2,649	Wilt Chamberlain, Philadelphia			
1966-67	2,775	Rick Barry, San Francisco			
1967-68	2,142	Dave Bing, Detroit			
1968-69	2,327	Elvin Hayes, San Diego			
1969-70	31.2[†]	Jerry West, Los Angeles			
1970-71	31.7[†]	Kareem Abdul-Jabbar, Milwaukee			
1971-72	34.8[†]	Kareem Abdul-Jabbar, Milwaukee			
1972-73	34.0[†]	Nate Archibald, K.C./Omaha			
1973-74	30.6[†]	Bob McAdoo, Buffalo			
1974-75	34.5[†]	Bob McAdoo, Buffalo			
1975-76	31.1[†]	Bob McAdoo, Buffalo			
1976-77	31.1[†]	Pete Maravich, New Orleans			
1977-78	27.2[†]	George Gervin, San Antonio			
1978-79	29.6[†]	George Gervin, San Antonio			

Top 10 NBA Career Scoring Leaders

Player	Pts.
Kareem Abdul-Jabbar	38,387
Wilt Chamberlain	31,419
Julius Erving	30,026
Moses Malone	29,580
Michael Jordan	29,277
Karl Malone	27,782
Dan Issel	27,482
Elvin Hayes	27,313
Oscar Robertson	26,710
George Gervin	26,595

*Selected by vote of NBA players until 1979–80; by writers and broadcasters since 1980–81.
[†]Based on average per game.
Source: National Basketball Association

NBA Career Leaders

Scoring Average (minimum 400 games or 10,000 points)

	G	FGM	FTM	Pts.	Avg.
Michael Jordan	930	10,962	6,798	29,277	31.5
Wilt Chamberlain	1,045	12,681	6,057	31,419	30.1
Elgin Baylor	846	8,693	5,763	23,149	27.4
Shaquille O'Neal	406	4,430	2,193	11,054	27.2
Jerry West	932	9,016	7,160	25,192	27.0
Bob Pettit	792	7,349	6,182	20,880	26.4
Karl Malone	1,061	10,290	7,133	27,782	26.2
Oscar Robertson	1,040	9,508	7,694	26,710	25.7
Dominique Wilkins	1,047	9,913	6,002	26,534	25.3
George Gervin	1,060	10,368	5,737	26,595	25.1

Field Goal Percentage (minimum 2,000 made)

	FGA	FGM	Pct.
Mark West	4,285	2,501	.584
Artis Gilmore	16,158	9,403	.582
Shaquille O'Neal	7,660	4,430	.578
Steve Johnson	4,965	2,841	.572
Darryl Dawkins	6,079	3,477	.572
James Donaldson	5,442	3,105	.571
Jeff Ruland	3,734	2,105	.564
Bobby Jones	7,953	4,451	.560
Kareem Abdul-Jabbar	28,307	15,837	.559
Kevin McHale	12,334	6,830	.554

Free Throw Percentage (minimum 1,200 made)

	FTA	FTM	Pct.
Mark Price	2,362	2,135	.904
Rick Barry	6,397	5,713	.893
Calvin Murphy	3,864	3,445	.892
Scott Skiles	1,741	1,548	.889
Larry Bird	4,471	3,960	.886
Bill Sharman	3,559	3,143	.883
Reggie Miller	5,037	4,416	.877
Ricky Pierce	3,871	3,389	.875
Billy Keller	1,378	1,202	.872
Jeff Hornacek	3,070	2,677	.872

Assists

John Stockton	12,713
Magic Johnson	10,141
Oscar Robertson	9,887
Isiah Thomas	9,061
Mark Jackson	7,538
Maurice Cheeks	7,392
Len Wilkens	7,211
Bob Cousy	6,955
Guy Rodgers	6,917
Kevin Johnson	6,687

Steals

John Stockton	2,620
Maurice Cheeks	2,310
Michael Jordan	2,306
Julius Erving	2,272
Clyde Drexler	2,207
Alvin Robertson	2,112
Derek Harper	1,913
Hakeem Olajuwon	1,895
Isiah Thomas	1,861
Don Buse	1,818

Personal Fouls

Kareem Abdul-Jabbar	4,657
Artis Gilmore	4,529
Robert Parish	4,443
Caldwell Jones	4,436
Buck Williams	4,267
Elvin Hayes	4,193
James Edwards	4,042
Jack Sikma	3,879
Hal Greer	3,855
Hakeem Olajuwon	3,847

Field Goals

Kareem Abdul-Jabbar	15,837
Wilt Chamberlain	12,681
Julius Erving	11,818
Elvin Hayes	10,976
Michael Jordan	10,962
Alex English	10,659
John Havlicek	10,513
Dan Issel	10,431
George Gervin	10,368
Karl Malone	10,290

Free Throws

Moses Malone	9,018
Oscar Robertson	7,694
Jerry West	7,160
Karl Malone	7,133
Dolph Schayes	6,979
Adrian Dantley	6,832
Michael Jordan	6,798
Kareem Abdul-Jabbar	6,712
Dan Issel	6,591
Julius Erving	6,256

Rebounds

Wilt Chamberlain	23,924
Bill Russell	21,620
Moses Malone	17,834
Kareem Abdul-Jabbar	17,440
Artis Gilmore	16,330
Elvin Hayes	16,279
Robert Parish	14,715
Nate Thurmond	14,464
Walt Bellamy	14,241
Wes Unseld	13,769

Source: National Basketball Association

Women's National Basketball Association

1998 Regular Season Standings

Eastern Conference	W	L	Pct.	GB	Western Conference	W	L	Pct.	GB
Cleveland	20	10	.667	–	Houston	27	3	.900	–
Charlotte	18	12	.600	2	Phoenix	19	11	.633	8
New York	18	12	.600	2	Los Angeles	12	18	.400	15
Detroit	17	13	.567	3	Sacramento	8	22	.267	19
Washington	3	27	.100	17	Utah	8	22	.267	19

Semifinals	Finals
Houston 85, at Charlotte 71 At Houston 77, Charlotte 61	At Phoenix 78, Cleveland 68 At Cleveland 67, Phoenix 66 Phoenix 71, at Cleveland 60	At Phoenix 54, Houston 51 At Houston 74, Phoenix 69 (OT) At Houston 80, Phoenix 71

American Basketball League

1997-98 Regular Season Standings

Eastern Conference	W	L	Pct.	GB	Western Conference	W	L	Pct.	GB
Columbus	36	8	.818	–	Portland	27	17	.613	–
New England	24	20	.545	13	Long Beach	26	18	.591	1
Atlanta	15	29	.340	21	San Jose	21	23	.477	5
Philadelphia	13	31	.295	23	Colorado	21	23	.477	6
					Seattle	15	29	.340	12

First Round	Semifinals	Finals
San Jose 80, at New England 78 At San Jose 83, New England 71 At Long Beach 96, Colorado 72 At Colorado 88, Long Beach 68 At Long Beach 92, Colorado 61	At Long Beach 72, Portland 62 Long Beach 70, at Portland 69 At Columbus 94, San Jose 88 Columbus 74, at San Jose 62	At Long Beach 65, Columbus 62 At Long Beach 71, Columbus 61 At Columbus 70, Long Beach 61 At Columbus 68, Long Beach 53 At Columbus 86, Long Beach 81

Baseball

Baseball, 1998! Let's go right to the highlights (take a deep breath):

Mark McGwire of the St. Louis Cardinals hit 70 home runs (70!) to set a new single-season home-run record. Sammy Sosa of the Chicago Cubs hit 66. David Wells of the New York Yankees pitched a perfect game against the Minnesota Twins. Kerry Wood of the Chicago Cubs, a 21-year-old genuine pheenom baseball pitcher, tied the National League record for strikeouts in a game with 20 Ks against the Houston Astros. The Baltimore Orioles' Cal Ripken Jr., healthy and uninjured, quietly and with no fanfare brought his consecutive-games-played streak to an end at 2,632 when he sat himself down on September 20 against the New York Yankees. Ken Griffey Jr. hit 56 home runs to lead the American League, batted .284 and drove in 146 runs, laying legitimate claim to being the Willie Mays of his generation. The New York Yankees won 114 regular-season games, setting an American League record, and for much of the season flirted with the idea of breaking the major-league record of 116 set by the Cubs in 1906.

The usual suspects of the 1990s won their divisions: The Atlanta Braves (NL East), Yankees (AL East), Cleveland Indians (AL Central),

Houston Astros (a late-'90s usual suspect, NL Central) and the San Diego Padres (NL West, and, all right, there was nothing usual about that). But in the AL West the Anaheim Angels and Texas Rangers staged an old-fashioned pennant race through the last weekend of the season before the Rangers came out on top. In the National League the Cubs, New York Mets and San Francisco Giants put the wild in Wild Card in a three-team race that needed a playoff game between the Cubs and the Giants before the Cubs claimed the spot on the day after the regular season was supposed to end. And finally, the Boston Red Sox played great baseball behind the steam-rolling Yankees, *didn't* swoon when the Toronto Blue Jays made a run at them, and won the American League Wild Card spot—thereby setting up the possibility of a Cubs-Red Sox World Series. Hey, it could happen.

Yes, it was sumkinda season. Wow!

Standing astride above it all, of course, was the Mark McGwire-Sammy Sosa home-run race. Before the season even started there was much talk that the planets had aligned correctly for someone (McGwire, namely) to take a serious run at Roger Maris's 61 homers in 1961. This was an expansion year, after all—the Arizona Diamondbacks joined the National League, Tampa Bay Devil Rays the American—and "major" league pitching was sure to feature too much minor-league throwing. Besides, McGwire had hit 58 the year before. The red-bearded St. Louis Cardinals' first baseman didn't disappoint. He hit a grand slam in his first game and was off to the races. It wasn't just that he hit home runs, it was the way he hit them. His massive forearms propelled the ball on long, majestic, sweeping arcs that deposited the cowhide into and beyond the far reaches of stadiums where no ball had dared go before. He turned batting practice into Must-See BP: 10-, 15-, 20 thousand people at a clip would show up at the stadiums he visited two hours before the game, trying to crowd themselves into left field for a raucous celebration of unbridled American Power. When he hit No. 62 on Sept. 8—an un-McGwire-like line shot that barely cleared the fence in the left-field corner—all of America, it seemed, stood and applauded.

And then there was Sammy Sosa, the Pride of the Dominican Republic. He was an improbable delight, having thrust himself onto the Big Stage in June by hitting 20 homers, the most ever for any month. Conventional wisdom insisted he would return to the pack after that, but . . . he didn't. Whenever it appeared he was about to fade, he'd come up with a couple, put the heat back on McGwire, who would then, it seemed, *always* respond with a few round-trippers of his own. And it couldn't have happened to two nicer

guys. At least that's what the country appeared to decide. McGwire, a divorced Dad, made sure his 10-year-old son was with him every step of the way as one of the Cardinals' bat boys. Sosa—ever gracious and self-deprecating—created an art form out of toiling in McGwire's shadow. He held the lead in the homer race only twice, for a grand total of about one hour and 45 minutes. His easy manner with the press, his sheer delight in the moment, his boundless joy in his own talent even served to rub off on McGwire, who for the first few months appeared to be the only person alive who wasn't enjoying America's Great Home-Run Derby. Which image will be remembered with more sweetness: McGwire lifting his son into the air after hitting No. 62 to break Maris's record, or McGwire and Sosa (poetically enough, McGwire's 62 came against the Cubs) embracing at home plate in respectful, grateful appreciation of each others' accomplishments?

So it was only fitting that they entered the final weekend of the season tied for the lead with 65 homers each. Well, fitting enough until McGwire hit five homers in the final three games to claim the record at an astounding SEVEN-OH! He was indeed The Man—just as "Slammin' Sammy Sosa" had been insisting all along.

Given the huge, warm fuzzy that baseball turned itself into in 1998—there was even actual talk that the fans had finally forgiven baseball for the disastrous, World-Series-canceling strike of 1994-1995—it seems almost a shame to mention that the business of baseball did, indeed, march forward.

Bud Selig, the owner of the Milwaukee Brewers, finally deleted the *acting* from in front of his title and became the Commissioner of Baseball. There was much discussion as to whether Mr. Selig would actually act (or, more precisely *do* anything) now that he was commissioner, but, after six leaderless years, the public-relations value alone of having a live body in the office was incalculable.

In June, the Los Angeles Dodgers traded all-star catcher Mike Piazza to the Florida Marlins for Gary Scheffield, Bobby Bonilla, Charles Johnson and Jim Eisenrach. The reason? Piazza, a free agent at the end of the season had balked at an $85 million contract offer from the Dodgers, insisting on something past $100 million. The Dodgers' new owners, News Corp.'s Fox, barely blinked. With little consultation with the Dodgers "baseball people," Fox made the deal.

The Marlins, meanwhile, were only too happy to oblige. After winning a World Series in 1997, owner H. Wayne Huizenga held a fire sale to get rid of all the high-priced players he had brought in to win said Series. Stating flatly that he couldn't make money in base-

World Series Results

Year	Winner		Loser		Attendance
1903	Boston (AL)	5	Pittsburgh (NL)	3	100,429
1904		No World Series played			
1905	New York (NL)	4	Philadelphia (AL)	1	91,723
1906	Chicago (AL)	4	Chicago (NL)	2	99,845
1907	Chicago (NL)	4	Detroit (AL)	0 1 tie	78,068
1908	Chicago (NL)	4	Detroit (AL)	1	62,232
1909	Pittsburgh (NL)	4	Detroit (AL)	3	145,205
1910	Philadelphia (AL)	4	Chicago (NL)	1	124,222
1911	Philadelphia (AL)	4	New York (NL)	2	179,851
1912	Boston (AL)	4	New York (NL)	3 1 tie	252,037
1913	Philadelphia (AL)	4	New York (NL)	1	151,000
1914	Boston (NL)	4	Philadelphia (AL)	0	111,009
1915	Boston (AL)	4	Philadelphia (NL)	1	143,351
1916	Boston (AL)	4	Brooklyn (NL)	1	162,859
1917	Chicago (AL)	4	New York (NL)	2	186,654
1918	Boston (AL)	4	Chicago (NL)	2	128,483
1919	Cincinnati (NL)	5	Chicago (AL)	3	236,928
1920	Cleveland (AL)	5	Brooklyn (NL)	2	178,737
1921	New York (NL)	5	New York (AL)	3	269,976
1922	New York (NL)	4	New York (AL)	0 1 tie	185,947
1923	New York (AL)	4	New York (NL)	2	301,430
1924	Washington (AL)	4	New York (NL)	3	283,665
1925	Pittsburgh (NL)	4	Washington (AL)	3	282,848
1926	St. Louis (NL)	4	New York (AL)	3	328,051
1927	New York (AL)	4	Pittsburgh (NL)	0	201,705
1928	New York (AL)	4	St. Louis (NL)	0	199,072
1929	Philadelphia (AL)	4	Chicago (NL)	1	190,490
1930	Philadelphia (AL)	4	St. Louis (NL)	2	212,619
1931	St. Louis (NL)	4	Philadelphia (AL)	3	231,567
1932	New York (AL)	4	Chicago (NL)	0	191,998
1933	New York (NL)	4	Washington (AL)	1	163,076
1934	St. Louis (NL)	4	Detroit (AL)	3	281,510
1935	Detroit (AL)	4	Chicago (NL)	2	286,672
1936	New York (AL)	4	New York (NL)	2	302,924
1937	New York (AL)	4	New York (NL)	1	238,142
1938	New York (AL)	4	Chicago (NL)	0	200,833
1939	New York (AL)	4	Cincinnati (NL)	0	183,849
1940	Cincinnati (NL)	4	Detroit (AL)	3	281,927
1941	New York (AL)	4	Brooklyn (NL)	1	235,773
1942	St. Louis (NL)	4	New York (AL)	1	277,101
1943	New York (AL)	4	St. Louis (NL)	1	277,312
1944	St. Louis (NL)	4	St. Louis (AL)	2	206,708
1945	Detroit (AL)	4	Chicago (NL)	3	333,457
1946	St. Louis (NL)	4	Boston (AL)	3	250,071
1947	New York (AL)	4	Brooklyn (NL)	3	389,763
1948	Cleveland (AL)	4	Boston (NL)	2	358,362
1949	New York (AL)	4	Brooklyn (NL)	1	236,716

Year	Winner		Loser		Attendance
1950	New York (AL)	4	Philadelphia (NL)	0	196,009
1951	New York (AL)	4	New York (NL)	2	341,977
1952	New York (AL)	4	Brooklyn (NL)	3	340,706
1953	New York (AL)	4	Brooklyn (NL)	2	307,350
1954	New York (NL)	4	Cleveland (AL)	0	251,507
1955	Brooklyn (NL)	4	New York (AL)	3	362,310
1956	New York (AL)	4	Brooklyn (NL)	3	345,903
1957	Milwaukee (NL)	4	New York (AL)	3	394,712
1958	New York (AL)	4	Milwaukee (NL)	3	393,909
1959	Los Angeles (NL)	4	Chicago (AL)	2	420,784
1960	Pittsburgh (NL)	4	New York (AL)	3	349,813
1961	New York (AL)	4	Cincinnati (NL)	1	223,247
1962	New York (AL)	4	San Francisco (NL)	3	376,864
1963	Los Angeles (NL)	4	New York (AL)	0	247,279
1964	St. Louis (NL)	4	New York (AL)	3	321,807
1965	Los Angeles (NL)	4	Minnesota (AL)	3	364,326
1966	Baltimore (AL)	4	Los Angeles (NL)	0	220,791
1967	St. Louis (NL)	4	Boston (AL)	3	304,085
1968	Detroit (AL)	4	St. Louis (NL)	3	379,670
1969	New York (NL)	4	Baltimore (AL)	1	272,378
1970	Baltimore (AL)	4	Cincinnati (NL)	1	253,183
1971	Pittsburgh (NL)	4	Baltimore (AL)	3	351,091
1972	Oakland (AL)	4	Cincinnati (NL)	3	363,149
1973	Oakland (AL)	4	New York (NL)	3	358,289
1974	Oakland (AL)	4	Los Angeles (NL)	1	260,004
1975	Cincinnati (NL)	4	Boston (AL)	3	308,272
1976	Cincinnati (NL)	4	New York (AL)	0	223,009
1977	New York (AL)	4	Los Angeles (NL)	2	337,708
1978	New York (AL)	4	Los Angeles (NL)	2	337,304
1979	Pittsburgh (NL)	4	Baltimore (AL)	3	367,597
1980	Philadelphia (NL)	4	Kansas City (AL)	2	324,516
1981	Los Angeles (NL)	4	New York (AL)	2	338,081
1982	St. Louis (NL)	4	Milwaukee (AL)	3	348,570
1983	Baltimore (AL)	4	Philadelphia (NL)	1	304,139
1984	Detroit (AL)	4	San Diego (NL)	1	271,820
1985	Kansas City (AL)	4	St. Louis (NL)	3	327,494
1986	New York (NL)	4	Boston (AL)	3	321,774
1987	Minnesota (AL)	4	St. Louis (NL)	3	387,178
1988	Los Angeles (NL)	4	Oakland (AL)	1	259,984
1989	Oakland (AL)	4	San Francisco (NL)	0	222,843
1990	Cincinnati (NL)	4	Oakland (AL)	0	208,544
1991	Minnesota (AL)	4	Atlanta (NL)	3	373,160
1992	Toronto (AL)	4	Atlanta (NL)	2	311,460
1993	Toronto (AL)	4	Philadelphia (NL)	2	344,394
1994		No World Series played			
1995	Atlanta (NL)	4	Cleveland (AL)	2	286,385
1996	New York (AL)	4	Atlanta (NL)	2	324,685
1997	Florida (NL)	4	Cleveland (AL)	3	403,617

Source: Office of the Commissioner of Baseball

World Series Most Valuable Player

1955	Johnny Podres, Brooklyn	1977	Reggie Jackson, New York (AL)
1956	Don Larsen, New York (AL)	1978	Bucky Dent, New York (AL)
1957	Lew Burdette, Milwaukee	1979	Willie Stargell, Pittsburgh
1958	Bob Turley, New York (AL)	1980	Mike Schmidt, Philadelphia
1959	Larry Sherry, Los Angeles	1981	Ron Cey, Pedro Guerrero, Steve Yeager,
1960	Bobby Richardson, New York (AL)		Los Angeles
1961	Whitey Ford, New York (AL)	1982	Darrell Porter, St. Louis
1962	Ralph Terry, New York (AL)	1983	Rick Dempsey, Baltimore
1963	Sandy Koufax, Los Angeles	1984	Alan Trammell, Detroit
1964	Bob Gibson, St. Louis	1985	Bret Saberhagen, Kansas City
1965	Sandy Koufax, Los Angeles	1986	Ray Knight, New York (NL)
1966	Frank Robinson, Baltimore	1987	Frank Viola, Minnesota
1967	Bob Gibson, St. Louis	1988	Orel Hershiser, Los Angeles
1968	Mickey Lolich, Detroit	1989	Dave Stewart, Oakland
1969	Donn Clendenon, New York (NL)	1990	Jose Rijo, Cincinnati
1970	Brooks Robinson, Baltimore	1991	Jack Morris, Minnesota
1971	Roberto Clemente, Pittsburgh	1992	Pat Borders, Toronto
1972	Gene Tenace, Oakland	1993	Paul Molitor, Toronto
1973	Reggie Jackson, Oakland	1994	No World Series played
1974	Rollie Fingers, Oakland	1995	Tom Glavine, Atlanta
1975	Pete Rose, Cincinnati	1996	John Wetteland, New York (AL)
1976	Johnny Bench, Cincinnati	1997	Livan Hernandez, Florida

Source: Office of the Commissioner of Baseball

All-Star Game Results

Date	Winner	Score	Date	Winner	Score
July 6, 1933	American	4-2	July 8, 1952	National	3-2
July 10, 1934	American	9-7	July 14, 1953	National	5-1
July 8, 1935	American	4-1	July 13, 1954	American	11-9
July 7, 1936	National	4-3	July 12, 1955	National	6-5*
July 7, 1937	American	8-3	July 10, 1956	National	7-3
July 6, 1938	National	4-1	July 9, 1957	American	6-5
July 11, 1939	American	3-1	July 8, 1958	American	4-3
July 9, 1940	National	4-0	July 7, 1959	National	5-4
July 8, 1941	American	7-5	Aug. 3, 1959	American	5-3
July 6, 1942	American	3-1	July 11, 1960	National	5-3
July 13, 1943	American	5-3	July 13, 1960	National	6-0
July 11, 1944	National	7-1	July 11, 1961	National	5-4*
1945	No game played		July 31, 1961	Tie	1-1**
July 9, 1946	American	12-0	July 10, 1962	National	3-1*
July 8, 1947	American	2-1	July 30, 1962	American	9-4
July 13, 1948	American	5-2	July 9, 1963	National	5-3
July 12, 1949	American	11-7	July 7, 1964	National	7-4
July 11, 1950	National	4-3*	July 13, 1965	National	6-5
July 10, 1951	National	8-3	July 12, 1966	National	2-1*

ball, he needed to bare-bones the payroll to make it an attractive sell. The Piazza deal took the last bit of fat from the Marlin carcass. The Marlins would go on to win 54 games, the lowest total by a a major-league team in 19 years and the lowest ever by a defending World Series champion. Piazza, meanwhile, would be traded within a week to the New York Mets. After a rocky honeymoon with the

New York fans, who expected him to produce a $100 million at bat every trip to the plate, Piazza settled in and helped keep the Mets in the Wild Card race through the final weekend. But there were no guarantees he wouldn't be wearing his fourth major-league uniform come Opening Day 1999.

Finally, an enterprising reporter noticed an interesting-looking bottle in McGwire's locker

Date	Winner	Score	Date	Winner	Score
July 11, 1967	National	2-1*	July 6, 1983	American	13-3
July 9, 1968	National	1-0	July 10, 1984	National	3-1
July 23, 1969	National	9-3	July 16, 1985	National	6-1
July 14, 1970	National	5-4*	July 15, 1986	American	3-2
July 13, 1971	American	6-4	July 14, 1987	National	2-0*
July 25, 1972	National	4-3	July 12, 1988	American	2-1
July 24, 1973	National	7-1	July 11, 1989	American	5-3
July 23, 1974	National	7-2	July 10, 1990	American	2-0
July 15, 1975	National	6-3	July 9, 1991	American	4-2
July 13, 1976	National	7-1	July 14, 1992	American	13-6
July 19, 1977	National	7-5	July 13, 1993	American	9-3
July 11, 1978	National	7-3	July 12, 1994	National	8-7
July 17, 1979	National	7-6	July 11, 1995	National	3-2
July 8, 1980	National	4-2	July 9, 1996	National	6-0
Aug. 9, 1981	National	5-4	July 8, 1997	American	3-1
July 13, 1982	National	4-1	July 7, 1998	American	13-8

Note: From 1959 to 1962, two all-star games were played.
*Extra innings.
**Game called because of rain after nine innings.
Source: Office of the Commissioner of Baseball

All-Star Game Most Valuable Player

Year	Player, team	Position	Year	Player, team	Position
1962 (1)	Maury Wills, L.A. (NL)	SS	1980	Ken Griffey, Cin.	LF
1962 (2)	*Leon Wagner, L.A. (AL)	LF	1981	*Gary Carter, Mon.	C
1963	*Willie Mays, S.F.	CF	1982	*Dave Concepcion, Cin.	SS
1964	Johnny Callison, Phi.	RF	1983	*Fred Lynn, CA	CF
1965	*Juan Marichal, S.F.	P	1984	*Gary Carter, Mon.	C
1966	*Brooks Robinson, Bal.	3B	1985	*LaMarr Hoyt, S.D.	P
1967	Tony Perez, Cin.	3B	1986	*Roger Clemens, Bos.	P
1968	*Willie Mays, S.F.	CF	1987	Tim Raines, Mon.	LF
1969	*Willie McCovey, S.F.	1B	1988	*Terry Steinbach, Oak.	C
1970	*Carl Yastrzemski, Bos.	CF-1B	1989	*Bo Jackson, K.C.	LF
1971	*Frank Robinson, Bal.	RF	1990	Julio Franco, TX	2B
1972	*Joe Morgan, Cin.	2B	1991	*Cal Ripken, Bal.	SS
1973	Bobby Bonds, S.F.	RF	1992	*Ken Griffey, Jr., Sea.	CF
1974	*Steve Garvey, L.A.	1B	1993	*Kirby Puckett, MN	LF
1975	Bill Madlock, Chi. (NL)	3B	1994	Fred McGriff, Atl.	1B
	Jon Matlack, N.Y. (NL)	P	1995	Jeff Conine, FL	OF
1976	*George Foster, Cin.	CF-RF	1996	*Mike Piazza, L.A.	C
1977	*Don Sutton, L.A.	P	1997	Sandy Alomar, Jr., Cleve.	C
1978	*Steve Garvey, L.A.	1B	1998	*Roberto Alomar, Bal.	2B
1979	*Dave Parker, Pit.	RF			

*Started game.
Source: Office of the Commissioner of Baseball

and discovered that it contained androstene-dione, an adrenal hormone produced naturally in men and women that is converted in the liver to testosterone. McGwire admitted he had been using it for almost a year, and pointed out correctly that it was not a substance banned by baseball. It is, however, banned by the Olympics, the NFL and the NCAA.

For a while there, The Great Drug Debate threatened to overshadow The Great Home-Run Derby. But McGwire—and Sosa, who said he didn't use "Andro" but did use creatine, a wildly popular protein booster—answered with their bats, 136 times. The fans, meanwhile answered with their wallets: more than 70 million times.

Hey, it was sumkinda season!

Steve McKee

Major League Baseball Regular Season Yearly Leaders

Batting Average

American League

1901: Nap Lajoie, Philadelphia .422
1902: Ed Delahanty, Washington .376
1903: Nap Lajoie, Cleveland .355
1904: Nap Lajoie, Cleveland .381
1905: Elmer Flick, Cleveland .308
1906: George Stone, St. Louis .358
1907: Ty Cobb, Detroit .350
1908: Ty Cobb, Detroit .324
1909: Ty Cobb, Detroit .377
1910: Ty Cobb, Detroit .385
1911: Ty Cobb, Detroit .420
1912: Ty Cobb, Detroit .410
1913: Ty Cobb, Detroit .390
1914: Ty Cobb, Detroit .368
1915: Ty Cobb, Detroit .369
1916: Tris Speaker, Cleveland .386
1917: Ty Cobb, Detroit .383
1918: Ty Cobb, Detroit .382
1919: Ty Cobb, Detroit .384
1920: George Sisler, St. Louis .407
1921: Harry Heilmann, Detroit .394
1922: George Sisler, St. Louis .420
1923: Harry Heilmann, Detroit .403
1924: Babe Ruth, New York .378
1925: Harry Heilmann, Detroit .393
1926: Heinie Manush, Detroit .378
1927: Harry Heilmann, Detroit .398
1928: Goose Goslin, Washington .379
1929: Lew Fonseca, Cleveland .369
1930: Al Simmons, Philadelphia .381
1931: Al Simmons, Philadelphia .390
1932: Dale Alexander, Detroit/Boston .367
1933: Jimmie Foxx, Philadelphia .356
1934: Lou Gehrig, New York .363
1935: Buddy Myer, Washington .349
1936: Luke Appling, Chicago .388
1937: Charlie Gehringer, Detroit .371
1938: Jimmie Foxx, Boston .349
1939: Joe DiMaggio, New York .381
1940: Joe DiMaggio, New York .352
1941: Ted Williams, Boston .406
1942: Ted Williams, Boston .356
1943: Luke Appling, Chicago .328
1944: Lou Boudreau, Cleveland .327
1945: George Stirnweiss, New York .309
1946: Mickey Vernon, Washington .353
1947: Ted Williams, Boston .343
1948: Ted Williams, Boston .369
1949: George Kell, Detroit .343
1950: Billy Goodman, Boston .354
1951: Ferris Fain, Philadelphia .344
1952: Ferris Fain, Philadelphia .327

1953: Mickey Vernon, Washington .337
1954: Bobby Avila, Cleveland .341
1955: Al Kaline, Detroit .340
1956: Mickey Mantle, New York .353
1957: Ted Williams, Boston .388
1958: Ted Williams, Boston .328
1959: Harvey Kuenn, Detroit .353
1960: Pete Runnels, Boston .320
1961: Norm Cash, Detroit .361
1962: Pete Runnels, Boston .326
1963: Carl Yastrzemski, Boston .321
1964: Tony Oliva, Minnesota .323
1965: Tony Oliva, Minnesota .321
1966: Frank Robinson, Baltimore .316
1967: Carl Yastrzemski, Boston .326
1968: Carl Yastrzemski, Boston .301
1969: Rod Carew, Minnesota .332
1970: Alex Johnson, California .329
1971: Tony Oliva, Minnesota .337
1972: Rod Carew, Minnesota .318
1973: Rod Carew, Minnesota .350
1974: Rod Carew, Minnesota .364
1975: Rod Carew, Minnesota .359
1976: George Brett, Kansas City .333
1977: Rod Carew, Minnesota .388
1978: Rod Carew, Minnesota .333
1979: Fred Lynn, Boston .333
1980: George Brett, Kansas City .390
1981: Carney Lansford, Boston .336
1982: Willie Wilson, Kansas City .332
1983: Wade Boggs, Boston .361
1984: Don Mattingly, New York .343
1985: Wade Boggs, Boston .368
1986: Wade Boggs, Boston .357
1987: Wade Boggs, Boston .363
1988: Wade Boggs, Boston .366
1989: Kirby Puckett, Minnesota .339
1990: George Brett, Kansas City .329
1991: Julio Franco, Texas .341
1992: Edgar Martinez, Seattle .343
1993: John Olerud, Toronto .363
1994: Paul O'Neill, New York .359
1995: Edgar Martinez, Seattle .356
1996: Alex Rodriguez, Seattle .358
1997: Frank Thomas, Chicago .347

National League

1876: Ross Barnes, Chicago .404
1877: Deacon White, Boston .385
1878: Abner Dalrymple, Milwaukee .356
1879: Cap Anson, Chicago .407
1880: George Gore, Chicago .365
1881: Cap Anson, Chicago .399
1882: Dan Brouthers, Buffalo .367
1883: Dan Brouthers, Buffalo .371

1884: Jim O'Rourke, Buffalo	.350	1941: Pete Reiser, Brooklyn	.343
1885: Roger Connor, New York	.371	1942: Ernie Lombardi, Boston	.330
1886: King Kelly, Chicago	.388	1943: Stan Musial, St. Louis	.357
1887: Cap Anson, Chicago	.421	1944: Dixie Walker, Brooklyn	.357
1888: Cap Anson, Chicago	.343	1945: Phil Cavarretta, Chicago	.355
1889: Dan Brouthers, Boston	.373	1946: Stan Musial, St. Louis	.365
1890: Jack Glasscock, New York	.336	1947: Harry Walker, St. Louis/Philadelphia	.363
1891: Billy Hamilton, Philadelphia	.338	1948: Stan Musial, St. Louis	.376
1892: Dan Brouthers, Brooklyn	.335	1949: Jackie Robinson, Brooklyn	.342
Cupid Childs, Cleveland	.335	1950: Stan Musial, St. Louis	.346
1893: Hugh Duffy, Boston	.378	1951: Stan Musial, St. Louis	.355
1894: Hugh Duffy, Boston	.438	1952: Stan Musial, St. Louis	.336
1895: Jesse Burkett, Cleveland	.423	1953: Carl Furillo, Brooklyn	.344
1896: Jesse Burkett, Cleveland	.410	1954: Willie Mays, New York	.345
1897: Willie Keeler, Baltimore	.432	1955: Richie Ashburn, Philadelphia	.338
1898: Willie Keeler, Baltimore	.379	1956: Hank Aaron, Milwaukee	.328
1899: Ed Delahanty, Philadelphia	.408	1957: Stan Musial, St. Louis	.351
1900: Honus Wagner, Pittsburgh	.381	1958: Richie Ashburn, Philadelphia	.350
1901: Jesse Burkett, St. Louis	.382	1959: Hank Aaron, Milwaukee	.355
1902: Ginger Beaumont, Pittsburgh	.357	1960: Dick Groat, Pittsburgh	.325
1903: Honus Wagner, Pittsburgh	.355	1961: Roberto Clemente, Pittsburgh	.351
1904: Honus Wagner, Pittsburgh	.349	1962: Tommy Davis, Los Angeles	.346
1905: Cy Seymour, Cincinnati	.377	1963: Tommy Davis, Los Angeles	.326
1906: Honus Wagner, Pittsburgh	.339	1964: Roberto Clemente, Pittsburgh	.339
1907: Honus Wagner, Pittsburgh	.350	1965: Roberto Clemente, Pittsburgh	.329
1908: Honus Wagner, Pittsburgh	.354	1966: Matty Alou, Pittsburgh	.342
1909: Honus Wagner, Pittsburgh	.339	1967: Roberto Clemente, Pittsburgh	.357
1910: Sherry Magee, Philadelphia	.331	1968: Pete Rose, Cincinnati	.335
1911: Honus Wagner, Pittsburgh	.334	1969: Pete Rose, Cincinnati	.348
1912: Heine Zimmerman, Chicago	.372	1970: Rico Carty, Atlanta	.366
1913: Jake Daubert, Brooklyn	.350	1971: Joe Torre, St. Louis	.363
1914: Jake Daubert, Brooklyn	.329	1972: Billy Williams, Chicago	.333
1915: Larry Doyle, New York	.320	1973: Pete Rose, Cincinnati	.338
1916: Hal Chase, Cincinnati	.339	1974: Ralph Garr, Atlanta	.353
1917: Edd Roush, Cincinnati	.341	1975: Bill Madlock, Chicago	.354
1918: Zack Wheat, Brooklyn	.335	1976: Bill Madlock, Chicago	.339
1919: Edd Roush, Cincinnati	.321	1977: Dave Parker, Pittsburgh	.338
1920: Rogers Hornsby, St. Louis	.370	1978: Dave Parker, Pittsburgh	.334
1921: Rogers Hornsby, St. Louis	.397	1979: Keith Hernandez, St. Louis	.344
1922: Rogers Hornsby, St. Louis	.401	1980: Bill Buckner, Chicago	.324
1923: Rogers Hornsby, St. Louis	.384	1981: Bill Madlock, Pittsburgh	.341
1924: Rogers Hornsby, St. Louis	.424	1982: Al Oliver, Montreal	.331
1925: Rogers Hornsby, St. Louis	.403	1983: Bill Madlock, Pittsburgh	.323
1926: Bubbles Hargrave, Cincinnati	.353	1984: Tony Gwynn, San Diego	.351
1927: Paul Waner, Pittsburgh	.380	1985: Willie McGee, St. Louis	.353
1928: Rogers Hornsby, Boston	.387	1986: Tim Raines, Montreal	.334
1929: Lefty O'Doul, Philadelphia	.398	1987: Tony Gwynn, San Diego	.370
1930: Bill Terry, New York	.401	1988: Tony Gwynn, San Diego	.313
1931: Chick Hafey, St. Louis	.349	1989: Tony Gwynn, San Diego	.336
1932: Lefty O'Doul, Brooklyn	.368	1990: Willie McGee, St. Louis	.335
1933: Chuck Klein, Philadelphia	.368	1991: Terry Pendleton, Atlanta	.319
1934: Paul Waner, Pittsburgh	.362	1992: Gary Sheffield, San Diego	.330
1935: Arky Vaughan, Pittsburgh	.385	1993: Andres Galarraga, Colorado	.370
1936: Paul Waner, Pittsburgh	.373	1994: Tony Gwynn, San Diego	.394
1937: Joe Medwick, St. Louis	.374	1995: Tony Gwynn, San Diego	.368
1938: Ernie Lombardi, Cincinnati	.342	1996: Tony Gwynn, San Diego	.353
1939: Johnny Mize, St. Louis	.349	1997: Tony Gwynn, San Diego	.372
1940: Debs Garms, Pittsburgh	.355	Note—Bases on balls counted as hits in 1887.	

Slugging Average

American League

1901: Nap Lajoie, Philadelphia	.635
1902: Ed Delahanty, Washington	.589
1903: Nap Lajoie, Cleveland	.533
1904: Nap Lajoie, Cleveland	.549
1905: Elmer Flick, Cleveland	.466
1906: George Stone, St. Louis	.496
1907: Ty Cobb, Detroit	.473
1908: Ty Cobb, Detroit	.475
1909: Ty Cobb, Detroit	.517
1910: Ty Cobb, Detroit	.554
1911: Ty Cobb, Detroit	.621
1912: Ty Cobb, Detroit	.586
1913: Joe Jackson, Cleveland	.551
1914: Ty Cobb, Detroit	.513
1915: Jack Fournier, Chicago	.491
1916: Tris Speaker, Cleveland	.502
1917: Ty Cobb, Detroit	.571
1918: Babe Ruth, Boston	.555
1919: Babe Ruth, Boston	.657
1920: Babe Ruth, New York	.847
1921: Babe Ruth, New York	.846
1922: Babe Ruth, New York	.672
1923: Babe Ruth, New York	.764
1924: Babe Ruth, New York	.739
1925: Ken Williams, St. Louis	.613
1926: Babe Ruth, New York	.737
1927: Babe Ruth, New York	.772
1928: Babe Ruth, New York	.709
1929: Babe Ruth, New York	.697
1930: Babe Ruth, New York	.732
1931: Babe Ruth, New York	.700
1932: Jimmie Foxx, Philadelphia	.749
1933: Jimmie Foxx, Philadelphia	.703
1934: Lou Gehrig, New York	.706
1935: Jimmie Foxx, Philadelphia	.636
1936: Lou Gehrig, New York	.696
1937: Joe DiMaggio, New York	.673
1938: Jimmie Foxx, Boston	.704
1939: Jimmie Foxx, Boston	.694
1940: Hank Greenberg, Detroit	.670
1941: Ted Williams, Boston	.735
1942: Ted Williams, Boston	.648
1943: Rudy York, Detroit	.527
1944: Bobby Doerr, Boston	.528
1945: George Stirnweiss, New York	.476
1946: Ted Williams, Boston	.667
1947: Ted Williams, Boston	.634
1948: Ted Williams, Boston	.615
1949: Ted Williams, Boston	.650
1950: Joe DiMaggio, New York	.585
1951: Ted Williams, Boston	.556
1952: Larry Doby, Cleveland	.541
1953: Al Rosen, Cleveland	.613
1954: Ted Williams, Boston	.635
1955: Mickey Mantle, New York	.611
1956: Mickey Mantle, New York	.705
1957: Ted Williams, Boston	.731
1958: Rocky Colavito, Cleveland	.620
1959: Al Kaline, Detroit	.530
1960: Roger Maris, New York	.581
1961: Mickey Mantle, New York	.687
1962: Mickey Mantle, New York	.605
1963: Harmon Killebrew, Minnesota	.555
1964: Boog Powell, Baltimore	.606
1965: Carl Yastrzemski, Boston	.536
1966: Frank Robinson, Baltimore	.637
1967: Carl Yastrzemski, Boston	.622
1968: Frank Howard, Washington	.552
1969: Reggie Jackson, Oakland	.608
1970: Carl Yastrzemski, Boston	.592
1971: Tony Oliva, Minnesota	.546
1972: Dick Allen, Chicago	.603
1973: Reggie Jackson, Oakland	.531
1974: Dick Allen, Chicago	.563
1975: Fred Lynn, Boston	.566
1976: Reggie Jackson, Baltimore	.502
1977: Jim Rice, Boston	.593
1978: Jim Rice, Boston	.600
1979: Fred Lynn, Boston	.637
1980: George Brett, Kansas City	.664
1981: Bobby Grich, California	.543
1982: Robin Yount, Milwaukee	.578
1983: George Brett, Kansas City	.563
1984: Harold Baines, Chicago	.541
1985: George Brett, Kansas City	.585
1986: Don Mattingly, New York	.573
1987: Mark McGwire, Oakland	.618
1988: Jose Canseco, Oakland	.569
1989: Ruben Sierra, Texas	.543
1990: Cecil Fielder, Detroit	.592
1991: Danny Tartabull, Kansas City	.593
1992: Mark McGwire, Oakland	.585
1993: Juan Gonzalez, Texas	.632
1994: Frank Thomas, Chicago	.729
1995: Albert Belle, Cleveland	.690
1996: Mark McGwire, Oakland	.730
1997: Ken Griffey Jr., Seattle	.646

National League

1900: Honus Wagner, Pittsburgh	.572
1901: Jimmy Sheckard, Brooklyn	.541
1902: Honus Wagner, Pittsburgh	.467
1903: Fred Clarke, Pittsburgh	.532
1904: Honus Wagner, Pittsburgh	.520
1905: Cy Seymour, Cincinnati	.559
1906: Harry Lumley, Brooklyn	.477
1907: Honus Wagner, Pittsburgh	.513
1908: Honus Wagner, Pittsburgh	.542
1909: Honus Wagner, Pittsburgh	.489
1910: Sherry Magee, Philadelphia	.507
1911: Frank Schulte, Chicago	.534
1912: Heinie Zimmerman, Chicago	.571
1913: Gavvy Cravath, Philadelphia	.568

1914: Sherry Magee, Philadelphia	.509	1972: Billy Williams, Chicago	.606
1915: Gavvy Cravath, Philadelphia	.510	1973: Willie Stargell, Pittsburgh	.646
1916: Zack Wheat, Brooklyn	.461	1974: Mike Schmidt, Philadelphia	.546
1917: Rogers Hornsby, St. Louis	.484	1975: Dave Parker, Pittsburgh	.541
1918: Edd Roush, Cincinnati	.455	1976: Joe Morgan, Cincinnati	.576
1919: Hy Myers, Brooklyn	.436	1977: George Foster, Cincinnati	.631
1920: Rogers Hornsby, St. Louis	.559	1978: Dave Parker, Pittsburgh	.585
1921: Rogers Hornsby, St. Louis	.659	1979: Dave Kingman, Chicago	.613
1922: Rogers Hornsby, St. Louis	.722	1980: Mike Schmidt, Philadelphia	.624
1923: Rogers Hornsby, St. Louis	.627	1981: Mike Schmidt, Philadelphia	.644
1924: Rogers Hornsby, St. Louis	.696	1982: Mike Schmidt, Philadelphia	.547
1925: Rogers Hornsby, St. Louis	.756	1983: Dale Murphy, Atlanta	.540
1926: Cy Williams, Philadelphia	.569	1984: Dale Murphy, Atlanta	.547
1927: Chick Hafey, St. Louis	.590	1985: Pedro Guerrero, Los Angeles	.577
1928: Rogers Hornsby, Boston	.632	1986: Mike Schmidt, Philadelphia	.547
1929: Rogers Hornsby, Chicago	.679	1987: Jack Clark, St. Louis	.597
1930: Hack Wilson, Chicago	.723	1988: Darryl Strawberry, New York	.545
1931: Chuck Klein, Philadelphia	.584	1989: Kevin Mitchell, San Francisco	.635
1932: Chuck Klein, Philadelphia	.646	1990: Barry Bonds, Pittsburgh	.565
1933: Chuck Klein, Philadelphia	.602	1991: Will Clark, San Francisco	.536
1934: Rip Collins, St. Louis	.615	1992: Barry Bonds, Pittsburgh	.624
1935: Arky Vaughan, Pittsburgh	.607	1993: Barry Bonds, San Francisco	.677
1936: Mel Ott, New York	.588	1994: Jeff Bagwell, Houston	.750
1937: Joe Medwick, St. Louis	.641	1995: Dante Bichette, Colorado	.620
1938: Johnny Mize, St. Louis	.614	1996: Ellis Burks, Colorado	.639
1939: Johnny Mize, St. Louis	.626	1997: Larry Walker, Colorado	.720
1940: Johnny Mize, St. Louis	.636		
1941: Pete Reiser, Brooklyn	.558		

Runs

American League

1942: Johnny Mize, New York	.521	1901: Nap Lajoie, Philadelphia	145
1943: Stan Musial, St. Louis	.562	1902: Dave Fultz, Philadelphia	110
1944: Stan Musial, St. Louis	.549	1903: Patsy Dougherty, Boston	108
1945: Tommy Holmes, Boston	.577	1904: Patsy Dougherty, Boston/New York	113
1946: Stan Musial, St. Louis	.587	1905: Harry Davis, Philadelphia	92
1947: Ralph Kiner, Pittsburgh	.639	1906: Elmer Flick, Cleveland	98
1948: Stan Musial, St. Louis	.702	1907: Sam Crawford, Detroit	102
1949: Ralph Kiner, Pittsburgh	.658	1908: Matty McIntyre, Detroit	105
1950: Stan Musial, St. Louis	.596	1909: Ty Cobb, Detroit	116
1951: Ralph Kiner, Pittsburgh	.627	1910: Ty Cobb, Detroit	106
1952: Stan Musial, St. Louis	.538	1911: Ty Cobb, Detroit	147
1953: Duke Snider, Brooklyn	.627	1912: Eddie Collins, Philadephia	137
1954: Willie Mays, New York	.667	1913: Eddie Collins, Philadelphia	125
1955: Willie Mays, New York	.659	1914: Eddie Collins, Philadelphia	122
1956: Duke Snider, Brooklyn	.598	1915: Ty Cobb, Detroit	144
1957: Willie Mays, New York	.626	1916: Ty Cobb, Detroit	113
1958: Ernie Banks, Chicago	.614	1917: Donie Bush, Detroit	112
1959: Hank Aaron, Milwaukee	.636	1918: Ray Chapman, Cleveland	84
1960: Frank Robinson, Cincinnati	.595	1919: Babe Ruth, Boston	103
1961: Frank Robinson, Cincinnati	.611	1920: Baby Ruth, New York	158
1962: Frank Robinson, Cincinnati	.624	1921: Babe Ruth, New York	177
1963: Hank Aaron, Milwaukee	.586	1922: George Sisler, St. Louis	134
1964: Willie Mays, San Francisco	.607	1923: Babe Ruth, New York	151
1965: Willie Mays, San Francisco	.645	1924: Babe Ruth, New York	143
1966: Dick Allen, Philadelphia	.632	1925: Johnny Mostil, Chicago	135
1967: Hank Aaron, Atlanta	.573	1926: Babe Ruth, New York	139
1968: Willie McCovey, San Francisco	.545	1927: Babe Ruth, New York	158
1969: Willie McCovey, San Francisco	.656	1928: Babe Ruth, New York	163
1970: Willie McCovey, San Francisco	.612	1929: Charlie Gehringer, Detroit	131
1971: Hank Aaron, Atlanta	.669		

1930: Al Simmons, Philadelphia	152
1931: Lou Gehrig, New York	163
1932: Jimmie Foxx, Philadelphia	151
1933: Lou Gehrig, New York	138
1934: Charlie Gehringer, Detroit	134
1935: Lou Gehrig, New York	125
1936: Lou Gehrig, New York	167
1937: Joe DiMaggio, New York	151
1938: Hank Greenberg, Detroit	144
1939: Red Rolfe, New York	139
1940: Ted Williams, Boston	134
1941: Ted Williams, Boston	135
1942: Ted Williams, Boston	141
1943: George Case, Washington	102
1944: George Stirnweiss, New York	125
1945: George Stirnweiss, New York	107
1946: Ted Williams, Boston	142
1947: Ted Williams, Boston	125
1948: Tommy Henrich, New York	138
1949: Ted Williams, Boston	150
1950: Dom DiMaggio, Boston	131
1951: Dom DiMaggio, Boston	113
1952: Larry Doby, Cleveland	104
1953: Al Rosen, Cleveland	115
1954: Mickey Mantle, New York	129
1955: Al Smith, Cleveland	123
1956: Mickey Mantle, New York	132
1957: Mickey Mantle, New York	121
1958: Mickey Mantle, New York	127
1959: Eddie Yost, Detroit	115
1960: Mickey Mantle, New York	119
1961: Mickey Mantle, New York	132
Roger Maris, New York	132
1962: Albie Pearson, Los Angeles	115
1963: Bob Allison, Minnesota	99
1964: Tony Oliva, Minnesota	109
1965: Zoilo Versalles, Minnesota	126
1966: Frank Robinson, Baltimore	122
1967: Carl Yastrzemski, Boston	112
1968: Dick McAuliffe, Detroit	95
1969: Reggie Jackson, Oakland	123
1970: Carl Yastrzemski, Boston	125
1971: Don Buford, Baltimore	99
1972: Bobby Murcer, New York	102
1973: Reggie Jackson, Oakland	99
1974: Carl Yastrzemski, Boston	93
1975: Fred Lynn, Boston	103
1976: Roy White, New York	104
1977: Rod Carew, Minnesota	128
1978: Ron LeFlore, Detroit	126
1979: Don Baylor, California	120
1980: Willie Wilson, Kansas City	133
1981: Rickey Henderson, Oakland	89
1982: Paul Molitor, Milwaukee	136
1983: Cal Ripken, Baltimore	121
1984: Dwight Evans, Boston	121
1985: Rickey Henderson, New York	146
1986: Rickey Henderson, New York	130

1987: Paul Molitor, Milwaukee	114
1988: Wade Boggs, Boston	128
1989: Wade Boggs, Boston	113
Rickey Henderson, New York/Oakland	113
1990: Rickey Henderson, Oakland	119
1991: Paul Molitor, Milwaukee	133
1992: Tony Phillips, Detroit	114
1993: Rafael Palmeiro, Texas	124
1994: Frank Thomas, Chicago	106
1995: Albert Belle, Cleveland	121
Edgar Martinez, Seattle	121
1996: Alex Rodriguez, Seattle	141
1997: Ken Griffey Jr., Seattle	125

National League

1900: Roy Thomas, Philadelphia	131
1901: Jesse Burkett, St. Louis	139
1902: Honus Wagner, Pittsburgh	105
1903: Ginger Beaumont, Pittsburgh	137
1904: George Browne, New York	99
1905: Mike Donlin, New York	124
1906: Honus Wagner, Pittsburgh	103
Frank Chance, Chicago	103
1907: Spike Shannon, New York	104
1908: Fred Tenney, New York	101
1909: Tommy Leach, Pittsburgh	126
1910: Sherry Magee, Philadelphia	110
1911: Jimmy Sheckard, Chicago	121
1912: Bob Bescher, Cincinnati	120
1913: Tommy Leach, Chicago	99
Max Carey, Pittsburgh	99
1914: George J. Burns, New York	100
1915: Gavvy Cravath, Philadelphia	89
1916: George J. Burns, New York	105
1917: George J. Burns, New York	103
1918: Heinie Groh, Cincinnati	88
1919: George J. Burns, New York	86
1920: George J. Burns, New York	115
1921: Rogers Hornsby, St. Louis	131
1922: Rogers Hornsby, St. Louis	141
1923: Ross Youngs, New York	121
1924: Frankie Frisch, New York	121
Rogers Hornsby, St. Louis	121
1925: Kiki Cuyler, Pittsburgh	144
1926: Kiki Cuyler, Pittsburgh	113
1927: Lloyd Waner, Pittsburgh	133
Rogers Hornsby, New York	133
1928: Paul Waner, Pittsburgh	142
1929: Rogers Hornsby, Chicago	156
1930: Chuck Klein, Philadelphia	158
1931: Bill Terry, New York	121
Chuck Klein, Philadelphia	121
1932: Chuck Klein, Philadelphia	152
1933: Pepper Martin, St. Louis	122
1934: Paul Waner, Pittsburgh	122
1935: Augie Galan, Chicago	133
1936: Arky Vaughan, Pittsburgh	122

1937: Joe Medwick, St. Louis	111
1938: Mel Ott, New York	116
1939: Bill Werber, Cincinnati	115
1940: Arky Vaughan, Pittsburgh	113
1941: Pete Reiser, Brooklyn	117
1942: Met Ott, New York	118
1943: Arky Vaughan, Brooklyn	112
1944: Bill Nicholson, Chicago	116
1945: Eddie Stanky, Brooklyn	128
1946: Stan Musial, St. Louis	124
1947: Johnny Mize, New York	137
1948: Stan Musial, St. Louis	135
1949: Pee Wee Reese, Brooklyn	132
1950: Earl Torgeson, Boston	120
1951: Stan Musial, St. Louis	124
Ralph Kiner, Pittsburgh	124
1952: Stan Musial, St. Louis	105
Solly Hemus, St. Louis	105
1953: Duke Snider, Brooklyn	132
1954: Stan Musial, St. Louis	120
Duke Snider, Brooklyn	120
1955: Duke Snider, Brooklyn	126
1956: Frank Robinson, Cincinnati	122
1957: Hank Aaron, Milwaukee	118
1958: Willie Mays, San Francisco	121
1959: Vada Pinson, Cincinnati	131
1960: Billy Bruton, Milwaukee	112
1961: Willie Mays, San Francisco	129
1962: Frank Robinson, Cincinnati	134
1963: Hank Aaron, Milwaukee	121
1964: Dick Allen, Philadelphia	125
1965: Tommy Harper, Cincinnati	126
1966: Felipe Alou, Atlanta	122
1967: Hank Aaron, Atlanta	113
Lou Brock, St. Louis	113
1968: Glenn Beckert, Chicago	98
1969: Bobby Bonds, San Francisco	120
Pete Rose, Cincinnati	120
1970: Billy Williams, Chicago	137
1971: Lou Brock, St. Louis	126
1972: Joe Morgan, Cincinnati	122
1973: Bobby Bonds, San Francisco	131
1974: Pete Rose, Cincinnati	110
1975: Pete Rose, Cincinnati	112
1976: Rose Rose, Cincinnati	130
1977: George Foster, Cincinnati	124
1978: Ivan DeJesus, Chicago	104
1979: Keith Hernandez, St. Louis	116
1980: Keith Hernandez, St. Louis	111
1981: Mike Schmidt, Philadelphia	78
1982: Lonnie Smith, St. Louis	120
1983: Tim Raines, Montreal	133
1984: Ryne Sandberg, Chicago	114
1985: Dale Murphy, Atlanta	118
1986: Tony Gwynn, San Diego	107
Von Hayes, Philadelphia	107
1987: Tim Raines, Montreal	123

1988: Brett Butler, San Francisco	109
1989: Will Clark, San Francisco	104
Howard Johnson, New York	104
Ryne Sandberg, Chicago	104
1990: Ryne Sandberg, Chicago	116
1991: Brett Butler, Los Angeles	112
1992: Barry Bonds, Pittsburgh	109
1993: Lenny Dykstra, Philadelphia	143
1994: Jeff Bagwell, Houston	104
1995: Craig Biggio, Houston	123
1996: Ellis Burks, Colorado	142
1997: Craig Biggio, Houston	146

Hits

American League

1901: Nap Lajoie, Philadelphia	229
1902: Charles Hickman, Boston/Cleveland	194
1903: Patsy Dougherty, Boston	195
1904: Nap Lajoie, Cleveland	211
1905: George Stone, St. Louis	187
1906: Nap Lajoie, Cleveland	214
1907: Ty Cobb, Detroit	212
1908: Ty Cobb, Detroit	188
1909: Ty Cobb, Detroit	216
1910: Nap Lajoie, Cleveland	227
1911: Ty Cobb, Detroit	248
1912: Ty Cobb, Detroit	227
1913: Joe Jackson, Cleveland	197
1914: Tris Speaker, Boston	193
1915: Ty Cobb, Detroit	208
1916: Tris Speaker, Cleveland	211
1917: Ty Cobb, Detroit	225
1918: George H. Burns, Philadelphia	178
1919: Ty Cobb, Detroit	191
Bobby Veach, Detroit	191
1920: George Sisler, St. Louis	257
1921: Harry Heilmann, Detroit	237
1922: George Sisler, St. Louis	246
1923: Charlie Jamieson, Cleveland	222
1924: Sam Rice, Washington	216
1925: Al Simmons, Philadelphia	253
1926: George H. Burns, Cleveland	216
Sam Rice, Washington	216
1927: Earle Combs, New York	231
1928: Heinie Manush, St. Louis	241
1929: Dale Alexander, Detroit	215
Charlie Gehringer, Detroit	215
1930: Johnny Hodapp, Cleveland	225
1931: Lou Gehrig, New York	211
1932: Al Simmons, Philadelphia	216
1933: Heinie Manush, Washington	221
1934: Charlie Gehringer, Detroit	214
1935: Joe Vosmik, Cleveland	216
1936: Earl Averill Sr., Cleveland	232
1937: Beau Bell, St. Louis	218
1938: Joe Vosmik, Boston	201

1939: Red Rolfe, New York	213
1940: Rip Radcliff, St. Louis	200
Barney McCosky, Detroit	200
Doc Cramer, Boston	200
1941: Cecil Travis, Washington	218
1942: Johnny Pesky, Boston	205
1943: Dick Wakefield, Detroit	200
1944: George Stirnweiss, New York	205
1945: George Stirnweiss, New York	195
1946: Johnny Pesky, Boston	208
1947: Johnny Pesky, Boston	207
1948: Bob Dillinger, St. Louis	207
1949: Dale Mitchell, Cleveland	203
1950: George Kell, Detroit	218
1951: George Kell, Detroit	191
1952: Nellie Fox, Chicago	192
1953: Harvey Kuenn, Detroit	209
1954: Nellie Fox, Chicago	201
Harvey Kuenn, Detroit	201
1955: Al Kaline, Detroit	200
1956: Harvey Kuenn, Detroit	196
1957: Nellie Fox, Chicago	196
1958: Nellie Fox, Chicago	187
1959: Harvey Kuenn, Detroit	198
1960: Minnie Minoso, Chicago	184
1961: Norm Cash, Detroit	193
1962: Bobby Richardson, New York	209
1963: Carl Yastrzemski, Boston	183
1964: Tony Oliva, Minnesota	217
1965: Tony Oliva, Minnesota	185
1966: Tony Oliva, Minnesota	191
1967: Carl Yastrzemski, Boston	189
1968: Bert Campaneris, Oakland	177
1969: Tony Oliva, Minnesota	197
1970: Tony Oliva, Minnesota	204
1971: Cesar Tovar, Minnesota	204
1972: Joe Rudi, Oakland	181
1973: Rod Carew, Minnesota	203
1974: Rod Carew, Minnesota	218
1975: George Brett, Kansas City	195
1976: George Brett, Kansas City	215
1977: Rod Carew, Minnesota	239
1978: Jim Rice, Boston	213
1979: George Brett, Kansas City	212
1980: Willie Wilson, Kansas City	230
1981: Rickey Henderson, Oakland	135
1982: Robin Yount, Milwaukee	210
1983: Cal Ripken, Baltimore	211
1984: Don Mattingly, New York	207
1985: Wade Boggs, Boston	240
1986: Don Mattingly, New York	238
1987: Kirby Puckett, Minnesota	207
Kevin Seitzer, Kansas City	207
1988: Kirby Puckett, Minnesota	234
1989: Kirby Puckett, Minnesota	215
1990: Rafael Palmeiro, Texas	191
1991: Paul Molitor, Milwaukee	216
1992: Kirby Puckett, Minnesota	210

1993: Paul Molitor, Toronto	211
1994: Kenny Lofton, Cleveland	160
1995: Lance Johnson, Chicago	186
1996: Paul Molitor, Minnesota	225
1997: Nomar Garciaparra, Boston	209

National League

1900: Willie Keeler, Brooklyn	208
1901: Jesse Burkett, St. Louis	228
1902: Ginger Beaumont, Pittsburgh	194
1903: Ginger Beaumont, Pittsburgh	209
1904: Ginger Beaumont, Pittsburgh	185
1905: Cy Seymour, Cincinnati	219
1906: Harry Steinfeldt, Chicago	176
1907: Ginger Beaumont, Boston	187
1908: Honus Wagner, Pittsburgh	201
1909: Larry Doyle, New York	172
1910: Honus Wagner, Pittsburgh	178
Bobby Byrne, Pittsburgh	178
1911: Doc Miller, Boston	192
1912: Heinie Zimmerman, Chicago	207
1913: Gavvy Cravath, Philadelphia	179
1914: Sherry Magee, Philadelphia	171
1915: Larry Doyle, New York	189
1916: Hal Chase, Cincinnati	184
1917: Heinie Groh, Cincinnati	182
1918: Charlie Hollocher, Chicago	161
1919: Ivy Olson, Brooklyn	164
1920: Rogers Hornsby, St. Louis	218
1921: Rogers Hornsby, St. Louis	235
1922: Rogers Hornsby, St. Louis	250
1923: Frankie Frisch, New York	223
1924: Rogers Hornsby, St. Louis	227
1925: Jim Bottomley, St. Louis	227
1926: Eddie Brown, Boston	201
1927: Paul Waner, Pittsburgh	237
1928: Fred Lindstrom, New York	231
1929: Lefty O'Doul, Philadelphia	254
1930: Bill Terry, New York	254
1931: Lloyd Waner, Pittsburgh	214
1932: Chuck Klein, Philadelphia	226
1933: Chuck Klein, Philadelphia	223
1934: Paul Waner, Pittsburgh	217
1935: Billy Herman, Chicago	227
1936: Joe Medwick, St. Louis	223
1937: Joe Medwick, St. Louis	237
1938: Frank McCormick, Cincinnati	209
1939: Frank McCormick, Cincinnati	209
1940: Stan Hack, Chicago	191
Frank McCormick, Cincinnati	191
1941: Stan Hack, Chicago	186
1942: Enos Slaughter, St. Louis	188
1943: Stan Musial, St. Louis	220
1944: Stan Musial, St. Louis	197
Phil Cavarretta, Chicago	197
1945: Tommy Holmes, Boston	224
1946: Stan Musial, St. Louis	228
1947: Tommy Holmes, Boston	191

1948: Stan Musial, St. Louis	230
1949: Stan Musial, St. Louis	207
1950: Duke Snider, Brooklyn	199
1951: Richie Ashburn, Philadelphia	221
1952: Stan Musial, St. Louis	194
1952: Richie Ashburn, Philadelphia	205
1954: Don Mueller, New York	212
1955: Ted Kluszewski, Cincinnati	192
1956: Hank Aaron, Milwaukee	200
1957: Red Schoendienst, New York/Milwaukee	200
1958: Richie Ashburn, Philadelphia	215
1959: Hank Aaron, Milwaukee	223
1960: Willie Mays, San Francisco	190
1961: Vada Pinson, Cincinnati	208
1962: Tommy Davis, Los Angeles	230
1963: Vada Pinson, Cincinnati	204
1964: Roberto Clemente, Pittsburgh	211
Curt Flood, St. Louis	211
1965: Pete Rose, Cincinnati	209
1966: Felipe Alou, Atlanta	218
1967: Roberto Clemente, Pittsburgh	209
1968: Felipe Alou, Atlanta	210
Pete Rose, Cincinnati	210
1969: Matty Alou, Pittsburgh	231
1970: Pete Rose, Cincinnati	205
Billy Williams, Chicago	205
1971: Joe Torre, St. Louis	230
1972: Pete Rose, Cincinnati	198
1973: Pete Rose, Cincinnati	230
1974: Ralph Garr, Atlanta	214
1975: Dave Cash, Philadelphia	213
1976: Pete Rose, Cincinnati	215
1977: Dave Parker, Pittsburgh	215
1978: Steve Garvey, Los Angeles	202
1979: Garry Templeton, St. Louis	211
1980: Steve Garvey, Los Angeles	200
1981: Pete Rose, Philadelphia	140
1982: Al Oliver, Montreal	204
1983: Jose Cruz, Houston	189
Andre Dawson, Montreal	189
1984: Tony Gwynn, San Diego	213
1985: Willie McGee, St. Louis	216
1986: Tony Gwynn, San Diego	211
1987: Tony Gwynn, San Diego	218
1988: Andres Galarraga, Montreal	184
1989: Tony Gwynn, San Diego	203
1990: Brett Butler, San Francisco	192
Lenny Dykstra, Philadelphia	192
1991: Terry Pendleton, Atlanta	187
1992: Terry Pendleton, Atlanta	199
Andy Van Slyke, Pittsburgh	199
1993: Lenny Dykstra, Philadelphia	194
1994: Tony Gwynn, San Diego	165
1995: Dante Bichette, Colorado*	197
Tony Gwynn, San Diego	197
1996: Lance Johnson, New York	227
1997: Tony Gwynn, San Diego	220

Home Runs

American League

1901: Nap Lajoie, Philadelphia	14
1902: Socks Seybold, Philadelphia	16
1903: Buck Freeman, Boston	13
1904: Harry Davis, Philadelphia	10
1905: Harry Davis, Philadelphia	8
1906: Harry Davis, Philadelphia	12
1907: Harry Davis, Philadelphia	8
1908: Sam Crawford, Detroit	7
1909: Ty Cobb, Detroit	9
1910: Jake Stahl, Boston	10
1911: Home Run Baker, Philadelphia	11
1912: Home Run Baker, Philadelphia	10
Tris Speaker, Boston	10
1913: Home Run Baker, Philadelphia	12
1914: Home Run Baker, Philadelphia	9
1915: Braggo Roth, Chicago/Cleveland	7
1916: Wally Pipp, New York	12
1917: Wally Pipp, New York	9
1918: Babe Ruth, Boston	11
Tilly Walker, Philadelphia	11
1919: Babe Ruth, Boston	29
1920: Babe Ruth, New York	54
1921: Babe Ruth, New York	59
1922: Ken Williams, St. Louis	39
1923: Babe Ruth, New York	41
1924: Babe Ruth, New York	46
1925: Bob Meusel, New York	33
1926: Babe Ruth, New York	47
1927: Babe Ruth, New York	60
1928: Babe Ruth, New York	54
1929: Babe Ruth, New York	46
1930: Babe Ruth, New York	49
1931: Babe Ruth, New York	46
Lou Gehrig, New York	46
1932: Jimmie Foxx, Philadelphia	58
1933: Jimmie Foxx, Philadelphia	48
1934: Lou Gehrig, New York	49
1935: Jimmie Foxx, Philadelphia	36
Hank Greenberg, Detroit	36
1936: Lou Gehrig, New York	49
1937: Joe DiMaggio, New York	46
1938: Hank Greenberg, Detroit	58
1939: Jimmie Foxx, Boston	35
1940: Hank Greenberg, Detroit	41
1941: Ted Williams, Boston	37
1942: Ted Williams, Boston	36
1943: Rudy York, Detroit	34
1944: Nick Etten, New York	22
1945: Vern Stephens, St. Louis	24
1946: Hank Greenberg, Detroit	44
1947: Ted Williams, Boston	32
1948: Joe DiMaggio, New York	39
1949: Ted Williams, Boston	43
1950: Al Rosen, Cleveland	37
1951: Gus Zernial, Chicago/Philadelphia	33

1952: Larry Doby, Cleveland	32	
1953: Al Rosen, Cleveland	43	
1954: Larry Doby, Cleveland	32	
1955: Mickey Mantle, New York	37	
1956: Mickey Mantle, New York	52	
1957: Roy Sievers, Washington	42	
1958: Mickey Mantle, New York	42	
1959: Rocky Colavito, Cleveland	42	
Harmon Killebrew, Washington	42	
1960: Mickey Mantle, New York	40	
1961: Roger Maris, New York	61	
1962: Harmon Killebrew, Minnesota	48	
1963: Harmon Killebrew, Minnesota	45	
1964: Harmon Killebrew, Minnesota	49	
1965: Tony Conigilaro, Boston	32	
1966: Frank Robinson, Baltimore	49	
1967: Harmon Killebrew, Minnesota	44	
Carl Yastrzemski, Boston	44	
1968: Frank Howard, Washington	44	
1969: Harmon Killebrew, Minnesota	49	
1970: Frank Howard, Washington	44	
1971: Bill Melton, Chicago	33	
1972: Dick Allen, Chicago	37	
1973: Reggie Jackson, Oakland	32	
1974: Dick Allen, Chicago	32	
1975: Reggie Jackson, Oakland	36	
George Scott, Milwaukee	36	
1976: Graig Nettles, New York	32	
1977: Jim Rice, Boston	39	
1978: Jim Rice, Boston	46	
1979: Gorman Thomas, Milwaukee	45	
1980: Reggie Jackson, New York	41	
Ben Oglivie, Milwaukee	41	
1981: Tony Armas, Oakland	22	
Dwight Evans, Boston	22	
Bobby Grich, California	22	
Eddie Murray, Baltimore	22	
1982: Reggie Jackson, California	39	
Gorman Thomas, Milwaukee	39	
1983: Jim Rice, Boston	39	
1984: Tony Armas, Boston	43	
1985: Darrell Evans, Detroit	40	
1986: Jesse Barfield, Toronto	40	
1987: Mark McGwire, Oakland	49	
1988: Jose Canseco, Oakland	42	
1989: Fred McGriff, Toronto	36	
1990: Cecil Fielder, Detroit	51	
1991: Jose Canseco, Oakland	44	
Cecil Fielder, Detroit	44	
1992: Juan Gonzalez, Texas	43	
1993: Juan Gonzalez, Texas	46	
1994: Ken Griffey, Jr., Seattle	40	
1995: Albert Belle, Cleveland	50	
1996: Mark McGwire, Oakland	52	
1997: Ken Griffey Jr., Seattle	56	

National League

1876: George Hall, Philadelphia	5

1877: George Shaffer, Louisville	3
1878: Paul Hines, Providence	4
1879: Charley Jones, Boston	9
1880: Jim O'Rourke, Boston	6
Harry Stovey, Worcester	6
1881: Dan Brouthers, Buffalo	8
1882: George Wood, Detroit	7
1883: Buck Ewing, New York	10
1884: Ned Williamson, Chicago	27
1885: Abner Dalrymple, Chicago	11
1886: Hardy Richardson, Detroit	11
1887: Roger Connor, New York	17
Billy O'Brien, Washington	17
1888: Roger Connor, New York	14
1889: Sam Thompson, Philadelphia	20
1890: Walt Wilmot, Chicago	14
1891: Harry Stovey, Boston	16
Mike Tiernan, New York	16
1892: Bug Holliday, Cincinnati	13
1893: Ed Delahanty, Philadelphia	19
1894: Hugh Duffy, Boston	18
Bobby Lowe, Boston	18
1895: Bill Joyce, Washington	17
1896: Ed Delahanty, Philadelphia	13
Sam Thompson, Philadelphia	13
1897: Nap Lajoie, Philadelphia	10
1898: Jimmy Collins, Boston	14
1899: Buck Freeman, Washington	25
1900: Herman Long, Boston	12
1901: Sam Crawford, Cincinnati	16
1902: Tommy Leach, Pittsburgh	6
1903: Jimmy Sheckard, Brooklyn	9
1904: Harry Lumley, Brooklyn	9
1905: Fred Odwell, Cincinnati	9
1906: Tim Jordan, Brooklyn	12
1907: Dave Brain, Boston	10
1908: Tim Jordan, Brooklyn	12
1909: Red Murray, New York	7
1910: Fred Beck, Boston	10
Frank Schulte, Chicago	10
1911: Frank Schulte, Chicago	21
1912: Heinie Zimmerman, Chicago	14
1913: Gavvy Cravath, Philadelphia	19
1914: Gavvy Cravath, Philadelphia	19
1915: Gavvy Cravath, Philadelphia	24
1916: Dave Robertson, New York	12
Cy Williams, Chicago	12
1917: Dave Robertson, New York	12
Gavvy Cravath, Philadelphia	12
1918: Gavvy Cravath, Philadelphia	8
1919: Gavvy Cravath, Philadelphia	12
1920: Cy Williams, Philadelphia	15
1921: George Kelly, New York	23
1922: Rogers Hornsby, St. Louis	42
1923: Cy Williams, Philadelphia	41
1924: Jack Fournier, Brooklyn	27
1925: Rogers Hornsby, St. Louis	39
1926: Hack Wilson, Chicago	21

1927: Hack Wilson, Chicago	30	
Cy Williams, Philadelphia	30	
1928: Hack Wilson, Chicago	31	
Jim Bottomley, St. Louis	31	
1929: Chuck Klein, Philadephia	43	
1930: Hack Wilson, Chicago	56	
1931: Chuck Klein, Philadelphia	31	
1932: Chuck Klein, Philadelphia	38	
Mel Ott, New York	38	
1933: Chuck Klein, Philadelphia	28	
1934: Rip Collins, St. Louis	35	
Mel Ott, New York	35	
1935: Wally Berger, Boston	34	
1936: Mel Ott, New York	33	
1937: Mel Ott, New York	31	
Joe Medwick, St. Louis	31	
1938: Mel Ott, New York	36	
1939: Johnny Mize, St. Louis	28	
1940: Johnny Mize, St. Louis	43	
1941: Dolf Camilli, Brooklyn	34	
1942: Mel Ott, New York	30	
1943: Bill Nicholson, Chicago	29	
1944: Bill Nicholson, Chicago	33	
1945: Tommy Holmes, Boston	28	
1946: Ralph Kiner, Pittsburgh	23	
1947: Ralph Kiner, Pittsburgh	51	
Johnny Mize, New York	51	
1948: Ralph Kiner, Pittsburgh	40	
Johnny Mize, New York	40	
1949: Ralph Kiner, Pittsburgh	54	
1950: Ralph Kiner, Pittsburgh	47	
1951: Ralph Kiner, Pittsburgh	42	
1952: Ralph Kiner, Pittsburgh	37	
Hank Sauer, Chicago	37	
1953: Eddie Mathews, Milwaukee	47	
1954: Ted Kluszewski, Cincinnati	49	
1955: Willie Mays, New York	51	
1956: Duke Snider, Brooklyn	43	
1957: Hank Aaron, Milwaukee	44	
1958: Ernie Banks, Chicago	47	
1959: Eddie Mathews, Milwaukee	46	
1960: Ernie Banks, Chicago	41	
1961: Orlando Cepeda, San Francisco	46	
1962: Willie Mays, San Francisco	49	
1963: Hank Aaron, Milwaukee	44	
Willie McCovey, San Francisco	44	
1964: Willie Mays, San Francisco	47	
1965: Willie Mays, San Francisco	52	
1966: Hank Aaron, Atlanta	44	
1967: Hank Aaron, Atlanta	39	
1968: Willie McCovey, San Francisco	36	
1969: Willie McCovey, San Francisco	45	
1970: Johnny Bench, Cincinnati	45	
1971: Willie Stargell, Pittsburgh	48	
1972: Johnny Bench, Cincinnati	40	
1973: Willie Stargell, Pittsburgh	44	
1974: Mike Schmidt, Philadelphia	36	
1975: Mike Schmidt, Philadelphia	38	

1976: Mike Schmidt, Philadelphia	38
1977: George Foster, Cincinnati	52
1978: George Foster, Cincinnati	40
1979: Dave Kingman, Chicago	48
1980: Mike Schmidt, Philadelphia	48
1981: Mike Schmidt, Philadelphia	31
1982: Dave Kingman, New York	37
1983: Mike Schmidt, Philadelphia	40
1984: Dale Murphy, Atlanta	36
Mike Schmidt, Philadelphia	36
1985: Dale Murphy, Atlanta	37
1986: Mike Schmidt, Philadelphia	37
1987: Andre Dawson, Chicago	49
1988: Darryl Strawberry, New York	39
1989: Kevin Mitchell, San Francisco	47
1990: Ryne Sandberg, Chicago	40
1991: Howard Johnson, New York	38
1992: Fred McGriff, San Diego	35
1993: Barry Bonds, San Francisco	46
1994: Matt Williams, San Francisco	43
1995: Dante Bichette, Colorado	40
1996: Andres Galarraga, Colorado	47
1997: Larry Walker, Colorado	49

Runs Batted In

American League

1907: Ty Cobb, Detroit	116
1908: Ty Cobb, Detroit	101
1909: Ty Cobb, Detroit	115
1910: Sam Crawford, Detroit	115
1911: Ty Cobb, Detroit	144
1912: Home Run Baker, Philadelphia	133
1913: Home Run Baker, Philadelphia	126
1914: Sam Crawford, Detroit	112
1915: Sam Crawford, Detroit	116
1916: Wally Pipp, New York	99
1917: Bobby Veach, Detroit	115
1918: George H. Burns, Philadelphia	74
Bobby Veach, Detroit	74
1919: Babe Ruth, Boston	112
1920: Babe Ruth, New York	137
1921: Babe Ruth, New York	171
1922: Ken Williams, St. Louis	155
1923: Babe Ruth, New York	131
1924: Goose Goslin, Washington	129
1925: Bob Meusel, New York	138
1926: Babe Ruth, New York	145
1927: Lou Gehrig, New York	175
1928: Babe Ruth, New York	142
Lou Gehrig, New York	142
1929: Al Simmons, Philadelphia	157
1930: Lou Gehrig, New York	174
1931: Lou Gehrig, New York	184
1932: Jimmie Foxx, Philadelphia	169
1933: Jimmie Foxx, Philadelphia	163
1934: Lou Gehrig, New York	165
1935: Hank Greenberg, Detroit	170

1936: Hal Trosky, Cleveland	162
1937: Hank Greenberg, Detroit	183
1938: Jimmie Foxx, Boston	175
1939: Ted Williams, Boston	145
1940: Hank Greenberg, Detroit	150
1941: Joe DiMaggio, New York	125
1942: Ted Williams, Boston	137
1943: Rudy York, Detroit	118
1944: Vern Stephens, St. Louis	109
1945: Nick Etten, New York	111
1946: Hank Greenberg, Detroit	127
1947: Ted Williams, Boston	114
1948: Joe DiMaggio, New York	155
1949: Ted Williams, Boston	159
Vern Stephens, Boston	159
1950: Walt Dropo, Boston	144
Vern Stephens, Boston	144
1951: Gus Zernial, Chicago-Philadelphia	129
1952: Al Rosen, Cleveland	105
1953: Al Rosen, Cleveland	145
1954: Larry Doby, Cleveland	126
1955: Ray Boone, Detroit	116
Jackie Jensen, Boston	116
1956: Mickey Mantle, New York	130
1957: Roy Sievers, Washington	114
1958: Jackie Jensen, Boston	122
1959: Jackie Jensen, Boston	112
1960: Roger Maris, New York	112
1961: Roger Maris, New York	142
1962: Harmon Killebrew, Minnesota	126
1963: Dick Stuart, Boston	118
1964: Brooks Robinson, Baltimore	118
1965: Rocky Colavito, Cleveland	108
1966: Frank Robinson, Baltimore	122
1967: Carl Yastrzemski, Boston	121
1968: Ken Harrelson, Boston	109
1969: Harmon Killebrew, Minnesota	140
1970: Frank Howard, Washington	126
1971: Harmon Killebrew, Minnesota	119
1972: Dick Allen, Chicago	113
1973: Reggie Jackson, Oakland	117
1974: Jeff Burroughs, Texas	118
1975: George Scott, Milwaukee	109
1976: Lee May, Baltimore	109
1977: Larry Hisle, Minnesota	119
1978: Jim Rice, Boston	139
1979: Don Baylor, California	139
1980: Cecil Cooper, Milwaukee	122
1981: Eddie Murray, Baltimore	78
1982: Hal McRae, Kansas City	133
1983: Cecil Cooper, Milwaukee	126
Jim Rice, Boston	126
1984: Tony Armas, Boston	123
1985: Don Mattingly, New York	145
1986: Joe Carter, Cleveland	121
1987: George Bell, Toronto	134
1988: Jose Canseco, Oakland	124
1989: Ruben Sierra, Texas	119

1990: Cecil Fielder, Detroit	132
1991: Cecil Fielder, Detroit	133
1992: Cecil Fielder, Detroit	124
1993: Albert Belle, Cleveland	129
1994: Kirby Puckett, Minnesota	112
1995: Albert Belle, Cleveland	126
Mo Vaughan, Boston	126
1996: Albert Belle, Cleveland	148
1997: Ken Griffey Jr., Seattle	147

National League

1907: Honus Wagner, Pittsburgh	91
1908: Honus Wagner, Pittsburgh	106
1909: Honus Wagner, Pittsburgh	102
1910: Sherry Magee, Philadelphia	116
1911: Frank Schulte, Chicago	121
1912: Heinie Zimmerman, Chicago	98
1913: Gavvy Cravath, Philadelphia	118
1914: Sherry Magee, Philadelphia	101
1915: Gavvy Cravath, Phildadelphia	118
1916: Hal Chase, Cincinnati	84
1917: Heinie Zimmerman, New York	100
1918: Fred Merkle, Chicago	71
1919: Hy Myers, Brooklyn	72
1920: George Kelly, New York	94
Rogers Hornsby, St. Louis	94
1921: Rogers Hornsby, St. Louis	126
1922: Rogers Hornsby, St. Louis	152
1923: Irish Meusel, New York	125
1924: George Kelly, New York	136
1925: Rogers Hornsby, St. Louis	143
1926: Jim Bottomley, St. Louis	120
1927: Paul Waner, Pittsburgh	131
1928: Jim Bottomley, St. Louis	136
1929: Hack Wilson, Chicago	159
1930: Hack Wilson, Chicago	190
1931: Chuck Klein, Philadelphia	121
1932: Don Hurst, Philadelphia	143
1933: Chuck Klein, Philadelphia	120
1934: Mel Ott, New York	135
1935: Wally Berger, Boston	130
1936: Joe Medwick, St. Louis	138
1937: Joe Medwick, St. Louis	154
1938: Joe Medwick, St. Louis	122
1939: Frank McCormick, Cincinnati	128
1940: Johnny Mize, St. Louis	137
1941: Dolf Camilli, Brooklyn	120
1942: Johnny Mize, New York	110
1943: Bill Nicholson, Chicago	128
1944: Bill Nicholson, Chicago	122
1945: Dixie Walker, Brooklyn	124
1946: Enos Slaughter, St. Louis	130
1947: Johnny Mize, New York	138
1948: Stan Musial, St. Louis	131
1949: Ralph Kiner, Pittsburgh	127
1950: Del Ennis, Philadelphia	126
1951: Monte Irvin, New York	121
1952: Hank Sauer, Chicago	121

1953: Roy Campanella, Brooklyn	142	1905: Jesse Tannehill, Boston	.710
1954: Ted Kluszewski, Cincinnati	141	1906: Eddie Plank, Philadephia	.760
1955: Duke Snider, Brooklyn	136	1907: Bill Donovan, Detroit	.862
1956: Stan Musial, St. Louis	109	1908: Ed Walsh, Sr., Chicago	.727
1957: Hank Aaron, Milwaukee	132	1909: George Mullin, Detroit	.784
1958: Ernie Banks, Chicago	129	1910: Chief Bender, Philadelphia	.821
1959: Ernie Banks, Chicago	143	1911: Chief Bender, Philadelphia	.773
1960: Hank Aaron, Milwaukee	126	1912: Joe Wood, Boston	.872
1961: Orlando Cepeda, San Francisco	142	1913: Walter Johnson, Washington	.837
1962: Tommy Davis, Los Angeles	153	1914: Chief Bender, Philadelphia	.850
1963: Hank Aaron, Milwaukee	130	1915: Joe Wood, Boston	.750
1964: Ken Boyer, St. Louis	119	1916: Ed Cicotte, Chicago	.682
1965: Deron Johnson, Cincinnati	130	1917: Reb Russell, Chicago	.750
1966: Hank Aaron, Atlanta	127	1918: Sam Jones, Boston	.762
1967: Orlando Cepeda, St. Louis	111	1919: Ed Cicotte, Chicago	.806
1968: Willie McCovey, San Francisco	105	1920: Jim Bagby, Sr., Cleveland	.721
1969: Willie McCovey, San Francisco	126	1921: Carl Mays, New York	.750
1970: Johnny Bench, Cincinnati	148	1922: Joe Bush, New York	.788
1971: Joe Torre, St. Louis	137	1923: Herb Pennock, New York	.760
1972: Johnny Bench, Cincinnati	125	1924: Walter Johnson, Washington	.767
1973: Willie Stargell, Pittsburgh	119	1925: Stan Coveleski, Washington	.800
1974: Johnny Bench, Cincinnati	129	1926: George Uhle, Cleveland	.711
1975: Greg Luzinski, Philadelphia	120	1927: Waite Hoyt, New York	.759
1976: George Foster, Cincinnati	121	1928: Alvin Crowder, St. Louis	.808
1977: George Foster, Cincinnati	149	1929: Lefty Grove, Philadephia	.769
1978: George Foster, Cincinnati	120	1930: Lefty Grove, Philadelphia	.848
1979: Dave Winfield, San Diego	118	1931: Lefty Grove, Philadelphia	.886
1980: Mike Schmidt, Philadelphia	121	1932: Johnny Allen, New York	.810
1981: Mike Schmidt, Philadelphia	91	1933: Lefty Grove, Philadelphia	.750
1982: Dale Murphy, Atlanta	109	1934: Lefty Gomez, New York	.839
Al Oliver, Montreal	109	1935: Eldon Auker, Detroit	.720
1983: Dale Murphy, Atlanta	121	1936: Monte Pearson, New York	.731
1984: Gary Carter, Montreal	106	1937: Johnny Allen, Cleveland	.938
Mike Schmidt, Philadelphia	106	1938: Red Ruffing, New York	.750
1985: Dave Parker, Cincinnati	125	1939: Lefty Grove, Boston	.789
1986: Mike Schmidt, Philadephia	119	1940: Schoolboy Rowe, Detroit	.842
1987: Andre Dawson, Chicago	137	1941: Lefty Gomez, New York	.750
1988: Will Clark, San Francisco	109	1942: Tiny Bonham, New York	.808
1989: Kevin Mitchell, San Francisco	125	1943: Spud Chandler, New York	.833
1990: Matt Williams, San Francisco	122	1944: Tex Hughson, Boston	.783
1991: Howard Johnson, New York	117	1945: Hal Newhouser, Detroit	.735
1992: Darren Daulton, Philadelphia	109	1946: Boo Ferriss, Boston	.806
1993: Barry Bonds, San Francisco	123	1947: Allie Reynolds, New York	.704
1994: Jeff Bagwell, Houston	116	1948: Jack Kramer, Boston	.783
1995: Dante Bichette, Colorado	128	1949: Ellis Kinder, Boston	.793
1996: Andres Galarraga, Colorado	150	1950: Vic Raschi, New York	.724
1997: Andres Galarraga, Colorado	140	1951: Bob Feller, Cleveland	.733

Note—Not compiled prior to 1907; officially adopted in 1920.

1952: Bobby Shantz, Philadelphia	.774
1953: Eddie Lopat, New York	.800
1954: Sandy Consuegra, Chicago	.842
1955: Tommy Byrne, New York	.762
1956: Whitey Ford, New York	.760
1957: Dick Donovan, Chicago	.727
Tom Sturdivant, New York	.727
1958: Bob Turley, New York	.750
1959: Bob Shaw, Chicago	.750
1960: Jim Perry, Cleveland	.643
1961: Whitey Ford, New York	.862

Pitching

Winning Percentage

American League

1901: Clark Griffith, Chicago	.774
1902: Bill Bernhard, Philadelphia/Cleveland	.783
1903: Cy Young, Boston	.757
1904: Jack Chesbro, New York	.759

1962: Ray Herbert, Chicago	.690
1963: Whitey Ford, New York	.774
1964: Wally Bunker, Baltimore	.792
1965: Mudcat Grant, Minnesota	.750
1966: Sonny Siebert, Cleveland	.667
1967: Joe Horlen, Chicago	.731
1968: Denny McLain, Detroit	.838
1969: Jim Palmer, Baltimore	.800
1970: Mike Cuellar, Baltimore	.750
1971: Dave McNally, Baltimore	.808
1972: Catfish Hunter, Oakland	.750
1973: Catfish Hunter, Oakland	.808
1974: Mike Cuellar, Baltimore	.688
1975: Mike Torrez, Baltimore	.690
1976: Bill Campbell, Minnesota	.773
1977: Paul Splittorff, Kansas City	.727
1978: Ron Guidry, New York	.893
1979: Mike Caldwell, Milwaukee	.727
1980: Steve Stone, Baltimore	.781
1981: Pete Vuckovich, Milwaukee	.778
1982: Pete Vuckovich, Milwaukee	.750
1983: Rich Dotson, Chicago	.759
1984: Doyle Alexander, Toronto	.739
1985: Ron Guidry, New York	.786
1986: Roger Clemens, Boston	.857
1987: Roger Clemens, Boston	.690
1988: Frank Viola, Minnesota	.774
1989: Bret Saberhagen, Kansas City	.793
1990: Bob Welch, Oakland	.818
1991: Scott Erickson, Minnesota	.714
1992: Mike Mussina, Baltimore	.783
1993: Jimmy Key, New York	.750
1994: Jason Bere, Chicago	.857
1995: Randy Johnson, Seattle	.900
1996: Charles Nagy, Cleveland	.773
1997: Randy Johnson, Seattle	.833

National League

1876: Al Spalding, Chicago	.783
1877: Tommy Bond, Boston	.646
1878: Tommy Bond, Boston	.678
1879: Monte Ward, Providence	.710
1880: Fred Goldsmith, Chicago	.880
1881: Hoss Radbourn, Providence	.694
1882: Larry Corcoran, Chicago	.675
1883: Jim McCormick, Cleveland	.675
1884: Hoss Radbourn, Providence	.833
1885: Mickey Welch, New York	.800
1886: Jocko Flynn, Chicago	.800
1887: Charlie Getzien, Detroit	.690
1888: Tim Keefe, New York	.745
1889: John Clarkson, Boston	.721
1890: Tom Lovett, Brooklyn	.744
1891: John Ewing, New York	.733
1892: Cy Young, Cleveland	.766
1893: Frank Killen, Pittsburgh	.773
1894: Jouett Meekin, New York	.791
1895: Bill Hoffer, Baltimore	.811

1896: Bill Hoffer, Baltimore	.788
1897: Fred Klobedanz, Boston	.788
1898: Ted Lewis, Boston	.765
1899: Jim Hughes, Brooklyn	.824
1900: Joe McGinnity, Brooklyn	.763
1901: Jack Chesbro, Pittsburgh	.700
1902: Jack Chesbro, Pittsburgh	.824
1903: Sam Leever, Pittsburgh	.781
1904: Joe McGinnity, New York	.814
1905: Sam Leever, Pittsburgh	.800
1906: Ed Reulbach, Chicago	.826
1907: Ed Reulbach, Chicago	.810
1908: Ed Reulbach, Chicago	.774
1909: Christy Mathewson, New York	.806
Howie Camnitz, Pittsburgh	.806
1910: King Cole, Chicago	.833
1911: Rube Marquard, New York	.774
1912: Claude Hendrix, Pittsburgh	.727
1913: Bert Humphries, Chicago	.800
1914: Bill James, Boston	.788
1915: Grover Alexander, Philadelphia	.756
1916: Tom Hughes, Boston	.842
1917: Ferdie Schupp, New York	.750
1918: Claude Hendrix, Chicago	.741
1919: Dutch Ruether, Cincinnati	.760
1920: Burleigh Grimes, Brooklyn	.676
1921: Bill Doak, St. Louis	.714
1922: Pete Donohue, Cincinnati	.667
1923: Dolf Luque, Cincinnati	.771
1924: Emil Yde, Pittsburgh	.842
1925: Willie Sherdel, St. Louis	.714
1926: Ray Kremer, Pittsburgh	.769
1927: Larry Benton, Boston/New York	.708
1928: Larry Benton, New York	.735
1929: Charlie Root, Chicago	.760
1930: Freddie Fitzsimmons, New York	.731
1931: Paul Derringer, St. Louis	.692
1932: Lon Warneke, Chicago	.786
1933: Ben Cantwell, Boston	.667
1934: Dizzy Dean, St. Louis	.811
1935: Bill Lee, Chicago	.769
1936: Carl Hubbell, New York	.813
1937: Carl Hubbell, New York	.733
1938: Bill Lee, Chicago	.710
1939: Paul Derringer, Cincinnati	.781
1940: Freddie Fitzsimmons, Brooklyn	.889
1941: Elmer Riddle, Cincinnati	.826
1942: Larry French, Brooklyn	.789
1943: Mort Cooper, St. Louis	.724
1944: Ted Wilks, St. Louis	.810
1945: Harry Brecheen, St. Louis	.789
1946: Murry Dickson, St. Louis	.714
1947: Larry Jansen, New York	.808
1948: Harry Brecheen, St. Louis	.741
1949: Preacher Roe, Brooklyn	.714
1950: Sal Maglie, New York	.818
1951: Preacher Roe, Brooklyn	.880
1952: Hoyt Wilhelm, New York	.833

1953: Carl Erskine, Brooklyn	.769	1979: Tom Seaver, Cincinnati	.727
1954: Johnny Antonelli, New York	.750	1980: Jim Bibby, Pittsburgh	.760
1955: Don Newcombe, Brooklyn	.800	1981: Tom Seaver, Cincinnati	.875
1956: Don Newcombe, Brooklyn	.794	1982: Phil Niekro, Atlanta	.810
1957: Bob Buhl, Milwaukee	.720	1983: John Denny, Philadephia	.760
1958: Warren Spahn, Milwaukee	.667	1984: Rick Sutcliffe, Chicago	.941
Lew Burdette, Milwaukee	.667	1985: Orel Hershiser, Los Angeles	.864
1959: Roy Face, Pittsburgh	.947	1986: Bob Ojeda, New York	.783
1960: Ernie Broglio, St. Louis	.700	1987: Dwight Gooden, New York	.682
1961: Johnny Podres, Los Angeles	.783	1988: David Cone, New York	.870
1962: Bob Purkey, Cincinnati	.821	1989: Mike Bielecki, Chicago	.720
1963: Ron Perranoski, Los Angeles	.842	1990: Doug Drabek, Pittsburgh	.786
1964: Sandy Koufax, Los Angeles	.792	1991: John Smiley, Pittsburgh	.714
1965: Sandy Koufax, Los Angeles	.765	Jose Rijo, Cincinnati	.714
1966: Juan Marichal, San Francisco	.806	1992: Bob Tewksbury, St. Louis	.762
1967: Dick Hughes, St. Louis	.727	1993: Mark Portugal, Houston	.818
1968: Steve Blass, Pittsburgh	.750	1994: Marvin Freeman, Colorado	.833
1969: Tom Seaver, New York	.781	1995: Greg Maddux, Atlanta	.905
1970: Bob Gibson, St. Louis	.767	1996: John Smoltz, Atlanta	.750
1971: Don Gullett, Cincinnati	.727	1997: Greg Maddux, Atlanta	.826
1972: Gary Nolan, Cincinnati	.750	Note—Based on 15 or more victories.	
1973: Tommy John, Los Angeles	.696	Note—1981 and 1994 percentages based on 10 or more	
1974: Andy Messersmith, Los Angeles	.769	victories.	
1975: Don Gullett, Cincinnati	.789		
1976: Steve Carlton, Philadelphia	.741	*Source: Society for American Baseball Research and*	
1977: John Candelaria, Pittsburgh	.800	*Total Baseball, the Official Encyclopedia of Major*	
1978: Gaylord Perry, San Diego	.778	*League Baseball*	

From Major League Baseball's Records Book
All-Time Leaders Through 1997 Season

Runs

1. Ty Cobb	2,246
2. Hank Aaron	2,174
Babe Ruth	2,174
4. Pete Rose	2,165
5. Willie Mays	2,062
6. Stan Musial	1,949
7. Rickey Henderson	1,913
8. Lou Gehrig	1,888
9. Tris Speaker	1,882
10. Mel Ott	1,859

Walks

1. Babe Ruth	2,056
2. Ted Williams	2,019
3. Joe Morgan	1,865
4. Carl Yastrzemski	1,845
5. Rickey Henderson	1,772
6. Mickey Mantle	1,733
7. Mel Ott	1,708
8. Eddie Yost	1,614
9. Darrell Evans	1,605
10. Stan Musial	1,599

Home Runs

1. Hank Aaron	755
2. Babe Ruth	714

3. Willie Mays	660
4. Frank Robinson	586
5. Harmon Killebrew	573
6. Reggie Jackson	563
7. Mike Schmidt	548
8. Mickey Mantle	536
9. Jimmie Foxx	534
10. Ted Williams	521
Willie McCovey	521

Grand Slam Home Runs

1. Lou Gehrig	23
2. Eddie Murray	19
3. Willie McCovey	18
4. Jimmie Foxx	17
Ted Williams	17
6. Hank Aaron	16
Babe Ruth	16
Dave Kingman	16
9. Gil Hodges	14
10. Joe DiMaggio	13
Ralph Kiner	13
George Foster	13

Runs Batted In (RBI)

1. Hank Aaron	2,297
2. Babe Ruth	2,213

3.	Lou Gehrig	1,995
4.	Stan Musial	1,951
5.	Ty Cobb	1,937
6.	Jimmie Foxx	1,922
7.	Eddie Murray	1,917
8.	Willie Mays	1,903
9.	Cap Anson	1,879
10.	Mel Ott	1,860

Stolen Bases

1.	Rickey Henderson	1,231
2.	Lou Brock	938
3.	Billy Hamilton	912
4.	Ty Cobb	892
5.	Tim Raines	795
6.	Vince Coleman	752
7.	Eddie Collins	744
8.	Arlie Latham	739
9.	Max Carey	738
10.	Honus Wagner	722

Strikeouts

| 1. | Reggie Jackson | 2,597 |
| 2. | Willie Stargell | 1,936 |

3.	Mike Schmidt	1,883
4.	Tony Perez	1,867
5.	Dave Kingman	1,816
6.	Bobby Bonds	1,757
7.	Dale Murphy	1,748
8.	Lou Brock	1,730
9.	Mickey Mantle	1,710
10.	Harmon Killebrew	1,699

At Bats

1.	Pete Rose	14,053
2.	Hank Aaron	12,364
3.	Carl Yastrzemski	11,988
4.	Ty Cobb	11,434
5.	Eddie Murray	11,336
6.	Robin Yount	11,008
7.	Dave Winfield	11,003
8.	Stan Musial	10,972
9.	Willie Mays	10,881
10.	Brooks Robinson	10,654

Source: Total Baseball, the Official Encyclopedia of Major League Baseball

Hockey

The National Hockey League acted globally during the 1997-1998 season, taking a 17-day, midseason break in February so the league's biggest stars could, for the first time, play on their respective home-country teams at the 1998 Olympics in Nagano, Japan.

The Detroit Red Wings, meanwhile, acted locally by winning their second consecutive Stanley Cup in June with a four-games-to-none icing of the Washington Capitals.

Give the league credit for gumption. By taking its much ballyhooed "Winter Break," the NHL was forced to stretch its season to eight and a half months, from an October 1 start to a June 16 final-game Stanley Cup finish. But the gamble appeared worth it. When the National Basketball Association sent the first U.S. "Dream Team" to the Barcelona Olympics in 1992, the league, by extension, enjoyed unprecedented success. And the Nagano tournament promised to be a competitive dream come true. Six teams— the United States, Canada, Russia, the Czech Republic, Sweden and Finland—all could lay serious claim to being the gold-medal favorite.

The reality was both more and less than anticipated. The Czech Republic, behind the otherworldly goaltending of the Buffalo Sabres' Dominik "The Terminator" Hasek, won the gold by beating Russia, 1-0. The game, and the outcome, was a dream come true for followers of international ice-hockey tradition.

But for the North Americans who follow hockey (read: all of Canada and small pockets of the United States) it was a nightmare. Team USA, the defending World Cup champions, never got its game together, was eliminated early and then was accused of trashing some rooms in the Olympic Village for good measure. Team Canada (playing with Wayne Gretzky but not Mark Messier, who was left off the squad) failed even to medal. Afterward, NHL Commissioner Gary Bettman said all the right things about the NHL's participation in Nagano. But, perhaps tellingly, as the 1998-1999 season was preparing to drop the puck, the league had made no commitment to participating in the 2002 Olympics, even though the Games are to be played in Salt Lake City, in the heart of North America.

Meanwhile, about that eight-and-a-half-month-long regular season. It was ... long. Only the dyed-in-the-woolest hockey fans weren't willing to admit that the defensive-oriented, clutch-and-grab, obstruction-filled style that permeated the league wasn't a threat to the game's viability. U.S. TV ratings on Fox were anemic. At 26 teams (and with more on the way) the league felt a little ... bloated. The Hartford (Connecticut) Whalers moved to North Carolina and became the Hurricanes and played in front of an enormous number of empty seats, throwing ice water on the league's continued push to move the game deeper into the U.S. Sunbelt.

And unless you were a hockey fan who happened to live in the Motor City or follow the Detroit Red Wings from afar, you likely found yourself feeling much like those North American Olympic fans felt in February: a little left out in the cold. The Scotty Bowman-coached Red Wings finished the regular season with only the third-best record in the league (and only the fourth-highest win total, at 44) but in the playoffs they pretty much had the run of the rink. None of their three series went the seven-game distance, and the Stanley Cup finals 4-0 victory over Washington was as much foregone conclusion as it was competition. Yes, three times during their playoff run the Red Wings were pressed into overtime. But they say that sometimes it's better to be lucky than good. Well, the Wings were both lucky and good: They won all three OT affairs.

A few of the competitive milestones reached by players in the regular season:

- Wayne Gretzky, New York Rangers, scored his 1,850th and 1,851st assist against The Mighty Ducks of Anaheim on October 26 to pass Gordie Howe's career points total of 1,850.
- Phil Housley, Washington Capitals, became just the second U.S.-born player to reach 1,000 points with an assist against the Edmonton Oilers on November 8.
- Mike Gartner, Phoenix Coyotes, netted

his 700th career goal against the Detroit Red Wings on December 14, the fifth player to reach the mark.

- Jari Kurri, Colorado Avalanche, scored his 600th career goal on December 23 against the Los Angeles Kings, solidifying his standing as the league's highest-scoring player born and raised outside North America.
- Dominik Hasek, Buffalo Sabres, notched his record-setting sixth shut out in one month with a 3-0 blanking of the Ottawa Senators on December 31. He would record 13 shutouts for the season, the most since Tony Esposito in 1969-1970. Hasek also would win the Vezina Trophy as the league's best goalie and the Hart Trophy as the league's Most Valuable Player.
- Dino Ciccarelli, Florida Panthers, reached the 600 goal plateau with a winner against the Detroit Red Wings on February 3.
- Rob Blake, Los Angeles Kings, won the James Norris Memorial Trophy as the league's best defenseman. He

led the NHL in goal scoring among defenders, with 23.

As noted, the playoffs belonged to the Detroit Red Wings. In the Stanley Cup round they beat the Washington Capitals 2-1, 5-4 (one of those overtime games), 2-1 and 4-1. Red Wing Steve Yzerman won the Conn Smythe Most Valuable Player award, leading all players in playoff scoring with six goals, 18 assists, for a total of 24 points in 22 games.

But a fine playoff supporting performance was posted by Dominik Hasek, about whom we have heard before. The Czech Republic/Buffalo Sabres netminder pushed his magical year deep into the playoffs. Does the man never tire? The Sabres beat the Philadelphia Flyers, four games to one, in the Eastern Conference quarterfinals, and twice "The Terminator" held Eric Lindros and the Flyers to one goal. Against the Montreal Canadiens, Hasek showed glimpses of being human, giving up nine goals in the first three games. Not that it mattered; the Sabres were still up

National Hockey League Regular Season 1997-98

Team Standings

Eastern Conference

Northeast Division

	GP	W	L	T	GF	GA	Pts.	Pct.*
Pittsburgh	82	40	24	18	228	188	98	.598
Boston	82	39	30	13	221	194	91	.555
Buffalo	82	36	29	17	211	187	89	.543
Montreal	82	37	32	13	235	208	87	.530
Ottawa	82	34	33	15	193	200	83	.506
Carolina	82	33	41	8	200	219	74	.451

Atlantic Division

	GP	W	L	T	GF	GA	Pts.	Pct.*
New Jersey	82	48	23	11	225	166	107	.652
Philadelphia	82	42	29	11	242	193	95	.579
Washington	82	40	30	12	219	202	92	.561
NY Islanders	82	30	41	11	212	225	71	.433
NY Rangers	82	25	39	18	197	231	68	.415
Florida	82	24	43	15	203	256	63	.384
Tampa Bay	82	17	55	10	151	269	44	.268

Western Conference

Central Division

	GP	W	L	T	GF	GA	Pts.	Pct.*
Dallas	82	49	22	11	242	167	109	.665
Detroit	82	44	23	15	250	196	103	.628
St. Louis	82	45	29	8	256	204	98	.598
Phoenix	82	35	35	12	224	227	82	.500
Chicago	82	30	39	13	192	199	73	.445
Toronto	82	30	43	9	194	237	69	.421

Pacific Division

	GP	W	L	T	GF	GA	Pts.	Pct.*
Colorado	82	39	26	17	231	205	95	.579
Los Angeles	82	38	33	11	227	225	87	.530
Edmonton	82	35	37	10	215	224	80	.488
San Jose	82	34	38	10	210	216	78	.476
Calgary	82	26	41	15	217	252	67	.409
Anaheim	82	26	43	13	205	261	65	.396
Vancouver	82	25	43	14	224	273	64	.390

*Percentage of actual points vs. possible points.

Results of All Playoff Series

Conference Quarterfinals (Best-of-seven series)

Eastern Conference

Series 'A'

April 22	Ottawa	2	at	New Jersey	1
April 24	Ottawa	1	at	New Jersey	3
April 26	New Jersey	1	at	Ottawa	2
April 28	New Jersey	3	at	Ottawa	4
April 30	Ottawa	1	at	New Jersey	3
May 2	New Jersey	1	at	Ottawa	3

(Ottawa won series 4-2)

Series 'B'

April 23	Montreal	3	at	Pittsburgh	2
April 25	Montreal	1	at	Pittsburgh	4
April 27	Pittsburgh	1	at	Montreal	3
April 29	Pittsburgh	6	at	Montreal	3
May 1	Montreal	5	at	Pittsburgh	2
May 3	Pittsburgh	0	at	Montreal	3

(Montreal won series 4-2)

Series 'C'

April 22	Buffalo	3	at	Philadelphia	2
April 24	Buffalo	2	at	Philadelphia	3
April 27	Philadelphia	1	at	Buffalo	6
April 29	Philadelphia	1	at	Buffalo	4
May 1	Buffalo	3	at	Philadelphia	2

(Buffalo won series 4-1)

Series 'D'

April 22	Boston	1	at	Washington	3
April 24	Boston	4	at	Washington	3
April 26	Washington	3	at	Boston	2
April 28	Washington	3	at	Boston	0
May 1	Boston	4	at	Washington	0
May 3	Washington	3	at	Boston	2

(Washington won series 4-2)

Western Conference

Series 'E'

April 22	San Jose	1	at	Dallas	4
April 24	San Jose	2	at	Dallas	5
April 26	Dallas	1	at	San Jose	4
April 28	Dallas	0	at	San Jose	1
April 30	San Jose	2	at	Dallas	3
May 2	Dallas	3	at	San Jose	2

(Dallas won series 4-2)

Series 'F'

April 22	Edmonton	3	at	Colorado	2
April 24	Edmonton	2	at	Colorado	5
April 26	Colorado	5	at	Edmonton	4
April 28	Colorado	3	at	Edmonton	1
April 30	Edmonton	3	at	Colorado	1
May 2	Colorado	0	at	Edmonton	2
May 4	Edmonton	4	at	Colorado	0

(Edmonton won series 4-3)

Series 'G'

April 22	Phoenix	3	at	Detroit	6
April 24	Phoenix	7	at	Detroit	4
April 26	Detroit	2	at	Phoenix	3
April 28	Detroit	4	at	Phoenix	2
April 30	Phoenix	1	at	Detroit	3
May 3	Detroit	5	at	Phoenix	2

(Detroit won series 4-2)

Series 'H'

April 23	Los Angeles	3	at	St. Louis	8
April 25	Los Angeles	1	at	St. Louis	2
April 27	St. Louis	4	at	Los Angeles	3
April 29	St. Louis	2	at	Los Angeles	1

(St. Louis won series 4-0)

3-0. In Game Four, when a letdown might have been understandable, Hasek held the Habs to a single goal in a 3-1 victory, which moved Buffalo into the Eastern Conference finals. There, finally, the magic ran out, in a four-games-to-two elimination by the Washington Capitals.

And then there was Scotty Bowman, the Red Wings' coach. On December 22, he became the only coach in NHL history to record at least 200 wins with each of three teams, turning the trick against the Boston Bruins in a 4-2 win. He was just getting started. By winning a second straight Stanley Cup with the Wings in June, he tied the legendary Toe Blake with eight career Stanley Cup championships.

Steve McKee

Conference Semifinals (Best-of-seven series)

Eastern Conference

Series 'I'

May 7	Ottawa	2	at	Washington	4
May 9	Ottawa	1	at	Washington	6
May 11	Washington	3	at	Ottawa	4
May 13	Washington	2	at	Ottawa	0
May 15	Ottawa	0	at	Washington	3

(Washington won series 4-1)

Series 'J'

May 8	Montreal	2	at	Buffalo	3
May 10	Montreal	3	at	Buffalo	6
May 12	Buffalo	5	at	Montreal	4
May 14	Buffalo	3	at	Montreal	1

(Buffalo won series 4-0)

Western Conference

Series 'K'

May 7	Edmonton	1	at	Dallas	3
May 9	Edmonton	2	at	Dallas	0
May 11	Dallas	1	at	Edmonton	0
May 13	Dallas	3	at	Edmonton	1
May 16	Edmonton	1	at	Dallas	2

(Dallas won series 4-1)

Series 'L'

May 8	St. Louis	4	at	Detroit	2
May 10	St. Louis	1	at	Detroit	6
May 12	Detroit	3	at	St. Louis	2
May 14	Detroit	5	at	St. Louis	2
May 17	St. Louis	3	at	Detroit	1
May 19	Detroit	6	at	St. Louis	1

(Detroit won series 4-2)

Conference Finals (Best-of-seven series)

Eastern Conference

Series 'M'

May 23	Buffalo	2	at	Washington	0
May 25	Buffalo	2	at	Washington	3
May 28	Washington	4	at	Buffalo	3
May 30	Washington	2	at	Buffalo	0
June 2	Buffalo	2	at	Washington	1
June 4	Washington	3	at	Buffalo	2

(Washington won series 4-2)

Western Conference

Series 'N'

May 24	Detroit	2	at	Dallas	0
May 26	Detroit	1	at	Dallas	3
May 29	Dallas	3	at	Detroit	5
May 31	Dallas	2	at	Detroit	3
June 3	Detroit	2	at	Dallas	3
June 5	Dallas	0	at	Detroit	2

(Detroit won series 4-2)

Stanley Cup Finals (Best-of-seven series)

Series 'O'

June 9	Washington	1	at	Detroit	2
June 11	Washington	4	at	Detroit	5
June 13	Detroit	2	at	Washington	1
June 16	Detroit	4	at	Washington	1

(Detroit won series 4-0)

Stanley Cup Winners

Year*	Winner		Finalist		Year	Winner		Finalist	
1918	Tor. Arenas	3	Van. Millionaires	2	1956	Montreal	4	Detroit	1
1919	No decision - series between Montreal				1957	Montreal	4	Boston	1
	and Seattle cancelled due to influenza				1958	Montreal	4	Boston	2
	epidemic; series tied 2-2 and 1 tie.				1959	Montreal	4	Toronto	1
1920	Ottawa	3	Seattle	2	1960	Montreal	4	Toronto	3
1921	Ottawa	3	Van. Millionaires	2	1961	Chicago	4	Detroit	2
1922	Tor. St. Pats	3	Van. Millionaires	2	1962	Toronto	4	Chicago	2
1923	Ottawa	2	Edm. Eskimos	0	1963	Toronto	4	Detroit	1
	Ottawa	3	Van. Maroons	1	1964	Toronto	4	Detroit	3
1924	Montreal	2	Calgary Tigers	0	1965	Montreal	4	Chicago	3
	Montreal	2	Van. Maroons	0	1966	Montreal	4	Detroit	2
1925	Victoria	3	Montreal	1	1967	Toronto	4	Montreal	2
1926	Mtl. Maroons	3	Victoria	1	1968	Montreal	4	St. Louis	0
1927	Ottawa	2	Boston	0**	1969	Montreal	4	St. Louis	0
1928	N.Y. Rangers	3	Mtl. Maroons	2	1970	Boston	4	St. Louis	0
1929	Boston	2	N.Y. Rangers	0	1971	Montreal	4	Chicago	3
1930	Montreal	2	Boston	0	1972	Boston	4	N.Y. Rangers	2
1931	Montreal	3	Chicago	2	1973	Montreal	4	Chicago	2
1932	Toronto	3	N.Y. Rangers	0	1974	Philadelphia	4	Boston	2
1933	N.Y. Rangers	3	Toronto	1	1975	Philadelphia	4	Buffalo Sabres	2
1934	Chicago	3	Detroit	1	1976	Montreal	4	Philadelphia	0
1935	Mtl. Maroons	3	Toronto	0	1977	Montreal	4	Boston	0
1936	Detroit	3	Toronto	1	1978	Montreal	4	Boston	2
1937	Detroit	3	N.Y. Rangers	2	1979	Montreal	4	N.Y. Rangers	1
1938	Chicago	3	Toronto	1	1980	N.Y. Islanders	4	Philadelphia	2
1939	Boston	4	Toronto	1	1981	N.Y. Islanders	4	Minnesota	1
1940	N.Y. Rangers	4	Toronto	2	1982	N.Y. Islanders	4	Vancouver	0
1941	Boston	4	Detroit	0	1983	N.Y. Islanders	4	Edmonton	0
1942	Toronto	4	Detroit	3	1984	Edmonton	4	N.Y. Islanders	1
1943	Detroit	4	Boston	0	1985	Edmonton	4	Philadelphia	1
1944	Montreal	4	Chicago	0	1986	Montreal	4	Calgary Flames	1
1945	Toronto	4	Detroit	3	1987	Edmonton	4	Philadelphia	3
1946	Montreal	4	Boston	1	1988	Edmonton	4	Boston	0
1947	Toronto	4	Montreal	2	1989	Calgary	4	Montreal	2
1948	Toronto	4	Detroit	0	1990	Edmonton	4	Boston	1
1949	Toronto	4	Detroit	0	1991	Pittsburgh	4	Minnesota	2
1950	Detroit	4	N.Y. Rangers	3	1992	Pittsburgh	4	Chicago	0
1951	Toronto	4	Montreal	1	1993	Montreal	4	Los Angeles	1
1952	Detroit	4	Montreal	0	1994	N.Y. Rangers	4	Vancouver	3
1953	Montreal	4	Boston	1	1995	New Jersey	4	Detroit	0
1954	Detroit	4	Montreal	3	1996	Colorado	4	Florida	0
1955	Detroit	4	Montreal	3	1997	Detroit	4	Philadelphia	0
					1998	Detroit	4	Washington	0

*The National Hockey League assumed control of Stanley Cup Competition after 1926.

**There were also 2 ties.

Source: National Hockey League

WINTER OLYMPICS

If you hold the Winter Olympics in Nagano, Japan, and nobody watches on American TV, did they really happen?

That was February's one-hand-clapping kind of question.

The Olympics were in fact held in Nagano, the eighteenth winter edition. And CBS did in fact broadcast the Games back to the United States. And, in fact, lots of people *did* watch— 40, 50, 60 million people at a clip each night. But those all important TV ratings were way down from the 1994 Tonya Harding–Nancy Kerrigan Brouhaha Games in Lillehammer, Norway, and, for that matter, CBS was hard put even to match the more modest ratings from its 1992 broadcast from Albertville, France. Perception is often the better part of reality, and it appears CBS will always be saddled with having broadcast the Olympics nobody watched.

The Games themselves were wonderful. By all accounts, the experience was a pleasant one, the people friendly, the locations exotic.

Some Games highlights:

Hermann "the Hermanator" Maier, the Austrian skiing sensation, airborne through a turn in the men's downhill, crashing through fences but arising unhurt in a snow bank. He returned just days later to win the super giant slalom and then won the giant slalom.

The United States's Picabo Street letting it all hang out to win the women's super giant slalom less than a year after tearing apart her knee.

Gordy Sheer and Chris Thorpe, and Mark Grimmette and Brian Martin of the United States bringing home America's first medals in luge, silver and bronze, respectively.

Artur Dmitriev of Russia becoming the first man to win two gold medals in pairs figure skating with two different partners.

Pasha Grishuk of Russia winning the gold with partner Yevgeny Platov, combining pure sex and pure athleticism inside some barely there costumes. Her Marylin Monroe *please-love-me* desperation was at once both chilling and mesmerizing.

Tara Lipinski and Michelle Kwan combining to create the Games' best pure competition in women's figure skating. Ms. Kwan, 17, was elegant, mature, nearly flawless—and a tad tentative. Ms. Lipinski, 15, was effervescent, athletic, all-girl—and held nothing back.

In any other year, Ms. Kwan wins. But before Ms. Lipinski had finished her long routine, it was clear she had triple-jumped her way to the top of the medal stand.

The players from the National Hockey League turning the hockey tournament into a Dream Team competition—but only for Czechoslovakia. The United States exited early and left in disgrace after trashing some athletes' village rooms. The Canadians didn't take any medals. That left the dreaming to the Czechs, who beat Russia for the gold, 1–0, behind the flawless goaltending of Dominik Hasek.

Women's hockey, in the Olympics for the first time, bringing the feel-good ending back home to North America. The U.S. beat Canada, 3–1, and both sides proved once and for all that these women can play. The postgame medals ceremony was suitably draped in red, white, blue and tears.

Now, about that TV coverage.

CBS paid $375 million for the rights to the telecast. The financial responsibilities were perhaps overwhelming, forcing CBS to bring the Games back to the United States in 10 and 12-minute chunks sliced between reams of commercials. Establishing rhythm was nearly impossible. The weather was awful, throwing the skiing schedule into complete disarray. Figure skating *practice* was covered extensively. As host, Jim Nance was smooth and competent, but he never seemed to click with the audience. And, finally, there was the totally befuddling 14-hour time difference between there and here.

To its credit, CBS came to play every night and demonstrated that it could rise to the occasion as needed. Its live coverage of the men's downhill, when Hermann Maier threw himself off the side of a mountain, was as compelling a moment of sports TV as you're likely ever to see. CBS's telling of the story was riveting, must-see TV.

The real winner of the TV game was TNT, the Time Warner cable network. With five afternoon hours to fill every weekday and with no pressure to create "signature" moments, TNT was free to do whatever it wanted. And that's what it did. A Japanese cooking show! A daily talk show on figure skating! Hours and hours of . . . curling? You bet, and it all worked.

Steve McKee

The Olympics

Winter Olympic Games

Year	Site	Attending Nations	Most Medals Won	# of Male Athletes	# of Female Athletes
1924	Chamonix, France	16	Norway (17)	281	13
1928	St. Moritz, Switzerland	25	Norway (15)	366	27
1932	Lake Placid, NY, USA	17	USA (12)	277	30
1936	Garmish-Partenkirchen, Germany	28	Norway (15)	680	76
1940	Canceled	–	–	–	–
1944	Canceled	–	–	–	–
1948	St. Moritz, Switzerland	28	Norway, Sweden, Switzerland (10)	636	77
1952	Oslo, Norway	30	Norway (16)	624	108
1956	Cortina d'Ampezzo, Italy	32	USSR (16)	687	132
1960	Squaw Valley, CA, USA	30	USSR (21)	521	144
1964	Innsbruck, Austria	36	USSR (25)	986	200
1968	Grenoble, France	37	Norway (14)	1,063	230
1972	Sapporo, Japan	35	USSR (16)	927	218
1976	Innsbruck, Austria	37	USSR (27)	1,013	218
1980	Lake Placid, NY, USA	37	East Germany (23)	1,012	271
1984	Sarajevo, Yugoslavia	49	USSR (25)	1,127	283
1988	Calgary, Canada	57	USSR (29)	1,270	364
1992	Albertville, France	64	Germany (26)	1,318	490
1994	Lillehammer, Norway	67	Norway (26)	1,302	542
1998	Nagano, Japan	72	Germany (29)	1,489	815

Gold Medalists

Biathlon–Men's 10 Kilometers
1980: Frank Ullrich, East Germany
1984: Eirik Kvalfoss, Norway
1988: Frank-Peter Roetsch, East Germany
1992: Mark Kirchner, Germany
1994: Serguei Tchepikov, Russia
1998: Ole Bjoerndalen, Norway

Biathlon–Men's 20 Kilometers
1960: Klas Lestander, Sweden
1964: Vladimir Melanin, USSR
1968: Magnar Solberg, Norway
1972: Magnar Solberg, Norway
1976: Nikolai Kruglov, USSR
1980: Anatoli Alyabiev, USSR
1984: Peter Angerer, West Germany
1988: Frank-Peter Roetsch, East Germany
1992: Yevgeny Redkine, Unified Team
1994: Serguei Tchepikov, Russia
1998: Halvard Hanevold, Norway

Biathlon–Men's 4 × 7.5-Kilometer Relay
1968: USSR
1972: USSR
1976: USSR
1980: USSR
1984: USSR
1988: USSR
1992: Germany
1994: Germany
1998: Germany

Biathlon–Women's 7.5 Kilometers
1992: Anfissa Restzova, Unified Team
1994: Myriam Bedard, Canada
1998: Galina Kukleva, Russia

Biathlon–Women's 15 Kilometers
1992: Antje Misersky, Germany
1994: Myriam Bedard, Canada
1998: Yekaterina Dafovska, Bulgaria

Biathlon–Women's 3-4 × 7.5-Kilometer Relay
1992: France
1998: Germany

Biathlon–Women's 30-Kilometer Relay
1994: Russia

Bobsled–Two-Man
1932: USA, Hubert Stevens, Curtis Stevens
1936: USA, Ivan Brown, Alan Washbound
1948: Switzerland, Felix Endrich, Friedrich Waller
1952: Germany, Andreas Ostler, Lorenz Nieberl
1956: Italy, Lamberto Dalla Costa, Giacomo Conti
1960:*
1964: Great Britain, Anthony Nash, Robin Dixon
1968: Italy, Eugenio Monti, Luciano De Paolis
1972: West Germany, Wolfgang Zimmerer, Peter
Utzschneider
1976: East Germany, Meinhard Nehmer, Bernhard
Germeshausen
1980: Switzerland, Erich Schaerer, Josef Benz
1984: East Germany, Wolfgang Hoppe, Dietmar Schauer-
hammer
1988: USSR, Ianis Kipours, Vladimir Kozlov
1992: Switzerland, Gustav Weder, Donat Acklin
1994: Switzerland, Gustav Weber, Donat Acklin
1998: Canada, Pierre Lueders, David MacEachern

_____
*Event not held.

Bobsled–Four-Man
1924: Switzerland
1928: USA
1932: USA
1936: Switzerland
1948: USA
1952: Germany
1956: Switzerland
1960:*
1964: Canada
1968: Italy
1972: Switzerland
1976: East Germany
1980: East Germany
1984: East Germany
1988: Switzerland
1992: Austria
1994: Germany
1998: Germany

_____
*Event not held.

Curling–Men's
1998: Switzerland

Curling–Women's
1998: Canada

Figure Skating–Men's Singles**
1908: Ulrich Salchow, Sweden
1920: Gillis Grafström, Sweden
1924: Gillis Grafström, Sweden
1928: Gillis Grafström, Sweden
1932: Karl Schafer, Austria

1936: Karl Schafer, Austria
1948: Richard Button, USA
1952: Richard Button, USA
1956: Hayes Alan Jenkins, USA
1960: David Jenkins, USA
1964: Manfred Schnelldörfer, West Germany
1968: Wolfgang Schwarz, Austria
1972: Ondrej Nepela, Czechoslovakia
1976: John Curry, Great Britain
1980: Robin Cousins, Great Britain
1984: Scott Hamilton, USA
1988: Brian Boitano, USA
1992: Viktor Petrenko, Unified Team
1994: Aleksei Urmanov, Russia
1998: Ilya Kulik, Russia

_____
**Before 1924 (the first separate Winter Games), figure skating
events were held when a rink was available.

Figure Skating–Women's Singles**
1908: Madge Syers, Great Britain
1920: Magda Julin-Mauroy, Sweden
1924: Herma Planck-Szabó, Austria
1928: Sonja Henie, Norway
1932: Sonja Henie, Norway
1936: Sonja Henie, Norway
1948: Barbara Ann Scott, Canada
1952: Jeannette Altwegg, Great Britain
1956: Tenley Albright, USA
1960: Carol Heiss, USA
1964: Sjoukje Dijkstra, Netherlands
1968: Peggy Fleming, USA
1972: Beatrix Schuba, Austria
1976: Dorothy Hamill, USA
1980: Anett Potzsch, East Germany
1984: Katarina Witt, East Germany
1988: Katarina Witt, East Germany
1992: Kristi Yamaguchi, USA
1994: Oksana Baiul, Ukraine
1998: Tara Lipinski, USA

_____
**Before 1924 (the first separate Winter Games), figure skating
events were held when a rink was available.

Figure Skating–Pairs**
1908: Germany, Anna Hubler, Heinrich Burger
1920: Finland, Ludovika Jakobsson-Eilers, Walter
Jakobsson
1924: Austria, Helene Engelmann, Alfred Berger
1928: France, Andree Joly, Pierre Brunet
1932: France, Andree Brunet-Joly, Pierre Brunet
1936: Germany, Maxi Herber, Ernst Baier
1948: Belgium, Micheline Lannoy, Pierre Baugniet
1952: West Germany, Ria Falk, Paul Falk
1956: Austria, Elisabeth Schwarz, Kurt Oppelt
1960: Canada, Barbara Wagner, Robert Paul
1964: USSR, Lyudmila Belousova, Oleg Protopopov
1968: USSR, Lyudmila Belousova, Oleg Protopopov
1972: USSR, Irina Rodnina, Aleksei Ulanov

1976: USSR, Irina Rodnina, Aleksandr Zaitsev
1980: USSR, Irina Rodnina, Aleksandr Zaitsev
1984: USSR, Elena Valova, Oleg Vassiliev
1988: USSR, Ekaterina Gordeeva, Sergei Grinkov
1992: Unified Team, Natalia Michkouteniok, Artur Dmitriev
1994: Russia, Ekaterina Gordeeva, Sergei Grinkov
1998: Russia, Oksana Kazakova, Artur Dmitriev
**Before 1924 (the first separate Winter Games), figure skating
events were held when a rink was available.

Figure Skating–Ice Dancing
1976: USSR, Ljudmila Pakhomova, Alexandr Gorshkov
1980: USSR, Natalia Linichuk, Gennadi Karponosov
1984: Great Britain, Jayne Torvill, Christopher Dean
1988: USSR, Natalia Bestemianova, Andrei Boukin
1992: Unified Team, Marina Klimova, Sergei Ponomarenko
1994: Russia, Oksana Grichtchuk, Yevgeny Platov
1998: Russia, Pasha Grishuk, Yevgeny Platov

Ice Hockey—Men's
1920: Canada
1924: Canada
1928: Canada
1932: Canada
1936: Great Britain
1948: Canada
1952: Canada
1956: USSR
1960: USA
1964: USSR
1968: USSR
1972: USSR
1976: USSR
1980: USA
1984: USSR
1988: USSR
1992: Unified Team
1994: Sweden
1998: Czech Republic

Ice Hockey–Women's
1998: USA

Luge–Men's Singles
1964: Thomas Kohler, East Germany
1968: Manfred Schmid, Austria
1972: Wolfgang Scheidl, East Germany
1976: Detlef Guenther, East Germany
1980: Bernhard Glass, East Germany
1984: Paul Hildgartner, Italy
1988: Jens Mueller, East Germany
1992: Georg Hackl, Germany
1994: Georg Hackl, Germany
1998: Georg Hackl, Germany

Luge–Men's Doubles
1964: Austria, Josef Feistmantl, Manfred Stengl
1968: East Germany, Klaus-M. Bonsack, Thomas Kohler
1972: Italy, Paul Hildgartner, Walter Plaikner
1976: East Germany, Hans Rinn, Norbert Hahn

1980: East Germany, Hans Rinn, Norbert Hahn
1984: West Germany, Hans Stangassinger, Franz
  Wembacher
1988: East Germany, Joerg Hoffmann, Jochen Pietzsch
1992: Germany, Stefan Krausse, Jan Behrendt
1994: Italy, Kurt Brugger, Wilfried Huber
1998: Germany, Stefan Krausse, Jan Behrendt

Luge–Women's Singles
1964: Ortrun Enderlein, East Germany
1968: Erica Lechner, Italy
1972: Anna-Maria Muller, East Germany
1976: Margit Schumann, East Germany
1980: Vera Zozulia, USSR
1984: Steffi Martin, East Germany
1988: Steffi Walter-Martin, East Germany
1992: Doris Neuner, Austria
1994: Gerda Weissensteiner, Italy
1998: Silke Kraushaar, Germany

Alpine Skiing–Men's Downhill
1948: Henri Oreiller, France
1952: Zeno Colo, Italy
1956: Toni Sailer, Austria
1960: Jean Vuarnet, France
1964: Egon Zimmermann, Austria
1968: Jean-Claude Killy, France
1972: Bernhard Russi, Switzerland
1976: Franz Klammer, Austria
1980: Leonhard Stock, Austria
1984: William Johnson, USA
1988: Pirmin Zurbriggen, Switzerland
1992: Patrick Ortlieb, Austria
1994: Tommy Moe, USA
1998: Jean-Luc Cretier, France

Alpine Skiing–Men's Slalom
1948: Edi Reinalter, Switzerland
1952: Othmar Schneider, Austria
1956: Toni Sailer, Austria
1960: Ernst Hinterseer, Austria
1964: Pepi Stiegler, Austria
1968: Jean-Claude Killy, France
1972: Francisco Fernandez Ochoa, Spain
1976: Piero Gros, Italy
1980: Ingemar Stenmark, Sweden
1984: Phil Mahre, USA
1988: Alberto Tomba, Italy
1992: Finn Christian Jagge, Norway
1994: Thomas Stangassinger, Austria
1998: Hans-Petter Buraas, Norway

Alpine Skiing–Men's Giant Slalom
1952: Stein Eriksen, Norway
1956: Toni Sailer, Austria
1960: Roger Staub, Switzerland
1964: François Bonlieu, France
1968: Jean-Claude Killy, France
1972: Gustav Thoni, Italy
1976: Heini Hemmi, Switzerland

1980: Ingemar Stenmark, Sweden
1984: Max Julen, Switzerland
1988: Alberto Tomba, Italy
1992: Alberto Tomba, Italy
1994: Markus Wasmeier, Germany
1998: Hermann Maier, Austria

Alpine Skiing–Men's Super Giant Slalom

1988: Franck Piccard, France
1992: Kjetil Andre Aamodt, Norway
1994: Markus Wasmeier, Germany
1998: Hermann Maier, Austria

Alpine Skiing–Men's Combined
(Downhill and Slalom)

1936: Franz Pfnur, Germany
1940-1944:*
1948: Henri Oreiller, France
1952-1984:*
1988: Hubert Strolz, Austria
1992: Josef Polig, Italy
1994: Lasse Kjus, Norway
1998: Mario Reiter, Austria

*Event not held.

Alpine Skiing–Women's Downhill

1948: Hedy Schlunegger, Switzerland
1952: Trude Jochum-Beiser, Austria
1956: Madeleine Berthod, Switzerland
1960: Heidi Biebl, West Germany
1964: Christl Haas, Austria
1968: Olga Pall, Austria
1972: Marie-Theres Nadig, Switzerland
1976: Rosi Mittermaier, West Germany
1980: Annemarie Moser-Pröll, Austria
1984: Michela Figini, Switzerland
1988: Marina Kiehl, West Germany
1992: Kerrin Lee-Gartner, Canada
1994: Katja Seizinger, Germany
1998: Katja Seizinger, Germany

Alpine Skiing–Women's Slalom

1948: Gretchen Fraser, USA
1952: Andrea Mead Lawrence, USA
1956: Renée Colliard, Switzerland
1960: Anne Heggtveit, Canada
1964: Christine Goitschel, France
1968: Marielle Goitschel, France
1972: Barbara Cochran, USA
1976: Rosi Mittermaier, West Germany
1980: Hanni Wenzel, Liechtenstein
1984: Paoletta Magoni, Italy
1988: Vreni Schneider, Switzerland
1992: Petra Kronberger, Austria
1994: Vreni Schneider, Switzerland
1998: Hilde Gerg, Germany

Alpine Skiing–Women's Giant Slalom

1952: Andrea Mead Lawrence, USA
1956: Ossi Reichert, West Germany

1960: Yvonne Ruegg, Switzerland
1964: Marielle Goitschel, France
1968: Nancy Greene, Canada
1972: Marie-Theres Nadig, Switzerland
1976: Kathy Kreiner, Canada
1980: Hanni Wenzel, Liechtenstein
1984: Debbie Armstrong, USA
1988: Vreni Schneider, Switzerland
1992: Pernilla Wiberg, Sweden
1994: Deborah Compagnoni, Italy
1998: Deborah Compagnoni, Italy

Alpine Skiing–Women's Super Giant Slalom

1988: Sigrid Wolf, Austria
1992: Deborah Campagnoni, Italy
1994: Diann Roffe-Steinrotter, USA
1998: Picabo Street, USA

Alpine Skiing–Women's Combined
(Downhill and Slalom)

1936: Christl Cranz, Germany
1940–1944:*
1948: Trude Beiser, Austria
1952–1984:*
1988: Anita Wachter, Austria
1992: Petra Kronberger, Austria
1994: Pernilla Wiberg, Sweden
1998: Katja Seizinger, Germany

*Event not held.

Freestyle Skiing–Men's Moguls

1992: Edgar Grospiron, France
1994: Jean-Luc Brassard, Canada
1998: Jonny Moseley, USA

Freestyle Skiing–Women's Moguls

1992: Donna Weinbrecht, USA
1994: Stine Lise Hattestad, Norway
1998: Tae Satoya, Japan

Men's Aerials

1994: Andreas Schoenbaechler, Switzerland
1998: Eric Bergoust, USA

Women's Aerials

1994: Lina Tcherjazova, Uzbekistan
1998: Nikki Stone, USA

Nordic Skiing–Men's 10-Kilometer Cross Country

1992: Vegard Ulvang, Norway
1994: Bjorn Daehlie, Norway
1998: Bjorn Dahlie, Norway

Nordic Skiing–Men's 15-Kilometer Cross Country

1924: Thorleif Haug, Norway
1928: Johan Grottumsbraaten, Norway
1932: Sven Utterstrom, Sweden
1936: Erik-August Larsson, Sweden
1948: Martin Lundstrom, Sweden
1952: Hallgeir Brenden, Norway
1956: Hallgeir Brenden, Norway
1960: Haakon Brusveen, Norway

1964: Eero Mantyranta, Finland
1968: Harald Gronningen, Norway
1972: Sven-Ake Lundbäck, Sweden
1976: Nikolai Bazhukov, USSR
1980: Thomas Wassberg, Sweden
1984: Gunde Anders Svan, Sweden
1988: Mikhail Deviatyarov, USSR
1992: Bjorn Daehlie, Norway
1994: Bjorn Daehlie, Norway
1998: Thomas Alsgaard, Norway

Nordic Skiing–Men's 30-Kilometer Cross Country
1956: Veikko Hakulinen, Finland
1960: Sixten Jernberg, Sweden
1964: Eero Mantyranta, Finland
1968: Franco Nones, Italian
1972: Vyacheslav Vedenine, USSR
1976: Sergei Saveliev, USSR
1980: Nikolai Zimiatov, USSR
1984: Nikolai Zimiatov, USSR
1988: Alexei Prokurorov, USSR
1992: Vegard Ulvang, Norway
1994: Thomas Alsgaard, Norway
1998: Mika Myllylae, Finland

Nordic Skiing–Men's 50-Kilometer Cross Country
1924: Thorleif Haug, Norway
1928: Per-Erik Hedlund, Sweden
1932: Veli Saarinen, Finland
1936: Elis Wiklund, Sweden
1948: Nils Karlsson, Sweden
1952: Veikko Hakulinen, Finland
1956: Sixten Jernberg, Sweden
1960: Kalevi Hamalainen, Finland
1964: Sixten Jernberg, Sweden
1968: Ole Ellefsaeter, Norway
1972: Pal Tyldum, Norway
1976: Ivar Formo, Norway
1980: Nikolai Zimiatov, USSR
1984: Thomas Wassberg, Sweden
1988: Gunde Anders Svan, Sweden
1992: Bjorn Daehlie, Norway
1994: Vladimir Smirnov, Kazakhstan
1998: Bjorn Dahlie, Norway

Nordic Skiing–Men's 4 × 10-Kilometer Relay
1936: Finland
1948: Sweden
1952: Finland
1956: USSR
1960: Finland
1964: Sweden
1968: Norway
1972: USSR
1976: Finland
1980: USSR
1984: Sweden
1988: Sweden
1992: Norway

1994: Italy
1998: Norway

Nordic Skiing–Women's 5-Kilometer Cross Country
1964: Claudia Boyarskikh, USSR
1968: Toini Gustafsson, Sweden
1972: Galina Kulakova, USSR
1976: Helena Takalo, Finland
1980: Raisa Smetanina, USSR
1984: Marja-L. Haemaelainen, Finland
1988: Marjo Matikainen, Finland
1992: Marjut Lukkarinen, Finland
1994: Lyubov Egorova, Russia
1998: Larissa Lazutina, Russia

Nordic Skiing–Women's 10-Kilometer Cross Country
1952: Lydia Wideman, Finland
1956: Lyubov Kosyreva, USSR
1960: Maria Gusakova, USSR
1964: Claudia Boyarskikh, USSR
1968: Toini Gustafsson, Sweden
1972: Galina Kulakova, USSR
1976: Raisa Smetanina, USSR
1980: Barbara Petzold, East Germany
1984: Marja-L. Haemaelainen, Finland
1988: Vida Ventsene, USSR
1992: Lyubov Egorova, Unified Team
1994: Lyubov Egorova, Russia
1998: Larissa Lazutina, Russia

Nordic Skiing–Women's 15-Kilometer Cross Country
1992: Lyubov Egorova, Unified Team
1994: Manuela Di Centa, Italy
1998: Olga Danilova, Russia

Nordic Skiing–Women's 20–30-Kilometer Cross Country
1984: Marja-L. Haemaelainen, Finland
1988: Tamara Tikhonova, USSR
1992: Stefania Belmondo, Italy
1994: Manuela Di Centa, Italy
1998: Yulia Tchepalova, Russia

Nordic Skiing–Women's 4 × 5-Kilometer Relay
1956: Finland
1960: Sweden
1964: USSR
1968: Norway
1972: USSR
1976: USSR
1980: East Germany
1984: Norway
1988: USSR
1992: Unified Team
1994: Russia
1998: Russia

Nordic Skiing–Men's 70-Meter Ski Jumping
1924: Jacob Tullin Thams, Norway
1928: Alf Andersen, Norway
1932: Birger Ruud, Norway
1936: Birger Ruud, Norway
1948: Petter Hugsted, Norway
1952: Arnfinn Bergmann, Norway
1956: Antti Hyvarinen, Finland
1960: Helmut Recknagel, East Germany
1964: Veikko Kankkonen, Finland
1968: Jiri Raska, Czechoslovakia
1972: Yukio Kasaya, Japan
1976: Hans-Georg Aschenbach, East Germany
1980: Anton Innauer, Austria
1984: Jens Weissflog, East Germany
1988: Matti Nykänen, Finland
1992: Ernst Vettori, Austria
1994: Espen Bredesen, Norway

Nordic Skiing–Men's 90-Meter Ski Jumping
1964: Toralf Engan, Norway
1968: Vladimir Beloussov, USSR
1972: Wojciech Fortuna, Poland
1976: Karl Schnabl, Austria
1980: Jouko Tormanen, Finland
1984: Matti Nykänen, Finland
1988: Matti Nykänen, Finland
1992: Toni Nieminen, Finland
1994: Jens Weissflog, Germany
1998: Jani Soininen, Finland

Nordic Skiing–Men's 120-Meter Ski Jumping
1998: Kazuyoshi Funaki, Japan

Nordic Skiing–Men's 90-Meter Team Ski Jumping
1988: Finland
1992: Finland
1994: Germany

Nordic Skiing–Men's 120-Meter Team Ski Jumping
1998: Japan

Nordic Skiing–Men's Combined
1924: Thorleif Haug, Norway
1928: Johan Grottumsbraaten, Norway
1932: Johan Grottumsbraaten, Norway
1936: Oddbjorn Hagen, Norway
1948: Heikki Hasu, Finland
1952: Simon Slattvik, Norway
1956: Sverre Stenersen, Norway
1960: Georg Thoma, West Germany
1964: Tormod Knutsen, Norway
1968: Franz Keller, West Germany
1972: Ulrich Wehling, East Germany
1976: Ulrich Wehling, East Germany
1980: Ulrich Wehling, East Germany
1984: Tom Sandberg, Norway
1988: Hippolyt Kempf, Switzerland

1992: Fabrice Guy, France
1994: Fred Barre Lundberg, Norway
1998: Bjarte Vik, Norway

Nordic Skiing–Men's Team Combined
1988: West Germany
1992: Japan
1994: Japan
1998: Norway

Long Track Speedskating–Men's 500 Meters
1924: Charles Jewtraw, USA
1928: Bernt Evensen, Norway
    Clas Thunberg, Finland [tie]
1932: John A. Shea, USA
1936: Ivar Ballangrud, Norway
1948: Finn Helgesen, Norway
1952: Kenneth Henry, USA
1956: Yevgeny Grishin, USSR
1960: Yevgeny Grishin, USSR
1964: Richard McDermott, USA
1968: Erhard Keller, West Germany
1972: Erhard Keller, West Germany
1976: Yevgeny Kulikov, USSR
1980: Eric Heiden, USA
1984: Sergei Fokitchev, USSR
1988: Jens-Uwe Mey, East Germany
1992: Jens-Uwe Mey, Germany
1994: Aleksandr Golubev, Russia
1998: Hiroyasu Shimizu, Japan

Long Track Speedskating–Men's 1,000 Meters
1976: Peter Mueller, USA
1980: Eric Heiden, USA
1984: Gaétan Boucher, Canada
1988: Nikolai Gouliaev, USSR
1992: Olaf Zinke, Germany
1994: Dan Jansen, USA
1998: Ids Postma, Netherlands

Long Track Speedskating–Men's 1,500 Meters
1924: Clas Thunberg, Finland
1928: Clas Thunberg, Finland
1932: John A. Shea, USA
1936: Charles Mathiesen, Norway
1948: Sverre Farstad, Norway
1952: Hjalmar Andersen, Norway
1956: Yevgeny Grishin, USSR
1960: Roald Aas, Norway
1964: Ants Antson, USSR
1968: Cornelis Verkerk, Netherlands
1972: Ard Schenk, Netherlands
1976: Jan-Egil Storholt, Norway
1980: Eric Heiden, USA
1984: Gaétan Boucher, Canada
1988: Andre Hoffmann, East Germany
1992: Johann Koss, Norway

1994: Johann Koss, Norway
1998: Adne Sondral, Norway

Long Track Speedskating–Men's 5,000 Meters
1924: Clas Thunberg, Finland
1928: Ivar Ballangrud, Norway
1932: Irving Jaffee, USA
1936: Ivar Ballangrud, Norway
1948: Reidar Liaklev, Norway
1952: Hjalmar Andersen, Norway
1956: Boris Shilkov, USSR
1960: Viktor Kosichkin, USSR
1964: Knut Johannesen, Norway
1968: Fred Anton Maier, Norway
1972: Ard Schenk, Netherlands
1976: Sten Stensen, Norway
1980: Eric Heiden, USA
1984: Sven Tomas Gustafson, Sweden
1988: Sven Tomas Gustafson, Sweden
1992: Geir Karlstad, Norway
1994: Johann Koss, Norway
1998: Gianni Romme, Netherlands

Long Track Speedskating–Men's 10,000 Meters
1924: Julius Skutnabb, Finland
1928: Event called off in the fifth race because of the bad
  condition of the ice.
1932: Irving Jaffee, USA
1936: Ivar Ballangrud, Norway
1948: Ake Seyffarth, Sweden
1952: Hjalmar Andersen, Norway
1956: Sigvard Ericsson, Sweden
1960: Knut Johannesen, Norway
1964: Jonny Nilsson, Sweden
1968: Johnny Hoglin, Sweden
1972: Ard Schenk, Netherlands
1976: Piet Kleine, Netherlands
1980: Eric Heiden, USA
1984: Igor Malkov, USSR
1988: Sven Tomas Gustafson, Sweden
1992: Bart Veldkamp, Netherlands
1994: Johann Koss, Norway
1998: Gianni Romme, Netherlands

Short Track Speedskating—Men's 500 Meters
1998: Takafumi Nishitani, Japan

Short Track Speedskating–Men's 1,000 Meters
1992: Kim Ki-Hoon, South Korea
1994: Kim Ki-Hoon, South Korea
1998: Kim Dong-sung, South Korea

Short Track Speedskating–Men's 5 Kilometers
Relay
1992: South Korea
1994: Italy
1998: Canada

Long Track Speedskating–Women's 500 Meters
1932: Jean Wilson, Canada
1936-1956:*
1960: Helga Haase, East Germany
1964: Lydia Skoblikova, USSR
1968: Lyudmila Titova, USSR
1972: Anne Henning, USA
1976: Sheila Young, USA
1980: Karin Enke, East Germany
1984: Christa Rothenburger, East Germany
1988: Bonnie Blair, USA
1992: Bonnie Blair, USA
1994: Bonnie Blair, USA
1998: Catriona LeMay Doan, Canada

———
*Event not held.

Long Track Speedskating–Women's 1,000 Meters
1932: Elizabeth Dubois, USA
1936-1956:*
1960: Klara Guseva, USSR
1964: Lydia Skoblikova, USSR
1968: Carolina Geijssen, Netherlands
1972: Monika Pflug, West Germany
1976: Tatiana Averina, USSR
1980: Natalia Petruseva, USSR
1984: Karin Kania-Enke, East Germany
1988: Christa Rothenburger, East Germany
1992: Bonnie Blair, USA
1994: Bonnie Blair, USA
1998: Marianne Timmer, Netherlands

———
*Event not held.

Long Track Speedskating–Women's 1,500 Meters
1932: Kit Klein, USA
1936-1956:*
1960: Lydia Skoblikova, USSR
1964: Lydia Skoblikova, USSR
1968: Kaija Mustonen, Finland
1972: Dianne Holum, USA
1976: Galina Stepanskaya, USSR
1980: Annie Borckink, Netherlands
1984: Karin Kania-Enke, East Germany
1988: Yvonne van Gennip, Netherlands
1992: Jacqueline Boerner, Germany
1994: Emese Hunyady, Austria
1998: Marianne Timmer, Netherlands

———
*Event not held.

Long Track Speedskating–Women's 3,000 Meters
1960: Lydia Skoblikova, USSR
1964: Lydia Skoblikova, USSR
1968: Johanna Schut, Netherlands
1972: Christina Baas-Kaiser, Netherlands
1976: Tatiana Averina, USSR
1980: Bjorg-Eva Jensen, Norway

1984: Andrea Schoene, East Germany
1988: Yvonne van Gennip, Netherlands
1992: Gunda Niemann, Germany
1994: Svetlana Bazhanova, Russia
1998: Gunda Niemann-Stirnemann, Germany

Long Track Speedskating–Women's 5,000 Meters
1988: Yvonne van Gennip, Netherlands
1998: Claudia Pechstein, Germany

Short Track Speedskating–Women's 500 Meters
1992: Cathy Turner, USA
1994: Cathy Turner, USA
1998: Annie Perreault, Canada

**Short Track Speedskating—Women's
1,000 Meters**
1998: Chun Lee-Kyung, South Korea

**Short Track Speedskating–Women's
3-Kilometer Relay**
1992: Canada
1994: South Korea
1998: South Korea

Snowboard—Men's Giant Slalom
1998: Ross Rebagliati, Canada

Snowboard—Men's Halfpipe
1998: Gian Simmen, Switzerland

Snowboard—Women's Giant Slalom
1998: Karine Ruby, France

Snowboard—Women's Halfpipe
1998: Nicola Thost, Germany

Summer Olympic Games

Year	Site	Attending Nations	Most Medals Won	# of Male Athletes	# of Female Athletes
1896	Athens, Greece	13	Greece (47)	311	0
1900	Paris, France	22	France (102)	1,319	11
1904	St. Louis, MO, USA	12	USA (238)	681	6
1906	Athens, Greece	20	France (40)	877	7
1908	London, England	23	Britain (145)	1,999	36
1912	Stockholm, Sweden	28	Sweden (65)	2,490	57
1916	Canceled	–	–	–	–
1920	Antwerp, Belgium	29	USA (96)	2,453	64
1924	Paris, France	44	USA (99)	2,956	136
1928	Amsterdam, Netherlands	46	USA (56)	2,724	290
1932	Los Angeles, CA, USA	37	USA (104)	1,281	127
1936	Berlin, Germany	49	Germany (89)	3,738	328
1940	Canceled	–	–	–	–
1944	Canceled	–	–	–	–
1948	London, England	59	USA (84)	3,714	385
1952	Helsinki, Finland	69	USA (76)	4,407	518
1956	Melbourne, Australia	67	USSR (98)	2,958	384
1960	Rome, Italy	83	USSR (103)	4,738	610
1964	Tokyo, Japan	93	USA (90)	4,457	683
1968	Mexico City, Mexico	112	USA (107)	4,750	781
1972	Munich, West Germany	122	USSR (99)	5,848	1,299
1976	Montreal, Canada	92	USSR (125)	4,834	1,251
1980	Moscow, USSR	81	USSR (195)	4,265	1,088
1984	Los Angeles, CA, USA	141	USA (174)	5,458	1,620
1988	Seoul, South Korea	159	USSR (132)	6,983	2,438
1992	Barcelona, Spain	172	The Unified Team (former Soviet Union republics) (112)	7,555	3,008
1996	Atlanta, GA, USA	197	USA (101)	6,596	3,785

Gold Medalists

Archery–Men's Individual
1972: John Williams, USA
1976: Darrell Pace, USA
1980: Tomi Poikolainen, Finland
1984: Darrell Pace, USA
1988: Jay Barrs, USA
1992: Sebastian Flute, France (70-meter)
1996: Justin Huish, USA

Archery–Men's Team
1988: South Korea
1992: Spain
1996: USA

Archery–Women's Individual
1972: Doreen Wilber, USA
1976: Luann Ryon, USA
1980: Keto Losaberidze, USSR
1984: Hyang-Soon Seo, South Korea
1988: Soo-Nyung Kim, South Korea
1992: Cho Youn-Jeong, South Korea (70 meter)
1996: Kim Kyung-Wook, South Korea

Archery–Women's Team
1988: South Korea
1992: South Korea
1996: South Korea

Badminton–Men's Singles
1992: Alan Budi Kusuma, Indonesia
1996: Poul-Erik Hoyer-Larsen, Denmark

Badminton–Men's Doubles
1992: South Korea, Kim Moon-Soo and Park Joo-Bong
1996: Indonesia, Ricky Subagja and Rexy Mainaky

Badminton–Women's Singles
1992: Susi Susanti, Indonesia
1996: Soo-Hyun Bang, South Korea

Badminton–Women's Doubles
1992: South Korea, Huang Hye Young, Chung So-Young
1996: China, Jun Gu and Fei Ge

Badminton–Mixed Doubles
1996: South Korea, Young-Ah Gil and Dung-Moon Kim

Baseball

1992: Cuba
1996: Cuba

Basketball—Men's Team

1904: USA
1936: USA
1948: USA
1952: USA
1956: USA
1960: USA
1964: USA
1968: USA
1972: USSR
1976: USA
1980: Yugoslavia
1984: USA
1988: USSR
1992: USA
1996: USA

Basketball—Women's Team

1976: USSR
1980: USSR
1984: USA
1988: USA
1992: Unified Team
1996: USA

Boxing—106 lbs. (Light Flyweight)

1968: Francisco Rodriguez, Venezuela
1972: Gyorgy Gedo, Hungary
1976: Jorge Hernandez, Cuba
1980: Shamil Sabyrov, USSR
1984: Paul Gonzales, USA
1988: Ivalio Hristov, Bulgaria
1992: Rogelio Marcelo, Cuba
1996: Daniel Petrov Bojilov, Bulgaria

Boxing—112 lbs. (Flyweight)

1904: George Finnegan, USA
1906–1912:*
1920: Frank Genaro, USA
1924: Fidel LaBarba, USA
1928: Antal Kocsis, Hungary
1932: Istvan Enekes, Hungary
1936: Willy Kaiser, West Germany
1948: Pascual Perez, Argentina
1952: Nathan Brooks, USA
1956: Terence Spinks, Great Britain
1960: Gyula Torok, Hungary
1964: Fernando Atzori, Italy
1968: Ricardo Delgado, Mexico
1972: Georgi Kostadinov, Bulgaria
1976: Leo Randolph, USA

*Event not held.

1980: Petr Lesov, Bulgaria
1984: Steven McCrory, USA
1988: Kwang-Sun Kim, South Korea
1992: Su-Choi-Chol, North Korea
1996: Maikro Romero, Cuba

Boxing—119 lbs. (Bantamweight)

1904: Oliver Kirk, USA
1906:*
1908: A. Henry Thomas, Great Britain
1912:*
1920: Clarence Walker, South Africa
1924: William Smith, South Africa
1928: Vittorio Tamagnimi, Italy
1932: Horace Gwynne, Canada
1936: Ulderico Sergo, Italy
1948: Tibor Csik, Hungary
1952: Pentti Hamalainen, Finland
1956: Wolfgang Behrendt, East Germany
1960: Oleg Grigoryev, USSR
1964: Takao Sakurai, Japan
1968: Valeri Sokolov, USSR
1972: Orlando Martinez, Cuba
1976: Yong-Jo Gu, North Korea
1980: Juan Hernandez, Cuba
1984: Maurizio Stecca, Italy
1988: Kennedy McKinney, USA
1992: Joel Casamayor, Cuba
1996: Istvan Kovacs, Hungary

*Event not held.

Boxing—125 lbs. (Featherweight)

1904: Oliver Kirk, USA
1906:*
1908: Richard Gunn, Great Britain
1912:*
1920: Paul Fritsch, France
1924: John "Jackie" Fields, USA
1928: Lambertus "Bep" van Klaveren, Netherlands
1932: Carmelo Robledo, Argentina
1936: Oscar Casanovas, Argentina
1948: Ernesto Formenti, Italy
1952: Jan Zachara, Czechoslovakia
1956: Vladimir Safronov, USSR
1960: Francesco Musso, Italy
1964: Stanislav Stepashkin, USSR
1968: Antonio Roldan, Mexico
1972: Boris Kuznetsov, USSR
1976: Angel Herrera, Cuba
1980: Rudi Fink, East Germany
1984: Meldrick Taylor, USA
1988: Giovanni Parisi, Italy
1992: Andreas Tews, Germany
1996: Somluck Kamsing, Thailand

*Event not held.

Boxing–132 lbs. (Lightweight)
1904: Harry Spanger, USA
1906:*
1908: Frederick Grace, Great Britain
1912:*
1920: Samuel Mosberg, USA
1924: Hans Nielsen, Denmark
1928: Carlo Orlandi, Italy
1932: Lawrence Stevens, South Africa
1936: Imre Harangi, Hungary
1948: Gerald Dreyer, South Africa
1952: Aureliano Bolognesi, Italy
1956: Richard McTaggart, Great Britain
1960: Kazimierz Pazdzior, Poland
1964: Jozef Grudzien, Poland
1968: Ronald Harris, USA
1972: Jan Szczepanski, Poland
1976: Howard Davis, USA
1980: Angel Herrera, Cuba
1984: Pernell Whitaker, USA
1988: Andreas Zuelow, East Germany
1992: Oscar De La Hoya, USA
1996: Hocine Soltani, Algeria

---
*Event not held.

Boxing–139 lbs. (Light Welterweight)
1952: Charles Adkins, USA
1956: Vladimir Yengibaryan, USSR
1960: Bohumil Nemecek, Czechoslovakia
1964: Jerzy Kulej, Poland
1968: Jerzy Kulej, Poland
1972: Ray Seales, USA
1976: "Sugar" Ray Leonard, USA
1980: Patrizio Oliva, Italy
1984: Jerry Page, USA
1988: Viatcheslav Janovski, USSR
1992: Hector Vinent, Cuba
1996: Hector Vinent, Cuba

Boxing–147 lbs. (Welterweight)
1904: Albert Young, USA
1906–1912:*
1920: Albert "Bert" Schneider, Canada
1924: Jean Delarge, Belgium
1928: Edward Morgan, New Zealand
1932: Edward Flynn, USA
1936: Sten Suvio, Finland
1948: Julius Torma, Czechoslovakia
1952: Zygmunt Chychla, Poland
1956: Nicolae Linca, Romania
1960: Giovanni Benvenuti, Italy
1964: Marian Kasprzyk, Poland
1968: Manfred Wolke, East Germany
1972: Emilio Correa, Cuba
1976: Jochen Bachfeld, East Germany
1980: Andres Aldama, Cuba

---
*Event not held.

1984: Mark Breland, USA
1988: Robert Wangila, Kenya
1992: Michael Carruth, Ireland
1996: Oleg Saitov, Russia

Boxing–156 lbs. (Light Middleweight)
1952: Laszlo Papp, Hungary
1956: Laszlo Papp, Hungary
1960: Wilbert McClure, USA
1964: Boris Lagutin, USSR
1968: Boris Lagutin, USSR
1972: Dieter Kottysch, West Germany
1976: Jerzy Rybicki, Poland
1980: Armando Martinez, Cuba
1984: Frank Tate, USA
1988: Si-Hun Park, South Korea
1992: Juan Lemus, Cuba
1996: David Reid, USA

Boxing–165 lbs. (Middleweight)
1904: Charles Mayer, USA
1906:*
1908: John Douglas, Great Britain
1912:*
1920: Harry Mallin, Great Britain
1924: Harry Mallin, Great Britain
1928: Piero Toscani, Italy
1932: Carmen Barth, USA
1936: Jean Despeaux, France
1948: Laszlo Papp, Hungary
1952: Floyd Patterson, USA
1956: Gennady Schatkov, USSR
1960: Edward Crook, USA
1964: Valeri Popenchenko, USSR
1968: Christopher Finnegan, Great Britain
1972: Vyacheslav Lemeschev, USSR
1976: Michael Spinks, USA
1980: Jose Gomez, Cuba
1984: Joon-Sup Shin, South Korea
1988: Henry Maske, East Germany
1992: Ariel Hernandez, Cuba
1996: Ariel Hernandez, Cuba

---
*Event not held.

Boxing–178 lbs. (Light Heavyweight)
1920: Edward Eagan, USA
1924: Harry Mitchell, Great Britain
1928: Victor Avendano, Argentina
1932: David Carstens, South Africa
1936: Roger Michelot, France
1948: George Hunter, South Africa
1952: Norvel Lee, USA
1956: James Boyd, USA
1960: Cassius Clay, USA
1964: Cosimo Pinto, Italy
1968: Dan Posnyak, USSR
1972: Mate Parlov, Yugoslavia

1976: Leon Spinks, USA
1980: Slobodan Kacar, Yugoslavia
1984: Anton Josipovic, Yugoslavia
1988: Andrew Maynard, USA
1992: Torsten May, Germany
1996: Vasilii Jirov, Kazakhkstan

Boxing–201 lbs. (Heavyweight)
1904: Samuel Berger, USA
1906:*
1908: A. L. Oldham, Great Britain
1912:*
1920: Ronald Rawson, Great Britain
1924: Ott von Porat, Norway
1928: Arturo Rodriguez Jurado, Argentina
1932: Santiago Lovell, Argentina
1936: Herbert Runge, Germany
1948: Rafael Iglesias, Argentina
1952: H. Edward Sanders, USA
1956: Peter Rademacher, USA
1960: Franco De Piccolo, Italy
1964: Joe Frazier, USA
1968: George Foreman, USA
1972: Teofilo Stevenson, Cuba
1976: Teofilo Stevenson, Cuba
1980: Teofilo Stevenson, Cuba
1984: Henry Tillman, USA
1988: Ray Mercer, USA
1992: Felix Savon, Cuba
1996: Felix Savon, Cuba

*Event not held.

Boxing–over 201 lbs. (Super Heavyweight)
1984: Tyrell Biggs, USA
1988: Lennox Lewis, Canada
1992: Roberto Balado, Cuba
1996: Vladimir Klichko, Ukraine

Canoe/Kayak–Men's Canadian Singles, 500 Meters
1976: Aleksandr Rogov, USSR
1980: Sergei Postrekhin, USSR
1984: Larry Cain, Canada
1988: Olaf Heukrodt, East Germany
1992: Nikolai Boukhalov, Bulgaria
1996: Martin Doktor, Czech Republic

Canoe/Kayak–Men's Canadian Singles, 1,000 Meters
1936: Francis Amyot, Canada
1948: Josef Holecek, Czechoslovakia
1952: Josef Holecek, Czechoslovakia
1956: Leon Rotman, Romania
1960: Janos Parti, Hungary
1964: Jurgen Eschert, East Germany
1968: Tibor Tatai, Hungary
1972: Ivan Patzaichin, Romania

1976: Matija Ljubek, Yugoslavia
1980: Liubomir Liubenov, Bulgaria
1984: Ulrich Eicke, West Germany
1988: Ivan Klementiev, USSR
1992: Nikolai Boukhalov, Bulgaria
1996: Martin Doktor, Czech Republic

Canoe/Kayak–Men's Canadian Singles, Slalom
1992: Lukas Pollert, Czechoslovakia
1996: Michael Martikan, Slovakia

Canoe/Kayak–Men's Canadian Pairs, 500 Meters
1976: USSR, Sergei Petrenko, Aleksandr Vonogradov
1980: Hungary, Laszlo Fultan, Istvan Vaskuti
1984: Yugoslavia, Matija Ljub, Mirko Nisovic
1988: USSR, Victor Reneiski, Nikolai Jouravski
1992: Unified Team, Alexandre Masseikov, Dmitri Dovgalenok
1996: Hungary, Csba Horvath, Gyorgy Kolonics

Canoe/Kayak–Men's Canadian Pairs, 1,000 Meters
1936: Czechoslovakia, Vladimir Syrovatka, Jan-Felix Brzak
1948: Czechoslovakia, Jan-Felix Brzak, Bohumil Kudrna
1952: Denmark, Bent Peder Rasch, Finn Haunstoft
1956: Romania, Alexe Dumitru, Simion Ismailciuc
1960: USSR, Leonid Geischtor, Sergei Makarenko
1964: USSR, Andrei Khimich, Stepan Oschepkov
1968: Romania, Ivan Patzaichin, Serahei Covaliov
1972: USSR, Vladas Chessyunas, Yuri Lobanov
1976: USSR, Sergei Petrenko, Aleksandr Vinogradov
1980: Romania, Ivan Patzaichin, Toma Simionov
1984: Romania, Ivan Potzaichin, Toma Simionov
1988: USSR, Victor Reneiski, Nikolai Jouravski
1992: Germany, Ulrich Papke, Ingo Spelly
1996: Germany, Andreas Dittmer, Gunar Kirchbach

Canoe/Kayak–Men's Canadian Pairs, Slalom
1992: USA, Scott Strausbaugh, Joe Jacobi
1996: France, Franck Adisson, Wilfrid Forgues

Canoe/Kayak–Men's Kayak Singles, 500 Meters
1976: Vasile Diba, Romania
1980: Vladimir Parfenovich, USSR
1984: Ian Ferguson, New Zealand
1988: Zsolt Gyulay, Hungary
1992: Mikko Yrjoe Kolehmainen, Finland
1996: Antonio Rossi, Italy

Canoe/Kayak–Men's Kayak Singles, 1,000 Meters
1936: Gregor Hradetzky, Austria
1948: Gert Fredriksson, Sweden
1952: Gert Fredriksson, Sweden
1956: Gert Fredriksson, Sweden
1960: Erik Hansen, Denmark
1964: Rolf Peterson, Sweden
1968: Mihaly Hesz, Hungary
1972: Aleksandr Shaparenko, USSR

1976: Rudiger Helm, East Germany
1980: Rudiger Helm, East Germany
1984: Alan Thompson, New Zealand
1988: Greg Barton, USA
1992: Clint Robinson, Australia
1996: Knut Holmann, Norway

Canoe/Kayak–Men's Kayak Singles, Slalom
1992: Pierpaolo Ferrazzi, Italy
1996: Oliver Fix, Germany

Canoe/Kayak–Men's Kayak Pairs, 500 Meters
1976: East Germany, Bernd Olbricht, Joachim Mattern
1980: USSR, Vladimir Parfenovich, Sergei Chukhrai
1984: New Zealand, Ian Ferguson, Paul McDonald
1988: New Zealand, Ian Ferguson, Paul MacDonald
1992: Germany, Kay Bluhm, Torsten Rene Gutsche
1996: Germany, Kay Bluhm, Torsten Rene Gutsche

Canoe/Kayak–Men's Kayak Pairs, 1,000 Meters
1936: Austria, Adolf Kainz, Alfons Dorfner
1948: Sweden, Hans Berglund, Lennart Klingstrom
1952: Finland, Kurt Wires, Yrjo Hietanen
1956: West Germany, Michel Scheuer, Meinrad Miltenberger
1960: Sweden, Gert Fredriksson, Sven-Olov Sjodelius
1964: Sweden, Sven-Olov Sjodelius, Gunnar Utterberg
1968: USSR, Aleksandr Shaparenko, Vladimir Morozov
1972: USSR, Nikolai Gorbachev, Viktor Kratassyuk
1976: USSR, Sergei Nagorny, Vladimir Romanovsky
1980: USSR, Vladimir Parfenovich, Sergei Chukhrai
1984: Canada, Hugh Fisher, Alwyn Morris
1988: USA, Greg Barton, Norman Bellingham
1992: Germany, Kay Bluhm, Torsten Rene Gutsche
1996: Italy, Antonio Rossi, Daniele Scarpa

Canoe/Kayak–Men's Kayak Pairs, 1,000 Meters
1964: USSR
1968: Norway
1972: USSR
1976: USSR
1980: East Germany
1984: New Zealand
1988: Hungary
1992: Germany
1996: Germany

Canoe/Kayak–Women's Kayak Singles, 500 Meters
1948: Karen Hoff, Denmark
1952: Sylvi Saimo, Finland
1956: Yelisaveta Dementyeva, USSR
1960: Antonina Seredina, USSR
1964: Lyudmila Khvedosyuk, USSR
1968: Lyudmila Pinayeva-Khvedosyuk, USSR
1972: Yulia Ryabchinskaya, USSR
1976: Carola Drechsler-Zirzow, East Germany
1980: Birgit Fischer, East Germany
1984: Agneta Andersson, Sweden
1988: Vania Guecheva, Bulgaria

1992: Birgit Schmidt, Germany
1996: Rita Koban, Hungary

Canoe/Kayak–Women's Kayak Singles, Slalom
1992: Elisabeth Micheler, Germany
1996: Stepanka Hilgertova, Czech Republic

Canoe/Kayak–Women's Kayak Pairs, 500 Meters
1960: USSR, Maria Chubina, Antonina Seredina
1964: West Germany, Roswitha Esser, Annemarie Zimmermann
1968: West Germany, Roswitha Esser, Annemarie Zimmermann
1972: USSR, Lyudmila Pinayeva-Khvedosyuk, Jekaterina Kuryshko
1976: USSR, Nina Popova, Galina Kreft
1980: East Germany, Carsta Genauss, Martina Bischof
1984: Sweden, Agneta Anderson, Anna Olsson
1988: East Germany, Birgit Schmidt, Anke Nothnagel
1992: Germany, Ramona Portwich, Anke Von Seck
1996: Sweden, Agneta Andersson, Susanne Gunnarsson

Canoe/Kayak–Women's Kayak Fours, 500 Meters
1984: Romania
1988: East Germany
1992: Hungary
1996: Germany

Cycling–Men's Individual Cross Country Mountain Biking
1996: Bart Jan Brentjens, Netherlands

Cycling–Men's 100-Kilometer Team Time Trial
1960: Italy
1964: Netherlands
1968: Netherlands
1972: USSR
1976: USSR
1980: USSR
1984: Italy
1988: East Germany
1992: Germany
1996:*

*Event not held.

Cycling–Men's Individual Time Trial
1996: Miguel Indurain, Spain

Cycling–Men's One-Kilometer Time Trial
1896: Paul Masson, France
1900–1904:*
1906: Francesco Verri, Italy
1908–1924:*
1928: Willy Falck Hansen, Denmark
1932: Edgar Gray, Australia
1936: Arie van Vliet, Netherlands
1948: Jacques Dupont, France

1952: Russell Mockridge, Australia
1956: Leandro Faggin, Italy
1960: Sante Gaiardoni, Italy
1964: Patrick Sercu, Belgium
1968: Pierre Trentin, France
1972: Niels Fredborg, Denmark
1976: Klaus Juergen Gruenke, East Germany
1980: Lothar Thoms, East Germany
1984: Fredy Schmidtke, West Germany
1988: Alexander Kirichenko, USSR
1992: Jose Moreno Perinan, Spain
1996: Florian Rousseau, France

---

*Event not held.

Cycling–Men's 4,000-Meter Individual Pursuit

1964: Jiri Daler, Czechoslovakia
1968: Daniel Rebillard, France
1972: Knut Knudsen, Norway
1976: Gregor Braun, West Germany
1980: Robert Dill-Bundi, Switzerland
1984: Steve Hegg, USA
1988: Gintaoutas Umaras, USSR
1992: Chris Boardman, Britain
1996: Andrea Collinelli, Italy

Cycling–Men's 4,000-Meter Team Pursuit

1908: Great Britain
1912:*
1920: Italy
1924: Italy
1928: Italy
1932: Italy
1936: France
1948: France
1952: Italy
1956: Italy
1960: Italy
1964: West Germany
1968: Denmark
1972: West Germany
1976: West Germany
1980: USSR
1984: Australia
1988: USSR
1992: Germany
1996: France

---

*Event not held.

Cycling–Men's Match Sprint

1896: Paul Masson, France
1900: Georges Taillandier, France
1904:*
1906: Francesco Verri, Italy
1908: Final was declared void because the time limit was exceeded.

1912:*
1920: Maurice Peeters, Netherlands
1924: Lucien Michard, France
1928: Roger Beaufrand, France
1932: Jacobus van Egmond, Netherlands
1936: Toni Merkens, Germany
1948: Mario Ghella, Italy
1952: Enzo Sacchi, Italy
1956: Michel Rousseau, France
1960: Sante Gaiardoni, Italy
1964: Giovanni Pettenella, Italy
1968: Daniel Morelon, France
1972: Daniel Morelon, France
1976: Anton Tkac, Czechoslovakia
1980: Lutz Hesslich, East Germany
1984: Mark Gorski, USA
1988: Lutz Hesslich, East Germany
1992: Jens Fiedler, Germany
1996: Jens Fiedler, Germany

---

*Event not held.

Cycling–Men's Individual Points Race

1984: Rogers Ilegems, Belgium
1988: Dan Frost, Denmark
1992: Giovanni Lombardi, Italy
1996: Silvio Martinello, Italy

Cycling–Men's Individual Road Race

1896: Aristidis Konstantinidis, Greece
1900–1904:*
1906: B. Vast, France
1908:*
1912: Rudolph Lewis, South Africa
1920: Harry Stenqvist, Sweden
1924: Armand Blanchonnet, France
1928: Henry Hansen, Denmark
1932: Attilio Pavesi, Italy
1936: Robert Charpentier, France
1948: Jose Beyaert, France
1952: Andre Noyelle, Belgium
1956: Ercole Baldini, Italy
1960: Viktor Kapitonov, USSR
1964: Mario Zanin, Italy
1968: Pierfranco Vianelli, Italy
1972: Hennie Kuiper, Netherlands
1976: Bernt Johansson, Sweden
1980: Sergei Sukhoruchenkov, USSR
1984: Alexi Grewal, USA
1988: Olaf Ludwig, East Germany
1992: Fabio Casartelli, Italy
1996: Pascal Richard, Switzerland

---

*Event not held.

Cycling–Women's Individual Cross Country Mountain Biking
1996: Paola Pezzo, Italy

Cycling–Women's Match Sprint
1988: Erika Salumae, USSR
1992: Erika Salumae, Estonia
1996: Felicia Ballanger, France

Cycling–Women's Individual Road Race
1984: Connie Carpenter-Phinney, USA
1988: Monique Knol, Netherlands
1992: Kathryn Watt, Australia
1996: Jeannie Longo-Ciprelli, France

Cycling–Women's 3,000-Meter Individual Pursuit
1992: Petra Rossner, Germany
1996: Antonella Bellutti, Italy

Cycling–Women's Individual Time Trial
1996: Zulfiya Zabirova, Russia

Cycling–Women's Individual Points Race
1996: Nathalie Lancien, France

Diving–Men's Platform
1904: George Sheldon, USA
1906: Gottlob Walz, Germany
1908: Hjalmar Johansson, Sweden
1912: Erik Adlerz, Sweden
1920: Clarence Pinkston, USA
1924: Albert White, USA
1932: Harold Smith, USA
1936: Marshall Wayne, USA
1948: Samuel Lee, USA
1952: Samuel Lee, USA
1956: Joaquin Capilla Perez, Mexico
1960: Robert Webster, USA
1964: Robert Webster, USA
1968: Klaus Dibiasi, Italy
1972: Klaus Dibiasi, Italy
1976: Klaus Dibiasi, Italy
1980: Falk Hoffmann, East Germany
1984: Gregory Louganis, USA
1988: Gregory Louganis, USA
1992: Sun Shuwei, China
1996: Dmitri Sautin, Russia

Diving–Men's Springboard
1908: Albert Zurner, Germany
1912: Paul Gunther, Germany
1920: Louis Kuehn, USA
1924: Albert White, USA
1928: Peter Desjardins, USA
1932: Michael Galitzen, USA
1936: Richard Degener, USA
1948: Bruce Harlan, USA
1952: David Browning, USA
1956: Robert Clotworthy, USA
1960: Gary Tobian, USA
1964: Kenneth Sitzberger, USA
1968: Bernie Wrightson, USA
1972: Vladimir Vasin, USSR
1976: Philip G. Boggs, USA
1980: Aleksandr Portnov, USSR
1984: Gregory Louganis, USA
1988: Gregory Louganis, USA
1992: Mark Lenzi, USA
1996: Xiong Ni, China

Diving–Women's Platform
1912: Greta Johanson, Sweden
1920: Stefani Fryland-Clausen, Denmark
1924: Caroline Smith, USA
1928: Elizabeth Pinkston-Becker, USA
1932: Dorothy Poynton, USA
1936: Dorothy Hill-Poynton, USA
1948: Victoria Draves, USA
1952: Patricia McCormick, USA
1956: Patricia McCormick, USA
1960: Ingrid Kramer, East Germany
1964: Lesley Bush, USA
1968: Milena Duchkova, Czechoslovakia
1972: Ulrika Knape, Sweden
1976: Elena Vaytsekhovskaya, USSR
1980: Martina Jaschke, East Germany
1984: Jihong Zhou, China
1988: Yanmei Xu, China
1992: Fu Mingxia, China
1996: Fu Mingxia, China

Diving–Women's Springboard
1920: Aileen Riggin, USA
1924: Elizabeth Becker, USA
1928: Helen Meany, USA
1932: Georgia Coleman, USA
1936: Marjorie Gestring, USA
1948: Victoria Draves, USA
1952: Patricia McCormick, USA
1956: Patricia McCormick, USA
1960: Ingrid Kramer, East Germany
1964: Ingrid Engel-Kramer, East Germany
1968: Sue Gossick, USA
1972: Micki King, USA
1976: Jennifer Chandler, USA
1980: Irina Kalinina, USSR
1984: Sylvie Bernier, Canada
1988: Min Gao, China
1992: Gao Min, China
1996: Fu Mingxia, China

Equestrian–Individual Dressage
1996: Isabell Werth, Germany

Equestrian–Team Dressage
1996: Germany

Equestrian–Individual Show Jumping
1900: Aime Haegeman, Belgium
1904–1908:*
1912: Jean Cariou, France
1920: Tommaso Lequio, Italy
1924: Alphonse Gemuseus, Switzerland
1928: Frantisek Ventura, Czechoslovakia
1932: Takeichi Nishi, Japan
1936: Kurt Hasse, Germany
1948: Humberto Mariles, Cortes, Mexico
1952: Pierre Jonqueres d'Oriola, France
1956: Hans-Gunter Winkler, West Germany
1960: Raimondo D'Inzeo, Italy
1964: Pierre Jonqueres d'Oriola, France
1968: William Steinkraus, USA
1972: Graziano Mancinelli, Italy
1976: Alwin Schockemoehle, West Germany
1980: Jan Kowalczyk, Poland
1984: Joe Fargis, USA
1988: Pierre Durand, France
1992: Ludger Beerbaum, Germany
1996: Ulrich Kirchhoff, Germany

―――――――
*Event not held.

Equestrian–Team Show Jumping
1912: Sweden
1920: Sweden
1924: Sweden
1928: Spain
1932: No nation completed the course with three riders.
1936: Germany
1948: Mexico
1952: Great Britain
1956: West Germany
1960: West Germany
1964: West Germany
1968: Canada
1972: West Germany
1976: France
1980: USSR
1984: USA
1988: West Germany
1992: Netherlands
1996: Germany

Equestrian–Individual Three-Day Event
1912: Axel Nordlander, Sweden
1920: Helmer Morner, Sweden
1924: Adolph van der Voort van Zijp, Netherlands
1928: Charles F. Pahud de Mortanges, Netherlands
1932: Charles F. Pahud de Mortanges, Netherlands
1936: Ludwig Stubbendorf, Germany

1948: Bernard Chevallier, France
1952: Hans von Blixen-Finecke, Jr., Sweden
1956: Petrus Kastenman, Sweden
1960: Lawrence Morgan, Australia
1964: Mauro Checcoli, Italy
1968: Jean-Jacques Guyon, France
1972: Richard Meade, Great Britain
1976: Edmund Coffin, USA
1980: Federico Euro Roman, Italy
1984: Mark Todd, New Zealand
1988: Mark Todd, New Zealand
1992: Matthew Ryan, Australia
1996: Blyth Tait, New Zealand

Equestrian–Team Three-Day Event
1912: Sweden
1920: Sweden
1924: Netherlands
1928: Netherlands
1932: USA
1936: Germany
1948: USA
1952: Sweden
1956: Great Britain
1960: Australia
1964: Italy
1968: Great Britain
1972: Great Britain
1976: USA
1980: USSR
1984: USA
1988: West Germany
1992: Australia
1996: Australia

Fencing–Men's Individual Épée
1900: Ramon Fonst, Cuba
1904: Ramon Fonst, Cuba
1906: Georges de la Falaise, France
1908: Gaston Alibert, France
1912: Paul Anspach, Belgium
1920: Armand Massard, France
1924: Charles Delporte, Belgium
1928: Lucien Gaudin, France
1932: Giancarlo Cornaggia-Medici, Italy
1936: Franco Riccardi, Italy
1948: Luigi Cantone, Italy
1952: Edoardo Mangiarotti, Italy
1956: Carlo Pavesi, Italy
1960: Giuseppe Delfino, Italy
1964: Grigori Kriss, USSR
1968: Gyozo Kulcsar, Hungary
1972: Csaba Fenyvesi, Hungary
1976: Alexander Pusch, West Germany
1980: Johan Harmenberg, Sweden
1984: Philippe Boisse, France
1988: Arnd Schmitt, West Germany

1992: Eric Srecki, France
1996: Aleksandr Beketov, Russia

Fencing–Men's Team Épée
1906: France
1908: France
1912: Belgium
1920: Italy
1924: France
1928: Italy
1932: France
1936: Italy
1948: France
1952: Italy
1956: Italy
1960: Italy
1964: Hungary
1968: Hungary
1972: Hungary
1976: Sweden
1980: France
1984: West Germany
1988: France
1992: Germany
1996: Italy

Fencing–Men's Individual Foil
1896: Emile Gravelotte, France
1900: Emile Coste, France
1904: Ramon Fonst, Cuba
1906: Georges Dillon-Kavanagh, France
1912: Nedo Nadi, Italy
1920: Nedo Nadi, Italy
1924: Roger Ducret, France
1928: Lucien Gaudin, France
1932: Gustavo Marzi, Italy
1936: Giulio Gaudini, Italy
1948: Jehan Buhan, France
1952: Christian d'Oriola, France
1956: Christian d'Oriola, France
1960: Viktor Zhdanovich, USSR
1964: Egon Franke, Poland
1968: Ion Drimba, Romania
1972: Witold Woyda, Poland
1976: Fabio dal Zotto, Italy
1980: Vladimir Smirnov, USSR
1984: Mauro Numa, Italy
1988: Stefano Cerioni, Italy
1992: Philippe Omnes, France
1996: Alessandro Puccini, Italy

Fencing–Men's Team Foil
1904: Cuba
1906–1912:*
1920: Italy
1924: France
1928: Italy

*Event not held.

1932: France
1936: Italy
1948: France
1952: France
1956: Italy
1960: USSR
1964: USSR
1968: France
1972: Poland
1976: West Germany
1980: France
1984: Italy
1988: USSR
1992: Germany
1996: Russia

Fencing–Men's Individual Sabre
1896: Jean Georgiadis, Greece
1900: Georges de la Falaise, France
1904: Manuel Diaz, Cuba
1906: Jean Georgiadis, Greece
1908: Jeno Fuchs, Hungary
1912: Jeno Fuchs, Hungary
1920: Nedo Nadi, Italy
1924: Sandor Posta, Hungary
1928: Odon Terstyanszky, Hungary
1932: Gyorgy Piller, Hungary
1936: Endre Kabos, Hungary
1948: Aladar Gerevich, Hungary
1952: Pal Kovacs, Hungary
1956: Rudolf Karpati, Hungary
1960: Rudolf Karpati, Hungary
1964: Tibor Pezsa, Hungary
1968: Jerzy Pawlowski, Poland
1972: Viktor Sidiak, USSR
1976: Viktor Krovopuskov, USSR
1980: Viktor Krovopuskov, USSR
1984: Jean-Francois Lamour, France
1988: Jean-Francois Lamour, France
1992: Bence Szabo, Hungary
1996: Stanislav Pozdnyakov, Russia

Fencing–Men's Team Sabre
1906: West Germany
1908: Hungary
1912: Hungary
1920: Italy
1924: Italy
1928: Hungary
1932: Hungary
1936: Hungary
1948: Hungary
1952: Hungary
1956: Hungary
1960: Hungary

1964: USSR
1968: USSR
1972: Italy
1976: USSR
1980: USSR
1984: Italy
1988: Hungary
1992: Unified Team
1996: Russia

Fencing–Women's Individual Épée
1996: Laurel Flessel, France

Fencing–Women's Team Épée
1996: France

Fencing–Women's Individual Foil
1924: Ellen Osiier, Denmark
1928: Helene Mayer, Germany
1932: Ellen Preis, Austria
1936: Ilona Elek, Hungary
1948: Ilona Elek, Hungary
1952: Irene Camber, Italy
1956: Gillian Sheen, Great Britain
1960: Heidi Schmid, West Germany
1964: Ildiko Ujlaki-Rejto, Hungary
1968: Yelena Novikova, USSR
1972: Antonella Lonzi-Ragno, Italy
1976: Ildiko Schwarzenberger-Tordasi, Hungary
1980: Pascale Trinquet-Hachin, France
1984: Jujie Luan, China
1988: Anja Fichtel, West Germany
1992: Giovanna Trillini, Italy
1996: Laura Badea, Romania

Fencing–Women's Team Foil
1960: USSR
1964: Hungary
1968: USSR
1972: USSR
1976: USSR
1980: France
1984: West Germany
1988: West Germany
1992: Italy
1996: Italy

Field Hockey–Men's Team
1908: Great Britain
1912:*
1920: Great Britain
1924:*
1928: India
1932: India
1936: India

*Event not held.

1948: India
1952: India
1956: India
1960: Pakistan
1964: India
1968: Pakistan
1972: West Germany
1976: New Zealand
1980: India
1984: Pakistan
1988: Great Britain
1992: Germany
1996: Netherlands

Field Hockey–Women's Team
1980: Zimbabwe
1984: Netherlands
1988: Australia
1992: Spain
1996: Australia

Gymnastics, Artistic–Men's Individual All-Around
(Combined Exercises)
1900: Gustave Sandras, France
1904: Julius Lenhart, Austria
1906: Pierre Paysse, France
1908: Alberto Braglia, Italy
1912: Alberto Braglia, Italy
1920: Georgio Zampori, Italy
1924: Leon Stukelj, Yugoslavia
1928: Georges Miez, Switzerland
1932: Romeo Neri, Italy
1936: Alfred Schwarzmann, Germany
1948: Veikko Huhtanen, Finland
1952: Viktor Chukarin, USSR
1956: Viktor Chukarin, USSR
1960: Boris Shakhlin, USSR
1964: Yukio Endo, Japan
1968: Sawao Kato, Japan
1972: Sawao Kato, Japan
1976: Nikolai Andrianov, USSR
1980: Aleksandr Dityatin, USSR
1984: Koji Gushiken, Japan
1988: Vladimir Artemov, USSR
1992: Vitali Chtcherbo, Belarus
1996: Li Xiaoshuang, China

Gymnastics, Artistic–Men's Team
(Combined Exercises)
1904: Philadelphia
1906: Norway
1908: Sweden
1912: Italy
1920: Italy
1924: Italy
1928: Switzerland
1932: Italy

1936: Germany
1948: Finland
1952: USSR
1956: USSR
1960: Japan
1964: Japan
1968: Japan
1972: Japan
1976: Japan
1980: USSR
1984: USA
1988: USSR
1992: Unified Team
1996: Russia

Gymnastics, Artistic–Men's Floor Exercise

1932: Istvan Pelle, Hungary
1936: Georges Miez, Switzerland
1948: Ferenc Pataki, Hungary
1952: William Thoresson, Sweden
1956: Valentin Muratov, USSR
1960: Nobuyuki Aihara, Japan
1964: Franco Menichelli, Italy
1968: Sawao Kato, Japan
1972: Nikolai Andrianov, USSR
1976: Nikolai Andrianov, USSR
1980: Roland Bruckner, East Germany
1984: Ning Li, China
1988: Serguei Kharihov, USSR
1992: Li Xiaoshuang, China
1996: Ioannis Melissanidis, Greece

Gymnastics, Artistic–Men's Horizontal Bar

1896: Hermann Weingartner, Germany
1900:*
1904: Anton Heida, USA
1906–1920: *
1924: Leon Stukelj, Yugoslavia
1928: Georges Miez, Switzerland
1932: Dallas Bixler, USA
1936: Aleksanteri Saarvala, Finland
1948: Josef Stalder, Switzerland
1952: Jack Gunthard, Switzerland
1956: Takashi Ono, Japan
1960: Takashi Ono, Japan
1964: Boris Shakhlin, USSR
1968: Akinori Nakayama, Japan
1972: Mitsuo Tsukahara, Japan
1976: Mitsuo Tsukahara, Japan
1980: Stoian Delchev, Bulgaria
1984: Shinji Morisue, Japan
1988: Vladimir Artemov, USSR
1992: Trent Dimas, USA
1996: Andreas Wecker, Germany

———————
*Event not held.

Gymnastics, Artistic–Men's Parallel Bars

1896: Alfred Flatow, Germany
1900:*
1904: George Eyser, USA
1908–1920:*
1924: August Guttinger, Switzerland
1928: Ladislav Vacha, Czechoslovakia
1932: Romeo Neri, Italy
1936: Konrad Frey, Germany
1948: Michael Reusch, Switzerland
1952: Hans Eugster, Switzerland
1956: Viktor Chukarin, USSR
1960: Boris Shakhlin, USSR
1964: Yukio Endo, Japan
1968: Akinori Nakayama, Japan
1972: Sawao Kato, Japan
1976: Sawao Kato, Japan
1980: Aleksandr Tkachyov, USSR
1984: Bart Conner, USA
1988: Vladimir Artemov, USSR
1992: Vitali Chtcherbo, Belarus
1996: Rustam Sharipov, Ukraine

———————
*Event not held.

Gymnastics, Artistic–Men's Pommel Horse

1896: Louis Zutter, Switzerland
1900:*
1904: Anton Heida, USA
1906–1920:*
1924: Josef Wilhelm, Switzerland
1928: Hermann Hanggi, Switzerland
1932: Istvan Pelle, Hungary
1936: Konrad Frey, Germany
1948: Paavo Aaltonen, Finland
1952: Viktor Chukarin, USSR
1956: Boris Shakhlin, USSR
1960: Eugen Ekman, Finland
1964: Miroslav Cerar, Yugoslavia
1968: Miroslav Cerar, Yugoslavia
1972: Viktor Klimenko, USSR
1976: Zoltan Magyar, Hungary
1980: Zoltan Magyar, Hungary
1984: Ning Li, China
1988: Dmitri Bilozertchev, USSR
1992: Vitali Chtcherbo, Belarus
1996: Donghua Li, Switzerland

———————
*Event not held.

Gymnastics, Artistic–Men's Still Rings

1896: Ioannis Metropoulos, Greece
1900:*
1904: Hermann Glass, USA
1906–1920:*
1924: Francesco Martino, Italy
1928: Leon Stukelj, Yugoslavia

———————
*Event not held.

1932: George Gulack, USA
1936: Alois Hudec, Czechoslovakia
1948: Karl Frei, Switzerland
1952: Grant Shaginyan, USSR
1956: Albert Azaryan, USSR
1960: Albert Azaryan, USSR
1964: Takuji Hayata, Japan
1968: Akinori Nakayama, Japan
1972: Akinori Nakayama, Japan
1976: Nikolai Andrianov, USSR
1980: Aleksandr Dityatin, USSR
1984: Koji Gushiken, Japan
1988: Holger Behrendt, East Germany
1992: Vitali Chtcherbo, Belarus
1996: Yuri Chechi, Italy

Gymnastics, Artistic–Men's Horse Vault
1896: Carl Schuhmann, Germany
1900:*
1904: George Eyser, USA
1906–1920:*
1924: Frank Kriz, USA
1928: Eugen Mack, Switzerland
1932: Savino Guglielmetti, Italy
1936: Alfred Schwarzmann, Germany
1948: Paavo Aaltonen, Finland
1952: Viktor Chukarin, USSR
1956: Helmut Bantz, West Germany
1960: Takashi Ono, Japan
1964: Haruhiro Yamashita, Japan
1968: Mikhail Voronin, USSR
1972: Klaus Koste, East Germany
1976: Nikolai Andrianov, USSR
1980: Nikolai Andrianov, USSR
1984: Yun Lou, China
1988: Yun Lou, China
1992: Vitali Chtcherbo, Belarus
1996: Alexei Nemov, Russia

———
*Event not held.

Gymnastics, Artistic–Women's Individual All-Around (Combined Exercises)
1952: Maria Gorokhovskaya, USSR
1956: Larissa Latynina, USSR
1960: Larissa Latynina, USSR
1964: Vera Caslavska, Czechoslovakia
1968: Vera Caslavska, Czechoslovakia
1972: Lyudmila Tourischeva, USSR
1976: Nadia Comaneci, Romania
1980: Yelena Davydova, USSR
1984: Mary Lou Retton, USA
1988: Elena Shoushounova, USSR
1992: Tatiana Goutsou, Ukraine
1996: Lilia Podkopayeva, Ukraine

Gymnastics, Artistic–Women's Team (Combined Exercises)
1928: Netherlands
1932:*
1936: Germany
1948: Czechoslovakia
1952: USSR
1956: USSR
1960: USSR
1964: USSR
1968: USSR
1972: USSR
1976: USSR
1980: USSR
1984: Romania
1988: USSR
1992: Unified Team
1996: USA

———
*Event not held.

Gymnastics, Artistic–Women's Balance Beam
1952: Nina Bocharova, USSR
1956: Agnes Keleti, Hungary
1960: Eva Bosakova, Czechoslovakia
1964: Vera Caslavska, Czechoslovakia
1968: Natalia Kutschinskaya, USSR
1972: Olga Korbut, USSR
1976: Nadia Comaneci, Romania
1980: Nadia Comaneci, Romania
1984: Simona Pauca, Romania
1988: Daniela Silivas, Romania
1992: Tatiana Lyssenko, Ukraine
1996: Shannon Miller, USA

Gymnastics, Artistic–Women's Floor Exercise
1952: Agnes Keleti, Hungary
1956: Agnes Keleti, Hungary
1960: Larissa Latynina, USSR
1964: Larissa Latynina, USSR
1968: Vera Caslavska, Czechoslovakia
1972: Olga Korbut, USSR
1976: Nelli Kim, USSR
1980: Nelli Kim, USSR
1984: Ecaterina Szabo, Romania
1988: Daniela Silivas, Romania
1992: Lavinia Milosovici, Romania
1996: Lilia Podkopayeva, Ukraine

Gymnastics, Artistic–Women's Uneven Bars
1952: Margit Korondi, Hungary
1956: Agnes Keleti, Hungary
1960: Polina Astakhova, USSR
1964: Polina Astakhova, USSR
1968: Vera Caslavska, Czechoslovakia
1972: Karin Janz, East Germany

1976: Nadia Comaneci, Romania
1980: Maxi Gnauck, East Germany
1984: Yanhong Ma, China
1988: Daniela Silivas, Romania
1992: Lu Li, China
1996: Svetlana Chorkina, Russia

Gymnastics, Artistic–Women's Horse Vault

1952: Yekaterina Kalinchuk, USSR
1956: Larissa Latynina, USSR
1960: Margarita Nikolayeva, USSR
1964: Vera Caslavska, Czechoslovakia
1968: Vera Caslavska, Czechoslovakia
1972: Karin Janz, East Germany
1976: Nelli Kim, USSR
1980: Natalia Shaposhnikova, USSR
1984: Ecaterina Szabo, Romania
1988: Svetlana Boguinskaia, USSR
1992: Henrietta Onodi, Hungary
1996: Simona Amanar, Romania

Gymnastics, Rhythmic–Women's Individual All-Around

1984: Lori Fung, Canada
1988: Marina Lobatch, USSR
1992: Alexandra Timoshenko, Ukraine
1996: Ekaterina Serebryanskaya, Ukraine

Gymnastics, Rhythmic–Women's Group All-Around

1996: Spain

Judo–Men's Extra Lightweight (Up to 60 kg)

1980: Thierry Rey, France
1984: Shinji Hosokawa, Japan
1988: Jae-Yup Kim, South Korea
1992: Nazim Gousseinov, Azerbaijan
1996: Tadahiro Nomura, Japan

Judo–Men's Half Lightweight (Up to 65 kg)

1980: Nikolai Solodukhin, USSR
1984: Yoshiyuki Matsuoka, Japan
1988: Kyung-Keun Lee, South Korea
1992: Rogerio Cardoso, Brazil
1996: Udo Quellmalz, Germany

Judo–Men's Lightweight (Up to 71 kg)

1964: Takehide Nakatani, Japan
1968:*
1972: Takao Kawaguchi, Japan
1976: Hector Rodriguez, Cuba
1980: Ezio Gamba, Italy
1984: Byeng-Keun Ahn, South Korea
1988: Marc Alexandre, France
1992: Toshihiko Koga, Japan
1996: Kenzo Nakamura, Japan

_____
*Event not held.

Judo–Men's Half Middleweight (Up to 78 kg)

1972: Toyokazu Nomura, Japan
1976: Vladimir Nevzorov, USSR
1980: Shota Khabareli, USSR
1984: Frank Wieneke, West Germany
1988: Waldemar Legien, Poland
1992: Hidehiko Yoshida, Japan
1996: Djamel Bouras, France

Judo–Men's Middleweight (Up to 86 kg)

1964: Isao Okano, Japan
1968:*
1972: Shinobu Sekine, Japan
1976: Isamu Sonoda, Japan
1980: Jurg Rothlisberger, Switzerland
1984: Peter Seisenbacher, Austria
1988: Peter Seisenbacher, Austria
1992: Waldemar Legien, Poland
1996: Jeon Ki-Young, South Korea

_____
*Event not held.

Judo–Men's Half Heavyweight (Up to 95 kg)

1972: Schota Chochoshvili, USSR
1976: Kazuhiro Ninomiya, Japan
1980: Robert van de Walle, Belgium
1984: Hyoung-Zoo Ha, South Korea
1988: Aurelio Miguel, Brazil
1992: Antal Kovacs, Hungary
1996: Pawel Nastula, Poland

Judo–Men's Heavyweight (Over 95 kg)

1964: Isao Inokuma, Japan
1968:*
1972: Wim Ruska, Netherlands
1976: Sergei Novikov, USSR
1980: Angelo Parisi, France
1984: Hitoshi Saito, Japan
1988: Hitoshi Saito, Japan
1992: David Khakhaleichvili, Georgia
1996: David Douillet, France

_____
*Event not held.

Judo–Men's Open Category

1964: Antonius Geesink, Netherlands
1968:*
1972: Wim Ruska, Netherlands
1976: Haruko Uemura, Japan
1980: Dietmar Lorenz, East Germany
1984: Yasuhiro Yamashita, Japan
1988–1996:*

_____
*Event not held.

Judo–Women's Extra Lightweight (Up to 48kg)
1992: Cécile Nowak, France
1996: Sun Hi Kye, North Korea

Judo–Women's Half Lightweight (Up to 52kg)
1992: Almudena Martinez, Spain
1996: Marie-Claire Restoux, France

Judo–Women's Lightweight (Up to 56kg)
1992: Miriam Blasco Soto, Spain
1996: Driulis Gonzalez, Cuba

Judo–Women's Half Middleweight (Up to 61kg)
1992: Catherine Fleury, France
1996: Yuko Emoto, Japan

Judo–Women's Middleweight (Up to 66kg)
1992: Odalis Reve Jimenez, Cuba
1996: Cho Min Sun, South Korea

Judo–Women's Half Heavyweight (Up to 72kg)
1992: Kim Mi-Jung, South Korea
1996: Ulla Werbrouck, Belgium

Judo–Women's Heavyweight (Over 72kg)
1992: Zhuang Xiaoyan, China
1996: Fuming Sun, China

Modern Pentathlon–Individual
1912: Gosta Lilliehook, Sweden
1920: Gustaf Dyrssen, Sweden
1924: Bo Lindman, Sweden
1928: Sven Thofelt, Sweden
1932: Johan Oxenstierna, Sweden
1936: Gotthard Handrick, Germany
1948: William Grut, Sweden
1952: Lars Hall, Sweden
1956: Lars Hall, Sweden
1960: Ferenc Nemeth, Hungary
1964: Ferenc Torok, Hungary
1968: Bjorn Ferm, Sweden
1972: Andras Balczo, Hungary
1976: Janusz Pyciak-Peciak, Poland
1980: Anatoli Starostin, USSR
1984: Daniele Masala, Italy
1988: Janos Martinek, Hungary
1992: Arkadiusz Skrzypaszek, Poland
1996: Aleksandr Parygin, Kazakhstan

Modern Pentathlon–Team
1952: Hungary
1956: USSR
1960: Hungary
1964: USSR
1968: Hungary
1972: USSR
1976: Great Britain
1980: USSR

1984: Italy
1988: Hungary
1992: Poland
1996:*

----

*Event not held.

Rowing–Men's Single Sculls
1900: Henri Barrelet, France
1904: Frank Greer, USA
1906: Gaston Delaplane, France
1908: Harry Blackstaffe, Great Britain
1912: William Kinnear, Great Britain
1920: John Kelly, Sr., USA
1924: Jack Beresford, Jr., Great Britain
1928: Henry Pearce, Australia
1932: Henry Pearce, Australia
1936: Gustav Schafer, Germany
1948: Mervyn Wood, Australia
1952: Yuri Tyukalov, USSR
1956: Vyacheslav Ivanov, USSR
1960: Vyacheslav Ivanov, USSR
1964: Vyacheslav Ivanov, USSR
1968: Henri Jan Wienese, Netherlands
1972: Yuri Malishev, USSR
1976: Pertti Karppinen, Finland
1980: Pertti Karppinen, Finland
1984: Pertti Karppinen, Finland
1988: Thomas Lange, East Germany
1992: Thomas Lange, Germany
1996: Xeno Mueller, Switzerland

Rowing–Men's Double Sculls
1904: USA, John Mulcahy, William Varley
1906–1912:*
1920: USA, John Kelly, Sr., Paul Costello
1924: USA, Paul Costello, John Kelly, Sr.
1928: USA, Paul Costello, Charles McIlvaine
1932: USA, Kenneth Myers, William E. Garrett Gilmore
1936: Great Britain, Jack Beresford, Jr., Leslie Southwood
1948: Great Britain, Richard Burnell, B. Herbert Bushnell
1952: Argentina, Tranquilo Cappozzo, Eduardo Guerrero
1956: USSR, Aleksandr Berkutov, Yuri Tyukalov
1960: Czechoslovakia, Vaclav Kozak, Pavel Schmidt
1964: USSR, Oleg Tyurin, Boris Dubrovski
1968: USSR, Anatoli Sass, Aleksandr Timoschinin
1972: USSR, Aleksandr Timoshinin, Gennady Korshikikov
1976: Norway, Frank Hansen, Alf Hansen
1980: East Germany, Joachim Dreifke, Kroppelien Klaus
1984: USA, Bradley Lewis, Paul Enquist
1988: Netherlands, Ronald Florijn, Nicolaas Rienks
1992: Australia, Stephen Hawkins, Peter Antonie
1996: Italy, Davide Tizzano, Agostino Abbagnale

----

*Event not held.

Rowing—Men's Lightweight Double Sculls
1996: Switzerland, Markus Gier, Michael Gier

Rowing—Men's Coxless Pairs
1908: Great Britain, J. R. K. Fenning, Gordon Thomson
1912–1920:*
1924: Netherlands, Antonie C. Beijnen, Wilhelm H. Rosingh
1928: Germany, Bruno Muller, Kurt Moeschter
1932: Great Britain, H.R. Arthur Edwards, Lewis Clive
1936: Germany, Willi Eichhorn, Hugo Strauss
1948: Great Britain, John Wilson, W. George Laurie
1952: USA, Charles Logg, Thomas Price
1956: USA, James Fifer, Duvall Hecht
1960: USSR, Valentin Boreiko, Oleg Golovanov
1964: Canada, George Hungerford, Roger Ch. Jackson
1968: East Germany, Jorg Lucke, Heinz-Jurgen Bothe
1972: East Germany, Siegfried Brietzke, Wolfgang Meyer
1976: East Germany, Jurgen Landvoigt, Bernd Landvoigt
1980: East Germany, Bernd Landvoigt, Jurgen Landvoigt
1984: Romania, Petru Iosub, Valer Toma
1988: Great Britain, Andrew Holmes, Steven Redgrave
1992: Great Britain, Steven Redgrave, Matthew Pinsent
1996: Great Britain, Steven Redgrave, Matthew Pinsent

_____
*Event not held.

Rowing—Men's Coxed Pairs
1900: Netherlands
1904:*
1906: Italy
1908–1912:*
1920: Italy
1924: Switzerland
1928: Switzerland
1932: USA
1936: Germany
1948: Denmark
1952: France
1956: USA
1960: West Germany
1964: USA
1968: Italy
1972: East Germany
1976: East Germany
1980: East Germany
1984: Italy
1988: Italy
1992: Great Britain
1996:*

_____
*Event not held.

Rowing—Men's Quadruple Sculls
1976: East Germany
1980: East Germany
1984: West Germany
1988: Italy
1992: Germany
1996: Germany

Rowing—Men's Coxless Fours
1904: USA
1906:*
1908: Great Britain
1912–1920:*
1924: Great Britain
1928: Great Britain
1932: Great Britain
1936: Germany
1948: Italy
1952: Yugoslavia
1956: Canada
1960: USA
1964: Denmark
1968: East Germany
1972: East Germany
1976: East Germany
1980: East Germany
1984: New Zealand
1988: East Germany
1992: Australia
1996: Australia

_____
*Event not held.

Rowing—Men's Coxed Fours
1900: France
1904:*
1906: Italy
1908:*
1912: Germany
1920: Switzerland
1924: Switzerland
1928: Italy
1932: Germany
1936: Germany
1948: USA
1952: Czechoslovakia
1956: Italy
1960: West Germany
1964: West Germany
1968: New Zealand
1972: West Germany
1976: USSR
1980: East Germany
1984: Great Britain
1988: East Germany
1992: Romania
1996:*

_____
*Event not held.

Rowing—Men's Lightweight Coxless Fours
1996: Denmark

Rowing–Men's Eight Oars

1900: USA
1904: USA
1906:*
1908: Great Britain
1912: Great Britain
1920: USA
1924: USA
1928: USA
1932: USA
1936: USA
1948: USA
1952: USA
1956: USA
1960: West Germany
1964: USA
1968: West Germany
1972: New Zealand
1976: East Germany
1980: East Germany
1984: Canada
1988: West Germany
1992: Canada
1996: Netherlands

---

*Event not held.

Rowing–Women's Single Sculls

1976: Christine Scheiblich, East Germany
1980: Sanda Toma, Romania
1984: Valeria Racila, Romania
1988: Jutta Behrendt, East Germany
1992: Elisabeta Lipa, Romania
1996: Yekaterina Khodotovich, Belarus

Rowing–Women's Double Sculls

1976: Bulgaria, Svetla Ozetova, Zdravko Yordanova-Barboulova
1980: USSR, Yelena Khloptseva, Larissa Popova
1984: Romania, Manoara Popescu, Elisabeta Oleniuc
1988: East Germany, Birgit Peter, Martina Schroeter
1992: Germany, Kerstin Koeppen, Kathrin Boron
1996: Canada, Marnie McBean, Kathleen Heddle

Rowing–Women's Coxless Pairs

1976: Bulgaria, Siika Kelbecheva-Barboulova, Stoyanka Grouicheva
1980: East Germany, Ute Steindorf, Cornelia Klier
1984: Romania, Rodica Arba, Elena Horvat
1988: Romania, Rodica Arba, Olga Homeghi
1992: Canada, Marnie McBean, Kathleen Heddle
1996: Australia, Megan Still, Kate Slatter

Rowing–Women's Coxless Fours

1992: Canada
1996:*

---

*Event not held.

Rowing–Women's Lightweight Double Sculls

1996: Romania, Constanta Burcica, Camelia Macoviciuc

Rowing–Women's Quadruple Sculls

1976: East Germany
1980: East Germany
1984: Romania
1988: East Germany
1992: Germany
1996: Germany

Rowing–Women's Coxed Fours

1976: East Germany
1980: East Germany
1984: Romania
1988: East Germany
1992–1996:*

---

*Event not held.

Rowing–Women's Eight Oars

1976: East Germany
1980: East Germany
1984: USA
1988: East Germany
1992: Canada
1996: Romania

Shooting–Men's Air Pistol

1988: Taniou Kiriakov, Bulgaria
1992: Wang Yifu, China
1996: Roberto DiDonna, Italy

Shooting–Men's Free Pistol

1896: Sumner Paine, USA
1900: Conrad Roderer, Switzerland
1904:*
1906: Georgios Orphanidis, Greece
1908:*
1912: Alfred Lane, USA
1920: Karl Frederick, USA
1924–1932:*
1936: Torsten Ullman, Sweden
1948: Edwin Vasquez Cam, Peru
1952: Huelet Benner, USA
1956: Pentti Linnosvuo, Finland
1960: Aleksei Gustchin, USSR
1964: Vaino Markkanen, Finland
1968: Grigori Kossykh, USSR
1972: Ragnar Skanaker, Sweden
1976: Uwe Potteck, East Germany
1980: Aleksandr Melentiev, USSR
1984: Haifeng Xu, China
1988: Sorin Babii, Romania
1992: Konstantine Loukachik, Belarus
1996: Boris Kokorev, Russia

---

*Event not held.

Shooting–Men's Rapid-Fire Pistol
1896: Jean Phrangoudis, Greece
1900: Marice Larrouy, France
1904:*
1906: Maurice Lecoq, France
1908: Paul Van Asbroeck, Belgium
1912: Alfred Lane, USA
1920: Guilherme Paraense, Brazil
1924: H. M. Bailey, USA
1928:*
1932: Renzo Morigi, Italy
1936: Cornelius Van Oyen, Germany
1948: Karoly Takacs, Hungary
1952: Karoly Takacs, Hungary
1956: Stefan Petrescu, Romania
1960: William McMillan, USA
1964: Pentti Linnosvuo, Finland
1968: Jozef Zapedzki, Poland
1972: Jozef Zapedzki, Poland
1976: Norbert Klaar, East Germany
1980: Corneliu Ion, Romania
1984: Takeo Kamachi, Japan
1988: Afanasi Kouzming, USSR
1992: Ralf Schumann, Germany
1996: Ralf Schumann, Germany

*Event not held.

Shooting–Men's Running Game Target
1900: Louis Debray, France
1904–1968:*
1972: Yakov Zhelezniak, USSR
1976: Aleksandr Gazov, USSR
1980: Igor Sokolov, USSR
1984: Yuwei Li, China
1988: Tor Heiestad, Norway
1992: Michael Jakosits, Germany
1996: Yang Ling, China

*Event not held.

Shooting–Men's Air Rifle
1984: Philippe Heberle, France
1988: Goran Maksimovic, Yugoslavia
1992: Iouri Fedkine, Russia
1996: Artem Khadzhibekov, Russia

Shooting–Men's Smallbore Free Rifle, Prone
1908: A. A. Carnell, Great Britain
1912: Frederick Hird, USA
1920: Lawrence A. Nuesslein, USA
1924: Pierre Coquelin De Lisle, France
1928:*
1932: Bertil Ronnmark, Sweden
1936: Willy Rogeberg, Norway
1948: Arthur Cook, USA

*Event not held.

1952: Iosif Sirbu, Romania
1956: Gerald R. Ouellette, Canada
1960: Peter Kohnke, West Germany
1964: Laszlo Hammerl, Hungary
1968: Jan Kurka, Czechoslovakia
1972: Ho-Jun Li, North Korea
1976: Karlheinz Smieszek, West Germany
1980: Karoly Vargo, Hungary
1984: Edward Etzel, USA
1988: Miroslav Varga, Czechoslovakia
1992: Eun-Chul Lee, South Korea
1996: Christian Klees, Germany

Shooting–Men's Smallbore Rifle, Three-Position
1952: Erling Kongshaug, Norway
1956: Anatoli Bogdanov, USSR
1960: Viktor Shamburkin, USSR
1964: Lones Wigger, USA
1968: Bernd Klingner, West Germany
1972: John Writer, USA
1976: Lanny Bassham, USA
1980: Viktor Vlasov, USSR
1984: Malcolm Cooper, Great Britain
1988: Malcolm Cooper, Great Britain
1992: Gratchia Petikian, Armenia
1996: Jean-Pierre Amat, France

Shooting–Olympic Trap (Open)
1900: Roger De Barbarin, France
1904:*
1906: Gerald Merlin, Great Britain, Sidney Merlin, Great Britain
1908: Walter H. Ewing, Canada
1912: James Graham, USA
1920: Mark Arie, USA
1924: Gyula Halasy, Hungary
1928–1948:*
1952: George P. Genereux, Canada
1956: Galliano Rossini, Italy
1960: Ion Dumitrescu, Romania
1964: Ennio Mattarelli, Italy
1968: John R. Braithwaite, Great Britain
1972: Angelo Scalzone, Italy
1976: Donald Haldeman, USA
1980: Luciano Giovannetti, Italy
1984: Luciano Giovannetti, Italy
1988: Dmitri Monakov, USSR
1992: Petr Hrdlicka, Czechoslovakia
1996: Michael Diamond, Australia

*Event not held.

Shooting–Men's Olympic Double Trap (Open)
1996: Russell Mark, Australia

Shooting–Olympic Skeet (Open)
1968: Yevgeny Petrov, USSR
1972: Konrad Wirnhier, West Germany
1976: Josef Panacek, Czechoslovakia
1980: Hans Kjeld Rasmussen, Denmark
1984: Matthew Dryke, USA
1988: Axel Wegner, East Germany
1992: Zhang Shan, China
1996: Ennio Falco, Italy

Shooting–Women's Air Pistol
1988: Jasna Sekaric, Yugoslavia
1992: Marina Logvinenko, Russia
1996: Olga Klochneva, Russia

Shooting–Women's Sport Pistol
1984: Linda Thom, Canada
1988: Nino Salukvadze, USSR
1992: Marina Logvinenko, Russia
1996: Li Duihong, China

Shooting–Women's Air Rifle
1984: Pat Spurgin, USA
1988: Irina Chilova, USSR
1992: Kab-Soon Yeo, South Korea
1996: Renata Mauer, Poland

Shooting–Women's Smallbore Rifle, Three-Position
1984: Xiao Xuan Wu, China
1988: Silvia Sperber, West Germany
1992: Launi Meili, USA
1996: Aleksandra Ivosev, Yugoslavia

Shooting–Women's Olympic Double Trap (Open)
1996: Kim Rhode, USA

Men's Soccer
1900: Great Britain
1904: Canada
1906: Denmark
1908: Great Britain
1912: Great Britain
1920: Belgium
1924: Uruguay
1928: Uruguay
1932:*
1936: Italy
1948: Sweden
1952: Hungary
1956: USSR
1960: Yugoslavia
1964: Hungary
1968: Hungary

*Event not held.

1972: Poland
1976: East Germany
1980: Czechoslovakia
1984: France
1988: USSR
1992: Spain
1996: Nigeria

Women's Soccer
1996: USA

Softball
1996: USA

Swimming–Men's 50-Meter Freestyle
1904: Zoltan von Halmay, Hungary
1906–1984:*
1988: Matthew Biondi, USA
1992: Aleksandr Popov, Russia
1996: Aleksandr Popov, Russia

*Event not held.

Swimming–Men's 100-Meter Freestyle
1896: Alfred Hajos, Hungary
1900:*
1904: Zoltan von Halmay, Hungary
1906: Charles Daniels, USA
1908: Charles Daniels, USA
1912: Duke Paoa Kahanamoku, USA
1920: Duke Paoa Kahanamoku, USA
1924: John Weissmuller, USA
1928: John Weissmuller, USA
1932: Yasuji Miyazaki, Japan
1936: Ferenc Csik, Hungary
1948: Walter Ris, USA
1952: Clarke Scholes, USA
1956: Jon Henricks, Australia
1960: John Devitt, Australia
1964: Don Schollander, USA
1968: Michael Wenden, Australia
1972: Mark Spitz, USA
1976: Jim Montgomery, USA
1980: Jorg Woithe, East Germany
1984: Ambrose Gaines, USA
1988: Matthew Biondi, USA
1992: Aleksandr Popov, Russia
1996: Aleksandr Popov, Russia

*Event not held.

Swimming–Men's 200-Meter Freestyle
1900: Frederick C. V. Lane, Australia
1904: Charles Daniels, USA
1906–1964:*

*Event not held.

1968: Michael Wenden, Australia
1972: Mark Spitz, USA
1976: Bruce Furniss, USA
1980: Sergei Kopliakov, USSR
1984: Michael Gross, West Germany
1988: Duncan Armstrong, Australia
1992: Evgueni Sadovyi, Russia
1996: Danyon Loader, New Zealand

Swimming–Men's 400-Meter Freestyle
1896: Paul Neumann, Australia
1900:*
1904: Charles Daniels, USA
1906: Otto Scheff, Austria
1908: Henry Taylor, Great Britain
1912: George Hodgson, Canada
1920: Norman Ross, USA
1924: John Weissmuller, USA
1928: Alberto Zorilla, Argentina
1932: Clarence Crabbe, USA
1936: Jack Medica, USA
1948: William Smith, USA
1952: Jean Boiteux, France
1956: Murray Rose, Australia
1960: Murray Rose, Australia
1964: Don Schollander, USA
1968: Michael Burton, USA
1972: Bradford Cooper, Australia
1976: Brian Goodell, USA
1980: Vladimir Salnikov, USSR
1984: George Dicarlo, USA
1988: Uwe Dassler, East Germany
1992: Evgueni Sadovyi, Russia
1996: Danyon Loader, New Zealand

*Event not held

Swimming–Men's 1,500-Meter Freestyle
1896: Alfred Hajos, Hungary
1900: John Jarvis, Great Britain
1904: Emil Rausch, Germany
1906: Henry Taylor, Great Britain
1908: Henry Taylor, Great Britain
1912: George Hodgson, Canada
1920: Norman Ross, USA
1924: Andrew Charlton, Australia
1928: Arne Borg, Sweden
1932: Kusuo Kitamura, Japan
1936: Noboru Terada, Japan
1948: James McLane, USA
1952: Ford Konno, USA
1956: Murray Rose, Australia
1960: John Konrads, Australia
1964: Robert Windle, Australia
1968: Michael Burton, USA
1972: Michael Burton, USA
1976: Brian Goodell, USA
1980: Vladimir Salnikov, USSR

1984: Michael O'Brien, USA
1988: Vladimir Salnikov, USSR
1992: Kieren Perkins, Australia
1996: Kieren Perkins, Australia

Swimming–Men's 100-Meter Backstroke
1904: Walter Brack, Germany
1906:*
1908: Arno Bieberstein, Germany
1912: Harry Hebner, USA
1920: Warren Paoa Kealoha, USA
1924: Warren Paoa Kealoha, USA
1928: George Kojac, USA
1932: Masaji Kiyokawa, Japan
1936: Adolf Kiefer, USA
1948: Allen Stack, USA
1952: Yoshinobu Oyakawa, USA
1956: David Theile, Australia
1960: David Theile, Australia
1964:*
1968: Roland Matthes, East Germany
1972: Roland Matthes, East Germany
1976: John Naber, USA
1980: Bengt Baron, Sweden
1984: Richard Carey, USA
1988: Daichi Suzuki, Japan
1992: Mark Tewksbury, Canada
1996: Jeff Rouse, USA

*Event not held.

Swimming–Men's 200-Meter Backstroke
1900: Ernst Hoppenberg, Germany
1904–1960:*
1964: Jed Graef, USA
1968: Roland Matthes, East Germany
1972: Roland Matthes, East Germany
1976: John Naber, USA
1980: Sandor Wladar, Hungary
1984: Richard Carey, USA
1988: Igor Polianski, USSR
1992: Martin Lopez-Zubero, Spain
1996: Brad Bridgewater, USA

*Event not held.

Swimming–Men's 100-Meter Breaststroke
1968: Donald McKenzie, USA
1972: Nobutaka Taguchi, Japan
1976: John Hencken, USA
1980: Dunkan Goodhew, Great Britain
1984: Steve Lundquist, USA
1988: Adrian Moorhouse, Great Britain
1992: Nelson Diebel, USA
1996: Fred DeBurghgraeve, Belgium

Swimming–Men's 200-Meter Breaststroke
1908: Frederick Holman, Great Britain

1912: Walther Bathe, Germany
1920: Hakan Malmroth, Sweden
1924: Robert Skelton, USA
1928: Yoshiyuki Tsuruta, Japan
1932: Yoshiyuki Tsuruta, Japan
1936: Tetsuo Hamuro, Japan
1948: Joseph Verdeur, USA
1952: John Davies, Australia
1956: Masaru Furukawa, Japan
1960: William Mulliken, USA
1964: Ian O'Brien, Australia
1968: Felipe Munoz, Mexico
1972: John Hencken, USA
1976: David Wilkie, Great Britain
1980: Robertas Zulpa, USSR
1984: Victor Davis, Canada
1988: Jozsef Szabo, Hungary
1992: Mike Barrowman, USA
1996: Norbert Rozsa, Hungary

Swimming–Men's 100-Meter Butterfly
1968: Douglas Russell, USA
1972: Mark Spitz, USA
1976: Matt Vogel, USA
1980: Par Arvidsson, Sweden
1984: Michael Gross, West Germany
1988: Anthony Nesty, Suriname
1992: Pablo Morales, USA
1996: Denis Pankratov, Russia

Swimming–Men's 200-Meter Butterfly
1956: William Yorzyk, USA
1960: Michael Troy, USA
1964: Kevin Berry, Australia
1968: Carl Robie, USA
1972: Mark Spitz, USA
1976: Mike Bruner, USA
1980: Sergei Fesenko, USSR
1984: Jon Sieben, Australia
1988: Michael Gross, West Germany
1992: Mel Stewart, USA
1996: Denis Pankratov, Russia

Swimming–Men's 200-Meter Individual Medley
1968: Charles Hickcox, USA
1972: Gunnar Larsson, Sweden
1976–1980:*
1984: Alex Baumann, Canada
1988: Tamas Darnyi, Hungary
1992: Tamas Darnyi, Hungary
1996: Attila Czene, Hungary

———————
*Event not held.

Swimming–Men's 400-Meter Individual Medley
1964: Richard Roth, USA
1968: Charles Hickcox, USA
1972: Gunnar Larsson, Sweden

1976: Rod Strachan, USA
1980: Aleksandr Sidorenko, USSR
1984: Alex Baumann, Canada
1988: Tamas Darnyi, Hungary
1992: Tamas Darnyi, Hungary
1996: Tom Dolan, USA

Swimming–Men's 4 × 100-Meter Freestyle Relay
1964: USA
1968: USA
1972: USA
1976–1980:*
1984: USA
1988: USA
1992: USA
1996: USA

———————
*Event not held.

Swimming–Men's 4 × 100-Meter Medley Relay
1960: USA
1964: USA
1968: USA
1972: USA
1976: USA
1980: Australia
1984: USA
1988: USA
1992: USA
1996: USA

Swimming–Men's 4 × 200-Meter Freestyle Relay
1906: Hungary
1908: Great Britain
1912: Australia
1920: USA
1924: USA
1928: USA
1932: Japan
1936: Japan
1948: USA
1952: USA
1956: Australia
1960: USA
1964: USA
1968: USA
1972: USA
1976: USA
1980: USSR
1984: USA
1988: USA
1992: Unified Team
1996: USA

Swimming–Women's 50-Meter Freestyle
1988: Kristin Otto, East Germany
1992: Yang Wenyi, China
1996: Amy Van Dyken, USA

Swimming–Women's 100-Meter Freestyle
1912: Fanny Durack, Australia
1920: Ethelda Bleibtrey, USA
1924: Ethel Lackie, USA
1928: Albina Osipowich, USA
1932: Helene Madison, USA
1936: Hendrika Mastenbroek, Netherlands
1948: Greta Andersen, Denmark
1952: Katalin Szoke, Hungary
1956: Dawn Fraser, Australia
1960: Dawn Fraser, Australia
1964: Dawn Fraser, Australia
1968: Jan Henne, USA
1972: Sandra Neilson, USA
1976: Kornelia Ender, East Germany
1980: Barbara Krause, East Germany
1984: Nancy Hogshead, USA
1988: Kristin Otto, East Germany
1992: Zhuang Yong, China
1996: Jingyi Le, China

Swimming–Women's 200-Meter Freestyle
1968: Debbie Meyer, USA
1972: Shane Gould, Australia
1976: Kornelia Ender, East Germany
1980: Barbara Krause, East Germany
1984: Mary Wayte, USA
1988: Heike Friedrich, East Germany
1992: Nicole Haislett, USA
1996: Claudia Poll, Costa Rica

Swimming–Women's 400-Meter Freestyle
1920: Ethelda Bleibtrey, USA
1924: Martha Norelius, USA
1928: Martha Norelius, USA
1932: Helene Madison, USA
1936: Hendrika Mastenbroek, Netherlands
1948: Ann Curtis, USA
1952: Valeria Gyenge, Hungary
1956: Lorraine Crapp, Australia
1960: Christine Von Saltza, USA
1964: Virginia Duenkel, USA
1968: Debbie Meyer, USA
1972: Shane Gould, Australia
1976: Petra Thuemer, East Germany
1980: Ines Diers, East Germany
1984: Tiffany Cohen, USA
1988: Janet Evans, USA
1992: Dagmar Hase, Germany
1996: Michelle Smith, Ireland

Swimming–Women's 800-Meter Freestyle
1968: Debbie Meyer, USA
1972: Keena Rothhammer, USA
1976: Petra Thuemer, East Germany
1980: Michelle Ford, Australia
1984: Tiffany Cohen, USA
1988: Janet Evans, USA

1992: Janet Evans, USA
1996: Brooke Bennett, USA

Swimming–Women's 100-Meter Backstroke
1924: Sybil Bauer, USA
1928: Maria Johanna Braun, Netherlands
1932: Eleanor Holm, USA
1936: Dina W. Senff, Netherlands
1948: Karen Margrete Harup, Denmark
1952: Joan Harrison, South Africa
1956: Judith Grinham, Great Britain
1960: Lynn Burke, USA
1964: Cathy Ferguson, USA
1968: Kaye Hall, USA
1972: Melissa Belote, USA
1976: Ulrike Richter, East Germany
1980: Rica Reinisch, East Germany
1984: Theresa Andrews, USA
1988: Kristin Otto, East Germany
1992: Kirsztina Egerszegi, Hungary
1996: Beth Botsford, USA

Swimming–Women's 200-Meter Backstroke
1968: Pokey Watson, USA
1972: Melissa Belote, USA
1976: Ulrike Richter, East Germany
1980: Rica Reinisch, East Germany
1984: Jolanda De Rover, Netherlands
1988: Krisztina Egerszegi, Hungary
1992: Krisztina Egerszegi, Hungary
1996: Krisztina Egerszegi, Hungary

Swimming–Women's 100-Meter Breaststroke
1968: Djurdjica Bjedov, Yugoslavia
1972: Catherine Carr, USA
1976: Hannelore Anke, East Germany
1980: Ute Geweniger, East Germany
1984: Petra Van Staveren, Netherlands
1988: Tania Dangalakova, Bulgaria
1992: Elena Roudkovskaïa, Belarus
1996: Penelope Heyns, South Africa

Swimming–Women's 200-Meter Breaststroke
1924: Lucy Morton, Great Britain
1928: Hilde Schrader, Germany
1932: Claire Dennis, Australia
1936: Hideko Maehata, Japan
1948: Petronella van Vliet, Netherlands
1952: Eva Szekely, Hungary
1956: Ursula Happe, West Germany
1960: Anita Lonsbrough, Great Britain
1964: Galina Prozumenshikova, USSR
1968: Sharon Wichman, USA
1972: Beverly Whitfield, Australia
1976: Marina Koshevaia, USSR
1980: Lina Kochushite, USSR
1984: Anne Ottenbrite, Canada

1988: Silke Hoerner, East Germany
1992: Kyoko Iwasaki, Japan
1996: Penelope Heyns, South Africa

Swimming–Women's 100-Meter Butterfly
1956: Shelley Mann, USA
1960: Carolyn Schuler, USA
1964: Sharon Stouder, USA
1968: Lynette McClements, Australia
1972: Mayumi Aoki, Japan
1976: Kornelia Ender, East Germany
1980: Caren Metschuck, East Germany
1984: Mary T. Meagher, USA
1988: Kristin Otto, East Germany
1992: Qian Hong, China
1996: Amy Van Dyken, USA

Swimming–Women's 200-Meter Butterfly
1968: Ada Kok, Netherlands
1972: Karen Moe, USA
1976: Andrea Pollack, East Germany
1980: Ines Geissler, East Germany
1984: Mary T. Meagher, USA
1988: Kathleen Nord, East Germany
1992: Summer Sanders, USA
1996: Susan O'Neill, Australia

Swimming–Women's 200-Meter Individual Medley
1968: Claudia Kolb, USA
1972: Shane Gould, Australia
1976-1980*
1984: Tracy Caulkins, USA
1988: Daniela Hunger, East Germany
1992: Lin Li, China
1996: Michelle Smith, Ireland

----
*Event not held.

Swimming–Women's 400-Meter Individual Medley
1964: Donna De Varona, USA
1968: Claudia Kolb, USA
1972: Gail Neall, Australia
1976: Ulrike Tauber, East Germany
1980: Petra Schneider, East Germany
1984: Tracy Caulkins, USA
1988: Janet Evans, USA
1992: Krisztina Egerszegi, Hungary
1996: Michelle Smith, Ireland

Swimming–Women's 4 × 100-Meter Freestyle Relay
1912: Great Britain
1920: USA
1924: USA
1928: USA

1932: USA
1936: Netherlands
1948: USA
1952: Hungary
1956: Australia
1960: USA
1964: USA
1968: USA
1972: USA
1976: USA
1980: East Germany
1984: USA
1988: East Germany
1992: USA
1996: USA

Swimming–Women's 4 × 100-Meter Medley Relay
1960: USA
1964: USA
1968: USA
1972: USA
1976: East Germany
1980: East Germany
1984: USA
1988: East Germany
1992: USA
1996: USA

Swimming–Women's 4 × 200-Meter Freestyle Relay
1996: USA

Synchronized Swimming–Solo
1984: Tracie Ruiz, USA
1988: Carolyn Waldo, Canada
1992: Kristen Babb-Sprague, USA
1996*

----
*Event not held.

Synchronized Swimming–Duet
1984: USA, Candy Costie, Tracie Ruiz
1988: Canada, Michelle Cameron, Carolyn Waldo
1992: USA, Karen Josephson, Sarah Josephson
1996*

----
*Event not held.

Synchronized Swimming–Team
1996: USA

Table Tennis–Men's Singles
1988: Nam-Kyu Yoo, South Korea
1992: Jan Waldner, Sweden
1996: Guoliang Liu, China

Table Tennis–Men's Doubles
1988: China, Longcan Chen, Qingguang Wei
1992: China, Lu Lin, Wang Tao
1996: China, Linghui Kung, Guoliang Liu

Table Tennis–Women's Singles
1988: Jing Chen, China
1992: Deng Yaping, China
1996: Deng Yaping, China

Table Tennis–Women's Doubles
1988: South Korea, Jung-Hwa Hyun, Young-Ja Yang
1992: China, Deng Yaping, Qiao Hong
1996: China, Deng Yaping, Qiao Hong

Team Handball–Men's Team
1936: Germany
1948:*
1952: Demonstration game only.
1956-1968:*
1972: Yugoslavia
1976: USSR
1980: East Germany
1984: Yugoslavia
1988: USSR
1992: Unified Team
1996: Croatia

_____
*Event not held.

Team Handball–Women's Team
1976: USSR
1980: USSR
1984: Yugoslavia
1988: South Korea
1992: South Korea
1996: Denmark

Tennis–Men's Singles
1896: John Boland, Great Britain
1900: Hugh Doherty, Great Britain
1904: Beals Wright, USA
1906: Max Decugis, France
1908: Josiah Ritchie, Great Britain, outdoor; Wentworth
  Gore, Great Britain, indoor
1912: Charles Winslow, South Africa, outdoor, Andre
  Govert, France, indoor
1920: Louis Raymond, South Africa
1924: Vincent Richards, USA
1928-1984:*
1988: Miloslav Mecir, Czechoslovakia
1992: Marc Rosset, Switzerland
1996: Andre Agassi, USA

_____
*Event not held.

Tennis–Men's Doubles
1896: Great Britain/Germany

1900: Great Britain
1904: USA
1906: France
1908: Great Britain, outdoor, Great Britain, indoor
1912: South Africa, outdoor, France, indoor
1920: Great Britain
1924: USA
1928-1984:*
1988: USA, Ken Flach, Robert Seguso
1992: Germany, Boris Becker, Michael Stich
1996: Australia, Todd Woodbridge, Mark Woodforde

_____
*Event not held.

Tennis–Women's Singles
1900: Charlotte Cooper, Great Britain
1904:*
1906: Esmee Simiriotou, Greece
1908: Dorothea Chambers, Great Britain, outdoor, Gwen
  Eastlake-Smith, Great Britain, indoor
1912: Maarguerite Broquedis, France, outdoor, Ethel
  Hannam, Great Britain, indoor
1920: Suzanne Lenglen, France
1924: Helen Wills, USA
1928-1984:*
1988: Steffi Graf, West Germany
1992: Jennifer Capriati, USA
1996: Lindsay Davenport, USA

_____
*Event not held.

Tennis–Women's Doubles
1920: Great Britain
1924: USA
1928-1984:*
1988: USA. Zina Garrison, Pam Shriver
1992: USA. Gigi Fernandez, Mary Joe Fernandez
1996: USA. Mary Joe Fernandez, Gigi Fernandez

_____
*Event not held.

Track and Field–Men's High Jump
1896: Ellery Clark, USA
1900: Irving Baxter, USA
1904: Samuel Jones, USA
1906: Con Leahy, Great Britain/Ireland
1908: Harry Porter, USA
1912: Alma Richards, USA
1920: Richmond Landon, USA
1924: Harold Osborn, USA
1928: Robert King, USA
1932: Duncan McNaughton, Canada
1936: Cornelius Johnson, USA
1948: John Winter, Australia
1952: Walter Davis, USA
1956: Charles Dumas, USA
1960: Robert Shavlakadze, USSR

1964: Valeri Brumel, USSR
1968: Dick Fosbury, USA
1972: Yuri Tarmak, USSR
1976: Jacek Wzsola, Poland
1980: Gerd Wessig, East Germany
1984: Dietmar Moegenburg, West Germany
1988: Guennadi Avdeenko, USSR
1992: Javier Sotomayor Sanabria, Cuba
1996: Charles Austin, USA

Track and Field–Men's Pole Vault
1896: William Hoyt, USA
1900: Irving Baxter, USA
1904: Charles Dvorak, USA
1906: Fernand Gonder, France
1908: Edward Cooke, USA, Alfred Gilbert, USA
1912: Harry Babcock, USA
1920: Frank Foss, USA
1924: Lee Barnes, USA
1928: Sabin Carr, USA
1932: William Miller, USA
1936: Earle Meadows, USA
1948: Guinn Smith, USA
1952: Robert Richards, USA
1956: Robert Richards, USA
1960: Donald Bragg, USA
1964: Fred Hansen, USA
1968: Bob Seagren, USA
1972: Wolfgang Nordwig, East Germany
1976: Tadeusz Slusarski, Poland
1980: Wladyslaw Kazakiewicz, Poland
1984: Pierre Quinon, France
1988: Sergei Bubka, USSR
1992: Maxim Tarassov, Russia
1996: Jean Galfione, France

Track and Field–Men's Long Jump
1896: Ellery Clark, USA
1900: Alvin Kraenzlein, USA
1904: Meyer Prinstein, USA
1906: Meyer Prinstein, USA
1908: Francis Irons, USA
1912: Albert Gutterson, USA
1920: William Petersson, Sweden
1924: William DeHart Hubbard, USA
1928: Edward Hamm, USA
1932: Edward Gordon, USA
1936: Jesse Owens, USA
1948: Willie Steele, USA
1952: Jerome Biffle, USA
1956: Greg Bell, USA
1960: Ralph Boston, USA
1964: Lynn Davies, Great Britain
1968: Bob Beamon, USA
1972: Randy Williams, USA
1976: Arnie Robinson, USA

1980: Lutz Dombrowski, East Germany
1984: Carl Lewis, USA
1988: Carl Lewis, USA
1992: Carl Lewis, USA
1996: Carl Lewis, USA

Track and Field–Men's Triple Jump
1896: James Connolly, USA
1900: Meyer Prinstein, USA
1904: Meyer Prinstein, USA
1906: Peter O'Connor, Great Britain/Ireland
1908: Timothy Ahearne, Great Britain/Ireland
1912: Gustaf Lindblom, Sweden
1920: Vilho Tuulos, Finland
1924: Anthony Winter, Australia
1928: Mikio Oda, Japan
1932: Chuhei Nambu, Japan
1936: Naoto Tajima, Japan
1948: Arne Ahman, Sweden
1952: Adhemar Ferreira da Silva, Brazil
1956: Adhemar Ferreira da Silva, Brazil
1960: Jozef Schmidt, Poland
1964: Jozef Schmidt, Poland
1968: Viktor Saneyev, USSR
1972: Viktor Saneyev, USSR
1976: Viktor Saneyev, USSR
1980: Jaak Uudmae, USSR
1984: Al Joyner, USA
1988: Hristo Markov, Bulgaria
1992: Mike Conley, USA
1996: Kenny Harrison, USA

Track and Field–Women's High Jump
1928: Ethel Catherwood, Canada
1932: Jean Shiley, USA
1936: Ibolya Csak, Hungary
1948: Alice Coachman, USA
1952: Esther Brand, South Africa
1956: Mildred McDaniel, USA
1960: Iolanda Balas, Romania
1964: Iolanda Balas, Romania
1968: Miloslava Rezkova, Czechoslovakia
1972: Ulrike Meyfarth, West Germany
1976: Rosemarie Ackermann, East Germany
1980: Sara Simeoni, Italy
1984: Ulrike Mayfarth, West Germany
1988: Louise Ritter, USA
1992: Heike Henkel, Germany
1996: Stefka Kostadinova, Bulgaria

Track and Field–Women's Long Jump
1948: Olga Gyarmati, Hungary
1952: Yvette Williams, New Zealand
1956: Elzbieta Krzesinska, Poland
1960: Vyera Krepkina, USSR
1964: Mary Rand, Great Britain
1968: Viorica Viscopoleanu, Romania

1972: Heidemarie Rosendahl, West Germany
1976: Angela Voigt, East Germany
1980: Tatiana Kolpakova, USSR
1984: Anisoara Cusmir-Stanciu, Romania
1988: Jackie Joyner-Kersee, USA
1992: Heike Dreschsler, Germany
1996: Chioma Ajunwa, Nigeria

Track and Field–Women's Triple Jump
1996: Inessa Kravets, Ukraine

Track and Field–Men's 100 Meters
1896: Thomas Burke, USA
1900: Francis Jarvis, USA
1904: Archie Hahn, USA
1906: Archie Hahn, USA
1908: Reginald Walker, South Africa
1912: Ralph Craig, USA
1920: Charles Paddock, USA
1924: Harold Abrahams, Great Britain
1928: Percy Williams, Canada
1932: Eddie Tolan, USA
1936: Jesse Owens, USA
1948: Harrison Dillard, USA
1952: Lindy Remigino, USA
1956: Robert Morrow, USA
1960: Armin Hary, West Germany
1964: Robert Hayes, USA
1968: Jim Hines, USA
1972: Valery Borsov, USSR
1976: Hasely Crawford, Trinidad and Tobago
1980: Allan Wells, Great Britain
1984: Carl Lewis, USA
1988: Carl Lewis, USA
1992: Linford Christie, Britain
1996: Donovan Bailey, Canada

Track and Field–Men's 200 Meters
1900: John Walter Tewksbury, USA
1904: Archie Hahn, USA
1906:*
1908: Robert Kerr, Canada
1912: Ralph Craig, USA
1920: Allen Woodring, USA
1924: Jackson Scholz, USA
1928: Percy Williams, Canada
1932: Eddie Tolan, USA
1936: Jesse Owens, USA
1948: Mel Patton, USA
1952: Andrew Stanfield, USA
1956: Robert Morrow, USA
1960: Livio Berruti, Italy
1964: Henry Carr, USA
1968: Tommie Smith, USA
1972: Valery Borsov, USSR
1976: Donald Quarrie, Jamaica

*Event not held.

1980: Pietro Mennea, Italy
1984: Carl Lewis, USA
1988: Joe DeLoach, USA
1992: Mike Marsh, USA
1996: Michael Johnson, USA

Track and Field–Men's 400 Meters
1896: Thomas Burke, USA
1900: Maxwell Long, USA
1904: Harry Hillman, USA
1906: Paul Pilgrim, USA
1908: Wyndham Halswelle, Great Britain
1912: Charles Reidpath, USA
1920: Bevil Rudd, South Africa
1924: Eric Liddell, Great Britain
1928: Raymond Barbuti, USA
1932: William Carr, USA
1936: Archie Williams, USA
1948: Arthur Wint, Jamaica
1952: George Rhoden, Jamaica
1956: Charles Jenkins, USA
1960: Otis Davis, USA
1964: Michael Larrabee, USA
1968: Lee Evans, USA
1972: Vincent Matthews, USA
1976: Alberto Juantorena, Cuba
1980: Viktor Markin, USSR
1984: Alonzo Babers, USA
1988: Steven Lewis, USA
1992: Quincy Watts, USA
1996: Michael Johnson, USA

Track and Field–Men's 800 Meters
1896: Edwin Flack, Australia
1900: Alfred Tysoe, Great Britain
1904: James Lightbody, USA
1906: Paul Pilgrim, USA
1908: Melvin Sheppard, USA
1912: James Meredith, USA
1920: Albert Hill, Great Britain
1924: Douglas Lowe, Great Britain
1928: Douglas Lowe, Great Britain
1932: Thomas Hampson, Great Britain
1936: John Woodruff, USA
1948: Malvin Whitfield, USA
1952: Malvin Whitfield, USA
1956: Tom Courtney, USA
1960: Peter Snell, New Zealand
1964: Peter Snell, New Zealand
1968: Ralph Doubell, Australia
1972: David Wottle, USA
1976: Alberto Juantorena, Cuba
1980: Steven Ovett, Great Britain
1984: Joaquim Cruz, Brazil
1988: Paul Ereng, Kenya
1992: William Tanui, Kenya
1996: Vebjoern Rodal, Norway

Track and Field–Men's 1,500 Meters

1896: Edwin Flack, Australia
1900: Charles Bennett, Great Britain
1904: James Lightbody, USA
1906: James Lightbody, USA
1908: Melvin Sheppard, USA
1912: Arnold Jackson, Great Britain
1920: Albert Hill, Great Britain
1924: Poavo Nurmi, Finland
1928: Harri Larva, Finland
1932: Luigi Beccali, Italy
1936: John Lovelock, New Zealand
1948: Henry Eriksson, Sweden
1952: Josef Barthel, Luxembourg
1956: Ron Delany, Ireland
1960: Herbert Elliott, Australia
1964: Peter Snell, New Zealand
1968: Kipchoge Keino, Kenya
1972: Kipchoge Keino, Kenya
1976: John Walker, New Zealand
1980: Sebastian Coe, Great Britain
1984: Sebastian Coe, Great Britain
1988: Peter Rono, Kenya
1992: Fermin Cacho Ruiz, Spain
1996: Noureddine Morceli, Algeria

Track and Field–Men's 5,000 Meters

1912: Johannes Kolehmainen, Finland
1920: Joseph Guillemot, France
1924: Paavo Nurmi, Finland
1928: Ville Ritola, Finland
1932: Lauri Lehtinen, Finland
1936: Gunnar Hockert, Finland
1948: Gaston Reiff, Belgium
1952: Emil Zatopek, Czechoslovakia
1956: Vladimir Kuts, USSR
1960: Murray Halberg, New Zealand
1964: Robert Schul, USA
1968: Mohamed Gammoudi, Tunisia
1972: Lasse Viren, Finland
1976: Lasse Viren, Finland
1980: Miruts Yifter, Ethiopia
1984: Said Aouita, Morocco
1988: John Ngugi, Kenya
1992: Dieter Baumann, Germany
1996: Venuste Niyongabo, Burundi

Track and Field–Men's 10,000 Meters

1912: Johannes Kolehmainen, Finland
1920: Paavo Nurmi, Finland
1924: Ville Ritola, Finland
1928: Paavo Nurmi, Finland
1932: Janusz Kusocinski, Poland
1936: Ilmari Salminen, Finland
1948: Emil Zatopek, Czechoslovakia
1952: Emil Zatopek, Czechoslovakia
1956: Vladmir Kuts, USSR
1960: Pyotr Bolotnikov, USSR

1964: William Mills, USA
1968: Naftali Temu, Kenya
1972: Lasse Viren, Finland
1976: Lasse Viren, Finland
1980: Miruts Yifter, Ethiopia
1984: Alberto Cova, Italy
1988: Brahim Boutaib, Morocco
1992: Khalid Skah, Morocco
1996: Haile Gebrselassie, Ethiopia

Track and Field–Men's Marathon

1896: Spyridon Louis, Greece
1900: Michel Theato, France
1904: Thomas Hicks, USA
1906: W. John Sherring, Canada
1908: John Hayes, USA
1912: Kenneth McArthur, South Africa
1920: Johannes Kolehmainen, Finland
1924: Albin Stenroos, Finland
1928: Boughera El Ouafi, France
1932: Juan Zabala, Argentina
1936: Kitei Son, Japan/South Korea
1948: Delfo Cabrera, Argentina
1952: Emil Zatopek, Czechoslovakia
1956: Alain Mimoun O'Kacha, France
1960: Abebe Bikila, Ethiopia
1964: Abebe Bikila, Ethiopia
1968: Mamo Wolde, Ethiopia
1972: Frank Shorter, USA
1976: Waldemar Cierpinski, East Germany
1980: Waldemar Cierpinski, East Germany
1984: Carlos Lopez, Portugal
1988: Gelindo Bordin, Italy
1992: Hwang Young-Cho, South Korea
1996: Josia Thugwane, South Africa

Track and Field–Men's 110-Meter Hurdles

1896: Thomas Curtis, USA
1900: Alvin Kraenzlein, USA
1904: Frederick Schule, USA
1906: Robert Leavitt, USA
1908: Forest Smithson, USA
1912: Frederick Kelly, USA
1920: Earl Thomson, Canada
1924: Daniel Kinsey, USA
1928: Sydney Atkinson, South Africa
1932: George Saling, USA
1936: Forrest Towns, USA
1948: William Porter, USA
1952: Harrison Dillard, USA
1956: Lee Calhoun, USA
1960: Lee Calhoun, USA
1964: Hayes Jones, USA
1968: Willie Davenport, USA
1972: Rod Milburn, USA
1976: Guy Drut, France
1980: Thomas Munkelt, East Germany
1984: Roger Kingdom, USA

1988: Roger Kingdom, USA
1992: Mark McKoy, Canada
1996: Allen Johnson, USA

Track and Field–Men's 400-Meter Hurdles
1900: John Walter Tewksbury, USA
1904: Harry Hillman, USA
1906:*
1908: Charles Bacon, USA
1912:*
1920: Frank Loomis, USA
1924: F. Morgan Taylor, USA
1928: David Burghley, Great Britain
1932: Robert Tisdall, Ireland
1936: Glenn Hardin, USA
1948: Roy Cochran, USA
1952: Charles Moore, USA
1956: Glenn Davis, USA
1960: Glenn Davis, USA
1964: Warren Cawley, USA
1968: David Hemery, Great Britain
1972: John Akii-Bua, Uganda
1976: Edwin Moses, USA
1980: Volker Beck, East Germany
1984: Edwin Moses, USA
1988: Andre Phillips, USA
1992: Kevin Young, USA
1996: Derrick Adkins, USA

*Event not held.

Track and Field–3,000 Meter Steeplechase
1900: George Orton, Canada
1904: James Lightbody, USA
1906:*
1908: Arthur Russell, Great Britain
1912:*
1920: Percy Hodge, Great Britain
1924: Ville Ritola, Finland
1928: Toivo Loukola, Finland
1932: Volmari Iso-Hollo, Finland
1936: Volmari Iso-Hollo, Finland
1948: Thore Sjostrand, Sweden
1952: Horace Ashenfelter, USA
1956: Christopher Brasher, Great Britain
1960: Zdzislaw Krzyszkowiak, Poland
1964: Gaston Roelants, Belgium
1968: Amos Biwott, Kenya
1972: Kipchoge Keino, Kenya
1976: Anders Garderud, Sweden
1980: Bronislav Malinovski, Poland
1984: Julius Korir, Kenya
1988: Julius Kariuki, Kenya
1992: Matthew Birir, Kenya
1996: Joseph Keter, Kenya

*Event not held.

Track and Field–Men's 4 × 100-Meter Relay
1912: Great Britain
1920: USA
1924: USA
1928: USA
1932: USA
1936: USA
1948: USA
1952: USA
1956: USA
1960: East Germany
1964: USA
1968: USA
1972: USA
1976: USA
1980: USSR
1984: USA
1988: USSR
1992: USA
1996: Canada

Track and Field–Men's 4 × 400-Meter Relay
1908: USA
1912: USA
1920: Great Britain
1924: USA
1928: USA
1932: USA
1936: Great Britain
1948: USA
1952: Jamaica
1956: USA
1960: USA
1964: USA
1968: USA
1972: Kenya
1976: USA
1980: USSR
1984: USA
1988: USA
1992: USA
1996: USA

Track and Field–Men's 20-Kilometer Walk
1956: Leonid Spirin, USSR
1960: Vladimir Golubnichi, USSR
1964: Kenneth Matthews, Great Britain
1968: Vladimir Golubnichi, USSR
1972: Peter Frenkel, East Germany
1976: Daniel Bautista, Mexico
1980: Maurizio Damilano, Italy
1984: Ernesto Canto, Mexico
1988: Jozef Pribilinec, Czechoslovakia
1992: Daniel Plaza Montero, Spain
1996: Jefferson Perez, Ecuador

Track and Field–Men's 50-Kilometer Walk
1932: Thomas Green, Great Britain
1936: H. Harold Whitlock, Great Britain
1948: John Ljunggren, Sweden
1952: Giuseppe Dordoni, Italy
1956: Norman Read, New Zealand
1960: Donald Thompson, Great Britain
1964: Abdon Pamich, Italy
1968: Christoph Hohne, East Germany
1972: Bernd Kannenberg, West Germany
1976:*
1980: Hartwig Gauder, East Germany
1984: Raul Gonzalez, Mexico
1988: Viacheslav Ivanenka, USSR
1992: Andrey Perlov, Russia
1996: Robert Korzeniowski, Poland

_____
*Event not held.

Track and Field–Women's 100 Meters
1928: Elizabeth Robinson, USA
1932: Stanislawa Walasiewicz, Poland
1936: Helen Stephens, USA
1948: Francina Blankers-Koen, Netherlands
1952: Marjorie Jackson, Australia
1956: Betty Cuthbert, Australia
1960: Wilma Rudolph, USA
1964: Wyomia Tyus, USA
1968: Wyomia Tyus, USA
1972: Renate Stecher, East Germany
1976: Annegret Richter, West Germany
1980: Lyudmila Kondratyeva, USSR
1984: Evelyn Ashford, USA
1988: Florence Griffith Joyner, USA
1992: Gail Devers, USA
1996: Gail Devers, USA

Track and Field–Women's 200 Meters
1948: Francina Blankers-Koen, Netherlands
1952: Marjorie Jackson, Australia
1956: Betty Cuthbert, Australia
1960: Wilma Rudolph, USA
1964: Edith McGuire, USA
1968: Irena Szewinska-Kirszenstein, Poland
1972: Renate Stecher, East Germany
1976: Barbel Eckert, East Germany
1980: Barbel Eckert Wockel, East Germany
1984: Valerie Brisco-Hooks, USA
1988: Florence Griffith Joyner, USA
1992: Gwen Torrence, USA
1996: Marie-José Pérec, France

Track and Field–Women's 400 Meters
1964: Betty Cuthbert, Australia
1968: Colette Besson, France
1972: Monika Zehrt, East Germany
1976: Irena Szewinska-Kirszenstein, Poland

1980: Marita Koch, East Germany
1984: Valerie Brisco-Hooks, USA
1988: Olga Bryzguina, USSR
1992: Marie-José Pérec, France
1996: Marie-José Pérec, France

Track and Field–Women's 800 Meters
1928: Lina Radke, Germany
1932–1956:*
1960: Lyudmila Shevtsova, USSR
1964: Ann Packer, Great Britain
1968: Madeline Manning, USA
1972: Hildegard Falck, West Germany
1976: Tatyana Kazankina, USSR
1980: Nadezhda Olizarenko, USSR
1984: Doina Melinte, Romania
1988: Sigrun Wodars, East Germany
1992: Ellen Van Langen, Netherlands
1996 Svetlana Masterkova, Russia

_____
*Event not held.

Track and Field–Women's 1,500 Meters
1972: Ljudmila Bragina, USSR
1976: Tatyana Kazankina, USSR
1980: Tatyana Kazankina, USSR
1984: Gabriella Dorio, Italy
1988: Paula Ivan, Romania
1992: Hassiba Boulmerka, Algeria
1996: Svetlana Masterkova, Russia

Track and Field–Women's 3,000 Meters
1984: Maricica Puica, Romania
1988: Tatiana Samolenko, USSR
1992: Elena Romanova, Russia
1996:*

_____
*Event not held.

Track and Field–Women's 5,000 Meters
1996: Wang Junxia, China

Track and Field–Women's 10,000 Meters
1988: Olga Bondarenko, USSR
1992: Derartu Tulu, Ethiopia
1996: Fernanda Ribeiro, Portugal

Track and Field–Women's Marathon
1984: Joan Benoit, USA
1988: Rosa Mota, Portugal
1992: Valentina Yegorova, Russia
1996: Fatuma Roba, Ethiopia

Track and Field–Women's 100-Meter Hurdles†
1932: Mildred "Babe" Didrikson, USA
1936: Trebisonda Valla, Italy

_____
†80-meter hurdles, 1932–1968.

1948: Francina Blankers-Koen, Netherlands
1952: Shirley De La Hunty-Strickland, Australia
1956: Shirley De La Hunty-Strickland, Australia
1960: Irina Press, USSR
1964: Karin Balzer, East Germany
1968: Maureen Caird, Australia
1972: Annelie Ehrhardt, East Germany
1976: Johanna Schaller, East Germany
1980: Vera Komisova, USSR
1984: Benita Fitzgerald-Brown, USA
1988: Jordanka Donkova, Bulgaria
1992: Paraskevi Patoulidou, Greece
1996: Ludmila Engquist, Sweden

Track and Field–Women's 400-Meter Hurdles
1984: Nawal El Moutawakel, Morocco
1988: Debra Flintoff-King, Australia
1992: Sally Gunnell, Britain
1996: Deon Hemmings, Jamaica

Track and Field–Women's 4 × 100-Meter Relay
1928: Canada
1932: USA
1936: USA
1948: Netherlands
1952: USA
1956: Australia
1960: USA
1964: Poland
1968: USA
1972: West Germany
1976: East Germany
1980: East Germany
1984: USA
1988: USA
1992: USA
1996: USA

Track and Field–Women's 4 × 400-Meter Relay
1972: East Germany
1976: East Germany
1980: USSR
1984: USA
1988: USSR
1992: Unified Team
1996: USA

Track and Field–Women's 10-Kilometer Walk
1992: Chen Yueling, China
1996: Yelena Nikolayeva, Russia

Track and Field–Men's Shot Put
1896: Robert Garrett, USA
1900: Richard Sheldon, USA
1904: Ralph Rose, USA
1906: Martin Sheridan, USA
1908: Ralph Rose, USA
1912: Patrick McDonald, USA

1920: Ville Porhola, Finland
1924: Clarence Houser, USA
1928: John Kuck, USA
1932: Leo Sexton, USA
1936: Hans Woellke, Germany
1948: Wilbur Thompson, USA
1952: Parry O'Brien, USA
1956: Parry O'Brien, USA
1960: William Nieder, USA
1964: Dallas Long, USA
1968: Randy Matson, USA
1972: Wladyslaw Komar, Poland
1976: Udo Beyer, East Germany
1980: Vladimir Kiselyov, USSR
1984: Alessandro Andrei, Italy
1988: Ulf Timmerman, East Germany
1992: Michael Stulce, USA
1996: Randy Barnes, USA

Track and Field–Men's Discus Throw
1896: Robert Garrett, USA
1900: Rudolf Bauer, Hungary
1904: Martin Sheridan, USA
1906: Martin Sheridan, USA
1908: Martin Sheridan, USA
1912: Armas Taipale, Finland
1920: Elmer Niklander, Finland
1924: Clarence Houser, USA
1928: Clarence Houser, USA
1932: John Anderson, USA
1936: Kenneth Carpenter, USA
1948: Adolfo Consolini, Italy
1952: Sim Iness, USA
1956: Al Oerter, USA
1960: Al Oerter, USA
1964: Al Oerter, USA
1968: Al Oerter, USA
1972: Ludvik Danek, Czechoslovakia
1976: Mac Wilkins, USA
1980: Viktor Rashchupkin, USSR
1984: Rolf Danneberg, West Germany
1988: Jurgen Schult, East Germany
1992: Robert Ubartas, Lithuania
1996: Lars Riedel, Germany

Track and Field–Men's Hammer Throw
1900: John Flanagan, USA
1904: John Flanagan, USA
1906:*
1908: John Flanagan, USA
1912: Matthew McGrath, USA
1920: Patrick Ryan, USA
1924: Frederick Tootell, USA
1928: Patrick O'Callaghan, Ireland
1932: Patrick O'Callaghan, Ireland

*Event not held.

1936: Karl Hein, Germany
1948: Imre Nemeth, Hungary
1952: Jozsef Csermak, Hungary
1956: Harold Connolly, USA
1960: Vasily Rudenkov, USSR
1964: Romuald Klim, USSR
1968: Gyula Zsivotzky, Hungary
1972: Anatoli Bondarchuk, USSR
1976: Yuriy Sedykh, USSR
1980: Yuriy Sedykh, USSR
1984: Juha Tiainen, Finland
1988: Serguei Litvinov, USSR
1992: Andrey Abduvaliyev, Tadzhikstan
1996: Balazs Kiss, Hungary

Track and Field–Men's Javelin Throw

1906: Eric Lemming, Sweden
1908: Eric Lemming, Sweden
1912: Eric Lemming, Sweden
1920: Jonni Myyra, Finland
1924: Jonni Myyra, Finland
1928: Erik Lundkvist, Sweden
1932: Matti Jarvinen, Finland
1936: Gerhard Stock, Great Britain
1948: Tapio Rautavaara, Finland
1952: Cyrus Young, USA
1956: Egil Danielsen, Norway
1960: Viktor Tsibulenko, USSR
1964: Pauli Nevala, Finland
1968: Janis Lusis, USSR
1972: Klaus Wolfermann, West Germany
1976: Miklos Nemeth, Hungary
1980: Dainis Kula, USSR
1984: Arto Harkonen, Finland
1988: Tapio Korjus, Finland
1992: Jan Zelezny, Czechoslovakia
1996: Jan Zelezny, Czech Republic

Track and Field–Men's Decathlon

1904: Thomas Kiely, Great Britain/Ireland
1906–1908:*
1912: James Thorpe, USA (previously disqualified, Jim Thorpe's medals were restored in 1982)
1920: Helge Lovland, Norway
1924: Harold Osborn, USA
1928: Paavo Yrjola, Finland
1932: James Bausch, USA
1936: Glenn Morris, USA
1948: Robert B. Mathias, USA
1952: Robert B. Mathias, USA
1956: Milton Campbell, USA
1960: Rafer Johnson, USA
1964: Willi Holdorf, West Germany
1968: Bill Toomey, USA
1972: Nikolai Avilov, USSR
1976: Bruce Jenner, USA

*Event not held

1980: Daley Thompson, Great Britain
1984: Daley Thompson, Great Britain
1988: Christian Schenk, East Germany
1992: Robert Zmelik, Czechoslovakia
1996: Dan O'Brien, USA

Track and Field–Women's Shot Put

1948: Micheline Ostermeyer, France
1952: Galina Zybina, USSR
1956: Tamara Tyshkevich, USSR
1960: Tamara Press, USSR
1964: Tamara Press, USSR
1968: Margitta Gummel-Helmbolt, East Germany
1972: Nadezhda Chizhova, USSR
1976: Ivanka Hristova, Bulgaria
1980: Ilona Slupianek, East Germany
1984: Claudia Losch, West Germany
1988: Natalia Lisovskaya, USSR
1992: Svetlana Kriveleva, Russia
1996: Astrid Kumbernuss, Germany

Track and Field–Women's Discus

1928: Halina Konopacka, Poland
1932: Lillian Copeland, USSR
1936: Gisela Mauermeyer, Germany
1948: Micheline Ostermeyer, France
1952: Nina Romaschkova, USSR
1956: Olga Fikotova, Czechoslovakia
1960: Nina Ponomaryeva-Romaschkova, USSR
1964: Tamara Press, USSR
1968: Lia Manoliu, Romania
1972: Faina Melnik, USSR
1976: Evelin Schlaak, East Germany
1980: Evelin Jahl-Schlaak, East Germany
1984: Ria Stalman, Netherlands
1988: Martina Hellmann, East Germany
1992: Maritza Marten Garcia, Cuba
1996: Ilke Wyludda, Germany

Track and Field–Women's Javelin

1932: Mildred "Babe" Didrikson, USA
1936: Tilly Fleischer, Germany
1948: Herma Bauma, Austria
1952: Dana Zatopkova, Czechoslovakia
1956: Inese Jaunzeme, USSR
1960: Elvira Ozolina, USSR
1964: Mihaela Penes, Romania
1968: Angela Nemeth, Hungary
1972: Ruth Fuchs, East Germany
1976: Ruth Fuchs, East Germany
1980: Maria Colon, Cuba
1984: Tessa Sanderson, Great Britain
1988: Petra Felke, East Germany
1992: Silke Renk, Germany
1996: Helia Rantanen, Finland

Track and Field–Women's Pentathlon

1964: Irina Press, USSR
1968: Ingrid Becker, West Germany

1972: Mary Peters, Great Britain
1976: Siegrun Siegl, East Germany
1980: Nadezhda Tkachenko, USSR
1984–1996:*

---

*Event not held

Track and Field–Women's Heptathlon
1984: Glynis Nunn, Australia
1988: Jackie Joyner-Kersee, USA
1992: Jackie Joyner-Kersee, USA
1996: Ghada Shouaa, Syria

Water Polo
1900: Great Britain
1904: USA
1906:*
1908: Great Britain
1912: Great Britain
1920: Great Britain
1924: France
1928: Germany
1932: Hungary
1936: Hungary
1948: Italy
1952: Hungary
1956: Hungary
1960: Italy
1964: Hungary
1968: Yugoslavia
1972: USSR
1976: Hungary
1980: USSR
1984: Yugoslavia
1988: Yugoslavia
1992: Italy
1996: Spain

*Event not held.

Weightlifting–52 kg
1972: Zygmunt Smalcerz, Poland
1976: Alexander Voronin, USSR
1980: Kanybek Osmonaliev, USSR
1984: Guoqiang Zeng, China
1988: Sevdalin Marinov, Bulgaria
1992: Ivan Ivanov, Bulgaria
1996: Halil Mutlu, Turkey (54 kg)

Weighlifting–56 kg
1948: Joseph De Pietro, USA
1952: Ivan Udodov, USSR
1956: Charles Vinci, USA
1960: Charles Vinci, USA
1964: Aleksei Vakhonin, USSR
1968: Mohammad Nassiri, Iran
1972: Imre Foldi, Hungary
1976: Norair Nourikian, Bulgaria
1980: Daniel Nunez, Cuba

1984: Shude Wu, China
1988: Oxen Mirzoian, USSR
1992: Chun Byung-Kwan, South Korea
1996: Tang Ningsheng, China (59 kg)

Weightlifting–60 kg
1920: Frans De Haes, Belgium
1924: Pierino Gabetti, Italy
1928: Franz Andrysek, Austria
1932: Raymond Suvigny, France
1936: Anthony Terlazzo, USA
1948: Mahmoud Fayad, Egypt
1952: Rafael Chimishkyan, USSR
1956: Isaac Berger, USA
1960: Yevgeny Minayev, USSR
1964: Yoshinobu Miyake, Japan
1968: Yoshinobu Miyake, Japan
1972: Norair Nurikjan, Bulgaria
1976: Nikolai Kolesnikov, USSR
1980: Viktor Mazin, USSR
1984: Weiqiang Chen, China
1988: Naim Suleymanoglu, Turkey
1992: Naim Suleymanoglu, Turkey
1996: Naim Suleymanoglu, Turkey (64 kg)

Weightlifting–67.5 kg
1920: Alfred Neuland, Estonia
1924: Edmond Decottignies, France
1928: Hans Haas, Austria
1932: Rene Duverger, France
1936: Robert Fein, Austria
1948: Ibrahim H. Shams, Egypt
1952: Tamio "Tommy" Kono, USA
1956: Igor Rybak, USSR
1960: Viktor Buschuyev, USSR ·
1964: Waldemar Baszanowski, Poland
1968: Waldemar Baszanowski, Poland
1972: Muckarbi Kirzhinov, USSR
1976: Zbigniew Kaczmarek, Poland
1980: Yanko Rusev, Bulgaria
1984: Yao Jingyuan, China
1988: Joachim Kunz, East Germany
1992: Israel Militossian, Armenia
1996: Xugang Zhan, China (70 kg)

Weightlifting–75 kg
1920: Henri Gance, France
1924: Carlo Galimberti, Italy
1928: Roger Francois, France
1932: Rudolf Ismayr, Germany
1936: Khadr Sayed El Touni, Egypt
1948: Frank Spellman, USA
1952: Peter George, USA
1956: Fyodor Bogdanovsky, USSR
1960: Aleksandr Kurynov, USSR
1964: Hans Zdazila, Czechoslovakia
1968: Viktor Kurentsov, USSR
1972: Yordan Bikow, Bulgaria

1976: Yordan Mitkov, Bulgaria
1980: Assen Zlatev, Bulgaria
1984: Karl-Heinz Radschinsky, West Germany
1988: Borislav Guidikov, Bulgaria
1992: Fedor Kassapu, Moldavia
1996: Pablo Lara, Cuba (76 kg)

Weightlifting–82.5 kg

1920: Ernest Cadine, France
1924: Charles Rigoulot, France
1928: El Sayed Nosseir, Egypt
1932: Louis Hostin, France
1936: Louis Hostin, France
1948: Stanley Stanczyk, USA
1952: Trofim Lomakin, USSR
1956: Tamio "Tommy" Kono, USA
1960: Ireneusz Palinski, Poland
1964: Rudolf Plukfelder, USSR
1968: Boris Selitsky, USSR
1972: Leif Jenssen, Norway
1976: Valeri Shary, USSR
1980: Yurik Vardanjan, USSR
1984: Petre Becheru, Romania
1988: Israil Arsamakov, USSR
1992: Pyrros Dimas, Greece
1996: Pyrros Dimas, Greece (83 kg)

Weightlifting–90 kg

1952: Norbert Schemansky, USA
1956: Arkadi Vorobyov, USSR
1960: Arkadi Vorobyov, USSR
1964: Vladimir Golovanov, USSR
1968: Kaarlo Kangasniemi, Finland
1972: Andon Nikolov, Bulgaria
1976: David Rigert, USSR
1980: Peter Baczaka, Hungary
1984: Nicu Vlad, Romania
1988: Anatoli Khrapatyi, USSR
1992: Kakhi Kakhiachvili, Russia
1996: Aleksey Petrov, Russia (91 kg)

Weightlifting–100 kg

1980: Ota Zaremba, Czechoslovakia
1984: Rolf Milser, West Germany
1988: Pavel Kouznetsov, USSR
1992: Victor Tregoubov, Russia
1996: Akakide Kakhiashvilis, Greece (99 kg)

Weightlifting–110 kg

1896: Launceston Elliott, Great Britain (one-hand lift),
    Viggo Jensen, Denmark (two-hand lift)
1900:*
1904: Oscar Paul Osthoff, USA (one-hand lift), Perikles
    Kakousis, Greece (two-hand lift)
1906: Josef Steinbach, Austria (one-hand lift), Dimitrios
    Tofalos, Great Britain (two-hand lift)
1908–1912:*

*Event not held.

1920: Filippo Bottino, Italy
1924: Giuseppe Tonani, Italy
1928: Josef Strassberger, Germany
1932: Jaroslav Skobla, Czechoslovakia
1936: Josef Manger, Germany
1948: John Davis, USA
1952: John Davis, USA
1956: Paul Anderson, USA
1960: Yuri Vlassov, USSR
1964: Leonid Zhabotinsky, USSR
1968: Leonid Schabotinski, USSR
1972: Jan Talts, USSR
1976: Valentin Khristov, Bulgaria
1980: Leonid Taranenko, USSR
1984: Norberto Oberburger, Italy
1988: Yuri Zakharevitch, USSR
1992: Ronny Weller, Germany
1996: Timur Taimazov, Ukraine (108 kg)

Weightlifting–Over 110 kg

1972: Vassili Alekseyev, USSR
1976: Vassili Alekseyev, USSR
1980: Sultan Rakhmanov, USSR
1984: Dean "Dinko" Lukin, Australia
1988: Alexandre Kourlovitch, USSR
1992: Alexandre Kourlovitch, Belarus
1996: Andrey Chemerkin, Russia (over 108 kg)

Wrestling, Freestyle–48 kg

1904: Robert Curry, USA
1906–1968:*
1972: Roman Dmitriev, USSR
1976: Hassan Issaev, Bulgaria
1980: Claudio Pollio, Italy
1984: Robert Weaver, USA
1988: Takashi Kobayashi, Japan
1992: Kim Il, North Korea
1996: Kim Il, North Korea

*Event not held.

Wrestling, Freestyle–52 kg

1904: George Mehnert, USA
1906–1936:*
1948: Lennart Viitala, Finland
1952: Hasan Gemici, Turkey
1956: Mirian Tsalkalamanidze, USSR
1960: Ahmet Bilek, Turkey
1964: Yoshikatsu Yoshida, Japan
1968: Shigeo Nakata, Japan
1972: Kiyomi Kato, Japan
1976: Yuji Takada, Japan
1980: Anatoli Beloglazov, USSR
1984: Saban Trstena, Yugoslavia
1988: Mitsuru Sato, Japan
1992: Li Hak-Son, South Korea
1996: Valentin Jordanov, Bulgaria

*Event not held.

Wrestling, Freestyle–57 kg
1904: Isaac Niflot, USA
1906:*
1908: George Mehnert, USA
1912–1920:*
1924: Kustaa Pihlajamaki, Finland
1928: Kaarlo Makinen, Finland
1932: Robert Pearce, USA
1936: Odon Zombori, Hungary
1948: Nasuh Akar, Turkey
1952: Shohachi Ishii, Japan
1956: Mustafa Dagistanli, Turkey
1960: Terrence McCann, USA
1964: Yojiro Uetake, Japan
1968: Yojiro Uetake, Japan
1972: Hideaki Yanagida, Japan
1976: Vladimir Umin, USSR
1980: Sergei Beloglazov, USSR
1984: Hideaki Tomiyama, Japan
1988: Sergei Beloglazov, USSR
1992: Alejandro Puerto, Cuba
1996: Kendall Cross, USA

---

*Event not held.

Wrestling, Freestyle–62 kg
1904: Benjamin Bradshaw, USA
1906:*
1908: George Dole, USA
1912:*
1920: Charles E. Ackerly, USA
1924: Robin Reed, USA
1928: Allie Morrison, USA
1932: Hermanni Pihlajamaki, Finland
1936: Kustaa Pihlajamaki, Finland
1948: Gazanfer Bilge, Turkey
1952: Bayram Sit, Turkey
1956: Shozo Sasahara, Japan
1960: Mustafa Dagistanli, Turkey
1964: Osamu Watanabe, Japan
1968: Masaaki Kaneko, Japan
1972: Sagalav Abdulbekov, USSR
1976: Yang Mo Yang, South Korea
1980: Magomedgasan Abushev, USSR
1984: Randy Lewis, USA
1988: John Smith, USA
1992: John Smith, USA
1996: Tom Brands, USA

---

*Event not held.

Wrestling, Freestyle–68 kg
1904: Otto Roehm, USA
1906:*
1908: George de Relwyskow, Great Britain
1912:*

---

*Event not held.

1920: Kalle Anttila, Finland
1924: Russell Vis, USA
1928: Osvald Kapp, Estonia
1932: Charles Pacome, France
1936: Karoly Karpati, Hungary
1948: Celal Atik, Turkey
1952: Olle Anderberg, Sweden
1956: Emamali Habibi, Iran
1960: Shelby Wilson, USA
1964: Enyu Waltschev, Bulgaria
1968: Abdollah Movahed Ardabili, Iran
1972: Dan Gable, USA
1976: Pavel Pinegin, USSR
1980: Saipulla Absaidov, USSR
1984: In-Tak Youh, South Korea
1988: Arsen Fadzaev, USSR
1992: Arsen Fadzaev, Russia
1996: Vadim Bogiyev, Russia

Wrestling, Freestyle–74 kg
1904: Charles Erickson, USA
1906–1920:*
1924: Hermann Gehri, Switzerland
1928: Arvo Haavisto, Finland
1932: Jack Van Bebber, USA
1936: Frank Lewis, USA
1948: Yasar Dogu, Turkey
1952: William Smith, USA
1956: Mitsuo Ikeda, Japan
1960: Douglas Blubaugh, USA
1964: Ismail Ogan, Turkey
1968: Mahmut Atalay, Turkey
1972: Wayne Wells, USA
1976: Ijichiro Date, Japan
1980: Valentin Raitchev, Bulgaria
1984: David Schultz, USA
1988: Kenneth Monday, USA
1992: Park Jang-Soon, South Korea
1996: Buvaysa Saytyev, Russia

---

*Event not held.

Wrestling, Freestyle–82 kg
1908: Stanley Bacon, Great Britain
1912:*
1920: Eino Leino, Finland
1924: Firtz Hagmann, Switzerland
1928: Ernst Kyburz, Switzerland
1932: Ivar Johansson, Sweden
1936: Emile Poilve, France
1948: Glen Brand, USA
1952: David Tsimakuridze, USSR
1956: Nikola Stantchev, Bulgaria
1960: Hasan Gungor, Turkey
1964: Prodan Gardschev, Bulgaria

---

*Event not held.

1968: Boris Gurevitch, USSR
1972: Levan Tediashvili, USSR
1976: John Peterson, USA
1980: Ismail Abilov, Bulgaria
1984: Mark Schultz, USA
1988: Myung-Woo Han, South Korea
1992: Kevin Jackson, USA
1996: Khadzhimurad Magomedov, Russia

Wrestling, Freestyle–90 kg
1920: Anders Larsson, Sweden
1924: John Spellman, USA
1928: Thure Sjostedt, Sweden
1932: Peter Mehringer, USA
1936: Knut Fridell, Sweden
1948: Henry Wittenberg, USA
1952: Wiking Palm, Sweden
1956: Gholam-Reza Takhti, Iran
1960: Ismet Atli, Turkey
1964: Aleksandr Medved, USSR
1968: Ahmet Ayik, Turkey
1972: Ben Peterson, USA
1976: Levan Tediashvili, USSR
1980: Sanasar Oganesyan, USSR
1984: Ed Banach, USA
1988: Makharbek Khadartsev, USSR
1992: Makharbek Khadartsev, Russia
1996: Rasull Khadem Azghadi, Iran

Wrestling, Freestyle–100 kg
1904: B. Hansen, USA
1906:*
1908: George C. O'Kelly, Great Britain/Ireland
1912:*
1920: Robert Roth, Switzerland
1924: Harry Steele, USA
1928: Johan Richtoff, Sweden
1932: Johan Richtoff, Sweden
1936: Kristjan Palusalu, Estonia
1948: Gyula Bobis, Hungary
1952: Arsen Mekokischvili, USSR
1956: Hamit Kaplan, Turkey
1960: Wilfried Dietrich, West Germany
1964: Aleksandr Ivanitsky, USSR
1968: Aleksandr Medved, USSR
1972: Ivan Yarygin, USSR
1976: Ivan Yarygin, USSR
1980: Ilya Mate, USSR
1984: Lou Banach, USA
1988: Vasile Puscasu, Romania
1992: Leri Khabelov, Georgia
1996: Kurt Angle, USA

*Event not held.

Wrestling, Freestyle–130 kg
1972: Aleksandr Medved, USSR
1976: Soslan Andiev, USSR
1980: Soslan Andiev, USSR
1984: Bruce Baumgartner, USA
1988: David Gobedjichvili, USSR
1992: Bruce Baumgartner, USA
1996: Mahmut Demir, Turkey

Wrestling, Greco-Roman–48 kg
1972: Gheorghe Berceanu, Romania
1976: Aleksei Shumakov, USSR
1980: Zaksylik Ushkempirov, USSR
1984: Vincenzo Maenza, Italy
1988: Vincenzo Maenza, Italy
1992: Oleg Koutherenko, Ukraine
1996: Sim Kwon Ho, South Korea

Wrestling, Greco-Roman–52 kg
1948: Pietro Lombardi, Italy
1952: Boris Gurevitch, USSR
1956: Nikolai Solovyov, USSR
1960: Dumitru Pirvulescu, Romania
1964: Tsutomu Hanahara, Japan
1968: Petar Kirov, Bulgaria
1972: Petar Kirov, Bulgaria
1976: Vitali Konstantinov, USSR
1980: Vakhtang Blagidze, USSR
1984: Atsuji Miyahara, Japan
1988: Jon Ronningen, Norway
1992: Jon Ronningen, Norway
1996: Armen Nazaryan, Armenia

Wrestling, Greco-Roman–57 kg
1924: Eduard Putsep, Estonia
1928: Kurt Leucht, Germany
1932: Jakob Brendel, Germany
1936: Marton Lorincz, Hungary
1948: Kurt Pettersen, Sweden
1952: Imre Hodos, Hungary
1956: Konstantin Vyrupayev, USSR
1960: Oleg Karavayev, USSR
1964: Masamitsu Ichiguchi, Japan
1968: Janos Varga, Hungary
1972: Rustem Kazakov, USSR
1976: Pertti Ukkola, Finland
1980: Shamil Serikov, USSR
1984: Pasquale Passarelli, West Germany
1988: Andras Sike, Hungary
1992: An Han-Bong, South Korea
1996: Yuriy Melnichenko, Kazakhstan

Wrestling, Greco-Roman–62 kg
1912: Kaarlo Koskelo, Finland
1920: Oskari Friman, Finland
1924: Kalle Anttila, Finland
1928: Voldemar Vali, Estonia
1932: Giovanni Gozzi, Italy

1936: Yasar Erkan, Turkey
1948: Mehmet Oktav, Turkey
1952: Jakov Punkin, USSR
1956: Rauno Makinen, Finland
1960: Muzahir Sille, Turkey
1964: Imre Polyak, Hungary
1968: Roman Rurua, USSR
1972: Georgi Markow, Bulgaria
1976: Kazimierz Lipien, Poland
1980: Stilianos Migiakis, Greece
1984: Weon-Kee Kim, South Korea
1988: Kamander Madjidov, USSR
1992: M. Akif Pirim, Turkey
1996: Wlodzimierz Zawadski, Poland

Wrestling, Greco-Roman–68 kg
1906: Rudolf Watzl, Austria
1908: Enrico Porro, Italy
1912: Eemil Vare, Finland
1920: Eemil Vare, Finland
1924: Oskari Friman, Finland
1928: Lajos Keresztes, Hungary
1932: Erik Malmberg, Sweden
1936: Lauri Koskela, Finland
1948: Gustav Freij, Sweden
1952: Schasam Safin, USSR
1956: Kyosti Lehtonen, Finland
1960: Avtandil Koridze, USSR
1964: Kazim Ayvaz, Turkey
1968: Munji Mumemura, Japan
1972: Schamil Khisamutdinov, USSR
1976: Suren Nalbandyan, USSR
1980: Stefan Rusu, Romania
1984: Vlado Lisjak, Yugoslavia
1988: Levon Djoulfalakian, USSR
1992: Attila Repka, Hungary
1996: Ryszard Wolny, Poland

Wrestling, Greco-Roman–74 kg
1932: Ivar Johansson, Sweden
1936: Rudolf Svedberg, Sweden
1948: Gosta Andersson, Sweden
1952: Mikos Szilvasi, Hungary
1956: Mithat Bayrak, Turkey
1960: Mithat Bayrak, Turkey
1964: Anatoli Kolesov, USSR
1968: Rudolf Vesper, East Germany
1972: Vitezslav Macha, Czechoslovakia
1976: Anatoli Bykov, USSR
1980: Ferenc Kocsis, Hungary
1984: Jouko Salomaki, Finland
1988: Young-Nam Kim, South Korea
1992: Mnatsakan Iskandarian, Armenia
1996: Feliberto Ascuy Aguilera, Cuba

Wrestling, Greco-Roman–82 kg
1906: Verner Weckman, Finland
1908: Frithiof Martensson, Sweden

1912: Claes Johanson, Sweden
1920: Carl Westergren, Sweden
1924: Edvard Westerlund, Finland
1928: Vaino Kokkinen, Finland
1932: Vaino Kokkinen, Finland
1936: Ivar Johansson, Sweden
1948: Axel Gronberg, Sweden
1952: Axel Gronberg, Sweden
1956: Givi Kartoziya, USSR
1960: Dimiter Dobrev, Bulgaria
1964: Branislav Simic, Yugoslavia
1968: Lothar Metz, East Germany
1972: Csaba Hegedus, Hungary
1976: Momir Petkovic, Yugoslavia
1980: Gennady Korban, USSR
1984: Ion Draica, Romania
1988: Mikhail Mamiachvili, USSR
1992: Peter Earkas, Hungary
1996: Humza Yerlikaya, Turkey

Wrestling, Greco-Roman–90 kg
1908: Verner Weckman, Finland
1912: no gold medalist
1920: Claes Johanson, Sweden
1924: Carl Westergren, Sweden
1928: Ibrahim Moustafa, Egypt
1932: Rudolf Svensson, Sweden
1936: Axel Cadier, Sweden
1948: Karl-Erik Nilsson, Sweden
1952: Kaelpo Grondahl, Finland
1956: Valentin Nikolayev, USSR
1960: Tevfik Kis, Turkey
1964: Bojan Radev, Bulgaria
1968: Bojan Radev, Bulgaria
1972: Valeri Rezantsev, USSR
1976: Valeri Rezantsev, USSR
1980: Norbert Noevenyi, Hungary
1984: Steven Fraser, USA
1988: Atanas Komchev, Bulgaria
1992: Maik Bullmann, Germany
1996: Vyacheslav Oleynyk, Ukraine

Wrestling, Greco-Roman–100 kg
1896: Carl Schuhmann, Germany
1900–1904:*
1906: Soren M. Jensen, Denmark
1908: Richard Weisz, Hungary
1912: Yrjo Saarela, Finland
1920: Adolf Lindfors, Finland
1924: Henri Deglane, France
1928: Rudolf Svensson, Sweden
1932: Carl Westergren, Sweden
1936: Kristjan Palusalu, Estonia
1948: Ahmet Kirecci, Turkey
1952: Johannes Kotkas, USSR
1956: Anatoli Parfenov, USSR

*Event not held.

1960: Ivan Bogdan, USSR
1964: Istvan Kozma, Hungary
1968: Istvan Kozma, Hungary
1972: Nicolae Martinescu, Romania
1976: Nikolai Bolboshin, USSR
1980: Georgi Raikov, Bulgaria
1984: Vasile Andrei, Romania
1988: Andrzej Wronski, Poland
1992: Hector Milian Perez, Cuba
1996: Andrzej Wronski, Poland

Wrestling, Greco-Roman–130 kg
1972: Anatoli Roshin, USSR
1976: Aleksandr Kolchinsky, USSR
1980: Aleksandr Kolchinsky, USSR
1984: Jeffrey Blatnick, USA
1988: Alexandre Karelin, USSR
1992: Alexander Karelin, Russia
1996: Aleksandr Karelin, Russia

Yachting–Men's 470
1976: West Germany, Frank Huebner, Harro Bode
1980: Brazil, Marcos Pinto Rizzo Soares, Eduardo Henrique Penido
1984: Spain, Jose Luis Doreste, Roberto Molina
1988: France, Thierry Peponnet, Luc Pillot
1992: Spain, Jordi Calafat, Francisco Sanchez
1996: Ukraine, Yevhen Braslavets, Ihor Matviyenko

Yachting–Women's 470
1988: USA, Allison Jolly, Lynne Jewell
1992: Spain, Theresa Zabell, Patricia Guerra
1996: Spain, Begona Via Dufresne, Theresa Zabell

Yachting–Finn
1924: Leon Huybrechts, Belgium
1928: Sven Thorell, Sweden
1932: Jacques Lebrun, France
1936: Daniel M. J. Kagchelland, Netherlands
1948: Paul Elvstrom, Denmark
1952: Paul Elvstrom, Denmark
1956: Paul Elvstrom, Denmark
1960: Paul Elvstrom, Denmark
1964: Wilhelm Kuhweide, West Germany
1968: Valentin Mankin, USSR
1972: Serge Maury, France
1976: Jochen Schumann, East Germany
1980: Esko Rechardt, Finland
1984: Russell Coutts, New Zealand
1988: Jose Luis Doreste, Spain
1992: Jose Van Der Ploeg, Spain
1996: Mateusz Kusznierewicz, Poland

Yachting–Europe
1992: Linda Anderson, Norway
1996: Kristine Roug, Denmark

Yachting–Flying Dutchman
1960: Norway, Peder Lunde Jr., Bjorn Bergvall
1964: New Zealand, Helmer Pedersen, Earle Wells
1968: Great Britain, Rodney Pattison, Iain S. MacDonald-Smith
1972: Great Britain, Rodney Pattison, Christopher Davies
1976: West Germany, Jorg Diesch, Eckart Diesch
1980: Spain, Alesandro Abascal, Miguel Noguer
1984: USA, Jonathan McKee, William Carl Buchan
1988: Denmark, Jorgen Bojsen-Moller, Christian Gronborg
1992: Spain, Luis Doreste, Domingo Manrique
1996:*

*Event not held.

Yachting–Division II Sailboard (Windgliding)
1984: Stephan Van Den Berg, Netherlands
1988: Bruce Kendall, New Zealand
1992: Franck David, France
1996:*

*Event not held.

Yachting–Women's Sailboard
1992: Barbara Kendall, New Zealand
1996:*

*Event not held.

Yachting–Soling
1972: USA
1976: Denmark
1980: Denmark
1984: USA
1988: East Germany
1992: Denmark
1996: Germany

Yachting–Star
1932: USA, Gilbert Gray, Andrew Libano
1936: Germany, Peter Bischoff, Hans-Joachim Weise
1948: USA, Hilary Smart, Paul Smart
1952: Italy, Agostino Straulino, Nicolo Rode
1956: USA, Herbert Williams, Lawrence Low
1960: USSR, Timir Pinegin, Fyodor Shutkov
1964: Bahamas, Durward Knowles, C. Cecil Cooke
1968: USA, Lowell North, Peter Barrett
1972: Australia, David Forbes, John Anderson
1976:*
1980: USSR, Valentin Mankin, Aleksandr Muzychenko
1984: USA, William E. Buchan, Stephen Erikson
1988: Great Britain, Michael McIntyre, Bryn Vaile
1992: USA, Mark Reynolds, Hal Haenel
1996: Brazil, Torben Grael, Marcelo Ferreira

*Event not held.

Yachting–Tornado
1976: Great Britain, Reginald White, John Osborn
1980: Brazil, Alexandre Welter, Lars Sigurd Bjorkstrom
1984: New Zealand, Rex Sellers, Christopher Timms
1988: France, Jean-Yves Le Deroff, Nicolas Henard
1992: France, Yves Loday, Nicolas Henard
1996: Spain, Jose Luis Ballester, Fernando Leon

Yachting–Tempest
1972: USSR, Valentin Mankin, Vitali Dyrdyra
1976: Sweden, John Albrechtson, Ingvar Hansson

Yachting–Laser
1996: Robert Scheidt, Brazil

Yachting–Women's Mistral
1996: Lai Shan Lee, Hong Kong

Yachting–Men's Mistral
1996: Nikolaos Kaklamanakis, Greece

Source: *The Olympic Factbook: A Spectator's Guide to the Winter Games* and *The Olympic Factbook: A Spectator's Guide to the Summer Games*, published by Visible Ink Press in Detroit, an official licensee of the U.S. Olympic Committee.

Olympics TV Ratings

Winter Olympics—Prime Time

Year	Site	Network	Average rating/share*	Number of households
1968	Grenoble	ABC	13.4/22	7,594,000
1972	Sapporo	NBC	17.2/28	10,681,000
1976	Innsbruck	ABC	21.7/34	15,103,000
1980	Lake Placid	ABC	23.6/37	18,007,000
1984	Sarajevo	ABC	18.2/28	15,252,000
1988	Calgary	ABC	19.3/30	17,100,000
1992	Albertville	CBS	18.7/29	17,260,000
1994	Lillehammer	CBS	27.8/42	26,187,600
1998	Nagano	CBS	16.3/26	15,974,000

Summer Olympics—Prime Time

Year	Site	Network	Average rating/share*	Number of households
1968	Mexico City	ABC	14.3/26	8,104,000
1972	Munich	ABC	25.0/45	15,525,000
1976	Montreal	ABC	24.8/48	17,260,000
1980	Moscow	U.S. Boycott	–	–
1984	Los Angeles	ABC	23.2/44	19,440,000
1988	Seoul	NBC	16.9/30	14,975,000
1992	Barcelona	NBC	17.5/34	16,130,000
1996	Atlanta	NBC	21.6/41	20,714,400

*The rating represents the percentage of all U.S. households with television sets watching the program. The share represents the percentage of all television sets in use at the time that were tuned to the program.
Source: Nielsen Media Research

World Cup

That quadrennial madness known as the World Cup of *futbol* visited itself upon France for 31 days in June and July, and guess what? Not only did the home team stun Brazil, 3–0, in the championship game, but the notoriously aloof French actually got excited about the whole thing and proved themselves a most congenial host.

Soccer Bleu!

Going in, this World Cup was supposed to be mere formality for defending champion Brazil. Led by the 21-year-old Ronaldo, twice proclaimed as the world's best soccer player, and a host of one-name teammates (Bebeto! Dunga! Taffarel!), the Brazilians were justly lauded for how magically they could play "the beautiful game." But they lost to Norway in group play, and after a convincing 5–1 win over Chile in the first elimination round, they needed to come from behind twice to beat Denmark, 3–2. Then, against a resurgent Netherlands squad in the semifinal, they needed the luck of the tie-break penalty-kick shootout after a 1–1 game to even *get* to the title game.

France, meanwhile, played like gangbusters in pool play, scoring nine goals and giving up just one in three games. But then the French team's offense deserted it. An overtime goal by Laurent Blanc saved the team, 1–0, against Norway in the Round of 16, the penalty-kick shootout got the French past Italy after 120 minutes of 0–0 quarterfinal play, and in the semifinal, they needed Liliam Thuram to score his first two international goals *ever* to get past Croatia, 2–1.

It was rumored before the title game that Ronaldo was unfit (and, indeed, after the game it was revealed he had had an epileptic seizure a few hours before the game). It didn't matter. The French defense exposed all the weaknesses of the wonderfully offensive Brazilians. Zinedine Zidane used his head twice to rocket corner kicks into the goal, and Emmanuel Petit added a third netter with time running out to claim France's first World Cup. And all of Gaul celebrated.

Some other Cup highlights, and one lowlight: Michael Owen, England's precocious 18-year-old, beat two Argentine defenders and the goalie on a 65-yard solo gallop from midfield to produce far and away the Cup's single greatest moment.

Chile snuck into the second round, with a 1–1–1 record, for the first time since 1962, and all of Santiago danced.

The Nigerians came into the tournament reputed to be in the same magically footed league as the Brazilians, but a much-anticipated Nigeria-Brazil quarterfinal was thwarted, 3–0, by Denmark and its blond-haired block of a goalie, Peter "The Terminator" Schmeichel.

Italy and England were both eliminated by penalty-kick shootouts—England for the third time, Italy for the second. Argentina, meanwhile, won its third shootout in three Cups. The randomness of the shootouts is beyond cruel, and the uproar they created was vocal. Don't be surprised if, at the 2002 Cup in Japan-South Korea, a tied title game is decided by the two teams playing until there is but one man standing.

Finally, the feigning of injuries by allegedly battered players trying to draw game expulsions for the equally alleged "perpetrators" reached absolutely absurd heights.

How did the Americans do? Poorly, and that's being kind. The Red, White and Blue came into France as a much touted "Best U.S. Squad Ever." It probably was—which only illuminated the huge gap between U.S. Soccer and even the world's better second- and third-tier teams.

The United States opened against Germany, a tough, veteran team with real title aspirations. The Germans took the Americans to *Kindergarten* in a 2–0 win. And with that the bottom fell out. Coach Steve Sampson reshuffled his starting side for game two, a match with Iran that fairly dripped with geopolitical significance. The game lived up to its billing, at least for the Iranians, becoming a sort of late '90s soccer version of the U.S. Miracle on Ice hockey triumph. Iran emerged victorious, beating The Great Satan, 2–1. The United States' third game, against Yugoslavia, was mere formality that Yugoslavia won, 2–0.

And with that the term "Ugly American" was redefined in a wallowing morass of finger-pointing. Steve Sampson quit, or was he fired? Some little-used veteran players complained openly and bitterly. Nobody came out a winner, and it was back to the drawing board for U.S. Soccer.

The real winners, in a roundabout way, were the Walt Disney Co. networks of ABC, ESPN and ESPN2 that broadcasted the World Cup. Their coverage was excellent, everything a great international sporting event could be but rarely is in the United States. The network troika did exactly what it promised it would do: point a camera at the action and get out of the way. This C-Span approach put all the emphasis where it should always be: on the games, all 64 of which were broadcast live in the United States. It didn't hurt, either, that each game was shown in 45-minute halves *uninterrupted by commercials*.

As advertised, Bob Ley and Seamus Mallon, who called all the U.S. games and the big-ticket matches, were terrific soccer announcers. Mr. Mallon in particular brings to his task a rich vocabulary never heard before in the sports booth. Roger Twibell, saddled with the "junior varsity" games, matched his voice perfectly to the emotions of the game. But it was Julie Foudy, a star on the U.S. women's world-dominant team, who was the

Cup's breakout TV star. A regular analyst on ESPN2's nightly "World Cup 2Nite" wrap-up show, Ms. Foudy was refreshing and candid and always knew how to pronounce the name of the guy from Romania.

Her problem is that she broke out to the maybe 400,000 ESPN2 households that bothered to tune in. Indeed, the networks' ratings were about half what they had been in 1994, when the Cup was in the United States. Univision, the Miami-based Spanish-language network, consistently outrated ESPN and ESPN2.

ABC/ESPN, which has publicly committed to the long haul of soccer's success in the United States, professed not to be worried. And they had a point. They had paid only about $22 million for the broadcast rights to the World Cup in France, and they likely turned a profit on their 230 hours of coverage. The question, of course, is can soccer be turned into a viable U.S. viewing sport—even for just one month every four years during the World Cup—in the absence of a competitive U.S. team? The answer is probably not. But should it ever happen, at least ABC/ESPN have already demonstrated they'll know how to cover it.

Steve McKee

The World Cup ⚽

Year	Champion	Runner-up	Score
1930	Uruguay	Argentina	4-2
1934	Italy	Czechoslovakia	2-1 (in overtime)
1938	Italy	Hungary	4-2
1950	Uruguay	Brazil	2-1
1954	West Germany	Hungary	3-2
1958	Brazil	Sweden	5-2
1962	Brazil	Czechoslovakia	3-1
1966	England	West Germany	4-2 (in overtime)
1970	Brazil	Italy	4-1
1974	West Germany	Holland	2-1
1978	Argentina	Holland	3-1 (in overtime)
1982	Italy	West Germany	3-1
1986	Argentina	West Germany	3-2
1990	West Germany	Argentina	1-0
1994	Brazil	Italy	0-0 (decided by penalty kicks, 3-2)
1998	France	Brazil	3-0

Source: FIFA-Féderation Internationale de Football Association

College Sports

Football Bowl Games

Rose Bowl
Pasadena, CA

Jan. 1, 1902	Michigan 49, Stanford 0
Jan. 1, 1916	Washington St. 14, Brown 0
Jan. 1, 1917	Oregon 14, Pennsylvania 0
Jan. 1, 1918	Mare Island 19, Camp Lewis 7
Jan. 1, 1919	Great Lakes 17, Mare Island 0
Jan. 1, 1920	Harvard 7, Oregon 6
Jan. 1, 1921	California 28, Ohio St. 0
Jan. 2, 1922	California 0, Wash. & Jeff. 0
Jan. 1, 1923	Southern Cal 14, Penn St. 3
Jan. 1, 1924	Navy 14, Washington 14
Jan. 1, 1925	Notre Dame 27, Stanford 10
Jan. 1, 1926	Alabama 20, Washington 19
Jan. 1, 1927	Alabama 7, Stanford 7
Jan. 2, 1928	Stanford 7, Pittsburgh 6
Jan. 1, 1929	Georgia Tech 8, California 7
Jan. 1, 1930	Southern Cal 47, Pittsburgh 14
Jan. 1, 1931	Alabama 24, Washington St. 0
Jan. 1, 1932	Southern Cal 21, Tulane 12
Jan. 2, 1933	Southern Cal 35, Pittsburgh 0
Jan. 1, 1934	Columbia 7, Stanford 0
Jan. 1, 1935	Alabama 29, Stanford 13
Jan. 1, 1936	Stanford 7, Southern Methodist 0
Jan. 1, 1937	Pittsburgh 21, Washington 0
Jan. 1, 1938	California 13, Alabama 0
Jan. 2, 1939	Southern Cal 7, Duke 3
Jan. 1, 1940	Southern Cal 14, Tennessee 0
Jan. 1, 1941	Stanford 21, Nebraska 13
Jan. 1, 1942	Oregon St. 20, Duke 16
Jan. 1, 1943	Georgia 9, UCLA 0
Jan. 1, 1944	Southern Cal 29, Washington 0
Jan. 1, 1945	Southern Cal 25, Tennessee 0
Jan. 1, 1946	Alabama 34, Southern Cal 14
Jan. 1, 1947	Illinois 45, UCLA 14
Jan. 1, 1948	Michigan 49, Southern Cal 0
Jan. 1, 1949	Northwestern 20, California 14
Jan. 2, 1950	Ohio St. 17, California 14
Jan. 1, 1951	Michigan 14, California 6
Jan. 1, 1952	Illinois 40, Stanford 7
Jan. 1, 1953	Southern Cal 7, Wisconsin 0
Jan. 1, 1954	Michigan St. 28, UCLA 20
Jan. 1, 1955	Ohio St. 20, Southern Cal 7
Jan. 2, 1956	Michigan St. 17, UCLA 14
Jan. 1, 1957	Iowa 35, Oregon St. 19
Jan. 1, 1958	Ohio St. 10, Oregon 7
Jan. 1, 1959	Iowa 38, California 12
Jan. 1, 1960	Washington 44, Wisconsin 8
Jan. 2, 1961	Washington 17, Minnesota 7
Jan. 1, 1962	Minnesota 21, UCLA 3
Jan. 1, 1963	Southern Cal 42, Wisconsin 37
Jan. 1, 1964	Illinois 17, Washington 7

Jan. 1, 1965	Michigan 34, Oregon St. 7
Jan. 1, 1966	UCLA 14, Michigan St. 12
Jan. 2, 1967	Purdue 14, Southern Cal 13
Jan. 1, 1968	Southern Cal 14, Indiana 3
Jan. 1, 1969	Ohio St. 27, Southern Cal 16
Jan. 1, 1970	Southern Cal 10, Michigan 3
Jan. 1, 1971	Stanford 27, Ohio St. 17
Jan. 1, 1972	Stanford 13, Michigan 12
Jan. 1, 1973	Southern Cal 42, Ohio St. 17
Jan. 1, 1974	Ohio St. 42, Southern Cal 21
Jan. 1, 1975	Southern Cal 18, Ohio St. 17
Jan. 1, 1976	UCLA 23, Ohio St. 10
Jan. 1, 1977	Southern Cal 14, Michigan 6
Jan. 2, 1978	Washington 27, Michigan 20
Jan. 1, 1979	Southern Cal 17, Michigan 10
Jan. 1, 1980	Southern Cal 17, Ohio St. 16
Jan. 1, 1981	Michigan 23, Washington 6
Jan. 1, 1982	Washington 28, Iowa 0
Jan. 1, 1983	UCLA 24, Michigan 14
Jan. 2, 1984	UCLA 45, Illinois 9
Jan. 1, 1985	Southern Cal 20, Ohio St. 17
Jan. 1, 1986	UCLA 45, Iowa 28
Jan. 1, 1987	Arizona St. 22, Michigan 15
Jan. 1, 1988	Michigan St. 20, Southern Cal 17
Jan. 2, 1989	Michigan 22, Southern Cal 14
Jan. 1, 1990	Southern Cal 17, Michigan 10
Jan. 1, 1991	Washington 46, Iowa 34
Jan. 1, 1992	Washington 34, Michigan 14
Jan. 1, 1993	Michigan 38, Washington 31
Jan. 1, 1994	Wisconsin 21, UCLA 16
Jan. 2, 1995	Penn St. 38, Oregon 20
Jan. 1, 1996	Southern Cal 41, Northwestern 32
Jan. 1, 1997	Ohio St. 20, Arizona St. 17
Jan. 1, 1998	Michigan 21, Washington St. 16

Orange Bowl
Miami, FL

Jan. 1, 1935	Bucknell 26, Miami (FL) 0
Jan. 1, 1936	Catholic 20, Mississippi 19
Jan. 1, 1937	Duquesne 13, Mississippi St. 12
Jan. 1, 1938	Auburn 6, Michigan St. 0
Jan. 2, 1939	Tennessee 17, Oklahoma 0
Jan. 1, 1940	Georgia Tech 21, Missouri 7
Jan. 1, 1941	Mississippi St. 14, Georgetown 7
Jan. 1, 1942	Georgia 40, Texas Christian 26
Jan. 1, 1943	Alabama 37, Boston College 21
Jan. 1, 1944	LSU 19, Texas A&M 14
Jan. 1, 1945	Tulsa 26, Georgia Tech 12
Jan. 1, 1946	Miami (FL) 13, Holy Cross 6
Jan. 1, 1947	Rice 8, Tennessee 0
Jan. 1, 1948	Georgia Tech 20, Kansas 14

Jan. 1, 1949	Texas 41, Georgia 28		Jan. 1, 1943	Tennessee 14, Tulsa 7
Jan. 2, 1950	Santa Clara 21, Kentucky 13		Jan. 1, 1944	Georgia Tech 20, Tulsa 18
Jan. 1, 1951	Clemson 15, Miami (FL) 14		Jan. 1, 1945	Duke 29, Alabama 26
Jan. 1, 1952	Georgia Tech 17, Baylor 14		Jan. 1, 1946	Oklahoma St. 33, St. Mary's (CA) 13
Jan. 1, 1953	Alabama 61, Syracuse 6		Jan. 1, 1947	Georgia 20, North Carolina 10
Jan. 1, 1954	Oklahoma 7, Maryland 0		Jan. 1, 1948	Texas 27, Alabama 7
Jan. 1, 1955	Duke 34, Nebraska 7		Jan. 1, 1949	Oklahoma 14, North Carolina 6
Jan. 2, 1956	Oklahoma 20, Maryland 6		Jan. 2, 1950	Oklahoma 35, LSU 0
Jan. 1, 1957	Colorado 27, Clemson 21		Jan. 1, 1951	Kentucky 13, Oklahoma 7
Jan. 1, 1958	Oklahoma 48, Duke 21		Jan. 1, 1952	Maryland 28, Tennessee 13
Jan. 1, 1959	Oklahoma 21, Syracuse 6		Jan. 1, 1953	Georgia Tech 24, Mississippi 7
Jan. 1, 1960	Georgia 14, Missouri 0		Jan. 1, 1954	Georgia Tech 42, West Virginia 19
Jan. 2, 1961	Missouri 21, Navy 14		Jan. 1, 1955	Navy 21, Mississippi 0
Jan. 1, 1962	LSU 25, Colorado 7		Jan. 2, 1956	Georgia Tech 7, Pittsburgh 0
Jan. 1, 1963	Alabama 17, Oklahoma 0		Jan. 1, 1957	Baylor 13, Tennessee 7
Jan. 1, 1964	Nebraska 13, Auburn 7		Jan. 1, 1958	Mississippi 39, Texas 7
Jan. 1, 1965	Texas 21, Alabama 17		Jan. 1, 1959	LSU 7, Clemson 0
Jan. 1, 1966	Alabama 39, Nebraska 28		Jan. 1, 1960	Mississippi 21, LSU 0
Jan. 2, 1967	Florida 27, Georgia Tech 12		Jan. 2, 1961	Mississippi 14, Rice 6
Jan. 1, 1968	Oklahoma 26, Tennessee 24		Jan. 1, 1962	Alabama 10, Arkansas 3
Jan. 1, 1969	Penn St. 15, Kansas 14		Jan. 1, 1963	Mississippi 17, Arkansas 13
Jan. 1, 1970	Penn St. 10, Missouri 3		Jan. 1, 1964	Alabama 12, Mississippi 7
Jan. 1, 1971	Nebraska 17, LSU 12		Jan. 1, 1965	LSU 13, Syracuse 10
Jan. 1, 1972	Nebraska 38, Alabama 6		Jan. 1, 1966	Missouri 20, Florida 18
Jan. 1, 1973	Nebraska 40, Notre Dame 6		Jan. 2, 1967	Alabama 34, Nebraska 7
Jan. 1, 1974	Penn St. 16, LSU 9		Jan. 1, 1968	LSU 20, Wyoming 13
Jan. 1, 1975	Notre Dame 13, Alabama 11		Jan. 1, 1969	Arkansas 16, Georgia 2
Jan. 1, 1976	Oklahoma 14, Michigan 6		Jan. 1, 1970	Mississippi 27, Arkansas 22
Jan. 1, 1977	Ohio St. 27, Colorado 10		Jan. 1, 1971	Tennessee 34, Air Force 13
Jan. 2, 1978	Arkansas 31, Oklahoma 6		Jan. 1, 1972	Oklahoma 40, Auburn 22
Jan. 1, 1979	Oklahoma 31, Nebraska 24		Dec. 31, 1972	Oklahoma 14, Penn St. 0
Jan. 1, 1980	Oklahoma 24, Florida St. 7		Dec. 31, 1973	Notre Dame 24, Alabama 23
Jan. 1, 1981	Oklahoma 18, Florida St. 17		Dec. 31, 1974	Nebraska 13, Florida 10
Jan. 1, 1982	Clemson 22, Nebraska 15		Dec. 31, 1975	Alabama 13, Penn St. 6
Jan. 1, 1983	Nebraska 21, LSU 20		Jan. 1, 1977	Pittsburgh 27, Georgia 3
Jan. 2, 1984	Miami (FL) 31, Nebraska 30		Jan. 2, 1978	Alabama 35, Ohio St. 6
Jan. 1, 1985	Washington 28, Oklahoma 17		Jan. 1, 1979	Alabama 14, Penn St. 7
Jan. 1, 1986	Oklahoma 25, Penn St. 10		Jan. 1, 1980	Alabama 24, Arkansas 9
Jan. 1, 1987	Oklahoma 42, Arkansas 8		Jan. 1, 1981	Georgia 17, Notre Dame 10
Jan. 1, 1988	Miami (FL) 20, Oklahoma 14		Jan. 1, 1982	Pittsburgh 24, Georgia 20
Jan. 2, 1989	Miami (FL) 23, Nebraska 3		Jan. 1, 1983	Penn St. 27, Georgia 23
Jan. 1, 1990	Notre Dame 21, Colorado 6		Jan. 2, 1984	Auburn 9, Michigan 7
Jan. 1, 1991	Colorado 10, Notre Dame 9		Jan. 1, 1985	Nebraska 28, LSU 10
Jan. 1, 1992	Miami (FL) 22, Nebraska 0		Jan. 1, 1986	Tennessee 35, Miami (FL) 7
Jan. 1, 1993	Florida St. 27, Nebraska 14		Jan. 1, 1987	Nebraska 30, LSU 15
Jan. 1, 1994	Florida St. 18, Nebraska 16		Jan. 1, 1988	Auburn 16, Syracuse 16
Jan. 1, 1995	Nebraska 24, Miami (FL) 17		Jan. 2, 1989	Florida St. 13, Auburn 7
Jan. 1, 1996	Florida St. 31, Notre Dame 26		Jan. 1, 1990	Miami (FL) 33, Alabama 25
Dec. 31, 1996	Nebraska 41, Virginia Tech 21		Jan. 1, 1991	Tennessee 23, Virginia 22
Jan. 2, 1998	Nebraska 42, Tennessee 17		Jan. 1, 1992	Notre Dame 39, Florida 28

Sugar Bowl

New Orleans, LA

Jan. 1, 1935	Tulane 20, Temple 14			
Jan. 1, 1936	Texas Christian 3, LSU 2			
Jan. 1, 1937	Santa Clara 21, LSU 14			
Jan. 1, 1938	Santa Clara 6, LSU 0			
Jan. 2, 1939	Texas Christian 15, Carnegie Mellon 7			
Jan. 1, 1940	Texas A&M 14, Tulane 13			
Jan. 1, 1941	Boston College 19, Tennessee 13			
Jan. 1, 1942	Fordham 2, Missouri 0			

Jan. 1, 1993	Alabama 34, Miami (FL) 13
Jan. 1, 1994	Florida 41, West Virginia 7
Jan. 2, 1995	Florida St. 23, Florida 17
Dec. 31, 1995	Virginia Tech 28, Texas 10
Jan. 2, 1997	Florida 52, Florida St. 20
Jan. 1, 1998	Florida St. 31, Ohio St. 14

Cotton Bowl

Dallas, TX

Jan. 1, 1937	Texas Christian 16, Marquette 6
Jan. 1, 1938	Rice 28, Colorado 14
Jan. 2, 1939	St. Mary's (CA) 20, Texas Tech 13

Jan. 1, 1940	Clemson 6, Boston College 3
Jan. 1, 1941	Texas A&M 13, Fordham 12
Jan. 1, 1942	Alabama 29, Texas A&M 21
Jan. 1, 1943	Texas 14, Georgia Tech 7
Jan. 1, 1944	Randolph Field 7, Texas 7
Jan. 1, 1945	Oklahoma St. 34, Texas Christian 0
Jan. 1, 1946	Texas 40, Missouri 27
Jan. 1, 1947	Arkansas 0, LSU 0
Jan. 1, 1948	Penn St. 13, Southern Methodist 13
Jan. 1, 1949	Southern Methodist 21, Oregon 13
Jan. 2, 1950	Rice 27, North Carolina 13
Jan. 1, 1951	Tennessee 20, Texas 14
Jan. 1, 1952	Kentucky 20, Texas Christian 7
Jan. 1, 1953	Texas 16, Tennessee 0
Jan. 1, 1954	Rice 28, Alabama 6
Jan. 1, 1955	Georgia Tech 14, Arkansas 6
Jan. 2, 1956	Mississippi 14, Texas Christian 13
Jan. 1, 1957	Texas Christian 28, Syracuse 27
Jan. 1, 1958	Navy 20, Rice 7
Jan. 1, 1959	Air Force 0, Texas Christian 0
Jan. 1, 1960	Syracuse 23, Texas 14
Jan. 2, 1961	Duke 7, Arkansas 6
Jan. 1, 1962	Texas 12, Mississippi 7
Jan. 1, 1963	LSU 13, Texas 0
Jan. 1, 1964	Texas 28, Navy 6
Jan. 1, 1965	Arkansas 10, Nebraska 7
Jan. 1, 1966	LSU 14, Arkansas 7
Dec. 31, 1966	Georgia 24, Southern Methodist 9
Jan. 1, 1968	Texas A&M 20, Alabama 16
Jan. 1, 1969	Texas 36, Tennessee 13
Jan. 1, 1970	Texas 21, Notre Dame 17
Jan. 1, 1971	Notre Dame 24, Texas 11
Jan. 1, 1972	Penn St. 30, Texas 6
Jan. 1, 1973	Texas 17, Alabama 13
Jan. 1, 1974	Nebraska 19, Texas 3
Jan. 1, 1975	Penn St. 41, Baylor 20
Jan. 1, 1976	Arkansas 31, Georgia 10
Jan. 1, 1977	Houston 30, Maryland 21
Jan. 2, 1978	Notre Dame 38, Texas 10
Jan. 1, 1979	Notre Dame 35, Houston 34
Jan. 1, 1980	Houston 17, Nebraska 14
Jan. 1, 1981	Alabama 30, Baylor 2
Jan. 1, 1982	Texas 14, Alabama 12
Jan. 1, 1983	Southern Methodist 7, Pittsburgh 3
Jan. 2, 1984	Georgia 10, Texas 9
Jan. 1, 1985	Boston College 45, Houston 28
Jan. 1, 1986	Texas A&M 36, Auburn 16
Jan. 1, 1987	Ohio St. 28, Texas A&M 12
Jan. 1, 1988	Texas A&M 35, Notre Dame 10
Jan. 2, 1989	UCLA 17, Arkansas 3
Jan. 1, 1990	Tennessee 31, Arkansas 27
Jan. 1, 1991	Miami (FL) 46, Texas 3
Jan. 1, 1992	Florida St. 10, Texas A&M 2
Jan. 1, 1993	Notre Dame 28, Texas A&M 3
Jan. 1, 1994	Notre Dame 24, Texas A&M 21
Jan. 2, 1995	Southern Cal 55, Texas Tech 14
Jan. 1, 1996	Colorado 38, Oregon 6
Jan. 1, 1997	Brigham Young 19, Kansas St. 15
Jan. 1, 1998	UCLA 29, Texas A&M 23

Gator Bowl
Jacksonville, FL

Jan. 1, 1946	Wake Forest 26, South Carolina 14
Jan. 1, 1947	Oklahoma 34, North Carolina St. 13
Jan. 1, 1948	Georgia 20, Maryland 20
Jan. 1, 1949	Clemson 24, Missouri 23
Jan. 2, 1950	Maryland 20, Missouri 7
Jan. 1, 1951	Wyoming 20, Wash. & Lee 7
Jan. 1, 1952	Miami (FL) 14, Clemson 0
Jan. 1, 1953	Florida 14, Tulsa 13
Jan. 1, 1954	Texas Tech 35, Auburn 13
Dec. 31, 1954	Auburn 33, Baylor 13
Dec. 31, 1955	Vanderbilt 25, Auburn 13
Dec. 29, 1956	Georgia Tech 21, Pittsburgh 14
Dec. 28, 1957	Tennessee 3, Texas A&M 0
Dec. 27, 1958	Mississippi 7, Florida 3
Jan. 2, 1960	Arkansas 14, Georgia Tech 7
Dec. 31, 1960	Florida 13, Baylor 12
Dec. 30, 1961	Penn St. 30, Georgia Tech 15
Dec. 29, 1962	Florida 17, Penn St. 7
Dec. 28, 1963	North Carolina 35, Air Force 0
Jan. 2, 1965	Florida St. 36, Oklahoma 19
Dec. 31, 1965	Georgia Tech 31, Texas Tech 21
Dec. 31, 1966	Tennessee 18, Syracuse 12
Dec. 30, 1967	Florida St. 17, Penn St. 17
Dec. 28, 1968	Missouri 35, Alabama 10
Dec. 27, 1969	Florida 14, Tennessee 13
Jan. 2, 1971	Auburn 35, Mississippi 28
Dec. 31, 1971	Georgia 7, North Carolina 3
Dec. 30, 1972	Auburn 24, Colorado 3
Dec. 29, 1973	Texas Tech 28, Tennessee 19
Dec. 30, 1974	Auburn 27, Texas 3
Dec. 29, 1975	Maryland 13, Florida 0
Dec. 27, 1976	Notre Dame 20, Penn St. 9
Dec. 30, 1977	Pittsburgh 34, Clemson 3
Dec. 29, 1978	Clemson 17, Ohio St. 15
Dec. 28, 1979	North Carolina 17, Michigan 15
Dec. 29, 1980	Pittsburgh 37, South Carolina 9
Dec. 28, 1981	North Carolina 31, Arkansas 27
Dec. 30, 1982	Florida St. 31, West Virginia 12
Dec. 30, 1983	Florida 14, Iowa 6
Dec. 28, 1984	Oklahoma St. 21, South Carolina 14
Dec. 30, 1985	Florida St. 34, Oklahoma St. 23
Dec. 27, 1986	Clemson 27, Stanford 21
Dec. 31, 1987	LSU 30, South Carolina 13
Jan. 1, 1989	Georgia 34, Michigan St. 27
Dec. 30, 1989	Clemson 27, West Virginia 7
Jan. 1, 1991	Michigan 35, Mississippi 3
Dec. 29, 1991	Oklahoma 48, Virginia 14
Dec. 31, 1992	Florida 27, North Carolina St. 10
Dec. 31, 1993	Alabama 24, North Carolina 10
Dec. 30, 1994	Tennessee 45, Virginia Tech 23
Jan.1, 1996	Syracuse 41, Clemson 0
Jan. 1, 1997	North Carolina 20, West Virginia 13
Jan.1, 1998	North Carolina 42, Virginia Tech 3

Florida Citrus Bowl
Orlando, FL

Jan. 1, 1947	Catawba 31, Maryville (TN) 6
Jan. 1, 1948	Catawba 7, Marshall 0
Jan. 1, 1949	Murray St. 21, Sul Ross St. 21
Jan. 2, 1950	St. Vincent 7, Emory & Henry 6
Jan. 1, 1951	Morris Harvey 35, Emory & Henry 14
Jan. 1, 1952	Stetson 35, Arkansas St. 20
Jan. 1, 1953	East Texas St. 33, Tennessee Tech 0
Jan. 1, 1954	Arkansas St. 7, East Texas St. 7
Jan. 1, 1955	Nebraska-Omaha 7, Eastern Ky. 6
Jan. 2, 1956	Juniata 6, Missouri Valley 6
Jan. 1, 1957	West Texas A&M 20, Southern Miss. 13
Jan. 1, 1958	East Texas St. 10, Southern Miss. 9
Jan. 1, 1960	Middle Tenn. St. 21, Presbyterian 12
Dec. 30, 1960	Citadel 27, Tennessee Tech 0
Dec. 29, 1961	Lamar 21, Middle Tenn. St. 14
Dec. 22, 1962	Houston 49, Miami (OH) 21
Dec. 28, 1963	Western Ky. 27, Coast Guard 0
Dec. 12, 1964	East Carolina 14, Massachusetts 13
Dec. 11, 1965	East Carolina 31, Maine 0
Dec. 10, 1966	Morgan St. 14, West Chester 6
Dec. 16, 1967	Tenn.-Martin 25, West Chester 8
Dec. 27, 1968	Richmond 49, Ohio 42
Dec. 26, 1969	Toledo 56, Davidson 33
Dec. 28, 1970	Toledo 40, William & Mary 12
Dec. 28, 1971	Toledo 28, Richmond 3
Dec. 29, 1972	Tampa 21, Kent 18
Dec. 22, 1973	Miami (OH) 16, Florida 7
Dec. 21, 1974	Miami (OH) 21, Georgia 10
Dec. 20, 1975	Miami (OH) 20, South Caro. 7
Dec. 18, 1976	Oklahoma St. 49, Brigham Young 21
Dec. 23, 1977	Florida St. 40, Texas Tech 17
Dec. 23, 1978	North Carolina St. 30, Pittsburgh 17
Dec. 22, 1979	LSU 34, Wake Forest 10
Dec. 20, 1980	Florida 35, Maryland 20
Dec. 19, 1981	Missouri 19, Southern Miss. 17
Dec. 18, 1982	Auburn 33, Boston College 26
Dec. 17, 1983	Tennessee 30, Maryland 23
Dec. 22, 1984	Florida St. 17, Georgia 17
Dec. 28, 1985	Ohio St. 10, Brigham Young 7
Jan. 1, 1987	Auburn 16, Southern Cal 7
Jan. 1, 1988	Clemson 35, Penn St. 10
Jan. 2, 1989	Clemson 13, Oklahoma 6
Jan. 1, 1990	Illinois 31, Virginia 21
Jan. 1, 1991	Georgia Tech 45, Nebraska 21
Jan. 1, 1992	California 37, Clemson 13
Jan. 1, 1993	Georgia 21, Ohio St. 14
Jan. 1, 1994	Penn St. 31, Tennessee 13
Jan. 2, 1995	Alabama 24, Ohio St. 17
Jan. 1, 1996	Tennessee 20, Ohio St. 14
Jan. 1, 1997	Tennessee 48, Northwestern 28
Jan. 1, 1998	Florida 21, Penn St. 6

Fiesta Bowl
Tempe, AZ

Dec. 27, 1971	Arizona St. 45, Florida St. 38
Dec. 23, 1972	Arizona St. 49, Missouri 35
Dec. 21, 1973	Arizona St. 28, Pittsburgh 7
Dec. 28, 1974	Oklahoma St. 16, Brigham Young 6
Dec. 26, 1975	Arizona St. 17, Nebraska 14
Dec. 25, 1976	Oklahoma 41, Wyoming 7
Dec. 25, 1977	Penn St. 42, Arizona St. 30
Dec. 25, 1978	Arkansas 10, UCLA 10
Dec. 25, 1979	Pittsburgh 16, Arizona 10
Dec. 26, 1980	Penn St. 31, Ohio St. 19
Jan. 1, 1982	Penn St. 26, Southern Cal 10
Jan. 1, 1983	Arizona St. 32, Oklahoma 21
Jan. 2, 1984	Ohio St. 28, Pittsburgh 23
Jan. 1, 1985	UCLA 39, Miami (FL) 37
Jan. 1, 1986	Michigan 27, Nebraska 23
Jan. 2, 1987	Penn St. 14, Miami (FL) 10
Jan. 1, 1988	Florida St. 31, Nebraska 28
Jan. 2, 1989	Notre Dame 34, West Virginia 21
Jan. 1, 1990	Florida St. 41, Nebraska 17
Jan. 1, 1991	Louisville 34, Alabama 7
Jan. 1, 1992	Penn St. 42, Tennessee 17
Jan. 1, 1993	Syracuse 26, Colorado 22
Jan. 1, 1994	Arizona 29, Miami (FL) 0
Jan. 2, 1995	Colorado 41, Notre Dame 24
Jan. 2, 1996	Nebraska 62, Florida 24
Jan. 1, 1997	Penn St. 38, Texas 15
Dec. 31, 1997	Kansas St. 35, Syracuse 18

Source: National Collegiate Athletic Association

Heisman Trophy Winners

Year	Heisman winner, Team, Position
1935	Jay Berwanger, Chicago, HB
1936	Larry Kelley, Yale, E
1937	Clint Frank,Yale, HB
1938	Davey O'Brien, Texas Christian, QB
1939	Nile Kinnick, Iowa, HB
1940	Tom Harmon, Michigan, HB
1941	Bruce Smith, Minnesota, HB
1942	Frank Sinkwich, Georgia, HB
1943	Angelo Bertelli, Notre Dame, QB
1944	Les Horvath, Ohio St., QB
1945	Doc Blanchard, Army, FB
1946	Glenn Davis, Army, HB
1947	Johnny Lujack, Notre Dame, QB
1948	Doak Walker, Southern Methodist, HB
1949	Leon Hart, Notre Dame, E
1950	Vic Janowicz, Ohio St., HB
1951	Dick Kazmeier, Princeton, HB
1952	Billy Vessels, Oklahoma, HB
1953	John Lattner, Notre Dame, HB
1954	Alan Ameche, Wisconsin, FB
1955	Howard Cassady, Ohio St., HB
1956	Paul Hornung, Notre Dame, QB
1957	John David Crow, Texas A&M, HB
1958	Pete Dawkins, Army, HB
1959	Billy Cannon, LSU, HB
1960	Joe Bellino, Navy, HB
1961	Ernie Davis, Syracuse, HB
1962	Terry Baker, Oregon St., QB
1963	Roger Staubach, Navy, QB
1964	John Huarte, Notre Dame, QB
1965	Mike Garrett, Southern Cal, HB
1966	Steve Spurrier, Florida, QB
1967	Gary Beban, UCLA, QB
1968	O.J. Simpson, Southern Cal, HB
1969	Steve Owens, Oklahoma, HB
1970	Jim Plunkett, Stanford, QB
1971	Pat Sullivan, Auburn, QB
1972	Johnny Rodgers, Nebraska, FL
1973	John Cappelletti, Penn St., HB
1974	Archie Griffin, Ohio St., HB
1975	Archie Griffin, Ohio St., HB
1976	Tony Dorsett, Pittsburgh, HB
1977	Earl Campbell, Texas, HB
1978	Billy Sims, Oklahoma, HB
1979	Charles White, Southern Cal, HB
1980	George Rogers, South Carolina, HB
1981	Marcus Allen, Southern Cal, HB
1982	Herschel Walker, Georgia, HB
1983	Mike Rozier, Nebraska, HB
1984	Doug Flutie, Boston College, QB
1985	Bo Jackson, Auburn, HB
1986	Vinny Testaverde, Miami (FL), QB
1987	Tim Brown, Notre Dame, WR
1988	Barry Sanders, Oklahoma St., RB
1989	Andre Ware, Houston, QB
1990	Ty Detmer, Brigham Young, QB
1991	Desmond Howard, Michigan, WR
1992	Gino Torretta, Miami (FL), QB
1993	Charlie Ward, Florida St., QB
1994	Rashaan Salaam, Colorado, RB
1995	Eddie George, Ohio St., RB
1996	Danny Wuerffel, Florida, QB
1997	Charles Woodson, Michigan, CB/WR

Source: National Collegiate Athletic Association

NCAA Basketball Tournament Most Outstanding Player Award

Year	Winner, team
1939	none selected
1940	Marvin Huffman, Indiana
1941	John Kotz, Wisconsin
1942	Howard Dallmar, Stanford
1943	Ken Sailors, Wyoming
1944	Arnold Ferrin, Utah
1945	Bob Kurland, Oklahoma St.
1946	Bob Kurland, Oklahoma St.
1947	George Kaftan, Holy Cross
1948	Alex Groza, Kentucky
1949	Alex Groza, Kentucky
1950	Irwin Dambrot, CCNY
1951	none selected
1952	Clyde Lovellette, Kansas
1953	B. H. Born, Kansas
1954	Tom Gola, La Salle
1955	Bill Russell, San Francisco
1956	Hal Lear, Temple
1957	Wilt Chamberlain, Kansas
1958	Elgin Baylor, Seattle
1959	Jerry West, West Virginia
1960	Jerry Lucas, Ohio St.
1961	Jerry Lucas, Ohio St.
1962	Paul Hogue, Cincinnati
1963	Art Heyman, Duke
1964	Walt Hazzard, UCLA
1965	Bill Bradley, Princeton
1966	Jerry Chambers, Utah
1967	Lew Alcindor, UCLA
1968	Lew Alcindor, UCLA
1969	Lew Alcindor, UCLA
1970	Sidney Wicks, UCLA
1971	Howard Porter, Villanova*
1972	Bill Walton, UCLA
1973	Bill Walton, UCLA
1974	David Thompson, N. Carolina St.
1975	Richard Washington, UCLA
1976	Kent Benson, Indiana
1977	Butch Lee, Marquette
1978	Jack Givens, Kentucky
1979	Earvin Johnson, Michigan St.
1980	Darrell Griffith, Louisville
1981	Isiah Thomas, Indiana
1982	James Worthy, North Carolina
1983	Akeem Olajuwon, Houston
1984	Patrick Ewing, Georgetown
1985	Ed Pinckney, Villanova
1986	Pervis Ellison, Louisville
1987	Keith Smart, Indiana
1988	Danny Manning, Kansas
1989	Glen Rice, Michigan
1990	Anderson Hunt, UNLV
1991	Christian Laettner, Duke
1992	Bobby Hurley, Duke
1993	Donald Williams, North Carolina
1994	Corliss Williamson, Arkansas
1995	Ed O'Bannon, UCLA
1996	Tony Delk, Kentucky
1997	Miles Simon, Arizona
1998	Jeff Sheppard, Kentucky

*Later vacated because player declared ineligible.

Source: National Collegiate Athletic Association

NCAA Basketball Championship Results

Year	Winner	Loser	Score	Championship total attendance
1939	Oregon	Ohio St.	46-33	15,025
1940	Indiana	Kansas	60-42	36,880
1941	Wisconsin	Washington St.	39-34	48,055
1942	Stanford	Dartmouth	53-38	24,372
1943	Wyoming	Georgetown	46-34	56,876
1944	Utah	Dartmouth	42-40*	59,369
1945	Oklahoma St.	New York U.	49-45	67,780
1946	Oklahoma St.	North Carolina	43-40	73,116
1947	Holy Cross	Oklahoma	58-47	72,959
1948	Kentucky	Baylor	58-42	72,523
1949	Kentucky	Oklahoma St.	46-36	66,077
1950	CCNY	Bradley	71-68	75,464
1951	Kentucky	Kansas St.	68-58	110,645
1952	Kansas	St. John's (NY)	80-63	115,712
1953	Indiana	Kansas	69-68	127,149
1954	La Salle	Bradley	92-76	115,391
1955	San Francisco	La Salle	77-63	116,983
1956	San Francisco	Iowa	83-71	132,513
1957	North Carolina	Kansas	54-53**	108,891
1958	Kentucky	Seattle	84-72	176,878
1959	California	West Virginia	71-70	161,809
1960	Ohio St.	California	75-55	155,491
1961	Cincinnati	Ohio St.	70-65*	169,520
1962	Cincinnati	Ohio St.	71-59	177,469
1963	Loyola (IL)	Cincinnati	60-58*	153,065
1964	UCLA	Duke	98-83	140,790
1965	UCLA	Michigan	91-80	140,673
1966	UTEP	Kentucky	72-65	140,925
1967	UCLA	Dayton	79-64	159,570
1968	UCLA	North Carolina	78-55	160,888
1969	UCLA	Purdue	92-72	165,712
1970	UCLA	Jacksonville	80-69	146,794
1971	UCLA	+Villanova	68-62	207,200
1972	UCLA	Florida St.	81-76	147,304
1973	UCLA	Memphis	87-66	163,160
1974	North Carolina St.	Marquette	76-64	154,112
1975	UCLA	Kentucky	92-85	183,857
1976	Indiana	Michigan	86-68	202,502
1977	Marquette	North Carolina	67-59	241,610
1978	Kentucky	Duke	94-88	227,149
1979	Michigan St.	Indiana St.	75-64	262,101
1980	Louisville	+UCLA	59-54	321,260
1981	Indiana	North Carolina	63-50	347,414
1982	North Carolina	Georgetown	63-62	427,251
1983	North Carolina St.	Houston	54-52	364,356
1984	Georgetown	Houston	84-75	397,481
1985	Villanova	Georgetown	66-64	422,519
1986	Louisville	Duke	72-69	499,704
1987	Indiana	Syracuse	74-73	645,744
1988	Kansas	Oklahoma	83-79	558,998
1989	Michigan	Seton Hall	80-79*	613,242
1990	UNLV	Duke	103-73	537,138
1991	Duke	Kansas	72-65	665,707
1992	Duke	Michigan	71-51	580,462
1993	North Carolina	Michigan	77-71	707,719
1994	Arkansas	Duke	76-72	578,007
1995	UCLA	Arkansas	89-78	539,440
1996	Kentucky	Syracuse	76-67	634,584
1997	Arizona	Kentucky	84-79	643,290
1998	Kentucky	Utah	78-69	682,530

*Overtime.
**Three overtimes.
+Later vacated because of ineligibility.
Source: National Collegiate Athletic Association

NCAA Women's Basketball Championship Results

Year	Winner	Score	Loser
1982	Louisiana Tech	76-62	Cheyney
1983	Southern Cal	69-67	Louisiana Tech
1984	Southern Cal	72-61	Tennessee
1985	Old Dominion	70-65	Georgia
1986	Texas	97-81	Southern Cal
1987	Tennessee	67-44	Louisiana Tech
1988	Louisiana Tech	56-54	Auburn
1989	Tennessee	76-60	Auburn
1990	Stanford	88-81	Auburn
1991	Tennessee	70-67*	Virginia
1992	Stanford	78-62	Western Kentucky
1993	Texas Tech	84-82	Ohio State
1994	North Carolina	60-59	Louisiana Tech
1995	Connecticut	70-64	Tennessee
1996	Tennessee	83-65	Georgia
1997	Tennessee	68-59	Old Dominion
1998	Tennessee	93-75	Louisiana Tech

NCAA Women's Basketball Most Outstanding Player Award

1982	—	Janice Lawrence, Louisiana Tech
1983	—	Cheryl Miller, Southern Cal
1984	—	Cheryl Miller, Southern Cal
1985	—	Tracy Claxton, Old Dominion
1986	—	Clarissa Davis, Texas
1987	—	Tonya Edwards, Tennessee
1988	—	Erica Westbrooks, Louisiana Tech
1989	—	Bridgette Gordon, Tennessee
1990	—	Jennifer Azzi, Stanford
1991	—	Dawn Staley, Virginia
1992	—	Molly Goodenbour, Stanford
1993	—	Sheryl Swoopes, Texas Tech
1994	—	Charlotte Smith, North Carolina
1995	—	Rebecca Lobo, Connecticut
1996	—	Michelle Marciniak, Tennessee
1997	—	Chamique Holdsclaw, Tennessee
1998	—	Chamique Holdsclaw, Tennessee

*Overtime.
Source: National Collegiate Athletic Association

Tennis

U.S. Open Champions—Men's Singles

YEAR	CHAMPION	RUNNER-UP
1881	Richard D. Sears (U.S.)	William E. Glyn (U.S.)
1882	Richard D. Sears (U.S.)	Clarence M. Clark (U.S.)
1883	Richard D. Sears (U.S.)	James Dwight (U.S.)
1884	Richard D. Sears (U.S.)	Howard A. Taylor (U.S.)
1885	Richard D. Sears (U.S.)	Godfrey M. Brinley (U.S.)
1886	Richard D. Sears (U.S.)	R. Livingston Beeckman (U.S.)
1887	Richard D. Sears (U.S.)	Henry W. Slocum, Jr. (U.S.)
1888	Henry W. Slocum, Jr. (U.S.)	Howard A. Taylor (U.S.)
1889	Henry W. Slocum, Jr. (U.S.)	Quincy Shaw (U.S.)
1890	Oliver S. Campbell (U.S.)	Henry W. Slocum, Jr. (U.S.)
1891	Oliver S. Campbell (U.S.)	Clarence Hobart (U.S.)
1892	Oliver S. Campbell (U.S.)	Fred H. Hovey (U.S.)
1893	Robert D. Wrenn (U.S.)	Fred H. Hovey (U.S.)
1894	Robert D. Wrenn (U.S.)	Manliffe Goodbody (Great Britain)
1895	Fred H. Hovey (U.S.)	Robert D. Wrenn (U.S.)
1896	Robert D. Wrenn (U.S.)	Fred H. Hovey (U.S.)
1897	Robert D. Wrenn (U.S.)	Wilberforce Eaves (Great Britain)
1898	Malcolm D. Whitman (U.S.)	Dwight F. Davis (U.S.)
1899	Malcolm D. Whitman (U.S.)	J. Parmly Paret (U.S.)
1900	Malcolm D. Whitman (U.S.)	William A. Larned (U.S.)
1901	William A. Larned (U.S.)	Beals C. Wright (U.S.)
1902	William A. Larned (U.S.)	Reginald F. Doherty (Great Britain)
1903	Hugh L. Doherty (Great Britain)	William A. Larned (U.S.)
1904	Holcombe Ward (U.S.)	William J. Clothier (U.S.)
1905	Beals C. Wright (U.S.)	Holcombe Ward (U.S.)
1906	William J. Clothier (U.S.)	Beals C. Wright (U.S.)
1907	William A. Larned (U.S.)	Robert LeRoy (U.S.)
1908	William A. Larned (U.S.)	Beals C. Wright (U.S.)
1909	William A. Larned (U.S.)	William J. Clothier (U.S.)
1910	William A. Larned (U.S.)	Thomas C. Bundy (U.S.)
1911	William A. Larned (U.S.)	Maurice E. McLoughlin (U.S.)
1912	Maurice E. McLoughlin (U.S.)	Wallace F. Johnson (U.S.)
1913	Maurice E. McLoughlin (U.S.)	Richard N. Williams (U.S.)
1914	Richard N. Williams (U.S.)	Maurice E. McLoughlin (U.S.)
1915	William M. Johnston (U.S.)	Maurice E. McLoughlin (U.S.)
1916	Richard N. Williams (U.S.)	William M. Johnston (U.S.)
1917	R. Lindley Murray (U.S.)	Nathaniel Niles (U.S.)
1918	R. Lindley Murray (U.S.)	William T. Tilden (U.S.)
1919	William M. Johnston (U.S.)	William T. Tilden (U.S.)
1920	William T. Tilden (U.S.)	William M. Johnston (U.S.)
1921	William T. Tilden (U.S.)	Wallace J. Johnson
1922	William T. Tilden (U.S.)	William M. Johnston (U.S.)
1923	William T. Tilden (U.S.)	William M. Johnston (U.S.)
1924	William T. Tilden (U.S.)	William M. Johnston (U.S.)
1925	William T. Tilden (U.S.)	William M. Johnston (U.S.)
1926	Rene Lacoste (France)	Jean Borotra (France)
1927	Rene Lacoste (France)	William T. Tilden (U.S.)
1928	Henri Cochet (France)	Francis T. Hunter (U.S.)
1929	William T. Tilden (U.S.)	Francis T. Hunter (U.S.)
1930	John H. Doeg (U.S.)	Francis X. Shields (U.S.)
1931	H. Ellsworth Vines (U.S.)	George M. Lott, Jr. (U.S.)
1932	H. Ellsworth Vines (U.S.)	Henri Cochet (France)
1933	Fred Perry (Great Britain)	John H. Crawford (Australia)
1934	Fred Perry (Great Britain)	Wilmer L. Allison (U.S.)
1935	Wilmer L. Allison (U.S.)	Sidney B. Wood (U.S.)
1936	Fred Perry (Great Britain)	J. Donald Budge (U.S.)
1937	J. Donald Budge (U.S.)	Gottfried von Cramm (Germany)
1938	J. Donald Budge (U.S.)	C. Gene Mako (U.S.)
1939	Robert Riggs (U.S.)	S. Welby van Horn (U.S.)

YEAR	CHAMPION	RUNNER-UP
1940	Donald McNeill (U.S.)	Robert Riggs (U.S.)
1941	Robert Riggs (U.S.)	Francis Kovacs, 2d (U.S.)
1942	Frederick Schroeder (U.S.)	Frank Parker (U.S.)
1943	Lt. Joseph R. Hunt (U.S.)	Seaman Jack Kramer (U.S.)
1944	Sgt. Frank Parker (U.S.)	William F. Talbert (U.S.)
1945	Sgt. Frank Parker (U.S.)	William F. Talbert (U.S.)
1946	Jack Kramer (U.S.)	Tom Brown, Jr. (U.S.)
1947	Jack Kramer (U.S.)	Frank Parker (U.S.)
1948	Richard A. Gonzalez (U.S.)	Eric W. Sturgess (South Africa)
1949	Richard A. Gonzalez (U.S.)	Fredrick Schroeder (U.S.)
1950	Arthur Larsen (U.S.)	Herbert Flam (U.S.)
1951	Frank Sedgman (Australia)	E. Victor Seixas, Jr. (U.S.)
1952	Frank Sedgman (Australia)	Gardnar Mulloy (U.S.)
1953	Tony Trabert (U.S.)	E. Victor Seixas, Jr. (U.S.)
1954	E. Victor Seixas, Jr. (U.S.)	Rex Hartwig (Australia)
1955	Tony Trabert (U.S.)	Ken Rosewall (Australia)
1956	Ken Rosewall (Australia)	Lewis Hoad (Australia)
1957	Malcolm J. Anderson (Australia)	Ashley J. Cooper (Australia)
1958	Ashley J. Cooper (Australia)	Malcolm J. Anderson (Australia)
1959	Neale Fraser (Australia)	Alejandro Olmedo (Peru)
1960	Neale Fraser (Australia)	Rod Laver (Australia)
1961	Roy Emerson (Australia)	Rod Laver (Australia)
1962	Rod Laver (Australia)	Roy Emerson (Australia)
1963	Rafael Osuna (Mexico)	Frank Froehling, III (U.S.)
1964	Roy Emerson (Australia)	Fred Stolle (Australia)
1965	Manuel Santana (Spain)	Cliff Drysdale (South Africa)
1966	Fred Stolle (Australia)	John Newcombe (Australia)
1967	John Newcombe (Australia)	Clark Graebner (U.S.)
1968	Arthur Ashe (U.S.)	Tom Okker (Netherlands)
1969	Rod Laver (Australia)	Tony Roche (Australia)
1970	Ken Rosewall (Australia)	Tony Roche (Australia)
1971	Stan Smith (U.S.)	Jan Kodes (Czechoslovakia)
1972	Ilie Nastase (Romania)	Arthur Ashe (U.S.)
1973	John Newcombe (Australia)	Jan Kodes (Czechoslovakia)
1974	Jimmy Connors (U.S.)	Ken Rosewall (Australia)
1975	Manuel Orantes (Spain)	Jimmy Connors (U.S.)
1976	Jimmy Connors (U.S.)	Bjorn Borg (Sweden)
1977	Guillermo Villas (Argentina)	Jimmy Connors (U.S.)
1978	Jimmy Connors (U.S.)	Bjorn Borg (Sweden)
1979	John McEnroe (U.S.)	Vitas Gerulaitis (U.S.)
1980	John McEnroe (U.S.)	Bjorn Borg (Sweden)
1981	John McEnroe (U.S.)	Bjorn Borg (Sweden)
1982	Jimmy Connors (U.S.)	Ivan Lendl (Czechoslovakia)
1983	Jimmy Connors (U.S.)	Ivan Lendl (Czechoslovakia)
1984	John McEnroe (U.S.)	Ivan Lendl (Czechoslovakia)
1985	Ivan Lendl (Czechoslovakia)	John McEnroe (U.S.)
1986	Ivan Lendl (Czechoslovakia)	Miloslav Mecir (Czechoslovakia)
1987	Ivan Lendl (Czechoslovakia)	Mats Wilander (Sweden)
1988	Mats Wilander (Sweden)	Ivan Lendl (Czechoslovakia)
1989	Boris Becker (West Germany)	Ivan Lendl (Czechoslovakia)
1990	Pete Sampras (U.S.)	Andre Agassi (U.S.)
1991	Stefan Edberg (Sweden)	Jim Courier (U.S.)
1992	Stefan Edberg (Sweden)	Pete Sampras (U.S.)
1993	Pete Sampras (U.S.)	Cedric Pioline (France)
1994	Andre Agassi (U.S.)	Michael Stich (Germany)
1995	Pete Sampras (U.S.)	Andre Agassi (U.S.)
1996	Pete Sampras (U.S.)	Michael Chang (U.S.)
1997	Patrick Rafter (Australia)	Greg Rusedski (Great Britain)
1998	Patrick Rafter (Australia)	Mark Philippoussis (Australia)

Source: U.S. Open

U.S. Open Champions—Women's Singles

YEAR	CHAMPION	RUNNER-UP
1887	Ellen Hansell (U.S.)	Laura Knight (U.S.)
1888	Bertha L. Townsend (U.S.)	Ellen Hansell (U.S.)
1889	Bertha L. Townsend (U.S.)	Lida D. Voorhes (U.S.)
1890	Ellen C. Roosevelt (U.S.)	Bertha L. Townsend (U.S.)
1891	Mabel Cahill (U.S.)	Ellen C. Roosevelt (U.S.)
1892	Mabel Cahill (U.S.)	Elisabeth Moore (U.S.)
1893	Aline Terry (U.S.)	Augusta Schultz (U.S.)
1894	Helen Hellwig (U.S.)	Aline Terry (U.S.)

YEAR	CHAMPION	RUNNER-UP
1895	Juliette Atkinson (U.S.)	Helen Hellwig (U.S.)
1896	Elisabeth Moore (U.S.)	Juliette Atkinson (U.S.)
1897	Juliette Atkinson (U.S.)	Elisabeth Moore (U.S.)
1898	Juliette Atkinson (U.S.)	Marion Jones (U.S.)
1899	Marion Jones (U.S.)	Maud Banks (U.S.)
1900	Myrtle McAteer (U.S.)	Edith Parker (U.S.)
1901	Elisabeth Moore (U.S.)	Myrtle McAteer (U.S.)
1902	Marion Jones (U.S.)	Elisabeth Moore (U.S.)
1903	Elisabeth Moore (U.S.)	Marion Jones (U.S.)
1904	May Sutton (U.S.)	Elisabeth Moore (U.S.)
1905	Elisabeth Moore (U.S.)	Helen Homans (U.S.)
1906	Helen Homans (U.S.)	Maud Barger-Wallach (U.S.)
1907	Evelyn Sears (U.S.)	Carrie Neely (U.S.)
1908	Maud Barger-Wallach (U.S.)	Evelyn Sears (U.S.)
1909	Hazel Hotchkiss (U.S.)	Maud Barger-Wallach (U.S.)
1910	Hazel Hotchkiss (U.S.)	Louise Hammond (U.S.)
1911	Hazel Hotchkiss (U.S.)	Florence Sutton (U.S.)
1912	Mary K. Browne (U.S.)	Eleonora Sears (U.S.)
1913	Mary K. Browne (U.S.)	Dorothy Green (U.S.)
1914	Mary K. Browne (U.S.)	Marie Wagner (U.S.)
1915	Molla Bjurstedt (Norway)	Hazel Hotchkiss Wightman (U.S.)
1916	Molla Bjurstedt (Norway)	Louise Hammond Raymond (U.S.)
1917	Molla Bjurstedt (Norway)	Marion Vanderhoef (U.S.)
1918	Molla Bjurstedt (Norway)	Eleanor E. Goss (U.S.)
1919	Hazel Hotchkiss Wightman (U.S.)	Marion Zinderstein (U.S.)
1920	Molla B. Mallory (U.S.)	Marion Zinderstein (U.S.)
1921	Molla B. Mallory (U.S.)	Mary K. Browne (U.S.)
1922	Molla B. Mallory (U.S.)	Helen Wills (U.S.)
1923	Helen Wills (U.S.)	Molla B. Mallory (U.S.)
1924	Helen Wills (U.S.)	Molla B. Mallory (U.S.)
1925	Helen Wills (U.S.)	Kathleen McKane (Great Britain)
1926	Molla B. Mallory (U.S.)	Elizabeth Ryan (U.S.)
1927	Helen Wills (U.S.)	Betty Nuthall (Great Britain)
1928	Helen Wills (U.S.)	Helen H. Jacobs (U.S.)
1929	Helen Wills (U.S.)	Phoebe Holcroft Watson (Great Britain)
1930	Betty Nuthall (Great Britain)	Anna McCune Harper (U.S.)
1931	Helen Wills Moody (U.S.)	Eileen Bennett Whitingstall (Great Britain)
1932	Helen H. Jacobs (U.S.)	Carolin A. Babcock (U.S.)
1933	Helen H. Jacobs (U.S.)	Helen Wills Moody (U.S.)
1934	Helen H. Jacobs (U.S.)	Sarah H. Palfrey (U.S.)
1935	Helen H. Jacobs (U.S.)	Sarah Palfrey Fabyan (U.S.)
1936	Alice Marble (U.S.)	Helen H. Jacobs (U.S.)
1937	Anita Lizana (Chile)	Jadwiga Jedrzejowska (Poland)
1938	Alice Marble (U.S.)	Nancye Wynne (Australia)
1939	Alice Marble (U.S.)	Helen H. Jacobs (U.S.)
1940	Alice Marble (U.S.)	Helen H. Jacobs (U.S.)
1941	Sarah Palfrey Cooke (U.S.)	Pauline Betz (U.S.)
1942	Pauline Betz (U.S.)	A. Louise Brough (U.S.)
1943	Pauline Betz (U.S.)	A. Louise Brough (U.S.)
1944	Pauline Betz (U.S.)	Margaret Osborne (U.S.)
1945	Sarah Palfrey Cooke (U.S.)	Pauline Betz (U.S.)
1946	Pauline Betz (U.S.)	Patricia Canning (U.S.)
1947	A. Louise Brough (U.S.)	Margaret Osborne (U.S.)
1948	Margaret Osborne duPont (U.S.)	A. Louise Brough (U.S.)
1949	Margaret Osborne duPont (U.S.)	Doris Hart (U.S.)
1950	Margaret Osborne duPont (U.S.)	Doris Hart (U.S.)
1951	Maureen Connolly (U.S.)	Shirley J. Fry (U.S.)
1952	Maureen Connolly (U.S.)	Doris Hart (U.S.)
1953	Maureen Connolly (U.S.)	Doris Hart (U.S.)
1954	Doris Hart (U.S.)	A. Louise Brough (U.S.)
1955	Doris Hart (U.S.)	Patricia Ward (Great Britain)
1956	Shirley J. Fry (U.S.)	Althea Gibson (U.S.)
1957	Althea Gibson (U.S.)	A. Louise Brough (U.S.)
1958	Althea Gibson (U.S.)	Darlene R. Hard (U.S.)
1959	Maria Bueno (Brazil)	Christine Truman (Great Britain)
1960	Darlene R. Hard (U.S.)	Maria Bueno (Brazil)
1961	Darlene R. Hard (U.S.)	Ann Haydon (Great Britain)
1962	Margaret Smith (Australia)	Darlene R. Hard (U.S.)
1963	Maria Bueno (Brazil)	Margaret Smith (Australia)
1964	Maria Bueno (Brazil)	Carole Caldwell Graebner (U.S.)
1965	Margaret Smith (Australia)	Billie Jean Moffitt (U.S.)
1966	Maria Bueno (Brazil)	Nancy Richey (U.S.)
1967	Billie Jean Moffitt King (U.S.)	Ann Haydon Jones (Great Britain)
1968	Virginia Wade (Great Britain)	Billie Jean King (U.S.)
1969	Margaret Smith Court (Australia)	Nancy Richey (U.S.)
1970	Margaret Smith Court (Australia)	Rosemary Casals (U.S.)
1971	Billie Jean King (U.S.)	Rosemary Casals (U.S.)
1972	Billie Jean King (U.S.)	Kerry Melville (Australia)

YEAR	CHAMPION	RUNNER-UP
1973	Margaret Smith Court (Australia)	Evonne Goolagong (Australia)
1974	Billie Jean King (U.S.)	Evonne Goolagong (Australia)
1975	Chris Evert (U.S.)	Evonne Goolagong (Australia)
1976	Chris Evert (U.S.)	Evonne Goolagong (Australia)
1977	Chris Evert (U.S.)	Wendy Turnbull (Australia)
1978	Chris Evert (U.S.)	Pam Shriver (U.S.)
1979	Tracy Austin (U.S.)	Chris Evert Lloyd (U.S.)
1980	Chris Evert Lloyd (U.S.)	Hana Mandlikova (Czechoslovakia)
1981	Tracy Austin (U.S.)	Martina Navratilova (U.S.)
1982	Chris Evert Lloyd (U.S.)	Hana Mandikova (Czechoslovakia)
1983	Martina Navratilova (U.S.)	Chris Evert Lloyd (U.S.)
1984	Martina Navratilova (U.S.)	Chris Evert Lloyd (U.S.)
1985	Hana Mandlikova (Czechoslovakia)	Martina Navratilova (U.S.)
1986	Martina Navratilova (U.S.)	Helena Sukova (Czechoslovakia)
1987	Martina Navratilova (U.S.)	Steffi Graf (West Germany)
1988	Steffi Graf (West Germany)	Gabriela Sabatini (Argentina)
1989	Steffi Graf (West Germany)	Martina Navratilova (U.S.)
1990	Gabriela Sabatini (Argentina)	Steffi Graf (West Germany)
1991	Monica Seles (Yugoslavia)	Martina Navratilova (U.S.)
1992	Monica Seles (Yugoslavia)	Arantxa Sanchez Vicario (Spain)
1993	Steffi Graf (Germany)	Helena Sukova (Czech Republic)
1994	Arantxa Sanchez Vicario (Spain)	Steffi Graf (Germany)
1995	Steffi Graf (Germany)	Monica Seles (U.S.)
1996	Steffi Graf (Germany)	Monica Seles (U.S.)
1997	Martina Hingis (Switzerland)	Venus Williams (U.S.)
1998	Lindsay Davenport (U.S.)	Martina Hingis (Switzerland)

Source: U.S. Open

U.S. Open Doubles Champions

Men's

1881: Clarence M. Clark–Fred W. Taylor
1882: Richard D. Sears–James Dwight
1883: Richard D. Sears–James Dwight
1884: Richard D. Sears–James Dwight
1885: Richard D. Sears–Joseph S. Clark
1886: Richard D. Sears–James Dwight
1887: Richard D. Sears–James Dwight
1888: Oliver S. Campbell–Valentine G. Hall
1889: Henry W. Slocum, Jr.–Howard A. Taylor
1890: Valentine G. Hall–Clarence Hobart
1891: Oliver S. Campbell–Robert Huntington, Jr.
1892: Oliver S. Campbell–Robert Huntington, Jr.
1893: Clarence Hobart–Fred H. Hovey
1894: Clarence Hobart–Fred H. Hovey
1895: Malcolm G. Chace–Robert D. Wrenn
1896: Carr B. Neel–Samuel R. Neel
1897: Leo E. Ware–George P. Sheldon, Jr.
1898: Leo E. Ware–George P. Sheldon, Jr.
1899: Holcombe Ward–Dwight F. Davis
1900: Holcombe Ward–Dwight F. Davis
1901: Holcombe Ward–Dwight F. Davis
1902: Reginald F. Doherty–Hugh L. Doherty
1903: Reginald F. Doherty–Hugh L. Doherty
1904: Holcombe Ward–Beals C. Wright
1905: Holcombe Ward–Beals C. Wright
1906: Holcombe Ward–Beals C. Wright
1907: Fred B. Alexander–Harold H. Hackett

1908: Fred B. Alexander–Harold H. Hackett
1909: Fred B. Alexander–Harold H. Hackett
1910: Fred B. Alexander–Harold H. Hackett
1911: Raymond D. Little–Gustave Touchard
1912: Maurice E. McLoughlin–Thomas C. Bundy
1913: Maurice E. McLoughlin–Thomas C. Bundy
1914: Maurice E. McLoughlin–Thomas C. Bundy
1915: William Johnston–Clarence Griffin
1916: William Johnston–Clarence Griffin
1917: Fred Alexander–Harold Throckmorton
1918: William Tilden, 2nd–Vincent Richards
1919: Norman E. Brookes–Gerald Patterson
1920: William Johnston–Clarence Griffin
1921: William Tilden, 2nd–Vincent Richards
1922: William Tilden, 2nd–Vincent Richards
1923: William Tilden, 2nd–Brian I.C. Norton
1924: Howard Kinsey–Robert Kinsey
1925: Richard Williams, 2nd–Vincent Richards
1926: Richard Williams, 2nd–Vincent Richards
1927: William Tilden, 2nd–Francis T. Hunter
1928: George M. Lott, Jr–John Hennessey
1929: George M. Lott, Jr.–John H. Doeg
1930: George M. Lott, Jr.–John H. Doeg
1931: Wilmer L. Allison–John Van Ryn
1932: H. Ellsworth Vines, Jr.–Keith Gledhill
1933: George M. Lott, Jr.–Lester R. Stoefen
1934: George M. Lott, Jr.–Lester R. Stoefen
1935: Wilmer L. Allison–John Van Ryn

1936: J. Donald Budge–C. Gene Mako
1937: Gottfried von Cramm–Henner Henkel
1938: J. Donald Budge–C. Gene Mako
1939: Adrian K. Quist–John E. Bromwich
1940: Jack Kramer–Frederick R. Schroeder, Jr.
1941: Jack Kramer–Frederick R. Schroeder, Jr.
1942: Lt. Gardnar Mulloy–William F. Talbert
1943: Jack Kramer–Frank A. Parker
1944: Lt. W. Donald McNeill–Robert Falkenburg
1945: Lt. Gardnar Mulloy–William F. Talbert
1946: Gardnar Mulloy–William F. Talbert
1947: Jack Kramer–Frederick R. Schroeder, Jr.
1948: Gardnar Mulloy–William F. Talbert
1949: John Bromwich–William Sidwell
1950: John Bromwich–Frank Sedgman
1951: Kenneth McGregor–Frank Sedgman
1952: Mervyn Rose–E. Victor Seixas, Jr.
1953: Rex Hartwig–Mervyn Rose
1954: E. Victor Seixas, Jr.–Tony Trabert
1955: Kosei Kamo–Atushi Miyagi
1956: Lewis Hoad–Kenneth Rosewall
1957: Ashley J. Cooper–Neale Fraser
1958: Alex Olmedo–Hamilton Richardson
1959: Neale Fraser–Roy Emerson
1960: Neale Fraser–Roy Emerson
1961: Charles McKinley–Dennis Ralston
1962: Rafael Osuna–Antonio Palafox
1963: Charles McKinley–Dennis Ralston
1964: Charles McKinley–Dennis Ralston
1965: Roy Emerson–Fred Stolle
1966: Roy Emerson–Fred Stolle
1967: John Newcombe–Tony Roche
1968: Robert Lutz–Stan Smith
1969: Ken Rosewall–Fred Stolle
1970: Pierre Barthes–Nikki Pilic
1971: John Newcombe–Roger Taylor
1972: Cliff Drysdale–Roger Taylor
1973: Owen Davidson–John Newcombe
1974: Robert Lutz–Stan Smith
1975: Jimmy Connors–Ilie Nastase
1976: Marty Riessen–Tom Okker
1977: Bob Hewitt–Frew McMillan
1978: Robert Lutz–Stan Smith
1979: John McEnroe–Peter Fleming
1980: Robert Lutz–Stan Smith
1981: John McEnroe–Peter Fleming
1982: Kevin Curren–Steve Denton
1983: John McEnroe–Peter Fleming
1984: John Fitzgerald–Tomas Smid
1985: Ken Flach–Robert Seguso
1986: Andres Gomez–Slobodan Zivojinovic
1987: Stefan Edberg–Anders Jarryd
1988: Sergio Casal–Emilio Sanchez
1989: John McEnroe–Mark Woodforde
1990: Pieter Aldrich–Danie Visser
1991: John Fitzgerald–Anders Jarryd
1992: Jim Grabb–Richey Reneberg
1993: Ken Flach–Rick Leach

1994: Jacco Eltingh–Paul Haarhuis
1995: Todd Woodbridge–Mark Woodforde
1996: Todd Woodbridge–Mark Woodforde
1997: Yevgeny Kafelnikov–Daniel Vacek
1998: Sandon Stolle–Cyril Suk

Women's

1889: Bertha Townsend–Margarette Ballard
1890: Ellen C. Roosevelt–Grace W. Roosevelt
1891: Mabel Cahill–Mrs. W. Fellowes Morgan
1892: Mabel E. Cahill–Adeline McKinlay
1893: Aline M. Terry–Hattie Butler
1894: Helen Hellwig–Juliette P. Atkinson
1895: Helen Hellwig–Juliette P. Atkinson
1896: Elisabeth H. Moore–Juliette P. Atkinson
1897: Juliette P. Atkinson–Kathleen Atkinson
1898: Juliette P. Atkinson–Kathleen Atkinson
1899: Jane W. Craven–Myrtle McAteer
1900: Edith Parker–Hallie Champlin
1901: Juliette P. Atkinson–Myrtle McAteer
1902: Juliette P. Atkinson–Marion Jones
1903: Elisabeth H. Moore–Carrie B. Neely
1904: May G. Sutton–Miriam Hall
1905: Helen Homans–Carrie B. Neely
1906: Mrs. L.S. Coe–Mrs. D.S. Platt
1907: Marie Wimer–Carrie B. Neely
1908: Evelyn Sears–Margaret Curtis
1909: Hazel V. Hotchkiss–Edith E. Rotch
1910: Hazel V. Hotchkiss–Edith E. Rotch
1911: Hazel V. Hotchkiss–Eleanora Sears
1912: Dorothy Green–Mary K. Browne
1913: Mary K. Browne–Mrs. R.H. Williams
1914: Mary K. Browne–Mrs. R.H. Williams
1915: Hazel Hotchkiss Wightman–Eleonora Sears
1916: Molla Bjurstedt–Eleanora Sears
1917: Molla Bjurstedt–Eleanora Sears
1918: Marion Zinderstein–Eleanor Goss
1919: Marion Zinderstein–Eleanor Goss
1920: Marion Zinderstein–Eleanor Goss
1921: Mary K. Browne–Mrs. R. H. Williams
1922: Marion Zinderstein Jessup–Helen N. Wills
1923: Kathleen McKane–Phyllis H. Covell
1924: Hazel Hotchkiss Wightman–Helen N. Wills
1925: Mary K. Browne–Helen N. Wills
1926: Elizabeth Ryan–Eleanor Goss
1927: Kathleen Godfree–Ermyntrude Harvey
1928: Hazel Hotchkiss Wightman–Helen N. Wills
1929: Phoebe Watson–Peggy S. Michell
1930: Betty Nuthall–Sarah Palfrey
1931: Betty Nuthall–Eileen B. Whitingstall
1932: Helen Jacobs–Sarah Palfrey
1933: Betty Nuthall–Freda James
1934: Helen Jacobs–Sarah Palfrey
1935: Helen Jacobs–Sarah Palfrey Fabyan
1936: Marjorie G. Van Ryn–Carolin Babcock
1937: Sarah Palfrey Fabyan–Alice Marble
1938: Sarah Palfrey Fabyan–Alice Marble
1939: Sarah Palfrey Fabyan–Alice Marble
1940: Sarah Palfrey Fabyan–Alice Marble

1941: Sarah Palfrey Fabyan–Margaret E. Osborne
1942: A. Louise Brough–Margaret E. Osborne
1943: A. Louise Brough–Margaret E. Osborne
1944: A. Louise Brough–Margaret E. Osborne
1945: A. Louise Brough–Margaret E. Osborne
1946: A. Louise Brough–Margaret E. Osborne
1947: A. Lousie Brough–Margaret E. Osborne
1948: A. Louise Brough–Margaret O. duPont
1949: A. Louise Brough–Margaret O. duPont
1950: A. Louise Brough–Margaret O. duPont
1951: Shirley Fry–Doris Hart
1952: Shirley Fry–Doris Hart
1953: Shirley Fry–Doris Hart
1954: Shirley Fry–Doris Hart
1955: A. Louise Brough–Margaret O. duPont
1956: A. Louise Brough–Margaret O. duPont
1957: A. Louise Brough–Margaret O. duPont
1958: Jeanne M. Arth–Darlene R. Hard
1959: Jeanne M. Arth–Darlene R. Hard
1960: Maria Bueno–Darlene R. Hard
1961: Darlene R. Hard–Lesley Turner
1962: Darlene R. Hard–Maria Bueno

1963: Robyn Ebbern–Margaret Smith
1964: Billie Jean Moffitt–Karen H. Susman
1965: Carole Caldwell Graebner–Nancy Richey
1966: Maria Bueno–Nancy Richey
1967: Rosemary Casals–Billie Jean King
1968: Maria Bueno–Margaret Smith Court
1969: Francoise Durr–Darlene R. Hard
1970: Margaret Smith Court–Judy Tegart Dalton
1971: Rosemary Casals–Judy Tegart Dalton
1972: Francoise Durr–Betty Stove
1973: Margaret Smith Court–Virginia Wade
1974: Rosemary Casals–Billie Jean King
1975: Margaret Smith Court–Virginia Wade
1976: Delina Boshoff–Ilana Kloss
1977: Martina Navratilova–Betty Stove
1978: Billie Jean King–Martina Navratilova
1979: Betty Stove–Wendy Turnbull
1980: Billie Jean King–Martina Navratilova
1981: Anne Smith–Kathy Jordan
1982: Rosemary Casals–Wendy Turnbull
1983: Pam Shriver–Martina Navratilova
1984: Pam Shriver–Martina Navratilova

U.S. Open Winners' Prize Money

	Singles		Doubles (per team)		
	Men	Women	Men	Women	Mixed
1980	$46,000	$46,000	$18,500	$18,500	$7,100
1981	66,000	66,000	26,400	26,400	9,680
1982	90,000	90,000	36,000	36,000	14,000
1983	120,000	120,000	48,000	48,000	17,000
1984	160,000	160,000	64,000	64,000	17,000
1985	187,500	187,500	65,000	65,000	19,000
1986	210,000	210,000	72,800	72,800	21,800
1987	250,000	250,000	86,667	86,667	26,160
1988	275,000	275,000	95,333	95,333	28,800
1989	300,000	300,000	104,000	104,000	34,000
1990	350,000	350,000	142,861	142,861	42,500
1991	400,000	400,000	163,500	163,500	46,500
1992	500,000	500,000	184,000	184,000	46,500
1993	535,000	535,000	200,000	200,000	46,500
1994	550,000	550,000	200,000	200,000	46,500
1995	575,000	575,000	210,000	210,000	50,000
1996	600,000	600,000	240,000	240,000	60,000
1997	650,000	650,000	300,000	300,000	100,000
1998	700,000	700,000	320,000	320,000	120,000

Source: U.S. Open

1985: Claudia Kohde-Kilsch–Helena Sukova
1986: Martina Navratilova–Pam Shriver
1987: Martina Navratilova–Pam Shriver
1988: Gigi Fernandez–Robin White
1989: Hana Mandlikova–Martina Navratilova
1990: Gigi Fernandez–Martina Navratilova
1991: Pam Shriver–Natalia Zvereva

1992: Gigi Fernandez–Natalia Zvereva
1993: Arantxa Sanchez Vicario–Helena Sukova
1994: Jana Novotna–Arantxa Sanchez Vicario
1995: Gigi Fernandez–Natasha Zvereva
1996: Gigi Fernandez–Natasha Zvereva
1997: Lindsay Davenport–Jana Novotna
1998: Martina Hingis–Jana Novotna

U.S. Open "Triple Crowns"

Thirty times in the history of the national championships, a player has accomplished the feat of winning all three possible titles in the same year—singles, doubles, and mixed doubles. This has been done by 21 players, 15 women and 6 men. Here are the three-championship winners:

1892: Mabel Cahill
1895: Juliette P. Atkinson
1909: Hazel Hotchkiss Wightman
1910: Hazel Hotchkiss Wightman
1911: Hazel Hotchkiss Wightman
1912: Mary K. Browne
1913: Mary K. Browne
1914: Mary K. Browne
1917: Molla Bjurstedt
1922: Bill Tilden
1923: Bill Tilden
1924: Helen N. Wills
1928: Helen N. Wills
1934: Helen H. Jacobs

1938: Don Budge, Alice Marble*
1939: Alice Marble
1940: Alice Marble
1941: Sarah Palfrey (Fabyan) Cooke
1947: Louise Brough
1950: Margaret O. duPont
1951: Frank Sedgman
1954: Vic Seixas, Doris Hart*
1956: Ken Rosewall
1959: Neale Fraser
1960: Neale Fraser
1967: Billie Jean King
1970: Margaret Smith Court
1987: Martina Navratilova

*Only twice have two players combined on a championship mixed doubles team and also won both of their own titles in singles and doubles, 1938 (Budge and Marble) and 1954 (Seixas and Hart).

Source: U.S. Open

Wimbledon Champions

YEAR	Men's	Women's	YEAR	Men's	Women's
1877	Spencer Gore		1897	Reggie Doherty	Blanche Bingley Hillyard
1878	Frank Hadow				
1879	John Hartley		1898	Reggie Doherty	Charlotte Cooper
1880	John Hartley		1899	Reggie Doherty	Blanche Bingley Hillyard
1881	William Renshaw				
1882	William Renshaw		1900	Reggie Doherty	Blanche Bingley Hillyard
1883	William Renshaw				
1884	William Renshaw	Maud Watson	1901	Arthur Gore	Charlotte Cooper Sterry
1885	William Renshaw	Maud Watson			
1886	William Renshaw	Blanche Bingley	1902	Laurie Doherty	Muriel Robb
1887	Herbert Lawford	Charlotte Dod	1903	Laurie Doherty	Dorothea Douglass
1888	Ernest Renshaw	Charlotte Dod	1904	Laurie Doherty	Dorothea Douglass
1889	William Renshaw	Blanche Bingley Hillyard	1905	Laurie Doherty	May Sutton
			1906	Laurie Doherty	Dorothea Douglass
1890	William Hamilton	Lena Rice	1907	Norman Brookes	May Sutton
1891	Wilfred Baddeley	Charlotte Dod	1908	Arthur Gore	Charlotte Cooper Sterry
1892	Wilfred Baddeley	Charlotte Dod			
1893	Joshua Pim	Charlotte Dod	1909	Arthur Gore	Dora Boothby
1894	Joshua Pim	Blanche Bingley Hillyard	1910	Anthony Wilding	Dorothea Lambert Chambers
1895	Wilfred Baddeley	Charlotte Cooper	1911	Anthony Wilding	Dorothea Lambert Chambers
1896	Harold Mahoney	Charlotte Cooper			

YEAR	Men's	Women's
1912	Anthony Wilding	Ethel Thomson Larcombe
1913	Anthony Wilding	Dorothea Lambert Chambers
1914	Norman Brookes	Dorothea Lambert Chambers
1915–1918	no tournament	
1919	Gerald Patterson	Suzanne Lenglen
1920	Bill Tilden	Suzanne Lenglen
1921	Bill Tilden	Suzanne Lenglen
1922	Gerald Patterson	Suzanne Lenglen
1923	William Johnston	Suzanne Lenglen
1924	Jean Borotra	Kathleen McKane
1925	Rene Lacoste	Suzanne Lenglen
1926	Jean Borotra	Kathleen McKane Godfree
1927	Henri Cochet	Helen Wills
1928	Rene Lacoste	Helen Wills
1929	Henri Cochet	Helen Wills
1930	Bill Tilden	Helen Wills Moody
1931	Sidney Wood	Cilly Aussem
1932	Ellsworth Vines	Helen Wills Moody
1933	Jack Crawford	Helen Wills Moody
1934	Fred Perry	Dorothy Round
1935	Fred Perry	Helen Wills Moody
1936	Fred Perry	Helen Jacobs
1937	Don Budge	Dorothy Round
1938	Don Budge	Helen Wills Moody
1939	Bobby Riggs	Alice Marble
1940–1945	no tournament	
1946	Yvon Petra	Pauline Betz
1947	Jack Kramer	Margaret Osborne
1948	Bob Falkenburg	Louise Brough
1949	Ted Schroeder	Louise Brough
1950	Budge Patty	Louise Brough
1951	Dick Savitt	Doris Hart
1952	Frank Sedgman	Maureen Connolly
1953	Vic Seixas	Maureen Connolly
1954	Jaroslav Drobny	Maureen Connolly
1955	Tony Trabert	Louise Brough
1956	Lew Hoad	Shirley Fry
1957	Lew Hoad	Althea Gibson
1958	Ashley Cooper	Althea Gibson
1959	Alex Olmedo	Maria Bueno
1960	Neale Fraser	Maria Bueno
1961	Rod Laver	Angela Mortimer
1962	Rod Laver	Karen Hantze Susman
1963	Chuck McKinley	Margaret Smith
1964	Roy Emerson	Maria Bueno
1965	Roy Emerson	Margaret Smith
1966	Manuel Santana	Billie Jean King
1967	John Newcombe	Billie Jean King
1968	Rod Laver	Billie Jean King
1969	Rod Laver	Ann Haydon Jones
1970	John Newcombe	Margaret Smith Court
1971	John Newcombe	Evonne Goolagong
1972	Stan Smith	Billie Jean King
1973	Jan Kodes	Billie Jean King
1974	Jimmy Connors	Chris Evert
1975	Arthur Ashe	Billie Jean King
1976	Bjorn Borg	Chris Evert
1977	Bjorn Borg	Virginia Wade
1978	Bjorn Borg	Martina Navratilova
1979	Bjorn Borg	Martina Navratilova
1980	Bjorn Borg	Evonne Goolagong Cawley
1981	John McEnroe	Chris Evert Lloyd
1982	Jimmy Connors	Martina Navratilova
1983	John McEnroe	Martina Navratilova
1984	John McEnroe	Martina Navratilova
1985	Boris Becker	Martina Navratilova
1986	Boris Becker	Martina Navratilova
1987	Pat Cash	Martina Navratilova
1988	Stefan Edberg	Steffi Graf
1989	Boris Becker	Steffi Graf
1990	Stefan Edberg	Martina Navratilova
1991	Michael Stich	Steffi Graf
1992	Andre Agassi	Steffi Graf
1993	Pete Sampras	Steffi Graf
1994	Pete Sampras	Conchita Martinez
1995	Pete Sampras	Steffi Graf
1996	Richard Krajicek	Steffi Graf
1997	Pete Sampras	Martina Hingis
1998	Pete Sampras	Jana Novotna

Source: Wimbledon Compendium

ATP Tour Prize Money Leaders

1968: Tony Roche	$63,504
1969: Rod Laver	$124,000
1970: Rod Laver	$201,453
1971: Rod Laver	$292,717
1972: Ilie Nastase	$176,000
1973: Ilie Nastase	$228,750
1974: Jimmy Connors	$285,490
1975: Arthur Ashe	$326,750
1976: Raul Ramirez	$484,343
1977: Guillermo Vilas	$766,065
1978: Eddie Dibbs	$575,273
1979: Bjorn Borg	$1,008,742
1980: John McEnroe	$972,369
1981: John McEnroe	$991,000
1982: Ivan Lendl	$2,028,850
1983: Ivan Lendl	$1,747,128
1984: John McEnroe	$2,026,109
1985: Ivan Lendl	$1,971,074
1986: Ivan Lendl	$1,987,537
1987: Ivan Lendl	$2,003,656

1988: Mats Wilander	$1,726,731	1994: Pete Sampras	$4,857,812
1989: Ivan Lendl	$2,344,367	1995: Pete Sampras	$5,415,066
1990: Pete Sampras	$2,900,057	1996: Boris Becker	$4,313,007
1991: David Wheaton	$2,479,239	1997: Pete Sampras	$6,498,311
1992: Michael Stich	$2,777,411		
1993: Pete Sampras	$4,579,325	*Source: ATP Tour*	

WTA Tour Prize Money Leaders

1974: Chris Evert	$107,485	1987: Steffi Graf	$1,063,785
1975: Chris Evert	$347,227	1988: Steffi Graf	$1,378,128
1976: Chris Evert	$319,565	1989: Steffi Graf	$1,963,905
1977: Chris Evert	$316,045	1990: Steffi Graf	$1,921,853
1978: Chris Evert	$454,486	1991: Monica Seles	$2,457,758
1979: Martina Navratilova	$618,698	1992: Monica Seles	$2,622,352
1980: Martina Navratilova	$749,250	1993: Steffi Graf	$2,821,337
1981: Martina Navratilova	$865,437	1994: Arantxa Sanchez Vicario	$2,943,665
1982: Martina Navratilova	$1,475,055	1995: Steffi Graf	$2,538,620
1983: Martina Navratilova	$1,456,030	1996: Steffi Graf	$2,665,706
1984: Martina Navratilova	$2,173,556	1997: Martina Hingis	$3,400,196
1985: Martina Navratilova	$1,328,829		
1986: Martina Navratilova	$1,905,841	*Source: Women's Tennis Association*	

Golf

U.S. Open Championship

1895: Horace Rawlins	1920: Edward Ray
1896: James Foulis	1921: James M. Barnes
1897: Joe Lloyd	1922: Gene Sarazen
1898: Fred Herd	1923: Robert T. Jones, Jr.
1899: Willie Smith	1924: Cyril Walker
1900: Harry Vardon	1925: William Macfarlane
1901: Willie Anderson	1926: Robert T. Jones, Jr.
1902: Laurence Auchterlonie	1927: Tommy Armour
1903: Willie Anderson	1928: Johnny Farrell
1904: Willie Anderson	1929: Robert T. Jones, Jr.
1905: Willie Anderson	1930: Robert T. Jones, Jr.
1906: Alex Smith	1931: Billy Burke
1907: Alex Ross	1932: Gene Sarazen
1908: Fred McLeod	1933: John Goodman
1909: George Sargent	1934: Olin Dutra
1910: Alex Smith	1935: Sam Parks, Jr.
1911: John J. McDermott	1936: Tony Manero
1912: John J. McDermott	1937: Ralph Guldahl
1913: Francis Ouimet	1938: Ralph Guldahl
1914: Walter Hagen	1939: Byron Nelson
1915: Jerome D. Travers	1940: Lawson Little
1916: Charles Evans, Jr.	1941: Craig Wood
1917–18: *	1942–45: *
1919: Walter Hagen	1946: Lloyd Mangrum

1947: Lew Worsham
1948: Ben Hogan
1949: Cary Middlecoff
1950: Ben Hogan
1951: Ben Hogan
1952: Julius Boros
1953: Ben Hogan
1954: Ed Furgol
1955: Jack Fleck
1956: Cary Middlecoff
1957: Dick Mayer
1958: Tommy Bolt
1959: Bill Casper, Jr.
1960: Arnold Palmer
1961: Gene Littler
1962: Jack Nicklaus
1963: Julius Boros
1964: Ken Venturi
1965: Gary Player
1966: Bill Casper, Jr.
1967: Jack Nicklaus
1968: Lee Trevino
1969: Orville Moody
1970: Tony Jacklin
1971: Lee Trevino
1972: Jack Nicklaus
1973: John Miller

1974: Hale Irwin
1975: Lou Graham
1976: Jerry Pate
1977: Hubert Green
1978: Andy North
1979: Hale Irwin
1980: Jack Nicklaus
1981: David Graham
1982: Tom Watson
1983: Larry Nelson
1984: Fuzzy Zoeller
1985: Andy North
1986: Raymond Floyd
1987: Scott Simpson
1988: Curtis Strange
1989: Curtis Strange
1990: Hale Irwin
1991: Payne Stewart
1992: Tom Kite
1993: Lee Janzen
1994: Ernie Els
1995: Corey Pavin
1996: Steve Jones
1997: Ernie Els
1998: Lee Janzen

*No championships.
Source: U.S. Golf Association

U.S. Women's Open Championship

1946: Patty Berg
1947: Betty Jameson
1948: Babe Didrikson Zaharias
1949: Louise Suggs
1950: Babe Didrikson Zaharias
1951: Betsy Rawls
1952: Louise Suggs
1953: Betsy Rawls
1954: Babe Didrikson Zaharias
1955: Fay Crocker
1956: Kathy Cornelius
1957: Betsy Rawls
1958: Mickey Wright
1959: Mickey Wright
1960: Betsy Rawls
1961: Mickey Wright
1962: Murle Lindstrom
1963: Mary Mills
1964: Mickey Wright
1965: Carol Mann
1966: Sandra Spuzich
1967: Catherine Lacoste
1968: Susie Maxwell Berning
1969: Donna Caponi
1970: Donna Caponi
1971: JoAnne Gunderson Carner
1972: Susie Maxwell Berning

1973: Susie Maxwell Berning
1974: Sandra Haynie
1975: Sandra Palmer
1976: JoAnne Gunderson Carner
1977: Hollis Stacy
1978: Hollis Stacy
1979: Jerilyn Britz
1980: Amy Alcott
1981: Pat Bradley
1982: Janet Alex
1983: Jan Stephenson
1984: Hollis Stacy
1985: Kathy (Baker) Guadagnino
1986: Jane Geddes
1987: Laura Davies
1988: Liselotte Neumann
1989: Betsy King
1990: Betsy King
1991: Meg Mallon
1992: Patty Sheehan
1993: Lauri Merten
1994: Patty Sheehan
1995: Annika Sorenstam
1996: Annika Sorenstam
1997: Alison Nicholas
1998: Se Ri Pak

Source: U.S. Golf Association

U.S. Senior Open Championship

1980: Roberto de Vicenzo
1981: Arnold Palmer
1982: Miller Barber
1983: Billy Casper
1984: Miller Barber
1985: Miller Barber
1986: Dale Douglass
1987: Gary Player
1988: Gary Player
1989: Orville Moody
1990: Lee Trevino

1991: Jack Nicklaus
1992: Larry Laoretti
1993: Jack Nicklaus
1994: Simon Hobday
1995: Tom Weiskopf
1996: Dave Stockton
1997: Graham Marsh
1998: Hale Irwin

Source: U.S. Golf Association

Masters Tournament Winners

Year Winner
1934: Horton Smith
1935: Gene Sarazen
1936: Horton Smith
1937: Byron Nelson
1938: Henry Picard
1939: Ralph Guldahl
1940: Jimmy Demaret
1941: Craig Wood
1942: Byron Nelson
1943:-1945:*
1946: Herman Keiser
1947: Jimmy Demaret
1948: Claude Harmon
1949: Sam Snead
1950: Jimmy Demaret
1951: Ben Hogan
1952: Sam Snead
1953: Ben Hogan
1954: Sam Snead
1955: Cary Middlecoff
1956: Jack Burke, Jr.
1957: Doug Ford
1958: Arnold Palmer
1959: Art Wall, Jr.
1960: Arnold Palmer
1961: Gary Player
1962: Arnold Palmer
1963: Jack Nicklaus
1964: Arnold Palmer
1965: Jack Nicklaus
1966: Jack Nicklaus

1967: Gay Brewer, Jr.
1968: Bob Goalby
1969: George Archer
1970: Billy Casper
1971: Charles Coody
1972: Jack Nicklaus
1973: Tommy Aaron
1974: Gary Player
1975: Jack Nicklaus
1976: Ray Floyd
1977: Tom Watson
1978: Gary Player
1979: Fuzzy Zoeller
1980: Seve Ballesteros
1981: Tom Watson
1982: Craig Stadler
1983: Seve Ballesteros
1984: Ben Crenshaw
1985: Bernhard Langer
1986: Jack Nicklaus
1987: Larry Mize
1988: Sandy Lyle
1989: Nick Faldo
1990: Nick Faldo
1991: Ian Woosnam
1992: Fred Couples
1993: Bernhard Langer
1994: Jose Maria Olazabal
1995: Ben Crenshaw
1996: Nick Faldo
1997: Tiger Woods
1998: Mark O'Meara

*No championship

Source: PGA Tour Media Guide

PGA Championship

Year   Winner
1916: James M. Barnes
1917-1918: *

*No Championship

1919: James M. Barnes
1920: Jock Hutchison
1921: Walter Hagen
1922: Gene Sarazen
1923: Gene Sarazen

1924: Walter Hagen
1925: Walter Hagen
1926: Walter Hagen
1927: Walter Hagen
1928: Leo Diegel
1929: Leo Diegel
1930: Tommy Armour
1931: Tom Creavy
1932: Olin Dutra
1933: Gene Sarazen
1934: Paul Runyan
1935: Johnny Revolta
1936: Denny Shute
1937: Denny Shute
1938: Paul Runyan
1939: Henry Picard
1940: Byron Nelson
1941: Vic Ghezzi
1942: Sam Snead
1943: *
1944: Bob Hamilton
1945: Byron Nelson
1946: Ben Hogan
1947: Jim Ferrier
1948: Ben Hogan
1949: Sam Snead
1950: Chandler Harper
1951: Sam Snead
1952: Jim Turnesa
1953: Walter Burkemo
1954: Chick Harbert
1955: Doug Ford
1956: Jack Burke
1957: Lionel Hebert
1958: Dow Finsterwald
1959: Bob Rosburg
1960: Jay Hebert
1961: Jerry Barber

1962: Gary Player
1963: Jack Nicklaus
1964: Bobby Nichols
1965: Dave Marr
1966: Al Geiberger
1967: Don January (69)
1968: Julius Boros
1969: Raymond Floyd
1970: Dave Stockton
1971: Jack Nicklaus
1972: Gary Player
1973: Jack Nicklaus
1974: Lee Trevino
1975: Jack Nicklaus
1976: Dave Stockton
1977: Lanny Wadkins
1978: John Mahaffey
1979: David Graham
1980: Jack Nicklaus
1981: Larry Nelson
1982: Raymond Floyd
1983: Hal Sutton
1984: Lee Trevino
1985: Hubert Green
1986: Bob Tway
1987: Larry Nelson
1988: Jeff Sluman
1989: Payne Stewart
1990: Wayne Grady
1991: John Daly
1992: Nick Price
1993: Paul Azinger
1994: Nick Price
1995: Steve Elkington
1996: Mark Brooks
1997: Davis Love III
1998: Vijay Singh

British Open

1860: Willie Park
(The first event was open only to professional golfers)
1861: Tom Morris, Sr.
(The second Open was open to amateurs also)
1862: Tom Morris, Sr.
1863: Willie Park
1864: Tom Morris, Sr.
1865: Andrew Strath
1866: Willie Park
1867: Tom Morris, Sr.
1868: Tom Morris, Jr.
1869: Tom Morris, Jr.
1870: Tom Morris, Jr.
1871: *
1872: Tom Morris, Jr.
1873: Tom Kidd

1874: Mungo Park
1875: Willie Park
1876: Bob Martin
1877: Jamie Anderson
1878: Jamie Anderson
1879: Jamie Anderson
1880: Robert Ferguson
1881: Robert Ferguson
1882: Robert Ferguson
1883: Willie Fernie
1884: Jack Simpson
1885: Bob Martin
1886: David Brown
1887: Willie Park, Jr.
1888: Jack Burns
1889: Willie Park, Jr.

1890: John Ball, Jr.	1948: Henry Cotton
1891: Hugh Kirkaldy	1949: Bobby Locke
1892: Harold H. Hilton	1950: Bobby Locke
1893: William Auchterlonie	1951: Max Faulkner
1894: John H. Taylor	1952: Bobby Locke
1895: John H. Taylor	1953: Ben Hogan
1896: Harry Vardon	1954: Peter Thomson
1897: Harold H. Hilton	1955: Peter Thomson
1898: Harry Vardon	1956: Peter Thomson
1899: Harry Vardon	1957: Bobby Locke
1900: John H. Taylor	1958: Peter Thomson
1901: James Braid	1959: Gary Player
1902: Alexander Herd	1960: Kel Nagle
1903: Harry Vardon	1961: Arnold Palmer
1904: Jack White	1962: Arnold Palmer
1905: James Braid	1963: Bob Charles
1906: James Braid	1964: Tony Lema
1907: Arnaud Massy	1965: Peter Thomson
1908: James Braid	1966: Jack Nicklaus
1909: John H. Taylor	1967: Roberto De Vicenzo
1910: James Braid	1968: Gary Player
1911: Harry Vardon	1969: Tony Jacklin
1912: Edward (Ted) Ray	1970: Jack Nicklaus
1913: John H. Taylor	1971: Lee Trevino
1914: Harry Vardon	1972: Lee Trevino
1915-1919: *	1973: Tom Weiskopf
1920: George Duncan	1974: Gary Player
1921: Jock Hutchison	1975: Tom Watson
1922: Walter Hagen	1976: Johnny Miller
1923: Arthur G. Havers	1977: Tom Watson
1924: Walter Hagen	1978: Jack Nicklaus
1925: James M. Barnes	1979: Seve Ballesteros
1926: Robert T. Jones, Jr.	1980: Tom Watson
1927: Robert T. Jones, Jr.	1981: Bill Rogers
1928: Walter Hagen	1982: Tom Watson
1929: Walter Hagen	1983: Tom Watson
1930: Robert T. Jones, Jr.	1984: Seve Ballesteros
1931: Tommy D. Armour	1985: Sandy Lyle
1932: Gene Sarazen	1986: Greg Norman
1933: Denny Shute	1987: Nick Faldo
1934: Henry Cotton	1988: Seve Ballesteros
1935: Alfred Perry	1989: Mark Calcavecchia
1936: Alfred Padgham	1990: Nick Faldo
1937: Henry Cotton	1991: Ian Baker-Finch
1938: R. A. Whitcombe	1992: Nick Faldo
1939: Richard Burton	1993: Greg Norman
1940-1945: *	1994: Nick Price
1946: Sam Snead	1995: John Daly
1947: Fred Daly	1996: Tom Lehman
	1997: Justin Leonard
*No Championship	1998: Mark O'Meara

Professional Golf Association: Leading Money-Winners

1934: Paul Runyan	$6,767	1938: Sam Snead	19,534
1935: Johnny Revolta	9,543	1939: Henry Picard	$10,303
1936: Horton Smith	7,682	1940: Ben Hogan	10,655
1937: Harry Cooper	14,138	1941: Ben Hogan	18,358

1942: Ben Hogan	13,143		1971: Jack Nicklaus	244,490
1943: No Statistics Compiled			1972: Jack Nicklaus	$320,542
1944: Byron Nelson (War Bonds)	$37,967		1973: Jack Nicklaus	308,362
1945: Byron Nelson (War Bonds)	63,335		1974: Johnny Miller	353,021
1946: Ben Hogan	42,556		1975: Jack Nicklaus	298,149
1947: Jimmy Demaret	27,936		1976: Jack Nicklaus	266,438
1948: Ben Hogan	32,112		1977: Tom Watson	310,653
1949: Sam Snead	31,593		1978: Tom Watson	362,428
1950: Sam Snead	35,758		1979: Tom Watson	462,636
1951: Lloyd Mangrum	26,088		1980: Tom Watson	530,808
1952: Julius Boros	37,032		1981: Tom Kite	375,698
1953: Lew Worsham	34,002		1982: Craig Stadler	446,462
1954: Bob Toski	65,819		1983: Hal Sutton	426,668
1955: Julius Boros	63,121		1984: Tom Watson	476,260
1956: Ted Kroll	72,835		1985: Curtis Strange	542,321
1957: Dick Mayer	65,835		1986: Greg Norman	653,296
1958: Arnold Palmer	42,607		1987: Curtis Strange	925,941
1959: Art Wall	53,167		1988: Curtis Strange	1,147,644
1960: Arnold Palmer	75,262		1989: Tom Kite	1,395,278
1961: Gary Player	64,540		1990: Greg Norman	1,165,477
1962: Arnold Palmer	81,448		1991: Corey Pavin	979,430
1963: Arnold Palmer	128,230		1992: Fred Couples	1,344,188
1964: Jack Nicklaus	113,284		1993: Nick Price	1,478,557
1965: Jack Nicklaus	140,752		1994: Nick Price	1,499,927
1966: Billy Casper	121,944		1995: Greg Norman	1,654,959
1967: Jack Nicklaus	188,998		1996: Tom Lehman	1,780,159
1968: Billy Casper	205,168		1997: Tiger Woods	2,066,833
1969: Frank Beard	164,707			
1970: Lee Trevino	157,037		*Source: PGA*	

Ladies Professional Golf Association: Leading Money Winners

1950: Babe Zaharias	$14,800		1975: Sandra Palmer	$76,374
1951: Babe Zaharias	15,087		1976: Judy Rankin	150,734
1952: Betsy Rawls	14,505		1977: Judy Rankin	122,890
1953: Louise Suggs	19,816		1978: Nancy Lopez	189,814
1954: Patty Berg	16,011		1979: Nancy Lopez	197,489
1955: Patty Berg	16,492		1980: Beth Daniel	231,000
1956: Marlene Hagge	20,235		1981: Beth Daniel	206,998
1957: Patty Berg	16,272		1982: JoAnne Carner	310,400
1958: Beverly Hanson	12,639		1983: JoAnne Carner	291,404
1959: Betsy Rawls	26,774		1984: Betsy King	266,771
1960: Louise Suggs	16,892		1985: Nancy Lopez	416,472
1961: Mickey Wright	22,236		1986: Pat Bradley	492,021
1962: Mickey Wright	21,641		1987: Ayako Okamoto	466,034
1963: Mickey Wright	31,269		1988: Sherri Turner	350,851
1964: Mickey Wright	29,800		1989: Betsy King	654,132
1965: Kathy Whitworth	28,658		1990: Beth Daniel	863,578
1966: Kathy Whitworth	33,517		1991: Pat Bradley	763,118
1967: Kathy Whitworth	32,937		1992: Dottie Mochrie	693,335
1968: Kathy Whitworth	48,379		1993: Betsy King	595,992
1969: Carol Mann	49,152		1994: Laura Davies	687,201
1970: Kathy Whitworth	30,235		1995: Annika Sorenstam	666,533
1971: Kathy Whitworth	41,181		1996: Karrie Webb	1,002,000
1972: Kathy Whitworth	65,063		1997: Annika Sorenstam	1,236,789
1973: Kathy Whitworth	82,864			
1974: JoAnne Carner	87,094		*Source: LPGA*	

Horse Racing

Winners of the Kentucky Derby

YEAR	HORSE	JOCKEY	YEAR	HORSE	JOCKEY
1875	Aristides	O. Lewis	1923	Zev	E. Sande
1876	Vagrant	B. Swim	1924	Black Gold	J. D. Mooney
1877	Baden-Baden	W. Walker	1925	Flying Ebony	E. Sande
1878	Day Star	J. Carter	1926	Bubbling Over	A. Johnson
1879	Lord Murphy	C. Shauer	1927	Whiskery	L. McAtee
1880	Fonso	G. Lewis	1928	Reigh Count	C. Lang
1881	Hindoo	J. McLaughlin	1929	Clyde Van Dusen	L. McAtee
1882	Apollo	B. Hurd	1930	Gallant Fox	E. Sande
1883	Leonatus	W. Donohue	1931	Twenty Grand	C. Kurtsinger
1884	Buchanan	I. Murphy	1932	Burgoo King	E. James
1885	Joe Cotton	E. Henderson	1933	Brokers Tip	D. Meade
1886	Ben Ali	P. Duffy	1934	Cavalcade	M. Garner
1887	Montrose	I. Lewis	1935	Omaha	W. Saunders
1888	Macbeth II	G. Covington	1936	Bold Venture	I. Hanford
1889	Spokane	T. Kiley	1937	War Admiral	C. Kurtsinger
1890	Riley	I. Murphy	1938	Lawrin	E. Arcaro
1891	Kingman	I. Murphy	1939	Johnstown	J. Stout
1892	Azra	A. Clayton	1940	Gallahadion	C. Bierman
1893	Lookout	E. Kunze	1941	Whirlaway	E. Arcaro
1894	Chant	F. Goodale	1942	Shut Out	W. Wright
1895	Halma	J. Perkins	1943	Count Fleet	J. Longden
1896	Ben Brush	W. Simms	1944	Pensive	C. McCreary
1897	Typhoon II	F. Garner	1945	Hoop Jr	E. Arcaro
1898	Plaudit	W. Simms	1946	Assault	W. Mehrtens
1899	Manuel	F. Taral	1947	Jet Pilot	E. Guerin
1900	Lieut. Gibson	J. Boland	1948	Citation	E. Arcaro
1901	His Eminence	J. Winkfield	1949	Ponder	S. Brooks
1902	Alan-a-Dale	J. Winkfield	1950	Middleground	W. Boland
1903	Judge Himes	H. Booker	1951	Count Turf	C. McCreary
1904	Elwood	F. Prior	1952	Hill Gail	E. Arcaro
1905	Agile	J. Martin	1953	Dark Star	H. Moreno
1906	Sir Huon	R. Troxler	1954	Determine	R. York
1907	Pink Star	A. Minder	1955	Swaps	W. Shoemaker
1908	Stone Street	A. Pickens	1956	Needles	D. Erb
1909	Wintergreen	V. Powers	1957	Iron Liege	B. Hartack
1910	Donau	F. Herbert	1958	Tim Tam	I. Valenzuela
1911	Meridian	G. Archibald	1959	Tomy Lee	W. Shoemaker
1912	Worth	C. H. Shilling	1960	Venetian Way	B. Hartack
1913	Donerail	R. Goose	1961	Carry Back	J. Sellers
1914	Old Rosebud	J. McCabe	1962	Decidedly	B. Hartack
1915	Regret	J. Notter	1963	Chateaugay	B. Baeza
1916	George Smith	J. Loftus	1964	Northern Dancer	B. Hartack
1917	Omar Khayyam	C. Borel	1965	Lucky Debonair	W. Shoemaker
1918	Exterminator	W. Knapp	1966	Kauai King	D. Brumfield
1919	Sir Barton	J. Loftus	1967	Proud Clarion	B. Ussery
1920	Paul Jones	T. Rice	1968	Forward Pass	I. Valenzuela
1921	Behave Yourself	C. Thompson	1969	Majestic Prince	B. Hartack
1922	Morvich	A. Johnson	1970	Dust Commander	M. Manganello

YEAR	HORSE	JOCKEY
1971	Canonero II	G. Avila
1972	Riva Ridge	R. Turcotte
1973	Secretariat	R. Turcotte
1974	Cannonade	A. Cordero, Jr.
1975	Foolish Pleasure	J. Vasquez
1976	Bold Forbes	A. Cordero, Jr.
1977	Seattle Slew	J. Cruguet
1978	Affirmed	S. Cauthen
1979	Spectacular Bid	R. Franklin
1980	Genuine Risk	J. Vasquez
1981	Pleasant Colony	J. Velasquez
1982	Gato Del Sol	E. Delahoussaye
1983	Sunny's Halo	E. Delahoussaye
1984	Swale	L. Pincay, Jr.
1985	Spend a Buck	A. Cordero, Jr.

YEAR	HORSE	JOCKEY
1986	Ferdinand	W. Shoemaker
1987	Alysheba	C. McCarron
1988	Winning Colors	G. Stevens
1989	Sunday Silence	P. Valenzuela
1990	Unbridled	C. Perret
1991	Strike the Gold	C. Antley
1992	Lil E. Tee	P. Day
1993	Sea Hero	J. Bailey
1994	Go for Gin	C. McCarron
1995	Thunder Gulch	G. Stevens
1996	Grindstone	J.D. Bailey
1997	Silver Charm	G. Stevens
1998	Real Quiet	K. Desormeaux

Source: Kentucky Derby Media Guide

Winners of the Preakness Stakes

YEAR	HORSE	JOCKEY
1873	Survivor	G. Barbee
1874	Culpepper	W. Donohue
1875	Tom Ochiltree	L. Hughes
1876	Shirley	G. Barbee
1877	Cloverbrook	C. Holloway
1878	Duke of Magenta	C. Holloway
1879	Harold	L. Hughes
1880	Grenada	L. Hughes
1881	Saunterer	T. Costello
1882	Vanguard	T. Costello
1883	Jacobus	G. Barbee
1884	Knight of Ellerslie	S. Fisher
1885	Tucumseh	J. McLaughlin
1886	The Bard	S. Fisher
1887	Dunboyne	W. Donohue
1888	Refund	F. Littlefield
1889	Buddhist	W. Anderson
1890	Montague	W. Martin
1894	Assignee	F. Taral
1895	Belmar	F. Taral
1896	Margrave	H. Griffin
1897	Paul Kauvar	Thorpe
1898	Sly Fox	W. Simms
1899	Half Time	R. Clawson
1900	Hindus	H. Spencer
1901	The Parader	Landry
1902	Old England	L. Jackson
1903	Flocarline	W. Gannon
1904	Bryn Mawr	E. Hildebrand
1905	Cairngorm	W Davis
1906	Whimsical	W. Miller
1907	Don Enrique	G. Mountain
1908	Royal Tourist	E. Dugan
1909	Effendi	W. Doyle
1910	Layminster	R. Estep
1911	Watervale	E. Dugan
1912	Colonel Holloway	C.Turner

YEAR	HORSE	JOCKEY
1913	Buskin	J. Butwell
1914	Holiday	A Schuttinger
1915	Rhine Maiden	D. Hoffman
1916	Damrosch	L. McAtee
1917	Kalitan	Ev. Haynes
1918	War Cloud	J. Loftus
1918	Jack Hare, Jr.	C. Peak
1919	Sir Barton	J. Loftus
1920	Man o' War	C. Kummer
1921	Broomspun	F. Coltiletti
1922	Pillory	L. Morris
1923	Vigil	B. Marinelli
1924	Nellie Morse	J. Merimee
1925	Coventry	C. Kummer
1926	Display	J. Maiben
1927	Bostonian	A. Abel
1928	Victorian	R. Workman
1929	Dr. Freeland	L. Schaefer
1930	Gallant Fox	E Sande
1931	Mate	G. Ellis
1932	Burgoo King	E. James
1933	Head Play	C. Kurtsinger
1934	High Quest	R. Jones
1935	Omaha	W. Saunders
1936	Bold Venture	G. Woolf
1937	War Admiral	C. Kurtsinger
1938	Dauber	M. Peters
1939	Challedon	G. Seabo
1940	Bimelech	F. A. Smith
1941	Whirlaway	E. Arcaro
1942	Alsab	B. James
1943	Count Fleet	J. Longden
1944	Pensive	C. McCreary
1945	Polynesian	W. D. Wright
1946	Assault	W. Mehrtens
1947	Faultless	D. Dobson
1948	Citation	E. Arcaro

YEAR	HORSE	JOCKEY	YEAR	HORSE	JOCKEY
1949	Capot	T. Atkinson	1974	Little Current	M. A. Rivera
1950	Hill Prince	E. Arcaro	1975	Master Derby	D. G. McHargue
1951	Bold	E. Arcaro	1976	Elocutionist	John Lively
1952	Blue Man	C. McCreary	1977	Seattle Slew	Jean Cruguet
1953	Native Dancer	E. Guerin	1978	Affirmed	Steve Cauthen
1954	Hasty Road	J. Adams	1979	Spectacular Bid	Ron Franklin
1955	Nashua	E. Arcaro	1980	Codex	Angel Cordero, Jr.
1956	Fabius	W. Hartack	1981	Pleasant Colony	Jorge Velasquez
1957	Bold Ruler	E. Arcaro	1982	Aloma's Ruler	Jack Kaenel
1958	Tim Tam	I. Valenzuela	1983	Deputed Testamony	Donald Miller, Jr.
1959	Royal Orbit	W. Harmatz	1984	Gate Dancer	Angel Cordero, Jr.
1960	Bally Ache	R. Ussery	1985	Tank's Prospect	Pat Day
1961	Carry Back	J. Sellers	1986	Snow Chief	Alex Solis
1962	Greek Money	J. L. Rotz	1987	Alysheba	Chris J. McCarron
1963	Candy Spots	W. Shoemaker	1988	Risen Star	Eddie Delahoussaye
1964	Northern Dancer	W. Hartack	1989	Sunday Silence	Patrick Valenzuela
1965	Tom Rolfe	R. Turcotte	1990	Summer Squall	Patrick Day
1966	Kauai King	D. Brumfield	1991	Hansel	Jerry Bailey
1967	Damascus	W. Shoemaker	1992	Pine Bluff	Chris J. McCarron
1968	Forward Pass	I. Valenzuela	1993	Prairie Bayou	Mike Smith
1969	Majestic Prince	W. Hartack	1994	Tabasco Cat	Pat Day
1970	Personality	E. Belmonte	1995	Timber Country	Pat Day
1971	Canonero II	G. Avila	1996	Louis Quatorze	Pat Day
1972	Bee Bee Bee	Eldon Nelson	1997	Silver Charm	Gary Stevens
1973	Secretariat	Ron Turcotte	1998	Real Quiet	Kent Desormeaux

Winners of the Belmont Stakes

YEAR	HORSE	JOCKEY	YEAR	HORSE	JOCKEY
1867	Ruthless	J. Gilpatrick	1894	Henry of Navarre	W. Simms
1868	General Duke	R. Swim	1895	Belmar	F. Taral
1869	Fenian	C. Miller	1896	Hastings	H. Griffin
1870	Kingfisher	E. Brown	1897	Scottish Chieftain	J. Scherrer
1871	Harry Basset	W. Miller	1898	Bowling Brook	F. Littlefield
1872	Joe Daniels	J. Rowe	1899	Jean Bereaud	R.R. Clawson
1873	Springbok	J. Rowe	1900	Ildrim	N. Turner
1874	Saxon	G. Barbee	1901	Commando	H. Spencer
1875	Calvin	R. Swim	1902	Masterman	J. Bullman
1876	Algerine	W. Donohue	1903	Africander	J. Bullman
1877	Cloverbrook	C. Holloway	1904	Delhi	G. Odom
1878	Duke of Magenta	L. Hughes	1905	Tanya	E. Hildebrand
1879	Spendthrift	S. Evans	1906	Burgomaster	L. Lyne
1880	Grenada	L. Hughes	1907	Peter Pan	G. Mountain
1881	Saunterer	T. Costello	1908	Colin	J. Notter
1882	Forester	J. McLaughlin	1909	Joe Madden	E. Dugan
1883	George Kinney	J. McLaughlin	1910	Sweep	J. Butwell
1884	Panique	J. McLaughlin	1911	no race	
1885	Tyrant	P. Duffy	1912	no race	
1886	Inspector B.	J. McLaughlin	1913	Price Eugene	R. Troxler
1887	Hanover	J. McLaughlin	1914	Luke McLuke	M. Buxton
1888	Sir Dixon	J. McLaughlin	1915	The Finn	G. Byrne
1889	Eric	W. Hayward	1916	Friar Rock	E. Haynes
1890	Burlington	S. Barnes	1917	Hourless	J. Butwell
1891	Foxford	E. Garrison	1918	Johren	F. Robinson
1892	Patron	W. Hayward	1919	Sir Barton	J. Loftus
1893	Commanche	W.Simms	1920	Man o' War	C. Kummer

YEAR	HORSE	JOCKEY	YEAR	HORSE	JOCKEY
1921	Grey Lag	E. Sande	1960	Celtic Ash	W. Hartack
1922	Pillory	C. H. Miller	1961	Sherluck	B. Baeza
1923	Zev	E. Sande	1962	Jaipur	W. Shoemaker
1924	Mad Play	E. Sande	1963	Chateaugay	B. Baeza
1925	American Flag	A. Johnson	1964	Quadrangle	M. Ycaza
1926	Crusader	A. Johnson	1965	Hail to All	J. Sellers
1927	Chance Shot	E. Sande	1966	Amberoid	W. Boland
1928	Vito	C. Kummer	1967	Damascus	W. Shoemaker
1929	Blue Larkspur	M. Garner	1968	Stage Door Johnny	H. Gustines
1930	Gallant Fox	E. Sande	1969	Arts and Letters	B. Baeza
1931	Twenty Grand	C. Kurtsinger	1970	High Echelon	J. L. Rotz
1932	Faireno	T. Malley	1971	Pass Catcher	W. Blum
1933	Hurryoff	M. Garner	1972	Riva Ridge	R. Turcotte
1934	Peace Chance	W. D. Wright	1973	Secretariat	R. Turcotte
1935	Omaha	W. Saunders	1974	Little Current	M. A. Rivera
1936	Granville	J. Stout	1975	Avatar	W. Shoemaker
1937	War Admiral	C. Kurtsinger	1976	Bold Forbes	A. Cordero Jr.
1938	Pasteurized	J. Stout	1977	Seattle Slew	J. Cruguet
1939	Johnstown	J. Stout	1978	Affirmed	S. Cauthen
1940	Bimelech	F.A. Smith	1979	Coastal	R. Hernandez
1941	Whirlaway	E. Arcaro	1980	Temperence Hill	E. Maple
1942	Shut Out	E. Arcaro	1981	Summing	G. Martens
1943	Count Fleet	J. Longden	1982	Conquistador Cielo	L. Pincay Jr.
1944	Bounding Home	G.L. Smith	1983	Caveat	L. Pincay Jr.
1945	Pavot	E. Arcaro	1984	Swale	L. Pincay Jr.
1946	Assault	W. Mehrtens	1985	Creme Fraiche	E. Maple
1947	Phalanx	R. Donoso	1986	Danzig Connection	C. J. McCarron
1948	Citation	E. Arcaro	1987	Bet Twice	C. Perret
1949	Capot	T. Atkinson	1988	Risen Star	E. Delahoussaye
1950	Middleground	W. Boland	1989	Easy Goer	P. Day
1951	Counterpoint	D. Gorman	1990	Go and Go	J.J. Kinane
1952	One Count	E. Arcaro	1991	Hansel	J.D. Bailey
1953	Native Dancer	E. Guerin	1992	A.P. Indy	E. Delahoussaye
1954	High Gun	E. Guerin	1993	Colonial Affair	J. A. Krone
1955	Nashua	E. Arcaro	1994	Tabasco Cat	P. Day
1956	Needles	D. Erb	1995	Thunder Gulch	G. L. Stevens
1957	Gallant Man	W. Shoemaker	1996	Editor's Note	R. Douglas
1958	Cavan	P. Anderson	1997	Touch Gold	C. McCarron
1959	Sword Dancer	W. Shoemaker	1998	Victory Gallop	G. Stevens

Triple Crown Winners

YEAR	HORSE	JOCKEY	TRAINER	OWNER	YEAR	HORSE	JOCKEY	TRAINER	OWNER
1919	Sir Barton	John Loftus	H. G. Bedwell	J. K. L. Ross	1946	Assault	Warren Mehrtens	Max Hirsch Hirsch	King Ranch
1930	Gallant Fox	Earl Sande	James Fitzsimmons	Belair Stud	1948	Citation	Eddie Arcaro	Ben A Jones	Calumet Farm
1935	Omaha	William Saunders	James Fitzsimmons	Belair Stud	1973	Secretariat	Ron Turcotte	Lucien Laurin	Meadow Stable
1937	War Admiral	Charley Kurtsinger	George Conway	Samuel D. Riddle	1977	Seattle Slew	Jean Cruget	William Turner, Jr.	Karen L. Taylor
1941	Whirlaway	Eddie Arcaro	Ben A. Jones	Calumet Farm	1978	Affirmed	Steve Cauthen	Lazaro S. Barrera	Harbor View Farm
1943	Count Fleet	John Longden	Don Cameron	Mrs. J.D. Hertz					

Top Money-Winning Jockeys

Year	Jockey	Amt. Won	Year	Jockey	Amt. Won
1954	W. Shoemaker	1,876,760	1978	D.G. McHargue	6,188,353
1955	E. Arcaro	1,864,796	1979	L. Pincay, Jr.	8,183,535
1956	W. Hartack	2,343,955	1980	C.J. McCarron	7,666,100
1957	W. Hartack	3,060,501	1981	C.J. McCarron	8,397,604
1958	W. Shoemaker	2,961,693	1982	A. Cordero, Jr.	9,702,520
1959	W. Shoemaker	2,843,133	1983	A. Cordero, Jr.	10,116,807
1960	W. Shoemaker	2,123,961	1984	C.J. McCarron	12,038,213
1961	W. Shoemaker	2,690,819	1985	L. Pincay, Jr.	13,415,049
1962	W. Shoemaker	2,916,844	1986	J.A. Santos	11,329,297
1963	W. Shoemaker	2,526,925	1987	J.A. Santos	12,407,355
1964	W. Shoemaker	2,649,553	1988	J.A. Santos	14,877,298
1965	B. Baeza	2,582,702	1989	J.A. Santos	13,847,003
1966	B. Baeza	2,951,022	1990	G.L. Stevens	13,881,198
1967	B. Baeza	3,088,888	1991	C.J. McCarron	14,456,073
1968	B. Baeza	2,835,108	1992	K.J. Desormeaux	14,193,006
1969	J. Velasquez	2,542,315	1993	M.E. Smith	14,008,148
1970	L. Pincay, Jr.	2,626,526	1994	M.E. Smith	9,985,703
1971	L. Pincay, Jr.	3,784,377	1995	J. Bailey	16,308,230
1972	L. Pincay, Jr.	3,225,827	1996	J. Bailey	17,064,409
1973	L. Pincay, Jr.	4,093,492	1997	J. Bailey	18,320,743
1974	L. Pincay, Jr.	4,251,060			
1975	B. Baeza	3,674,398			
1976	A. Cordero, Jr.	4,709,500			
1977	S. Cauthen	6,151,750			

Sources: Daily Racing Form and Equibase Co.

Auto Racing

Indianapolis 500 Winners ⚑⚑

Year	Winner	Speed (mph)	Year	Winner	Speed (mph)
1911	Ray Harroun	74.602	1957	Sam Hanks	135.601
1912	Joe Dawson	78.719	1958	Jimmy Bryan	133.791
1913	Jules Goux	75.933	1959	Rodger Ward	135.857
1914	Rene Thomas	82.474	1960	Jim Rathmann	138.767
1915	Ralph DePalma	89.840	1961	A. J. Foyt	139.131
1916	Dario Resta	84.001	1962	Rodger Ward	140.293
1917–18	Race not held due to World War I		1963	Parnelli Jones	143.137
1919	Howard Wilcox	88.050	1964	A. J. Foyt	147.350
1920	Gaston Chevrolet	88.618	1965	Jimmy Clark	150.686
1921	Tommy Milton	89.621	1966	Graham Hill	144.317
1922	Jimmy Murphy	94.484	1967	A. J. Foyt	151.207
1923	Tommy Milton	90.954	1968	Bobby Unser	152.882
1924	L. L. Corum, Joe Boyer	98.234	1969	Mario Andretti	156.867
1925	Pete DePaolo	101.127	1970	Al Unser	155.749
1926	Frank Lockhart	95.904	1971	Al Unser	157.735
1927	George Souders	97.545	1972	Mark Donohue	162.962
1928	Louis Meyer	99.482	1973	Gordon Johncock	159.036
1929	Ray Keech	97.585	1974	Johnny Rutherford	158.589
1930	Billy Arnold	100.448	1975	Bobby Unser	149.213
1931	Louis Schneider	96.629	1976	Johnny Rutherford	148.725
1932	Fred Frame	104.144	1977	A. J. Foyt	161.331
1933	Louis Meyer	104.162	1978	Al Unser	161.363
1934	Bill Cummings	104.863	1979	Rick Mears	158.899
1935	Kelly Petillo	106.240	1980	Johnny Rutherford	142.862
1936	Louis Meyer	109.069	1981	Bobby Unser	139.084
1937	Wilbur Shaw	113.580	1982	Gordon Johncock	162.029
1938	Floyd Roberts	117.200	1983	Tom Sneva	162.117
1939	Wilbur Shaw	115.035	1984	Rick Mears	163.612
1940	Wilbur Shaw	114.277	1985	Danny Sullivan	152.982
1941	Floyd Davis, Mauri Rose	115.117	1986	Bobby Rahal	170.722
1942–45	Race not held due to World War II		1987	Al Unser	162.175
1946	George Robson	114.820	1988	Rick Mears	144.809
1947	Mauri Rose	116.338	1989	Emerson Fittipaldi	167.581
1948	Mauri Rose	119.814	1990	Arie Luyendyk	185.981
1949	Bill Holland	121.327	1991	Rick Mears	176.457
1950	Johnnie Parsons	124.002	1992	Al Unser, Jr.	134.479
1951	Lee Wallard	126.244	1993	Emerson Fittipaldi	157.207
1952	Troy Ruttman	128.922	1994	Al Unser, Jr.	160.872
1953	Bill Vukovich	128.740	1995	Jacques Villeneuve	153.616
1954	Bill Vukovich	130.840	1996	Buddy Lazier	147.956
1955	Bob Sweikert	128.209	1997	Arie Luyendyk	145.857
1956	Pat Flaherty	128.490	1998	Eddie Cheever	145.155

Source: Indianapolis Motor Speedway

Speedway Money

Year	Purse	Winner
1960	$369,150	$110,000
1961	400,000	117,975
1962	426,152	125,015
1963	494,030	148,513
1964	506,575	153,650
1965	628,399	186,621
1966	691,808	156,297
1967	734,634	171,227
1968	712,269	177,523
1969	805,127	205,727
1970	1,000,002	271,697
1971	1,001,604	238,454
1972	1,011,848	218,767
1973	1,006,105	236,022
1974	1,015,686	245,031
1975	1,001,321	214,031
1976	1,037,755	256,121
1977	1,116,807	259,791
1978	1,145,225	290,383
1979	1,271,954	270,401
1980	1,503,225	318,819
1981	1,609,375	299,124
1982	2,067,475	290,609
1983	2,411,450	385,886
1984	2,795,899	434,061
1985	3,271,025	517,662
1986	4,001,450	581,062
1987	4,490,375	526,762
1988	5,025,400	809,853
1989	5,723,725	1,001,604
1990	6,325,803	1,090,940
1991	7,009,150	1,219,704
1992	7,527,450	1,244,184
1993	7,681,300	1,155,304
1994	7,864,800	1,373,813
1995	8,063,550	1,312,019
1996	8,114,600	1,367,854
1997	8,634,450	1,553,650
1998	8,722,150	1,433,000

Source: Indianapolis Motor Speedway

Top Indianapolis 500 Winners

Winner	Years
A. J. Foyt	1961, 1964, 1967, 1977
Rick Mears	1979, 1984, 1988, 1991
Al Unser, Sr.	1970, 1971, 1978, 1987
Louis Meyer	1928, 1933, 1936
Mauri Rose	1941, 1947, 1948
Johnny Rutherford	1974, 1976, 1980
Wilbur Shaw	1937, 1939, 1940
Bobby Unser	1968, 1976, 1981

Source: Indianapolis Motor Speedway

NASCAR Winston Cup Champions

Year	Driver
1949	Red Byron
1950	Bill Rexford
1951	Herb Thomas
1952	Tim Flock
1953	Herb Thomas
1954	Lee Petty
1955	Tim Flock
1956	Buck Baker
1957	Buck Baker
1958	Lee Petty
1959	Lee Petty
1960	Rex White
1961	Ned Jarrett
1962	Joe Weatherly
1963	Joe Weatherly
1964	Richard Petty
1965	Ned Jarrett
1966	David Pearson
1967	Richard Petty
1968	David Pearson
1969	David Pearson
1970	Bobby Isaac
1971	Richard Petty
1972	Richard Petty
1973	Benny Parsons
1974	Richard Petty
1975	Richard Petty
1976	Cale Yarborough
1977	Cale Yarborough
1978	Cale Yarborough
1979	Richard Petty
1980	Dale Earnhardt
1981	Darrel Waltrip
1982	Darrel Waltrip
1983	Bobby Allison
1984	Terry Labonte
1985	Darrel Waltrip
1986	Dale Earnhardt
1987	Dale Earnhardt
1988	Bill Elliott
1989	Rusty Wallace
1990	Dale Earnhardt
1991	Dale Earnhardt
1992	Alan Kulwicki
1993	Dale Earnhardt
1994	Dale Earnhardt
1995	Jeff Gordon
1996	Terry Labonte
1997	Jeff Gordon

Heavyweight Boxing Champions

	Winner	Opponent	Site of Championship
Aug. 29, 1885	John L. Sullivan (Wins Vacant World Title)	Dominick McCaffrey	Cincinnati
Sept. 7, 1892	James J. Corbett	John L. Sullivan	New Orleans
March 17, 1897	Bob Fitzsimmons	James J. Corbett	Carson City, NV
June 9, 1899	James J. Jeffries	Bob Fitzsimmons	Brooklyn, NY
July 3, 1905	Marvin Hart (Wins Vacant World Title)	Jack Root	Reno
Feb. 23, 1906	Tommy Burns	Marvin Hart	Los Angeles
Dec. 26, 1908	Jack Johnson	Tommy Burns	Sydney
April 5, 1915	Jess Willard	Jack Johnson	Havana
July 4, 1919	Jack Dempsey	Jess Willard	Toledo, OH
Sept. 23, 1926	Gene Tunney	Jack Dempsey	Philadelphia
June 12, 1930	Max Schmeling (Wins Vacant World Title)	Jack Sharkey	Bronx, NY
June 21, 1932	Jack Sharkey	Max Schmeling	Long Island City, NY
June 29, 1933	Primo Carnera	Jack Sharkey	Long Island City, NY
June 14, 1934	Max Baer	Primo Carnera	Long Island City,NY
June 13, 1935	James J. Braddock	Max Baer	Long Island City, NY
June 22, 1937	Joe Louis	James J. Braddock	Chicago
June 22, 1949	Ezzard Charles (Wins Vacant World Title)	Jersey Joe Walcott	Chicago
July 18, 1951	Jersey Joe Walcott	Ezzard Charles	Pittsburgh
Sept. 23, 1952	Rocky Marciano	Jersey Joe Walcott	Philadelphia
Nov. 30, 1956	Floyd Patterson (Wins Vacant World Title)	Archie Moore	Chicago
June 26, 1959	Ingemar Johansson	Floyd Patterson	Bronx, NY
June 20, 1960	Floyd Patterson	Ingemar Johansson	New York City
Sept. 25, 1962	Sonny Liston	Floyd Patterson	Chicago
Feb. 25, 1964	Cassius Clay*	Sonny Liston	Miami Beach
March 5, 1965	Ernie Terrell (Wins Vacant World Boxing Association Title)	Eddie Machen	Chicago
Feb. 6, 1967	Muhammad Ali (Unifies World Title)	Ernie Terrell	Houston
March 4, 1968	Joe Frazier (Wins Vacant New York World Title)	Buster Mathis	New York City
April 27, 1968	Jimmy Ellis (Wins Vacant WBA Title)	Jerry Quarry	Oakland, CA
Feb. 16, 1970	Joe Frazier (Unifies World Title)	Jimmy Ellis	New York City
Jan. 22, 1973	George Foreman	Joe Frazier	Kingston, Jamaica
Oct. 30, 1974	Muhammad Ali	George Foreman	Kinshasa, Zaire
Feb. 15, 1978	Leon Spinks	Muhammad Ali	Las Vegas
June 9, 1978	Larry Holmes (Wins World Boxing Council Title)	Ken Norton**	Las Vegas
Sept. 15, 1978	Muhammad Ali (Regains WBA Title)	Leon Spinks	New Orleans
Oct. 20, 1979	John Tate (Wins Vacant WBA Title)	Gerrie Coetzee	Pretoria, South Africa
March 31, 1980	Mike Weaver (Wins WBA Title)	John Tate	Knoxville, TN
Dec. 10, 1982	Michael Dokes (Wins WBA Title)	Mike Weaver	Las Vegas
Sept. 23, 1983	Gerrie Coetzee (Wins WBA Title)	Michael Dokes	Richfield, OH

	Winner	Opponent	Site of Championship
March 9, 1984	Tim Witherspoon (Wins Vacant WBC Title)	Greg Page	Las Vegas
Aug. 31, 1984	Pinklon Thomas (Wins WBC Title)	Tim Witherspoon	Las Vegas
Dec. 1, 1984	Greg Page (Wins WBA Title)	Gerrie Coetzee	Sun City
April 29, 1985	Tony Tubbs (Wins WBA Title)	Greg Page	Buffalo
Sept. 21, 1985	Michael Spinks (Wins International Boxing Federation Title)	Larry Holmes[†]	Las Vegas
Jan. 17, 1986	Tim Witherspoon (Wins WBA Title)	Tony Tubbs	Atlanta
March 22, 1986	Trevor Berbick (Wins WBC Title)	Pinklon Thomas	Las Vegas
Nov. 22, 1986	Mike Tyson (Wins WBC Title)	Trevor Berbick	Las Vegas
Dec. 12, 1986	Bonecrusher Smith (Wins WBA Title)	Tim Witherspoon	New York City
March 7, 1987	Mike Tyson (Wins WBA Title)	Bonecrusher Smith	Las Vegas
May 30, 1987	Tony Tucker (Wins Vacant IBF Title)	Buster Douglas	Las Vegas
Aug. 1, 1987	Mike Tyson (Wins IBF Title; Unifies World Title)	Tony Tucker	Las Vegas
Feb. 11, 1990	Buster Douglas (Wins World Title)	Mike Tyson	Tokyo
Oct. 25, 1990	Evander Holyfield (Wins World Title)	Buster Douglas	Las Vegas
Nov. 13, 1992	Riddick Bowe (Wins World Title)	Evander Holyfield	Las Vegas
Nov. 6, 1993	Evander Holyfield (Regains WBA, IBF Titles)	Riddick Bowe	Las Vegas
April 22, 1994	Michael Moorer (Wins WBA, IBF Titles)	Evander Holyfield	Las Vegas
Sept. 24, 1994	Oliver McCall (Wins WBC Title)	Lennox Lewis[‡]	London
Nov. 5, 1994	George Foreman (Regains WBA Title; Wins IBF Title)	Michael Moorer	Las Vegas
April 8, 1995	Bruce Seldon (Wins Vacant WBA Title)	Tony Tucker	Las Vegas
Sept. 2, 1995	Frank Bruno (Wins WBC Title)	Oliver McCall	London
Dec. 9, 1995	Frans Botha (Wins Vacant IBF Title)	Axel Schulz	Stuttgart, Germany
March 16, 1996	Mike Tyson (Regains WBC Title)	Frank Bruno	Las Vegas
June 22, 1996	Michael Moorer (Regains Vacant IBF Title)	Axel Schulz	Dortmund, Germany
Sept. 7, 1996	Mike Tyson (Regains WBA Title)	Bruce Seldon	Las Vegas
Nov. 9, 1996	Evander Holyfield (Regains WBA Title)	Mike Tyson	Las Vegas
Feb. 7, 1997	Lennox Lewis (Regains WBC Title)	Oliver McCall	Las Vegas
Nov. 8, 1997	Evander Holyfield (Regains IBF Title)	Michael Moorer	Las Vegas

*Immediately after winning the title, Clay changed his name to Muhammad Ali
**Norton had been named WBC champion following his victory over Jimmy Young in November 1977
[†]After vacating the WBC title, Holmes had been named IBF champion following his November 1983 victory over Marvis Frazier
[‡]Lewis had been named WBC champion following his victory over Razor Ruddock in October 1992

Source: The Ring Magazine

Running Marathons

New York City Marathon Winners

Men	Time	Women	Time
1970: Gary Muhrche	2:31:38	NO WINNER	
1971: Norman Higgins	2:22:54	Beth Bonner	2:55:22
1972: Sheldon Karlin	2:27:52	Nina Kuscsik	3:08:41
1973: Tom Fleming	2:21:54	Nina Kuscsik	2:57:07
1974: Norbert Sander	2:26:30	Kathrine Switzer	3:07:29
1975: Tom Fleming	2:19:27	Kin Merritt	2:46:14
1976: Bill Rodgers	2:10:10	Miki Gorman	2:39:11
1977: Bill Rodgers	2:11:38	Miki Gorman	2:43:10
1978: Bill Rodgers	2:12:12	Grete Waitz	2:32:30
1979: Bill Rodgers	2:11:42	Grete Waitz	2:27:33
1980: Alberto Salazar	2:09:41	Grete Waitz	2:25:42
1981: Alberto Salazar	2:08:13	Allison Roe	2:25:29
1982: Alberto Salazar	2:09:29	Grete Waitz	2:27:14
1983: Rod Dixon	2:08:59	Grete Waitz	2:27:00
1984: Orlando Pizzolato	2:14:53	Grete Waitz	2:29:30
1985: Orlando Pizzolato	2:11:34	Grete Waitz	2:28:34
1986: Gianni Poli	2:11:06	Grete Waitz	2:28:06
1987: Ibrahim Hussein	2:11:01	Priscilla Welch	2:30:17
1988: Steve Jones	2:08:20	Grete Waitz	2:28:07
1989: Juma Ikangaa	2:08:01	Ingrid Kristiansen	2:25:30
1990: Douglas Wakiihuri	2:12:39	Wenda Panfil	2:30:45
1991: Salvador Garcia	2:09:28	Liz McColgan	2:27:00
1992: Willie Mtolo	2:09:29	Lisa Ondieki	2:24:40
1993: Andres Espinosa	2:10:04	Uta Pippig	2:26:24
1994: German Silva	2:11:21	Tegla Loroupe	2:27:37
1995: German Silva	2:10:00	Tegla Loroupe	2:28:06
1996: Giacomo Leone	2:09:54	Anuta Catuna	2:28:18
1997: John Kagwe	2:08:12	Franziska Rochat-Moser	2:28:43

Source: New York Road Runners Club

Boston Marathon Champions

Men's Open	Time
1897: John J. McDermott	2:55:10
1898: Ronald J. MacDonald	2:42:00
1899: Lawrence J. Brignolia	2:54:38
1900: John Peter Caffery	2:39:44
1901: John Peter Caffery	2:29:23
1902: Sammy Mellor	2:43:12
1903: John C. Lorden	2:41:29
1904: Michael Spring	2:38:04
1905: Fred Lorz	2:38:25
1906: Timothy Ford	2:45:45
1907: Tom Longboat	2:24:24
1908: Thomas Morrissey	2:25:43
1909: Henri Renaud	2:53:36
1910: Fred S. Cameron	2:28:52
1911: Clarence H. DeMar	2:21:39
1912: Mike Ryan	2:21:18
1913: Fritz Carlson	2:25:14
1914: James Duffy	2:25:01
1915: Edouard Fabre	2:31:41
1916: Arthur Roth	2:27:16
1917: Bill Kennedy	2:28:37
1918: Camp DevenA	2:24:53
1919: Carl Linde	2:29:13
1920: Peter Trivoulides	2:29:31
1921: Frank Zuna	2:18:57
1922: Clarence H. DeMar	2:18:10
1923: Clarence H. DeMar	2:23:37
1924: Clarence H. DeMar	2:29:40
1925: Charles Mellor	2:33:00
1926: Johnny Miles	2:25:40
1927: Clarence H. DeMar	2:40:22
1928: Clarence H. DeMar	2:37:07
1929: Johnny Miles	2:33:08
1930: Clarence H. DeMar	2:34:48
1931: James P. Henigan	2:46:45
1932: Paul deBruyn	2:33:36
1933: Leslie S. Pawso	2:31:01
1934: Dave Komonen	2:32:53
1935: John A. Kelley	2:32:07
1936: Ellison M. Brown	2:33:40
1937: Walter Young	2:33:20
1938: Leslie S. Pawson	2:35:34
1939: Ellison M. Brown	2:28:51
1940: Gerard Cote	2:28:28
1941: Leslie S. Pawson	2:30:38
1942: Bernard Joseph Smith	2:26:51
1943: Gerard Cote	2:28:25
1944: Gerard Cote	2:31:50
1945: John A. Kelley	2:30:40
1946: Stylianos Kyriakides	2:29:27
1947: Yun Bok	2:25:39
1948: Gerard Cote	2:31:02
1949: Karl Gosta Leandersson	2:31:50

	Time
1950: Kee Yong Ham	2:32:39
1951: Shigeki Tanaka	2:27:45
1952: Doroteo Flores	2:31:53
1953: Keizo Yamada,	2:18:51
1954: Veikko Karvonen	2:20:39
1955: Hideo Hamamura	2:18:22
1956: Antti Viskari	2:14:14
1957: John J. Kelley	2:20:05
1958: Franjo Mihalic	2:25:54
1959: Eino Oksanen	2:22:42
1960: Paavo Kotil	2:20:54
1961: Eino Oksanen	2:23:39
1962: Eino Oksanen	2:23:48
1963: Aurele Vandendriessche	2:18:58
1964: Aurele Vandendriessche	2:19:59
1965: Morio Shigematsu	2:16:33
1966: Kenji Kimihara	2:17:11
1967: David C. McKenzie	2:15:45
1968: Amby Burfoot	2:22:17
1969: Yoshiaki Unetani	2:13:49
1970: Ron Hill, Cheshird	2:10:30
1971: Alvaro Mejia	2:18:45
1972: Olavi Suomalainend	2:15:39
1973: Jon P. Andersonn	2:16:03
1974: Neil Cusack	2:13:39
1975: Bill Rodgers	2:09:55
1976: Jack Fultz	2:20:19
1977: Jerome P. Drayton	2:14:46
1978: Bill Rodgers	2:10:13
1979: Bill Rodgers	2:09:27
1980: Bill Rodgers	2:12:11
1981: Toshihiko Seko	2:09:26
1982: Alberto B. Salazar	2:08:52
1983: Gregory A. Meyer	2:09:00
1984: Geoff Smith	2:10:34
1985: Geoff Smith	2:14:05
1986: Robert de Castella	2:07:51
1987: Toshihiko Seko	2:11:50
1988: Ibrahim Hussein	2:08:43
1989: Abebe Mekonnen	2:09:06
1990: Gelindo Bordin	2:08:19
1991: Ibrahim Hussein	2:11:06
1992: Ibrahim Hussein	2:08:14
1993: Cosmas Ndet	2:09:33
1994: Cosmas Ndet	2:07:15
1995: Cosmas Ndeti	2:09:22
1996: Moses Tanui	2:09:15
1997: Lameck Aguta	2:10:34
1998: Moses Tanui	2:07:34

Women's Open	Time
1966: Roberta Gibb—Unofficial	3:21:40
1967: Roberta Gibb—Unofficial	3:27:17
1968: Roberta Gibb—Unofficial	3:30:00

1969: Sara Mae Berman—Unofficial	3:22:46	1984: Lorraine Moller	2:29:28
1970: Sara Mae Berman—Unofficial	3:05:07	1985: Lisa Larsen Weidenbach	2:34:06
1971: Sara Mae Berman—Unofficial	3:08:30	1986: Ingrid Kristiansen	2:24:55
1972: Nina L. Kuscsik	3:10:26	1987: Rosa Mota	2:25:21
1973: Jacqueline A. Hansen	3:05:59	1988: Rosa Mota	2:24:30
1974: Miki Gorman	2:47:11	1989: Ingrid Kristiansen	2:24:33
1975: Liane Winte	2:42:24	1990: Rosa Mota	2:25:24
1976: Kim Merritt	2:47:10	1991: Wanda Panfil	2:24:18
1977: Miki Gorman	2:48:33	1992: Olga Markova	2:23:43
1978: Gayle Barron	2:44:52	1993: Olga Markova	2:25:27
1979: Joan Benoi	2:35:15	1994: Uta Pippig	2:21:45
1980: Jacqueline Gareau	2:34:28	1995: Uta Pippig	2:25:11
1981: Allison Roe	2:26:46	1996: Uta Pippig	2:27:12
1982: Charlotte Tesk	2:29:33	1997: Fatuma Roba	2:26:23
1983: Joan Benoit	2:22:43	1998: Fatuma Roba	2:23:21

Fastest Marathons

Men

Time	Runner, Country	Site	Date
2:06:50	Belayneh Dinsamo, Ethiopia	Rotterdam	April 17, 1988
2:07:02	Sammy Lelei, Kenya	Berlin	Sept. 24, 1995
2:07:07	Ahmed Salah, Djibouti	Rotterdam	April 17, 1988
2:07:10	Khalid Khannouchi, Morocco	Chicago	Oct. 19, 1997
2:07:12	Carlos Lopes, Portugal	Rotterdam	April 20, 1985
2:07:13	Steve Jones, Great Britain	Chicago	Oct. 20, 1985
2:07:15	Cosmos Ndeti, Kenya	Boston	April 18, 1994
2:07:19	Andreas Espinosa, Mexico	Boston	April 18, 1994
2:07:20	Vincent Rousseau, Belgium	Berlin	Sept. 24, 1995
2:07:27	Fabian Roncero, Spain	Rotterdam	April 19, 1998

Women

Time	Runner, Country	Site	Date
2:20:47	Tegla Loroupe, Kenya	Rotterdam	April 19, 1998
2:21:06	Ingrid Kristiansen, Norway	London	April 21, 1985
2:21:21	Joan Benoit Samuelson, USA	Chicago	Oct. 20, 1985
2:21:45	Uta Pippig, Germany	Boston	April 18, 1994
2:22:07	Tegla Loroupe, Kenya	Rotterdam	April 20, 1998
2:22:43	Joan Benoit, Samuelson, USA	Boston	April 18, 1983
2:22:48	Ingrid Kristiansen, Norway	London	May 10, 1987
2:23:05	Ingrid Kristiansen, Norway	Chicago	Oct. 20, 1985
2:23:21	Fatuma Roba, Ethiopia	Boston	April 20, 1998
2:23:29	Rosa Mota, Portugal	Chicago	Oct. 20, 1985

Most Popular Participation Sports

Number of Persons Who Participated More Than Once, Seven Years of Age and Older (In millions)

	Sport	1985	1990	1995	1996	1997
1	Exercise Walking	41.5	71.4	70.3	73.3	76.3
2	Swimming	73.3	67.5	61.5	60.2	59.5
3	Exercising with Equipment	32.1	35.3	44.3	47.8	47.9
4	Camping	46.4	46.2	42.8	44.7	46.6
5	Bicycle Riding	50.7	55.3	56.3	53.3	45.1
6	Bowling	35.7	40.1	41.9	42.9	44.8
7	Fishing	–	46.9	44.2	45.6	44.7
8	Billiards/Pool	23.0	28.1	31.1	34.5	37.0
9	Basketball	19.5	26.3	30.1	33.3	30.7
10	Hiking	21.1	22.0	25.0	26.5	28.4
11	Boating (Motor/Power)	26.6	28.6	26.8	28.8	27.2
12	Inline Skating	–	3.6	23.9	25.5	26.6
13	Aerobic Exercising	23.9	23.3	23.1	24.1	26.3
14	Golf	18.5	23.0	24.0	23.1	26.2
15	Running/Jogging	26.3	23.8	20.6	22.2	21.7
16	Dart Throwing	9.4	16.4	19.8	21.3	21.4
17	Volleyball	20.1	23.2	18.0	18.5	17.8
18	Hunting with Firearms	–	18.5	17.4	19.3	17.0
19	Softball	21.6	20.1	17.6	19.9	16.3
20	Mountain Biking	–	–	–	–	16.0
21	Baseball	12.8	15.6	15.7	14.8	14.1
22	Soccer	8.6	10.9	12.0	13.9	13.7
23	Target Shooting	–	12.8	13.9	15.7	13.5
24	Backpack/Wilderness Camp	–	–	–	–	12.0
25	Football	–	–	12.1	11.6	11.9

Source: National Sporting Goods Association

INDEX